RECONFIGURABLE COMPUTING

The Morgan Kaufmann Series in Systems on Silicon

Series Editor: Wayne Wolf, Georgia Institute of Technology

Coming Soon ...

RECONFIGURABLE COMPUTING
THE THEORY AND PRACTICE OF FPGA-BASED COMPUTATION

Edited by

Scott Hauck and André DeHon

AMSTERDAM • BOSTON • HEIDELBERG • LONDON
NEW YORK • OXFORD • PARIS • SAN DIEGO
SAN FRANCISCO • SYDNEY • TOKYO

Morgan Kaufmann is an imprint of Elsevier

MORGAN KAUFMANN PUBLISHERS

Publisher:	Denise E. M. Penrose
Senior Acquisitions Editor:	Charles B. Glaser
Publishing Services Manager:	George Morrison
Project Manager:	Marilyn E. Rash
Assistant Editors:	Michele Cronin, Matthew Cater
Copyeditor:	Dianne Wood
Proofreader:	Jodie Allen
Indexer:	Steve Rath
Cover Image:	© istockphoto
Typesetting:	diacriTech
Illustration Formatting:	diacriTech
Interior Printer:	Maple-Vail Book Manufacturing Group
Cover Printer:	Phoenix Color Corp.

Morgan Kaufmann Publishers is an imprint of Elsevier.
30 Corporate Drive, Suite 400, Burlington, MA 01803-4255

This book is printed on acid-free paper.

Library of Congress Cataloging-in-Publication Data
Reconfigurable computing: the theory and practice of FPGA-based computation/edited by
   Scott Hauck, André DeHon.
   p. cm. — (Systems on silicon)
   Includes bibliographical references and index.
   ISBN 978-0-12-370522-8 (alk. paper)
   1. Adaptive computing systems. 2. Field-programmable gate arrays. I. Hauck, Scott.
   II. DeHon, André.
QA76.9.A3R43 2008   2007029773

For information on all Morgan Kaufmann publications,
visit our Web site at *www.mkp.com* or *www.books.elsevier.com*.

Printed in the United States
08 09 10 11 12   10 9 8 7 6 5 4 3 2 1

CONTENTS

6   Programming FPGA Applications in VHDL   129

7   Compiling C for Spatial Computing   155

LIST OF CONTRIBUTORS

Rajeevan Amirtharajah, Department of Electrical and Computer Engineering, University of California–Davis, Davis, California (Chapter 24)

Vaughn Betz, Altera Corporation, San Jose, California (Chapter 14)

Robert W. Brodersen, Department of Electrical Engineering and Computer Science, University of California–Berkeley, Berkeley, California (Chapter 8)

Timothy J. Callahan, School of Computer Science, Carnegie Mellon University, Pittsburgh, Pennsylvania (Chapter 7)

Eylon Caspi, Tabula, Inc., Santa Clara, California (Chapter 9)

Chen Chang, Department of Mathematics and Department of Electrical Engineering and Computer Sciences, University of California–Berkeley, Berkeley, California (Chapter 8)

Mark L. Chang, Electrical and Computer Engineering, Franklin W. Olin College of Engineering, Needham, Massachusetts (Chapter 1)

Wang Chen, Department of Electrical and Computer Engineering, Northeastern University, Boston, Massachusetts (Chapter 32)

Young H. Cho, Open Acceleration Systems Research, Chatsworth, California (Chapter 28)

Michael Chu, DRC Computer, Sunnyvale, California (Chapter 9)

Katherine Compton, Department of Electrical and Computer Engineering, University of Wisconsin–Madison, Madison, Wisconsin (Chapters 4 and 11)

Jason Cong, Department of Computer Science, California NanoSystems Institute, University of California–Los Angeles, Los Angeles, California (Chapter 13)

George A. Constantinides, Department of Electrical and Electronic Engineering, Imperial College, London, United Kingdom (Chapter 23)

André DeHon, Department of Electrical and Systems Engineering, University of Pennsylvania, Philadelphia, Pennsylvania (Chapters 5, 6, 7, 9, 11, 36, 37, and 38)

Chris Dick, Advanced Systems Technology Group, DSP Division of Xilinx, Inc., San Jose, California (Chapter 25)

Carl Ebeling, Department of Computer Science and Engineering, University of Washington, Seattle, Washington (Chapter 17)

Ken Eguro, Department of Electrical Engineering, University of Washington, Seattle, Washington (Chapter 20)

Diana Franklin, Computer Science Department, California Polytechnic State University, San Luis Obispo, California (Chapter 35)

Thomas W. Fry, Samsung, Global Strategy Group, Seoul, South Korea (Chapter 27)

Maya B. Gokhale, Lawrence Livermore National Laboratory, Livermore, California (Chapter 10)

Steven A. Guccione, Cmpware, Inc., Austin, Texas (Chapters 3 and 19)

Scott Hauck, Department of Electrical Engineering, University of Washington, Seattle, Washington (Chapters 20 and 27)

K. Scott Hemmert, Computation, Computers, Information and Mathematics Center, Sandia National Laboratories, Albuquerque, New Mexico (Chapter 31)

Randy Huang, Tabula, Inc., Santa Clara, California (Chapter 9)

Brad L. Hutchings, Department of Electrical and Computer Engineering, Brigham Young University, Provo, Utah (Chapters 12 and 21)

Nachiket Kapre, Department of Computer Science, California Institute of Technology, Pasadena, California (Chapter 6)

Andreas Koch, Department of Computer Science, Embedded Systems and Applications Group, Technische Universität of Darmstadt, Darmstadt, Germany (Chapter 15)

Miriam Leeser, Department of Electrical and Computer Engineering, Northeastern University, Boston, Massachusetts (Chapter 32)

John W. Lockwood, Department of Computer Science and Engineering, Washington University in St. Louis, St. Louis, Missouri; and Department of Electrical Engineering, Stanford University, Stanford, California (Chapter 34)

Wayne Luk, Department of Computing, Imperial College, London, United Kingdom (Chapter 22)

Sharad Malik, Department of Electrical Engineering, Princeton University, Princeton, New Jersey (Chapter 29)

Yury Markovskiy, Department of Electrical Engineering and Computer Sciences, University of California–Berkeley, Berkeley, California (Chapter 9)

Margaret Martonosi, Department of Electrical Engineering, Princeton University, Princeton, New Jersey (Chapter 29)

Larry McMurchie, Synplicity Corporation, Sunnyvale, California (Chapter 17)

Brent E. Nelson, Department of Electrical and Computer Engineering, Brigham Young University, Provo, Utah (Chapters 12 and 21)

Peichen Pan, Magma Design Automation, Inc., San Jose, California (Chapter 13)

Oliver Pell, Department of Computing, Imperial College, London, United Kingdom (Chapter 22)

Stylianos Perissakis, Department of Electrical Engineering and Computer Sciences, University of California–Berkeley, Berkeley, California (Chapter 9)

Laura Pozzi, Faculty of Informatics, University of Lugano, Lugano, Switzerland (Chapter 9)

Brian C. Richards, Department of Electrical Engineering and Computer Sciences, University of California–Berkeley, Berkeley, California (Chapter 8)

Eduardo Sanchez, School of Computer and Communication Sciences, Ecole Polytechnique Fédérale de Lausanne; and Reconfigurable and Embedded Digital Systems Institute, Haute Ecole d'Ingénierie et de Gestion du Canton de Vaud, Lausanne, Switzerland (Chapter 33)

Lesley Shannon, School of Engineering Science, Simon Fraser University, Burnaby, BC, Canada (Chapter 2)

Satnam Singh, Programming Principles and Tools Group, Microsoft Research, Cambridge, United Kingdom (Chapter 16)

Greg Stitt, Department of Computer Science and Engineering, University of California–Riverside, Riverside, California (Chapter 26)

Russell Tessier, Department of Computer and Electrical Engineering, University of Massachusetts, Amherst, Massachusetts (Chapter 30)

Keith D. Underwood, Computation, Computers, Information and Mathematics Center, Sandia National Laboratories, Albuquerque, New Mexico (Chapter 31)

Andres Upegui, Logic Systems Laboratory, School of Computer and Communication Sciences, École Polytechnique Fédérale de Lausanne, Lausanne, Switzerland (Chapter 33)

Frank Vahid, Department of Computer Science and Engineering, University of California–Riverside, Riverside, California (Chapter 26)

John Wawrzynek, Department of Electrical Engineering and Computer Sciences, University of California–Berkeley, Berkeley, California (Chapters 8 and 9)

Nicholas Weaver, International Computer Science Institute, Berkeley, California (Chapter 18)

Joseph Yeh, Lincoln Laboratory, Massachusetts Institute of Technology, Lexington, Massachusetts (Chapter 9)

Peixin Zhong, Department of Electrical and Computer Engineering, Michigan State University, East Lansing, Michigan (Chapter 29)

PREFACE

In the two decades since field-programmable gate arrays (FPGAs) were introduced, they have radically changed the way digital logic is designed and deployed. By marrying the high performance of application-specific integrated circuits (ASICs) and the flexibility of microprocessors, FPGAs have made possible entirely new types of applications. This has helped FPGAs supplant both ASICs and digital signal processors (DSPs) in some traditional roles.

To make the most of this unique combination of performance and flexibility, designers need to be aware of both hardware and software issues. Thus, an FPGA user must think not only about the gates needed to perform a computation but also about the software flow that supports the design process. The goal of this book is to help designers become comfortable with these issues, and thus be able to exploit the vast opportunities possible with reconfigurable logic.

We have written *Reconfigurable Computing* as a tutorial and as a reference on the wide range of concepts that designers must understand to make the best use of FPGAs and related reconfigurable chips—including FPGA architectures, FPGA logic applications, and FPGA CAD tools—and the skills they must have for optimizing a computation. It is targeted particularly toward those who view FPGAs not just as cheap, slow ASIC gates or as a means of prototyping before the "real" hardware is created, but are interested in evaluating or embracing the substantial advantages reprogrammable devices offer over other technologies. However, readers who focus primarily on ASIC- or CPU-based implementations will learn how FPGAs can be a useful addition to their normal skill set. For some traditional designers this book may even serve as an entry point into a completely new way of handling their design problems.

Because we focus on both hardware and software systems, we expect readers to have a certain level of familiarity with each technology. On the hardware side, we assume that readers have a basic knowledge of digital logic design, including understanding concepts such as gates (including multiplexers, flip-flops, and RAM), binary number systems, and simple logic optimization. Knowledge of hardware description languages, such as Verilog or VHDL, is also helpful. We also assume that readers have basic knowledge of computer programming, including simple data structures and algorithms. In sum, this book is appropriate for most readers with a background in electrical engineering, computer science, or computer engineering. It can also be used as a text in an upper-level undergraduate or introductory graduate course within any of these disciplines.

No one book can hope to cover every possible aspect of FPGAs exhaustively. Entire books could be (and have been) written about each of the concepts that are discussed in the individual chapters here. Our goal is to provide a good working knowledge of these concepts, as well as abundant references for those who wish to dig deeper.

Reconfigurable Computing: The Theory and Practice of FPGA-Based Computation is divided into six major parts—hardware, programming, compilation/ mapping, application development, case studies, and future trends. Once the introduction has been read, the parts can be covered in any order. Alternatively, readers can pick and choose which parts they wish to cover. For example, a reader who wants to focus on CAD for FPGAs might skip hardware and application development, while a reader who is interested mostly in the use of FPGAs might focus primarily on application development.

Part V is made up of self-contained overviews of specific, important applications, which can be covered in any order or can be sprinkled throughout a course syllabus. The part introduction lists the chapters and concepts relevant to each case study and so can be used as a guide for the reader or instructor in selecting relevant examples.

One final consideration is an explanation of how this book was written. Some books are created by a single author or a set of coauthors who must stretch to cover all aspects of a given topic. Alternatively, an edited text can bring together contributors from each of the topic areas, typically by bundling together standalone research papers. Our book is a bit of a hybrid. It was constructed from an overall outline developed by the primary authors, Scott Hauck and André DeHon. The chapters on the chosen topics were then written by noted experts in these areas, and were carefully edited to ensure their integration into a cohesive whole. Our hope is that this brings the benefits of both styles of traditional texts, with the reader learning from the main experts on each topic, yet still delivering a well-integrated text.

Acknowledgments

While Scott and André handled the technical editing, this book also benefited from the careful help from the team at Elsevier/Morgan Kaufmann. Wayne Wolf first proposed the concept of this book to us. Chuck Glaser, ably assisted by Michele Cronin and Matthew Cater, was instrumental in resurrecting the project after it had languished in the concept stage for several years and in pushing it through to completion. Just as important were the efforts of the production group at Elsevier/Morgan Kaufmann who did an excellent job of copyediting, proofreading, integrating text and graphics, laying out, and all the hundreds of little details crucial to bringing a book together into a polished whole. This was especially true for a book like this, with such a large list of contributors. Specifically, Marilyn E. Rash helped drive the whole production process and was supported by Dianne Wood, Jodie Allen, and Steve Rath. Without their help there is no way this monumental task ever would have been finished. A big thank you to all.

Scott Hauck
André DeHon

INTRODUCTION

In the computer and electronics world, we are used to two different ways of performing computation: hardware and software. Computer hardware, such as application-specific integrated circuits (ASICs), provides highly optimized resources for quickly performing critical tasks, but it is permanently configured to only one application via a multimillion-dollar design and fabrication effort. Computer software provides the flexibility to change applications and perform a huge number of different tasks, but is orders of magnitude worse than ASIC implementations in terms of performance, silicon area efficiency, and power usage.

Field-programmable gate arrays (FPGAs) are truly revolutionary devices that blend the benefits of both hardware and software. They implement circuits just like hardware, providing huge power, area, and performance benefits over software, yet can be reprogrammed cheaply and easily to implement a wide range of tasks. Just like computer hardware, FPGAs implement computations spatially, simultaneously computing millions of operations in resources distributed across a silicon chip. Such systems can be hundreds of times faster than microprocessor-based designs. However, unlike in ASICs, these computations are programmed into the chip, not permanently frozen by the manufacturing process. This means that an FPGA-based system can be programmed and reprogrammed many times.

Sometimes reprogramming is merely a bug fix to correct faulty behavior, or it is used to add a new feature. Other times, it may be carried out to reconfigure a generic computation engine for a new task, or even to reconfigure a device during operation to allow a single piece of silicon to simultaneously do the work of numerous special-purpose chips.

However, merging the benefits of both hardware and software does come at a price. FPGAs provide nearly all of the benefits of software flexibility and development models, and nearly all of the benefits of hardware efficiency—but not quite. Compared to a microprocessor, these devices are typically several orders of magnitude faster and more power efficient, but creating efficient programs for them is more complex. Typically, FPGAs are useful only for operations that process large streams of data, such as signal processing, networking, and the like. Compared to ASICs, they may be 5 to 25 times worse in terms of area, delay, and performance. However, while an ASIC design may take months to years to develop and have a multimillion-dollar price tag, an FPGA design might only take days to create and cost tens to hundreds of dollars. For systems that do not require the absolute highest achievable performance or power efficiency, an FPGA's development simplicity and the ability to easily fix bugs and upgrade functionality make them a compelling design alternative. For many tasks, and particularly for beginning electronics designers, FPGAs are the ideal choice.

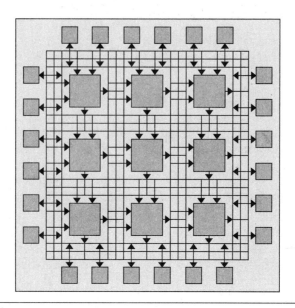

FIGURE I.1 ■ An abstract view of an FPGA; logic cells are embedded in a general routing structure.

Figure I.1 illustrates the internal workings of a field-programmable gate array, which is made up of logic blocks embedded in a general routing structure. This *array* of logic *gates* is the *G* and *A* in *FPGA*. The logic blocks contain processing elements for performing simple combinational logic, as well as flip-flops for implementing sequential logic. Because the logic units are often just simple memories, any Boolean combinational function of perhaps five or six inputs can be implemented in each logic block. The general routing structure allows arbitrary wiring, so the logical elements can be connected in the desired manner.

Because of this generality and flexibility, an FPGA can implement very complex circuits. Current devices can compute functions on the order of millions of basic gates, running at speeds in the hundreds of Megahertz. To boost speed and capacity, additional, special elements can be embedded into the array, such as large memories, multipliers, fast-carry logic for arithmetic and logic functions, and even complete microprocessors. With these predefined, fixed-logic units, which are fabricated into the silicon, FPGAs are capable of implementing complete systems in a single programmable device.

The logic and routing elements in an FPGA are controlled by programming points, which may be based on antifuse, Flash, or SRAM technology. For reconfigurable computing, SRAM-based FPGAs are the preferred option, and in fact are the primary style of FPGA devices in the electronics industry as a whole. In these devices, every routing choice and every logic function is controlled by a simple memory bit. With all of its memory bits programmed, by way of a configuration file or bitstream, an FPGA can be configured to implement the user's desired function. Thus, the configuration can be carried out quickly and without permanent fabrication steps, allowing customization at the user's electronics bench, or even in the final end product. This is why FPGAs are *field programmable*, and why they differ from mask-programmable devices, which have their functionality fixed by masks during fabrication.

Because customizing an FPGA merely involves storing values to memory locations, similarly to compiling and then loading a program onto a computer, the creation of an FPGA-based circuit is a simple process of creating a bitstream to load into the device (see Figure I.2). Although there are tools to do this from software languages, schematics, and other formats, FPGA designers typically start with an application written in a hardware description language (HDL) such as Verilog or VHDL. This abstract design is optimized to fit into the FPGA's available logic through a series of steps: Logic synthesis converts high-level logic constructs and behavioral code into logic gates, followed by technology mapping to separate the gates into groupings that best match the FPGA's logic resources. Next, placement assigns the logic groupings to specific logic blocks and routing determines the interconnect resources that will carry the user's signals. Finally, bitstream generation creates a binary file that sets all of the FPGA's programming points to configure the logic blocks and routing resources appropriately.

After a design has been compiled, we can program the FPGA to perform a specified computation simply by loading the bitstream into it. Typically either a host microprocessor/microcontroller downloads the bitstream to the device, or an EPROM programmed with the bitstream is connected to the FPGA's configuration port. Either way, the appropriate bitstream must be loaded every time the FPGA is powered up, as well as any time the user wants to change the circuitry when it is running. Once the FPGA is configured, it operates as a custom piece of digital logic.

Because of the FPGA's dual nature—combining the flexibility of software with the performance of hardware—an FPGA designer must think differently from designers who use other devices. Software developers typically write sequential programs that exploit a microprocessor's ability to rapidly step through a series of instructions. In contrast, a high-quality FPGA design requires thinking about spatial parallelism—that is, simultaneously using multiple resources spread across a chip to yield a huge amount of computation.

Hardware designers have an advantage because they already think in terms of hardware implementations; even so, the flexibility of FPGAs gives them new opportunities generally not available in ASICs and other fixed devices. Field-programmable gate array designs can be rapidly developed and deployed, and even reprogrammed in the field with new functionality. Thus, they do not demand the huge design teams and validation efforts required for ASICs. Also, the ability to change the configuration, even when the device is running, yields new opportunities, such as computations that optimize themselves to specific demands on a second-by-second basis, or even time multiplexing a very large design onto a much smaller FPGA. However, because FPGAs are noticeably slower and have lower capacity than ASICs, designers must carefully optimize their design to the target device.

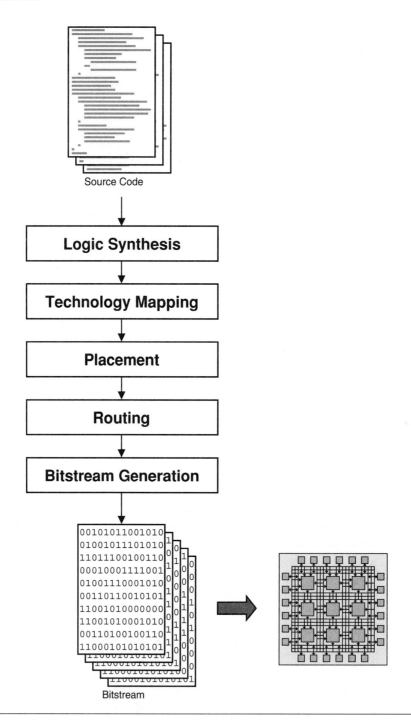

FIGURE I.2 ■ A typical FPGA mapping flow.

FPGAs are a very flexible medium, with unique opportunities and challenges. The goal of *Reconfigurable Computing: The Theory and Practice of FPGA-Based Computation* is to introduce all facets of FPGA-based systems—both positive and problematic. It is organized into six major parts:

- Part I introduces the hardware devices, covering both generic FPGAs and those specifically optimized for reconfigurable computing (Chapters 1 through 4).
- Part II focuses on programming reconfigurable computing systems, considering both their programming languages and programming models (Chapters 5 through 12).
- Part III focuses on the software mapping flow for FPGAs, including each of the basic CAD steps of Figure I.2 (Chapters 13 through 20).
- Part IV is devoted to application design, covering ways to make the most efficient use of FPGA logic (Chapters 21 through 26). This part can be viewed as a finishing school for FPGA designers because it highlights ways in which application development on an FPGA is different from both software programming and ASIC design.
- Part V is a set of case studies that show complete applications of reconfigurable logic (Chapters 27 through 35).
- Part VI contains more advanced topics, such as theoretical models and metric for reconfigurable computing, as well as defect and fault tolerance and the possible synergies between reconfigurable computing and nanotechnology (Chapters 36 through 38).

As the 38 chapters that follow will show, the challenges that FPGAs present are significant. However, the effort entailed in surmounting them is far outweighed by the unique opportunities these devices offer to the field of computing technology.

PART I

RECONFIGURABLE COMPUTING HARDWARE

At a fundamental level, reconfigurable computing is the process of best exploiting the potential of reconfigurable hardware. Although a complete system must include compilation software and high-performance applications, the best place to begin to understand reconfigurable computing is at the chip level, as it is the abilities and limitations of chips that crucially influence all of a system's steps. However, the reverse is true as well—reconfigurable devices are designed primarily as a target for the applications that will be developed, and a chip that does not efficiently support important applications, or that cannot be effectively targeted by automatic design mapping flows, will not be successful.

Reconfigurable computing has been driven largely by the development of commodity field-programmable gate arrays (FPGAs). Standard FPGAs are somewhat of a mixed blessing for this field. On the one hand, they represent a source of commodity parts, offering cheap and fast programmable silicon on some of the most advanced fabrication processes available anywhere. On the other hand, they are not optimized for reconfigurable computing for the simple reason that the vast majority of FPGA customers use them as cheap, low-quality application-specific integrated circuits (ASICs) with rapid time to market. Thus, these devices are never quite what the reconfigurable computing user might want, but they are close enough. Chapter 1 covers commercial FPGA architectures in depth, providing an overview of the underlying technology for virtually all generally available reconfigurable computing systems.

Because FPGAs are not optimized toward reconfigurable computing, there have been many attempts to build better silicon devices for this community. Chapter 2 details many of them. The focus of the new architectures might be the inclusion of larger functional blocks to speed up important computations, tight connectivity to a host processor to set up a coprocessing model, fast reconfiguration features to reduce the time to change configurations, or other concepts. However, as of now, no such system is commercially viable, largely because

- The demand for reconfigurable computing chips is much smaller than that for the FPGA community as a whole, reducing economies of scale.
- FPGA manufacturers have access to cutting-edge fabrication processes, while reconfigurable computing chips typically are one to two process generations behind.

For these reasons, a reconfigurable computing chip is at a significant cost, performance, and electrical power-consumption disadvantage compared to a commodity FPGA. Thus, the architectural advantages of a reconfigurable computing-specific device must be huge to make up for the problems of less economies of scale and fabrication process lag. It seems likely that eventually a company with a reconfigurable computing-specific chip will be successful; however, so far there appears to have been only failures.

Although programmable chips are important, most reconfigurable computing users need more. A real system generally requires large memories, input/output (I/O) ports to hook to various data streams, microprocessors or microprocessor interfaces to coordinate operation, and mechanisms for configuring and reconfiguring the device. Chapter 3 considers such complete systems, chronicling the development of reconfigurable computing boards.

Chapters 1 through 3 present a good overview of most reconfigurable systems hardware, but one topic requires special consideration: the reconfiguration subsystems within devices. In the first FPGAs, configuration data was loaded slowly and sequentially, configuring the entire chip for a given computation. For glue logic and ASIC replacement, this was sufficient because FPGAs needed to be configured only once, at power-up; however, in many situations the device may need to be reconfigured more often. In the extreme, a single computation might be broken into multiple configurations, with the FPGA loading new configurations during the normal execution of that circuit. In this case, the speed of reconfiguration is important. Chapter 4 focuses on the configuration memory subsystems within an FPGA, considering the challenges of fast reconfiguration and showing some ways to greatly improve reconfiguration speed.

CHAPTER 1

DEVICE ARCHITECTURE

Mark L. Chang
Electrical and Computer Engineering
Franklin W. Olin College of Engineering

The best race car drivers understand how their cars work. The best architects know how carpenters, bricklayers, and electricians do their jobs. And the best programmers know how the hardware they are programming does computation. Knowing how your device works, "down to the metal," is essential for efficient utilization of available resources.

In this chapter, we take a look inside the package to discover the basic hardware elements that make up a typical field-programmable gate array (FPGA). We'll talk about how computation happens in an FPGA—from the blocks that do the computation to the interconnect that shuttles data from one place to another. We'll talk about how these building blocks fit together in terms of FPGA architecture. And, of course, because programmability (as well as reprogrammability) is part of what makes an FPGA so useful, we'll spend some time on that, too. Finally, we'll take an in-depth look at the architectures of some commercially available FPGAs in Section 1.5, Case Studies.

We won't be covering many of the research architectures from universities and industry—we'll save that for later. We also won't be talking much about how you successfully program these things to make them useful parts of a computational platform. That, too, is later in the book.

What you *will* learn is what's "under the hood" of a typical commercial FPGA so that you will become more comfortable using it as a platform for solving problems and performing computations. The first step in our journey starts with how computation in an FPGA is done.

1.1 LOGIC—THE COMPUTATIONAL FABRIC

Think of your typical desktop computer. Inside the case, among other things, are storage and communication devices (hard drives and network cards), memory, and, of course, the central processing unit, or CPU, where most of the computation happens. The FPGA plays a similar role in a reconfigurable computing platform, but we're going to break it down.

In very general terms, there are only two types of resources in an FPGA: *logic* and *interconnect*. Logic is where we do things like arithmetic, 1+1=2, and logical functions, if (ready) x=1 else x=0. Interconnect is how we get data (like the results of the previous computations) from one node of computation to another. Let's focus on logic first.

1.1.1 Logic Elements

From your digital logic and computer architecture background, you know that any computation can be represented as a Boolean equation (and in some cases as a Boolean equation where inputs are dependent on past results—don't worry, FPGAs can hold state, too). In turn, any Boolean equation can be expressed as a truth table. From these humble beginnings, we can build complex structures that can do arithmetic, such as adders and multipliers, as well as decision-making structures that can evaluate conditional statements, such as the classic if-then-else. Combining these, we can describe elaborate algorithms *simply by using truth tables*.

From this basic observation of digital logic, we see the truth table as the computational heart of the FPGA. More specifically, one hardware element that can easily implement a truth table is the lookup table, or LUT. From a circuit implementation perspective, a LUT can be formed simply from an N:1 (N-to-one) multiplexer and an N-bit memory. From the perspective of our previous discussion, a LUT simply enumerates a truth table. Therefore, using LUTs gives an FPGA the generality to implement arbitrary digital logic. Figure 1.1 shows a typical N-input lookup table that we might find in today's FPGAs. In fact, almost all commercial FPGAs have settled on the LUT as their basic building block.

The LUT can compute any function of N inputs by simply programming the lookup table with the truth table of the function we want to implement. As shown in the figure, if we wanted to implement a 3-input exclusive-or (XOR) function with our 3-input LUT (often referred to as a 3-LUT), we would assign values to the lookup table memory such that the pattern of select bits chooses the correct row's "answer." Thus, every "row" would yield a result of 0 except in the four cases where the XOR of the three select lines yields 1.

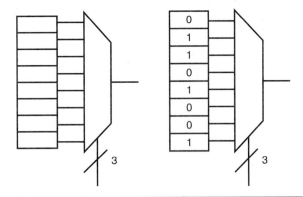

FIGURE 1.1 ▪ A 3-LUT schematic (a) and the corresponding 3-LUT symbol and truth table (b) for a logical XOR.

Of course, more complicated functions, and functions of a larger number of inputs, can be implemented by aggregating several lookup tables together. For example, one can organize a single 3-LUT into an 8×1 ROM, and if the values of the lookup table are reprogrammable, an 8×1 RAM. But the basic building block, the lookup table, remains the same.

Although the LUT has more or less been chosen as the smallest computational unit in commercially available FPGAs, the size of the lookup table in each logic block has been widely investigated [1]. On the one hand, larger lookup tables would allow for more complex logic to be performed per logic block, thus reducing the wiring delay between blocks as fewer blocks would be needed. However, the penalty paid would be slower LUTs, because of the requirement of larger multiplexers, and an increased chance of waste if not all of the functionality of the larger LUTs were to be used. On the other hand, smaller lookup tables may require a design to consume a larger number of logic blocks, thus increasing wiring delay between blocks while reducing per–logic block delay.

Current empirical studies have shown that the 4-LUT structure makes the best trade-off between area and delay for a wide range of benchmark circuits. Of course, as FPGA computing evolves into wider arenas, this result may need to be revisited. In fact, as of this writing, Xilinx has released the Virtex-5 SRAM-based FPGA with a 6-LUT architecture.

The question of the number of LUTs per logic block has also been investigated [2], with empirical evidence suggesting that grouping more than one 4-LUT into a single logic block may improve area and delay. Many current commercial FPGAs incorporate a number of 4-LUTs into each logic block to take advantage of this observation.

Investigations into both LUT size and number of LUTs per block begin to address the larger question of computational *granularity* in an FPGA. On one end of the spectrum, the rather simple structure of a small lookup table (e.g., 2-LUT) represents *fine-grained* computational capability. Toward the other end, *coarse-grained*, one can envision larger computational blocks, such as full 8-bit arithmetic logic units (ALUs), more typical of CPUs. As in the case of lookup table sizing, finer-grained blocks may be more adept at bit-level manipulations and arithmetic, but require combining several to implement larger pieces of logic. Contrast that with coarser-grained blocks, which may be more optimal for datapath-oriented computations that work with standard "word" sizes (8/16/32 bits) but are wasteful when implementing very simple logical operations. Current industry practice has been to strike a balance in granularity by using rather fine-grained 4-LUT architectures and augmenting them with coarser-grained heterogeneous elements, such as multipliers, as described in the Extended Logic Elements section later in this chapter.

Now that we have chosen the logic block, we must ask ourselves if this is sufficient to implement all of the functionality we want in our FPGA. Indeed, it is not. With just LUTs, there is no way for an FPGA to maintain any sense of state, and therefore we are prohibited from implementing any form of sequential, or state-holding, logic. To remedy this situation, we will add a simple single-bit storage element in our base logic block in the form of a D flip-flop.

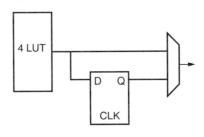

FIGURE 1.2 ■ A simple lookup table logic block.

Now our logic block looks something like Figure 1.2. The output multiplexer selects a result either from the function generated by the lookup table or from the stored bit in the D flip-flop. In reality, this logic block bears a very close resemblance to those in some commercial FPGAs.

1.1.2   Programmability

Looking at our logic block in Figure 1.2, it is a simple task to identify all the programmable points. These include the contents of the 4-LUT, the select signal for the output multiplexer, and the initial state of the D flip-flop. Most current commercial FPGAs use volatile static-RAM (SRAM) bits connected to configuration points to configure the FPGA. Thus, simply writing a value to each configuration bit sets the configuration of the entire FPGA.

In our logic block, the 4-LUT would be made up of 16 SRAM bits, one per output; the multiplexer would use a single SRAM bit; and the D flip-flop initialization value could also be held in a single SRAM bit. How these SRAM bits are initialized in the context of the rest of the FPGA will be the subject of later sections.

1.2   THE ARRAY AND INTERCONNECT

With the LUT and D flip-flop, we begin to define what is commonly known as the *logic block*, or *function block*, of an FPGA. Now that we have an understanding of how computation is performed in an FPGA at the single logic block level, we turn our focus to how these computation blocks can be tiled and connected together to form the fabric that is our FPGA.

Current popular FPGAs implement what is often called *island-style* architecture. As shown in Figure 1.3, this design has logic blocks tiled in a two-dimensional array and interconnected in some fashion. The logic blocks form the islands and "float" in a sea of interconnect.

With this array architecture, computations are performed spatially in the fabric of the FPGA. Large computations are broken into 4-LUT-sized pieces and mapped into physical logic blocks in the array. The interconnect is configured to route signals between logic blocks appropriately. With enough logic blocks, we can make our FPGAs perform any kind of computation we desire.

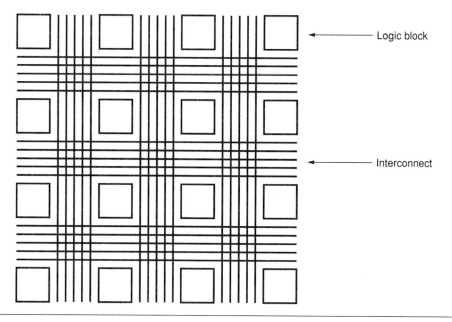

FIGURE 1.3 ■ The island-style FPGA architecture. The interconnect shown here is not representative of structures actually used.

1.2.1 Interconnect Structures

Figure 1.3 does not tell the whole story. The interconnect structure shown is not representative of any structures used in actual FPGAs, but is more of a cartoon placeholder. This section introduces the interconnect structures present in many of today's FPGAs, first by considering a small area of interconnection and then expanding out to understand the need for different styles of interconnect. We start with the simplest case of nearest-neighbor communication.

Nearest neighbor

Nearest-neighbor communication is as simple as it sounds. Looking at a 2×2 array of logic blocks in Figure 1.4, one can see that the only needs in this neighborhood are input and output connections in each direction: north, south, east, and west. This allows each logic block to communicate directly with each of its immediate neighbors.

Figure 1.4 is an example of one of the simplest routing architectures possible. While it may seem nearly degenerate, it has been used in some (now obsolete) commercial FPGAs. Of course, although this is a simple solution, this structure suffers from severe delay and connectivity issues. Imagine, instead of a 2×2 array, a 1024×1024 array. With only nearest-neighbor connectivity, the delay scales linearly with distance because the signal must go through many cells (and many switches) to reach its final destination.

From a connectivity standpoint, without the ability to bypass logic blocks in the routing structure, all routes that are more than a single hop away require

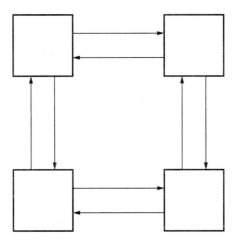

FIGURE 1.4 ▪ Nearest-neighbor connectivity.

traversing a logic block. With only one bidirectional pair in each direction, this limits the number of logic block signals that may cross. Signals that are passing through must not overlap signals that are being actively consumed and produced.

Because of these limitations, the nearest-neighbor structure is rarely used *exclusively*, but it is almost always available in current FPGAs, often augmented with some of the techniques that follow.

Segmented

As we add complexity, we begin to move away from the pure logic block architecture that we've developed thus far. Most current FPGA architectures look less like Figure 1.3 and more like Figure 1.5.

In Figure 1.5 we introduce the connection block and the switch box. Here the routing structure is more generic and meshlike. The logic block accesses nearby communication resources through the connection block, which connects logic block input and output terminals to routing resources through programmable switches, or multiplexers. The connection block (detailed in Figure 1.6) allows logic block inputs and outputs to be assigned to arbitrary horizontal and vertical tracks, increasing routing flexibility.

The switch block appears where horizontal and vertical routing tracks converge as shown in Figure 1.7. In the most general sense, it is simply a matrix of programmable switches that allow a signal on a track to connect to another track. Depending on the design of the switch block, this connection could be, for example, to turn the corner in either direction or to continue straight. The design of switch blocks is an entire area of research by itself and has produced many varied designs that exhibit varying degrees of connectivity and efficiency [3–5]. A detailed discussion of this research is beyond the scope of this book.

With this slightly modified architecture, the concept of a segmented interconnect becomes more clear. Nearest-neighbor routing can still be accomplished, albeit through a pair of connect blocks and a switch block. However, for

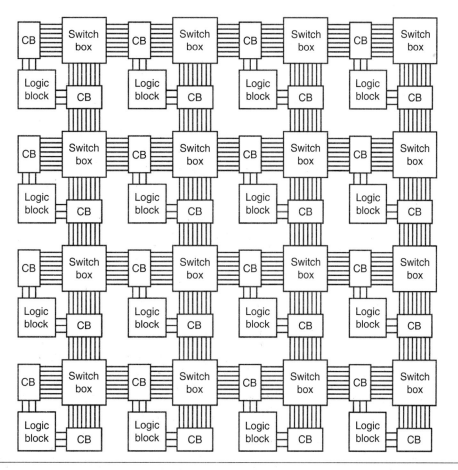

FIGURE 1.5 ■ An island-style architecture with connect blocks and switch boxes to support more complex routing structures. (The difference in relative sizes of the blocks is for visual differentiation.)

signals that need to travel longer distances, individual segments can be switched together in a switch block to connect distant logic blocks together. Think of it as a way to emulate long signal paths that can span arbitrary distances. The result is a long wire that actually comprises shorter "segments."

This interconnect architecture alone does not radically improve on the delay characteristics of the nearest-neighbor interconnect structure. However, the introduction of connection blocks and switch boxes separates the interconnect from the logic, allowing long-distance routing to be accomplished without consuming logic block resources.

To improve on our structure, we introduce longer-length wires. For instance, consider a wire that spans one logic block as being of length-1 (L1). In some segmented routing architectures, longer wires may be present to allow signals to travel greater distances more efficiently. These segments may be

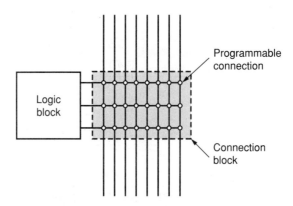

FIGURE 1.6 ▪ Detail of a connection block.

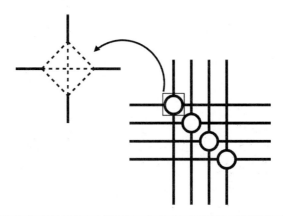

FIGURE 1.7 ▪ An example of a common switch block architecture.

length-4 (L4), length-8 (L8), and so on. The switch blocks (and erhaps more embedded switches) become points where signals can switch from shorter to longer segments. This feature allows signal delay to be less than $O(N)$ when covering a distance of N logic blocks by reducing the number of intermediate switches in the signal path.

Figure 1.8 illustrates augmenting the single-segment interconnect with two additional lengths: direct-connect between logic blocks and length-2 (L2) lines. The direct-connect lines leave general routing resources free for other uses, and L2 lines allow signals to travel longer distances for roughly the same amount of switch delay. This interconnect architecture closely matches that of the Xilinx XC4000 series of commercial FPGAs.

Hierarchical

A slightly different approach to reducing the delay of long wires uses a hierarchical approach. Consider the structure in Figure 1.9. At the lowest level of hierarchy, 2×2 arrays of logic blocks are grouped together as a single cluster.

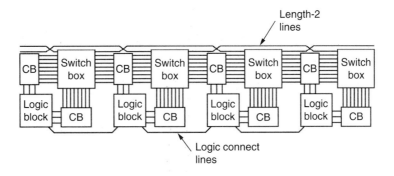

FIGURE 1.8 ■ Local (direct) connections and L2 connections augmenting a switched interconnect.

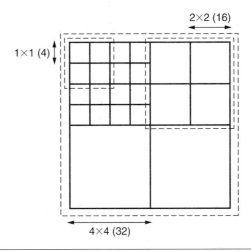

FIGURE 1.9 ■ Hierarchical routing used by long wires to connect clusters of logic blocks.

Within this block, local, nearest-neighbor routing is all that is available. In turn, a 2 × 2 cluster of these clusters is formed that encompasses 16 logic blocks. At this level of hierarchy, longer wires at the boundary of the smaller, 2 × 2 clusters, connect each cluster of four logic blocks to the other clusters in the higher-level grouping. This is repeated in higher levels of hierarchy, with larger clusters and longer wires.

The pattern of interconnect just described exploits the assumption that a well-designed (and well-placed) circuit has mostly local connections and only a limited number of connections that need to travel long distances. By providing fewer resources at the higher levels of hierarchy, this interconnect architecture remains area-efficient while preserving some long-length wires to minimize the delay of signals that need to cross large distances.

As in the segmented architecture, the connection points that connect one level of routing hierarchy to another can be anywhere in the interconnect structure. New points in the existing switch blocks may be created, or completely independent switching sites elsewhere in the interconnect can be created specifically for the purpose of moving between hierarchy levels.

1.2.2 Programmability

As with the logic blocks in a typical commercial FPGA, each switch point in the interconnect structure is programmable. Within the connection block, programmable multiplexers select which routing track each logic block's input and output terminals map to; in the switch block, the junction between vertical and horizontal routing tracks is switched through a programmable switch; and, finally, switching between routing tracks of different segment lengths or hierarchy levels is accomplished, again through programmable switches.

For all of these programmable points, as in the logic block, modern FPGAs use SRAM bits to hold the user-defined configuration values. More discussion of these configuration bits comes later in this chapter.

1.2.3 Summary

Programmable routing resources are the natural counterpart to the logic resources in an FPGA. Where the logic performs the arithmetic and logical computations, the interconnection fabric takes the results output from logic blocks and routes them as inputs to other logic blocks. By tiling logic blocks together and connecting them through a series of programmable interconnects as described here, an FPGA can implement complex digital circuits. The true nature of *spatial computing* is realized by spreading the computation across the physical area of an FPGA.

Today's commercial FPGAs typically use bits of each of these interconnect architectures to provide a smooth and flexible set of routing resources. In actual implementation, segmentation and hierarchy may not always exhibit the logarithmic scaling seen in our examples. In modern FPGAs, the silicon area consumed by interconnect greatly dominates the area dedicated to logic. Anecdotally, 90 percent of the available silicon is interconnect whereas only 10 percent is logic. With this imbalance, it is clear that interconnect architecture is increasingly important, especially from a delay perspective.

1.3 EXTENDING LOGIC

With a logic block like the one shown in Figure 1.2, tiled in a two-dimensional array with a supporting interconnect structure, we can implement any combinational and sequential logic. Our only constraint is area in terms of the number of available logic blocks. While this is comprehensive, it is far from optimal. In this section, we investigate how FPGA architects have augmented this simple design to increase performance.

1.3.1 Extended Logic Elements

Modern FPGA interconnect architectures have matured to include much more than simple nearest-neighbor connectivity to give increased performance for common applications. Likewise, the basic logic elements have been augmented to increase performance for common operations such as arithmetic functions and data storage.

Fast carry chain

One fundamental operation that the FPGA is likely to perform is an addition. From the basic logic block, it is apparent that we can implement a full-adder structure with two logic blocks given at least a 3-LUT. One logic block is configured to compute the sum, and one is configured to compute the carry. Cascading N pairs of logic blocks together will yield a simple N-bit full adder.

As you may already know from digital arithmetic, the critical path of this type of addition comes not from the computation of the sum bits but rather from the rippling of the carry signal from lower-order bits to higher-order bits (see Figure 1.10). This path starts with the low-order primary inputs, goes through the logic block, out into the interconnect, into the adjacent logic block, and so on. Delay is accumulated at every switch point along the way.

One clever way to increase speed is to shortcut the carry chain between adjacent logic blocks. We can accomplish this by providing a dedicated, minimally switched path from the output of the logic block computing the carry signal to the adjacent higher-order logic block pair. This carry chain will not need to be routed on the general interconnect network. By adding a minimal amount of overhead (wires), we dramatically speed up the addition operation.

This feature does force some constraints on the spatial layout of a multibit addition. If, for instance, the dedicated fast carry chain only goes vertically, along columns of logic blocks, all additions must be oriented along the carry chain to take advantage of this dedicated resource. Additionally, to save switching area, the dedicated carry chain may not be a bidirectional path, which further restricts the physical layout to be oriented vertically and dictates the order of the bits relative to one another. The fast carry-chain of the Xilinx XC4000E is shown in Figure 1.11. Note that the bidirectional fast carry-chain wires are arranged along the columns while the horizontal lines are unidirectional. This allows large adder structures to be placed in a zig-zag pattern in the array and still make use of the dedicated carry-chain interconnect.

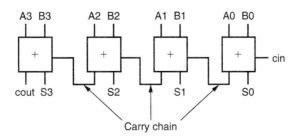

FIGURE 1.10 ■ A simple 4-bit full adder.

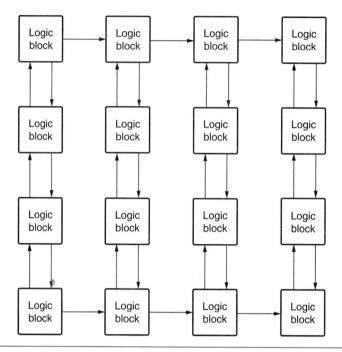

FIGURE 1.11 ▪ The Xilinx XC4000E fast carry chain. (*Source:* Adapted from [6], Figure 11, p. 6-18.)

The fast carry-chain logic is now commonplace in commercial FPGAs, with the physical design constraints at this point completely abstracted away by the tools provided by manufacturers. The success of this optimization relies on the toolset's ability to identify additions in the designer's circuit description and then use the dedicated logic. With today's tools, this kind of optimization is nearly transparent to the end user.

Multipliers

If addition is commonplace in algorithms, multiplication is certainly not rare. Several implementations are available if we wish to use general logic block resources to build our multipliers. From the area-efficient iterative shift-accumulate method to the area-consumptive array multiplier, we can use logic blocks to either compute additions or store intermediate values. While we can certainly implement a multiplication, we can do so only with a large delay penalty, or a large logic block footprint, depending on our implementation. In essence, our logic blocks *aren't very efficient* at performing a multiplication.

Instead of doing it with logic blocks, why not build *real* multipliers outside, but still connected to, the general FPGA fabric? Then, instead of inefficiently using simple LUTs to implement a multiply, we can route the values that need to be multiplied to actual multipliers implemented in silicon. How does this save space and time? Recall that FPGAs trade speed and power for configurability when compared to their ASIC (application-specific integrated circuit) counterparts. If you asked a VLSI designer to implement a fast multiplier out of transistors any way she wanted, it would take up far less silicon area, be much faster, and consume less power than we could ever manage using LUTs.

The result is that, for a small price in silicon area, we can offload the otherwise area-prohibitive multiplication onto dedicated hardware that does it much better. Of course, just like fast carry chains, multipliers impose important design considerations and physical constraints, but we add one more option for computation to our palette of operations. It is now just a matter of good design and good tools to make an efficient design. Like fast carry chains, multipliers are commonplace in modern FPGAs.

RAM

Another area that has seen some customization beyond the general FPGA fabric is in the area of on-chip data storage. While logic blocks can individually provide a few bits of storage via the lookup table structure—and, in aggregate, many bits—they are far from an efficient use of FPGA resources. Like the fast carry chain and the "hard" multiplier, FPGA architectures have given their users generous amounts of on-chip RAM that can be accessed from the general FPGA fabric.

Static RAM cells are extremely small and, when physically distributed throughout the FPGA, can be very useful for many algorithms. By grouping many static RAM cells into banks of memory, designers can implement large ROMs for extremely fast lookup table computations and constant-coefficient operations, and large RAMs for buffering, queuing, and basic scratch use—all with the convenience of a simple clocking strategy and the speed gained by avoiding off-chip communication to an external memory. Today's FPGAs provide anywhere from kilobits to megabits of dedicated RAM.

Processor blocks

Tying all these blocks together, most commercial FPGAs now offer entire dedicated processors in the FPGA, sometimes even more than one. In a general sense, FPGAs are extremely efficient at implementing raw computational pipelines, exploiting nonstandard bit widths, and providing data and functional parallelism. The inclusion of dedicated CPUs recognizes the fact that algorithm flows that are very procedural and contain a high degree of branching do not lend themselves readily to acceleration using FPGAs.

Entire CPU blocks can now be found in high-end FPGA devices. At the time of this writing, these CPUs are on the scale of 300 MHz PowerPC devices, complete, without floating-point units. They are capable of running an entire embedded operating system, and some are even able to reprogram the FPGA fabric around them.

The CPU cores are not nearly as easily exploited as the carry chains, multipliers, and on-chip RAMs, but they represent a distinct shift toward making FPGAs more "platform"-oriented. With a traditional CPU on board (and perhaps up to four), a single FPGA can serve nearly as an entire "system-on-a-chip"—the holy grail of system integrators and embedded device manufacturers. With standard programming languages and toolchains available to developers, an entire project might indeed be implemented with a single-chip solution, dramatically reducing cost and time to market.

1.3.2 Summary

In the end, modern commercially available FPGAs provide a rich variety of basic, and not so basic, computational building blocks. With much more than simple lookup tables, the task for the FPGA architect is to decide in what proportion to provide these resources and how they should be connected. The task of the hardware designer is then to fully understand the capabilities of the target FPGAs to create designs that exploit their potential.

The common thread among these extended logical elements is that they provide critical functionality that cannot be implemented very efficiently in the general FPGA fabric. As much as the technology drives FPGA architectures, applications provide a much needed push. If multiplies were rare, it wouldn't make sense to waste silicon space on a "hard" multiplier. As FPGAs become more heterogeneous in nature, and become useful computational platforms in new application domains, we can expect to see even more varied blocks in the next generation of devices.

1.4 CONFIGURATION

One of the defining features of an FPGA is its ability to act as "blank hardware" for the end user. Providing more performance than pure software implementations on general-purpose processors, and more flexibility than a fixed-function ASIC solution, relies on the FPGA being a reconfigurable device. In this section, we will discuss the different approaches and technologies used to provide programmability in an FPGA.

Each configurable element in an FPGA requires 1 bit of storage to maintain a user-defined configuration. For a simple LUT-based FPGA, these programmable locations generally include the contents of the logic block and the connectivity of the routing fabric. Configuration of the FPGA is accomplished through programming the storage bits connected to these programmable locations according to user definitions. For the lookup tables, this translates into filling it with 1s and 0s. For the routing fabric, programming enables and disables switches along wiring paths.

The configuration can be thought of as a flat binary file whose contents map, bit for bit, to the programmable bits in the FPGA. This *bitstream* is generated by the vendor-specific tools after a hardware design is finalized. While its exact format is generally not publicly known, the larger the FPGA, the larger the bitstream becomes.

Of course, there are many known methods for storing a single bit of binary information. We discuss the most popular methods used for FPGAs next.

1.4.1 SRAM

As discussed in previous sections, the most widely used method for storing configuration information in commercially available FPGAs is volatile static RAM, or SRAM. This method has been made popular because it provides fast and infinite reconfiguration in a well-known technology.

Drawbacks to SRAM come in the form of power consumption and data volatility. Compared to the other technologies described in this section, the SRAM cell is large (6–12 transistors) and dissipates significant static power because of leakage current. Another significant drawback is that SRAM does not maintain its contents without power, which means that at power-up the FPGA is not configured and must be programmed using off-chip logic and storage. This can be accomplished with a nonvolatile memory store to hold the configuration and a micro-controller to perform the programming procedure. While this may seem to be a trivial task, it adds to the component count and complexity of a design and prevents the SRAM-based FPGA from being a truly single-chip solution.

1.4.2 Flash Memory

Although less popular than SRAM, several families of devices use Flash memory to hold configuration information. Flash memory is different from SRAM in that it is nonvolatile and can only be written a finite number of times.

The nonvolatility of Flash memory means that the data written to it remains when power is removed. In contrast with SRAM-based FPGAs, the FPGA remains configured with user-defined logic even through power cycles and does not require extra storage or hardware to program at boot-up. In essence, a Flash-based FPGA can be ready immediately.

A Flash memory cell can also be made with fewer transistors compared to an SRAM cell. This design can yield lower static power consumption as there are fewer transistors to contribute to leakage current.

Drawbacks to using Flash memory to store FPGA configuration information stem from the techniques necessary to write to it. As mentioned, Flash memory has a limited write cycle lifetime and often has slower write speeds than SRAM. The number of write cycles varies by technology, but is typically hundreds of thousands to millions. Additionally, most Flash write techniques require higher voltages compared to normal circuits; they require additional off-chip circuitry or structures such as charge pumps on-chip to be able to perform a Flash write.

1.4.3 Antifuse

A third approach to achieving programmability is antifuse technology. Antifuse, as its name suggests, is a metal-based link that behaves the opposite of a fuse. The antifuse link is normally open (i.e., unconnected). A programming procedure that involves either a high-current programmer or a laser melts the link to form an electrical connection across it—in essence, creating a wire or a short-circuit between the antifuse endpoints.

Antifuse has several advantages and one clear disadvantage, which is that it is not reprogrammable. Once a link is fused, it has undergone a physical transformation that cannot be reversed. FPGAs based on this technology are generally considered one-time programmable (OTP). This severely limits their flexibility in terms of reconfigurable computing and nearly eliminates this technology for use in prototyping environments.

However, there are some distinct advantages to using antifuse in an FPGA platform. First, the antifuse link can be made very small, compared to the large multi-transistor SRAM cell, and does not require any transistors. This results in very low propagation delays across links and zero static power consumption, as there is no longer any transistor leakage current. Antifuse links are also not susceptible to high-energy radiation particles that induce errors known as single-event upsets, making them more likely candidates for space and military applications.

1.4.4 Summary

There are several well-known methods for storing user-defined configuration data in an FPGA. We have reviewed the three most common in this section. Each has its strengths and weaknesses, and all can be found in current commercial FPGA products.

Regardless of the technology used to store or convey configuration data, the idea remains the same. From vendor-specific tools, a device-specific programming bitstream is created and used either to program an SRAM or Flash memory, or to describe the pattern of antifuse links to be used. In the end, the user-defined configuration is reflected in the FPGA, bringing to reality part of the vision of reconfigurable computing.

1.5 CASE STUDIES

If you've read everything thus far, the FPGA should no longer seem like a magical computational black box. In fact, you should have a good grasp of the components that make up modern commercial FPGAs and how they are put together. In this section, we'll take it one step further and solidify the abstractions by taking a look at two real commercial architectures—the Altera Stratix and the Xilinx Virtex-II Pro—and linking the ideas introduced earlier in this chapter with concrete industry implementations.

Although these devices represent near-current technologies, having been introduced in 2002, they are not the latest generation of devices from their respective manufacturers. The reason for choosing them over more cutting-edge examples is in part due to the level of documentation available at the time of this writing. As is often the case, detailed architecture information is not available as soon as a product is released and may never be available depending on the manufacturer.

Finally, the devices discussed here are much more complex than we have space to describe. The myriad ways modern devices can be used to perform computation and the countless hardware and software features that allow you to create powerful and efficient designs are all part of a larger, more advanced dialog. So if something seems particularly interesting, we encourage you to grab a copy of the device handbook(s) and dig a little deeper.

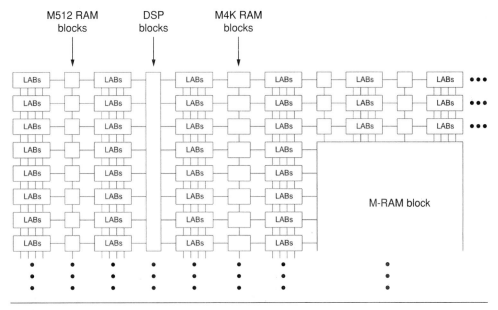

FIGURE 1.12 ■ Altera Stratix block diagram. (*Source:* Adapted from [7], Chapter 2, p. 2-2.)

1.5.1 Altera Stratix

We begin by taking a look at the Altera Stratix FPGA. Much of the information presented here is adapted from the July 2005 edition of the *Altera Stratix Device Handbook* (available online at *http://www.altera.com*).

The Stratix is an SRAM-based island-style FPGA containing many heterogeneous computational elements. The basic logical tile is the logic array block (LAB), which consists of 10 logic elements (LEs). The LABs are tiled across the device in rows and columns with a multilevel interconnect bringing together logic, memory, and other resources. Memory is provided through TriMatrix memory structures, which consist of three memory block sizes—M512, M4K, and M-RAM—each with its own unique properties. Additional computational resources are provided in DSP blocks, which can efficiently perform multiplication and accumulation. These resources are shown in a high-level block diagram in Figure 1.12.

Logic architecture

The smallest logical block in the array is the LE, shown in Figure 1.13. The general architecture of the LE is very similar to the structure that we introduced earlier—a single 4-LUT function generator and a programmable register as a state-holding element. In the Altera LE, you can see additional components to facilitate driving the interconnect (*right* side of Figure 1.12), setting and clearing the programmable register, choosing from several programmable clocks, and propagating the carry chain.

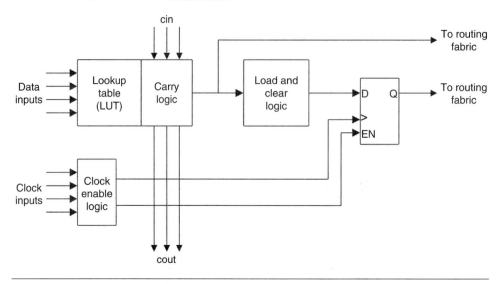

FIGURE 1.13 ▪ Simplified Altera Stratix logic element. (*Source:* Adapted from [7], Chapter 2, p. 2-5.)

Because the LEs are simple structures that may appear tens of thousands of times in a single device, Altera groups them into LABs. The LAB is then the basic structure that is tiled into an array and connected via the routing structure. Each LAB consists of 10 LEs, all LE carry chains, LAB-wide control signals, and several local interconnection lines. In the largest device, the EP1S80, there are 101 LAB rows and 91 LAB columns, yielding a total of 79,040 LEs. This is fewer than would be expected given the number of rows and columns because of the presence of the TriMatrix memory structures and DSP blocks embedded in the array.

As shown in Figure 1.14, the LAB structure is dominated, at least conceptually, by interconnect. The local interconnect allows LEs in the same LAB to send signals to one another without using the general interconnect. Neighboring LABs, RAM blocks, and DSP blocks can also drive the local interconnect through direct links. Finally, the general interconnect (both horizontal and vertical channels) can drive the local interconnect. This high degree of connectivity is the lowest level of a rich, multilevel routing fabric.

The Stratix has three types of memory blocks—M512, M4K, and M-RAM—collectively dubbed TriMatrix memory. The largest distinction between these blocks is their size and number in a given device. Generally speaking, they can be configured in a number of ways, including single-port RAM, dual-port RAM, shift-register, FIFO, and ROM table. These memories can optionally include parity bits and have registered inputs and outputs.

The M512 RAM block is nominally organized as a 32×18-bit memory; the M4K RAM as a 128×36-bit memory; and the M-RAM as a $4K \times 144$-bit memory. Additionally, each block can be configured for a variety of widths depending on the needs of the user. The different-sized memories throughout the array provide

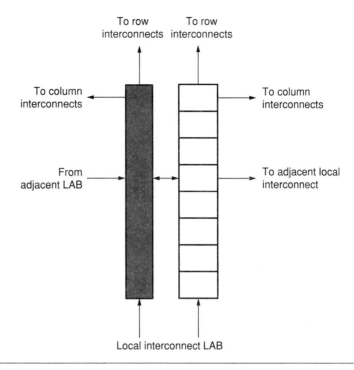

FIGURE 1.14 ■ Simplified Altera Stratix LAB structure. (*Source:* Adapted from [8], Chapter 2, p. 2-4.)

an efficient mapping of variable-sized memory designs to the device. In total, on the EP1S80 there are over 7 million memory bits available for use, divided into 767 M512 blocks, 364 M4K blocks, and 9 M-RAM blocks.

The final element of logic present in the Altera Stratix is the DSP block. Each device has two columns of DSP blocks that are designed to help implement DSP-type functions, such as finite-impulse response (FIR) and infinite-impulse response (IIR) filters and fast Fourier transforms (FFT), without using the general logic resources of the LEs. The common computational function required in these operations is often a multiplication and an accumulation. Each DSP block can be configured by the user to support a single 36×36-bit multiplication, four 18×18-bit multiplications, or eight 9×9-bit multiplications, in addition to an optional accumulation phase. In the EP1S80, there are 22 total DSP blocks.

Routing architecture

The Altera Stratix provides an interconnect system dubbed MultiTrack that connects all the elements just discussed using routing lines of varying fixed lengths. Along the row (horizontal) dimension, the routing resources include direct connections left and right between blocks (LABs, RAMs, and DSP) and interconnects of lengths 4, 8, and 24 that traverse either 4, 8, or 24 blocks left and right, respectively. A detailed depiction of an R4 interconnect at a single

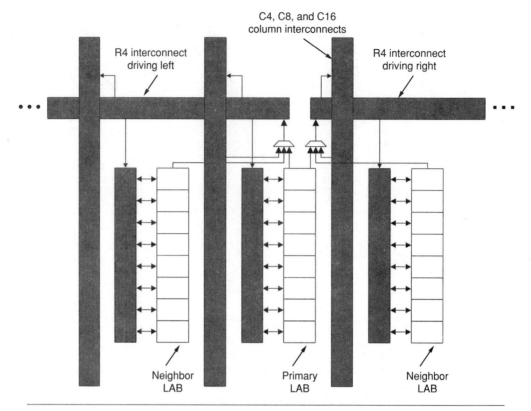

FIGURE 1.15 ▪ Simplified Altera Stratix MultiTrack interconnect. (*Source:* Adapted from [7], Chapter 2, p. 2-14.)

LAB is shown in Figure 1.15. The R4 interconnect shown spans 4 blocks, left to right. The relative sizing of blocks in the Stratix allows the R4 interconnect to span four LABs; three LABs and one M512 RAM; two LABs and one M4K RAM; or two LABs and one DSP block, in either direction.

This structure is repeated for every LAB in the row (i.e., every LAB has its own set of dedicated R4 interconnects driving left and right). R4 interconnects can drive C4 and C16 interconnects to propagate signals vertically to different rows. They can also drive R24 interconnects to efficiently travel long distances.

The R8 interconnects are identical to the R4 interconnects except that they span 8 blocks instead of 4 and only connect to R8 and C8 interconnects. By design, the R8 interconnect is faster than two R4 interconnects joined together. The R24 interconnect provides the fastest long-distance interconnection. It is similar to the R4 and R8 interconnects, but does not connect directly to the LAB local interconnects. Instead, it is connected to row and column interconnects at every fourth LAB and only communicates to LAB local interconnects through R4 and C4 routes. R24 interconnections connect with all interconnection routes except L8s.

In the column (vertical) dimension, the resources are very similar. They include LUT chain and register chain direct connections and interconnects of lengths 4, 8, and 16 that traverse 4, 8, or 16 blocks up and down, respectively. The LAB local interconnects found in row routing resources are mirrored through LUT chain and register chain interconnects. The LUT chain connects the combinatorial output of one LE to the fast input of the LE directly below it without consuming general routing resources. The register chain connects the register output of one LE to the register input of another LE to implement fast shift registers.

Finally, although this discussion was LAB-centric, all blocks connect to the MultiTrack row and column interconnect using a direct connection similar to the LAB local connection interfaces. These direct connection blocks also support fast direct communication to neighboring LABs.

1.5.2 Xilinx Virtex-II Pro

Launched and shipped right behind the Altera Stratix, the Xilinx Virtex-II Pro FPGA was the flagship product of Xilinx, Inc. for much of 2002 and 2003. A good deal of the information that is presented here is adapted from "Module 2 (Functional Description)" of the October 2005 edition of *Xilinx Virtex-II Pro™ and Virtex-II Pro X™ Platform FPGA Handbook* (available at *http://www.xilinx.com*).

The Virtex-II Pro is an SRAM-based island-style FPGA with several heterogeneous computational elements interconnected through a complex routing matrix. The basic logic tile is the configurable logic block (CLB), consisting of four *slices* and two 3-state buffers. These CLBs are tiled across the device in rows and columns with a segmented, hierarchical interconnect tying all the resources together. Dedicated memory blocks, SelectRAM+, are spread throughout the device. Additional computational resources are provided in dedicated 18×18-bit multiplier blocks.

Logic architecture

The smallest piece of logic from the perspective of the interconnect structure is the CLB. Shown in Figure 1.16, it consists of four equivalent *slices* organized into two columns of two slices each with independent carry chains and a common shift chain. Each slice connects to the general routing fabric through a configurable switch matrix and to each other in the CLB through a fast local interconnect.

Each slice comprises primarily two 4-LUT function generators, two programmable registers for state holding, and fast carry logic. The slice also contains extra multiplexers (MUXFx and MUXF5) to allow a single slice to be configured for wide logic functions of up to eight inputs. A handful of other gates provide extra functionality in the slice, including an XOR gate to complete a 2-bit full adder in a single slice, an AND gate to improve multiplier implementations in the logic fabric, and an OR gate to facilitate implementation of sum-of-products chains.

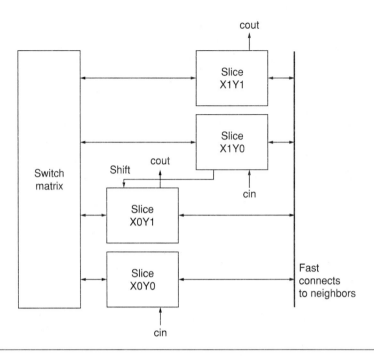

FIGURE 1.16 ▪ Xilinx Virtex-II Pro configurable CLB. (*Source:* Adapted from [8], Figure 32, p. 35.)

In the largest Virtex-II Pro device, the XC2VP100, there are 120 rows and 94 columns of CLBs. This translates into 44,096 individual slices and 88,192 4-LUTs—comparable to the largest Stratix device. In addition to these general configurable logic resources, the Virtex-II Pro provides dedicated RAM in the form of block SelectRAM+. Organized into multiple columns throughout the device, each block SelectRAM+ provides 18 Kb of independently clocked, true dual-port synchronous RAM. It supports a variety of configurations, including single- and dual-port access in various aspect ratios. In the largest device there are 444 blocks of block SelectRAM+ organized into 16 columns, yielding a total of 8,183,808 bits of memory.

Complementing the general logic resources are a number of 18×18-bit 2's complement signed multiplier blocks. Like the DSP blocks in the Altera Stratix, these multiplier structures are designed for DSP-type operations, including FIR, IIR, FFT, and others, which often require multiply-accumulate structures. As shown in Figure 1.17, each 18×18 multiplier block is closely associated with an 18Kb block SelectRAM+. The use of the multiplier/block SelectRAM+ memory, with an accumulator implemented in LUTs, allows the implementation of efficient multiply-accumulate structures. Again, in the largest device, just as with block SelectRAM+, there are 16 columns yielding a total of 444 18×18-bit multiplier blocks.

Finally, the Virtex-II Pro has one unique feature that has been carried into newer products and can also be found in competing Altera products. Embedded

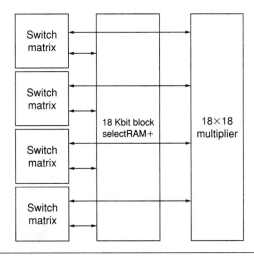

FIGURE 1.17 ■ Virtex-II Pro multiplier/block SelectRAM+ organization. (*Source:* Adapted from [8], Figure 53, p. 48.)

in the silicon of the FPGA, much like the multiplier and block SelectRAM+ structures, are up to four IBM PowerPC 405-D5 CPU cores. These cores can operate up to 300+ MHz and communicate with surrounding CLB fabric, block SelectRAM+, and general interconnect through dedicated interface logic. On-chip memory (OCM) controllers allow the PowerPC core to use block Select-RAM+ as small instruction and data memories if no off-chip memories are available.

The presence of a complete, standard microprocessor that has the ability to interface at a very low level with general FPGA resources allows unique, system-on-a-chip designs to be implemented with only a single FPGA device. For example, the CPU core can execute housekeeping tasks that are neither time-critical nor well suited to implementation in LUTs.

Routing architecture

The Xilinx Virtex-II Pro provides a segmented, hierarchical routing structure that connects to the heterogeneous fabric of elements through a switch matrix block. The routing resources (dubbed Active Interconnect) are physically located in horizontal and vertical routing channels between each switch matrix and look quite different from the Altera Stratix interconnect structures.

The routing resources available between any two adjacent switch matrix rows or columns are shown in Figure 1.18, with the switch matrix block shown in black. These resources include, from top to bottom, the following:

- 24 long lines that span the full height and width of the device.
- 120 hex lines that route to every third or sixth block away in all four directions.

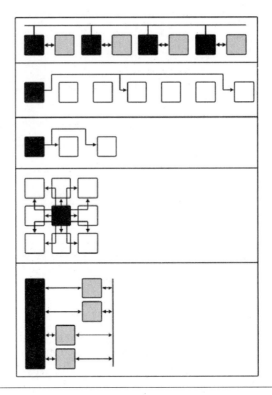

FIGURE 1.18 ■ Xilinx Virtex-II Pro routing resources. (*Source:* Adapted from [7], Figure 54, p. 45.)

- 40 double lines that route to every first or second block away in all four directions.
- 16 direct connect routes that route to all immediate neighbors.
- 8 fast-connect lines in each CLB that connect LUT inputs and outputs.

1.6   SUMMARY

This chapter presented the basic inner workings of FPGAs. We introduced the basic idea of lookup table computation, explained the need for dedicated computational blocks, and described common interconnection strategies. We learned how these devices maintain generality and programmability while providing performance through dedicated hardware blocks. We investigated a number of ways to program and maintain user-defined configuration information. Finally, we tied it all together with brief overviews of two popular commercial architectures, the Altera Stratix and the Xilinx Virtex-II Pro.

Now that we have introduced the basic technology that serves as the foundation of reconfigurable computing, we will begin to build on the FPGA to create reconfigurable devices and systems. The following chapters will discuss how to efficiently conceptualize computations spatially rather than procedurally, and the algorithms necessary to go from a user-specified design to configuration data. Finally, we'll look into some application domains that have successfully exploited the power of reconfigurable computing.

References

[1] J. Rose, A. E. Gamal, A Sangiovanni-Vincentelli. Architecture of field-programmable gate arrays. *Proceedings of the IEEE* 81(7), July 1993.

[2] P. Chow, et al. The design of an SRAM-based field-programmable gate array—Part 1: Architecture. *IEEE Transactions on VLSI Systems* 7(2), June 1999.

[3] H. Fan, J. Liu, Y. L. Wu, C. C. Cheung. On optimum switch box designs for 2-D FPGAs. *Proceedings of the 38th ACM/SIGDA Design Automation Conference (DAC)*, June 2001.

[4] ———. On optimal hyperuniversal and rearrangeable switch box designs. *IEEE Transactions on Computer-Aided Design of Integrated Circuits and Systems* 22(12), December 2003.

[5] H. Schmidt, V. Chandra. FPGA switch block layout and evaluation. *IEEE International Symposium on Field-Programmable Gate Arrays*, February 2002.

[6] Xilinx, Inc. *Xilinx XC4000E and XC4000X Series Field-Programmable Gate Arrays, Product Specification* (Version 1.6), May 1999.

[7] Altera Corp. *Altera Stratix™ Device Handbook*, July 2005.

[8] Xilinx, Inc. *Xilinx Virtex-II Pro™ and Virtex-II Pro™ Platform FPGA Handbook*, October 2005.

CHAPTER 2

RECONFIGURABLE COMPUTING ARCHITECTURES

Lesley Shannon
School of Engineering Science
Simon Fraser University

There has been considerable research into possible reconfigurable computing architectures. Alternatives range from systems constructed using standard off-the-shelf field-programmable gate arrays (FPGAs) to systems constructed using custom-designed chips. Standard FPGAs benefit from the economies of scale; however, custom chips promise a higher speed and density for custom-computing tasks. This chapter explores different design choices made for reconfigurable computing architectures and how these choices affect both operation and performance. Questions we will discuss include:

- Should the reconfigurable fabric be instantiated as a separate coprocessor or integrated as a functional unit (see Instruction augmentation subsection of Section 5.2.2)
- What is the appropriate granularity (Chapter 36) for the reconfigurable fabric?

Computing applications generally consist of both control flow and dataflow. General-purpose processors have been designed with a control plane and a data plane to support these two requirements. All reconfigurable computers have a reconfigurable fabric component that is used to implement at least a portion of the dataflow component of an application.

In this discussion, the reconfigurable fabric in its entirety will be referred to as the *reconfigurable processing fabric*, or RPF. The RPF may be statically or dynamically reconfigurable, where *a static* RPF is only configured between application runs and a *dynamic* RPF may be updated during an application's execution.

In general, the reconfigurable fabric is relatively symmetrical and can be broken down into similar tiles or cells that have the same functionality. These blocks will be referred to as *processing elements*, or PEs. Ideally, the RPF is used to implement computationally intensive kernels in an application that will achieve significant performance improvement from the pipelining and parallelism available in the RPF. The kernels are called *virtual instruction configurations*, or VICs, and we will discuss possible RPF architectures for implementing them in the following section.

2.1 RECONFIGURABLE PROCESSING FABRIC ARCHITECTURES

One of the defining characteristics of a reconfigurable computing architecture is the type of reconfigurable fabric used in the RPF. Different systems have quite different granularities. They range from fine-grained fabrics that manipulate data at the bit level similarly to commercial FPGA fabrics, to coarse-grained fabrics that manipulate groups of bits via complex functional units such as ALUs (arithmetic logic units) and multipliers. The remainder of this section will provide examples of these architectures, highlighting their advantages and disadvantages.

2.1.1 Fine-grained

Fine-grained architectures offer the benefit of allowing designers to implement bit manipulation tasks without wasting reconfigurable resources. However, for large and complex calculations, numerous fine-grained PEs are required to implement a basic computation. This results in much slower clock rates than are possible if the calculations could be mapped to fewer, coarse-grained PEs. Fine-grained architectures may also limit the number of VICs that can be concurrently stored in the RPF because of capacity limits.

Garp's nonsymmetrical RPF

The BRASS Research Group designed the Garp reconfigurable processor as an MIPS processor and on-chip cache combined with an RPF [14]. The RPF is composed of an array of PEs, as shown in Figure 2.1. Unlike most RPF architectures, not all of the PEs (drawn as rounded squares in the array) are the same. There is one control PE in each row (illustrated as the dark gray square in the leftmost column) that provides communication between the RPF and external resources. For example, the control block can be used to generate an interrupt for the main processor or to initiate memory transactions. The remaining PEs (illustrated as light gray squares) in the array are used for data processing and modeled after the configurable logic blocks (CLBs) in the Xilinx 4000 series [13]. The number of columns of PEs is fixed at 24, with the middle 16 PEs dedicated to providing memory access for the RPF. The 3 extra PEs on the left and the 4 extra PEs on the right in Figure 2.1 are used for operations such as overflow, error checking, status checking, and wider data sizes.

The number of rows in the RPF is not fixed by the architecture, but is typically at least 32 [13]. A wire network is provided between rows and columns, but the only way to switch wires is through logic blocks, as there are no connections from one wire to another. Each PE operates at the bit level on two bits of data, performing the same operation on both bits based on the assumption that a large fraction of most configurations will be used for multibit operations. By creating identical configurations for both bits, the configuration size and time can be reduced but only at the expense of flexibility [13].

The loading of configurations into an RPF with a fine-grained fabric is extremely costly relative to coarse-grained architectures. For example, each PE

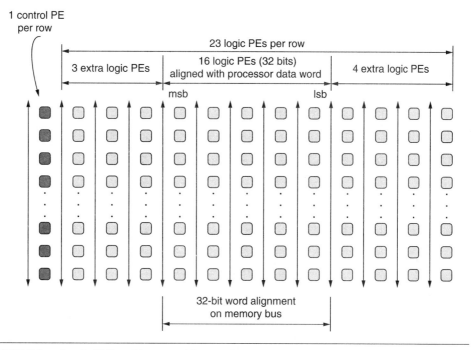

FIGURE 2.1 ■ Garp's RPF architecture. (*Source:* Adapted from [13].)

in Garp's RPF requires 64 configuration bits (8 bytes) to specify the sources of inputs, the PE's function, and any wires to be driven by the PE [13]. So, if there are only 32 rows in the RPF, 6144 bytes are required to load the configuration. While this may not seem significant given that the configuration bitstream of a commercial FPGA is on the order of megabytes (MB), it is considerable relative to a traditional CPU's context switch. For example, if the bit path to external memory from the Garp is assumed to be 128 bits, loading the full configuration takes 384 sequential memory accesses.

Garp's RPF architecture supports partial array configuration and is dynamically reconfigurable during application execution (i.e., a *dynamic* RPF). Garp's RPF architecture allows only one VIC to be stored on the RPF at a time. However, up to four different full RPF VIC configurations can be stored in the on-chip cache [13]. The VICs can then be swapped in and out of the RPF as they are needed for the application.

The loading and execution of configurations on the reconfigurable array is always under the control of a program running on the main (MIPS) processor. When the main processor initiates a computation on the RPF, an iteration counter in the RPF is set to a predetermined value. The configuration executes until the iteration counter reaches zero, at which point the RPF stalls. The MIPS-II instruction set has been extended to provide the necessary support to the RPF [13].

Originally, the user was required to write configurations in a textual language that is similar to an assembler. The user had to explicitly assign data and operations to rows and columns. This source code was fed through a program called the *configurator* to generate a representation for the configuration as a collection of bits in a text file. The rest of the user's source code could then be written in C, where the configuration was referenced using a character array initializer. This required some further assembly language programming to invoke the Garp instructions that interfaced with the reconfigurable array. Since then, considerable compiler work has been done on this architecture, and the user is now able to program the entire application in a high-level language (HLL) [14] (see Chapter 7).

2.1.2 Coarse-grained

For the purpose of this discussion, we describe coarse-grained architectures as those that use a bus interconnect and PEs that perform more than just bitwise operations, such as ALUs and multipliers. Examples include PipeRench and RaPiD (which is discussed later in this chapter).

PipeRench

The PipeRench RPF architecture [6], as shown in Figure 2.2, is an ALU-based system with a specialized reconfiguration strategy (Chapter 4). It is used as a coprocessor to a host microprocessor for most applications, although applications such as PGP and JPEG can be run on PipeRench in their entirety [8]. The architecture was designed in response to concerns that standard FPGAs do not provide reasonable forward compatibility, compilation time, or sufficient hardware to implement large kernels in a scalable and portable manner [6].

The PipeRench RPF uses pipelined configuration, first described by Goldstein et al. [6], where the reconfigurable fabric is divided into physical pipeline stages that can be reconfigured individually. Thus, the resulting RPF architecture is both partially and dynamically reconfigurable. PipeRench's compiler is able to compile the static design into a set of "virtual" stages such that each virtual stage can be mapped to any physical pipeline stage in the RPF. The complete set of virtual stages can then be mapped onto the actual number of physical stages available in the pipeline. Figure 2.3 illustrates how the virtual pipeline stages of an application can be mapped onto a PipeRench architecture with three physical pipeline stages.

A pipeline stage can be loaded during each cycle, but all cyclic dependencies must fit within a single stage. This limits the types of computations the array can support, because many computations contain cycles with multiple operations. Furthermore, since configuration of a pipeline stage can occur concurrent to execution of another pipeline stage, there is no performance degradation due to reconfiguration.

A row of PEs is used to create a physical stage of the pipeline, also called a physical stripe, as shown in Figure 2.2. The configuration word, or VIC, used to configure a physical stripe is also known as a virtual stripe. Before a physical

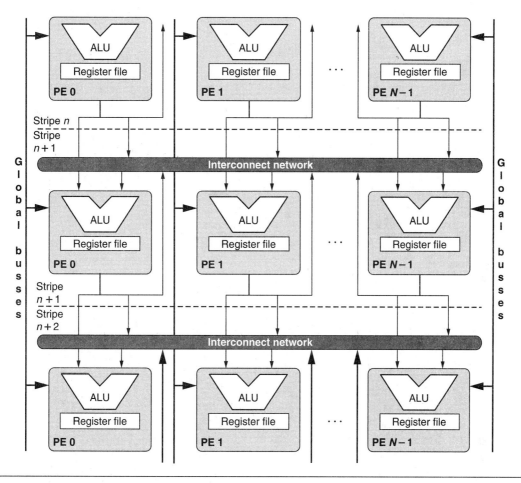

FIGURE 2.2 ■ PipeRench architecture: PEs and interconnect. (*Source:* Adapted from [6].)

stripe is configured with a new virtual stripe, the state of the present virtual stripe, if any, must be stored outside the fabric so it can be restored when the virtual stripe is returned to the fabric. The physical stripes are all identical so that any virtual stripe can be placed onto any physical stripe in the pipeline. The interconnect between adjacent stripes is a full crossbar, which enables the output of any PE in one stage to be used as the input of any PE in the adjacent stage [6].

The PEs for PipeRench are composed of an ALU and a pass register file. The pass register file is required as there can be no unregistered data transmitted over the interconnect network between stripes, creating pipelined interstripe connections. One register in the pass register file is specifically dedicated to intrastripe feedback. An 8-bit PE granularity was chosen to optimize the performance of a suite of kernels [6].

It has been suggested that reconfigurable fabric is well suited to stream-based functions (see Chapter 5, Section 5.1.2) and custom instructions [6]. Although

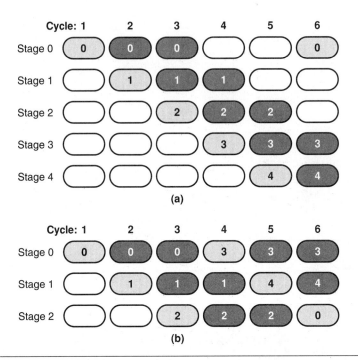

FIGURE 2.3 ■ The virtual pipeline stages of an application (a). The light gray blocks represent the configuration of a pipeline stage; the dark gray blocks represent its execution. The mapping of virtual pipeline stages to three physical pipeline stages (b). The physical pipeline stages are labeled each cycle with the virtual pipeline stage being executed. (*Source:* Adapted from [6].)

the first version of PipeRench was implemented as an attached processor, the next was designed as a coprocessor so that it would be more tightly coupled with the host processor [6]. However, the developers of PipeRench argue against making the RPF a functional unit on the host processor. They state that this could "restrict the applicability of the reconfigurable unit by disallowing state to be stored in the fabric and in some cases by disallowing direct access to memory, essentially eliminating their usefulness for stream-based processing" [6].

PipeRench uses a set of CAD tools to synthesize a stripe based on the parameters N, B, and P, where N is the number of PEs in the stripe, B is the width in bits of each PE, and P is the number of registers in a PE's pass register file. By adjusting these parameters, PipeRench's creators were able to choose a set of values that provides the best performance according to a set of benchmarks [6]. Their CAD tools are able to achieve an acceptable placement of the stripes on the architecture, but fail to achieve a reasonable interconnect routing, which has to be optimized by hand.

The user also has to describe the kernels to be executed on the PipeRench architecture using the *Dataflow Intermediate Language* (DIL), a single-assignment C-like language created for the architecture. DIL is intended for use by programmers and as an intermediate language for any high-level language compiler that targets PipeRench architectures [6]. Obviously, applications have to be recompiled, and probably even redesigned, to run on PipeRench.

2.2   RPF INTEGRATION INTO TRADITIONAL COMPUTING SYSTEMS

Whereas the RPF in a reconfigurable computing device dictates the programmable logic resources, a full reconfigurable computing system typically also has a microprocessor, memory, and possibly other structures. One defining characteristic of reconfigurable computing chips is the integration, or lack of integration, of the RPF with a host CPU.

As shown in Figure 2.4, there are multiple ways to integrate an RPF into a computing system's memory hierarchy. The different memory components of the system are drawn as shaded rectangles, where the darker shading indicates a tighter coupling of the memory component to the processor. The types of RPF integration for these computing systems are illustrated as rounded

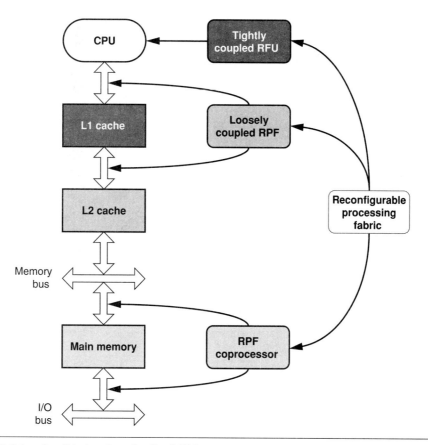

FIGURE 2.4 ■ Possible locations for the RPF in the memory hierarchy. (*Source:* Adapted from [6].)

rectangles, where the darker shading indicates a tighter coupling of the RPF to the processor. Some systems have the RPF as a separate processor [2–7]; however, most applications require a microprocessor somewhere to handle complex control. In fact, some separate reconfigurable computing platforms are actually defined to include a host processor that interfaces with the RPF [1]. Unfortunately, when the RPF is integrated into the computing system as an independent coprocessor, the limited bandwidth between CPU and reconfigurable logic can be a significant performance bottleneck.

Other systems include an RPF as an extra functional unit coupled with a more traditional processor core on one chip [8–24]. How tightly the RPF is coupled with the processor's control plane varies.

2.2.1 Independent Reconfigurable Coprocessor Architectures

Figure 2.5 illustrates a reconfigurable computing architecture with an independent RPF [1–7]. In these systems, the RPF has no direct data transfer links to the processor. Instead, all data communication takes place through main memory. The host processor, or a separate configuration controller, loads a configuration into the RPF and places operands for the VIC into the main memory. The RPF can then perform the computation and return the results back to main memory.

Since independent coprocessor RPFs are separate from the traditional processor, the integration of the RPF into existing computer systems is simplified. Unfortunately, this also limits the bandwidth and increases the latency of transmissions between the RPF and traditional processing systems. For this reason, independent coprocessor RPFs are well suited only to applications where the RPF can act independently from the processor. Examples include data-streaming applications with significant digital signal processing, such as multimedia applications like image compression and decompression, and encryption.

RaPiD

One example of an RPF coprocessor is the *Reconfigurable Pipelined Datapaths* [4], or *RaPiD*, class of architectures. RaPiD's RPF can be used as an independent

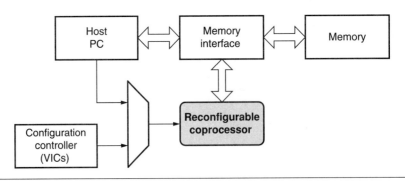

FIGURE 2.5 ■ A reconfigurable computing system with an independent reconfigurable coprocessor.

coprocessor or integrated with a traditional computing system as shown in Figure 2.5. RaPiD is designed for applications that have very repetitive pipelined computations that are typically represented as nested loops [5]. The underlying architecture is comparable to a super-scalar processor with numerous PEs and instruction generation decoupled from external memory but with no cache, no centralized register file, and no crossbar interconnect, as shown in Figure 2.6.

Memory access is controlled by the *stream generator*, which uses first-in-first-out (FIFOs), or *streams* (Chapter 5, Sections 5.1.2 and 5.2.1), to obtain and transfer data from external memory via the memory interface, as shown in Figure 2.7. Each stream has an associated address generator, and the individual address patterns are generated statically at compile time [5]. The actual reads and writes

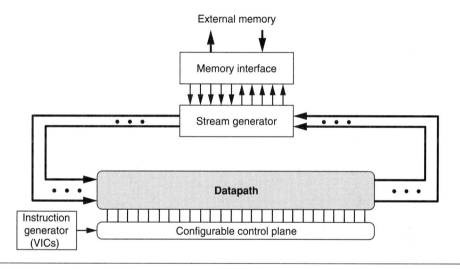

FIGURE 2.6 ■ A block diagram of the RaPiD architecture (*Source:* Adapted from [5].)

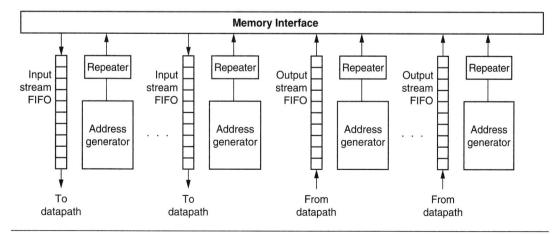

FIGURE 2.7 ■ RaPiD's stream generator. (*Source:* Adapted from [5].)

from the FIFOs are triggered by instruction bits at runtime. If the datapath's required input data is not available (i.e., the input FIFO is empty) or if the output data cannot be stored (i.e., the output FIFO is full), then the datapath will stall. Fast access to memory is therefore important to limit the number of stalls that occur. Using a fast static RAM (SRAM), combined with techniques, such as interleaving and out-of-order memory accesses, reduces the probability of having to stall the datapath [5].

The actual architecture of RaPiD's datapath is determined at fabrication time and is dictated by the class of applications that will be using the RaPiD RPF. This is done by varying the PE structure and the data width, and by choosing between fixed-point or floating-point data for numerical operations. The ability to change the PE's structure is fundamental to RaPiD architectures, with the complexity of the PE ranging from a simple general-purpose register to a multi-output booth-encoded multiplier with a configurable shifter [5].

The RaPiD datapath consists of numerous PEs, as shown in Figure 2.8. The creators of RaPiD chose to benchmark an architecture with a rather complex PE consisting of ALUs, RAMs, general-purpose registers, and a multiplier to provide reasonable performance [5]. The coarse-grained architecture was chosen because it theoretically allows simpler programming and better density [5]. Furthermore, the datapath can be dynamically reconfigured (i.e., a dynamic RPF) during the application's execution.

Instead of using a crossbar interconnect, the PEs are connected by a more area-efficient linear-segmented bus structure and bus connectors, as shown in Figure 2.8. The linear bus structure significantly reduces the control overhead—from the 95 to 98 percent required by FPGAs to 67 percent [5]. Since

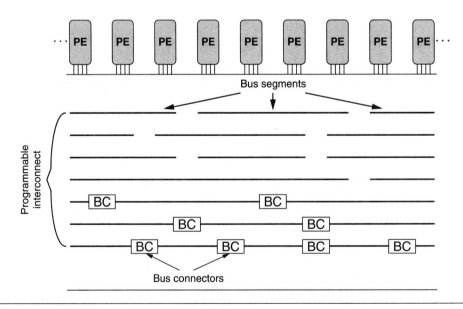

FIGURE 2.8 ▪ An overview of RaPiD's datapath. (*Source:* Adapted from [5].)

the processor performance was benchmarked for a rather complex PE, the datapath was composed of only 16 PEs [5].

Each operation performed in the datapath is determined by a set of control bits, and the outputs are a data word plus status bits. These status bits enable data-dependent control. There are both *hard* control bits and *soft* control bits. As the hard control bits are for static configuration and are field programmable via SRAM bits, they are time consuming to set. They are normally initialized at the beginning of an application and include the tristate drivers and the programmable routing bus connectors, which can also be programmed to include pipelined delays for the datapath. The soft control bits can be dynamically configured because they are generated efficiently and affect multiplexers and ALU operations. Approximately 25 percent of the control bits are soft [5].

The instruction generator generates soft control bits in the form of VICs for the configurable control plane, as shown in Figure 2.9. The RaPiD system is built around the assumption that there is regularity in the computations. In other words, most of its processing time is spent within nested loops, as opposed to initialization, boundary processing, or completion [5], so the soft control bits are generated by a small programmable controller as a short instruction word (i.e., a VIC).

The programmable controller is optimized to execute nested loop structures. For each nested loop, the user's original code is statically compiled to remove all conditionals on loop variables and expanded to generate static instructions for loops [5]. The innermost loop can then often be packed into a single VIC with a count indicating how many times the VIC should be issued. One VIC can also be used to control more than one operation in more than one pipeline stage [5]. Figure 2.10(a) shows a snippet of code that includes conditional statements (if and for). This same functionality is shown in terms of static instructions in Figure 2.10(b).

As there are often parallel loop nests in applications, the instruction generator has multiple programmable controllers running in parallel (see Figure 2.9) [5]. Although this causes synchronization concerns, the appropriate status bits exist to provide the necessary handshaking. The VICs from each controller are

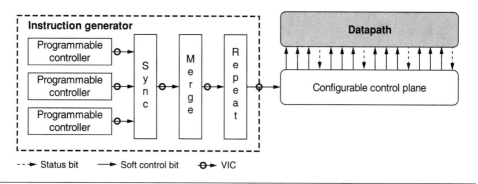

FIGURE 2.9 ■ RaPiD's instruction generator. (*Source:* Adapted from [5].)

```
for (i=0; i<10; i++)                Execute 10 times
{                                   {
    for(j=0; j<16; j++)
    {
        if(j==0)                        Execute once:           // j==0 case
            load data;                      load data;
        else if(j < 8)                  Execute six times:      // 0<j<8 case
            x = x + y;                      x = x + y;
        else                            Execute eight times:    // 7<j<16 case
            z = y * z;                      z = y * z;
    }
}                                   }
        (a)                                     (b)
```

FIGURE 2.10 ▪ Original code (a) and pseudo-code (b) for static instruction implementation of the original code.

synchronized to ensure proper coordination between the parallel loops and then merged to generate the configurable control plane for the entire datapath [5].

There are obvious benefits to RaPiD, but it is not easily programmed: The programmer must use a specialized language and compiler designed specifically for RaPiD. This allows the designer to specify the application in such a way as to obtain better hardware utilization [5]. However, this class of architecture is not well suited to highly irregular computations with complex addressing patterns, little reuse of data, or an absence of fine-grained parallelism, which do not map well to RaPiD's datapath [5].

It is interesting to note that while RaPiD was implemented as a stand-alone processor, its creators suggest that it would be better to combine RaPiD with an RISC engine on the same chip so that it would have a larger application space [5]. The RISC processor could control the overall computation flow, and RaPiD could speed up the compute-intensive kernels found in the application. The developers also suggest that better performance could be achieved if RaPiD were a special functional unit as opposed to a coprocessor, because it would be more closely bound to the general-purpose processor [5]. These are the types of architecture we will be discussing in the following section.

2.2.2 Processor + RPF Architectures

As opposed to the independent coprocessor model, other systems more tightly couple the RPF with the host processor on the same chip; in some cases, the RPF is loosely coupled with the processor as an independent functional unit. Such architectures typically allow direct access to the RPF from the processor as well as independent access to memory, as do the Garp architecture [13] and the Chameleon system [20] (to be discussed in the following section). Alternatively, we can couple the RPF more tightly with the processor. For example, in architectures, such as Chimaera [18] (to be discussed later in this chapter), the

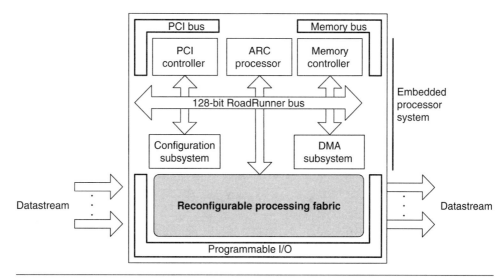

FIGURE 2.11 ■ Chameleon's RCP architecture. (*Source:* Adapted from a figure obtained off of Chameleon System's home page, which is no longer available.)

RPF is incorporated as a reconfigurable functional unit (RFU) (see Instruction augmentation subsection in Section 5.2.2) within the processor itself.

Loosely coupled RPF and processor architecture
The commercial Reconfigurable Communications Processor (RCP) was created by Chameleon Systems Inc. [20]. It combined an embedded processor subsystem with an RPF via a proprietary shared bus architecture, known as the RoadRunner bus (Figure 2.11). The RPF had direct access to the processor as well as direct memory access (DMA). The reconfigurable fabric also had a programmable I/O interface so that users could process off-chip I/O independent of the rest of the embedded on-chip processing system. This provided more flexibility for the RPF than in typical reconfigurable computing architectures, where the RPF generally had access only to the processor and memory.

The Chameleon architecture was able to provide improved price/performance relative to the highest-performing DSPs of its time, but its RCP consumed more power because of the RPF. After 2002, there was little mention of Chameleon or its RCP. Conceptually, the product was an interesting idea, but it failed to corner a product niche during the electronics market downturn.

Tightly coupled RPF and processor
Figure 2.12 illustrates a traditional processor's datapath architecture with the RPF integrated as an RFU. Such systems tightly couple the RFU to the central processing unit's (CPU) datapath similarly to the technology of traditional CPU functional units (FUs), such as the ALU, the multiplier, and the FPU. In some cases, these architectures only provide RFU access to input data from the register file in the same way as the traditional CPU FUs (Chimaera [18], PRISC

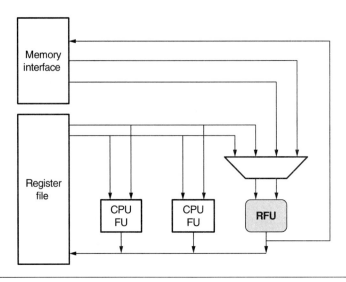

FIGURE 2.12 ▪ The datapath of the processor + RFU architecture.

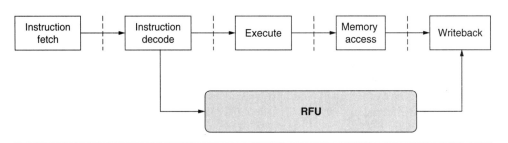

FIGURE 2.13 ▪ An example of a pipeline of a processor with an RFU. (*Source:* Adapted from [16].)

[11], etc.). Other architectures allow the RFU to access data stored in the local cache/memory directly (e.g., OneChip [16]). Many of them can have multiple VICs instantiated in the RFU at once, enabling designers to accelerate multiple software instructions at the same time.

For reconfigurable computing architectures in which the RFU is tightly coupled with the processing core, the processor pipeline must be updated as shown in Figure 2.13. VICs in the RFU typically run during the *execute* stage (and possibly the *memory* stage) of the pipeline. Some of these processors are capable of running VICs in parallel with instructions that use more traditional processor resources, such as the ALU or FPU, and even support out-of-order execution (OneChip [16], Chimaera [18]).

Chimaera
The Chimaera architecture [18], shown in Figure 2.14, was developed at Northwestern University. Its developers created a C compiler that could create

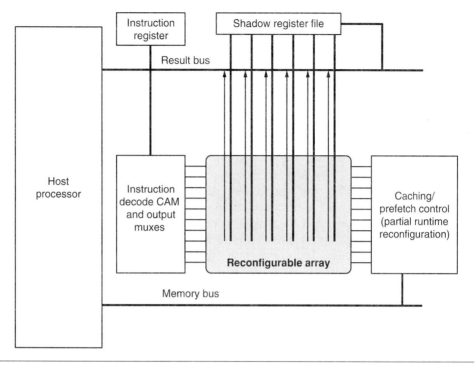

FIGURE 2.14 ■ Overview of the Chimaera architecture. (*Source:* Adapted from [18].)

specialized instructions for their RFU, known as RFUOPs (VICs for the purpose of our discussion) [19]. These custom instructions are created on a per application basis and have direct access to the processor's register file. Furthermore, commonly used VICs can be cached for easy reloading so that the processor does not have to stall while the RFU is configured [19].

The RFU is structured as a reconfigurable array (RA) of PEs, where any VIC occupies an integer number of rows. Influenced by the Triptych FPGA [18], the Altera Flex 8000 series, and the PRISC architecture [11], the array structure is FPGA-like to support computationally intensive kernels. Each PE in a row operates on 1 bit, with each row containing the same number of PEs as the size of the processor's memory word. The RFU can be partially configured so that multiple VICs can be cached in it at any given time. When an instruction is to be written to the RFU and there are no empty rows, the VIC that is overwritten is chosen such that configurations of the RFU will be minimized [19].

Another benefit of the Chimaera architecture is that it allows for speculative execution of VICs. Any VIC that is loaded in the RFU speculatively executes each cycle. If one of them is actually executed, the resulting value is stored at the writeback stage; otherwise, it is ignored and discarded. The RFU also supports multi-input operations, so that any VIC occupying one row will execute in a single clock cycle and with the appropriate data dependencies. Assuming that data dependencies are not an issue, multi-cycle operations can execute without pipelining stalls [19].

When a VIC is detected at the decode stage of the pipeline, a check is made of the RFU to determine if it is already loaded. If it is not loaded, a check is made of the VIC cache. If the VIC instruction is not in either of these locations, it must be loaded from memory to reconfigure the necessary rows of the RFU. In that case the microprocessor will stall. This is time consuming because, although the precise configuration timing requirements are not specified, the objective is to minimize the number of configurations of the RFU performed from memory [19].

Chimaera has the benefit of a high-level design language for the user. It also has the same style interface as that of a normal stand-alone processor, which means that the architecture is able to provide extra functionality to improve performance, without complicating the design process. The idea is to treat the RFU as a cache for instructions as opposed to logic and then to assume that the majority of the functionality required for the algorithm will be supplied by the microprocessor [18]. In this way, the RFU can be used to accelerate the program's computationally intensive kernels. Integrating the RPF as an RFU within the processor has increased the bandwidth for communication between the two [18]. However, because the RFU cannot access memory directly, it is overly dependent on the host processor to fetch and store operands.

2.3 SUMMARY AND FUTURE WORK

In this chapter, we discussed key characteristics of reconfigurable computing architectures and their tradeoffs; specifically: (1) how the RPF should be coupled into the system, and (2) what the nature of the RPF should be. Fine-grained fabrics allow users to perform bitwise operations without wasting reconfigurable resources, whereas basic multibit computations can be mapped to fewer coarse-grained modules and run at a faster clock rate.

The coupling of the RPF with a traditional processor affects both its ability to do independent computation and the rate at which data can be transferred from the processor itself. Independent reconfigurable coprocessors are easily added to a traditional processing system and can operate independently from the processor. However, this loose coupling increases the latency and decreases the communication bandwidth between the processor and the RPF. In contrast, tightly coupling the RPF to the processor facilitates communication and data transfers, but limits the RFP's independence. In tightly coupled architectures, the RPF is often part of the processor's pipeline, potentially stalling execution until the VIC is completed. Loosely coupled RPFs try to offer the best of both worlds: sufficient independence from the main processor to prevent pipeline stalls combined with reasonable bandwidth for inter-processor/RPF communications.

One important challenge in developing reconfigurable computing architectures is to create CAD tools and programming environments that enable designers to use HLLS. This would allow designers to abstract the low-level hardware of the RPF and to simplify programming the architecture, while still achieving speedup over a traditional processor. Another significant challenge is how to evaluate reconfigurable computing architectures. There is no equivalent to the Spec Benchmark [25] set for such evaluation. Furthermore, as these architectures may have different programming models or limited compiler support, designers are not easily able to run the same benchmark on multiple architectures for a standard comparison.

That Chameleon, and many other reconfigurable computing startup companies in similar market niches, was forced to close its doors during the electronic market downturn in the early 2000s illustrates an interesting aspect of reconfigurable computing as a whole. Even though, theoretically, special-purpose reconfigurable computing chips are a compelling technology, to date they have failed to achieve commercial success and there have been numerous failures. Many popular arguments have been used to justify this failure—they are too power-hungry; an effective high-level programming environment has not been developed; no one has identified a "killer" application to justify the design cost of using them—but no definitive answer exists. As it becomes increasingly difficult to improve the performance of traditional processor architectures, the possibility that reconfigurable computing architectures may yet find their place in the world of commercial success increases.

Despite the lack of significant market success to date, reconfigurable computing is still an area of significant ongoing research and commercial interest. For example, Rapport Inc.'s Kilocore design is a commercial derivative of the PipeRench architecture. As of 2007, Rapport was offering 256 PE components organized as 16 stripes, each composed of 16 8-bit PEs, and it has plans to expand its offerings to components containing thousands of PEs.

References

[1] J. M. Arnold. The Splash 2 software environment. *Proceedings of the IEEE Symposium on Field-Programmable Custom Computing Machines*, April 1993.

[2] M. Wazlowski, L. Agarwal, T. Lee, A. Smith, E. Lam, P. Athanas, H. Silverman, S. Ghosh. PRISM-II compiler and architecture. *Proceedings of the IEEE Symposium on Field-Programmable Custom Computing Machines*, April 1993.

[3] M. J. Wirthlin, B. L. Hutchings. A dynamic instruction set computer. *Proceedings of the IEEE Symposium on Field-Programmable Custom Computing Machines*, April 1995.

[4] C. Ebeling, D. C. Cronquist, P. Franklin. RaPiD: Reconfigurable Pipelined Datapath. *Proceedings of the Sixth International Workshop on Field-Programmable Logic and Applications*, Springer-Verlag, September 1996.

[5] D. Cronquist, P. Franklin, C. Fisher, M. Figueroa, C. Ebeling. Architecture design of reconfigurable pipelined datapaths. *Proceedings of the 20th Anniversary Conference on Advanced Research in VLSI*, March 1999.

[6] S. Goldstein, H. Schmit, M. Moe, M. Budiu, S. Cadambi, R. R. Taylor, R. Laufer. PipeRench: A coprocessor for streaming multimedia acceleration. *Proceedings of the 26th International Symposium on Computer Architecture*, May 1999.

[7] H. Schmit. Incremental reconfiguration for pipelined applications. *Proceedings of the IEEE Symposium on Field-Programmable Custom Computing Machines*, April 1997.

[8] Y. Chou, P. Pillai, H. Schmit, J. Shen. PipeRench implementation of the instruction path coprocessor. *Proceedings of the 33rd International Symposium on Microarchitecture*, December 2000.

[9] M. J. Wirthlin, B. L. Hutchings, K. L. Gilson. The nano processor: A low resource reconfigurable processor. *Proceedings of the IEEE Symposium on Field-Programmable Custom Computing Machines*, April 1994.

[10] M. Budiu. Application-specific hardware: Computing without CPUs. *Fourth CMU Symposium on Computer Systems*, October 2001.

[11] R. Razdan, M. Smith. A high-performance microarchitecture with hardware-programmable functional units. *Proceedings of the 27th Annual IEEE/ACM International Symposium on Microarchitecture*, November 1994.

[12] B. Kastrup, A. Bink, J. Hoogerbrugge. ConCISe: A compiler-driven CPLD-based instruction set accelerator. *Proceedings of the IEEE Symposium on Field-Programmable Custom Computing Machines*, April 1999.

[13] J. Hauser, J. Wawrzynek. Garp: A MIPS processor with a reconfigurable coprocessor. *Proceedings of the IEEE Symposium on Field-Programmable Custom Computing Machines*, April 1997.

[14] T. J. Callahan, J. R. Hauser, J. Wawrzynek. The Garp architecture and C compiler. *Computer*, April 2000.

[15] R. D. Wittig, P. Chow. OneChip: An FPGA processor with reconfigurable logic. *Proceedings of the IEEE Symposium on Field-Programmable Custom Computing Machines*, March 1996.

[16] J. E. Carrillo, E. P. Chow. The effect of reconfigurable units in superscalar processors. *Proceedings of the Ninth ACM International Symposium on Field-Programmable Gate Arrays*, February 2001.

[17] C. R. Rupp, M. Landguth, T. Garverick, E. Gomersall, H. Holt, J. A. Arnold, M. Gokhale. The NAPA adaptive processing architecture. *Proceedings of the IEEE Symposium on Field-Programmable Custom Computing Machines*, April 1998.

[18] S. Hauck, T. W. Fry, M. Hosier, J. P. Kao. The Chimaera reconfigurable functional unit. *Proceedings of the IEEE Symposium on Field-Programmable Custom Computing Machines*, April 1997.

[19] Z. A. Ye, A. Moshovos, S. Hauck, P. Banerjee. CHIMAERA: A high-performance architecture with a tightly coupled reconfigurable functional unit. *Proceedings of the 27th International Symposium on Computer Architecture*, June 2000.

[20] D. Wilson. Chameleon takes on FPGAs, ASICs. *Electronic Business Asia, EDN Online Magazine* (*http://www.edn.com/article/CA50551.html?partner=enews*), October 2000.

[21] P. Graham, B. Nelson. Reconfigurable processors for high-performance, embedded digital signal processing. *Proceedings of the Ninth International Workshop on Field-Programmable Logic and Applications*, August 1999.

[22] B. Salefski, L. Caglar. Reconfigurable computing in wireless. *Proceedings of the Design Automation Conference*, June 2001.

[23] T. Bijlsma, P. T. Wolkotte, G. J. M. Smit. An optimal architecture for a DDC. *Proceedings of the 20th IEEE International Parallel and Distributed Processing Symposium (IPDPS'06)—12th Reconfigurable Architecture Workshop (RAW 2006)*, April 2006.

[24] A. A. Chien, J. H. Byun. Safe and protected execution for the Morph/AMRM reconfigurable processor. *Proceedings of the IEEE Symposium on Field-Programmable Custom Computing Machines*, April 1999.

[25] Standard Performance Evaluation Corp. Spec Benchmarks (*http://www.spec.org*).

CHAPTER 3

RECONFIGURABLE COMPUTING SYSTEMS

Steven A. Guccione

Cmpware, Inc.

Like most technologies, reconfigurable computing systems are built on a variety of existing technologies and techniques. It is always difficult to pinpoint the exact moment a new area of technology comes into existence or even to pinpoint which is the first system in a new class of machines. Popular scientific history often gives simple accounts of individuals and projects that represent a turning point for a particular technology, but in reality the story is usually more complicated. A number of individuals may arrive at similar conclusions, at very nearly the same time, and the details of their research are nearly always different. It is in the investigation of these details that a better understanding of the technology, and its development, can be reached.

While it is satisfying to say that Thomas Edison invented the lightbulb in 1879, the real story is much more complex and much more interesting. Such is the case with reconfigurable computing hardware systems, as it is with most technologies. In the short time that these systems have been in existence, a relatively large number of them, developed by many highly trained and talented individuals from diverse fields, have evolved very quickly. In approximately a decade the number of implemented reconfigurable systems went from a small handful to hundreds.

The large number of exotic high-performance systems designed and built over a very short time makes this area particularly difficult to document, but there is also a problem specific to them. Much of the work was done inside various government agencies, particularly in the United States, and was never published. In these cases, all that can be relied on is currently available records and publications.

3.1 EARLY SYSTEMS

The generally agreed on criterion for a reconfigurable computing system is that it be built from reconfigurable computing devices such as field-programmable gate arrays (FPGAs) or FPGA-like devices. In general, these devices must be reprogrammable and permit hardwarelike levels of performance, if not hardwarelike structures. Moreover, they should permit orders of magnitude speedup over traditional microprocessors for similar clock speeds, silicon

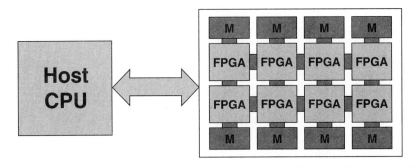

FIGURE 3.1 ▪ The traditional processor/coprocessor arrangement for reconfigurable computing hardware.

area, and technology. Most significantly, however, the system must be reprogrammable and able to perform with a variety of applications. Systems that use a fixed hardware design, even if they use reconfigurable computing elements, are viewed more as using this design in place of traditional hardware for cost savings or convenience. It is in the ability to use reconfigurable devices for more general-purpose computing that makes them "reconfigurable."

Reconfigurable systems are likewise distinguished from other cellular multiprocessor systems. Array processors, in particular Single Instruction Multiple Data Processors (SIMDs), are considered architecturally distinct from reconfigurable machines, in spite of many similarities. This distinction arises primarily from the programming techniques. Array processors tend to have either a shared or dedicated instruction sequencer and take standard instruction-style programming code. Reconfigurable machines tend to be programmed spatially, with different physical regions of the device being configured at different times. This necessarily means that they will be slower to reprogram than cellular multiprocessor systems but should be more flexible and achieve higher performance for a given silicon area.

One of the earliest acknowledged reconfigurable computing machines, although it is frequently referenced under "distributed computing," is the Fixed-Plus-Variable (F+V) computer developed by Estrin and his colleagues at the University of California at Los Angeles in the mid-1960s [17–20]. The F+V consisted of a standard processor unit that controlled many other "variable" units. It had several limitations, including the need to manually change wiring as part of the reconfiguration process, but it did offer relatively mature software tools for its time. Generally because of its use of reconfigurable computing concepts, the F+V system is acknowledged to be the forerunner of modern reconfigurable computing architectures.

After the F+V, there was a gap of nearly two decades before more modern reconfigurable computing systems began to be explored. The rise of the modern era began in the mid-1980s, when commercially available FPGA devices from companies such as Xilinx and Altera as well as several smaller companies became widely available.

These devices were generally based around small lookup tables (LUTs) and a programmable interconnection network. The LUTs were typically 8- or 16-bit memories configured to implement arbitrary logic functions, taking their inputs from and sending their outputs to a programmable interconnection network. While this network could not provide arbitrary interconnections, software tools were usually able to produce operational digital circuits for a wide range of popular designs.

Even by 1990, however, the largest FPGA devices supported designs on the order of 10K logic gates. This is a very small number and barely suitable for a parallel multiplier circuit. Even worse, the FPGAs were in competition with modern microprocessors, which were doubling in performance every 18 months and providing a simpler programming model, more mature tools, and a larger base of experienced users. For these reasons, the early work in reconfigurable systems necessarily concentrated on two areas, often simultaneously:

- The systems would have to use relatively large numbers of FPGAs, sometimes hundreds, to achieve sufficient computing power to be of use when compared to microprocessor-based systems.
- They would attack problems that were naturally ill suited to modern microprocessors, including bit-oriented algorithms that did not map efficiently to word-oriented microprocessors and highly structured and repetitive algorithms such as graphics that mapped well to the hardwarelike structures of reconfigurable systems.

The 1990s also marked the beginning of an explosive growth in circuit density following Moore's Law, with a doubling in FPGA density approximately every 18 months. As the density increased, the typical application went from simple interface or "glue" logic circuits to more complex designs, eventually supporting large custom coprocessors, typically for digital signal processing (DSP) or other data-intensive applications. With large, high-quality, commercially available FPGA devices now in use, and with the ongoing rapid increase in density, FPGA-based reconfigurable computing machines quickly became widely available.

3.2 PAM, VCC, AND SPLASH

In the late 1980s, PAM, VCC, and Splash—three significant general-purpose systems using multiple FPGAs—were designed and built. They were similar in that they used multiple FPGAs, communicated to a host computer across a standard system bus, and were aimed squarely at reconfigurable computing.

3.2.1 PAM

The Programmable Active Memories (PAM) project at Digital Equipment Corporation (DEC) initially used four Xilinx XC3000-series FPGAs as shown in Figure 3.2 [8]. The original Perle-0 board contained 25 Xilinx XC3090 devices

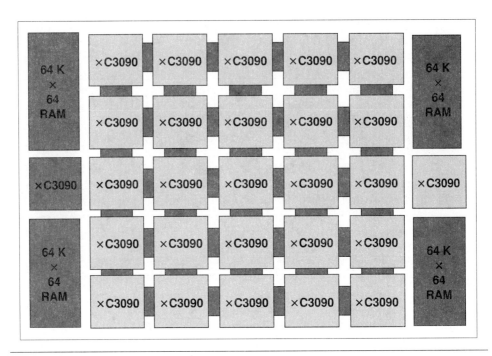

FIGURE 3.2 ▪ Digital Equipment Corporation's PAM Perle-0.

in a 5×5 array, attached to which were four independent banks of fast static RAM (SRAM), arranged as 64K $\times$ 64 bits, which were controlled by an additional two XC3090 FPGA devices. This wide and fast memory provided the FPGA array with high bandwidth. The Perle-0 was quickly upgraded to the more recent XC4000 series. As the size of the available XC4000-series devices grew, the PAM family used a smaller array of FPGA devices, eventually settling on 2×2.

Based at the DEC research lab, the PAM project ran for over a decade and continued in spite of the acquisition of DEC by Compaq and then the later acquisition of Compaq by Hewlett-Packard. PAM, in its various versions, plugged into the standard PCI bus in a PC or workstation and was marked by a relatively large number of interesting applications as well as some groundbreaking work in software tools. It was made available commercially and became a popular research platform.

3.2.2 Virtual Computer

The Virtual Computer from the Virtual Computer Corporation (VCC) was perhaps the first commercially available reconfigurable computing platform. Its original version was an array of Xilinx XC4010 devices and I-Cube programmable interconnect devices in a checkerboard pattern, with the I-Cube devices essentially serving as a crossbar switch as shown in Figure 3.3 [11]. The topology of the interconnection for these large FPGA arrays was an important issue at this time: With a logic density of approximately 10K gates and input/output (I/O) pins on the order of 200, a major concern was communication across FPGAs. The I-Cube

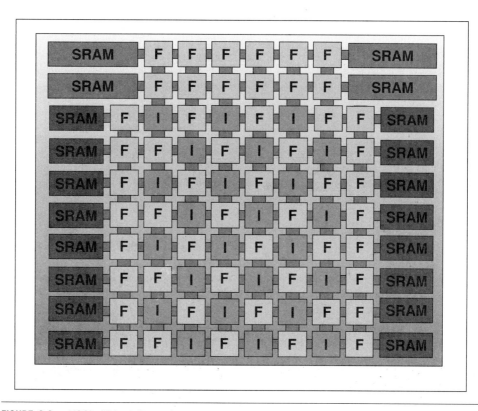

FIGURE 3.3 ■ VCC's Virtual Computer.

devices were perceived as providing more flexibility, although each switch had to be programmed, which increased the design complexity.

The first Virtual Computer used an 8×8 array of alternating FPGA and I-Cube devices. The exception was on the left and right sides of the array, which exclusively used FPGAs, which consumed 40 Xilinx XC4010 FPGAs and 24 I-Cubes. Along the left and right sides were 16 banks of independent $16 \times 8K$ dual-ported SRAM, and attached to the top row were 4 more banks of standard single-ported $256K \times 32$ bits SRAM controlled by an additional 12 Xilinx XC4010 FPGAs. While this system was large and relatively expensive, and had limited software support, VCC went on to offer several families of reconfigurable systems over the next decade and a half.

3.2.3 Splash

The Splash system, from the Supercomputer Research Center (SRC) at the Institute for Defense Analysis, was perhaps the largest and most heavily used of these early systems [22, 23, 27]. Splash was a linear array consisting of XC3000-series Xilinx devices interfacing to a host system via a PCI bus. Multiple boards could be hosted in a single system, and multiple systems could be connected together. Although the Splash system was primarily built and used by the Department of

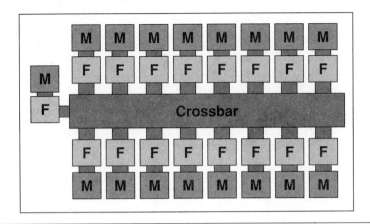

FIGURE 3.4 ▪ SRC's Splash 2.

Defense, a large amount of information on it was made available. A Splash 2 system quickly followed and was made commercially available from Annapolis Microsystems [30].

The Splash 2 board consisted of two rows of eight Xilinx XC4010 devices, each with a small local memory attached as shown in Figure 3.4. These 16 FPGA/memory pairs were connected to a crossbar switch, with another dedicated FPGA/memory pair used as a controller for the rest of the system. Much of the work using Splash concentrated on defense applications such as cryptography and pattern matching, but the associated tools effort was also notable, particularly some of the earliest high-level language (HLL) to hardware description language (HDL) translation software targeting reconfigurable machines [4]. Specifically, the data parallel C compiler and its debug tools and libraries provided reconfigurable systems with a new level of software support.

PAM, VCC, and Splash represent the early large-scale reconfigurable computing systems that emerged in the late 1980s. They each had a relatively long lifetime and were upgraded with new FPGAs as denser versions became available. Also of interest is the origin of each system. One was primarily a military effort (Splash), another emerged from a corporate research lab (PAM), and the third was from a small commercial company (Virtual Computer). It was this sort of widespread appeal that was to characterize the rapid expansion of reconfigurable computing systems during the 1990s.

3.3 SMALL-SCALE RECONFIGURABLE SYSTEMS

PAM, VCC, and Splash were large and relatively expensive machines. Because a single high-density FPGA device could cost several thousand dollars, their circuit boards were perhaps some of the most expensive built at that time. Around 1990, a cost of approximately $1 per reconfigurable logic gate in a reconfigurable system was not unusual. Of course, this cost dropped rapidly as FPGAs of higher densities and lower prices became available.

Because of their cost, the use of FPGAs was somewhat limited, and none of these systems achieved widespread success as consumer products. While work on them was ongoing, smaller-scale FPGAs were beginning to appear that would have a major impact on the direction of the field, especially because their rapidly increasing density meant that the large multichip systems of yesterday would very soon fit within a single device.

3.3.1 PRISM

One of the smaller-scale experiments with reconfigurable computing was PRISM, developed at Brown University [5]. This was an unusual project in that it used a single small FPGA as a coprocessor in a larger distributed system. This distributed processor/coprocessor arrangement was unique for its time and would reappear many years later in more mainstream reconfigurable supercomputers. It permitted small but often complex calculations to be offloaded from the central processing unit (CPU) to the reconfigurable coprocessor. The circuits implemented in the coprocessor may not have been large, but the tighter coupling to the processor gave this architecture an advantage in places where larger and more expensive arrays would not have been appropriate.

Also of note are PRISM's software development tools. Its compiler technology used was advanced for its era and was one of the earlier experiments in high-level language programming of reconfigurable systems. In particular, it addressed a more fine-grained form of coprocessing where the host CPU and the reconfigurable coprocessor shared the workload. Larger systems tended to have vastly more powerful reconfigurable units and often used the host only for simple control, input/output, and display. The workload was seldom shared with the host CPU in any meaningful way in these larger systems.

3.3.2 CAL and XC6200

Perhaps the most interesting project of this era came from Algotronix, a small Scottish company with connections to the University of Edinburgh [28], which created its own FPGA exclusively targeted at reconfigurable computing [1]. The Configurable Array Logic (CAL) featured very simple logic cells compared to other commercial FPGAs. What was unique about CAL was that each cell could be individually addressed and reconfigured dynamically—something that no other FPGA device at the time could manage. CAL also featured a fairly standard bus interface that permitted it to be easily used with a microprocessor in a coprocessor arrangement. Algotronix also offered some fairly traditional graphical tools to program CAL, as well as a small board containing multiple CAL devices.

While CAL was unique and influential, it was not until the acquisition of Algotronix by Xilinx in the early 1990s that its ideas would become more widespread. Xilinx began development of a second-generation CAL device it called the XC6200 [12]. Many of its features were the same as those of the earlier CAL devices, but the backing of Xilinx gave the XC6200 a high level of acceptance, at least in the research community.

Perhaps the most groundbreaking aspect of CAL, and later the XC6200 family, was largely nontechnical. Because these devices supported fine-grained and dynamic reconfiguration, they required that the configuration bitstream be openly documented. Thus, all of the internal details of the logic circuitry and the configuration process were fully documented and made publicly available. Unlike other programmable hardware, the internal programming codes for most FPGAs have never been published, largely for historical and practical reasons.

3.3.3 Cloning

Early in the history of FPGAs, there was some concern that lower-cost "cloned" FPGA devices could be made by third parties. For instance, a company could produce a device that was functionally identical to a Xilinx XC4000 and sell it to Xilinx customers. This was common practice for older and smaller silicon devices and was sometimes encouraged by manufacturers. However, the large investment FPGA vendors had in software tools and silicon intellectual property made them resistant to releasing any more information than necessary about their silicon architectures. Also, as long as the high-level design tools were available for a reasonable price and worked well, most users did not have any particular need to examine an FPGA device's internal workings.

Today it is unlikely that a device as complex as an FPGA could be "cloned." Even if the technical challenges could be overcome, legal barriers to using such intellectual property probably could not be successfully challenged.

Another concern of some customers was that knowledge of the internal workings of FPGA devices could permit their designs to be compromised. While most people familiar with the issues tended to dismiss the idea of reverse-engineering, especially as FPGAs have increased in size, it was still a concern to some customers.

For these reasons, FPGA bitstreams have traditionally been, and still remain, a tightly held trade secret. The XC6200 broke ranks by publicizing its configuration data and permitting a new level of experimentation with tools and applications that could make use of these powerful new modes of operation. Commercial success for the XC6200 would be elusive in the fiercely competitive and rapidly changing FPGA market of the 1990s, but it remained a favorite of researchers even long after its cancellation by Xilinx.

3.4 CIRCUIT EMULATION

One of the early large-scale uses of reconfigurable logic was for circuit emulation. Because FPGAs can, in theory, implement any arbitrary digital logic circuit, some people realized that they could be used as a form of simulation accelerator. At the time, digital circuit simulation had become a bottleneck in the design process. As integrated circuit designs became larger and more complex, the time necessary to simulate them also grew. Without accurate simulation, design errors inevitably crept into the final design, often requiring another expensive and time-consuming redesign cycle. In spite of the high cost of FPGA devices, the ability to quickly and accurately evaluate the function of large and complex digital circuits became very valuable. Also, for chip designs that included programmable processors (or that were the processors themselves), an FPGA-based prototype provided a development platform for testing the software that would eventually run on the production device.

Interestingly, the larger and more complex the circuit, the more difficult and time consuming simulation became and the more valuable FPGA-based emulation would be to designers. For this reason, some of the largest and most expensive FPGA-based machines have traditionally been digital circuit emulators. Some purists may point out that such machines were highly application specific and did not necessarily constitute reconfigurable computing. While these machines did often simulate only a single design in their lifetimes, they were usually reconfigured as much as several times per day to perform different functions. Also, in some cases users would go on to realize that the emulation platforms could be employed for more general-purpose computing.

Emulation using reconfigurable logic quickly became popular, with very large-scale systems becoming commercially available in rapid succession. PiE and QuickTurn in the United States announced their machines, as did the smaller InCA in Europe. The machines were very similar, all attempting to put as many high-density FPGAs as possible into a single system. Because they were highly scalable, and their densities and prices were changing rapidly, it is difficult to gauge what a typical large FPGA emulation system would be. However, a system on the order of 1 million programmable logic gates built from devices with approximately a 10K-gate capacity would be representative of a large, but early FPGA emulation. While large and expensive, these systems were very valuable to integrated circuit designers, who knew the high cost of designs with bugs. One place in particular where they had a large impact was in the design of microprocessors.

3.4.1 AMD/Intel

Because microprocessors were very complex and had strict deadlines to meet, emulation became very important at places such as Advanced Micro Devices (AMD) and Intel. And because the new microprocessor parts often had to be compatible with older models, emulation was a very good way to guarantee that systems would be compatible across generations. One event in the 1990s would help further drive emulator popularity. AMD and Intel began a decades-long competition to produce the latest high-performance device compatible with a x86 instruction set for the desktop PC market.

Initially, AMD was in the "follower" position and was attempting to create functionally identical versions of Intel devices. This was no small challenge, and with new products being released almost yearly, the value to AMD of getting a functionally correct Intel work-alike device as soon as possible was very high.

Emulators played a very large role in verifying the functional correctness of the AMD designs against the Intel device. While the emulated designs would run at perhaps a few hundred kilohertz as compared to the tens of megahertz of the final silicon devices, being able to run test vectors at this rate, and even eventually booting entire operating systems, was crucial in proving the compatibility of these microprocessor designs.

Emulation is still widely used in digital design, but the increasing size and decreasing cost of FPGA devices has led to a smaller market for very large emulation machines such as the ones offered by QuickTurn and PiE. In fact, QuickTurn and PiE merged in 1993 after a short legal battle. The merged company was acquired in 1998 by Cadence, a CAD software vendor.

3.4.2 Virtual Wires

Although emulation was largely a commercial endeavor, one research project in this area warrants special mention—the Virtual Wires Project (see Chapter 30, Logic Emulation on Multi-FPGA Systems) at M.I.T., which produced an emulator that helped overcome one of the most serious limitations of emulators of the time [6]. Whereas the logic density of FPGAs grew rapidly, chip-to-chip interconnect soon became the limiting factor in large, multi-FPGA designs such as emulation. In fact, many emulated designs used only a fraction of the logic in the FPGAs while consuming all of the input/output resources. Then along came Virtual Wires with a pin multiplexing scheme to share I/O pins on FPGA devices transparently, permitting their higher utilization. This technology would be licensed to another logic emulation company, Ikos, which would eventually be bought by another of the large CAD software vendors, Mentor Graphics.

Emulation had perhaps two major impacts on reconfigurable computing. First, it was an early large-scale user of reconfigurable logic that was commercially successful. This helped drive similar work in the field. Perhaps just as important, many of the researchers involved in the emulation work saw the value of more general-purpose computing using reconfigurable logic and would go on to lead advancements in other areas of reconfigurable systems.

3.5 ACCELERATING TECHNOLOGY

After the success of digital circuit emulators and the research results of the early systems, reconfigurable computing was poised to expand. Three factors helped drive this expansion. First, the ever-increasing density of FPGA devices was making larger and larger amounts of reconfigurable logic available at an increasingly lower price. In just a few short years, the million-gate systems that took several large boards could be built with a single device. This in itself led to widespread experimentation with reconfigurable computing as dozens of research projects at universities and research labs across the globe sprang up.

The second factor is one that has become more obvious in retrospect. By the mid-1990s the decades-long increase in microprocessor computing power was beginning to ebb. Late in the decade, it was clear that manufacturing technology constraints, power consumption issues, and architectural limitations such as memory performance were bringing an end to the long era of microprocessor dominance. In the past, new solutions to high-performance computing had had to contend with the yearly appearance of a new microprocessor with double the performance of the previous generation and a consumer-friendly price. This made it difficult for custom high-performance systems to be competitive. With the end of the steep growth in microprocessor performance in sight, however, other solutions to high performance were beginning to look more attractive. Reconfigurable computing technology happened to be emerging just at this critical juncture and would be considered by many as a top contender for the future of high-performance computing.

The third factor was the Department of Defense's new funding program, named Adaptive Computing Systems (ACS), which invested more than $100 million in reconfigurable computing research during the mid- to late 1990s. It is always difficult to judge the effect of such a program, but it is clear that ACS not only led to an increased level of research in this field but also provided a useful forum for researchers, both academically and commercially. While the program funded exclusively U.S. researchers, it also appears to have spurred reconfigurable computing research in other places, particularly the United Kingdom and Japan [31,32].

The era of expansion in reconfigurable computing technology was marked by a rapid growth in the number of systems being constructed. An accurate count of projects in this area is difficult, but certainly dozens and perhaps hundreds of reconfigurable systems were constructed at this time [25]. However, the increased density of FPGA devices led to a shift away from large, expensive systems like those of the first generation and toward smaller systems, often containing a single FPGA device on a standard board to be plugged into a personal computer or workstation.

The new systems tended to be primarily for research and were more often than not hobbled by two problems. First, the tools to program a reconfigurable computing platform were not standardized and often amounted to two completely decoupled design flows. Hardware design tools provided by the FPGA vendor were used to construct a circuit in the FPGA coprocessor, while standard software development tools were used to program the host PC or workstation. This hardware/software codesign style was inefficient and inflexible, and required highly skilled engineers. For those reasons, although there were a few notable software and tools projects at this time, they were more the exception than the rule. None achieved widespread popularity.

3.5.1 Teramac

Among the projects to come out of this era, Teramac [3,14], a product of the Hewlett-Packard research laboratories, bears special mention, for three reasons. First, it went against the trend by creating a large multi-FPGA machine. Second, it straddled different markets by being aimed at both circuit emulation and reconfigurable computing. Lastly, it was constructed of custom-integrated circuits instead of commercially available FPGA devices.

Teramac was originally designed to perform emulation for a large microprocessor design that was being developed jointly by Hewlett-Packard and Intel. It was to be the first 64-bit Intel processor and at the time went by the name "Merced." The joint Intel/HP project was announced in 1994 and was expected to produce its first silicon device by 1999.

All of this was taking place just as large circuit emulators from vendors such as QuickTurn were emerging as the new tools for large microprocessor development. The HP/Intel venture decided to also produce its own emulator, which would not use commercial FPGAs but rather an HP custom-designed reconfigurable logic device [2]. This was not as unusual an idea as it may seem. Intel and HP certainly had the resources to produce such a machine, and the current FPGA-based offerings were far from perfect.

The three biggest problems associated with emulators at this time were cost, low circuit density, and tools. In fact, the tools problem was perhaps the most severe of the three. Large designs needed massive computing resources on their own to be converted into configuration bitstreams for the many FPGA devices. If we assume that the emulator hardware consisted of hundreds of FPGA devices, each taking several hours of time on a standard personal computer or workstation to produce a configuration bitstream, it is clear that a large computational resource was required just to produce the data used by the emulator.

This part of design and test was often the bottleneck, and there appeared to be little that could be done to accelerate the process. Additionally, commercial FPGA devices were aimed at a more general-purpose logic design market and were not explicitly aimed at emulation. A special-purpose device more tailored to the needs of circuit emulation could provide the higher density and performance required by emulation users.

Teramac was announced in 1995 and had some unique features. First, it successfully overcame many of the limitations of the commercial FPGA devices of that era. Its custom FPGA (called Plasma) focused on fast compilation times via very flexible crossbar-based interconnects. This was in contrast to commercial FPGA's focus on logic density and performance, and it meant that the placement and routing of a design for a single Plasma device took seconds, not minutes to hours. Perhaps more interesting, Plasma made good use of defect tolerance. Boards and devices that would otherwise have been thrown away could be used in the Teramac; an analysis phase would test the system to log defects and permit the faulty portions of the system to be bypassed. While regular array architectures such as FPGAs lend themselves naturally to such defect and fault tolerance, it had not traditionally been used in commercial reconfigurable logic devices.

In addition to its emulation duties, Teramac was used for applications such as image processing, bioinformatics, search, and CAD, making it a true reconfigurable computing platform. However, while Teramac was successful, the chip it was built to emulate, the IA-64 family, was somewhat less so. The IA-64 devices were late to market, but they did eventually ship and found their way

FIGURE 3.5 ■ A Hewlett-Packard Laboratories Teramac board.

into commercial products—just not enough to justify the massive investment by HP and Intel, which would not jointly produce other architectures. Thus, Teramac became an early casualty of the HP/Intel microprocessor design partnership. Figure 3.5 shows a picture of one of the boards from a Teramac system.

3.6 RECONFIGURABLE SUPERCOMPUTING

While the number of small reconfigurable coprocessing boards would continue to proliferate as commercial FPGA devices became denser and cheaper, other new hardware architectures were produced to address the needs of large-scale supercomputer users. Unlike the earlier generation of boards and systems that sought to put as much reconfigurable logic as possible into a single unified system, these machines took a different approach. In general, they were traditional multiprocessor systems, but each processing node in them consisted of a very powerful commercial desktop microprocessor combined with a large commercial FPGA device. Another factor that made these systems unique is that they were all offered by mainstream commercial vendors. By 2005 the three largest makers of traditional supercomputer systems—Cray Research, SRC, and Silicon Graphics—were all producing systems of this type.

3.6.1   Cray, SRC, and Silicon Graphics

The first reconfigurable supercomputing machine from Cray, the XD1, is based on a chassis of 12 processing nodes, with each node consisting of an AMD Opteron processor. Up to 6 reconfigurable computing processing nodes, based on the Xilinx Virtex-4 devices, can also be configured in each chassis, and up to 12 chassis can be combined in a single cabinet, with multiple cabinets making larger systems. Hundreds of processing nodes can be easily configured with this approach.

SRC, a company with historic connections to Cray, takes a more aggressive approach to reconfigurable computing [34]. Both of their multiprocessor systems feature traditional processor and reconfigurable processing units that share a common buslike structure and may be mixed in various configurations [21]. Like the Cray system, the SRC machines also use large Xilinx Virtex-series FPGAs and x86-family desktop processors. SRC also offers smaller personal workstation systems for development.

Finally, Silicon Graphics offers its Reconfigurable Application-Specific Processor (RASP) family of systems [36], which also use high-density Xilinx Virtex FPGAs as its reconfigurable computing elements, but in dual-device configurations on a "blade"-style module. These are very small boards that can be plugged into large racks, often with the system still operating. They interface to the more traditional Silicon Graphics workstation and multiprocessor systems, which also use high-performance desktop microprocessors but are based on the MIPS architecture.

The Cray, SRC, and Silicon Graphics machines point to a clear direction for large-scale reconfigurable computing systems. They combine a more distributed array of FPGA elements with an emphasis on floating-point arithmetic. As FPGA densities continue to increase, the ability to perform large floating-point calculations, even multiple floating-point calculations, in a single device becomes significant. Also, as the performance of commodity microprocessors remains plateaued, it is likely that acceleration techniques such as those used in these reconfigurable machines will continue to be used.

3.6.2   The CMX-2X

A discussion of distributed, floating-point FPGA-based supercomputing would not be complete without a mention of the CM-2X [13]. This machine predates the current crop of reconfigurable supercomputers by over a decade and consists of a Connection Machine 2 from Thinking Machines supplemented with FPGA coprocessors instead of the standard floating-point devices typically used. The CM-2X was a defense-related project, and little information is available on it. However, along with the PRISM system, it is clearly the forerunner of this family of distributed multiprocessor reconfigurable supercomputers.

3.7   NON-FPGA RESEARCH

Although the vast majority of reconfigurable computing systems were based on commercially available FPGA devices, there are some notable exceptions. A small number of projects designed and built custom-reconfigurable silicon devices as the basis of their designs [7, 15, 16, 24, 26, 33, 35]. The general trend was to replace the smaller-grained LUTs in the FPGA architecture with coarser-grained structures more amenable to computing. Typically this meant arithmetic logic units (ALUs) that mapped more closely to traditional programming languages.

Such a coarser-grained approach raises the issue of categorizing non-FPGA devices. Large numbers of ALU-like structures quickly begin to resemble multiprocessors or very long instruction word (VLIW) machines more than they do FPGAs. The way routing is performed may further differentiate non-FPGA from FPGA devices. In general, non-FPGAs are computation, not circuit, oriented. They can easily produce the larger and more complex circuits used by typical arithmetic-based computations, but may not be able to efficiently implement arbitrary digital logic functions.

These systems may have broken new and interesting ground, but the problem with them may ultimately be a practical one. Because commercial FPGAs are very popular, they tend to use the latest silicon processes and are very efficiently designed. The software support for such devices is also decidedly nontrivial. To produce a custom reconfigurable computing device that can compete with both the dense, efficient circuitry and the large body of available software tools of modern FPGAs is a daunting prospect. Given these barriers, no serious contenders to commercial FPGAs as the basis for reconfigurable computing machines have arisen. While the ideas behind these novel architectures are sound and the advantages tangible, it has proved difficult to offer them as a viable alternative to FPGA-based reconfigurable systems.

3.8   OTHER SYSTEM ISSUES

In spite of nearly two decades of intensive research and commercial activity, and the potential to provide orders of magnitude performance, reconfigurable logic-based computing systems have not yet begun to displace conventional systems in any significant way. There are perhaps many factors in this lack of acceptance, but technical details at the hardware level certainly appear to be one of the most serious.

One unavoidable architectural problem involves the necessary use of reconfigurable logic in a processor/coprocessor arrangement, which ties an inherently serial host system to the high-performance and highly parallel reconfigurable processing unit. This connection is necessarily made across a system bus of some sort, which is guaranteed to serialize access to the coprocessor. Thus, the reconfigurable coprocessor can only be "fed" data at a relatively low and fixed rate. Such a drawback resembles the "von Neumann bottleneck" in conventional uniprocessor systems, where access to memory over a similar bus restricts performance. In the case of reconfigurable systems, the bus interface is the same but the processor is connected to the reconfigurable unit instead of to a memory unit.

By a similar analogy, Amdahl's Law states that an algorithm's parallel performance is eventually dominated by its serial portions. If, for instance, an algorithm is 90 percent parallelizable, the limit on speedup is 10. This implies that even if the parallel portion of the algorithm can be executed in zero time, the serial portion will still take the same fixed amount of time to execute. Similarly, no matter how much work can be offloaded to the reconfigurable coprocessors, the portions that cannot will tend to dominate the computation time.

In this sense, the same problems that limit the ability to parallelize algorithms also limit the ability to use reconfigurable computing. While there are other issues that limit acceptance of reconfigurable systems, including the lack of mature software development tools and competition from other, more conventional architectures, the basic inability to exploit the parallelism in general-purpose reconfigurable computing will always be a serious concern.

The conventional desktop or server approaches to reconfigurable systems have their difficulties, but reconfigurable computing may still find an agreeable environment in embedded systems, which tend to have streaming data inputs and outputs and may not be at the mercy of the bandwidth of existing system buses. In addition, there may be other attractive features of reconfigurable logic in such embedded systems, including lower overall power consumption and the ability to dynamically adapt to external conditions.

3.9 THE FUTURE OF RECONFIGURABLE SYSTEMS

There appear to be some clear trends in the relatively brief, but active, history of reconfigurable computing. Commercial FPGA devices have continued to be dominant in such systems, but FPGA architectures are also evolving, beginning to incorporate coarser-grained resources. Block memory units and multiplier units have become standard, and even multiple microprocessor cores have found their way onto FPGA devices. Morover, this trend has been mirrored in the coarser-grained research efforts in more recent reconfigurable logic devices. Clearly there is a trend toward coarser-grained elements, as well as a heterogeneous variety of elements.

Perhaps in a related way, large-scale high-performance computing, or supercomputing, has clearly embraced reconfigurable logic. Reconfigurable computing appears to be the path to the higher levels of performance desired by these architectures, particularly as traditional microprocessor architectures have reached a performance plateau. Still, while the manufacturers of supercomputing equipment have clearly embraced reconfigurable computing, it remains to be seen if end users will do so as well.

References

[1] Algotronix, Ltd. *CAL1024 Datasheet*, 1990.

[2] R. Amerson, R. Carter, W. Culbertson, P. Kuekes, G. Snider. Plasma: An FPGA for million gate systems. *Proceedings of the ACM/SIGDA Fourth International Symposium on Field-Programmable Gate Arrays*, February 1996.

[3] R. Amerson, R. Carter, W. Culbertson, P. Kuekes, G. Snider. Teramac-configurable custom computing. *IEEE Symposium on FPGAs for Custom Computing Machines*, April 1995.

[4] J. M. Arnold. The Splash 2 software environment. *Proceedings of the IEEE Workshop on FPGAs for Custom Computing Machines*, April 1993.

[5] P. M. Athanas, H. F. Silverman. Processor reconfiguration through instruction-set metamorphosis. *IEEE Computer* 26(3), March 1993.

[6] J. A. Babb, R. Tessier, A. Agarwal. Virtual wires: Overcoming pin limitations in FPGA-based logic emulators. *Proceedings of the IEEE Workshop on FPGAs for Custom Computing Machines*, April 1993.

[7] V. Baumgarten, F. May, A. Nuckel, M. Vorbach, M. Weinhardt. PACT XPP—A self-reconfigurable data processing architecture. *First International Conference on Engineering of Reconfigurable Systems and Algorithms (ERSA)*, Las Vegas, June 25–28, 2001.

[8] P. Bertin, D. Roncin, J. Vuillemin. Introduction to programmable active memories. *Technical Report 3*, DEC Paris Research Laboratory, 1989.

[9] D. H. Brown Assoc. Cray XD1 brings high-bandwidth supercomputing to the mid-market (*http://www.cray.com/downloads/dhbrown_crayxd1_oct2004.pdf*), October 2004.

[10] D. A. Buell, K. L. Pocek, eds. *Proceedings of the IEEE Workshop on FPGAs for Custom Computing Machines*, IEEE Computer Society Press, 1993.

[11] S. Casselman. Virtual computing and the virtual computer. *IEEE Workshop on FPGAs for Custom Computing Machines*, April 1993.

[12] S. Churcher, T. Kean, B. Wilkie. XC6200 FASTMAP^{TM} processor interface. *Proceedings of the Fifth International Workshop on Field-Programmable Logic and Applications, FPL 1995*, August/September 1995.

[13] S. A. Cuccaro, C. F. Reese. The CM-2X: A hybrid CM-2/Xilinx prototype. *IEEE Workshop of FPGAs for Custom Computing*, April 1993.

[14] W. B. Culbertson, R. Amerson, R. J. Carter, P. J. Kuekes, G. Snider. Teramac configurable custom computer. *Field-Programmable Gate Arrays (FPGAs) for Fast Board Development and Reconfigurable Computing, Proceedings of International Society of Optical Engineering*, October 1995.

[15] C. Ebeling, D. C. Cronquist, P. Franklin. RaPiD—Reconfigurable pipelined datapath. *Field-Programmable Logic: Smart Applications, New Paradigms and Compilers*, R. W. Hartenstein, M. Glesner, eds., Springer-Verlag, September 1996.

[16] C. Ebeling, D. C. Cronquist, P. Franklin, J. Secosky, S. G. Berg. Mapping applications to the rapid configurable architecture. *IEEE Symposium on FPGAs for Custom Computing Machines*, April 1997.

[17] G. Estrin. Organization of computer systems—The fixed plus variable structure computer. *Proceedings of the Western Joint Computer Conference*, May 1960.

[18] G. Estrin, B. Bussell, R. Turn, J. Bibb. Parallel processing in a restructurable computer system. *IEEE Transactions on Electronic Computers* 12(5), December 1963.

[19] G. Estrin, R. Turn. Automatic assignment of computations in a variable structure computer system. *IEEE Transactions on Electronic Computers* 12(5), December 1963.

[20] G. Estrin, C. R. Viswanathan. Organization of a "fixed-plus-variable" structure computer for eigenvalues and eigenvectors of real symmetric matrices. *Journal of the ACM* 9(1), January 1962.

[21] O. D. Fidanci, D. Poznanovic, K. Gaj, T. El-Ghazawi, N. Alexandritis. Performance overhead in a hybrid reconfigurable computer. *Reconfigurable Architecture Workshop*, April 2003.

[22] M. Gokhale, W. Holmes, A. Kosper, D. Kunze, D. Lopresti, S. Lucas, R. Minnich, P. Olsen. SPLASH: A reconfigurable linear logic array. *International Conference on Parallel Processing*, 1990.

[23] M. Gokhale, A. Kosper, S. Lucas, R. Minnich. The logic description generator. *Proceedings of the International Conference on Application Specific Array Processing*, 1990.

[24] S. C. Goldstein, H. Schmit, M. Budiu, S. Cadambi, M. Moe, R. Taylor. PipeRench: A reconfigurable architecture and compiler. *IEEE Computer* 33(4), April 2000.

[25] S. A. Guccione. List of FPGA-based computing machines (*http://www.io.com/~guccione/HW_list.html*), 1994.

[26] R. W. Hartenstein, M. Herz, T. Hoffmann, U. Nageldinger. Using the KressArray for configurable computing. *Proceedings of the International Society of Optical Engineering Conference on Configurable Computing: Technology and Applications*, November 1998.

[27] M. W. Holmes, A. Kosper, S. Lucas, R. Minnich, D. Sweely. Building and using a highly parallel programmable logic array. *IEEE Computer* 24(1), January 1991.

[28] T. A. Kean. *Configurable Logic: A Dynamically Programmable Cellular Architecture and Its VLSI Implementation*, Ph.D. thesis, University of Edinburgh, January 1989.

[29] T. A. Kean. Déjà vu, all over again. *IEEE Design and Test of Computers* 22(2), March/April 2005.

[30] J. T. McHenry, R. L. Donaldson. WILDFIRE custom configurable computer. *Field Programmable Gate Arrays (FPGAs) for Fast Board Development and Reconfigurable Computing, Proceedings of the International Society of Optical Engineering*, October 1995.

[31] T. Miyazaki, T. Murooka, M. Katayama, A. Takahara. Transmutable telecom system and its application. *IEEE Symposium on FPGAs for Custom Computing Machines*, April 1999.

[32] T. Miyazaki, K. Shirakawa, M. Katayama, T. Murooka, A. Takahara. A transmutable telecom system. *Field-Programmable Logic: From FPGAs to Computing Paradigms*, Springer-Verlag, August/September 1998.

[33] M. Moe, H. Schmit, S. Copen Goldstein. Characterization and parameterization of a pipeline reconfigurable FPGA. *IEEE Symposium on FPGAs for Custom Computing Machines*, April 1998.

[34] D. S. Poznanovic. Application development on the SRC Computers, Inc. systems. *Proceedings of the 19th IEEE International Parallel and Distributed Processing Symposium*, 2005.

[35] H. Schmit, D. Whelihan, A. Tsai, M. Moe, B. Levine, R. Reed Taylor. PipeRench: A virtualized programmable datapath in 0.18 micron technology. *Proceedings of the IEEE Custom Integrated Circuits Conference*, 2002.

[36] Silicon Graphics, Inc. Extraordinary acceleration of workflows with reconfigurable application-specific computing from SGI (*http://www.sgi.com/pdfs/3721.pdf*), 2004.

CHAPTER 4

RECONFIGURATION MANAGEMENT

Katherine Compton
Department of Electrical and Computer Engineering
University of Wisconsin–Madison

The flexibility of reconfigurable devices allows them to be customized to a wide variety of applications. Even individual applications can benefit from reconfigurability by using the hardware to perform different tasks at different times. If not all of an application's configurations fit on the hardware simultaneously, they can be swapped in and out as needed. In some cases, the circuitry implemented on reconfigurable hardware can also be optimized based on specific runtime conditions, further improving system efficiency. The process of reconfiguring the hardware at runtime, whether to accelerate different applications or different parts of an individual application, is (unsurprisingly) called *runtime reconfiguration* (RTR).

Unfortunately, although RTR can increase hardware utilization, it can also introduce significant *reconfiguration overhead*. Reconfiguring the hardware, depending on its capacity and design, can be very time consuming. Modern high-end FPGAs can have tens of millions of configuration points, and writing this information can require on the order of hundreds of milliseconds [3, 54]. In a reconfigurable computing system, where the compute-intensive portions of applications are implemented on reconfigurable hardware, computation and reconfiguration are mutually exclusive operations. Thus, time spent reconfiguring is time lost in terms of application acceleration. Studies estimate that, in some cases, reconfiguration time alone occupies approximately 25 to 98 percent of the total execution time of a reconfigurable computing application [36, 42, 50, 51]. Therefore, management and minimization of reconfiguration overhead to maximize the performance of reconfigurable computing systems is essential.

We first discuss the process of reconfiguration in Section 4.1 and then present different configuration architectures, including those designed specifically to help reduce reconfiguration overhead, in Section 4.2. Section 4.3 discusses the different issues in and approaches to managing the reconfiguration process to minimize reconfiguration overhead and maximize the benefit of hardware acceleration. Section 4.4 focuses on techniques that specifically reduce the configuration transfer time when a reconfiguration is required. Finally, Section 4.5 discusses configuration encryption to maintain intellectual property security in reconfigurable computing systems.

4.1   RECONFIGURATION

In reconfigurable devices, such as field-programmable gate arrays (FPGAs), logic and routing resources are controlled by reprogrammable memory locations, such as SRAM or Flash RAM. Boolean values held in these memory bits control whether certain wires are connected and what functionality is implemented by a particular piece of logic. The process of loading the Boolean values into these memory locations is called *reconfiguration*. A specific sequence of 1s and 0s for particular memory locations in hardware defines a specific circuit and is called a *configuration* for a given hardware task. Runtime reconfiguration therefore involves reconfiguring the device (loading a new set of 1s and 0s) with a different configuration (a specific sequence of 1s and 0s) from the one previously loaded in the reconfigurable hardware (RH). The configurations themselves are created by CAD software based on both the circuit design to be implemented and the architecture of the implementing RH. The architectural information is required for the design tools to know which configuration bits control which resources and what effect a 1 has versus a 0 in each of the configuration bit locations.

Once generated by the CAD tools, configurations are generally stored in a memory structure external to the RH. In some cases, configurations are stored in main memory and a CPU acts as the go-between, transferring them from memory to the RH as needed. In other cases, configurations are stored in a programmable ROM and a *configuration controller* loads the data directly from the ROM in the RH, potentially at the request of a central processing unit (CPU). The configuration controller and the ROM may be incorporated into the same device, such as the specialized configuration controllers marketed by various FPGA companies [3, 55], or they may be part of a user-designed custom device. Figure 4.1 shows a block diagram of a system using a configuration controller triggered by a CPU to reconfigure the RH (in this case, an FPGA). The configuration controller essentially implements a finite-state machine (FSM) that, based on the configuration requested by the CPU, generates the sequence of addresses needed to read the appropriate data sequence for that configuration out of the ROM.

4.2   CONFIGURATION ARCHITECTURES

A configuration architecture is the underlying physical circuitry that loads configuration data during reconfiguration, and holds it at the correct locations. Configuration architectures can range from simple serial shift chains, as discussed in the next section, to addressable structures that can manipulate configuration information after it is loaded. Some researchers have developed methods to emulate more complex configuration architectures on existing commercial designs, using a combination of hardware and software to provide advanced configuration functionalities. These approaches are discussed in Section 4.3.4.

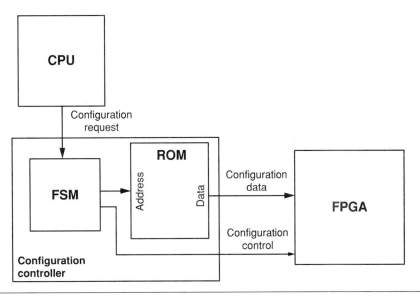

FIGURE 4.1 ■ Configuration data can be transferred to an FPGA by a specialized configuration controller containing nonvolatile ROM memory; the reconfiguration process can be triggered by a CPU.

4.2.1   Single-context

The single-context FPGA has been the most common choice in commercial designs, though there are exceptions. In this type of FPGA, configuration information is loaded into the programmable array through a serial shift chain, as shown in Figure 4.2.

Internally, the configuration architecture may actually be addressable, similar to a standard RAM device or the partially reconfigurable designs discussed in Section 4.2.3, but this would be an implementation detail hidden from the FPGA user. Addressable configuration architectures generally require fewer transistors per SRAM cell than serially programmed architectures, reducing the area required for configuration memory. In this case, an internal-state machine would control writing serially received data to locations in the array.

The Xilinx Virtex family of FPGAs have addressable configuration locations, but have a single-context configuration mode [54]. In these FPGAs, configuration data is divided up into addressable blocks called "frames," each of which corresponds to part of a column of reconfigurable resources. During reconfiguration, the configuration data is shifted into the frame data input register (FDRI) and from there written to a configuration memory location specified by the frame address register (FAR). For single-context configuration mode, this address starts at 0 and is automatically incremented each time a new frame is loaded. This allows the device to appear externally as a single-context device despite the addressability of the configuration information.

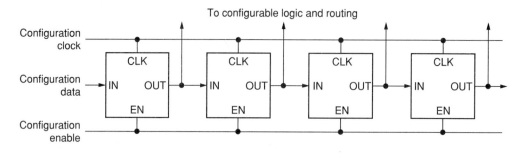

FIGURE 4.2 ■ Serially programmed FPGAs shift in configuration data. Each cell shown contains one SRAM bit of programming data. The clock controls shifting during configuration.

The benefit of serially programmed devices is that they require few pins for configuration, potentially simplifying board-level design. However, the entire chip must be reprogrammed for any change to the configuration data because the data cannot be selectively "reused" on the chip. For example, a large part of the structure of an encryption application may be independent of the chosen key, with only a relatively small portion optimized on a per-key basis. Ideally, only the key-dependent parts are reconfigured and the key-independent parts remain untouched when the key changes. However, a single-context design requires all configuration data to be rewritten during configuration, even if it is with the same values. A relatively minor change to the configuration data becomes a full reconfiguration process, replete with the associated delays.

The number of configuration cycles can be somewhat reduced in single-context devices by widening the configuration path. The Altera Stratix-II [3] and the Xilinx Virtex-II [54] receive either a single bit or a byte of configuration information per configuration clock cycle. The designer then chooses between the two modes by weighing the board-level design impact against the performance impact. As the larger Stratix II devices currently require more than 4MB of configuration data, with a maximum configuration clock speed of 100 MHz, the ability to configure in eight times fewer cycles can be significant. Newer Xilinx devices, such as the Virtex-5, allow a configuration data bus up to 32 bits wide [55].

4.2.2   Multi-context

For RTR systems, the overhead of serial programming may be prohibitive. An attractive alternative may be to provide storage in the device for multiple configurations simultaneously, facilitating configuration prefetching and fast reconfiguration. A *multi-context* device (sometimes called "time-multiplexed") contains multiple planes (contexts) of configuration data. Each configuration point of the device is controlled by a multiplexer that chooses between the context planes. Two configuration points for a 4-context device are shown in Figure 4.3. Several time-multiplexed FPGA architectures have been proposed, including Time-Multiplexed [47], DPGA [17], Dharma [11], and Morphosys [45].

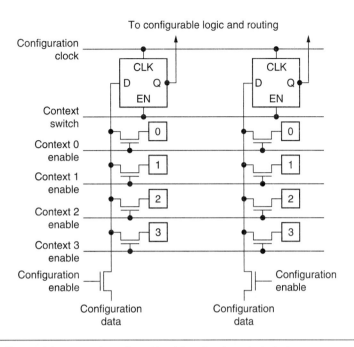

FIGURE 4.3 ■ Two multi-contexted configuration bits of a 4-context device.

Multi-context devices have two main benefits over single-context devices. First, they permit background loading of configuration data during circuit operation, overlapping computation with reconfiguration. Second, they can switch between stored configurations quickly—some in a single clock cycle— dramatically reducing reconfiguration overhead if the next configuration is present in one of the alternate contexts. However, if the next needed configuration is not present, there is still a significant penalty while the data is loaded. For that reason, either all needed contexts must fit in the available hardware or some control must determine when contexts should be loaded in order to minimize the number of wasted cycles stalling while reconfiguration completes. This type of control is discussed in Section 4.3.2.

One of the drawbacks of multi-contexted architectures is that the additional configuration data and required multiplexing occupies valuable area that could otherwise be used for logic or routing. Therefore, although multi-contexting can facilitate the use of an FPGA as virtual hardware, the *physical* capacity of a multi-contexted FPGA device is less than that of a single-context device of the same area. For example, a 4-context device has only 80 percent of the "active area" (simultaneously usable logic/routing resources) that a single-context device occupying the same fixed silicon area has [17]. A multi-context device limited to one active and one inactive context (a single SRAM plus a flip-flop) would have the advantages of background loading and fast context switching coupled with a lower area overhead, but it may not be appropriate if several different contexts are frequently reused.

Another drawback of multi-contexted devices is a direct consequence of its ability to perform a reconfiguration of the full device in a single cycle: spikes in dynamic power consumption. All configuration points are loaded from context memory simultaneously, and potentially the majority of configuration locations may be changed from 0 to 1 or vice versa. Switching many locations in a single cycle results in a significant momentary increase in dynamic power, which may violate system power constraints.

Finally, if any state-storing component of the FPGA is not connected to the configuration information, as may be true for flip-flops, its state will not be restored when switching back to the previous context. However, this issue can also be seen as a feature because it facilitates communication between configurations in other contexts by leaving partial results in place across configurations [27].

4.2.3 Partially Reconfigurable

Because not all configurations require the entire chip area, we might reduce reconfiguration time if we reloaded data only to those areas that actually must change. In partially reconfigurable devices, the configuration memory is addressable, similar to traditional RAM structures. If configurations are smaller than the full device, partial reconfiguration can decrease reconfiguration time by limiting reconfiguration to the resources used by a given configuration and, therefore, the amount of configuration data to transfer. Partial reconfiguration can also allow multiple independent configurations to be swapped in and out of hardware independently, as one configuration can be selectively replaced on the chip while another is left intact. Furthermore, we can leverage the addressability to modify only part of a configuration already located on the chip if some of its structure matches a new configuration that we wish to load. For example, in an encryption circuit the bulk of the configuration may remain the same when the key is changed, and only a few resources may need to change based on the new key value. Partial reconfiguration can allow the system to reconfigure only those changed resources instead of the full circuit.

The Xilinx 6200 FPGA [53] was an early partially reconfigurable device where each logic block could be programmed individually. It therefore became a platform for a great deal of study of configuration architectures and RTR. Current partially reconfigurable commercial FPGAs include the Atmel AT40K [5] and the Xilinx Virtex FPGA family [54, 55]. The Virtex series is more coarsely reconfigurable than the 6200. Instead of addressing each logic block independently, it reconfigures logic blocks in groups called frames. In the Virtex-II, a frame corresponds to part of a full column of resources and the size of the frame increases with the number of logic block rows in the device. In the Virtex 5, frames are a fixed size of 41 32-bit words (regardless of device size) that represent a partial column of resources.

Although partially reconfigurable designs provide a great deal more flexibility for RTR systems, they can still stuffer from potential problems. First, if configurations occupy large areas of the device, the time saved transmitting configuration data may be outweighed by the time spent transmitting configuration addresses.

In this case, a serially programmed FPGA may be more appropriate. Second, and more critical to RTR systems, partial configurations are generally fixed to specific locations on the device. If two independent configurations are implemented in overlapping hardware locations, they cannot operate simultaneously. One method of mitigating this issue is to view configuration placement as a three-dimensional floorplanning problem, with the third dimension representing time [6]. Configurations then occupy some three-dimensional volume of space based on physical location and time of use, allowing the floorplanner to determine the best two-dimensional placement to avoid time-related (three-dimensional) conflicts. Unfortunately, this technique cannot guarantee nonoverlapping configurations if the full configuration sequence is not known at compile time—a major problem in multitasking systems. The next section discusses advanced configuration architectures that eliminate configuration placement conflicts.

4.2.4 Relocation and Defragmentation

As previously discussed, conflicts between configuration locations can limit the effectiveness of partially reconfigurable architectures. To remove these conflicts, configurations should not be associated with fixed device locations. Relocation is a technique permitting configurations to be moved to different compatible device locations within the array, based where free area is available. Figure 4.4(a) shows a device loaded with configurations A, B, and C in sequence, each assigned to a free area. Figure 4.4(b) shows configurations A and B removed, and configuration D relocated and programmed onto the array.

The composition of the reconfigurable hardware can complicate this process in three critical ways. First, if the device's logic or routing is heterogeneous, relocation becomes less flexible, or even impossible, as a configuration may require resources located in only one or a few array locations. For example, in devices with hierarchical routing, different routing connections are available at different locations in the array. However, if heterogeneity is restricted to a repeating pattern, configurations can be relocated distances corresponding to some multiple of the distance of the repeat. To the relocated configuration, resources will be located in the same relative position as in the original placement.

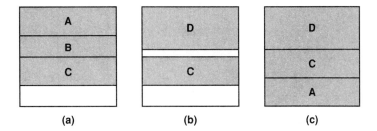

| (a) | (b) | (c) |

FIGURE 4.4 ■ Three configurations have been programmed on the hardware (a). In (b), A and B have been removed, and D has been relocated/configured to an available area, causing fragmentation. Defragmentation relocates configuration C to make room for configuration A when it is again needed, this time to a new location in the array (c).

Second, the external pin connections to the reconfigurable hardware fabric are fixed either at fabrication (reconfigurable hardware cores in a system-on-a-chip) or at board-level design (discrete FPGA components). If a configuration is relocated, its connections to the required I/O pins must be rerouted to maintain the proper connections. One solution to this problem is to use a communication network that itself has fixed pin connections but provides internal interfaces at multiple array locations to allow configurations to have the same communication connections regardless of position [14, 50]. This type of structure is known as *virtualized I/O* and can in some cases be emulated by using reconfigurable resources to implement a static communication structure and including the communication interfaces in individual dynamic configurations [7]. However, configurations must still be relocated such that they can still connect to the communication bus.

Third, a two-dimensional architecture can exacerbate the previous two problems, but particularly complicating virtualized I/O. If a configuration can be relocated both horizontally and vertically, the virtualized I/O must potentially distribute signals to all locations in the array. Furthermore, a two-dimensional architecture increases the possibilities for relocation, as we can consider not only configuration shifting but also rotation, which requires manipulating configuration information related to routing [14]. More relocation possibilities leads to a more complex relocation process and possibly increased configuration overhead.

A partially reconfigurable architecture designed specifically with relocation support should therefore require a homogeneous logic architecture, a bus-based communication structure, and a one-dimensional organization to simplify the relocation process [31, 50]. The one-dimensional architecture means that a configuration must use complete rows, even if it only needs a portion of a row. As device sizes increase, using rows as atomic reconfiguration units may become inefficient. Instead, the fabric can be split into multiple one-dimensional fabrics to retain the relocation benefits while preserving a reasonably sized atomic unit. The Virtex-5 device uses this approach [55].

One of the architectures designed for relocation [14] uses a "staging area" equivalent in size to one row of configuration data, which is similar in approach to the column-wise frame-based configuration method of the Xilinx Virtex family introduced in Section 4.2.1 and discussed in Section 4.2.3 [54]. The staging area is filled one configuration word at a time; then the entire row of data is simultaneously written to the architecture at a location computed with a base address of the top row of the configuration combined with an offset indicating the position of the current row relative to the top configuration row. The choice of the base location can be made by a special circuit that monitors empty locations on the hardware, or by software. When combined with the proper software as described in Section 4.3.2, this configuration architecture has been shown to reduce reconfiguration overhead by 85 percent over a single-context device [31].

Even if an architecture allows relocation, fragmentation of the usable resources can decrease its effectiveness. Like memory fragmentation, swapping configurations in and out of different places in the hardware can result in a situation where various locations in the array may be unused, but there may not be enough contiguous space available to load a configuration. In this case, if the configurations can be defragmented, the new configuration can be loaded into the array without having to remove any of the configurations already on the device. Figure 4.4(b) shows an example of an array that has become fragmented, and Figure 4.4(c) shows how defragmentation can allow a configuration to be configured without having to remove an existing one. A simple approach to this problem is to remove all configurations, then reconfigure the array with the removed ones, this time relocating them to contiguous locations to eliminate fragmentation. However, this process involves significant communication overhead between fabric and configuration memory. Alternately, the reconfigurable hardware can move configurations internally, avoiding the need to communicate with configuration memory. The R/D FPGA [14, 31] provides both relocation and defragmentation ability, which together provide a 90 percent reduction in reconfiguration overhead compared to a single-context FPGA.

A configuration controller for one-dimensional hardware, such as the R/D FPGA, that specifically supports relocation and defragmentation may simply need to keep track of occupied and unoccupied locations, or request this information as needed from the hardware itself. The controller can determine locations for incoming configurations using a first-fit or best-fit method, similar to general memory allocation [7, 14]. Defragmentation, which is easy for the one-dimensional case, can be triggered when sufficient free area is available but is broken up into fragments too small to fit an incoming configuration. If there is insufficient free area, one or more configurations can be removed to make room, as described in Section 4.3.2.

4.2.5 Pipeline Reconfigurable

Pipeline reconfigurable arrays use a series of physical pipeline stages to implement the virtual pipeline stages of configurations. A virtual pipeline stage can be relocated to any physical pipeline stage, and the number of virtual stages is generally not constrained by the number of physical stages. The most well-known pipeline reconfigurable architecture is PipeRench [19], which is designed to implement deeply pipelined configurations, subdivided into a set of virtual pipeline stages. At runtime, the virtual pipeline stages are assigned to physical pipeline stage computation units. These units are arranged in a unidirectional ring, as shown in Figure 4.5(a). Although pipeline stages may be implemented in different physical locations over time, the virtual pipeline *appears* fixed to its own pipeline stages, with each stage receiving input from its predecessor and generating output to its successor. PipeRench permits pipeline stages to be configured in a single cycle to speed execution.

Pipeline reconfiguration eliminates many of the difficulties of using reconfigurable hardware as virtual hardware, but places restrictions on the circuits that can be implemented as information can only propagate forward through the pipeline stages, and any feedback connections must be completely contained within a single stage. Figure 4.5(b) shows a 4-stage virtual pipeline implemented on a 3-stage physical architecture.

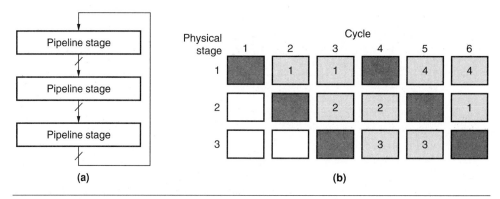

(a)   **(b)**

FIGURE 4.5 ▪ A pipeline reconfigurable architecture with three physical stages (a). A 3-stage physical pipeline implementing a 4-stage virtual pipeline (b). Numbers within physical pipeline stages indicate the implemented virtual pipeline stage. Shaded stages are reconfiguring for the given cycle.

4.2.6 Block Reconfigurable

Block reconfigurable arrays can share characteristics with any of the previously described configuration architectures. However, rather than providing one large reconfigurable fabric, they are made up of multiple discrete blocks that can be used independently. For these purposes, "block" should not be confused with "logic block" in an FPGA. In this case each independent block can contain many logic resources. An individual configuration may occupy one or more blocks, but blocks may not be subdivided between configurations. Blocks are connected either through a crossbar structure [39] or a bus/network [10], as shown in Figure 4.6. Although this would seem to describe any architecture formed from multiple connected FPGAs or FPGA cores, block reconfigurable devices have the ability to relocate configurations to different blocks at runtime. For this reason, the blocks of reconfigurable logic in this style of architecture have also been referred to as "swappable logic units" (SLU) [55]. In the SLU architecture, a block reconfigurable design is implemented as an abstraction layer on top of a partially reconfigurable architecture to facilitate runtime relocation.

The SCORE reconfigurable architecture model [10] is a block reconfigurable design where the reconfigurable blocks are referred to as "pages" to evoke a virtual memory view of the reconfigurable hardware. Any virtual page can be implemented on any physical page, and computation pages are loaded as needed. Once configured, pages communicate with one another using datastreams over a scalable hierarchical network.

A heterogeneous multiprocessor may fit the block reconfigurable model, provided multiple blocks of reconfigurable hardware are present and configurations can be relocated between the blocks for computational flexibility. These architectures may contain a single communication network used by the configurable blocks and other resources such as microprocessors and custom circuitry. Although the Pleiades reconfigurable architecture [1] has some of these features (a heterogeneous multiprocessor with multiple reconfigurable blocks),

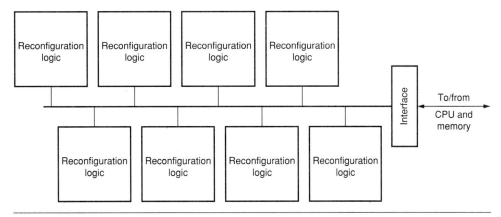

FIGURE 4.6 ■ In a block reconfigurable device, configurations can be relocated to any of the interconnected and equivalent blocks of reconfigurable logic.

computations are preassigned to specific resources, violating one of the requirements of the block reconfigurable category.

4.2.7 Summary

This section presented a variety of configuration architectures, each optimized for a different type of reconfiguration. The single-context device is the simplest in terms of configuration process and interface, and it is the most popular for current commercial devices. Partial reconfiguration, which allows reconfiguration of parts of the device (leaving the rest untouched), can reduce the amount of configuration data that must be transferred but is hampered by configuration placement conflicts. Partially reconfigurable designs augmented with relocation and defragmentation, as well as block reconfigurable designs, avoid this issue by allowing configurations to be placed at different locations from the ones originally assigned. Likewise, pipeline reconfigurable devices allow pipeline stages to be relocated but prohibit interstage feedback connections. Finally, multi-contexted devices provide a method for single-cycle device reconfiguration but at the cost of decreased computation resources for a given area and a dramatic increase in power consumption during context changes.

The more advanced reconfiguration architectures, such as relocation, defragmentation, and multi-contexting, have been popular for some time in the research community as tools essential for effective reconfigurable computing systems. However, such devices have not yet gained a significant market foothold because of the limited demand for fast reconfiguration capabilities. Instead, most FPGAs are currently used as drop-in ASIC replacements or as infrequently reconfigured hardware modified only for firmware updates. To provide devices at a competitive cost, most FPGA vendors forgo the more innovated configuration architectures in favor of a simpler single-context design. Although Xilinx, one of the most prominent FPGA vendors, offers partial reconfiguration in its Virtex families, design support is still somewhat limited, relocation and defragmentation are not supported, and a single-context interface is still provided to cater to users who do not require partial reconfiguration. Even so, as reconfigurable computing becomes a more common practice, spurred perhaps by the difficulty of continued clock speed increases for general-purpose processors, demand for innovative configuration architectures will increase in order to maximize the benefits of reconfigurable computing.

4.3   MANAGING THE RECONFIGURATION PROCESS

Reconfigurable computing systems swap configurations in and out of hardware at runtime, a process controlled by software, hardware, or a combination of both. Although a system can simply load a configuration whenever it is needed, and unload it when hardware execution is complete, this can cause a significant reconfiguration overhead: while the configuration is loading, the controlling application or thread cannot compute. Also, if the hardware is currently in use by another thread or process, the requesting application or thread must wait until the hardware is idle or until enough area is free to even begin the reconfiguration process, leading to further stalling. Ideally, configurations are loaded in advance of when they are needed and those likely to be reused in the near future should be cached on the hardware.

The following sections discuss several aspects of reconfiguration control, including choosing the configurations to load, and when and where on the hardware to load them.

4.3.1   Configuration Grouping

Single-context and multi-context FPGAs may have more resources available at once than are usable by a single configuration. Reconfiguration overhead can be reduced by grouping configurations that are likely to be used one after another into a single larger configuration. Algorithms proposed to perform this grouping include simulated annealing and a clustering approach [31]. They examine the overall application control flow to predict configurations that should be grouped together. The loading of a grouped configuration involves not only the currently needed configuration but also those most likely to be used after. Therefore, if the next configuration requested is already present on the device, no reconfiguration is necessary, reducing reconfiguration overhead. With configuration grouping, a configuration will appear in at least one group, and possibly several, depending on application behavior and the configuration's relationship to other configurations.

This approach is primarily appropriate for single-application systems, as configuration grouping is a compile-time operation. However, it could also be used in a multitasking system with a multi-context device. In this case, the configuration grouping would still be performed at compile time for individual applications, and the choice of which configuration groups to load and when would be a runtime operation, as described in the next section.

4.3.2 Configuration Caching

In a single-context device, the loading of one configuration overwrites all configuration data in the FPGA. Thus, context grouping implicitly decides what operations will coexist within the device at any point. In a multi-context or partially reconfigurable architecture, reconfiguration only overwrites a portion of the configuration data, allowing other configurations to be retained elsewhere. With configuration caching, the goal is to keep configurations on the hardware if they are likely to be reused in the near future. If there is enough free area on the device to fit a requested configuration, it is simply loaded, but if there is insufficient space, the configuration controller must select one or more "victim" configurations to remove from the hardware to free the required area. This process is simplified from the point of view of the controller if the device does not support relocation, as the victim configurations are simply any that overlap with the incoming one. However, this will generally result in a high reconfiguration overhead, as the removed configurations could be needed again in the near future, requiring another reconfiguration.

If the device supports relocation and defragmentation, or multiple contexts, the controller may have a variety of potential victims to choose from that will free the needed area. In some cases, general caching approaches may be used. These approaches assume a fixed-sized data block. However, in a partially reconfigurable device the size of the block to load can vary because configurations can each use differing amounts of resources. The caching algorithm must therefore consider the impact of variable-sized blocks.

One algorithm uses a penalty-based approach that considers both the configuration's size and how recently it was used [31]. When a configuration is first loaded, its "credit" is set to its size. When one or more configurations must be removed to make room for an incoming one, the configuration with the lowest credit is chosen, and the credit values of the remaining configurations are lowered by the credit value of the removed one. For the R/D FPGA design [14], penalty-based caching consistently results in a lower reconfiguration overhead than a simple least recently used (LRU) approach and 90 percent less overhead than a single-context configuration architecture. A configuration controller for a multi-context device must select which context to overwrite when a new context not already in the device is requested [14]. Because each context is the same size, general caching techniques, such as LRU, have been used.

4.3.3 Configuration Scheduling

Configurations can be loaded simply as they are requested, but this may result in significant overhead if the software stalls while waiting for reconfiguration to complete [50]. If instead the system can request configurations in advance of when they are needed, a process called *prefetching*, reconfiguration may proceed concurrent with software execution until the hardware is actually required. The challenge, however, is to ensure that prefetched configurations will not be ejected from the hardware by other prefetching operations before they can be used. For example, Figure 4.7 shows a flow graph for an application containing both

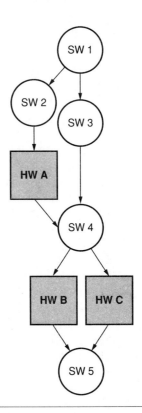

FIGURE 4.7 ■ An example reconfigurable computing application flow graph, containing both hardware and software components.

hardware and software components. Configuration A can safely begin loading at the beginning of the flow graph, provided that the application represented by the flow graph is the only one using the reconfigurable hardware. On the other hand, after the first branch rejoins at software block 4, it is unclear whether configuration B or configuration C will be needed next. If both potential branches have equal probability, the next configuration should not be loaded until after program flow determines the correct branch.

For static scheduling, prefetching commands may be inserted by the compiler based on static analysis of the application flow graph [23], and have been shown to reduce reconfiguration overhead up to a factor of 2. A more dynamic approach uses a Markov model to predict the next configuration that will be needed for a partially reconfigurable architecture with relocation and defragmentation [33]. Combining this approach with configuration caching results in a reconfiguration overhead reduction of a factor of 2 over configuration caching alone. Adding compiler "hints" to dynamic prediction achieves still better results.

Some dynamic approaches use the dataflow graph to determine when a given configuration is valid for execution [37, 39]. In these cases, nodes of the flow graph may be scheduled only if their ancestors have completed execution. This approach works even if multiple applications are executing concurrently in the system and also works in systems implementing hardware tasks as independent "hardware threads" [4, 43].

Other approaches do not consider the actual flow graphs of applications, but instead use system status and current resource demand to allocate reconfigurable hardware to different configurations over time. Window-based scheduling periodically chooses the configurations to be implemented in hardware for the next "window" of time. This approach treats scheduling as a series of static problems yet still accommodates dynamic system behavior. One window-based scheduler uses a multi-constraint knapsack approach to choose configurations providing the best benefit (speedup) to the system as a whole based on configuration requests in the past window period. This technique was shown to increase overall *system* throughput by at least 20 percent relative to a processor without reconfigurable hardware [57].

In true multitasking systems load may not be consistent, with demand for the reconfigurable resources varying over time. This has led to more complex scheduling techniques that also consider modifying configurations based on available resources to take advantage of numerous resources when possible or to fit in limited resources when necessary [37, 40, 41, 57]. Another possibility is to permit a software alternative for configurations to avoid stalls if the hardware resources are in high demand [16, 34, 41, 57]. This approach allows dynamic binding of computations to hardware or software, where only the most beneficial configurations are actually implemented in hardware. Real-time systems similarly must choose tasks at runtime for hardware implementation based on real-time requirements (task priority, arrival and execution time, and deadlines), rejecting remaining tasks to software or possibly dropping them entirely [46].

4.3.4 Software-based Relocation and Defragmentation

Systems that do not support relocation and defragmentation at the configuration architecture level may support it at the software level to gain some of the associated benefits. However, this can be computationally intense for two-dimensional architectures. Finding a possible location for an arbitrarily shaped configuration can require an exhaustive search, which may incur a greater overhead penalty than the configuration penalty it seeks to avoid. Restricting configurations to rectangular shapes simplifies the process somewhat, though it is still a two-dimensional bin-packing problem. One approach to solving this problem is to maintain a list of empty spaces in the device and search it whenever a new configuration is to be loaded [6, 21, 48]. In either case, when the controller removes a configuration from the hardware, it can update the list based on the freed area. The "best" empty location to implement the incoming configuration can be chosen based on algorithms similar to one-dimensional packing, such as first-fit or best-fit.

When there are no empty locations that can fit the incoming configuration, the configuration controller can defragment the hardware to consolidate empty space, or remove an existing configuration. Like two-dimensional relocation, two-dimensional defragmentation is very complex. It can be implemented by removing all configurations from the hardware and then successively reloading each one using one of the two-dimensional relocation techniques described previously. Alternately, a reconfiguration controller can use a technique specifically designed for two-dimensional defragmentation that rearranges only a subset of configurations, and dynamically schedules their movements in an effort to minimize disruption of those in execution [18].

A critical problem in supporting relocation, whether for the one-dimensional or the two-dimensional case, is rerouting the connections between a relocated configuration and the (nonrelocated) I/O pins. As discussed in Section 4.2.4, a virtualized I/O structure simplifies this problem, though virtualized I/O for two-dimensional architectures may be infeasibly large. However, if the architecture does not have virtualized I/O, either these signals must be rerouted at runtime [49] or the configurations must be modified to emulate virtualized I/O by having a specific movable interface to a nonrelocatable communications structure [7].

4.3.5   Context Switching

Unfortunately, some of the same terminology in the reconfigurable computing area is used to refer to different concepts. In this section, "context switch" does not refer to switching between planes of configuration data in a multicontext device. Instead, it refers to the suspend/resume behavior of processors (and potentially their associated reconfigurable logic) when multitasking. A few studies have discussed supporting suspend/resume of hardware operations as a way to support hardware multitasking [24, 44]. In these systems, long-running configurations may be interrupted to allow other configurations to proceed, and later be resumed to complete computation. Although the configuration state can be resumed by reloading the required configuration, the flip-flop values and the values stored in embedded RAM blocks are not necessarily part of the configuration, and therefore may require additional steps to save their state.

Reconfigurable hardware context switches may mirror processor context switches to facilitate hardware control by ensuring that the "owning" process is active and ready to receive results. The host processor may stall or wait while the reconfigurable hardware is active [43], or it may continue with parallel operations that are not dependent on the hardware's results [1, 24, 43].

4.4   REDUCING CONFIGURATION TRANSFER TIME

The various techniques described previously can reduce the number of times we have to reconfigure the hardware, or attempt to hide the configuration latency, but the actual time required to transfer a given configuration can also be reduced. One hardware-based technique already discussed in Section 4.2.3, partial reconfiguration, permits configuring only those parts of the hardware that are needed. The remainder of the chip does not need to be configured, and therefore configuration data for these other areas does not need to be transferred. The next few sections present a number of other methods used to reduce the configuration transfer time, in most cases by reducing the amount of data transferred.

4.4.1 Architectural Approaches

The design of the reconfigurable architecture itself can affect the time required to configure it. For example, a coarse-grained architecture containing primarily fixed functional units will generally require fewer configuration bits for the same functionality than does a fine-grained LUT-based architecture [25]. Another architectural design feature that can impact reconfiguration times is the width of the configuration path. Section 4.2.1 discussed how a serially programmed FPGA can be programmed $8\times$ faster if configuration data is loaded a byte per cycle instead of a bit per cycle. In cases where the reconfigurable hardware is located on the same chip as the configuration memory, a very wide path between them may be possible, drastically reducing reconfiguration time. For example, the R/D architecture [14] can have a wide enough path to an on-chip configuration cache to allow the entire staging area to be loaded in a single cycle.

4.4.2 Configuration Compression

Compression is a widely used method in general-purpose computing and networking to reduce data transfer times by reducing the number of bits transferred. Compression can also reduce the amount of configuration data transmitted to reconfigurable hardware, leading to a corresponding decrease in reconfiguration time. The first proposed configuration compression technique [22] targeted the Xilinx 6200-series FPGA [53], which, as discussed in Section 4.2.3, is partially reconfigurable at a very fine-grained level, addressing individual logic cells by their row and column. The 6200 includes two "wildcard registers," equal in bit width to the row and column addresses, which act as masks on the configuration addresses. This allows one piece of configuration data to be written to more than one location. Essentially, 0s in the wildcard register retain the configuration address bits for those locations, whereas 1s indicate that all possible combinations of values in those specific locations should be addressed. By treating wildcard register value generation as a logic minimization problem, configuration data is compressed by an average factor of four for the Xilinx 6200 [22].

An expansion of these efforts exploits the fact that not all configuration bits in a logic cell are used by all configurations [30]. In many cases, a number of bits in a logic cell configuration can be considered "don't-care" values and can be programmed either with a 1 or a 0 without affecting the configuration's functionality. This allows configuration data to be manipulated to increase the achievable compression rates by about a factor of 2. Although the wildcarding and don't-care approaches are effective, they are specific to a discontinued architecture. More recent studies [15, 32] examine the use of a variety of standard compression techniques that achieve up to a compression factor of 4 on more modern architectures.

Configuration compression is not merely an academic pursuit. Both Altera's and Xilinx's design tools can generate compressed configurations [3, 55]. The compressed configurations are stored in a separate configuration controller that decompresses them as they are sent to the FPGA. However, this form of compression only reduces configuration storage requirements and does not decrease the size of configuration data sent to the FPGA. Compressed configurations can, however, be loaded directly onto Stratix-II devices in some configuration modes, and decompressed on the FPGA itself.

4.4.3   Configuration Data Reuse

At times, only a portion of a configuration must be updated, such as the key-specific hardware in an encryption configuration. Rather than resend the full configuration information, a partially reconfigurable device allows just the changed portions to be sent. Circuits can be designed specifically to use partial reconfiguration to customize them based on constant values not known until runtime [58]. However, even less directly related configurations may also have configuration data in common. Certain computation or communication patterns may be common to several configurations, such as the use of adder structures, emphasis on near-neighbor routing instead of long-distance routing, and the like [20]. Similarly, there may be "default" values for configuration bits for unused resources, and two configurations may have used as well as unused resources in common. These commonalities can decrease the amount of "new" configuration data required to implement the next configuration, particularly if configuration data reuse is a factor in the design of the configurations. The degree of similarity is increased with a decrease in the granularity of reconfiguration (there are fewer ways for small sets of bits to differ than for large sets to differ) and can result in a decrease in configuration data by approximately 35 to 40 percent [35].

4.5   CONFIGURATION SECURITY

In most of this book, we view the programmability of an FPGA as an inherent advantage that provides a circuit implementation platform or a multi-purpose acceleration engine. However, this flexibility also increases the potential for intellectual property theft compared to custom ASIC hardware. SRAM-based FPGAs (the focus of this chapter), have volatile configuration memory; to retain configuration data, a battery must provide a constant power supply to the configuration bits. This configuration data is stored in memory (RAM or a PROM) external to the FPGA, and is loaded into the FPGA at power-up. Someone monitoring the wires between these structures could capture the configuration data flowing from memory to the reconfigurable device. They could then duplicate the circuit simply by loading that data onto a new chip. Design firms that create FPGA-based hardware want to protect their work (which may have required significant design time) and prevent reverse-engineering of their designs.

To discourage their unauthorized copying, FPGA configurations can be watermarked with a special signature based on the circuit designer and the purchasing customer [28]. Of course, the design can still be copied and reverse-engineered, but the watermark can help identify the source of the unauthorized copies.

Design security can also be provided by encrypting configuration data to obscure the employed design techniques and/or functionality [26]. Many FPGA vendors now support configuration encryption with special on-chip decryption hardware. The Xilinx Virtex-II, for example, uses triple-key DES [54], and Altera's Stratix-II [3], Actel's ProASIC3 [2], and Lattice's ECP2 [29] all support 128-bit AES configuration encryption. In all cases, the keys are stored in the FPGA, and encrypted configurations may only be loaded if they were encrypted with the same key as that stored in the device. For a Virtex-II device, a battery must be attached to the proper pins to retain the key when the device is not powered. In contrast, the Stratix-II, ECP2, and ProASIC3 devices use nonvolatile memory for key storage, eliminating the need for a separate battery.

For systems that do not require runtime reconfiguration, the opportunity to copy a design can be reduced in end-products by not transmitting the configuration data on probeable wires. Antifuse and Flash FPGAs, based on nonvolatile configuration memory structures, inherently retain configuration data on-chip once configured, avoiding the need to transfer the information for systems not using runtime reconfiguration.

4.6 SUMMARY

The difficulty of clock speed increases and power consumption concerns motivate reconfigurable computing as an important technique to advance digital design, implementing compute-intensive application tasks in reconfigurable hardware. However, the performance and power penalty of reconfiguration has the real potential to overwhelm its benefits. This chapter discussed a variety of methods proposed and used to reduce and in some cases remove reconfiguration overhead, including various configuration architecture designs, scheduling and caching techniques, and ways to reduce the configuration data size.

In many cases, several approaches can be combined to further reduce the overhead. For example, relocation and defragmentation architectural features facilitate advanced configuration scheduling mechanisms that load configurations in advance of their use to minimize processor stall time during reconfiguration. Likewise, a configuration cache can be combined with a relocation- and defragmentation-enabled design that uses a staging area, providing a wide path to configuration memory to decrease transfer time. This in turn can be combined with wildcarding to allow multiple identical rows or columns to be configured simultaneously. Such combined methods allow reconfigurable computing system designers to effectively minimize reconfiguration overhead and to provide the full benefit of reconfigurable computing in future computing systems.

References

[1] A. Abnous, H. Zhang, M. Wan, G. Varghese, V. Prabhu, J. Rabaey. The Pleiades architecture. *Application of Programmable DSPs in Mobile Communications*, A. Gatherer, A. Auslander, eds., Wiley, 2002.

[2] Actel Corp. *ProASIC3 Flash Family FPGAs*. Actel Corp., Mountain View, CA, 2006.

[3] Altera, Inc. *Stratix-II™ Device Handbook, Volumes 1 and 2*, Altera, Inc., San Jose, 2005.

[4] D. Andrews, D. Niehaus, R. Jidin. Implementing the thread programming model on hybrid FPGA/CPU computational components. *Workshop on Embedded Processor Architectures of the International Symposium on Computer Architecture*, 2004.

[5] Atmel Corp. *AT40K Series FPGA Interactive Architecture Guide*. Atmel Corp., San Jose, 1999.

[6] K. Bazargan, R. Kastner, M. Sarrafzadeh. Fast template placement for reconfigurable computing systems. *IEEE Design and Test, Special Issue on Reconfigurable Computing* 17(1), 2000.

[7] G. Brebner, O. Diessel. Chip-based reconfigurable task management. *International Conference on Field Programmable Logic and Applications*, 2001.

[8] J. Burns, A. Donlin, J. Hogg, S. Singh, M. de Wit. A dynamic reconfiguration runtime system. *IEEE Symposium on FPGAs for Custom Computing Machines*, 1997.

[9] J. M. P. Cardoso, M. Weinhardt. From C programs to the Configure-Execute model. *Design, Automation, and Test in Europe*, 2003.

[10] E. Caspi, A. DeHon, J. Wawrzynek. A streaming multithreaded model. *Third Workshop on Media and Stream Processors*, 2001.

[11] D. Chang, M. Marek-Sadowska. Partitioning sequential circuits on dynamically reconfigurable FPGAs. *IEEE Transactions on Computers* 48(6), 1999.

[12] M. C.-T. Chao, G.-M. Wu, I.-H.-R. Jiang, Y.-W. Chang. A clustering- and probability-based approach for time-multiplexed FPGA partitioning. *IEEE/ACM International Conference on Computer-Aided Design*, 1999.

[13] M. M. Chu. *Dynamic Runtime Scheduler Support for SCORE*, Master's thesis, University of California, Berkeley, 2000.

[14] K. Compton, Z. Li, J. Cooley, S. Knol, S. Hauck. Configuration relocation and defragmentation for runtime reconfigurable systems. *IEEE Transactions on VLSI* 10(3), June 2002.

[15] A. Dandalis, V. K. Prasanna. Configuration compression for FPGA-based embedded systems. *Proceedings of the ACM/SIGDA International Symposium on Field-Programmable Gate Arrays*, 2001.

[16] M. Dales. Managing a reconfigurable processor in a general purpose workstation environment. *Conference on Design, Automation, and Test in Europe*, 2003.

[17] A. DeHon. DPGA utilization and application. *Proceedings of the ACM/SIGDA International Symposium on Field Programmable Gate Arrays*, 1996.

[18] O. Diessel, H. E. Gindy, M. Middendorf, H. Schmeck, B. Schmidt. Dynamic scheduling of tasks on partially reconfigurable FPGAs. *IEE Proceedings—Computers and Digital Techniques, Special Issue on Reconfigurable Systems* 147(3), 2000.

[19] S. C. Goldstein, H. Schmit, M. Budiu, S. Cadambi, M. Moe, R. R. Taylor. PipeRench: A reconfigurable architecture and compiler. *IEEE Computer* 33(4), April 2000.

[20] J. D. Hadley, B. L. Hutchings. Design methodologies for partially reconfigured systems. *IEEE Symposium on FPGAs for Custom Computing Machines*, 1995.

[21] M. Handa, R. Vemuri. An efficient algorithm for finding empty space for online FPGA placement. *Design Automation Conference*, 2004.

[22] S. Hauck, Z. Li, E. J. Schwabe. Configuration compression for the Xilinx XC6200 FPGA. *IEEE Symposium on FPGAs for Custom Computing Machines*, 1998.

[23] S. Hauck. Configuration prefetch for single context reconfigurable coprocessors. *ACM/SIGDA International Symposium on Field-Programmable Gate Arrays*, 1998.

[24] J. R. Hauser. *Augmenting a Microprocessor with Reconfigurable Hardware*, Ph.D. thesis, University of California, Berkeley, 2000.

[25] Z. Huang, S. Malik. Managing dynamic reconfiguration overhead in systems-on-a-chip design using reconfigurable datapaths and optimized interconnection networks. *Design, Automation, and Test in Europe*, 2001.

[26] T. Kean. Cryptographic rights management of FPGA intellectual property cores. *International Symposium on Field-Programmable Gate Arrays*, 2002.

[27] A. Khan, N. Miyamoto, T. Ohkawa, A. Jamak, S. Kita, K. Kotani, T. Ohmi. An approach to realize time-sharing of flip-flops in time-multiplexed FPGAs. *IEEE International Conference on Field-Programmable Technology*, 2004.

[28] J. Lach, W. H. Mangione-Smith, M. Potkonjak. Fingerprinting techniques for field-programmable gate array intellectual property protection. *IEEE Transactions on Computer-Aided Design of Integrated Circuits and Systems* 20(10), 2001.

[29] Lattice Semiconductor Corp. *LatticeECP2 Family Data Sheet*, Lattice Semiconductor Corp., Hillsboro, OR, 2006.

[30] Z. Li, S. Hauck. Don't care discovery for FPGA configuration compression. *ACM/SIGDA International Symposium on Field-Programmable Gate Arrays*, 1999.

[31] Z. Li, K. Compton, S. Hauck. Configuration caching for FPGAs. *IEEE Symposium on FPGAs for Custom Computing Machines*, 2000.

[32] Z. Li, S. Hauck. Configuration compression for Virtex FPGAs. *IEEE Symposium on FPGAs for Custom Computing Machines*, 2001.

[33] Z. Li, S. Hauck. Configuration prefetching techniques for partial reconfigurable coprocessor with relocation and defragmentation. *ACM/SIGDA International Symposium on Field-Programmable Gate Arrays*, 2002.

[34] R. Lysecky, F. Valid. A configurable logic architecture for dynamic hardware/software partitioning. *Design, Automation, and Test in Europe*, 2004.

[35] U. Malik, O. Diessel. On the placement and granularity of FPGA configurations. *IEEE International Conference on Field-Programmable Technology*, 2004.

[36] W. H. Mangione-Smith. ATR from UCLA. Personal communication, 1999.

[37] Y. Markovskiy, E. Caspi, R. Huang, J. Yeh, M. Chu, J. Wawrzynek, A. DeHon. Analysis of quasi-static scheduling techniques in a virtualized reconfigurable machine. *ACM/SIGDA International Symposium on Field-Programmable Gate Arrays*, 2002.

[38] J. Noguera, R. M. Badia. HW/SW codesign techniques for dynamically reconfigurable architectures. *IEEE Transactions on VLSI Systems* 10(4), 2002.

[39] J. Noguera, R. M. Badia. Multitasking on reconfigurable architectures: Microarchitecture support and dynamic scheduling. *ACM Transactions on Embedded Computing Systems* 3(2), May 2004.

[40] V. Nollet, P. Coene, D. Verkest, S. Vernalde, R. Lauwereins. Designing an operating system for a heterogeneous reconfigurable SoC. *Reconfigurable Architecture Workshop*, 2003.

[41] H. Quinn, L. S. King, M. Leeser, W. Meleis. Runtime assignment of reconfigurable hardware components for image processing pipelines. *IEEE Symposium on Field-Programmable Custom Computing Machines*, 2003.

[42] J. Resano, D. Mozos, F. Catthoor. A hybrid prefetch scheduling heuristic to minimize at runtime the reconfiguration overhead of dynamically reconfigurable hardware. *Design, Automation, and Test in Europe*, 2005.

[43] C. R. Rupp, M. Landguth, T. Garverick, E. Gomersall, H. Holt, J. M. Arnold, M. Gokhale. The NAPA adaptive processing architecture. *IEEE Symposium on FPGAs for Custom Computing Machines*, 1998.

[44] H. Simmler, L. Levinson, R. Männer. Multitasking on FPGA coprocessors. *International Conference on Field-Programmable Logic and Applications*, 2000.

[45] H. Singh, G. Lu, M.-H. Lee, F. Kurdahi, N. Bagherzadeh, E. Filho, R. Mastre. MorphoSys: Case study of a reconfigurable computing system targeting multimedia applications. *Design Automation Conference*, 2000.

[46] C. Steiger, H. Walder, M. Platzner. Operating systems for reconfigurable embedded platforms: Online scheduling of real-time tasks. *IEEE Transactions on Computers* 53(11), 2004.

[47] S. Trimberger, D. Carberry, A. Johnson, J. Wong. A time-multiplexed FPGA. *IEEE Symposium on FPGAs for Custom Computing Machines*, 1997.

[48] H. Walder, M. Platzner. Non-preemptive multitasking on FPGAs: Task placement and footprint transform. *International Conference on Engineering of Reconfigurable Systems and Architectures*, 2002.

[49] G. Wigley, D. Kearney. The first real operating system for reconfigurable computing. *Australasian Computer Systems Architecture Conference*, 2001.

[50] M. J. Wirthlin, B. L. Hutchings. A dynamic instruction set computer. *IEEE Symposium on FPGAs for Custom Computing Machines*, 1995.

[51] M. J. Wirthlin, B. L. Hutchings. Sequencing run-time reconfigured hardware with software. *ACM/SIGDA International Symposium on Field-Programmable Gate Arrays*, 1996.

[52] G.-M. Wu, J.-M. Lin, Y.-W. Chang. Generic ILP-based approaches for time-multiplexed FPGA partitioning. *IEEE Transactions on Computer-Aided Design of Integrated Circuits and Systems* 20(10), 2001.

[53] Xilinx, Inc. *XC6200 Field Programmable Gate Arrays Product Description*, Xilinx, Inc., San Jose, 1997.

[54] Xilinx, Inc. *Virtex-II Platform FPGAs: Complete Data Sheet*, Xilinx, Inc., San Jose, 2004.

[55] Xilinx, Inc. *Virtex-5 FPGA Configuration User Guide*, Xilinx, Inc., San Jose, 2006.

[56] G. Brebner. The swappable logic unit: A paradigm for virtual hardware, *IEEE Symposium on FPGAs for Custom Computing Machines*, 1997.

[57] W. Fu, K. Compton. An execution environment for reconfigurable computing. *IEEE Symposium on Field-Programmable Custom Computing Machines*, 2005.

[58] M. Wirthlin, B. Hutchings. Improving functional density through run-time constant propagation. *ACM/SIGDA International Symposium on Field-Programmable Gate Arrays*, 86–92, 1997.

PART II

PROGRAMMING RECONFIGURABLE SYSTEMS

As suggested in the Introduction, field-programmable gate arrays (FPGAs) and reconfigurable architectures have both the postfabrication programmability of software and the spatial parallelism of hardware. To fully exploit them, we need models and programming approaches that support the software's programmability, including infrastructure and runtime support to allow the configuration to change over time. In addition to temporal reprogrammability, the reconfigurable programming systems must simultaneously deal with spatial issues normally associated only with hardware (e.g., physical placement of computations and timing of functional units).

To illustrate how we can program reconfigurable systems, the chapters in this part of the book describe the current state of the art in approaching and capturing designs for FPGAs and reconfigurable architectures. Chapter 5 reviews compute models and organizations suitable for reconfigurable applications, Chapters 6 through 10 and Chapter 12 explore different design entry points for reconfigurable applications, and Chapters 11 and 12 examine infrastructural support issues, including operating and runtime systems and debuggers.

The flexibility of FPGAs and reconfigurable architectures, as well as their dual hardware/software nature, means that the old computational models we are familiar with for hardware or software may not be the most effective for reasoning about reconfigurable designs. Furthermore, the design space for reconfigurable solutions is much larger than those most of us are used to navigating. Chapter 5 explores some useful models for capturing and conceptualizing reconfigurable applications and a variety of system architectures for providing efficient implementations. A clear conceptual model of the parallelism in the application, how to expose it, and how to exploit it make up an invaluable starting point for describing the application in a concrete programming language.

Chapter 6 provides an introduction to VHDL as an example of a Register transfer level (RTL) hardware description language. A software designer might think of VHDL as a semi-portable assembly language for reconfigurable designs; it provides fine control of hardware and parallelism, but it demands that the designer manage quite a number of low-level details. Many of the higher-level programming approaches still use VHDL as an intermediate mapping stage on the way to a reconfigurable configuration.

Chapter 7 turns to more software-friendly approaches and shows how programs written in C can automatically be translated into reconfigurable hardware designs. Today, we cannot expect to obtain good performance from arbitrary C code with no concern for the capabilities of the reconfigurable architecture and compiler. However, with an appreciation for what reconfigurable architectures can do, an appropriate system architecture, and an understanding of the capabilities of the C compiler, it is possible to effectively develop and optimize reconfigurable applications in C.

Chapters 8 and 9 discuss two examples of programming systems that support streaming dataflow compute models (Section 5.1.3). These models, too, provide a higher-level approach to reconfigurable design than VHDL, offering greater opportunities for automated design scalability. Chapter 8 describes how we can apply the SDF (Synchronous Dataflow) model (Section 5.1.3) using Simulink, illustrating how methodology and suitable libraries can raise the abstraction for design construction. These techniques can readily be adopted by today's system designers. At the same time, the Simulink integration example shows how reconfigurable design can leverage popular system analysis tools such as MATLAB.

Chapter 9 describes a more custom and automated experimental design flow that supports application scalability for dynamic streaming dataflow applications (Section 5.1.3). It illustrates how many system architectures (Section 5.2) come together to support efficient and automated mapping of designs to reconfigurable computing platforms, and it offers a vision of how integrated programming systems for reconfigurable platforms might evolve.

Many efficient reconfigurable applications are naturally data parallel (Section 5.1.5) and are efficiently implemented with a Single Instruction Multiple Data (SIMD) or vector organization. Chapter 10 describes data parallel programming approaches customized for reconfigurable compilation.

In Chapter 12 we see an example of a rich generator language, JHDL, which provides even lower-level control of structure than VHDL, but does so with the full programming power of a conventional software language, Java. Thus, it provides a high-level platform from which to develop highly tuned designs. It also provides rich support for the construction of custom tools for reconfigurable design optimization.

As reconfigurable computers emerge as platforms for creating and delivering software, we must develop software support normally associated only with general-purpose processors, including operating systems, runtime support, and interactive debuggers. Chapter 11 describes the growing demands for reconfigurable operating systems, highlighting some of the early work along this path and pointing out important directions for the future. JHDL (Chapter 12) is notable for its support for interactive debugging and the extensible programming environment it provides, including hooks for software modules that interact with reconfigurable designs.

CHAPTER 5

COMPUTE MODELS AND SYSTEM ARCHITECTURES

André DeHon
Department of Electrical and Systems Engineering
University of Pennsylvania

Field-programmable gate array (FPGA) and reconfigurable architectures provide enormous raw computing power and tremendous flexibility. How do we best exploit this opportunity and bring it to bear on particular computing tasks? When we do take advantage of the flexibility, and how do we ensure correctness? How do we preserve and reuse our designs as technology continues to advance? The raw size and flexibility of today's devices and systems make these questions daunting to consider and intractable to approach in an undisciplined manner. In this chapter, we review models and organizational styles for large-scale, highly parallel computing resources and emphasize how they can be used in the organization of reconfigurable computers.

A modern FPGA has hundreds of thousands of independently configured bit-processing units and hundreds of memories. Today's multi-FPGA systems and future single-chip FPGAs raise these numbers to millions of bit-processing units and thousands or tens of thousands of memories. Furthermore, configurable interconnect allows us to arrange these resources in almost any manner. This gives us the power to adapt the computation to a particular task. Now that we have that power, what do we do with it?

Developing large software applications is a known hard problem, and managing resources and computations in highly parallel systems is, notoriously, even harder. Without care, our parallel computations may behave differently on each execution, producing nondeterministic results, some of which may be erroneous, and some executions may lead to deadlock. Unconstrained, the additional flexibility that comes with parallelism increases the complexity of application development and verification.

Considering both the limits of the human mind and the desire to achieve reasonably low time-to-solution periods, we cannot afford to custom-tailor each 4-LUT and each memory. With industry producing new devices according to Moore's Law, we cannot afford to design for 100,000 4-LUTs one year, discard the design, and then redesign for 200,000 4-LUTs three years later when the next part becomes available. Nor can we afford to reason about the interaction of every individual 4-LUT with every other—a number of interactions that grows quadratically with resource count.

The good news is that, while there is almost unbounded freedom in how we might solve problems, there are a small number of high-level organizational strategies that suffice to describe and efficiently implement most computing tasks. To bridge the semantic gap between applications and FPGA resources, we should think about two abstractions:

- *Compute models*—high-level models of the flow of computation in an application, useful for capturing parallelism and reasoning about correctness of implementations.
- *System architectures*—high-level strategies for organizing resources, managing the parallelism in the implementation, and facilitating optimization and design scaling.

Within each system architecture, there remains considerable flexibility to tailor the computing resources to the particular task, exploiting the flexibility of the architecture's reconfigurability. The compute model provides high-level constraints and guidance for conceptualizing the problem, reasoning about its correctness, and supporting manual and automated optimization. Chosen properly, the compute model naturally captures the parallelism of the application, making it easier to reason about its description and mapping.

A diversity of compute models and system architectures is needed to capture the diversity of natural organizations and implementations of tasks. Nonetheless, evidence to date suggests that there are only a modest number, perhaps tens of each, necessary to do this. Mismatches between the compute model and the task increase the complexity and awkwardness of the design and limit scalability. However, a good designers will be aware of the variety of compute models and system architectures and judiciously select the ones that naturally match her problem.

For decades, software engineers have faced the problem of managing complexity in large, highly concurrent software systems. *Software architectures* [1] were developed as one of the organizational tools to manage the complexity and to guide the design of these systems. The *system architectures* identified here are a deliberate expansion and adaptation of software architecture for reconfigurable computing, and many of the challenges are identical. However, the additional flexibility of reconfigurable architectures opens up design options and tradeoffs not typically present in the conventional multiprocessor systems for which software architectures have been traditionally targeted.

The two main sections in this chapter introduce, respectively, compute models and system architectures relevant to reconfigurable computing. For the reader approaching these topics for the first time, it may make sense to read the introductory sections, giving the detailed sections only a cursory review, for a high-level understanding of why we need a variety of models and architectures. As one delves further into reconfigurable designs or has a particular application in mind to solve, the in-depth sections can serve as a reference guide and provide deeper consideration of the merits and suitability of each approach.

5.1 COMPUTE MODELS

Figure 5.1 provides a taxonomy of the major compute models discussed and refined in this chapter. The leftmost branch is a set of models organized around the flow of data between operators; in these we think about the computation as a graph of computational operators and we reason about the correctness and assembly of operation in terms of data arrival at the operators, the function performed on the data, and the result produced and forwarded to other operators. The rightmost branch is a set of models organized around synchronous steps for the entire machine; here we think about the computation as a sequence of, perhaps parallel, operations performing transformation to global state.

At the top of the figure is a generic multi-threaded model or, formally, a model such as Hoare's Communicating Sequential Processes (CSP) [2]. All of the models below can be seen as refinements and stylizations on it. The multi-threaded model gives little guidance to the programmer on how to organize and design programs. Consequently, each of the refinements takes a stronger stand on how computation and parallelism are organized and how we manage synchronization. In many cases the refined models come with greater opportunities for optimization and stronger verification guarantees.

As we will see, system architectures are typically built on some of the same distinctions identified here in compute models (e.g., sequential control versus dataflow). However, there is not necessarily a one-to-one matching between the compute model used for capturing and reasoning about the application and the system architecture used for implementation. For example, modern superscalar microprocessors efficiently execute sequential instructions streams using dataflow techniques (e.g., Tomasulo [3]), and digital signal processors (DSPs) execute synchronous dataflow graphs as a sequence of instructions.

5.1.1 Challenges

When approaching a problem, we want to know how to implement the desired computation correctly, with the least effort, while exploiting the available

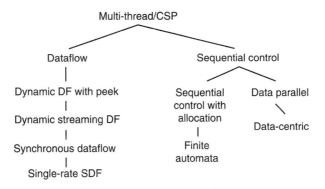

FIGURE 5.1 ■ Overview of compute models.

hardware capabilities on current and future machines. We can decompose this into specific challenges in selecting a compute model and developing the implementation:

■ How do we think about composing the application?
■ How does the compute model naturally lead to efficient, spatial solutions?
■ How does the compute model support design (de)composition?
■ How do we conceptualize parallelism?
■ How do we trade area for time in the compute model?
■ How do we reason about correctness?
■ How do we deal with technology effects and adapt to technology changes?
■ How does the compute model provide or guarantee determinacy?
■ How do we avoid deadlock?
■ What can we compute?
■ How complex is it to optimize or validate properties of the application?

The first thing the compute model gives us is a way to think about the application. For example: Should we think of the application as a sequence of operations that need to be performed (sequential control)? As applying an operation to a set of independent data items (data parallel)? As a set of transformations on a data sequence (streaming dataflow)? To the extent these questions provide a natural way to describe the application, they make it easier to compose the application, identify the natural parallelism, and reason about correctness and transformations. Ideally, the compute model acts as part of the bridge between the application and the reconfigurable platform, providing a modest semantic gap between the application and the system architecture. The system architecture then brings to bear a large set of knowledge, accumulated across many applications, about how to efficiently bridge the gap between the compute model and the reconfigurable platform.

Reconfigurable platforms are most efficient when we can arrange for each resource to do the same thing over and over, and keep most of the resources active doing exactly the work needed for the computation. The compute model should allow us to capture computations that can exploit this; further, it should encourage the developer to express applications in a manner amenable to this kind of computation. The restrictions and stylizations in some compute models may limit the freedom in expressing an algorithm. However, limiting expressive freedom that would lead to poor reconfigurable solutions is one of the ways that a good compute model provides assistance and guidance. If the limitations make a solution hard to express, that can be good guidance that the solution approach is not well suited to a reconfigurable platform or that the compute model is not the natural choice for the task.

A good compute model helps us decompose a problem into components that can be designed and validated independently. This helps avoid the quadratic explosion in complexity arising from potentially interacting resources, and even avoid the linear cost necessary if we had to program each resource independently. Sequential control models may focus on sequences of subroutines; dataflow models, on composition of functions; and streaming dataflow models, on hierarchical operator graphs.

Important to identify early is where the parallelism exists in an application. Is it between data items (data parallelism), between coarse-grained tasks (task parallelism), between operators in a task (instruction-level parallelism), or within low-level arithmetic and binary operations (bit-level parallelism)? Identifying and exposing these opportunities assists area-time tradeoffs: On small, economical platforms, we can tune a task for the modest area at the expense of longer runtime, while on larger platforms we might exploit the additional area to reduce compute time. Parallelism shows up implicitly or explicitly in each compute model, and a good match in parallelism will facilitate successful application scaling.

One of the most important tools provided by each compute model is a way to reason about correctness, which ultimately facilitates scaling, implementation adaptation, and optimization because it defines what transformations are possible without impacting correctness. In a sequential control model we identify the visible state on each step and reason about the changes in it; in a streaming dataflow model we reason about the output sequence of a computational graph.

With rapidly advancing technology, the size, speed, and energy of computing primitives (e.g., gates, wires, memories) are changing continually as they move from platform to platform. Sometimes they move together, with compute, interconnect, and memory speeds all growing uniformly smaller. Often, however, they change at different rates. As vendors have optimized memory for density and logic for speed, relative speeds have diverged, and, as we reach into the deep submicron regime, interconnect scales more slowly than compute. As a result, simply moving an old design to a new platform is unlikely to optimally exploit it. With increasing interconnect delays, perhaps the design needs more pipelining to distant locations; with slower memories, perhaps it needs more parallel memory blocks servicing a compute block. The compute model helps us understand the transformations permissible for the design, which may point to techniques the system architecture can employ for tolerating changes in constituent delays. Stall signals, for example, allow sequential control to slow down only when uncommon operations run at slower speeds than the scaled speed of the rest of the logic; data presence (see Data presence subsection of Section 5.2.1) allows streaming dataflow computations to tolerate variable delays within and between operators.

Given the same set of inputs, we might want our computation to produce the same outputs. That is, we often want our computation to be *deterministic*. Certainly, if the result of the computation differs each time it is performed, it becomes harder to debug our application or demonstrate its correctness. This can be a mild problem with sequential applications, where dependence on dynamic effects (e.g., dynamically allocated addresses) may change the program behavior; it becomes acute in concurrent systems. If there is variability in the relative timing of operations, the order of events can change, and without care this may result in different visible application behavior.

Further, as we scale to different hardware capacities, we may exploit different amounts of concurrency and deliberately change the order of primitive events. Nonetheless, we might want to guarantee that the application remains deterministic, providing the same results for any legal parallelism. Some compute models with limited constraints may not be able to guarantee such determinacy but place this burden on the individual programmer. Most, however, come with disciplines that the developer can use to provide determinism, and some come with a sufficient set of model restrictions to automatically guarantee it.

Still, sometimes we want or need nondeterminism to deal with variations in the outside world (e.g., waiting for human input) or with deliberate variations to avoid bad behavior (e.g., randomized algorithms). Sometimes, too, there are multiple "correct" results and it is efficient to allow the system to select any of them, perhaps in a way that looks nondeterministic to the application as a whole. The point here is that nondeterminism always adds complexity to construction and validation, so it should be used sparingly and with care [4]

When dealing with shared or limited resources or variable operations in concurrent systems, we must also watch out for *deadlock*; in other words, we must watch for cases where the system may enter a state that prevents it from making forward progress. Often deadlock occurs when we attempt to give exclusive access to resources in an application. If a set of tasks end up waiting for each other—that is, the task set has a dependent cycle waiting for resources—the tasks can become deadlocked and the application will never complete. This can happen in purely deterministic computations, but should be at least identified by reasonably testing if the paths through the code are largely data independent. However, if the paths are largely data dependent, and deadlock only occurs for certain data values, identifying it with *ad hoc* testing can be difficult. When resource allocation and sequencing are nondeterministic, avoiding deadlock can be even more tricky. For these reasons, it is necessary to carefully guarantee that none of the legal, nondeterministic choices leads to a deadlock situation.

Computational theory gives us a well-developed set of models for computation. The Church–Turing Thesis [5–7] suggests that there is a very robust class of computing models that are all equivalent to the Turing Machine or the Lambda Calculus model. In fact, most of the models discussed here are Turing Complete. However, some refinements, such as synchronous dataflow (see Synchronous dataflow subsection of Section 5.1.3) or finite-state sequential control (see Finite state subsection of Section 5.1.4) models, are specifically less powerful. As will be noted, these restricted models give up expressive power in order to gain more powerful optimization and analysis.

We want to be able to say that an application always has certain properties. Ideally, we can verify that our expression of the application is correct, or, more specifically, that our captured algorithm is deterministic or that it can never deadlock. Further, to facilitate automated optimization and area–time scaling, we must guarantee that any changes made to the implementation preserve determinism and freedom from deadlock. Thus, we are ultimately concerned with the computational tractability of verification and optimization. In Turing–Complete compute models, where anything is allowed, verification and general optimization can be *undecidable*; that is, without solving the *halting problem* it is not possible to analyze the design and say whether or not it is correct, determinate, or deadlock free. In more restricted models, verification or optimization may be *decidable* but *NP-hard*, meaning that we know of no polynomial time solutions to perform the optimization. And in even more restricted models, verification and optimization may be polynomial time. Consequently, we have a trade-off between the expressiveness and the strength of automation we can bring to bear on the problem, which suggests that the designer carefully select compute models that are expressive enough for her problem but not unnecessarily so.

5.1.2 Common Primitives

Two common primitives useful for defining and reasoning about compute models are *functions* and *objects*.

Function

A *function* is simply a deterministic, mathematical function that maps each finite input to a finite output:

$$Y = [y_0, y_1, \ldots, y_n] = f(X = [x_0, x_1, \ldots, x_m])$$

A function depends on no hidden state but only the input arguments to it, and it modifies no state values. Examples include addition, square root, and discrete-cosine transform (DCT). Functions can be composed, and the result is another function. For example:

$$y = (f \circ g)(x) = f(g(x))$$

Functions are interesting as a building block for several reasons:

- Functions are a useful formal primitive for defining computational models.
- Functional operations can be a tool or clue to parallelism—since functions do not modify state, they may be evaluated in parallel; evaluation of functions on different data can often be heavily pipelined.
- Functions can be a tool or guide to recurrent computations—those that show up regularly in the description of a computation are candidates for computational blocks that can be profitably implemented in spatial reconfigurable logic.

Transform or object

We can associate state with a function in order to create a common building block we can think of as a *transform*, or a primitive version of an *object*. In signal processing, we might think of a general transform as taking a sequence of inputs and computing outputs based on them as well as on some finite state from the previous output:

$$Y_i = f(X_i, Y_{i-1})$$

In an *object-oriented* model, we might think of the object, O, being the combination of state, $O.s$, and a function, $O.f$, with each invocation evaluating the function on the input and the state and returning an output and a new state value:

$$Y, O.s_i = O.f(X, O.s_{i-1})$$

Examples of transforms include accumulators, finite-impulse response filters (FIRs), infinite impulse response filters (IIRs), and linear-feedback shift registers (LFSRs).

This primitive object or transform is more powerful than a pure function, but the inclusion of state may restrict its freedom of usage and implementation. As described, the state is finite, and each object can be viewed as a finite automata. The model says that the sequential invocations of an object see the state from the previous invocation; this demands that we complete the function's evaluation before starting the next invocation—or, at least, that we provide an implementation that produces the same net output sequence and state updates as though we had done so. For simple functions (e.g., LFSRs) or those where the state can be maintained without computation (e.g., FIRs), we can still pipeline the operation heavily. However, for complex functions (e.g., IIRs) the state feedback may limit our ability to heavily pipeline the object.

Nonetheless, object state is owned by the object, so evaluation of an object affects no others. Consequently, distinct objects with a complete set of inputs can evaluate in parallel; they impact each other only by communicating values between them. Further, objects with the same function may be able to share the same hardware to create commonality. This is useful both for enabling area–time trade-offs and for keeping a spatial datapath active in repeatedly performing the same operations. If sequential dependencies within an operator limit pipelining and we have many objects of the same type, it may be possible to C-slow the function evaluation (Chapter 18) to use the same hardware to service multiple objects.

In rich object-oriented models, we may associate additional capabilities with objects. We will introduce some of these as we explore more powerful compute models in the following sections.

5.1.3   Dataflow

We begin our detailed discussion of compute models with the left branch in Figure 5.1. In these models, we reason about the computation based on the flow of data. Computations are performed by *operators*, which can be either functions or objects as defined previously. We connect the operators into a graph, linking the output data from one to the input data of another. When its inputs arrive,

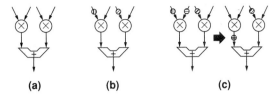

FIGURE 5.2 ■ Computation on a dataflow graph: (a) graph without inputs, (b) graph with partial inputs, and (c) arrival of matched input on left ×-operator allows it to evaluate and compute its output.

an operator can evaluate, produce its outputs, and send them to any operators connected to it (see Figure 5.2).

The dataflow graph exposes considerable parallelism and freedom in evaluation permitted to an implementation. The links capture the communication and dependence structure of the computation explicitly.

There is a large hierarchy of dataflow models with different flexibilities and challenges. For example, the simple models can be easily mapped to spatial, reconfigurable computation. The more flexible and powerful models are more complicated to implement efficiently, and make it difficult to guarantee correctness. However, for some applications, these more powerful models may be essential to efficiently describing and executing an application.

Single-rate synchronous dataflow
One of the most primitive dataflow models is that of a static graph of operators. The graph is created once, before the application executes, and persists unchanged throughout execution. In contrast, in the Streaming dataflow with allocation subsection (see page 102), we will consider models that allow the dataflow graph to change as part of the computation. We call the persistent edges between operators *streams* or *pipes*, as they deliver a sequence of values from a single producer to a single consumer, and we identify each value carried over these streams as a *token*. Such a graph of operators can itself be viewed as an operator, so this provides a model for composition of more powerful operators from more primitive functions and objects (see Figure 5.3). Computationally, this still provides the power of a finite automata, but the dataflow view is often a more natural way to describe, compose, and reason about the computation.

Synchronous dataflow
In single-rate synchronous dataflow, we assume that each transform operator takes in a single set of input tokens and produces a single set of output tokens. It is a simple generalization to allow the model to take in multiple tokens on a single stream link or to produce multiple tokens on an output stream link for one logical evaluation of the function. For example, a down-sample operator might read two inputs and only output one value, discarding every other input token. The number of inputs received from each input stream, or outputs produced on each output stream, can be different; for example, an operator might read two A tokens for every B token. However, as long as there are a constant number of

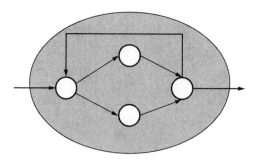

FIGURE 5.3 ▪ A single-rate static dataflow graph.

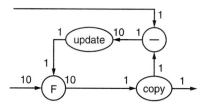

FIGURE 5.4 ▪ A multirate dataflow graph.

tokens consumed from each input stream and tokens produced on each output stream on each such evaluation, the model retains the same power as before, but it now allows us to efficiently express multirate streaming applications; that is, some loops in the dataflow graph can operate at much lower frequency than others.

An inner loop might execute on every input to the graph, while an outer loop might perform updates only once every 10 inputs as shown in Figure 5.4. The numbers on the operator I/Os in Figure 5.4 indicate the rate of I/O consumption or production. The update module produces a single output every 10 tokens; the F function consumes a single input from update every tenth data input and output token; and the copy and subtract units each produce a single set of output tokens for each set of input tokens.

This is the Synchronous Dataflow (SDF) model [8], and it retains the same computational power of a finite automata. However, it allows multirate designs to be expressed more efficiently, explicitly identifying the relative operating rates of each of the computational functions in the graph. An implementation can use this information when provisioning operators and scheduling the sharing of physical resources. The computation is completely deterministic, and it is possible to automatically identify when operator rates are mismatched, leading to deadlock, and to automatically identify any buffering necessary during execution [9].

Dynamic streaming dataflow
Synchronous dataflow retains analysis simplicity because there is no data dependence in the consumption or production of tokens. Every evaluation of an object consumes and produces the same number of tokens regardless of the data.

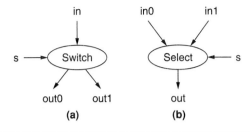

FIGURE 5.5 ■ The dynamic dataflow primitives—*switch* (a) and *select* (b).

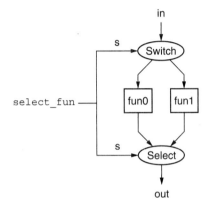

FIGURE 5.6 ■ Data-driven function selection in the dataflow model.

A more general model allows the production of input and output tokens to depend on the object state or the values of the inputs. We can fully capture this additional power by adding the *switch* and *select* operators, shown in Figure 5.5, to a persistent object graph.

In the figure, these two operators are data dependent, producing data on only one output, or consuming the inputs selectively, based on an input value. Equivalently, this can be captured by generalizing the notion of an object to allow its state to determine the token consumption and production actually performed on each evaluation. This allows us to efficiently deal with data-dependent cases, such as the following:

- Performing different operations based on the data (Figure 5.6).
- Varying the rate of the output relative to the input, such as in a compressor or decompresser (e.g., Huffman encoder).
- Iterating a computation a variable number of times to yield convergence (e.g., Newton–Raphson method for finding roots of equations).

In some cases these operations can be data independent, but only at the expense of more work (e.g., evaluating both functions in Figure 5.6 and then discarding one result). However, if no constant bound can be placed on the iterations (e.g., the number of cycles required for convergence), data dependence is a necessity, not just an efficiency optimization.

The addition of data-dependent operators changes the power of the streaming dataflow, making it more difficult to analyze statically. The computation remains deterministic, but data-dependent production and consumption rates on operators necessitate reasoning about the streams as first-in-first-out (FIFO) token buffers. The addition of unbounded buffers between operators is sufficient to make the model Turing Complete, and it is no longer always possible to determine the FIFO buffers' required capacity. If the implementation buffer capacity is too small, the application may artificially deadlock. This demands either that the developer identify the necessary buffer size to avoid deadlock for each application or that the implementation provide dynamic support to allow arbitrary buffer expansion at runtime [10].

Dynamic Streaming Dataflow with Peeks
So far, we have demanded that the object evaluate based on a valid set of input tokens. In the data-dependent case, we allowed the value of the present tokens to determine which other tokens were consumed. We can further allow the operator to perform an action or modify state based on the absence of a token; that is, we can allow it to *peek* to see if an input is present. For example, a merge unit might have two inputs and forward either token to its output whenever there is some input present. As the merge unit example suggests, this creates new freedom for efficient evaluation but also introduces nondeterminism. The operator can now behave differently based on the arrival timing of its inputs. The data-dependent streaming dataflow model discussed earlier only introduced concern about deadlock but remained deterministic. The Dynamic Streaming Dataflow with Peeks model forces the developer to manage determinacy.

Streaming dataflow with allocation
The parallelism in the application is, in general, data dependent. Consequently, it can be useful for the operator dataflow graph to evolve on the basis of the data in a computation. In a telecommunications application, the number and type (e.g., voice, data) of connections change over time. Each channel has its own noise characteristics, perhaps requiring filter complexity (e.g., number of taps, length of echo cancellation) different from the others'. To accommodate these changes in the computational demand of an application over time, we must change the dataflow operator graph. We could force the graph construction to a different compute model and stay with graph evaluation as one of the models reviewed earlier. Alternately, we must expand the compute model with the ability to create new operators and link them into the graph.

The key addition now is for our operators to be able to perform instantiation (e.g., new) of operators and streams and to be able to connect them. Even if operators remain finite state, instantiation provides the ability to create unbounded state by growing the object graph to unbounded size, with arbitrary data structures implemented as subgraphs. This provides a more efficient path to achieving Turing Completeness than the unbounded buffers in dynamic streaming dataflow.

While powerful, dynamic allocation means that the logical graph is changing during execution, and with dynamically changing computational graphs, it is no longer possible to optimize, schedule, place, and route them before execution. As a result, dynamic allocation gives us a model for the application to change during execution that can exploit the capabilities of a reconfigurable computing platform. However, it can also force a need for reconfiguration during execution, so allocation should be used with care. If it is infrequent, and allocated objects are long-lived, the cost of runtime management and reconfiguration can be amortized out over long usage periods.

General dataflow

Once we add allocation of operators, the model becomes powerful enough to be used as general dataflow computation. Some dataflow models do not treat operators or links as persistent (e.g., Arvind and Nikhil [11] and Culler et al. [12]). Rather, the dataflow is instantiated during a function or object call, used once, and then it is disposed. This does not change the model, but it does change the relative rate of allocation versus dataflow usage in a significant way. On typical reconfigurable platforms, dataflow construction is expensive, making it more difficult to efficiently map models that dispose of and reconstruct dataflow. For efficient execution on a reconfigurable platform, the compiler must discover opportunities to create dataflow operator graphs and reuse them across many invocations.

5.1.4 Sequential Control

The most widely used models for capturing and reasoning about algorithms are based on some form of sequential operation, including popular programming languages (e.g., C, Java, Fortran), control structures for hardware (finite-state machines), and formal models of computation (Deterministic Finite Automata, Sequential Turing Machines). The basic idea behind these models is that computations are defined as a sequence of primitive operations performed on some data state. The primitive operations define how state is transformed, including the state that determines which primitive operation(s) to execute next. Simple, concrete embodiments of this include sequential Instruction Set Architecture (ISA) processor models [13], but the state transforms can be much larger, may be coarse grained, and may include substantial parallelism on each sequential step.

Sequential control allows us to decompose a problem into simple, primitive operations. One thing happens at a time, making it relatively easy to reason about what each operation can do to the state.

Execution where only one primitive operation occurs at a time does not take full advantage of spatial reconfigurable architectures, leaving almost all the hardware idle as operations are sequentialized. Coarse-grained sequential operations that perform complex functions on large amounts of data may provide sufficient parallelism to match the reconfigurable hardware. While strict sequentialization of operations defines the intended results in the model, careful analysis can often reconstruct a data dependence graph (Chapter 7), essentially the dataflow graph (see Section 5.1.3), to allow several operations to proceed in parallel and at the same time maintaining the sequential model semantics. Still, care must be taken in the sequential expression to avoid introducing false dependencies that inhibit parallelism. In general, the sequential expression can be a poor match for the parallel capabilities, and sequential models tend to lead the designer away from good reconfigurable implementations. There are, however, characteristics of our computations that sequential control may capture well at a high level.

- Data-dependent calculations are naturally captured with branching. Sequential control here allows us to express the selection of the computation we need to perform on the data.
- Phased computations where the algorithm does widely different things at different times may also be captured well with sequential control. If each phase requires widely different computation, spatially supporting them all at once may leave much of the reconfigurable hardware idle during the calculation. Transitions between phases gives us a way of expressing and identifying points in the program where it may be useful to reconfigure the hardware for the different portions of the task, instantiating only the relevant hardware for each phase.

Finite state
The simplest models of sequential control operate with a finite amount of state and are computationally equivalent to finite automata. Given this, verification of optimized computations can be performed in polynomial time with state reachability [14].

Sequential control with allocation
In more powerful models of sequential computation, we allow operations that allocate additional memory (e.g., `malloc`, `new`). Coupled with data-dependent branching, this allows the computation to allocate an unbounded amount of state, making the model Turing Complete, which in turn means that we cannot generally prove a bound on the amount of memory the application may require to run to completion.

Single memory pool
As noted earlier (see Section 5.1.2), because of an object's internal state we must carefully sequence the operations on it. We can think of each logical memory pool in a sequential model as an object with state so every operation on a single memory can be dependent on every other. If static analysis cannot prove that two users of the memory operator modify disjoint state in the memory, the operations must be sequentialized to preserve sequential correctness. In single-memory compute models, such as the C programming language or a traditional ISA execution environment, all memory operations must be sequentialized. This

sequentialization significantly limits the parallelism a compiler can extract from a single-thread, single-memory compute model. Consequently, large C programs that have not been carefully written to avoid these dependencies can be difficult or impossible to parallelize. Nonetheless, aggressive compilers can sometimes succeed in decomposing the monolithic memory into disjoint memory pools (e.g., Babb et al. [15]).

5.1.5 Data Parallel

Some applications are naturally captured as performing identical transformations on a set of independent data items. For example, we may need to perform the same color–space conversion to every pixel in an image, or perform the same match test to every data item in a database. Even though we could express such a task as a sequential loop over all the data items, it is often difficult for a compiler to prove the independence of each data item transform, and it can be tricky for the developer to identify which loop operations allow independent computation. Therefore, it is often useful to have an explicitly data parallel model that allows us to reason about and express algorithms as a sequence of transformations on aggregate datasets.

Once the desired computation is captured as a sequence of independent, identical, potentially parallelizable operations, we have considerable freedom in implementation for area–time tradeoffs. The computation can be rendered spatially and kept active as a heavily pipelined vector unit (see Vector coprocessors subsection of Section 5.2.4). Additional, parallel units can be allocated as the dataset demands and the platform permits.

The model typically remains sequential at the core and can suffer from artificial parallelism limits based on the provided sequential model. In particular, it may be hard to determine cases where multiple, independent data parallel operations can occur simultaneously. Although the parallelism on a single operation is limited by the size of the aggregate data item, the data parallel model does give general high-level guidance to the developer that often trends in the right direction for efficient spatial realizations.

5.1.6 Data-centric

In the streaming dataflow model, the designer thinks of the application as a transformation graph with data generally flowing through operators with fixed state. For some applications, such as physical simulations, it makes sense to turn that around and think about the operators and their state as the primary data structure, and reason about the computation as transformations on the operator state. For a network flow problem, we might construct the graph for the network; each operator maintains state to represent the flow through its links and the accumulating overflow at the node, and each operator sends tokens over the edges between operators to reroute flow. At each sequential step we may allow each operator to process a set of inputs and send a set of outputs. At a high level the operation is data parallel, with each operator performing its node update operation; however, locally the computation may be data and state dependent. High-level data parallel instructions to the operators can sequence phases of the computation (e.g., preflow and push phases in network flow).

Applications that regularly visit many nodes on large graphs of data are a natural source of parallelism. Even if the nodes are not identical, there are usually only a small number of different node types, providing an opportunity for sharing of spatial operators. Without strict dataflow communication ordering, additional disciplines may be necessary to maintain determinacy. Efficient execution may require load balancing and sharing if graph nodes have low or widely varying activity factors.

5.1.7 Multi-threaded

A widely used model for parallelism is multi-threading or some form of CSP [2]. Basically the model is a collection of sequential control processes with communication links between them, either as direct communication edges or as shared memory. Multi-threading is a very general model and, in fact, any of the models presented so far could be seen as subsets of it.

The problem with multi-threading is that it is too general and powerful to provide guidance for application development and correct implementation. It permits the expression of solutions that are difficult to reason about, and it provides little guidance on good solutions and guaranteeing determinism [4]. How should the application be divided into threads? How do the threads synchronize with each other? How do we guarantee determinism and avoid deadlock? In our streaming dataflow model, we think of each thread, the operators, as transforms on the data flowing through them, and we synchronize based on token flow; in our data parallel model, we think of each thread as a separate data item and update each in lockstep; in our data-centric model, we think of each thread as an active object in the graph, performing updates on barrier-synchronized steps.

When faced with applications that demand more power than is available in a more restricted model, we should think about the power actually necessary for our application and the extent to which we can define a restricted discipline for using the multi-threaded model that answers the questions the model does not answer for us. What do our threads and operators represent? What is the synchronization discipline? What is our basis for reasoning about determinacy, deadlock, and correctness?

5.1.8 Other Compute Models

The compute models reviewed here are by no means exhaustive. From the start, we want to emphasize the need to consider multiple models and choose the one most natural for the application. The set just described are useful in reasoning about the architectures and applications developed in this book and may be most helpful for reasoning about reconfigurable applications. Nonetheless, as we master these models and encounter applications that match poorly with them, we should look for others that further ease the conceptualization of an application. (For other summaries of compute models see Lee and Sangiovanni-Vincentelli [16] and Lee and Neuendorffer [17].)

5.2 SYSTEM ARCHITECTURES

Whereas the compute model helped us understand the natural composition and parallelism in the application, the system architecture deals primarily with how we organize the implementation. As noted (introduction to Section 5.1), applications in a compute model may be mapped to any of several system architectures. The choice of architecture will depend on technology costs and resource availability compared to the application resource and performance requirements. For example, a platform that is very small compared to the size of the task drives serialization in the implementation, which may favor sequential control. Even here, though, we have important decisions to make about the level at which the sequential control is exercised (e.g., coarse-grained phasing) (see Phased reconfiguration manager subsection of Section 5.2.2) versus cycle-by-cycle sequencing (see FSMD, VLIW datapath control, and Processor subsections of Section 5.2.2).

Figure 5.7 is an overview of the system architectures, and their variants, covered in this section. To help the designer easily identify those that may be relevant to his or her specific problem, we open the description of each one by identifying the major problem or challenge it addresses.

5.2.1 Streaming Dataflow

We best exploit a reconfigurable platform when we can spatially arrange specialized computational pipelines and keep them each actively working on useful computation at a high cycle rate. How do we organize computations that can exploit this efficient use and arrange for data to feed the pipelines?

In the simplest case, we can use one of the streaming dataflow compute models (Section 5.1.3) directly as a guide for system implementation; that is,

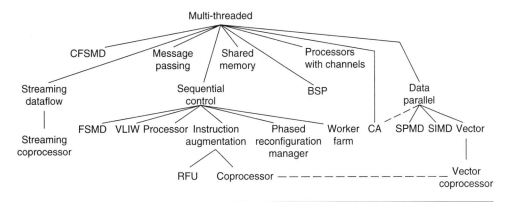

FIGURE 5.7 ■ Overview of system architectures.

we can map each operator to its own physical datapath and interconnect them all via configured interconnect. The efficiency of spatial pipelines on FPGAs and reconfigurable architectures makes this attractive. Further, the streaming model shows where in the detailed, cycle-by-cycle behavior of operations we have the implementation freedom to adapt to target platform delays. This architecture is known as *Pipe and Filter* in the literature [1]. Chapters 8 and 9 describe applications and programming that use it.

In the remainder of this section, we highlight four detailed techniques that are often useful in implementing streaming dataflow architectures.

Data presence

Direct connections of pipelined datapaths may pose challenges to guaranteeing the proper streaming dataflow semantics, offering efficient implementations, or allowing composition. These challenges include:

- Configured interconnect paths between operator datapaths may be long and can vary on the basis of platform, implementation technology, and operator placement. Long interconnect paths may limit the speed of operation.
- Different implementations of an operator may operate at different rates, and we want to be able to interchange these implementations without redesigning the implementations for all of the operators that interact with this operator.
- In dynamic dataflow models, an operator may not be able to consume an input, or produce an output, on every cycle of operation.

To promote easy and efficient operator composition, we can associate a "data present" signal with each data item. We design the physical functional units so that they can stall while waiting for the required inputs to be present. This decouples the clock cycle for interconnect and compute from the logical alignment of data, allowing us to pipeline the datapaths and the interconnect paths between them without changing the meaning of our computation. In many cases, we need to treat the interconnect paths as FIFO queues between operators; further, we can use back-pressure to indicate when a stream link between operators is full and so the upstream operator must wait before producing additional results.

The discipline makes the implementation of an operator independent of the implementation of others with which it communicates, allowing each to run at its desired clock rate even as all of them are composed together to build a larger system. This permits a variety of composite implementations:

- Operators and interconnect can all be designed to a single target clock frequency.
- Operators may run on separate clocks that are based on a common base frequency.
- Operators and interconnect may run fully asynchronously, handshaking locally.

- Operators may use a Globally Asynchronous, Locally Synchronous (GALS) model, with local operator clocks and asynchronous handshaking between operators.

It is still necessary to pay attention to the length of logical cycles in the original streaming dataflow graph; a loop in the graph may force sequential evaluation of all the graph's operators. Even though we can physically pipeline the operators and the links, the logical alignment of data may force the operators to effectively operate at lower rates, leaving the datapaths and interconnect inactive on most cycles. Such dependencies may motivate sequential sharing of operators or the resources inside them.

Datapath sharing
Ultimately, we must fit our entire dataflow graph onto our physical platform. For efficiency, we hope all of the hardware allocated to the dataflow graph is put to productive use on each cycle. Following are specific scenarios we may need to address:

- The substrate may not be large enough to hold the entire dataflow graph spatially.
- Multirate dataflow graphs may leave some operators idle while others are busy.
- Cyclic dependencies in the dataflow graph may make it impossible to keep all the operators active simultaneously.

To use the datapath hardware efficiently in cases such as these, it is often useful to share a physical datapath among multiple operators. In the simplest case, we share identical operators so that the datapath remains the same, only adding the unique state associated with each of the operators. In more complicated cases, we might generalize the datapath so that it can implement two or more types of operators.

When we share operators, we need to identify which data inputs are associated with which logical operator. This can be simply orchestrated by scheduling and pipelining for static-rate operators, but for dynamic operators and variable implementation delays, it may be necessary to further tag the data with information that identifies the logical operator for which it is destined.

Streaming coprocessors
With extreme variation in operator frequencies, large numbers of operators, and very small platforms, operator sharing may not be sufficient to provide an efficient solution. Here, even allocating a single datapath for a particular hardware type may leave the datapath highly underutilized or it may still demand more area than the platform provides.

In these more extreme cases, it is often useful to schedule the low-rate operators onto an embedded or attached processor (see Processor subsection of Section 5.2.2). By augmenting the processor with streaming instructions, processor-mapped operators can communicate efficiently with streaming dataflow. Data destined for active operators can be forwarded spatially, while data intended for inactive operators can be queued in memory. Data presence allows the processor tasks to operate without knowing the size of the reconfigurable platform or the residency of operators. Data presence on stream reads by the processor can be used like a memory stall, tolerating varying implementation delay on the reconfigurable platform or triggering an operator swap, similar to a thread swap on an I/O or virtual memory page miss.

Interconnect sharing

In spatial computations, interconnect often consumes a substantial portion of the hardware area and can often be a performance bottleneck. Consequently, we should always be concerned about using the interconnect efficiently. A direct, configured connection between a source and a sink can be inefficient when

- The link between operators is used infrequently because of a slow datapath or a low-rate operator relative to the rest of the computation.
- Because of dynamic data dependence, the communication rate on many links is highly variable.

To optimize interconnect in these cases it may be possible to reduce the interconnect requirements on these interconnect links by sharing them. Links can be shared in a variety of ways, including shared bus, pipelined ring, and network-on-a-chip. These can be statically scheduled in data-independent cases and in data-dependent cases with low communication variability, or dynamically managed when the data-dependence produces high variability.

5.2.2 Sequential Control

While sequential control is familiar and heavily used for highly sequential machines and algorithms, it is most interesting to us as a way to organize synchronization and control of a large set of spatially parallel operators, particularly when

- The compute task is too large to fit spatially onto the available computing resources, so we must share the resources in time.
- Data dependencies result in low utilization of the datapath, so we can share resources to produce a smaller design with little or no impact on compute time.

Even when we start with a dataflow or data-centric computation, it may be useful to control the implementation, or parts of it, in sequential manner; this is especially true when we share spatial operators in time to economize on space.

A common idiom is to

1. Start with the computation data dependence graph (e.g., Figure 5.8(a) or Figure 5.2) based on the description in the compute model.
2. Identify a base set of datapath elements that can implement all the operators in the computation graph.

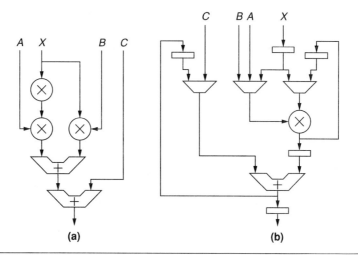

FIGURE 5.8 ■ A dataflow graph for $y = Ax^2 + Bx + C$ with three multiplies and two adds (a); a shared datapath (b) with a single multiplier and adder with state registers and multiplexors.

3. Schedule the operators in the compute graph onto the datapath elements.
4. Add data storage and interconnect to hold intermediate operator state and forward data between the locations where producing and consuming operations are performed.

In the simplest case, we might allocate a single datapath element for every operator in the compute graph. While there is no sharing in this case, it may still be necessary to control when the elements should sample their inputs and produce outputs. This can be done in a purely dataflow manner as suggested in the Data presence subsection of Section 5.2.1; however, for modest blocks in a single clocking domain with predictable datapath timing, it can be more efficient to centrally control the operators, sending control signals to each datapath element from a central control unit.

In the more general case, we have fewer datapath elements than operators and must orchestrate the sharing of those elements and interconnect. Intermediate values in the original computational graph that are not consumed in the cycle immediately following production, or immediately after being routed from the source to the destination, are stored temporarily in memories (see Figure 5.8). Object state that persists through the computation must be stored in memory or registers and routed to the associated datapath when the operator has its turn to use the datapath.

Within this paradigm, the key piece of freedom is the selection of the base datapath elements and the assignment of operators to them. This selection is where we can exploit area–time tradeoffs, allocating more spatial datapath elements as we have more area available and want to reduce the time for computation; it is also where we have opportunities to instantiate highly specialized operators that are matched to the needs of a particular task (e.g., Chapter 22).

The design community has identified a number of stylized forms for sequential control over the years. In the remainder of this section, we highlight a number of organizations and note when they may be useful for managing reconfigurable resources.

FSMD

Once we have selected the operators, assigned them to datapath elements, and scheduled the operations, we still need some way to implement the central control that manages resource sharing and orchestrates the routing of intermediate data among datapath elements.

One common way to support this control is to build a finite-state machine (FSM) that controls the operation of the datapath; this is called a Finite-State Machine with Datapath (FSMD) [18]. The FSM controller can assert the various controls (e.g., multiplexer selections, load or read/write enables, datapath operation selection) on each cycle and provide cycle-by-cycle sequencing of them (see Figure 5.9). Further, the FSM can take inputs from the datapath and, based on their data, branch to different control sequences.

A data-dependent operator might be internally implemented as an FSMD, with the state transitions in the FSM controlling the input consumption and output production (see Dynamic streaming dataflow subsection of Section 5.1.3, or Section 5.1.6).

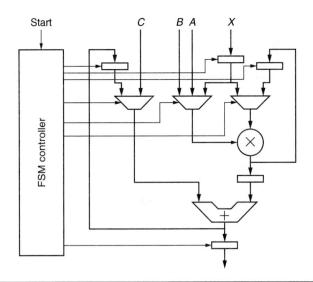

FIGURE 5.9 ▪ FSMD for a single multiply and add datapath for quadratic equation evaluation.

VLIW datapath control

While we can build a custom FSMD for each application, the FSMD form does not, itself, provide disciplined organizations for state storage and data routing, nor does it suggest any organizing principles for managing the control of each datapath. As a result:

- With heavy sharing there is a proliferation of intermediate state that needs to be managed.
- With many datapath operators, state memories, and switched interconnect, there is a proliferation of control signals that must be distributed to these compute, memory, and interconnect elements.
- For generality, robustness to change, and the opportunity to deploy the datapath for multiple tasks, it may be useful to be able to change the control sequencing without rebuilding the entire controller.

One stylization for sequential control is the Very Long Instruction Word (VLIW) model, which in its most primitive form is closely related to Horizontal Microcode [19]. In VLIW we start with the collection of datapath elements as before. These can be homogeneous or heterogeneous and provisioned according to the needs of the task. We then add one or more memory banks to hold inputs to each datapath element, and we add switched interconnect between the datapath elements and the memories. The controls to the memories, datapath elements, and interconnect become the long instruction word, to which we allocate a wide memory, perhaps distributing it with the memory cells and memory outputs local to the compute, interconnect, and memory elements they control (see Figure 5.10). To issue an "instruction" (see Chapter 36), the controller sends a single instruction address to the wide memory, and the memory output tells every datapath element, memory, and interconnect switch how it

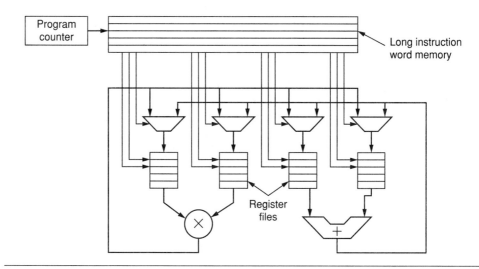

FIGURE 5.10 ■ VLIW-style control of a single multiply and add datapath.

should be configured on that cycle of operation. Typically, the datapath is configured to send one or a few bits back to the controller that can be used to select the next instruction address to allow data-dependent branching.

When VLIW was first introduced for general-purpose processing (e.g., Ellis [20]), the datapath elements used were generic (e.g., ALUs, FPUs, load/store units), of modest size, and fairly homogeneous. With FPGAs and reconfigurable architectures, we have the opportunity to select the datapath elements based on the task, make them highly specialized, and potentially even make them fairly coarse grained (e.g., a DCT step, motion estimation step, or AES encryption step).

Processor
The FSMD and, to some extent, VLIW control both assume that there are common datapaths that can be shared, and both allow multiple, concurrent operations to exploit the spatial parallelism available on an FPGA or reconfigurable device. However, for some computations our premium may be space saving rather than operation performance. That is, overall system performance may depend on this operator fitting onto the platform and being performed infrequently, but the time the operator takes may have little impact on it.

A conventional, sequential processor or microcontroller with a single arithmetic logic unit (ALU) is the extreme end of sharing, where we

1. Allocate a single, universal datapath element.
2. Decompose all operators into sequences of operations on this primitive datapath element.
3. Provide state storage for all intermediates between the cycle of production and the cycle of consumption, including storage for all object state.
4. Define a narrow instruction to control the datapath element and state storage.
5. Provide a sequencer and branch unit to sequence the instructions on the datapath in a potentially data-dependent manner.

Because this allocates minimal area to computation and interconnect, the total area for the computation can be very compact; however, compactness comes at the expense of most of the resources going to control, instruction, and state management. As a result, only a tiny fraction of the consumed computational resources go directly to implementing the application (see Chapter 36).

If heavy serialization to economize area is what we need for an entire task, a dedicated processor is certainly more efficient than a processor configured on top of an FPGA. Nonetheless, there are a few scenarios where a processor configured on top of an FPGA might be reasonable. Such scenarios would typically exploit the flexibility of either building a particularly specialized and lightweight processor for a specific task and/or embedding one in a flexible and highly integrated manner alongside a much larger computation implemented using a more spatial implementation architecture.

When we have multirate computations (e.g., Synchronous Dataflow model subsection of Section 5.1.3), some operators may execute at much lower rates than others. To balance the system and achieve maximum application performance in a limited area, we typically allocate space to operators in proportion to the fraction of the total computation they perform. As a result, we may end up with some very infrequent operators that are needed to complete the task but can afford to operate very slowly. If there is a dedicated, attached processor, perhaps these operators can be run there; if not, or if the flexibility to place the processor datapath for this operator local to other computations is important, it may be worthwhile to implement the operator as a configured processor.

Instruction augmentation

For resource sharing, a sequential controller is often necessary to direct the use of specialized datapaths. Sometimes this takes the form of a mix of irregular, low-throughput tasks that do not need to be executed quickly along with some very regular computations that are critical to performance. Manifestations of this need include:

- We need to sequence a modest amount of FPGA or reconfigurable logic.
- The computation contains a few operations that account for most of the time, embedded in a large amount of irregular tasks necessary to define the complete computation.

A processor is an efficient, programmable, and well-understood sequential controller. Consequently, it is often useful as the base design for a sequential controller. This is common enough that many platforms provide a dedicated processor attached to an FPGA or reconfigurable array (Chapter 2). It is also useful enough that this may be one of the motivations to employ a custom, configured processor.

One way to provide the coupling between the processor and the FPGA array is to treat the functions provided by the FPGA as additional instructions that augment the processor's base instructions. The processor's execution model of issuing instructions and expecting them to be performed in sequence remains intact, but the set of instructions it can issue are enlarged by the configured array. The FPGA instructions can potentially be very powerful, performing the equivalent of hundreds of base processor instructions in a single invocation. This can be particularly effective when a few such powerful instructions can cover the bulk of the execution time in the task. The processor serves as the application glue, sequencing these dominant operations and orchestrating the movement of data to connect them.

Functional Unit model   One way to implement instruction augmentation is to provide a reconfigurable functional unit (RFU) (e.g., Razdan and Smith [21], Hauck et al. [22], and the Tightly coupled RPF and processor subsection of Section 2.2.2); that is, we treat the reconfigurable array just like any other functional unit

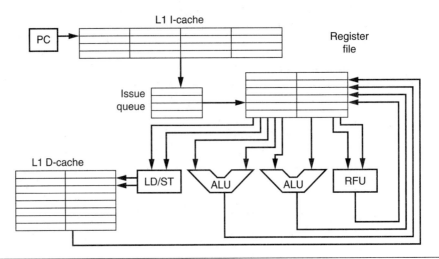

FIGURE 5.11 ■ A super-scalar processor with an RFU.

in the processor (see Figures 2.12 and 5.11). The processor issues instructions to it, feeding it data from the register file, and the array returns the result to a register. Normal processor issue and scoreboarding mechanisms can be used to accommodate variable delay in the array operation. The Functional Unit model may be particularly useful in specializing a configured processor to a particular application, where the custom functional units each perform a single function. It can also be used for coupling a custom processor to a reconfigurable array. One variant is to allocate a set of opcodes in the instruction for the reconfigurable function unit so that the processor instruction can call out different array operations.

The Functional Unit model is easily integrated into a conventional processor pipeline. However, it provides limited I/O between the processor and the array and demands that the reconfigurable operation be a function, preserving no internal state. This potentially limits the use of the array, by preventing the allocation of large, coarse-grained operations on it.

Coprocessor model Another way to implement instruction augmentation is to treat the reconfigurable array as a coprocessor (e.g., Callahan et al. [23]—see Figure 5.12), with the processor performing explicit data moves to and from it and directing it to perform specific operations. The coprocessor model allows the array to hold its state and places data close to it. This makes it possible to push larger portions of the computation onto the array, only communicating data back to the processor at large operation boundaries. The I/O to a single operation can be sequenced over several cycles, which allows greater flexibility in operator granularity.

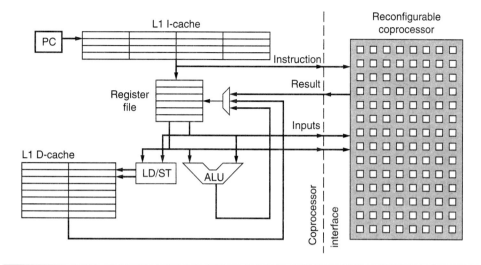

FIGURE 5.12 ■ A scalar processor with a reconfigurable coprocessor.

Phased reconfiguration manager

In the preceding sections, we shared the FPGA or the reconfigurable array resources in time in a fine-grained manner by scheduling operators on a cycle-by-cycle basis onto the datapath elements. This works when we have common operator types that permit sharing, or when we can generalize the datapath element to support many operators. In order to realize this we added additional circuitry to the design to flexibly route data between the datapath elements and to sequence the sharing. These additional resources did not contribute computation to the original task and so were pure overhead. However, since our hardware is reconfigurable, in some cases it is possible to reconfigure it and perform this sharing at a coarser granularity with less overhead. Since reconfiguration is often slow, this is viable only when we can arrange for the array to be used for a long period of time in a single configuration, such as when tasks operate in phases, performing distinct computations for long times. For this to be useful the "long time" in a configuration should be long compared to the time required to perform the reconfiguration (see Section 4.2 and Chapter 9).

In these cases, sequentialization is very coarse grained. We can nonetheless still think of the sequencing as a sequential control application, with each state potentially representing a different configuration of the array. The sequential controller monitors the execution to detect the end of the phase, implements configuration, and may even perform state-dependent branching. Sequential control can be realized with many of the architectures previously discussed (e.g., FSM, processor, instruction augmentation).

Worker farm

Sometimes we may have a set of dependent operations where each one runs for a large and variable amount of time. For example, Unix/Linux `make` rules specify

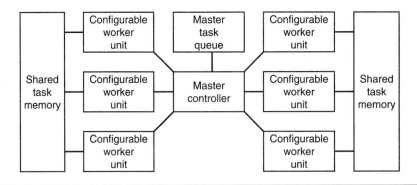

FIGURE 5.13 ▪ A worker farm.

a coarse-grained, dependent task set, and clustered multiprocessors exploit this parallelism with parallel `make` utilities such as `pmake` [24]. The variable runtime means that predetermined assignments of operations to hardware resources can be very inefficient.

We can exploit the reconfigurable hardware in these cases by organizing resources as a set of *workers*, which actually process jobs, and a central *manager*, which is responsible for assigning operations to them, potentially coordinating data movement and reconfiguration (see Figure 5.13). Here, the manager might

1. Maintain a queue of ready tasks.
2. Issue the first ready task to execute on a free worker.
3. Continue issuing tasks to workers until there are no free workers.
4. Wait for one or more workers to signal completion.
5. As tasks complete, put any tasks they enable on the ready queue.
6. Loop back to step 2.

Operations are enabled in dataflow form as they are completed. If the tasks are largely homogeneous or taken from a small set of types, the workers may be identical or taken from a small set of datapath configurations. If they are long running and highly heterogeneous, it may make sense to reconfigure them to each task; when the reconfigurable array supports it, this might include partial reconfiguration (see Section 4.2.3) of the array to customize each worker for its next task.

5.2.3 Bulk Synchronous Parallelism

In our sequential control architectures, we had a central controller telling every datapath element what to do. This guaranteed that the datapath elements moved forward in a synchronized manner. However, if the work required by each datapath is highly data dependent, a centralized locus of control may become inefficient. Consequently, we often allow the local datapathsto have independent control but still want to guarantee that they remain synchronized at some coarser granularity. In particular, we might want to ensure that one set of tasks completes before another begins.

Bulk Synchronous Parallelism (BSP) [25] can be seen as a variant that keeps the synchronization centralized but distributes the datapath sequencing. In BSP, independent units of computation progress independently, with the local computations punctuated by periodic barrier synchronization events. Each local computation announces when it reaches the barrier and waits for a global acknowledgment that all local tasks have reached it before proceeding.

The barrier is an efficient technique for supporting data-dependent, time-variable operations in each task while still providing strong synchronization guarantees. An alternate would be to statically determine the length of each epoch and have local tasks that complete their epoch early wait until the static epoch duration completes. If the runtime of each task varies widely based on data or potential resource contention, the static bound necessary to guarantee correctness may be excessively long compared to the common case local task completion time.

Further, if the local tasks are Turing Complete, it may not be possible to even identify such a static upper bound on the timing between barriers. The expense of the barrier is that it requires $\Omega(\log(N))$ time to perform the synchronization in the ideal case, where wire delays are negligible, and $O(\sqrt{N})$ or $O(\sqrt[3]{N})$ time in realistic 2-space or 3-space physical implementations for the barrier to complete. This suggests efficient operation only when the computational work between barriers is at least as large as this barrier synchronization time.

A BSP architecture can be appropriate for implementing data-centric computations (Section 5.1.6). Often objects communicate over their connected graph links. For many applications it is useful to guarantee that each object processes one round of method invocations before starting the next round. Barriers between rounds allow the operator to know when it has received all the invocations associated with a single round and can safely advance [26].

5.2.4   Data Parallel

As the Data Parallel Compute model suggests, sometimes computation can be organized as a set of computations applied, mostly independently, to a large set of data (see Section 5.1.5). This gives us both parallelism and regularity that a reconfigurable implementation can exploit. We want to be able to use this parallelism in a scalable manner, allocating more or less hardware as the platform permits.

A number of stylized architectures support data parallel computations and can be tuned for varying amounts of parallelism. The remainder of this section highlights three architectures and one technique for interfacing and controlling data parallel computation with more general computation.

Single program, multiple data

Although it is sometimes useful to apply the same basic operations to each component piece of data, these operations can be highly data dependent and can benefit from independent, local control. However, even though they are locally independent, it may be useful to guarantee that a set of operations on the data completes before continuing with the next operation set.

SPMD (single program, multiple data) is an organizational structure that follows the high-level Data Parallel model with minimum stylization within each data parallel task. Essentially, we have a collection of independent threads or control units that happen to be performing the same operation on different datasets. Individual independent threads can, themselves, be implemented as one of the system architectures described here. They are typically synchronized periodically in BSP fashion (Section 5.2.3).

Single-instruction multiple data

Control and instructions for a datapath can become expensive. Thus, if the data dependence for data parallel operations can be kept low, it is beneficial to share instructions and control across a large set of datapaths.

SIMD (single-instruction multiple data) architectures control the hardware operations on a cycle-by-cycle basis similarly to our sequential control architectures (Section 5.2.2). However, instead of a heterogeneous set of datapath elements, each potentially receiving unique operations, a single, common instruction is delivered to all of them. Each element has its own data and performs the sequence of instructions on it. Communication between datapath elements is also supported with common instructions to orchestrate data movement.

SIMD architectures can be more compact per processing element than VLIW architectures, because they do not need to store separate instructions for each compute, memory, or interconnect block. However, since SIMD architectures force all datapath elements to perform the same operation simultaneously, the SIMD datapath elements are efficiently utilized only on much more stylized and limited computations (see Chapter 36).

Chapter 10 describes a particular SIMD system in more detail, including an approach to SIMD compilation for FPGAs.

Vector

The motivation for vector architectures is similar to that for SIMD: When operations are sufficiently regular and data independent, they admit implementations that economize on resources by sharing instructions and associated control. Vector architectures particularly exploit the fact that datapath operations often have long latencies and can be pipelined so that calculations on many, independent data items can reuse the datapath at high throughput.

In a vector organization, a sequential controller issues data parallel instructions across a logical dataset. Here, we think of supplying vectors of component data, rather than individual words, as our inputs and outputs of instructions. The instructions perform operations similarly to a sequential processor on the pairwise components of vector inputs. Rather than the data living with the datapath elements, as is typical in SIMD, the vector data is normally kept in central memory banks and vector register files and is routed to the datapath elements. The vector instructions then specify where to find vector inputs and where to return vector results. The data parallel operation on these vectors can be performed in sequence on a highly pipelined vector functional unit, in parallel on a set of parallel functional units, or as a sequentialized set of parallel batches based on the area allocated.

On reconfigurable platforms, we can construct highly specialized vector functional units for each task. Thus, a vector control unit can be augmented with specialized vector pipelines just as a processor can be augmented with configurable instructions in an Instruction Augmentation architecture (see Instruction augmentation subsection of Section 5.2.2). Here we are operating on vectors of data rather than on individual scalar data elements. As with other models, we can identify the coarse-grained, data parallel operations required in the task and allocate a suitable set of functional units for them. The vector control unit then issues instructions to perform the data routing and sequencing to connect the operations running on the vector functional units (see Figure 5.14).

Vector coprocessors

As noted earlier, we often have a mix of irregular computations and more regular stylized computations (see Instruction augmentation subsection of Section 5.2.2). This is certainly true when exploiting highly stylized, data parallel computations using vector or SIMD architectures.

The Coprocessor model (see Coprocessor model subsection of Section 5.2.2) provides one stylized way to add configurable vector units to a base processor architecture (e.g., Wawrzynek et al. [27] and Jacob and Chow [28]). Here, the vector operations become coprocessor instructions. The processor can remain scalar, with normal instructions and register files, with the configurable vector unit maintaining all the vector states local to the configurable array. The vector

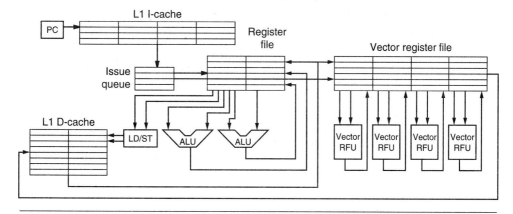

FIGURE 5.14 ■ A super-scalar processor with vector functional units.

coprocessor can keep multiple vector operations in flight, using scoreboarding on memory or vector registers to enforce sequential semantics on the sequentially issued vector operations.

5.2.5 Cellular Automata

Although spatial computation organizations offer great parallelism, they also demand that the spatially distributed datapaths communicate with each other. For large computations, the physical latency between distant operations can be large; further, the worst-case, cross-chip latencies actually grow relative to cycle rates as technology scales. Considerable, nonlocal traffic can slow the computation both because of round-trip latencies and because of limited available cross-chip bandwidth.

Cellular automata (CA) suggest a pattern for organizing computations as a line (one dimension), mesh (two dimensions), or cube (three dimensions) of regular operators with nearest-neighbor communication (see Figure 5.15). The operators run logically in lockstep, sampling the state of adjacent operators and updating their own. The regularity of identical operators makes it easy to scale to larger spatial designs. Moreover, nearest-neighbor communication eases layout and guarantees that communication does not limit overall design performance. A CA can be seen as a very stylized data-centric (see Section 5.1.6) computation in which the parallel operators have a restricted, regular communication pattern.

The restriction for nearest-neighbor communication may seem extreme, but it naturally shows up in many physical world simulations. Because physical interactions are also primarily nearest neighbor, the topology of the physical problem often maps directly to that of a regular CA. Examples of physical simulations include discrete-time solutions to wave, diffusion, Navier–Stokes, or Maxwell's equations (see Chapter 32). Perhaps the simplest and most well-known CA is Conway's game of "Life" [29]. It is even possible to implement CAD optimizations,

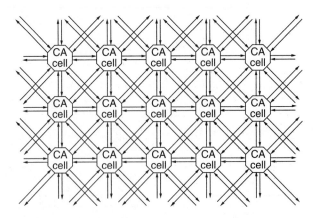

FIGURE 5.15 ■ Two-dimensional cellular automata.

such as placement, using CAs (e.g., Wrighton and DeHon [30]; also mentioned briefly in Chapters 9 and 20).

Folded CA
CAs can be highly efficient, but the size of the fully spatial design depends on the size of the problem. Thus, for large problem sizes the fully spatial CA can be too large for an affordable reconfigurable platform.

Since the CA is based on an array of identical operators and regular communication, it can be efficiently folded onto smaller physical platforms (e.g., Margolus [31] and Kobori et al. [32]). At one virtualization extreme we can build a single, physical CA cell processor and stream through the state of the virtual cells in series, using the single physical cell to implement all cells. The access pattern for the data is regular and predetermined, allowing efficient use of memory bandwidth. Plus, all the data communications are local, which means that we can readily program data buffering so that all data is available at the cell as needed on a single pass through the memory. We can also implement a single row (or column) of the CA and scan through one row (or column) at a time. In fact, we can choose just about any number of physical cells to implement—up to half the number in the logical array—and achieve a linear speedup of the computation. Chapter 32 describes a particular, folded mapping for a finite-difference, time-domain solution of Maxwell's equations.

5.2.6 Multi-threaded

The architectures discussed previously all place restrictions and stylizations on the computation to allow efficient implementation. Nonetheless, particular restrictions may not match with the needs of some applications and, consequently, may not provide the most efficient implementation support.

As suggested with compute models, multi-threading can be seen as the most general organization (Section 5.1.7). It provides great expressiveness, but at the cost of little guidance to the designer in how to exploit that expressiveness and guarantee correctness of implementation. This expressiveness can also make it expensive to support the full generality of the model on reconfigurable hardware.

In the remainder of this section, we review some common multi-threaded organizations and the benefits and caveats they entail.

Communicating FSMs with datapaths
Earlier we noted that an FSMD is a stylized way to control the operation of a datapath (see FSMD subsection of Section 5.2.2). For very large designs, a central controller may become a performance bottleneck for the following reasons:

- Central control may lead to unnecessary state explosion in a central controller.
- Sending control signals across a large system to a central controller and distributing control back from it may result in long latencies and slow operating rates.

One alternative to a single controller is decomposing the system into a number of independent FSMDs that communicate with each other. In this way, in addition to its own datapath controls, the FSM controller for each FSMD now contains inputs and outputs to one or more of the other FSMDs through which it coordinates synchronization. Thus, each FSM controller can be simpler and faster than the single, monolithic controller, and each can branch independently. However, the designer must be careful to manage the coordination of the FSMs so that they do not deadlock or otherwise transition into inconsistent states.

Technically, a composition of finite automata is still a finite automata, and it is possible to compute the composite automata in order to prove properties of the composite system. The state space of the composed automata can be as large as the product set of the state space of the individual automata. In some cases this state explosion can become intractably large for practical verification.

Processors with channels

In the Processor subsection of Section 5.2.2, we saw the motivation for an operator or several operators to run on a processor or, more likely, a processor controller with a specialized datapath. For similar reasons that motivate the communicating finite-state machines with datapaths (CFSMD) described in the previous section, it may not make sense to centrally control this collection of processors.

Here, too, we decompose the computation into a collection of augmented processor datapaths that coordinate with each other through direct links. Special instructions allow the processor to poll information from input channels and place information on output channels.

Message passing

When we connect processors or FSMs with communication channels, we often find it inefficient to commit dedicated, point-to-point links.

- The data rate on point-to-point channels between processors, operators, or FSMDs can often be too low to merit a dedicated channel.
- Dedicating point-to-point channels between processors, operators, or FSMDs can be too expensive for an implementation.
- Individual units of control may only need to communicate infrequently.

Rather than keep a channel open at all times, operators can share a common communication infrastructure (e.g., bus, pipelined ring, network-on-a-chip) and send their coordination information tagged with the identity or location of the recipient—in other words, send messages.

Shared memory

Multiple operators cooperating on a task may need infrequent access to a large set of shared state. When we exploit parallelism, these operators may be running on different parts of a physical platform yet need to access shared data pools.

When possible, it is best to give ownership of state to a single operator and let it provide coordinated access to it. This approach avoids a host of synchronization problems that can make parallel execution particularly troublesome. If the state is small and infrequently changed, and when several operators need regular access to it, it can make sense to allow each to have its own copy and allow coordination operations to change the data across them. However, when the state is large and infrequently accessed, such as with a large database, it is sometimes efficient to allow multiple physical processing elements to access a single, shared memory pool to avoid replicating the data and to allow data communication to be deferred until it is needed. This can allow each processing element to extract just the information it needs without burdening the others with knowing which information will be needed by which processing element.

In the general case, we may share memory pools between small sets of physical processing elements. Unlike with homogeneous multiprocessors, there is generally little reason to have a single, large, shared memory pool across all the processing elements in a reconfigurable computer. The configurability of our reconfigurable designs allows us to limit sharing based on the shape of communications in the application.

5.2.7 Hierarchical Composition

In this chapter we described most system architectures as homogeneous entities. However, in general we can consider them each as levels in a hierarchy. For example, it may make sense to use FSMD (see FSMD subsection of Section 5.2.2) or vector coprocessor (see Vector coprocessors subsection of Section 5.2.4) nodes to implement the dataflow operators in a streaming dataflow system architecture (Section 5.2.1). Further, to model and coordinate changes in the composition of the dataflow network over time, it may make sense to model each of the dataflow configurations as a state in a very coarse-grained FSM (see Phased reconfiguration manager subsection of Section 5.2.2). With a variety of system architectures, rich implementation options within each, and their hierarchical compositions, we have a broad and powerful set of techniques to exploit the flexibility in reconfigurable computing platforms.

References

[1] M. Shaw, D. Garlan. *Software Architecture: Perspectives on an Emerging Discipline*, Prentice-Hall, 1996.

[2] C. A. R. Hoare. *Communicating Sequential Processes*, International Series in Computer Science, Prentice-Hall, 1985.

[3] R. M. Tomasulo. An efficient algorithm for exploiting multiple arithmetic units. *IBM Journal of Research and Development*, 1967.

[4] E. A. Lee. The problem with threads. *IEEE Computer* 36(5), May 2006.

[5] S. Kleene. Recursive predicates and quantifiers. *Transactions of the American Mathematical Society* 53(1), 1943.

[6] A. M. Turing. On computable numbers, with an application to the entscheidungs problem. *Proceedings of the London Mathematical Society* 42(2), 1937.

[7] A. Church. An unsolvable problem of elementary number theory. *American Journal of Mathematics* 58, 1936.

[8] E. A. Lee, D. G. Messerschmitt. Synchronous dataflow. *Proceedings of the IEEE* 75(9), September 1987.

[9] S. S. Bhattacharyya, P. K. Murthy, E. A. Lee. *Software Synthesis from Dataflow Graphs* (Synchronous Dataflow chapter), Kluwer Academic, 1996.

[10] T. M. Parks. *Bounded Scheduling of Process Networks*, UCB/ERLl95-105, University of California at Berkeley, 1995.

[11] Arvind, R. S. Nikhil. Executing a program on the MIT tagged-token dataflow architecture. *IEEE Transactions on Computers* 39(3), March 1990.

[12] D. E. Culler, S. C. Goldstein, K. E. Schauser, T. von Eicken. TAM—a compiler-controlled threaded abstract machine. *Journal of Parallel and Distributed Computing*, June 1993.

[13] J. Hennessy, D. Patterson. *Computer Architecture: A Quantitative Approach*, 3rd ed., Morgan Kaufmann, 2002.

[14] S. Devadas, Hi-K. T. Ma, R. Newton. On the verification of sequential machines at differing levels of abstraction. *IEEE Transactions on Computer-Aided Design of Integrated Circuits and Systems* 7(6), June 1988.

[15] J. Babb, M. Rinard, C. A. Moriz, W. Lee, M. Frank, R. Barua, S. Amarasinghe. Parallelizing applications into silicon. *Proceedings of the IEEE Symposium on Field-Programmable Custom Computing Machines*, 1999.

[16] E. Lee, A. Sangiovanni-Vincentelli. A framework for comparing models of computation. *IEEE Transactions on Computer-Aided Design of Integrated Circuits and Systems* 17(12), December 1998.

[17] E. Lee, S. Neuendorffer. Concurrent models of computation for embedded software. *IEEE Proceedings—Computers and Digital Techniques* 152(2), March 2005.

[18] D. Gajski, L. Ramachandran. Introduction to high-level synthesis. *IEEE Design and Test of Computers* 11(4), 1994.

[19] J. Fisher. Trace scheduling: A technique for global microcode compaction. *IEEE Transactions on Computers* 30(7), 1981.

[20] J. R. Ellis. *Bulldog: A Compiler for VLIW Architectures*, MIT Press, 1986.

[21] R. Razdan, M. D. Smith. A high-performance microarchitecture with hardware-programmable functional units. *Proceedings of the 27th Annual International Symposium on Microarchitecture*, November 1994.

[22] S. Hauck, T. Fry, M. Hosler, J. Kao. The chimaera reconfigurable functional unit. *Proceedings of the IEEE Symposium on FPGAs for Custom Computing Machines*, April 1997.

[23] T. Callahan, J. Hauser, J. Wawrzynek. The Garp architecture and C compiler. *IEEE Computer* 33(4), April 2000.

[24] E. H. Baalbergen. Design and implementation of parallel make. *Computing Systems* 1(2), 1988.

[25] L. G. Valliant. A bridging model for parallel computation. *Communications of the ACM* 33(8), August 1990.

[26] M. deLorimier, N. Kapre, N. Mehta, D. Rizzo, I. Eslick, R. Rubin, T. E. Uribe, T. F. Knight, Jr., A. DeHon. GraphStep: A system architecture for sparse-graph algorithms. *Proceedings of the IEEE Symposium on Field-Programmable Custom Computing Machines*, 2006.

[27] J. Wawrzynek, K. Asanovic, B. Kingsbury, J. Beck, D. Johnson, N. Morgan. Spert-II: A vector microprocessor system. *IEEE Computer*, March 1996.

[28] J. A. Jacob, P. Chow. Memory interfacing and instruction specification for reconfigurable processors. *Proceedings of the ACM/SIGDA International Symposium on Field-Programmable Gate Arrays*, February 1999.

[29] M. Gardner. The fantastic combinations of John Conway's new solitaire game "Life." *Scientific American* 223, October 1970.

[30] M. Wrighton, A. DeHon. Hardware-assisted simulated annealing with application for fast FPGA placement. *Proceedings of the ACM/SIGDA International Symposium on Field-Programmable Gate Arrays*, February 2003.

[31] N. Margolus. An FPGA architecture for DRAM-based systolic computations. *Proceedings of the IEEE Symposium on FPGAs for Custom Computing Machines*, 1997.

[32] T. Kobori, T. Maruyama, T. Hoshino. A cellular automata system with FPGA. *Proceedings of the IEEE Symposium on Field-Programmable Custom Computing Machines*, 2001.

CHAPTER 6

PROGRAMMING FPGA APPLICATIONS IN VHDL

Nachiket Kapre
Department of Computer Science
California Institute of Technology
André DeHon
Department of Electrical and Systems Engineering
University of Pennsylvania

Modern field-programmable gate arrays (FPGAs) contain hundreds of thousands of lookup tables (LUTs), hundreds of embedded memories, and hundreds of multipliers connected through a programmable interconnect fabric. Obviously it is intractable to program the FPGA at the granularity of these individual elements. However, with modern synthesis and layout tools, it is possible to describe a design simply by writing logical expressions, a level higher than gates, and letting the tools do the rest. Register transfer level (RTL) design is a popular discipline for describing these logical expressions. It allows the designer to express the design by describing the logic between each pair of register stages. This allows her to carefully control register-to-register logic depth while freeing her from selecting the actual gates and their mapping to the FPGA. Very High-Speed Integrated Circuit Hardware Description Language (VHDL) is one popular programming language that supports RTL hardware descriptions.

VHDL enjoys widespread popularity among designers in the industry, along with its close cousin, Verilog. Indeed, almost all modern CAD tools that perform simulation, synthesis, and layout support both. Verilog differs from VHDL primarily in the syntax it uses (VHDL is derived from Ada; Verilog, from C), but both languages are IEEE standards and are periodically reviewed to reflect changing industry realities and expectations.

VHDL is a strongly typed, Ada-based programming language that includes special constructs and semantics for describing concurrency at the hardware level. These concurrency constructs are new for most programmers and can be a source of confusion for beginners. In the following sections, we provide a tutorial overview of how to express and compose synchronous designs in VHDL. Through examples, we highlight the control one can exercise in VHDL to direct proper synthesis of hardware. We first look at how VHDL can be used to describe a design structurally as a composition of sub-circuits. We then show how to express hardware in RTL form. Next we illustrate how hardware can be generated parametrically in a programmable manner. Finally we outline the basic tool and workflow for developing VHDL designs.

This chapter is by no means a complete discussion of all VHDL language features. For a more comprehensive treatment of language syntax and coding style the reader is referred to the work of Ashenden [1, 2] and the appropriate vendor manuals (e.g., Xilinx, Inc. [3]).

6.1   VHDL PROGRAMMING

Programming in VHDL is quite different from programming in C because of its concurrent semantics. However, it does have several similarities with object-oriented languages like C++ and Java (e.g., encapsulation and interfaces). These common principles should help beginners understand the basic structure of the language and help them relate to hardware-specific VHDL constructs. In this section, we describe a few simple design elements in VHDL to outline key language features and illustrate important programming concepts.

We first show how to program a 2-input multiplexer using a structural abstraction. We then program a 4-input multiplexer using RTL semantics. Next we illustrate the use of parametric hardware generation by creating a 16-bit wide, 4-input multiplexer using a 1-bit, 4-input multiplexer from the previous example. Then we combine structural and RTL styles in a finite-state machine (FSM) datapath example to show how to use them in the same design. This final example introduces the programming of FSMs in VHDL.

6.1.1   Structural Description

To describe a multiplexer structurally, we first decompose it into primitive gates derived from its Boolean equations. Each gate is *instantiated* individually and then connected to others. We can think of a structural decomposition as a textual representation of a schematic or as subroutines in a conventional programming language such as C. As with schematic capture, a structural decomposition permits code for a recurring design element to be shared. This means that we can design an element once and instantiate it as many times as required. Unlike schematic capture, a textual structural description can be modified and updated easily with a text editor. Moreover, a hierarchical decomposition allows the designer to manage the complexity of a large hardware design by breaking it up into individual, manageable pieces. Listing 6.1 and Figure 6.1 illustrate the following important concepts.

Listing **6.1** ▪ A structural 2-input multiplexer.

```
1 library ieee;
2 use ieee.std_logic_1164. all;
3
4 — this is the entity declaration for the 2-input mux
5 — it is a list of ports into the module.
```

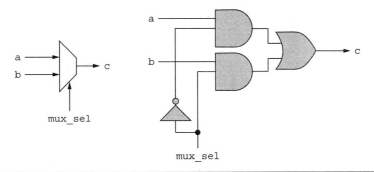

FIGURE 6.1 ■ A structural 2-input multiplexer.

```
 6 entity mux2 is
 7 port (
 8    a : in std_logic;
 9    b : in std_logic;
10    mux_sel : in std_logic;
11    c : out std_logic
12 );
13 end;
14
15 — this is where the structure of the multiplexer is defined
16 architecture struct of mux2 is
17
18 — all components that will be used in the structure
19 — need to be declared before use.
20 component notgate is
21 port (
22    a : in std_logic;
23    b : out std_logic
24 );
25 end component;
26
27 component andgate is
28 port (
29    a : in std_logic;
30    b : in std_logic;
31    c : out std_logic
32 );
33 end component;
34
35 component orgate is
36 port (
37    a : in std_logic;
38    b : in std_logic;
39    c : out std_logic
40 );
41 end component;
42
43 — internal signals/wires used to connect the components
44 — also need to be declared here.
```

```
45 signal muxsel_inverted_sig : std_logic;
46
47 signal sela_sig : std_logic;
48 signal selb_sig : std_logic;
49
50 — this signifies the start of the structural code
51 begin
52
53 — instantiation of the inverter
54 inverter_inst_0 : notgate
55 port map (
56    a => mux_sel,
57    b => muxsel_inverted_sig
58 );
59
60 — instantiation of the and gate
61 and_inst_a : andgate
62 port map (
63    a => a,
64    b => muxsel_inverted_sig,
65    c => sela_sig
66 );
67
68 — another instantiation of the and gate
69 and_inst_b : andgate
70 port map (
71    a => b,
72    b => mux_sel,
73    c => selb_sig
74 );
75
76 or_inst : orgate
77 port map (
78    a => sela_sig,
79    b => selb_sig,
80    c => c
81 );
82
83 end;
```

1. VHDL files typically start by including the IEEE library and certain important packages like `std_logic_1164` (Listing 6.1, lines 1–2) that permit the use of type `std_logic` and Boolean operations on it. Additional packages such as `std_logic_arith` and `std_logic_unsigned` are often included for supporting arithmetic operations.

2. The VHDL description of a hardware module requires an `entity` declaration (Listing 6.1, lines 6–13) that specifies the interface of the module with the outside world. It is an enumeration of the interface ports. The declaration also provides additional information about the ports such as their direction (in/out), data type, bit width, and endianness. An entity declaration in VHDL is analogous to an interface definition in Java or a function header declaration in C.

3. Almost all VHDL signals and ports use the data type `std_logic` and `std_logic_vector`. These data types define how VHDL models electrical behavior of signals, which we discuss in the Multivalued logic subsection of Section 6.1.5. The vector `std_logic_vector` allows declaration of buses that are bundled together. We will see its use in a subsequent example.

4. While an entity specifies the interface of a hardware module, its internal structure and function are enclosed within the `architecture` definition (Listing 6.1, lines 16–83).

5. In a structural description of a module, the constituent submodules are declared, instantiated, and connected to each other. Each submodule needs to be first declared in the `component` declaration (Listing 6.1, lines 20–25). This is merely a copy of the entity declaration where only the submodule's interface is specified. Once the components are declared, they can then be instantiated (Listing 6.1, lines 54–58). Each instance of the component is unique, and a component can have multiple instances (Listing 6.1, lines 61 and 69). The instantiated components are connected to each other via internal signals by a process called *port mapping* (Listing 6.1, lines 55–58). Port mapping is performed on a signal-by-signal basis using the => symbol. It is analogous to assembling a set of integrated circuits (ICs) on a breadboard and wiring up the connections between the IC pins using jumper wires. Observe the similarity between the schematic representation of the multiplexer and the structural VHDL in the example.

6. Notice in the example that the component for the AND gate is reused for each AND gate in the design (Listing 6.1, lines 61–66 and 69–74). This is one of the benefits of a structural representation—it permits reuse of existing code for recurring design elements and helps reduce total code size.

7. The submodules used in Listing 6.1 are primitives supported in the vendor library. In a larger design that is a collection of several multiplexers, the different multiplexers can be declared, instantiated, and connected to each other as required. A design can have several such levels of structural hierarchy. Hierarchy is a fairly common technique for design composition.

6.1.2 RTL Description

The multiplexer's RTL description can be specified much more succinctly than its corresponding structural representation. In RTL, logic is organized as transformations on data bits between register stages. By selecting the number of pipeline stages wisely, the designer can create a high-performance, high-speed hardware implementation, and by carefully deciding the degree of resource sharing, the size of the mapped design can be controlled as well. RTL provides the designer with sufficient low-level control to allow her to create an implementation that meets her specifications.

For the VHDL description, we still need the logical equations that define the multiplexer, but these can now be represented directly as equations, from which a synthesis tool *infers* the actual gates. The tool tries to choose the gates on the basis of user-specified design criteria such as high speed or small area.

Listing 6.2 shows how to write a 4-input multiplexer with registered outputs (Listing 6.1 simply showed a 2-input multiplexer without a register).

1. As before, we start with the package and entity declarations (Listing 6.2, lines 6–18).

2. The RTL description of the VHDL entity is enclosed in the **architecture** block (Listing 6.2, lines 20–52). The logic equations and registers that are part of the RTL description are written here. Earlier, we used the **architecture** block to write the structural port-mapping statements.

Listing 6.2 ■ RTL for a 4-input multiplexer.

```
 1 — library and package includes
 2 library ieee;
 3 use ieee.std_logic_1164.all;
 4
 5 — entity declaration for the 4-input multiplexer
 6 entity mux4 is
 7 port (
 8     clk : in std_logic;
 9     reset : in std_logic;
10     a : in std_logic;
11     b : in std_logic;
12     c : in std_logic;
13     d : in std_logic;
14     — notice the use of the type vector.
15     mux_sel : in std_logic_vector (1 downto 0);
16     e : out std_logic
17 );
18 end;
19
20 — RTL description of the multiplexer is defined here
21 architecture rtl of mux4 is
22
23 — internal signals used in the multiplexer are
24 — declared here before use
25 signal e_c : std_logic;
26
27 — indicates start of the actual RTL code
28 begin
29
30 — concurrent signal assignment
31 — the multiplexer functionality is described
32 — at a level above gates
33 e_c <= a when mux_sel="00" else
34     b when mux_sel="01" else
35     c when mux_sel="10" else
36     d;
37
38 — sequential signal assignment
```

```
39 process (clk, reset)
40 begin
41
42 — action under reset
43 if (reset = '1') then
44    e <= '0';
45 — action under rising clock edge
46 elsif (clk' EVENT and clk='1') then
47    e <= e_c;
48 end if;
49
50 end process;
51
52 end;
```

3. In the structural example, we saw how signals were used as wires for connecting component ports. In VHDL, signals are also used for representing logic. A signal can be defined as a function of one or more signals. The assignment operation is represented by the symbol <=, which is analogous to the = operation in C; however, the manner in which signals are assigned values is quite different from C.

4. As before, a signal needs to be declared before the **begin** statement (Listing 6.2, line 25). Each signal is defined using a signal assignment statement that describes the logic that drives it. A signal assignment statement can be either concurrent or sequential.

5. A concurrent signal assignment is used to describe the logic equation for the multiplexer (Listing 6.2, lines 33–36). Concurrent statements are written inside the **begin-end** statements of the **architecture** block but outside any **process** blocks (Listing 6.2, lines 39–50). For simulation purposes, a concurrent statement can be thought of as being evaluated in parallel with other concurrent statements.

6. In the listing, a sequential assignment describes a register (Listing 6.2, lines 39–50). The behavior of the register under reset and a rising edge of the clock is defined between the **begin-end** statements of the **process** block, which is itself enclosed within the **begin-end** statements of the **architecture** block (Listing 6.2, lines 21–52). A **process** block is executed only when any signal on its *sensitivity list* (e.g., clk and reset signals in Listing 6.2, line 39) changes value.

As their name suggests, sequential assignment statements enclosed within a **process** block are executed sequentially. A process is suspended when it finishes evaluating all of the statements it can inside the block, and signals are assigned values only at that time. Additionally, during evaluation of a **process** block, a signal retains the same logical value it had when the process began execution. This can be a potential source of confusion for new programmers. In Listing 6.6, we show how to write combinational logic using sequential statements.

7. Notice the compactness with which the multiplexer was described in Listing 6.2 (52 lines of RTL code versus 83 for structural). This is one of the key benefits of RTL over purely structural descriptions.

6.1.3 Parametric Hardware Generation

VHDL allows the designer to generate hardware as a function of some changeable parameter. This is a useful technique for code reuse when we need several variants of an element in the same design (e.g., an 8-bit and 16-bit adder in the same design). Certain design parameters are often not known until late in the design cycle, and some can change as the design specification evolves to meet customer requirements. It might also be necessary to perform a parametric design space exploration based on certain variables before deciding on the final architecture. These issues can be resolved with VHDL **generic**s.

The generics are specified at the start of the entity declaration. In the simplest form, VHDL allows the designer to write signals as vectors of parametric width. More advanced uses of parametric hardware generation employ **generate** statements, and **generate** loops can be used to create multiple copies of a repeating logic block.

In Listing 6.3 and Figure 6.2, we illustrate the use of parametric hardware generation using a multibit 4-input multiplexer. The width of the multiplexer is defined by a generic DATA_WIDTH (Listing 6.3, lines 8–13), which sets the range of the vectors in the interface and is later used as the termination value in the **generate** loop (Listing 6.3, lines 47–61). DATA_WIDTH copies of the 4-input multiplexer described in Listing 6.2 are instantiated and connected to the interface ports appropriately (Listing 6.3, lines 54–59).

Listing 6.3 ▪ Parametric generation of a multibit 4-input multiplexer.

```
1  — library and package includes
2  library ieee;
3  use ieee.std_logic_1164.all;
4
5  — entity declaration of the multiplexer array
6  entity mux4_array is
7  — definition of the generic for this entity
8  generic (
9     — here 16 is the default value
10    — it can be redefined during
11    — instantiation, or during synthesis
12    DATA_WIDTH : integer := 16
13 );
14 port (
15    clk : in std_logic;
16    reset : in std_logic;
17    — notice the use of generic for constraining the vector length
18    a : in std_logic_vector(DATA_WIDTH-1 downto 0);
19    b : in std_logic_vector(DATA_WIDTH-1 downto 0);
20    c : in std_logic_vector(DATA_WIDTH-1 downto 0);
21    d : in std_logic_vector(DATA_WIDTH-1 downto 0);
```

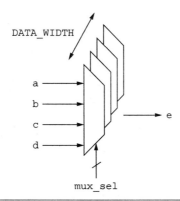

FIGURE 6.2 ■ Parametric generation of a multibit 4-input multiplexer.

```
22    mux_sel : in std_logic_vector(1 downto 0);
23    e : out std_logic_vector(DATA_WIDTH-1 downto 0)
24 );
25 end;
26
27 — the parametric code is enclosed within the architecture block
28 architecture parametric of mux4_array is
29
30 — like structural VHDL, the component being used needs to be declared here
31 component mux4 is
32 port (
33    clk : in std_logic;
34    reset : in std_logic;
35    a : in std_logic;
36    b : in std_logic;
37    c : in std_logic;
38    d : in std_logic;
39    mux_sel : in std_logic_vector(1 downto 0);
40    e : out std_logic
41 );
42 end component;
43
44 begin
45
46 — loop for generating a programmable number of mux4 instances
47 bitslices_gen : for i in 0 to DATA_WIDTH-1 generate
48    inst_mux : mux4
49    port map (
50       clk => clk,
51       reset => reset,
52       — notice the use of loop variable i for indexing
53       — into the array
54       a => a(i),
55       b => b(i),
56       c => c(i),
57       d => d(i),
58       mux_sel => mux_sel,
```

```
59        e => e(i)
60    );
61 end generate bitslices_gen;
62
63 end;
```

6.1.4   Finite-state Machine Datapath Example

In Listing 6.4, we design a time-shared datapath that computes $Ax^2 + Bx + C$ using only one multiplier and one adder. The design is naturally separated into state machine controller and datapath components. The controller and the datapath are designed using RTL and composed together structurally. The multiplier, the adder, and the associated multiplexers and registers are part of the datapath, whereas the control signals for the datapath multiplexers (Listing 6.4, lines 80–82) and registers (Listing 6.4, lines 84–86) are generated by the controller. Figure 6.3 shows the structural decomposition and the associated VHDL code. We can see that the control signals are connected from the controller to the datapath in the structural VHDL representation.

Listing 6.4 ■ A structural representation of the FSM datapath design.

```
 1  — library and package includes
 2  library ieee;
 3  use ieee.std_logic_1164.all;
 4  use ieee.std_logic_unsigned.all;
 5
 6  — entity declaration of the state-machine controller
 7  entity fsm_datapath is
 8  port (
 9      — system signals
10      clk : in std_logic;
11      reset : in std_logic;
12
13      — input interface
14      start : in std_logic;
15      A : in std_logic_vector(3 downto 0);
16      B : in std_logic_vector(3 downto 0);
17      C : in std_logic_vector(3 downto 0);
18      x : in std_logic_vector(3 downto 0);
19
20      — output interface
21      output_valid : out std_logic;
22      result : out std_logic_vector(12 downto 0)
23  );
24  end;
25
26  architecture struct of fsm_datapath is
27
28  component fsm is
29  port (
30      — system signals
```

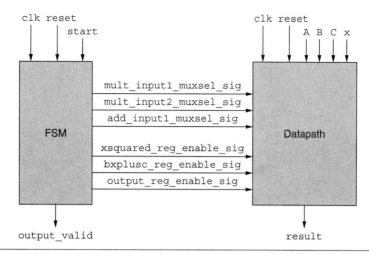

FIGURE 6.3 ■ A structural representation of the FSM datapath design.

```
31    clk : in std_logic;
32    reset : in std_logic;
33
34    — start the computation
35    start : in std_logic;
36
37    — datapath multiplexer select
38    mult_input1_muxsel : out std_logic_vector(1 downto 0);
39    mult_input2_muxsel : out std_logic;
40    add_input1_muxsel : out std_logic;
41
42    — register enables
43    xsquared_reg_enable : out std_logic;
44    bxplusc_reg_enable : out std_logic;
45    output_reg_enable : out std_logic;
46
47    — indicate output is valid
48    output_valid : out std_logic
49  );
50  end component;
51
52  component datapath is
53  port (
54    — system signals
55    clk : in std_logic;
56    reset : in std_logic;
57
58    — input operands
59    A : in std_logic_vector(3 downto 0);
60    B : in std_logic_vector(3 downto 0);
61    C : in std_logic_vector(3 downto 0);
62    x : in std_logic_vector(3 downto 0);
63
```

```
64      — datapath multiplexer select
65      mult_input1_muxsel : in std_logic_vector(1 downto 0);
66      mult_input2_muxsel : in std_logic;
67      add_input1_muxsel : in std_logic;
68
69      — register enables
70      xsquared_reg_enable : in std_logic;
71      bxplusc_reg_enable : in std_logic;
72      output_reg_enable : in std_logic;
73
74      — output data
75      result : out std_logic_vector(12 downto 0)
76   );
77   end component;
78
79   — internal wires for connecting the components
80   signal mult_input1_muxsel_sig : std_logic_vector(1 downto 0);
81   signal mult_input2_muxsel_sig : std_logic;
82   signal add_input1_muxsel_sig : std_logic;
83
84   signal xsquared_reg_enable_sig : std_logic;
85   signal bxplusc_reg_enable_sig : std_logic;
86   signal output_reg_enable_sig : std_logic;
87
88   — start component instantion and wiring
89   begin
90
91   datapath_inst : datapath
92   port map (
93
94      — system signals
95      clk => clk,
96      reset => reset,
97
98      — input operands
99      A => A,
100     B => B,
101     C => C,
102     x => x,
103
104     — datapath multiplexer select
105     mult_input1_muxsel => mult_input1_muxsel_sig,
106     mult_input2_muxsel => mult_input2_muxsel_sig,
107     add_input1_muxsel => add_input1_muxsel_sig,
108
109     — register enables
110     xsquared_reg_enable => xsquared_reg_enable_sig,
111     bxplusc_reg_enable => bxplusc_reg_enable_sig,
112     output_reg_enable => output_reg_enable_sig,
113
114     — output data
115     result => result
116  );
117
```

```
118 fsm_inst : fsm
119 port map (
120    — system signals
121    clk => clk,
122    reset => reset,
123
124    — start the computation
125    start => start,
126
127    — datapath multiplexer select
128    mult_input1_muxsel => mult_input1_muxsel_sig,
129    mult_input2_muxsel => mult_input2_muxsel_sig,
130    add_input1_muxsel => add_input1_muxsel_sig,
131
132    — register enables
133    xsquared_reg_enable => xsquared_reg_enable_sig,
134    bxplusc_reg_enable => bxplusc_reg_enable_sig,
135    output_reg_enable => output_reg_enable_sig,
136
137    — indicate output is valid
138    output_valid => output_valid
139 );
140
141 end;
```

We use the RTL form to describe the datapath, and we use a combination of concurrent and sequential statements for this purpose. The structure of the datapath is shown in Listing 6.5 and Figure 6.4.

Listing 6.5 ■ A time-shared datapath for computing $Ax^2 + Bx + C$.

```
1  — include the unsigned package to support arithmetic operations.
2  library ieee;
3  use ieee.std_logic_1164.all;
4  use ieee.std_logic_unsigned.all;
5
6  — describes the interface to the datapath,
7  — with its operands and control signals listed.
8  entity datapath is
9  port (
10    — system signals
11    clk : in std_logic;
12    reset : in std_logic;
13
14    — input operands
15    A : in std_logic_vector(3 downto 0);
16    B : in std_logic_vector(3 downto 0);
17    C : in std_logic_vector(3 downto 0);
18    x : in std_logic_vector(3 downto 0);
19
```

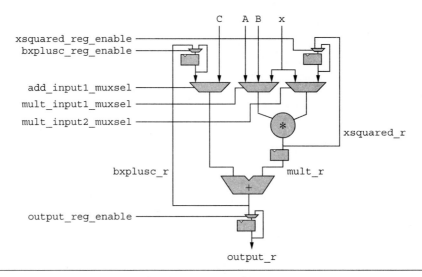

xsquared_reg_enable
bxplusc_reg_enable

add_input1_muxsel
mult_input1_muxsel
mult_input2_muxsel

xsquared_r

bxplusc_r   mult_r

output_reg_enable

output_r

C   A B   x

FIGURE 6.4 ▪ A time-shared datapath for computing $Ax^2 + Bx + C$.

```
20      — datapath multiplexer select
21      mult_input1_muxsel : in std_logic_vector(1 downto 0);
22      mult_input2_muxsel : in std_logic;
23      add_input1_muxsel : in std_logic;
24
25      — register enables
26      xsquared_reg_enable : in std_logic;
27      bxplusc_reg_enable : in std_logic;
28      output_reg_enable : in std_logic;
29
30      — output data
31      result : out std_logic_vector(12 downto 0)
32   );
33 end;
34
35   architecture rtl of datapath is
36
37   — notice the different bitwidths on each signal
38   — these precisions have been carefully selected
39   — based on the multiply/add operations and input
40   — bitwidths
41   signal mux_0_c : std_logic_vector(3 downto 0);
42   signal mux_1_c : std_logic_vector(7 downto 0);
43   — mux_1_c needs 8 bits of precision due to
44   — x–squared at the input
45   signal mux_2_c : std_logic_vector(8 downto 0);
46   — mux_2_c needs 9 bits of precision due to
47   — precision of Bx+C
48
49   signal mult_c : std_logic_vector(11 downto 0);
50   — product of 8-bit and 4-bit inputs is 12-bit
51
```

```
52  signal add_c : std_logic_vector(12 downto 0);
53  — sum of 12-bit and 9-bit inputs is 13-bits with overflow
54
55  signal mult_r : std_logic_vector(11 downto 0);
56  signal output_r : std_logic_vector(12 downto 0);
57  signal bxplusc_r : std_logic_vector(8 downto 0);
58  signal xsquared_r : std_logic_vector(7 downto 0);
59
60
61  begin
62
63  — concurrent statements to describe the multiplexers
64  mux_0_c <= A when mult_input1_muxsel = "00" else
65            B when mult_input1_muxsel = "01" else
66            x;
67
68  mux_1_c <= "0000"&x when mult_input2_muxsel = '0' else
69            xsquared_r;
70
71  mux_2_c <= "00000"&C when add_input1_muxsel = '0' else
72            bxplusc_r;
73
74  — multiplier
75  mult_c <= mux_0_c * mux_1_c;
76
77  — adder
78  — the extra 0s at the MSB of the inputs are
79  — to capture overflow bit in the result
80  add_c <= ("0000"&mux_2_c) + ('0'&mult_r);
81
82  — define all registers
83  all_registers : process(clk, reset)
84  begin
85
86  if (reset= '1') then
87
88     mult_r <= (others=>'0');
89     xsquared_r <= (others=>'0');
90     bxplusc_r <= (others=>'0');
91     output_r <= (others=>'0');
92
93  elsif (clk' EVENT and clk='1') then
94
95     — infer simple register
96     mult_r <= mult_c;
97
98     — notice that we are not specifying
99     — the else condition. the synthesis tool will
100    — infer a latch for this case. if enable is
101    — low, previous value will be retained.
102    if (xsquared_reg_enable='1') then
103       xsquared_r <= mult_c(7 downto 0);
104    end if;
105
```

```
106    if (bxplusc_reg_enable='1') then
107        bxplusc_r <= add_c(8 downto 0);
108    end if;
109
110    if (output_reg_enable='1') then
111        output_r <= add_c;
112    end if;
113
114 end if;
115 end process;
116
117 — drive the output with a simple wire from the register
118 result <= output_r;
119
120 end;
```

Included in this datapath design is the special package `std_logic_unsigned` (Listing 6.5, line 4), which allows us to express arithmetic operations using high-level symbols (+ and *) on signals of type `std_logic_vector`. These functions are defined in the package. The package also helps us infer the right kind of arithmetic units (e.g., signed or unsigned). VHDL supports the signed data type for arithmetic operations.

Notice that we must carefully specify the precision required for all internal signals (Listing 6.5, lines 37–58). We must also pad extra 0s when the input signal precision is smaller than that of the operator (Listing 6.5, lines 68–69). The concatenation operator `&` in VHDL further allows us to combine the right mix of signals to enter the datapath as required by the design. This low-level control makes VHDL suitable for designers seeking to customize their designs to the problem.

We represent the multiplexers, multipliers, and adders using concurrent statements (Listing 6.5, lines 63–80), which are evaluated in parallel and inferred as combinational logic blocks. Note that all three multiplexers evaluate their inputs simultaneously. Concurrent statements allow the designer to capture this hardware-level concurrency in VHDL. Also note, however, that there is a dataflow dependency between the multiplexers and the multiplier (as well as the multiplexer and the adder). These dependencies are converted into wires that connect the appropriate logic blocks together, but each logic block continues to evaluate its inputs in parallel. The dataflow dependency only means that signal changes are propagated to the downstream multiplier input after a suitable delay for the multiplexer evaluation (see Delta delay subsection of Section 6.1.5 for more information on this delay).

We express the registers in the design using sequential statements inside the **process** block (Listing 6.5, lines 83–115). Most registers have a conditional signal assignment (Listing 6.5, lines 102–104). Notice the absence of an **else** statement or a default value on the rising clock edge. This implies that the signal retains its previous value if the condition for assignment is not satisfied. VHDL automatically infers feedback from the output to the multiplexer at the register input. If the **else** is present or if a default value is specified, no feedback will be inferred. This can be seen in Listing 6.6 (signals in the next-state decoder process have default values, avoiding inference of feedback paths).

To design the state machine controller, we first create a time sequence of operations that must be performed to obtain the final result. This gives us a cycle-by-cycle schedule for how the datapath elements are shared between the different operations. Each of these cycles is represented by a state, which is then decoded into multiplexer select and register enable signals for the datapath. The VHDL for this state machine is written in an RTL form specialized for state machines. It is shown in Listing 6.6 and illustrated in Figure 6.5.

Listing 6.6 ■ A state machine for generating control signals for the time-shared datapath.

```
1   — library and package includes
2   library ieee;
3   use ieee.std_logic_1164.all;
4
5   — entity declaration of the state-machine controller
6   entity fsm is
7   port (
8       — system signals
9       clk : in std_logic;
10      reset : in std_logic;
11
12      — start the computation
13      start : in std_logic;
14
15      — datapath multiplexer select
16      mult_input1_muxsel : out std_logic_vector(1 downto 0);
17      mult_input2_muxsel : out std_logic;
18      add_input1_muxsel : out std_logic;
19
20      — register enables
21      xsquared_reg_enable : out std_logic;
22      bxplusc_reg_enable : out std_logic;
23      output_reg_enable : out std_logic;
24
25      — indicate output is valid
26      output_valid : out std_logic
27  );
28  end;
29
30  — state-machine code is enclosed is defined inside this architecture block
31  architecture behav of fsm is
32
33  — define an enumerated type for state
34  type state_type is (IDLE, COMPUTE_BX, COMPUTE_BXPLUSC_AND_XSQR,
35              COMPUTE_AXSQR, COMPUTE_ASQRPLUSBXPLUSC, ASSERT_OUTPUT);
```

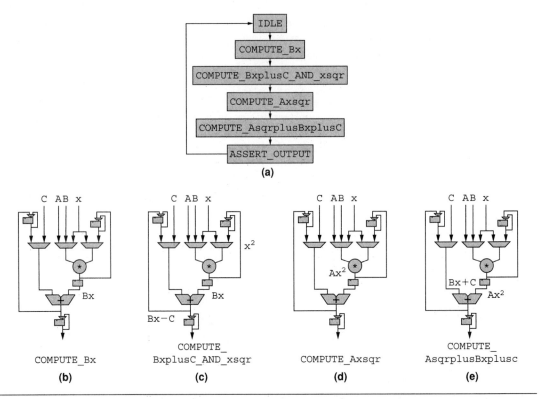

FIGURE 6.5 ▪ A state machine for generating control signals for the time-shared datapath. Labels on wires show dataflow steps in calculation.

```
36   signal state_c : state_type;
37   signal state_r : state_type;
38
39   — internal signals
40   signal mult_input1_muxsel_c : std_logic_vector(1 downto 0);
41   signal mult_input2_muxsel_c : std_logic;
42   signal add_input1_muxsel_c : std_logic;
43   signal xsquared_reg_enable_c : std_logic;
44   signal bxplusc_reg_enable_c : std_logic;
45   signal output_reg_enable_c : std_logic;
46   signal output_valid_c : std_logic;
47
48   — start the signal assignments
49   begin
50
51   — logic to compute the next state of the state machine
52   — also generate the control signals [only combinational, right now]
53   next_state_decoder : process(state_r, start)
54   begin
55
56   — given initial values for all signals
57   mult_input1_muxsel_c <= "00";
58   mult_input2_muxsel_c <= '0';
```

```
59   add_input1_muxsel_c <= '0';
60   xsquared_reg_enable_c <= '0';
61   bxplusc_reg_enable_c <= '0';
62   output_reg_enable_c <= '0';
63   output_valid_c <= '0';
64   state_c <= IDLE;
65
66   — specify state transistions
67   — update state variable
68   — update the control signals
69   case state_r is
70     when IDLE =>
71
72         — conditional state transition
73         if (start='1') then
74
75             state_c <= COMPUTE_BX;
76
77             mult_input1_muxsel_c <= "01"; — select B
78             mult_input2_muxsel_c <= '0'; — select x
79
80     end if;
81
82     when COMPUTE_BX =>
83
84     — unconditional state transition
85     state_c <= COMPUTE_BXPLUSC_AND_XSQR;
86
87     mult_input1_muxsel_c <= "10"; — select x
88     mult_input2_muxsel_c <= '0'; — select x
89     xsquared_reg_enable_c <= '1'; — save x*x
90     bxplusc_reg_enable_c <= '1'; — save Bx+C
91     add_input1_muxsel_c <= '1'; — select C
92
93   when COMPUTE_BXPLUSC_AND_XSQR =>
94
95     state_c <= COMPUTE_AXSQR;
96
97     mult_input1_muxsel_c <= "00"; — select A
98     mult_input2_muxsel_c <= '1'; — select xsqr
99
100  when COMPUTE_AXSQR =>
101
102    state_c <= COMPUTE_ASQRPLUSBXPLUSC;
103
104    add_input1_muxsel_c <= '1'; — select Bx+C
105    output_reg_enable_c <= '1';
106
107  when COMPUTE_ASQRPLUSBXPLUSC =>
108
109    state_c  <= ASSERT_OUTPUT;
110    output_valid_c <= '1';
111
112  when ASSERT_OUTPUT =>
113
```

```
114     state_c <= IDLE;
115
116  end case;
117
118  end process;
119
120  — describe the registers that hold the state bits
121  — the actual bits will be inferred by the
122  — synthesis tool from the symbolic states
123  state_register : process(clk, reset)
124  begin
125
126  if (reset = '1') then
127     state_r <= IDLE;
128  elsif (clk' EVENT and clk='1') then
129     state_r <= state_c;
130  end if;
131
132  end process;
133
134  — register the control signals generated during state transitions
135  output_logic : process(clk, reset)
136  begin
137
138  if (reset = '1') then
139
140     mult_input1_muxsel <= "00";
141     mult_input2_muxsel <= '0';
142     add_input1_muxsel <= '0';
143     xsquared_reg_enable <= '0';
144     bxplusc_reg_enable <= '0';
145     output_reg_enable <= '0';
146     output_valid <= '0';
147
148  elsif (clk EVENT and clk='1') then
149
150     mult_input1_muxsel <= mult_input1_muxsel_c;
151     mult_input2_muxsel <= mult_input2_muxsel_c;
152     add_input1_muxsel <= add_input1_muxsel_c;
153     xsquared_reg_enable <= xsquared_reg_enable_c;
154     bxplusc_reg_enable <= bxplusc_reg_enable_c;
155     output_reg_enable <= output_reg_enable_c;
156     output_valid <= output_valid_c;
157
158  end if;
159
160  end process;
161
162  end;
```

By encoding the state of the controller with an enumerated data type (Listing 6.6, lines 34–36), we can defer the actual encoding of the state bits until the synthesis stage. The synthesis tool then assigns a bit encoding to optimize logic. It is easier to verify the operation of the state machine using symbolic states. It is also easier to update and modify symbolic state machine code.

In the next-state decoder (Listing 6.6, lines 53–118), we enumerate all possible states of the state machine and define state transitions from each of them. These transitions are expressed as conditions under which the state changes.

We use the **process** block for describing purely combinational logic in the next-state decoder of the state machine (Listing 6.6, lines 53–118). Previously, we used **process** for describing only registers (Listing 6.2, lines 39–50). This shows how we can write combinational logic here as well. In this listing, notice that the same signal is assigned values multiple times in the **process** block (signal `mult_input1_muxsel_c` in Listing 6.6, lines 57, 77, 87, and 97). As the statements are evaluated sequentially, the last signal assignment statement to be evaluated is considered valid, superseding all previous assignments. During execution of sequential statements in a process, for purposes of determining new signal values all signals are considered to have the same value they had at the start of the process. Signals that are assigned values inside the process will acquire those values only when process execution is complete—that is, **process** suspends. It is in this aspect that the VHDL sequential semantics are different from those of a conventional programming language (e.g., C). Figure 6.6 shows similar code written in C and VHDL to illustrate how the different execution semantics lead to different answers.

In Listing 6.6, all signals are assigned a value at the beginning of the process. By design, only one **when** subblock of the **case** statement will be evaluated, which means that only those signals that have assignments inside the valid **when** subblock will get new values (Listing 6.6, line 77, 87, or 97 will execute; line 57 will execute in all cases). According to the VHDL sequential signal assignment rule, these new assignments will hold when the process suspends. Other signals will simply carry the default values they were assigned at the start. This avoids the inference of feedback that we saw earlier (refer to Listing 6.2).

```
1 process(clk)                               1 int updatecounter(int counter){
2 begin                                      2        counter++;
3                                            3
4        if(clk 'EVENT'and clk='1') then     4        if(counter==10)
5                counter <= counter + 1;     5          counter = 0;
6                if(counter=10)              6
7                        counter <= 0;       7        return counter;
8                end if;                     8 }
9        end if;                             9
10                                          10 // updatecounter(9) returns 0
11 end process;
12
13 — if counter=9 at start of process,
14 — when process suspends, counter=10.
                 (a)                                        (b)
```

FIGURE 6.6 ■ Comparison of sequential VHDL (a) and C (b) assignment semantics.

6.1.5 Advanced Topics

Delta delay

VHDL uses an event-driven simulation model. A signal is evaluated only when an event—that is, a signal transition associated with the input signals—has occurred. Once a statement is evaluated, its associated signal needs to be assigned the newly generated value. However, this is not done right away so as to keep the evaluations of other statements from using this new value immediately, potentially leading to inconsistent results.

Remember that in VHDL all concurrent statements are evaluated in parallel. Hence, to keep the simulation consistent VHDL uses delta delay, in which the newly generated value is scheduled as an event at the following delta. (A delta is simply a logical delay used in the simulator and not a physical delay of the circuit.) The simulator will generate as many deltas as required depending on the logical depth of the circuit and its input transitions. Once all events for a given delta are exhausted, the simulator proceeds to the earliest delta at which the next event exists. Physical time in the simulator is advanced only when no more events are left to be processed at the last delta at the current physical time. Sometimes the simulator is unable to advance its physical time because of asynchronous, combinational feedback loops that continue generating new events at incremental deltas. Such loops should be avoided when programming VHDL, and modern synchronous simulation and synthesis tools usually warn the designer if such a loop is detected.

Multivalued logic

Another electrical behavior is modeled in VHDL using the multivalued logic type `std_logic`. It allows a signal to have different kinds of electrical states, apart from a Boolean 0 or 1, which are required for modeling tristate drivers, multiple simultaneous drivers (usually a design error), uninitialized signals, and weak drivers.

6.2   HARDWARE COMPILATION FLOW

To fully understand how VHDL fits into the design process, we expand the FPGA compilation process shown in Figure I.2. Our flow is shown in Figure 6.7.

1. The hardware designer begins the design-engineering process with a problem specification—that is, a functional description of the problem along with additional performance and area constraints that the implementation must meet.

2. Based on this specification and the inherent problem structure, the designer identifies an appropriate system architecture to use for the implementation. We saw different kinds of system architectures in Chapter 5.

3. The designer writes VHDL code to describe this design using structural and RTL styles that we saw earlier in this chapter.

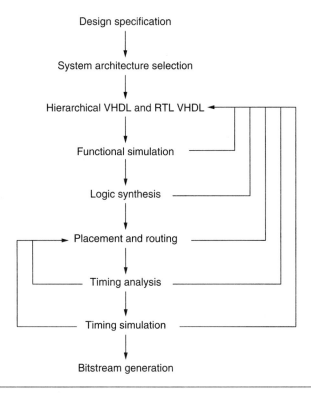

System architecture selection

Hierarchical VHDL and RTL VHDL

Functional simulation

Logic synthesis

Placement and routing

Timing analysis

Timing simulation

Bitstream generation

FIGURE 6.7 ■ FPGA compilation flow.

4. Once the VHDL is written, the designer needs to first check if her VHDL meets functional specifications, using a suitable testbench that can be written in VHDL itself. The testbench and the design are run in a logic-level simulator. The testbench generates appropriate test vectors for the design and verifies the result. This is typically an iterative process, and the designer continues to refine the VHDL design until the functional specification is met.

5. After verifying correctness, the designer then proceeds to the FPGA back-end phase, a multistage (and iterative) process. It starts with synthesis, where the synthesis tool converts the VHDL description of the design (excluding the testbench) into a logic-level FPGA netlist. This netlist is generated by first inferring hardware from VHDL code and then optimizing it through several state-of-the-art algorithms—for example, logic minimization, retiming (Chapter 18), covering (Chapter 13), and sharing to meet timing and area constraints. Constraints can be specified as a separate input to the tool by the user.

6. The designer uses backend tools to perform placement (Chapter 14) and routing (Chapter 17) on the synthesized logic elements to map them to an actual physical device (logic elements are assigned physical LUTs while the wires between them are mapped to the interconnect fabric). This is typically the most time-consuming step of the backend process. The designer can help direct these tools using additional constraints (see Section 6.2.1) either to improve the quality of the final mapped design or to reduce the compilation time needed.

7. Once the design is placed and routed, the designer can perform static timing analysis to ensure that the timing constraints are met. FPGA tools can also write out a post place and route timing annotated VHDL netlist for a timing simulation that models logic and interconnect delays accurately. Specific timing requirements not covered in the simple static timing analysis can then be simulated and checked.

8. If the designer is satisfied with the performance of her implemented hardware, the tools generate a programming file for the FPGA device (Chapter 19).

6.2.1   Constraints

Constraints are an indispensable tool directive that a designer can use to help her designs meet required specifications. They can be used to direct the synthesis tools in optimizing the design for either high-speed operation or low-area implementation (these are usually conflicting goals). For example, the designer can specify a frequency target that Synplify Pro (a synthesis tool) must meet using the following timing constraint.

```
set option -frequency 300.000
```

This sets the target frequency for the compilation to be 300 MHz. Similarly, designers can provide timing constraints for the placement and routing phases as well.

```
TIMESPEC "clock signal name"=3.3ns;
```

More important, a designer can give physical floorplanning constraints to direct the placement and routing algorithms to use a specified region on the chip.

```
INST "*" AREA GROUP = "dummy name";
AREA GROUP "dummy_name" RANGE = SLICE X0Y0:SLICE X100Y100;
```

Here we create a group `dummy_name` containing all hardware elements in the design using wildcards (*). Then we specify a rectangular box from 0,0 to 100,100 on the FPGA. The units are measured in `SLICE`s; a `SLICE` is a cluster of a few, usually four, Xilinx FPGA LUTs. The proper selection of these constraint values is typically based on intuition and can be refined with designer experience. Placement constraints, such as the one in the previous code snippet, are vendor and device specific, but each vendor typically has analogous constraints for each device.

6.3 LIMITATIONS OF VHDL

Although VHDL currently enjoys a healthy market share, there are several limitations and drawbacks in the language:

- VHDL syntax is verbose, extremely cumbersome, and requires several lines of code to describe even simple logic elements (e.g., a register typically requires four to ten lines of code).
- Hardware needs to be described at a very low level of abstraction (i.e., RTL). The programmer is responsible for specifying the logic that goes between each register stage, which can become a significant programming challenge for large irregular designs with thousands of registers and unique logic between register stages.
- As technology and FPGA architectures evolve, the optimal amount of pipelining required to meet the desired cycle time changes. Because RTL is written for a specific number of registers in the logic path, it needs to be rewritten when the number of register stages changes. In other words, the amount of logic between register stages must be modified accordingly.
- Low-level descriptions also make it hard for synthesis tools to optimize and schedule logic. Programmer bias disallows optimizations that might have otherwise been possible in a more flexible description.
- Hardware described in VHDL suffers from the additional drawback of significantly long verification times. It is known that equivalent simulation-specific, cycle-accurate models written in C, C++, Java, or other higher-level language can be simulated 10 to 100 times faster than in VHDL. Verification is a significant portion of the design cycle, and there is demand to contain the time spent on it.

In subsequent chapters, we will see other high-level languages that address many of these limitations (e.g., Chapters 7, 9, and 10). In many cases, however, these languages use VHDL as an intermediate target in their mapping flow.

References

[1] P. Ashenden. *The Designer's Guide to VHDL*, 2nd ed., Morgan Kaufmann, 2002.
[2] P. Ashenden. *The Student's Guide to VHDL*, Morgan Kaufmann, 1998.
[3] *Development System Reference Guide*, Xilinx, Inc.

CHAPTER 7

COMPILING C FOR SPATIAL COMPUTING

Timothy J. Callahan
School of Computer Science
Carnegie Mellon University

André DeHon
Department of Electrical and Systems Engineering
University of Pennsylvania

This chapter describes techniques for compiling from C or similar languages to reconfigurable architectures. We will first briefly describe the benefits of this approach and the contexts where it is most useful. Then we will describe in detail the algorithms and their technical limitations and challenges.

For the discussion in this chapter, we assume the presence of a microprocessor coupled with the reconfigurable fabric (RF). This eases adaptation in several ways and is particularly useful when supporting a mix of irregular control tasks (best suited to the microprocessor) and compute-intensive, high-throughput tasks (best suited to the RF), as described in the Processor subsection of Section 5.2.2.

The original C code can be partitioned between the central processing unit (CPU) and the RF at several granularities, including procedures, compound loops, inner loops, and blocks. The algorithms described in this chapter apply to any of these cases. The appropriate granularity for a particular system will depend on the hardware available and the particular costs involved in communication between the CPU and the RF and will not be treated in this chapter.

For most of this section we will assume that the source code, both before and after the designer's target-specific efforts to improve performance via hints in comments or pragmas, will be legal C code as defined by the ISO standard [9]. However, at the end we will overview some methods for integrating blocks designed via HDL or schematic capture into a C program.

The benefits to having a full, pushbutton path that starts from C and that can put at least some of the application on the reconfigurable hardware follow.

- There are many more C programmers than hardware designers, and writing an algorithm in C is typically faster than in an HDL.
- There is a large existing code base even for embedded applications, with at least the reference version written in C.
- Working with a single description of the entire program makes it easy for the designer or compiler to quickly explore the tradeoffs of different hardware/software partitionings. Also, it allows both hardware (HW) and

software (SW) versions to be created so that the operating system can choose at runtime which is better (see Chapter 11).

- Designers can start with automatic compilation, and then focus their efforts on improving a few loops while benefiting from the compiler's speedup on the remainder. Furthermore, with the compiler's support the designer's required effort is reduced in many cases to simply restructuring the code or embedding simple compiler directives in the form of comments or #pragma syntax.
- The code can be easily tested on a conventional microprocessor for correctness.

This chapter will be of direct value to those interested in compilation for spatial computing from a sequential language. More generally, it will give an application writer an understanding of the power and limitations of the state of the art of such compilers—and thereby how to write high-performance code quickly.

7.1   OVERVIEW OF HOW C CODE RUNS ON SPATIAL HARDWARE

This section provides a quick overview of how C code can be implemented on a reconfigurable fabric. It assumes basic familiarity with C. The approaches used are simple and far from optimal, but easy to understand. The detailed algorithms of how a compiler does this construction will follow.

In the figures that follow (e.g., Figure 7.1), the gray rectangles represent registers. For simplicity, the global clock is not shown. An arrow from the side toward the register indicates a load enable signal. The hardware appears at the operator level, not at the gate/CLB level.

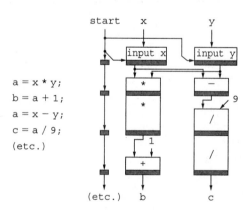

```
a = x * y;
b = a + 1;
a = x - y;
c = a / 9;
(etc.)
```

FIGURE 7.1 ▪ Straight-line code.

7.1.1 Data Connections between Operations

The simplest components of C code to start with are sequences of straight-line arithmetic and logical statements. A sequence effectively tells us the set of primitive operations that make up the computation and how those operations are linked together—that is, they tell us how the outputs of one operation become inputs to other operations.

In a C program, the statements execute in order. A statement can define a variable, and subsequent statements using that variable get its last defined value. This is how value definitions are connected to their use(s)—the most recent assignment to a variable is the one that is used by a subsequent statement.

With spatial computation, each operation is implemented as a function unit (or *module*) and a producer is connected to its consumer(s) by a direct physical connection. Even if two different C statements assign to the same program variable, they are treated as different variables internally. In the example in Figure 7.1, the two definitions of variable *a*, while sequential in the C program, are actually independent and can be performed in parallel spatially. This is one step in the direction of exploiting the unlimited parallelism of spatial hardware, where we wish to reduce unnecessary ordering of operations as much as possible and keep only the necessary ordering.

Because we are implementing the computation spatially and in parallel, the actual compute datapaths are always instantiated, ready to perform their operations. It is sometimes necessary to inform the modules when their inputs are available and when they should actually perform their actions. The chain of registers on the left of Figure 7.1 acts as a very simple sequencer. In this particular example, the registers simply count off how many cycles are required to compute all of the results. A '1' bit is fed from the `start` signal, kicking off the sequencer and latching values into the input modules. The input modules hold the input values constant during execution of this unit of computation. When a 1 bit appears at `finish`, the final values are ready to pass on.

Mixed operations of different complexity (e.g., adders and multipliers) may take different amounts of time to complete. For efficient operation, rather than slowing all operators down to the latency of the slowest one, it is often worthwhile to decompose slower operators into multiple cycles, potentially pipelining them internally. In this example, multiply and divide are split into two stages requiring two cycles, while add and subtract require just one cycle each.

Throughout this section, we employ a timing discipline where values are held constant until the end of their block schedule. If a module's output register is shown at level P in the schedule, and the overall schedule length is SL, then the output of that module is guaranteed to be correct and stable from cycles P through SL of that specific block execution (where cycle 0 is when the `start` signal is raised).

7.1.2 Memory

Memory loads and stores pose additional complications beyond simple arithmetic and logical operations, in that their effects are not just local. In particular,

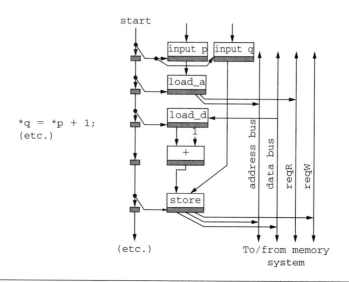

FIGURE 7.2 ■ Implementation of memory accesses.

memory can be used to perform dynamic interconnect between operations, and we must be careful to preserve the original communication semantics of the C program. A "memory" function unit has local input and output connections to other function units as normal, but also has connections to global shared address, data, and control buses. These connect each memory node to the same shared memory system.

Memory access operations must be scheduled on a particular cycle both to allow sharing among memory operations and to preserve sequential C semantics. Without scheduled coordination, two modules can attempt to drive the address or data bus simultaneously. The simple controller triggers each memory access at the correct time so that no clashes arise on either the address or the data buses. Memory access must be scheduled after its input values are ready. The compiler is also responsible for scheduling memory accesses in a way that ensures that each pair that might access the same memory location is performed in the correct relative program order.

The example in Figure 7.2 shows how a load node is split into a `load_a`, which sends the address and load request, and a `load_d` (or *load continuation*), which grabs the data when it comes back. The example assumes a load latency of just one cycle. If the memory system takes extra time to return the load data, as in the case of a cache miss, there must also be a `stall` signal factored into the sequencer to freeze execution of the subcircuit; this is *not* shown in the figure.

7.1.3 If-then-else Using Multiplexers

Simple if-then-else statements can be merged into a single subcircuit by performing the operations along both branches and then using multiplexers to

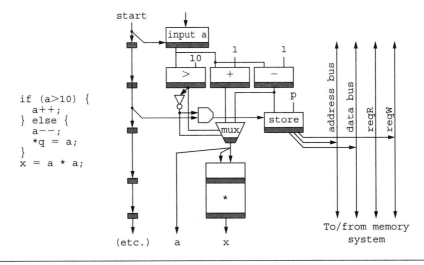

FIGURE 7.3 ■ If-conversion: Combining if-then-else using predicates and multiplexers.

select the correct version of each variable for use in subsequent computation. This removes the branch; instead, the comparison result is used as a *predicate* to choose the correct variable for later use, as with variable a in the example in Figure 7.3. In the figure the predicates are the result of the comparison a > 10 and its inverse, which say whether the then or the else branch is taken. In general, a predicate is always a Boolean value—the result of a comparison, or a Boolean function of multiple comparisons, as occurs when nested if-then-else statements are reduced. switch statements and even forward goto statements can be implemented using similar techniques.

If the then or else contains a side-effect-causing operation, such as the store in Figure 7.3, that operation's cycle trigger must be ANDed with the predicate under which it should execute.

7.1.4 Actual Control Flow

To map C code containing more than just simple if-then-else control flow to the reconfigurable fabric, some real control flow is needed. Control flow means that there may be multiple subcircuits on the RF; only one is active at a time; and the transition from one to another subcircuit is guided by the values that are computed by the ongoing computation. This is spatial computation's implementation of a conditional branch.

The control flow is implemented with the control bit: When it reaches the end of a subcircuit, it is directed to the start of the next subcircuit to execute. When a subcircuit has multiple successors, a predicate controls which one receives the control bit. In Figure 7.4, we see the explicit branch either to a subcircuit performing the then computation or to the one performing the else computation. Subcircuit SC1 computes the condition a > 10, and the result determines

```
if (a>10) {
    a++;
} else {
    a--;
}
x = a ^ 7;
(etc.)
```

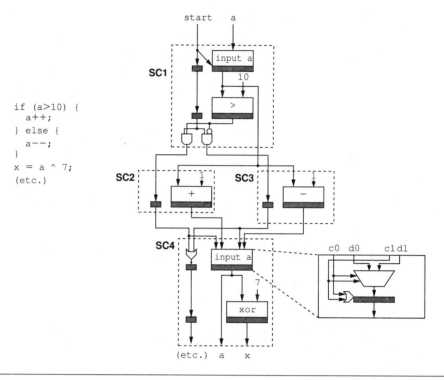

FIGURE 7.4 ▪ Actual control flow.

whether the control bit goes to SC2 or SC3; then one or the other gets the control bit and executes. Control flow paths then merge at SC4, where a control bit from either SC2 or SC3 starts SC4's execution. Note that the source of the control bit entering SC4 also controls whether SC2's or SC3's final version of a is latched at the start of SC4 (note in Figure 7.4 the expansion of input a).

Subcircuits as small as those shown in Figure 7.4 would not typically be created by the compiler; instead, they would likely be merged as shown earlier. However, if SC2 and SC3 had very different execution lengths, it would be worthwhile to keep them separate like this. If, for example, one had 1-cycle latency and the other 13-cycle, we would only experience the 13-cycle latency when that path was taken. In contrast, when uneven paths are combined into one subcircuit, we pay the worst-case latency every execution.

A subcircuit that has a single predecessor actually does not require input modules, assuming in our implementation that the predecessor subcircuit holds its outputs constant until it is activated again. This simplification is shown in SC2 and SC3 of Figure 7.4.

A loop is implemented simply by control branching back to the top of itself or to some other, earlier subcircuit.

7.1.5 Optimizing the Common Path

We have seen two extremes: (1) combining all the computation in an if-then-else nest and (2) doing no combining and keeping all branches. But the key to getting the best performance from limited spatial hardware is *selectively* merging the computation on the common path(s) (to remove the subcircuit-to-subcircuit latency and to expose operation parallelism) while excluding computation on the rarely taken paths (so that it doesn't get in the way of the common case).

In Figure 7.5 we see the same code as in Figure 7.4, but we have merged the computation along the path with the increment. However, we have excluded the path with the decrement. The compiler chose to merge the computation along the path with the increment (SC1 → SC2 → SC4 from Figure 7.4) into one subcircuit because a test run (or the programmer) told it that that path was more commonly executed. Because reentering the merged increment path is not allowed, we needed to copy the XOR computation for the decrement path.

Merging the common path allowed the compiler to schedule the comparison and the addition in parallel, reducing computation time to three cycles. The schedule for the common case is also better than that for the case where all blocks were merged, as in that case we needed a multiplexer to merge the results from the decrement path, and that would add an extra step between the addition and the XOR. In the general case, the benefit of excluding a rare path could be even greater: Consider if the decrement were instead a multiplication, or even a

```
if (a>10) {
  a++;
} else {
  a--;
}
x = a ^ 7;
(etc.)
```

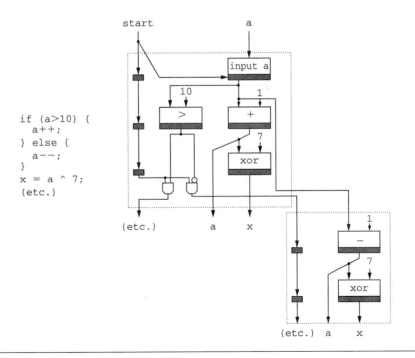

FIGURE 7.5 ■ Optimizing the common path.

long chain of operations. In that case, if that rare path were included, it would force a much longer schedule.

In this case, when the execution flow exits the common path and continues to the excluded path, the total time will be five cycles, longer than the four cycles that would have resulted if decrement had been included. Many 3-cycle executions with a few 5-cycle executions are better than all 4-cycle executions—again, optimizing the common path.

A system might also choose to implement rarely taken paths as normal software on the CPU. This would ease the demand for resources on the reconfigurable fabric and allow implementation of a loop or procedure that otherwise would not fit. This approach is also beneficial when the excluded path includes an operation, such as a library call, that cannot be implemented directly on the RF. However, the cost of transferring control to the CPU for a rare path, when it does happen, must be considered.

7.1.6   Summary and Challenges

In this section we sketched how C can be implemented spatially and began to illustrate optimizations for parallelism that are the key to extracting high performance from spatial hardware, even when the spatial hardware runs at a slower clock rate than the CPU. We also illustrated context-specific optimization, which allows us to highly specialize the computation to the common case execution of the application, further increasing parallelism and reducing the computation required. Nonetheless, these simple techniques leave us with spatial designs that can be inefficient and that underutilize our reconfigurable fabric. These inefficiencies include:

- *Not pipelining:* Sequential paths prevent us from reusing our spatial hardware at its full capacity; spatial operators sit idle for most of the cycles in a block. To fully use the capabilities of the reconfigurable hardware, datapaths should be pipelined for rapid reuse.
- *Memory:* Sequential dependencies among memory access operations limit available parallelism.
- *Operator size and specialization:* The reconfigurable fabric can provide hardware tailored to the compute needs (e.g., just the right datapath width, specialized around compile time constants), but specific information about operator size is often not immediately apparent in the original C program.

The following sections show how we can address many of the simple translation scheme's limitations.

7.2   AUTOMATIC COMPILATION

A particular compiler flow is largely determined by the system architecture. Here we will assume that fairly large pieces of code will be migrated to the reconfigurable fabric—a loop or perhaps even a complete procedure. There is little difference in the algorithms between granularities at this level.

We assume a standard C compiler frontend that parses the source files (see Figure 7.6(a)) and performs further processing until the intermediate representation consists of a *control flow graph* (CFG) for each procedure. A CFG consists of *basic blocks*, each containing an ordered list of simple instructions and connected by control edges indicating a possible branch from the end of one basic block to the start of another, as shown in Figure 7.6(b). By definition, entry to a basic block occurs only at the beginning, exits occur only at the end, and all instructions inside the basic block execute once the block is entered.

Within each basic block, complex expressions are broken up by introducing compiler temporary variables so that each simple instruction contains just one operation. This list of simple instructions in each basic block resembles assembly code to some degree, but is of a higher level: variables (including compiler temporaries) are used instead of explicit registers, and all type information is still available. Many optimizations are performed on this representation to reduce the number of instructions by, for example, constant propagation, constant folding, and common subexpression elimination. (See Aho et al. [1] or Muchnick [13] for related background.)

The frontend also provides some standard analyses. Of particular interest here is live variable analysis, which indicates whether or not the current contents of a variable need to be preserved for a possible future use.

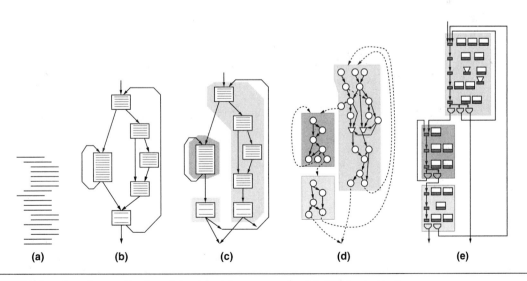

(a)   (b)   (c)   (d)   (e)

FIGURE 7.6 ■ Overall compiler flow: (a) original C source code, (b) CFG basic blocks, (c) clustering of basic blocks into hyperblocks, (d) construction of the DFG, and (e) circuit generation from the DFG.

After frontend processing produces an optimized CFG for each procedure, we start compilation steps specific to reconfigurable computing:

- *HW/SW partitioning:* This is very system dependent, and its discussion is deferred until section 7.3.1.
- *HW/HW clustering of the CFG basic blocks into hyperblocks:* illustrated in Figure 7.6(c) and discussed in section 7.2.1.
- *Building the dataflow graph (DFG) for each hyperblock:* illustrated in Figure 7.6(d) and discussed in section 7.2.2.
- *DFG optimization:* discussed in section 7.2.3.
- *Generating the circuit from the DFGs:* This involves module mapping (packing one or more DFG nodes into a single-cycle macro function unit), scheduling, connecting hyperblock subcircuits, and other related tasks; illustrated in Figure 7.6(e), which leaves out data connections, and discussed in section 7.2.4.

After we go over these steps, we will describe some uses and variations in Section 7.3.

7.2.1 Hyperblocks

Because basic blocks are limited to straight-line control flow between branches, they are often quite small and limit our opportunities for parallelism. As we saw in the previous section, we can often convert if-then-else constructs into dataflow using multiplexers. These composite blocks, or *hyperblocks*, have a single entry point at the top and one or more exits. All branches within the hyperblock are eliminated by using predicates and multiplexers. Each hyperblock becomes a subcircuit, as shown earlier.

To form hyperblocks, the compiler starts with the basic block CFG. It then combines blocks along commonly taken paths—for example, the right group in Figure 7.6(c), excluding rarely taken paths. A single basic block can always be a hyperblock. To respect the single top-entry requirement, *tail duplication* is required to eliminate an edge that otherwise would reenter the hyperblock; that edge is redirected to a copy of its original target. For example, the bottom basic block in Figure 7.6(b) is duplicated in Figure 7.6(c).

The hyperblock was originally constructed by Mahlke and colleagues [12] for compiling to VLIW (very long instruction word) processors (see VLIW datapath control subsection of Section 5.2.2), although the clustering heuristics they developed are not necessarily effective here. In particular, VLIW processors have a fixed instruction issue width; once this is saturated, adding additional parallel paths may extend the schedule and hurt the performance of the common case. With spatial computing, we have no limit on per-cycle operation parallelism, so it is often beneficial to make "fatter" hyperblocks by including more parallel paths from the CFG.

7.2.2 Building a Dataflow Graph for a Hyperblock

Here we focus on constructing a DFG (dataflow graph) from the set of basic blocks in a hyperblock. The DFG is a "stepping stone" between the original software specification and the final spatial hardware implementation. The compiler performs many important tasks in building it:

- Control dependence within the hyperblock is converted to data dependence: Internal conditional branches are eliminated through the introduction of predicates (Boolean values indicating the "taken" path through the computation). The only remaining conditional branches are exits out of the hyperblock.
- Data producer–consumer relationships are made explicit via data edges in the graph; also, because a new DFG node is created for each definition, variable renaming is effectively performed, which eliminates false dependencies.
- Any remaining ordering constraints between individual operations, particularly memory operations, are also made explicit through ordering edges.

These actions convert the sequential ordering of instructions to a partial order of DFG nodes, exposing parallelism. In addition, maximal control speculation is employed so that all safe operations execute every iteration, removing dependencies between predicate calculations and those operations, breaking critical paths, and further increasing operation parallelism. Finally, the DFG is an ideal representation with which to perform many additional optimizations, described next.

The DFG is composed of nodes and edges:

- *Nodes:* These include constants, inputs to the hyperblock, simple computational operations having no side effects (such as addition), memory accesses, and exit nodes. Exit nodes are associated with an outgoing control edge from one hyperblock to another; when an exit node's predicate input is true, it causes a control transfer to the target hyperblock recorded on the node. The exit node also defines which live data values should be transferred to the successor hyperblock, as indicated by liveness edges.
- *Edges:* These are directed edges between the nodes and are of three types: data edges, indicating producer–consumer relationships; ordering edges, indicating an ordering constraint between two nodes such as memory operations; and liveness edges. Liveness edges go only to exit nodes. They indicate the set of values that are live-out at that hyperblock exit and thus must be copied out—that is, transferred to the successor hyperblock or back to the CPU. Each liveness edge is annotated with the name of the variable because, in general, the variable cannot be deduced from the source DFG node (a single node may be the source for different variables at different exits). These edges are necessary because the set of live variables to be transferred typically differs at each exit. Also, the source DFG node for a given variable can be different at different exits.

Top-level build algorithms

We build the DFG from the basic block CFG for each hyperblock. The algorithm for building the DFG performs a single forward pass, visiting each basic block in the hyperblock in an order such that each basic block is visited only after all its predecessors have been visited. Then, when visiting each basic block, the simple instructions are visited in sequence. This forward pass builds all of the DFG nodes, including nodes directly translated from instructions as well as predicate calculation nodes and mux (multiplexer) nodes inserted to implement predicated execution. The forward pass also builds all data and ordering edges.

Building data edges

When a node is constructed, the compiler creates data edges to its inputs using the `lastDefs` data structure. Throughout the forward pass, this table is kept up to date regarding which node produced the last definition of each variable; there is at most one such definition at any point. We show an example in Figure 7.7.

At the start of processing a hyperblock's entry basic block, the `lastDefs` list is initialized with an input node associated with each live variable, as with `y:n1` in the example.

Whenever an instruction assigns to a variable, `lastDefs` is updated. In our example, y++ in BB1 uses the current value of y, n1 as the source for the incoming edge to the new add node, n4; then the `lastDefs` list is updated so that the new value of y is available from n4.

A copy—an assignment from one variable to another—requires no action other than updating the `lastDefs` list (see for example x=y in BB1 in Figure 7.7). A new entry for x is made in the `lastDefs` list, x:n1, just using the current entry for y. Similar for z=y, although at that point the entry for y is different so a different source node is given to z. This has the effect of performing

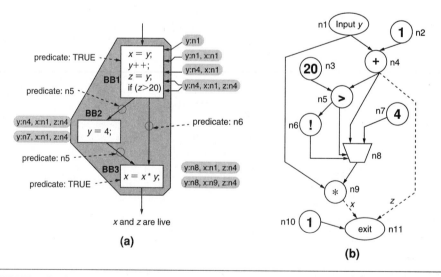

FIGURE 7.7 ■ Basic blocks selection for the hyperblock: (a) the state of the `lastDefs` list at various points in the process; (b) the resulting DFG.

copy propagation and constant propagation for free while building the DFG. At the end of processing each basic block, the final `lastDefs` list is recorded.

For a nonentry basic block B with a single predecessor in the hyperblock, the predecessor's final `lastDefs` list is used as the starting `lastDefs` list for processing B. This occurs from the end of BB1 to the start of BB2.

Building muxes

At a basic block with $N > 1$ incoming CFG edges, a given variable may have differing definitions arriving via the edges as indicated by the predecessors' respective final `lastDefs` lists. In such cases, an unencoded mux is constructed in the DFG to route the appropriate definition to subsequent consumers. An unencoded mux has N data inputs and N Boolean select inputs—only one of the select inputs can be true—and the corresponding data input is routed to the output. The N data inputs to the mux are from the data source nodes from the arriving `lastDefs` lists; the select input corresponding to each of the N data inputs is the predicate for that arriving edge. The data output of the mux structure becomes the definition of the variable entered in the `lastDefs` list for the start of processing that basic block. This occurs for y entering BB3, where the compiler inserts mux n8 to select between sources n4 and n7, and then makes n8 the new entry for y. Because the entries for x and z are the same, however, no mux is built for either of them.

Predicates

At the beginning of processing each basic block, a node calculating that block's predicate is built if necessary and the predicate source is recorded to be used as input for nodes that cannot be executed speculatively (e.g., stores). The predicate for the hyperblock entry block is TRUE. For each other basic block, the predicate is built as the OR of the predicate sources of all incoming edges. When there is just one incoming edge, the calculation degenerates to just using that edge's predicate.

At the end of processing a basic block, a predicate is built if necessary and recorded for each outgoing edge. For a basic block ending in a conditional branch, an edge's predicate is built as its source block's predicate, ANDed with the branch condition under which that edge is taken. For a basic block ending in an unconditional branch, the edge predicate on the single outgoing edge is just the same as the block's predicate. After forming predicates for a nested if-then-else, it may be possible to simplify them; for example, a block may be (p1 AND p2) OR (p1 AND not p2), which can be reduced to just (p1) by rules of Boolean logic.

Ordering edges

To help build ordering edges, the compiler maintains lists of all loads and stores seen along any path from the entry of the hyperblock to the current point. At the start of processing the hyperblock, the lists are initialized as empty. At the end of processing each basic block, the state of the lists at that point is recorded. At the start of any nonentry basic block, the starting lists are simply calculated: For a basic block with a single predecessor, the predecessor's lists are copied; when there are multiple predecessors, the respective lists are unioned.

When building a new load, construct an ordering edge from each upstream store to the new load, and then the load is added to the seen_loads list. When a new store is built, an ordering edge is constructed from each node on both the seen_loads and seen_stores lists to the new store and the store is added to the seen_stores list. This step is very conservative; for example, it adds an ordering edge from a store to each subsequent load even if the load is from a different array. Later phases use dependency information to remove ordering edges that are not necessary—that is, when it is guaranteed that the two accesses cannot refer to the same memory location.

Live variables at exits

This phase determines, for each exit, which values must be copied out to the next hyperblock or CPU when that exit is taken. For each such variable, a liveness edge is constructed from the node responsible for the last definition, as found in the lastDefs list, to the DFG exit node.

If the variable is live at that exit, there will be an entry for it in lastDefs at the point of exit. The indicated DFG node is the one providing the value for the variable, so the edge is constructed from that node to the exit DFG node.

Figure 7.8 shows an example of a swap. There are two exits from the first hyperblock, at one of which a and b are swapped—this results purely from

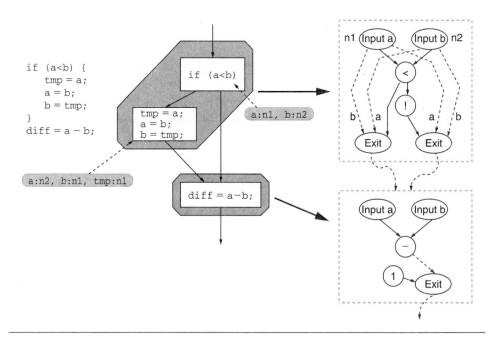

FIGURE 7.8 ▪ Code, hyperblock formation, and resulting DFGs.

`lastDefs` list processing. The figure shows the differing contents of the `lastDefs` lists at the different exits. In one case, a's source is n1 (input a); in the other, its source is n2 (input b). Later, when the compiler translates the DFGs to subcircuit implementations, it will also form connections from the appropriate liveness edge sources in the first hyperbock to the input nodes in the second hyperblock.

Scalar variables in memory
If the address of a scalar variable is taken at some point by the C language & operator, it may be written or read through a pointer access. In this case, in general the variable must reside in memory. When direct accesses to the variable are interspersed with pointer accesses, we can't be sure when the pointer access might be accessing that variable without further analysis. Thus, we must keep the memory version of the variable up to date. When this situation occurs, each use of the variable requires an explicit load from memory, and each definition requires a store. Going to memory for each variable access is obviously detrimental to performance, especially on a reconfigurable fabric, so later optimizations attempt to eliminate or reduce the number of such accesses.

7.2.3 DFG Optimization

Optimizations have been performed by the compiler frontend before DFG construction even starts. More optimizations are performed during construction, some of them coming automatically in the construction process, such as constant and copy propagation. Finally, after the DFG is completed, the compiler performs many optimizations, often performing the same ones multiple times, and sometimes iterating a set of different optimizations until no further improvement occurs. We will review a few of these optimizations in the following subsections. (More detail can be found in other references; see the work of Budiu [4] and Callahan [5].) These optimizations consider the scope of the DFG (i.e., each hyperblock), which is larger than each basic block but smaller than the entire procedure.

Constant folding
Constant folding is simply the reduction of expressions of compile time constants to the equivalent constants. Its most obvious benefit is that it removes operations from the DFG and ultimately reduces area and latency in the subcircuit. A second benefit is that constant folding can enable operator specialization for other operations. (See Chapter 22.)

Figure 7.9 shows a simple example of constant folding. The important part of this example is observing how this opportunity for optimization occurs only after hyperblock formation, because the definition of x in B3 no longer interferes with constant propagation and constant folding in B1-B2-B4. This effect is not limited to constant folding, but has the potential to improve all optimizations described here.

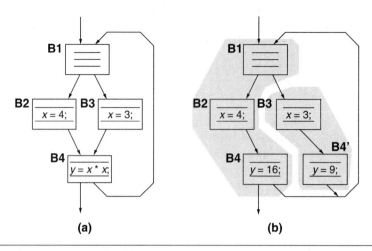

FIGURE 7.9 ▪ The commonly taken path in the loop is B1-B2-B4 (a). Hyperblock formation (b)—tail duplication occurs with basic block B4. This enables constant propagation and then constant folding for the expressions x*x, although this is actually done after conversion to the DFG.

Identity simplification

This can be considered a special case of constant folding, that is, finding cases where the operator can be eliminated because one of the inputs is a *specific* constant. Integer operations that add or subtract zero, shift by zero, or multiply by one are eliminated. Similar optimizations exist for Boolean predicate operations: If either an OR or an AND has a constant input, it can be eliminated by replacing it either with a constant or with a pass-through from the other input.

Strength reduction

This replaces one operator with another operator (or operators) having less overall latency/area. For example, replace x*2 with x+x or x<<1. Again, this is often based on having a specific constant input. Sometimes, equivalent implementations occur whether we do operator-level strength reduction or bit-level specialization, but it does not hurt to have multiple attacks. Multiplication by a constant is an important example because it occurs so often and because a general multiplication function unit can be expensive on a reconfigurable fabric. The expression x*7 can be expressed as (x<<2)+(x<<1)+x, but even better as (x<<3)-x.

Dead node elimination

A cleanup pass eliminates nodes that are "dead"—that is, those that are not "live." A node is live when it is required for proper execution if (1) it has side effects (i.e., it is a store or an exit), or (2) its data output is used by another "live" node, including the case where the node supplies a live-out value to an exit node. The algorithm starts by marking as live all nodes with side effects: stores and exits. Then it marks as live any node whose data output is used by any other "live" node, and so on. Only data and liveness edges need to be traversed.

Once no more nodes can be marked as live, any remaining nodes not marked as such are known to be dead and can be safely removed.

Common subexpression elimination

Common subexpression elimination (CSE) is a well-known optimization for identifying and removing redundant computation—that is, the same operation is performed on the same operands. When a node has the same operands as another, it is immediately obvious from the structure of the graph. All simple operator nodes are subject to elimination, as are all nodes introduced to support predicated execution (Boolean calculations and muxes). Store and exit node types are not considered for elimination. Loads can be considered if additional analysis is done (see Memory access optimization subsection later).

Boolean value identification

The C language defines signed and unsigned integer data types of various sizes, but ISO C does not contain a Boolean data type [9]. Although the result of a comparison is defined to be either 0 or 1, the type of the result is a signed integer—typically 32 bits. However, no information is lost if only a single bit is used to carry the result. This can be exploited to advantage in hardware. Therefore, it is useful to identify as "Boolean" those operations guaranteed to produce only 0 or 1. When necessary for non-Boolean uses, Boolean values can be converted back to standard C type by zero-padding.

The algorithm identifies "base case" Boolean-producing nodes: comparisons, constant 0, and constant 1. Then it forward-propagates the Boolean property to nodes that have an opcode that preserves the Boolean property and that also have all inputs already flagged as Boolean. Opcodes that preserve the Boolean property include bitwise AND, OR, and XOR, as well as muxes. Opcodes that do not preserve the Boolean property include bitwise NOT and addition. However, all predicate calculations are marked as Boolean when they are constructed, including NOT operators.

For a compilation flow that eventually goes through commercial logic synthesis tools, many of the excess bits being trimmed would be trimmed eventually anyway. However, if the compiler needs to make decisions based on hardware area estimates—for example, for hardware/software partitioning—it is useful to have more accurate information about required bus and function unit width earlier in the compiler flow. This is also a motivation for the next two analyses.

Type-based operator size reduction

ISO C semantics [9] dictate that arithmetic and logical operations involving type `char` and/or `short` operands must be performed at the precision of type `int`. Figure 7.10 shows the implicit type conversions.

During initial DFG construction, all three casts are faithfully translated to DFG nodes. But since the destination's representation size of `short` (say 16 bits) is less than that of `int` (say 32 bits), the upper bits of the addition are discarded. Thus, a 16-bit adder will give the same result as a 32-bit adder in all cases, so in the intermediate representation we can signify that just a 16-bit adder

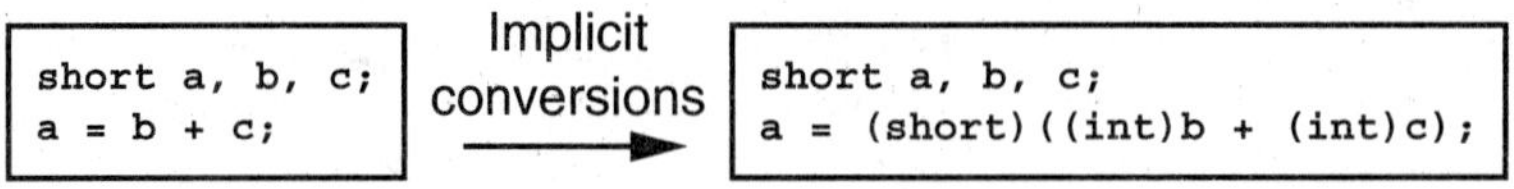

FIGURE 7.10 ▪ Implicit type conversions.

is required. This in turn means that the addition uses just the lower 16 bits of each operand; thus, reducing the size of one operator may enable the size reduction of others. There also may be type conversions on the operands that can be eliminated, as shown in the figure. Besides the obvious savings in area and operator size for the addition, there are additional savings in this example: eliminating the two sign-extending type conversions on b and c.

Dataflow analysis-based operator size reduction
More detailed dataflow analyses can be performed to find the number of bits actually required by variables and operators. They may be based on range—for example, i within the loop for (i = 0; i < 100; i++). They may also be bit level: propagating forward information about bits fixed at 0 or 1 and propagating backward information about bits not used (e.g., Budiu et al. [3]).

Memory access optimization
The handling of memory access ordering occurs in three phases:

1. The compiler conservatively adds ordering edges between pairs of memory accesses during DFG construction.
2. After DFG construction, the compiler tries to find and remove false ordering edges. Considering each pair of memory accesses connected by an ordering edge, it applies a series of tests. If any test can prove that the two operations can never access the same location during the same iteration, that ordering edge is removed. These various tests are based on array index analysis, pointer analysis, and simple testing of fixed locations (e.g., &a and &b).
3. Although removing false ordering edges is useful in itself because it exposes more parallelism and typically results in a shorter schedule, there are also many optimizations based on ordering edges that will see improved results.

Space does not allow the description of all memory optimizations that have been developed (see Callahan [5] or Budiu and Goldstein [2] for more examples), so just one will be presented here as an example.

Removing redundant loads
Consider this simple C code snippet:

```
a = *p;
*q = b;
c = *p;
```

Originally, there will be ordering edges from the first load to the store and from the store to the second load. But if subsequent pointer analysis can guarantee that p and q can never point to the same location, those ordering edges will be removed.

The existence or absence of ordering edges is then used in the following optimization. Two loads can be reduced to one if (1) they definitely access the same location, and (2) there is no intervening store that might modify that location. Both of these requirements can be determined directly from the DFG.

To check (1), the compiler checks if the addresses of the two loads come from the same node (this assumes that common subexpression elimination has been run, which would ensure that equivalent addresses come from the same node). To check (2), we need to check for an intervening store. If there is a path from one of the loads to any store, and from that store to the other load, via ordering edges, then that store is intervening and represents a possible modification of that memory location. If both requirements hold—(1) same location and (2) no intervening store—then one of the loads can be eliminated, and its consumers can use the output of the other load. In this example, the store to *q was originally intervening, but is no longer after removal of the ordering edges.

7.2.4 From DFG to Reconfigurable Fabric

At this point we have an optimized DFG for each hyperblock. The final translation involves mapping DFG nodes to modules, scheduling each module to a specific timestep, and creating the simple sequencer, resulting in an actual subcircuit (RTL HDL description) for each hyperblock. Then, finally, connections are made among the sequencers and modules from different hyperblock subcircuits to complete the overall circuit.

Packing operations into clock cycles

A CPU cannot exploit the fact that a simple logical AND requires much less latency to complete than an integer addition; both take one cycle. But with spatial computing, we can pack multiple low-latency operations into a clock period (i.e., between registers) [6]. A typical example is predicate calculation, which consists of 1-bit Boolean calculations—a large subgraph of these can be performed in the time it takes to do one 32-bit addition. Another case is two successive ripple-carry adders because the latencies of their carry chains largely overlap. Additional opportunities arise from the context-specific optimization of each operation allowed by spatial computing (Chapter 22), which can greatly reduce the latency of a specific operation. On the other hand, long latency operations, such as multiplication, are typically split into stages across multiple cycles, and these stages are not considered for combining as noted before.

For simplicity it is useful to assume a target clock period from the start to get an even "packing," even if the reconfigurable platform supports a variable clock period. For systems with a fixed clock period, the upper bound is a hard limit. If the final circuit has a combinational path with latency exceeding the clock period, then some portion of the design flow must be rerun, either with more conservative decisions (for example, with operation packing) or with higher priority given to the failing paths. With a variable clock period, mistakes can be accommodated.

After this grouping, rather than a graph of operator nodes, we have a graph of modules, each of which implements one or more original DFG nodes (or a stage of a multi-cycle operation). Each module has a register at its output.

Scheduling

Scheduling a module-mapped DFG is straightforward using list scheduling. The output of list scheduling is, for each module m, an assigned slot $\sigma(m)$ when it *starts* computing. A module m's outputs are available to other modules starting at $\sigma(m) + \text{lat}(m)$, where $\text{lat}(m)$ is the latency (in clock cycles) of m (a multi-cycle operation is scheduled as a unit). In most cases this latency is one clock.

List scheduling maintains three lists of modules, and each module is a member of exactly one list. The three lists are:

- `scheduled`: modules that have already been assigned a slot. This is initialized to the input modules, all scheduled at slot 0.
- `ready`: modules whose sources have all been scheduled.
- `notready`: modules that have one or more sources not yet scheduled.

Then the list-scheduling algorithm iterates as follows until all modules have been scheduled:

1. Choose a module m from the `ready` list based on some priority heuristic.
2. Set S to the earliest cycle on which m can be scheduled, considering only when m's inputs are first all available.
3. If m has a resource conflict at slot S with any already scheduled module, increment S and go to step 3.
4. Schedule m in slot S and put it on `scheduled`.
5. Check m's successors and move them as appropriate from `notready` to `ready`.
6. If any nodes remain on `ready`, go to step 1.

Only memory operations can encounter a resource conflict in step 3, arising from the use of shared address and/or memory data buses. In contrast, any simple (nonmemory) module is scheduled as soon as all its inputs are available. Note that most such simple modules are not "actively" scheduled—they don't have an activation input from the sequencer. These passive modules simply compute a result each cycle whether or not their inputs are valid. After scheduling, the total schedule length is known, so the sequencer can be built to count off the cycles and trigger those modules that need it. The output of the final sequencer stage is ANDed with the predicate values for each exit node to create the appropriate outgoing control bit. Also, the source of each liveness edge to each exit node is translated to the appropriate connection to the input module in the destination subcircuit.

Pipelined scheduling

Here we will briefly give an idea of how pipelined scheduling works. Only hyperblocks branching to themselves to form a self-loop are considered. In the final implementation, the key difference is that with pipelined scheduling the calculation of the control bit that is fed back to the top of the sequencer is produced not at the end of the schedule but somewhere in the middle. The result is that there are multiple '1' control bits shifting through the sequencer simultaneously, corresponding to the fact that multiple iterations of the loop are executing in an overlapped fashion. The compiler must now watch out for resource conflicts between successive iterations when scheduling the loop. The spacing between successive iterations is limited by either loop-carried data or memory dependencies, or by resource requirements. Further details are available in works by Callahan [5, 8].

Connecting memory nodes to the memory ports
Recall that each load node is split into a `load_a`, for sending the request and address, and a `load_d`, for receiving the data. Our circuit diagrams have implied that shared access to the memory port uses buses driven by tristate buffers, which some FPGAs have. But this approach could run out of tristate buffers or could restrict placement options. An alternative is to use an unencoded mux to drive each input to the shared port. For example, a mux might replace the address bus; when a memory module asserts a request to its control line of the mux, its address is routed to the mux output and to the memory port. The load data bus returning data from memory does not need any active routing; it is driven only by the memory port and fans out to all of the `load_d` modules, one of which will latch the result. However, additional buffering may be required to avoid timing problems when fanout is large.

What next?
Although we have shown the implementations as schematics, what we actually have at this point is a structural (RTL) description in an HDL such as Verilog or VHDL (Chapter 6). In a system with a commercial FPGA as its reconfigurable fabric, there is likely a fixed wrapper circuit that handles the details of connections between the compiler-generated circuit and the FPGA pins connected to the CPU and external memory. The wrapper and compiled circuit together are fed through commercial tools to perform the gate-level optimizing, mapping, placing, and routing.

7.3 USES AND VARIATIONS OF C COMPILATION TO HARDWARE

Now that we have covered the technical aspects of compiling C to hardware, we will return to higher-level programming and system-level design.

7.3.1 Automatic HW/SW Partitioning

Once we have a common source language, here C, and compilation tools that can compile a program, or parts of it, to either the CPU or the reconfigurable fabric, the remaining problem is to partition the program between the two resources. This partitioning can be performed manually, with the user adding annotations about where to run blocks of code (e.g., loops, procedures), automatically, with the compiler making all the decisions, or some combination of the two.

Even when partitioning is manual, the use of a common source language allows rapid exploration of the design space of different HW/SW mappings. The program can be written and debugged entirely on the CPU and the programmer need only modify the allocation directives to move code onto the hardware or to change which code is allocated to it. Profiling can help the user converge on a good split.

Nonetheless, in the purely manual case the program developed ends up tuned to a specific machine, with a specific amount of hardware, specific relative speeds for the RF and the CPU, and communication between the two. Ideally, we have a single source program to run on multiple hardware platforms with varying hardware and performance. An intermediate solution is for the directives to *suggest* which software blocks might be most profitable on the RF, then to allow the compiler, perhaps with runtime feedback, to decide which of the suggested set to actually run on the hardware based on performance benefits and capacity.

Ultimately, the compiler and runtime system should take full responsibility for determining the right code and granularity to move to the reconfigurable fabric. This is an active area of research and development. Chapter 26 discusses issues and techniques for hardware/software partitioning in more detail.

The Garp C compiler [5,7] provides an example of automatic partitioning. It starts by marking all loops as candidates for the reconfigurable fabric. Then, for each loop, it removes any paths from this candidate that include operations not supported on the array (removed paths are executed in software on the CPU). The compiler further trims the less taken paths in the loop until the remaining loop paths fit on the fabric capacity. Finally, it trims paths to improve performance. At this point, if any paths remain in the candidate loop, the compiler evaluates HW versus SW performance for the loop, considering the overhead costs for paths switching between HW and SW. If a loop is faster on the CPU, it is given a completely SW implementation. The Garp hardware supports fast configuration loads, and it caches configurations in the array, so there is a hard bound to the size of each loop but no limit on the number of accelerated loops.

For conventional FPGAs that do not support fast configuration swaps, it may be necessary to allocate all hardware logic at startup and keep them resident throughout operation. In these cases, the bound is on the total capacity of all hardware allocated to the RF, not just a single loop. The compiler may start with all feasible candidates, as in the Garp C compiler case, but then must select a subset that fits in the available capacity and maximizes performance.

7.3.2 Programmer Assistance

Useful code changes

As Section 7.2.4 shows, the compiler does many things to try to expose parallelism and optimize the implementation. However, discovering many of the optimization opportunities requires very sophisticated analysis by the compiler, and sometimes it simply cannot prove that a particular optimization is always safe. Consequently, there are many ways a programmer might restructure or modify the application code to assist the compiler and achieve better performance on the target system. Some of these transformations have been studied to some degree in a research setting, but have not yet been fully automated in production compilers.

Loop interchange, reversal, and other transforms A loop nest can be altered in ways that still obey all required scalar and memory dependencies but that improve performance. For example, a compiler may automatically exploit memory accesses that are unit stride (A[0], A[1], A[2], ...) by streaming or prefetching. Even without explicit stream fetch support, unit stride accesses will improve cache locality, so the programmer should strive for them within the innermost loops. From one iteration to the next, loop interchange typically affects the loop-carried dependencies of the innermost loop; this impacts how effectively the block can be pipelined. If the programmer can structure the loop nest so that the innermost loop has no loop-carried dependencies, pipelining will be very effective. When the unit of HW implementation is an inner loop, another consideration is the overhead of switching between SW and HW execution. To reduce the relative cost of the overhead, it is best if possible to interchange the loops so that the innermost loops have high loop counts—as long as this does not adversely affect other aspects such as cache performance, unit stride, or loop-carried dependencies.

Loop fusion and fission Loop fusion is the combining of successive loops with identical bounds. This can remove memory accesses if the second loop loads values written by the first loop; instead, the value can be passed directly within the fused loop. The reverse, loop fission (splitting one loop into two), can also be useful when the original loop cannot fit in its entirety on the reconfigurable resources. Afterward, the two halves can each fit, but not at the same time, so temporary arrays may need to be introduced to store data produced in the first half and used in the second.

Local arrays When an array is local to a procedure and of fixed size, it is relatively easy for the compiler to do the "smart thing" and implement it using a memory block on the FPGA fabric. But if the program instead uses `malloc`'d or global arrays as temporaries, it is very challenging to safely convert them to local arrays. Thus, changing the code to use local arrays wherever possible can be very useful because on-FPGA memory blocks have much lower latency to/from the computation unit and can be accessed in parallel with each other.

Control structure Most compliers keep the loop, procedure, and block structure in the original code. As noted previously, common heuristics for hardware/software partitioning select loop bodies or procedures as candidates for hardware implementation. If the loop is too large, it may not be feasible on the array. If the loop is too small, it might not make good use of the array's parallelism. The programmer can often assist the compiler by sizing and organizing loops, procedures, and blocks that make good candidates for hardware allocation.

Address indirection   As noted in Section 7.2.3, whenever the address of a variable is taken, the compiler must make conservative assumptions about when the value will be updated, forcing additional sequentialization and increasing memory traffic. Consequently, address indirection and pass-by-reference should be used judiciously with the realization that it can inhibit compiler optimizations. Note that this unfortunate effect can also occur when a global scalar variable is visible beyond the file in which it is declared; with separate compilation, the compiler must assume that code in some other file takes the address of the variable and passes it back as a pointer. Therefore, declaring file-global variables as static helps as well.

Declaration of data sizes   On CPUs there is often little advantage to using a narrow data word. Except for low-cost embedded systems, all processors have at least 32-bit words, with high-performance processors trending to 64 bit; even DSPs and embedded processors can typically assume CPUs with at least 16-bit words. Consequently, there is little incentive to software programmers to pay much attention to the actual range of data used. However, in fine-grained reconfigurable fabrics, such as field-programmable gate arrays (FPGAs), narrow data words can be implemented with less area and, sometimes, with less delay. As noted in Section 7.2.3, the compiler can make use of narrower type declarations (e.g., `short`, `char`) to reduce operator size.

Useful annotations

A programmer annotation gives the compiler a guarantee about a certain property of the program, which typically allows the compiler to make more aggressive optimizations; however, if the programmer is in error and the guarantee does not hold in all cases, incorrect program behavior may result. Some annotations can be expressed as assertions. If the assertion fails, the program will terminate, signaling the user (hopefully, the programmer) that the assertion was violated. The compiler knows that when execution continues past the assertion, certain properties must hold.

Annotations and assertions can be used as ways to communicate information to the compiler that it is not capable of inferring itself. In this way they may be an alternative to very advanced compiler analysis, or a complement when the analysis is simply intractable. Following are two examples of useful annotations:

- *Pointer independence:* declaring that a pair of pointers will never point to the same location, so that an ordering edge between accesses using those pointers can always be removed safely.
- *Absence of loop-carried memory dependences:* declaring that the memory operations in different iterations of the loop are always independent (to

different locations), which typically allows much greater overlap and greater performance when using pipelined scheduling.

Integrating operator-level modules

Even when writing C code for CPUs, the compiler does not always generate optimal machine code, and it is occasionally necessary to write assembly code for key routines. Similarly, when the C compiler does not provide the tight implementations of which the RF is capable, it may be necessary to provide a direct hardware implementation. Here, the "assembly" may be a VHDL (Chapter 6) implementation of a function or a piece of dataflow. As in the assembly language case, the developer can start with a pure C program profile, the code, and then judiciously spend his customization effort on the code's most performance-critical regions.

It is fairly easy to integrate a custom operation into the flow we have described. The designer simply needs to create the module via HDL or schematic capture, and tell the compiler the latency, in cycles, of the design. The operation can be accessed from C source code using function call syntax, instantiated, and scheduled in parallel with other "native" C operations in the hyperblock. For example, in this code snippet:

```
x = bitreverse(a);
y = a ^ b;
z = x + y;
```

the `bitreverse` module would have one cycle latency and could be scheduled in parallel with the XOR (`^`) module.

The power of this approach is greatly increased with a *module generator*. In this case, the HDL module is not just copied from a library; instead, it is dynamically generated by the compiler. This allows constant arguments to the module instantiation to specialize it, for example,

```
X = bit_reverse_range(a,8,15);
```

which will generate a module that will reverse the bits of a from bit 8 to bit 15 to produce x. A detailed interface between compiler and dynamic module generator is described in work by Koch [10] (see also Chapter 15).

It is useful to always have a functionally equivalent software implementation of each custom operation in order to enable testing of the overall application in a pure software environment. This is required, for example, when adding hand-designed HDL modules in the SRC Computers compiler [14].

Integrating large blocks

Another method for integrating a hand-designed circuit with an otherwise C-compiled program is to treat it as its own hyperblock subcircuit within the compiler, allowing it to manage its own sequencing. The HDL implementation of the custom block in this case receives a `start` control bit, like any other hyperblock, and must send a `finish` control bit when done. This allows the designer to incorporate custom blocks that have variable latency (e.g., an iterative divider or a greatest-common-divisor computation). The programmer could use function call syntax to instantiate this larger block as well, but, the compiler would prevent the function from being merged with other blocks into a larger hyperblock.

7.4 SUMMARY

After a decade of research, C compilation for reconfigurable computers is now commercially available in many forms (e.g., SRC Computers [14] and Lau and colleagues [11]). While today's commercial compilers cannot generally compile arbitrary ISO C code or take arbitrary C code and expect to fully extract the performance of the reconfigurable fabric, they have closed the gap so that nontrivial code acceleration is possible with minor programmer effort. A developer can use the C compiler to rapidly get applications running on a suitable reconfigurable platform. C code developed or tuned with an understanding of the reconfigurable platform and the capabilities of the compiler can achieve higher performance. Although today's C compilers do not free the reconfigurable developer from understanding good application and system architectures, they can allow her to focus her efforts.

C compilation and optimization remain an active area of research, and we expect to see continuing improvements over time. Many opportunities exist for innovative research on aggressive optimization techniques and development of more automated optimizing complier flows.

References

[1] A. V. Aho, R. Sethi, J. D. Ullman. *Compilers, Principles, Techniques, and Tools*, Addison-Wesley, 1986.

[2] M. Budiu, S. Copen Goldstein. Optimizing memory accesses for spatial computation. *International ACM/IEEE Symposium on Code Generation and Optimization*, March 2003.

[3] M. Budiu, M. Sakr, K. Walker, S. Copen Goldstein. Bit value inference: Detecting and exploiting narrow bit-width computations. *European Conference on Parallel Processing*, Springer-Verlag, 2000.

[4] M. Budiu. *Spatial Computation*, Ph.D. thesis, Carnegie-Mellon University, December 2003 (technical report CMU-CS-03-217).

[5] T. J. Callahan. *Automatic Compilation of C for Hybrid Reconfigurable Architectures*, Ph.D. thesis, University of California, Berkeley, December 2002.

[6] T. J. Callahan, P. Chong, A. DeHon, J. Wawrzynek. Rapid module mapping and placement for FPGAs. *Proceedings of the ACM/SIGDA International Symposium on Field Programmable Gate Arrays*, 1998.

[7] T. Callahan, J. Hauser, J. Wawrzynek. The Garp architecture and C compiler. *IEEE Computer* 33(4), April 2000.

[8] T. Callahan, J. Wawrzynek. Adapting software pipelining for reconfigurable computing. *Proceedings of the International Conference on Compilers, Architecture, and Synthesis for Embedded Systems (CASES)*, 2000.

[9] P. Harbison, G. L. Steele. *C, A Reference Manual*, 4th ed. Prentice-Hall, 1995.

[10] A. Koch. Compilation for adaptive computing systems using complex parameter-ized hardware objects. *Journal of Supercomputing* 21(2), 2002.

[11] D. Lau, O Pritchard, P. Molson. Automated generation of hardware accelerators with direct memory access from ANSI/ISO standard C functions. *Proceedings of the IEEE Symposium on Field-Programmable Custom Computing Machines*, April 2006.

[12] S. A. Mahlke, D. C. Lin, W. Y. Chen, R. E. Hank, R. A. Bringmann. Effective compiler support for predicated execution using the hyperblock. *Proceedings of the 25th Annual International Symposium on Microarchitecture*, 1992.

[13] S. S. Muchnick. *Advanced Compiler Design and Implementation*. Morgan Kaufmann, 1997.

[14] SRC Computers. *SRC Carte C Programming Environment v2.2 Guide*, Colorado Springs, 2007.

CHAPTER 8

PROGRAMMING STREAMING FPGA APPLICATIONS USING BLOCK DIAGRAMS IN SIMULINK

Brian C. Richards, Chen Chang, John Wawrzynek,
Robert W. Brodersen
Department of Electrical Engineering and Computer Science
University of California–Berkeley

Although a system designer can use hardware description languages, such as VHDL (Chapter 6) and Verilog to program field-programmable gate arrays (FPGAs), the algorithm developer typically uses higher-level descriptions to refine an algorithm. As a result, an algorithm described in a language such as Matlab or C is frequently reentered by hand by the system designer, after which the two descriptions must be verified and refined manually. This can be time consuming.

To avoid reentering a design when translating from a high-level simulation language to HDL, the algorithm developer can describe a system from the beginning using block diagrams in Matlab Simulink [1]. Other block diagram environments can be used in a similar way, but the tight integration of Simulink with the widely used Matlab simulation environment allows developers to use familiar data analysis tools to study the resulting designs. With Simulink, a single design description can be prepared by the algorithm developer and refined jointly with the system architect using a common design environment.

The single design entry is enabled by a library of Simulink operator primitives that have a direct mapping to HDL, using matching Simulink and HDL models that are cycle accurate and bit accurate between both domains. Examples and compilation environments include System Generator from Xilinx [2], Synplify DSP from Synplicity [3], and the HDL Coder from The Mathworks [1]. Using such a library, nearly any synchronous multirate system can be described, with high confidence that the result can be mapped to an FPGA given adequate resources.

In this chapter, a high-performance image-processing system is described using Simulink and mapped to an FPGA-based platform using a design flow built around the Xilinx System Generator tools. The system implements edge detection in real time on a digitized video stream and produces a corresponding video stream labeling the edges. The edges can then be viewed on a high-resolution monitor. This design demonstrates how to describe a high-performance parallel datapath, implement control subsystems, and interface to external devices, including embedded processors.

8.1 DESIGNING HIGH-PERFORMANCE DATAPATHS USING STREAM-BASED OPERATORS

Within Simulink we employ a Synchronous Dataflow computational model (SDF), described in the Synchronous dataflow subsection of Section 5.1.3. Each operator is executed once per clock cycle, consuming input values and producing new output values once per clock tick. This discipline is well suited for stream-based design, encouraging both the algorithm designer and the system architect to describe efficient datapaths with minimal idle operations.

Clock signals and corresponding clock enable signals do not appear in the Simulink block diagrams using the System Generator libraries, but are automatically generated when an FPGA design is compiled. To support multirate systems, the System Generator library includes up-sample and down-sample blocks to mark the boundaries of different clock domains. When compiled to an FPGA, clock enable signals for each clock domain are automatically generated.

All System Generator components offer compile time parameters, allowing the designer to control data types and refine the behavior of the block. Hierarchical blocks, or *subsystems* in Simulink, can also have user-defined parameters, called *mask parameters*. These can be included in block property expressions within that subsystem to provide a means of generating a variety of behaviors from a single Simulink description. Typical mask parameters include data type and precision specification and block latency to control pipeline stage insertion. For more advanced library development efforts, the mask parameters can be used by a Matlab program to create a custom schematic at compile time.

The System Generator library supports fixed-point or Boolean data types for mapping to FPGAs. Fixed-point data types include signed and unsigned values, with bit width and decimal point location as parameters. In most cases, the output data types are inferred automatically at compile time, although many blocks offer parameters to define them explicitly.

Pipeline operators are explicitly placed into a design either by inserting delay blocks or by defining a delay parameter in selected functional blocks. Although the designer is responsible for balancing pipeline operators, libraries of high-level components have been developed and reused to hide pipeline-balancing details from the algorithm developer.

The Simulink approach allows us to describe highly concurrent SDF systems where many operators—perhaps the entire dataflow path—can operate simultaneously. With modern FPGAs, it is possible to implement these systems with thousands of simultaneous operators running at the system clock rate with little or no control logic, allowing complex, high-performance algorithms to be implemented.

8.2 AN IMAGE-PROCESSING DESIGN DRIVER

The goal of the edge detection design driver is to generate a binary bit mask from a video source operating at up to a 200 MHz pixel rate, identifying where likely edges are in an image. The raw color video is read from a neighboring FPGA over a parallel link, and the image intensity is then calculated, after which two 3×3 convolutional Sobel operator filters identify horizontal and vertical edges; the sum of their absolute values indicates the relative strength of a feature edge in an image. A runtime programmable gain (variable multiplier) followed by an adjustable threshold maps the resulting pixel stream to binary levels to indicate if a given pixel is labeled as an edge of a visible feature. The resulting video mask is then optionally mixed with the original color image and displayed on a monitor.

Before designing the datapaths in the edge detection system, the data and control specification for the video stream sources and sinks must be defined. By convention, stream-based architectures are implemented by pairing data samples with corresponding control tags and maintaining this pairing through the architecture. For this example, the video datastreams may have varying data types as the signals are processed whereas the control tags are synchronization signals that track the pipeline delays in the video stream. The input video stream and output display stream represent color pixel data using 16 bits—5 bits for red, 6 bits for green, and 5 bits for blue unsigned pixel intensity values. Intermediate values might represent video data as 8-bit grayscale intensity values or as 1-bit threshold detection mask values.

As the datastreams flow through the signal-processing datapath, the operators execute at a constant 100 MHz sample rate, with varying pipeline delays through the system. The data, however, may arrive at less than 100 MHz, requiring a corresponding `enable` signal (see the discussion in Data presence subsection of Section 5.2.1) to tag valid data. Additionally, `hsync`, `vsync`, and `msync` signals are defined to be true for the first pixel of each row, frame, and movie sequence, respectively, allowing a large variety of video stream formats to be supported by the same design.

Once a streaming format has been specified, library components can be developed that forward a video stream through a variety of operators to create higher-level functions while maintaining valid, pipeline-delayed synchronization signals. For blocks with a pipeline latency that is determined by mask parameters, the synchronization signals must also be delayed based on the mask parameters so that the resulting synchronization signals match the processed datastream.

8.2.1 Converting RGB Video to Grayscale

The first step in this example is to generate a grayscale video stream from the RGB input data. The data is converted to intensity using the NTSC RGB-to-Y matrix:

$$Y = 0.3 \times \text{red} + 0.59 \times \text{green} + 0.11 \times \text{blue}$$

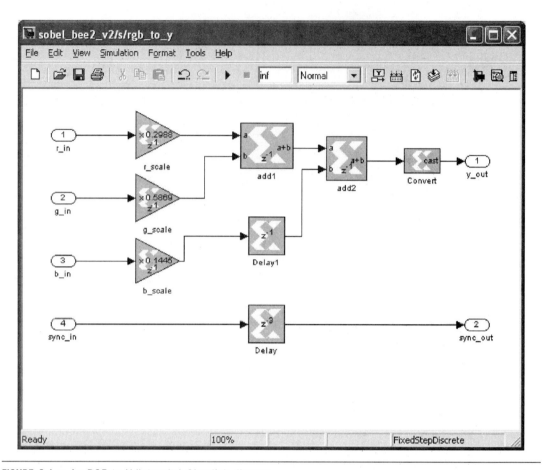

FIGURE 8.1 ▪ An RGB-to-Y (intensity) Simulink diagram.

This formula is implemented explicitly as a block diagram, shown in Figure 8.1, using constant gain blocks followed by adders. The constant multiplication values are defined as floating-point values and are converted to fixed point according to mask parameters in the gain model. This allows the precision of the multiplication to be defined separately from the gain, leaving the synthesis tools to choose an implementation. The scaled results are then summed with an explicit adder tree.

Note that if the first adder introduces a latency of adder_delay clock cycles, the b input to the second adder, add2, must also be delayed by adder_delay cycles to maintain the cycle alignment of the RGB data. Both the Delay1 block and the add1 block have a subsystem mask parameter defining the delay that the block will introduce, provided by the mask parameter dialog as shown in Figure 8.2. Similarly, the synchronization signals must be delayed by three cycles corresponding to one cycle for the gain blocks, one cycle for the first adder,

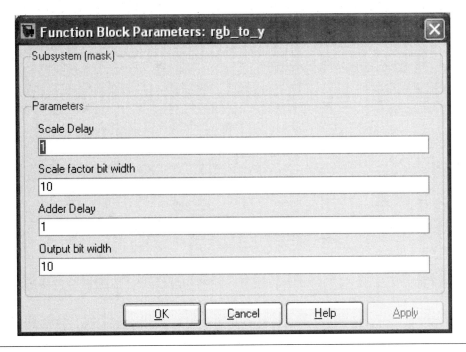

FIGURE 8.2 ■ A dialog describing mask parameters for the `rgb_to_y` block.

and one cycle for the second adder. By designing subsystems with configurable delays and data precision parameters, library components can be developed to encourage reuse of design elements.

8.2.2 Two-dimensional Video Filtering

The next major block following the RGB-to-grayscale conversion is the edge detection filter itself (Figure 8.3), consisting of two pixel row delay lines, two 3×3 kernels, and a simplified magnitude detector. The delay lines store the two rows of pixels preceding the current row of video data, providing three streams of vertically aligned pixels that are connected to the two 3×3 filters—the first one detecting horizontal edges and the second detecting vertical edges. These filters produce two signed fixed-point streams of pixel values, approximating the edge gradients in the source video image.

On every clock cycle, two 3×3 convolution kernels must be calculated, requiring several parallel operators. The operators implement the following convolution kernels:

Sobel X Gradient:

-1	0	$+1$
-2	0	$+2$
-1	0	$+1$

Sobel Y Gradient:

$+1$	$+2$	$+1$
0	0	0
-1	-2	-1

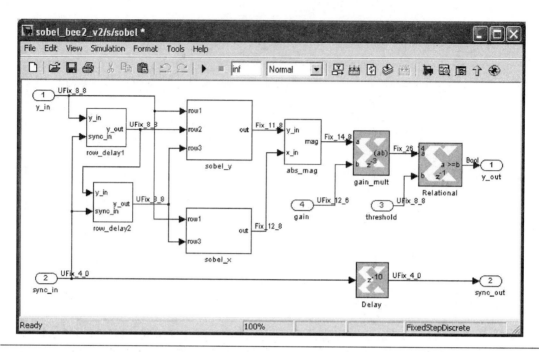

FIGURE 8.3 ■ The Sobel edge detection filter, processing an 8-bit video datastream to produce a stream of Boolean values indicating edges in the image.

To support arbitrary kernels, the designer can choose to implement the Sobel operators using constant multiplier or gain blocks followed by a tree of adders. For this example, the subcircuits for the *x*- and *y*-gradient operators are hand-optimized so that the nonzero multipliers for both convolution kernels are implemented with a single hardwired shift operation using a power-of-2 scale block. The results are then summed explicitly, using a tree of add or subtract operators, as shown in Figures 8.4 and 8.5.

Note that the interconnect in Figures 8.4 and 8.5 is shown with the data types displayed. For the most part, these are assigned automatically, with the input data types propagated and the output data types and bit widths inferred to avoid overflow or underflow of signed and unsigned data types. The bit widths can be coerced to different data types and widths using casting or reinterpret blocks, and by selecting saturation, truncation, and wraparound options available to several of the operator blocks. The designer must exercise care to verify that such adjustments to a design do not change the behavior of the algorithm.

Through these Simulink features a high-level algorithm designer can directly explore the impact of such data type manipulation on a particular algorithm.

Once the horizontal and vertical intensity gradients are calculated for the neighborhood around a given pixel, the likelihood that the pixel is near the boundary of a feature can be calculated. To label a pixel as a likely edge of a feature in the image, the magnitude of the gradients is approximated and the

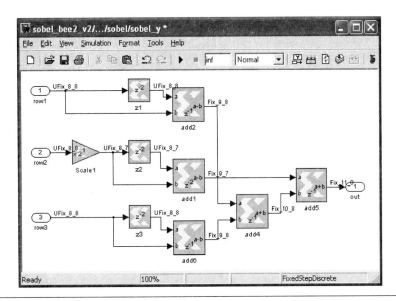

FIGURE 8.4 ■ The `sobel_y` block for estimating the horizontal gradient in the source image.

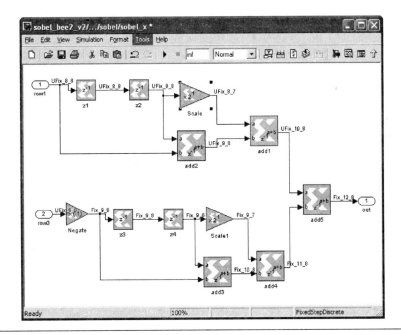

FIGURE 8.5 ■ The `sobel_x` block for estimating the vertical gradient in the source image.

resulting nonnegative value is scaled and compared to a given threshold. The magnitude is approximated by summing the absolute values of the horizontal and vertical edge gradients, which, although simpler than the exact magnitude calculation, gives a result adequate for our applications.

A multiplier and a comparator follow the magnitude function to adjust the sensitivity to image noise and lighting changes, respectively, resulting in a 1-bit mask that is nonzero if the input pixel is determined to be near the edge of a feature. To allow the user to adjust the gain and threshold values interactively, the values are connected to gain and threshold input ports on the filter (see Figure 8.6).

To display the resulting edge mask, an overlay datapath follows the edge mask stream, allowing the mask to be recombined with the input RGB (red, green, blue) signal in a variety of ways to demonstrate the functionality of the system in real time. The overlay input is read as a 2-bit value, where the LSB 0 bit selects whether the background of the image is black or the original RGB, and the LSB 1 bit selects whether or not the mask is displayed as a white overlay on the background. Three of these mixer subsystems are used in the main video-filtering subsystem, one for each of the red, green, and blue video source components.

The three stream-based filtering subsystems are combined into a single subsystem, with color video in and color video out, as shown in Figure 8.7. Note that the color data fed straight through to the red, green, and blue mixers is delayed. The delay, 13 clock cycles in this case, corresponds to the pipeline delay through both

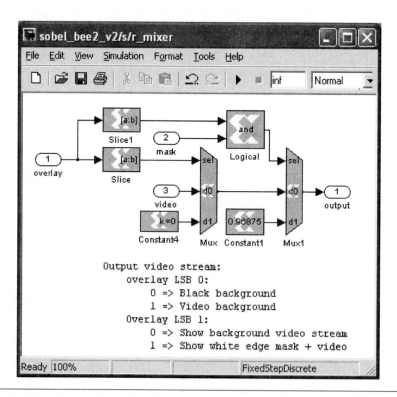

FIGURE 8.6 ■ One of three video mixers for choosing displays of the filtered results.

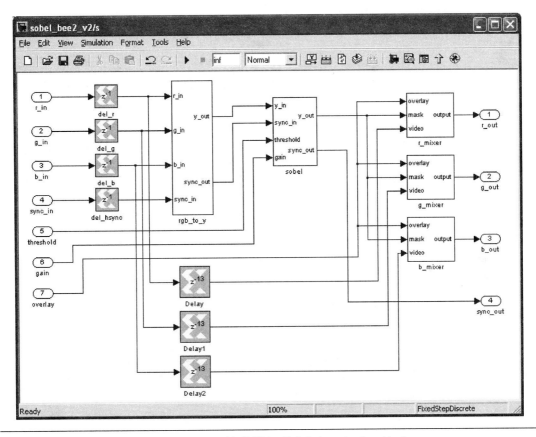

FIGURE 8.7 ■ The main filtering subsystem, with RGB-to-*Y*, Sobel, and mixer blocks.

the `rgb_to_y` block and the Sobel edge detection filter itself. This is to ensure that the background original image data is aligned with the corresponding pixel results from the filter. The sync signals are also delayed, but this is propagated through the filtering blocks and does not require additional delays.

8.2.3   Mapping the Video Filter to the BEE2 FPGA Platform

Our design, up to this point, is platform independent—any Xilinx component supported by the System Generator commercial design flow can be targeted. The next step is to map the design to the BEE2 platform—a multiple-FPGA design, developed at UC Berkeley [4], that contains memory to store a stream of video data and an HDMI interface to output that data to a high-resolution monitor.

For the Sobel edge detection design, some ports are for video datastreams and others are for control over runtime parameters. The three user-controllable inputs to the filtering subsystem, threshold, gain, and overlay are connected to external input ports, for connection to the top-level testbench. The filter, included as a subsystem of this testbench design, is shown in Figures 8.8 and 8.9. So far, the library primitives used in the filter are independent of both the type of FPGA that will be used and the target testing platform containing the FPGA.

To support targeting the filter to the BEE2 FPGA platform for real-time testing, a set of libraries and utilities from the BEE Platform Studio, also developed at Berkeley, is used [5]. Several types of library blocks are available to assist with platform mapping, including simple I/O, high-performance I/O, and microprocessor register and memory interfaces.

The strategy for using the Simulink blocks to map a design to an FPGA assumes that a clear boundary is defined to determine which operators are mapped to the FPGA hardware and which are for simulation only. The commercial tools and design flows for generating FPGA bit files assume that there are input and output library blocks that appear to Simulink as, respectively, double-precision to fixed-point conversion and fixed-point to double type conversion blocks. For simulation purposes, these blocks allow the hardware

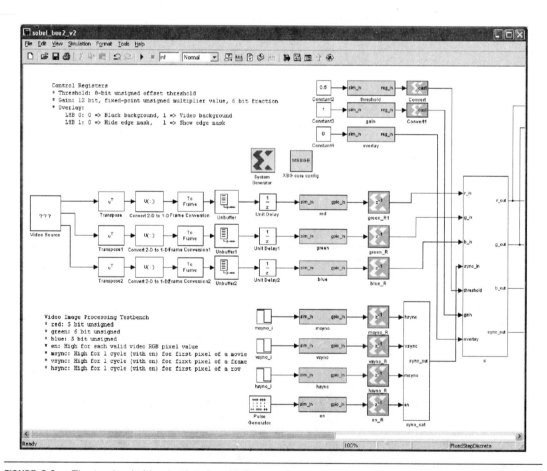

FIGURE 8.8 ▪ The top-level video testbench, with input, microprocessor register, and configuration blocks.

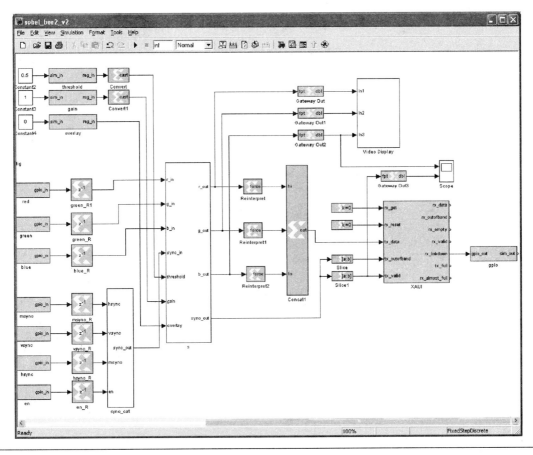

FIGURE 8.9 ■ The output section of the top-level testbench, with a 10G XAUI interface block.

description to be simulated with a software testbench to verify basic functionality before mapping the design to hardware. They also allow the designer to assign the FPGA pin locations for the final configuration files.

The BEE Platform Studio (BPS) [5] provides additional I/O blocks that allow the designer to select pin locations symbolically, choosing pins that are hardwired to other FPGAs, LEDs, and external connections on the platform. The designer is only required to select a platform by setting BPS block parameters, and does not need to keep track of I/O pin locations. This feature allows the designer to experiment with architectural tradeoffs without becoming a hardware expert.

In addition to the basic I/O abstractions, the BPS allows high-performance or analog I/O devices to be designed into a system using high-level abstractions. For the video-testing example, a 10 Gbit XAUI I/O block is used to output the color video stream to platform-specific external interfaces. The designer selects the port to be used on the actual platform from a pulldown menu of available names, hiding most implementation details.

A third category of platform-specific I/O enables communication with embedded microprocessors, such as the Xilinx MicroBlaze soft processor core or the embedded PowerPC available on several FPGAs. Rather than describe the details of the microprocessor subsystem, the designer simply selects which processor on a given platform will be used and a preconfigured platform-specific microprocessor subsystem is then generated and included in the FPGA configuration files. For the video filter example, three microprocessor registers are assigned and connected to the threshold, gain, and overlap inputs to the filter using general-purpose I/O (GPIO) blocks. When the BPS design flow is run, these CPU register blocks are mapped to GPIO registers on the selected platform, and C header files are created to define the memory addresses for the registers.

8.3   SPECIFYING CONTROL IN SIMULINK

On the one hand, Simulink is well suited to describing highly pipelined stream-based systems with minimal control overhead, such as the video with synchronization signals described in the earlier video filter example. These designs assume that each dataflow operator is essentially running in parallel, at the full clock rate. On the other hand, control tasks, such as state machines, tend to be inherently sequential and can be more challenging to describe efficiently in Simulink. Approaches to describing control include:

- Counters, registers, and logic to describe controllers
- Matlab M-code descriptions of control blocks
- VHDL or Verilog hand-coded or compiled descriptions
- Embedded microprocessors

To explore the design of control along with a stream-based datapath, consider the implementation of a synchronous delay line based on a single-port memory. The approach described here is to alternate between writing two data samples and reading two data samples on consecutive clock cycles. A simpler design could be implemented using dual-port memory on an FPGA, but the one we are using allows custom SOC designs to use higher-density single-port memory blocks.

8.3.1   Explicit Controller Design with Simulink Blocks

The complete synchronous delay line is shown in Figure 8.10. The control in this case is designed around a counter block, where the least significant bit selects between the two words read or written from the memory on a given cycle and the upper counter bits determine the memory address. In addition to the counter, control-related blocks include *slice* blocks to select bit fields and Boolean *logic* blocks. For this design, the block diagram is effective for describing control, but minor changes to the controller can require substantial redesign.

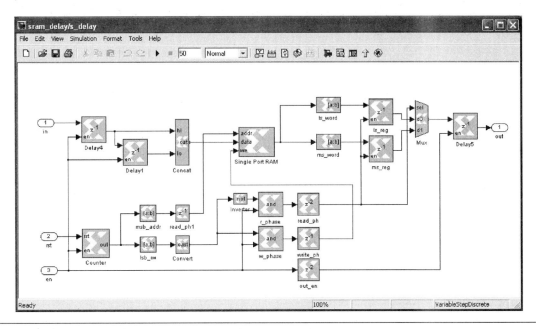

FIGURE 8.10 ■ A simple datapath with associated explicit control.

8.3.2 Controller Design Using the Matlab M Language

For a more symbolic description of the synchronous delay line controller, the designer can use the Matlab "M" language to define the behavior of a block, with the same controller described previously written as a Matlab function. Consider the code in Listing 8.1 that is saved in the file sram_delay_cntl.m.

Listing 8.1 ■ The delay line controller described with the Matlab function sram_delay_cntl.m.

```
function [addr, we, sel] = sram_delay_cntl(rst, en, counter_bits, counter_max)
% sram_delay_cntl -- MCode implementation block.
% Author: Brian Richards, 11/16/2005, U. C. Berkeley
%
% The following Function Parameter Bindings should be declared in
% the MCode block Parameters (sample integer values are given):
%    {'counter_bits', 9, 'counter_max', 5}

% Define all registers as persistent variables.
persistent count,
    count = xl_state(0, {xlUnsigned, counter_bits, 0});
persistent addr_reg,
    addr_reg = xl_state(0, {xlUnsigned, counter_bits-1, 0});
persistent we_reg,    we_reg   = xl_state(0, {xlBoolean});
persistent sel_reg_1, sel_reg_1 = xl_state(0, {xlBoolean});
persistent sel_reg_2, sel_reg_2 = xl_state(0, {xlBoolean});

% Delay the counter output, and split the lsb from
% the upper bits.
```

```
addr = addr_reg;
addr_reg = xl_slice(count, counter_bits-1, 1);
count_lsb = xfix({xlBoolean}, xl_slice(count, 0, 0));

% Write-enable logic
we = we_reg;
we_reg = count_lsb & en;

% MSB-LSB select logic
sel = sel_reg_2;
sel_reg_2 = sel_reg_1;
sel_reg_1 = ~count_lsb & en;

% Update the address counter:
if (rst | (en & (count == counter_max)))
    count = 0;
elseif (en)
    count = count + 1;
else
    count = count;
end
```

To add the preceding controller to a design, the Xilinx M-code block can be dragged from the Simulink library browser and added to the subsystem. A dialog box then asks the designer to select the file containing the M source code, and the block `sram_delay_cntl` is automatically created and added to the system (see Figure 8.11).

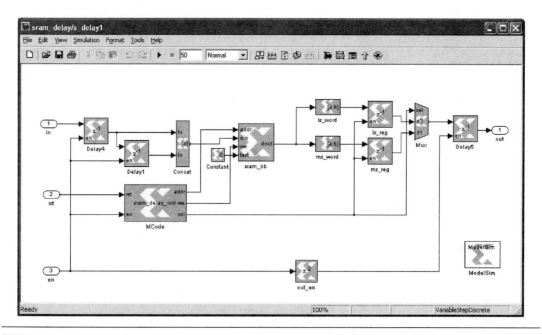

FIGURE 8.11 ▪ A simple datapath using a controller described in Matlab code.

There are several advantages to using the M-code description compared to its explicit block diagram equivalent. First, large, complex state machines can be described and documented efficiently using the sequential M language. Second, the resulting design will typically run faster in Simulink because many fine-grained blocks are replaced by a single block. Third, the design is mapped to an FPGA by generating an equivalent VHDL RTL description and synthesizing the resulting controller; the synthesis tools can produce different results depending on power, area, and speed constraints, and can optimize for different FPGA families.

8.3.3 Controller Design Using VHDL or Verilog

As in the M language approach just described, a controller can also be described with a *black box* containing VHDL or Verilog source code. This approach can be used for both control and datapath subsystems and has the benefit of allowing IP to be included in a Simulink design.

The VHDL or Verilog subsystems must be written according to design conventions to ensure that the subsystem can be mapped to hardware. Clocks and enables, for example, do not appear on the generated Simulink block, but must be defined in pairs (e.g., `clk_sg`, `ce_sg`) for each implied data rate in the system. Simulink designs that use these VHDL or Verilog subsystems can be verified by cosimulation between Simulink and an external HDL simulator, such as Modelsim [6]. Ultimately, the same description can be mapped to hardware, assuming that the hardware description is synthesizable.

8.3.4 Controller Design Using Embedded Microprocessors

The most elaborate controller for an FPGA is the embedded microprocessor. In this case, control can be defined by running compiled or interpreted programs on the microprocessor. On the BEE2 platform, a tiny shell can be used interactively to control datapath settings, or a custom C-based program can be built using automatically generated header files to symbolically reference hardware devices.

A controller implemented using an embedded microprocessor is often much slower than the associated datapath hardware, perhaps taking several clock cycles to change control parameters. This is useful for adjusting parameters that do not change frequently, such as threshold, gain, and overlay in the Sobel filter. The BEE Platform Studio design flow uses the Xilinx Embedded Development Kit (EDK) to generate a controller running a command line shell, which allows the user to read and modify configuration registers and memory blocks within the FPGA design. Depending on the platform, this controller can be accessed via a serial port, a network connection, or another interface port.

The same embedded controller can also serve as a source or sink for low-bandwidth datastreams. An example of a user-friendly interface to such a source or sink is a set of Linux 4.2 kernel extensions developed as part of the BEE operating system, BORPH [7]. BORPH defines the notion of a hardware process, where a bit file and associated interface information is encapsulated in an executable .bof file. When launched from the Linux command line, a software process is started that programs and then communicates with the embedded processor on a selected FPGA. To the end user, hardware sources and sinks in Simulink are mapped to Linux files or pipes, including standard input and standard output. These file interfaces can then be accessed as software streams to read from or write to a stream-based FPGA design for debugging purposes or for applications with low-bandwidth continuous datastreams.

8.4   COMPONENT REUSE: LIBRARIES OF SIMPLE AND COMPLEX SUBSYSTEMS

In the previous sections, low-level primitives were described for implementing simple datapath and control subsystems and mapping them to FPGAs. To make this methodology attractive to the algorithm developer and system architect, all of these capabilities are combined to create reusable library components, which can be parameterized for a variety of applications; many of them have been tested in a variety of applications.

8.4.1   Signal-processing Primitives

One example of a rich library developed for the BPS is the Astronomy library, which was codeveloped by UC Berkeley and the Space Sciences Laboratory [8,9] for use in a variety of high-performance radio astronomy applications. In its simplest form, this library comprises a variety of complex-valued operators based on Xilinx System Generator real-valued primitives. These blocks are implemented as Simulink subsystems with optional parameters defining latency or data type constraints.

8.4.2   Tiled Subsystems

To enable the development of more sophisticated library components, Simulink supports the use of Matlab M language programs to create or modify the schematic within a subsystem based on parameters passed to the block. With the Simulink Mask Editor, initialization code can be added to a subsystem to place other Simulink blocks and to add interconnect to define a broad range of implementations for a single library component.

Figure 8.12 illustrates an example of a tiled cell, the biplex_core FFT block, which accepts several implementation parameters. The first parameters define the size and precision of the FFT operator, followed by the quantization behavior (truncation or rounding) and the overflow behavior of adders (saturation or wrapping). The pipeline latencies of addition and multiplication operators are also user selectable within the subsystem.

Automatically tiled library components can conditionally use different subsystems, and can have multiple tiling dimensions. An alternative to the stream-based biplex_core block shown in Figure 8.13, a parallel FFT implementation,

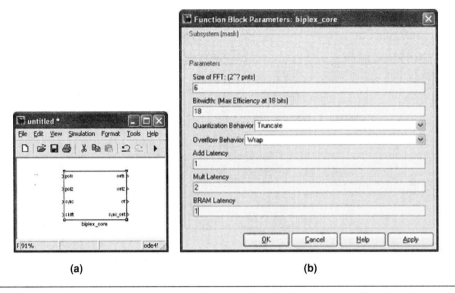

(a)   (b)

FIGURE 8.12 ■ The `biplex_core` dual-channel FFT block (a), with the parameter dialog box (b).

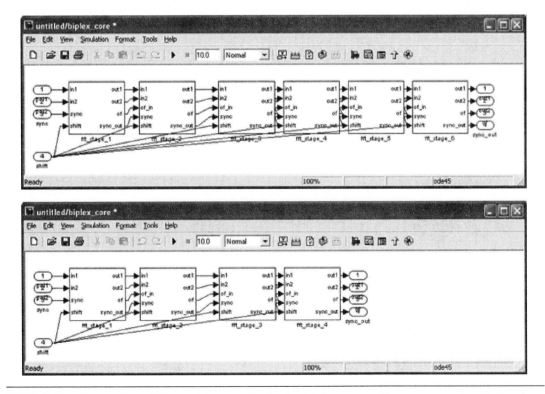

FIGURE 8.13 ■ Two versions of the model schematic for the `biplex_core` library component, with the size of the FFT set to 6 (2^6) and 4 (2^4). The schematic changes dynamically as the parameter is adjusted.

is also available, where the number of I/O ports changes with the FFT size parameter. An 8-input, 8-output version is illustrated in Figure 8.14. The parallel FFT tiles butterfly subsystems in two dimensions and includes parameterized pipeline registers so that the designer can explore speed versus pipeline latency tradeoffs.

In addition to the FFT, other commonly used high-level components include a poly-phase filter bank (PFB), data delay and reordering blocks, adder trees, correlator functions, and FIR filter implementations. Combining these platform-independent subsystems with the BPS I/O and processor interface library described in Section 8.2.3, an algorithm designer can take an active roll in the architectural development of high-performance stream-based signal-processing applications.

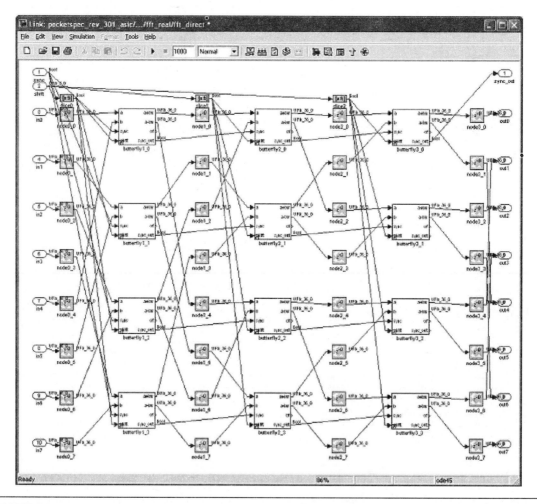

FIGURE 8.14 ▪ An automatically generated 8-channel parallel FFT from the `fft_direct` library component.

8.5 SUMMARY

This chapter described the use of Simulink as a common design framework for both algorithm and architecture development, with an automated path to program FPGA platforms. This capability, combined with a rich library of high-performance parameterized stream-based DSP components, allows new applications to be developed and tested quickly.

The real-time Sobel video edge detection described in this chapter runs on the BEE2 platform, shown in Figure 8.15, which has a dedicated LCD monitor

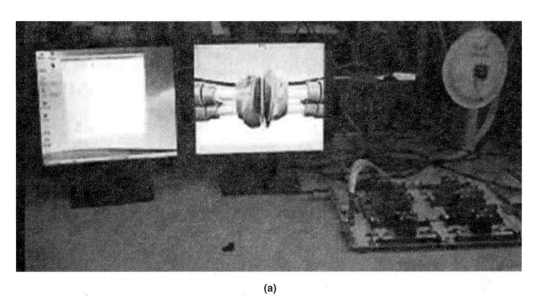

(a)

(b)   (c)

FIGURE 8.15 ■ (a) The Sobel edge detection filter running on the BEE2, showing the BEE2 console and video output on two LCD displays, with (b, c) two examples of edge detection results based on interactive user configuration from the console.

connected to it. Two filtered video samples are shown, with edges displayed with and without the original source color video image.

For more information on the BPS and related software, visit *http://bee2. eecs.berkeley.edu*, and for examples of high-performance stream-based library components, see the Casper Project [9].

Acknowledgments This work was funded in part by C2S2, the MARCO Focus Center for Circuit and System Solutions, under MARCO contract 2003-CT-888, and by Berkeley Wireless Research Center (BWRC) member companies (*bwrc.eecs.berkeley.edu*). The BEE Platform Studio development was done jointly with the Casper group at the Space Sciences Laboratory (*ssl.berkeley.edu/casper*).

References

[1] *http://www.mathworks.com.*

[2] *http://www.xilinx.com.*

[3] *http://www.synplicity.com.*

[4] C. Chang, J. Wawrzynek, R. W. Brodersen. BEE2: A high-end reconfigurable computing system. *IEEE Design and Test of Computers* 22(2), March/April 2005.

[5] C. Chang. *Design and Applications of a Reconfigurable Computing System for High Performance Digital Signal Processing*, Ph.D. thesis, University of California, Berkeley, 2005.

[6] *http://www.mentor.com.*

[7] K. Camera, H. K.-H. So, R. W. Brodersen. An integrated debugging environment for reprogrammble hardware systems. *Sixth International Symposium on Automated and Analysis-Driven Debugging*, September, 2005.

[8] A. Parsons et al. PetaOp/Second FPGA signal processing for SETI and radio astronomy. *Asilomar Conference on Signals, Systems, and Computers*, November 2006.

[9] *http://casper.berkeley.edu/papers/asilomar_2006.pdf.*

CHAPTER 9

STREAM COMPUTATIONS ORGANIZED FOR RECONFIGURABLE EXECUTION

André DeHon
Department of Electrical and Systems Engineering
University of Pennsylvania

Yury Markovskiy, Eylon Caspi, Michael Chu,
Randy Huang, Stylianos Perissakis, Laura Pozzi,
Joseph Yeh, John Wawrzynek
Department of Electrical Engineering and Computer Sciences
University of California–Berkeley

SCORE is a programming model for reconfigurable computing designed for application longevity and scalability, based on a streaming dataflow compute model (Section 5.1.3) and employing several system architectures (Section 5.2) to support scalability. The compute model allows us to abstract away hardware details such as platform capacity (e.g., number of lookup tables [LUTs]) and the detailed cycle-by-cycle timing of hardware implementation. This allows a single application description to automatically run faster on larger hardware or to fit onto smaller hardware. The abstraction of platform size and clock cycle timing makes SCORE a higher-level programming model than RTL-level descriptions such as VHDL (Chapter 6). The streaming dataflow model allows high concurrency and natural task descriptions for a large class of streaming applications, including signal and image processing.

Figure 9.1 shows one of the key scaling forms enabled. We capture the computation as a streaming dataflow graph of persistent operators (Section 5.1.2) abstracted from a particular platform (Figure 9.1(a)). On small hardware platforms, we use a phased reconfiguration manager (Phased reconfiguration manager subsection of Section 5.2.2) to implement the task as a sequence of configurations on the available hardware (Figure 9.1(b)). For larger platforms, more operators can be placed spatially, exploiting greater concurrency to reduce runtime (Figure 9.1(c)).

To achieve scalability, Stream Computations Organized for Reconfigurable Execution (SCORE) allows and encourages the programmer to ignore the hardware capacity of a particular platform and focus on capturing the fully spatial, streaming dataflow graph. A combination of the compiler and the runtime system must decompose and schedule the application onto a variety of hardware capacities. To support late-bound, runtime adaptation to various hardware platforms, the SCORE runtime employs a paged reconfiguration discipline (Section 9.2.4).

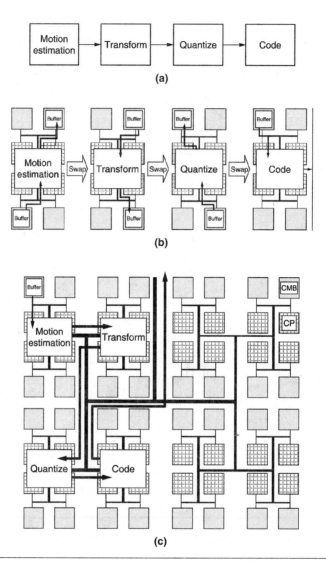

FIGURE 9.1 ▪ Score application and sequential versus fully spatial execution: (a) a video compression task, (b) a capacity-limited sequential implementation, and (c) a fully spatial implementation on SCORE hardware.

In implementing this model, we must

- Provide concrete programming language instantiations for describing SCORE applications (Section 9.1).
- Select and employ suitable system architectures to implement the application and support area–time trade-offs for scalability (Section 9.2).
- Compile between the programming language description of the application and the runtime system architectures (Section 9.3).
- Provide runtime support for the tasks that must be performed during execution (Section 9.4).

The SCORE programming model demonstrates how compute model and system architectures come together to efficiently support a class of streaming applications.

9.1   PROGRAMMING

The specific compute model SCORE supports is Dynamic Streaming Dataflow with Allocation but without peeks (Dynamic streaming dataflow and Streaming dataflow with allocation subsections of Section 5.1.3), making it fully deterministic. Programs are composed by linking together operators (functions or objects, Section 5.1.2) and memory segments with first-in-first-out (FIFO) stream links (Section 5.1.3). Operators themselves can be described by their behavior or composed structurally as a graph.

Any number of languages that obey streaming dataflow semantics can be defined to program SCORE computations. The key requirements are to capture operators with appropriate dataflow input/output (I/O) interfaces and to allow operator compositions.

SCORE can be programmed with conventional programming languages (e.g., C++, Java) by defining stylized language subsets and library support to describe and compose SCORE operators. In Section 9.1.2, we show how to use C++ for dynamic composition.

In a multi-threaded language, such as Java or C++, with an appropriate thread package, a SCORE operator would be an independent thread that communicates with the rest of the program only through single-reader, single-writer I/O streams. Specifically, SCORE does not have a global, shared memory abstraction among operators (Single Memory Pool, Section 5.1.4). An operator may *own* a chunk of the address space (a memory segment) during operation and return it after it has completed, but no two operators may own a piece of memory simultaneously.

Alternately, SCORE programming could use a modern system-level design language, such as System C [1], as long as the communication library provides suitable dataflow communication semantics. To focus on the necessary semantics during SCORE development, we define an intermediate register transfer level (RTL) language to describe SCORE operators and their composition (Section 9.1.1). We view this intermediate language, TDF, as a device-independent, assembly language target on the way to platform-specific executable operators.

9.1.1   Task Description Format

Task Description Format (TDF) is basically an RTL-level operator description with special syntax for handling input and output datastreams from the operator [7, 22]. Common datapath operators can be described using a C-like syntax. For example, Figure 9.2 shows how an FIR computation might be implemented in TDF. Operators may have parameters whose values are bound at operator instantiation time; parameters are identified with the keyword `param`. In the

```
fir4(param signed[8] w0, param signed[8] w1,
     param signed[8] w2, param signed[8] w3,
     // param's bound at instantiation time
     input unsigned[8] x,
     output unsigned[20] y)
{
     state only(x): // "fire" when x present
     {
       // assignment to output y denotes a stream write
       y = w0*x + w1*x@1 + w2*x@2 + w3*x@3;
       // x@n notation picks out nth previous value for
       //   x on input stream.
       //   (this notation is patterned after Silage [2])
       goto only; // loop in this state
     }
}
```

FIGURE 9.2 ▪ A TDF specification of 4-TAP FIR (a static rate operator).

FIR example, the coefficient weights are parameters; these are specified when the operator is created, and the values persist as long as the operator is used. The FIR reads from a single input stream (x) and produces a single output stream (y); the assignment to y denotes the stream write. The behavior of the state is gated on the arrival of the next x input value, producing a new y output for each such input.

To allow dynamic-rate dataflow (Dynamic streaming dataflow subsection of Section 5.1.3), the basic form of a behavioral TDF operator is that of a finite-state machine (FSM) (Finite State, Section 5.1.4), in which each state specifies the inputs that must be present before it can fire. Once the inputs arrive, the operator consumes them, and the FSM may choose to change states based on the input data consumed. A simple merge operator is shown in Figure 9.3 to demonstrate how the state machine can also be used to allow data-dependent consumption of input values. (Note: This version has been simplified for illustration; it does not properly handle the end-of-stream condition.) Output value production can be conditioned as illustrated in the uniq example shown in Figure 9.4. Together, data-dependent input consumption and output production allow the user to specify arbitrary, deterministic, dynamic-rate operators.

Of course, the FSM gives the user the semantic power to describe heavily sequential and complex, control-oriented operators. Nonetheless, the programmer should avoid sequentialization and complex control when possible, as operators with many states are less likely to use spatial computing resources efficiently. Larger operators can be composed structurally from smaller operators in a straightforward manner, as shown in Figure 9.5.

9.1.2 C++ Integration and Composition

With a suitable stream implementation and interface code, SCORE operators can be instantiated by and used with a conventional, multi-threaded programming

```
signed[w] merge(param unsigned[6] w,
                // can use parameters to define data width
                input signed[w] a,
                input signed[w] b)
{

  signed[w] tmpA; // define local state inside the operator
  signed[w] tmpB;
  // states used here to show dynamic data consumption
  state start(a,b): // requires inputs on both a and b to be
                    //    available in order to evaluate
   {
     // assignments to local variables have C-like semantics
     tmpA=a;  tmpB=b;
     if (tmpA<tmpB) { merge=tmpA;
                        goto replaceA; }
     else { merge=tmpB;
           goto replaceB; }
     // note: assignment to function name signifies a write to the
     //  output stream which is returned from operator instantiation
   }
  state replaceA(a): // requires availability of only input a
   {
     tmpA=a;
     if (tmpA<tmpB) { merge=tmpA;
                        goto replaceA; }
     else { merge=tmpB;goto replaceB; }
   }
  state replaceB(b): // requires availability of only input b
   {
     tmpB=b;
     if (tmpA<tmpB) { merge=tmpA;
                        goto replaceA; }
     else { merge=tmpB; goto replaceB; }
   }
}
```

FIGURE 9.3 ■ A TDF specification of `merge` operator (a dynamic input rate operator).

language. Figure 9.6 shows an example C++ program that uses the `merge` and `uniq` operators defined in Figures 9.3 and 9.4. Note that SCORE operator instantiation and composition can be performed in C++ code. Once created, the operators behave as independently running threads, operating in parallel with the main C++ execution thread. In general, a SCORE operator will run until its input streams are closed or its output streams are released (i.e., the stream is deallocated with a `free`-like operation).

After primitive behavioral (or leaf) operators have been defined (e.g., in TDF or some other suitable form) and compiled into their hardware-level implementation, large programs can be composed entirely in a conventional programming language as just described and illustrated in Figure 9.6. If one thinks of TDF as a portable assembly language for critical computational building blocks, then this language binding allows a high-level language to compose these building blocks

```
// uniq behaves like the unix command of the same name;
//  it filters an input stream, removing any adjacent, duplicate
//  entries before passing them on to the output stream.
signed[w] uniq(param unsigned[6] w,
               input signed[w] x)
{
   signed[w] lastx;
   state start(x):
     { lastx=x; uniq=x; goto loop; }
   state loop(x):
     {
       if (x=!lastx)
         { lastx=x; uniq=x; }
      goto loop;
     }
}
```

FIGURE 9.4 ■ A TDF specification of `uniq` operator (a dynamic output rate operator).

```
merge3uniq(param unsigned[6] n,
           input signed[n] a,
           input signed[n] b,
           input signed[n] c,
           output signed[n] o)
{
       signed [n] t;
       t=merge(n,merge(n,a,b),c);
       o=uniq(n,t);
}
```

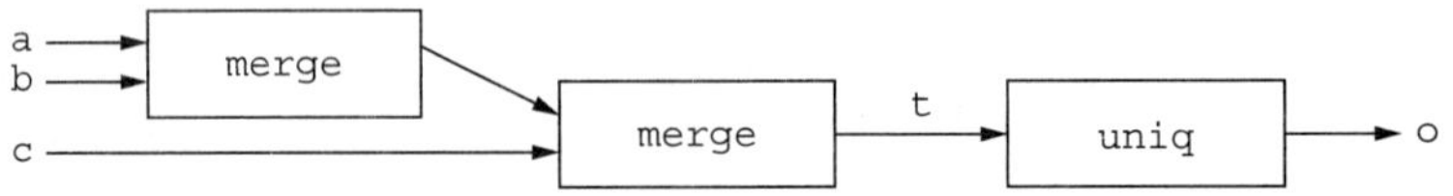

FIGURE 9.5 ■ The TDF compositional operator.

in much the same way that assembly language kernels are composed using high-level languages in order to efficiently program early DSPs and supercomputers. The instantiation parameters for TDF operators allow the definition of generic operators that can be highly customized to the needs of the application.

9.2 SYSTEM ARCHITECTURE AND EXECUTION PATTERNS

To support the SCORE programming model efficiently, implementations are based on several system architectures and execution design patterns (e.g., DeHon et al. [3]). In this section, we highlight how these architectures are used and introduce additional execution patterns.

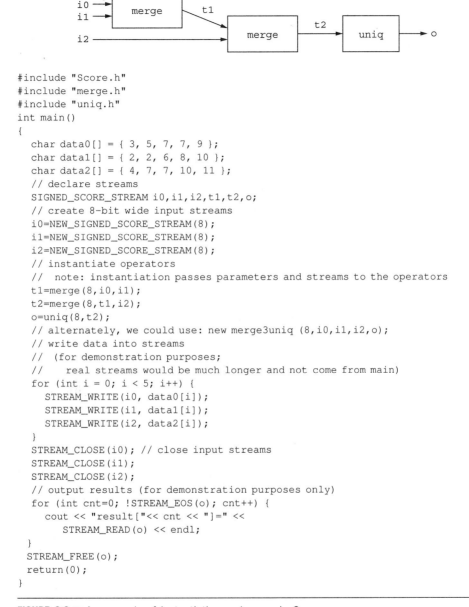

```
#include "Score.h"
#include "merge.h"
#include "uniq.h"
int main()
{
  char data0[] = { 3, 5, 7, 7, 9 };
  char data1[] = { 2, 2, 6, 8, 10 };
  char data2[] = { 4, 7, 7, 10, 11 };
  // declare streams
  SIGNED_SCORE_STREAM i0,i1,i2,t1,t2,o;
  // create 8-bit wide input streams
  i0=NEW_SIGNED_SCORE_STREAM(8);
  i1=NEW_SIGNED_SCORE_STREAM(8);
  i2=NEW_SIGNED_SCORE_STREAM(8);
  // instantiate operators
  // note: instantiation passes parameters and streams to the operators
  t1=merge(8,i0,i1);
  t2=merge(8,t1,i2);
  o=uniq(8,t2);
  // alternately, we could use: new merge3uniq (8,i0,i1,i2,o);
  // write data into streams
  // (for demonstration purposes;
  //    real streams would be much longer and not come from main)
  for (int i = 0; i < 5; i++) {
    STREAM_WRITE(i0, data0[i]);
    STREAM_WRITE(i1, data1[i]);
    STREAM_WRITE(i2, data2[i]);
  }
  STREAM_CLOSE(i0); // close input streams
  STREAM_CLOSE(i1);
  STREAM_CLOSE(i2);
  // output results (for demonstration purposes only)
  for (int cnt=0; !STREAM_EOS(o); cnt++) {
    cout << "result["<< cnt << "]=" <<
        STREAM_READ(o) << endl;
  }
  STREAM_FREE(o);
  return(0);
}
```

FIGURE 9.6 ■ An example of instantiation and usage in C++.

9.2.1 Stream Support

SCORE heavily leverages the stream abstraction (Chapter 5, Section 5.1.3) for communication between operators. The streamed data can be assigned to a buffer if the producer and consumer are not coresident (see Figure 9.1(b));

if they are coresident, the data can be assigned to physical networking (see Figure 9.1(c)). Further, any number of mechanisms (e.g., shared bus, packet-switched network, time-multiplexed network, configured links) can implement the stream based on data rate, predictability, and platform capabilities. Once data communication is organized as a stream, the platform knows which data to prefetch and how to package it to or from memory.

When a SCORE implementation physically implements streams as wires between dynamic-rate operators, data presence (Data presence subsection of Section 5.2.1) tags allow us to abstract out dynamic data rates or delays. While data presence allows producers to signal consumers that data are not ready, it is often useful to signal the opposite direction as well; consequently, we also implement a *back-pressure* signal, which allows the consumer to inform the producer that it is not ready to consume additional inputs. We can further place queues between the producer and the consumer to decouple their cycle-by-cycle firing.

When the consumer is not ready, produced values accumulate in the queue, allowing the producer to continue operation; if there are stored values in the queue, the consumer can continue to operate while the producer is stalled as well. Queues are of finite size, so a full queue also uses back-pressure to stall an attached producer. In dynamic data rate operations where queue size cannot be bounded (Dynamic streaming dataflow subsection of Section 5.1.3), the hardware signals the OS when queues fill, and the OS may need to allocate additional queue capacity at runtime to prevent deadlock [4].

9.2.2 Phased Reconfiguration

When the operator graph is too large for the platform, it is necessary to share the physical hardware in time (see Figures 9.1(b) and 9.7). For a reconfigurable platform, this can be done by changing the configuration overtime, to implement the

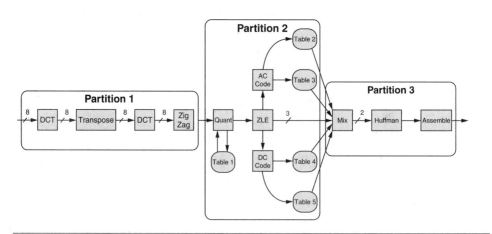

FIGURE 9.7 ■ Partitioning of a JPEG image encoder to match platform capacity.

graph in pieces (Phased reconfiguration manager subsection of Section 5.2.2). Reconfiguration, however, can be an expensive operation requiring many cycles. To minimize its overhead cost, we want to run each operator for many cycles between reconfigurations. In particular, if we can ensure that each operation runs for a large number of cycles compared to the reconfiguration time, then we can make the overhead for reconfiguration small ($T_{run-before-reconfig}$ >> T_{config}). Streaming data with large queues helps us achieve this. We can queue up a large number of data items that will keep the operator busy. We then reconfigure the operator, compute on the queued data, and, if the consumer is not coresident, queue up the results (Figure 9.1(b)). When the input queue is empty or the output queue is full, we reconfigure to the next set of operators.

9.2.3 Sequential versus Parallel

When the platform contains both processors and reconfigurable logic, it is possible to assign some operators to the processor(s) (Processor subsection of Section 5.2.2) and some to the reconfigurable fabric. We can compile SCORE operators either to processor instructions or to reconfigurable configurations, and we can even save both implementations as part of the program executable. At load time or runtime, low-throughput operators can be assigned to the sequential processor(s), while high-throughput logic can be assigned to the reconfigurable fabric. As the size of the reconfigurable fabric grows, more operators can be implemented spatially on it.

Phased reconfiguration can be ineffective when mutually dependent cycles are large compared to the size of the platform. Processors are designed to time-multiplex their hardware at a fine granularity; thus, one way to fit large operator cycles onto the platform is to push lower throughput operators onto the processor until the cycle is contained.

We interface the processor to the reconfigurable array using a streaming coprocessor arrangement (Streaming Coprocessors, Section 5.2.1). The processor can write data into stream FIFOs to go to the reconfigurable array coprocessor, and it reads data back from them. This decouples the cycle-by-cycle operation of the reconfigurable array from the processor, abstracting the relative timing of the two units. In the case where the reconfigurable array can be occupied (e.g., allocated to another operator or task), this reduces coresidence requirements between operators on the array and processor. As a result, the options for the array size to vary among platform implementations increase.

9.2.4 Fixed-size and Standard I/O Page

To allow the platform size to vary with the implementation platform, it is necessary to perform placement at load time or runtime based on the amount of physical hardware and the time-multiplexed schedule. If we had to place everything at the LUT level, we would have a very large placement problem. Further, if we allowed partial reconfiguration in order to efficiently support the fact that different operators may need to be resident for different amounts of time, we would have a fragmentation and bin-packing problem [5], as different operators take up different space and have different footprints. We can simplify the runtime problem by using a discipline of fixed-size pages that have a standard I/O interface.

First, we decide on a particular page size (e.g., 512 4-LUTs) for the architecture. At compile time, we organize operators into standard page-size blocks so that we can perform the intrapage placement and routing offline at compile time. At runtime, we simply place pages and perform interpage routing. The runtime placement problem is simplified because all pages are identically sized and interchangeable. Furthermore, because pages are typically 100 to 1000 4-LUTs, the runtime placement problem is two to three orders of magnitude smaller than LUT-level placement. Unfortunately, fixed-size pages may incur internal fragmentation, leaving some resources in each page unused. Brebner's SLU is an early example of this pattern [6].

Note that this is the same basic approach used in virtual memory, where we do not manage every bit or even every word independently, but instead gather a fixed number of words into a page and manage (e.g., map and swap) them as a group. In both cases, this reduces the overhead associated with page mapping considerably.

9.3   COMPILATION

We have developed a complete compilation flow from TDF to conventional FPGAs using Verilog (an HDL similar to VHDL—see Chapter 6) as an intermediate form (Figure 9.8) [7]. The TDF compiler, `tdfc`, automatically generates RTL Verilog to efficiently implement the streaming constructs of the TDF language, including flow control checking, stream buffering in queues, and stream pipelining. The TDF compiler also maps between abstract operators of arbitrary size and the fixed-size pages supported at runtime by the system architecture.

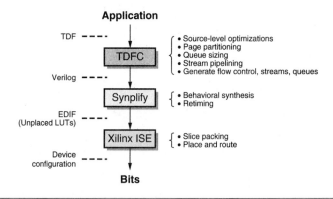

FIGURE 9.8 ■ TDF compilation flow targeting an FPGA.

The compiler then emits a netlist of pages for compilation by a commercial backend FPGA synthesis, place, and route flow.

Because SCORE streams abstract the number of clock cycles between operators, we can pipeline both the interconnect between operators and the operator datapaths. To pipeline operators, the compiler adds registers to the input and output streams and employs retiming (Chapter 18) to redistribute the registers into the operator logic.

To accommodate the wide range of operator sizes that the programmer may produce, the compiler must perform operator packing and splitting in order to target any particular, fixed-size page. Our previous experience suggests that most user-written leaf operators require fewer than 512 4-LUTs, which means that page packing will be adequate to reshape most applications. Many large operators are feedforward pipelines (e.g., DCT, IDCT), which can be easily decomposed using directional cuts in the dataflow. For the general case, it is necessary to decompose large state machines to fit them onto small pages. This could be done by starting with individual states and clustering state logic and datapaths, obeying the page area and I/O bound. To minimize delay, the goal is to group states that typically execute together so as to minimize the frequency of state transitions that cross the page boundary. Clustering techniques such as those described by Li et al. [8] can be employed for this general clustering case.

9.4 RUNTIME

To support the late-bound task and platform mapping integral to SCORE's power and scalability, we must perform scheduling, placement, and routing no earlier than load time. In this section, we highlight how these tasks can all be performed quickly at load time or runtime.

9.4.1 Scheduling

We support SCORE's virtualization model in the presence of late-bound platform mapping with a load-time and runtime scheduler. We do not know the capacity of the platform until load time; consequently, we cannot partition the graph into sets of pages that fit on the platform before then. Further, because operators have dynamic execution times and dynamic consumption and production rates, the relative execution time of each operator cannot be known with certainty until execution. To support SCORE efficiently, we must be able to:

- Quickly partition the page graph into platform-feasible components (within milliseconds).
- Produce a high-quality schedule—that is, one that minimizes the time to run the task (minimizes the make span).
- Minimize the sequential handling required for managing reconfiguration and advancing the schedule.

In the simplest cases, we partition the graph once, at load time, when the program starts and never again. In this way, we amortize the cost of partitioning across the entire application runtime (Figure 9.9). If the application will run for seconds, we can afford tens of milliseconds for this scheduling operation while keeping the overhead small. If we can decrease the scheduling time, then it will be possible to run even shorter jobs efficiently. In more advanced cases, the graph may change during execution, or the execution rates of operators may change in a data-dependent way. In such cases, it might be useful to repartition and reschedule the graph during execution. The shorter we can make the partitioning time, the more frequently we can afford to invoke the partitioner without paying a large overhead.

We have developed a series of schedulers to address these issues [9–12]. Our highest-quality scheduler (shown in Figure 9.10) is quasi-static and load-time based [10], and operates in two phases: (1) load-time partitioning and (2) runtime schedule advancement. At application load-time, the scheduler partitions the page-level dataflow graph into platform-feasible subgraphs. This partition can use feedback information on operator and stream activity rates based on previous program runs. The load-time partitioning heuristic requires only a few hundred thousand processor cycles (e.g., submillisecond time on gigahertz processors) for graphs with up to one hundred operators [12].

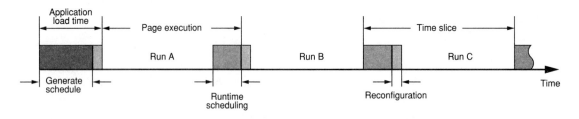

FIGURE 9.9 ■ An application execution timeline.

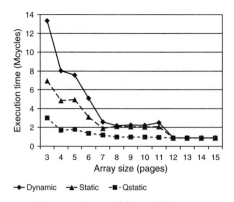

FIGURE 9.10 ■ JPEG decoder scaling: Total execution time is compared among fully dynamic, fully static, and quasi-static schedulers.

The result is a schedule for the phased reconfiguration. During execution, the runtime system advances the computed schedule by reconfiguring the array at regular intervals (Phased reconfiguration manager subsection of Section 5.2.2). The schedule computed at load time specifies a nominal period for each schedule timeslice. Additionally, the system monitors execution to determine when the current configuration can no longer make forward progress (e.g., all input buffers are empty or all output buffers are full) and dynamically triggers early phase termination and schedule advancement.

9.4.2 Placement

Using the fixed-size and standard I/O pages discipline (Section 9.2.4) we immediately reduce the size of the placement task by two to three orders of magnitude. Nonetheless, the placement task may still take too long when run using conventional single-processor-based placers at reconfiguration time or even load time. Fortunately, once we have a spatially parallel reconfigurable computing platform, we can use the platform itself to perform placement substantially faster. In Wrighton and DeHon [13] and Wrighton [14], we show how to perform simulated annealing spatially with reconfigurable logic; we can place a graph with 1000 movable elements in roughly 1 million cycles. Even if we only ran the placement engine at 100 MHz, this would mean that we could perform placement in 10 ms. If each page held 512 4-LUTs, this would correspond to platforms with half a million 4-LUTs.

The key idea for spatial simulated annealing is to build a placement engine on top of the reconfigurable platform. If we make each page large enough, then it can act as a cellular placement cell. As a placement cell, it holds a candidate, logical page and negotiates exchanges with its nearest neighbors (i.e., cellular automata system architecture Section 5.2.5). A pair of adjacent pages will swap logical pages if they estimate that the swap will produce a superior placement (e.g., shorter wire lengths) or if the randomness in the simulated annealing process suggests attempting the swap anyway. All pages can be paired up and can negotiate swaps in parallel, allowing many moves per swap epoch.

By pairing up only neighbors, we can guarantee minimizing the interconnect for this placement engine and keep the cycle times short. Because there is one cellular placement cell for every page site on the device, the hardware and parallelism in the placement engine scales exactly to the size of the placement problem that needs to be solved. Wrighton and DeHon [13] estimate that 400 4-LUTs are adequate to implement a 100 MHz cellular placement cell on Xilinx Virtex-II–generation hardware [15]; this suggests that SCORE platforms with 512 LUT pages will be able to perform their own placement.

9.4.3 Routing

Once the pages have been placed, we must perform interpage routing. Again, we can exploit the fact that we have a spatially parallel computing platform to route tasks in 100,000 to 1 million cycles [16]. Here, we augment the interpage network with additional logic to allow it to identify all free paths between a source node and a sink node in parallel. This permits a flooding search (e.g., Figure 9.11) to find a free path in the time it takes to propagate a signal across the network rather than the time it takes to perform a sequential search on a large graph structure in memory. Consequently, each new path can be added in tens of cycles rather than the tens of thousands of cycles required by the best software routers.

Using randomization, rip-up, and multiple restarts, this approach can even perform congestion negotiation and achieve comparable quality to PathFinder [17] (Chapter 17), the state-of-the-art software-routing algorithm for FPGAs [18, 19]. With word-wide (e.g., 16-bit) datapaths for the interpage network, the additional area overhead for this augmented network is less than 30 percent when network routing channels are switch-area limited; the augmented network adds only control wires, so it has almost no area overhead when network-routing channels are wire dominated.

An alternate approach is to employ a packet-switched network for interpage routing (see Marescaux et al. [20] and Kapre et al. [21]) to avoid the need to compute and configure the network. Packet switches are generally much larger and have higher latency than configured switches, but they may be able to handle multirate and dynamic traffic more efficiently.

Figure 9.11 shows the result of a path search for a route from node 4 to node 2. Light thick lines show preexisting routes; dark thick lines show the free paths explored between source and sink. At the crossover switchbox (labeled "XXX"), only a single switch is found by both source- and sink-initiated searches.

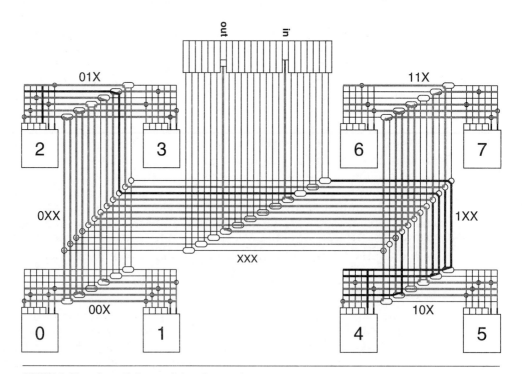

FIGURE 9.11 ▪ A spatially parallel path search.

9.5 HIGHLIGHTS

SCORE compilation has automatically mapped image-processing applications (e.g., wavelet, JPEG, MPEG) to streamed implementations that exceed 100 MHz sample throughput on a Virtex-II Pro XC2VP70-7 [12]. In comparable technology, a 4-page SCORE design outperforms a Pentium-3 (500 MHz) by 10 times on JPEG compression. Mapped design performance scales to deliver larger speedup with additional pages (see Figure 9.10).

For further details on SCORE, see DeHon et al. [12] and Caspi et al. [22].

References

[1] Open System C Initiative. *System C 2.1 Language Reference Manual*, May 2005 (*http://www.systemc.org*).

[2] D. Genin, J. Rabaey, P. Hilfinger, C. Scheers, H. DeMan. DSP specification using the SILAGE language. *Proceedings of the IEEE ICASSP Conference*, April 1990.

[3] A. DeHon, J. Adams, M. deLorimier, N. Kapre, Y. Matsuda, H. Naeimi, M. Vanier, M. Wrighton. Design patterns for reconfigurable computing. *Proceedings of the IEEE Symposium on Field-Programmable Custom Computing Machines*, April 2004.

[4] T. M. Parks. *Bounded Scheduling of Process Networks*, UCB/ERL95–105, University of California, Berkeley, 1995.

[5] K. Bazargan, R. Kastner, M. Sarrafzadeh. Fast template placement for reconfigurable computing systems. *IEEE Design and Test of Computers* 17(1), January–March 2000.

[6] G. Brebner. The swapable logic unit: A paradigm for virtual hardware. *Proceedings of the IEEE Symposium on FPGAs for Custom Computing Machines*, April 1997.

[7] E. Caspi. *Design Automation for Streaming Systems*, Ph.D. thesis, University of California, Berkeley, 2005.

[8] Z. Li, K. Compton, S. Hauck. Configuration caching techniques for FPGAs. *Proceedings of the IEEE Symposium on Field-Programmable Custom Computing Machines*, 2000.

[9] M. Chu. *Dynamic Runtime Scheduler Support for SCORE*, Master's thesis, University of California, Berkeley, December 2000.

[10] Y. Markovskiy, E. Caspi, R. Huang, J. Yeh, M. Chu, J. Wawrzynek, A. DeHon. Analysis of quasi-static scheduling techniques in a virtualized reconfigurable machine. *Proceedings of the International Symposium on Field-Programmable Gate Arrays*, February 2002.

[11] Y. Markovskiy. *Quasi-Static Scheduling for SCORE*, Master's thesis, University of California, Berkeley, December 2004.

[12] A. DeHon, Y. Markovskiy, E. Caspi, M. Chu, R. Huang, S. Perissakis, L. Pozzi, J. Yeh, J. Wawrzynek. Stream computations organized for reconfigurable execution. *Journal of Microprocessors and Microsystems* 30(6), September 2006.

[13] M. Wrighton, A. DeHon. Hardware-assisted simulated annealing with application for fast FPGA placement. *Proceedings of the International Symposium on Field-Programmable Gate Arrays*, February 2003.

[14] M. Wrighton. *A Spatial Approach to FPGA Cell Placement by Simulated Annealing*, Master's thesis, California Institute of Technology, June 2003.

[15] Xilinx, Inc. *Xilinx Virtex-II 1.5V Platform FPGAs Data Sheet*, San Jose, July 2002.

[16] A. DeHon, R. Huang, J. Wawrzynek. Hardware-assisted fast routing. *Proceedings of the IEEE Symposium on Field-Programmable Custom Computing Machines*, April 2002.

[17] L. McMurchie, C. Ebeling. PathFinder: A negotiation-based performance-driven router for FPGAs. *Proceedings of the International Symposium on Field-Programmable Gate Arrays*, February 1995.

[18] R. Huang, J. Wawrzynek, A. DeHon. Stochastic, spatial routing for hypergraphs, trees, and meshes. *Proceedings of the International Symposium on Field-Programmable Gate Arrays*, February 2003.

[19] A. DeHon, R. Huang, J. Wawrzynek. Stochastic spatial routing for reconfigurable networks. *Journal of Microprocessors and Microsystems* 30(6), September 2006.

[20] T. Marescaux, V. Nollet, J.-Y. Mignolet, A. Bartic, W. Moffat, P. Avasare, P. Coene, D. Verkest, S. Vernalde, R. Lauwereins. Run-time support for heterogeneous multitasking on reconfigurable SOCs. *INTEGRATION, The VLSI Journal* 38(1), October 2004.

[21] N. Kapre, N. Mehta, M. deLorimier, R. Rubin, H. Barnor, M. J. Wilson, M. Wrighton, A. DeHon. Packet-switched vs. time-multiplexed FPGA overlay networks. *Proceedings of the IEEE Symposium on Field-Programmable Custom Computing Machines*, April 2006.

[22] E. Caspi, M. Chu, R. Huang, N. Weaver, J. Yeh, J. Wawrzynek, A. DeHon. Stream Computations Organized for Reconfigurable Execution (SCORE): Introduction and tutorial (*http://www.cs.berkeley.edu/projects/brass/documents/score_tutorial.html*); a short version appears in *FPL '2000* (Lecture Notes in Computer Science, 1896), 2000.

CHAPTER 10

PROGRAMMING DATA PARALLEL FPGA APPLICATIONS USING THE SIMD/VECTOR MODEL

Maya B. Gokhale
Lawrence Livermore National Laboratory

In the Single Instruction Multiple Data (SIMD) model, aggregate operations on arrays and vectors can be mapped to arrays of function units. A single instruction stream is dispatched from a control unit to the function units, which operate in lockstep on the data sequences. Reconfigurable hardware is well suited to perform SIMD (also called *vector* or *data parallel*) computation (see Section 5.1.5). Groups of lookup tables (LUTs) can be configured as function units, and the data local to each unit can be stored in distributed memories. This chapter explores parallel processing on reconfigurable computers using the SIMD/vector model.

Reconfigurable computers can exploit parallelism at many different levels of granularity, from coarse-grained parallel tasks to fine-grained instruction-level parallelism. The massive amount of parallelism available in the reconfigurable computer more than compensates for its slow clock rate—one-tenth the clock rate of modern microprocessors. Raw spatial parallelism is plentiful in reconfigurable processors, especially those based on FPGAs. The challenge is to partition and map the application onto the inherently parallel fabric of lookup tables, DSP blocks, and memories. Parallel activities can be explicitly described and scheduled by the programmer or hardware designer, or can be inferred through analysis of the source code. SIMD/vector parallelism is very well suited to the spatial parallelism of FPGAs and other coarse-grained arithmetic logic units (ALU) arrays. In this programming model, aggregate data such as vectors and matrices are processed in parallel on arrays of function units.

10.1 SIMD COMPUTING ON FPGAS: AN EXAMPLE

As an introduction to SIMD computing on FPGAs, Figure 10.1 shows an SIMD array customized to perform two vector operations. A vector A is scaled by a constant factor, and then the dot product $A \cdot B = \Sigma a_i \times b_i$ of vectors A and B is performed. In this example, the number of SIMD processors is equal to the size of the vectors. Each processor holds one element of A and one of B. There is an additional storage location in each processor to hold the result of the $\times$ operation.

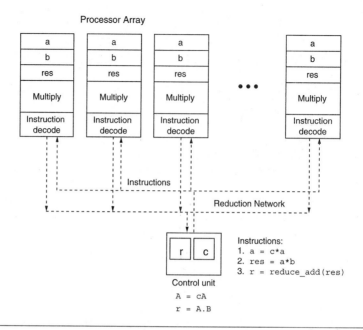

FIGURE 10.1 ▪ An SIMD dot-product machine.

The control unit generates the instruction stream. An instruction can be executed on the control unit itself, on each processor of the processor array, or cooperatively on both. In this example, the control unit sends the constant c as part of the first multiply instruction. The constant appears as an immediate operand in the instruction to each processor. Next the control unit sends the second multiply instruction to the processor array, and all processors perform the operation res=a*b. The final instruction performs a *reduction*, a global combining operation, in which each processor sends its instance of res into the reduction network. Because the operation is a global sum, all the res instances are summed and the result is stored in the control unit variable r. While the example shows the control unit sending three separate instructions to the processor array, on an FPGA it is very possible that the controller will send a single instruction that results in a multi-cycle sequence of multiply operations followed by the global sum.

In this idealized example, the number of processors exactly matches the size of the vectors. In real applications, there are many different vectors of different sizes. The vectors must be distributed to the processors in blocks, and each processor must multiply subvectors of elements. If the number of processors doesn't evenly divide the vector size, some processors must remain inactive when the tail ends of the vectors are multiplied. Each processor must keep a subaccumulation, and, when the entire vector has been processed, the global sum is performed over the partial sums. When the processor array is on an FPGA, the compiler must synthesize state machines (FSMD subsection of Section 5.2.2) to control the sequence of operations and iterate over the blocks of data. Designing algorithms for reconfigurable computers in the SIMD model in the face of these real-world complicating factors will be addressed in Section 10.4.

10.2 SIMD PROCESSING ARCHITECTURES

SIMD/vector machines were among the first parallel processors to be designed. From the days of the Iliac IV, with 64 processing elements (PEs) receiving instructions from a control processor, this parallel-processing architecture has gone through myriad incarnations. Notable among SIMD arrays are the Connection Machine, which had thousands of simple PEs operating in synchrony [1], as well as DAP and MasPar (late 1980s [2]). The Terasys Integrated Circuit [3] and the Clearspeed SIMD array [4] both included an SIMD processing array on a single integrated circuit.

Historically, supercomputers with dedicated floating-point function units used for processing arrays and vectors were called vector supercomputers, while massively parallel, highly interconnected arrays of function units were referred to as SIMD, or data parallel. More recently, as small arrays of function units have been incorporated into the architecture of scalar processors, the terms *SIMD*, *vector*, and *data parallel* have become interchangeable. This is especially apropos to reconfigurable computers, in which arbitrary numbers and types of function units may be used with many different kinds of interconnect patterns.

An SIMD processing array, illustrated in Figure 10.2, consists of a collection of identical processing elements operating in lockstep. The PEs all execute exactly the same instruction, which is broadcast to them from a control unit, or "sequencer," as indicated by the dotted lines in the figure. Each PE has a local memory from which to fetch data operands and store results. On an SIMD array, control flow instructions, such as branching, conditional branch, and subroutine call, are executed on the control unit.

Data-dependent branching represents a particular challenge when different instances of the data are resident in each PE's memory. Depending on the data value, some PEs might evaluate the branch predicate to true and others to false. Because they all must execute the same instruction at the same time, each PE has a predicate mask flag (the M in the corner of each ALU) indicating whether the PE should execute or ignore the current instruction.

The PE sets the predicate mask to the result of evaluating the predicate on its data items, and then either executes subsequent instructions or is inactive. The control unit can reset PEs to the active mode by issuing "unconditional" instructions to them, directing them to ignore the predicate mask. The notion of predicated instructions, which is essential to SIMD processing, is also used in some microprocessor instruction sets [5], particularly in wide-word explicitly parallel architectures.

In SIMD processing, PEs exchange data synchronously. The PE interconnection network may be arranged as a linear array, as in Figure 10.2, or as a two-dimensional (or even three-dimensional) mesh or torus. In addition to

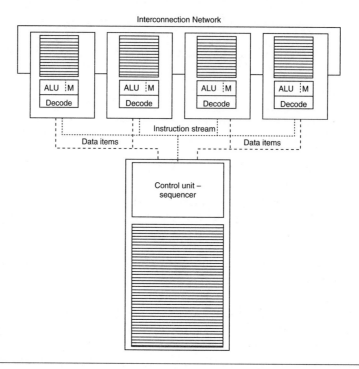

FIGURE 10.2 ■ An SIMD processing array.

nearest-neighbor communication (illustrated with solid lines in the figure), data parallel arrays usually include global combining networks for global reduction (sum, product, min, max, and logical) operations. The control unit can retrieve data from the memory of individual PEs and can also receive the result of the global combining operations (dashed lines in the figure).

A global combining network is illustrated in Figure 10.3, which shows a network organized as a binary tree with a combining operator at each interior tree node. Global combining networks can be used for any associative operation. With parallel tree operations, an $O(n)$ operation is reduced to $O(\log(n))$.

10.3 DATA PARALLEL LANGUAGES

High-level data parallel languages for SIMD machines were popularized in the late 1980s with the emergence of the Connection Machines CM-1, CM-2, and CM-5, and were adopted by other vendors. In the CM approach, a base language such as Fortran or C was extended with new keywords, syntax, and semantics. In the C* language, a data parallel extension to ANSI C, new data type modifiers mono and poly were introduced. A mono variable resides in the control unit memory, while a poly variable occupies memory local to each PE,

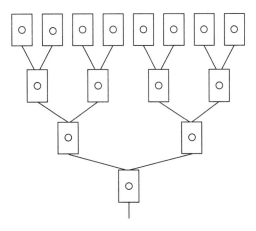

FIGURE 10.3 ■ A global sum network.

implicitly defining a vector or higher-dimension array. Operation on a `mono` variable is performed on the control unit, while a `poly` expression is evaluated independently on each PE.

Also in the 1980s, new syntax and intrinsic functions were introduced to express global combining operations, inter-PE communication, and unconditional execution.

Declaration of `poly` variables in most data parallel languages implicitly defines an aggregate object whose length is the number of PEs in the physical array. Unfortunately, most datasets do not conform in size or shape to the physical PE array, and therefore the programmer must arrange the data arrays in blocks distributed among the PEs' memories, and then loop over the blocks on each PE. The Connection Machines, however, supported "virtual" processors in microcode. The programmer could define an array of processing elements larger than the size of the physical PE array that better matched the size of the datasets, and microcode in each PE looped over the block of data in its memory.

10.4 RECONFIGURABLE COMPUTERS FOR SIMD/VECTOR PROCESSING

In contrast to specific physical implementations of SIMD arrays in silicon, a large variety of data parallel machines may be mapped onto FPGA-based reconfigurable computers. The data parallel model maps naturally to the physical structure of FPGAs, with dedicated hardware blocks of arithmetic units and memories tiled regularly in a two-dimensional array, as well as a flexible interconnect. In addition, there are many degrees of freedom in an FPGA implementation. The data parallel engine can be customized to the datasets being processed in terms of geometry (one versus multidimensional arrays), interconnect (linear, mesh, torus), and even PE instruction set.

An early experiment in data parallel computing on FPGAs was the dbC project [6] in which a data parallel language was compiled onto the Splash 2 reconfigurable logic array [7]. dbC was modeled on the Connection Machines' C* language. Like C*, dbC included the `mono` and `poly` data type modifiers to denote data on the control unit and SIMD array, respectively.

The size of the SIMD array could be specified at the language level by setting a predefined variable to the number of PEs. The linear array thus defined was automatically partitioned among the 16 FPGAs of the Splash system.

Instructions were broadcast to the FPGAs from the Sun workstation host, which served as the control unit. Unlike conventional SIMD arrays, the PE instruction set was not fixed. Rather, the compiler created a unique instruction set for each dbC program, generating a behavioral VHDL module (see Chapter 6) that was synthesized through the normal CAD tool flow. An instruction, rather than being a simple arithmetic or load/store operation, was synthesized as a predicated block. This could be a simple basic block—a straight-line sequence of code with a single entry and a single exit. If the C code contained `if` statements, the compiler transformed control dependence into data dependence [8], creating sequential predicated blocks that contained first the true branch and then the false branch of the `if`. Thus, a single instruction dispatched from the control unit to the SIMD array could result in a multi-clock-cycle block of logic executing a predicated hyperblock.

To exploit the flexibility of FPGAs to perform arithmetic on arbitrary bit-length operands, dbC allowed `poly` variables to be of user-specified bit length. dbC extended C integer data types by permitting C bit field syntax to be used to define the bit length of signed and unsigned integer variables. This ability was particularly valuable on early FPGAs with limited logic and interconnect. The arithmetic units synthesized within the SIMD PE were customized to the precision required, and the programmer specified that precision by the choice of data types.

In keeping with the SIMD interprocessor communication model, a runtime hardware library was built to implement global communications instructions such as min/max and a small set of logic operations, which were performed bit-serially by the Splash 2 control FPGA.

The dbC language and compiler thus combined a parallel language, traditional compiler transformations, and a simple form of hardware synthesis to generate a control program and FPGA bitstream for the Splash system.

To illustrate the dbC data parallel language and its mapping onto FPGAs, Figure 10.4 expands on the vector multiply example in Section 10.2. Line 3 illustrates the use of bit field syntax to define a new data type, a 24-bit integer, `my_int`. DBC_net_shape (line 6) is a predefined variable used to set the number of processors and their shape. (On Splash, the shape was limited to a linear array.) The vector multiply is divided into two sections. First there is a loop over the blocks of vectors resident on each PE (lines 31–34). The control unit handles the loop control and iteratively issues instructions in the loop body to the SIMD array. The += operation on line 33 is executed by each PE and accumulates the partial product into the `poly` variable `res`.

```
1    #define ISIZE 24
2
3    typedef poly int my_int:ISIZE;
4
5    /* specify 64 processors in a linear array */
6    unsigned in DBC_net_shape[1] = {64};
7
8    /* Each PE can hold up to 500 elements of the vector,
9       so maximum vector size is 500*64                 */
10
11   #define VEC_MAX 500
12   void main() {
13
14     /* vectors A, B, res are on each PE */
15     poly my_int A[VEC_MAX];
16     poly my_int B[VEC_MAX];
17     poly my_int res[VEC_MAX];
18
19     /* r, c, and vec_size are on the control unit */
20     mono unsigned long long int r;
21     mono int c;
22     mono int vec_size;
23     int i;
24
25     /* first initialize vec_size, vectors A and B, constant c */
26
27     /* next, compute vector multiply on the vector elements up to
28        the index that evenly divide the total number of PEs.    */
29
30     res = 0;
31     for (i=0; i<vec_size/DBC_nproc; i++) {
32       A[i] = A[i] * c;
33       res += A[i] * B[i];
34     }
35
36     /* now multiply the remaining elements of the vectors */
37
38     if (DBC_iproc < vec_size % DBC_nproc) {
39       A[i] = A[i] * c;
40       res += A[i]*B[i];
41     }
42
43     r += res;
44
45     /* continue computation */
46
47   }
```

FIGURE 10.4 ■ A vector multiply program in dbC.

The second section of code finishes the multiplication of final residue, potentially on a smaller number of PEs (lines 38–41). The if statement on line 38 sets the predicate mask bit to true in each PE whose processor number is less than the number of remaining elements of the vectors, and to false in all the other

PEs. The comparison of `vec_size` to `DBC_nproc` involves only `mono` variables and so is performed on the control unit and sent to the PE array as a constant in the instruction. Line 43 is a global accumulation of intermediate results from each PE into the control unit variable `r`.

There are some unique aspects to compiling SIMD algorithms to FPGA-based reconfigurable computers. For one, the compiler can synthesize an instruction set customized to the application. In our example, there need be only three instructions:

- `A[i] = A[i] * c; res += A[i] * b[i];`
- mask bit ← DBC iproc < vec size % DBC nproc
- `r += res;`

For another, the ALU can be customized to the operations used in the code. In this example, only a 24-bit multiplier, adder, and comparator are required. If different precision is needed, the PE can be resynthesized. In fact, if floating-point data types are necessary, floating-point, rather than integer arithmetic units can be instantiated. Finally, the PE array can be easily resynthesized to hold more or fewer PEs.

10.5   VARIATIONS OF SIMD/VECTOR COMPUTING

The SIMD programming model is attractive in its simplicity of parallel operation. There is a single instruction stream; inter-PE communication is global and synchronous; and the global reduction operations allow operations across the entire PE array. However, SIMD also has some deficiencies. Often there are cases in which some PEs perform slightly different operations than others, particularly with boundary conditions. The SIMD model requires that all PEs participate in all alternatives. This can result in poor performance in the presence of deeply nested `if` statements, as the instruction stream follows all possible control flows. For this reason, SIMD processing is often used in conjunction with other programming models on reconfigurable computers.

10.5.1   Multiple SIMD Engines

It is possible to map multiple SIMD engines onto an FPGA, with a controller for each engine synthesized in the reconfigurable logic. Such a system is illustrated in Figure 10.5. This capability was offered by the Fabric-based System [9], and demonstrated on a system-on-a-chip using the Altera Excalibur FPGA. In this framework, the on-chip microprocessor controls a flexible, runtime reconfigurable computing fabric of mesh-connected processing cells. Each cell has a separate local data memory and a small program memory that holds DSP-like microcode instructions. In SIMD mode, a group of cells all contain the same program and are sequenced through it by a customized control unit that is also in the reconfigurable logic.

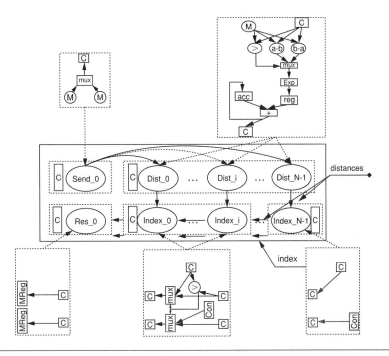

FIGURE 10.5 ■ An extended SIMD architecture.

The fabric illustrated in Figure 10.5 shows a multi-SIMD implementation of a compute-intensive kernel of the K-Means clustering algorithm. In this iterative data-mining algorithm, the dataset is partitioned into a predetermined number of classes. Initially, elements of the dataset are randomly assigned to classes, and a center C_i (where i ranges over the number of classes) of each class is computed. Then, for each element E_j (j ranges over the number of data elements) and each class C_i, the distance between E_j and C_i is computed. E_j is moved to the class closest to it in the distance metric, and the process repeats either for a fixed number of iterations or until there is no change from the previous iteration. In the example, the distance metric is $|E_j - C_i|$ (i.e., the absolute value [10] is used).

This design (Figure 10.5) implements the distance calculation, in which the distance between E_j and C_i is computed, and finds the class closest to each element E_j. There are five cell types—send, distance calculation, two for index calculation, and receive—each with its own control unit (labeled "C" in the figure). The "Dist" SIMD engine controls the distance calculation PEs; the "Index" SIMD engine, the index calculation PEs. The last index calculation has its own controller because its interconnect is slightly different from the others. Similarly, the send and receive cells have unique datapaths, so each has a dedicated controller.

In the figure, the computation is parallelized across classes, with one distance/index pair per class. A microprocessor controls the outer K-Means loop and updates class centers by loading new values into the Send_0 cell's local memory. Send_0 reads from one of two memories and sends the data element out its communication channel. This allows the microprocessor to load one memory while the fabric is computing with the other. The distance calculation cells compute the distance between the pixel and the class centers. Their datapath is shown in the upper right box. The index calculation cells calculate the index of the class having the minimum distance to the pixel (the middle and right boxes at the bottom). The receive cell (Res_0) stores the class index corresponding to the minimum distance. It accepts data from two channels and writes into two memories.

Thus, an efficient parallel architecture for the K-Means clustering algorithm combines two SIMD arrays with three additional specialized processing units and a control microprocessor.

10.5.2 A Multi-SIMD Coarse-grained Array

In addition to FPGA-based data parallel systems, the Morphosys system [11] was designed as a coarse-grained SIMD array. Morphosys was an 8×8 array of reconfigurable logic cells controlled by a small RISC processor. Each row or column of the array operated in SIMD mode, executing the same instruction on different data instances. The RISC processor could dynamically load configurations into the array on a row/column granularity. This versatility in data parallelism and dynamic reconfiguration made it possible to map a combination of data parallel and control parallel algorithms onto Morphosys.

10.5.3 SPMD Model

A popular generalization of SIMD is the Single Program Multiple Data (SPMD) model (see Single program multiple data subsection of Section 5.2.4 and [12]) in which all processes independently execute the same program and can take different paths through it. SPMD differs from SIMD in that, rather than execute a global, synchronized communication step, programs use send/receive message passing to communicate with each other, and may employ other synchronization primitives such as barrier synchronization, in which each process waits at the barrier until all processes have reached it in their control flow.

SPMD is most common in parallel processing clusters. However, elements of it have also been adapted to FPGA computing. For example, in the Streams-C language, a CSP-like [13] parallel programming language for FPGAs [14], the programmer can define a parallel processor composed of an "array of processes," with each having the same hardware logic and control program, operating independently from the others, and using unidirectional channels to communicate.

10.6 PIPELINED SIMD/VECTOR PROCESSING

Pipeline processing can often be incorporated into SIMD/vector reconfigurable computing. This technique in essence synthesizes customized vector units that are replicated on the FPGA. Pipelined SIMD processing is especially beneficial on

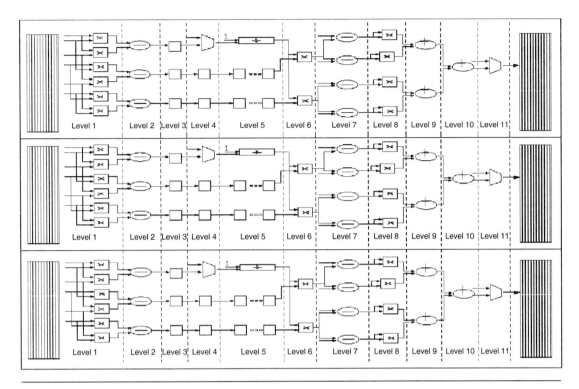

FIGURE 10.6 ■ SIMD with pipelined vector units.

FPGAs when complex arithmetic operations such as floating-point calculations must be performed.

Figure 10.6 shows an SIMD pipelined processing system in reconfigurable logic [15] having three PEs. Three pipelines are instantiated, with each receiving input parameters from a local memory and returning results to another memory. Each pipeline has 11 stages of floating-point operations, and each floating-point operation is, in turn, pipelined, resulting in a 43-stage pipeline. This pipeline implements the inner loop of a Monte Carlo simulation of radiative heat transfer in a two-dimensional chamber. In this case, three single-precision floating-point pipelines could be accommodated on a Xilinx Virtex-II Pro 100.

10.7 SUMMARY

In the SIMD/vector model, a tightly coupled ensemble of processors execute a single instruction stream issued by a control unit. The model can be synthesized onto an FPGA fabric. Having programmable hardware makes it possible to synthesize an instruction set tailored to the specific computations in the application. Customized data widths are naturally accommodated, as there is no fixed-width

ALU. Global combining operations utilizing parallel prefix networks can also be synthesized.

On FPGAs, the SIMD/vector model can be flexibly extended. Collections of SIMD subunits can be assembled and interconnected. This permits portions of the application that map naturally to the SIMD programming model to use it while still allowing other more irregular, control flow-dominated code to be synthesized on the same device. Pipeline processing can also be incorporated into the SIMD/vector processor, increasing the spatial parallelism available to the application.

Acknowledgments   The contributions of Christophe Wolinski to Section 10.5 and of Jan Frigo to Section 10.6 are gratefully acknowledged.

References

[1] W. D. Hillis. *The Connection Machine*, MIT Press, 1989.

[2] R. M. Hord. *Parallel Supercomputing in SIMD Architectures*, CRC Press, 1990.

[3] M. Gokhale, B. Holmes, K. Iobst. Processing in memory: The Terasys massively parallel PIM array. *IEEE Computer* 23–31, 1995.

[4] Clearspeed. *http://www.clearspeed.com/*.

[5] D. I. August, et al. Integrated predicated and speculative execution in the IMPACT EPIC architecture. *International Symposium on Computer Architecture*, 1998.

[6] M. Gokhale, B. Schott. Data parallel C on a reconfigurable logic array. *Journal of Supercomputing* 9(3), 1995.

[7] D. A. Buell, J. M. Arnold, W. J. Kleinfelder (eds.). *Splash 2: FPGAs in a Custom Computing Machine*, Wiley-IEEE Computer Society Press, 1996.

[8] J. R. Allen, K. Kennedy, C. Porterfield, J. Warren. Conversion of control dependence to data dependence. *Proceedings of the 10th ACM SIGACT-SIGPLAN Symposium on Principles of Programming Languages*, 1983.

[9] C. Wolinski, M. Gokhale, K. McCabe. *Polymorphous Fabric-based Systems: Model, Tools, Applications*, Elsevier Science, 2003.

[10] M. Leeser, P. Belanovic, M. Estlick, M. Gokhale, J. Szymanski, J. Theiler. Applying reconfigurable hardware to the analysis of multispectral and hyperspectral imagery. *Proceedings SPIE* 4480, 2001.

[11] H. Singh, M.-H. Lee, G. Lu, F. J. Kurdahi, N. Bagherzadeh, E. M. C. Filho. Morphosys: An integrated reconfigurable system for data-parallel and computation-intensive applications. *IEEE Transactions on Computers* 49(5), 2000.

[12] T. G. Mattson, B. A. Sanders, B. Massingill. *Patterns for Parallel Programming*, Addison-Wesley, 2004.

[13] C. A. R. Hoare. *Communicating Sequential Processes*, Prentice-Hall, 1985.

[14] M. B. Gokhale, J. M. Stone, J. Arnold, M. Kalinowski. Stream-oriented FPGA computing in the Streams-C high level language. *IEEE International Symposium on FPGAs for Custom Computing Machines*, April 2000.

[15] M. Gokhale, J. Frigo, C. Ahrens, J. L. Tripp, R. Minnich. Monte Carlo radiative heat transfer simulation on a reconfigurable computer: An evaluation. *Proceedings Field-Programmable Logic and Applications (FPL)*, 2004.

CHAPTER 11

OPERATING SYSTEM SUPPORT FOR RECONFIGURABLE COMPUTING

Katherine Compton
Department of Electrical and Computer Engineering
University of Wisconsin–Madison

André DeHon
Department of Electrical and Systems Engineering
University of Pennsylvania

As part of the evolution of the field of reconfigurable computing, researchers are increasingly focusing their attention on the issues of integrating reconfigurable computing into multipurpose or general-purpose compute environments. Operating systems (OSs) fill two key roles in computing: simplifying the programming interface through an abstracted programming model and managing shared resources [40]. Both are critical to reconfigurable computing systems, which have in the past suffered from the stigma of programming difficulty as well as from a general focus on single-application systems and nonscalable, nonportable designs.

An operating system, coupled with the proper compilation environment, can simplify the programming of reconfigurable computing systems by providing a well-defined, well-documented compute model that abstracts the structure and capacity of the underlying hardware. This model may explicitly provide constructs for defining hardware tasks (the parts of the application implemented in reconfigurable logic). Alternately, it may be agnostic to the implementation medium. Like the compute fabric, the communication structures between tasks can be abstracted by the compute model to simplify the design process.

Reconfigurable hardware in a reconfigurable computing system is explicitly intended to be a shared resource. Even in a single-application system, hardware may be shared within the application to accelerate different tasks at different times. In a multitasking system, different threads of computation may vie for the hardware resources. The operating system arbitrates hardware use both within and across applications. Furthermore, the OS also provides protection and security to prevent a maliciously or poorly programmed application from compromising the system. Through isolation, the operating system also provides a safe environment where applications can be debugged and inspected without concern that buggy code will affect system stability.

The demands on an operating system for reconfigurable computing include

- Abstraction of the capacity and composition of reconfigurable hardware resources.
- Scheduling use of shared resources across processes.
- Methods for communication and synchronization among hardware tasks and software.
- Protection of the tasks of one process (hardware and software) from those of another.

This chapter discusses the above concepts in terms of both key roles of an operating system: the programmer's view and the management of shared resources.

11.1 HISTORY

Although the concept of operating system support for reconfigurable computing has existed since at least 1996 [6], the idea languished for a time, not quite gaining popular momentum. A significant barrier to operating system development for reconfigurable computing has been the lack of a standard reconfigurable computing hardware platform as a focus for commercial and academic development.

With much of reconfigurable computing research focused on specialized scientific computers or embedded systems, researchers were willing to forgo the abstraction/virtualization benefits provided by an operating system. Instead, application designers (who frequently were the hardware/system designers) would include hardware management operations in their application, explicitly deciding when and where to load particular operations. Manual management leveraged the designer's understanding of the application to provide potentially better performance than an OS layer, discouraging many researchers from dedicating valuable research time to finding a more generic (but possibly less optimized) solution. Yet these systems too would benefit from operating system support to attract a broader group of application designers uninterested in every hardware detail or in micromanaging its use. Even those with suitable hardware backgrounds could then focus their efforts on application (instead of hardware) details.

The increase in demand for operating system support is mirrored, in part, by the increase in complexity of embedded systems and applications. Many single-function devices of the past have evolved into multifunction devices. Cell phones, for example, not only provide basic voice communication, but also capture pictures and video, replay video and audio, browse the Internet, communicate with other electronic devices, and support gaming. A device may execute several of these applications over time, giving it a "general-purpose" flavor within an "embedded" body. Reconfigurable hardware is attractive for devices such as this because of its flexibility to reconfigure to accelerate a variety of applications. The compute-intensive computations of an application execute in hardware to operate faster, using less power (battery) than even an embedded instruction-based processor [34,41].

Even a single-function device may require many different compute-intensive operations. For example, a digital audio player may need to perform error checking, Huffman decoding, IDCT, and other tasks. The reconfigurable hardware that accelerates these operations may, because of cost considerations, be too small to fit all hardware tasks simultaneously. However, an operating system can automatically reconfigure it to implement each task in sequence, as shown in Figure 11.1 (and discussed in Chapters 4, 5, and 9), allowing applications to execute all hardware tasks as if they were persistent in hardware. This provides the application programmer with a virtualized hardware view not hampered by low-level details.

Another contributor to the growing demand for OS support for reconfigurable computing is the increasing difficulty of providing clock speed increases to general-purpose processors [1]. This problem is causing researchers to more closely investigate the potential benefit of reconfigurable computing in general-purpose computers in order to boost performance for compute-intensive applications, including multimedia and communications applications. Using reconfigurable computing in a general-purpose machine requires more

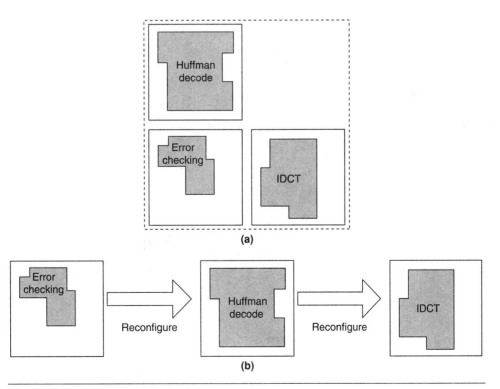

FIGURE 11.1 ■ The abstraction of a large virtual hardware capacity (a) can be implemented on more limited hardware resources using runtime reconfiguration (b).

sophisticated resource management than can be expected from individual applications, further driving the need for OS support.

11.2 ABSTRACTED HARDWARE RESOURCES

The official Commodore *Programmer's Reference Guide* for the C64 computer, originally published in 1982, provides programmers with a great deal of information [10]. For example, it contains a table of the memory map of the C64, including the memory location of the BASIC ROM, the memory-mapped screen output, other memory-mapped I/O, and available program memory locations. It even provides the pinouts of the C64's I/O ports and a schematic of the motherboard—as information to a *programmer*. Much like the preceding evolution of abstracted programming models for mainframe computers [28], increased complexity in personal computing systems later both enabled and required an increase in abstraction.

Today's programming texts do not provide explicit hardware details; instead, for example, they instruct on the use of system calls to provide I/O. One can write an application in a high-level language such as Java or C without knowing even what processor it will run on or how much memory the system will have. For some time, the average software programmer has not needed an understanding of underlying hardware.[1]

To ease programmer burden, the OS provides an abstracted view of hardware—a simpler *virtual* machine as the target for the application. In this virtual machine, the programmer may use library or system calls that provide standardized interfaces to interact with a wide variety of I/O, such as the screen, storage units, and other peripherals. The virtual machine also gives the programmer the appearance of isolation, effectively providing the illusion of dedicated use of the computer's resources [47]. Furthermore, specific details of system resources, such as their quantity and speed, are abstracted. In reality, the operating system is managing these limited physical resources both to allow sharing and to avoid conflicts between applications, each of which was designed as if it were the only one in the system and as if resources were unbounded.

The section that follows discusses the abstraction provided to the programmer by the reconfigurable computing operating system.

11.2.1 Programming Model

Reconfigurable computing provides a mechanism for parallel computation. In some cases, compute-intensive tasks in a sequential application are converted to hardware to capture instruction- or data-level parallelism within the sequential framework. In others, the application is designed explicitly for parallel execution

---

[1] Embedded systems, some graphics, and other specialized programmers may still require some knowledge of hardware to target specific customized architectures or to meet stringent performance requirements.

throughout, with many concurrent hardware (and software) tasks. Chapter 5, Section 5.1, discusses a variety of compute models for reconfigurable computing.

The application developer, the compiler, or the runtime environment can create multiple interchangeable implementations for a task using a separable interface and implementation. This separation is analogous to the delineation between interface and architecture in VHDL (Chapter 6), or the interface and implementation in Java or C++. The operating system can use the interchangeable implementations to bind the computation to a specific resource at runtime, as discussed in Section 11.3. Compiled applications may be a combination of software components and either abstracted hardware components (which undergo the final steps of compilation/synthesis at install time or runtime) or configuration bitstreams that represent hardware tasks.

Depending on the development environment, designers may explicitly partition their application between hardware and software components, or the compiler may automatically partition a high-level application description (Chapter 26). If explicitly partitioned, the hardware components may be specified in a hardware description language (HDL) or in a high-level language with added constructs to specify parallelism, communication, variable bit width, or other hardware-specific features (e.g., Chapter 7).

Implicit partitioning facilitates application portability, as added language constructs for explicit partitioning may not be available for different systems, and hardware descriptions, while more portable than postsynthesis designs, may still depend on specific hardware features. Automatic partitioning and synthesis at compilation time allows an application description to be easily recompiled for different systems (provided that tool support is available).

Because software programmers are not usually hardware designers, and automatic compilation from a high-level language to hardware does not always provide acceptable results, reusable libraries can provide a balance between ease of specification and result quality. Developers can use library calls to perform compute-intensive operations without concerning themselves with how the operation is actually implemented (hardware versus software, hardware and software details). Libraries can contain efficient hardware implementations, potentially at multiple area/performance tradeoff points, and, possibly, software alternatives for a set of related operations [29, 45]. Static linking to such a library could significantly increase application distribution size if multiple implementation options were included to support different execution platforms or to provide runtime binding (as discussed in Section 11.3). A dynamically linked library (DLL) could ameliorate this problem if it were reused by other applications.

A final approach is to use description languages designed to be agnostic to the eventual implementation in hardware, software, or a mix of the two [13, 22]. Much of the automatic partitioning work focuses on high-level languages normally used in software programming, which were created for inherently sequential compute structures (instruction-based processors). Depending on the hardware design, a reconfigurable computing platform has the potential to provide much more parallelism at a variety of levels difficult to describe using a software-centric approach. (These concepts are discussed in more detail in Chapter 5.)

Within an application, the programmer or compiler instantiates a hardware task as a virtual resource and later applies it to the suitable input data. When the operating system scheduler (Section 11.4) decides to allocate hardware to the task, it loads that task onto hardware. For best performance, a single hardware task can (and should) execute repeatedly on successive input data. Depending on the extent of runtime support, the operating system could instantiate multiple copies of the task to increase captured parallelism or time-multiplex multiple tasks if hardware resources are limited, as discussed in Section 11.3. This detail should be abstracted from the user, however, as the amount of resources available for the task can be based on runtime system state, which is likely unknown at design time. One approach (discussed in Chapter 9) is to design the application for *maximum possible* parallelism, with the operating system automatically time-multiplexing the different tasks if insufficient resources are available for the full application simultaneously [13].

11.3   FLEXIBLE BINDING

Because reconfigurable computing systems are inherently flexible, they allow the operating system greater freedom in managing shared resources. The operating system can perform flexible binding of tasks to different types of resources (hardware/software) and, for those bound to hardware, can perform a runtime tradeoff between resource use and performance. Flexible binding allows a single application to be implemented using different resources on different computing platforms, or even on the same platform at different times. Install-time binding decisions are based on the physical characteristics of the system (e.g., the number of programmable resources or memories). Runtime binding, on the other hand, uses information about the physical characteristics along with the current system state (e.g., number of running tasks) to make implementation decisions.

11.3.1   Install Time Binding

Install time binding involves the compilation of applications to a generic representation analogous to an intermediate representation in software compilation. Final synthesis of the generic representation occurs at install time based on the specific resource types available on the system. Install time binding is therefore important to the prevailing economic model of computer purchasing: Spending more money does not (generally) allow one to run *different* applications but rather the *same* applications *better*. Likewise, reconfigurable computing machines should be available at multiple price points, with the capacity/performance/power efficiency of their resources increasing in relation to cost.

Applications running on a more expensive, more powerful machine should perform better than those running on a base machine—but they should still *run* on that base machine. In keeping with this economic discussion, if the reconfigurable hardware in a computer is upgraded, the applications may require reinstallation to leverage the new resources. Depending on the level of abstraction of the specification, this may require CAD processing, which should be performed quickly (and potentially in the background when the system is idle) to avoid system slowdown, as discussed in Section 11.3.3 and Chapter 20. An alternate form of install time binding is dynamic linking to precompiled libraries of hardware (and software) task implementations [29]. Libraries can be compiled for different platforms and distributed with the OS as part of the hardware drivers.

11.3.2 Runtime Binding

Runtime binding is based on both physical characteristics and current system state, and may be performed as part of the scheduling process (Section 11.4). It modifies a task's implementation based on the resources allocated to it during scheduling. The most simple form of runtime binding supports relocation of hardware tasks to different regions of the hardware resources. Relocation (discussed in more detail in Chapter 4) facilitates concurrent residency and/or operation of multiple hardware tasks. It also affects task communication, discussed in Section 11.5.

Another form of runtime binding allows a given task to execute in either hardware or software depending on scheduling decisions [14, 29, 31], discussed in Section 11.4.3. Systems that permit dynamic binding can avoid stalling for hardware availability by proceeding with a software alternative for the task. Dynamic hardware/software binding at runtime requires either a task executable capable of running on hardware or software (e.g., [22]) or a pair of interchangeable hardware and software implementations [13, 14, 29]. To facilitate application design and debug, the two components should have identical functional behavior.

Runtime binding can allow hardware tasks to expand or contract to make use of the resources allocated to them by the scheduler, as discussed in Section 11.4. This ability allows tasks to be implemented on a variety of architectures, from low capacity to high capacity, to promote portability. Hardware tasks can also be modified based on system load, occupying fewer resources in a system under heavy load and more in a system under light load, as shown in Figure 11.2. In (a), task A is using fewer resources because of increased demand by other tasks. In (b), task A rebounds to more resources after task B is no longer needed. Task A's data rate is improved in (b) by the increased parallelism.

A task can occupy fewer resources by time-multiplexing its functionality, or more resources by unrolling or replicating [13]. Time-multiplexing a task requires storage to hold intermediate results between the temporal partitions. Performing time-multiplexing or expansion at runtime can be quite expensive, potentially involving a modified CAD flow, as discussed next in Section 11.3.3. Alternately, implementations at multiple area–performance (or power) tradeoffs can be created at compilation time, eliminating transformation overhead at runtime [14, 29].

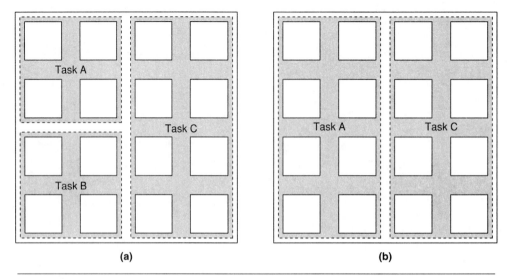

FIGURE 11.2 ■ Flexible binding allows tasks to use a different number of resources based on hardware capacity and resource availability. In this example, Task A can either occupy less area at the expense of performance (a), or achieve a higher data rate at the expense of area (b).

Although a specific palette of implementations reduces OS complexity, it also limits the possibilities of customizing the hardware task to the exact hardware resources available.

11.3.3   Fast CAD for Flexible Binding

Modifying a hardware task after application distribution may require that one or more CAD operations, such as placement, be applied at install time or runtime [13, 39, 43, 44] (e.g., Section 9.4). Unfortunately, CAD algorithms, depending on the problem size, can be quite slow. Chapter 20 discusses a number of fast CAD approaches for hardware task implementation motivated in part by flexible binding. Some possible solutions to accelerating install time or runtime CAD processes include

- Trading solution quality for speed in the CAD process (less optimized solutions).
- Accelerating CAD algorithms in hardware (i.e., implementing CAD hardware tasks on the target reconfigurable computing system).
- Abstracting some of the hardware detail to simplify the problem (applying algorithms to larger blocks of structures, where intragroup CAD decisions are fixed at compile time, and only intergroup CAD decisions are required at install time or runtime, as discussed in Chapter 4 and Section 9.2.4).
- Using a compile time CAD process to generate static information about the hardware task that can be used to accelerate later CAD operations (marking areas of the circuit for replication or time-multiplexing).

11.4 SCHEDULING

Scheduling determines what tasks should use hardware when, and may also decide how many resources (and what type) to allocate to each. These decisions may be made at compile time based on static application information, at runtime based on dynamic system status, or at a combination of the two. The scheduling goals may include maximizing application or system performance, minimizing power consumption, or meeting real-time deadlines. Achieving these goals also requires minimizing the reconfiguration overhead, as discussed in Chapter 4.

Schedulers that include resource allocation also perform flexible binding (Section 11.3), choosing specific resources to implement a given task and potentially altering that task to fit the resources. Flexible binding complicates the scheduler's decision process by expanding the search space. However, expanding the search space with flexible binding also opens the door to scheduling solutions that would otherwise not be possible.

11.4.1 On-demand Scheduling

One of the simplest forms of runtime scheduling is servicing hardware resource requests in the order received, reconfiguring as needed, and queuing requests that cannot yet be serviced [6]. When an application calls a hardware task, its request is sent to the operating system. If the task is preconfigured on hardware, it executes; otherwise, it must be loaded into hardware (configured) prior to execution. If all hardware resources are allocated and in use, the system will queue waiting requests until the resources are freed.

Hardware requests are generally blocking, forcing the requestor to busy-wait until the hardware is available. Then the task is configured and finally executes. Busy-waiting can contribute significantly to reconfigurable computing overhead, as discussed in Chapter 4, but the system (with an appropriate compute model) can use a sleep/wake approach instead of busy-waiting to allow nonblocking threads or processes to use the compute resources in the meantime, hiding some of the configuration latency. Furthermore, runtime binding, discussed in Section 11.3, allows threads or processes that might otherwise be blocked waiting for hardware availability to execute in software instead.

11.4.2 Static Scheduling

Static scheduling relies on analyzed, profiled, or annotated application behavior to determine when an application should request that each hardware task be configured [23, 26, 27]. Static schedulers operate "offline" and thus have a more global view of the task requirements and are able to search a greater expanse of the solution space than a dynamic (online) scheduler. Brute-force or Monte Carlo approaches may therefore be feasible for static schedulers even if prohibitively slow for dynamic scheduling. A static scheduler can also attempt to load hardware tasks prior to their execution to minimize configuration overhead (a technique known as prefetching [24]).

For static scheduling to be profitable, however, both the application task set and resource availability must be highly predictable. An offline schedule does not have access to runtime information and therefore cannot adapt to the current system load. This can prevent the static schedule from computing a good coschedule of multiple independent tasks. Further, if the static schedule is wrong about which tasks must run next, prefetching can actually be detrimental to performance, forcing needed configurations to be evicted and performing extra, unnecessary reconfigurations.

11.4.3 Dynamic Scheduling

Dynamic schedulers use runtime information to aid scheduling. Data-dependent application behavior, system load, and the characteristics of other executing applications can therefore all contribute to (and complicate) schedule computation. Although single-application behavior may be statically predictable in some cases, the interferences arising from multiple simultaneously executing applications lead to an explicitly nondeterministic interleaving of hardware task calls from different applications.

As a simplification, some schedulers use a window-based approach, dividing time into windows and solving the scheduling problem for each [14, 27, 31]. Figure 11.3 illustrates the timing of window-based scheduling. Once the scheduler determines which tasks should be implemented in hardware, the hardware must be reconfigured to implement them. After reconfiguration, the hardware can execute until the next reconfiguration phase in the following window. To minimize the impact of scheduling overhead, the window should be "large" compared to the time required to compute the schedule and perform reconfiguration. However, it should also be small enough to capture current system behavior for use in the scheduling decision. Statistics from the previous interval (or multiple previous intervals) provide recent behavior information to the scheduler.

A "frontier" dynamic scheduler [27] uses application dataflow and task execution information from the previous interval (such as which tasks executed and at what data rate) to compute the new schedule for the next interval. Input data availability and allocatable output space information are requirements for task scheduling and are used to compute the relative priority of tasks. The scheduler can use resource availability and information on data rate (of the considered task

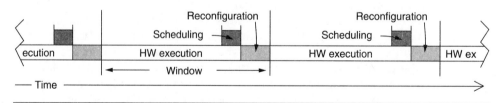

FIGURE 11.3 ■ A dynamic scheduler can divide time into a series of windows, each with its own scheduling problem.

and ones it communicates with) to choose a flexible binding implementation. This approach matches a streaming communication approach (Chapter 9), where good scheduling is necessary to minimize the buffering requirements between tasks. Flexible binding allows the frontier scheduler to time-multiplex or replicate tasks to balance the data rate between one task and those adjacent [27].

Runtime information, such as the frequency of task use in the prior interval and task performance information, also can be used without considering the dataflow of the executing applications. In each window, hardware resources can be treated as a knapsack, which the scheduler tries to pack with the greatest overall value [14]. Each task is assigned a "value" based on performance or power consumption and a "cost" based on hardware area requirements. Tasks not scheduled to hardware execute with lower performance in software to avoid starving less valued tasks. By including multiple implementations of a task with different values/costs, the scheduler can also use dynamic binding to adapt task implementations based on resource availability/demand [14, 27]. The knapsack problem can be solved either heuristically or, if the problem size is small enough, exactly.

11.4.4 Quasi-static Scheduling

A purely dynamic scheduler only considers information available at runtime and loses the opportunity to optimize based on known application characteristics. In contrast, quasi-static scheduling combines dynamic system and application information with static application analysis. Using dynamic management with static analysis enables the scheduler to more accurately predict near-future hardware task needs (and, just as important, which tasks will *not* be needed) [24, 27]. Quasi-static scheduling also accelerates the scheduling process by reducing the dynamic scheduler's burden.

For example, static analysis can provide the ordering of tasks within an application, timing estimates for when the tasks will be executed relative to one another, data rate analysis of different possible time-multiplexing/replications of the tasks, and intertask communication resource requirements. The runtime scheduler can then use dynamic scheduling techniques, but prune the solution space based on static analysis information to arrive at an improved solution more quickly. Dynamic scheduling can also allow otherwise statically scheduled applications to reuse hardware tasks configured for other applications to reduce configuration costs [35].

11.4.5 Real-time Scheduling

Scheduling for real-time systems considers task deadlines rather than general performance. Hard deadlines must be met within the specified time or the system has failed. An example of a hard deadline would be triggering operation of strictly timed automotive engine components. Soft deadlines must be generally met for acceptable use, but missing one or even a few is not mission-critical. An example of missing a soft deadline would be dropping a frame in real-time video.

Missing a soft deadline may not invalidate the computation, but it may degrade the application in some way. This type of operation is common in embedded systems. Indeed, real-time systems and their operating systems are the focus of much research [20, 23].

One approach to implementing reconfigurable real-time systems is to leverage the vast real-time research effort by wrapping hardware tasks with a thread interface [4]. Such a system includes a generic hardware-based scheduler for both hardware and software threads using whatever scheduling algorithm is implemented within it. Synchronization details of this approach are presented in Section 11.6.1.

Alternately, the scheduling algorithm can be tailored specifically to reconfigurable computing, using information about hardware capacity, task hardware requirements, and task configuration time in addition to deadline information [39, 43]. For example, tasks that can fit in a currently available area are more likely to be guaranteed to meet a deadline than are those that require reconfiguration due to reconfiguration overhead. If sufficient resources are free, but are distributed throughout the hardware, defragmentation may be required (see Chapter 4) to consolidate sufficient free space for the incoming task.

The time required for this process affects the ability of the system to meet the task's deadline. If free space is not available even with defragmentation, the task may be rejected or its deadline not guaranteed. The task could meet the deadline if one or more other tasks executing on hardware complete with enough time left to permit configuration and execution of the new task before its deadline expires. Alternately, a task implemented in hardware may be preempted (see next section) in favor of an incoming task if the latter has higher priority [43].

11.4.6 Preemption

A scheduler may use preemption to reallocate hardware to a "more desirable" task, whether based on meeting specific deadlines in a real-time system, based on the relative priority of different tasks in a performance-based system, or to allow a more balanced use of hardware in the presence of long-executing tasks [2, 18, 31, 43]. The configuration data for a given task holds some of the required information, such as circuit structure, and possibly initial values for embedded memories. However, any values in state-holding elements that change in response to hardware operation are not included. Therefore, the complete "saved state" for preempting a hardware task is a combination of its configuration data and the current values of any state-holding elements modified during execution. Provided a hardware interface to this information is available, the operating system can read the current state to store in memory and later load it back into hardware when needed.

Preemption is complicated by flexible binding if the implementation saved does not match the implementation resumed. The sizes of configuration data and the number of state-holding elements may not match between different implementations. Therefore, systems supporting flexible binding and preemption must save an abstracted view of task state.

11.5 COMMUNICATION

A key feature of communication abstractions is that they are, in fact, abstractions. Although certain abstractions may map well to specific hardware architectures (and vice versa), the use of one in particular does not necessarily require a particular hardware structure (or vice versa). For example, a message-passing abstraction could be implemented on a shared memory architecture, or a shared memory abstraction could be implemented on top of a message-passing architecture. Library calls and the compilation environment map communication abstractions to the actual implementation, and the operating system manages the implementation. The abstractions, however, allow the programmer to ignore implementation details and focus on efficient specification. The following subsections discuss a number of abstractions and their operating system requirements, along with other communication issues requiring operating system intervention.

11.5.1 Communication Styles

When our applications are composed from multiple, concurrent tasks (e.g., threads, hardware tasks, software tasks, operators), the tasks must often exchange intermediate data in order to solve the entire problem. Specifying this communication can be highly error prone and performance critical. The form in which the communication is specified should match both the natural compute model (see Section 5.1) for the application and the nature of the communication required.

Shared memory

Shared memory is an implicit form of communication motivated by certain implementations where tasks share a common memory pool (Single memory pool subsection of Section 5.1.4) and address space, or share a mapped portion of an address space (Section 11.5.2). Here, the semantics are that each task sees the same image of memory. If one task writes to the image, another should be able to see the values written to the memory. In this way, the memory addresses serve as named locations through which values can be exchanged among tasks.

Uniprocessor operating system developers see shared memory as a particularly efficient way of communicating between tasks. In multithreaded environments where tasks are interleaved in time on the same processor, shared memory segments within the single memory hierarchy allow multiple tasks to share data without an explicit need for data to be copied between the routines. This can minimize the overhead for data communication between tasks. Without caches, shared bus multiprocessing systems with a common main memory would exhibit a similar efficiency. Local caches potentially complicate the picture. However, good architecture and engineering can maintain this abstraction efficiently in the common case, at the cost of additional hardware to support cache coherence.

A reconfigurable computing architecture may nevertheless more closely mirror, at the chip or board level, the organization of a large, distributed memory system.

Here, data may actually need to be copied between distant memories, complicating the shared memory abstraction. The result is both significant hardware overhead to support the model and, often, significant communication time overhead beyond what would be required to move the data between the producer and the consumer. Furthermore, synchronization between shared memory threads/tasks (Section 11.6.1) is a common source of application errors, leading some to question the viability of this model for capturing larger-scale parallelism [21, 36].

Method calls

As the previous section suggested, word-level shared memory is a very low-level form of implicit communication that is prone to synchronization issues. Implementing the abstraction can increase hardware requirements in architectures containing distributed memories. In modern object-oriented systems, particularly when each object may itself be an independent thread, a higher-level communication technique is method calls between objects or operators (see Section 5.1.2). The method call on the object explicitly states the intended destination for the data; further, the object method provides additional semantic information to the receiver about what the data means. As long as object methods are serialized on each object, method invocation can be atomic, providing a natural mechanism for consistent updates to object state. In some cases, method calls can eliminate the need for a hardware task to communicate directly with memory, allowing many lightweight, reconfigurable operators to avoid the expense of a memory interface unit.

When the destination object is running on hardware that is physically distinct from the sending object, the method invocation, and the communication in general, requires data to be routed from the sending to the receiving hardware. This is true even in a shared memory implementation—the method call style simply makes this communication explicit. However, when the objects share the same physical memory, method call communication can still occur through shared memory.

Message passing (discussed in the Message passing subsection of Section 5.2.6) is a form of method call communication, as is remote procedure call [30]. MPI [38] is a well-developed standard for message passing, and reconfigurable computers have been built to interface with standard MPI communications [32]. However, MPI itself is fairly heavyweight, and its overhead may be too high for finer-grained composition of tasks and operators. Lighter-weight message passing designed for on-chip reconfigurable applications has been developed [31], as have remote procedure call interfaces for symmetric use between processors and reconfigurable logic [8].

Streams

While method invocation is an explicit communication mechanism, it is still dynamic and does not provide the OS with advanced warning about which tasks will communicate and when. Further, the actual graph of communication remains implicit in the object call structure. A more explicit form of communication is to represent the graph structure for task communications and share that information with the operating system. This is similar to the use of pipes or streams in conventional software multi-threading to represent persistent communication links between communicating threads. The reconfigurable computing dataflow models in Section 5.1.3, and the streaming dataflow programming approaches in Chapters 8 and 9 provide some ways to capture these communication graphs. Data-centric compute models (Section 5.1.6) do so as well.

Streams (pipes, channels) are persistent, unidirectional links between tasks (software or hardware) that pass data or control information. Tasks receive available data from one or more input streams and write the results of their computation to one or more output streams [9, 13]. A stream may buffer data in a FIFO manner between the producer and consumer to allow them to run independently of each other and minimize the effects of both reconfiguration and communication latency. Figure 11.4 is an example that shows abstract use of streams (a) and its implementation on a streaming architecture (b). Sections 5.1.3 and 5.2.1 and Chapter 9 present in-depth discussions of streaming models and architectures.

Because the structure of communication (producer–consumer) is explicit, the operating system is able to more easily make intelligent decisions about where to place tasks to promote physical locality, and the scheduler is able to better choose when to run them. For example, if a stream between a producer and consumer is empty or near empty, the scheduler knows that it is more profitable to run the producer than the consumer. A very full stream would imply the opposite.

The persistence of abstract streams allows us to separate the part of communication that specifies the location (source/destination) of data from the part

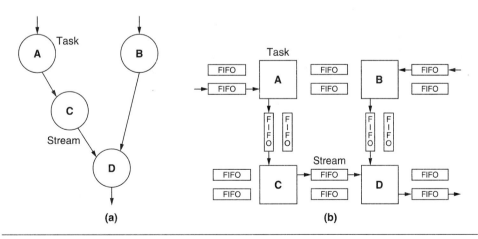

(a)   **(b)**

FIGURE 11.4 ■ A stream abstraction defines application dataflow (a); a streaming architecture can implement the streams between tasks using FIFOs (b).

that provides or uses it. For regular communications, this brings the destination specification out of the inner loop of communication, reducing communication overhead. For spatial, reconfigurable datapaths, it allows a stronger correlation between the abstraction and implementation of communication between currently-executing hardware tasks, reducing overhead. The stream can be implemented with simple wires, or a FIFO, between the producer and consumer. Nonetheless, although specifying, allocating, and setting up the stream can be expensive, for heavily used, persistent communications, the long use over time amortizes the cost of stream setup. Short communication sequences or communications to short-lived tasks may not be able to amortize this cost and may be better served with a different communication scheme.

Stream abstraction can be implemented efficiently on a variety of physical communication structures. It can be supported efficiently on a shared memory system with the use of a well-designed and well-tested queue object library that encapsulates the explicit synchronization necessary to implement the stream. Encapsulation is a huge benefit in that it allows one highly trained system programmer to work out a robust locking discipline that can then be used by other programmers with less (or no) experience with synchronization primitives. Stream data can be packed into efficient, longer messages on packet-switched, message-passing systems, or it can be supported by concurrent direct memory access (DMA) data transfers. A message-passing implementation of a stream abstraction can also be extended across the Internet using TCP/IP connections. As noted earlier in this section and elaborated in Chapter 9, when the source and the sink are coresident, the stream can reduce to a direct, configured connection between tasks, requiring minimum hardware and latency overhead during operation.

11.5.2 Virtual Memory

Software applications for general-purpose systems use a virtual memory abstraction, enabled by a combination of hardware and software, to simplify the programming model and to provide isolation (protection) from other processes. Reconfigurable computing systems require this abstraction for the same reasons.

To avoid the complexities of virtual address translation in reconfigurable hardware, the reconfigurable computing system designer may place the burden of memory communication on host processor resources, which already support virtual memory. When the reconfigurable unit is tightly coupled with a processor, it can explicitly share the processor's memory management unit (MMU) [18]. Alternately, the processor can perform memory accesses for a hardware task, feeding data to the task through a dedicated buffer structure [15]. The drawback of using the processor in this fashion is a lack of efficiency. The processor is consigned to acting as an overqualified memory controller, which reduces its availability for parallel computation.

To leverage the processor's address translation capability (including translation lookaside buffer [TLB] miss processing and page fault handling) and at the same time remove the processor from the inner memory access loop, a DMA-style approach can be used. The processor provides hardware with translated physical addresses for the needed virtual addresses. User hardware should not, however, be able to issue these accesses directly, as it could potentially issue memory requests to other physical addresses outside the task's virtual memory space. An architectural solution to this problem is to add one or more hardware memory address generators that are guaranteed to abide by the virtual memory abstraction. The address generator may require the processor to translate all addresses, or it potentially can combine offsets from the hardware task with a translated page or segment base address to further reduce processor involvement.

Finally, a dedicated hardware MMU can directly translate virtual addresses to physical ones [16, 42]. It maintains its own copy of the TLB for address lookups. TLB misses can be handled either by the hardware MMU itself or by interrupting a processor to walk the page table. In this arrangement, page faults are handled by the operating system, which updates the hardware MMU's TLB based on the result.

11.5.3   I/O

Finally, in addition to communicating with other tasks, a hardware task may need to communicate with system I/O. Libraries abstract the hardware interfaces for the programmer [11] (as discussed in Chapter 8). However, I/O standards are continually evolving and can do so during the lifetime of a given application. The operating system, through I/O device drivers, can support changing I/O standards by providing these libraries in dynamically linked form so that they can be updated and expanded without requiring any changes to the applications in order to use them.

11.5.4   Uncertain Communication Latency

Communication between tasks (and memory) is subject to uncertain latencies for a number of reasons. One common example in many traditional computing systems is the uncertain latency of memory access due to location in the memory hierarchy and memory contention. Reconfigurable computing systems share this problem. However, those that support flexible binding (Section 11.3) are subject to additional sources of uncertainty, as different implementations of a given task have different data rates. Even given the same implementation of a hardware task, its location on hardware can affect the latency of communication between it and other tasks. Depending on the physical implementation of the routing network between physical task locations, some locations may be "closer" than others.

Although this could create variable clock rates depending on task locations, the problem is easily addressed using pipelined interconnect and data presence (discussed in the Data presence subsection of Section 5.2.1 and in Chapter 9). The same set of data presence techniques also support flexible binding where a task implemented in hardware can have a much higher data rate than one implemented in software.

11.6   SYNCHRONIZATION

Reconfigurable computing applications are generally concurrent, executing one or more hardware tasks in parallel along with one or more software tasks. Therefore, they require synchronization between tasks. A number of factors complicate synchronization in reconfigurable computing. First, reconfigurable computing applications can leverage a variety of parallelism types (instruction-level, data-level, task-level, pipeline-level) to a greater degree than software-only applications can, as discussed in Chapter 5. More parallelism exacerbates the already difficult process of concurrent programming [33]. Furthermore, runtime binding and placement can affect communication source/destination locations and task data rate even after program specification and compilation. Given this degree of parallelism and uncertainty, effective synchronization techniques are critical to reconfigurable computing application design and performance.

These effects are mitigated to some extent by the fact that reconfigurable computations and data often use distinct resources with less potential sharing; this can often clarify the synchronization required and permits more coarse-grained resource locking. Depending on the abstraction employed, synchronization may be controlled explicitly by the programmer or implicitly by the operating system or underlying hardware.

11.6.1   Explicit Synchronization

Synchronization between tasks can be performed explicitly through abstractions similar or identical to those used in software-only multi-threaded programming. This approach is particularly appealing in embedded systems, where application designers may have used a shared memory multi-threaded model more widely than the average general-purpose computer programmer would have. As in software-only shared memory applications, constructs such as locks and semaphores can protect access to shared resources to avoid race conditions.

We can impose thread-style interfaces on hardware tasks [4, 7, 42]. The thread interface requests/releases a semaphore and forces hardware to stall or sleep while waiting to acquire one. Memory structures within the hardware must be augmented with a table to hold semaphore information. This has the advantage of hiding details of the hardware task implementation from the communicating thread but at the cost of logic overhead to interface hardware with the shared memory pool that holds the synchronization address.

11.6.2   Implicit Synchronization

Low-level, thread-style synchronization, already prone to design error and debug difficulty, is likely to become even more difficult to implement correctly as the degree of parallelism required to achieve demanded performance increases [21, 36]. Instead, designers could turn to abstractions that provide more explicit parallelism with implicit synchronization.

To efficiently use our reconfigurable resources, we typically provide them with large blocks of data at a time contained in contiguous memory addresses (e.g., an image frame). Thus, it is natural to give exclusive ownership of a memory block to a hardware task during its execution. By combining this locking with the instantiation semantics for the operation, we can automate locking to prevent the programmer from having to manage it explicitly. This can even be supported by hardware using a scoreboarding technique similar to the ones used to prevent hazards in aggressive processor pipelines [19].

Synchronization is implicit in all forms of dataflow (Chapter 5, Section 5.1.3). The semantics of its operation are based on data arrival, not sequential timing, which makes proper synchronization the job of the compiler, the hardware, and the runtime system rather than the programmer. In streaming dataflow, stream data comes with data presence information (see Section 11.5.1 and Chapter 9). In general dataflow, I-structures allow fine-grained synchronization and concurrent cooperation on common data structures [5].

11.6.3 Deadlock Prevention

Whether synchronization is implicit or explicit, the need for it in a concurrent application presents the unfortunate opportunity for deadlock. Essentially, one or more tasks in the application may not be able to continue because they are waiting on other tasks. When the waiting set forms a cycle, the system will never be able to make forward progress. However, because deadlock can arise only when a task needs exclusive access to multiple resources simultaneously, many hardware tasks will work on a single, coarse-grained set of data at a time, avoiding this issue. Nonetheless, it is common for a hardware task to need multiple resources (e.g., one or more input buffers and an output buffer).

A common method to prevent deadlock is to force tasks to acquire all of their resources in a canonically ordered sequence. This way we avoid deadlock by never creating a cyclic dependence that could lead to it. With implicit and higher-level locking, runtime support mechanisms can provide the ordering guarantee. This demands that we establish a canonical ordering for all resources that might be locked, both in hardware and in memory locations, and use it uniformly throughout the system.

11.7 PROTECTION

Modern computing systems all share a need for protection from processes (intentionally or unintentionally) interfering with one another. This protection is critical for dealing with not only maliciously coded applications but also poorly programmed ones. During the application development process, isolation is critical because it allows designers to test and inspect their implementations. Development is significantly more complicated if bugs can bring down the development system, destroying state information critical to the debugging process. The same need for protection holds for reconfigurable computing systems. The operating system must prevent processes from using hardware inappropriately or from interfering with or intercepting communication between tasks (hardware or software) of other processes. Some of these responsibilities fall to the scheduler—preventing task resource starvation is one example; others fall to the hardware allocator (which may be part of the scheduler); still others fall to the system's hardware interface.

11.7.1 Hardware Protection

Implementing user tasks as hardware circuits in the reconfigurable fabric introduces a major security flaw unfathomable to the average software user or developer. Depending on the underlying hardware design, a hardware task can cause a short circuit, permanently damaging the computing system. Therefore, either the hardware structure itself must prevent the possibility of short circuits [3, 46] or the operating system must screen user hardware and prohibit any implementations that cannot be proven to be free of short circuits.

Even if an individual task does not cause a short circuit, incorrectly allocating hardware resources to more than one task can create one. That is why the allocation process must physically separate tasks [44]. Figure 11.5 shows a generic FPGA architecture with resources allocated to two different tasks (separated by the heavy dashed line). Wires shown in bold cross the boundaries between tasks, causing potential conflicts. Resources that cross task boundaries can be allocated to no more than one task unless they are part of intertask communication (discussed in the next section). This restriction also prevents maliciously designed tasks from "snooping" communication paths to which they should not have access (also discussed in the next section).

General FPGA structures complicate the task interference problem by having large numbers of extremely flexible routing structures that may span large distances in the hardware. In contrast, some architectures designed specifically for

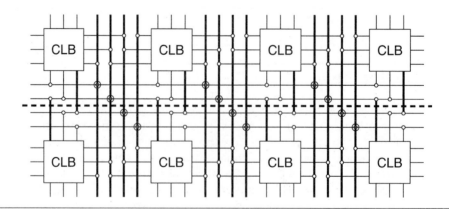

FIGURE 11.5 ■ A generic FPGA architecture may have resources (*bold lines*) that cross the boundary (*dashed line*) between two hardware tasks.

reconfigurable computing, such as SCORE (Chapter 9 and [13]) and PipeRench (Chapter 2, Section 2.1.2, and [17]), are composed of sets of reconfigurable logic (pages/blocks/stages) that are more self-contained, and are the atomic hardware unit for task allocation. Restricted, well-structured connections between these blocks simplify the problem of preventing cross-task interference.

11.7.2 Intertask Communication

As discussed in Section 11.5.2, virtual memory provides each process with a separate address space, preventing one process from accessing the memory space of another. For the same reason, we must provide similar isolation for other forms of communication.

Point-to-point communication, too, can provide isolation if we can guarantee that tasks can only access communication paths owned by their process. The programming model may support this view, but simply trusting it would be equivalent to trusting that compilers will not allow hackers to create viruses. The system (hardware and operating system) must ensure that the isolation model is enforced.

To provide isolation, the system could allow only indirect intertask communication through shared virtual memory [15, 16]. However, this approach can introduce significant communication latencies if both tasks are present in hardware close to one another, but communicate through a relatively distant memory hierarchy acting as intermediary. Safe direct on-hardware intertask communication can be implemented by treating intertask communication routing as special resources that cannot be self-allocated by a hardware task description. Instead, the operating system must allocate these resources when configuring the related tasks onto hardware [13]. By removing user control over allocation of these resources, the isolation the programming model provides is implemented by the operating system. This is much like how only the OS is allowed to manipulate the page tables and TLBs that support the virtual memory abstraction.

11.7.3 Task Configuration Protection

The loading of tasks into hardware must be restricted to the operating system to ensure that the OS has an accurate view of hardware for scheduling/allocation decisions and to enforce hardware and communication protection as discussed previously. Hardware communication paths must therefore be accessible only to OS kernel-level processes. An operating system can isolate task addressability by employing a model akin to virtual memory, where each process can address its own tasks only. Any tables of task information used by the operating system in this case include the process ID as part of the task ID. Any requests for task access are within the user task ID space. Isolation not only prevents processes from triggering the execution, reconfiguring, removing, or altering of tasks from another process, but it also reinforces the abstraction that processes have the hardware to themselves.

11.8 SUMMARY

The primary role of the operating system is to provide abstraction. Abstraction benefits the application designer in the following ways:

- By simplifying the design process to remove the burden of low-level details.
- By allowing the application to run on various hardware platforms and capacities.
- By implementing a virtual machine for each application to prevent interference between them.

This chapter presented the needs, opportunities, benefits, and techniques surrounding the abstraction of reconfigurable resources. It also showed how abstraction affects the application specification process, and discussed the issues involved in implementing these abstractions in the operating system and architecture of the reconfigurable computing system.

References

[1] V. Agarwal, M. S. Hrishikesh, S. W. Keckler, D. Buger. Clock rate versus IPC: The end of the road for conventional microarchitectures. *International Conference on Computer Architecture*, 2000.

[2] A. Ahmadinia, C. Bobda, D. Koch, M. Majer, J. Teich. Task scheduling for heterogeneous reconfigurable computers. *Symposium on Integrated Circuits and System Design*, 2004.

[3] R. Amerson, R. Carter, W. Culbertson, P. Kuekes, G. Snider, L. Albertson. Plasma: An FPGA for million gate systems. *ACM International Symposium on Field-Programmable Gate Arrays*, 1996.

[4] D. Andrews, D. Niehaus, R. Jidin. Implementing the thread programming model on hybrid FPGA/CPU computational components. *Workshop on Embedded Processor Architectures, International Symposium on Computer Architecture*, 2004.

[5] Arvind, R. S. Nikhil, K. Pingali. I-Structures: Data structures for parallel computing. *Proceedings of the Workshop on Graph Reduction*, 1986.

[6] G. Brebner. A virtual hardware operating system for the Xilinx XC6200. *International Workshop on Field-Programmable Logic and Applications*, 1996.

[7] G. Brebner. Multithreading for logic-centric systems. *International Conference on Field-Programmable Logic and Applications*, 2002.

[8] M. Budiu, M. Mishra, A. Bharambe, S. C. Goldstein. Peer-to-peer hardware–software interfaces for reconfigurable fabrics. *IEEE Symposium on Field-Programmable Custom Computing Machines*, 2002.

[9] M. Butts, A. M. Jones, P. Wasson. A structural object programming model, architecture, chip and tools for reconfigurable computing. *IEEE Symposium on Field-Programmable Custom Computing Machines*, 2007.

[10] Commodore Business Machines. *Commodore 64: Programmer's Reference Guide*, H. W. Sams, 1982.

[11] C. Chang, J. Wawrzynek, R. W. Brodersen. BEE2: A high-end reconfigurable computing system. *IEEE Design and Test of Computers* 22(2), 2005.

[12] M. Dales. Managing a reconfigurable processor in a general purpose workstation environment. *Design, Automation and Test in Europe*, 2003.

[13] A. DeHon, Y. Markovskiy, E. Caspi, M. Chu, R. Huang, S. Perissakis, L. Pozzi, J. Yeh, J. Wawrzynek. Stream computations organized for reconfigurable execution. *Microprocessors and Microsystems* 30, September 2006.

[14] W. Fu, K. Compton. An execution environment for reconfigurable computing. *IEEE Symposium on Field-Programmable Custom Computing Machines*, 2005.

[15] W. Fu, K. Compton. A simulation platform for reconfigurable computing research. *International Conference on Field-Programmable Logic and Applications*, August 2006.

[16] P. Garcia, K. Compton. A reconfigurable hardware interface for a modern computing system. *IEEE Symposium on Field-Programmable Custom Computing Machines*, 2007.

[17] S. C. Goldstein, H. Schmit, M. Moe, M. Budiu, S. Cadambi, R. R. Taylor, R. Laufer. PipeRench: A coprocessor for streaming multimedia acceleration. *International Symposium on Computer Architecture*, May 1999.

[18] J. R. Hauser. *Augmenting a Microprocessor with Reconfigurable Hardware*, Ph.D. thesis, University of California, Berkeley, 2000.

[19] J. A. Jacob, P. Chow. Memory interfacing and instruction specification for reconfigurable processors. *ACM/SIGDA International Symposium on Field-Programmable Gate Arrays*, 1999.

[20] H. Koptez. *Real-Time Systems: Design Principles for Distributed Embedded Applications*, Kluwer Academic Publishers, 1997.

[21] E. Lee. The problem with threads. *Computer* 39(5), May 2006.

[22] B. Levine, H. Schmit. Efficient application representation for HASTE: Hybrid architectures with a single, transformable executable. *IEEE Symposium on Field-Programmable Custom Computing Machines*, 2003.

[23] Z. Li, K. Compton, S. Hauck. Configuration caching management techniques for reconfigurable computing. *IEEE Symposium on FPGAs for Custom Computing Machines*, 2000.

[24] Z. Li, S. Hauck. Configuration prefetching techniques for partial reconfigurable coprocessor with relocation and defragmentation. *ACM/SIGDA Symposium on Field-Programmable Gate Arrays*, 2002.

[25] J. W. S. Liu. *Real Time Systems*, Prentice-Hall, 2000.

[26] R. Maestre, F. J. Kurdahi, M. Fernández, R. Hermida, N. Bagherzadeh, H. Singh. A framework for reconfigurable computing: Task scheduling and context management. *IEEE Transactions on VLSI* 9(6), December 2001.

[27] Y. Markovskiy, E. Caspi, R. Huang, J. Yeh, M. Chu, J. Wawrzynek, A. DeHon. Analysis of quasi-static scheduling techniques in a virtualized reconfigurable machine. *ACM/SIGDA International Symposium on Field-Programmable Gate Arrays*, 2002.

[28] G. H. Mealy. The functional structure of OS/360, Part I: Introductory survey. *IBM Systems Journal* 6(1), 1966.

[29] N. Moore, A. Conti, M. Leeser, L. S. King. Writing portable applications that dynamically bind at run time to reconfigurable hardware. *IEEE Symposium on Field-Programmable Custom Computing Machines*, 2007.

[30] B. J. Nelson. *Remote Procedure Call*, Xerox Palo Alto Research Center technical report, 1981.

[31] V. Nollet, P. Coene, D. Verkest, S. Vernalde, R. Lauwereins. Designing an operating system for a heterogeneous reconfigurable SoC. *Proceedings of the Reconfigurable Architectures Workshop*, 2003.

[32] A. Patel, C. A. Madill, M. Saldana, C. Comis, R. Pomes, P. Chow. A scalable FPGA-based multiprocessor. *IEEE Symposium on Field-Programmable Custom Computing Machines*, 2006.

[33] S. Qadeer, D. Wu. KISS: Keep It Simple and Sequential. *ACM SIGPLAN Conference on Programming Language Design and Implementation*, 2004.

[34] J. Rabaey. Reconfigurable processing: The solution to low-power programmable DSP. *Proceedings of ICASSP*, April 1997.

[35] J. Resano, D. Mozos, F. Catthoor. A hybrid prefetch scheduling heuristic to minimize at runtime the reconfiguration overhead of dynamically reconfigurable hardware. *Design, Automation, and Test in Europe*, 2005.

[36] S. Singh. Integrating FPGAs in high-performance computing: Programming models for parallel systems—the programmer's perspective. *ACM/SIGDA International Symposium on Field-Programmable Gate Arrays*, 2007.

[37] G. Snider, B. Shackleford, R. J. Carter. Attacking the semantic gap between application programming languages and configurable hardware. *International Symposium on Field-Programmable Gate Arrays*, 2001.

[38] M. Snir, W. Gropp. *MPI: The Complete Reference*, 2nd ed., MIT Press, 1998.

[39] C. Steiger, H. Walder, M. Platzner. Operating systems for reconfigurable embedded platforms: Online scheduling of real-time tasks. *IEEE Transactions on Computers* 53(11), 2004.

[40] A. S. Tanenbaum. *Modern Operating Systems*, Prentice-Hall, 1992.

[41] R. Tessier, W. Burleson. Reconfigurable computing and digital signal processing: A survey. *Journal of VLSI Signal Processing* 28(1–2), 2001.

[42] M. Vuletic, L. Pozzi, P. Hauck. Seamless hardware-software integration in reconfigurable computing systems. *IEEE Design and Test of Computers* 22(2 N), 2005.

[43] H. Walder, M. Platzner. Online scheduling for block-partitioned reconfigurable devices. *Design, Automation and Test in Europe*, 2003.

[44] G. Wigley, D. Kearney. The development of an operating system for reconfigurable computing. *IEEE Symposium on Field-Programmable Custom Computing Machines*, 2001.

[45] M. J. Wirthlin, B. L. Hutchings. A dynamic instruction set computer. *IEEE Symposium on FPGAs for Custom Computing Machines*, 1995.

[46] Xilinx. *XC6200 FPGA Advanced Product Specification*, June 1996.

[47] B. Ylvisaker, B. Van Essen, C. Ebeling. A type architecture for hybrid micro-parallel computers. *IEEE Symposium on Field-Programmable Custom Computing Machines*, 2006.

CHAPTER 12

THE JHDL DESIGN AND DEBUG SYSTEM

Brent Nelson, Brad Hutchings
Department of Electrical and Computer Engineering
Brigham Young University

JHDL [1, 8] is a CAD environment developed at Brigham Young University for the design, debug, and runtime control of configurable computing applications based on field-programmable gate array (FPGA) technology. Developed roughly between 1997 and 2003 it was made available under an open-source license (*http://www.jhdl.org*) in approximately 2000. The term *JHDL* can refer to one of two things: (1) the JHDL circuit design language itself, or (2) the JHDL CAD system. The JHDL language is a text-based design language for algorithmic construction of structured circuits that is embedded within the Java programming language. JHDL designs are created as Java programs that access JHDL libraries to generate circuits. Within the JHDL CAD environment, circuits can be simulated, netlisted, and downloaded to the reconfigurable computing platform for execution and testing. Additional CAD tools can be built on top of the JHDL infrastructure to support higher-level circuit construction, optimization, and debugging tasks. One of the most unique features of JHDL is its runtime environment, which provides a unified simulator/hardware debugger that can be used to debug and validate a circuit through either simulation or hardware execution, and which contains many features normally found only in source-level software debuggers.

12.1 JHDL BACKGROUND AND MOTIVATION

Historically, FPGA designers have used CAD tools from three sources to develop their designs. The early tools were derived from application-specific integrated circuit (ASIC) tool flows such as schematic capture, HDL synthesis, and so on. Some were invented as new languages or language dialects specifically for FPGA design [4]. Finally, some designers have used general-purpose programming languages (GPLs) to describe FPGA circuitry [3, 9]. Although there are good reasons behind all three tool approaches, the case for using GPLs for FPGA design is quite compelling. Compared to the other two alternatives (schematic capture and HDL synthesis), GPLs are much more accessible to a larger set of users and can be applied to a much broader set of problems. In addition, GPL programming environments are less expensive, more widely available, and more mature (less buggy) than the other two alternatives.

Within the realm of GPL-based design tools, a range of approaches as well as design abstraction levels can be (and have been) supported. Sea Cucumber [11] is representative of high-level tools that *compile* standard programming language descriptions into hardware. In this case, the tie to GPLs is simply that the input specification syntax used is based on a GPL. A different approach is represented by *structural* design languages that leverage GPL language constructs to assist the user in creating a circuit from a set of building blocks (gates, wires, etc.).

JHDL is an *embedded design language* based on the Java GPL and is a structural design tool. Embedded languages like JHDL are specialized application programming interfaces (APIs) where user-defined classes and function overloading are carefully used to create the illusion of a customized circuit design language within the GPL environment. APIs allow designers to build circuits by declaring interfaces and interconnecting gates and modules, all in a structural way. Embedding does this without making any modifications to existing language syntax, which is an important point because modifying the GPL syntax negates most of the advantages of the embedding approach. Examples of past embedded languages include PAMDC [2] and Spyder [9].

As a structural design tool, JHDL constructs circuits from library primitives with the help of provided Java methods (subroutines) and module generators whose execution produces a circuit graph. This graph is then available for manipulation, including simulation and netlisting. In this era of behavioral synthesis, why are we still interested in structural design? There are three answers to this question. First, when working with FPGAs, structural design techniques often still result in circuits that are substantially smaller and faster than those developed using only behavioral synthesis tools. Second, for many applications found in the reconfigurable computing arena (especially where control over circuit placement is required), structural capture is simply a faster, easier to learn, and more effective way to design an application. Thus, it has a place in any high-performance FPGA design tool kit. Third, the circuit graph produced by the execution of a JHDL description is amenable to a variety of modifications prior to netlisting. For example, it can be programmatically modified to insert debug support features, it can be instrumented to support runtime profiling and monitoring of the final hardware, and it can be modified to support checkpointing (extraction of the hardware computation's state for later restoration) and therefore support context switching of designs on and off a configurable computing platform. None of these features are as readily performed using other approaches, especially behavioral synthesis approaches.

An overview of the design process for JHDL-based design is presented in Figure 12.1. As shown, a collection of JHDL class libraries provides the foundation for all JHDL designs. These libraries contain, at a minimum, Java classes representing primitive circuit elements. Layered on top of the device primitives library are additional libraries that contain subroutines to programmatically generate higher-level circuits from the primitives (known variously as *module generators*). A user creates a JHDL design by writing a Java program that instances these library primitives or calls the module generator subroutines that, in turn, instance primitives.

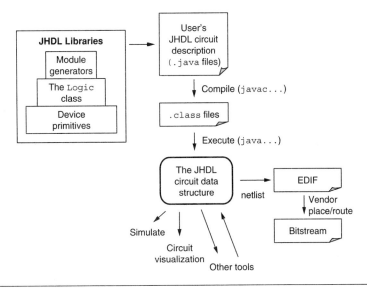

FIGURE 12.1 ■ An overview of the design process and the JHDL system.

Once a JHDL Java program has been written and compiled to a set of class files, it may be executed. The result is an in-memory data structure representing the constructed circuit in the form of a graph, in which nodes represent circuit elements and wires, and arcs represent connections between them. As shown in Figure 12.1, once this data structure has been built, various CAD tools can be applied to it to accomplish simulation, netlisting, or other desired activities. Of interest is that tools can be used to modify the JHDL circuit data structure prior to netlisting or simulation. This is shown in the figure by the arrow leading from "Other tools" up to "The JHDL circuit data structure." These modifications can be for purposes of adding debug or in-circuit monitoring features, and so on.

12.2 THE JHDL DESIGN LANGUAGE

As noted, because JHDL is *embedded*, two mechanisms are used to create the illusion of it as a customized circuit design language: classes and function overloading. The predefined classes provided by JHDL represent primitives, such as gates and wires, so one design method is to simply create instances of these primitives using the Java new construct. Beyond this, function overloading provides a higher level of design abstraction by allowing the designer to call parameterized functions that build the desired circuit out of primitive objects. This section describes these levels of JHDL design from a circuit designer's perspective.

12.2.1 Level-1 Design: Primitive Instantiation

The JHDL primitives library shown in Figure 12.1 is simply a package of Java classes where each class corresponds to a circuit primitive (e.g., AND, OR). Given such a library, the lowest level of JHDL design is to instance primitives from it using new.

Listing 12.1 shows a simple design built by instantiating primitives. The first two lines import general JHDL libraries needed by all designs. The third import makes the primitives from JHDL's Xilinx Virtex library available for use in the construction of this design.

The mux class is next declared by subclassing (extending) the JHDL Logic class. The interface ports (the named inputs and outputs for the cell) are declared using the CellInterface mechanism where, for example, in ("sel", 1) declares an input port named sel that is of width 1 and out ("q", 1) declares an output port named q that is also of width 1.

Listing 12.1 ▪ Multiplexer example using primitive instantiation.

```
import byucc.jhdl.base.*;
import byucc.jhdl.Logic.*;
import byucc.jhdl.Xilinx.Virtex.*;

// This cell is a Java class called 'mux'
public class mux extends Logic {

  // Declare the cell's ports
  public static CellInterface[] cell_interface = {
    in("a", 1),
    in("b", 1),
    in("sel", 1),
    out ("q", 1),
  };

  // This is the mux's constructor
  public mux(Node parent, Wire aw, Wire bw, Wire selw, Wire qw) {
    super(parent);
    connect("a", aw); connect("b", bw);
    connect("sel", selw); connect("q", qw);

    // The code below this point is the 'body' of the cell and builds
    //   it from primitive wire and gate objects.

    // Declare and construct local wires
    Wire a1 = new Xwire(this, 1, "a1");
    Wire a2 = new Xwire(this, 1, "a2");
    Wire selbar = new Xwire(this, 1, "selbar");

    // Invert signal "sel"
    new inv(this, selw, selbar);
    // Form AND gates
    new and2(this, aw, selbar, a1);
    new and2(this, bw, sel, a2);

    // Form OR gate for final output
    new or2(this, a1, a2, qw);
  }
}
```

The declaration of the constructor for the `mux` class comes next. This is a standard Java constructor method that can be called to construct a new instance of `mux`. The `connect()` calls associate a given wire with a specific port; for example, the wire parameter `aw` is associated with (connected to) port `a`.

The last section of the constructor instantiates the wires and gates needed to implement the multiplexer logic using Java `new...` calls. The objects being created to build the circuit are implemented by Java classes from the `byucc.jhdl.Xilinx.Virtex` package and represent wires and logic gates.

The problem with using primitive instantiation, as just described, is that the resulting design is specific to a particular primitive library (the example above relies on the `byucc.jhdl.Xilinx.Virtex` package). Designing this way limits the portability of the design between technologies, even when it is based on building blocks as simple as individual Boolean gates. Another problem with this design style is that it was specifically written for a multiplexer that has single-bit inputs and outputs—in essence, it is a fixed netlist. The `Logic` class overcomes these limitations.

12.2.2 Level-2 Design: Using the `Logic` Class and Its Provided Methods

The `Logic` class consists of a large collection of subroutines that can be called to create user logic. Listing 12.2 shows the design of the same multiplexer (Listing 12.1) written using methods of the `Logic` class. The difference between this and the previous design is that at the bottom of the constructor, rather than primitive instantiation, this version uses method calls to build the MUX circuit. These methods are available for our use because the `mux` class extends the predefined `Logic` class. In Listing 12.2, the changes from the previous MUX example are underlined, to show how the portion of the code that actually builds the logic has been changed.

Listing 12.2 ■ MUX example written using `Logic` class.

```
import byucc.jhdl.base.*;
import byucc.jhdl.Logic.*;
import byucc.jhdl.Xilinx.Virtex.*;

// This cell is a Java class called 'mux'
public class mux extends Logic {

  // Declare the cell's ports
  public static CellInterface[] cell_interface = {
    in("a", 1),
    in("b", 1),
    in("sel", 1),
    out("q", 1),
  };

  // This is the mux's constructor
  public mux(Node parent, Wire aw, Wire bw, Wire selw, Wire qw) {
    super(parent);
```

```
connect("a", aw); connect("b", bw);
connect("sel", selw); connect("q", qw);

// The code below this point is the 'body' of the cell and builds
//   it from Logic class subroutine calls.

or_o(this, and(aw, not(selw)), and(bw, sel), qw);
  }
}
```

Invoking `and (a,b)` calls `byucc.jhdl.Logic.and(a,b)`, which is a subroutine that builds the desired logic (an AND gate) and returns a reference (pointer) to the output wire it created for the gate. This wire can then be used as an input to the `or_o()` call, which creates a 2-input OR gate.[1]

In addition to less verbosity, tremendous power derives from using methods (subroutines) to build circuitry in this manner. OR methods with as many inputs as desired can be created to accommodate any size OR gate and can be written to accommodate input/output wires of any width. Thus, the overloaded `or()` subroutine can handle requests for 2-input OR gates with single-bit inputs/outputs as well as requests for 8-input OR gates with 32-bit inputs/outputs.

The `Logic` class methods accomplish this using JHDL `Techmapper` classes. Figure 12.2 shows that when user code calls a `Logic` method, that method ultimately calls a `Techmapper` class object to do a technology-specific implementation of the logic it has determined should be built, and the `Techmapper` object ultimately maps the resulting logic to technology-specific primitives. This means that designs created using `Logic` class methods are completely technology independent—retargeting a design created using `Logic` to a different technology is as simple as instructing the `Logic` class object to call on a different technology's `Techmapper`. To date, `Techmapper`s have been written at Brigham Young University for the Xilinx: 4K, Virtex, Virtex-II, and Virtex-II Pro technologies.

The `Logic` class contains methods to build gates, wires, registers, memories, multiplexers, adders, subtracters, and shifters, as well as methods for manipulating wires: concatenation, slicing, and so forth. Users are encouraged to use the `Logic` style of Listing 12.2 instead of the primitive style of Listing 12.1 whenever possible, as primitive instantiation is typically used only for taking advantage of device-specific features such as clock managers and memories.

---

[1] Note that some of the function calls have an `an_o` suffix. Functions with this suffix instantiate the gate using the provided input and output wires. Functions without this suffix instantiate both the gate and an output wire that is connected to it. In either case, the output wire is returned by the function. This approach reduces verbosity by eliminating the need to declare and construct intermediate wires.

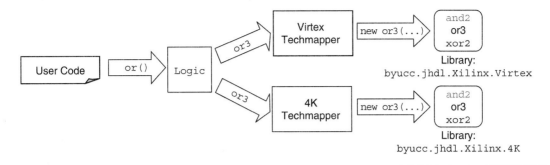

FIGURE 12.2 ■ The relationship of user code, `Logic` class methods, and `Techmapper` objects.

12.2.3 Level-3 Design: Programmatic Circuit Generation (Module Generators)

The creation of programmatic circuit generators (module generators) is a natural extension of the techniques employed by the `Logic` class. That is, Java-based subroutines that intelligently create complex hardware modules based on build time–supplied parameters can be created by any JHDL user. A very simple example that illustrates parameterized design is shown in Listing 12.3.

Listing 12.3 ■ n-bit full adder example.

```
// This design assumes the existence of a FullAdder JHDL design
//   which it instances repeatedly to build an n-bit adder.
import byucc.jhdl.base.*;
import byucc.jhdl.Logic.*;
public class NBitAdder extends Logic {
  public static CellInterface[] cell_interface = {
    param("n", INTEGER),
    in("a", "n"),
    in("b", "n"),
    out("sum", "n+1")
  };

  public NBitAdder(Node parent, Wire a, Wire b, Wire sum) {
    super(parent); // Always call super-constructor
    int width = a.getWidth(); // Get the width of the 'a' wire
    bind("n", width);
    connect("a", a);   connect("b", b);   connect("sum", sum);

    // Create intermediate carry wires as a multi-bit wire
    Wire carries = wire(width);

    // Build and connect together needed full adders
    // The gw() method calls pull individual bits
    //   out of multi-bit wires.  The gnd() method returns
    //   a single constant '0' wire.
```

```
    for (int i=0; i < width; i++) {
      if (i==0)
        new FullAdder(this, a.gw(i), b.gw(i), gnd(),
                   sum.gw(i), carries.gw(0));
      else
        new FullAdder(this, a.gw(i), b.gw(i), carries.gw(i-1),
                   sum.gw(i), carries.gw(i));
    }
    buf_o(carries.gw(width-1), sum.gw(width));
  }
}
```

This is an `NBitAdder` design[2] that programmatically constructs a multibit adder using previously designed full adder cells (not shown). In its `CellInterface` declaration, the first line, `param("n", INTEGER)`, declares a parameter n that is of type `integer` (similar to a generic in VHDL—see Section 6.1.3). More precisely, n is declared to be an instance of the Java class `INTEGER`. All port declarations in the `CellInterface` then use n or n+1 as their width. When `NBitAdder` is constructed, the `bind()` call binds the value of n to the width of the a wire. Based on this information, `connect()` calls will verify that the wires passed in to the constructor are the correct width for the ports they are being connected to. Finally, the ripple-carry adder body is constructed using a Java `for` loop that creates and interconnects `FullAdder` cells. The final `buf_o()` call connects the top carry-out bit to the most significant bit of the sum.

`NBitAdder` is a trivial example of a module generator, that is, a circuit that can be parameterized according to some set of criteria. Listing 12.4 is a slightly more complex version of the `NBitAdder` design that has been parameterized for pipelining (additions to the original design have been underlined in the source code). Here a single Boolean parameter `"pipe"` is passed into the cell constructor method to control whether a pipeline register is to be placed on the adder output. The main difference between this and the previous design is that the last few lines of the constructor body connect the adder outputs to the cell's outputs through either a register or a buffer, based on the value of the `"pipe"` parameter.

Listing 12.4 ▪ n-bit full adder with optional pipelining.

```
... // Same imports as previous NBitAdder design
public class NBitAdder extends Logic {
  public static CellInterface[] cell_interface = {
    ... // Same ports as previous NBitAdder design
  };

  public NBitAdder(Node parent, Wire a, Wire b, Wire sum, Boolean pipe) {
```

---

[2] The `Logic` class contains a family of multibit adder constructor methods that would normally be called instead of this example design. Nevertheless, this design is presented here to illustrate module generator-like concepts in JHDL.

```
... // Main constructor body  same as previous NBitAdder design
Wire tmpsum;

// New code is below
// If desired, insert pipeline latch
if (pipe)
  (reg_o(tmpsum, sum);
else
  buf_o(tmpsum, sum);
}
}
```

On the surface this is similar to what can be accomplished through the use of VHDL generics: the `for-generate` and `if-generate` statements. However, parameterized circuit generation is limited in VHDL, consisting of very simple conditional circuit instantiations that are controlled by a small subset of the language dedicated solely to this purpose. In JHDL, the entire Java language can be brought to bear on this problem and sophisticated algorithms can be used to generate circuits. JHDL module generators exist for counters, comparators, accumulators, arithmetic units (multipliers, dividers, floating-point units, digit serial units), decoders, shift registers, and memories. These have employed, as a part of the module generators' calculations, simple timing and area estimation techniques, recursive tree search computations, file I/O, and the like. Such module generators have been parameterized for features such as number format, rounding/saturation/truncation modes, pipelining granularity, constant encoding methods, and resource usage (serial versus parallel implementation).

12.2.4   JHDL Is a Structural Design Language

Structural design often improves the performance of configurable computing applications because many applications that are FPGA based can benefit from manual placement of at least some parts of the design. Effective manual placement can be achieved only if the overall organization of the circuit is well understood—it is very difficult to manually place circuitry generated by behavioral synthesis.

Placement attributes can be attached to JHDL primitive circuit objects as string properties, to be interpreted by backend tools. To simplify the attaching of these attributes when `Logic` methods are used in circuit building, the `Logic` class also contains a placement API to help in the tasks of (1) mapping gates to lookup tables (LUTs), ALUs, or other atomic FPGA cells, and (2) specifying the relative placement of those cells. For example, to force a collection of gates that implement a 3-input, 1-output logic function into a single LUT, the `map()` call can be used as in:

```
map(a, b, ci, s );
```

This will force the cone of logic with `a`, `b`, and `ci` as inputs and with `s` as output into a single primitive (a LUT for most FPGA technologies). Then that primitive can be placed by specifying the location of *its output wire* in a `place()` call:

```
place( s, "R0C0.F" );
```

Note that these methods *do not* create logic themselves, but rather pack already created logic into LUTs, which they then physically place. The use of these method calls is technology specific, so a technology-specific `Techmapper` is used to determine their interpretation for the target technology at build time. This placement API acts as a window of opportunity for the user to obtain design assistance from the `Techmapper`. For example, when `map()` is called, the `Techmapper` checks the network of gates for validity (i.e., intermediate fanin or fanout to the network), and, when the circuit is fully constructed, it resolves all placement hints and reports any placement conflicts. In this way placement errors can be detected at the *front* of the tool chain rather than during place and route, which helps minimize design cycles.[3]

12.2.5   JHDL Is a Programmatic Circuit Design Language

That JHDL is also a programmatic circuit design language is perhaps the most powerful and unique feature of GPL-based circuit generation techniques. The key point is that a JHDL description, once compiled, *is* an executable Java program; it is the execution of that Java program that constructs the circuit. This gives JHDL significant advantages over HDL descriptions, which must be *parsed* by a synthesizer and a corresponding circuit then constructed.

With JHDL there is no separation between the code that represents the circuit itself and any code that might be executed to help determine how best to generate it—all of the code in a JHDL description is executable Java. In a language like JHDL there is a very clear separation between circuit generation and computation: Module instantiation is circuit generation and everything else is computation. In contrast, all code written in a VHDL or Verilog design (excepting simulation testbenches) *is* the circuit description—there is no provision for code that can be executed apart from it. This presents difficulties when computations are required, prior to circuit construction, to determine how best to generate the circuit.

At one time, designers often resorted to macro preprocessors with Verilog code to provide `for-generate-` and `if-generate`-like functionality for their designs. Similarly, some designers (including our own students) have often written C or C++ circuit generators that generate VHDL or Verilog code as output in order to work around the lack of an effective compile time computational capability in conventional HDLs. In contrast, JHDL and other GPL-based embedded languages avoid such workarounds because they provide a clean mechanism

---

[3] In contrast, VHDL annotation approaches for placement are nonstandard and differ from tool to tool (see Section 6.2.1). Also, VHDL placement directives are passed through to the backend tools without performing any error checking such as described previously.

for freely intermixing computational code with circuit descriptions—all based on the general-purpose computational power of the underlying GPL. One could say that languages like JHDL don't need a formal elaboration step as VHDL and Verilog do. Or one could say that the *entire* circuit construction process in JHDL is an elaboration step, albeit a much more powerful one than that provided by HDLs.

Finally, there is no *synthesizable subset* of JHDL, and thus there is no possibility for a mismatch between simulation and synthesis results due to differing CAD tools' interpretation of the description. The same circuit is constructed each time the JHDL code is executed regardless of whether it is intended for simulation or for netlisting.

12.3 THE JHDL CAD SYSTEM

As Figure 12.1 showed, the execution of a compiled JHDL design creates an in-memory structural representation of the JHDL circuit. This is a classical circuit graph where Java objects represent the cells and wires in the circuit and pointers between these objects represent connections and hierarchical parent–child relationships. The figure also showed that this circuit data structure is the entry point for the JHDL CAD system, meaning that all CAD functions and tasks, such as simulation and netlisting, use the circuit data structure via an API provided for this purpose. The result is that it is straightforward to write Java-based CAD tools for interacting with and manipulating the circuit data structure (and therefore the circuit).

12.3.1 Testbenches in JHDL

Because a JHDL design is a Java program, it needs a `main()` routine. It is the program's `main()` routine that usually acts as a testbench for JHDL designs. Listing 12.5 shows such a `main()` testbench that, like most JHDL testbenches, does three things:

- First, it creates an `HWSystem` object that is the top-level container object for the circuit and contains the simulator and netlister objects. The entire user design (testbench and device under test) exists as a child node of `HWSystem` in the resulting JHDL object hierarchy.

Listing 12.5 ■ A sample JHDL testbench.

```
import ...;    // Import needed packages

// Declare testbench class
public class tb_myCell extends Logic implements TestBench {

  static HWSystem hw;   // Declare a HWSystem
  private int aVal, bVal, cinVal; // Declare some private variables
```

```
// The main() routine for this Java program
public static void main(String argv[]) {
  // Step 1: build a HWSystem
  hw = new HWSystem();  // Build a HWSystem
  // Step 2: Build an instance of this testbench
  tb_myCell tb = new tb_myCell(hw, ...); // Pass in some params
  // Step 3: Do something with the circuit now that the testbench
  // and DUT are built.  We can do any one of:
  // 1. Start a simulation
  // 2. Netlist the circuit
  // 3. Traverse or modify the circuit data structure
  // 4. Start a GUI-based CAD system
  // We will do the last - create a GUI-based CAD system
  // Create a new instance of cvt (the Circuit Visualization Tool)
  new cvt( tb );
}

// The constructor for this testbench
public tb_myCell (Node parent, ...);  // Not all params shown
  super(parent);

  // Step 1: Specify (create) a TechMapper for Virtex
  setDefaultTechMapper(new VirtexTechMapper(true));

  // Step 2: Build wires to connect to DUT
  an = wire(1,"an");   bn = wire(1,"bn");   cinn = wire(1, "cinn");
  sn = wire(1,"sn");   coutn = wire(1,"coutn");

  // Step 3: Build mycell (the DUT)
  myCell dut = new myCell(this, an, bn, cinn, sn, coutn, "myCell");
  }
}
```

- Second, as shown in Listing 12.5, it creates a testbench object (which in turn creates the device under test).
- Third, once the JHDL circuit data structure has been created, the `main()` routine can do one of a number of things: (1) start a batch simulation, (2) call on the netlister to netlist the design, or (3) create a GUI-based interface to enable the user to interactively work with the circuit. In Listing 12.5, the `main()` routine starts up `cvt`, a graphical environment for viewing the circuit, simulation, and netlisting.

12.3.2   The cvt Class

Class `cvt` is a GUI-based system with widgets for navigating the design hierarchy, starting a simulation of the circuit, generating a netlist of the circuit, and so forth. The actual simulation and netlisting classes are accessed via the `HWSystem` class, and `cvt` makes calls into it to satisfy user requests. The `cvt` class implements a standard event-driven GUI system based on Swing, distributed as a part of the JHDL language. Swing was chosen for its portability and availability on all

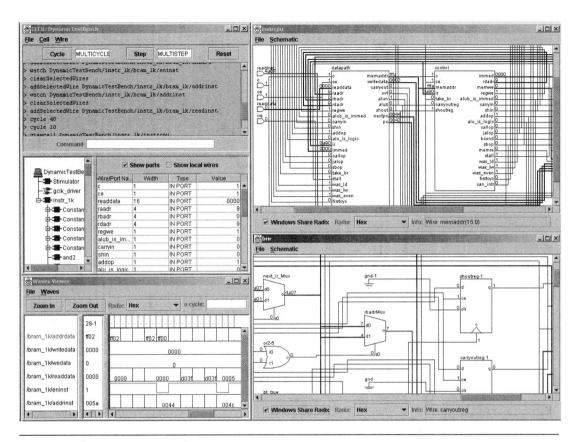

FIGURE 12.3 ■ The JHDL cvt GUI.

platforms. Class cvt uses the built-in Swing event mechanism for its own internal communication.

Figure 12.3 shows a screenshot of the cvt GUI. In the upper left is a text console window where commands may be typed. Menus and buttons above largely duplicate what can be entered in the window. Below the console is a hierarchy navigation tool. On the left is a hierarchy browser; on the right is a list of ports for the currently selected cell along with their current values (if a simulation is in progress). Beneath the browser is a waveform viewer; and on the lower right half of the figure are two different schematic viewers. This screenshot shows that the various parts of the GUI are all contained in a single pane but each can be broken out into an individually sized window if desired.

Unlike with most CAD tools, there is no *standard* JHDL CAD system. Rather, the circuit data structure API provides a mechanism for any program a user might write to interact with the circuit. The cvt class is simply one such example. Examples of other programs include stand-alone simulators and netlisters.

Many of the debugging experiments described later in this chapter were carried out by writing custom CAD tools to interact with the circuit data structure API. For example, a number of tools have been written that modify the circuit prior to netlisting by, for example, inserting clock managers or other special-purpose circuitry into the user's design. These tools have also instrumented designs for debug by adding scan chains to them. Finally, complete software applications that interact with the circuit during simulation and execution have been created. This last point is a unique feature of JHDL—once the circuit has been built, application software can be written that communicates with the design via the `HWSystem` API. This allows the complete application (software and hardware) to be deployed as a single Java program.

12.4 JHDL'S HARDWARE MODE

JHDL supports hardware-in-the-loop debugging with what is called *hardware mode*. Hardware mode is based on the observation that much of the data created when a JHDL circuit is built and simulated is also useful in the actual hardware debug process.

Figure 12.4 shows JHDL's dual simulation/hardware execution environment. When initially simulating a design (*left* side of figure), the simulation/runtime API provides `cvt` and simulator access to the JHDL circuit graph.

After the design's configuration bitstream is created, hardware debugging can take place using hardware mode (on the right of Figure 12.4). Loading a JHDL design in `cvt` now performs two steps: (1) the JHDL design is constructed as usual to create the internal circuit representation, and (2) the bitstream is configured onto the specified FPGA platform. Using the same `cvt` GUI as before, the user can advance execution of the design via the simulator control buttons or via commands on the command line. However, instead of cycling the simulator, these actions cause `cvt` to send clocking commands to the FPGA platform through the board's driver. After a clock command is executed, the state of the FPGA platform is retrieved using readback and *back-annotated into the JHDL circuit data structure*.

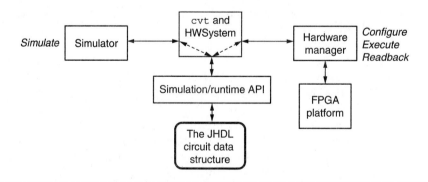

FIGURE 12.4 ■ The JHDL unified simulation/hardware execution environment.

The simulator is then used to compute the steady state of all combinational nodes in the circuit as a function of these state values, and a complete picture of the hardware execution state is now present in the JHDL circuit data structure. As a result, `cvt` can query and display the state of the circuit as normal, just as it would if the circuit were being simulated. In this case, however, it displays hardware signal values rather than simulated signal values.

JHDL's hardware mode is readily adapted to new hardware platforms given programmatic methods that exist for communicating with the board. The following capabilities are required for adaptation:

- *Configuration:* This is needed to configure the FPGA(s) on the hardware platform with bitstreams.
- *Clock control:* One or more subroutines are required to single- or multistep the clock on the board.
- *Readback:* This is necessary to read back the state from the FPGA(s) on the board.[4]

Given these capabilities, JHDL can easily be extended to communicate with the board for hardware mode operation.[5] This is achieved by modifying a thin layer of Java translation code so that standard JHDL methods can communicate with the specific C-based device driver subroutines for the board.

12.5 ADVANCED JHDL CAPABILITIES

A variety of design and debug tools have been built on top of JHDL. A few of these are described in the following sections.

12.5.1 Dynamic Testbenches

Some of the power of JHDL derives from its extensive use of the Java feature called *reflection*. The Java reflection API provides a set of methods that a Java program can use to examine the structure of a Java `.class` file. By reflecting on a Java class, a program can determine the names and type signatures of all methods in it and, if desired, dynamically load the class file and construct an object of the class.

---

[4] To date, JHDL supports hardware mode only on Xilinx platforms, because they contain a readback capability. Experiments have also been done to determine the cost of adding a scan chain to user designs for this purpose when readback is not available [12].

[5] An additional capability would also prove very useful—loading state into the FPGA. In the case of Xilinx FPGAs (the focus of the JHDL hardware mode work), this can be done by modifying the configuration bitstream appropriately and then reconfiguring the FPGA with that bitstream. Thus, this capability is not listed as a strict requirement in the list. A number of the debug experiments described in the next section performed bitstream modification to load state into an FPGA, but would have benefited from a simpler mechanism that did not require a reconfiguration of the FPGA.

The JHDL `dtb` class is a general-purpose testbench tool that uses reflection to automatically perform testbench functions, eliminating the need, in most cases, for the user to write code for constructing the testbench. The user runs `dtb` and specifies the name of the circuit to be constructed on the command line. `dtb` examines the corresponding file (`FullAdder.class`, for example) using reflection to determine the parameters required by its constructor. It then creates the necessary wires and calls the constructor to build an instance of the specified class, connecting it to the wires it created. When `dtb` is used, the `dtb` object itself performs all of the services required of a testbench. For example, it examines the constructed circuit, determines the clocking required, and sets up the clock for simulation. In addition, when everything has been constructed, it brings up `cvt` so that design simulation and netlisting can proceed as usual. All that is required of the user is to provide the simulation stimulus either interactively or via a script.

12.5.2 Behavioral Synthesis

Sea Cucumber [11] is a behavioral synthesis tool that was built on top of the JHDL framework and accepts a behavioral description written in Java that is compiled into bytecodes by any standard Java compiler. It parses these byte codes, discovers instruction-level parallelism, performs other common optimizations, and then synthesizes a circuit by invoking calls to the JHDL Logic library. Advantages provided by the JHDL framework include access to JHDL visualization and debugging tools to verify Sea Cucumber designs and access to JHDL netlisting modules so that the synthesized JHDL circuitry can be converted into netlists for place and route by vendor software. In fact, all of the previously mentioned JHDL features are available to Sea Cucumber, including hardware mode, dynamic test benches, and the like.

A behavioral debugger, also developed in conjunction with Sea Cucumber [7], allows the user to debug fully optimized code in the context of the original user description. It does this by traversing the JHDL circuit structure to retrieve circuit values and presenting them to the user in the context of the JHDL CAD framework.

12.5.3 Advanced Debugging Capabilities

Much of the power of JHDL comes by exploiting a single FPGA feature (read-back) to access internal FPGA state and present the data to the user in some form. Because of this enhanced visibility, the current JHDL debugging environment has proved to be effective for verifying and debugging large, complex applications. However, much more powerful debugging capabilities can be achieved if a small part of the FPGA is reconfigured to implement supplemental circuitry to aid debug and validation. This is similar in spirit to the "-g" flag used in conventional software compilation where the compiler can enable debugging by inserting additional code. Because FPGA hardware is reconfigurable, any inserted debugging circuitry can be removed when the application is ready for deployment.

Some of the advanced debugging features that are possible via embedded debug circuitry include:

- Signals can be automatically routed to external I/O pins for viewing.
- Unused FPGA circuitry and memory can be used to implement "probe" circuits that sample and store circuit activity during circuit execution.
- Unused FPGA hardware can be used to implement complex, real-time hardware breakpoints.

As long as designers must manually modify their designs in order to embed debug circuitry, these powerful techniques may go unused. The best way to overcome this is to automate the process of synthesizing and embedding debug circuitry into user circuitry—a task best performed directly by the CAD tool environment. The ability to use a debugging tool as an integrated part of the design environment, tied to the original design specification and accessed using standard user interfaces, makes this a powerful and convenient way to develop and verify a design.

As a part of DARPA-funded research at Brigham Young University, researchers investigated a variety of advanced debug mechanisms using JHDL, all of them were aimed at providing a debug system with capabilities similar to those found in software development systems and that are significantly easier to use than manual methods. A few of these mechanisms are described in the following subsections.

Debug circuitry synthesis

In software debugging using the *gdb* symbolic debugger or similar tools, it is not uncommon for the user to temporarily change variable values as a way of determining how the program would behave *if* the variable had that different value. The work described by Graham [6] demonstrated a similar capability for hardware. First, JHDL was used to perform a readback of the FPGA's state. Changes were then made to the bitstream to reflect the user's choice for the new circuit state, and the bitstream was configured back into the FPGA. Upon resumption, the system was seen to continue execution from the previous point but with changed state values.

As another example, in the work described by Graham et al. [5], JHDL and JBits were used together to modify FPGA design bitstreams on the fly in order to rewire embedded logic analyzers to user logic in a placed-and-routed design—all within a few seconds of a mouse click. The collected data could then be viewed in the original design environment using the built-in JHDL GUI framework.

When these features first appeared in JHDL, there were no equivalent commercial debugging tools available. However, with the passage of time, commercial offerings have improved, incorporating some of the features of the original JHDL system. Altera's SignalTap and Xilinx's ChipScope now provide convenient ways to integrate customized logic analyzers into user designs (these are implemented with unused programmable circuitry), and offer separate tools that emulate a logic analyzer display on the PC's monitor. However, JHDL still differs from these products in the level of integration it provides (the debug environment *is* the design environment). Perhaps Synplicity's Identify tool comes closest to JHDL in this regard because it provides the ability to view some circuit behavior in the original VHDL context. Still, none of the commercial offerings allow the user to simultaneously integrate logic analyzers, display these results in the original design environment, and modify the current state of the circuit during debug.

Checkpointing, context switching, and remote access

Checkpointing is defined as saving the state of a computation in a way that the computation can later be restarted from that same point. It is often used in software to allow a long-running computation such as a simulation to be restarted from a known point if, for example, the system it is running on goes down. The concept of readback can easily be extended to extract the state of the entire FPGA platform.

Once this is done, checkpointing of FPGA-based computations can be supported. To do this, the JHDL `HWSystem` was augmented not only to retrieve the state of the FPGA but also to retrieve the state of all memory elements on the hardware platform (FIFOs and memories) and save that information to disk. Later, the state could be retrieved from disk and loaded back onto the FPGA platform, whereupon execution would continue from the time of the checkpoint. What is important is that a *simulation* checkpoint could be loaded onto the FPGA platform and *hardware execution* could be continued from that point. Likewise, a *hardware execution* checkpoint could be loaded into JHDL and a *simulation* continued from that point. With the availability of checkpointing in JHDL, it then became possible to time-share an FPGA platform using context switching (swapping an application off the platform to make room for another). Experiments conducted at Brigham Young University on checkpointing and context switching are described by Landaker et al. [10], to which the interested reader is referred for more information and results.

Finally, JHDL was also modified to permit remote access to an FPGA platform. In this work, the `cvt` and `HWSystem` classes were extended to include a client–server capability so that hardware mode communications with an FPGA platform could be conducted over a network.

12.6 SUMMARY

JHDL is currently in use in a variety of research projects, from module generators systems to behavioral synthesis systems to microarchitectural simulation systems. By providing a framework for the construction, simulation, netlisting, and hardware debug of FPGA-based designs, JHDL allows researchers to focus on tasks other than recreating the infrastructure that JHDL provides. Of particular importance in this regard, is that JHDL provides a target for use by synthesis tools with its primitive libraries and its `Logic` and `Techmapper` classes.

JHDL has been in use since approximately 1998 and was released under an open-source license (*http://www.jhdl.org*) in approximately 2000. Potential users can download either compiled JAR files of the JHDL system, or they can download and build JHDL from sources themselves. Documentation on the JHDL system is provided as well.

References

[1] P. Bellows, B. L. Hutchings. JHDL—An HDL for reconfigurable systems. *Proceedings of IEEE Workshop on FPGAs for Custom Computing Machines*, April 1998.

[2] P. Bertin, D. Roncin, J. Vuillemin. Programmable active memories: A performance assessment. In G. Borriello, C. Ebeling (eds.). *Research on Integrated Systems: Proceedings of the 1993 Symposium*, 1993.

[3] P. Bertin, H. Touati. PAM programming environments: Practice and experience. In D. A. Buell, K. L. Pocek (eds.). *Proceedings of IEEE Workshop on FPGAs for Custom Computing Machines*, April 1994.

[4] D. Galloway. The transmogrifier C hardware description language and compiler for FPGAs. *Proceedings of IEEE Workshop on FPGAs for Custom Computing Machines*, April 1995.

[5] P. Graham, B. Nelson, B. Hutchings. Instrumenting bitstreams for debugging FPGA circuits. *Proceedings of the IEEE Symposium on Field-Programmable Custom Computing Machines*, April 2001.

[6] P. S. Graham. *Logical Hardware Debuggers for FPGA-Based Systems,* Ph.D. thesis, Brigham Young University, 2001.

[7] K. S. Hemmert, J. L. Tripp, B. L. Hutchings, P. A. Jackson. Source level debugger for the Sea Cucumber synthesizing compiler. *Proceedings of the IEEE Symposium on Field-Programmable Custom Computing Machines*, April 2003.

[8] B. L. Hutchings, P. Bellows, J. Hawkins, S. Hemmert, B. Nelson, M. Rytting. A CAD suite for high-performance FPGA design. *Proceedings of IEEE Workshop on FPGAs for Custom Computing Machines*, April 1999.

[9] C. Iseli, E. Sanchez. A C++ compiler for FPGA custom execution units synthesis. *Proceedings of IEEE Workshop on FPGAs for Custom Computing Machines*, April 1995.

[10] W. J. Landaker, M. J. Wirthlin, B. L. Hutchings. Multitasking hardware on the SLAAC1-V reconfigurable computing system. *Proceedings of the 12th International Workshop on Field-Programmable Logic and Applications*, Springer-Verlag, September 2002.

[11] J. L. Tripp, P. A. Jackson, B. L. Hutchings. Sea Cucumber: A synthesizing compiler for FPGAs. *Proceedings of the 12th International Workshop on Field-Programmable Logic and Applications*, Springer-Verlag, September 2002.

[12] T. Wheeler, P. Graham, B. Nelson, B. Hutchings. Using design-level scan to improve FPGA design observability and controllability for functional verification. *Proceedings of the 11th International Workshop on Field-Programmable Logic and Applications*, Springer-Verlag, August/September 2001.

PART III

MAPPING DESIGNS TO RECONFIGURABLE PLATFORMS

The chapters that follow cover the key mapping steps unique to field-programmable gate arrays (FPGAs) and reconfigurable targets. These steps include technology mapping to the primitive FPGA programmable gates (Chapter 13), placement of these gates (Chapters 14 through 16), routing of the interconnect between gates (Chapter 17), retiming of registers in the design (Chapter 18), and bitstream generation (Chapter 19). A final chapter summarizes a number of approaches to accelerating various stages of the mapping process (Chapter 20).

Placement is a difficult mapping problem, but is critical to the performance of the resulting reconfigurable design. As a result, it can be very slow, limiting the rate of the edit–compile–debug loop for reconfigurable application development, and the designs it produces may have longer cycle times than we would like. For these reasons, in addition to the general-purpose algorithms for placement covered in Chapter 14, algorithms that are highly optimized to exploit the regularity of datapaths are discussed in Chapter 15, and constructive approaches to layout are treated in Chapter 16. These more specialized approaches can significantly reduce placement runtime and often deliver placements that allow faster design operation.

As Chapters 13 through 20 demonstrate, there is a well-developed set of approaches and tools for programming reconfigurable applications. However, the tools are always slower than we might like them to be, especially as FPGA capacities continue to grow with Moore's Law. Moreover, the designs they produce are often too large or too slow, and the level at which we must program them is often lower than optimal. These deficiencies present ample opportunities for innovation and improvement in software support for reconfigurable systems.

For the designer who works on reconfiguration issues, the following chapters provide a look under the covers at the tools used to map designs and at the problems they must solve. It is important to understand which problems the tools are and are not solving and how well they can be expected to work. An understanding of the mapping flow and algorithms often helps the designer appreciate why tools may not produce the quality of results expected and how the design could be optimized to obtain better results. Similarly, understanding the problems that the tools are solving helps the designer understand the trade-offs associated with higher- or lower-level designs and how to mix and match design levels to obtain the desired quality of results with minimal effort.

For the tool or software developer, this part covers the key steps in a traditional tool flow and summarizes the key algorithms used to map reconfigurable designs. With this knowledge the developer can rapidly assimilate conventional approaches and options and thus prepare to explore opportunities to improve quality of results, reduce tool time, or increase automation and raise the configurable design's level of abstraction.

CHAPTER 13

TECHNOLOGY MAPPING

Jason Cong
Department of Computer Science
California NanoSystems Institute
University of California–Los Angeles

Peichen Pan
Magma Design Automation, Inc.

Technology mapping is an essential step in an field-programmable gate array (FPGA) design flow. It is the process of converting a network of technology-independent logic gates into a network comprising logic cells on the target FPGA device. Technology mapping has a significant impact on the quality of the final FPGA implementation.

Technology-mapping algorithms have been proposed for optimizing area [29, 36, 58, 65], timing [9, 12, 13, 19, 21, 37, 58], power [2, 8, 34, 45, 52, 71], and routability [3, 67]. Mapping algorithms can be classified into those for general networks [13, 16] and those for special ones such as treelike networks [35, 36]. Algorithms for special networks may be applied to general ones through partitioning, with a possible reduction in solution quality.

Technology-mapping algorithms can be *structural* or *functional*. A structural mapping algorithm does not modify the input network other than to duplicate logic [12, 13]. It reduces technology mapping to a covering problem in which the technology-independent logic gates in the input network are covered with logic cones such that each cone can be implemented using one logic cell—for example, a K-input lookup table (K-LUT)—for LUT-based FPGAs. Figure 13.1 is an example of structural mapping. The logic gates in the original network (a) are covered with three logic cones, each with at most three inputs, as indicated (b). Note that node i is included in two cones and will be duplicated. The corresponding mapping solution (c) comprises three 3-LUTs.

A functional mapping algorithm, on the other hand, treats technology mapping in its general form as a problem of Boolean transformation/decomposition of the input network into a set of interconnected logic cells [15, 48, 58, 60]. It mixes Boolean optimization with covering. Functional mapping algorithms tend to be time consuming, which limits their use to small designs or to small portions of a design.

Note: This work is partially supported by the National Science Foundation under grant number CCF 0530261.

Recent advances in technology mapping try to combine mapping with other steps in the design flow. Such integrated mapping algorithms have the potential to explore a larger solution space than is possible with just technology mapping and thus have the potential to arrive at mapping solutions with better quality. For example, algorithms have been proposed to combine logic synthesis with covering to overcome the limitations of pure structural mapping [11, 22, 57].

13.1   STRUCTURAL MAPPING ALGORITHMS

Technology mapping is part of a logic synthesis flow, which typically consists of three steps. First, the initial network is optimized using technology-independent optimization techniques such as node extraction/substitution and don't-care optimization [33]. Second, the optimized network is decomposed into one consisting of 2-input gates plus inverters (that is, the network is *2-bounded*) to increase flexibility in mapping [12, 36]. Third, the actual mapping takes place, with the goal of covering the 2-bounded network with K-LUTs while optimizing one or more objectives. In the remaining discussion, we assume that the input network is 2-bounded.

A logic network can be represented as a graph where the nodes represent logic gates, primary inputs (PIs), and primary outputs (POs). The edges represent the interconnects or wires. A *cut* of a node v is a set of nodes in the input network such that every path from the primary inputs or sequential element outputs to v contains at least one node in the set. A *K-cut* is a cut with at most K nodes. For example, $\{a, b, z\}$ is a 3-cut for the node y in the network in Figure 13.1(a). Given a K-cut for v, we can obtain a K-LUT for v by collapsing the gates in the logic cone between the nodes in the cut, v, including v itself. For the 3-cut $\{a, b, z\}$ for y, the 3-LUT for y in Figure 13.1(c) is derived from the corresponding cone indicated for y in Figure 13.1(b).

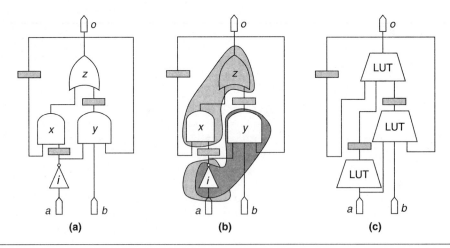

(a)   (b)   (c)

FIGURE 13.1 ■ Structural technology mapping: (a) original network, (b) covering, and (c) mapping solution.

Most structural mapping algorithms are based on the dynamic programming technique. They typically consist of the following steps:

1. Cut generation/enumeration
2. Cut ranking
3. Cut selection
4. Final mapping solution generation

Cut generation obtains one or more cuts that will be used to generate LUTs; it is discussed in the next section. Cut ranking evaluates the cuts obtained in cut generation to see how good they are based on the mapping objectives. It assigns a label or cost to each cut by visiting the nodes in a topological order from PIs to POs. Cut selection picks a cut with the best label for each node and is typically done in reverse topological order from POs to PIs. Cut ranking and selection may be carried out multiple times to refine solution quality.

After the final cut selection, a mapping solution is generated using the selected cuts. In this step, the nodes are visited in the reverse topological order, starting from POs and going back to PIs. At each node, a cut with the best label is selected and the corresponding LUT is added to the solution. Next, the nodes that drive the LUT are visited. This process is repeated until only PIs are left. At that point, a complete mapping solution is obtained.

13.1.1 Cut Generation

Early mapping algorithms combine cut generation and selection to determine one or a few "good" cuts for each node. The most successful example is the FlowMap algorithm, which finds a single cut with optimal mapping depth at each node via max-flow computation [16]. It computes the optimal mapping depth of each node in a topological order from PIs to POs, and at each node uses a max-flow formulation to test whether that node can have the same optimal mapping depth as the maximum depth of its input nodes. If not, the depth is set to one greater than the input nodes' maximum depth. It is shown that these are the only two possible mapping depths. The FlowMap algorithm was the first polynomial time algorithm to find a depth-optimal mapping solution for LUT-based FPGAs.

In practice, K, the number of inputs of the LUTs, is a small constant typically ranging between 3 and 6. It becomes practical to enumerate all K-cuts for each node. With all cuts available, we have additional flexibility in selecting cuts to optimize the mapping solution.

Cuts can be generated by a traversal of the nodes in a combinational network (or the combinational portion of a sequential network) from PIs to POs in a topological order [29, 67]. Let $\Phi(v)$ denote the set of all K-cuts for a node v. For a PI, $\Phi(v)$ contains only the trivial cut consisting of the node itself, that is, $\Phi(v) = \{\{v\}\}$. For a non-PI node v with two fanin nodes, u_1 and u_2, $\Phi(v)$ can be computed by merging the sets of cuts of u_1 and u_2 as follows:

$$\Phi(v) = \{\{v\} \cup \{c_1 \cup c_2 | c_1 \in \Phi(u_1),\, c_2 \in \Phi(u_2),\, |c_1 \cup c_2|\} <= K\} \qquad (13.1)$$

In other words, the set of cuts of v is obtained by the pairwise union of the cuts of its fanin nodes and then the elimination of those cuts with more than K nodes. Note that the trivial cut is added to the set. This is necessary so the nodes driven by v can include v in their cuts.

13.1.2   Area-oriented Mapping

For LUT mapping, the area of a mapping solution can be measured by the total number of LUTs. It has been shown that finding an area-optimal mapping solution is NP-hard [35]. Therefore, it is unlikely that there is an accurate way to rank cuts for area. The difficulty of precise area estimation is mainly due to the existence of multiple fanout nodes. In fact, for treelike networks, area-optimal mapping solutions can be determined in polynomial time [35].

Cong et al. [29] proposed the concept of *effective area* as a way to rank and select cuts for area. A similar concept, *area flow*, was later proposed by Manohararajah et al. [55]. Intuition regarding effective area is to distribute the area for a multi-fanout node to its fanout nodes so that logic sharing and reconvergence can be considered during area cost propagation. Effective areas are computed in a topological order from PIs to POs. The effective area $a(v)$ of a PI node v is set to zero. Equation 13.2 is used to compute the effective area of a cut:

$$a(c) = \left(\Sigma_{u \in c}\left[a(u)/|output(u)|\right]\right) + A_c \qquad (13.2)$$

where A_c is the area of the LUT corresponding to the cut c. The area cost of a non-PI node can then be set to the minimum effective area of its cuts: $a(v) = \min\{a(c)|\forall u \in \Phi(v)\}$.

It should be pointed out that effective area may not account for the situation where the node may be duplicated in a mapping solution. In the example shown in Figure 13.2, with $K = 3$, the LUT for w is introduced solely for the LUT for v. However, in effective area computation, only one-half is counted for v, and as a result the LUT for w is undercounted. In this example, the sum of effective area of the POs is 2.5 whereas the mapping solution has three LUTs. In general, effective area is a lower bound of the actual area.

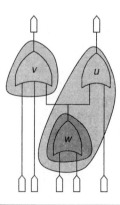

FIGURE 13.2 ■ Inaccuracy in effective area.

The PRAETOR algorithm [29] is an area-oriented mapping algorithm that ranks cuts using effective area. It further improves the basic mapping framework with a number of area reduction techniques. One such technique is to encourage the use of common subcuts. A cut for a fanout of a node v induces a cut for v (perhaps the trivial cut consisting of v itself). If two fanouts of v induce different cuts for v, the most likely result will be an area increase due to the need to duplicate v and possibly some of its predecessor nodes. To alleviate this problem, PRAETOR sorts and selects cuts with the same effective area in a predetermined order to avoid arbitrary selection. It assigns an integer ID to each node and then sorts all cuts with the same effective area according to the lexicographic order based on the IDs of the nodes in the cuts. The first cut with minimum effective area for each node is selected.

Another area reduction technique introduced in PRAETOR is to carry out cut selection twice. The nodes with LUTs selected in the first pass are declared nonduplicable and can only be covered by LUTs for themselves in the second pass. This encourages selection of cuts with less duplication. As an example, suppose that in the first pass of cut selection, the mapping solution shown in Figure 13.3(a), with four LUTs, is selected. In the second pass, the LUT containing v and u_1 is excluded from consideration for u_1. This exclusion will also encourage the selection of the cut that results in the LUT containing a for u_1. As a result, the mapping algorithm generates, in the second pass, the mapping solution in Figure 13.3(b), with only three LUTs. Experimental results show that PRAETOR can significantly improve area over previous algorithms.

The IMap algorithm proposed by Manohararajah et al. [55] is another mapping algorithm targeting area optimization. It introduced two enhancements: (1) iteration between cut ranking and cut selection multiple times, and (2) adjustment of the area costs between successive iterations using history information. In the effective area formula (equation 13.2), the fanout count of u in the initial network, $|output(u)|$, is used to estimate the fanout count of the LUT rooted at u in the mapping solution. In the IMap algorithm between iterations, the fanout

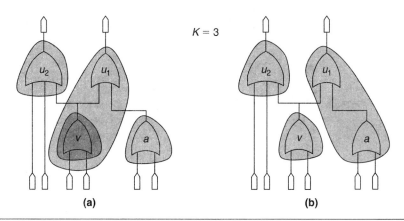

| (a) | (b) |

FIGURE 13.3 ■ Effect of excluding cuts across nonduplicable nodes: (a) initial mapping solution, and (b) improved solution with better area.

count estimation is updated by using a weighted combination of the estimated and the real fanout counts in previous iterations. As a result, equation 13.2 becomes $a(c) = (\Sigma_{u \in c} [a(u)/estimated\_fc(u)]) + A_c$, where $estimated\_fc(u)$ denotes the estimated fanout count for the current iteration.

Ling et al. [54] proposed a mixed structural and functional area-mapping algorithm that starts with a mapping solution (e.g., generated by a structural mapping algorithm). The key idea is a Boolean satisfiability (SAT) formulation for the problem of mapping a small circuit with up to ten inputs into the smallest possible number of LUTs. The algorithm iteratively selects a small logic cone to remap to fewer LUTs using an SAT solver. It is shown that for some highly structured (albeit small) designs, area can be improved significantly.

Most area optimization techniques are heuristic. A natural question is how close the mapping solutions obtained using existing mapping algorithms are from optimal. Cong and Minkovich [24] constructed a set of designs with known optimal area-mapping solutions, called LEKO (logic synthesis examples with known optimal bounds) examples, and tried existing academic algorithms and commercial tools on them. The average gap from optimal varied from 5 to 23 percent. From LEKO examples, they further derived LEKU (logic synthesis examples with known upper bounds) examples that require both logic optimization and mapping. Existing algorithms perform poorly on LEKU examples, with an average optimality gap of more than 70 times. This indicates that more research is needed in area-oriented mapping and optimization.

13.1.3 Performance-driven Mapping

The FlowMap algorithm and its derivatives can find a mapping solution with optimal depth. Recent advances in delay mapping focus on achieving the best performance with minimal area.

Exact layout information is not available during technology mapping in a typical FPGA design flow. Mapping algorithms usually ignore routing delays and try to optimize the total cell delays on the longest combinational paths in the mapping solution.

Most delay optimal mapping algorithms use the labeling scheme introduced in the FlowMap algorithm to rank and select cuts. The label of a PI is set to zero, assuming that the signal arrives at the beginning of the clock edge. After the labels for all the nodes in the fanin cone of a node v are found, the label of a cut c of v is determined using the formula in equation 13.3:

$$l(c) = \max\{l(u) + D_c | \forall u \in c\} \qquad (13.3)$$

where D_c is the delay of the LUT corresponding to c. Intuitively, $l(c)$ is the best arrival time at v if it is covered using the LUT generated from c. The label of v is then the smallest label among all of its cuts: $l(v) = \min\{l(c) | \forall c \in \Phi(v)\}$.

DAOmap [9] is a mapping algorithm that guarantees optimal delay while at the same time minimizing the area. It introduces three key techniques to optimize area without degrading timing. First, it enhances effective area computation to make it better avoid node duplication. Second, it applies area optimization techniques on noncritical paths. Last, it uses an iterative cut selection procedure to explore and perturb the solution space to improve solution quality.

DAOmap first picks cuts with the minimum label for each node. From those, it then picks one with minimum effective area. Furthermore, when there is positive slack, which is the difference between required time and arrival time at a node, it picks a cut with as small an area cost as possible under the condition that the timing increase does not exceed the slack.

Recognizing the heuristic nature of effective area computation, DAOmap also employs the technique of multiple passes of cut selection. Moreover, it adjusts area costs based on input sharing to encourage using nodes that have already been contained in selected cuts. This reduces the chance that a newly picked cut cuts into the interior of existing LUTs. Between successive iterations of cut selection, DAOmap also adjusts area cost to encourage selecting cuts containing nodes with a large number of fanouts in previous iterations. There are a few other secondary techniques used in DAOmap. The interested reader is referred to Chen and Cong [9] for details.

Based on the results reported, DAOmap can improve the area by about 13 percent on a large set of academic and industrial designs while maintaining optimal depths. It is also many times faster than previous mapping algorithms based on max-flow computation, mainly because of efficient implementation of cut enumeration.

A recent delay optimal mapping algorithm introduced several techniques to improve area while preserving performance [57]. Like DAOmap, this algorithm goes through several passes of cut selection, with each pass selecting cuts with better areas among the cuts that do not degrade timing. It is also based on the concept of effective area (or area flow). However, it does cut selection from PIs to POs instead of from POs to PIs, as in most other algorithms. With this processing order, the algorithm tries to use timing slacks on nodes close to PIs to reduce area cost. This is based on the observation that logic is typically denser when close to PIs, so slack relaxation is more effective for nodes closer to PIs. Experimental data shows 7 percent better area over DAOmap for the same optimal depths.

13.1.4 Power-aware Mapping

Power has become a major concern for FPGAs [51, 68]. Dynamic power dissipation in FPGAs results from charging and discharging capacitances. It is determined by the switching activities and the load capacitance of the LUT outputs and can be captured by equation 13.4:

$$P = \frac{1}{2}\Sigma_v C_v \cdot f_v \cdot V^2 \tag{13.4}$$

where C_v is the output load capacitance of node v, f_v is the switching activity of node v, and V is the supply voltage. Given a fixed supply voltage, power consumption in a mapped netlist is determined by switching activities and load capacitance of the LUT outputs.

Because technology mapping for power is NP-hard [34], a number of heuristic algorithms have been proposed. Most power-aware mapping algorithms try to reduce switching activities by hiding nodes with high switching activities inside LUTs, hence leaving LUTs with small output-switching activities in the mapped netlist.

Anderson and Najm [2] proposed a mapping algorithm to reduce switching activities and minimize logic duplication. Logic duplication is necessary to optimize timing and area, but can potentially increase power consumption. The algorithm uses the following power-aware cost function to rank cuts: $Cost(c) = l(c) + \beta \cdot P(c) + \gamma \cdot R(c)$, where $l(c)$ is the depth label of the cut c as given in equation 13.3 and $P(c)$ and $R(c)$ are the power and replication costs of the cut, respectively. The weighting factors β and γ can be used to bias the three cost terms. Anderson and Najm suggest a very small β to get a depth-optimal mapping solution with minimal power.

Power cost $P(c)$ is defined in such a way that it encourages absorbing high-activity connections inside LUTs. The replication cost tries to discourage logic duplication on timing noncritical paths. Power savings of over 14 percent were reported over timing-oriented mapping algorithms when both targeted optimal depths. When the mapping depth was relaxed by one level over optimal, additional power reduction of about 8 percent for 4-LUTs and 10 percent for 5-LUTs was reported.

One serious limitation of the power-based ranking in Anderson and Najm [2] is that it cannot account for multiple fanouts and reconvergence, which are common in most practical designs. Chen et al. [8] proposed a low-power technology-mapping algorithm based on an improved power-aware ranking in equation 13.5:

$$P(c) = (\Sigma_{u \in c} [P(u)/|output(u)|]) + U_c \qquad (13.5)$$

where U_c is a cost function that tries to capture power contributed by the cut c itself. Experimental results show that this algorithm outperforms previous power-aware mapping algorithms. It has also been extended to handle dual supply voltage FPGA architectures.

13.2   INTEGRATED MAPPING ALGORITHMS

Technology mapping is a step in the middle of an FPGA design flow. Technology-independent optimization is carried out before mapping; placement is carried out after. Sequential optimization such as retiming can be carried out before or after mapping. A separate approach can miss the best overall solutions even if we can solve each individual step optimally. In the section that follows we discuss mapping algorithms that combine mapping with other steps in the design flow.

13.2.1   Simultaneous Logic Synthesis, Mapping

Technology-independent Boolean optimizations carried out prior to technology mapping can significantly impact the mapping solution. During technology-independent optimization, we have the freedom to change the network structures, but accurate estimation of their impact on mapping is not available. During technology mapping, we can achieve optimal or close to optimal solutions using the algorithms discussed in Section 13.1. However, we are stuck with a fixed network. It is desirable to capture the interactions between logic optimization and mapping to arrive at a solution with better quality.

Lossless synthesis has been proposed by Mishchenko et al. [57] as a way to consider technology-independent optimization during mapping. It is based on the concept of *choice networks*, which is similar to the concept of mapping graphs [11, 49]. A choice network contains choice nodes that encode functionally equivalent but structurally different alternatives. The algorithm operates on a simple yet powerful data structure called *AIG*, which is a network of AND2 and INV gates. A combination of SAT and simulation techniques is used to detect functionally equivalent points in different networks and compress them to form one choice network.

Figure 13.4 illustrates the construction of a network with choices from two equivalent networks with different structures. The nodes x_1 and x_2 in the two networks are functionally equivalent. They are combined in an equivalence class in the choice network, and an arbitrary member (x_1 in this case) is set as the class representative. Note that p does not lead to a choice because its implementation is structurally the same in both networks. Similarly, o does not lead to a choice node.

Rather than try to come up with one "good" optimized network before mapping, the algorithm proposed by Mishchenko et al. [57] accumulates choices by combining intermediate networks seen during logic synthesis to generate a network with many choices. In a sense, it does not make judgments on the goodness of the intermediate networks but defers that decision to the mapping phase, when the best combination of these choices is selected. In the final mapping solution, different sections may come from different intermediate networks. For example, the timing-critical sections of the final mapping solution may come

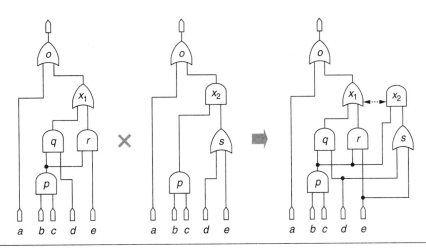

FIGURE 13.4 ■ Combining networks to create a choice network.

from networks optimized for timing, while the timing noncritical sections of the final mapping solution may come from networks optimized for area.

For mapping on choice networks, cut generation and cut ranking are extended to choice nodes. For example, the set of cuts of a choice node is simply the union of the sets of cuts of all of that node's fanin nodes. Similarly, the label of a choice node is the smallest one among the labels of its fanin nodes. The rest of the approach is similar to a conventional mapping algorithm. Results reported by Mishchenko et al. [57] show that both timing and area can be improved by over 7 percent on a set of benchmark designs compared to applying mapping to just one "optimized" network.

13.2.2 Integrated Retiming, Mapping

Retiming (discussed in Chapter 18) is an optimization technique that relocates flip-flops (FFs) in a network while preserving functionality of the network [50]. Retiming can shift FF boundaries and change the timing. If retiming is applied after mapping, mapping may optimize the wrong paths because the critical paths seen during mapping may not be critical after the FFs are repositioned. On the other hand, if retiming is applied before mapping, it will be carried out using less accurate timing information because it is applied to an unmapped network. In either approach, the impact of retiming on cut generation cannot be accounted for.

The network in Figure 13.5(a) is derived from the design in Figure 13.1(a) by retiming the FFs at the outputs of y and i to their inputs. After the retiming, all gates can be covered with one 3-LUT, as indicated in (a). The corresponding mapping solution is shown in (b). This mapping solution is obviously better than the one in Figure 13.1(c) in both area and timing.

Pan and Liu [63] proposed a polynomial time-mapping algorithm that can find a solution with the best cycle time in the combined solution space of

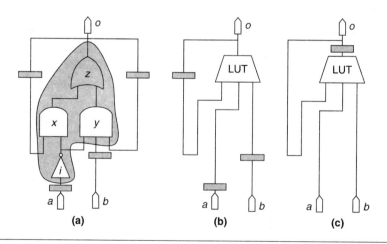

FIGURE 13.5 ▪ Retiming, mapping: (a) retiming and covering, (b) mapping solution, and (c) retimed solution.

retiming and mapping. In other words, the solution obtained is the best among all possible ways of retiming and mapping a network. Improved algorithms were later proposed that significantly reduce runtime while preserving the optimality of the final mapping solution [25, 27]. These algorithms, like the FlowMap algorithm, are all based on max-flow computation.

A cut enumeration-based algorithm for integrated retiming and mapping was proposed by Pan and Lin [61]. In it, cut generation is extended to go across FF boundaries to generate sequential cuts. In a network with FFs, a gate may go through zero or more FFs in addition to logic gates before reaching gate v. To capture this information, an element in a cut for a node v is represented as a pair consisting of the driving node u and the number of FFs d on the paths from u to v, denoted by u^d. Note that one node may reach another node through paths with different FF counts. In that case, the node will appear in the cut multiple times with different values of d. For example, for the cone in Figure 13.5(a), the corresponding cut is $\{z^1, a^1, b^1\}$. Pan and Lin [61] suggested an iterative procedure to determine the sequential cuts for all nodes.

To consider retiming effect, the concept of labels is extended using sequential arrival times [62, 63]. The label of a cut c is now defined as follows:

$$l(c) = \max\{l(u) - d \cdot \phi + D_c | \forall u^d \in c\} \qquad (13.6)$$

where ϕ is the target cycle time and D_c is the delay of the LUT corresponding to c. The combinationl cut formula (equation 13.3) can be viewed as a special case of equation 13.6 when $d = 0$. As in combinational mapping algorithms, the label of a gate v is the minimum of the labels of its cuts: $l(v) = \min\{l(c) | \forall c \in \Phi(v)\}$. The label of each PI is zero, and the label for each PO is that of its driver.

Pan and Lin's algorithm finds the labels for cuts and nodes through successive approximation by going through the nodes in the initial network in passes. After the labels for all nodes are computed and the target cycle time is determined to be achievable, the next step is to generate a mapping solution. As in the combinational case, a mapped network is constructed starting from POs and going backward. At each node v, the algorithm selects one of the cuts that realize the node's label and then moves on to select a cut for u if u^d is in the cut selected for v. On the interconnection from u to v, d FFs are inserted. To obtain the final mapping solution with a cycle time of ϕ, the algorithm retimes the LUT for each non-PI/PO node v by $\lceil l(v)/\phi \rceil - 1$. For the initial network in Figure 13.1(a), the final mapping solution with optimal cycle time generated by the algorithm is shown in Figure 13.5(c). Experimental results show that the algorithm is very efficient and consistently produces mapping solutions with better performance than combinational depth optimal mapping followed by optimal retiming.

13.2.3 Placement-driven Mapping

One drawback of the conventional mapping flow is the lack of accurate timing information on interconnects. Most algorithms use logic depth to measure timing. However, optimal-depth mapping solutions may not always be good after placement. To overcome this problem, we need to combine mapping with placement so that mapping can see more accurate interconnect information.

A number of algorithms try to carry out placement and mapping simultaneously [3, 6, 53, 59, 69]. For example, the MIS-pga algorithm of Murgai et al. [59] performs iterative logic optimization and placement. Chen et al. [6] proposed an algorithm that tightly couples technology mapping and placement by mapping each cell and placing it at the same time. In practice, such integrated approaches suffer a serious limitation: Because of the complexity of the combined problem, simple mapping, placement techniques are employed. As a result, the benefit of the combined approach is diminished.

Another approach is to iterate between mapping and placement (or placement refinement). Here, the design is first mapped and placed. Then the netlist is back-annotated and remapped under the given placement. This process can be repeated until a satisfactory solution is found. Figure 13.6 outlines the major steps in the iterative mapping and placement algorithm proposed by Lin et al. [53]. The key step is placement-driven remapping. The remapping step may make the placement illegal—for example, it may place more than one cell at the same location. If this happens, the placement needs to be legalized and refined.

Lin et al.'s algorithm [53] uses table lookup to estimate interconnect delays based on placement locations. Given two locations, it looks up the estimated delay in a prestored table for the wiring between the two locations. This is more accurate and realistic than the "fixed" interconnect delays used in earlier layout-based mapping algorithms [56, 72].

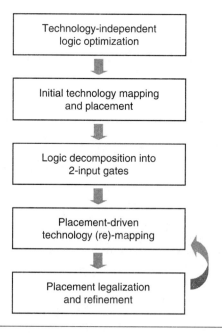

FIGURE 13.6 ▪ Iterative mapping, placement.

One difficulty in placement-driven mapping is that the placement may not become legal because of cell overlaps. Another is that timing predicted in the labeling phase may be unrealizable because of congestion in the new mapping solution. Congestion means that many LUTs are assigned to a small region, which requires many cell relocations to legalize the placement, which in turn, perturbs the placement and eventually the timing. To overcome this problem, the algorithm employs an iterative process with multiple passes of cut selection. Each pass uses the cell congestion information gathered during previous iterations to guide the mapping decisions. Several techniques have been proposed to relieve congestion. One is a hierarchical area control scheme to evaluate the local congestion cost, in which the chip is divided into bins with different granularities. Area increase is tallied in bins, and penalty costs are given to bins with area overflows.

Once a mapping solution is generated, the algorithm invokes timing-driven legalization that moves overlapping cells to empty locations in their neighborhood based on the timing slack available to the cells. Finally, a simulated annealing-based placement refinement phase is carried out to improve performance. Experimental results show that the algorithm can improve timing by more than 12 percent, with minimal area penalty due to remapping.

13.3 MAPPING ALGORITHMS FOR HETEROGENEOUS RESOURCES

Up to this point, we have assumed that all logic cells are LUTs with a uniform input size K. In reality, commercial FPGA architectures contain heterogeneous resources (e.g., LUTs of different input sizes, embedded memory, and PLA-like logic cells). We briefly summarize mapping algorithms that target or take advantage of such architectural features.

13.3.1 Mapping to LUTs of Different Input Sizes

There are a number of commercial FPGA architectures that support LUTs with multiple input sizes on the same device. Mapping algorithms have been proposed to optimize area [29, 39, 40, 43] and timing [30, 32].

In the special case of tree networks, Korupolu et al. [43] presented a polynomial area optimal algorithm. For general networks, the PRAETOR algorithm discussed in Section 13.1.2 can be applied to these architectures by assigning different area costs for LUTs with different input sizes.

For timing optimization, the algorithm proposed by Cong and Xu [30] is an extension of FlowMap. Like FlowMap, it is also based on flow computation and can be cast in the cut enumeration framework. Assume that there are two types of LUTs with input sizes K_1 and K_2, and delays d_1 and d_2, where $K_1 < K_2$, $d_1 < d_2$. We can enumerate all K_2-cuts. When labeling a cut, we can set its delay to d_1 or d_2 depending on its size. With this simple modification, an algorithm for homogeneous LUT architectures can be used for architectures with different LUT sizes.

When there are resource bounds on available LUTs of different sizes, the mapping problem becomes NP-hard. Assuming that there can be at most r K_2-LUTs, a heuristic algorithm was proposed that starts out by finding a mapping solution without considering resource bounds [31]. If the current mapping solution meets the resource bound, it stops. If not, it increases d_2, the delay of K_2-LUTs, and solves the unconstrained version again, which should lead to another mapping solution with a decreased number of K_2-LUTs. This process is repeated until the resource bound is met.

13.3.2 Mapping to Complex Logic Blocks

FPGA devices typically contain additional logic that, together with LUTs, can form complex *programmable logic blocks* (PLBs). PLBs can implement complex logic functions. Figure 13.7 shows two PLBs that consist of LUTs and logic gates and can implement functions of up to nine inputs.

A simple approach to PLB mapping is to map the initial network to the constituent cells inside the PLBs. For example, for a device with the PLB in Figure 13.7(a), we can first map the initial network to 3-LUTs and 4-LUTs. Afterwards, the LUTs are clustered to obtain a network of PLBs. Such a two-step approach is obviously suboptimal.

Recent approaches try to map directly to PLBs [13, 23, 47, 65]. The cut enumeration framework can still be used after enhancements. Because a PLB can have more inputs than a typical LUT, a node may have too many cuts. Intelligent cut pruning, using techniques such as those proposed by Chatterjee et al. [5] and Ling et al. [54], is necessary to avoid long runtime and memory explosion. Unlike in the case of LUTs, a PLB has limited functional capability in that it cannot implement all of the functions of its inputs. For example, the PLB in Figure 13.7(b) can implement all functions of up to five inputs, but it can only implement some of the functions with six inputs. An essential step in PLB mapping is Boolean matching, which, given a cut, decides if the corresponding logic cone can be implemented by a PLB.

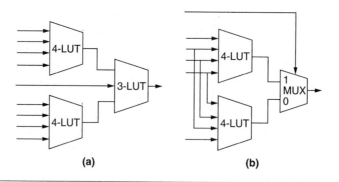

(a)   (b)

FIGURE 13.7 ■ Two PLB examples.

Algorithms for Boolean matching for PLBs can be classified into two categories: decomposition based [13, 23] and satisfiability (SAT) based [25, 54, 65]. Decomposition-based Boolean matching tries to decompose the input function according to the structure of the target PLB using functional decomposition. Cong and Hwang [23] proposed matching procedures for a wide variety of common PLBs.

A drawback of decomposition-based Boolean matching is that each PLB needs a specialized matching procedure. Decomposition-based Boolean matching can also be slow and memory intensive because of extensive use of BDD operations. On the other hand, SAT-based Boolean matching encodes the function, the target PLB, and their matching in a Boolean expression in conjunctive normal form (CNF). Then it leverages an efficient SAT solver (e.g., the one proposed by Moskewicz et al. [58]) to check whether the PLB can be configured to implement the function. The size of the CNF expression can have significant impact on the runtime of an SAT-based matching algorithm. An improved SAT formulation with smaller expressions was proposed recently by Cong and Minkovich [25].

13.3.3 Mapping Logic to Embedded Memory Blocks

On-chip memory has become a common feature of high-performance FPGAs. Dedicated embedded memory blocks (EMBs) can be used to improve clock frequencies and lower costs for large designs that require memory. If a design does not need all the available EMBs, unused ones can be employed to implement logic, which essentially turns them into large multi-input multi-output LUTs.

EMBs usually have configurable widths and depths, so they can be used to implement functions with different numbers of inputs/outputs. For example, a 2K-bit memory with configurations 2048×1, 1024×2, and 512×4 can be used to implement an 11-input/1-output, 10-input/2-output, or 9-input/4-output logic function, respectively.

Mapping logic to EMBs is typically done as a postprocessing step after LUT mapping. These algorithms start with an optimized LUT-mapping solution and then pack groups of LUTs into unused EMBs [26, 70]. The SMAP algorithm [70] maps one EMB at a time. It begins by selecting a seed node. A fanin cone of the seed node is generated by finding a d-feasible cut that covers as many nodes as possible, where d is the bit width of the address line of the target EMB. Because d is considerably large, flow-based cut generation is used. After the cone is generated, the output selection process selects signals to be the EMB outputs. Output selection tries to select a set of signals so that the resulting EMB can eliminate as many LUTs as possible. This is done by assigning each node a score that reflects the number of eliminated nodes if the node is selected. The w highest-scoring nodes are selected as the EMB outputs, where w is the number of outputs of the target EMB.

The selection of the seed node is critical for this method. The algorithm tests each candidate node and selects the one that leads to the maximum number of eliminated LUTs. Heuristics were introduced to consider EMBs with different configurations and to preserve timing.

Another algorithm, EMB_Pack, proposed by Cong and Xu [26], takes a slightly different approach. It finds the logic to map to EMBs altogether instead of one at a time, as in SMAP, which can potentially find better mapping.

13.3.4 Mapping to Macrocells

Complex programmable logic devices (CPLDs) are a class of programmable logic devices that are more coarse grained than typical FPGAs. Each CPLD logic cell (called Pterm block) is essentially a programmable logic array (PLA) that consists of a set of product terms (Pterms) with multiple outputs. A Pterm block can be characterized by a 3-tuple (k, m, p) where k is the number of inputs, p is the number of outputs, and m is the number of Pterms for the block. The input size k is typically much larger than that of FPGA logic cells.

Relatively speaking, there is much less mapping work reported for CPLDs. A fast heuristic partition method for PLA-based structures was presented by Hasan et al. [38]. The DDMap algorithm [42] adapts a LUT mapper for CPLD mapping. It uses wide cuts to form big LUTs and decomposes the big LUTs into Pterms allowed in the target CPLD. Packing is used to form multi-output Pterm cells. An area-oriented mapping algorithm was proposed for CPLDs by Anderson and Brown [1]. Cong et al. [20] investigated an FPGA architecture consisting of single-output Pterm blocks, and proposed a timing-oriented mapping algorithm.

PLAmap is a timing-oriented mapping algorithm for CPLDs [7]. Like the LUT mapping algorithms discussed earlier, it has a labeling phase and a mapping phase. In the labeling phase, it tries to find the minimal mapping depth for each node using a logic cell $(k, m, 1)$—that is, a single-output Pterm block, assuming that each logic cell has one unit delay. The labeling procedure is based on Lawler et al.'s clustering algorithm [46]. Let l be the largest label of the nodes in the fanin cone of a node. The algorithm forms a cluster for the node by grouping it with all nodes in its fanin cone with the label l. If the cluster can be implemented by a $(k, m, 1)$ cell, the node is assigned the label l; otherwise, the node gets the label $l + 1$ with a cluster consisting of the node itself. Note that this is a heuristic in that the label may not be the best because of the so-called *non-monotone property* [7]. The mapping phase is done in reverse topological order from the POs. The algorithm tries to merge the clusters generated in the labeling phase to form (k, m, p) cells whenever possible. Cluster merging is done in such a way that duplication is minimized and the labels of the POs do not exceed the performance target. Experimental results show that PLAmap outperforms commercial tools and other algorithms with no (or a very small) area penalty.

Pterm blocks or macrocells are suitable for implementing wide-fanin, low-density logic, such as finite-state machines. They can potentially complement fine-grained LUTs to improve both performance and utilization. Device architectures with a mixture of LUTs and Pterm blocks or macrocells have been suggested to take advantage of different types of logic cells. Technology mapping algorithms have been proposed for such hybrid architectures [41, 42, 44].

13.4 SUMMARY

This chapter discussed technology mapping algorithms for FPGAs. Emphasis was placed on state-of-the-art algorithms that have been, or most likely will be, reduced to practice. We discussed mapping algorithms for different objectives, such as area, timing, and power, as well as mapping algorithms that take advantage of heterogeneous resources in modern FPGA devices.

FPGA technology mapping has been and continues to be a subject of active research. A general trend is to integrate technology mapping with other steps in the FPGA design flow to improve the quality of final implementations (e.g., combining mapping and clustering [10]).

As semiconductor technologies advance, new FPGA architecture features are being introduced to improve area utilization, performance, and power consumption. For example, architectures have been introduced or proposed that use large LUTs (much larger than traditional 4-/5-LUTs) or multiple supply voltages. New mapping techniques are being developed to take advantage of these architecture features.

References

[1] J. H. Anderson, S. D. Brown. Technology mapping for large complex PLDs. *ACM/IEEE Design Automation Conference*, 1998.

[2] J. H. Anderson, F. N. Najm. Power-aware technology mapping for LUT-based FPGAs. *IEEE International Conference on Field-Programmable Technology*, 2002.

[3] N. Bhat, D. D. Hill. Routable technology mapping for LUT FPGAs. *IEEE International Conference on Computer Design*, 1992.

[4] S. C. Chang, M. Marek-Sodowska, T. Hwang. Technology mapping for LUT FPGA based on decomposition of binary decision diagrams. *IEEE Transactions on Computer-Aided Design of Integrated Circuits and Systems*, 15(10), October 1996.

[5] S. Chatterjee, A. Mishchenko, R. Brayton. Factor cuts. *International Conference on Computer-Aided Design*, 2006

[6] C. Chen, Y. Tsay, Y. Hwang, T. Wu, Y. Lin. Combining technology mapping, placement for delay-optimization in FPGA designs. *International Conference on Computer-Aided Design*, 1993.

[7] D. Chen, J. Cong, M. Ercegovac, Z. Huang. Performance-driven mapping for CPLD architectures. *IEEE Transactions on Computer-Aided Design of Integrated Circuits and Systems* 22(10), October 2003.

[8] D. Chen, J. Cong, F. Li, L. He. Low-power technology mapping for FPGA architectures with dual supply voltages. *International Symposium on Field-Programmable Gate Arrays*, February 2004.

[9] D. Chen., J. Cong. DAOmap: A depth-optimal area optimization mapping algorithm for FPGA designs. *International Conference on Computer-Aided Design*, 2004.

[10] D. Chen, J. Cong, J. Lin. Optimal simultaneous mapping, clustering for FPGA delay optimization. *ACM/IEEE Design Automation Conference*, 2006.

[11] G. Chen, J. Cong. Simultaneous logic decomposition with technology mapping in FPGA designs. *International Symposium on Field-Programmable Gate Arrays*, 2001.

[12] K. C. Chen, J. Cong, Y. Ding, A. B. Kahng, P. Trajmar. DAGmap: Graph-based FPGA technology mapping for delay optimization. *IEEE Design and Test of Computers* 9(3), September 1992.

[13] M. Chikodikar, S. Laddha, A. Sirasao. A technology mapper for Xilinx FPGAs. *Tenth International Conference on VLSI Design*, January 1997.

[14] J. Cong, Y. Ding. An optimal technology-mapping algorithm for delay optimization in lookup table–based FPGA designs. *International Conference on Computer-Aided Design*, November 1992.

[15] J. Cong, Y. Ding. Beyond the combinatorial limit in depth minimization for LUT-based FPGA designs. *International Conference on Computer-Aided Design*, 1993.

[16] J. Cong, Y. Ding. FlowMap: An Optimal technology-mapping algorithm for delay optimization in lookup table–based FPGA designs. *IEEE Transactions on Computer-Aided Design of Integrated Circuits and Systems* 13(1), January 1994.

[17] J. Cong, Y. Ding. On area/depth trade-off in LUT-based FPGA technology mapping. *IEEE Transactions on VLSI Systems* 2(2), 1994.

[18] J. Cong, Y. Ding. Combinational logic synthesis for LUT-based field-programmable gate arrays. *ACM Transactions on Design Automation of Electronic Systems* 1(2), April 1996.

[19] J. Cong, Y. Ding. T. Gao, K. C. Chen. LUT-base, FPGA technology mapping under arbitrary net-delay model. *Computers and Graphics* 18(4), 1994.

[20] J. Cong, H. Huang, X. Yuan. Technology mapping and architecture evaluation for k/m-macrocell-based FPGAs. *ACM Transactions on Design Automation of Electronic Systems*, January 2005.

[21] J. Cong, Y. Hwang. Simultaneous depth and area minimization in LUT-based FPGA mapping. *International Symposium on Field-Programmable Gate Arrays*, February 1995.

[22] J. Cong, Y. Hwang. Structural gate decomposition for depth-optimal technology mapping in LUT-based FPGA design. *Design Automation Conference*, 1996.

[23] J. Cong, Y. Hwang. Boolean matching for LUT-based logic blocks with applications to architecture evaluation and technology mapping. *IEEE Transactions on Computer-Aided Design of Integrated Circuits and Systems* 20(9), 2001.

[24] J. Cong, K. Minkovich. Optimality study of logic synthesis for LUT-based FPGAs. *International Symposium on Field-Programmable Gate Arrays*, February 2006.

[25] J. Cong, K. Minkovich. Improved SAT-based Boolean matching using implicants for LUT-based FPGAs. *International Symposium on Field-Programmable Gate Arrays*, February 2007.

[26] J. Cong, S. Xu. Technology mapping for FPGAs with embedded memory blocks. *International Symposium on Field-Programmable Gate Arrays*, 1998.

[27] J. Cong, C Wu. FPGA Synthesis with retiming and pipelining for clock period minimization of sequential circuits, *Design Automation Conference,* 1997.

[28] J. Cong, C Wu. Optimal FPGA mapping, retiming with efficient initial state computation. *Design Automation Conference,* 1998.

[29] J. Cong, C. Wu, Y. Ding. Cut ranking and pruning: Enabling a general, efficient FPGA mapping solution. *International Symposium on Field-Programmable Gate Arrays*, February 1999.

[30] J. Cong, S. Xu. Delay-optimal technology mapping for FPGAs with heterogeneous LUTs. *Design Automation Conference*, 1998.

[31] J. Cong, S. Xu. Delay-oriented technology mapping for heterogeneous FPGAs with bounded resources. *International Conference on Computer-Aided Design*, 1998.

[32] J. Cong, S. Xu. Performance-driven technology mapping for heterogeneous FPGAs. *IEEE Transactions on Computer-Aided Design of Integrated Circuits and Systems* 19(11), November 2000.

[33] G. De Micheli. *Synthesis: Optimization of Digital Circuits*, McGraw-Hill, 1994.

[34] A. H. Farrahi, M. Sarrafzadeh. FPGA technology mapping for power minimization. *International Workshop on Field-Programmable Logic and Applications*, 1994.

[35] A. Farrahi, M. Sarrafzadeh. Complexity of the lookup-table minimization problem for FPGA technology mapping. *IEEE Transactions on Computer-Aided Design of Integrated Circuits and Systems* 13(11), November 1994.

[36] R. J. Francis et al. Chortle-CRF: Fast technology mapping for lookup table–based FPGAs. *Design Automation Conference*, 1991.

[37] R. J. Francis, J. Rose, Z. Vranesic. Technology mapping for lookup table–based FPGAs for performance. *International Conference on Computer-Aided Design*, November 1991.

[38] Z. Hasan, D. Harrison, M. Ciesielski. A fast partition method for PLA-based FPGAs. *IEEE Design and Test of Computers*, December 1992.

[39] J. He, J. Rose. Technology mapping for heterogeneous FPGAs. *International Symposium on Field-Programmable Gate Arrays,* 1994.

[40] M. Inuani, J. Saul. Resynthesis in technology mapping for heterogeneous FPGAs. *International Conference on Computer-Aided Design*, 1998.

[41] A. Kaviani, S. Brown. Technology-mapping issues for an FPGA with lookup tables, PLA-like blocks. *International Symposium on Field-Programmable Gate Arrays,* 2000.

[42] J. L. Kouloheris. *Empirical Study of the Effect of Cell Granularity on FPGA Density, Performance*, Ph.D. thesis, Stanford University, 1993.

[43] M. R. Korupolu, K. K. Lee, D. F. Wong. Exact tree-based FPGA technology mapping for logic blocks with independent LUTs. *Design Automation Conference,* 1998.

[44] S. Krishnamoorthy, R. Tessier. Technology-mapping algorithms for Hybrid FPGAs containing lookup tables, PLAs. *IEEE Transactions on Computer-Aided Design of Integrated Circuits and Systems* 22(5), May 2003.

[45] J. Lamoureux, S. J. E. Wilton. On the interaction between power-aware FPGA CAD algorithms. *IEEE International Conference on Computer-Aided Design*, November 2003.

[46] E. L. Lawler, K. N. Levitt, J. Turner. Module clustering to minimize delay in digital networks. *Transactions on Computers* 18(1), 1969.

[47] K. Lee, D. Wong. An exact tree-based, structural technology-mapping algorithm for configurable logic blocks in FPGAs. *International Conference on Computer-Aided Design*, 1999.

[48] C. Legl, B. Wurth, K. Eckl. A Boolean approach to performance-directed technology mapping for LUT-based FPGA designs. *Design Automation Conference*, June 1996.

[49] E. Lehman, Y. Watanabe, J. Grodstein, H. Harkness. Logic decomposition during technology mapping. *IEEE Transactions on Computer-Aided Design of Integrated Circuits and Systems* 16(8), 1997.

[50] C. E. Leiserson, J. B. Saxe. Retiming synchronous circuitry. *Algorithmica* 6, 1991.

[51] F. Li, D. Chen, L. He, J. Cong. Architecture evaluation for power-efficient FPGAs. *International Symposium on Field-Programmable Gate Arrays*, February 2003.

[52] H. Li, S. Katkoori, W. K. Mak. Power minimization algorithms for LUT-based FPGA technology mapping. *ACM Transactions on Design Automation of Electronic Systems* 9(1), January 2004.

[53] J. Lin, A. Jagannathan, J. Cong. Placement-driven technology mapping for LUT-based FPGAs. *International Symposium on Field-Programmable Gate Arrays*, February 2003.

[54] A. Ling, D. Singh, S. Brown. FPGA technology mapping: A study of optimality. *Design Automation Conference*, 2005.

[55] V. Manohararajah, S. D. Brown, Z. G. Vranesic. Heuristics for area minimization in LUT-based FPGA technology mapping. *International Workshop on Logic Synthesis*, 2004.

[56] A. Mathur, C. L. Liu. Performance-driven technology mapping for lookup table–based FPGAs using the general delay model. *International Workshop on Field-Programmable Gate Arrays*, February 1994.

[57] A. Mishchenko, S. Chatterjee, R. Brayton. Improvements to technology mapping for LUT-based FPGAs. *International Symposium on Field-Programmable Gate Arrays*, 2006.

[58] M. Moskewicz, C. Madigan, Y. Zhao, L. Zhang, S. Malik. Chaff: Engineering an efficient SAT solver. *Design Automation Conference*, 2001.

[59] R. Murgai et al. Improved logic synthesis algorithms for table lookup architectures. *International Conference on Computer-Aided Design*, November 1991.

[60] R. Murgai et al. Performance directed synthesis for table lookup programmable gate arrays. *International Conference on Computer-Aided Design*, November 1991.

[61] P. Pan, C. C. Lin. A new retiming-based technology-mapping algorithm for LUT-based FPGAs. *International Symposium on Field-Programmable Gate Arrays*, 1998.

[62] P. Pan, C. L. Liu. Technology mapping of sequential circuits for LUT-based FPGAs for performance. *International Symposium on Field-Programmable Gate Arrays*, 1996.

[63] P. Pan, C. L. Liu. Optimal clock period FPGA technology mapping for sequential circuits. *Design Automation Conference*, June 1996.

[64] P. Pan, C. L. Liu. Optimal clock period FPGA technology mapping for sequential circuits. *ACM Transactions on Design Automation of Electronic Systems* 3(3), 1998.

[65] S. Safarpour, A. Veneris, G. Baeckler, R. Yuan. Efficient SAT-based Boolean matching for FPGA technology mapping. *Design Automation Conference*, July 2006.

[66] P. Sawkar, D. Thomas. Technology mapping for table lookup–based field-programmable gate arrays. *ACM/SIGDA Workshop on Field-Programmable Gate Arrays*, February 1992.

[67] M. Schlag, J. Kong, P. K. Chan. Routability-driven technology mapping for lookup table–based FPGAs. *IEEE Transactions on Computer-Aided Design of Integrated Circuits and Systems* 13(1), 1994.

[68] L. Shang, A. Kaviani, K. Bathala. Dynamic power consumption in Virtex-II FPGA family. *International Symposium on Field-Programmable Gate Arrays*, February 2002.

[69] N. Togawa, M. Sato, T. Ohtsuki. Maple: A simultaneous technology mapping, placement, and global routing algorithm for field-programmable gate arrays. *International Conference on Computer-Aided Design*, 1994.

[70] S. Wilton. SMAP: Heterogeneous technology mapping for area reduction in FPGAs with embedded memory arrays. *International Symposium on Field-Programmable Gate Arrays*, 1998.

[71] Z. H. Wang, E. C. Liu, J. Lai, T. C. Wang. Power minimization in LUT-based FPGA technology mapping. *Asia South Pacific Design Automation Conference*, 2001.

[72] H. Yang, D. F. Wong. Edge-map: Optimal performance-driven technology mapping for iterative LUT-based FPGA designs. *International Conference on Computer-Aided Design*, November 1994.

FPGA PLACEMENT

One thing that stands out in this book's contents: While most individual steps in the compilation flow are covered in a single chapter, placement is covered in three—Chapters 14 through 16. Placement is actually just the problem of assigning specific logic computations to individual logic blocks in the architecture, so why does it merit a longer treatment than, say, FPGA routing? There are at least two reasons.

One reason is historical: Until relatively recently, the placement problem was small enough that structured approaches were possible. These included hand placement, which produced higher-quality results than automatic placement. In contrast, for a problem such as routing, FPGA routers were very fast and efficient, and thus hand-routing was almost never done.

A second reason is that fundamentally different approaches can be taken to solve the placement problem. Do we view the design as an unstructured pile of gates to be scattered across the FPGA's surface, or is there an inherent structure that can be leveraged? And, if we use the computation's structure to drive the placement process, how do we handle portions of the computation, such as control, that likely do not have such an easily determined structure?

These considerations have given rise to several ways of performing FPGA placement, which are represented by the three chapters that follow. In Chapter 14 we consider general-purpose FPGA placement. Such systems, using complex optimization techniques, treat the designer's circuit as essentially an unstructured collection of gates. These are packed together into logic blocks and placed in the array, guided almost exclusively by the design's local connectivity information. Higher-level information, such as the design hierarchy or the regularity in multibit operations, is largely ignored. Thus, these techniques can handle any possible placement problem. Moreover, they serve as a good starting point, as other approaches that rely on more structure in the netlist generally do not work for unstructured designs, and so there must always be some way for unstructured netlists to be processed.

Chapter 15 considers datapath placement. Most designs for an FPGA consist of a large, highly structured datapath and a small, unstructured control system. The datapath is built from multibit function units, such as adders and multipliers, where the computation is fairly similar for each bit of the operands. Datapath-oriented placers can automatically leverage this information to improve the resulting placement quality.

An alternative to fully automatic placement, whether for random logic or for datapaths, is to provide ways for the user to guide the placement process. For example, the user generally knows what portions of the design should be kept together, where the critical paths are, and how these critical paths should be laid out. Chapter 16 considers such systems, in which placement is more a user-guided process than a fully automated algorithm. Whereas the size of modern FPGA designs, and the increasing quality of placers, is making this approach less attractive over time, constructive placement of critical subsystems is still a valid alternative.

CHAPTER 14

PLACEMENT FOR GENERAL-PURPOSE FPGAS

Vaughn Betz
Altera Corporation

Placement follows technology mapping in the CAD flow and chooses a location for each block in a circuit. This chapter describes "general-purpose" placement approaches; these techniques can be used with any circuit targeting the commercial field-programmable gate arrays (FPGAs) in widespread use today. After defining the placement problem and optimization goals, the chapter describes the clustering algorithms that are frequently used in conjunction with placement tools. Three different classes of placement algorithms are then detailed: simulated annealing, partition based, and analytic. The chapter concludes with suggestions for further reading and open challenges in FPGA placement.

14.1 THE FPGA PLACEMENT PROBLEM

An FPGA placement algorithm takes two basic inputs: (1) a netlist specifying the functional blocks to be implemented and the connections between them, and (2) a device map indicating which functional unit can be placed at each location. The algorithm selects a legal location for each block such that the circuit wiring is optimized. Figure 14.1 illustrates the FPGA placement problem. Both the legality constraints and the optimization metric (what constitutes a "good" arrangement of functional blocks) depend on the FPGA architecture being targeted.

A good placement is extremely important for FPGA designs—without a high-quality placement, a circuit generally cannot be successfully routed. Even if the circuit does route, a poor placement will still lead to a lower maximum operating speed and increased power consumption. At the same time, finding a good placement for a circuit is a challenging problem. A large commercial FPGA contains approximately 500,000 functional blocks, leading to approximately 500,000! possible placements. Exhaustive evaluation of the placement solution space is therefore impossible. Furthermore, placement is a computationally hard problem, so there are no known algorithms that produce optimal results in practical central processing unit (CPU) time. Consequently, the development of fast and effective heuristic placement algorithms is a very important research area.

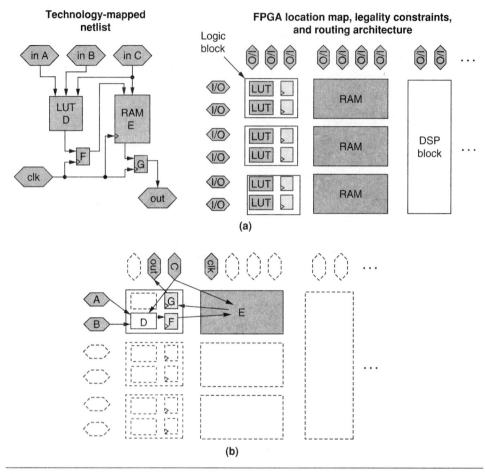

FIGURE 14.1 ■ Placement overview: (a) inputs to the placement algorithm, and (b) placement algorithm output—the location of each block.

14.1.1   Device Legality Constraints

The fact that all resources are prefabricated in an FPGA leads to a variety of placement legality constraints:

■ A legal placement must place a functional block only in a location on the chip that can accommodate it. For example, a RAM block must be placed in a RAM location, and a lookup table (LUT) must be placed in a LUT location.
■ Usually there are legality constraints on groups of functional blocks. In Altera's Stratix-II FPGAs, for example, a *logic block* contains 16 LUTs and 16 registers [1]. However, there are limits on the number of clock signals, clock enable signals, and routing inputs to the logic block. Consequently, not every grouping of 16 LUTs and 16 registers constitutes

a legal logic block, and the placement algorithm must ensure that it does not produce illegal logic blocks.

- Some groups of functional blocks must be placed in a specific relative orientation so that they can make use of special, dedicated routing resources. The simplest example of this constraint is arithmetic logic cells—in order to use the dedicated carry-chain hardware available in an FPGA, the logic cells forming a carry chain must be placed adjacent to each other in the sequence required by the carry structure.
- There are other detailed legality constraints, such as a limit on the number of global clocking resources in each area of the device, which commercial FPGA placement algorithms must respect.[1]

14.1.2 Optimization Goals

The basic goal of an FPGA placement algorithm is to locate functional blocks such that the interconnect required to route the signals between them is minimized. As Figure 14.2 illustrates, the routing required to connect two blocks is a function not only of the distance between them but also of the FPGA architecture. Figure 14.2(a) shows the wiring required to connect two blocks in different relative positions in a Stratix-II FPGA. Stratix-II is an *island-style* FPGA [3] that contains routing segments that span 4, 16, and 24 logic blocks. Programmable switches allow routing segments in the same direction (horizontal or vertical) to be connected at their endpoints to create longer routes. Other programmable switches allow some horizontal routing segments to connect to vertical routing segments where they cross and vice versa. In an island-style FPGA, the amount of wiring required to connect two functional blocks is roughly proportional to the Manhattan distance between them.

Figure 14.2(b) shows that the wiring required by the same placements in an FPGA with a *hierarchical* routing architecture (in this case the Altera APEX family [4]) is quite different. For hierarchical FPGAs, the amount of wiring required to connect two functional blocks is proportional to the number of levels of the routing hierarchy that must be traversed to connect them. Note that even the ranking of placement choices is different between APEX and Stratix-II—in Stratix-II placements, *A* and *C* are best, while in APEX placements, *A* and *B* are best. Clearly FPGA placement algorithms must have a model of the routing architecture they target in order to achieve good results.

FPGA placement tools can broadly be divided into *routability-driven* and *timing-driven* algorithms. Routability-driven algorithms try to create a placement that minimizes the total interconnect required, as this increases the probability of successfully routing the design. Since FPGA interconnect is prefabricated, the amount of interconnect in each region of a device is fixed, and a placement that requires more interconnect in a device region than that region contains cannot be routed. Consequently, some routability-driven placement algorithms

---

[1] Researchers wishing to target their CAD tools to industrial FPGAs can obtain a full list of the legality constraints in Altera FPGAs from the Quartus University Interface Program [2].

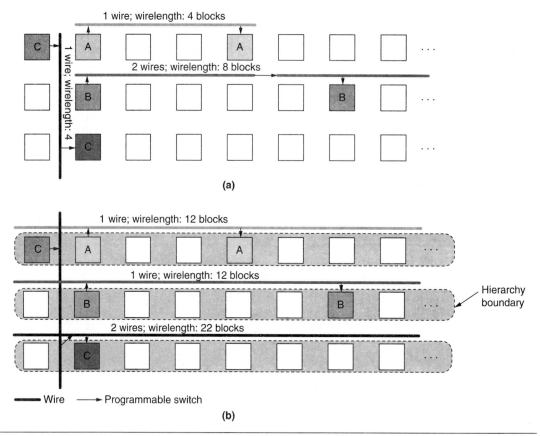

FIGURE 14.2 ■ Influence of the routing architecture on wirelength for a given placement: (a) sample routings on a Stratix-II FPGA (island style), and (b) sample routings on an APEX FPGA (hierarchical).

minimize not only the total wiring required by the design but also the amount of *routing congestion*. Routing congestion occurs when the interconnect demand approaches or exceeds the fabricated wiring capacity in some part of the FPGA.

In addition to optimizing for routability, timing-driven algorithms use timing analysis [5] to identify critical paths and/or connections and to optimize the delay of those connections. Since most delays in an FPGA are due to the programmable interconnect, timing-driven placement can achieve a large improvement in circuit speed over routability-driven approaches.

Some recent FPGA placement algorithms attempt to minimize power consumption as well.

14.1.3 Designer Placement Directives

Commercial FPGA placement tools allow designers to control the placement of some or all of the design logic at various levels of abstraction. Obeying the placement directives specified by a designer while still choosing good locations for the unconstrained and partially constrained blocks is a challenging problem, but one on which little has been published.

Figure 14.3 illustrates the common types of placement directives. The most restrictive specifies the *exact location* of a block. Typical uses of this directive are to lock down the design I/Os at the locations required by the circuit board or to lock down the elements of a performance-critical intellectual property (IP) core. A less restrictive directive forces blocks to go into a specific two-dimensional area, or *fixed region*. This directive allows a designer to guide the placement tool to a good high-level floorplan while still allowing automatic optimization of the placement details. One can specify the *relative location* of several blocks, but let the placement tool choose exactly where to locate the block group. This directive is useful for library components where a designer knows a good placement of the component blocks relative to each other. A *floating region* specifies that some logic should be placed within a tight region but that the placement tool can choose where that region should be on the device.

One must take care when specifying placement directives, as fixing portions of the placement ineffectively will reduce result quality versus a fully automatic placement. Modern placement tools produce high-quality results, and generally

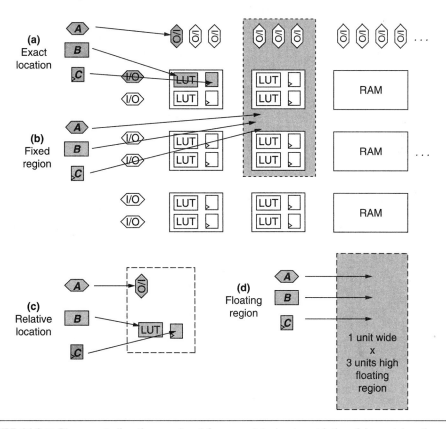

FIGURE 14.3 ■ Placement directives, ordered from most to least restrictive: (a) exact location, (b) fixed region, (c) relative location, and (d) floating region.

it is very difficult for a designer to specify placement directives on irregular logic that lead to a better solution than the placement tool would find without guidance. Placement directives have more value for regular structures, since humans are better than conventional CAD tools at recognizing regular logic patterns and matching them to a highly optimized regular placement. For examples of the use of placement directives, see Chapter 16.

14.2 CLUSTERING

A common companion to FPGA placement algorithms is a bottom-up clustering step that runs before the main placement algorithm to group-related circuit elements together into clusters. Clustering reduces the number of blocks to place, improving the runtime of the main placement algorithm. In addition, one normally chooses a cluster size that corresponds to a natural boundary in the FPGA architecture, such as a logic block. This allows the clustering algorithm to deal with many of the device legality constraints by ensuring that each cluster forms a legal logic (or RAM or DSP) block, and it simplifies legality checking for the main placement algorithm.

The most common FPGA clustering formulation transforms a netlist of logic elements into a netlist of logic blocks. In most FPGA architectures each logic element consists of a LUT plus a register, and each logic block has the capacity to implement up to N logic elements. As well, logic blocks have a limit on the number of input signals that can be brought in from the programmable routing and on the number of different control signals, such as register clocks, that can be used.

The typical clustering goals are:

- To achieve high density by minimizing the number of clusters (i.e., logic blocks) required to implement a circuit.
- To improve circuit speed by localizing time-critical connections within a cluster so they can be completed with fast local routing.
- To reduce wiring demand in the FPGA by grouping related logic in each cluster.

The RASP system [6] includes one of the first logic block clustering algorithms. It performs maximum weighted matching on a graph where edge weights between logic elements reflect the desirability of clustering them. Logic elements that cannot be legally clustered have no edge between them, while those connected by timing-critical connections or with a large number of common signals have edges with high weights.

RASP has the attractive feature of simultaneously choosing all clusters of two logic elements to maximize the total weight of edges contained within the clusters. By recursively repeating the algorithm, one can create larger clusters, at least when the cluster capacity is a power of 2. The first matching produces a netlist of size-2 clusters; a matching on the size-2 cluster netlist produces size-4 clusters, and so on. The RASP clustering algorithm has a high computational complexity of $O(n^3)$, where n is the number of logic elements in the circuit. This prevents it from scaling to large problems.

The VPack algorithm [3] takes the opposite approach to that of RASP—it creates one cluster of the desired size (e.g., seven logic elements) before moving on to create the next cluster. VPack first chooses a *seed* logic element for a new cluster and then greedily packs the logic element with the highest *attraction* to the current cluster until no more can be legally added. The attraction function is the number of nets that connect to both the logic element in question and the current cluster. VPack has a computational complexity of $O(k_{max}n)$ where k_{max} is the maximum fanout of any net in the design, so it scales well to large problems.

Many algorithms that use the same basic procedure as VPack, but different attraction functions, have been published. The T-VPack algorithm by Marquardt et al. [3,7] is a timing-driven enhancement of VPack where the attraction function for a logic element, L, to cluster C becomes

$$Attraction(L) = 0.75 \cdot \sum_{j \in conn(L,C)} criticality(j) + 0.25 \cdot \frac{|Nets(L) \cap Nets(C)|}{MaxNets} \qquad (14.1)$$

The first term in equation 14.1 gives higher attraction to logic elements that are connected to the current cluster by timing-critical connections, while the second term is taken from VPack and favors grouping together logic elements with many common signals. To find the criticality of each connection, a timing analysis is performed with a simple delay model to determine each connection's timing *slack*. The slack of a connection [5] is defined as the amount of delay that can be added to that connection before some path through it limits the circuit speed. The *criticality* of a connection, j, is then given by

$$criticality(j) = 1 - \frac{slack(j)}{D_{max}} \qquad (14.2)$$

where D_{max} is the delay of the longest path in the circuit. Connections on the critical path (i.e., with no timing slack) have a criticality of 1, while connections with a large amount of slack have a criticality near 0.

Somewhat surprisingly, T-VPack improves not only circuit speed over VPack but also reduces the amount of programmable routing required between clusters. By absorbing more connections within clusters, T-VPack is able to capture more nets entirely within a cluster, which reduces wiring demand between logic blocks.

The iRAC [8] clustering algorithm uses an attraction function that favors the absorption of small nets within a cluster:

$$Attraction(L, C) = \sum_{i \in Nets(L) \cap Nets(C)} k(i, L, C) \cdot \frac{[1 + pins\_in\_cluster(i, C)]}{|pins(i)|}$$

$$k(i, L, C) = \begin{cases} 10, \text{ if adding } L \text{ to } C \text{ would absorb net } i \text{ within } C \\ \\ 1, \text{otherwise} \end{cases} \qquad (14.3)$$

The attraction function (equation 14.3) weights nets more heavily with a small number of terminals outside the cluster, and also gives a ten-times attraction bonus to any net that would be immediately absorbed by adding block L to the cluster. By reducing the number of nets to be routed between logic blocks, iRAC achieves an improvement in routability over T-VPack.

Lamoureaux and Wilton [9] have developed a power-aware enhancement of T-VPack. They modify equation 14.1 by adding a power minimization term that weights each connection from block L to cluster C by its *switching activity*. The switching activity of a signal is the number of times it is expected to change state per second. The power minimization term favors the absorption of nets that frequently switch logic states, resulting in lower capacitance for these nets and lower overall dynamic power.

14.3 SIMULATED ANNEALING FOR PLACEMENT

Simulated annealing is the most widely used placement algorithm for FPGAs. It mimics the annealing procedure by which strong metal alloys are created—initially blocks can move fairly freely, but as the *temperature* drops they gradually freeze into a high-quality placement [10].

Figure 14.4 shows the basic flow of simulated annealing for placement. First an initial placement is generated. This initial placement is generally of low quality, and is often created simply by assigning each block to the first legal location found. The placement is then iteratively improved by proposing and evaluating placement perturbations, or *moves*. A placement perturbation is proposed by a *move generator*, generally by moving a small number of blocks to new locations. A *cost function* is used to evaluate the impact of each proposed move.

Moves that reduce cost are always accepted, or committed to the placement, while those that increase cost are accepted with probability

$$e^{-\frac{\Delta Cost}{T}}$$

where T is the current *temperature*. This function ensures that moves that increase the cost by an amount that is small compared to the current temperature are likely to be accepted, while moves that increase the cost by an amount much larger than the current temperature are not. Accepting some moves that increase the cost helps escape local minima and produces a higher-quality final placement. At the start of the anneal, temperature is high; it gradually decreases according to the *annealing schedule*. This schedule also controls how many moves are performed between temperature updates and when the placement is considered sufficiently optimized that the anneal should end.

Two key strengths of simulated annealing that make it well suited to FPGA placement are:

1. One can enforce all the legality constraints imposed by the FPGA architecture fairly directly. The two basic techniques are to forbid the creation of illegal placements in the move generator or to add a penalty cost to illegal placements.

```
P = InitialPlacement ();
T = InitialTemperature ();

while (ExitCriterion () == False) {
    while (InnerLoopCriterion () == False) { /* One temperature */
        P_new = PerturbPlacementViaMove (P);
        ΔCost = Cost (P_new) - Cost (P);
        r = random (0,1);
        if (r < e^-ΔCost/T) {
            P = P_new ; /* Accept move */
        }
    }   /* End one temperature */
    T = UpdateTemp (T);
}
```

FIGURE 14.4 ■ Pseudo-code of a generic simulated annealing placement algorithm. (*Source*: Adapted from [13].)

2. By creating an appropriate cost function, one can directly model the impact of the FPGA routing architecture on circuit delay and routing congestion.

14.3.1 VPR and Related Annealing Algorithms

VPR [3,11,12] is a popular timing-driven simulated annealing placement tool. It is usually used in conjunction with T-VPack, or a similar clustering algorithm, that preclusters the logic elements into legal logic blocks. One of VPR's main features is that it can automatically adapt to different FPGA architectures so long as they employ island-style routing.

VPR's annealing schedule is based on parameters computed during placement rather than on fixed starting and ending temperatures and a fixed cooling rate. This adaptive annealing schedule generates high-quality results across a wide range of design sizes, FPGA architectures, and cost functions, making it preferable to more "hardcoded" schedules. VPR sets the *InitialTemperature* to 20 times the cost change of the average move, and the *ExitCriterion* is met when the temperature is less than 0.5 percent of the cost divided by the number of nets in the circuit. The fraction of moves that are accepted at each temperature, α, is monitored throughout the anneal.

Lam and Delosme [14] showed that simulated annealing makes the largest improvements to a placement when α is near 44 percent. Consequently, VPR rapidly decreases the temperature when α is significantly above or below 44 percent and slowly decreases it when α is near 44 percent in order to spend the majority of the annealing time in the most productive range. The move generator used by VPR to find placement perturbations also varies as the anneal progresses in order to keep α near 44 percent. When a block is picked for a move, its new proposed location will always be within a window with a Manhattan radius of *range limit* blocks. Initially, the range limit is the size of the entire chip, allowing a block to move anywhere in the device in one move.

As the anneal progresses, the range limit shrinks so that the moves proposed are smaller local improvements, since these are the most likely moves to be accepted as the placement converges to an increasingly high-quality solution. More specifically, whenever the temperature is updated in Figure 14.4, VPR also updates the range limit according to

$$range\_limit\ (new) = range\_limit\ (old) \cdot (1 - 0.44 - \alpha) \qquad (14.4)$$

VPR's cost function [12] also has some ability to adapt to different FPGA architectures:

$$
\begin{aligned}
Cost = (1 - \lambda) \sum_{i \in\ AllNets} q(i) \left[\frac{bb_x(i)}{C_{av,x}(i)} + \frac{bb_y(i)}{C_{av,y}(i)} \right] \\
+ \lambda \sum_{j \in\ AllConnections} Criticality(j) \cdot Delay(j)
\end{aligned}
\qquad (14.5)
$$

The first term in equation 14.5 causes the placement algorithm to optimize an estimate of the routed wirelength, normalized to the average wiring capacity in each region of the FPGA. The wirelength needed to route each net i is estimated as the bounding box span (bb_x and bb_y) in each direction, multiplied by a fanout-based correction factor, $q(i)$. As Figure 14.5(a) illustrates, the bounding box of a net is simply the smallest rectangle that encloses all the net terminals. Figure 14.5(b) shows that for higher fanout nets, the bounding box span underpredicts the wiring needed. For the eight-terminal net shown, the sum of bb_x and bb_y is 10 units, but even a best-case routing requires 11 units of wire. $q(i)$ is 1 for two- and three-terminal nets and slowly increases with net terminal count to compensate for this underprediction [16].

The corrected bounding box span is a reasonable estimate of the routed wirelength for an island-style FPGA that contains at least some short wiring segments that span only a few logic blocks. Most recent commercial FPGAs, including the Altera Stratix and Xilinx Virtex [15] families, meet this condition. Equation 14.5 does not contain a good estimate of wirelength for other FPGA types, such as hierarchical FPGAs, so this cost function would not perform well with them.

Some FPGAs have differing amounts of routing available in the vertical direction compared to the horizontal direction, or in different regions of the chip. For example, a Stratix-II FPGA has 1.6 times as much horizontal as vertical routing, and some routing is not available over the large 576-kbit RAM blocks. Therefore, the routing capacity is not uniform everywhere in the device. In such cases, it is beneficial to move wiring demand to the more routing-rich direction or regions. Accordingly, the cost function of equation 14.5 scales the estimated wiring in each direction by the average routing capacity over the net bounding box in that direction. Figure 14.5(a) shows an example computation.

The second term in equation 14.5 optimizes timing by favoring placements in which timing-critical connections have the potential to be routed with low delay. To evaluate the second term quickly, VPR needs to be able to rapidly estimate the delay of a connection. It makes use of the fact that the delay between two points in an island-style FPGA is primarily a function of the distance between them. Before placement begins, VPR precomputes a table of best-case routing

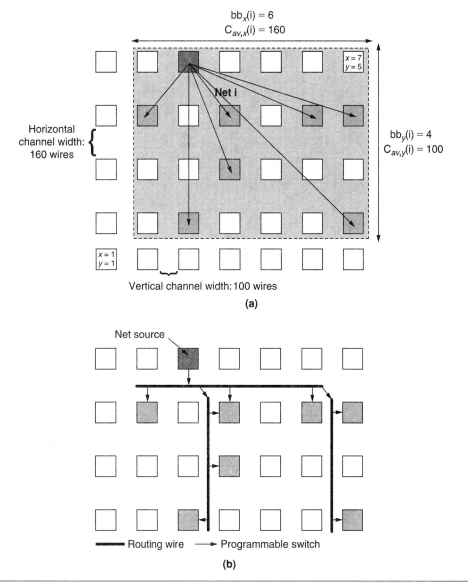

FIGURE 14.5 ■ An example wirelength cost computation: (a) net bounding box and average channel capacity; (b) best-case routing, with a wirelength of 11.

delays for every possible distance between pairs of points. The delay table entries are computed by invoking a router with each possible $(\Delta x, \Delta x)$—the router finds the fastest path between the two endpoints.

Periodically (generally once per temperature) VPR computes the delay of every connection given the current placement and then performs a timing analysis to find each connection's slack. Equation 14.2 computes the criticality of each connection given its slack. Consequently, VPR's estimate of which connections are critical changes as placement progresses, and timing optimization can move from one part of the circuit to another.

One of the important features of VPR's cost function is that, with appropriate coding, the cost change caused by the motion of a constant number of blocks can be computed in constant time. This enables many moves to be evaluated during the placement of a large circuit, which is one of the keys to obtaining a high-quality placement with simulated annealing. The overall computational complexity of VPR is $O(n^{1.33})$ [3], where n is the number of functional blocks to be placed, allowing VPR to scale well to large circuits.

Many enhancements have been made to the original VPR algorithm. The PATH algorithm by Kong [17] uses a new timing criticality formulation in which the criticality of a connection is a function of the slacks of all the paths passing through it, rather than just a function of the worst (smallest) slack. This technique increases the cost function weighting on connections with many critical or near-critical paths, which is beneficial because a move that reduces the delay of such a connection can improve many important timing paths simultaneously. On average, PATH reduces critical path delay by 15 percent compared to VPR.

The SCPlace algorithm [18] enhances VPR so that a portion of the moves are *fragment moves* in which a single logic element is moved instead of an entire logic block. This allows the placement algorithm to modify the initial clustering to shorten connections that are now seen to be poorly localized. Fragment moves improve both circuit timing and wirelength.

Sankar and Rose [19] explored a trade-off between reduced result quality and extremely low placement runtimes. Instead of simply clustering logic elements into logic blocks, their *hierarchical annealing* algorithm clusters logic blocks twice into larger units, as shown in Figure 14.6. The first-level clustering creates

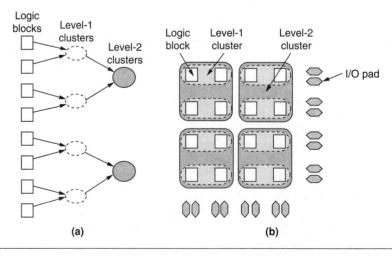

FIGURE 14.6 ■ An overview of hierarchical annealing: (a) multilevel clustering, and (b) placement of large clusters followed by unclustering and placement refinement.

clusters that each contain approximately 64 logic blocks, and the second-level clustering groups four level-1 clusters into each level-2 cluster. Placement of a netlist of level-2 clusters is very fast because there are relatively few blocks to place. To make placement of the level-2 clusters even faster, Sankar and Rose [19] use a greedy (temperature = 0 anneal) iterative improvement algorithm, seeded with a fast constructive (instead of random) placement. Once placement of the level-2 clusters is complete, a level-1 initial placement is created by locating each level-1 cluster inside the boundary of the level-2 cluster that contained it.

The placement of level-1 clusters is refined by a temperature-0 anneal. The clusters are then replaced by their constituent logic blocks and the placement of each logic block is fine-tuned with a *low-temperature* anneal. The initial temperature for this anneal is selected so that only moves that reduce cost or increase it a small amount are allowed; consequently, the initial placement solution has a large impact on the final placement. For very fast CPU times this algorithm significantly outperforms VPR in achieved wirelength, but it lags behind VPR for longer permissible CPU times.

Lamoureaux and Wilton [9] modified VPR's cost function by adding a third term, *PowerCost*, to equation 14.5.

$$PowerCost = \sum_{i \in AllNets} q(i) \left[bb_x(i) + bb_y(i) \right] \cdot Activity(i) \qquad (14.6)$$

where *Activity(i)* is the average number of times net i transitions per second. This additional cost term reduces circuit power by focusing more effort on localizing rapidly transitioning nets.

14.3.2 Simultaneous Placement and Routing with Annealing

Instead of relying on fast heuristics to estimate placement routability and timing, some algorithms use a router to obtain a partial or complete routing for each placement proposed during the anneal. These algorithms can directly extract wiring usage, congestion, and timing from the circuit routing, so their cost functions can be very detailed. Another of their advantages is that one can develop a placement algorithm that automatically adapts to a wider class of FPGA architectures, since fewer (or ideally no) assumptions about the device-routing architecture need to be incorporated into the cost function. The disadvantage of using a router in the cost function is CPU time. Evaluating the cost change after each move is very CPU intensive, making it difficult to evaluate enough moves to obtain high-quality placements for large circuits in a reasonable time.

PROXI [20] is a timing-driven FPGA placement algorithm that uses a router to compute its cost function. The PROXI cost function is a weighted sum of the number of unrouted nets and the delay of the circuit critical path. After each placement perturbation, PROXI rips up all of the nets connected to blocks that have moved and reroutes them via a fast, directed-search maze router [21].

To improve CPU time, PROXI allows the maze router to explore only a small portion of the routing fabric at high temperatures—if no unblocked routing path is found quickly, the net is left unrouted. At lower temperatures, the placement is of higher quality and the router is allowed to explore a larger portion of the routing fabric. After each net is rerouted, the critical path is recomputed incrementally. PROXI produces high-quality results, but requires high CPU time.

Independence [22] is an FPGA placement tool that can effectively target a wide variety of FPGA routing architectures. It is purely routability-driven, and its cost function monitors both the amount of wiring used by the placement and the routing congestion:

$$Cost = \sum_{i \in Nets} Routing\,Resources\,(i) + \lambda$$
$$\sum_{k \in Routing\,Resources} \max\,(Occupancy\,(k) - Capacity\,(k),\,0) \qquad (14.7)$$

The λ parameter in equation 14.7 is a heuristic weighting factor. Independence uses the PathFinder routing algorithm [23] to find new routes for all affected nets after each move. Instead of leaving nets unrouted when there is no unblocked path, PathFinder allows *wire congestion* by routing two nets on the same routing resource. Such a routing is not legal; however, by summing the overuse of all the routing resources in the FPGA, Independence can directly monitor the amount of routing congestion implicit in the current placement. The Independence cost function monitors not only routing congestion but also the total wirelength used by the router to create a smoother cost function that is easier for the annealer to optimize. Independence produces high-quality results on a wide variety of FPGA architectures, including both island style and hierarchical, but it requires very high CPU time.

14.4   PARTITION-BASED PLACEMENT

Another popular placement approach recursively partitions the circuit netlist and assigns each partition to a different physical region in the FPGA. Usually each partitioning step divides a previous (larger) partition into two pieces, or *bipartitions* the component, although some algorithms perform *multiway partitioning* to produce a larger number of circuit partitions in each step. Partitioning algorithms attempt to minimize the number of nets that are cut, or that cross, between partitions. Since each partition of the circuit will be assigned to a different region of the FPGA, partition-based placement minimizes the number of nets leaving each region and hence indirectly optimizes the amount of wiring required by the design. Partition-based placement can leverage the availability of high-quality, CPU-efficient partitioning algorithms, making this approach scalable to large problems. However, for some FPGA architectures, partition-based placement suffers from the disadvantage that it does not directly optimize the circuit timing or the amount of routing required by the placement.

Hierarchical FPGAs are good candidates for partition-based placement, since their routing architectures create natural partitioning cut lines. Hutton et al. [24] describe a commercial placement algorithm for the Altera Apex 20K family that recursively partitions the circuit along the cut lines formed by the routing hierarchy, as shown in Figure 14.7. This algorithm is made timing-driven by heavily weighting connections with low slack during each partitioning phase and by partitioning to minimize weighted cut size. This encourages partitioning solutions in which timing-critical connections can be routed using the fast routing available within the lower levels of the routing hierarchy. To improve the prediction of the critical path, the delay estimate for each connection is a function of (1) the number of hierarchy boundaries the net must traverse because of the known partition cuts at the higher levels of the routing hierarchy, and (2) statistical estimates of how many hierarchy boundaries the connection will cross at future partitioning steps.

Recursive partitioning has also been used for placement in island-style FPGAs. ALTOR [25] was originally developed for standard cell circuits, but was adapted to FPGAs and widely used in FPGA research. Figure 14.8 shows the sequence of cut lines used by ALTOR to target an island-style FPGA—note that the sequence is quite different from that used with a hierarchical FPGA. In an island-style FPGA, blocks separated by a short Manhattan distance can be connected with a small amount of routing. Consequently, the cut lines are designed to divide the FPGA into ever-shrinking squares—the fewer signals that must leave each square, the less interconnect required.

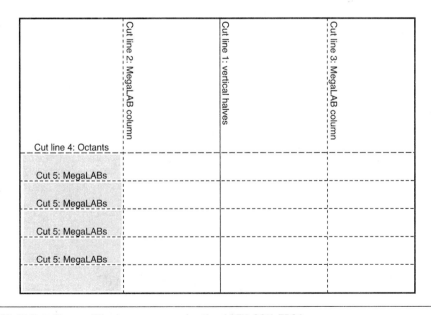

FIGURE 14.7 ■ The partitioning sequence for the APEX 20K FPGA.

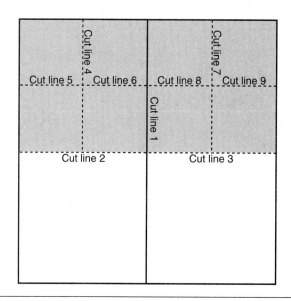

FIGURE 14.8 ■ The partitioning sequence for an island-style FPGA.

ALTOR's first cut line divides the chip into two halves vertically. The second cut line divides the left half of the circuit into upper left and lower left quarters. The third cut line divides the right half of the circuit in the same way. When partitioning along the third cut line, ALTOR uses *terminal propagation* [26] from the left half of the chip, which is already partitioned into an upper and lower quarter, to bias the partitioning of the right half. For example, the net shown in Figure 14.9 has one terminal in the right half of the chip and one terminal in the upper left corner. During partitioning along cut line 3, this net is considered to have a fixed terminal in the upper partition, which will bias the partitioner to keep the free terminal of this net in the partition above cut line 3. Terminal propagation reduces final wirelength by optimizing the placement of the terminals of nets that have been cut in some partitioning step.

Maidee et al. [27] developed a timing-driven placement algorithm for island-style FPGAs that employs both partitioning and annealing. Before partitioning begins, the VPR router is used to generate a table of net delay versus distance spanned by the net that takes into account the FPGA routing architecture. As partitioning proceeds, the algorithm records the minimum length each net can achieve given the current number of partitioning boundaries it crosses. The delay corresponding to each net's span is retrieved from the net delay versus span table, and a timing analysis is performed to identify critical connections.

Timing-critical connections to terminals outside the region being partitioned act as anchor points during each partitioning. This forces the other end of the connection to be allocated to the partition that allows the critical connection to be short. Once partitioning has proceeded to the point that each region contains only a few cells, any overfilled regions are legalized with a greedy movement

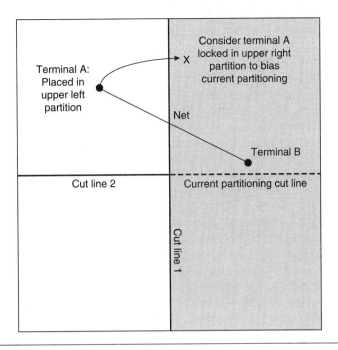

FIGURE 14.9 ■ An example of terminal propagation.

heuristic. Finally, the VPR annealing algorithm is invoked with a low starting temperature to "fine-tune" the placement. This fine-tuning step allows blocks to move anywhere in the device, so early placement decisions made by the partitioner, when little information about the critical paths or the final wirelength of each net was available, can be reversed. This algorithm achieves wirelength and speed results comparable to those of a full VPR anneal, with significantly reduced CPU time.

14.5 ANALYTIC PLACEMENT

Analytic algorithms are based on creating a smooth function of a placement that approximates routed wirelength. Efficient numerical techniques are used to find the global minimum of this function; if the function approximates wirelength well, this solution is a placement with good wirelength. However, this global minimum is usually an illegal placement, so constraints and heuristics must be applied to guide the algorithm to a legal solution.

While analytic placement approaches are popular for ASICs, few exist for FPGAs, likely due to the more difficult FPGA placement legality constraints. The Negotiated Analytic Placement (NAP) algorithm from Chan and Schlag [28] targets FPGAs and has several novel features, including some that make it suitable for implementation on multiple processors in parallel.

14.6   FURTHER READING AND OPEN CHALLENGES

While this chapter has focused on placement algorithms specifically designed for FPGAs, there is also a great deal of literature on placement for custom-manufactured integrated circuits, much of which is relevant to FPGAs. For a recent overview of general placement algorithms, see Cong et al. [29]. This chapter also treated placement as separate from synthesis. Recent commercial and academic tools incorporate *physical synthesis*, however, where portions of the circuit are resynthesized as placement proceeds and more information about critical paths becomes available. For an overview of FPGA physical synthesis and its interaction with placement, see Hutton and Betz [13].

The greatest challenge facing FPGA placement is the need to produce high-quality placements for ever-larger circuits. FPGA capacity doubles every two to three years, doubling the size of the placement problem at the same rate. In addition, uniprocessor speed is no longer increasing as quickly as it did in the past, which means that single processor speed will increase by less than two times in the same period. In order to maintain the fast time to market and ease of use historically provided by FPGAs, placement algorithms cannot be allowed to take ever more CPU time. There is thus a compelling need for algorithms that are very scalable yet still produce high-quality results.

The roadmap for future microprocessors indicates that the number of independent processors, or cores, on a single chip will increase rapidly in the coming years. Consequently, most engineers will have parallel computers on their desktops. Part of the solution to the problem of keeping FPGA placement times reasonable may be to find techniques and algorithms to exploit parallel processing without sacrificing result quality.

References

[1] D. Lewis, E. Ahmed, G. Baeckler. The Stratix-II routing and logic architecture. *Proceedings of the 13th ACM International Symposium on Field-Programmable Gate Arrays,* 2005.

[2] The Quartus University Interface Program (*www.altera.com/education/univ/research/unv-quip.html*).

[3] V. Betz., J. Rose, A. Marquardt. *Architecture and CAD for Deep-Submicron FPGAs,* Kluwer, February 1999.

[4] R. Cliff, et al. A next generation architecture optimized for high density system level integration. *Proceedings of the 21st IEEE Custom Integrated Circuits Conference,* 1999.

[5] R. Hitchcock, G. Smith, D. Cheng. Timing analysis of computer hardware. *IBM Journal of Research and Development,* January 1983.

[6] J. Cong, J. Peck, Y. Ding. RASP: A general logic synthesis system for SRAM-based FPGAs. *Proceedings of the Fifth International Symposium on Field-Programmable Gate Arrays,* 1996.

[7] A. Marquardt, V. Betz, J. Rose. Using cluster-based logic blocks and timing-driven packing to improve FPGA speed and density. *Proceedings of the Seventh International Symposium on Field-Programmable Gate Arrays,* 1999.

[8] A. Singh, M. Marek-Sadowska. Efficient circuit clustering for area and power reduction in FPGAs. *Proceedings of the International Symposium on Field-Programmable Gate Arrays*, 2002.

[9] J. Lamoureaux, S. Wilton. On the interaction between power-aware FPGA CAD algorithms. *Proceedings of the International Symposium on Computer-Aided Design*, 2003.

[10] S. Kirkpatrick, C. Gelatt, M. Vecchi. Optimization by simulated annealing. *Science* 2(20), May 1983.

[11] V. Betz, J. Rose. VPR: A new packing, placement and routing tool for FPGA research. *Proceedings of the Seventh International Conference on Field-Programmable Logic and Applications*, 1997.

[12] A. Marquardt, V. Betz, J. Rose. Timing-driven placement for FPGAs. *Proceedings of the International Symposium on Field-Programmable Gate Arrays*, 2000.

[13] M. Hutton, V. Betz. *Electronic Design Automation for Integrated Circuits Handbook*, Taylor and Francis, eds. (Chapter 13), CRC Press, 2006.

[14] J. Lam, J. Delosme. Performance of a new annealing schedule. *Design Automation Conference*, 1988.

[15] *Virtex Family Datasheet (www.xilinx.com)*.

[16] C. Cheng. RISA: Accurate and efficient placement routability modeling. *Proceedings of the International Conference on Computer-Aided Design*, 1994.

[17] T. Kong. A novel net weighting algorithm for timing-driven placement. *Proceedings of the International Conference on Computer-Aided Design*, 2002.

[18] G. Chen, J. Cong. Simultaneous timing driven clustering and placement for FPGAs. *Proceedings of the International Conference on Field-Programmable Logic and Applications*, 2004.

[19] Y. Sankar, J. Rose. Trading quality for compile time: Ultra-fast placement for FPGAs. *Proceedings of the International Symposium on Field-Programmable Gate Arrays*, 1999.

[20] S. K. Nag, R. A. Rutenbar. Performance-driven simultaneous placement and routing for FPGAs. *IEEE Transactions on Computer-Aided Design*, June 1998.

[21] Y. C. Lee. An algorithm for path connections and applications. *IRE Transactions on Electronic Computing*, September 1961.

[22] A. Sharma, C. Ebeling, S. Hauck. Architecture-adaptive routability-driven placement for FPGAs. *Proceedings of the International Symposium on Field-Programmable Logic and Applications*, 2005.

[23] L. McMurchie, C. Ebeling. PathFinder: A negotiation-based performance-driven router for FPGAs. *Proceedings of the Fifth International Symposium on Field-Programmable Gate Arrays*, 1995.

[24] M. Hutton, K. Adibsamii, A. Leaver. Adaptive delay estimation for partitioning-driven PLD placement. *IEEE Transactions on VLSI* 11(1), February 2003.

[25] J. Rose, W. Snelgrove, Z. Vranesic. ALTOR: An automatic standard cell layout program. *Proceedings of the Canadian Conference on VLSI*, January 1985.

[26] A. Dunlop, B. Kernighan. A procedure for placement of standard-cell VLSI circuits. *IEEE Transactions on Computer-Aided Design*, January 1985.

[27] M. Maidee, C. Ababei, K. Bazargan. Fast timing-driven partitioning-based placement for island style field-programmable gate arrays. *Design Automation Conference*, 2003.

[28] P. Chan, M. Schlag. Parallel placement for field-programmable gate arrays. *Proceedings of the 11th International Symposium on Field-Programmable Gate Arrays*, 2003.

[29] J. Cong, J. Shinnerl, M. Xie, T. Kong, X. Yuan. Large-scale circuit placement. *ACM Transactions on Design Automation of Electronic Systems*, April 2005.

CHAPTER 15

DATAPATH COMPOSITION

Andreas Koch
Department of Computer Science
Embedded Systems and Applications Group
Technische Universität of Darmstadt, Germany

As shown in Chapter 14, a wide variety of algorithms can be employed for placing arbitrary netlists on various reconfigurable fabrics. To achieve this generality, the input netlists are treated as random collections of primitive elements (gates, lookup tables [LUTs], flip-flops) and interconnections. These approaches do not attempt to exploit any kind of structure that might be present in their input circuits. Many practically relevant circuits, however, do exhibit regularities in their composition (e.g., by following a classical bit-sliced design). Since the days of manual full-custom ASIC design ("polygon pushing"), regularity in circuit *structure* has been exploited with great success to derive a corresponding regular circuit *layout*—for example, by abutment of replicated bit-slice layouts.

This chapter describes the application of this idea to efficient layout of regular bit-sliced datapaths on reconfigurable fabrics. It will begin by considering how to characterize, extract, and preserve regularities at different abstraction levels. The next steps describe the datapath composition tool flow and address issues such as mapping dataflow operators to hardware units and arranging these in an abutting regular layout. We will also cover how quality can be improved even further by judiciously dissolving regularity boundaries in parts of the datapath performing cross-boundary optimization, and finally reregularizing the optimized circuit.

15.1 FUNDAMENTALS

With the increasing use of reconfigurable devices as core processing units in adaptive computer systems, the architecture and implementation of high-performance compute units on reconfigurable fabrics becomes ever more important. A *datapath* is one architectural style of realizing a given computation (Figure 15.1(a)) in hardware. It is often described as the number of interconnected *operators* in the form of a dataflow graph (DFG) or control dataflow graph (CDFG), shown in Figure 15.1(b). The execution of the operators is orchestrated by a supervising *controller* (Figure 15.1(c)). The controller is generally not considered part of the datapath, but together the datapath and controller form a *compute unit*. For purposes of this discussion, we will assume that we are processing a CDFG but will concentrate on its dataflow part.

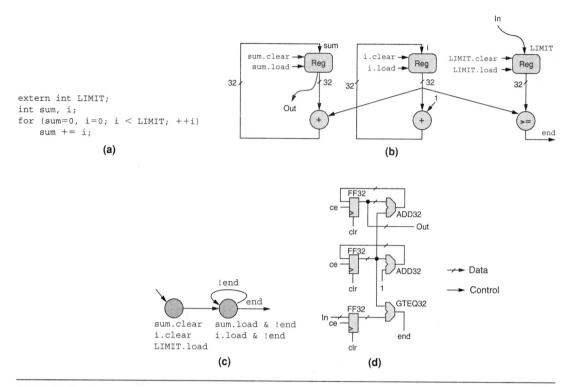

```
extern int LIMIT;
int sum, i;
for (sum=0, i=0; i < LIMIT; ++i)
    sum += i;
```

(a)

FIGURE 15.1 ▪ From computation to realization.

The datapath is created in hardware by mapping the CDFG operators to *hardware operators*, or HWOPs (see Figure 15.1(d)). Generally, HWOPs have multibit *data* inputs and outputs for the operand(s) and result(s) (e.g., ADD32 HWOPs). Some may also have *control* inputs (e.g., the load and clear signals of the FF32 HWOPs) or outputs (e.g., for indicating certain conditions such as the GTEQ32 output). These control signals are generally much narrower than bused data signals, often only a single bit wide. In some cases, an HWOP is available in several different *implementations*, all having the same function but differing, for example, in their area/speed characteristics or layout shape.

15.1.1 Regularity

The multibit-wide HWOPs are often assembled by repeatedly instantiating and interconnecting narrower template circuits in an adjacent fashion until the specific HWOP's desired bit width is reached (Figure 15.2). These template circuits will be called *master slices* here, while their instances are generally referred to as *bit slices*. We will further extend this terminology to call areas where the same master slice has been instantiated a number of times a *zone*, and a sequence of zones is termed a *stack*. Together, these concepts describe an HWOP as a *regular* circuit.

Such a structure has a natural direction of *dataflow* (horizontally in the case of Figure 15.2). When processing word-wide data, the individual bits of the

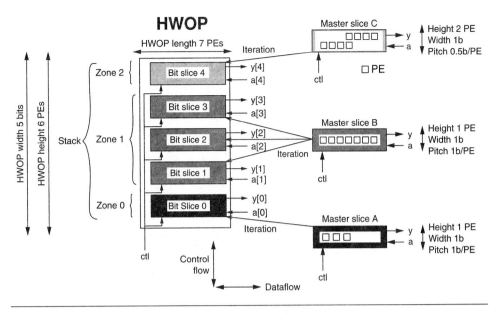

FIGURE 15.2 ■ Regular HWOP structure.

words are arranged orthogonally to the direction of dataflow (in the figure, vertically). With few exceptions (e.g., bus-wide logic gates), the position of individual bits is not arbitrary but follows an ordering from least significant (LSB) to most significant (MSB). For example, stacking ripple-carry full-adder bit slices generally has the first slice process the LSB and the last slice process the MSB. Ports on the master slice (e.g., a, y) do not have a bit significance of their own. Only after instantiating the masters as bit slices can the significance be derived from their iteration number (e.g., port a on the bottommost slice will have a significance of 0; the one above that, 1, etc.).

For describing the characteristics of elements such as HWOPs, bit slices, and master slices, four quantities are useful. Any of these elements may process multiple bits from a single word, with the logical *width* being the largest number of such bits. *Height* and *length* refer to the bounding box of the element layout on the target device. They are specified in device-dependent units, such as processing elements (PEs), cells, configurable logic blocks (CLBs), and the like. The *pitch* of a master slice is the width divided by the height—essentially, the number of output bits per unit height. To reduce interconnect lengths, all HWOPs in the datapath should have the same pitch and the LSBs of all data nets should be vertically aligned.

Regularity in datapaths does not appear just in the replicated logic elements but also in commonly occurring interconnect patterns (Figure 15.3):

Data nets are generally multibit buses that carry operands and results between HWOPs, where they are connected to data ports (e.g., op1, op2). Each signal in the bus has an associated bit significance and generally connects to the HWOP at a data port with the same significance. Shifts and permutations occur only rarely [23].

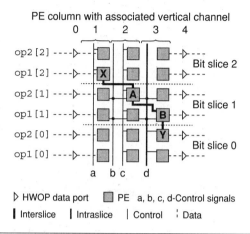

FIGURE 15.3 ▪ Regular interconnection patterns.

Control nets are generally narrower, often only a single bit wide. In general, they connect an HWOP to a controller but not to another HWOP in the datapath. Control signals attach to the HWOP at control ports. In many cases, a control signal connects to the same control port in all bit slices of a zone. With our assumption of horizontal dataflow, in the following discussion control signals are assumed to run vertically.

Interslice nets run between separate bit slices in the same HWOP, thus vertically crossing slice boundaries (e.g., B–Y, A–X). Most commonly, they connect neighboring bit slices, but these may have different master slices, particularly near the top and bottom of a stack. An example of an interslice net is the carry net running between full-adder bit slices.

Intraslice nets connect individual logic elements within a bit slice (e.g., A–B). Since the internals of a bit slice are considered random logic, these nets do not follow specific interconnection patterns.

An example of a unified representation for both block and interconnect regularity, the Abstract Physical Model (APM), is proposed by Ye and De Micheli [22].

15.1.2 Datapath Layout

With these concepts in place, we can now consider the anatomy of our compute unit in greater detail (Figure 15.4(a)). The datapath will have a *regular* area, where pitch-matched HWOPs with a common direction of increasing bit significance process horizontal, LSB-aligned dataflows. Outside this area, HWOPs may contain *irregular* parts (e.g., carry initialization, overflow detection, or, for complex sequential HWOPs, even local controllers). The global controller for the compute unit is also placed outside the regular area. Generally, control nets are routed vertically across the regular area. This chapter does not address the handling of the controller, but concentrates on the datapath

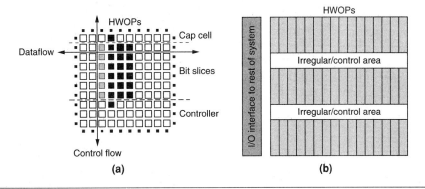

FIGURE 15.4 ■ Common datapath layouts: (a) classical linear and (b) multistripe.

instead. The controller can be placed via techniques such as those presented in Chapter 14.

Given these constraints, the best arrangement for minimizing interconnect lengths and delays for a small number of HWOPs will generally be linear. This approach has been exploited by devices like Garp [4], which realize such topologies directly in their chip architecture. However, once the number of HWOPs grows, the datapath generally needs to be wrapped into multiple stripes of HWOPs (Figure 15.4(b)).

15.2   TOOL FLOW OVERVIEW

Multiple steps are required to actually compose the datapath from individual HWOPs. These steps can be broadly grouped into the following categories:

Module generation: The HWOPs are often realized by procedural descriptions in the form of module generators (see Section 15.4). Thus, at some point in the flow other tools will interact with the library of module generators either to retrieve data *about* appropriately parametrized module instances or (later in the process) to generate the actual netlists. Often these netlists are already annotated with module-local relative placement information.

Mapping: The operators in the computation are mapped from the CDFG to the HWOPs realizing them in hardware. Beyond a straight 1:1 mapping, this can be performed in 1:M (if an operator requires multiple HWOPs) or N:1 fashion (if multiple operators can be combined into the same HWOP). The mapping calculated here need not be final, but can be altered in later flow steps. In some cases, the mapping step can also choose among multiple different HWOP implementations for an operator. This is sometimes called the *module selection* step.

Placement: HWOPs are assigned to actual PEs on the target device fabric. Similarly to the mapping step, *N*:1 and 1:*M* assignments are possible here. In the first case, a PE is so complex that it can implement multiple HWOPs at the same time. In the second case, each HWOP needs to be realized using multiple PEs. This is usually the case when targeting fine-grained devices such as field-programmable gate arrays (FPGAs).

Compaction: This is the altering of the HWOPs' structure after mapping (before or after placement). It generally indicates optimizing across HWOP boundaries. For example, it might merge connected adjacent HWOPs into a more compact/faster, but functionally identical, hardware block. This optimized block is then treated as any other HWOP in the datapath.

Not all of the flows discussed next perform all of these steps, and their execution order can vary. Additionally, some steps may be repeated.

Certain combinations are also possible. For example, in some flows placement and the mapping of operators to HWOPs occur simultaneously. For coarse-grained targets, operators can be mapped to HWOPs that are placeable in the same PE. For fine-grained devices, HWOP implementations can be selected whose layouts fit together with minimal area.

15.3   THE IMPACT OF DEVICE ARCHITECTURE

The tool flow required for creating a datapath on a reconfigurable fabric of PEs is highly dependent on the target device architecture. For coarse-grained target devices, the operators of the computation can often be mapped to PEs in a one-to-one fashion. On a fine-grained device, the operators have to be assembled from individual PEs.

Bit-sliced is not the only way to realize HWOPs. They may as well be completely irregular internally, or they may be monolithic (Figure 15.5). In both cases, many of the optimizations described in Section 15.7 that affect the internal structure of HWOPs are not be applicable. However, the techniques for processing multiple HWOPs at the datapath level (Section 15.6) remain relevant.

If the reconfigurable fabric has a linear or a two-dimensional matrix structure (Figure 15.6(a–c)), this can be exploited to efficiently map the regular

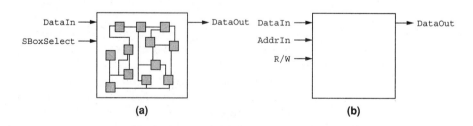

FIGURE 15.5 ▪ Non-bit-sliced HWOPs: (a) irregular and (b) monolithic.

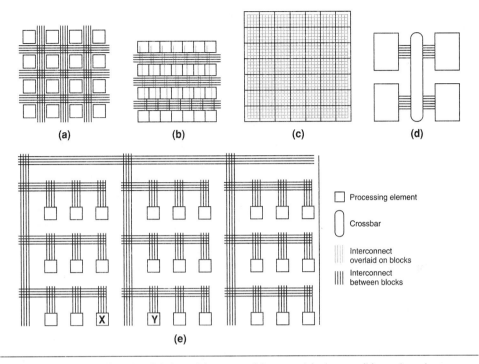

FIGURE 15.6 ■ Reconfigurable fabric architectures: (a) symmetrical array, (b) row-based, (c) sea-of-gates, (d) hierarchical PLD, and (e) hierarchical FPGA.

datapath structure to a corresponding regular geometric layout. For other kinds of target devices—for example, those having fully hierarchical structures (d–e in Figure 15.6)—algorithms optimizing for geometric arrangement are unsuitable, because geometrically adjacent blocks on the device might not actually be neighbors in the interconnect network (Figure 15.6(e), PEs X and Y). While other techniques such as hierarchical partitioning and clustering [19] could be used instead, they no longer attempt to take advantage of the datapath regularity.

15.3.1 Architecture Irregularities

Even in seemingly regular fabrics, irregularities often occur at the detail level. Consider, for example, the logic block structure of the Xilinx XC4000 FPGA (Figure 15.7). The base architecture of this device is a symmetrical array of CLBs, each of which contains two 4-LUTs and registers. However, each CLB also provides an additional 3-LUT. While very useful (e.g., for the efficient implementation of 4-input multiplexers or 5-input functions within a single CLB), the 3-LUT impedes the regularity in that it is no longer possible to realize two instances of a master slice that uses the 3-LUT within a single CLB. Also, when using the 3-LUT it is no longer possible to employ the registers in the CLB independently from the 4-LUTs: Only one of the registers can be directly connected to a CLB external port (DIN); the other one is not reachable from the outside.

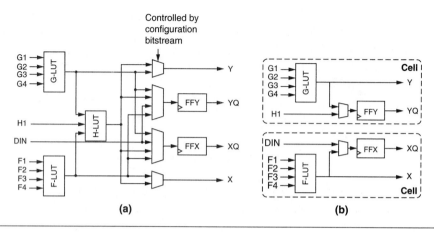

FIGURE 15.7 ▪ Regularizing an existing device architecture: (a) the real structure of the Xilinx XC4000 CLB and (b) the simplified regular structure.

These irregularities can be alleviated by disregarding the 3-LUT for regular logic, using it solely to make the other register accessible via the H1 port. As a result, each CLB can now be used to implement two fully regular bit slices, with the registers accessible both from inside and outside the bit slice.

Interconnect features also have an effect on datapath placement style. The physical direction of bit significances on the fabric is sometimes dictated by the running order of fast carry wires, which, on most devices is fixed. Also, high fanout control signals (e.g., the select signal of wide multiplexers) can be distributed across an entire HWOP by special long-distance interconnects. For example, on the Xilinx Virtex series of chips, so-called vertical long lines connect to all PEs on both sides of a vertical routing channel and are thus ideally suited for control routing. As will be shown in the following section, tool flows for datapaths can take advantage of all these features for efficient layout.

15.4   THE INTERFACE TO MODULE GENERATORS

As in many hardware design flows, individual hardware cells (in our case, the circuits used as HWOPs), are retrieved from a library. Instead of static cells, however, a more flexible approach uses procedural module generators to tailor these circuits to fit current requirements. For example, a multiplier might have eight pipeline stages in one context and only four in another, matching it to the latency/clock speed of the rest of the datapath. No longer a passive collection of cell descriptions, the library now becomes *active*: It accepts a set of constraints from another part of the flow and delivers a matching circuit.

The very flexibility of these parametrized generators complicates their integration with the rest of the tool flow: Other tools need not only the circuit description in the form of a (possibly preplaced) netlist but also data *about* this specific instance. Different tools are interested in different aspects of the circuit. This plethora of cell *views*, combined with the sheer volume of the design space covered by each parametrized generator, precludes a simple enumeration of all alternatives. Thus, the traditional static library data files, holding tables of delays, bounding boxes, and the like, for a set of fixed parameter values, become impractical.

The Flexible API for Module-based Environments (FLAME) [11] is one approach to overcoming these difficulties. It consists of three major components: (1) the communications interface between the generator library and the other flow tools, (2) the design data model, and (3) the library specification.

A reference realization of a FLAME-based generator library exists in the form of the Generic Library for Adaptive Computing Environments (GLACE) [14]. This package has successfully been used in the COMRADE compiler [7], which compiles C into hybrid hardware/software applications for adaptive computer systems. GLACE uses a Java-based FLAME implementation, but could be called from other languages using the Java Native Interface (JNI).

15.4.1 The Flow Interface

The communications infrastructure and API provided by the FLAME Manager (Figure 15.8) replace static library files with an active function call–based interface. Clients in the main design flow can thus enter into a dialog with the module libraries and retrieve data specific to the actual parameter values of the current instance. In GLACE, the client queries accepted by the FLAME Manager are forwarded to the circuit generation code [6], resulting in the retrieval of circuit characteristics, or the creation of actual netlists.

15.4.2 The Data Model

The information exchanged in this manner just described is represented using the FLAME design data model. This model is partitioned into a number of task-specific views: A frontend compiler might request a "behavior" view to determine which functions are available for a given target technology. Later on, it could

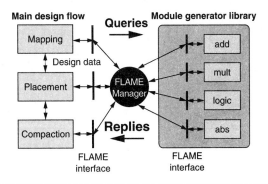

FIGURE 15.8 ■ FLAME system overview.

query for a "synthesis" view to retrieve area and timing characteristics for a specific module instance. Additional views include "topology" for layout shapes and port pitch, and "netlist," "placed," and "mapped" views describing the circuit itself. For the latter, standard formats such as EDIF are encapsulated inside the FLAME messages.

15.4.3   The Library Specification

The FLAME library specification describes a set of behaviors and interfaces. One or more of these can be attached to a hardware cell to precisely define its function for automatic use by another tool. For example, the cell of a runtime controllable adder/subtractor might have both the addition and subtraction behaviors attached. The interface carefully distinguishes between the logical (e.g., the operands of the adder) and the physical perspective (e.g., clock ports and clock enable signals). Furthermore, a FLAME interface extends beyond port specifications such as width and data type to the control characteristics of the cell. This can cover "start" and "done" signals as well as mode switches (e.g., alternating between addition and subtraction). By considering all of these aspects, another tool can choose the cell most applicable to a given task and automatically drive it correctly from the central datapath controller.

15.4.4   The Intra-module Layout

For efficiency, most module generators create circuits whose internal PEs have already been preplaced. In this case, the module generators and the datapath placement tools must agree on a set of common layout conventions. Otherwise, the regular target layout described in Section 15.1.1 will not be achievable.

Figure 15.9 shows such a regular layout, along with the FLAME description of its topology, using an unsigned 8-bit multiplier from GLACE as an example.

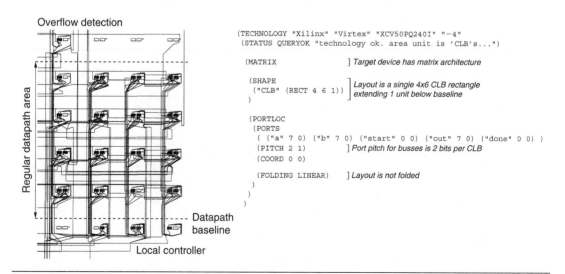

FIGURE 15.9 ■ Module topology and FLAME reply.

The layout has the LSBs of the operand and result data busses aligned at a common baseline. This sequential HWOP has two irregular components, which are placed below and above the regular datapath region. For that reason, in order to preserve regularity within the stack, we had to leave extra space on the top and/or bottom to accommodate any irregularities (such as overflow detection, sign handling, etc.). All buses are spaced with a pitch of 2 bits per CLB of layout height.

15.5 THE MAPPING

Mapping techniques can be distinguished by whether they map in N:1 fashion (i.e., *multiple* CDFG operators into a single HWOP) or map (at least initially) in 1:1 fashion.

15.5.1 1:1 Mapping

Here each CDFG operator is considered individually. However, trade-off decisions can still occur with regard to the different HWOP alternatives for it:

Area/delay trade-offs can be performed to allow the selection of smaller but slower HWOPs for operations that are not on the critical path of the computation.

Topology matching can be performed to match the heights of the HWOPs across the datapath (Figure 15.10(a)). This can be necessary when a few HWOPs in the datapath are significantly wider than the rest (e.g., 64-bit modules in

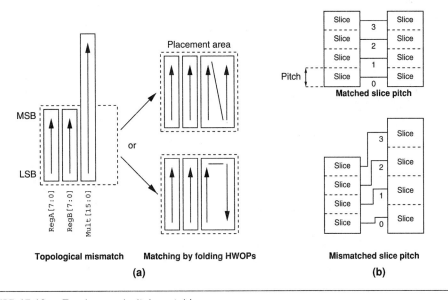

FIGURE 15.10 ■ Topology and pitch matching.

a mostly 32-bit datapath). Here regularity can be traded for area efficiency by selecting implementations for these modules that have been folded, doubling the length but halving the height.

Pitch matching occurs if modules in the library are available only with a limited number of pitch values. The goal here is to compose the datapath with the least number of pitch mismatches (Figure 15.10(b)).

Various techniques can be employed to solve these optimization problems. Since in general no single *best* solution exists for complex cases, it is practical to use an algorithm that can generate sets of good (Pareto-optimal) solutions. The SDI system [10] used a genetic algorithm in the floorplanning step to perform these calculations.

However, this approach is only applicable if a very flexible module library exists that actually gives the optimization heuristics some leeway to operate. This was the case with the PARAMOG library used in SDI, but the effort to implement this degree of flexibility is significant. More current module libraries, such as GLACE, often provide a smaller variety of implementations (generally just one) for each operator, allowing the replacement of complex heuristics with just a few simple rules for pitch and topology matching.

15.5.2 *N*:1 Mapping

In this approach, multiple operators can be mapped to a single HWOP, often using a tree-covering approach. The initial CDFG is split into a forest of trees (Figure 15.11) using techniques that splitt at multi-fanout nodes (between B and D,F) and possibly partially duplicate the operator cones rooted at the multi-fanout node (duplicating A into A,A′). While this limited approach no longer optimally solves the *graph*-covering problem, it is necessary in order to avoid the NP-completeness of computing the latter.

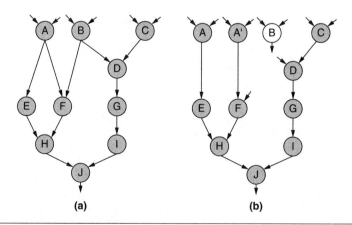

(a)   (b)

FIGURE 15.11 ■ Conversion of CDFG to a forest of trees: (a) input dataflow graph and (b) forest of dataflow trees.

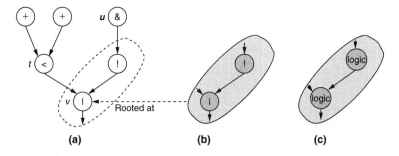

FIGURE 15.12 ■ Covering operator trees using patterns: (a) the dataflow tree, (b) the HWOP pattern P, and (c) HWOP equivalence class pattern C.

GAMA [3] employs a linear time algorithm using dynamic programming to cover the operator trees with HWOPs (Figure 15.12). This algorithm, which has its origin in the code generation steps of compilers, treats the operator(s) realizable by each HWOP as a *pattern*. Patterns are described as productions in a grammar, from which a code generator-generator creates the actual tree-covering code.

For each operator tree, the covering proceeds from the leaf nodes toward the root, applying all matching patterns that can be locally rooted at the currently examined node (v in the example, roots pattern P). A cost function computing delay and area characteristics determines the desirability of using the current pattern at this point. It is based on the cost of the currently tried pattern plus the previously computed costs (dynamic programming) of the fanin nodes to the pattern (u, v in the example). The "best" pattern covering each node/subtree is then selected using heuristics that either do a straight area minimization or attempt to additionally minimize delays. This best solution is then stored in the local root node, and the covering proceeds to the next node. Once the tree's root node has been matched with a best pattern, the final covering can be retrieved by starting with the root pattern and then processing the current pattern's fanin nodes. At each of these fanin nodes, the best pattern selection stored there is retrieved. This phase of the algorithm thus works recursively toward the leaves.

The algorithm has some limitations that *must* be worked around:

■ First, tree covering in this fashion relies on the principle of optimality, where the combination of optimal solutions to subproblems leads to an optimal solution of the entire problem. This is indeed achievable when optimizing for minimal area. However, when attempting to minimize delays the timing criticality of operators can vary depending on later covering decisions. Thus, at the time of decision the criticality of the current node is not known.

To mitigate this issue, GAMA attempts to estimate the criticality using an initial purely delay-oriented covering pass. Then the final covering proceeds in an area-minimizing fashion until the currently accumulated

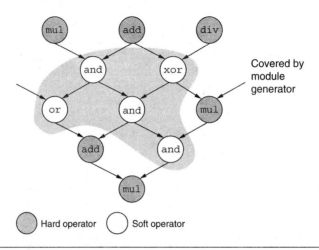

Covered by module generator

⬤ Hard operator   ◯ Soft operator

FIGURE 15.13 ▪ Subgraph covering with flexible generator.

delay at a node exceeds its estimate. At this stage, the cost function is switched from area to delay minimization.

▪ Second, the runtime of the algorithm depends linearly on the number of patterns in the grammar (which equal different modules in the library). When the PEs of the target device are very flexible (e.g., LUT based), they can implement a wide spectrum of CDFG primitive operators (e.g., AND, OR, INV, ADD, SUB, combinations ...). Without further refinement to the approach, a straight description of this flexibility in the grammar will lead to an explosion in the number of rules. However, in practice, many operators are *equivalent* for mapping purposes. For example, all 2-input logic operators map in exactly the same way in all patterns in which they occur. This fact can be exploited by defining equivalence classes for all operators (e.g., logic, additive) and then defining the grammar rules in terms of these classes (C in Figure 15.13). Combined with the factoring out of common subpatterns, this significantly reduces the complexity of the grammar.

15.5.3 The Combined Approach

A completely different approach maps some operators in a 1:1 fashion and others in an *N*:1 fashion. This combination employs powerful module generators that can generate regular modules covering entire subgraphs of the CDFG. As an example, the LogicGen tool [20] can handle arbitrary multibit logical expressions, including shifts and permutations, with optional registering of the outputs. It extracts a regular structure from the input operators and synthesizes logic-optimized bit slices using SIS [16], which are then preplaced in a regular layout. To apply LogicGen, the CDFG is searched for the largest subgraphs of plain logic modules. Each of these clusters is then handed to the tool in its entirety, allowing it to exploit reconvergent fanouts, factorization, and the like. All operators in the cluster are thus covered by a single, LogicGen-created HWOP. Operators that are not amenable to traditional logic optimizations, such as arithmetic and memories that are usually implemented on device-specific blocks, are then mapped into corresponding HWOPs in a 1:1 manner by dedicated module generators.

15.6   PLACEMENT

The HWOPs resulting from mapping have to be placed on the device fabric. This can happen either during mapping or in a separate step afterward. Placement approaches can be classified into three groups according to the nature of the generated placement (see Figure 15.14). Purely linear techniques create a one-dimensional arrangement of HWOPs in a single stripe. Others compute a placement consisting of multiple stripes, which is sometimes referred to as 1.5 dimensional or constrained two dimensional. A last group of algorithms generates arbitrary two dimensional arrangements, an approach closely related to the classical floorplanning or macro-module scenarios in ASIC tool flows.

15.6.1   Linear Placement

An example of linear placement, GAMA [3], performs a one-dimensional placement simultaneously with the mapping step (see Figure 15.15(a)). It assumes that the external I/Os to the datapath are located on only one side of the stripe (at the right in the figure). The roots of all subtrees are placed toward this I/O side, with the root of the entire HWOP tree directly adjacent to the I/Os (op3 in the figure). Furthermore, the HWOPs within a subtree are all placed contiguously, which means that (at least initially) HWOPs from different subtrees (here op1 and op2) will not be intermingled in the placement. The placement algorithm thus consists of recursively deciding in which linear order to place the fanin HWOPs of a node.

Note that the placement order *does* affect the routing delay between different HWOPs (Figures 15.15(b) and (c)). The timing estimates calculated in this fashion are used in the cost function guiding the mapping (covering the trees

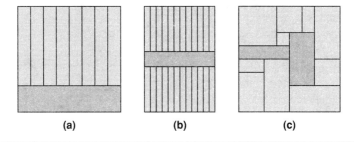

(a)   (b)   (c)

FIGURE 15.14 ■ Placements styles: (a) linear, (b) constrained two dimensional, and (c) full two dimensional.

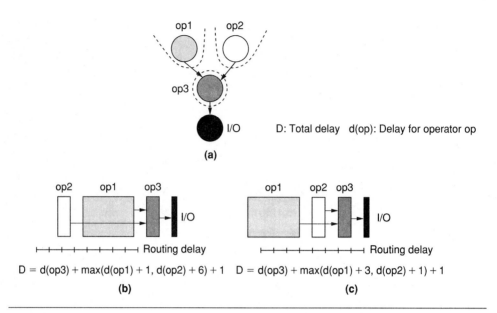

(a)

D: Total delay   d(op): Delay for operator op

$D = d(op3) + \max(d(op1) + 1, d(op2) + 6) + 1$

(b)

$D = d(op3) + \max(d(op1) + 3, d(op2) + 1) + 1$

(c)

FIGURE 15.15 ▪ Simultaneous tree covering and placement.

with HWOP patterns). The different trees of the forest (into which the CDFG has already been split) are placed in the stripe using a greedy algorithm that aims to place critical path trees close to each other. After this purely constructive initial placement, a greedy clustering algorithm can move HWOPs globally, across subtree and tree boundaries, in a further attempt to reduce routing delays. In practice, however, the quality gains achievable using this simple cleanup pass are negligible.

The techniques proposed by Ababei and Bazargan [1] are an example of a separate postmapping linear placement step, which employs two core algorithms to quickly determine linear placements in polynomial time. The first, shown in Figure 15.16(a), tries to heuristically compute a minimum bandwidth/minimum wirelength placement by transforming a matrix representation of the input circuit into band form and reflecting the transformation steps in HWOP swaps. This algorithm is applicable to general CDFGs.

The second, faster algorithm (Figure 15.16(b)) gives even better results, but is limited to operating on trees (similarly to GAMA). It proceeds topdown, recursively placing the nodes in a linear arrangement. The root is placed in the middle; the left subtree of the root, to the left; and the right subtree, to the right. The order in which the nodes are visited depends on the summed lengths of all HWOPs in the subtrees rooted at each node (this is called the *volume* of a node): Nodes rooting smaller volume subtrees are visited first, placing them closer to the root. In Figure 15.16, the length of all HWOPs is assumed to be 1.

In a refinement, Ababei and Bazargan [1] then extend the techniques for partial reconfiguration: A sequence of CDFGs is arranged so that previously placed

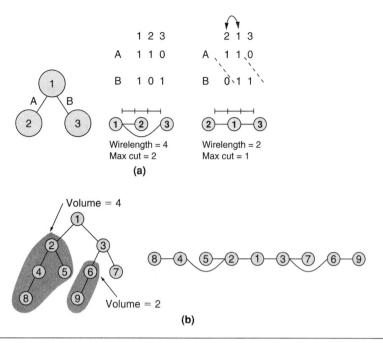

FIGURE 15.16 ■ Postmapping linear placement.

HWOPs and their interconnect can be reused in succeeding configurations, thus reducing the amount of configuration data. In the (albeit limited) experiments, up to 74 percent of HWOPs and 36 percent of inter-HWOP connectivity could be reused between configurations. However, with increased reuse, the delays and wirelengths began to deteriorate over independent placements (without reuse).

Other techniques that have been applied to compose linear stripes of HWOPs are spectral partitioning [13], genetic algorithms [10], and quadratic placement [22]. In the last case, it was determined that the quadratic placement needed to be postprocessed for by computing the optimal arrangement of HWOPs in a small window (less than or equal to five HWOPs long) using exact methods (e.g., exhaustive search, branch/bound). The process is then repeated, sliding the window across the stripe, until no further improvement can be realized.

15.6.2 Constrained Two-dimensional Placement

With the focus on linear datapath structures, published work on constrained two-dimensional or 1.5-dimensional datapath placement is sparse. Some limited results are reported by Thorns [18]: The CLAP tool first performs a clustering procedure similar to that in VPack [2] to determine the HWOPs to fit into each stripe. Then the horizontal arrangement of HWOPs inside a stripe, as well as the vertical and horizontal arrangements of entire stripes, is optimized using different moves in an adaptive simulated annealing algorithm [2], resulting in the constrained layout shown in Figure 15.14. Again, only a limited set of benchmarks was evaluated for CLAP. However, even for a small 28-module datapath, the constrained two-dimensional approach reduced the delay by more than 20 percent over a linear placement created using a GAMA-like technique.

15.6.3   Two-dimensional Placement

A full two-dimensional placement is generally not applicable to the datapath structures discussed previously. However, if the target device architecture does not impose a specific ordering of bit significances (for example, when no hardwired carry logic is present), two-dimensional placement can be performed by treating the HWOPs as conventional macro blocks. A family of such placement algorithms has been described for the tools TS-FP [5] and Frontier [17] (Figure 15.17). Both distinguish between *hard* macros, with fixed rectangular shape, and *soft* macros, with a malleable shape. In both cases, the algorithms partition the device fabric into a number of *bins*, whose size depends on the area of the largest hard macro present in the input circuit. Smaller macros are then clustered up to the bin size to avoid wasting intrabin area.

This clustering process takes into account a number of factors: the compatibility of the macro shapes inside a bin (shapes in bin must geometrically fit in the bin bounding box), the relative size of the cluster compared to the entire circuit, the relative size of the blocks in the cluster, and the connectivity of the macros in the cluster. If, after clustering, the number of clusters exceeds the number of available bins, the size of the bins is increased and the clustering process is repeated. The clusters are then assigned to individual bins using standard placement techniques.

Intrabin placement is now performed constructively. TS-FP places hard macros from right to left by abutment, leaving the left side of the bin free for

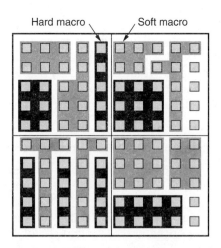

FIGURE 15.17 ■ Bin-based two-dimensional HWOP floorplanning.

soft macros. Frontier (shown in Figure 15.17) spreads the hard macros horizontally across the entire length of a bin, leaving the unused space *between* them for the soft macros. These are then placed in the free regions. TS-FP performs a geometrical minimax matching, reshaping the logic of each soft macro to fit into available space while attempting to keep the macros' initial internal placement intact. Frontier uses a simpler approach, laying a snakelike pattern across the free space, filled by sequentially selecting from the soft macro an unassigned PE that leads to the minimal overall wirelength. To improve routability, Frontier additionally employs a final low-temperature annealing pass for the PEs in the soft macros. These are allowed to move across macro and bin boundaries. The annealing start temperature is set sufficiently high to allow perturbation of the layout but low enough to ensure that the basic bin structure is kept intact.

15.7 COMPACTION

In a 1:1 mapping of simple CDFG operators (for example, trivial logic gates) to HWOPs, the PEs inside an HWOP are often not used to their full capacity. This inefficiency is worse when coarse-grained PEs are being targeted, and it accumulates across all HWOPs implementing simple operators. Figure 15.18 shows an example of this in which the functionality of a 2-input multiplexer described using simple logic HWOPs requires three PEs—even though it would completely fit in a single PE.

Compaction dissolves the boundaries of selected HWOPs and optimizes their contents as a whole, resulting in the creation of a new super-HWOP that realizes all of the original functions in a smaller/faster fashion. The procedure can generally be split into four phases:

1. Select the HWOPs to merge and compact.
2. Analyze regularity across the selected HWOPs to derive new master slices.
3. Optimize the newly discovered master slices.

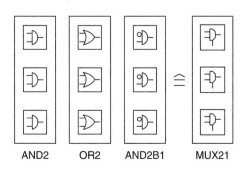

FIGURE 15.18 ■ Wasted space in the layout of very simple HWOPs.

4. Construct the super-HWOP by instantiating and placing the optimized master slices according to the regular inter-HWOP structure discovered previously.

15.7.1 Selecting HWOPs for Compaction

Two approaches have been proposed for selecting candidate HWOPs for compaction. Early work, such as the Structured Design Implementation (SDI) approach [8–10], aimed to keep a precomputed one-dimensional placement intact and so only considered connected *neighboring* HWOPs to compact. However, more recent research [21, 23] shows that better area efficiency is achievable by selecting candidates purely based on their connectivity, independent of any placement.

Additionally, depending on the actual optimization procedures to be performed on the selected candidates certain HWOPs, despite being connected and adjacently placed, might later be unsuitable for compaction. For commonly used optimization methods, this category generally includes HWOPs exploiting target device–specific features such as hardwired carry chains or fixed-function blocks (e.g., multipliers or memory blocks). Thus, their enclosing HWOPs are exempt from compaction.

15.7.2 Regularity Analysis

Since compaction is a regularity-preserving transformation, regularity aspects have to be considered both in its preparation and while it is taking place. Although methods exist to determine regular patterns in arbitrary circuits [12,15], it is much more efficient to keep track of this data from the moment of HWOP circuit generation. The method developed by Ye and colleagues [21,23] requires knowledge of the netlists at the bit slice level. SDI, supported by the powerful PARAMOG module generator library, goes beyond that by explicitly describing both regularity (in the model described in Section 15.1.1) and hierarchy (using master slice/bit slice relationships).

Based on the detailed data, SDI can consider more complicated structures for regular compaction. Figure 15.19 shows how it can isolate two new master slices and their instances from the HWOPs ALU and LSHR under compaction, even though the number of bit slices between these HWOPS differs. The inter-HWOP regularity consists of a 2-zone stack. The top zone holds a single instance of a newly discovered master slice, which consists of the original master slices ALU4, TOPDWN, and DWN. The second zone has two instances of a new master slice, which consists of ALU4 and two instances DWN. Ye and colleagues' technique [23] would not attempt to merge these two HWOPs, as it can only compact HWOPs with the same number of bit slices.

15.7.3 Optimization Techniques

The core of compaction lies in the intermodule optimizations applied to the super-HWOP constructed by merging the original HWOPs. Here, Ye and

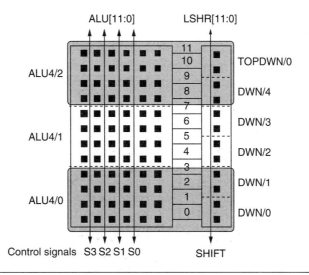

FIGURE 15.19 ■ Extracting inter-HWOP regularity.

colleagues' approach [23] performs two additional steps compared to SDI: word-wide transformations that affect entire HWOPs followed by exploiting the context (external signals) of the HWOPs under compaction. The main processing step of both SDI and the system of Ye et al. [23], however, consists of applying traditional logic synthesis and optimization algorithms at the bit slice level.

Word-level optimization

Word-level optimizations, which in Ye and colleagues' approach [23] were performed manually, alter the datapath from the structure described in the original CDFG. Two of the transformations are shown in Figure 15.20. The first, shown in Figure 15.20(a), tentatively collapses trees of multiplexers into a single wide multiplexer, modifying the select logic appropriately. If this replacement requires more area than the original version, the original version is retained. This transformation cannot be performed by optimizing at the slice level, because the multiplexer select logic is not part of the regular area holding the bit slices.

The second transformation, shown in Figure 15.20(b), is called operation reordering. It attempts to reduce area by restructuring individual multiplexers. A subcircuit, in which a multiplexer selects a single result from multiple identical operator instances, is turned into a form where multiple multiplexers select from a set of inputs feeding a single operator instance. Under the assumption that a multiplexer is smaller than the operator, this reduces area. Note, however, that this is not always the case: In many fine-grained architectures that combine LUTs and arithmetic carry logic within a logic block, both multiplexers and adders/subtractors may occupy the same number of logic blocks.

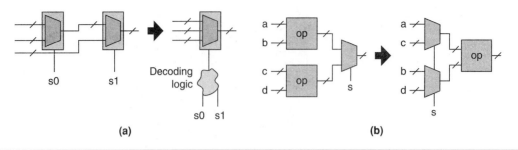

FIGURE 15.20 ▪ Word-level optimizations performed by Ye et al. [23].

Furthermore, the second transformation is problematical in that it loses parallelism between the original multiple operator instances. Consider the following scenario: The operator instances 1 and 2 have data-dependent execution times t_1 and t_2, and the select input arrives at t_s after the operands of the operators. In the original case, both computations would be speculatively performed in parallel. The delay of the entire structure is then $\max(t_s, t_1)$ if the result of the first operator is selected, and $\max(t_s, t_2)$ otherwise. In effect, the delay of the select input hides part of the operator delay. In the reordered form, the operator can begin computation only *after* the select input has become valid, leading to total delays of $t_s + t_1$ and $t_s + t_2$, respectively.

The ramifications of such a transformation can be appraised to their full extent only when *building* the CDFG in the first place—for example, when considering instruction-level parallelism in a hardware compiler. At the same time, the multiplexer tree collapsing could also be performed, dispensing with a special optimization pass later in the design flow. Instead, the CDFG would contain generic multiplexer operator nodes with a varying number of inputs. During the mapping step, the module library would determine the best realization for each operator, also considering global issues such as the criticality of their signal paths.

Context-sensitive optimization

The tool flow designed by Ye and colleagues [23] then performs an additional suite of optimizations that also considers the super-HWOP in the *context* of the surrounding datapath (Figure 15.21). To this end, it partitions the super-HWOP into m-bit-wide *superslices*, each of which may thus consist of multiple bit slices. Next, the external ports of each superslice are examined for certain connectivity patterns and the presence of constant values. The actual optimizations are then performed in this superslice-specific context.

Constant inputs are absorbed for each of the superslices (Figure 15.21(a)). Similarly, nets that connect slice inputs directly to outputs are also pulled into the slice (Figure 15.21(b)). Multiple slice inputs all sourced by the same external signal are replaced by a single input that fans out to the original internal sinks (Figure 15.21(c)).

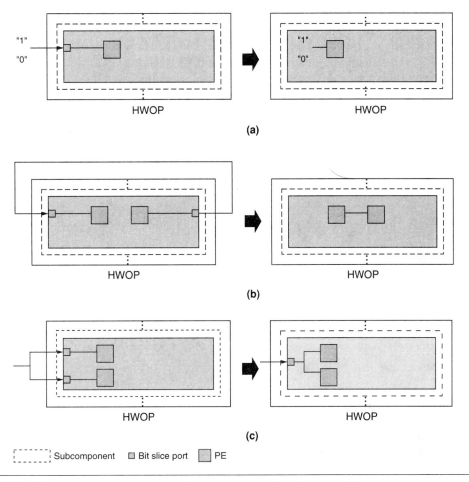

FIGURE 15.21 ■ Context-sensitive optimizations performed by Ye et al. [23].

These transformations occur *only* if all bit slices within a superslice have *identical* context (e.g., all bit slice input ports a within a superslice have the constant value 0 applied from the outside). Otherwise, the superslice is left unchanged.

The quantity m is thus a control for the internal regularity of the super-HWOP. With $m = 1$, the super-HWOP is partitioned into *width* superslices, each consisting only of a single 1-bit-wide bit slice. Each of these narrow super-slices is thus affected by only very limited context: A superslice's single bit slice can be perfectly matched to its context (e.g., allowing the absorption of even irregular constant input patterns into each slice) in the super-HWOP. However, while allowing a large degree of optimization, this setting of $m = 1$ potentially introduces significant irregularity into the optimized super-HWOP (it may end up consisting of completely different bit slices). At the other extreme, with $m = width$, the super-HWOP is covered by a single superslice containing m 1-bit-wide bit slices. Here optimization will occur only if the context affects *all* bit slices within the single superslice identically. Thus, even the optimized super-HWOP will be completely regular (composed only of identical bit slices). With the context required to be identical for more bit slices, however, fewer optimization opportunities arise. In Ye and colleagues' approach [23], a value of $m = 4$ is suggested as a good trade-off between widespread optimization and the preservation of a regular structure.

In effect, the idea of superslices is similar to the *zone* concept introduced in Section 15.5.1, although zones, with their variable granularity, remain more flexible than superslices, with their fixed granularity.

Logic optimization

In logic optimization, the netlists of the HWOPs under compaction are merged into HWOP-spanning bit slices (possibly newly discovered, as discussed in Section 15.7.2). The resulting larger merged netlists are then passed to conventional logic synthesis tools that can exploit the additional optimization opportunities resulting from them.

In addition to this slice-internal optimization, the system of Ye and colleagues [23] can specialize the bit slices by considering the constant *external* inputs and connections that were discovered in the context-sensitive analysis pass.

15.7.4   Building the Super-HWOP

The optimization phase of compaction changes the circuit structure. Thus, any regular placement created by a generator is invalidated. Ye and colleagues' tool flow [23], which concentrates on measuring regularity and area overheads, does not perform the further processing steps itself. Instead, the resulting optimized bit-slice netlists are passed to standard place-and-route tools for further handling. In contrast, Structured Design Implementation (SDI), additionally aiming at delay minimization, attempts to restore a regular placement for the optimized super-HWOP. This *micro-placement* step, shown in Figure 15.22, exploits regularity by operating at the master slice level. The results are then automatically replicated across the entire super-HWOP according to its zone structure.

Microplacement operates on cells (LUT and FF blocks), and proceeds in two phases:

1. The placement of cells horizontally, grouped into columns (Figure 15.22(a)). This is performed across all master slices, ensuring that cells sharing a control net are located adjacently to a vertical routing channel. Such an arrangement allows the efficient routing of high-fanout control nets on vertical long lines. Analogously, cells on interslice nets are horizontally aligned to allow short-distance routing. The remaining cells are placed in a timing-driven fashion, using estimates for the as yet unknown vertical position. This placement phase optimizes the super-HWOP in the geometric context of the datapath by constraining the master slice I/O ports to the appropriate sides of the layout.

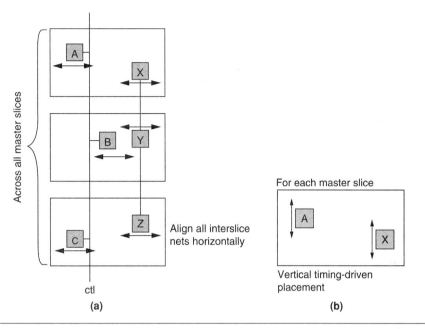

FIGURE 15.22 ■ Horizontal and vertical microplacement to restore regularity to compacted super-HWOP.

2. The placement of cells within the columns vertically (Figure 15.22(b)). This step looks across master slice boundaries only initially when performing a timing analysis on the entire super-HWOP. After annotating the timing criticalities calculated in this manner on the master slice ports, each master slice is placed independently in a purely timing-driven fashion. The timing model used here models the intricacies of the target device routing network and leads to measurably better results than simple Manhattan distances.

Since the microplacement results are replicated according to the regular structure previously determined for the super-HWOP, it is advantageous to employ high-quality algorithms. To this end, SDI uses a combination of well-converging heuristics and exact integer linear programming (ILP)-based methods. The latter are feasible because of the separation of the placement problem into horizontal and vertical phases, and the relatively small circuit size of the master slices (compared to the entire super-HWOP).

15.7.5 Discussion

Implementing a circuit in a regular bit-sliced fashion is generally associated with some area overhead compared to synthesizing/optimizing the circuit in an irregular flat manner. The reason is that the bit-slice boundaries prevent the exploitation of cross-slice optimization opportunities. The system devised by Ye and colleagues [23], with its additional interslice optimizations, observed area overheads of between 0 percent and 7.4 percent for superslice granularity values of $m = 1$ (fully irregular) and $m = 32$ (fully regular with a width of 32 bits), respectively. For SDI, which lacks these optimizations, area increases of up to 17 percent were observed over the flat solution. However, by scrupulously maintaining a regular structure, SDI was able to reduce the total delay in the circuit by up to 33 percent over the flat implementation. A combination of the interslice optimizations of Ye and colleagues [23] with the microplacement of SDI appears to be promising to achieve further gains.

15.8 SUMMARY AND FUTURE WORK

This chapter presented an overview of some of the many issues to consider when realizing datapaths on reconfigurable logic devices. The aspect of *regularity* is a crucial one and must be considered both at the level of the target device architecture and during the operation of the EDA tools. Module generators are an efficient means to actually create the circuits making up the datapath. However, in addition they must offer sufficient metadata to the rest of the tool flow as a base for effective transformation and optimization steps.

With increasing requirements on datapath performance, tool flows and algorithms must keep up with improvements in device architectures. All of the techniques described here have the potential for further refinement. Refinement opportunities include module generators that better support specialization, floorplanning with constrained two-dimensional placement, and a compaction technique in which the best of these refinements is combined.

References

[1] C. Ababei, K. Bazargan. Non-contiguous linear placement for reconfigurable fabrics. *Proceedings of the of the Reconfigurable Architectures Workshop*, 2004.

[2] V. Betz, J. Rose, A. Marquardt. *Architecture and CAD for Deep-Submicron FPGAs*, Kluwer, 1999.

[3] T. J. Callahan, P. Chong, A. DeHon, J. Wawrzynek. Fast module mapping and placement for datapaths in FPGAs. *Proceedings of the of the International Symposium on Field-Programmable Gate Arrays*, 1998.

[4] T. Callahan, R. Hauser, J. Wawrzynek. The GARP architecture and C compiler. *IEEE Computer* 33(4), 2000.

[5] J. M. Emmert, D. Bhati. A methodology for fast FPGA floorplanning. *Proceedings of the International Symposium on Field-Programmable Gate Arrays*, 1999.

[6] B. Hutchings, P. Bellows. J. Hawkins, S. Hemmert. A CAD suite for high-performance FPGA design. *Proceedings of the of the IEEE Symposium on Field-Programmable Custom Computing Machines*, 1999.

[7] N. Kasprzyk, A. Koch. High-level-language compilation for reconfigurable computers. *Proceedings of the International Conference on Reconfigurable Communication-centric SoCs*, 2005.

[8] A. Koch. Module compaction in FPGA-based regular datapaths. *Proceedings of the Design Automation Conference*, 1996.

[9] A. Koch. Structured design implementation—A strategy for implementing regular datapaths on FPGAs. *Proceedings of the International Symposium on Field-Programmable Gate Arrays*, 1996.

[10] A. Koch. *Regular Datapaths on Field-Programmable Gate Arrays.* CS doctoral thesis, technical, University of Braunschweig, 1997.

[11] A. Koch. On tool integration in high-performance FPGA design flows. *Proceedings of the International Conference on Field-Programmable Logic and Applications*, 1999.

[12] T. Kutzschebauch, L. Stok. Regularity-driven logic synthesis. *Proceedings of the International Conference on Computer-Aided Design*, 2000

[13] J. Li, J. Lillis, L. T. Liu, C. K. Cheng. New spectral linear placement and clustering approach. *Proceedings of the Design Automation Conference*, 1996.

[14] T. Neumann, A. Koch. A generic library for adaptive computing environments. *Proceedings of the International Conference on Field-Programmable Logic and Applications*, 2001.

[15] R. Nijssen, J. Jess. Two-dimensional datapath regularity extraction. *Proceedings of the ACM SIGDA Physical Design Workshop*, 1996.

[16] E. M. Sentovich, K. J. Singh, L. Lavagno, C. Moon, et al. SIS: A system for sequential circuit synthesis. *EECS Memorandum No. UCB/ERL M92/41*, University of California, Berkeley, 1992.

[17] R. Tessier. Frontier: A fast placement system for FPGAs. *Proceedings of the International Conference on VLSI*, 1999.

[18] F. Thorns. *CLAP—Clustering and placement.* Diploma thesis, Technical University of Braunschweig, 2003.

[19] C. C. Vi, D. Lewis. Area-speed trade-offs for hierarchical field-programmable gate arrays. *Proceedings of the International Symposium on Field-Programmable Gate Arrays*, 1996.

[20] C. Wewetzer. *A Universal Generator for Logic Circuits on FPGAs.* Diploma thesis, Technical University of Braunschweig, 2005.

[21] A. G. Ye. *Field-Programmable Gate Array Architectures and Algorithms Optimized for Implementing Datapath Circuits.* Doctoral thesis, University of Toronto, 2004.

[22] T. T. Ye, G. De Micheli. Data path placement with regularity. *Proceedings of the International Conference on Computer-Aided Design*, 2000.

[23] A. G. Ye, J. Rose, D. Lewis. Synthesizing datapath circuits for FPGAs with emphasis on area minimization. *Proceedings of the International Conference on Field-Programmable Technology*, 2002.

[24] A. G. Ye, J. Rose. Measuring and utilizing the correlation between signal connectivity and signal positioning for FPGAs containing multibit building blocks. *Proceedings of the International Conference on Field-Programmable Logic and Applications*, 2005.

CHAPTER 16

SPECIFYING CIRCUIT LAYOUT ON FPGAs

Satnam Singh
Programming Principles and Tools Group
Microsoft Research Cambridge

Typically, the layout of a circuit implemented on a field-programmable gate array (FPGA) is computed automatically by vendor design tools. This computation often results in an acceptable mapping of logical wires in the design onto actual physical routing resources on the FPGA that meets the designer's performance requirements. Instead of relying on automated tools, however, a designer could try to use an FPGA by explicitly stating the configuration of individual logic blocks and explicitly specifying the routing between them. One almost never needs to program an FPGA at this basic and raw level, and often the proprietary nature of programming information makes it difficult or impossible to take this approach. Still, the FPGA design flow provides a powerful set of abstractions that allow a designer to think in terms of structural circuit netlists, which can be automatically converted into programming information for FPGAs. Structural netlists are abstracted further by the synthesis flow, which allows designers to think of circuit functions in an algorithmic or sequential manner.

16.1 THE PROBLEM

Although it is just about tractable for humans to explicitly specify the layout of some mapped circuits on an FPGA, explicitly specifying the routing is extremely difficult because of the complex nature of the wiring resources. A screen snapshot of some of these resources on a Xilinx FPGA is shown in Figure 16.1. As one can see there are simply too many wires and interconnection options for a human to economically make routing decisions. However, providing layout hints or even explicit layout for only the logic blocks is a reasonable approach, because designers often have good intuition about a desirable layout but little intuition about how to use the underlying routing resources. By specifying some aspects of the layout, the tools can produce a faster circuit than is possible with purely automatic approaches [4]. The ability to specify layout helps with other operations like dynamic reconfiguration [3].

A design that contains a mixture of manually and automatically placed blocks is shown in Figure 16.2. The rectangular block is the core of the Xilinx Micro-Blaze soft processor, which is designed with explicit layout specification for each gate. The other blocks are components, such as the system bus and peripherals,

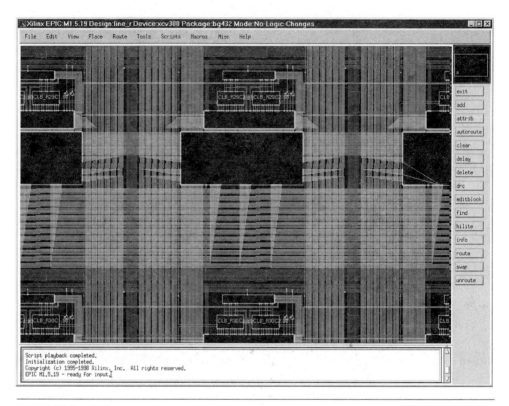

FIGURE 16.1 ■ FPGA routing resources.

that are designed without explicit layout specification—the placer automatically decides where to put these gates. Many of Xilinx's Core Generator IP core blocks are designed with explicit layout information. By giving a good layout for a circuit, one can indirectly control performance by influencing wiring that contributes to the critical path. Also, by providing user-specified placement information for small blocks that will be reused for many designs, the upfront design effort can be worthwhile.

An automatic placement algorithm can often find an acceptable placement that meets the design requirements for speed, area, power, and so forth. However, when such an algorithm cannot find a good placement—or any placement at all—there is often little the designer can do. In these situations it would be desirable either to allow the designer to influence the placement by adding extra information or to allow her to partly or completely specify the layout of her circuit. For circuits that need very high performance or that need to be very compact, often only a user-specified layout can achieve the required results. For example, the design shown in Figure 16.3 has been automatically placed and routed without any user-specified layout information. The same design can be augmented with user-specified layout information to produce the layout shown in Figure 16.4, which performs approximately 30 percent faster.

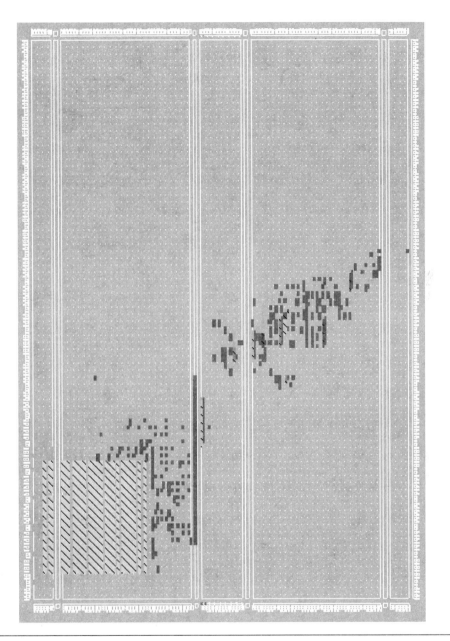

FIGURE 16.2 ■ An example of manually and automatically placed blocks.

Providing explicit layout information can also reduce the runtime of FPGA implementation tools, mainly because of the reduction in work for the automatic router. This is particularly important for uses of reconfigurable computing that create custom circuit designs for each problem instance, when placement and routing tool runtimes are part of the system's execution time (see Chapter 5).

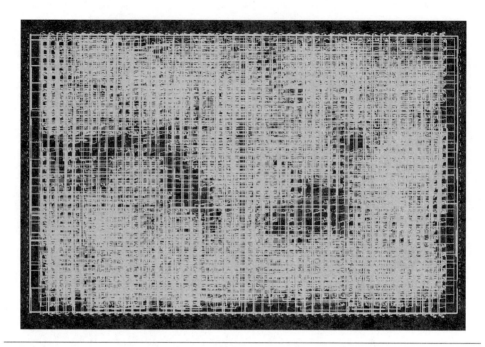

FIGURE 16.3 ■ A design with no explicit layout (automatic place and route).

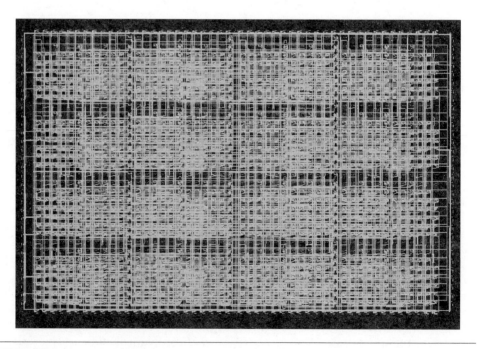

FIGURE 16.4 ■ A design with totally explicit layout.

An important reason for explicitly specifying absolute or relative layout is to support runtime reconfiguration, which is much easier to perform if the system knows the shape and location of circuits to be swapped in and out or updated in place.

This chapter reviews various techniques for specifying the layout of circuits for FPGAs. We illustrate our examples using Xilinx's FPGA technology, which provides an accessible mechanism for specifying circuit layout.

16.2 EXPLICIT CARTESIAN LAYOUT SPECIFICATION

Explicit Cartesian layout specification involves specifying the location of some or all logic elements using a two-dimensional coordinate system. One form of explicit layout involves giving an absolute location for each gate in the mapped netlist. This approach is not common because it does not permit the specification of reusable layouts, which can be replicated throughout the FPGA, and such descriptions may be unnecessarily specific to a particular FPGA chip or family. A more common approach is the relative layout specification.

Xilinx's placement tools can take user-specified layout information either as absolute or as relative locations. Relative locations identify the bottom left corner of a block of logic. Blocks may be placed relative to each other in a hierarchical fashion.

The layout of a gate or block is achieved by attaching a special attribute called LOC for absolute layouts and RLOC for relative layouts. The VHDL code in Figure 16.5 illustrates the design of a 1-bit adder in which two of the gates have their relative layout explicitly specified.

In the figure, the attribute mechanism of VHDL is used to attach a relative layout attribute to two instances: one for an xor gate and the other for an or gate. The RLOC attribute specifies the relative location of the CLB that will be used to realize a given gate. One may further specify the specific lookup table (LUT) within the CLB or omit this specification to allow the placer to make the choice.

```
architecture structural of adder is
    signal xor1_out, and1_out, and2_out, or1_out : std_logic;
    attribute RLOC of xor1 is "X2Y5" ;
    attribute RLOC of or1 is "X3Y4" ;
begin
    xor1: xorg port map (in1 =>a, in2 => b, out1 => xor1_out);
    xor2: xorg port map (in1 => xor1_out, in2 => cin, out1 => sum);
    and1: andg port map (in1 => a, in2 => b, out1   => and1_out);
    or1: org port map (in1 => a, in2 => b, out1   => or1_out);
    and2: andg port map (in1 => cin, in2 => or1_out, out1   => and2_out);
    or2: org port map (in1 => and1_out, in2 => and2_out, out1   => cout);
end structural;
```

FIGURE 16.5 ■ An example of explicit layout in VHDL.

Explicit layout works well for small circuits that are not parameterized and for VHDL and Verilog descriptions that do not make use of statements like `for . . . generate`. In parameterized circuits, layout specifications become quite complex, with location specifications becoming difficult to comprehend layout calculation expressions. Because layout specifications are string attributes, one has the extra complexity of performing integer index calculations and then converting them into their string representation. This is often too tedious to be practical. The difficulty of working with explicit Cartesian layout specifications has led to the development of various systems to specify layout at a higher level of abstraction.

16.3 ALGEBRAIC LAYOUT SPECIFICATION

Algebraic layout specification typically does not involve Cartesian coordinates. Instead, one specifies the geometric relationship between one circuit and another. These specifications (or constraints) are gathered together, and a *deterministic* layout can then be *calculated*. Techniques such as this have been shown to work for parameterized circuits, circuits with irregular layouts, and recursively defined circuit layouts. Such descriptions are also slightly less tightly coupled to a specific FPGA architecture or family. In this section we describe how algebraic layout specifications work in the Lava system [1]. Several other systems are based on similar principles.

Lava is based on the concept of *circuit combinators*, which are calculations that take circuits as inputs and deliver a circuit as a result; essentially, they are procedures that compute on circuit descriptions. One important design decision in Lava is the coupling of the description of circuit behavior and that of circuit layout by using circuit combinators that compose both behavior and layout. This works well when the circuit layout description can use the same patterns as those of the circuit behavior. When this is not the case, one can directly use Cartesian coordinates.

One important combinator is the serial composition combinator. This combinator, written as an infix operator >->, takes two circuits R and S as arguments and delivers a circuit comprising R with its output connected to the input of S. Furthermore, R is laid out to the left of S, which matches a left-to-right dataflow.

Figure 16.6 shows the composition of an AND2 and an INV gate. Each gate or circuit starts life in its own coordinate system. The basic gates each have a height and width of one unit. The serial composition combinator sees that the circuit on the left has a width of one and then translates the circuit on the right by one unit. These algebraic descriptions can be arbitrarily nested. When the system needs to produce a VHDL or EDIF netlist, the algebraic specifications are computed and a netlist that contains RLOCs is automatically generated.

Notice, now that layout has been combined with behavior, that there is a need for several kinds of serial composition combinators. Those for right-to-left (<-<), bottom-to-top (^), and top-to-bottom (V) layout are all supported by Lava.

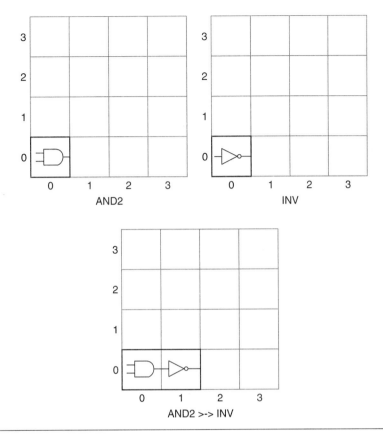

FIGURE 16.6 ■ Layout calculation.

Figure 16.7 shows the layout produced by the Lava circuit expression AND2 >->
FD clk, which serially composes an AND2 gate with an FD component (a flip-flop).

In the Xilinx device, a LUT–flip-flop pair is called a *slice*. AND2 and a flip-flop
(FD) each have a width and height of one unit, or slice, causing the FD flip-
flop to be mapped to a slice to the right of the slice containing the function generator for the AND2 gate. Such a process is very inefficient. To allow circuits
to be composed but mapped to the same location we can use the serial overlay
operator, written as >|>. This is illustrated on the right side of Figure 16.7 and
shows both the AND2 gate and the FD flip-flop mapped to the same location.

The circuit tiles presented so far have only one-dimensional dataflow. Four-
sided tiles allow us to specify dataflow horizontally and vertically. Rather than
introduce a new basic tile, a 4-sided tile can be represented in terms of a 2-sided
tile. This is done by considering the 4-sided tile as a function that maps a pair of
input values to a pair of output values. Each element of each pair corresponds to
a face of the tile, as shown in Figure 16.8. We can now define a below combinator,
which places one tile below another (r below s is shown in the middle of the

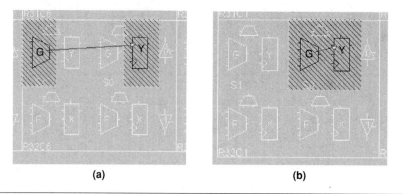

FIGURE 16.7 ■ The overlay combinator: (a) AND2 >-> FD clk; (b) AND2 >I> FD clk.

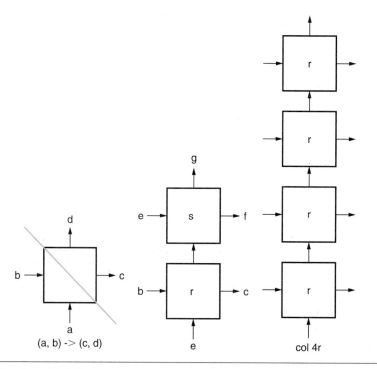

FIGURE 16.8 ■ Four-sided tiles.

figure). The col combinator replicates a tile vertically (`col 4 r` is shown on the right of the figure).

A concrete example of the col combinator is shown in Figure 16.9. The col combinator acts on a 1-bit adder circuit that takes a pair as input (the carry-in [`cin`] and another pair of values to be added) and delivers a pair as its output

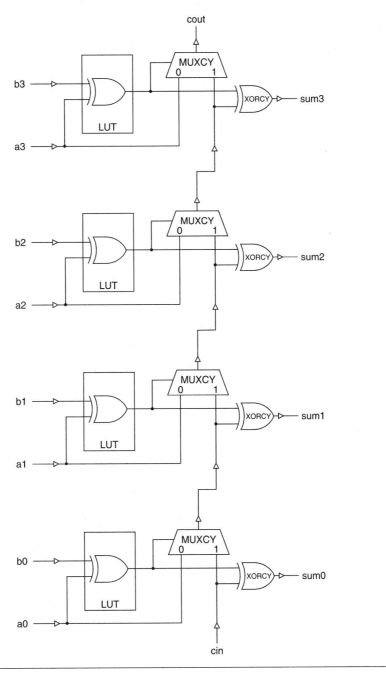

FIGURE 16.9 ■ A col 4 1-bit adder.

(the sum and the carry-out [cout]). It will connect the carry-out of each stage to the carry-in of the next stage. Furthermore, it will vertically stack the 1-bit adders.

The actual FPGA layout produced for col 8 oneBitAdder is shown in Figure 16.10. In this case the automatic placement tools would have produced the same layout because the carry chain would have constrained a vertical alignment for the circuit. Through combinations of these regular abutment techniques, very complex but regular circuits can be efficiently created.

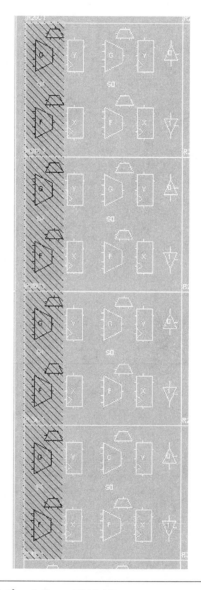

FIGURE 16.10 ■ FPGA layout of col 8 oneBitAdder.

16.3.1 Case Study: Batcher's Bitonic Sorter

This section presents the layout specification of a high-speed parallel sorter that would have been difficult to lay out using explicit Cartesian coordinates. We show how to build complex structures incrementally by composing the layout of subcomponents using simple operators. The use of hierarchy achieves complex layout structures that would have been difficult or tedious to produce otherwise and impossible to produce in a compositional manner.

The objective is to build a parallel sorter from a parallel merger, as shown in Figure 16.11. A parallel merger takes two sublists of numbers where each sublist is sorted and produces a completely sorted list of numbers as its output. All inputs and outputs are shifted in, in parallel rather than serially. Furthermore, for performance reasons the sorter should have the same floorplan as shown in the figure.

This parallel sorter uses a two-sorter as its building block, which is shown fully placed in Figure 16.12. This circuit has left-to-right dataflow. Although the >=> combinator is also a serial composition combinator, it does not have any layout semantics because it is used to compose wiring circuits (which are not subject to layout directives).

The two-sorter in Figure 16.12 has been carefully designed to have a rectangular footprint because we will want to tile many of these circuits together vertically and horizontally to produce a compact and high-performance sorter network.

Another important combinator we will use in our sorter design is the two-combinator, which makes two copies of a circuit r, one of which works on the bottom half of the input and the other on the top half of the input, as illustrated in Figure 16.13. Furthermore, the second copy of r should be placed vertically on top of the first copy. The two combinator can be defined as

```
two r = halve >-> par [r,r] >-> unhalve
```

which says halve the input, use two copies of r in parallel (stacked vertically) on the halved input, and then take the result and unhalve it.

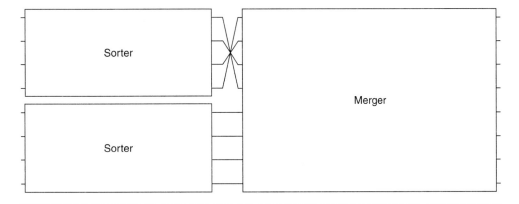

FIGURE 16.11 ■ The recursive structure of a sorter.

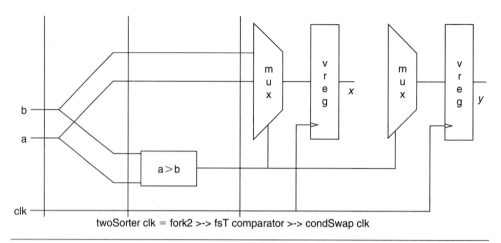

twoSorter clk = fork2 >-> fsT comparator >-> condSwap clk

FIGURE 16.12 ▪ Two-sorter layout and behavior specification.

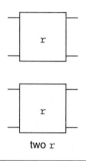

two r

FIGURE 16.13 ▪ The two-combinator.

Interleave (ilv) is another combining form that uses two copies of the same circuit. This combinator has the property that the bottom circuit processes the inputs at even positions and the top circuit processes the inputs at odd positions. It can be defined as

```
ilv r = unriffle >-> two r >-> riffle
```

An instance of ilv r for an 8-input bus is shown in Figure 16.14. The related evens combinator chops the input list into pairs and then applies copies of the same circuit to each input.

Given these ingredients, we can give a recursive description of a parallel merger butterfly circuit:

```
bfly r 1 = r
bfly r n = ilv (bfly r (n-1)) >-> evens r
```

A bitonic merger of degree 3 is shown in Figure 16.15, which not only describes how to compose the behavior of elements to form a merger circuit, but also

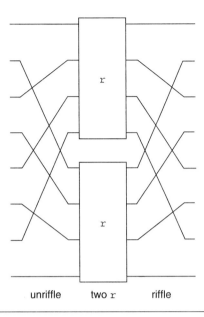

unriffle   two r   riffle

FIGURE 16.14 ■ The `ilv` combinator.

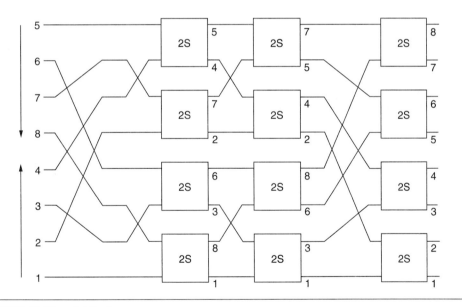

FIGURE 16.15 ■ A bitonic merger.

specifies the *layout* of the merger circuit using algebraic layout specifications. This circuit is a bitonic merger that can merge its inputs as long as one half of the input is increasing in the opposite order from the other half, as shown in the figure.

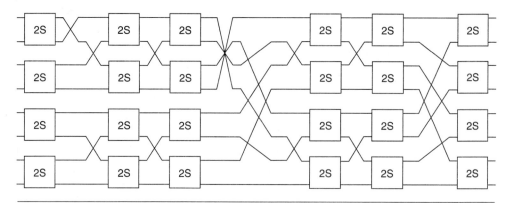

FIGURE 16.16 ▪ Sorter recursion and layout for 8 inputs.

Now that we have our merger, we can recursively unfold the pictorial specification in of the sorter layout to produce the design and layout in Figure 16.16 (for 8 inputs). This layout can be specified using the following combinators:

```
sortB cmp 1 = cmp
sorB cmp n
= two (sortB cmp (n-1)) >->
  pair >-> snD reverse >-> unpair >->
  butterfly cmp n
```

In the figure the description uses two subsorters to produce a bitonic input for a merger (shown on the right).

The 8-input description can be evaluated to produce an EDIF or VHDL netlist containing RLOC specifications for every gate. The FPGA layout of a degree-5 sorter (32 inputs) with 16-bit numbers is shown in Figure 16.17 on a Xilinx Virtex-II device. The resulting netlist is the same but with the layout information removed. It is shown in Figure 16.18. The netlist with the layout information leads to an implementation that is approximately 50 percent faster, and a 64-input sorter leads to a 75 percent speed improvement.

The case study just outlined shows how a complicated and recursive layout can be described in a feasible manner using algebraic layout combinators rather than explicit Cartesian coordinates.

16.4 LAYOUT VERIFICATION FOR PARAMETERIZED DESIGNS

A common problem with parameterized layout descriptions (especially those based on Cartesian coordinates) is that designer errors can produce bad layouts that cannot be realized on the target FPGAs—for example, the layout specification may try to map too many logic gates into the same location. Such errors

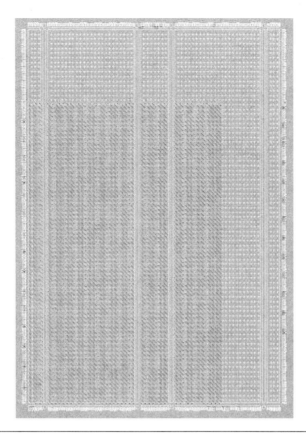

FIGURE 16.17 ■ The sorter FPGA layout (32 16-bit inputs).

make the production of IP cores that rely on layout very difficult and time consuming.

For a nonparameterized design, this is not much of an issue: The developer can check if the design maps, places, and routes. However, for a parameterized design it is usually impractical to check every possible combination of parameters to ensure that each one leads to a valid layout. A recent, interesting approach for layout verification involves theorem provers to statically analyze and formally verify that a design is free of layout errors. This is the approach taken by Pell [2] in his Quartz declarative block composition system, which uses a special hardware description notation that can be formally analyzed with the Isabelle theorem prover. The Quartz system works on algebraic layout combinators similar to those presented in the previous section.

The Quartz system verifies layout correctness by checking for validity, containment, and intersection. Validity ensures that the size function of a block always evaluates to a positive result. Containment ensures that for all parameter values all subblocks stay within the bounding box of the overall circuit. The intersection property checks for badly overlapping blocks.

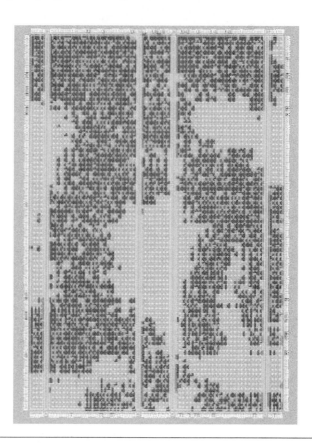

FIGURE 16.18 ■ The sorter with layout information removed.

16.5 SUMMARY

User specification of the layout of circuits for FPGAs is sometimes necessary to meet performance requirements, to reduce area, or to facilitate dynamic reconfiguration. While a user-defined layout is impractical for many complete designs because of complexity or time-to-market constraints, optimizing the most critical blocks of a circuit can have significant benefits, especially for reusable IP blocks and vendor libraries.

Some vendor tools provide the ability to specify the layout of gates or composite blocks through either absolute or relative Cartesian coordinates. However, these tools are tedious to use and error prone, particularly for parameterized circuits. Various systems have adopted algebraic layout specifications that use geometric relationships between blocks instead of coordinate values. Such descriptions work well for irregular and recursive layouts, as demonstrated by the recursive parallel sorter in this chapter. However, one may still specify illegal layouts for parameterized circuits, and no satisfactory technique exists for finding them. A promising approach is the use of theorem provers to statically analyze algebraic layout descriptions to ensure that they have no layout errors for any given permutation of parameters.

References

[1] P. Bjesse, K. Claessen, M. Sheeran, S. Singh. Lava: Hardware design in Haskell. *International Conference on Functional Programming (ICFP)*, Springer-Verlag, 1998.

[2] O. Pell. Verification of FPGA layout generators in higher order logic. *Journal of Automated Reasoning* 37(1–2), August 2006.

[3] P. J. Roxby, S. Singh. Rapid construction of partial configuration datastreams from high level constructs using JBits. *Field Programmable Logic (FPL)*, Springer-Verlag, 2001.

[4] S. Singh. Death of the RLOC. *Field-Programmable Custom Computing Machines (FCCM)*, April 2000.

CHAPTER 17

PATHFINDER: A NEGOTIATION-BASED, PERFORMANCE-DRIVEN ROUTER FOR FPGAS

Larry McMurchie
Synplicity Corporation

Carl Ebeling
Department of Computer Science and Engineering
University of Washington

Routing is a crucial step in the mapping of circuits to field-programmable gate arrays (FPGAs). For large circuits that utilize many FPGA resources, it can be very difficult and time consuming to successfully route all of the signals. Additionally, the performance of the mapped circuit depends on routing critical and near-critical paths with minimum interconnect delays. One disadvantage of FPGAs is that they are slower than their ASIC counterparts, so it is important to squeeze out every possible nanosecond of delay in the routing.

The first goal, a complete routing of all signals, is difficult to achieve in FPGAs because of the hard constraints on routing resources. Unlike ASICs and printed circuit boards (PCBs), FPGAs have a fixed amount of interconnect. The usual approach in placement is to minimize the wiring resources anticipated for routing signals. Although this reduces the overall demand for resources, signals inevitably compete for the same resources during routing. The challenge is to find a way to allocate resources so that all signals can be routed. The second goal, minimizing delay, requires the use of minimum-delay routes for signals, which can be expensive in terms of routing resources, especially for high-fanout signals. Thus, the solution to the entire routing problem requires the simultaneous solution of two interacting and often competing subproblems.

Early solutions to the FPGA routing problem were based on the considerable literature on routing in the context of ASICs and gate arrays. The problem of routing FPGAs bears a considerable resemblance to the problem of global routing for custom integrated circuit design, where signals are assigned to channels. However, the two problems differ in several fundamental respects. First, routing resources in FPGAs are discrete and scarce while they are relatively continuous in custom integrated circuits (ICs). For this reason FPGAs require an integrated approach using both global and detailed routing. A second difference is that global routing for custom ICs is based on an undirected graph embedded in Cartesian space (i.e., a two-dimensional grid). In FPGAs the switches are often directional, and the routing resources connect arbitrary (but fixed) locations, requiring a directed graph that may not be embedded in Cartesian space. Both of these distinctions are important, as they prevent direct application of much of the previous work in routing.

By far, the most common approach to global routing of custom ICs is a shortest-path algorithm with obstacle avoidance. By itself, this technique usually yields many unroutable nets that must be rerouted by hand. A plethora of rip-up and retry approaches have been proposed to remedy this deficiency [1–3]. The basic problem with rip-up and retry is that the success of a route is dependent not just on the choice of nets to reroute but also on the order in which rerouting is done. Delay is usually factored into the standard rip-up and retry approach by ordering the nets to be routed such that critical nets are routed most directly [4–6].

To make the FPGA routing problem tractable, nearly all of the routing schemes in the literature incorporate features of the underlying architecture. Palczewski [7] describes a maze router with rip-up and reroute targeting the Xilinx 4000 series. In this work the structure of the plane-parallel switchbox in the 4000 series is exploited in conjunction with an A* search. Brown et al. [4] employ an architecture model consisting of channels, switchboxes, connection matrices, and logic blocks. A global router balances channel densities and a detailed router generates families of explicit paths within channels to resolve congestion. These approaches, as well as others, obtain some of their success by exploiting the features of a particular architecture model. The problem is that new architectures become constrained by the restrictions of such existing routing algorithms.

17.1 THE HISTORY OF PATHFINDER

PathFinder was used initially in the development of the Triptych FPGA architecture [8–10]. In fact, Triptych, with its heavy reliance on effective placement and routing tools, was a catalyst for the development of the PathFinder algorithm— a perfect example of "necessity being the mother of invention." As part of an FPGA architecture exploration tool called Emerald [11], PathFinder was also employed in the development of an FPGA under development by IBM in the mid-1990s. This was particularly appropriate because PathFinder is inherently architecture independent. That experience showed that PathFinder was indeed an improvement over other FPGA routers available at the time.

The PathFinder algorithm was adopted and carefully implemented by Betz and Rose in the very popular versatile place and route (VPR) FPGA tool suite [12, 13], which has been widely used for academic and industry research. The Toronto place-and-route challenge [14] was established as a way to compare different FPGA placement and routing algorithms. Since the contest was established in 1997, the champion has been either VPR's implementation of PathFinder or SC-PathFinder, implemented at the University of California–Santa Cruz. Although companies are reluctant to divulge the details of their design tools, it is clear that some version of the PathFinder algorithm is currently used by virtually all commercial FPGA routers.

17.2   THE PATHFINDER ALGORITHM

17.2.1   The Circuit Graph Model

One of the key features of PathFinder is its architecture independence, which derives from the use of a simple underlying graph representation of FPGA architectures. This model allows PathFinder to be adapted to virtually any architecture and thus used to explore new architectures with very little startup cost. Once an architecture has been decided on, PathFinder can be specialized to it for improved results and performance.

The routing resources in an FPGA and their connections are represented by the directed graph $G = (V, E)$. The set of vertices V corresponds to the electrical nodes or wires in the FPGA architecture, and the edges E correspond to the switches that connect these nodes. An example of this graph model is shown in Figure 17.1 for a version of the Triptych FPGA cell. Note that devices are represented only implicitly by the wires connected to their terminals. That is, routing from one device terminal to another is routing between the wires connected to those terminals.

Associated with each node n in the architecture is a base cost b_n that represents the relative cost of using that node. This cost is typically proportional to the length of the wire, although other measures like capacitance or number of fanins and fanouts are also possible. Each node also has a delay d_n, which may or may not be the same as b_n.

Given a signal i in a circuit mapped onto the FPGA, the signal net N_i is the set of terminals, including the source terminal s_i and sinks t_{ij}. N_i forms a subset of V. A solution to the routing problem for signal i is the directed routing tree RT_i embedded in G and connecting the source s_i to all of its sinks t_{ij}.

17.2.2   A Negotiated Congestion Router

We assume that the reader is familiar with Djikstra's shortest-path graph algorithm [15–17], which is at the core of many routing algorithms. Note that in our formulation costs are associated with nodes, not edges. This changes the basic

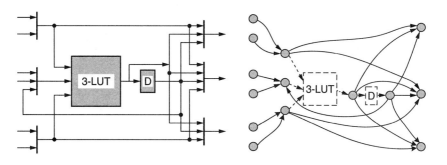

FIGURE 17.1 ■ The circuit for a Triptych FPGA cell is represented in PathFinder by the graph at the right.

shortest-path algorithm only slightly by redefining the cost of a path from node n_i to node n_j as the sum of the node costs along the path, including the starting and ending nodes.

Routing algorithms differ primarily in the cost function applied to the routing resources and in how individual applications of the shortest-path algorithm are used to successfully route all the signals of a netlist onto the graph representing the architecture. We ignore the issue of fanout in our initial presentation and assume that each signal is a simple route from source to a single sink.

A naive routing algorithm proceeds by applying the shortest-path algorithm to each signal in order, with the cost of a node defined as

$$c_n = b_n \tag{17.1}$$

Resources already used by previous routes are not available to later routes. It is clear that the order in which signals are routed is crucial, as later routes have many fewer available routing resources. Some algorithms perform rip-up and retry when later routes cannot find a path. Selected early routes that are blocking are ripped up and rerouted later—in essence, adaptively changing the order in which signals are routed.

The very simple example in Figure 17.2 shows how this naive algorithm can fail. There are three signals, 1, 2, and 3, to be routed from the sources $S_1, S_2,$ and S_3 to their respective sinks $D_1, D_2,$ and D_3. The ovals represent partial paths through one or more nodes, annotated with the associated costs. Ignoring congestion, the minimum-cost path for each signal would use node B. If the naive obstacle avoidance routing scheme is used, the order in which the signals are routed becomes crucial: Routing in the order 1, 2, 3 fails, and the minimum-cost routing solution will be found only when starting with signal 2.

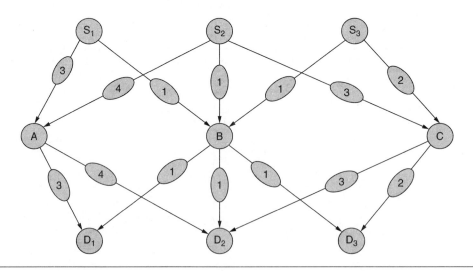

FIGURE 17.2 ▪ First-order congestion.

This problem can be solved by introducing negotiated congestion avoidance, first suggested by Nair [18] by extending the cost of using a given node n in a route to

$$c_n = b_n \cdot p_n \qquad (17.2)$$

where b_n is the base cost of using n, and p_n is a function of the number of other signals presently using n (p_n is often called the "present-sharing" term). Note that in the naive router, $p_n = 1$ if no other signals are using n, and infinity otherwise. In the negotiated congestion algorithm, p_n is set initially to 1 and all signals are routed. This allows each signal to be routed as if no other signals were present. The cost of sharing is then increased, and all nets are ripped up and rerouted in turn. This iterative process continues, with the cost of sharing increasing at each iteration until all signals have been successfully routed. The idea is that the cost of a congested node will increase and that signals that have other alternatives will eventually find other paths, leaving the node to the signal that needs it most. p_n is a function of the iteration i and the number of signals sharing a node k. The definition of p_n is a key tuning parameter of PathFinder.

The negotiated congestion avoidance algorithm solves the problem of Figure 17.2. During the first iteration, p_n is initialized to 1, and consequently no penalty is imposed for the use of n regardless of how many signals occupy it. Thus, in the first iteration all three signals share B. When the sharing function p_n increases sufficiently, signal 1 will find that a route through node A gives a lower cost than a route through the congested node B. During an even later iteration signal 3 will find that a route through node C gives a lower cost than that through B. This scheme of negotiation for routing resources depends on a relatively gradual increase in the cost of sharing nodes. If the increase is too abrupt, signals may be forced to take high-cost routes that lead to other congestion. Just as in the standard rip-up and retry scheme, the ordering becomes important.

While iterative negotiated congestion routing with the cost function of equation 17.2 can optimally route simple "first-order" routing problems like that in Figure 17.2, it fails on more complex "second-order" routing problems like that shown in Figure 17.3. Again we need to route three signals, one from each source to the corresponding sink. Let us first consider this example from the standpoint of obstacle avoidance with rip-up and retry. Assume that we start with the routing order (1, 2, 3). Signal 1 routes through node B, and signals 2 and 3 share node C. For rip-up and retry to succeed, both signals 1 and 2 would have to be rerouted, with signal 2 rerouted first. Because signal 1 does not use a congested node, determining that it needs to be rerouted is in general difficult.

This second-order congestion problem cannot be solved using p_n alone. Signal 2 will never choose node B because the present sharing costs for nodes B and C are the same, with B used by signal 1 and C used by signal 3. Since the path through C is cheaper, it is always chosen. PathFinder solves this by extending the cost function with a "history" term, h_n:

$$c_n = (b_n + h_n) \cdot p_n \qquad (17.3)$$

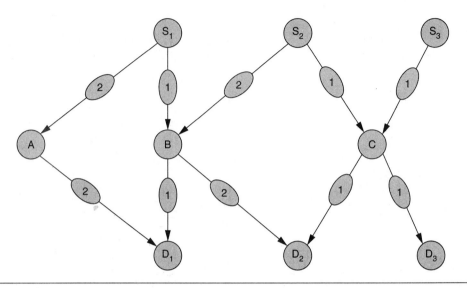

FIGURE 17.3 ■ Second-order congestion.

Unlike p_n, h_n "remembers" the congestion that has occurred on node n during previous routing iterations. That is, the history term is updated after each routing iteration; any node shared by multiple signals has its history term increased by some amount. The effect of h_n is to permanently increase the cost of using congested nodes so that routes through other nodes are attempted. Without this term, as soon as signals stop sharing a node, its cost drops to the base cost and it again becomes attractive. This leads to oscillations where signals switch back and forth between nodes but never resolve the congestion problem. The addition of the history term is a key difference between PathFinder and Nair's routing algorithm [18].

The term h_n allows the problem in Figure 17.3 to be routed successfully. On each iteration that node C is shared, h_n is increased slightly. When signal 2 switches to using node B, the cost of node C remains elevated. Now the history cost of node B rises because it is shared by signals 1 and 2. Eventually signal 1 will route through node A. Note that, depending on the base costs and how p_n and h_n are defined, signal 2 may switch back and forth between nodes B and C several times before the history costs of both are sufficiently high to force signal 1 onto node A.

The history term h_n is updated whenever a node n has shared signals. The size of δ_h, the amount by which h_n is increased, and how this depends on k, the number of sharing signals, are tunable parameters. If δ_h is too small, many iterations may be required to resolve the congestion; if it is too large, some solutions may not be found. Additionally, the relationship between p_n and h_n is very important. For example, it can be important to give the history term a chance to solve congestion before forcing the issue with p_n.

The details of the Negotiated Congestion algorithm are given in Figure 17.4. The while loop at line 2 executes the routing iterations until a solution has been

```
iteration ← 0                                                          1
While shared resources exist                                          2
    Iteration ← iteration + 1                                         3
    Loop over all signals i (signal router)                           4
        Rip up routing tree RTᵢ                                       5
        RTᵢ ← sᵢ                                                      6
        Loop until all sinks tᵢⱼ have been found                      7
            Initialize priority queue PQ to RTᵢ at cost 0             8
            Loop until new tᵢⱼ is found                               9
                Remove lowest cost node m from PQ                    10
                Loop over fanouts n of node m                        11
                    Add n to PQ at cost Pᵢₘ + cₙ                     12
                end loop                                             13
            end loop                                                 14
            Loop over nodes n in path tᵢⱼ to sᵢ (backtrace)          15
                Update cₙ                                            16
                Add n to RTᵢ                                         17
            end loop                                                 18
        end loop                                                     19
    end loop                                                         20
    Loop over all nodes nᵢ shared by multiple signals                21
        hᵢ ← hᵢ + δ(k)                                               22
    end loop                                                         23
end while                                                            24
```

FIGURE 17.4 ■ Negotiated Congestion algorithm.

found. The signal router loop at line 4 iterates over all signals in the netlist, ripping up and rerouting the nets one at a time. The routing tree RT_i is the set of nodes used to route signal i. To reroute a signal, the routing tree is reset to be just the signal's source.

The priority queue is used to implement the breadth-first search of Djikstra's algorithm. At each iteration of the loop of line 9, the lowest-cost node is taken from the priority queue. It is generally best to order the nodes with the same cost according to when they were inserted into the queue, with the newest nodes being extracted first. The cost used when inserting a new node in the priority queue at line 12 is

$$P_{im} + c_n \tag{17.4}$$

where P_{im} is the cost of the current partial path from the source, and c_n is the cost of using node n.

A signal is routed one sink at a time using Djikstra's breadth-first algorithm. When the search finds a sink, the nodes on the path from the source to it are added to RT_i. This is done by back-tracing the search path to the source. The search is then restarted with the priority queue being initialized with all the nodes already in RT_i. In this way, all the nodes on routes to previously found sinks are used as potential sources for routes to subsequent sinks. This algorithm for constructing the routing tree is similar to Prim's algorithm for determining a minimum spanning tree over an undirected graph, and it is identical to one suggested by Takahashi and Matsuyama [19] for constructing a tree embedded in an undirected graph. The quality of the points chosen by the algorithm is an open question for directed graphs; however, finding optimum (or even near-optimum) points is not essential for the router to be successful in adjusting costs to eliminate congestion.

The VPR router [12] reduces the cost of reinitializing the priority queue for each fanout by observing that for large-fanout nets, most of the paths found in searching for the previous fanout remain valid, especially if the segment added to the routing tree is relatively small. Thus, the search continues from the previous state after the new segment has been added to the routing tree. Because of the way Djikstra's algorithm ignores nodes after they have been visited once, this optimization must be implemented carefully to avoid expensive routing trees for high-fanout nets. Other algorithms for forming the fanout tree are possible. For example, there are times when routing to the most distant sink first results in a better routing tree.

At the end of each iteration, the history cost of each node shared by multiple signals is updated. The δ added to the history cost is generally a function of k, the number of signals sharing the node.

17.2.3   The Negotiated Congestion/Delay Router

To introduce delay into the Negotiated Congestion algorithm, we redefine the cost of using node n when routing a signal from s_i to t_{ij} as

$$C_n = A_{ij}d_n + (1 - A_{ij})c_n \qquad (17.5)$$

where c_n is defined in equation 17.3 and A_{ij} is the slack ratio:

$$A_{ij} = D_{ij}/D_{\max} \qquad (17.6)$$

where D_{ij} is the delay of the longest delay (register–register) path containing the signal segment (s_i, t_{ij}), and $D_{\max}$ is the maximum delay over all paths (i.e., the critical-path delay). Thus, $0 < A_{ij} \leq 1$. (This standard definition of slack ratio is easily extended to include circuit inputs and outputs with timing constraints as well as circuits with multiple clocks.)

Because path delay is made up of both device and wire delay, and the router can only control the wire delay, a more accurate formulation for A_{ij} is

$$A_{ij} = (D_{ij} - Ddev_{ij})/(D_{\max} - Ddev_{ij}) \qquad (17.7)$$

where $Ddev_{ij}$ is the path delay from node i to node j attributable to devices, and $D_{ij} - Ddev_{ij}$ is thus the wire delay on the path from node i to node j. With equation 17.7, paths with the same path delay but greater wire delay pay more attention to delay and less to congestion.

The first term of equation 17.5 is the delay-sensitive term; the second term is congestion sensitive. Equations 17.5, 17.6, and 17.7 are the keys to providing the appropriate mix of minimum-cost and minimum-delay trees. If a particular source/sink pair lies on the critical-path, then $A_{ij} = 1$ and the cost of node n

is just the delay term; hence a minimum-delay route is used and congestion is ignored. In practice, A_{ij} is limited to a maximum value such as 0.9 or 0.95 so that congestion is not completely ignored. If a source/sink pair belongs to a path whose delay is much smaller than the critical-path, then A_{ij} is small and the congestion term dominates, resulting in a route that avoids congestion at the expense of extra delay.

To accommodate delay, the basic Negotiated Congestion algorithm of Figure 17.4 is changed as follows. For the first iteration, all A_{ij} are initialized to 1 and minimum-delay routes are found for every signal. This yields the smallest possible critical-path delay. All A_{ij} are recomputed after every routing iteration using the critical-path delay and the delays incurred by signals on that iteration.

The sinks of each signal are now routed in decreasing A_{ij} order. This allows the most timing-constrained sinks to determine the coarse structure of the routing tree with no interference from less constrained paths.

The priority queue (line 8 in Figure 17.4) is initialized by inserting each node of RT_i with the cost $A_{ij}\sum_k d_k$, where the n_k are nodes on the path from the source n_i to node n_j. This initializes the nodes already in the partial routing tree with the weighted path delay from the source.

The router completes when no more shared resources exist. Note that by recalculating all A_{ij}, we have kept a tight rein on the critical-path. Over the course of the routing iterations, the critical-path increases only to the extent required to resolve congestion. This approach is fundamentally different from other schemes [4, 5] that attempt to resolve congestion first and then reduce delay by rerouting critical nets.

The PathFinder algorithm is particularly powerful for asymmetric architectures that have a range of slow and fast wires. By making the slower wires lower cost, the negotiation algorithm automatically assigns critical signals to the fast wires as needed and noncritical signals to the slow wires.

17.2.4 Applying A* to PathFinder

Djikstra's shortest-path algorithm performs an expensive breadth-first search of the graph. This search has an $O(n^2)$ running time for two-dimensional circuit structures, where n is the length of the path. The A* heuristic [20] is a technique that uses additional information about the cost of paths in the graph to bound the size of the search. The cost of a partial path becomes the cost of the partial path plus the estimated cost from the end of the partial path to the destination. If this estimated cost is a lower bound on the actual cost, then the search will provide an optimal solution. If the estimated cost is accurate, then the search becomes a depth-first search with $O(n)$ running time.

In applying A* to PathFinder, both the cost and the delay of paths in the graph must be estimated. We modify equation 17.4 as follows:

$$C_n = P_{im} + A_{ij}(d_n + Dest_{nj}) + (1 - A_{ij})(c_n + Cest_{nj}) \tag{17.8}$$

where $Dest_{nj}$ and $Cest_{nj}$ are the estimated delay and cost, respectively, of the minimum-delay route from n to sink j.

To use the A* heuristic, the router must know the destination in order to determine the estimated cost. Instead of letting the breadth-first router find the closest destination when there are multiple fanouts, the path length estimates are used to sort the fanouts from closest to furthest and the routing is performed in this order.

In many FPGAs, such as those that are standard island style, the cost and delay of routes can be estimated based on the locations of the source and destination using the geometry of the layout. A more general and accurate method is to use the shortest-path algorithm to create a complete "distance table" that contains the cost estimate of the minimum-delay route from every node to all potential sinks. This is only feasible, however, for relatively small architectures or for coarse-grained architectures that have many fewer nodes than fine-grained FPGAs. To reduce the table size, clustering can be used and estimates stored for the cost/delay between clusters [21]. If the cost/delay between two clusters is taken as the minimum cost/delay between any two nodes in the two clusters, it represents a true lower bound. Clustering has been reported to reduce the size of the distance table by a factor of 100 while slowing the search only by a factor of 2 [21].

In the early iterations of PathFinder, when sharing is ignored, the full advantage of A* is obtained. That is, if the cost/delay estimates are accurate, a depth-first search is achieved. As the cost of sharing rises, however, the cost estimates, which do not include the sharing costs, become less and less accurate and the search becomes less efficient.

In experiments with PathFinder and A*, Swartz et al. [22] used a multiplicative direction factor α to inflate the path estimate. In effect, α determines how aggressively the router drives toward the target sink. An α of 1.0 corresponds to true A* and is guaranteed to find the shortest source/sink connection. Swartz et al. determined that an α of 1.5 gave the best results for large circuits, with no measurable degradation in the quality of the resulting routing. However, note that the cost function had only a congestion term and no delay term. Tessier also experimented with accelerating routing with even more aggressive use of the A* search [23, 24].

17.3 ENHANCEMENTS AND EXTENSIONS TO PATHFINDER

Many research papers have discussed extensions and optimizations of the PathFinder algorithm. First and foremost is the work by Betz and Rose on VPR [12], which for the past eight years has been a widely used vehicle for academic and industrial research into FPGA architectures and CAD. We discuss here some of the more salient ideas that have been applied to PathFinder.

17.3.1 Incremental Rerouting

A common optimization suggested in the original PathFinder paper [8] is to limit the rip-up and rerouting of signals in an iteration only to those that use shared resources. Intuitively, this reduces the amount of "wasted" effort that goes into rerouting signals that always take the same path. The argument is that if a signal does not use a shared resource, it will take the same path as it did before, because history costs can only rise and thus no other path can become cheaper. This argument fails where p_n becomes smaller as sharing signals reroute around a congested node. Experience shows that this optimization increases the number of routing iterations, but reduces the total running time substantially, with negligible impact on the quality of the solution found.

17.3.2 The Cost Function

There are many ways to tune PathFinder for specific architectures or to achieve specific goals. Many variations of the cost function have been described that change how the three cost terms b_n, p_n, and h_n are computed and combined. The essential feature of the cost function is that h_n is a function of the history of the congestion of the node and that p_n is a function of the current congestion. The rates at which h_n and p_n increase can be tuned; increasing them quickly, for example, decreases the number of iterations required but also decreases the quality of the solution. The history term may include a decay function on the assumption that the more recent history is more valid than the distant past. This is particularly important when PathFinder is used in an integrated place-and-route tool [21, 25].

The PathFinder cost function can also be modified to include both short-path and long-path delay terms [26]. For long paths, delay is minimized by using the PathFinder cost function. For short paths, however, the cost function is changed to find a path with a target delay, not the minimum delay. This changes the underlying shortest-path problem considerably and requires an accurate "look-ahead" function that predicts the remaining delay to the destination so that the router can opportunistically add the appropriate extra delay.

17.3.3 Resource Cost

Determining the base cost of routing resources is harder than it appears. The shortest-path algorithm attempts to minimize the total cost of a solution, so minimizing the cost should also minimize congestion. The typical cost function used by routers is the length of the wire, which is a good heuristic for typical architectures where the number of available wires is inversely proportional to their individual lengths. A better heuristic is to base the cost of a wire on the expected routing demand for it. This can be approximated by routing a set of placed benchmarks onto an architecture and measuring wire by wire the routing demand. Another method is to perform a large number of random routes using a typical Rent's wirelength distribution through the architecture and again measuring the overall use of each wire. In this formulation, wire costs are initialized to 1, raised à la PathFinder according to wire usage, and converge to some constant value.

Delay is an approximation that is often used for cost as it is typically closely related to wirelength and relative demand. It also simplifies the cost function for the integrated congestion and delay router.

17.3.4   The Relationship of PathFinder to Lagrangian Relaxation

The PathFinder algorithm is very similar to Lagrangian relaxation for finding an optimal routing subject to congestion and delay constraints [27–29]. In Lagrangian relaxation, the constraints are relaxed by multiplying them by a vector of Lagrangian multipliers and adding them to the objective function to be minimized. The solution to a Lagrangian formulation with a specific set of Lagrangian multipliers provides an approximate solution to the original minimization problem. An iterative procedure that modifies the Lagrangian multipliers is used to find increasingly better solutions. A subgradient method is used to update the multipliers. Intuitively, the multipliers are increased or decreased depending on the extent to which the corresponding constraint is satisfied.

A Lagrangian relaxation method proceeds somewhat differently from the PathFinder algorithm. The multipliers operate much like PathFinder's history term, but there is no corresponding present-sharing term p_n. While the history term is monotonically nondecreasing, the Lagrangian multipliers can both increase and decrease depending on how well the corresponding constraint is satisfied. The amount by which the multipliers are adjusted in Lagrangian relaxation is also decreased with each iteration.

17.3.5   Circuit Graph Extensions

The simple circuit graph model is very general, but there are some specific circuit structures that require extensions. This section describes some solutions for these.

Symmetric device inputs

Lookup tables (LUTs) are the prime example of FPGA devices whose pins are "permutable." That is, the inputs to a LUT can be swapped arbitrarily by permuting the table's contents. Other devices like adders also have symmetric inputs. In the simple graph model, a signal is routed to a specific input terminal and there is no way to specify a route to one of a set of terminals.

Symmetric inputs are easily accommodated in the graph model by adding "pseudo-multiplexers" on the inputs of the LUT. These are shown as dashed nodes at the top of Figure 17.5. Signal sinks can be arbitrarily assigned to the LUT inputs and routed in the usual way. After the routing solution has been found, the pseudo-multiplexers are removed and implemented "virtually" by permuting the LUT table contents appropriately. In the example of Figure 17.5, the signals $a, b,$ and c are routed to the LUT inputs $A, B,$ and C, respectively, using the pseudo-multiplexers as shown with bold lines. This routing is then used to permute the LUT inputs as shown on the right by modifying the LUT contents.

De-multiplexers

A de-multiplexer is a device that can connect its input to at most one of several outputs. Each output connection is represented as an edge in the circuit graph shown in Figure 17.6. Wire fanout, of course, is not constrained, and there is no way in the graph model to specify a constraint on the number of fanouts that can be used. This case is handled by a special counter that counts the number of the edges that are used. If more than one edge is being used, the

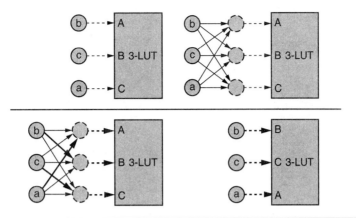

FIGURE 17.5 ■ Symmetric device inputs are handled by inserting pseudo-multiplexers.

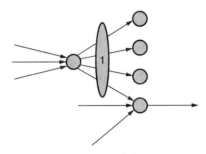

FIGURE 17.6 ■ De-multiplexers are handled by negotiating for the fanouts of the de-multiplexer.

de-multiplexer is being shared in much the same way that wires can be shared by signals. A PathFinder cost function can be applied with both a sharing and a history component so that the single fanout used is determined by means of negotiation.

Bidirectional switches

Edges in the graph model, which represent connections, are directional. This models multiplexer-based architectures directly. Transistors that are often used to construct configurable interconnects are bidirectional. These bidirectional switches simply translate to two directional edges in the graph. The router uses at most one of the edges, which induces a logical direction on the switch. That is, when a switch is turned on in a configuration, it is being driven by an output from one side to the other.

17.4 PARALLEL PATHFINDER

A typical large FPGA design has many thousands of signals. If separate signals could be routed in parallel, the degree of parallelism would be limited only by the number of signals to be routed and the number of processors available. The difficulty, of course, is that the route taken by each signal depends on the knowledge of other signal routes, as routing resources cannot be shared. Although parallel implementations of global standard cell routers exist, the problem for FPGAs becomes much harder because the routing resources are discrete and fixed.

Because the routing of separate signals in an FPGA is tightly coupled, it might appear that a parallel approach to routing FPGAs would not be possible given that knowledge of other signal locations is necessary to find a feasible route. This is the case in a typical maze router, which uses rip-up and reroute to resolve conflicts. In PathFinder, however, there is no restriction on the number of signals that can occupy a resource simultaneously during routing. Instead, the cost of using congested resources is the mechanism used to resolve resource conflicts. If the congestion costs are decentralized in a parallel environment, the concerns are how and when they will be updated and whether the update method will be acceptable in terms of the number of processors effectively utilized and the quality of the resulting routing.

In Chan et al. [30] a distributed memory multiprocessor implementation of the PathFinder algorithm is described. Each processor has a private local memory and is connected in a network. Processors communicate with each other by sending and receiving messages via Unix socket communication. A complete copy of the routing resource graph, including first- and second-order congestion costs, is kept and maintained by each processor. The signals in a netlist to be routed are statically assigned to processors such that each processor has about the same number of sinks to be routed. No attempt is made to assign signals to processors based on locality.

Processors route signals asynchronously and thus communicate updated congestion costs asynchronously. There is no guarantee of the order or the timing of the arrival of such congestion cost updates, resulting in a source of indeterminism. Processors are allowed to proceed to successive iterations without waiting for others, although a limit of a few iterations of separation is generally employed.

It is conceded that, because of latency, this parallel routing algorithm may not converge. Imagine a scenario in which two signals being routed by two different processors vie for the same resource. Message latency or merely concurrency may cause the two signals to oscillate between routing iterations, because each processor knows where the other processor's signal was in the last iteration but not in the current one. Such cases generally occur during the last iterations of a route. At that point, Chan and colleagues [30] reduce the multiprocessor implementation to a single-processor implementation in order to resolve the congestion.

This parallel implementation was tested on a set of benchmarks ranging from 118 to 1542 signal nets on the Xilinx 4000 architecture. Speedups ranged from 1.6 to 2.2 times for two processors and 2.3 to 3.8 times for four processors. For nearly all benchmarks, no additional speedups are obtained for more than four processors. The performance of the benchmarks (in terms of delay or clock rate) was shown to vary minimally with increasing numbers of processors.

This initial implementation of a parallel form of PathFinder is significant in that it demonstrates appreciable speedups while employing a rather simple computational framework. Because of the inherent approximations of congestion cost and its gradual increase, PathFinder exhibits good qualities for parallelism in a framework where congestion costs are communicated asynchronously, as they become available. It may result (as shown by Chan et al. [30]) in an increased number of iterations to converge, but is able to employ more multiple loosely connected processors to good advantage.

17.5 OTHER APPLICATIONS OF THE PATHFINDER ALGORITHM

PathFinder has been used to incrementally reroute signals around faults in cluster-based FPGAs [31]. This rerouting uses the accumulated history costs acquired by the initial routing to quickly find a new routing solution when nodes and edges in the circuit graph have been removed because of faults.

QuickRoute [32] extends PathFinder to handle pipelined routing structures. The key idea in QuickRoute is to change Djikstra's shortest-path algorithm to allow nodes to be visited more than once, by paths with different latencies. This causes many more overlapping paths to be explored, but the negotiated congestion avoidance of PathFinder still performs well.

Several groups have applied PathFinder to the problem of scheduling the communication in computing graphs to coarse-grained architectures or multiprocessors [33–35]. In this application of PathFinder, the routing becomes a space–time problem.

17.6 SUMMARY

The widespread use of PathFinder by commercial FPGA routers and university research efforts alike is a testimonial to its robustness.

Several key facets of the algorithm make it attractive. However, its primary advantage is the iterative nature of resolving congestion, using both current as well as historical resource use in the formulation of the cost function. By very gradually increasing cost due to both usages, the routing search space is thoroughly explored. Routing with other objective functions, delay in particular, is easily integrated into the cost function. A primary feature implicit in PathFinder (that distinguishes it from previous efforts) is the allowance of nonphysically feasible intermediate states—for example, shared resources—while converging to a physically feasible final state. Finally, by being grounded in a directed graph representation, PathFinder is very adaptable to changing FPGA architectures as well as other problems that can be abstracted to a directed graph.

In the future we see the routing problem as being an increasingly dominant hurdle in the use of FPGAs with millions of resources. To reduce the runtime, more investigation will be required to effectively parallelize PathFinder, making use of additional computational resources. Given the growing focus on other objectives such as power consumption, it is likely that we will see experimentation with other cost function formulations as well.

Acknowledgments   We wish to thank Gaetano Borriello for initial discussions about routing when PathFinder was being applied to the Triptych architecture, and Steven Yee for his help in constructing detailed descriptions of the Xilinx architectures. We also thank Pak Chan and Martine Schlag for sharing the results on parallel PathFinder.

References

[1] W. A. Dees, R. J. Smith. Performance of interconnection rip-up and reroute strategies. *Design Automation Conference*, 1981.

[2] R. Linsker. An iterative-improvement penalty-function-driven wire routing system. *IBM J. Res. Development* 28(5), 1984.

[3] J. Cohn, D. Garrod, R. Rutenbar, L. Carley. Koan/anagram II: New tools for device-level analog placement and routing. *IEEE Journal of Solid-State Circuits* 26(3), 1991.

[4] S. Brown, J. Rose, Z. Vranesic. A detailed router for field-programmable gate arrays. *IEEE Transactions on Computer-Aided Design of Integrated Circuits and Systems* 11(5), 1992.

[5] J. Frankle. Iterative and adaptive slack allocation for performance-driven layout and FPGA routing. *Design Automation Conference*, 1992.

[6] M. J. Alexander, J. P. Cohoon, J. L. Ganley, G. Robins. An architecture-independent approach to FPGA routing based on multi-weighted graphs. *Proceedings of the Conference on European Design Automation*, 1994.

[7] M. Palczewski. Plane parallel a maze router and its application to FPGAs. *Design Automation Conference*, 1992.

[8] L. McMurchie, C. Ebeling. A negotiation-based performance-driven router for FPGAs. *Proceedings of the 1995 ACM Third International Symposium on Field-Programmable Gate Arrays Aided Design*, 1995.

[9] G. Borriello, C. Ebeling, S. Hauck, S. Burns. The triptych FPGA architecture. *IEEE Transactions on Very Large Scale Integration (VLSI) Systems* 3(4), 1995.

[10] C. Ebeling, L. McMurchie, S. Hauck, S. Burns. Placement and routing tools for the triptych FPGA. *IEEE Transactions on Very Large Scale Integration (VLSI) Systems* 3(4), 1995.

[11] D. C. Cronquist, L. McMurchie. Emerald: An architecture-driven tool compiler for FPGAs. *Proceedings of the Fourth ACM International Symposium on Field-Programmable Gate Arrays*, 1996.

[12] V. Betz, J. Rose. VPR: A new packing, placement and routing tool for FPGA research. *Proceedings of the Seventh International Workshop on Field-Programmable Logic and Applications*. Springer-Verlag, 1997.

[13] V. Betz, J. Rose, A. Marquardt. *Architecture and CAD for deep-submicron FPGAs*. Kluwer Academic, 1999.

[14] V. Betz. The FPGA place-and-route challenge (*www.eecg.toronto.edu/vaughn/challenge/challenge.html*).

[15] E. W. Dijkstra. A note on two problems in connexion with graphs. *Numerische Mathematik* 1(1), December 1959.

[16] E. Moore. The shortest path through a maze. *International Symposium on the Theory of Switching*, April 1959.

[17] C. Y. Lee. An algorithm for path connections and its applications. *IRE Transactions on Electronic Computers* 10, September 1961.

[18] R. Nair. A simple yet effective technique for global wiring. *IEEE Transactions on Computer-Aided Design of Integrated Circuits and Systems* 6(2), 1987.

[19] H. Takahashi, A. Matsuyama. An approximate solution for the Steiner problem in graphs. *Math. Japonica* 24(6), 1980.

[20] P. Hart, N. Nilsson, B. Raphael. A formal basis for the heuristic determination of minimum cost paths. *IEEE Transactions on Systems Science and Cybernetics*, 1968.

[21] A. Sharma. *Place and Route Techniques for FPGA Architecture Advancement*, Ph.D. thesis, University of Washington, 2005.

[22] J. S. Swartz, V. Betz, J. Rose. A fast routability-driven router for FPGAs. *Proceedings of the ACM/SIGDA Ssixth International Symposium on Field-Programmable Gate Arrays*, 1998.

[23] R. G. Tessier. Negotiated A* routing for FPGAs. *Fifth Canadian Workshop on Field-Programmable Logic*, 1998.

[24] R. G. Tessier. *Fast Place and Route Approaches for FPGAs*, Ph.D. thesis, MIT, 1999.

[25] A. Sharma, S. Hauck, C. Ebeling. Architecture-adaptive routability-driven placement for FPGAs. *International Conference on Field-Programmable Logic and Applications*, 2005.

[26] R. Fung, V. Betz, W. Chow. Simultaneous short-path and long-path timing optimization for FPGAs. *IEEE/ACM International Conference on Computer Aided Design*, 2004.

[27] S. Lee, Y. Cheon, M. D. F. Wong. A min-cost flow based detailed router for FPGAs. *International Conference on Computer-Aided Design*, 2003.

[28] S. Lee, M. Wong. Timing-driven routing for FPGAs based on Lagrangian relaxation. *IEEE Transactions on Computer-Aided Design of Integrated Circuits and Systems* 22(4), 2003.

[29] M. M. Ozdal, M. D. F. Wong. Simultaneous escape routing and layer assignment for dense PCBs. *Proceedings of the 2004 IEEE/ACM International Conference on Computer-Aided Design*, 2004.

[30] P. K. Chan, M. D. F. Schlag, C. Ebeling, L. McMurchie. Distributed-memory parallel routing for field-programmable gate arrays. *IEEE Transactions on Computer-Aided Design of Integrated Circuits and Systems* 19(8), August 2000.

[31] V. Lakamraju, R. Tessier. Tolerating operational faults in cluster-based FPGAs. *Proceedings of the 2000 ACM/SIGDA Eighth International Symposium on Field-Programmable Gate Arrays*, 2000.

[32] S. Li, C. Ebeling. QuickRoute: A fast routing algorithm for pipelined architectures. *IEEE International Conference on Field-Programmable Technology*, 2004.

[33] B. Mei, S. Vernalde, D. Verkest, H. De Man, R. Lauwereins. Exploiting loop-level parallelism on coarse-grained reconfigurable architectures using modulo scheduling. *Design, Automation and Test in Europe*, 2003.

[34] J. Cook, L. Baugh, D. Gottlieb, N. Carter. Mapping computation kernels to clustered programmable reconfigurable processors. *IEEE International Conference on Field-Programmable Technology*, 2003.

[35] L.-Y. Lin, C.-Y. Wang, P.-J. Huang, C.-C. Chou, J.-Y. Jou. Communication-driven task binding for multiprocessor with latency insensitive network-on-chip. *Proceedings of the 2005 Conference on Asia South Pacific Design Automation*, 2005.

CHAPTER 18

RETIMING, REPIPELINING, AND C-SLOW RETIMING

Nicholas Weaver
International Computer Science Institute

Although pipelining is a huge benefit in field-programmable gate array (FPGA) designs, and may be required on some FPGA fabrics [5, 10, 12], it is often difficult for a designer to manage and balance pipeline stages and to insert the necessary delays to meet design requirements.

Leiserson et al. [4] were the first to propose *retiming*, an automatic process to relocate pipeline stages to balance a design. Their algorithm, in $O(n^2 lg(n))$ time, can rebalance a design so that the critical path is optimally pipelined. In addition, two modifications, *repipelining* and *C-slow retiming*, can add additional pipeline stages to a design to further improve the critical path.

The key idea is simple: If the number of registers around every cycle in the design does not change, the end-to-end symantics do not change. Thus, retiming attempts to solve two primary constraints: All paths longer than the desired critical path are registered, and the number of registers around every cycle is unchanged.

This optimization is useful for conventional FPGAs but absolutely essential for fixed-frequency FPGA architectures, which are devices that contain large numbers of registers and are designed to operate at a fixed, but very high, frequency, often by pipelining the interconnect as well as the computation.

To meet the array's fixed frequency, a design must ensure that every path is properly registered. Repipelining or C-slow retiming enables a design to be transformed to meet this constraint. Without automated repipelining or C-slow retiming, the designer must manually ensure that all pipeline constraints are met by the design.

Retiming operates by determining an optimal placement for existing registers, while repipelining and C-slowing add registers before the retiming process begins. After retiming, the design should be optimally (or near-optimally) balanced, with no pipeline stage requiring significantly more time than any other stage.

Section 18.1 describes the basic retiming operation and the retiming algorithm and its semantics. Then Section 18.2 discusses repipelining and C-slowing: two different techniques for adding registers. Repipelining improves feedforward designs by adding additional pipelining stages, while C-slowing creates an interleaved design by replacing every register with a sequence of C registers. Both of these transformations increase throughput but also increase latency.

Section 18.3 surveys the various implementations, beginning with Leiserson's original algorithm and concluding with both academic and commercial tools. Section 18.4 discusses implementing retiming for fixed-frequency arrays. Unlike general FPGAs, fixed-frequency FPGAs require retiming in order to match user designs with architectural constraints. Finally, Section 18.5 discusses an interesting side effect of *C*-slowing: the creation of interleaved, multi-threaded architectures. We conclude in Section 18.6 with a discussion of the reasons that retiming is not a ubiquitous optimization in FPGA tool flows.

18.1 RETIMING: CONCEPTS, ALGORITHM, AND RESTRICTIONS

The goal of retiming is to move the pipeline registers in a design into the optimal position. Figure 18.1 shows a trivial example. In this design, the nodes represent logic delays (a), with the inputs and outputs passing through mandatory, fixed registers. The critical path is 5, and the input and output registers cannot be moved. Figure 18.1(b) shows the same graph after retiming. The critical path is reduced from 5 to 4, but the I/O semantics have not changed, as three cycles are still required for a datum to proceed from input to output.

As can be seen, the initial design has a critical path of 5 between the internal register and the output. If the internal register could be moved forward, the critical path would be shortened to 4. However, the feedback loop would then be incorrect. Thus, in addition to moving the register forward, another register would need to be added to the feedback loop, resulting in the final design.

Additionally, even if the last node is removed, it could never have a critical path lower than 4 because of the feedback loop. There is no mechanism that can reduce the critical path of a single-cycle feedback loop by moving registers: Only additional registers can speed such a design.

Retiming's objective is to automate this process: For a graph representing a circuit, with combinational delays as nodes and integer weights on the edges, find a new assignment of edge weights that meets a targeted critical path or fail if the critical path cannot be met. Leiserson's retiming algorithm is guaranteed to find such an assignment, if it exists, that both minimizes the critical path and ensures that around every loop in the design the number of registers always remains the same. It is this second constraint, ensuring that all feedback loops

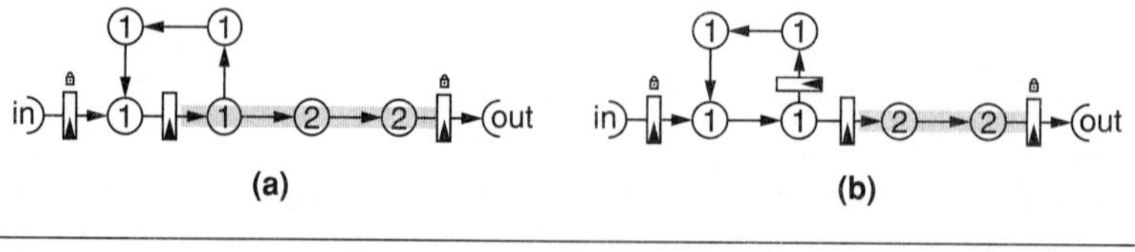

(a)   (b)

FIGURE 18.1 ■ A small graph before retiming (a) and the same graph after retiming (b).

TABLE 18.1 ■ The constraint system used by the retiming procsess

Condition normal edge from $u \rightarrow v$	Constraint $r(u) - r(v) \leq w(e)$
Edge from $u \rightarrow v$ must be registered	$r(u) - r(v) \leq w(e) - 1$
Edge from $u \rightarrow v$ can never be registered	$r(u) - r(v) \leq 0$ and $r(v) - r(u) \leq 0$
Critical paths must be registered	$r(u) - r(v) \leq W(u,v) - 1$ for all u, v such that $D(u,v) > P$

are unchanged, which ensures that retiming doesn't change the semantics of the circuit. In Table 18.1, $r(u)$ is the lag computed for each node (which is used to determine the final number of registers on each edge), $w(e)$ is the initial number of registers on an edge, $W(u,v)$ is the minimum number of registers between u and v, and $D(u,v)$ is the critical path between u and v.

Leiserson's algorithm takes the graph as input and then adds an additional node representing the external world, with appropriate edges added to account for all I/Os. This additional node is necessary to ensure that the circuit's global I/O semantics are unchanged by retiming.

Two matrices are then calculated, W and D, that represent the number of registers and critical path between every pair of nodes in the graph. These matrices are necessary because retiming operates by ensuring that at least one register exists on every path that is longer than the critical path in the design.

Each node also has a lag value r that is calculated by the algorithm and used to change the number of registers that will be placed on any given edge. Conventional retiming does not change the design semantics: All input and output timings remain unchanged while minor design constraints are imposed on the use of FPGA features. More details and formal proofs of correctness can be found in Leiserson's original paper [4].

The algorithm works as follows:

1. Start with the circuit as a directed graph. Every node represents a computational element, with each element having a computational delay. Each edge can have zero or more registers as a weight w. Add an additional dummy node with 0 delay, with an edge from every output and to every input. This additional node is to ensure that from every input to every output the number of registers is unchanged and therefore the data input to output timing is unaffected.

2. Calculate W and D. D is the critical path for every node to every other node, and W is the initial number of registers along this path. This requires solving the all-pairs shortest-path problem, of which the optimal algorithm, by Dijkstra, requires $O(n^2 lg(n))$ time. This dominates the asymptotic running time of the algorithm.

3. Choose a target critical path and create the constraints, as summarized in Table 18.1. Each node has a lag value r, which will eventually specify the *change* in the number of registers between each node. Initialize all nodes to have a lag of 0.

4. Since all constraints are pairwise integer inequalities, the Bellman–Ford constraint solver is guaranteed to find a solution if one exists or to terminate if not. The Bellman–Ford algorithm performs N iterations (N = the number of constraints to solve). In each iteration, every constraint is examined. If a constraint is already satisfied, nothing happens. Otherwise, $r(u)$ or $r(v)$ is decremented to meet the particular constraint. Once an iteration occurs where no values change, the algorithm has found a solution. If there is no solution, after N iterations the algorithm terminates with a failure.

5. If the constraint solver fails to find a solution, or a tighter critical path is desired, choose a new critical path and return to step 3.

6. With the final set of constraints, a new set of registers is constructed for each edge, $w' \cdot w'(e) = w(e) - r(u) + r(v)$.

A graphical example of the algorithm's results is shown in Figure 18.1. The initial graph has a critical path of 5, which is clearly nonoptimal. After retiming, the graph has a critical path of 4, but the I/O semantics have not changed, as any input will still require three cycles to affect the output. To determine whether a critical path P can be achieved, the retiming algorithm creates a series of constraints to calculate the lag on each node (Table 18.1).

The primary constraints ensure correctness: No edge will have a negative number of registers, while every cycle will always contain the original number of registers. All I/O passes through the intermediate node, ensuring that input and output timings do not change. These constraints can be modified so that a particular line will contain no registers, or a mandatory minimum number of registers, to meet architectural constraints without changing the complexity of the equations. But it is the final constraint, that all critical paths above a predetermined delay P are registered, that gives this optimization its effectiveness.

If the constraint system has a solution, the new lag assignments for all nodes will allocate registers properly to meet the critical path P. But if there is no solution, there cannot be an assignment of registers that meets P. Thus, the common usage is to find the minimum P where the constraints are all met.

In general, multiple constraint-solving attempts are made to search for the minimum critical path P. The constraints for P are the final retimed design. There are two ways to speed up this process. First, if the Bellman–Ford algorithm can find a solution, it usually converges very quickly. Thus, if there is no solution that satisfies P, it is usually effective to abandon the Bellman–Ford algorithm early after $0.1N$ iterations rather than N iterations. This seems to have no impact on the quality of results, yet it can greatly speed up searching for the minimum P that can be satisfied in the design.

A second optimization is to use the last computed set of constraints as a starting point. In conventional retiming, the Bellman–Ford process is invoked multiple times to find the lowest satisfiable critical path. In contrast, fixed-frequency repipelining or *C*-slow retiming uses Bellman–Ford to discover the minimum number of additional registers needed to satisfy the constraints. In both cases, keeping the last failed or successful solution in the data structure provides a starting point that can significantly speed up the process if a solution exists.

Retiming in this way imposes only minimal design limitations: Because it applies only to synchronous circuits, there can be no asynchronous resets or similar elements. A synchronous global reset imposes too many constraints to allow effective retiming. Local synchronous resets and enables only produce small, self loops that have no effect on the correct operation of the algorithm.

Most other design features can be accommodated simply by adding appropriate constraints. For example, an FPGA with a tristate bus cannot have registers placed on this bus. A constraint that says that all edges crossing the bus can never be registered ($r(u) - r(v) \leq 0$ and $r(v) - r(u) \leq 0$) ensures this. Likewise, an embedded memory with a mandatory output flip-flop can have a constraint ($r(u) - r(v) \leq w(e) - 1$) that ensures that at least one register is placed on this output.

Memories themselves can be retimed similarly to any other element in the design, with dual-ported memories treated as a single node for retiming purposes. Memories that are synthesized with a negative clock edge (to create the design illusion of asynchronicity) can be either unchanged or switched to operate on the positive edge with constraints to mandate the placement of registers.

Some FPGA designs have registers with predefined initial values. If retiming is allowed to move these registers, the proper initial values must be calculated such that the circuit still produces the same behavior.

In an ASIC model, all flip-flops start in an undefined state, and the designer must create a small state machine in order to reset the design. FPGAs, however, have all flip-flops start in a known, user-defined state, and when a dedicated global reset is applied the flip-flops are reset to it. This has serious implications in retiming.

If the decision is made to utilize the ASIC model, retiming is free to safely ignore initial conditions because explicit reset logic in state machines will still operate correctly—this is reflected in the I/O semantics. However, without the ability to violate the initial conditions with an ASIC-style model, retiming quality often suffers as additional logic is required or limits are placed on where flip-flops may be moved in a design.

In practice, performing retiming with initial conditions is NP-hard. Cong and Wu [3] have developed an algorithm that computes initial states by restricting the design to forward retiming only so that it propagates the information and registers forward throughout the computation. This is because solving initial states for all registers moved forward is straightforward, but backward movement is NP hard as it reduces to satisfiability.

Additionally, global set/reset imposes a huge constraint on retiming. An asynchronous set/reset can never be retimed (retiming cannot modify an asynchronous circut) while a synchronous set/reset just imposes too high a fanout.

An important question is how to deal with multiple clocks. If the interfaces between the clock domains are registered by clocks from both domains, it is a simple process to retime the domains separately, with mandatory registers

TABLE 18.2 ■ The results of retiming four benchmarks

Benchmark	Unretimed	Automatically retimed
AES core	48 MHz	47 MHz
Smith/Waterman	43 MHz	40 MHz
Synthetic datapath	51 MHz	54 MHz
LEON processor	23 MHz	25 MHz

on the domain crossings—the constraints placed on the I/Os ensure correct and consistent timing through the interface. Yet without this design constraint, retiming across multiple clock domains is very hard, and there does not appear to be any clean automatic solution.

Table 18.2 shows the results for a particular retiming tool [13]—the Xilinx Virtex family of FPGAs—on four benchmark circuits: an AES core, a Smith/Waterman systolic cell, a synthetic microprocessor datapath, and the LEON-I synthesized SPARC core. This tool does not use a perfectly accurate delay model and has to place registers after retiming, so it sometimes creates slightly suboptimal results.

The biggest problem with retiming is that it is of limited benefit to a well-balanced design. As mentioned earlier, if the clock cycle is defined by a single-cycle feedback loop, retiming can never improve the design, as moving the register around the feedback loop produces no effect.

Thus, for example, the Smith–Waterman example in Table 18.2 does not benefit from retiming. The Smith–Waterman benchmark design consists of a series of repeated identical systolic cells that implement the Smith–Waterman sequence alignment algorithm. The cells each contain a single-cycle feedback loop, which cannot be optimized. The AES encryption algorithm also consists of a single-cycle feedback loop. In this case, the initial design used a negative-edge Block-RAM to implement the *S*-boxes, which the retiming tool converted to a positive edge memory with a "must register" constraint.

Nevertheless, retiming can still be a benefit if the design consists of multiple feedback loops (such as the synthetic microprocessor datapath or the LEON SPARC–compatible microprocessor core) or an initially unbalanced pipeline. Still, for well-designed circuits, even complex ones, retiming is often only a slight benefit, as engineers have considerable experience designing reasonably optimized feedback loops.

The key benefit to retiming occurs when more registers can be added to the design along the critical path. We will discuss two techniques, repipelining and *C*-slow retiming, which first add a large number of registers that general retiming can then move into the optimal location.

18.2 REPIPELINING AND *C*-SLOW RETIMING

The biggest limitation of retiming is that it simply cannot improve a design beyond the design-dependent limit produced by an optimal placement of registers along the critical path. As mentioned earlier, if the critical path is defined by a single-cycle feedback loop, retiming will completely fail as an optimization. Likewise, if a design is already well balanced, changing the register placement produces no improvement. As was seen in the four reasonably optimized benchmarks (refer to Table 18.2), this is often the case.

Repipelining and *C*-slow retiming are tranformations designed to add registers in a predictible matter that a designer can account for, which retiming can then move to optimize the design. Repipelining adds registers to the beginning or end of the design, changing the pipeline latency but no other semantics. *C*-slow retiming creates an interleaved design by replacing every register with a sequence of *C* registers.

18.2.1 Repipelining

Repipelining is a minor extension to retiming that can increase the clock frequency for feedforward computations at the cost of additional latency through more pipeline registers. Unlike *C*-slow retiming, repipelining is only beneficial when a computation's critical path contains no feedback loops.

Feedforward computations, those that contain no feedback loops, are commonly seen in DSP kernels and other tasks. For example, the discrete cosine transform (DCT), the fast Fourier transform (FFT), and finite impulse response filters (FIRs) can all be constructed as feedforward pipelines.

Repipelining is derived from retiming in one of two ways, both of which create semantically equivalent results. The first involves adding additional pipeline stages to the start of the computation and allowing retiming to rebalance the delays and create an absolute number of additional stages. The second involves decoupling the inputs and outputs to allow the retimer to add additional pipelining. Although these techniques operate in slightly different ways, they both provide extra registers for the retimer to then move and they produce roughly equivalent results.

If the designer wishes to add *P* pipeline stages to a design, all inputs simply have *P* delays added before retiming proceeds. Because retiming will develop an optimum placement for the resulting design, the new design contains *P* additional pipeline stages that are scattered throughout the computation. If a CAD tool supports retiming but not repipelining, the designer can simply add the registers to the input of the design manually and let the tool determine the optimum placement.

Another option is to simply remove the cycle between all outputs and inputs, with additional constraints to ensure that all outputs share an output lag, with all inputs sharing a different input lag. This way, the inputs and outputs are all synchronized but retiming can add an arbitrary number of additional pipeline registers between them. To place a limit on these registers, an additional constraint must be added to ensure that for a single I/O pair no more than *P* pipeline registers are added. Depending on the other constraints in the retiming process, this may add fewer than *P* additional pipeline stages, but will never add more than *P*.

Repipelining adds additional cycles of latency to the design, but otherwise retains the rest of the circuit's behavior. Thus, it produces the same results and the same relative timing on the outputs (e.g., if input *B* is supposed to be presented three cycles after input *A*, or output *C* is produced two cycles after output *D*, these relative timings remain unchanged). It is only the data-in to data-out timing that is affected.

Unfortunately, repipelining can only improve feedforward designs or designs where the feedback loop is not on the critical path. If performance is limited by a feedback loop, repipelining offers no benefit over normal retiming.

Repipelining is designed to improve throughput, but will almost always make overall latency worse. Although the increased pipelining will boost the clock rate (and thus reduce some of the delay from unbalanced clocked paths), the delay from additional flip-flops on the input-to-output paths typically overwhelms this improvement and the resulting design will take longer to produce a result for an individual input.

This is a fundamental trade-off in repipelining and *C*-slow retiming. While ordinary retiming improves both latency and throughput, repipelining and *C*-slow retiming generally improve throughput at the cost of additional latency due to the additional pipeline stages required.

18.2.2   *C*-slow Retiming

Unlike repipelining, *C*-slow retiming can enhance designs that contain feedback loops. *C*-slowing enhances retiming simply by replacing every register with a sequence of *C* separate registers before retiming occurs; the resulting design operates on *C* distinct execution tasks. Because all registers are duplicated, the computation proceeds in a round-robin fashion, as illustrated in Figure 18.2.

In this example, which is 2-slow, the design interleaves between two computations. On the first clock cycle, it accepts the first input for the first stream of execution. On the second clock cycle, it accepts the first input for the second stream, and on the third it accepts the second input for the first stream. Because of the interleaved nature of the design, the two streams of execution will *never* interfere. On odd clock cycles, the first stream of execution accepts input; on even clock cycles, the second stream accepts input.

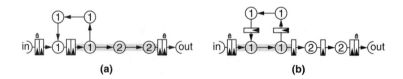

(a)   (b)

FIGURE 18.2 ■ The example from Figure 18.1, converted to 2-slow operation (a). The critical path remains unchanged, but the design now operates on two independent streams in a round-robin fashion. The design retimed (b). By taking advantage of the extra flip-flops, the critical path has been reduced from 5 to 2.

The easiest way to utilize a *C*-slowed block is to simply multiplex and de-multiplex *C* separate datastreams. However, a more sophisticated interface may be desired depending on the application (as described in Section 18.5).

One possible interface is to register all inputs and outputs of a *C*-slowed block. Because of the additional edges retiming creates to track I/Os and to ensure a consistent interface, every stream of execution presents all outputs at the same time, with all inputs registered on the next cycle. If part of the design is *C*-slowed, but all parts operate on the same clock, the result can be retimed as a complete whole and still preserve all other semantics.

One way to think of *C*-slowing is as a threaded design, with an overall system clock and with each stream having a "stream clock" of $1/C$—each stream is completely independent. However, *C*-slowing imposes some more significant FPGA design constraints, as summarized in Table 18.3. Register clock enables and resets must be expressed as logic features, since each independent thread must have an independent reset or enable. Thus, they can remain features in the design but cannot be implemented by current FPGAs using native enables and resets. Other specialized features, such as Xilinx SRL16s (a mode where a LUT is used as a 16-bit shift register), cannot be utilized in a *C*-slow design for the same reason.

One important challenge is how to properly *C*-slow memory blocks. In cases where the *C*-slowed design is used to support *N* independent computations, one needs the illusion that each stream of execution is completely independent and unchanged. To create this illusion, the memory capacity must be increased by a factor of *C*, with additional address lines driven by a thread counter. This ensures that each stream of execution enjoys a completely separate memory space.

For dual-ported memories, this potentially enables a greater freedom in retiming: The two ports can have different lags as long as the difference in lag is less than *C*. After retiming, the difference is added to the appropriate port's thread counter, which ensures that each stream of execution will read and write to both ports in order while enabling slightly more freedom for retiming to proceed.

C-slowing normally guarantees that all streams view independent memories. However, a designer may desire shared memory common to all streams. Such

TABLE 18.3 ■ The effects of various FPGA features on retiming, repipelining, and *C*-slowing

FPGA feature	Effect on retiming	Effect on repipelining	Effect on *C*-slowing
Asynchronous global set/reset	Forbidden	Forbidden	Forbidden
Synchronous global set/reset	Effectively forbidden	Effectively forbidden	Forbidden
Asynchronous local set/reset	Forbidden	Forbidden	Forbidden
Synchronous local set/reset	Allowed	Allowed	Express as logic
Clock enables	Allowed	Allowed	Express as logic
Tristate buffers	Allowed	Allowed	Allowed
Memories	Allowed	Allowed	Increase size
SRL16	Allowed	Allowed	Express as logic
Multiple clock domains	Design restrictions	Design restrictions	Design restrictions

memories could be embedded in a design, but the designer would need to consider how multiple streams would affect the semantics and would need to notify any automatic tool to treat the memory in a special manner. Beyond this, there are no other semantic effects imposed by *C*-slow retiming.

C-slowing significantly improves throughput, but it can only apply to tasks where there are at least *C* independent threads of execution and where throughput is the primary goal. The reason is that *C*-slowing makes the latency substantially worse. This trade-off brings up a fundimental observation: Latency is a property of the design and computational fabric whereas throughput is a property derived from cost. Both repipelining and *C*-slow retiming can be applied only when there is sufficient task-level parallelism, in the form of either a feed-forward pipeline (repipelining) or independent tasks (*C*-slowing).

Table 18.4 shows the difference that *C*-slowing can make in four designs. While the retiming tool alone was unable to improve the AES or Smith Waterman designs, *C*-slowing substantially increased throughput, improving the clock rate by 80–95 percent! However, latency for individual tasks was made worse, resulting in significantly slower clock rates for individual tasks.

Latency can be improved only up to a given point for a design through conventional retiming. Once the latency limit is met, no amount of optimization, save a major redesign or an improvement in the FPGA fabric, has any effect. This often appears in cryptographic contexts, where feedback mode–based encryption (such as CFB) requires the complete processing of each block before the next can be processed.

In contrast, throughput is actually a part of a throughput/cost metric: throughput/area, throughput/dollar, or throughput/joule. This is because independent task throughput can be added via replication, creating independent modules that perform the same function, as well as *C*-slowing. When sufficient parallelism exists, and costs are not constrained, simply throwing more resources at the problem is sufficient to improve the design to meet desired goals.

One open question on *C*-slowing is its effect in a low-power environment. Higher throughput, achieved through high-speed clocking, naturally increases the power consumption of a design, just as replicating units for higher throughput increases power consumption. In both cases, if lower power is desired, the higher-throughput design can be modified to save power by reducing the clock rate and operating voltage.

Unlike the replicated case, the question of whether a *C*-slowed design would offer power savings if both frequency and voltage were reduced is highly design

TABLE 18.4 ■ The effect of *C*-slowing on four benchmarks

Benchmark	Initial clock	*C*-factor	*C*-slow clock	Stream clock
AES encryption	48 MHz	4-slow	87 MHz	21 MHz
Smith/Waterman	43 MHz	3-slow	84 MHz	28 MHz
Synthetic datapath	51 MHz	3-slow	91 MHz	30 MHz
LEON processor core	23 MHz	2-slow	46 MHz	23 MHz

and usage dependent. Although the finer pipelining allows the frequency and the voltage to be scaled back to a significant degree while maintaining throughput, the activity factor of each signal may now be considerably higher. Because each of the C streams of execution is completely independent, it is safe to assume that every wire will probably have a significantly higher activity factor that increases power consumption.

Whether the initial design before C-slowing has a comparable activity factor is highly input and design dependent. If the initial design's activity factor is low, C-slowing will significantly increase power consumption. But if that factor is high, C-slowing will not increase it. Thus, although the C-slowing transformation may have a minor affect on worst-case power (and can even result in significant savings through voltage scaling), the impact on average-case power may be substantial.

18.3 IMPLEMENTATIONS OF RETIMING

Three significant academic retiming tools have been developed for FPGAs. The first, by Cong and Wu [3], combines retiming with technology mapping. This approach enables retiming to occur before placement without adding undue constraints on the placer, because the retimed registers are packed with their associated logic. The disadvantage is a lack of precision, as delays can only be crudely estimated before placement. This tool is unsuitable for significant C-slowing, which creates significantly more registers that can pose problems with logic packing and placement.

The second tool, developed by Singh and Brown [6], combines retiming with placement, operating by modifying the placement algorithm to be aware that retiming is occurring and then modifying the retiming portion to enable permutation of the placement as retiming proceeds. Singh and Brown demonstrate how the combination of placement and retiming performs significantly better than retiming either before or after placement.

The simplified FPGA model used by Singh and Brown has a logic block where the flip-flop cannot be used independently of the LUT, constraining the ability of postplacement retiming to allocate new registers. Thus, the need to permute the placement to allocate registers is significantly exacerbated in their target architecture.

The third tool, developed by Weaver et al. [13], performs retiming after placement but before routing, taking advantage of the (mostly) independent register operation available on Xilinx FPGAs. (It would not apply to most Altera FPGAs.) It too also supports C-slowing.

Some commercial HDL synthesis tools, notably the Synopsys FPGA compiler [9] and Synplify [8], also support retiming. Because this retiming occurs fairly early in the mapping and optimization processes, it suffers from a lack of precision regarding placement and routing delays. The Amplify tool [10] can produce a higher-quality retiming because it contains placement information. Since these tools attempt to maintain the FPGA model of initial conditions, both on startup and in the face of a global reset signal, considerable logic is added to the design.

18.4   RETIMING ON FIXED-FREQUENCY FPGAs

Fixed-frequency FPGAs differ from conventional FPGAs in that they have an intrinsic clock rate and commonly include pipelined interconnect and other design features to enable very high-speed operations. However, this fixed frequency demands a design modification to support the pipeline stages it requires.

Retiming for fixed-frequency FPGAs, unlike that for their conventional counterparts, does not require the creation of a global critical path constraint, as simply ensuring that all local requirements are met guarantees that the final design meets the architecture's required delay constraints. Instead, retiming attempts to solve these local constraints by ensuring that every path through the interconnect meets the delay requirements inherent in the FPGA. Once these local constraints are met, the final design will operate at the FPGA's intrinsic clock frequency.

Because there are no longer any global constraints, the W and D matrices are not created. A fixed-frequency FPGA does not require the global constraints, so having only to solve a set of local constraints requires linear, not quadratic, memory and $O(n^2)$, rather than $O(n^2 lg(n))$, execution time. This speeds the process considerably.

Additionally, only a single invocation of the constraint solver is necessary to determine whether the current level of pipelining can meet the constraints imposed by the target architecture. Unfortunately, most designs do not possess sufficient pipelining to meet these constraints, instead requiring a significant level of repipelining or *C*-slow retiming to do so. The level necessary can be discovered in two ways.

The first approach is simply to allow the user to specify a desired level of repipelining or *C*-slowing. The retiming system then adds the specified number of delays and attempts to solve the system. If a solution is discovered, it is used. Otherwise, the user is notified that the design must be repipelined or retimed to a greater degree to meet the array's clock cycle. The second approach requires searching to find the minimal level of repipelining or *C*-slowing necessary to meet the constraints. Although this necessitates multiple iterations of the constraint solver, fixed-frequency retiming only requires local constraints. Without having to check the global constraints, this process proceeds quickly. The resulting level of repipelining or *C*-slowing is then reported to the user.

Fixed-frequency FPGAs require retiming considerably later in the tool flow. It is impossible to create a valid retiming until routing delays are known. Since the constraints required invariably depend on placement, the final retiming process must occur afterwards. Some arrays, such as HSRA [10], have deterministic routing structures that enable retiming to be performed either before or after routing. Other interconnect structures, such as SFRA [12], lack deterministic routing and require that retiming be performed only after routing.

Finally, the fact that fixed-frequency arrays may use considerably more pipelining than conventional arrays makes retiming registers a significant architectural feature. Because these delay chains [10], either on inputs or on outputs, are programmable, the array can implement longer ones. A common occurrence after aggressive *C*-slow retiming is a design with several signals requiring considerable delay. Therefore, dedicated resources to implement these features are effectively required to create a viable fixed-frequency FPGA.

18.5 *C*-SLOWING AS MULTI-THREADING

There have been numerous multi-threaded architecture designs, but all share a common theme: increasing system throughput by enabling multiple streams of execution, or threads, to operate simultaneously. These architectures generally fall into four classes: context switching always without bypassing (HEP [7] and Tera [2]), context switching on event (Intel IXP) [14], interleaved multi-threaded, and symmetric multi-threaded (SMT) [11]. The ideal goal of all of them is to increase system throughput by operating on multiple streams of execution.

The general concept of *C*-slow retiming can be applied to highly complex designs, including microprocessors. Unlike a simple FIR filter bank or an encryption algorithm, it is not a simple matter of inserting registers and balancing delays. Nevertheless, the changes necessary are comparatively small and the benefits substantial: producing a simple, statically scheduled, higher clock rate, multi-threaded architecture that is semantically equivalent to an interleaved-multi-threaded architecture, alternating between a fixed number of threads in a round-robin fashion to create the illusion of a multiprocessor system.

C-slowing requires three minor architectural changes: enlarging and modifying the register file and TLB, replacing the cache and memory interface, and slightly modifying the interrupt semantics. Beyond that, it is simply a matter of replacing every pipeline register in both the control logic and the datapath with *C* registers and then moving the registers to balance the delays, as is traditional in the *C*-slow retiming transformation and can be performed by an automatic tool. The resulting design, as expected, has full multi-threaded semantics and improved throughput because of a significantly higher clock rate. Figure 18.3 shows how this transformation can operate.

The biggest complications in *C*-slowing a microprocessor are selecting the implementation semantics for the various memories through the design. The first type keeps the traditional *C*-slow semantics of complete independence, where each thread sees a completely independent view, usually by duplication. This applies to the register file and most of the state registers in the system. This occurs automatically if *C*-slowing is performed by a tool, because it represents the normal semantics for *C*-slowed memory.

The second is completely shared memory, where every thread sees the same memory, such as the caches and main memory of the system. Most such memories exist in the non-*C*-slowed portion and so are unaffected by an automatic tool.

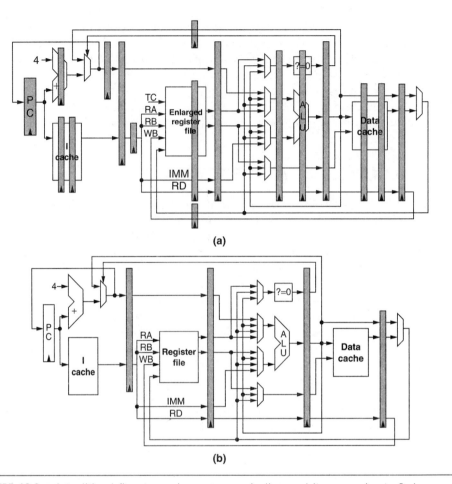

(a)

(b)

FIGURE 18.3 ▪ A traditional five-stage microprocessor pipeline, and its conversion to 3-slow operation.

The third is dynamically shared, where a hardware thread ID or a software thread context ID is tagged to each entry, with only the valid tags used. This breaks the automatic *C*-slow semantics and is best employed for branch predictors and similar caches. Such memories need to be constructed manually, but offer potential efficiency advantages as they do not need to increase in size. Because they cannot be constructed automatically they may be subject to interference or synergistic effects between threads.

The biggest architectural changes are to the register file: It needs to be increased by a factor of *C*, with a hardware thread counter to select which group of registers is being accessed. Now each thread will see an independent set of registers, with all reads and writes for the different threads going to separate memory locations. Apart from the thread selection and natural enlargement, the only piece remaining is to pipeline the register access. If necessary, the

C independently accessed sections can be banked so that the register file can operate at a higher clock frequency.

Naturally, this linearly increases the size of the register file, but pipelining the new larger file is not difficult since each thread accesses a disjoint register set, allowing staggered access to the banks if desired. This matches the automatic memory transformations that *C*-slowing creates: increasing the size and ensuring that each task has an independent view of memory.

To maintain the illusion that the different threads are running on completely different processors, it is important that each thread have an independent translation of memory. The easiest solution is to apply the same transformations to the TLB that were applied to the register file: increasing the size by *C*, with each thread accessing its own set, and pipelining access. Again, this is the natural result of applying the *C*-slow semantics from an automatic tool.

The other option is to tag each TLB entry. The interference effect may be significant if the associativity or size of the TLB is low. In such a case, and considering the generally small size of most TLBs, increasing the size (although perhaps by less than a factor of *C*) is advisable. Software thread ID tags are preferable to hardware ID tags because they reduce the cost of context switching if a shared TLB is used and may also provide some synergistic effects. In either case, a shared TLB requires interlocking between TLB writes to prevent synchronization bugs.

If the caches are physically addressed, it is simply a matter of pipelining access to improve throughput without splitting memory. Because of the interlocked execution of the threads and the pipelined nature of the modified caches, no additional coherency mechanisms are required except to interlock any existing test-and-set or atomic read/write instructions between the threads to ensure that each instruction has time to be completed.

Such cache modifications occur outside the *C*-slow semantics, suggesting that the cache needs to be changed manually. This means that the cache and memory controller must be manually updated to support pipelined access from the distinct threads, and must exist outside of the *C*-slowed core itself.

Unfortunately, virtually addressed caches are significantly more complicated: They require that each tag include thread ownership (to prevent one thread from viewing another's version of memory) and that a record of virtual-to-physical mappings be maintained to ensure coherency between threads. These complications suggest that a physically addressed cache would be superior when *C*-slowing a microprocessor to produce a simple multi-threaded design. A virtually addressed cache is one of the few structures that do not have a natural *C*-slow representation or that can easily exist outside a *C*-slowed core.

The rest of the machine state registers, being both loaded and read, are automatically separated by the *C*-slow transformation. This ensures that each thread will have a completely independent set of machine registers. Combined with the distinct registers and TLB tagging, each thread will see an independent processor.

The only other portion that needs to be changed is the interrupt semantics. Just as the rest of the control logic is pipelined, with control registers duplicated, the same transformations need to be applied to the interrupt logic. Thus, every external interrupt is interpreted by the rules corresponding to *every* virtual processor running in the pipeline. Yet, since the control registers are duplicated, the OS can enforce policies where different interrupts are handled by different execution streams. Similarly, internally driven interrupts (such as traps or watchdog timers), when *C*-slowed, are independent between threads, as *C*-slowing ensures that each thread sees only its own interrupts.

In this way, the OS can ensure that one virtual thread receives one set of externally sourced interrupts while another receives a different set. This also suggests that interrupts be presented to all threads of execution, enabling each thread (or even multiple threads) to service the appropriate interrupt.

The resulting design has full multi-threaded semantics, with each of *C* threads being independent. Because *C*-slowing can improve the clock rate (by two times in the case of the LEON benchmark), this can easily and substantially improve the throughput of a very complex design.

18.6 WHY ISN'T RETIMING UBIQUITOUS?

An interesting question is why retiming is not heavily used in FPGA tool flows. Although some FPGA vendors [1] and CAD vendors [8] support retiming, it is not universally available, and even when it is, it is usually optional.

There are three major factors that limit the general adoption of retiming: It interacts poorly with many critical FPGA features; it can only optimize poor implementations yet is not a substitute for good implementation; and it is computationally intensive.

As mentioned earlier, retiming does not work well with initial conditions or global resets—features that FPGA designers have traditionally relied on. Likewise, BlockRAMs, hardware clock eEnables, and other features can pin registers, limiting the ability of a retiming tool to move them. For these reasons, many FPGA designs *cannot* be effectively retimed.

A related observation is that retiming helps only poor designs and, moreover, only fixes one common deficiency of a poor design, not all of them. Additionally, if the designer has enough savvy to work around the limitations of retiming, he will probably produce a naturally well-balanced design.

Finally, although retiming is a polynomial time algorithm, its still superlinear. As designs continue to grow in size, $O(n^2 lg(n))$ can still be too long for many uses. This is especially problematic as the Moore's Law scaling for FPGAs is currently greater than that for single-threaded microprocessors.

References

[1] Altera Quartus II eda (*http://www.altera.com/*).
[2] R. Alverson, D. Callahan, D. Cummings, B. Koblenz, A. Porterfield, B. Smith. The Tera computer system. *Proceedings of the 1990 International Conference on Supercomputing*, 1990.

[3] J. Cong, C. Wu. Optimal FPGA mapping and retiming with efficient initial state computation. *Design Automation Conference*, 1998.

[4] C. Leiserson, F. Rose, J. Saxe. Optimizing synchronous circuitry by retiming. *Third Caltech Conference On VLSI*, March 1993.

[5] H. Schmit. Incremental reconfiguration for pipelined applications. *Proceedings of the IEEE Symposium on Field-Programmable Gate Arrays for Custom Computing Machines*, April 1997.

[6] D. P. Singh, S. D. Brown. Integrated retiming and placement for field-programmable gate arrays. *Tenth ACM International Symposium on Field-Programmable Gate Arrays*, 2002.

[7] B. J. Smith. Architecture and applications of the HEP multiprocessor computer system. Advances in laser scanning technology. *SPIE Proceedings* 298, Society for Photo-Optical Instrumentation Engineers, 1981.

[8] Synplify pro (*http://www.synplicity.com//products//synplifypro//index.html*).

[9] Synopsys, Inc. Synopsis FPGA Compiler II (*http://www.synopsys.com*).

[10] W. Tsu, K. Macy, A. Joshi, R. Huang, N. Walker, T. Tung, O. Rowhani, V. George, J. Wawrzynek, A. DeHon. HSRA: High-speed, hierarchical synchronous reconfigurable array. *Proceedings of the International Symposium on Field-Programmable Gate Arrays*, February 1999.

[11] D. M. Tullsen, S. J. Eggers, H. M. Levy. Simultaneous multi-threading: Maximizing on-chip parallelism. *Proceedings 22nd Annual International Symposium on Computer Architecture*, June 1995.

[12] N. Weaver, J. Hauser, J. Wawrzynek. The SFRA: A corner-turn FPGA architecture. *Twelfth International Symposium on Field-Programmable Gate Arrays*, 2004.

[13] N. Weaver, Y. Markovskiy, Y. Patel, J. Wawrzynek. Postplacement *C*-slow retiming for the Xilinx-Virtex FPGA. *Eleventh ACM International Symposium on Field-Programmable Gate Arrays*, 2003.

[14] Intel Corporation. The Intel IXP network processor. *Intel Technology Journal* 6(3), August 2002.

CHAPTER 19

CONFIGURATION BITSTREAM GENERATION

Steven A. Guccione
Cmpware, Inc.

While a reconfigurable logic device shares some of the characteristics of a fixed hardware device and some of a programmable instruction set processor, the details of the underlying architecture and how it is programmed are what distinguish these machines. Both a reconfigurable logic device and an instruction set processor are programmable by "software," but the internal organization and use of this software are quite different. In an instruction set processor, the programming is a set of binary codes that are incrementally fed into the device during operation. These codes actually carry out a form of reconfiguration inside the processor. The arithmetic and logic unit(s) (ALU) is configured to perform a requested function and various control multiplexers (MUXes) that control the internal flow of data are set. In the instruction set machine, these hardware components are relatively small and fixed and the system is reconfigured on a cycle-by-cycle basis. The processor itself changes its internal logic and routing on every cycle based on the input of these binary codes.

In a processor, the binary codes—the processor's machine language—are fairly rigid and correspond to sequential "instructions." The sequence of these instructions to implement a program is often generated by some higher-level automatic tool such as a high-level language (HLL) compiler from a language such as Java, C, or C++. But they may, in reality, come from any source. What is important is that the collection of binary data fits this rigid format. The collection of binary data goes by many names, most typically an "executable" file or even more generally a "binary program."

A reconfigurable logic device, or field-programmable gate array (FPGA), is based on a very different structure than that of an instruction set machine. It is composed of a two-dimensional array of programmable logic elements joined together by some programmable interconnection network. The most significant difference between FPGA and the instruction set architecture is that the FPGA is typically intended to be programmed as a complete unit, with the various internal components acting together in parallel. While the structure of its binary programming (or configuration) data is every bit as rigid as that of an instruction set processor, the data are used spatially rather than sequentially.

In other words, the binary data used to program the reconfigurable logic device are loaded into the device's internal units before the device is placed in its operating mode, and typically, no changes are made to the data while the device is operating. There are some significant exceptions to this rule: The configuration data may in fact be changed while a device is operational, but this is somewhat akin to "self-modifying code" in instruction set architectures. This is a very powerful technique, but carries with it significant challenges.

The collection of binary data used to program the reconfigurable logic device is most commonly referred to as a "bitstream," although this is somewhat misleading because the data are no more bit oriented than that of an instruction set processor and there is generally no "streaming." While in an instruction set processor the configuration data are in fact continuously streamed into the internal units, they are typically loaded into the reconfigurable logic device only once during an initial setup phase. For historical reasons, the somewhat undescriptive "bitstream" has become the standard term.

As much as the binary instruction set interface describes and defines the architecture and functionality of the instruction set machine, the structure of the reconfigurable logic configuration data bitstream defines the architecture and functionality of the FPGA. Its format, however, currently suffers from a somewhat interesting handicap. While the format of the programming data of instruction set architectures is freely published, this is almost never the case with reconfigurable logic devices. Almost all of them that are sold by major manufacturers are based on a "closed" bitstream architecture.

The underlying structure of the data in the configuration bitstream is regarded by these companies as a trade secret for reasons that are historical and not entirely clear. In the early days of reconfigurable logic devices, the underlying architecture was also a trade secret, so publishing the configuration bitstream format would have given too many clues about it. It is presumed that this was to keep competitors from taking ideas about an architecture, or perhaps even "cloning" it and providing a hardware-compatible device. It also may have reassured nervous FPGA users that, if the bitstream format was a secret, then presumably their logic designs would be difficult to reverse-engineer.

While theft and cloning of device hardware do not appear to be a potential problem today, bitstream formats are still, perhaps out of habit alone, treated as trade secrets by the major manufacturers. This is a shame because it prohibits interesting experimentation with new tools and techniques by third parties. But this is perhaps only of interest to a very small number of people. The vast majority of users of commercial reconfigurable logic devices are happy to use the vendor-supplied tools and have little or no interest in the device's internal structure as long as the logic design functions as specified. However, for those interested in the architecture of reconfigurable logic devices, trade secrecy is an important subject.

While exact examples from popular industry devices are not possible because of this secrecy, much is publicly known about the underlying architectures, the general way a bitstream is generated, and how it operates when loaded into a device.

19.1 THE BITSTREAM

The bitstream spatially represents the configuration data of a large collection of small, relatively simple hardware components. Thus, we can identify these components and discuss the ways in which the bitstream is used to produce a working digital circuit in a reconfigurable logic device. Although there is really no limit to the types of units possible in a reconfigurable logic device, two basic structures make up the microarchitecture of most modern FPGAs. These are the lookup table (LUT) and the switch box.

The LUT is essentially a very small memory element, typically with 16 bits of bit-oriented storage. Some early FPGAs used smaller 8-bit LUTs, and other more exotic architectures used non-LUT structures. In general, however, the vast majority of commercial FPGA devices sold over the last decade use the 16-bit LUT as a primary logic building block.

The functionality of LUTs is very simple. Binary data are loaded into them to produce some Boolean function. In the case of the 16-bit LUT, there are four inputs, which can produce any arbitrary 4-input Boolean logic function. For instance, to provide the AND function of all four inputs, each bit in the memory except the bit at address A(1,1,1,1) is loaded with a binary 0 and the A(1,1,1,1) bit is loaded with a 1. The address inputs of the LUT are used as the inputs to the logic function, with the output of the LUT providing the output of the logic function. Figure 19.1 illustrates this mapping of a 2-input LUT to a 2-input AND gate.

While the LUTs provide the logic for the circuit, the switch boxes provide the interconnection. These switch boxes are typically made up of multiplexers in various regular configurations. These multiplexers are controlled by bits of memory that select the inputs and send them to the multiplexer's outputs. Figure 19.2 shows a typical configurable interconnect element constructed using a multiplexer.

The multiplexer inputs in Figure 19.2 are controlled by two memory elements that are set during configuration. They select which input value is sent to the output. By connectiong large numbers of elements of this type, an interconnection

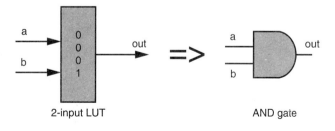

2-input LUT   AND gate

FIGURE 19.1 ■ A 2-input LUT configured as an AND gate.

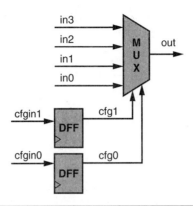

FIGURE 19.2 ▪ A configurable 4-input multiplexer used in routing.

network of the kind typically used to construct modern reconfigurable logic devices can be made.

In various topologies, the ouputs of the multiplexers in the switch boxes feed the address inputs of the LUTs; the outptus of the LUTs, in turn, feed the inputs of the switch box multiplexers. This provides a basic reprogrammable architecture capable of producing arbitrary logic functions, as well as the ability to interconnect these functions in a variety of ways. How complex a circuit a given reconfigurable logic device can implement is based on both the number of LUTs and the size and complexity of the interconnection fabric.

In fact, the topology of the interconnect fabric and the implementation of the switch boxes is perhaps the defining characteristic of an FPGA architecture. Older FPGAs had a limited silicon area and few metal layers to supply wires. For this reason, the LUTs were typically "islands" of logic, with the interconnect wires running in the "channels" between them. Where these channels intersected were the switch boxes. How many wires to use and how to configure the switch boxes were the main work of the FPGA architect. Balancing the cost of more wires with the needs of typical digital circuit was important to making a cost-effective device that would be commercially successful. Covering as many potential circuit designs as possible at as high a speed as possible, but with the smallest silicon area, is still the challenge FPGA device architects must confront.

In later silicon process generations, however, more metal layers were available, which resulted in a much higher ratio of wires to logic in FPGAs. Where older generations of FPGAs often had a scarcity of interconnection resources, more modern FPGA devices seldom encounter circuits they are unable to implement because of a lack of routing resources. And these wires now tend to run on top of the logic rather than in channels, which has led to higher circuit densities, a tighter integration between the switch boxes and the logic, and faster interconnect.

The configuration bitstream data for the routing are essentially the multiplexer inputs in these switch boxes. The memory for these MUX inputs tends to be individual memory elements such as flip-flops scattered around the device as needed, establishing the basic bitstream for the FPGA: the LUT data plus the bits to control the routing multiplexers.

While the multiplexer and switch boxes are the basic elements of modern FPGA devices, many other components are possible. One of the more popular is a configurable input/output block, or IOB. An IOB is typically connected to the end of one of the wires in the routing system on one side and to a physical device pin on the other. It is then configured to define the type of pin used by this device: either input or output. More complex IOBs can configure pin voltages and even parameters such as capacitance, and some even provide higher-level support for various serial communication protocols. Much like switch boxes, the configuration bitstream data for the IOBs are some collection of bits used to set flip-flops within them to select these features.

In addition to IOBs, other, more special-purpose units have turned up in later generations of FPGA devices. Two prominent examples are block memory and multiplier units. Block memory (BlockRAM) is simply relatively large RAM units that are usually on the order of 1K bits but can be implemented in any number of ways. The actual data bits may be part of the bitstream, which initializes the BlockRAM upon power-up. To reduce the size of the bitstream, however, this data may be absent and internal circuitry may be required to reset and initialize the BlockRAM.

In addition to the internal data, the BlockRAM is typically interfaced to the switch boxes in various ways. Its location and interfacing to the interconnection network is a major architectural decision in modern reconfigurable logic device design.

Because the multiplication function has become more popular in FPGA designs and because FPGAs are so inefficient at implementing such circuits, the addition of hardwired multiplier units into modern FPGA devices has been increasing. These units typically have no internal state or configuration, but are interfaced to the interconnection network in a manner similar to the BlockRAM interface. As with the BlockRAM, where to locate these resources and how many to include are major architectural decisions that can have a large impact on the size and efficiency of modern FPGAs.

Many other features also find control bits in the FPGA bitstream. Some of these are global control related to configuration and reconfiguration; others are ID codes and error-checking information such as cyclic redundancy check codes. How these features are implented is very architecture dependent and can vary widely from device family to device family. One common feature is basic control for bit-level storage elements, often in the form of flip-flops on the LUT output. Various control bits often set circuit parameters such as the flip-flop type (D, JK, T) or the clock edge trigger type (rising or falling edge). The ability to chage the flip-flop into a transparent D-type latch is also a popular option. Each of these bits also contributes to the configuration data, with one set of flip-flop configuration settings per LUT being typical.

Finally, while the items just discussed are the major standard units used to construct modern FPGA devices and define the configuration bitstream, there

TABLE 19.1 ■ Configuration bitstream sizes

Year	Device	Bits
1986	XC2018	18 Kbits
1988	XC3090	64 Kbits
1990	XC4013	248 Kbits
1994	XC4025	422 Kbits
1996	XC4028	668 Kbits
1998	XCV1000	6.1 Mbits
2000	XCV3200	16 Mbits
2003	XC2V8000	29 Mbits

is no limit to the types of circuits and configurations possible. For example, an interest in analog FPGAs has resulted in unique architectures to perform analog signal processing. Also, some coarser-grained reconfigurable logic devices have moved up in granularity from LUTs to ALUs, and these devices have somewhat different bitstream structures. Other architectures have gone in the other direction toward extremely fine-grained architectures. One notable device, the Xilinx XC6200, has a logic cell that is essentially a 2-input multiplexer. The balance of routing and logic in these devices has made them less attractive than coarser-grained devices, but they have not been reevaluated in the context of the denser routing available with newer multilayer metal processes and so may yet have some promise.

As FPGA devices themselves have grown, so has the size of the configuration bitstreams. In fact, bitstream size can be a reasonable gauge of the size and complexity of the underlying device, which can be useful because it is a single number that is readily available. Table 19.1 gives some representative sizes of various bitstreams from members of the Xilinx family of FPGAs and the approximate dates they were introduced.

19.2 DOWNLOADING MECHANISMS

The FPGA configuration bitstream is typically saved externally in a nonvolatile memory such as an EPROM. The data are usually loaded into the device shortly after the initial power-up sequence, most often bit-serially. (This loading mechanism may be the reason that many engineers perceive the configuration data as a "stream of bits.") The reason for serial loading is primarily one of cost and convenience. Since there is usually no particular hurry in loading the FPGA configuration data on power-up, using a single physical device pin for this data is the simplest, cheapest approach. Once the data are fully loaded, this pin may even be put into service as a standard I/O pin, thus preventing the configuration downloading mechanism from consuming valuable I/O resources on the device.

A serial configuration download is the norm, but some FPGA devices have a parallel download mode that typically permits the use of eight I/O pins to download configuration data in parallel. This may be helpful for designs that use an 8-bit memory device and for applications where reprogramming is common and speed is important—often the case when an FPGA is controlled by a host processor in a coprocessor arrangement. As with the serial approach, the pins may be returned to regular I/O duty once downloading is complete.

One place where such high-bandwidth configuration is useful is in the device test in the factory. Testing FPGA devices after manufacture can be a very expensive task, mostly because of time spent attached to the test equipment. Thus, decreasing the configuration download time by a factor of eight may result in the FPGA manufacturer requiring substantially fewer pieces of test equipment, which can result in a significant cost savings during manufacture. Anecdotal evidence suggests that high-speed download is driven mostly by increased test efficiency and not by any customer requirements related to runtime reconfiguration.

One type of device that is based on nonvolatile memory bears mention here. Rather than using RAM and flip-flops as the internal logic and control, commercially available devices from companies such as Actel use nonvolatile Flash-style internal configuration memory. These devices are programmed once and do not require reloading of configuration data on power-up, which can be important in systems that must be powered-up quickly. Such devices also tend to be more resistant to soft errors that can occur in volatile RAM devices. This makes them especially popular in harsh environments such as space and military applications.

19.3 SOFTWARE TO GENERATE CONFIGURATION DATA

The software used to generate configuration bitstream data for FPGA devices is perhaps some of the most complex available. It usually consists of many layers of functionality and can run on the largest workstations for hours or even days to produce the output for a single design. While the details of this software are beyond the scope of this chapter, some of the way the software generates this bitstream will be briefly discussed in this section.

The top-level input to the FPGA design software is most often a hardware description language (HDL) or a graphical circuit design created with a schematic capture package. This representation is usually then translated into a low-level description more closely related to the implementation technology. A common choice for this intermediate format is EDIF (Electronic Design Interchange Format). This translation is fairly generic and such tools are widely available from a variety of software vendors.

The EDIF description is still not suitable for directly programming the reconfigurable logic device. In the typical FPGA, the underlying circuit must be "mapped" onto the array of LUTs and switch boxes. While the actual implementation may vary, the two basic processes for getting such abstract circuit descriptions into a physical representation of FPGA configuration data are placement/routing and mapping. Figure 19.3 shows the basic flow of this process.

Mapping refers to taking general logic descriptions and converting them into the bits used to fill in a LUT. This is sometimes referred to as "packing," because

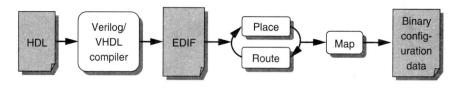

FIGURE 19.3 ▪ The tool flow for producing the configuration bitstream.

several small logic gates are often "packed" into a single LUT. There is also a notion of placement that decides which LUT should receive the data, but this may also be considered a part of the mapping process.

Once the values for the LUTs have been decided, software can begin to decide how to interconnect the LUTs in a process called "routing." There are many algorithms of varying sophistication to perform routing, and factors such as circuit timing may be taken into account in the process. The result of the routing procedure is eventually used to supply the configuration data for the switch boxes.

Of course, this description is highly simplified, and mapping and routing can take place in various interleaved phases and can be optimized in a wide variety of ways. Still, this is the essential process used to produce the configuration bitstream. Finally, data for configuring the IOBs are typically input in some form that is aware of the particular package being used for the FPGA device. Once all of this data have been defined and collected, they can be written out to a single file containing the configuration bitstream.

As mentioned, FPGA configuration bitstream formats have almost always been proprietary. For this reason, the only tools available to perform bitstream generation tasks have been those supplied by the device manufacturer. The one notable exception is the Xilinx XC6200, which had an "open" bitstream. One of the XC6200's software tools was an application program interface (API) that permitted users to create configuration data or to even directly alter the config-uration of an XC6200 in operation mode. Some of this technology was trans-ferred to more mainstream Xilinx FPGAs and is available from Xilinx as a toolkit called JBits.

JBits is a Java API into the configuration bitstream for the XC4000 and Virtex device families. With JBits, the actual values on LUTs and switch box settings, as well as all other microarchitectural components, could be directly programmed. While the control data could be used to produce a traditional bitstream file, they could also be accessed directly and changed dynamically. The JBits API not only permitted dynamic reconfiguration of the FPGA but also permitted third-party tools to be built for these devices for the first time. JBits was very popular with researchers and users with exotic design requirements, but it never achieved popular use as a mainstream tool, although many of its related toolkit components, including the debug tool and partial reconfiguration support, have found their way into more mainstream software.

19.4 SUMMARY

While the generation of bitstream data to configure an FPGA device is a very common activity, there has been very little information available on the details of either the configuration bitstream or the underlying FPGA architecture. Thus, the FPGA can best be viewed as a collection of microarchitecture components, chiefly LUTs and switch boxes. These components are configured by writing data to the LUT values and to control memories associated with the switch boxes. Setting these bits to various values results in custom digital circuits.

A variety of tools and techniques are used to program reconfigurable logic devices, but all must eventually produce the relatively small configuration "bitstream" data the devices require. This data is in as rigid a format as any binary execution data for a microprocessor, but this format is typically proprietary and unpublished. While direct examination of actual commercial bitstream data is largely impossible, the general structure and the microarchitecture components configured by this data can be examined, at least in the abstract.

References

[1] Xilinx, Inc. *Virtex Data Sheet*, Xilinx, Inc., 1998.
[2] S. A. Guccione, D. Levi, P. Sundararajan. JBits: A Java-based interface for reconfigurable computing. *Second Annual Military and Aerospace Applications of Programmable Devices and Technologies Conference (MAPLD)*, Laurel, MD, September 1999.
[3] E. Lechner, S. A. Guccione. The Java environment for reconfigurable computing. *Proceedings of the Seventh International Workshop on Field-Programmable Logic and Applications*, September 1997.
[4] Xilinx, Inc. *XAPP151: Virtex Series Configuration Architecture User Guide (version 1.7)*, (*http://direct.xilinx.com/bvdocs/appnotes/xapp151.pdf*), October 20, 2004.
[5] P. Alfke. *FPGA Configuration Guidelines (version 1.1)* (*http://direct.xilinx.com/bvdocs/appnotes/xapp090.pdf*), November 24, 1997.
[6] Xilinx, Inc. *XC6200 Field-Programmable Gate Arrays*, Xilinx, Inc., 1997.
[7] V. Betz, J. Rose. VPR: A new packing, placement, and routing tool for FPGA research. *Proceedings of the Seventh International Workshop on Field-Programmable Logic and Applications*, September 1997.
[8] Xilinx, Inc. *JBits 2.8 SDK for Virtex*, Xilinx Inc., 1999.

FAST COMPILATION TECHNIQUES

Ken Eguro, Scott Hauck
Department of Electrical Engineering
University of Washington

Most users rely on sophisticated CAD tools to implement their circuits on field-programmable gate arrays (FPGAs). Unfortunately, since each of these tools must perform reasonably complex optimization, the entire process can take a long time. Although fairly slow compilation is fine for the majority of current FPGA users, there are many situations that demand more efficient techniques. Looking into the future, we see that faster CAD tools will become necessary for many different reasons.

FPGA scaling. Modern reconfigurable devices have a much larger capacity compared to those from even a few years ago, and this trend is expected to continue. To handle the dramatic increase in problem size, while maintaining current usability and compilation times, smarter and more efficient techniques are required.

Hardware prototyping and logic emulation systems. These are very large multi-FPGA systems used for design verification during the development of other complex hardware devices such as next-generation processors. They present a challenging CAD problem both because of the sheer number of FPGAs in the system and because the compilation time for the design is part of the user's debug cycle. That is, the CAD tool time directly affects the usability of the system as a whole.

Instance-specific design. Instance-specific designs are applications where a given circuit can only solve one particular occurrence of a problem. Because of this, every individual hardware implementation must be created and mapped as the problems are presented. Thus, the true solution time for any specific example includes the netlist compilation time.

Runtime netlist compilation. Reconfigurable computing systems are often constructed with an FPGA or an array of FPGAs alongside a conventional processor. Multiple programs could be running in the system simultaneously, each potentially sharing the reconfigurable fabric. In some of the most aggressive systems, portions of a program are individually mapped to the FPGA while the instructions are in flight. This creates a need for almost real-time compilation techniques.

For each of these systems, the runtime of the CAD tools is a clear concern. In this chapter, we consider each scenario and cover techniques to accelerate the various steps in the mapping flow. These techniques range from fairly cost-neutral optimizations that speed the CAD flow without greatly impacting circuit quality to more aggressive optimizations that can significantly accelerate compilation time but also appreciably degrade mapping quality.

FPGA scaling

The mere scaling of VLSI technology itself has created part of the burden for conventional FPGA CAD tools. Fulfilling Moore's Law, improvements in lithography and manufacturing techniques have radically increased the capabilities of integrated circuits over the last four decades. Of course, just as these advancements have increased the performance of desktop computers, they have increased the logic capacity of FPGAs. Correspondingly, the size of desired applications has also increased. Because of this simultaneous scaling across the industry, reconfigurable devices and their applications become physically larger at approximately the same rate that general-purpose processors become faster.

Unfortunately, this does not mean that the time required to compile a modern FPGA design on a modern processor stays the same. Over a particular period of time, desktop computers and compute servers will become twice as fast and, concurrently, FPGA architectures and user circuits will double in size. Since the complexity of many classical design compilation techniques scale super-linearly with problem size, however, the relative runtime for mapping contemporary applications using contemporary machines will naturally rise.

To continue to provide reasonable design compilation time across multiple FPGA generations, changes must be made to prevent a gap between available computational power and netlist compilation complexity. However, although application engineers depend on compilation times of at most a few hours to meet fast production timelines, they also have expectations about the usable logic block density and achievable clock frequency for their applications. Thus, any algorithmic improvements or architectural changes made to speed up the mapping process cannot come at the cost of dramatically increased critical-path timing or reduced mapping density.

Hardware prototyping and logic emulation systems

The issue of nonscalable compilation is even more obvious in large prototyping or logic emulation systems. These devices integrate multiple FPGAs into a single system, harnessing tens to thousands. As Chapter 30 discusses in more detail, the fundamental size of typical circuits on these architectures suggests fast mapping techniques. However, even more critical, the compilation time of the netlists themselves may become a limiting factor in the basic usefulness of the entire system.

Hardware prototyping is often employed for many reasons. One of the greatest advantages of hardware emulation over software simulation is its extremely fast validation time. During the design and debug cycle of hardware development, hundreds of thousands of test vectors may be applied to ensure that a given implementation complies with design specifications. Although an FPGA-based prototyping system cannot be expected to achieve anywhere near the clock rate of the dedicated final product, the sheer volume of tests that need to be performed every time a change is made to the system makes software simulation too slow to have inside the engineering design loop. That said, software simulation code can easily accommodate design updates and, more important, the changes have a predictable compilation time of minutes to hours, not hours to days. Still, since reconfigurable logic emulation systems maintain such a runtime advantage over software simulation, prototyping designers are willing to exchange some of the classical FPGA metrics of implementation quality, critical-path timing, and logical density for faster and more predictable compilation time.

Instance-specific design
Similar to logic emulation systems, the netlist compilation time of instance-specific circuits can greatly affect the overall value of an FPGA-based implementation. For example, although Boolean satisfiability is NP-complete, the massive parallelism offered by reconfigurable fabrics can often solve these problems extremely quickly—potentially on the order of milliseconds (see Chapter 29). Unfortunately, these FPGA implementations are equation-specific, so the time required to solve any given SAT problem is not determined by the vanishingly short runtime of the actual mapped circuit running on a reconfigurable device, but instead is dominated by the compilation time required to obtain the programming bitstream in the first place—potentially on the order of hours.

Because of this reliance on netlist compilation, the Boolean satisfiability problem differs strongly from more traditional reconfigurable computing applications for two reasons.

First, if we disregard compilation time, FPGA-based SAT solvers can obtain two to three orders of magnitude better performance than software-based solutions. Thus, the critical path and, by extension, the overall quality of the mapping in the classical sense are virtually irrelevant. As long as compilation results in *any* valid mapping, the vast majority of the performance benefit will be maintained. While some effort is required to reliably produce routable circuits, we can make huge concessions in terms of circuit quality in the name of speeding compilation. Mappings that are quickly produced, but possibly slow, will still drastically improve the overall solution runtime.

Second, features of the SAT problem itself suggest that application-specific approaches might be worthwhile. For example, because SAT solvers typically have very structured forms, fast SAT-specific CAD tools can be created. One possibility is the use of preplaced and prerouted SAT-specialized macros that simply need to be assembled together to create the overall system. To extend the concept of application-specialized tuning to its logical end, architectural changes can even be made to the reconfigurable fabric itself to make the device particularly amenable to simple, fast mapping techniques. That said, the large engineering effort this would involve must be weighed against the possible benefits.

Runtime netlist compilation
All reconfigurable computing systems have a certain amount of overhead that eats away at their performance benefit. Although kernel execution might be blindingly fast once started on the reconfigurable logic, its overall benefit is limited by the

need to profile operations, transfer data, and configure or reconfigure the FPGA. Reconfigurable computing systems that use dynamically compiled applications have the additional burden of runtime netlist compilation. These systems only map application kernels to the hardware during actual system execution, in the hope that runtime data, such as system loads, resource availability, and execution profiles, can improve the resultant speedups provided by the hardware. Their almost real-time requirements demand the absolutely fastest compilation techniques. Thus, even more so than instance-specific designs, these systems are only concerned with compilation speed.

Mapping stages

When evaluating mapping techniques for high-speed circuit compilation, we have to remember that the individual tools are part of a larger system. Therefore, any quality degradation in an early stage may not only limit the performance of the final mapping, but also make subsequent compilation problems more difficult. If these later mapping phases are more difficult, they may require a longer runtime, overwhelming the speedups achieved in earlier steps. For example, a poor-quality placement obtained very quickly will likely make the routing problem harder. Since we are interested in reducing the runtime of the compilation phase as a whole, we must ensure that we do not simply trade placement runtime for routing runtime. We may even run the risk of increasing total compilation time, since a very poor placement might be impossible to route, necessitating an additional placement and routing attempt.

Although logic synthesis, technology mapping, and logic block packing are considered absolutely necessary parts of a modern, general-use FPGA compiler flow, the majority of research into fast compilation has been focused on efficient placement and routing techniques. Not only do the placement and routing phases make up a large portion of the overall mapping runtime, in some cases the other steps can be considered either unsuitable or unnecessary to accelerate. Sometimes high-level synthesis and technology mapping may be unnecessary because designs are assumed to be implemented in low-level languages, or it is assumed that they can be performed offline and thus outside the task's critical path. Furthermore, although logic synthesis and technology mapping can be very difficult problems by themselves, they are also common to all hardware CAD tools—not just FPGA-based technologies. On the other hand, placement and routing tools for reconfigurable devices have to deal with architectural restrictions not present in conventional standard cell tools, and thus generally must be accelerated with unique approaches.

20.1 ACCELERATING CLASSICAL TECHNIQUES

An obvious starting point to improve the runtime of netlist compilation is to make minor algorithmic changes to accelerate the classical techniques already in use. For example, simulated annealing placement has some obvious parameters that can be changed to reduce overall runtime. The initial annealing temperature can be lowered, the freezing point can be increased, the cooling schedule can be accelerated, or the number of moves per iteration can be reduced. These approaches all tend to speed up the annealing, but at some cost to placement quality.

20.1.1 Accelerating Simulated Annealing

Because of the adaptive nature of modern simulated annealing temperature schemes, any changes made to the structure of the cooling schedule itself can have unreliable runtime behavior. Not only have the settings of initial and final temperatures been carefully selected to thoroughly explore the solution space, changing these values may dramatically affect final placement quality while still not guaranteeing satisfactorily shorter runtime.

As described in Chapter 14, VPR updates the current temperature based on the fraction of moves accepted out of those attempted during a given iteration. Thus, decreasing the initial temperature cuts off the phase in which sweeping changes can easily occur early in the annealing. Simply starting the system at a lower initial temperature may cause the annealing to compensate by lingering longer at moderately high temperatures. Similarly, modifying the cooling schedule to migrate toward freezing faster fundamentally goes against the basic premise of simulated annealing itself. This will have an unpredictable, and likely undesirable, effect on solution quality.

It is generally accepted that the most predictable way to scale simulated annealing effort is by manipulating the number of moves attempted per temperature iteration. For example, in VPR the number of moves in a given iteration is always based on the size of the input netlist: $O(n^{1.33})$. The annealing effort is simply adjusted by scaling up or down the multiplicative constant portion of this value. In VPR, the "fast" placement option simply divides the default value by 10, which in testing indeed reduces the overall placement time by a factor of 10 while affecting final circuit quality by less than 10 percent [3]. Furthermore, as shown by Mulpuri and Hauck [12], simply changing the number of moves per iteration allows a continuous and relatively predictable spectrum of placement effort versus placement quality results.

Haldar and colleagues [11] exploited a very similar phenomenon to reduce mapping time by distributing the simulated annealing effort across multiple processors. In the strictest sense, simulated annealing is very difficult to parallelize because it attempts sequential changes to a given placement in order to slowly improve the overall wirelength. To be most faithful to this process while attempting multiple changes simultaneously, different processors must try non-overlapping changes to the system; otherwise, multiple processors may try to move the same block to two different locations or two different blocks to the same location. Not only is this type of coordination typically very difficult to enforce, it also generally requires a large amount of communication between processors. Since all processors begin each move operating on the same placement, they all must communicate any changes that are made after each step. However, a slightly less faithful but far simpler approach can take advantage of the idea that reducing the number of moves attempted per temperature iteration can gracefully reduce runtime.

In this case, all of the processors agree upon a single placement to begin a temperature iteration. At this point, though, each processor performs simulated annealing independently of the others. To reduce the overall runtime, given N processors, each only attempts $1/N$ of the originally intended moves per iteration. At the end of the iteration, the placements discovered by all of the processors are compared and the best one is broadcasted to the rest for use during the next iteration. This greatly reduces the communication overhead and produces nearly linear speedup for two to four processors while reducing placement quality by only 10 to 25 percent [11].

Wrighton and DeHon [19] also parallelized the simulated annealing process, but approached the problem in a completely different manner. In this case, instead of attempting to develop parallel software, they actually configure an FPGA to find its own placement for a netlist. They divide a large array into distinct processing elements that will each keep track of one node in a small netlist. In their testing, the logic required to trace the inputs and outputs of a single LUT required approximately 400 LUTs. Because every processing element represents the logic held at a single location in the array, a large emulation system consisting of approximately 400 FPGAs can place a netlist for one device at a time, or one large FPGA can place a netlist requiring approximately 1/400 of the array.

Each processing element is responsible for keeping track of both the block in the netlist currently mapped to that location and the position of the sinks of the net sourced by this block. During a given timestep, each processing element determines the wirelength of its output net by evaluating the location of all of its sinks; the entire system is then perturbed in parallel by allowing each location to negotiate a possible swap with its neighbors. Just as in conventional simulated annealing, good moves are always accepted and bad moves are accepted with a probability dependent on the annealing temperature and how much worse the move makes the system as a whole. Similarly, although swaps can only be made one nearest neighbor to another, any block can eventually migrate to any other location in the array through multiple swaps. The system avoids having two blocks attempt to occupy the same location by always negotiating swaps pairwise.

As shown in Figure 20.1, a block negotiates a swap with each of its neighbors in turn. Phases 1 and 2 may swap blocks to the left or right, while phases 3 and 4 may swap with a neighbor above or below.

We should note that although very similar to the classical simulated annealing model, this arrangement does not necessarily calculate placement cost in the same way. The net bounding box calculated at each timestep cannot take into account the potential simultaneous movement of all the other blocks to which it is connected. That said, whatever inaccuracies might be introduced by this computation difference are relatively small.

Of much greater importance is the problem caused by communication bandwidth. It is possible that in a given timestep every processing element decides to swap with its neighbor. If this is the case, the location of all sinks will change.

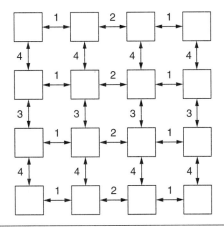

FIGURE 20.1 ■ Swap negotiation in hardware-assisted placement. (*Source*: Based on an illustration in Wrighton and DeHon [19]).

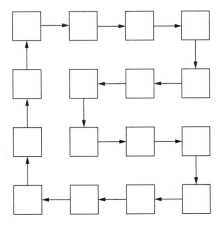

FIGURE 20.2 ■ Location update chain. (*Source*: Based on an illustration in Wrighton and DeHon [19]).

To keep completely consistent recordkeeping with conventional simulated annealing, this requires each processing element to notify its nets' sources of the block's new location. Of course, this creates a huge communication overhead. However, this can be avoided if the processing elements are allowed to calculate wirelength based on stale location information.

As shown in Figure 20.2, instead of a huge broadcast each time a block is relocated, position information marches through the system in a linear fashion. As blocks are moved during the annealing process, new positions for each one are communicated to other blocks via a dedicated location update chain. Thus, if the system has N processing elements, it might take N clock cycles before all relevant processing elements see the new placement of that block. Since the processing elements are still calculating further moves, this means up to N cycles of stale data. Because of these inaccuracies, compared with a fast VPR run, this hardware-based simulated annealing system generally requires 36 percent more routing tracks to implement the same circuits. However, it also is three to four orders of magnitude faster.

As mentioned earlier, classical simulated annealing techniques have been very carefully tuned to produce high-quality placements. Most of the methodologies we have covered to accelerate simulated annealing rely on reducing the number of moves attempted. Thus, while they can produce reasonable placements quickly for current circuits, they do not necessarily perform well for all applications.

Mulpuri and Hauck [12] demonstrated that, while we may be able to reduce the number of moves per temperature iteration by a factor of 10 with little effect on routability, if we continue to reduce the placement effort, the quality of the placement drops off severely. The conclusion to be drawn is that, acceleration approaches, although reasonable for dealing with FPGA scaling in the short term, are not a permanent solution. Applying them on increasing netlist and device sizes will eventually lead to worse and worse placements, and, furthermore, they simply do not have the capability to produce useable placements quickly enough for either runtime netlist compilation or most instance-specific circuits.

On the other hand, hardware-assisted simulated annealing seems far more promising. Although this technique introduces some inaccuracy in cost calculation because of both simultaneously negotiated moves and stale location information, the effect of these factors is relatively predictable. The error introduced by simultaneous moves will always be relatively small because all swaps are performed between nearest neighbors. Also, the error introduced by stale location information scales linearly with netlist size. This means not only that such information will likely cause the placement quality to degrade gracefully but also that we can reduce this inaccuracy relatively easily by adding additional update paths, perhaps even a bidirectional communication network that quickly informs both forward and backward neighbors of a moved element. Since we hope that the majority of nets will cover a relatively small area, this should considerably reduce inaccurate cost calculation due to stale location information.

These trade-offs make hardware-assisted annealing an interesting possibility. Although it may impose a significant quality cost, that cost may not grow with increased system capacity, and it may be one of the only approaches that provide the drastic speedups necessary for both runtime netlist compilation and instance-specific circuits. This may make it of particular interest for future nanotechnology systems (see Chapter 38).

20.1.2 Accelerating PathFinder

Just as in placement, minor alterations can be made to classical routing algorithms to improve their runtime. Some extremely simple modifications may speed routing without affecting overall quality, or they may reduce routability in a graceful and predictable manner. Swartz et al. [15] suggest sorting the nets to be routed in order of decreasing fanout instead of simply arbitrarily. Although high fanout nets generally make up a small fraction of a circuit, they typically monopolize a large portion of the routing runtime. By routing these comparatively difficult nets first in a given iteration, they may be presented with the lowest congestion cost and thus take the most direct and easily found paths. Lower fanout nets tend to be more localized, so they can deal with congestion more easily and their search time is comparatively smaller. This tends to speed overall routing, but since no changes are made to the actual search algorithm, it is not expected to affect routability.

Conversely, Swartz et al. [15] also suggest scaling present sharing and history costs more quickly between routing iterations. As discussed in Chapter 17, PathFinder gradually increases the cost of using congested nodes to discourage sharing over multiple iterations. Increasing present sharing and history costs more aggressively emphasizes removing congestion over route exploration. This may potentially decrease achievable routability, but the system may converge on a legal routing more quickly.

One of the most effective changes that can be made to conventional Dijkstra-based routing approaches is limiting the expansion of the search. Ignoring congestion, in most island-style FPGAs it is unnecessary for a given net to use routing resources outside the bounding box formed by its terminals. Of course, congestion must be resolved to obtain a feasible mapping, but given the routing-rich nature of modern reconfigurable devices, and assuming that routing is performed on a reasonable placement, the area formed by a net's bounding box is most likely to be used.

However, traditional Dijkstra's searches expand from the source of a net evenly in all directions. Given that the source of a 2-terminal net must lie on the edge of the bounding box, this is obviously wasteful since, again ignoring congestion costs, the search essentially progresses as concentric rings—most of which lie in the incorrect direction for finding the sink. As shown in Figure 20.3, it is unlikely that a useful route will require such a meandering path. If we would like to find

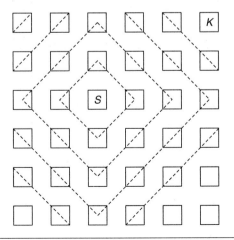

FIGURE 20.3 ■ A conventional routing search wave.

a route between blocks *S* and *K*, it is most likely that we will be able to find a direct route between them. Thus, we should direct the majority of our efforts upward and to the right before exploring downward or to the left. As described in Chapter 17, this is the motivation for adding A^* enhancements to the PathFinder algorithm. However, this concept can be taken even further by formally preventing searches from extending very far beyond the net's bounding box.

According to Betz et al. [3], a reasonable fixed limitation can prevent an exploration from visiting routing channels more than three steps outside of a net's bounding box. Although this technique may degrade routability under conditions of very high congestion, such situations may not be encountered. An architecture might have sufficient resources so that high-stress routing situations are never created, particularly in scenarios where the user is willing to reduce the amount of logic mapped to an FPGA to improve compilation runtimes.

Slightly more difficult to manage is the case of multi-terminal nets. Although the scope of a multisink search as a whole may be limited by the net's bounding box, this only alleviates one source of typically unnecessary exploration. PathFinder generally sorts the sinks of a multi-terminal net by Manhattan distance. However, each time a sink is discovered, the search for the next sink is restarted based on the entire routing tree found up to that point. As shown in Figure 20.4, this creates a wide search ring that is explored and reexplored each time a new sink is discovered, which is particularly problematic for high-fanout nets.

If we consider the new sink and the closest portion of the existing routing tree to be almost a 2-terminal net by itself, we can further reduce the amount of extraneous exploration. Swartz et al. [15] suggest splitting the bounding box of multi-terminal nets into gridlike bins. As shown in Figure 20.5, after a sink is found, a new search is launched for the next furthest sink, but explorations are only started from the portion of the routing tree contained in the bin closest to the new target. In our example, after a route to *K*1 is found, only the portion

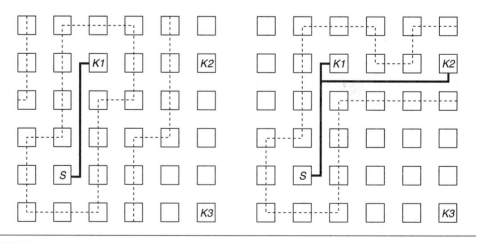

FIGURE 20.4 ▪ PathFinder exploration and multi-terminal nets.

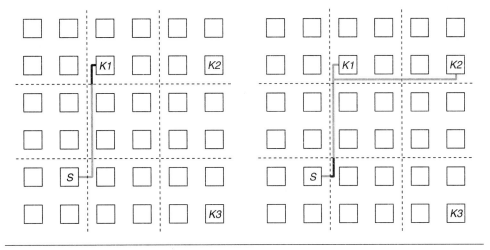

FIGURE 20.5 ■ Multi-terminal nets and region segmentation.

of the existing path in the topmost bin is used to launch a search for *K2*. The process of restricting the initialization of the search is repeated to find a route to *K3*. This may result in slightly longer branches, but, again, it is not an issue in low-stress routing situations.

Although potentially very effective, all of these techniques only attempt to improve the time required to route a single net. As described in Chapter 17, however, the PathFinder algorithm is relatively amenable to parallel processing. Chan et al. [7] showed that we can simply split the nets of a given circuit among multiple processors and allow each to route its nets mostly independently of the others. Similarly to what happens in parallel simulated annealing, complete faithfulness to the original PathFinder algorithm requires a large amount of communication bandwidth. This is because we have no guarantees that one processor will not attempt to route a signal on the same wire as another processor during a given iteration unless they are in constant communication with each other. However, because PathFinder already has a mechanism to discourage the overuse of routing resources between different nets over multiple iterations, such continuous communication is unnecessary. We can allow multiple processors to operate independently of one another for an entire routing iteration.

When all processors have routed all of their nets, we can simply determine which nodes were accidentally shared by different processors and increase their present sharing and history costs appropriately. Just as it discourages sharing between nets in classical single-processor PathFinder, this gradually discourages sharing between different processors over multiple iterations. We are using the built-in conflict-resolution mechanism in a slightly different way, but this allows us to reduce the communication overhead considerably. That said, after we have resolved the large-scale congestion in the system, the last few routing iterations likely must be performed on a single processor using conventional PathFinder.

Overall, these techniques are extremely effective on modern FPGAs. Most of today's reconfigurable architectures include a wealth of routing resources that are sufficient for a wide range of applications. Because of this, all of these approaches to accelerating PathFinder-style routing produce good results. Ordering of nets, fast growth of present sharing and history costs, and limiting the scope of exploration to net bounding boxes are common in modern FPGA routing tools. Unfortunately, however, they are still not fast enough for the most demanding applications such as runtime netlist compilation. Even the parallel technique outlined here has an unavoidable serial component. Thus, while such techniques may be adequate to produce results for next-generation FPGAs or hardware prototyping systems, they must be much faster if we are to make runtime netlist compilation practical.

20.2 ALTERNATIVE ALGORITHMS

Although classical mapping techniques have proven that they can achieve high-quality results, there is a limit to their acceleration through conventional means if we want to maintain acceptable quality for many applications. For example, in the case of placement the number of moves attempted in the inner loop of simulated annealing can only be reduced to a certain point before solution quality is no longer acceptable. While the runtime on a single processor can be cut by a factor of 10 with relatively little change in terms of routability or critical-path timing, even such modest degradation may not meet the most demanding design constraints. Furthermore, as discussed earlier, attempting to scale this technique beyond the $10x$ point generally results in markedly lower quality because the algorithm simply does not have sufficient time to adequately explore the solution space. To achieve further runtime improvements without resorting to potentially complex parallel implementations and without abandoning solution quality, we must make fundamental algorithmic changes.

20.2.1 Multiphase Solutions

One of the most popular ways to accelerate placement is to break the process into multiple phases, each handled by a different algorithm. Although many techniques use this method, a common thread among them all is that large-scale optimization is performed first by a fast but relatively imprecise algorithm. Slower, more accurate algorithms are reserved for local, small-scale refinement as a secondary step. A good example of this approach is shown in papers such as that by Xu and Kalid [20]. Here, the authors use a quadratic technique to obtain a rough placement and then work toward a better solution with a short simulated annealing phase.

In quadratic placement, the connections between blocks in the netlist are converted into linear equations, any valid solution to which indicates the position of each block. A good placement solution is found by solving the matrix equations while attempting to minimize another function: the sum of the squared wirelength for each net. Unfortunately, one of the problems with this approach is that, in order for the equations to be solved quickly, they must be unconstrained. Thus, the placements found directly from the quadratic solver will likely have many blocks that overlap.

Xu and Kalid [20] identify these overlapping cells and, over multiple iterations, slowly add equations that force them to move apart. This is a comparatively fast process, but the additional placement legalization factors are added somewhat arbitrarily. Thus, although the quadratic placement might have gotten all of the blocks in roughly the correct area, there is still quite a bit of room for wirelength and timing improvements.

In contrast, while simulated annealing produces very good results, much of the runtime is devoted to simply making sense of a random initial placement. By combining the two approaches, and starting a low-temperature annealing only after we obtain a reasonable initial placement from the quadratic solver phase, we can drastically reduce runtime and still maintain the majority of the solution quality. Similar approaches can substitute force-directed placement for large-scale optimization or completely greedy optimization for small-scale improvement [12].

Another way to quickly obtain relatively high-quality initial placements is with partitioning-based approaches. As mentioned in Chapter 14, although recursive bipartitioning can be performed very quickly, reducing the number of signals cut by the partitions is not necessarily the same thing as minimizing wirelength or critical path delay. A similar but more sophisticated method is also discussed in Chapter 14. In hierarchical placement, as described by Sankar and Rose [13], the logical resources of a reconfigurable architecture are roughly divided into K separate regions. Multiple clustering steps then assign the netlist blocks into groups of approximately the correct size for the K logical areas. At this point, the clusters themselves can be moved around via annealing, assuming that all of the blocks in a cluster are at the center of the region.

This annealing can be performed very quickly since the number of clusters is relatively small compared to the number of logic blocks in the netlist. We can obtain a relatively good logic block-level placement by taking the cluster-level placement and decomposing it. Here, we can take each cluster in turn and arbitrarily place every block somewhere within the region assigned to it earlier. This initial placement can then be refined with a low-temperature annealing.

Purely mechanical clustering techniques are not the only way to group related logic together and obtain rough placements very quickly. In fact, the initial design specification itself holds valuable information concerning how the circuit is constructed and how it might best be laid out. Unfortunately, this knowledge is typically lost in the conventional tool flow. Regardless of whether they are using a high-level or low-level hardware description language, the organizational methods of humans naturally form top-level designs by connecting multiple large modules together. These large modules are, in turn, also created from lower-level modules. However, information about the overall design organization is generally not passed down through logical synthesis and technology mapping tools.

Packing, placement, and routing are typically performed on a completely flattened netlist of basic logic blocks. However, as suggested in works by Gehring and Ludwig and colleagues [10] and Callahan et al. [6], for example, for most applications this innate hierarchy can suggest which pieces are heavily interconnected and should be kept close together during the mapping process. Furthermore, information about multiple instances of the same module can be used to speed the physical design process.

The datapath-oriented methodology described in Chapter 15 uses a closely related concept to help design highly structured computations. In datapath composition, the entire CAD toolflow, from initial algorithm specification to floorplanning to placement, is centered on building coarse-grained objects that have obvious, simple relationships to one another. The entire computation is built from regular, snap-together tiles that can be arranged in essentially the same order in which they appear in the input dataflow graph. Although many applications simply do not fit the restrictive nature of the datapath computation model, applications that can be implemented in this way benefit greatly from the highly regular structures these tools create.

There may not be as much regularity in most applications, but we can still use organizational information to accelerate both placement and routing. At the very least, such information provides some top-level hints to reasonable clustering boundaries and can be used to roughly floorplan large designs. In some sense, this is exactly the aim of hierarchical placement, although it attempts to accomplish this without any a priori knowledge. Extending this idea, for very large systems we can use these natural boundaries to create multiple, more or less independent top-level placement problems. Even if we place each of the large system-level modules serially on a single processor, it is likely that, because of nonlinear growth in problem complexity, the total runtime will still be smaller than if we had performed one large, unified placement.

We can also employ implicit organizational information on a smaller scale in a bottom-up fashion. For example, many modern FPGAs contain dedicated fast carry-chain logic between neighboring cells. To use these structures, however, the cells must be placed in consecutive vertical logic block locations. If we were to begin with a random initial placement for a multibit adder, we would probably not find the optimal single-column placement despite the fact that, based on higher-level information, the best organization is obvious. Such very common operations can be identified and then preplaced and routed with known good solutions. These blocks then become hard macros. Less common or larger calculations can be identified and turned into soft macros. As suggested by projects such as Tessier's [17], using the high-level knowledge of macros within a hierarchical-style placement tool can improve runtime by a factor of up to 50 without affecting solution quality.

Still, while macro identification can significantly improve placement runtime, its effect on routing runtime is likely negligible. Soft macros still need to be routed because each instance may be of a different shape. Furthermore, although hard macros do not need to be repeatedly routed, and may be relatively common, their nets represent a small portion of the overall runtime because they are typically short and are simple to route. Rather, to substantially improve routing runtime we need to address the nets that consume the largest portion of the computational effort—high-fanout nets. As discussed earlier, multi-terminal nets present a host of problems for routers such as PathFinder. In many circuits, the routing time for one or two extremely high-fanout nets can be a significant portion of the overall routing runtime. However, this effort might be unnecessary since, even though these nets are ripped up and rerouted in every iteration, they go nearly everywhere within their bounding box. This means that virtually all legal routing scenarios will create a relatively even distribution of traffic within this region and none are markedly better than any other. For this reason, we can easily route these high-fanout nets once at the beginning of the routing phase and then exclude them from following a conventional PathFinder run without seriously affecting overall routability. At the very least, if we do not want to put these nets completely outside the control of PathFinder congestion resolution, we can rip up and reroute them less frequently, perhaps every other or every third iteration.

Regardless of how the placement and routing problem is divided into simpler subproblems, multiphase approaches are the most promising way to deal with the issues associated with FPGA technology scaling. Of course, when possible it is best to gather implicit hierarchical information directly from the source hardware description language specification. This not only allows us to create both hard and soft macros very easily, but gives strong hints regarding how large designs might be floorplanned. That said, we may not have information regarding high-level module organization. In these cases we can fall back on hierarchical or partitioning placement techniques to make subsequent annealing problems much more manageable. All of these placement methodologies scale very well, and they represent algorithms that can solve the most pressing issues presented by growing reconfigurable devices and netlists.

When applicable, constructive techniques, such as the datapath-oriented methodology described in Chapter 15, or macro-based approaches can be very useful for mapping hardware prototyping systems and instance-specific circuits. These methodologies naturally produce reasonable placements very quickly. Because hardware emulation systems and instance-specific circuits do not necessarily need optimal area or timing results, these techniques often produce placements that can be used directly without the need for subsequent refinement steps.

20.2.2 Incremental Place and Route

Incremental placement and routing techniques attempt to reduce compilation time by combining and extending the same ideas exploited by multiphase compilation approaches: (1) begin with a known reasonable placement and (2) avoid ripping up and rerouting as many nets as possible.

In many situations, multiple similar versions of a given circuit might be placed and routed several times. In the case of hardware emulation, for example, it is unlikely that large portions of the circuit will change between consecutive designs. Far more likely is that small bug fixes or local modifications will be made to specific portions of the circuit, leaving the vast majority of the design completely unchanged. Incremental placement and routing methodologies identify those portions of a circuit that have not changed from a previous mapping and attempt to integrate the changed portions in the least disruptive manner. This allows successive design updates to be compiled very quickly and minimizes the likelihood of dramatic changes to the characteristics of the resultant mapping.

The key to incremental mapping techniques is to modify an existing placement as little as possible while still finding good locations for newly introduced parts. The largest hurdle to this is merely finding a legal placement for all new blocks. If the changes reduce the overall size of the resulting circuit, any new logic blocks can simply fit into the void left by the old section. However, if the overall design becomes larger, the mapping process is more complex. Although the extra blocks can simply be dropped into any available location on the chip, this will probably result in poor timing and routability. Thus, incremental mapping techniques generally use simple algorithms to slightly move blocks and make vacant locations migrate toward the modified sections of the circuit.

The most basic approaches, such as those described by Choy et al. [4], determine where the closest empty logic block locations are and then simply slide intervening blocks toward these vacancies to create space where it is needed. Singh and Brown [14] use a slightly more sophisticated approach that employs a stochastic hill-climbing methodology, similar to a restricted simulated annealing run. This algorithm takes into account where additional resources are needed, the estimated critical path of the circuit, and the estimated required wirelength. In this way, logic blocks along noncritical paths will preferentially be moved to make room for the added logic.

Incremental techniques not only speed up the placement process, but can accelerate routing as well. Because so much of the placement is not disturbed, the nets associated with those logic blocks do not necessarily have to be rerouted. Initially, the algorithm can attempt to route only the nets associated with new or moved logic blocks. If this fails, or produces unacceptable timing results, the algorithm can slowly rip up nets that travel through congested or heavily used areas and try again. Either way, it will likely need to reroute only a very small portion of the overall circuit.

Unfortunately, there are many situations in which we do not have the prior information necessary to use incremental mapping techniques. For example, the very first compilation of a netlist must be performed from scratch. Furthermore, it is a good idea to periodically perform a complete placement and routing run, because applying multiple local piecework changes, one on top of another, can eventually lead to disappointing global results. However, as mentioned earlier, incremental compilation is ideal for hardware prototyping systems because they are typically updated very frequently with minor changes. This behavior also occurs in many other development scenarios, which is why incremental compilation is a common technique to accelerate the engineering/debugging design loop.

However, there are some situations in which it is very difficult to apply incremental approaches. For example, these techniques rely on the ability to determine what portions of a circuit do or do not change between design revisions. Not only can merely finding these similarities be a difficult problem, we must also be able to carefully control how high-level synthesis, technology mapping, and logic block packing are performed. These portions of the mapping process must be aware when incremental placement and routing is going to be attempted, and when major changes have been made to the netlist and placement and routing should be attempted from scratch.

20.3 EFFECT OF ARCHITECTURE

Although we have considered many algorithmic changes that can improve compilation runtime, we should also consider the underlying reasons that the FPGA mapping problem is so difficult. Compared to standard cell designs, FPGAs are much more restrictive because the logic and routing are fixed. Technology mapping must target the lookup tables (LUTs) and small computational cores available on a given device, placement must deliver a legal arrangement that coincides with the array of provided logic blocks, and routing must contend with a fixed topology of communication resources.

For these reasons, the underlying architecture of a reconfigurable device strongly affects the complexity of design compilation. For example, routing on a device that had an infinite number of extremely fast and flexible wires in the communication network would be easy. Every signal could simply take its shortest preferred path, and routing could be performed in a single Dijkstra's pass. Furthermore, placement would also be obvious on such an architecture since even a completely arbitrary arrangement could meet design constraints. Granted, real-world physical limitations prevent us from developing such a perfect device, but we can reduce the necessary CAD effort with smart architectural design that emphasizes ease of compilation—potentially even over logic capacity and clock speed.

The Plasma architecture [2] is a good example of designing an FPGA explicitly for simple mapping. Plasma was developed as part of the Teramac project [1]—an extremely large reconfigurable computing system slated to contain hundreds or thousands of individual FPGAs. Even given that a large design would be separated into smaller pieces that could be mapped onto individual FPGAs, contemporary commercial reconfigurable devices required tens of minutes to complete placement and routing for each chip. To further compound this issue, even after placement was completed once, there was no guarantee that all of the signals could be successfully routed, so the entire process might have to be repeated. This meant that a design that utilized thousands of conventional FPGAs could require days or weeks of overall compilation time. For the Teramac system to be useful in applications such as hardware prototyping, in which design changes might be made on a daily or even hourly basis, mapping had to be orders of magnitude faster. Thus, the Plasma FPGA architecture was designed explicitly with fast mapping in mind.

Although Plasma differed from contemporary commercial FPGAs in several key ways, its most important distinction was high connectivity. Plasma was built from 6-input, 2-output logic blocks connected hierarchically by two levels of crossbars. As seen in Figure 20.6, logic blocks are separated into groups of 16 that are connected by a full crossbar that spans half the width of the chip. These groups are then connected to other groups by a central partial crossbar. The central vertical lines span a quarter of the height of the array, but have the capability to be connected together to span the entire distance. Since full crossbars would

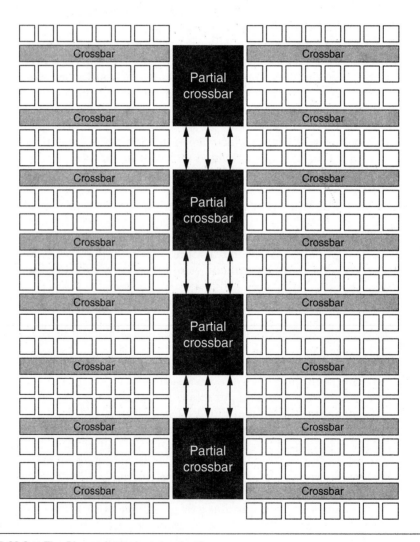

FIGURE 20.6 ■ The Plasma interconnect network.

have been prohibitively large, the developers used empirical testing to determine what level of connectivity was typically used in representational benchmarks. In addition to high internal connectivity, Plasma also contained an unusually large number of off-chip I/O pins.

Although this extremely dense routing fabric consumed 90 percent of the overall area, and its reliance on very long wires reduced the maximum operating frequency considerably, placement and routing could reliably be performed on the order of seconds on existing workstations. Given Teramac's target applications, the dramatic increase in compilation speed and the extremely consistent place and route success rate was considered to be more important than logical density or execution clock frequency.

Of course, not all applications can make such an extreme trade-off between ease of compilation and general usability metrics. However, manipulating the architecture of an FPGA does not necessarily require dramatically altering the characteristics of the device. For example, it is possible to make small changes to the interconnect to make routing simpler. One possibility is using a track domain architecture, which restricts the structure of the switch boxes in an island-style FPGA.

As shown in Figure 20.7, the connectivity of an architecture's switch boxes can affect routability. While each wire in both the top and bottom switch boxes have the same number of fanouts, the top switch box allows tracks to switch wire domains, eventually migrating to any track through multiple switch points.

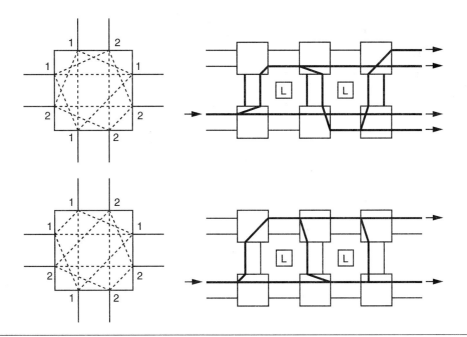

FIGURE 20.7 ■ Switch box style and routability.

This allows a signal coming in on one wire on the left of the top architecture to reach all four wires exiting the right. However, the symmetric switch box shown on the bottom does not allow tracks to switch wire domains and forces a signal to travel along a single class of wire. This means that a signal coming in from the left of the bottom architecture can only reach two of the four wires exiting to the right. Although this may reduce the flexibility of the routing fabric somewhat [18], potentially requiring more wires to achieve the same level of routability [8], this effect is relatively minor.

Even though we may need to increase the channel width of our architecture because of the restrictive nature of track domain switch boxes, routing on this type of FPGA can be dramatically faster than on more flexible systems. As shown by Cabral et al. [5], since the routing resources on track domain FPGAs are split into M different classes of wire, routing becomes a parallel problem. First, N processors are each assigned a small number of track domains from a given architecture. Then the nets from a circuit placed onto the architecture are simply split into N groups. Because each track domain is isolated from every other due to the nature of the architecture, each processor can perform normal PathFinder routing without fear that the paths found by one processor will interfere with the paths found by another. When a processor cannot route a signal on its allotted routing resources, it is given an additional unassigned track domain. Although load balancing between processors and track domains is somewhat of a problem, this technique has shown linear or even super-linear speedup with a very small penalty to routability. In this case, Cabral and colleagues [5] were able to solve the problems encountered by the parallel routing approaches that were discussed earlier by modifying the architecture itself.

Another way to modify the physical FPGA to speed routing is by offering specialized hardware to allow the device to route its own circuits. Although similar to the approach discussed earlier in which simulated annealing is implemented on a generic FPGA to accelerate the placement of its own circuits, DeHon et al. [9] suggest that by modifying the actual switch points internal to an FPGA, we can create a specialized FPGA that can assist a host processor to perform PathFinder-like routing by performing its own Dijkstra searches. In this type of architecture, the switch points have additional hardware that gives them the ability to remember the inputs and outputs currently being used when the FPGA is put into a special compilation time-only "routing search" mode.

After the placement of a given circuit is found, we configure the FPGA to perform routing on itself. This begins by clearing the occupancy markers on all of the switch points. During the routing phase, the host processor requests that each net in turn drive a signal from its source, which helps discover a path to each of its sinks. Every time this signal encounters a switching element, the switch allows the signal to propagate though unallocated resources but prevents it from continuing along occupied segments. In this way, the device explores all possible paths virtually instantaneously. When a route is found between the source and a sink, the switch point occupancy markers along this path are updated to reflect the "taken" status of these resources. When a route cannot be found for a given net, because all of the legal paths have been occupied by earlier nets, the system simply victimizes a random previously routed path and rips it up until the blocked net can successfully route. Nets are continuously routed and ripped up in this round-robin fashion until all nets have been routed. Although this approach does not have the same sophistication as PathFinder, the experiments by DeHon and colleagues [9] show that hardware-assisted routing can obtain extremely similar track counts (only 1 to 2 additional tracks) with 4 to 6 orders of magnitude speedup in terms of runtime on the largest benchmarks.

Of course, modifying an FPGA architecture can involve a great deal of engineering effort. For example, while hardware-assisted routing is one of the only approaches that is fast enough to make runtime netlist compilation feasible, it involves completely redesigning the communication network. That said, not all of our architecture modifications need to be that drastic. For example, commercial FPGA manufacturers have already made modifications to their architectures that accelerate routing. As mentioned earlier, commercial FPGAs offer a resource-rich, flexible routing fabric to support a wide range of applications. Their high bandwidth and connectivity naturally make the routing problem simpler and much faster to solve. Following this logic, it seems natural that FPGAs might switch to track domain architectures in the future. While such devices require only minor layout changes that slightly affect overall system routability, they enable very simple parallel routing algorithms to be used. This becomes more and more important as reconfigurable devices scale and as multi-threaded and multicore processors gain popularity.

20.4 SUMMARY

In this chapter we explored many techniques to accelerate FPGA placement and routing. Ultimately, all of them have restrictions, benefits, and drawbacks. This means that our applications, architectures, and design constraints must dictate which methodologies can and should be used. Several of the approaches do not provide acceptable runtime given problem constraints, while some may not offer sufficient implementation quality. Some techniques may not scale adequately to address our issues, while we may not have the necessary information to use others.

FPGA scaling. Although classical block-level simulated annealing techniques have been the cornerstone of FPGA CAD tools for decades, these methodologies must eventually be replaced. Hierarchical and macro-based techniques seem to scale much more gracefully while preserving the large-scale characteristics of high-quality simulated annealing. On the other hand, routing will likely depend on PathFinder and other negotiated congestion techniques for quite some time. That said, for compilation time to keep pace given newer and larger devices, FPGA developers need to make some architectural changes that simplify the routing problem. Track domain systems seem to be a natural solution given that modern desktops and workstations offer multiple types of parallel processing resources.

Hardware prototyping and logic emulation systems. While these systems benefit greatly from incremental mapping techniques, they still require fast place and route algorithms when compilation needs to be performed from scratch. Hardware-assisted placement seems an obvious choice that can take full advantage of the multichip arrays present in these large devices. Furthermore, since optimal critical-path timing is not essential and application source code is generally available to provide hierarchical information, datapath and macro-based approaches can be very effective.

Instance-specific designs. Datapath and macro-based approaches are even more important to instance-specific circuits because they cannot take advantage of many other techniques. However, the limited scope of these problems and the dramatic speedup made possible by these systems also make specialized architectures attractive. While the overhead imposed by architectures such as Plasma may not be practical for most commercial devices, these drawbacks are far less important to instance-specific circuits given the significant CAD tool benefits.

Runtime netlist compilation. Reconfigurable computing systems that require runtime netlist compilation present an incredibly demanding real-time compilation problem. Correspondingly, these systems require the most aggressive architectural approaches to make this possible. Radical system-wide modifications that provide huge amounts of routing resources significantly simplify the placement problem. However, just providing more bandwidth does not necessarily accelerate the routing process. These systems need to provide communication channels that either do not need to be negotiated or, through hardware-assisted routing, can automatically negotiate their own connections. An open question is whether the advantages of runtime netlist compilation are worth the attendant costs and complexities they introduce.

References

[1] R. Amerson, R. Carter, W. Culbertson, P. Kuekes, G. Snider. Teramac—configurable custom computing. *Proceedings of the IEEE Symposium on FPGAs for Custom Computing Machines*, 1995.

[2] R. Amerson, R. Carter, W. Culbertson, P. Kuekes, G. Snider, L. Albertson. Plasma: An FPGA for million gate systems. *Proceedings of ACM Symposium on Field-Programmable Gate Arrays*, 1996.

[3] V. Betz, J. Rose, A. Marquardt. *Architecture and CAD for Deep-Submicron FPGAs*, Kluwer Academic, 1999.

[4] C. Choy, T. Cheung, K. Wong. Incremental layout placement modification algorithm. *IEEE Transactions on Computer-Aided Design* 15(4), April 1996.

[5] L. Cabral, J. Aude, N. Maculan. TDR: A distributed-memory parallel routing algorithm for FPGAs. *Proceedings of International Conference on Field-Programmable Logic and Applications*, 2002.

[6] T. Callahan, P. Chong, A. Dehon, J. Wawrynek. Fast module mapping and placement for datapaths in FPGAs. *Proceedings of ACM Symposium on Field-Programmable Gate Arrays*, 1998.

[7] P. Chan, M.D.F. Schlag, C. Ebeling. Distributed-memory parallel routing for field-programmable gate arrays. *IEEE Transactions on Computer-Aided Design* 19(8), August 2000.

[8] Y. Chang, D. F. Wong, C. K. Wong. Universal switch modules for FPGA design. *ACM Transactions on Design Automation of Electronic Systems* 1(1), January 1996.

[9] A. DeHon, R. Huang, J. Wawrzynek. Hardware-assisted fast routing. *Proceedings of the IEEE Symposium on FPGAs for Custom Computing Machines*, 2002.

[10] S. Gehring, S. Ludwig. Fast integrated tools for circuit design with FPGAs. *Proceedings of ACM Symposium on Field-Programmable Gate Arrays*, 1998.

[11] M. Haldar, M. A. Nayak, A. Choudhary, P. Banerjee. Parallel algorithms for FPGA placement. *Proceedings of the Great Lakes Symposium on VLSI*, 2000.

[12] C. Mulpuri, S. Hauck. Runtime and quality trade-offs in FPGA placement and routing. *Proceedings of ACM Symposium on Field-Programmable Gate Arrays*, 2001.

[13] Y. Sankar, J. Rose. Trading quality for compile time: Ultra-fast placement for FPGAs. *Proceedings of ACM Symposium on Field-Programmable Gate Arrays*, 1999.

[14] D. Singh, S. Brown. Incremental placement for layout-driven optimizations on FPGAs. *Proceedings of the IEEE/ACM International Conference on Computer-Aided Design*, 2002.

[15] J. Swartz, V. Betz, J. Rose. A fast routability-driven router for FPGAs. *Proceedings of the ACM Symposium on Field-Programmable Gate Arrays*, 1998.

[16] R. Tessier. Negotiated A* routing for FPGAs. *Proceedings of the Canadian Workshop on Field-Programmable Devices*, 1998.

[17] R. Tessier. Fast placement approaches for FPGAs. *Transactions on Design Automation of Electronic Systems* 7(2), April 2002.

[18] S. Wilton. *Architecture and Algorithms for Field-Programmable Gate Arrays with Embedded Memory*, Ph.D. thesis, University of Toronto, 1997.

[19] M. Wrighton, A. DeHon. Hardware-assisted simulated annealing with application for fast FPGA placement. *Proceedings of the ACM Symposium on Field-Programmable Gate Arrays*, 2003.

[20] Y. Xu, M.A.S. Kalid. QPF: Efficient quadratic placement for FPGAs. *Proceedings of the International Conference on Field-Programmable Logic and Applications*, 2005.

PART IV

APPLICATION DEVELOPMENT

Creating an efficient FPGA-based computation is similar to creating any other hardware. A designer carefully optimizes his or her computation to the needs of the underlying technology, exploiting the parallelism available while meeting resource and performance constraints. These designs are typically written in a hardware description language (HDL), such as Verilog, and CAD tools are then used to create the final implementation.

Field-programmable gate arrays (FPGAs) do have unique constraints and opportunities that must be understood in order for this technology to be employed most effectively. The resource mix is fixed, and the devices are never quite fast enough or have high enough capacity for what we want to do. However, because the chips are reprogrammable we can change the system in response to bugs or functionality upgrades, or even change the computation as it executes.

Because of the unique restrictions and opportunities inherent in FPGAs, a set of approaches to application development have proven critical to exploiting these devices to the fullest. Many of them are covered in the chapters that follow. Although not every FPGA-based application will use each of the approaches, a true FPGA expert will make them all part of his or her repertoire.

Some of the most challenging questions in the design process come at the very beginning of a new project: Are FPGAs a good match for the application? If so, what problems must be considered and overcome? Will runtime reconfiguration be part of the solution? Will fixed- or floating-point computation be used? Chapter 21 focuses on this level of design, covering the important issues that arise when we first consider an application and the problems that must be avoided or solved. It also offers a quick overview of application development. Chapters 22 through 26 delve into individual concerns in more detail.

FPGAs are unique in their potential to be more efficient than even ASICs for some types of problems: Because the circuit design is completely programmable, we can create a custom circuit not just for a given problem but for a specific problem *instance*. Imagine, for example, that we are creating an engine for solving Boolean equations (e.g., a SAT solver, discussed in Chapter 29 in Part V). In an ASIC design, we would create a generic engine capable of handling any possible Boolean equation because each use of the chip would be for a different equation. In an FPGA-based system, the equation can be folded into the circuit mapping itself, creating a custom FPGA mapping optimized to solving that Boolean equation and no other. As long as there is a CPU available to dynamically create a new FPGA bitstream each time a new Boolean equation must be solved, a much more aggressively optimized design can be created. However, because this means that the time to create the new mapping is part of system execution, fast mapping algorithms are often the key (Chapter 20). This concept of instance-specific circuits is covered in Chapter 22.

In most cases, the time to create a completely new mapping in response to a specific problem instance is too long. Indeed, if it takes longer to create the custom circuit than for a generic circuit to solve the problem, the generic circuit is the better choice. However, more restricted versions of this style of optimization are still valuable. Consider a simple FIR filter, which involves multiplication of an incoming datastream with a set of constant coefficients. We could use a completely generic multiplier to handle the constant * variable computation. However, the bits of the constant are known in advance, so many parts of this multiplication can be simplified out. Multipliers, for example, generally compute a set of partial products—the result of multiplying one input with a single bit of the other input. These partial products are then added together. If the constant coefficient provided that single bit for a partial product, we can know at mapping creation time whether that partial product will be 0 or equal to the variable input—no hardware is necessary to create it. Also, in cases where the partial product is a 0, we no longer need to add it into the final result. In general, the use of constant inputs to a computation can significantly improve most metrics in FPGA mapping quality. These techniques, called constant propagation and partial evaluation, are covered in Chapter 22.

Number formats in FPGAs are another significant concern. For microprocessor-based systems we are used to treating everything as a 64-bit integer or an IEEE-format floating-point value. Because the underlying hardware is hardcoded to efficiently support these specific number formats, any other format is unlikely to be useful. However, in an FPGA we custom create the datapath. Thus, using a 64-bit adder on values that are at most 18 bits in length is wasteful because each bit position consumes one or more lookup tables (LUTs) in the device.

For this reason, an FPGA designer will carefully consider the required wordlength of the numbers in the system, hoping to shave off some bits of precision and thus reduce the hardware requirements of the design.

Fractional values, such as π or fractions of a second, are more problematic. In many cases, we can use a fixed-point format. We might use numbers in the range of $0 \ldots 31$ to represent the values from 0 to $\frac{31}{32}$ in steps of $\frac{1}{32}$ by just remembering that the number is actually scaled by a factor of 32. Techniques for addressing each of the concerns just mentioned are treated in Chapter 23.

Sometimes these optimizations simply are not possible, particularly for signals that require a high dynamic range (i.e., they must represent both very large and very small values simultaneously), so we need to use a floating-point format. This means that each operation will consume significantly more resources than its integer or fixed-point alternatives will. Chapter 31 in Part V covers floating-point operations on FPGAs in detail.

Once the number format is decided, it is important to determine how best to perform the actual computation. For many applications, particularly those from signal processing, the computation will involve a large number of constant coefficient multiplications and subsequent addition operations, such as in finite impulse response (FIR) filters. While these can be carried out in the normal, parallel adders and multipliers from standard hardware design, the LUT-based logic of an FPGA allows an even more efficient implementation. By converting to a bit–serial dataflow and storing the appropriate combination of constants into the LUTs in the FPGA, the multiply–accumulate operation can be compressed to a small table lookup and an addition. This technique, called distributed arithmetic, is covered in Chapter 24. It is capable of providing very efficient FPGA-based implementations of important classes of digital signal processing (DSP) and similar operations.

Complex mathematical operations such as sine, cosine, division, and square root, though less common than multiply–add, are still important in many applications. In some cases they can be handled by table lookup, with a table of precomputed results stored in memories inside the FPGA or in attached chips. However, as the size of the operand(s) for these functions grows, the size of the memory explodes, limiting this technique's effectiveness. A particularly efficient alternative in FPGA logic is the CORDIC algorithm. By the careful creation of an iterative circuit, FPGAs can efficiently compute many of these complex functions. The full details of the CORDIC algorithm, and its implementation in FPGAs, are covered in Chapter 25.

A final concern is the coupling of both FPGAs and central processing units (CPUs). In early systems, FPGAs were often deployed together with microprocessors or microcontrollers, either by placing an FPGA card in a host PC or by placing both resources on a single circuit board. With modern FPGAs, which can contain complete microprocessors (either by mapping their logic into LUTs or embedding a complete microprocessor into the chip's silicon layout), the coupling of CPUs and FPGAs is even more attractive. The key driver is the relative advantages of each technology. FPGAs can provide very high performance for streaming applications with a lot of data parallelism—if we have to apply the same repetitive transformation to a large amount of data, an FPGA's performance is generally very high. However, for more sequential operations FPGAs are a poor choice. Sometimes long sequences of operations, with little or no opportunity for parallelism, come up in the control of the overall system. Also, exceptional cases do occur and must be handled—for example, the failure of a component, using denormal numbers in floating point, or interfacing to command-based peripherals. In each case a CPU is a much better choice for those portions of a computation. As a result, for many computations the best answer is to use the FPGA for the data-parallel kernels and a CPU for all the other operations. This process of segmenting a complete computation into software/CPU portions and hardware/FPGA portions is the focus of Chapter 26.

CHAPTER 21

IMPLEMENTING APPLICATIONS WITH FPGAS

Brad L. Hutchings, Brent E. Nelson
Department of Electrical and Computer Engineering
Brigham Young University

Developers can choose various devices when implementing electronic systems: field-programmable gate arrays (FPGAs), microprocessors, and other standard products such as ASSPs, and custom chips or application-specific integrated circuits (ASICs). This chapter discusses how FPGAs compare to other digital devices, outlines the considerations that will help designers to determine when FPGAs are appropriate for a specific application, and presents implementation strategies that exploit features specific to FPGAs.

The chapter is divided into four major sections. Section 21.1 discusses the strengths and weaknesses of FPGAs, relative to other available devices. Section 21.2 suggests when FPGA devices are suitable choices for specific applications/ algorithms, based upon their I/O and computation requirements. Section 21.3 discusses general implementation strategies appropriate for FPGA devices. Then Section 21.4 discusses FPGA-specific arithmetic design techniques.

21.1 STRENGTHS AND WEAKNESSES OF FPGAs

Developers can choose from three general classes of devices when implementing an algorithm or application: microprocessor, FPGA, or ASIC (for simplicity, ASSPs are not considered here). This section provides a brief summary of the advantages and disadvantages of these devices in terms of time to market, cost, development time, power consumption, and debug and verification.

21.1.1 Time to Market

Time to market is often touted as one of the FPGA's biggest strengths, at least relative to ASICs. With an ASIC, from specification to product requires (at least): (1) design, (2) verification, (3) fabrication, (4) packaging, and (5) device test. In addition, software development requires access to the ASIC device (or an emulation of such) before it can be verified and completed. As immediately available standard devices, FPGAs have already been fabricated, packaged, and tested by the vendor, thereby eliminating at least four months from time to market.

More difficult to quantify but perhaps more important are: (1) refabrications (respins) caused by either errors in the design or late changes to the specification, due to a change in an evolving standard, for example, and (2) software development schedules that depend on access to the ASIC. Both of these items impact product production schedules; a respin can easily consume an additional four months, and early access to hardware can greatly accelerate software development and debug, particularly for the embedded software that communicates directly with the device.

In light of these considerations, a conservative estimate of the time-to-market advantage of FPGAs relative to ASICs is 6 to 12 months. Such a reduction is significant; in consumer electronics markets, many products have only a 24-month lifecycle.

21.1.2   Cost

Per device, FPGAs can be much less expensive than ASICs, especially in lower volumes, because the nonrecurring costs of FPGA fabrication are borne by many users. However, because of their reprogrammability, FPGAs require much more silicon area to implement equivalent functionality. Thus, at the highest volumes possible in consumer electronics, FPGA device cost will eventually exceed ASIC device cost.

21.1.3   Development Time

FPGA application development is most often approached as hardware design: applications are described in Verilog or VHDL, simulated to determine correctness, and synthesized using commercial logic synthesis tools. Commercial tools are available that synthesize behavioral programs written in sequential languages such as C to FPGAs. However, in most cases, much better performance and higher densities are achieved using HDLs, because they allow the user to directly describe and exploit the intrinsic parallelism available in an application. Exploiting application parallelism is the single best way to achieve high FPGA performance. However, designing highly parallel implementations of applications in HDLs requires significantly more development effort than software development with conventional sequential programming languages such as Java or C++.

21.1.4   Power Consumption

FPGAs consume more power than ASICs simply because programmability requires many more transistors, relative to a customized integrated circuit (IC). FPGAs may consume more or less power than a microprocessor or digital signal processor (DSP), depending on the application.

21.1.5   Debug and Verification

FPGAs are developed with standard hardware design techniques and tools. Coded in VHDL or Verilog and synthesized, FPGA designs can be debugged in simulators just as typical ASIC designs are. However, many designers verify their designs directly, by downloading them into an FPGA and testing them in a system. With this approach the application can be tested at speed (a million times faster than simulation) in the actual operating environment, where it is exposed to real-world conditions. If thorough, this testing provides a stronger form of functional verification than simulation. However, debugging applications in an FPGA can be difficult because vendor tools provide much less observability and controllability than, for example, an hardware description language (HDL) simulator.

21.1.6 FPGAs and Microprocessors

As discussed previously, FPGAs are most often contrasted with custom ASICs. However, if a programmable solution is dictated because of changing application requirements or other factors, it is important to study the application carefully to determine if it is possible to meet performance requirements with a programmable processor—microprocessor or DSP. Code development for programmable processors requires much less effort than that required for FPGAs or ASICs, because developing software with sequential languages such as C or Java is much less taxing than writing parallel descriptions with Verilog or VHDL. Moreover, the coding and debugging environments for programmable processors are far richer than their HDL counterparts. Microprocessors are also generally much less expensive than FPGAs. If the microprocessor can meet application requirements (performance, power, etc.), it is almost always the best choice.

In general, FPGAs are well suited to applications that demand extremely high performance and reprogrammability, for interfacing components that communicate with many other devices (so-called glue-logic) and for implementing hardware systems at volumes that make their economies of scale feasible. They are less well suited to products that will be produced at the highest possible volumes or for systems that must run at the lowest possible power.

21.2 APPLICATION CHARACTERISTICS AND PERFORMANCE

Application performance is largely determined by the computational and I/O requirements of the system. Computational requirements dictate how much hardware parallelism can be used to increase performance. I/O system limitations and requirements determine how much performance can actually be exploited from the parallel hardware.

21.2.1 Computational Characteristics and Performance

FPGAs can outperform today's processors only by exploiting massive amounts of parallelism. Their technology has always suffered from a significant clock-rate disadvantage; FPGA clock rates have always been slower than CPU clock rates by about a factor of 10. This remains true today, with clock rates for FPGAs limited to about 300 to 350 MHz and CPUs operating at approximately 3 GHz. As a result, FPGAs must perform at least 10 times the computational work per cycle to perform on par with processors. To be a compelling alternative, an FPGA-based solution should exceed the performance of a processor-based solution by 5 to 10 times and hence must actually perform 50 to 100 times the computational work per clock cycle. This kind of performance is feasible only if the target application exhibits a corresponding amount of exploitable parallelism.

The guideline of 5 to 10 times is suggested for two main reasons. First of all, prior to actual implementation, it is difficult or impossible to foresee the impact of various system and I/O issues on eventual performance. In our experience, 5 times can quickly become 2 times or less as various system and algorithmic issues arise during implementation. Second, application development for FPGAs is much more difficult than conventional software development. For that reason, the additional development effort must be carefully weighed against the potential performance advantages. A guideline of 5 to 10 times provides some insurance that any FPGA-specific performance advantages will not completely vanish during the implementation phase.

Ultimately, the intrinsic characteristics of the application place an upper bound on FPGA performance. They determine how much raw parallelism exists, how exploitable it is, and how fast the clock can operate. A review of the literature [3–6, 11, 16, 19–21, 23, 26, 28] shows that the application characteristics that have the most impact on application performance are: data parallelism, amenability to pipelining, data element size and arithmetic complexity, and simple control requirements.

Data parallelism

Large datasets with few or no data dependencies are ideal for FPGA implementation for two reasons: (1) They enable high performance because many computations can occur concurrently, and (2) they allow operations to be extensively rescheduled. As previously mentioned, concurrency is extremely important because FPGA applications must be able to achieve 50 to 100 times the operations per clock cycle of a microprocessor to be competitive. The ability to reschedule computations is also important because it makes it feasible to tailor the circuit design to FPGA hardware and achieve higher performance. For example, computations can be scheduled to maximize data reuse to increase performance and reduce memory bandwidth requirements. Image-processing algorithms with their attendant data parallelism have been among the highest-performing algorithms mapped to FPGA devices.

Data element size and arithmetic complexity

Data element size and arithmetic complexity are important because they strongly influence circuit size and speed. For applications with large amounts of exploitable parallelism, the upper limit on this parallelism is often determined by how many operations can be performed concurrently on the FPGA device. Larger data elements and greater arithmetic complexity lead to larger and fewer computational elements and less parallelism. Moreover, larger and more complex circuits exhibit more delay that slows clock rate and impacts performance. Not surprisingly, representing data with the fewest possible bits and performing computation with the simplest operators generally lead to the highest performance. Designing high-performance applications in FPGAs almost always involves a precision/performance trade-off.

Pipelining

Pipelining is essential to achieving high performance in FPGAs. Because FPGA performance is limited primarily by interconnect delay, pipelining (inserting registers on long circuit pathways) is an essential way to improve clock rate (and therefore throughput) at the cost of latency. In addition, pipelining allows computational operations to be overlapped in time and leads to more parallelism in the implementation. Generally speaking, because pipelining is used extensively throughout FPGA-based designs, applications must be able to tolerate some latency (via pipelining) to be suitable candidates for FPGA implementation.

Simple control requirements

FPGAs achieve the highest performance if all operations can be statically scheduled as much as possible (this is true of many technologies). Put simply, it takes time to make decisions and decision-making circuitry is often on the critical path for many algorithms. Replacing runtime decision circuitry with static control eliminates circuitry and speeds up execution. It makes it much easier to construct circuit pipelines that are heavily utilized with few or no pipeline bubbles. In addition, statically scheduled controllers require less circuitry, making room for more datapath operators, for example. In general, datasets with few or no dependencies often have simple control requirements.

21.2.2 I/O and Performance

As mentioned previously, FPGA clock rates are at least one order of magnitude slower than those of CPUs. Thus, significant parallelism (either data parallelism or pipelining) is required for an FPGA to be an attractive alternative to a CPU. However, I/O performance is just as important: Data must be transmitted at rates that can keep all of the parallel hardware busy.

Algorithms can be loosely grouped into two categories: I/O bound and compute bound [17, 18]. At the simplest level, if the number of I/O operations is equal to or greater than the number of calculations in the computation, the computation is said to be I/O bound. To increase its performance requires an increase in memory bandwidth—doing more computation in parallel will have no effect. Conversely, if the number of computations is greater than the number of I/O operations, computational parallelism may provide a speedup.

A simple example of this, provided by Kung [18], is matrix–matrix multiplication. The total number of I/Os in the computation, for n-by-n matrices, is $3n^2$—each matrix must be read and the product written back. The total number of computations to be done, however, is n^3. Thus, this computation is compute bound. In contrast, matrix–matrix addition requires $3n^2$ I/Os and $3n^2$ calculations and is thus I/O bound. Another way to see this is to note that each source element read from memory in a matrix–matrix multiplication is used n times and each result is produced using n multiply–accumulate operations. In matrix–matrix addition, each element fetched from memory is used only once and each result is produced from only a single addition.

Carefully coordinating data transfer, I/O movement, and computation order is crucial to achieving enough parallelism to provide effective speedup. The entire field of systolic array design is based on the concepts of (1) arranging the I/O and computation in a compute-bound application so that each data element fetched from memory is reused multiple times, and (2) keeping many processing elements busy operating in parallel on that data.

FPGAs offer a wide variety of memory elements that can be used to coordinate I/O and computation: flip-flops to provide single-bit storage (10,000s of bits); LUT-based RAM to provide many small blocks of randomly distributed memory (100,000s of bits); and larger RAM or ROM memories (1,000,000s of bits). Some vendors' FPGAs contain multiple sizes of random access memories, and these memories are often easily configured into special-purpose structures such as dynamic-length shift registers, content-addressable memories (CAMs), and so forth. In addition to these types of on-chip memory, most FPGA platforms provide off-chip memory as well.

Increasing the I/O bandwidth to memory is usually critical in harnessing the parallelism inherent in a computation. That is, after some point, further multiplying the number of processing elements (PEs) in a design (to increase parallelism) usually requires a corresponding increase in I/O. This additional I/O can often be provided by the many on-chip memories in a typical modern FPGA. The work of Graham and Nelson [8] describes a series of early experiments to map time-delay SONAR beam forming to an FPGA platform where memory bandwidth was the limiting factor in design speedup. While the data to be processed were an infinite stream of large data blocks, many of the other data structures in the computation were not large (e.g., coefficients, delay values). In this computation, it was not *the total amount of memory* that limited the speedup but rather the *number of memory ports available*. Thus, the use of multiple small memories in parallel were able to provide the needed bandwidth.

The availability of many small memories in today's FPGAs further supports the idea of trading off computation for table lookup. Conventional FPGA fabrics are based on a foundation of 4-input LUTs; in addition, larger on-chip memories can be used to support larger lookup structures. Because the memories already exist on chip, unlike in ASIC technology, using them adds no additional cost to the system. A common approach in FPGA-based design, therefore, is to evaluate which parts of the system's computations might lend themselves to table lookup and use the available RAM blocks for these lookups.

In summary, the performance of FPGA-based applications is largely determined by how much exploitable parallelism is available, and by the ability of the system to provide data to keep the parallel hardware operational.

21.3 GENERAL IMPLEMENTATION STRATEGIES FOR FPGA-BASED SYSTEMS

In contrast with other programmable technologies such as microprocessors or DSPs, FPGAs provide an extremely rich and complex set of implementation alternatives. Designers have complete control over arithmetic schemes and number representation and can, for example, trade precision for performance. In addition, reprogrammable, SRAM-based FPGAs can be configured any number of times to provide additional implementation flexibility for further tailoring the implementation to lower cost and make better use of the device.

There are two general configuration strategies for FPGAs: configure-once, where the application consists of a single configuration that is downloaded for the duration of the application's operation, and runtime reconfiguration (RTR), where the application consists of multiple configurations that are "swapped" in and out as the application operates [14].

21.3.1 Configure-once

Configure-once (during operation) is the simplest and most common way to implement applications with reconfigurable logic. The distinctive feature of configure-once applications is that they consist of a single system-wide configuration. Prior to operation, the FPGAs comprising the reconfigurable resource are loaded with their respective configurations. Once operation commences, they remain in this configuration until the application completes. This approach is very similar to using an ASIC for application acceleration. From the application point of view, it matters little whether the hardware used to accelerate the application is an FPGA or a custom ASIC because it remains constant throughout its operation.

The configure-once approach can also be applied to reconfigurable applications to achieve significant acceleration. There are classes of applications, for example, where the input data varies but remains constant for hours, days, or longer. In some cases, data-specific optimizations can be applied to the application circuitry and lead to dramatic speedup. Of course, when the data changes, the circuit-specific optimizations need to be reapplied and the bitstream regenerated. Applications of this sort consist of two elements: (1) the FPGA and system hardware, and (2) an application-specific compiler that regenerates the bitstream whenever the application-specific data changes. This approach has been used, for example, to accelerate SNORT, a popular packet filter used to improve network security [13]. SNORT data consists of regular expressions that detect malicious packets by their content. It is relatively static, and new regular expressions are occasionally added as new attacks are detected. The application-specific compiler translates these regular expressions into FPGA hardware that matches packets many times faster than software SNORT. When new regular expressions are added to the SNORT database, the compiler is rerun and a new configuration is created and downloaded to the FPGA.

21.3.2 Runtime Reconfiguration

Whereas configure-once applications statically allocate logic for the duration of an application, RTR applications use a dynamic allocation scheme that re-allocates hardware at runtime. Each application consists of *multiple* configurations per FPGA, with each one implementing some fraction of it. Whereas a configure-once application configures the FPGA once before execution, an RTR application typically reconfigures it many times during the normal operation.

There are two basic approaches that can be used to implement RTR applications: *global* and *local* (sometimes referred to as partial configuration in the literature). Both techniques use multiple configurations for a single application, and both reconfigure the FPGA during application execution. The principal difference between the two is the way the dynamic hardware is allocated.

Global RTR

Global RTR allocates *all* (FPGA) hardware resources in each configuration step. More specifically, global RTR applications are divided into distinct temporal phases, with each phase implemented as a single system-wide configuration that occupies all system FPGA resources. At runtime, the application steps through each phase by loading all of the system FPGAs with the appropriate configuration data associated with a given phase.

Local RTR

Local RTR takes an even more flexible approach to reconfiguration than does global RTR. As the name implies, these applications *locally* (or selectively) reconfigure subsets of the logic as they execute. Local RTR applications may configure any percentage of the reconfigurable resources at any time, individual FPGAs may be configured, or even single FPGA devices may themselves be partially reconfigured on demand. This flexibility allows hardware resources to be tailored to the runtime profile of the application with finer granularity than that possible with global RTR. Whereas global RTR approaches implement the execution process by loading relatively large, global application partitions, local RTR applications need load only the necessary functionality at each point in time. This can reduce the amount of time spent downloading configurations and can lead to a more efficient runtime hardware allocation.

The organization of local RTR applications is based more on a *functional* division of labor than the phased partitioning used by global RTR applications. Typically, local RTR applications are implemented by functionally partitioning an application into a set of fine-grained operations. These operations need not be temporally exclusive—many of them may be active at one time. This is in direct contrast to global RTR, where only one configuration (per FPGA) may be active at any given time. Still, with local RTR it is important to organize the operations such that idle circuitry is eliminated or greatly reduced. Each operation is implemented as a distinct circuit module, and these circuit modules are then downloaded to the FPGAs as necessary during operation. Note that, unlike global RTR, several of these operations may be loaded simultaneously, and each may consume any portion of the system FPGA resources.

RTR applications

Runtime Reconfigured Artificial Neural Network (RRANN) is an early example of a global RTR application [7]. RRANN divided the back-propagation algorithm (used to train neural networks) into three temporally exclusive configurations that were loaded into the FPGA in rapid succession during operation. It demonstrated a 500 percent increase in density by eliminating idle circuitry in individual algorithm phases.

RRANN was followed up with RRANN-2 [9], an application using local RTR. Like RRANN, the algorithm was still divided into three distinct phases. However, unlike the earlier version, the phases were carefully designed so that they shared common circuitry, which was placed and routed into identical physical locations for each phase. Initially, only the first configuration was loaded; thereafter, the common circuitry remained resident and only circuit differences were loaded during operation. This reduced configuration overhead by 25 percent over the global RTR approach.

The Dynamic Instruction Set Computer (DISC) [29] used local RTR to create a sequential control processor with a very small fixed core that remained resident at all times. This resident core was augmented by circuit modules that were dynamically loaded as required by the application. DISC was used to implement an image-processing application that consisted of various filtering operations. At runtime, the circuit modules were loaded as necessary. Although the application used all of the filtering circuit modules, it did not require all of them to be loaded simultaneously. Thus, DISC loaded circuit modules on demand as required. Only a few active circuit modules were ever resident at any time, allowing the application to fit in a much smaller device than possible with global RTR.

21.3.3 Summary of Implementation Issues

Of the two general implementation techniques, configure-once is the simplest and is best supported by commercially available tool flows. This is not surprising, as all FPGA CAD tools are derivations of conventional ASIC CAD flows. While the two RTR implementation approaches (local and global) can provide significant performance and capacity advantages, they are much more challenging to employ, primarily because of a lack of specific tool support.

The designer's primary task when implementing global RTR applications is to temporally divide the application into roughly equal-size partitions to efficiently use reconfigurable resources. This is largely a manual process—although the academic community has produced some partitioning tools, no commercial offerings are currently available. The main disadvantage of global RTR is the need for equal-size partitions. If it is not possible to evenly partition the application, inefficient use of FPGA resources will result.

The main advantage of local RTR over global RTR is that it uses fine-grained functional operators that may make more efficient use of FPGA resources. This is important for applications that are not easily divided into equal-size temporally exclusive circuit partitions. However, partitioning a local RTR design may require an inordinate amount of designer effort. For example, unlike global

RTR, where circuit interfaces typically remain fixed between configurations, local RTR allows these interfaces to change with each configuration. When circuit configurations become small enough for multiple configurations to fit into a single device, the designer needs to ensure that all configurations will *interface* correctly one with another. Moreover, the designer may have to ensure not only structural compliance but *physical* compliance as well. That is, when the designer creates circuit configurations that do not occupy an entire FPGA, he or she will have to ensure that the physical footprint of each is compatible with that of others that may be loaded concurrently.

21.4 IMPLEMENTING ARITHMETIC IN FPGAs

Almost since their invention, FPGAs have employed dedicated circuitry to accelerate arithmetic computation. In earlier devices, dedicated circuitry sped up the propagation of carry signals for ripple-carry, full-adder blocks. Later devices added dedicated multipliers, DSP function blocks, and more complex fixed-function circuitry. The presence of such dedicated circuitry can dramatically improve arithmetic performance, but also restricts designers to a very small subset of choices when implementing arithmetic.

Well-known approaches such as carry-look-ahead, carry-save, signed-digit, and so on, generally do not apply to FPGAs. Though these techniques are commonly used to create very high-performance arithmetic blocks in custom ICs, they are not competitive when applied to FPGAs simply because they cannot access the faster, dedicated circuitry and must be constructed using slower, general-purpose user logic. Instead, FPGA designers accelerate arithmetic in one of two ways with FPGAs: (1) using dedicated blocks if they fit the needs of the application, and (2) avoiding the computation entirely, if possible. Designers apply the second option by, for example, replacing full-blown floating-point computation with simpler, though not equivalent, fixed-point, or block floating-point, computations. In some cases, they can eliminate multiplication entirely with constant propagation. Of course, the feasibility of replacing slower, complex functions with simpler, faster ones is application dependent.

21.4.1 Fixed-point Number Representation and Arithmetic

A fixed-point number representation is simply an integer representation with an implied binary point, usually in 2's complement format to enable the representation of both positive and negative values. A common way of describing the structure of a fixed-point number is to use a tuple: n, m, where n is the number of bits to the left of the binary point and m is the number of bits to the right. A 16.0 format would thus be a standard 16-bit integer; a 3.2 format fixed-point number would have a total of 5 bits with 3 to the left of the implied binary point and 2 to the right. A range of numbers from $+1$ to $-1A$ is common in digital signal-processing applications. Such a representation might be of the form 1.9, where the largest number is 0.111111111 = 0.99810 and the smallest is 1.000000000 = −1₁₀. As can be seen, fixed-point arithmetic exactly follows the rules learned in grade school, where lining up the implied binary point is required for performing addition or subtraction.

When designing with fixed-point values, one must keep track of the number format on each wire; such bookkeeping is one of the design costs associated with fixed-point design. At any point in a computation, either truncation or rounding can be used to reduce the number of bits to the right of the binary point, the effect being to simply reduce the precision with which the number is represented.

21.4.2 Floating-point Arithmetic

Floating-point arithmetic overcomes many of the challenges of fixed-point arithmetic but at increased circuit cost and possibly reduced precision. The most common format for a floating-point number is of the form *seeeeffffff*, where *s* is a sign bit, *eeeee* is an exponent, and *ffffff* is the mantissa. In the IEEE standard for single-precision floating point, the number of exponent bits is 8 and the number of mantissa bits is 23, but nonstandard sizes and formats have also been used in FPGA work [2, 24].

IEEE reserves various combinations of exponent and mantissa to represent special values: zero, not a number (NAN), infinity (+8 and −8), and so on. It supports denormalized numbers (no leading implied 1 in the mantissa) and flags them using a special exponent value. Finally, the IEEE specification describes four rounding modes. Because supporting all special case number representations and rounding modes in hardware can be very expensive, FPGA-based floating-point support often omits some of them in the interest of reducing complexity and increasing performance.

For a given number of bits, floating point provides extended *range* to a computation at the expense of *accuracy*. An IEEE single-precision floating-point number allocates 23 bits to the mantissa, giving an effective mantissa of only 24 bits when the implied 1 is considered. The advantage of floating point is that its exponent allows for the representation of numbers across a broad range (IEEE normalized single-precision values range from $\approx \pm 3 \times 10^{38}$ to $\approx \pm 1 \times 10^{-38}$). Conversely, while a 32-bit fixed-point representation (1.31 format) has a range of only −1 to $\approx +1$, it can represent some values within that range much more accurately than a floating-point format can—for example, numbers close to +1 such as 0.11111111111111111111111111111111. However, for numbers very close to +0, the fixed-point representation would have many leading zeroes, and thus would have *less* precision than the competing floating-point representation.

An important characteristic of floating point is its auto-scaling behavior. After every floating-point operation, the result is normalized and the exponent adjusted accordingly. No work on the part of the designer is required in this respect (although significant hardware resources are used). Thus, it is useful in cases where the range of intermediate values cannot be bounded by the designer and therefore where fixed point is unsuitable.

The use of floating point in FPGA-based design has been the topic of much research over the past decade. Early papers, such as Ligon and colleagues [15] and Shirazi et al. [24], focused on the cost of floating point and demonstrated that small floating-point formats as well as single-precision formats could be eventually implemented using FPGA technology. Later work, such as that by Bellows and Hutchings [1] and Roesler and Nelson [22], demonstrated novel ways of leveraging FPGA-specific features to more efficiently implement floating-point modules. Finally, Underwood [27] argued that the capabilities of FPGA-based platforms for performing floating point would eventually surpass those of standard computing systems.

All of the research just mentioned contains size and performance estimates for floating-point modules on FPGAs at the time they were published. Clever design techniques and growing FPGA densities and clock rates continually combine to produce smaller, faster floating-point circuits on FPGAs. At the time of this writing, floating-point module libraries are available from a number of sources, both commercial and academic.

21.4.3 Block Floating Point

Block floating point (BFP) is an alternative to fixed-point and floating-point arithmetic that allows entire blocks of data to share a single exponent. Fixed-point arithmetic is then performed on a block of data with periodic rescaling of its data values. A typical use of block floating point is as follows:

1. The largest value in a block of data is located, a corresponding exponent is chosen, and that value's fractional part is normalized to that exponent.
2. The mantissas of all other values in the block are adjusted to use the same exponent as that largest value.
3. The exponent is dropped and fixed-point arithmetic proceeds on the resulting values in the data block.
4. As the computation proceeds, renormalization of the entire block of data occurs—after every individual computation, only when a value overflows, or after a succession of computations.

The key is that BFP allows for growth in the range of values in the data block while retaining the low cost of fixed-point computations. Block floating point has found extensive use in fast Fourier transform (FFT) computations where an input block (such as from an A/D converter) may have a limited range of values, the data is processed in stages, and stage boundaries provide natural renormalization locations.

21.4.4 Constant Folding and Data-oriented Specialization

As mentioned Section 21.3.2, when the data for a computation changes, an FPGA can be readily reconfigured to take advantage of that change. As a simple example of data folding, consider the operation: $a = ?b$, where a and b are 4-bit

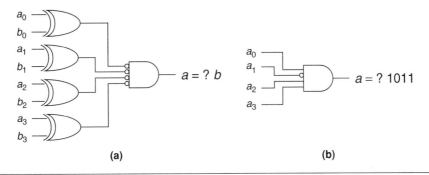

FIGURE 21.1 ■ Two comparator implementations: (a) with and (b) without constant folding.

numbers. Figure 21.1 shows two implementations of a comparator. On the left
(a) is a conventional comparator; on the right (b) is a comparator that may be
used when b is known ($b = 1011$). Implementation (a) requires three 4-LUTs to
implement while implementation (b) requires just one. Such logic-level constant
folding is usually performed by synthesis tools.

A more complex example is given by Wirthlin [30], who proposed a method
for creating constant coefficient multipliers. When one constant to a multiplier
was known, a custom multiplier consuming far fewer resources than a general multiplier could usually be created. Wirthlin's manipulations [30], going
far beyond what logic optimization performed, created a custom structure for a
given multiplier instance based on specific characteristics of the constant.

Hemmert et al. [10] offer an even more complex example in which a pipeline
of image morphology processing stages was created, each of which could perform one image morphology step (e.g., one iteration in an erosion operation).
The LUT contents in each pipeline stage controlled the stage's operation; thus,
reconfiguring a stage required modifying only LUT programming. A compiler
was then created to convert programs, written in a special image morphology
language, into the data required to customize each pipeline stage's operation.

When a new image morphology program was compiled, a new bitstream for
the FPGA could be created in a second or two (by directly modifying the original
bitstream) and reconfigured onto the platform. This provided a way to create a
custom computing solution on a per-program basis with turnarounds on the
order of a few seconds. In each case, the original morphology program that was
compiled provided the constant data that was folded into the design.

Additional examples in the literature show the power of constant folding.
However, its use typically requires specialized CAD support. Slade and Nelson
[25] argue that a fundamentally different approach to CAD for FPGAs is the
solution to providing generalized support for such data-specific specialization.
They advocate the use of JHDL [1, 12] to provide deployment time support for
data-specific modifications to an operating FPGA-based system.

In summary, FPGAs provide architectural features that can accelerate simple arithmetic operations such as fixed-point addition and multiplication.

Floating-point operations can be accelerated using block floating point or by reducing the number of bits to represent floating-point values. Finally, constants can be propagated into arithmetic circuits to reduce circuit area and accelerate arithmetic performance.

21.5 SUMMARY

FPGAs provide a flexible, high-performance, and reprogrammable means for implementing a variety of electronic applications. Because of their reprogrammability, they are well suited to applications that require some form of direct reprogrammability, and to situations where reprogrammability can be used indirectly to increase reuse and thereby reduce device cost or count. FPGAs achieve the highest performance when the application can be implemented as many parallel hardware units operating in parallel, and where the aggregate I/O requirements for these parallel units can be reasonably met by the overall system. Most FPGA applications are described using HDLs because HDL tools and synthesis software are mature and well developed, and because, for now, they provide the best means for describing applications in a highly parallel manner.

Once FPGAs are determined to be a suitable choice, there are several ways to tailor the system design to exploit their reprogrammability by reconfiguring them at runtime or by compiling specific, temporary application-specific data into the FPGA circuitry. Performance can be further enhanced by crafting arithmetic circuitry to work around FPGA limitations and to exploit the FPGA's special arithmetic features. Finally, FPGAs provide additional debug and verification methods that are not available in ASICs and that enable debug and verification to occur in a system and at speed.

In summary, FPGAs combine the advantages and disadvantages of microprocessors and ASICs. On the positive side, they can provide high performance that is achievable only with custom hardware, they are reprogrammable, and they can be purchased in volume as a fully tested, standard product. On the negative side, they remain largely inaccessible to the software community; moreover, high-performance application development requires hardware design and the use of standard synthesis tools and Verilog or VHDL.

References

[1] P. Bellows, B. L. Hutchings. JHDL—An HDL for reconfigurable systems. *Proceedings of IEEE Workshop on FPGAs for Custom Computing Machines*, April 1998.
[2] B. Catanzaro, B. Nelson. Higher radix floating-point representations for FPGA-based arithmetic. *Proceedings of the IEEE Symposium on FPGAs for Custom Computing Machines*, April 2005.
[3] W. Culbertson, R. Amerson, R. Carter, P. Kuekes, G. Snider. Exploring architectures for volume visualization on the Teramac custom computer. *Proceedings of IEEE Workshop on FPGAs for Custom Computing Machines*, April 1996.

[4] A. Dandalis, V. K. Prasanna. Fast parallel implementation of DFT using configurable devices. Field-programmable logic: Smart applications, new paradigms, and compilers. *Proceedings 6th International Workshop on Field-Programmable Logic and Applications*, Springer-Verlag, 1997.

[5] C. H. Dick, F. Harris. FIR filtering with FPGAs using quadrature sigma-delta modulation encoding. Field-programmable logic: Smart applications, new paradigms, and compilers. *Proceedings 6th International Workshop on Field-Programmable Logic and Applications*, Springer-Verlag 1996.

[6] C. Dick. Computing the discrete Fourier transform on FPGA-based systolic arrays. *ACM/SIGDA International Symposium on Field-Programmable Gate Arrays*, February 1996.

[7] J. G. Eldredge, B. L. Hutchings. Density enhancement of a neural network using FPGAs and runtime reconfiguration. *Proceedings of the IEEE Workshop on FPGAs for Custom Computing Machines*, April 1994.

[8] P. Graham, B. Nelson. FPGA-based sonar processing. *ACM/SIGDA International Symposium on Field-Programmable Gate Arrays*, February 1998.

[9] J. D. Hadley, B. L. Hutchings. Design methodologies for partially reconfigured systems. *Proceedings of the IEEE Workshop on FPGAs for Custom Computing Machines*, April 1995.

[10] S. Hemmert, B. Hutchings, A. Malvi. An application-specific compiler for high-speed binary image morphology. *Proceedings of the the 9th Annual IEEE Symposium on Field-Programmable Custom Computing Machines*, 2001.

[11] R. Hudson, D. Lehn, P. Athanas. A runtime reconfigurable engine for image interpolation. In *Proceedings of the IEEE Symposium on FPGAs for Custom Computing Machines*, IEEE, April 1998.

[12] B. L. Hutchings, P. Bellows, J. Hawkins, S. Hemmert, B. Nelson, M. Rytting. A CAD suite for high-performance FPGA design. *Proceedings of the IEEE Workshop on FPGAs for Custom Computing Machines*, April 1999.

[13] B. L. Hutchings, R. Franklin, D. Carver. Assisting network intrusion detection with reconfigurable hardware. *Proceedings of the IEEE Symposium on FPGAs for Custom Computing Machines*, IEEE, April 2002.

[14] B. L. Hutchings, M. J. Wirthlin. Implementation approaches for reconfigurable logic applications. *Field-Programmable Logic and Applications*, August 1995.

[15] W. B. Ligon III, S. McMillan, G. Monn, K. Schoonover, F. Stivers, K. D. Underwood. A re-evaluation of the practicality of floating-point operations on FPGAs. *Proceedings of the IEEE Symposium on FPGAs for Custom Computing Machines*, 1998.

[16] W. E. King, T. H. Drayer, R. W. Conners, P. Araman. Using MORPH in an industrial machine vision system. *Proceedings of the IEEE Workshop on FPGAs for Custom Computing Machines*, April 1996.

[17] H. T. Kung. Why Systolic Architectures? *IEEE Computer* 15(1), 1982.

[18] S. Y. Kung. *VLSI Array Processors*, Prentice-Hall, 1988.

[19] T. Moeller, D. R. Martinez. Field-programmable gate array based radar front-end digital signal processing. *Proceedings of the IEEE Workshop on FPGAs for Custom Computing Machines*, April 1999.

[20] G. Panneerselvam, P. J. W. Graumann, L. E. Turner. Implementation of fast Fourier transforms and discrete cosine transforms in FPGAs. *Fifth International Workshop on Field-Programmable Logic and Applications*, September 1995.

[21] R. J. Petersen. *An Assessment of the Suitability of Reconfigurable Systems for Digital Signal Processing*, Master's thesis, Brigham Young University, 1995.

[22] E. Roesler, B. Nelson. Novel optimizations for hardware floating-point units in a modern FPGA architecture. *Proceedings of the 12th International Workshop on Field-Programmable Logic and Applications*, August 2002.

[23] N. Shirazi, P. M. Athanas, A. L. Abbott. Implementation of a 2D fast Fourier transform on an FPGA-based custom computing machine. *Fifth International Workshop on Field-Programmable Logic and Applications*, September 1995.

[24] N. Shirazi, A. Walters, P. Athanas. Quantitative analysis of floating point arithmetic on FPGA-based custom computing machines. *Proceedings of the IEEE Workshop on FPGAs for Custom Computing Machines*, April 1995.

[25] A. Slade, B. Nelson. Reconfigurable computing application frameworks. *Proceedings of the IEEE Symposium on Field-Programmable Custom Computing Machines*, April 2003.

[26] L. E. Turner, P. J. W. Graumann, S. G. Gibb. Bit-serial FIR filters with CSD coefficients for FPGAs. *Fifth International Workshop on Field-Programmable Logic and Applications*, September 1995.

[27] K. Underwood. FPGAs vs. CPUs: Trends in peak floating-point performance. *Proceedings of the ACM/SIGDA 12th International Symposium on Field-Programmable Gate Arrays*, 2004.

[28] J. E. Vuillemin. On computing power. Programming languages and system architectures. *Lecture Notes in Computer Science*, vol. 781, Springer-Verlag, 1994.

[29] M. J. Wirthlin, B. L. Hutchings (eds). A dynamic instruction set computer. *Proceedings of the IEEE Workshop on FPGAs for Custom Computing Machines*, April 1995.

[30] M. J. Wirthlin. Constant coefficient multiplication using look-up tables. *Journal of VLSI Signal Processing* 36, 2004.

CHAPTER 22

INSTANCE-SPECIFIC DESIGN

Oliver Pell, Wayne Luk
Department of Computing
Imperial College, London

This chapter covers instance-specific design, an optimization technique involving effective exploitation of information specific to an instance of a generic design description. Here we introduce different types of instance-specific designs with examples. We then describe partial evaluation, a systematic method for producing instance-specific designs that can be automated. Our treatment covers the application of partial evaluation to hardware design in general, and to field-programmable gate arrays (FPGAs) in particular.

22.1 INSTANCE-SPECIFIC DESIGN

FPGAs are an effective way to implement designs in computationally intensive datapath-oriented applications such as cryptography, digital signal processing, and network processing. The main alternative implementation technologies in these application areas are general-purpose processors, digital signal processors, and application-specific integrated circuits (ASICs).

ASICs are integrated circuits designed to implement a single application directly in fixed hardware. Because they are specialized to a single application, they can be very efficient, with reduced resource usage and power consumption over processor-based software implementations. Reconfigurable logic offers similar advantages over general-purpose processors. However, the overhead of providing general-purpose logic and routing resources means that FPGA-based systems typically provide lower density and performance than ASICs. Still, reconfigurable logic can provide a level of specialization beyond what is possible for an ASIC: optimizing circuits not just for a particular problem but for a particular *instance* of it. For example, an encryption application can create custom FPGA mappings every time a new password is given, allowing any password to be supported yet providing very highly optimized circuitry.

The basic concept of instance-specific design is to optimize a circuit for a particular computation. This can allow a reduction in area and/or an increase in processing speed by sacrificing the flexibility of the circuit. It is important to distinguish between the FPGA itself, which is inherently flexible and can be reconfigured to suit any application by loading a new bitstream, and the current configuration of the chip, which may have a certain level of flexibility in processing its inputs.

One common way of achieving instance-specific designs automatically is constant folding (Section 22.2.3), which involves propagating static input values through a circuit to eliminate unnecessary logic. Thus, in our encryption example, an exclusive-or (XOR) gate with one input driven by a password bit can be replaced with a wire or an inverter because the value of that bit is known for each specific password.

To produce an instance-specific design, one first needs a means of providing a particular instance for a given design. In the previous encryption example, if all the passwords are known at design time, an instance-specific design specialized for each password can be produced, say by constant propagation followed by the usual tools such as placement (Chapter 14), routing (Chapter 17), and bitstream generation (Chapter 19).

At runtime, a processor is often used to control the configuration of the FPGA by the appropriate bitstream at the right moment to support a particular password. However, if the passwords are known only at runtime, then the designer has to decide whether the benefits of having instance-specific designs outweigh the time to produce them, since, for instance, current place and route tools often take a long time to complete and their use is usually not recommended at runtime. Fortunately for some applications, differences between instances are so small that they can be generated realistically using runtime partial evaluation (Section 22.2).

The ability to implement specialized designs, while at the same time providing flexibility by allowing different specialized designs to be loaded onto a device, can make reconfigurable logic more effective at implementing some applications than what is possible with ASICs. For other applications, performance improvements from optimizing designs to a particular problem instance can help shift the price/performance ratio away from ASICs and toward FPGAs. Specializing a Data Encryption Standard (DES) crypto-processor, for example, can save 60 percent in area, while replacing general multipliers with constant coefficient versions can save area and lead to speedups of two to four times. Instance-specific designs can also consume lower power. Bit-width optimization of digital filters, for example, has been shown to reduce power consumption by up to 98 percent [2].

Changing an instance-specific design at runtime is generally much slower than changing the inputs of a general circuit, because a new (or partial) configuration must be loaded. Because this may take many tens or hundreds of milliseconds, it is important to carefully choose how a design is specialized.

22.1.1 Taxonomy

Types of instance-specific optimizations

We can divide the different approaches to optimizing a design for a particular problem instance into three main categories. Table 22.1 lists some examples of the different categories used.

Constant folding Constant folding is the process of eliminating unnecessary logic that computes functions with some inputs that never change or that

TABLE 22.1 ▪ Examples of the uses of instance-specific designs

	Purpose	Example use	Impact
Constant folding	Optimize logic for static inputs	Key-specific DES	60% area reduction
Function adaptation	Optimize for desired quality of result	Accuracy-guaranteed bit-width optimization [4]	26% area reduction, 12% latency reduction
Architecture adaptation	Achieve a specified performance, area, or power target	Custom instruction processors [3]	72% decrease in runtime for 3% more area

change only rarely. This logic can be specialized to increase performance and reduce area. Examples of circuits that can benefit from constant folding will be seen later, and a more detailed description of the technique can be found in Section 22.2.3.

Function adaptation Function adaptation is the process of altering a circuit's function to achieve a specific quality of result. Typically this involves varying the number of bits used to represent data values or switching between floating-point and fixed-point arithmetic functions. It can also involve adding or removing parts of processing units that affect accuracy—for example, adding or removing stages from a CORDIC circuit. Word-length optimization can be treated automatically (Chapter 23), modifying a circuit's area to meet particular accuracy constraints.

Architecture adaptation Architecture adaptation alters the way in which a circuit computes a result while keeping the overall function the same. This can entail introducing additional parallelism to increase speed, serializing existing parallel processing units to save area, or refining processing capabilities to exploit some expected characteristics of the input data. Custom instruction processors (see Figure 22.4 later) are one example of the latter type of architecture adaptation.

22.1.2 ▪ Approaches

Instance-specific circuits can be produced either by specializing a general-purpose circuit or by starting directly from a "template" that must be instantiated for a particular problem instance before use, as shown in Figure 22.1. Specialization has the advantage that it can often be performed automatically, using techniques such as partial evaluation (Section 22.2). The template approach probably requires the manual design of a template circuit substantially different from the general-purpose architecture, but it can possibly provide a greater level of optimization than what is possible through specializing a general-purpose circuit. It can also offer the advantage that the hardware compilation process may need to be

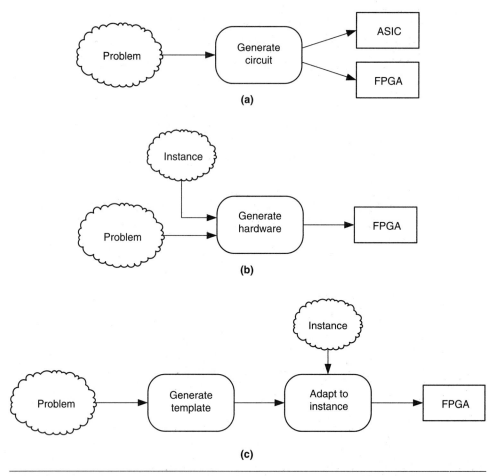

FIGURE 22.1 ■ General-purpose hardware (a) can be implemented using FPGAs or ASICs. Instance information (b) can be incorporated at hardware generation to produce a specialized circuit. "Template" hardware (c) can be generated and then instantiated for particular problem instances. The reason for the differences between (b) and (c) are that, in (b) the time-consuming process of hardware compilation must be executed for each instance while in (c) hardware compilation may only need to be run once, after which the final circuit bitstream can be amended.

executed only once, with instance-specific information being annotated directly into the bitstream.

In both cases, one or more instance-specific designs will be produced that can be converted into bitstreams through the FPGA design flow (see chapters in Part III). The appropriate bitstream can then be used to configure an FPGA, usually under the control of a general-purpose processor; during the reconfiguration process the FPGA will usually not be able to process data, although some partially reconfigurable devices can support the reconfiguration of some of its resources, while some of its other resources stay operational.

22.1.3 Examples of Instance-specific Designs

The benefits of instance-specific design can be illustrated by considering a few examples of its use. In this section we present three examples of specialization by constant folding into an existing design, and two examples of architecture adaptation.

Constant coefficient multipliers

If using standard logic cells, multipliers are relatively expensive to implement on FPGAs. A standard combinational multiplier ANDs each bit of input B with all bits of input A (to perform the multiply by 0/1); an adder is then used to sum together the partial products. When one coefficient of the multiplication is constant, however, the required area can be reduced dramatically. The AND functions are unnecessary because multiplying by a fixed 0 or 1 is trivial, and the adders can be eliminated for bits of B that are 0 (and thus have a partial product of 0). Constant coefficient multiplication is a useful operation in many signal-processing applications.

Finite impulse response (FIR) filters contain a set of multiply–add cells that multiply the value of the input signal across a number of cycles with filter coefficients and then sum these values. The multiplier coefficients are properties of the filter and do not change with the input data, but only need adjusting when different filter properties are required. Thus, the generic multipliers in a FIR filter circuit can often be replaced by smaller constant coefficient multipliers. (see Figure 22.2).

Another application that requires multipliers with constant coefficients is conversion from RGB to YUV video signals. This is a matrix multiplication operation where one matrix is constant, allowing specialized multipliers to be used.

Key-specific crypto-processors

Cryptographic algorithms are often designed for efficient implementation in both hardware and software. Block ciphers, such as DES and its successor Advanced Encryption Standard (AES), have regular algorithmic structures consisting of simple operations, such as XOR and bit permutation, that are efficiently implemented in hardware.

The DES algorithm consists of 16 "rounds," or processing stages, that can be pipelined for parallel operation. Blocks of 64-bit data are input to the array along with a 56-bit key and processed through each round, with the same key required to decrypt the data at the other end of the communication channel. A single DES round is illustrated in Figure 22.3.

In typical operation it is likely that a crypto-processor is used to process large blocks of data with the same key—for example, when transferring data between a single sender and receiver in a network or encrypting a large file to be saved to disk. It is therefore expected that, in contrast to the data input, the key value will change very slowly.

The shaded area of Figure 22.3 is key generator circuitry that generates the round key from the master key and then uses it as an input to a set of 2-input XOR functions across the data bits.

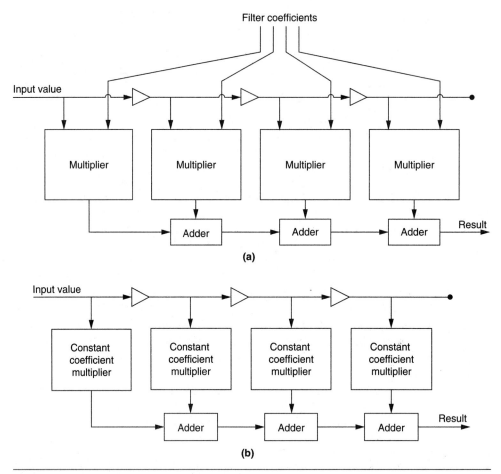

FIGURE 22.2 ▪ FIR filters utilizing (a) general multipliers with variable filter coefficients and (b) instance-specific multipliers specialized to filter coefficients.

When the key value is known, the key generation circuitry can be eliminated and the XOR functions replaced with either wires or inverters [5]. In fact, these inverters can be merged into the substitution stage, eliminating the inverter logic as well [11]. Key-specific crypto-processors can exhibit much higher throughput than general versions, even outperforming ASIC implementations. Area savings are also significant—a relatively simple specialization of a placed DES description can yield area savings of 60 percent when implemented on a Xilinx Virtex FPGA [9].

Network intrusion detection
Network Intrusion Detection Systems (NIDS) perform deep packet inspection on network packets to identify malicious attacks. Normally, these systems are implemented in software, but on high-speed networks software alone is often unable to process all traffic at the full data rate.

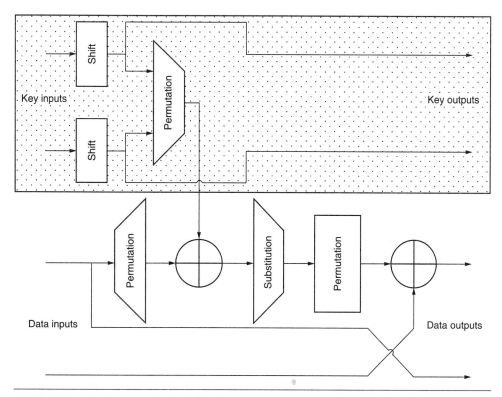

FIGURE 22.3 ■ A single round of a DES circuit. The shaded area contains key expansion circuitry that can be eliminated in a key-specific DES circuit, allowing the XOR function to be optimized.

The SNORT open source NDIS (see *http://www.snort.org*) uses a rule-based language to detect abnormal network activities. It contains thousands of rules, more than 80 percent of which contain signatures that must be matched against packet contents. Eighty percent of the CPU time for SNORT is consumed by this string-matching task [6]. String matching can be done efficiently in hardware and in particular can be easily optimized for particular search strings. While network data might be expected to arrive at high speed, the rule set changes much more slowly, so string-matching circuitry on FPGAs can be customized to match particular signatures. Section 22.2.5 illustrates in more detail how an instance-specific pattern matcher can be constructed. Further information about instance-specific designs for SAT solving applications can be found in Chapter 29.

Customizable instruction processors
General-purpose instruction processors are very flexible computational devices. Application-specific instruction processors, in contrast, have been customized to perform particularly well in a particular application area. This is a form of architecture adaptation that can improve performance for particular problem instances while maintaining the flexibility of the overall system.

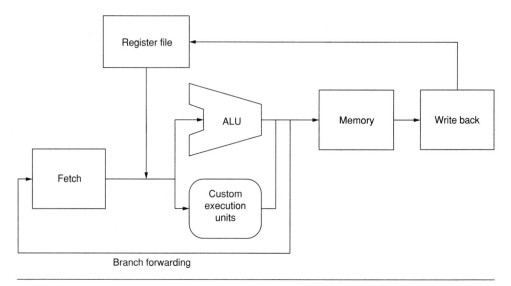

FIGURE 22.4 ▪ A simplified architecture of a custom instruction processor. The standard arithmetic and logic operations are augmented by custom execution units that can accelerate particular applications.

Figure 22.4 illustrates the architecture of a simple custom instruction processor that has standard arithmetic and logic functions implemented by a standard ALU. These functions can be supported by additional custom execution units to accelerate particular applications. The automatic identification of instructions that can benefit from the custom execution units is a topic of active research [1]. Further information about partitioning sequential and parallel programs for software and hardware execution can be found in Chapter 26.

22.2 PARTIAL EVALUATION

Partial evaluation is a process that automates specialization in software or hardware. In both cases the motivation is the same: to produce a design that runs faster than the original. In software, partial evaluation can be thought of as a combination of constant folding, loop unrolling, function inlining, and interprocedural analyses; in hardware, constant folding is mainly used as an optimization method.

Partial evaluation is accomplished by detecting fragments of hardware that depend exclusively on variables with fixed values and then optimizing the hardware logic to reduce its area or even eliminate it totally from the design by precomputing the result.

22.2.1 Motivation

Partial evaluation can simplify logic, and thus reduce area and increase performance. Figure 22.5 illustrates its impact on a 2-input XOR function. When both inputs are dynamic, the logical function must be implemented; however, when one input is known, a partial evaluator can simplify the circuit. If one input is fixed high, the XOR functions as an inverter and so can be replaced by a 1-input NOT gate; if the input is fixed low, the XOR serves as a wire and the logic can be completely eliminated.

Constant folding propagates constants through a circuit and can substantially simplify logic functions. This can both reduce area (by allowing functions to be implemented using fewer LUTs) and increase performance (by reducing the number of logic levels between registers).

In this chapter we highlight two related uses of partial evaluation for circuits. The first, at the beginning of Section 22.2.4, optimizes generic circuit descriptions for improved performance. That is, circuits are described using clear and easily maintainable but nonoptimal design patterns, which are then automatically optimized during synthesis. The second, in the middle of Section 22.2.4, specializes general circuits when some inputs are static, such as constant coefficient arithmetic.

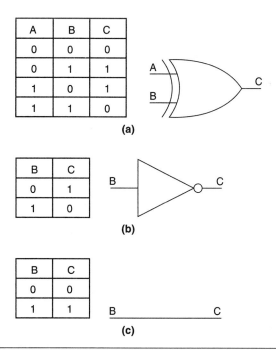

FIGURE 22.5 ■ Partial evaluation of an XOR gate. (a) A 2-input XOR function can be specialized, when input A is to become static: (b) an inverter when A is true or (c) a wire when A is false.

22.2.2   Process of Specialization

Consider a general circuit C producing output R, whose inputs are partitioned into two sets S and D.

$$R = C(S,D)$$

This circuit can be specialized for a particular set of S inputs such that it computes the same result for all possible inputs D:

$$R = C_{S=X}(D)$$

A partial evaluator is an algorithm that, when supplied with values for the set of inputs S and the circuit C, produces a specialized circuit $C_{S=X}$.

$$C_{S=X} = \mathbf{P}(C,S,X)$$

where S is the set of static inputs that are known at compile time, and D is the set of dynamic inputs. The importance of partial evaluation is that the specialized circuit computes precisely the same result as the original circuit, though it may require less hardware to do so.

Relating this framework to the XOR gate example, $R = \text{XOR}(A,B)$, with $S = \{A\}$ and $D = \{B\}$, the two possible simplified functions can be described as

$$R = \text{XOR}_{A=X}(B)$$

for the two possible values of A.

$$\text{XOR}_{A=0} = \text{P}(\text{XOR},A,0) = \text{NOT}(B)$$
$$\text{XOR}_{A=1} = \text{P}(\text{XOR},A,1) = B$$

22.2.3   Partial Evaluation in Practice

Constant folding in logical expressions

Partial evaluation of logic is well understood and has been used to simplify circuit logic for many years. Figure 22.6 gives a simple partial evaluation function, $P(S)[[X]]$, for optimizing Boolean logic expressions expressed using *not*, *and*, and *or* connectives. The function is parameterized by a set S of pairs mapping static variables to their values and a Boolean expression X represented as a tree.

The function is defined recursively on the structure of Boolean expressions. Cases (1), (2), and (3) are base conditions, indicating that partial evaluation of the Boolean constants True and False always has no effect, and partial evaluation of a variable a returns either the constant value of that variable (if it is contained within the static inputs) or the variable name if it is not static (i.e., remains dynamic).

Case (4) defines partial evaluation of a single-input *not* function. If the subexpression evaluates to logical truth or falsity, this is inverted by the conditional

```
(1) P(S)[[True]]       = True

(2) P(S)[[ False ]]    = False

(3) P(S)[[ a ]]        = if a ∈ dom(S) then P(S)[[ S(a) ]] else a

(4) P(S)[[ ¬ x ]]      = Let y = P(S)[[ x ]]
                         If y == True then False
                         Else if y == False then True
                         Else ¬ y

(5) P(S)[[ x & y ]]    = Let x' = P(S)[[ x ]]
                         Let y' = P(S)[[ y ]]
                         if(x' == False || y' == False) then False
                         Else if x' == True then y'
                         Else if y' == True Then x'
                         Else x' & y'

(6) P(S)[[ x+y ]]      = Let x' = P(S)[[ x ]]
                         Let y' = P(S)[[ y ]]
                         If(x' == True || y' == True) then True
                         Else if x' == False then y'
                         Else if y' == False then x'
                         Else x+y
```

FIGURE 22.6 ■ A partial evaluation algorithm for simplifying Boolean logic expressions.

check. Otherwise, the partially evaluated subexpression is returned with the *not* operation.

Cases (5) and (6) define partial evaluation of 2-input *and* and *or* functions. The process is the same: Simplify the subexpressions, precompute the function result if possible, and, if not, return the function with simplified arguments.

As an example, consider the application of this algorithm to the simplification of the XOR function in Figure 22.5. XOR can be described in terms of basic Boolean operators as

$$a \text{ xor } b = (a \,\&\, \neg b) + (\neg a \,\&\, b)$$

Partially evaluating when a is asserted, the function is executed:

$$\text{(i)} \quad P(\{a \rightarrow \text{True}\})[[(a \,\&\, \neg b) + (\neg a \,\&\, b)]]$$

Case (6) for simplifying logical-or is used, and the two subexpressions are partially evaluated separately:

$$\text{(ii)} \quad P(\{a \rightarrow \text{True}\})[[a \,\&\, \neg b]]$$
$$\text{(iii)} \quad P(\{a \rightarrow \text{True}\})[[\neg a \,\&\, b]]$$

Both (ii) and (iii) are partially evaluated by the case for logical-and. For (ii) the two subexpressions are first evaluated as

$$\text{(iv)} \quad P(\{a \rightarrow \text{True}\})[[a]] = \text{True}$$
$$\text{(v)} \quad P(\{a \rightarrow \text{True}\})[[\neg b]] = \neg b$$

In (iv), the variable a is within the static inputs S and thus is simplified to True, while $\neg b$ is unchanged because it does not contain a. The results from partially evaluating (iii) are similar:

(vi) $P(\{a \rightarrow \text{True}\})[[\neg a]] = P(\{a \rightarrow \text{True}\})[[\neg \text{True}]] = \text{False}$

(vii) $P(\{a \rightarrow \text{True}\})[[b]] = b$

Equipped with the simplified subexpressions, the expression $a \,\&\, \neg b$ is simplified to $\neg b$ and the expression $\neg a \,\&\, b$ is simplified to False. At the top level this gives a logical-or: $\neg b + \text{False}$:

(viii) $P(\{a \rightarrow \text{True}\})[[\neg b + \text{False}]] = \neg b$

The XOR function reduces to a single inverter; if supplied with $\{a \rightarrow \text{False}\}$ the partial evaluation function instead returns just b, indicating the simple wire. This is consistent with the truth tables in Figure 22.5.

The partial evaluation function just given is quite simple and does not capture all possible optimizations. For example, the logic function $a + \neg a$ always evaluates to True, regardless of the value of a; however, this expression will not be simplified by this function.

Unnecessary logic removal

Another optimization that can be carried out during partial evaluation is removal of dead logic in a design, which does not affect any output and thus is unnecessary. This is a very important optimization because it allows generic hardware blocks computing many functions to be used in designs, with unused functions pruned during synthesis.

As an algorithmic process, logic removal is quite simple and can be formulated in a number of different ways. One of the simplest is to identify each gate whose output is unconnected and eliminate it. By recursively applying this rule we can eliminate acyclic dead logic.

22.2.4   Partial Evaluation of a Multiplier

Optimizing a simple description

Figure 22.7 shows a shift–add circuit designed for a Xilinx architecture to compute the 3-bit multiplication of two 3-bit inputs. This circuit appears semi-regular, with x and y inputs propagating horizontally and vertically through a triangular array of processing cells. Each processing cell has common features; however, it contains slightly different logic depending on its position in the array.

Creating and maintaining a circuit description that contains and correctly connects the different types of cell is quite complicated. A simpler approach is to exploit the regularity to describe the circuit as an array of a single type of cell that is then partially evaluated during synthesis to produce the circuit in Figure 22.7.

The general cell of the multiplier can be described as shown in Figure 22.8. This cell implements a multiplication operation for 1 bit of x and 1 bit of y,

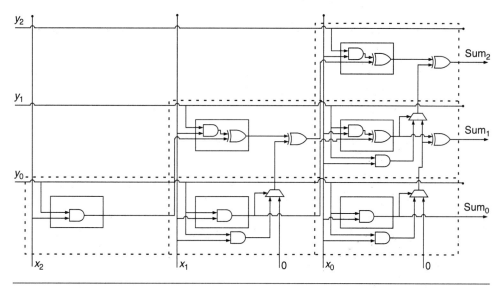

FIGURE 22.7 ■ A shift–add multiplier circuit that takes two 3-bit inputs and produces a 3-bit output.

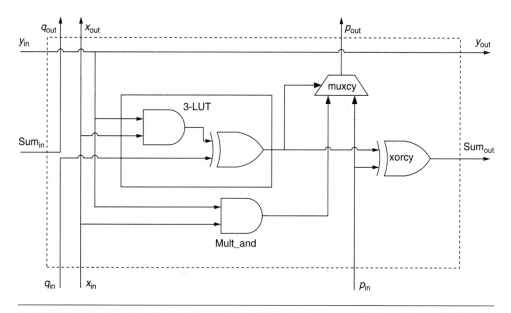

FIGURE 22.8 ■ This cell design can be replicated in a grid arrangement to create a multiplier.

producing sum and carry-out bits, and can be arranged in a grid to generate a multiplication circuit identical in function to that shown in Figure 22.8. These cells can be implemented densely on Xilinx architectures by using the specialized `mult_and`, `xorcy`, and `muxcy` components in each slice.

Partial evaluation can automatically produce the optimized multiplication circuitry from the initial regular description. The four components within each cell each have their own logical formula. In the case of `mult_and`, `xorcy`, and `muxcy`, no simplification is possible unless we can totally eliminate these functions, because these are fixed resources on the device, compared with the LUT, which can flexibly implement any 4-input function.

The logic of the standard cell can be represented as

$$LUT_{out} = (Y_{in} \& X_{in}) \operatorname{xor} Q_{in} = (\neg (Y_{in} \& X_{in}) \& Q_{in}) + ((Y_{in} \& X_{in}) \& \neg Q_{in})$$
$$AND_{out} = (Y_{in} \& X_{in})$$
$$P_{out} = (LUT_{out} \& P_{in}) + (\neg LUT_{out} \& AND_{out})$$
$$SUM_{out} = (\neg LUT_{out} \& P_{in}) + (LUT_{out} \& \neg P_{in})$$

This logic can be simplified by two operations: removing unconnected logic and constant folding to optimize the logic that remains. Removal of disconnected logic transforms the grid into the triangular array, while constant folding can be performed by the partial evaluation function introduced in Figure 22.6.

For example, for the cells along the bottom in Figure 22.8, inputs Q_{in} and P_{in} are all zero. This allows the LUT contents to be optimized by

$$LUT_{out}' = P(\{Q_{in} \rightarrow \text{False}, SUM_{in} \rightarrow \text{False}, P_{in} \rightarrow \text{False}\})$$
$$[[(\neg(Y_{in} \& X_{in}) \& Q_{in}) + ((Y_{in} \& X_{in}) \& \neg Q_{in})]] = (Y_{in} \& X_{in})$$

The function attempts to partially evaluate both branches of the OR expression. On the left branch, $\neg(Y_{in} \& X_{in})$ cannot be further optimized and so is left intact; however, Q_{in} is known to be false, so the entire left branch must be false and thus is eliminated. On the right branch, $\neg Q_{in}$ is evaluated to true and eliminated from the expression, leaving $(Y_{in} \& X_{in})$ as the simplified function for the LUT contents.

AND_{out} cannot be simplified because both Y_{in} and X_{in} are unknown. Neither can P_{out} because, although it can be partially optimized (because P_{in} is false), it is a fixed component available on the FPGA that cannot be simplified. Partial evaluation of SUM_{out} does succeed in eliminating logic:

$$SUM_{out}' = P(\{Q_{in} \rightarrow \text{False}, SUM_{in} \rightarrow \text{False}, P_{in} \rightarrow \text{False}\})$$
$$[[(\neg LUT_{out} \& P_{in}) + (LUT_{out} \& \neg P_{in})]] = LUT_{out}$$

The result of this partial evaluation is that the bottom cells of the multiplier are optimized to remove the unnecessary `xorcy` component and to simplify the 3-input LUT function into a basic 2-input AND function.

Functional specialization for constant inputs
If some of the input values to the multiplication circuit are known statically, we can apply constant folding to eliminate further logic. For example, assume that x_1 is static and always zero. Partially evaluating the cell logic under the new assumption that $\{X_{in} \rightarrow \text{False}\}$ we find that the entire cell can be eliminated and replaced with pure routing. The simplified cell is shown in Figure 22.9.

Because a single bit of the x input is shared with an entire column of the multiplier, this specialized cell can be used for the full column, replacing all the logic with routing, as shown in Figure 22.10; this arrangement in turn allows optimizations to be applied to the second LUT in the final column to eliminate the XOR function (not shown in the figure so that the routing can be seen).

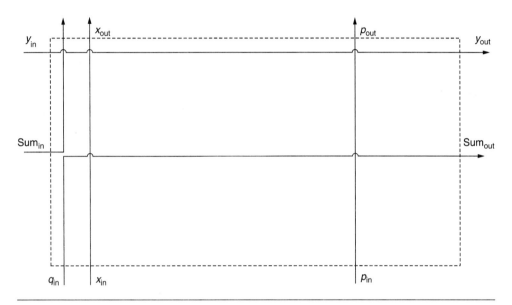

FIGURE 22.9 ■ The impact of partial evaluation on multiplier cell logic when X_{in} = False.

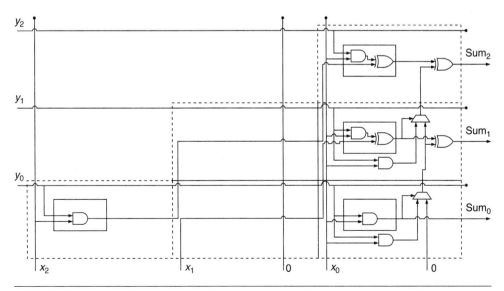

FIGURE 22.10 ■ Multiplier circuit specialized by eliminating the center column when x_i is always zero.

When an x value is known to be true, partial evaluation can still carry out some optimizations. However, it does not offer the significant advantages that result when x is false. The LUT can again be optimized to a 2-input function and the `mult_and` component can be eliminated. This is not very significant, however—the `mult_and` component is already present on the device, so no area is saved, and it is utilized in parallel with the (slower) LUT so there is also no performance gain.

Geometric specialization

High-performance FPGA designs often include layout information to produce good placements with low routing delays (see Chapter 17). Specialization of placed designs may lead to nonoptimal results if the placement is not updated to reflect eliminated logic. Automatic placement is not affected, since partial evaluation is usually carried out at the synthesis stage prior to placement and routing. However, when hand-placed designs are specialized, the effect can be to introduce unnecessary delays by failing to compact components. These gaps can also prevent effective use of freed logic because it is fragmented among other components. To ensure a good placement of specialized designs it is necessary to optimize placement information, compacting the circuit. This can be achieved in a framework that allows partial evaluation prior to placement position generation [8] or by describing circuit layouts in a way that adapts when the circuit is specialized [12].

22.2.5 Partial Evaluation at Runtime

Pattern matching is a relatively simple operation that can be performed efficiently in hardware. It is useful in a range of fields but is of particular interest in networking for inspecting the contents of data packets.

Figure 22.11 illustrates a simple general pattern matcher made up of a repeating bit-level matcher cell. Each cell contains a pattern and a mask value, which can be loaded separately from the data to be matched. Input data is streamed in 1 bit per cycle; if the mask value for a particular bit position is set, the cell for that position checks the current data value against the bit pattern.

The pattern matcher requires one LUT and three registers for each bit in the data pattern. However, it is likely that the pattern and mask values will change much more slowly than the data input, so it is reasonable to investigate the potential for partial evaluation to optimize this circuit for fixed patterns.

When the pattern and mask are fixed, the registers storing their values can be eliminated and the logic in the LUTs can be optimized. Figure 22.12 shows how the pattern matcher can be optimized for a pattern of "10X1" (the third pattern bit is a "don't care," as specified by the mask of "1101"). This circuit uses fewer registers and three LUTs rather than four. The significance of this particular way of optimizing is that the pattern matcher's structure has mostly been maintained and thus this specialization can be carried out at runtime.

Changes to the mask require routing changes—complex, though far from impossible at runtime; however, the pattern to be matched can be changed merely by updating the LUT contents.

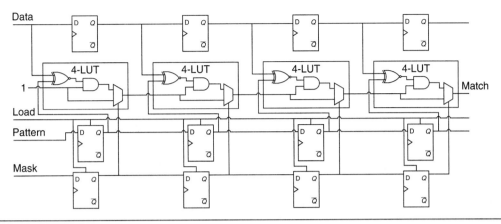

FIGURE 22.11 ■ A general bit-level pattern matcher, shown for 4-bit patterns. The pattern matcher circuit is controlled by a pattern and a mask, which can be loaded by asserting the load signal. If the mask bit is set for a particular position, the matcher will attempt to detect a match between the pattern bit and the data bit.

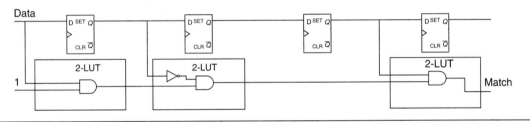

FIGURE 22.12 ■ An instance-specific pattern matcher optimized for a mask of `1101` and pattern of `10X1` requires only three LUTs and four registers.

22.2.6 FPGA-specific Concerns

LUT mapping

Recall the pattern matcher example from the previous section, where we showed one partial evaluation of the circuit for a particular pattern. In this case partial evaluation significantly simplified the contents of each LUT, from a 4-input function to a much simpler 2-input function.

It is important that, in contrast to ASICs, there is often no performance advantage to be gained by reducing the complexity of logic functions in an FPGA unless the number of LUTs required to implement those functions is reduced. The propagation delay of a LUT is independent of the function it implements; thus, there is no gain in reducing a 4-input function to a 2-input function within the same LUT (although it does allow routing resources to be freed for other uses).

For runtime specialization, it may be desirable to maintain much of the original circuit structure. However, when partial evaluation is carried out at compile time it should be performed before logic is mapped to LUTs, giving more scope for improvements in circuit area and performance. Figure 22.13 shows that the

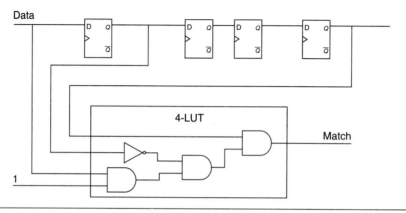

FIGURE 22.13 ▪ The instance-specific pattern matcher from Figure 22.12 can be implemented using a single 4-LUT rather than three 2-LUTs.

specialized pattern matcher can indeed be implemented using one 4-LUT rather than three 2-LUTs, with higher performance and lower area requirements than the version partially evaluated at runtime.

In fact, the static 1-input can also be eliminated from this LUT; however, it has been left to indicate that this LUT structure can be used as part of a chain in a larger pattern matcher.

Static resources

As alluded to in the multiplier example, the existence of specific resources on an FPGA in addition to LUTs, such as carry chain logic, poses a problem for automatic partial evaluation algorithms. Not only can this logic not be simplified (for example, the xorcy gate cannot be replaced with an inverter), in some cases it cannot be eliminated at all because of routing constraints (carry signals must propagate through muxcy multiplexers, for example, regardless of necessity).

Furthermore, it is often important to maintain use of the dedicated carry chain, even though significantly simpler logic could perhaps be generated after partial evaluation, because the carry chain is designed to propagate carry signals very quickly—and much faster than the general routing fabric.

Verification of runtime specialization

Dynamic specialization at runtime poses additional verification problems over and above verification of an original design. While a circuit may have been verified through extensive simulation or formal methods prior to synthesis, when it is specialized at runtime it is possible for new errors to be introduced.

To avoid this it is necessary to ensure that the algorithms that apply partial evaluation at runtime have themselves been verified. Formal proof is an appropriate methodology for this problem, since it is necessary to check a generic property of the algorithm applied to all circuits rather than any particular specialization operation.

Although formal verification has been applied to partial evaluation algorithms for specialization of FPGA circuits [7, 14], it remains a relatively unexplored area.

22.3 SUMMARY

This chapter described instance-specific design, which offers the opportunity to exploit the reconfigurable nature of FPGAs to improve performance by tailoring circuits to particular problem instances. It can be broadly categorized into three techniques: constant folding, which can be applied when some inputs are static; function adaptation, which alters the function of circuitry to produce a certain quality of result; and architecture adaptation, in which the circuit architecture is adapted without affecting its functional behavior.

The level of automation that can be applied varies among these approaches. Constant folding can often be carried out automatically using partial evaluation techniques. Function adaptation can be performed by varying bit widths and arithmetic methods in parameterized IP cores. Tools, such as Quartz (for low-level design) [12] or ASC (for stream architectures) [10], can produce highly parameterized circuit cores where design parameters can be traded off against each other to achieve the desired requirements in area, speed, and power consumption. Architecture adaptation, such as adding additional processing units to instruction processors, is typically much less automated. The designer must create separate implementations of the different architectures, optimizing each of them somewhat independently.

References

[1] K. Atasu, R. Dimond, O. Mencer, W. Luk, C. Özturan, G. Dündar. Optimizing instruction-set extensible processors under data bandwidth constraints. *Proceedings of Design, Automation and Test in Europe Conference*, 2007.

[2] G. A. Constantinides. Perturbation analysis for word-length optimization. *Proceedings of the IEEE Symposium on Field-Programmable Custom Computing Machines*, 2003.

[3] R. Dimond, O. Mencer, W. Luk. Application-specific customisation of multi-threaded soft processors. *IEE Proceedings on Computers and Digital Techniques*, May 2006.

[4] D. Lee, A. Abdul Gaffar, R.C.C. Cheung, O. Mencer, W. Luk, G. A. Constantinides. Accuracy guaranteed bit-width optimization. *IEEE Transactions on Computer-Aided Design of Integrated Circuits and Systems*, October 2006.

[5] J. Leonard, W. Magione-Smith. A case study of partially evaluated hardware circuits: Key-specific DES. *Proceedings of the International Workshop on Field-Programmable Logic and Applications*, 1997.

[6] E. P. Markatos, S. Antonatos, M. Polychronakis, K. G. Anagnostakis. Exclusion-based signature matching for intrusion detection. *Proceedings of IASTED International Conference on Communication and Computer Networks*, 2002.

[7] S. McKeever, W. Luk. Provably-correct hardware compilation tools based on pass separation techniques. *Formal Aspects of Computing*, June 2006.

[8] S. McKeever, W. Luk, A. Derbyshire. Towards verifying parametrised hardware libraries with relative placement information. *Proceedings of the 36th IEEE Hawaii International Conference on System Sciences*, 2003.

[9] S. McKeever, W. Luk, A. Derbyshire. Compiling hardware descriptions with relative placement information for parameterised libraries. *Proceedings of International Conference on Formal Methods in Computer-Aided Design*, LNCS 2517, 2002.

[10] O. Mencer. ASC: A stream compiler for computing with FPGAs. *IEEE Transactions on Computer-Aided Design*, August 2006.

[11] C. Patterson. High performance DES encryption in Virtex FPGAs using JBits. *Proceedings of the IEEE Symposium on Field-Programmable Custom Computing Machines*, 2000.

[12] O. Pell, W. Luk. Compiling higher-order polymorphic hardware descriptions into parametrised VHDL libraries with flexible placement information. *Proceedings of the International Workshop on Field-Programmable Logic and Applications*, 2006.

[13] O. Pell, W. Luk. Quartz: A framework for correct and efficient reconfigurable design. *Proceedings of the International Conference on Reconfigurable Computing and FPGAs*, 2005.

[14] K. W. Susanto, T. Melham. Formally analyzed dynamic synthesis of hardware. *Journal of Supercomputing* 19(1), 2001.

CHAPTER 23

PRECISION ANALYSIS FOR FIXED-POINT COMPUTATION

George A. Constantinides
Department of Electrical and Electronic Engineering
Imperial College, London

Many values in a computation are naturally represented by integers, which have very efficient hardware implementations; basic operations are relatively cheap, and they map well to an FPGA's underlying hardware. However, some computations naturally result in fractional values, that is, numbers where part or all of the value are less than 1—for example, 0.25, 3.25, and π—or that are so large that representation as integers is too costly—for example, 10^{120}. Handling these values is a significant concern because the hardware necessary to compute on *scaled* values can be significant in speed, power consumption, and area.

In arithmetic for reconfigurable computing designs, it is common to employ fixed point instead of floating point to represent scaled values. This chapter explores the reason for this design decision and the associated analysis that must be performed in order to choose an appropriate fixed-point representation for a particular design. Since designs for reconfigurable logic can be customized for particular applications, it is appropriate to fit the number system to the underlying application properties.

23.1 FIXED-POINT NUMBER SYSTEM

In general-purpose computing, floating-point representations are most commonly used for the representation of numbers containing fractional components. The floating-point representations standardized by the IEEE [22] have several advantages, the foremost being portability across different computational platforms.

In general, we may consider a floating-point number $X[t]$ at time t as made up of two components: a signed mantissa $M[t]$ and a signed exponent $E[t]$ (see equation 23.1). Within this representation, the ratio of the largest positive value of X to the smallest positive value of X varies exponentially with the exponent $E[t]$ and hence doubly exponentially with the number of bits used to store the exponent. As a result, it is possible to store a wide dynamic range with only a few bits of exponent, while the mantissa maintains the precision of the representation across that range by dividing the corresponding interval for each exponent into equally spaced representable values.

$$X[t] = M[t] \cdot 2^{E[t]} \qquad (23.1)$$

However, the flexibility of the floating-point number system comes at a price. Addition or subtraction of two floating-point numbers requires the alignment of radix ("decimal") points, typically resulting in a large, slow, and power-hungry barrel shifter. In a general-purpose computer, this is a minor concern compared to the need to easily support a wide range of applications. This is why processors designed for general-purpose computing typically have a built-in floating-point unit.

In embedded applications, where power consumption and silicon area are of significant concern, the fixed-point alternative is more often used [24]. We can consider fixed point as a degenerate case of floating point, where the exponent is fixed and cannot vary with time (i.e., $E[t] = E$). The fixing of the exponent eliminates the need for a variable alignment and thus the need for a barrel shifter in addition and subtraction. In fact, basic mathematical operations on fixed-point values are essentially identical to those on integer values. However, compared to floating point, the dynamic range of the representation is reduced because the range of representable values varies only singly exponentially with the number of bits used to represent the mantissa.

When implementing arithmetic in reconfigurable logic, the fixed-point number system becomes even more attractive. If a low-area fixed-point implementation can be achieved, space on the device can be freed for other logic. Moreover, the absence of hardware support for barrel shifters in current-generation reconfigurable logic devices results in an even higher area and power overhead compared to that in fully custom or ASIC technologies.

23.1.1 Multiple-wordlength Paradigm

For simplicity we will restrict ourselves to 2's complement representations, although the techniques presented in this chapter apply similarly to most other common representations. Also, we will use dataflow graphs, also known as signal flow graphs in the digital signal processing (DSP) community, as a simple underlying model of computation [12]. In a dataflow graph, each atomic computation is represented by a vertex $v \in V$, and dataflow between these nodes is represented by a set of directed edges $S \subseteq V \times V$. To be consistent with the terminology used in the signal-processing community, we will refer to an element of S as a *signal*; the terms *signal* and *variable* are used interchangeably.

The multiple-wordlength paradigm is a design approach that tries to fit the precision of each part of a datapath to the precision requirements of the algorithm [8]. It can be best introduced by comparison to more traditional fixed-point and floating-point implementations. Each 2's complement signal $j \in S$ in a multiple-wordlength implementation of a dataflow graph (V, S) has two parameters n_j and p_j, as illustrated in Figure 23.1(a). The parameter n_j represents the

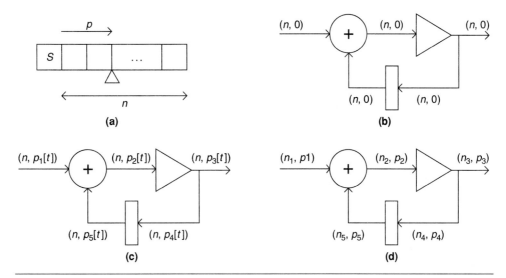

FIGURE 23.1 ■ The multiple-wordlength paradigm: (a) signal parameters ("s" indicates a sign bit); (b) fixed point; (c) floating point; (d) multiple wordlength. The triangle represents a constant coefficient multiplication, or "gain"; the rectangle represents a register, or unit sample delay.

number of bits in the representation of the signal (excluding the sign bit, by convention), and the parameter p_j represents the displacement of the binary point from the least significant bit (LSB) side of the sign bit toward the LSB. Note that there are no restrictions on p_j; the binary point could lie outside the number representation (i.e., $p_j < 0$ or $p_j > n_j$).

A simple fixed-point implementation is illustrated in Figure 23.1(b). Each signal j in this dataflow graph representing a recursive DSP algorithm is annotated with a tuple (n_j, p_j) representing the wordlength scaling of the signal. In this implementation, all signals have the same wordlength and scaling, although shift operations are often incorporated in fixed-point designs in order to provide an element of scaling control [25]. Figure 23.1(c) shows a standard floating-point implementation, where the scaling of each signal is a function of time.

A single systemwide wordlength is common to both fixed and floating point. This is a result of historical implementation on single, or multiple, predesigned arithmetic units. In FPGAs the situation is quite different. Different operations are generally computed in different hardware resources, and each of these computations can be built to any size desired. Such freedom points to an alternative implementation style, shown in Figure 23.1(d). This multiple-wordlength implementation style inherits the speed, area, and power advantages of traditional fixed-point implementations, since the computation is fixed point with respect to each individual computational unit. However, by potentially allowing each signal in the original specification to be encoded by binary words with different scaling and wordlength, the degrees of freedom in design are significantly increased.

23.1.2 Optimization for Multiple Wordlength

Now that we have established the possibility of using multiple scalings and wordlengths for different variables, two questions arise: How can we optimize the scalings and wordlengths in a design to match the computation being performed, and what are the potential benefits from doing so? For FPGA-based implementation, the benefits have been shown to be significant: Area savings of up to 45 percent [8] and 80 percent [15] have been reported compared to the use of a single wordlength across the entire circuit. The main substance of this chapter is to describe suitable scaling and wordlength optimization procedures to achieve such savings.

Section 23.2 shows that we can determine the appropriate scaling for a signal from an estimation of its peak value over time. One of two main techniques—simulation based and analytical—is then introduced to perform this peak estimation. While an analytical approach provides a tight bound on the peak signal value, it is limited to computations exhibiting certain mathematical properties. For computations outside this class, an analytical technique tends to be pessimistic, and so simulation-based methods are commonly used.

Section 23.3 focuses on determining the wordlength for each signal in the computation. The fundamental issue is that, because of roundoff or truncation, the wordlength of different signals in the system can have different impacts on both the implementation area and the error observed at the computation output. Thus, any wordlength optimization system needs to perform a balancing act between these two factors when allocating wordlength to signals. The goal of the work presented in this section is to allocate wordlength so as to minimize the area of the resulting circuit while maintaining an acceptable computational accuracy at the output of the circuit.

23.2 PEAK VALUE ESTIMATION

The physical representation of an intermediate result in a bit-parallel implementation of an algorithm consists of a finite set of bits, usually encoded using 2's complement representation. To make efficient use of the resources, it is essential to select an appropriate *scaling* for each signal. Such a scaling should ensure that the representation is not overly wasteful in catering to rare or impossibly large values and that overflow errors, which lead to low arithmetic quality, do not occur often.

To determine an appropriate scaling, it is necessary to determine the peak value that each signal can reach. Given a peak value P, a power-of-two scaling p is selected with $p = \lfloor \log_2 P \rfloor + 1$, since power-of-two multiplication is free in a hardware implementation.

For some algorithms, it is possible to estimate the peak value that each signal could reach using analytic means. In the next section, such techniques for two different classes of system are discussed. The alternative, to use simulation to determine the peak signal value, is described in the following section.

Also discussed are some hybrid techniques that aim to combine the advantages of both approaches.

23.2.1 Analytic Peak Estimation

If the DSP algorithm under consideration is a linear time-invariant system, it is possible to find a tight analytic bound on the peak value reachable by every signal in it. This is the problem addressed in the section immediately following. If, on the other hand, the system is nonlinear or time varying, such an approach cannot be used. If the algorithm is nonrecursive—that is, the dataflow graph does not contain any feedback loops—data range propagation may be used to determine an analytic bound on the peak value of each signal. However, this approach, described in the next section, cannot be guaranteed to produce a tight bound.

Linear time-invariant systems

A linear time-invariant (LTI) system is one that obeys the distinct properties of linearity and time invariance. A *linear system* is one that obeys superposition—that is, if its output is the sequence $y_1[t]$ in response to input $x_1[t]$, and is $y_2[t]$ in response to input $x_2[t]$, then it will be $\alpha y_1[t] + \beta y_2[t]$ in response to input $\alpha x_1[t] + \beta x_2[t]$. A *time-invariant* system is one that, given the input $x[t]$ and the corresponding output $y[t]$, will provide output $y[t - t_0]$ a given input $x[t - t_0]$. In other words, shifting the input sequence in time merely shifts the output sequence by the same amount.

From a practical perspective, any computation made entirely of addition, constant coefficient multiplication, and delay operations is guaranteed to be LTI. This class of algorithms, while restricted, is extremely important; it contains all the fundamental building blocks of DSP, such as finite impulse response (FIR) and infinite impulse response (IIR) filters, together with transformations such as the discrete cosine transform (DCT), the fast Fourier transform (FFT), and many color–space conversions.

The remainder of this section assumes a basic knowledge of digital signal processing, in particular the z-transform and transfer functions. For the unfamiliar reader, Mitra [32] provides an excellent introduction. Readers unconcerned with the mechanics of peak estimation for LTI systems may simply take it as read that for such systems it is possible to obtain tight analytic bounds on peak signal values.

Transfer function calculation   The analytical scaling rules derived in this section rely on a knowledge of system transfer functions. A transfer function of a discrete-time LTI system between any given I/O pair is defined to be the z-transform of the sequence produced at that output, in response to a unit impulse at that input [32]; these transfer functions may be expressed as the ratio of two polynomials in z^{-1}. The transfer function from each primary input to each signal must be calculated for signal-scaling purposes. This section considers the practical problem of transfer function calculation from a dataflow graph.

Given a dataflow graph $G(V, S)$, let $V_I \subseteq V$ be the set of input nodes, $V_O \subseteq V$ be the set of output nodes, and $V_D \subseteq V$ be the set of unit sample delay nodes. For signal scaling, a matrix of transfer functions $H(z)$ is required, with elements $h_{iv}(z)$ for $i \in V_I$ and $v \in V$ representing the transfer function from the primary input i to the output of node v.

Calculation of transfer functions for nonrecursive systems is a simple task, leading to a matrix of polynomials in z^{-1}; a straightforward algorithm is presented by Constantinides et al. [12]. For recursive systems, it is necessary to identify a subset $V_c \subseteq V$ of nodes whose outputs correspond to a system *state*. In this context, a state set consists of a set of nodes that, if removed from the dataflow graph, would break all feedback loops. Once such a state set has been identified, transfer functions can easily be expressed in terms of the outputs of these nodes using algorithms suitable for nonrecursive computations.

Let $S(z)$ be a z-domain matrix representing the transfer function from each input signal to the output of each of these state nodes. The transfer functions from each input to each state node output may be expressed as in equation 23.2, where A and B are matrices of polynomials in z^{-1}. Each of these matrices represents a z-domain relationship once the feedback has been broken at the outputs of state nodes. $A(z)$ represents the transfer functions between state nodes and state nodes, and $B(z)$ represents the transfer functions between primary inputs and state nodes.

$$S(z) = AS(z) + B(z) \qquad (23.2)$$

$$H(z) = CS(z) + D(z) \qquad (23.3)$$

The matrices $C(z)$ and $D(z)$ are also matrices of polynomials in z^{-1}. $C(z)$ represents the z-domain relationship between state node outputs and the outputs of all nodes. $D(z)$ represents the z-domain relationship between primary inputs and the outputs of all nodes.

It is clear that $S(z)$ may be expressed as a matrix of rational functions (equation 23.4), where I is the identity matrix of appropriate size. This allows the transfer function matrix $H(z)$ to be calculated directly from equation 23.3.

$$S(z) = (I - A)^{-1}B \qquad (23.4)$$

Example   Consider the simple dataflow graph from Section 23.1.1, shown in Figure 23.1. Clearly, removal of any one of the four internal nodes (adder, gain, delay, or the signal branch) from it will break the feedback loop. Let us arbitrarily choose the adder node as a state node and choose the gain coefficient to be 0.1. The polynomial matrices $A(z)$ to $D(z)$ may then be calculated (equation 23.5).

$$\begin{aligned}
A(z) &= 0.1z^{-1} \\
B(z) &= 1 \\
C(z) &= [0 \ 1 \ 0.1 \ 0.1 \ 0.1 \ 0.1z^{-1}]^T \\
D(z) &= [1 \ 0 \ 0 \ 0 \ 0 \ 0]^T
\end{aligned} \qquad (23.5)$$

Calculation of $S(z)$ may then proceed following equation 23.4, yielding equation 23.6. Finally, the matrix $H(z)$ can be constructed following equation 23.3, giving equation 23.7.

$$S(z) = 1/(1 - 0.1z^{-1}) \tag{23.6}$$

$$H(z) = [1 \; 1/(1 - 0.1z^{-1}) \; 0.1/(1 - 0.1z^{-1}) \; 0.1/(1 - 0.1z^{-1}) \; 0.1/(1 - 0.1z^{-1})$$
$$0.1z^{-1}/(1 - 0.1z^{-1})]^T \tag{23.7}$$

The runtime of this algorithm grows significantly with the number of *state signals* $|V_c|$, and so selecting a small set of state signals is important. A simple approach is to select all of the delay elements in a circuit, assuming that it has no combinational cycles. Alternatively, techniques such as Levy and Low's [30] can be employed.

Scaling with transfer functions   To produce the smallest fixed-point implementation, it is desirable to utilize as much as possible of the full dynamic range provided by each internal signal representation. The first step of the optimization process is therefore to choose the smallest possible value of p_j for each signal $j \in S$ in order to guarantee no overflow.

Consider a dataflow graph $G(V, S)$, annotated with wordlengths $\boldsymbol{n}$ and scalings $\boldsymbol{p}$. Recall that $V_I \subseteq V$ denotes the set of input nodes, and let us say that each such node reaches peak signal values of $\pm M_i (M_i > 0)$ for $i \in V_I$. Let $H(z)$ be the scaling transfer function matrix defined before, with the associated impulse response matrix $h[t]$ related to the transfer function matrix through the component-wise inverse z-transform. Then the worst-case peak value P_j reached by any signal $j \in S$ is given by maximizing the well-known convolution sum (equation 23.8) [32], where $x_i[t]$ is the value of the input $i \in V_I$ at time index t.

Solving this maximization problem provides the input sequence given in equation 23.9, and allowing $N_{ij} \to \infty$ leads to the peak response at signal j given in equation 23.10. Here sgn( ) is the signum function (equation 23.11).

$$P_j = \pm \sum_{i \in V_I} \max_{x_i[t']} \left(\sum_{t=0}^{N_{ij}-1} x_i\left[t'-t\right] h_{ij}[t] \right) \tag{23.8}$$

$$x_i[t] = M_i \, \mathrm{sgn}\left(h_{ij}\left\lfloor N_{ij} - t - 1 \right\rfloor\right) \tag{23.9}$$

$$P_j = \sum_{i \in V_I} M_i \sum_{t=0}^{\infty} \left| h_{ij}[t] \right| \tag{23.10}$$

$$\mathrm{sgn}(x) = \begin{cases} 1, & x \geq 0 \\ -1, & \text{otherwise} \end{cases} \tag{23.11}$$

This worst-case approach leads to the concept of l_1 scaling, defined in the following paragraphs.

The l_1-norm of a transfer function $H(z)$ is given by equation 23.12, where $Z^{-1}\{\ \}$ denotes the inverse z-transform.

$$l_1\{H(z)\} = \sum_{t=0}^{\infty} Z^{-1}\{H(z)\}[t] \tag{23.12}$$

A dataflow graph $G(V, S)$ annotated with wordlengths $\boldsymbol{n}$ and scalings $\boldsymbol{p}$ is said to be l_1-scaled} if equation 23.13 holds for all signals $j \in S$.

$$p_j = \left\lfloor \log_2 \left(\sum_{i \in V_I} M_i l_1\{h_{ij}(z)\} \right) \right\rfloor + 1 \tag{23.13}$$

The important point about an l_1-scaled algorithm is that the scalings used are *optimal* in the following sense. If any scaling is reduced lower than its value from equation 23.13, it is possible for overflow to result on that variable. If any scaling is increased beyond its value from equation 23.13, the area of the resulting implementation increases or stays the same without any matching improvement in arithmetic quality observable at the algorithm outputs.

Data range propagation

If the algorithm under consideration is not linear or time invariant, one mechanism for estimating the peak value reached by each signal is to consider the propagation of data ranges through the computation graph. This is generally possible only for nonrecursive algorithms.

Forward propagation   A naive way of approaching this problem is to examine the binary-point position that "naturally" results from each hardware operator. Such an approach, illustrated here, is an option in the Xilinx System Generator tool [20].

In the dataflow graph shown in Figure 23.2, if we consider that each input has a range $(-1, 1)$, then we require a binary-point location of $p = 0$ at each input. Let us consider each of the adders in turn. Adder a1 adds two inputs with $p = 0$ and therefore produces an output with $p = \max(0, 0) + 1 = 1$. Adder a2 adds one input with $p = 0$ and one with $p = 1$, and therefore produces an output with $p = \max(0, 1) + 1 = 2$. Similarly, the output of a3 has $p = 3$, and the output of a4 has $p = 4$. While we have successfully determined a binary-point location for each signal that will not lead to overflow, the disadvantage of this approach

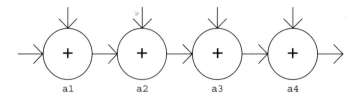

FIGURE 23.2 ▪ A dataflow graph representing a string of additions.

should be clear. The range of values reachable by the system output is actually $5*(-1,1) = (-5,5)$, so $p = 3$ is sufficient; $p = 4$ is an overkill of one MSB.

A solution to this problem that has been used in practice is to propagate data ranges rather than binary-point locations [4, 40]. To understand this approach in practice, let us apply the technique to the example of Figure 23.2. The output of adder a1 is a subset of $(-2,2)$ and thus is assigned $p = 1$; the output of adder a2 is a subset of $(-3,3)$ and is thus assigned $p = 2$; the output of adder a3 is a subset of $(-4,4)$ and is thus assigned $p = 3$; and the output of adder a4 is a subset of $(-5,5)$ and is thus also assigned $p = 3$. For this simple example, the problem of peak value detection has been solved to optimality.

However, such a tight solution is not always possible with data range propagation. Under circumstances where the dataflow graph contains one or more branches (fork nodes), which later reconverge, such a "local" approach to range propagation can be overly pessimistic. As an example, consider the computation graph representing a constant coefficient multiplication on complex numbers shown in Figure 23.3.

In the figure, each signal has been labeled with a propagated range, assuming that the primary inputs have range $(-0.6, 0.6)$. Under this approach, both outputs require $p = 2$. However, such ranges are overly pessimistic. The upper output in Figure 23.3 has the value $y_1 = 2.1x_1 - 1.8(x_1 + x_2) = 0.3x_1 - 1.8x_2$. Thus, its range can also be calculated as $0.3(-0.6, 0.6) - 1.8(-0.6, 0.6) = (-1.26, 1.26)$. A similar calculation for the lower output provides a range of $(-1.2, 1.2)$. By examining the global system behavior, we can therefore see that in reality $p = 1$ is sufficient for both outputs.

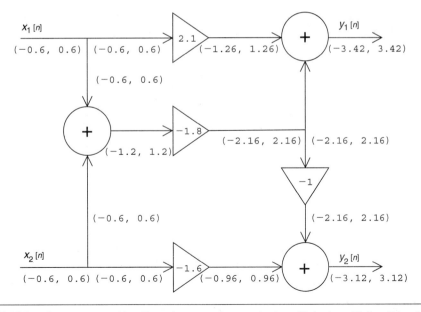

FIGURE 23.3 ■ Range propagation through a complex constant coefficient multiplier. Triangles represent (real) constant coefficient multiplication.

Note that the analytic scheme described previously for linear time-invariant systems would calculate the tighter bound in this case.

In summary, range propagation techniques may provide larger bounds on signal values than are absolutely necessary. This problem is seen *in extremis* with recursive computation graphs. In these cases, it is generally impossible to use range propagation to place a finite bound on signal values, even in cases when such a finite bound can analytically be shown to exist. Under these circumstances, it is standard practice to use some form of simulation to estimate the peak value of signals.

23.2.2 Simulation-based Peak Estimation

A completely different approach to peak estimation is to use simulation—that is, to actually run the algorithm with one or more provided input datasets and measure the peak values reached by each signal.

In its simplest form, the simulation approach consists of measuring the peak signal value P_j reached by a signal $j \in S$ and then setting $p = \lfloor \log_2 kP_j \rfloor + 1$, where $k > 1$ is a user-supplied "safety factor" (typically 2 to 4). Thus, it is ensured that no overflow will occur so long as the signal value does not exceed kP_j when excited by a different input sequence. Particular care must therefore be taken to select an appropriate test sequence.

Kim et al. [25] extend the simulation approach by considering more complex forms of the safety factor. In particular, it is possible to extract information from the simulation relating to the class of probability density function followed by each signal. A histogram of the data values for each signal is built, and from it the distribution is classified as unimodal or multimodal, symmetric or nonsymmetric, and zero mean or nonzero mean. Different forms of safety factor are applied in each case.

Simulation approaches are appropriate for nonlinear or time-varying systems, for which data range propagation, described in Section 23.1.2, provides overly pessimistic results (such as for recursive systems). The main drawback of simulation-based approaches is the significant dependence on the input dataset used for simulation; moreover, usually no general guidelines can be given for how to select an appropriate input. These approaches can, of course, be combined with the analytical techniques of Section 23.2.1 [13].

There has been some recent work [34] aiming to put the derivation of safety factors on a sound theoretical footing by using the statistical theory of extreme value distributions [26]. It is known that the distribution of the sum of a large number of statistically independent identically distributed (i.i.d.) random variables approaches the Gaussian distribution (the Central Limit Theorem). What is less well known is that the (scaled) maximum value of a large number of i.i.d. variables also approaches one of three possible distributions, no matter the distribution of the variables themselves. These are the Gumbel, Fréchet, and Weibull distributions [26]. Using this property, and making an assumption on the type of distribution converged to (Özer and colleagues [34] assume Gumbel), provides a statistically sound way of estimating the safety factor required for a given arbitrarily small probability of overflow.

23.2.3 Summary of Peak Estimation

The optimization of a bit-parallel fixed-point datapath can be split into the two problems of determining an appropriate scaling and determining an appropriate wordlength for each signal. We have discussed the first of these two problems in detail. It has been shown that in the case of LTI systems, tight analytic bounds can be placed on the scaling required. Analytic scaling is also possible for non-LTI systems, at the cost of tightness in the bound—disastrously so in the case of recursive systems. The alternative to the analytical approach is the use of simulation on trusted input datasets; some progress has recently been made on the issue of statistically sound simulation-based peak determination.

23.3 WORDLENGTH OPTIMIZATION

Once a scaling has been determined, it is necessary to find an appropriate wordlength for each signal. While optimizing the scaling usually improves circuit quality without changing circuit functionality (assuming no overflows occur), wordlength optimization trades circuit quality (area, delay, power) for result accuracy. The major problem in wordlength optimization is to determine the error at system outputs for a given set of wordlengths and scalings of all internal variables. We will call this problem *error estimation*. Once a technique for error estimation has been selected, the wordlength selection problem reduces to utilizing the known area and error models within a constrained optimization setting: Find the minimum area implementation satisfying certain constraints on arithmetic error at each system output.

The majority of this section is taken up with the problem of error estimation (Section 23.3.1). Following on from this discussion, the problem of area modeling is addressed. Optimization techniques suitable for solving the wordlength determination problem are introduced (Section 23.3.2), with some discussion of the problem's inherent computational complexity.

23.3.1 Error Estimation and Area Models

Traditionally, much of the research on estimating the effects of truncation and roundoff noise in fixed-point systems has focused on DSP uniprocessors. This leads to certain constraints and assumptions on quantization errors—for example, that the wordlength of all signals is the same, that quantization is performed after multiplication, and that the wordlength before quantization is much greater than that following it [36]. The multiple-wordlength paradigm allows a more general design space to be explored, free from these constraints.

The effect of using finite register length in fixed-point systems has been studied for some time. Oppenheim and Weinstein [36] and Liu [29] lay down standard models for quantization errors and error propagation through LTI systems based on a linearization of signal truncation or rounding. Error signals, assumed to be uniformly distributed, uncorrelated with each other and with themselves over time, are added whenever a truncation occurs. This approximate model has served very well because quantization error power is dramatically affected by wordlength in a uniform wordlength structure, decreasing at approximately 6 dB per bit. This means that it is not necessary to have highly accurate models of quantization error power in order to predict the required signal width [35]. In a multiple-wordlength circuit, the implementation error power may be adjusted much more finely, and so the resulting implementation tends to be more sensitive to errors in estimation. This has led to a simple refinement of the model, which will be discussed soon.

The most generally applicable method for error estimation is simulation: Simulate the system with a given "representative" input and measure the deviation at the system outputs when compared to an accurate simulation (usually "accurate" means IEEE double-precision floating point [22]). Indeed, this is the approach taken by several systems [6, 27]. Unfortunately, simulation suffers from several drawbacks, some of which correspond to the equivalent simulation drawbacks discussed in Section 23.2, and some of which are peculiar to the error estimation problem.

First, there is the problem of dependence on the chosen "representative" input dataset. Second, there is the problem of speed: Simulation runs can take a significant amount of time, and during an optimization procedure a large number of simulation runs may be needed. Third, even the "accurate" simulation will have errors induced by finite wordlength effects that, depending on the system, may not be negligible.

We will be using signal-to-noise ratio (SNR), sometimes referred to as signal-to-quantization-noise ratio (SQNR), as a generally accepted metric for measuring the quality of a fixed-point algorithm implementation [32] (although other measures, such as maximum instantaneous error, exist). Conceptually, the output sequence at each system output resulting from a particular finite-precision implementation can be subtracted from the equivalent sequence resulting from an infinite-precision implementation. The difference is known as the *fixed-point error*.

The ratio of the output power (i.e., the sum of squared signal values) resulting from an infinite precision implementation to the fixed-point error power of a specific implementation defines the SNR. For the purposes of this chapter, the signal power at each output is fixed because it is determined by a combination of the input signal statistics and the dataflow graph $G(V, S)$. To explore different implementations of the dataflow graph, it is therefore sufficient to concentrate on noise estimation, which is the subject of this section.

The approach taken to wordlength optimization should depend on the mathematical properties of the system under investigation. After briefly considering simulation-based estimation, we will examine analytic or semi-analytic techniques that may be applied to certain classes of system. Next we will describe one such method, which may be used to obtain high-quality results for linear time-invariant algorithms. Then we will generalize this approach to nonlinear systems containing only differentiable nonlinear components.

Simulation-based methods

Simulation-based methods for wordlength optimization were first established at Seoul National University, and some of them have been integrated into the Signal Processing Worksystem of Cadence.

In Kim et al. [25] and Kum and Sung [27], the search space is reduced by grouping together all variables involved in a multiply–add operation and optimizing them as a single-wordlength "block." Within each block, the Oppenheim model of quantization noise is applied [35].

Although simulation is almost certainly the most widespread mechanism for estimating the impact of a given choice of wordlength, it suffers from the drawbacks discussed earlier. Indeed, the dependence of the result on the input dataset, while widely acknowledged, is rarely considered in depth. The class of algorithm for which simulation forms a suitable mechanism has also remained unclear. Recently, Alippi [1] proposed an analytical framework within which the question of simulation input dependence can be addressed. A mechanism for understanding the perturbation of Lebesgue-measurable functions, an extremely wide class of algorithmic behavior, has been proposed that uses the theory of randomized algorithms. The essential contribution of this work, for the purposes of fixed-point analysis, has been to demonstrate that simulation is an appropriate mechanism for analyzing fixed-point error. Moreover, Alippi [1] provides a theoretically sound guideline on the number of simulations required in order to be confident, to within a certain probability, that the SNR is within a given limit (alternative signal quality metrics are also Lebesgue measurable and hence can be used as well).

An analytic technique for linear time-invariant systems

We will first address error estimation for LTI systems. An appropriate noise model for truncation of LSBs is described in the subsection that follows. It is then shown that the noise injected through truncation can be analytically propagated through the system in order to measure the effect of such noise on system outputs.

Noise model A common assumption in DSP design is that signal quantization (rounding or truncation) occurs only after a multiplication or multiply-accumulate operation. This corresponds to a uniprocessor viewpoint, where the result of an n-bit signal multiplied by an n-bit coefficient needs to be stored in an n-bit register. The result of such a multiplication is an $n' = 2n$-bit word, which must therefore be quantized down to n bits. Considering signal truncation, the least area-expensive method of quantization [18], the lowest value of the truncation error in 2's complement with $p = 0$, is $2^{-n'} - 2^{-n} \approx -2^{-n}$, and the highest value is 0 (2's complement truncation error is always nonpositive).

It has been observed that values between these values tend to be equally likely to occur in practice, so long as the $2n$-bit signal has sufficient dynamic range [29, 36]. This observation leads to the formulation of a uniform distribution model [36] for the noise of variance $\sigma^2 = 2^{-2n}/12$ for the standard normalization of $p = 0$. It has also been observed that, under the same conditions, the spectrum of such errors tends to be white because there is little correlation between low-order bits over time even if there is a correlation between high-order bits. Similarly, different truncations occurring at different points within the implementation structure tend to be uncorrelated.

When considering a multiple-wordlength implementation, or truncation at different points within the datapath, some researchers have opted to carry the uniform distribution model over to the new implementation style [25]. However, there are associated inaccuracies involved in such an approach [7]. First, quantizations from n' bits to n bits, where $n' \approx n$, will suffer in accuracy because of the discretization of the error probability density function; for example, if $p = 0$, $n' = 2$, $n = 1$, then the only possible error values are 0 and $-1/4$. Second, in such cases the lower bound on error can no longer be simplified in the preceding manner because $2^{-n'} - 2^{-n} \approx -2^{-n}$ no longer holds.

These two issues may be resolved by considering a discrete probability distribution for the injected error signal. For 2's complement arithmetic, the truncation error injection signal $e[t]$ caused by truncation from (n', p) to (n, p) is bounded by equation 23.14.

$$-2^p \left(2^{-n} - 2^{-n'} \right) \le e[t] \le 0 \tag{23.14}$$

It is assumed that each possible value of $e[t]$ has equal probability, as discussed earlier. For 2's complement truncation, there is nonzero mean $E\{e[t]\}$ (equation 23.15) and variance σ_e^2 (equation 23.16).

$$E\{e[t]\} = -\frac{1}{2^{n'-n}} \sum_{i=0}^{2^{n'-n}-1} i \cdot 2^{p-n} = -2^{p-1}\left(2^{-n} - 2^{-n'}\right) \tag{23.15}$$

$$\sigma_e^2 = \frac{1}{2^{n'-n}} \sum_{i=0}^{2^{n'-n}-1} \left(i \cdot 2^{p-n'}\right)^2 - E^2\{e[t]\} = \frac{1}{12} 2^{2p}\left(2^{-2n} - 2^{-2n'}\right) \tag{23.16}$$

Note that for $n_1 \gg n_2$ and $p = 0$, equation 23.16 simplifies to $\sigma_e^2 \approx 1/12 \; 2^{-2n}$, which is the well-known predicted error variance of Oppenheim and Schafer [35] for a model with continuous probability density function.

Noise propagation and power estimation If it is our aim to optimize the wordlengths used in a design, then it is important to be able to predict the arithmetic quality observable at the design outputs. Given a set of wordlengths and scalings, it is possible to use the truncation model described in the previous section to predict the variance of each injection input. For each signal $j \in S$, a straightforward application of equation 23.16 may be used, with n_1 equal to the "natural" full-precision wordlength produced by the source component, $n_2 = n_j$, and $p = p_j$.

By constructing noise sources in this manner for the entire dataflow graph, a set $F = \{(\sigma_p^2, R_p)\}$ of injection input variances σ_p^2, and their associated transfer function to each primary output $R_p(z)$, can be constructed. From this set it is possible to predict the nature of the noise appearing at the system primary outputs, which is the quality metric of importance to the user. Since the noise sources have a white spectrum and are uncorrelated with each other, it is possible to use L_2 scaling to predict the noise power at the system outputs. The L_2 norm of a transfer function $H(z)$ is defined in equation 23.17, where Z^{-1} denotes the inverse z-transform. It can be shown that the noise variance E_k at output k is given by equation 23.18.

$$L_2\{H(z)\} = \left(\sum_{n=0}^{\infty} \left| Z^{-1}\{H(z)\}[n] \right|^2 \right)^{1/2} \tag{23.17}$$

$$E_k = \sum_{(\sigma^2, R) \in F} \sigma^2 L_2{}^2\{R_k\} \tag{23.18}$$

A hybrid approach for nonlinear differentiable systems

With some modification, some of the results from the preceding section can be carried over to the more general class of nonlinear time-varying systems containing only differentiable nonlinearities. In this section we address one possible approach to this problem, deriving from the type of small-signal analysis typically used in analogue electronics [12, 38].

Perturbation analysis   To make some of the analytical results on error sensitivity for LTI systems applicable to nonlinear systems, the first step is to linearize these systems. The assumption is made that the quantization errors induced by rounding or truncation are sufficiently small not to affect the system's macroscopic behavior. Under such circumstances, each system component can be locally linearized or replaced by its "small-signal equivalent" [38] in order to determine the output behavior under a given rounding scheme.

We will consider one such n-input component, the differentiable function $Y[t] = f(X_1[t], X_2[t], \ldots, X_n[t])$, where t is a time index. If we denote by $x_i[t]$ a small perturbation on variable $X_i[t]$, then a first-order Taylor approximation for the induced perturbation $y[t]$ on $Y[t]$ is given by equation 23.19.

$$y[t] \approx x_1[t] \left. \frac{\partial f}{\partial X_1} \right|_t + \ldots + x_n[t] \left. \frac{\partial f}{\partial X_n} \right|_t \tag{23.19}$$

Note that this approximation is linear in each x_i but that the coefficients may vary with time index t because, in general, $\partial f / \partial X_1$ is a function of $X_1, X_2, \ldots, X_n$. Thus, by applying such an approximation, we have produced a linear time-varying small-signal model for a nonlinear time-invariant component. Such an analysis is readily extended to a time-varying component by expressing $Y[t] = f(t, X_1[t], X_2[t], \ldots, X_n[t])$.

The linearity of the resulting model allows us to predict the error at system outputs due to *any* linear scaling of a small perturbation of signal $j \in S$ analytically, given the simulation-obtained error from a *single* such perturbation instance at j, which can be obtained by a single simulation run. Thus, this method can be considered to be a hybrid analytic/simulation error analysis [15].

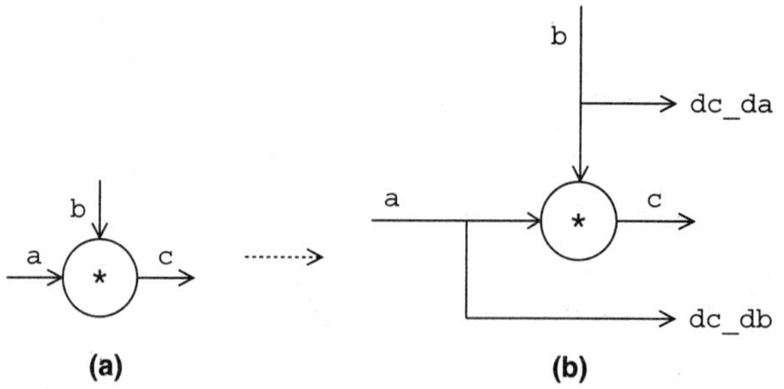

FIGURE 23.4 ■ A local graph transformation to insert derivative monitors: (a) multiplier node; (b) with derivative monitors.

Derivative monitors   To construct the small-signal model, we must first evaluate the differential coefficients of the Taylor series model for nonlinear components.

In general, methods must be introduced to calculate the differential of each nonlinear node type. This is performed by applying a graph transformation to the dataflow graph, introducing the necessary extra nodes and outputs to do this calculation.

The general multiplier is the only nonlinear component considered explicitly in this section, although the approach is general; the graph transformation for multipliers is illustrated in Figure 23.4. Since $f(X_1, X_2) = X_1 X_2$, $\partial f / \partial X_1 = X_2$ and $\partial f / \partial X_2 = X_1$.

After insertion of the monitors (dc_da and dc_db, which capture the derivatives of c with respect to a and b, respectively), a simulation may be performed to write the derivatives to appropriate data files to be used by the linearization process, which is described next.

Linearization   Our aim is to construct a small-signal model, which can be simulated to determine the sensitivity to rounding errors. Once we have obtained the derivative monitors, the construction of the small-signal model may proceed, again through graph transformation. All linear components (adder, constant coefficient multiplier, fork, delay, primary input, primary output) remain unchanged as a result of the linearization process. Each nonlinear component is replaced by its first-order Taylor model. Additional primary inputs are added to the dataflow graph to read the Taylor coefficients from the derivative monitor files created by the previous large-signal simulation.

As an example, the Taylor expansion transformation for the multiplier node is illustrated in Figure 23.5. The inputs dc_da and dc_db are themselves time-varying sequences, derived from the previous step of the procedure. Note that the graph portion of Figure 23.5(b) still contains multiplier "nonlinear" components, although one input of each multiplier node is now external to the model. This absence of feedback ensures linearity, although not time invariance.

Noise injection   In Section 23.3.1, L_2 scaling was used to analytically estimate the noise variance at a system output through scaling of the (analytically

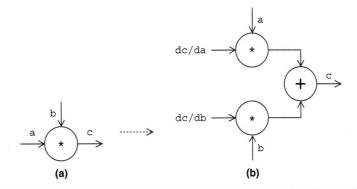

FIGURE 23.5 ■ A local graph transformation to produce a small-signal model: (a) multiplier node; (b) first-order Taylor model.

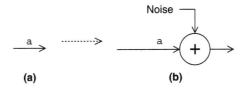

FIGURE 23.6 ■ A local graph transformation to inject perturbations: (a) original signal; (b) with noise injection.

derived) noise variance injected at each point of quantization. Such a purely analytic technique can be used only for LTI systems. In this section we discuss an extension of the approach for nonlinear systems.

Because the small-signal model is linear, if an output exhibits variance V when excited by an error of variance σ^2 injected into a given signal, then the output will exhibit variance αV when excited by a signal of variance $\alpha\sigma^2$ injected into the same signal ($\alpha \geq 0$). Herein lies the strength of the proposed linearization procedure: If the output response to a noise of known variance can be determined *once only* through simulation, this response can be scaled with analytically derived coefficients in order to estimate the response to any rounding or truncation scheme.

Thus, the next step of the procedure is to transform the graph through the introduction of an additional adder node, and associated signals, and then simulate the graph with a known noise. In our case, to simulate truncation of a 2's complement signal, the noise is independent and identically distributed with a uniform distribution over the range $[-2\sqrt{3}, 0]$, chosen to have unit variance ($1/12(2\sqrt{3})^2 = 1$), in this way making the measured output response an unscaled "sensitivity" measure. The graph transformation of inserting a noise injection is shown in Figure 23.6. One of these transformations is applied to a distinct copy of the linearized graph for each signal in the dataflow graph, after which zeros are propagated from the *original* primary inputs, to finalize the small-signal model. This is a special case of constant propagation [2] that leads to significantly faster simulation results for nontrivial dataflow graphs.

The entire process is illustrated for a simple dataflow graph in Figure 23.7. The original graph is shown in (a). The perturbation analysis will be performed for the signals marked (*) and (**). After inserting derivative monitors

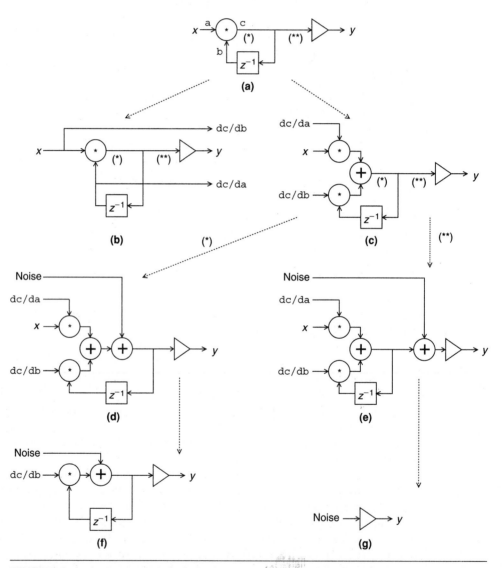

FIGURE 23.7 ■ An example of perturbation analysis: (a) original dataflow graph; (b) transformed dataflow graph; (c) linearized dataflow graph; (d) variant for (*) signal; (e) variant for (**) signal; (f) simplified graph for (*) signal; (g) simplified graph for (**) signal.

for nonlinear components, the transformed DFG is shown in (b). The linearized DFG is shown in (c), and its two variants for the signals (*) and (**) are illustrated in (d) and (e), respectively. Finally, the corresponding simplified DFGs after zero propagation are shown in (f) and (g), respectively.

High-level area models

To implement a multiple-wordlength system, component libraries must be available to support multiple-wordlength arithmetic. These libraries can then be instantiated by the synthesis system and must be modeled in terms of area consumption to provide the wordlength optimization procedure with a cost metric.

Integer arithmetic libraries are available from FPGA vendors (e.g., Xilinx Coregen or Altera LPM macros). Parameterizable macros for standard arithmetic functions operating on integer arithmetic form the basis of the multiple-wordlength libraries synthesized to by wordlength optimization tools such as Right-Size [15] and Synoptix [8]. Blocks from each of these vendors may have slightly different cost parameters, but the general approach described in this section is applicable across all of them. Example external interfaces of multiple-wordlength library blocks for constant coefficient multipliers (`gain`) and adders (`add`) written in VHDL are shown in Listing 23.1 [23].

Listing 23.1 ■ Constant coefficient multipliers (`gain`) and adders (`add`) written in VHDL.

```
ENTITY gain IS
  GENERIC( INWIDTH, OUTWIDTH, NULLMSBS, COEFWIDTH : INTEGER;
          COEF : std_logic_vector( COEFWIDTH downto 0 ) );
  PORT( data : IN std_logic_vector( INWIDTH downto 0 );
        result : OUT std_logic_vector( OUTWIDTH downto 0 ) );
END gain;

ENTITY add IS
  GENERIC( AWIDTH, BWIDTH, BSHL, OUTWIDTH, NULLMSBS : INTEGER );
  PORT( dataa : IN std_logic_vector( AWIDTH downto 0 );
        datab : IN std_logic_vector( BWIDTH downto 0 );
        result : OUT std_logic_vector( OUTWIDTH downto 0 ) );
END add;
```

As well as an individually parameterizable wordlength for each input and output port, each library block has a NULLMSBS parameter that indicates how many most significant bits (MSBs) of the operation result are to be ignored (the converse of sign extension). Thus, each operation result can be considered to be made up of zero or more MSBs that are ignored, followed by one or more data bits, followed by zero or more LSBs that may be truncated depending on the OUTWIDTH parameter. For the adder library block, there is an additional BSHL generic that accounts for the alignment necessary for addition operands. BSHL represents the number of bits by which the datab input must be conceptually shifted left to align it with the dataa input. Note that, because this is fixed-point arithmetic, there is no physical shifting involved; the data is simply aligned in a skewed manner, as shown in Figure 23.8. Note, too, that `dataa` and `datab` are permuted as necessary to ensure that `BSHL` is always nonnegative.

In the figure, (a) shows that the MSB of input b protrudes beyond that of input a and that all the output bits are drawn from the core integer addition of the overlap. Figure 23.8(b) shows that the MSB of input a protrudes beyond that of input b and that all output bits are drawn from the core integer addition of the overlap. Figure 23.8(c) shows that the MSB of input b protrudes beyond that of input a but that some of the output bits are drawn from the LSB overhang of input a and are thus produced "free." Figure 23.8(d) shows that the MSB of input a protrudes beyond that of input b but that some of the output bits

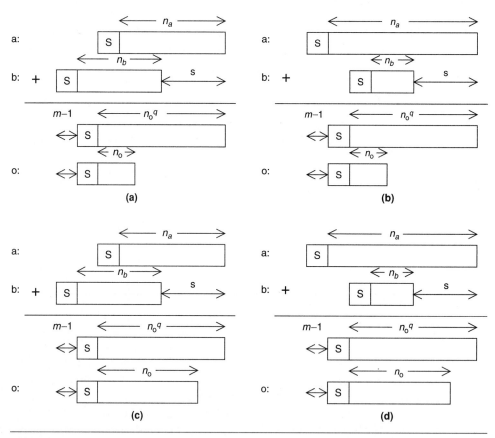

FIGURE 23.8 ■ Four multiple-wordlength adder formats arising in practice: (a) MSB of input b protruding beyond MSB of input a; (b) MSB of input a protruding beyond MSB of input b; (c) MSB of input b protruding beyond MSB of input a, with "free" output bits; (d) MSB input a protruding beyond MSB of input b, with "free" output bits. (s denotes the value of the BSHL generic; m denotes the value of the NULLMSBS generic.)

are drawn from the LSB overhang of input a and are thus produced "free." In each case, the upper result shows the "error-free" wordlength n_o^q without further truncation, whereas the lower result shows the wordlength n_o after potential further truncation.

Each of the library block parameters has an impact on the area resources consumed by the overall system implementation. It is generally assumed when constructing a cost model that each operator in the dataflow graph will map to a separate hardware resource and that the area cost of wiring is negligible [17]. These assumptions (relaxed by Constantinides et al. [12]) simplify the construction of an area cost model. It is sufficient to estimate separately the area consumed by each computation node and then sum the resulting estimates. In reality, of course, logic synthesis, performed after wordlength optimization, is likely to result in some logic optimization between the boundaries of two connected library elements. This may result in lower area than estimated, but experience shows that these deviations from the area model are small.

The area model for a multiple-wordlength adder is reasonably straightforward. A ripple-carry architecture is used [21] since FPGAs provide good support for fast ripple-carry implementations. The only area-consuming component is the core (integer) adder constructed from the vendor library. This adder has a width of max(AWIDTH – BSHL, BWIDTH) – NULLMSBS + 2 bits. Depending on the FPGA architecture in question, each bit may not consume the same area; however, because some bits are required for the result port whereas others may be needed only for carry propagation, their sum outputs remain unconnected and therefore the sum circuitry is optimized away by logic synthesis. The cost model thus has two parameters k_1 and k_2, corresponding to the area cost of a sum-and-carry full adder and to the area cost of a carry-only full adder, respectively. The area of an adder is expressed in equation 23.20.

$$A_{\text{add}}(\text{AWIDTH, BWIDTH, BSHL, NULLMSBS, OUTWIDTH})$$
$$= k_1(\text{OUTWIDTH} + 1) + k_2(\max(\text{AWIDTHBSHL, BWIDTH}) \qquad (23.20)$$
$$- \text{NULLMSBS} - \text{OUTWIDTH} + 1)$$

Area estimation for general multipliers can proceed in a similarly straightforward way. However, the equivalent problem for constant coefficient multipliers is significantly more problematic. A constant coefficient multiplier is typically implemented as a series of additions through a recoding scheme such as the classic Booth technique [3]. This implementation style causes the area consumption to be highly dependent on the coefficient value. In addition, the exact implementation scheme used by the vendor integer arithmetic libraries is known only to the vendor.

A simple area model has been proposed (equation 23.21) and the coefficient values k_3 and k_4 have been determined through the synthesis of several hundred multipliers of different coefficient values and widths [12]. The model has then been fitted to this data using a least-squares approach. Note that the model does not account for NULLMSBS because, for a properly scaled coefficient,

NULLMSBS ≤ 1 for a constant coefficient multiplier and therefore has little impact on area consumption.

$$A_{\text{gain}}(\text{INWIDTH, OUTWIDTH, COEFWIDTH}) = k_3 \text{COEFWIDTH}(\text{INWIDTH} + 1)$$
$$+ k_4(\text{INWIDTH} + \text{COEFWIDTH} - \text{OUTWIDTH}) \qquad (23.21)$$

More detailed area models for components are discussed by Chang and Hauck [14].

23.3.2 Search Techniques

A heuristic search procedure

Because the wordlength optimization problem is NP-hard [16], several heuristic approaches have been developed to find feasible wordlength vectors having small, though not necessarily optimal, area consumption. An example heuristic is shown in Listing 23.2. After performing binary-point estimation using the techniques of Section 23.2, the algorithm determines the minimum uniform wordlength satisfying all error constraints. The design at this stage corresponds to a standard uniform wordlength design with implicit power-of-two scaling, such as may be used for an optimized uniprocessor-based implementation. Each wordlength is then scaled up by a factor $k > 1$, which represents a bound on the largest value that any wordlength in the final design may reach (in the Synoptix implementation of this algorithm [8], $k = 2$ has been used).

The resulting structure forms a starting point from which one signal wordlength is reduced by one bit on each iteration. The signal wordlength to reduce is decided in each iteration by reducing each wordlength in turn until it violates an output noise constraint (Listing 23.2). At this point there is likely to have been some pay-off in reduced area, and the signal whose wordlength reduction provided the largest pay-off is chosen. Each signal's wordlength is explored using a binary search.

Listing 23.2 ■ Algorithm wordlength falling.

```
Input: A Dataflow Graph G(V, S) and binary-point vector p.
Output: An optimized wordlength vector n.
begin
  Let the elements of S be denoted as S = { j₁, j₂, ..., j|S| }
  Determine u, the minimum uniform wordlength satisfying error
    criteria
  Set n ← 1ku
  do
    currentcost ← AREA(n)
    foreach jᵢ ∈ S do
      bestmin ← currentcost
      Set w to the smallest positive value where the error criteria
        are satisfied for wordlength [n₁ ... nᵢ₋₁ w nᵢ₊₁ ... n|S|]
      Set minval ← AREA([n₁ ... nᵢ₋₁ w nᵢ₊₁ ... n|S|])
      if minval < bestmin, set bestsig ← i and bestmin ← minval
    end foreach
```

```
  if bestmin < currentcost
    n_bestsig ← n_bestsig − 1
  while bestmin < currentcost
end
```

Alternative search procedures

The algorithm described in Section 23.3.1 is a heuristic; it does not guarantee to produce the optimum area cost for a given set of error constraints. A technique to discover the true optimum-wordlength vectors has also been proposed [10] that uses integer linear programming (ILP) to model the constraint space and objective functions. This technique was able to demonstrate that the heuristic from Section 23.1.1 provides good-quality results for the small benchmark problems addressed by both approaches. Like all NP-hard problems [16], however, finding the optimum solution becomes computationally infeasible for large problem sizes. The methodology of Constantinides et al. [10] is applicable only for very small practical problems and is thus more of a theoretical than practical interest.

Several other heuristic search procedures have been proposed in the literature, and we will review some of the more interesting ones (further comparisons are made in the brief survey by Cantin et al. [6]).

An approach used by Kum and Sung [27] is based on the intuition that the error observable at a system output reduces monotonically with each wordlength in that system. This is a plausible conjecture, but is not always the case. Indeed, it was shown independently by Constantinides [9] and Lehtinen and Renfors [31] that this conjecture may be violated in practical situations. Nevertheless, if we accept it for the moment, a natural search procedure becomes apparent. We may divide the search into two phases. In the first phase, the system is simulated with all but one variable having a very large precision (e.g., double precision floating point). In this way, we can find the point at which the output constraints are violated because of quantization on this variable alone. Repeating this for all variables provides, under the conjecture, a lower bound on each element of the wordlength vector. The second phase of the algorithm is invoked if the constraints are violated when these lower bounds are used as the wordlength vector. In this case, the precision of all variables is increased by an equal number of bits until the constraints are satisfied. A variation on the second phase is to exhaustively explore all possibilities above this lower bound, until the constraints are satisfied [27].

The common meta-heuristics of simulated annealing and genetic algorithms have been used for this problem—for example, by Chang and Hauck [14]—(using a linear combination of area and error as an objective function [28,40]). While there are practical advantages to using tried-and-tested meta-heuristics for combinatorial problems, the smooth nature of the constraints and objectives, as outlined previously, means that it is likely that better results can be obtained within a fixed computation time budget by using application-specific heuristic techniques.

23.4 SUMMARY

This chapter introduced the fundamental problems of designing optimized fixed-point arithmetic circuits in custom hardware, including FPGA devices. The fixed-point number system is of widespread interest in the FPGA community because of the highly efficient arithmetic implementations possible when compared to what can be achieved with floating-point arithmetic. However, much more than with floating point, working with fixed point requires designers to have a good grasp of the numerical robustness issues involved with their designs. Performing such design by hand is tedious and error prone, which has motivated the development of automatic procedures, some of which have been described in this chapter.

The freedom in custom hardware to use multiple wordlengths in a design creates the possibility of shaping the circuit datapath to the requirements of the algorithm, leading to low-area, high-speed, and low-power implementations. This emerging paradigm throws up a new challenge, however: wordlength optimization.

This chapter demonstrated that wordlength determination can be considered as a constrained optimization, and suitable models were presented for FPGA-based bit-parallel implementations, together with signal-to-noise ratio of linear time-invariant and differentiable nonlinear time-varying systems. In each case, we described at least one error estimation procedure in depth and discussed related procedures and their advantages and disadvantages.

We will now consider some fruitful avenues for further research in this field, broken down into MSB-side optimization, error modeling, and search procedures.

The work discussed in Section 23.2 either avoids overflow completely (e.g., l_1-scaling) or reduces the probability of overflow to an arbitrary level (e.g., extreme value theory) without considering the effect of overflow on signal-to-noise ratio or other accuracy metrics. In algorithms where the worst-case variable range is much larger than the average-case range, it may make sense to save area by allowing rare overflow and its consequent reduction in arithmetic accuracy. This problem was discussed by Constantinides et al. [11] using a simple model of the error induced by overflow, based on approximating all signals by Gaussian random variables. The results achieved were weakened, however, by an inability of the proposed method to accurately estimate the correlations between overflow errors at different points within the algorithm. Further work could provide much stronger bounds.

The analytical error-modeling approaches discussed in Section 23.3.1 can adequately deal with linear time-invariant systems or with time-varying systems containing only differentiable nonlinearities. This still leaves open the problem of adequately modeling systems containing nondifferentiable nonlinearities. This is a serious omission, as it includes any algorithm containing conditionally executed statements, where the condition is a logical expression containing variables generated by the algorithm itself (in the case where the variables are external inputs, this can be viewed as a time-varying differentiable system). Further work incorporating the results from the analysis of nonlinear dynamical systems is likely to shed new light here.

Both heuristic and optimal search procedures were discussed in Section 23.3.2. One of the limitations of the optimal approach from Constantinides et al. [10] is that is has relied on coercing inherently nonlinear constraints into a linear form, resulting in a large ILP problem. Branch-and-bound, or other combinatorial search procedures, on top of bounding procedures from the more general field of nonlinear mathematical programming may be able to provide optimal results for significantly larger problems. Further effort is also called for in the development of heuristic search procedures. None of the heuristics presented thus far can guarantee a bounded distance to optimality, although under certain error metrics the wordlength optimization problem is approximatible in this sense. It would be useful to concentrate efforts on heuristics that do provide these guarantees.

It is my belief that, apart from a practical design problem, the problem of wordlength optimization has much to offer in terms of understanding the numerical properties of algorithms. The earliest contributions to this subject can be traced back to two giants of computing, Alan Turing [39] and John von Neumann [33]. At the time, IEEE standard floating point was nonexistent, and it was necessary to carefully design the architecture around the algorithm. FPGA-based computing has reopened this method of design by giving an unprecedented degree of freedom in the implementation of numerical algorithms.

References

[1] C. Alippi. Randomized algorithms: A system-level poly-time analysis of robust computation. *IEEE Transactions on Computers* 51(7), 2002.

[2] A. V. Aho, R. Sethi, J. D. Ullman. *Compilers: Principles, Techniques and Tools*, Addison-Wesley, 1986.

[3] A. D. Booth. A signed binary multiplication technique. *Quarterly Journal Mechanical Applications of Mathematics* 4(2), 1951.

[4] A. Benedetti, P. Perona. Bit-width optimization for configurable DSPs by multi-interval analysis. *Proceedings of the 34th Asilomar Conference on Signals, Systems and Computers*, 2000.

[5] M.-A. Cantin, Y. Savaria, P. Lavoie. An automatic word length determination method. *Proceedings of the IEEE International Symposium on Circuits and Systems*, 2001.

[6] M.-A. Cantin, Y. Savaria, P. Lavoie. A comparison of automatic word length optimization procedures. *Proceedings of the IEEE International Symposium on Circuits and Systems*, 2002.

[7] G. A. Constantinides, P. Y. K. Cheung, W. Luk. Truncation noise in fixed-point SFGs. *IEE Electronics Letters* 35(23), November 1999.

[8] G. A. Constantinides, P. Y. K. Cheung, W. Luk. The multiple wordlength paradigm. *Proceedings of the IEEE Symposium on Field-Programmable Custom Computing Machines*, April–May 2001.

[9] G. A. Constantinides. *High-level Synthesis and Wordlength Optimization for Digital Signal Processing Systems*, Ph.D. thesis, University of London, 2001.

[10] G. A. Constantinides, P. Y. K. Cheung, W. Luk. Optimum wordlength allocation. *Proceedings of the IEEE Symposium on Field-Programmable Custom Computing Machines*, April 2002.

[11] G. A. Constantinides, P. Y. K. Cheung, W. Luk. Synthesis of saturation arithmetic architectures. *ACM Transactions on Design Automation of Electronic Systems* 8(3), 2003.

[12] G. A. Constantinides, P. Y. K. Cheung, W. Luk. *Synthesis and Optimization of DSP Algorithms*, Kluwer Academic, 2004.

[13] M. Chang, S. Hauck. Precis: A design-time precision analysis tool. *Proceedings of the IEEE Symposium on Field-Programmable Custom Computing Machines*, 2002.

[14] M. Chang, S. Hauck. Automated least-significant bit datapath optimization for FPGAs. *Proceedings of the IEEE Symposium on Field-Programmable Custom Computing Machines*, 2004.

[15] G. A. Constantinides. wordlength optimization for differentiable nonlinear systems. *ACM Transactions on Design Automation for Electronic Systems*, January 2006.

[16] G. A. Constantinides, G. J. Woeginger. The complexity of multiple wordlength assignment. *Applied Mathematics Letters* 15, 2002.

[17] G. DeMicheli. *Synthesis and Optimization of Digital Circuits*, McGraw-Hill, 1994.

[18] P. D. Fiore. Lazy rounding. *Proceedings of the IEEE Workshop on Signal Processing Systems*, 1998.

[19] C. Fang, T. Chen, R. Rutenbar. Floating-point error analysis based on affine arithmetic. *Proceedings of the IEEE International Conference on Acoustics, Speech, and Signal Processing*, 2003.

[20] J. Hwang, B. Milne, N. Shirazi, J. Stroomer. System level tools for DSP in FPGAs. In R. Woods and G. Brebner, eds., *Processing Field Programmable Logic*, Springer-Verlag, 2001.

[21] K. Hwang. *Computer Arithmetic: Principles, Architecture and Design*, Wiley, 1979.

[22] *IEEE Standard for Binary Floating-point Arithmetic* (ANSI/IEEE Standard 991), 1986.

[23] *IEEE Standard for VHDL Register Transfer Level (RTL) Synthesis* (IEEE Standard 1076.6), 1999.

[24] C. Inacio, D. Ombres. The DSP decision: Fixed point or floating? *IEEE Spectrum* 33(9), September 1996.

[25] S. Kim, K. Kum, W. Sung. Fixed-point optimization utility for C and C++ based digital signal processing programs. *IEEE Transactions on Circuits and Systems II* 45(11), November 1998.

[26] S. Kotz, S. Nadarajah. *Extreme Value Distributions: Theory and Applications*, Imperial College Press, 2000.

[27] K.-I. Kum, W. Sung. Combined wordlength optimization and high-level synthesis of digital signal processing systems. *IEEE Transactions on Computer-Aided Design* 20(8), August 2001.

[28] D.-U. Lee, A. Gaffar, R. Cheung, O. Mencer, W. Luk, G. A. Constantinides. Accuracy guaranteed bit-width optimization. *IEEE Transactions on Computer-Aided Design of Integrated Circuits and Systems*, 2006.

[29] B. Liu. Effect of finite word length on the accuracy of digital filters—A review. *IEEE Transactions on Circuit Theory* 18(6), 1971.

[30] H. Levy, D. W. Low. A contraction algorithm for finding small cycle cutsets. *Journal of Algorithms* 9, 1988.

[31] V. Lehtinen, M. Renfors. Truncation noise analysis of noise shaping DSP systems with application to CIC decimators. *Proceedings of the European Signal Processing Conference*, 2002.

[32] S. K. Mitra. *Digital Signal Processing*, McGraw-Hill, 1998.

[33] J. von Neumann, H. H. Goldstine. Numerical inverting of matrices of high order. *Bulletin of the American Mathematics Society* 53, 1947.

[34] E. Özer, A. Nisbet, D. Gregg. Stochastic bit-width approximation using extreme value theory for customizable processors. *Proceedings of the International Conference on Compiler Construction*, 2004.

[35] A. V. Oppenheim, R. W. Schafer. *Digital Signal Processing*, Prentice-Hall, 1975.

[36] A. V. Oppenheim, C. J. Weinstein. Effects of finite register length in digital filtering and the fast fourier transform. *IEEE Proceedings* 60(8), 1972.

[37] W. Sung, K. Kum. Simulation-based wordlength optimization method for fixed-point digital signal processing systems. *IEEE Transactions on Signal Processing* 43(12), December 1995.

[38] A. S. Sedra, K. C. Smith. *Microelectronic Circuits*, Saunders, 1991.

[39] A. Turing. Rounding-off errors in matrix processes. *Quarterly Journal of Mechanics* 1, 1948.

[40] S. A. Wadekar, A. C. Parker. Accuracy sensitive wordlength selection for algorithm optimization. *Proceedings of the International Conference on Computer Design*, October 1998.

CHAPTER 24

DISTRIBUTED ARITHMETIC

Rajeevan Amirtharajah
Department of Electrical and Computer Engineering
University of California–Davis

Distributed arithmetic (DA) [1, 2] is a computation algorithm that performs multiplication using precomputed lookup tables (LUTs) instead of logic. It is well suited to implementation on homogeneous field-programmable gate arrays (FPGAs) because of its high utilization of the available LUTs. It may also have advantages for modern heterogeneous FPGAs that contain built-in multipliers because it is area efficient for implementing long digital filters. DA targets the sum-of-products (or vector dot product) operation, and many digital signal processing (DSP) tasks such as filter implementation, matrix multiplication, and frequency transformation can be reduced to one or more sum-of-products computations.

24.1 THEORY

The theory behind DA is based on reorganizing the vector dot product operation around the binary representation of the vector elements [2]. Suppose that X is the vector of input samples and A is a constant vector of filter coefficients, corresponding to the taps of a finite impulse response (FIR) filter. Vectors X and A each consist of M elements X_k and A_k. The dot product y of X and A (corresponding to the convolution of X with the FIR impulse response) can be written as

$$y = \sum_{k=0}^{M-1} A_k X_k \tag{24.1}$$

We can represent each element of the input sample vector X in N-bit 2's complement notation. Then equation 24.1 can be expressed as

$$y = \sum_{k=0}^{M-1} A_k \left[-b_{k(N-1)} 2^{N-1} + \sum_{n=0}^{N-2} b_{kn} 2^n \right] \tag{24.2}$$

where $b_{k(N-1)}$ is the sign bit of the input sample X_k in N-bit 2's complement notation, and b_{kn} is the nth bit of input sample X_k. The possible values of b_{ki}

are either 0 or 1. Equation 24.2 can be further rearranged into equation 24.3 by multiplying out the factors and changing the order of the summation:

$$y = -\sum_{k=0}^{M-1} A_k b_{k(N-1)} 2^{N-1} + \sum_{n=0}^{N-2} \left[\sum_{k=0}^{M-1} A_k b_{kn} \right] 2^n = Z_{sign} + Z_{n1} \qquad (24.3)$$

Consider each term in the brackets of the second summation in equation 24.3, labeled Z_{n0} in the following:

$$Z_{n0} = \sum_{k=0}^{M-1} A_k b_{kn} \qquad (24.4)$$

where term Z_{n0} has 2^M possible values because b_{kn} is either 1 or 0. Therefore, each summation term $A_k b_{kn}$ can have the value of either A_k or 0. Instead of using a multiplier to compute any of these 2^M possible values whenever necessary, we can precompute them and store them in a LUT with depth 2^M. The contents of the LUT are then addressed directly by the bit-serial input data, $[b_{0n}, b_{1n}, b_{2n}, \ldots b_{Mn}]$, corresponding to the nth bits of each element X_k of input vector X. Multiplication by the factor 2^n in equation 24.3 can be realized by a shifter and the addressed LUT contents shifted and accumulated to form term Z_{n1} in $(N-1)$ cycles.

The sign term Z_{sign} can be handled in the same way with additional circuitry to implement subtraction; it takes one additional clock cycle. The final result y is formed after N cycles. Note that, if the filter length is greater than the bit width of the input data (i.e., $M > N$), DA computes the final result in fewer cycles than an implementation using a single multiply–accumulate functional unit. However, because the size of the LUT grows exponentially in the number of vector elements (2^M), most practical implementations use multiple LUTs and adders to combine partial dot products into the final result.

24.2 DA IMPLEMENTATION

A simple DA implementation is shown in Figure 24.1. It requires a 16-bit shift register for the input vector, a 16-entry LUT, an adder/subtractor, and an accumulator (`Result`) for the output. The x2 operation is handled purely by wiring. This unit is a direct implementation of the DA algorithm described in the preceding section, and it is capable of computing the dot product of a 4-element vector X and a constant 4-element vector A.

In the figure the four 4-bit-wide elements of X are fed into the address decoder in most significant bit (MSB) first order to select the appropriate LUT row contents. The selected content is added with the left-shifted version of the previous RESULT value to form the current RESULT value. Ts is the sign bit timing signal that controls the add/subtract operation; when Ts is high, the current LUT content is subtracted from the left-shifted version of the previous result. The final vector dot product is obtained in four cycles. Shifting in the bit vector

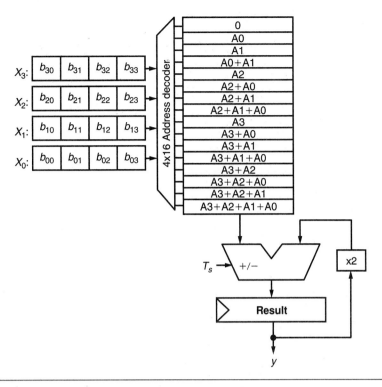

FIGURE 24.1 ▪ A simple implementation of distributed arithmetic.

least significant bit (LSB) first also produces the correct final value and has the advantage of eliminating long carry propagations when accumulating the intermediate results.

The only modifications to Figure 24.1 required for this alternative are to reverse the bits of vector X_{in}, the shift register, and replace the left shift by 1 bit and the right shift by 1 bit. Various other modifications to this structure are possible. For example, the input sample shift register can be serial in/serial out or parallel in/serial out depending on the application.

LUT size can be a determining factor in the total hardware cost of a DA implementation. It is possible to modify the structure in Figure 24.1 to reduce the table size by a factor of 2. To achieve this reduction, consider a different representation of the input data samples X_k:

$$X_k = \frac{1}{2}[X_k - (-X_k)] \tag{24.5}$$

The 2's complement representation of the negative of X_k can be expressed as

$$-X_k = -\overline{b}_{k(N-1)}2^{N-1} + \sum_{n=0}^{N-2}\overline{b}_{kn}2^n + 1 \tag{24.6}$$

where each bit of X_k has been complemented and a 1 has been added to the complemented bits. Plugging equation 24.6 into equation 24.5 yields

$$X_k = \frac{1}{2}\left[-\left(b_{k(N-1)} - \overline{b}_{k(N-1)}\right)2^{N-1} + \sum_{n=0}^{N-2}\left(b_{kn} - \overline{b}_{kn}\right)2^n - 1\right] \qquad (24.7)$$

Each difference term $\left(b_{kn} - \overline{b}_{kn}\right)$ (for $n = 0$ to $N-1$) in equation 24.7 can take on values of $+1$ or -1. This alternate representation for X_k is convenient because, in the resulting summation for the dot product, each linear combination of A_k has a corresponding negative linear combination. Only one of these combinations needs to be stored in the LUT, with the negative being applied during operation using the subtractor. Substituting equation 24.7 into equation 24.1 and rearranging terms yields the following new expression for the result of the dot product y:

$$y = \sum_{n=0}^{N-1} Q(b_n) + Q(0) \qquad (24.8)$$

where

$$Q(b_n) = \frac{1}{2}\sum_{k=0}^{M-1} A_k \left(b_{kn} - \overline{b}_{kn}\right)2^n, \quad n \neq N-1 \qquad (24.9a)$$

$$Q(b_{N-1}) = -\frac{1}{2}\sum_{k=0}^{M-1} A_k \left(b_{k(N-1)} - \overline{b}_{k(N-1)}\right)2^{N-1}, \quad n = N-1 \qquad (24.9b)$$

$$Q(0) = -\frac{1}{2}\sum_{k=0}^{M-1} A_k \qquad (24.9c)$$

Note that the expressions for $Q(b_n)$ and $Q(b_{N-1})$ have 2^{M-1} possible magnitudes, with signs determined by the input bits, and that the computation of y requires an additional register to hold the constant term $Q(0)$. This leads to the reduced DA memory implementation shown in Figure 24.2, where the exclusive-or (XOR) gates are required to recode the addresses to access the appropriate LUT row and to control the timing of the sign bit into the adder/subtractor. The XOR gates, the initial condition register for $Q(0)$, and a 2-input multiplexer are the only additional hardware required to reduce the memory size by a factor of 2.

The implementations in both Figures 24.1 and 24.2 require N clock cycles to compute the final result, although additional cycles may be needed to match the throughput of the DA unit to other functional units in the system for a particular application. In Section 24.3 we will discuss mapping these basic structures onto FPGA fabrics. We will address the issue of performance improvement (by reducing the number of required clock cycles and increasing the clock frequency) in Section 24.4.

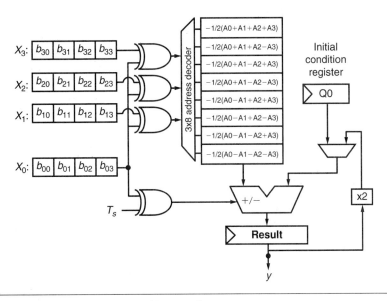

FIGURE 24.2 ■ Reduced DA memory implementation.

24.3 MAPPING DA ONTO FPGAs

Consider mapping a 16-tap FIR filter ($M = 16$) operating on 16-bit data ($N = 16$) onto an FPGA fabric based on 4-input LUTs. As discussed earlier, DA's primary drawback is that the size of the LUTs grows exponentially in the number of filter coefficients (or filter taps). If we want to use 16-bit data to represent the precomputed values, we need $16 \times 2^{16} = 1$ Mbit of memory. To limit this growth, long filters can be partitioned into several smaller DA units whose outputs are then combined using a tree of 2-input adders, as shown in Figure 24.3. This partitions the 16 filter taps A_0 to A_{15} among four DA units, each of which incorporates N 1-bit-wide 4-input LUTs.

The partitioning is chosen to correspond to the LUT size of the individual logic elements or CLBs. If the filter taps are symmetric (which they often are for typical signal-processing applications), the memory size can be reduced by a further factor of 2 by summing the appropriate elements of the input vector X_k using serial addition and using the bits of the resulting sum to address the LUTs. In addition to the serial adder hardware, this memory reduction comes at the expense of an additional clock cycle of latency before the final result is valid.

As CMOS technology has scaled and the complexity of individual CLBs has increased with succeeding FPGA generations, the hardware cost of implementing our example filter has shrunk dramatically. Based on an early implementation of an 8-tap, 8-bit filter using DA on a Xilinx 3042 FPGA [3], our example would consume approximately 120 CLBs, including control logic, even using the

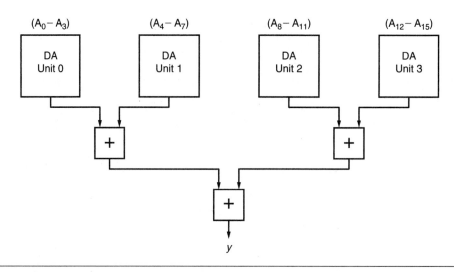

FIGURE 24.3 ▪ A 16-tap FIR filter mapped onto multiple DA units.

symmetry of the filter coefficients to reduce the memory requirements. This would consume roughly the entire FPGA chip. Resource usage would be dominated by the input shift registers (60 CLBs) since this older FPGA architecture only allowed the local CLB flip-flops to be used in a shift configuration.

In contrast, a recent FPGA architecture encompasses four logic "slices" in each CLB, where two slices each roughly correspond to an entire CLB in the older architecture [6]. Because LUTs in Xilinx Spartan-3E FPGAs can be configured as 16×1 shift registers, the number of CLB resources to implement the data memory for DA is drastically reduced. Each logic slice also contains carry propagation logic for efficient implementation of adder circuits, which can be used to increase the speed of DA computation, as will be shown later. Implementing the example filter on a Spartan-3E FPGA requires approximately 113 slices, corresponding to 29 CLBs. This is under 12 percent of the total number of slices available in the smallest member of the 3S100E FPGA family.

Further enhancements to the architecture building blocks may allow for more efficient DA implementation in the future. For example, the potential of heterogeneous or coarse-grained FPGAs to support DA more efficiently by incorporating small adders and accumulators directly in the CLB is currently being explored [7].

24.4 IMPROVING DA PERFORMANCE

Two approaches can be taken to improve DA performance on an FPGA platform. First, the design can be modified to reduce the number of cycles required to compute the final result. Second, the cycle time can be decreased by reducing the number of logic stages in the critical path of the computation. Examples of both approaches will be discussed in this section.

A simple approach to speeding up DA computation is to recognize that multiple bits from each input vector element X_k can be used to address multiple LUTs in each clock cycle (because addition is associative, we can perform the sum in equation 24.3 using any combination of partial sums that is convenient). This leads to an architecture like the one shown in Figure 24.4, which uses 2 bits of the input data vector elements at a time. The LUTs are identical because they contain the same linear combinations of filter coefficients A_k. The LUT outputs must be scaled by the correct exponent of 2 to maintain the significance of the bits added to the accumulated result (the x2 unit in Figure 24.4). Only two cycles are required to compute the result y for this implementation, instead of four cycles for the implementation in Figure 24.2. For longer bit-width input data, this idea can be extended to using more bits at a time.

The modification just described provides the benefit of a linear decrease in the number of clock cycles at the expense of a linear increase in LUT memory size. In addition, the number of inputs and the bit width of the adder/subtractor must increase. Mapping this approach onto an FPGA involves a trade-off between the routing resources consumed and the speed of the computation, as the input data bit vectors must be divided into subwords and distributed to multiple CLBs. In addition, multiple LUT outputs must be accumulated at a single destination to form the result, which consumes further routing.

Following a derivation similar to that presented by White [2], we can analyze this trade-off quantitatively. Suppose that we are implementing an M-tap filter

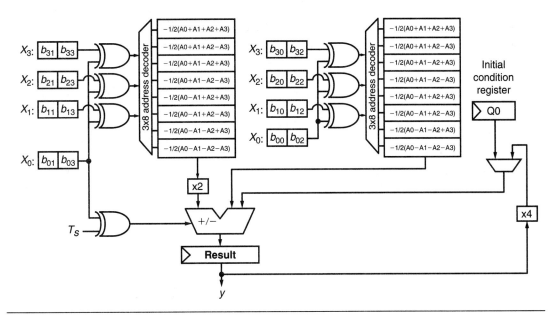

FIGURE 24.4 ■ Two-bit-at-a-time reduced memory DA implementation.

using an N-bit number representation and that the computation is proceeding L bits at a time. Further suppose that the LUT data is W bits wide. Computing the result requires that, in each cycle, MN bits are shifted in and WL bits are read out, and N/L clock cycles must pass. The number of wires N_W is therefore

$$N_W = \frac{MN}{N/L} + WL = (M + W)L \qquad (24.10\text{a})$$

If we define the relative importance of minimizing routing resources to minimizing latency as the ratio r, then

$$r = \frac{N/L}{N_W} = \frac{N}{(M + W)L^2} \qquad (24.10\text{b})$$

and we can find the L that satisfies our design criterion of relative importance r:

$$L = \left\lceil \sqrt{\frac{N}{r(M + W)}} \right\rceil \qquad (24.10\text{c})$$

Now suppose that an application demands low latency and that routing resources are not too tightly constrained; then, for $r = 2$, 32-bit input data ($N = 32$), a 4-tap FIR filter ($M = 4$), and 4-bit LUT data ($W = 4$); this yields $L = 2$. The desired DA implementation takes the input data 2 bits at a time to address the LUTs, completing a dot product computation in 16 cycles.

In addition to exploiting parallelism to speed up the DA computation, it is possible to employ various levels of pipelining. As we saw in Figure 24.1, the critical path involves decoding the address presented by the data shift registers, accessing the row from the LUT, and propagating the carry through the adder/subtractor while meeting the setup time constraints for the accumulator. If the implementation spans multiple CLBs, there is a potentially significant interconnect delay in this critical path in addition to the combinational logic delay. An obvious way to pipeline the simple implementation is to make the LUT synchronous and latch the outputs before they are fed to the adder/subtractor.

An alternative approach is to use carry save addition to reduce the carry propagation chain in the critical path [8]. The key modification to Figure 24.1 is to use a different structure for the adder/subtractor and to perform the computation in LSB first order. Instead of using a carry propagate adder to accumulate the entire result in one clock cycle, the adder/subtractor is pipelined at the bit level and the sum and carry outputs are stored in flip-flops at each cycle. Each full adder takes one input bit from the LUT output and one from the sum output of the next most significant full adder, automatically accounting for the x2 scaling required in Figure 24.1. Assuming that the accumulator is wider than N bits, after N clock cycles the least significant N bits of the final result are stored in the LSBs of the accumulator while the remaining MSBs require one more carry propagating addition to produce the final result. This operation adds one extra clock cycle to the latency of the DA computation.

Most modern FPGA fabrics have dedicated paths for high-speed carry propagation. Given that most DA designs require accumulators with not too many more than N bits, the final carry propagation is typically not the critical path for the entire computation. The throughput is determined by the speed of the carry save addition in the accumulator.

Although using carry save addition at the single-bit level results in the greatest speed improvement, it is also the most resource intensive in terms of logic slices and CLBs. A speed versus area trade-off can be achieved by partitioning the adder/subtractor into multiple subcircuits, each of which propagates a carry across p bits ($p = 1$ in the example just described). Speedup factors of at least 1.5 have been observed over the traditional design shown in Figure 24.1 [8].

24.5 AN APPLICATION OF DA ON AN FPGA

In addition to FIR filters, a common DA application on FPGAs is acceleration of frequency transformations such as the discrete cosine transform (DCT), which is a critical component of the MPEG video compression and JPEG image compression standards. The two-dimensional DCT can be implemented as two one-dimensional DCTs and a matrix transposition. Each DCT can be implemented as a matrix–vector multiplication, which is easy to implement on an FPGA using DA because it can be decomposed into a set of vector dot products.

In one example, using DA instead of multiply–accumulate for the DCT resulted in a factor of 2.4 reduction in area for the FPGA implementation (on a Xilinx XC6200 FPGA) [9]. Using DA and pipelining of the routing to improve the algorithm performance, this implementation was fast enough to process VGA resolution images (640 × 480 pixels) at 25 frames per second—approximately four times faster than a full software implementation running on a microprocessor. The entire two-dimensional DCT consumed a 64 × 78 array of logic blocks on the chip (about 30 percent of the total FPGA area) and the DA portions of the DCT consumed 3648 logic blocks, or about 70 percent of the two-dimensional DCT total. The average utilization of each logic block for the DA components was 61 percent. This high level of utilization was a result of careful floorplanning in addition to DA's inherent suitability to FPGA implementation.

References

[1] Xilinx, Inc. *The Role of Distributed Arithmetic in FPGA-based Signal Processing*, Xilinx, Inc. (*http://www.xilinx.com/appnotes/theory1.pdf*), January 2006.

[2] S. A. White. Applications of distributed arithmetic to digital signal processing: A tutorial review. IEEE *ASSP Magazine* 6(3), July 1989.

[3] L. Mintzer. FIR filters with field-programmable gate arrays. *Journal of VLSI Signal Processing* 6, 1993.

[4] G. Roslin. A guide to using field-programmable gate arrays (FPGAs) for application-specific digital signal processing performance. Xilinx white paper, 1995.

[5] W. Wolf. *FPGA-based System Design* (Modern Semiconductor Design Series), Prentice-Hall, 2004.

[6] Xilinx, Inc. *Spartan-3E FPGA Family: Complete Data Sheet*, DS312 (v2.0) (*http://www.xilinx.com*), November 2005.

[7] B. Calhoun, F. Honore, A. Chandrakasan. A leakage reduction methodology for distributed MTCMOS. *IEEE Journal of Solid-State Circuits* 39(5), May 2004.

[8] R. Grover, W. Shang, Q. Li. A faster distributed arithmetic architecture for FPGAs. *Proceedings of the 10th ACM International Symposium on Field-Programmable Gate Arrays*, February 2002.

[9] R. Woods, D. Trainor, J.-P. Heron. Applying an XC6200 to real-time image processing. *IEEE Design & Test of Computers* 15(1), January/March 1998.

CHAPTER 25

CORDIC ARCHITECTURES FOR FPGA COMPUTING

Chris Dick
Advanced Systems Technology Group
DSP Division of Xilinx, Inc.

Because field-programmable gate arrays (FPGAs) are often used for realizing complex mathematical calculations, the FPGA designer is in need of a set of math libraries to support such implementations. The literature is rich with algorithmic options for evaluating the type of math functions (e.g., sine, cosine, sinh, cosh, arctangent, atan2, logarithms) that are typically found in a math library for general-purpose and DSP processors. The enormous flexibility of the FPGA coupled with the vast suite of algorithmic options for computing math functions can make the development of an FPGA math library a challenging task.

Common approaches to evaluating math functions include polynomial approximation-based techniques [13] and Newton-style iterations [13], to name a couple. One of the most useful and flexible approaches available to the hardware designer for developing high-performance computing hardware is the CORDIC (COordinate Rotation DIgital Computer) algorithm.

CORDIC is unparalleled in its ability to encapsulate a diversity of math functions in one basic set of iterations. It can be viewed as the Swiss Army Knife, so to speak, of arithmetic—that is, a single hardware architecture, with very minimal control overhead, having the ability to compute sine, cosine, cosh, sinh, atan2, square root, and polar-to-rectangular and rectangular-to-polar conversions, to name only a few functions.

It is in coordinate transformations that the algorithm comes into its own. In both, multi-operand input and multi-element output vectors are involved. There are a plethora of alternatives for realizing, say, division in an FPGA, and most of the CORDIC alternatives provide good hardware efficiency. However, the algorithm remains unrivaled when it comes to processing multi-element I/O vectors, as is the case when converting from Cartesian to polar coordinates or vice versa. CORDIC falls into the class of shift-and-add algorithms—it is a multiplierless method dominated by additions. FPGAs are very efficient at realizing arbitrary precision adders, and so the CORDIC algorithm is in many ways a natural fit for course-grained FPGA architectures such as the Xilinx Virtex-4 family of devices [41].

This chapter begins with a brief tutorial overview of the CORDIC algorithm. Because most hardware realizations of CORDIC employ fixed-point arithmetic, design considerations for quantizing the datapath and selecting a suitable number of iterations are provided. Approaches for architecting FPGA CORDIC processors are then presented. Various options are discussed that highlight the use of FPGA features such as embedded multipliers, embedded multiply–accumulator (MACC) tiles, and logic fabric to deliver hardware realizations that provide various trade-offs between throughput, latency, logic fabric utilization, and numerical accuracy. A brief overview of the System Generator [38] design flow used to produce our implementations is also provided. Design considerations for producing very high throughput (450–500 MHz) implementations in Virtex-4 [41] devices are presented as well.

25.1   CORDIC ALGORITHM

The CORDIC algorithm was first published by Volder [35] in 1959 as a technique for efficiently implementing the trigonometric functions required for real-time aircraft navigation. Since first being published, the method has been extensively analyzed and extended to the point where a very rich set of functions is accessible from the one basic set of equations. The algorithm is dominated by bit shifts and additions and so was an ideal match for early-generation computing technology in which multiplication and division were expensive in terms of computation time and physical resources. Volder essentially presented iterative techniques for performing translations between Cartesian and polar coordinate systems (*vectoring mode*), and a method for realizing a plane rotation (*rotation mode*) using a series of arithmetic shifts and adds.

Since its publication, the CORDIC algorithm has been applied to many different applications and has been used as the cornerstone of the arithmetic engine in many VLSI signal-processing implementations [34]. It has been used extensively for computing various types of transforms, including the fast Fourier transform (FFT) [10,11], the discrete cosine transform [4], and the discrete Hartley transform [3]. And it has found widespread use in realizing various classes of digital filters, including Kalman filters [31], adaptive lattice structures [21], and adaptive nulling [30]. A large body of work has been published on CORDIC-based approaches for implementing various types of linear algebra operations, including singular value decomposition (SVD) [1], Given's rotations [30], and QRD-RLS (recursive least squares) filtering [14].

A brief tutorial style treatment of the basic algorithm is provided here; its FPGA implementation will be discussed in subsequent sections.

25.1.1   Rotation Mode

The CORDIC algorithm has two basic modes: vectoring and rotation. These can be applied in several coordinate systems, including circular, hyperbolic, and linear, to compute various functions such as atan2, sine, cosine, and even division. We begin our treatment by considering the problem of constructing an efficient method to realize a plane rotation of the vector (x_s, y_s) through an angle θ to produce a vector (x_f, y_f), as shown in Figure 25.1.

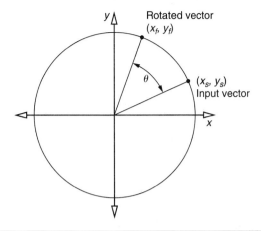

FIGURE 25.1 ■ Plane rotation of the vector (x_s, y_s) through an angle θ.

The rotation is formally captured in matrix form by equation 25.1.

$$\begin{bmatrix} x_f \\ y_f \end{bmatrix} = \begin{bmatrix} \cos\theta & -\sin\theta \\ \sin\theta & \cos\theta \end{bmatrix} \begin{bmatrix} x_s \\ y_s \end{bmatrix} = ROT(\theta) \begin{bmatrix} x_s \\ y_s \end{bmatrix} \qquad (25.1)$$

which can be expanded to the set of equations in equation 25.2.

$$\begin{aligned} x_f &= x_s \cos\theta - y_s \sin\theta \\ y_f &= x_s \sin\theta + y_s \cos\theta \end{aligned} \qquad (25.2)$$

The development of a simplified approach for producing rotation through the angle θ begins by considering it not as one lumped operation but as the result of a series of smaller rotations, or *micro-rotations*, through the set of angles α_i where

$$\theta = \sum_{i=0}^{\infty} \alpha_i \qquad (25.3)$$

The rotation can now be cast as a product of smaller rotations, or

$$ROT(\theta) = \prod_{i} ROT(\alpha_i) \qquad (25.4)$$

If these values α_i are carefully chosen, we can provide a very efficient computation structure. Equation 25.2 can be modified to reflect a micro-rotation $ROT(\alpha_i)$, leading to equation 25.5.

$$\begin{aligned} x_{i+1} &= x_i \cos\alpha_i - y_i \sin\alpha_i \\ y_{i+1} &= x_i \sin\alpha_i + y_i \cos\alpha_i \end{aligned} \qquad (25.5)$$

where $(x_0, y_0) = (x_s, y_s)$. Factoring permits the equations to be expressed as

$$\begin{aligned} x_{i+1} &= \cos\alpha_i (x_i - y_i \tan\alpha_i) \\ y_{i+1} &= \cos\alpha_i (y_i + x_i \tan\alpha_i) \end{aligned} \qquad (25.6)$$

which positions the iterative update as the product of two procedures: a scaling by the $\cos\alpha_i$ term and a similarity transformation, or scaled rotation.

The next significant step that leads to an algorithm that lends itself to an efficient hardware realization is to place restrictions on the values that α_i can take. If

$$\alpha_i = \tan^{-1}\left(\sigma_i 2^{-i}\right) \tag{25.7}$$

where $\sigma_i \in \{-1, +1\}$, then equation 25.6 can be written as

$$
\begin{aligned}
x_{i+1} &= \cos\alpha_i \left(x_i - \sigma_i y_i 2^{-i}\right) \\
y_{i+1} &= \cos\alpha_i \left(y_i + \sigma_i x_i 2^{-i}\right)
\end{aligned}
\tag{25.8}
$$

The purpose of σ_i will be explained shortly.

With the exception of the scaling term, these equations can be implemented using only additions, subtractions, and shifts. In the set of equations that are typically presented as the CORDIC iterations, and following the lead of Volder [35], the scaling term is usually excluded from the defining equations to produce the modified set of equations

$$
\begin{aligned}
x_{i+1} &= x_i - \sigma_i y_i 2^{-i} \\
y_{i+1} &= y_i + \sigma_i x_i 2^{-i}
\end{aligned}
\tag{25.9}
$$

To determine the value of these σ_i we introduce a new variable, z (the *angle* variable). The recurrence on z is defined by equation 25.10.

$$z_{i+1} = z_i - \sigma_i \tan^{-1}\left(2^{-i}\right) \tag{25.10}$$

If the z variable is initialized with the desired angle of rotation θ—that is, z_0—it can be driven to 0 by conditionally adding or subtracting terms of the form $\tan^{-1}\left(2^{-i}\right)$ from the state variable z. The conditioning is captured by the term σ_i as a test on the sign of the current state of the angle variable z_i—that is,

$$\sigma_i = \begin{cases} 1 & \text{if } z_i \geq 0 \\ -1 & \text{if } z_i < 0 \end{cases} \tag{25.11}$$

Driving z to 0 is actually an iterative process for decomposing θ into a weighted linear combination of terms of the form $\tan^{-1}\left(2^{-i}\right)$. As z goes to 0, the vector (x_0, y_0) experiences a sequence of micro-rotation extensions that in the limit $n \to \infty$ converge to the coordinates (x_f, y_f).

The complete algorithm is summarized in equation 25.12.

$$
\begin{aligned}
i &= 0 \\
x_0 &= x_s \\
y_0 &= y_s \\
z_0 &= \theta \\
x_{i+1} &= x_i - \sigma_i y_i 2^{-i} \\
y_{i+1} &= y_i + \sigma_i x_i 2^{-i} \\
z_{i+1} &= z_i - \sigma_i \tan^{-1}\left(2^{-i}\right) \\
\sigma_i &= \begin{cases} 1 & \text{if } z_i \geq 0 \\ -1 & \text{if } z_i < 0 \end{cases}
\end{aligned}
\tag{25.12}
$$

which is easily realized in hardware because of the simple nature of the arithmetic required. The only complex function is the $\tan^{-1}$, which can be pre-computed and stored in a memory.

Because of the manner in which the updates are directed, this mode of the CORDIC algorithm is sometimes referred to as the *z-reduction mode*. Figure 25.2 shows the signal flow graph for the algorithm. Observe the butterfly-style architecture in the cross-addition update.

25.1.2 Scaling Considerations

Because the scaling term $\cos \alpha_i$ has not been carried over into equation 25.12, the input vector (x_0, y_0) not only undergoes a rotation but also experiences scaling or growth by a factor $1/\cos \alpha_i$ at each iteration. That is,

$$
\begin{aligned}
R_{i+1} = K_{c,i} R_i &= \frac{1}{\cos \alpha_i} R_i = \left(1 + \sigma_i^2 2^{-2i}\right)^{1/2} R_i \\
&= \left(1 + 2^{-2i}\right)^{1/2} R_i
\end{aligned}
\tag{25.13}
$$

where $R_i = |x_i + jy_i|$ designates the modulus of the vector at iteration i, and the subscript c associates the scaling constant with the *circular* coordinate system.

Figure 25.3 illustrates the growth process at each of the intermediate CORDIC iterations as (x_0, y_0), which is translated to its final location (x_f, y_f). For an infinite number of iterations the scaling factor is

$$
K_c = \prod_{i=0}^{\infty} \left(1 + 2^{-2i}\right)^{1/2} \approx 1.6468
\tag{25.14}
$$

It should also be noted that, since $\sigma_i \in \{-1, +1\}$, the scaling term is a constant that is independent of the angle of rotation.

As captured by equation 25.4, the angle of rotation θ is decomposed into an infinite number of elemental angles α_i, which implies that an infinite number of iterations is theoretically required. In practice, a finite number of iterations, n, is selected to make the system realizable in software or hardware. Application of n iterations translates (x_0, y_0) to (x_n, y_n) rather than to (x_f, y_f)

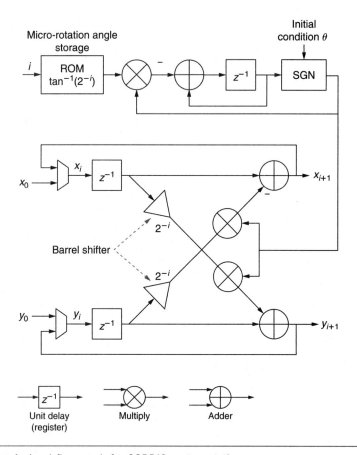

FIGURE 25.2 ■ A signal flow graph for CORDIC vector rotation.

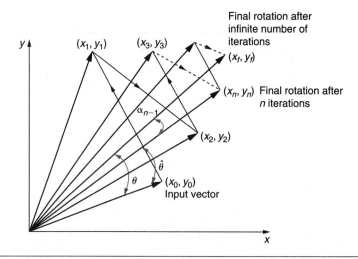

FIGURE 25.3 ■ Each iteration of a CORDIC rotation introduces vector growth by a factor of
$\frac{1}{\cos \alpha_i} = \left(1 + \sigma_i^2 2^{-2i}\right)^{1/2}$.

as shown in Figure 25.3. The rotation error $\left|\arg\left(x_f + jy_f\right) - \arg\left(x_n + jy_n\right)\right|$ has an upper bound of α_{n-1}, which is the smallest term in the weighted linear expansion of θ.

For an *infinite-precision* arithmetic implementation of the system of equations, each iteration contributes one additional effective fractional bit to the result. Most hardware implementations of the CORDIC algorithm are realized using fixed-point arithmetic, and, as will be discussed soon, the relationship between the number of effective output binary result digits is very different from that of a floating-point realization of the algorithm.

25.1.3 Vectoring Mode

The CORDIC vectoring mode is most commonly used for implementing a conversion from a rectangular to a polar coordinate system. In contrast to rotation mode, where Z is driven to 0, in the vectoring mode the initial vector (x_0, y_0) is rotated until the y component is driven to 0. The modification to the basic algorithm required to accomplish this goal is to direct the iterations using the sign of y_i. As the y variable is reduced, the corresponding angle of rotation is accumulated in the z register. The complete vectoring algorithm is captured by equation 25.15.

$$
\begin{aligned}
i &= 0 \\
x_0 &= x_s \\
y_0 &= y_s \\
z_0 &= 0 \\
x_{i+1} &= x_i - \sigma_i y_i 2^{-i} \\
y_{i+1} &= y_i + \sigma_i x_i 2^{-i} \\
z_{i+1} &= z_i - \sigma_i \tan^{-1}\left(2^{-i}\right) \\
\sigma_i &= \begin{cases} 1 & \text{if } y_i < 0 \\ -1 & \text{if } y_i \geq 0 \end{cases}
\end{aligned}
\tag{25.15}
$$

This CORDIC mode is commonly referred to as *y-reduction* mode.

Figure 25.4 shows the results of a CORDIC vector mode simulation for $\arg(x_s + jy_s) = 7\pi/8$ and $|x_s + jy_s| = 1$. The top plot (a) shows the true angle of the input vector (solid line) overlaid with $\arg(x_i + jy_i), i = 1, \ldots, 16$. We note the oscillatory behavior of (x_i, y_i) about the true value of the angle. Overdamped or underdamped behavior will be produced depending on the system initial conditions. The lower plot (b) shows, for this case of initial conditions, how rapidly the algorithm can converge toward the correct solution. In fact, for many practical applications, a *short* CORDIC (small number of iterations) produces acceptable performance.

For example, in a 16-QAM (quadrature amplitude modulation) carrier recovery circuit [29] employing a Costas Loop [23], a 5-iteration CORDIC usually provides adequate performance [12].

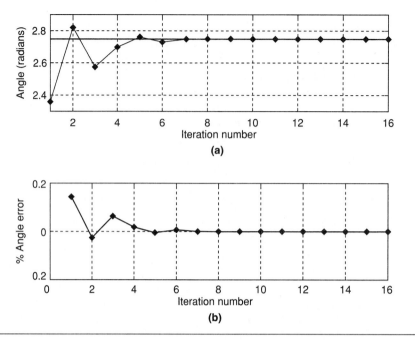

FIGURE 25.4 ▪ Convergence of CORDIC vectoring. The top plot (a) shows the true angle of the input vector $\arg(x_s + jy_s)$ (solid line) overlaid with $\arg(x_i + jy_i)$, $i = 1,\ldots,16$. The bottom plot (b) is the percentage angle error as a function of the iteration number.

25.1.4   Multiple Coordinate Systems and a Unified Description

Alternative versions of the CORDIC engine can be defined under the circular, hyperbolic, and linear coordinate systems [13]. These use a computation similar to that of the basic CORDIC algorithm, but can provide additional functions. It is possible to capture the vectoring and rotation modes of the CORDIC algorithm in all three coordinate systems using a single set of unified equations. To do this a new variable, m, is introduced to identify the coordinate system so that

$$m = \begin{cases} +1 & \text{circular coordinates} \\ 0 & \text{linear coordinates} \\ -1 & \text{hyperbolic coordinates} \end{cases} \tag{25.16}$$

The unified micro-rotation is

$$\begin{aligned} x_{i+1} &= x_i - m\sigma_i y_i 2^{-i} \\ y_{i+1} &= y_i + \sigma_i x_i 2^{-i} \end{aligned} \tag{25.17}$$

$$z_{i+1} = \begin{cases} z_i - \sigma_i \tan^{-1}\left(2^{-i}\right) & \text{if } m = 1 \\ z_i - \sigma_i \tan \text{h}^{-1}\left(2^{-i}\right) & \text{if } m = -1 \\ z_i - \sigma_i \left(2^{-i}\right) & \text{if } m = 0 \end{cases}$$

The scaling factor is $K_{m,i} = \left(1 + m2^{-2i}\right)^{1/2}$.

TABLE 25.1 ■ Functions computed by a CORDIC processor for the circular ($m = 1$), hyperbolic ($m = -1$), and linear ($m = 0$) coordinate systems

Coordinate system	Rotation/vectoring	Initialization	Result vector
1	Rotation	$x_0 = x_s$	$x_n = K_{1,n} \cdot (x_s \cos\theta - y_s \sin\theta)$
		$y_0 = y_s$	$y_n = K_{1,n} \cdot (y_s \cos\theta + x_s \sin\theta)$
		$z_0 = \theta$	$z_n = 0$
		$x_0 = 1/K_{1,n}$	$x_n = \cos\theta$
		$y_0 = 0$	$y_n = \sin\theta$
		$z_0 = \theta$	$z_n = 0$
1	Vectoring	$x_0 = x_s$	$x_n = K_{1,n} \cdot \operatorname{sgn}(x_0) \cdot \left(\sqrt{x^2 + y^2}\right)$
		$y_0 = y_s$	$y_n = 0$
		$z_0 = \theta$	$z_n = \theta + \tan^{-1}(y_s/x_s)$
0	Rotation	$x_0 = x_s$	$x_n = x_s$
		$y_0 = y_s$	$y_n = y_s + x_s y_s$
		$z_0 = z_s$	$z_n = 0$
0	Vectoring	$x_0 = x_s$	$x_n = x_s$
		$y_0 = y_s$	$y_n = 0$
		$z_0 = z_s$	$z_n = z_s + y_s/x_s$
-1	Rotation	$x_0 = x_s$	$x_n = K_{-1,n} \cdot (x_s \cosh\theta + y_s \sinh\theta)$
		$y_0 = y_s$	$y_n = K_{-1,n} \cdot (y_s \cosh\theta + x_s \sinh\theta)$
		$z_0 = \theta$	$z_n = 0$
		$x_0 = 1/K_{-1,n}$	$x_n = \cosh\theta$
		$y_0 = 0$	$y_n = \sinh\theta$
		$z_0 = \theta$	$z_n = 0$
-1	Vectoring	$x_0 = x_s$	$x_n = K_{-1,n} \cdot \operatorname{sgn}(x_0) \cdot \left(\sqrt{x^2 - y^2}\right)$
		$y_0 = y_s$	$y_n = 0$
		$z_0 = \theta$	$z_n = \theta + \tanh^{-1}(y_s/x_s)$

TABLE 25.2 ■ CORDIC shift sequences, ranges of convergence, and scale factor bound for circular, linear, and hyperbolic coordinate systems

Coordinate system	Shift sequence	Convergence	Scale factor
m	$s_{m,i}$	θ_{MAX}	$K_m \ (n \to \infty)$
1	$0, 1, 2, 3, 4, \ldots, i, \ldots$	≈ 1.74	≈ 1.64676
0	$1, 2, 3, 4, 5, \ldots, i{+}1, \ldots$	1.0	1.0
-1	$1, 2, 3, 4, 4, 5, \ldots$*	≈ 1.13	≈ 0.83816

∗ For $m = -1$, the following iterations are repeated: $\{4, 13, 40, 121, \ldots, k, 3k+1, \ldots\}$.

Operating the two modes in the three coordinate systems, in combination with suitable initialization of the algorithm variables, generates a rich set of functions, shown in Table 25.1. Table 25.2 summarizes the shift sequences, maximum angle of convergence θ_{MAX} (elaborated on in a later section), and scaling function for the three coordinate systems. Note that each system requires slightly different shift sequences (the sequence of i values).

25.1.5 Computational Accuracy

One of the first design requirements for the fixed-point arithmetic implementation of a CORDIC processor is to define the numerical precision requirements of the datapath. This includes defining the numeric representation for the input operands and the processing engine internal registers, in addition to the number of micro-rotations that will be required to achieve a specified numerical quality of result. To guide this process it is useful to have an appreciation for the sources of computation noise in CORDIC arithmetic. While CORDIC processing can be realized with floating-point arithmetic [2, 7], we will restrict our discussion to fixed-point arithmetic implementations, as they are the most commonly used numeric type employed in FPGA realizations.

Two primary noise sources are to be considered. One is associated with the weighted and finite linear combination of elemental angles that are used to represent the desired angle of rotation θ; the second source is associated with the rounding of the datapath variables x, y, and z. These noise sources are referred to as the *angle approximation* and the *rounding error*, respectively.

Angle approximation error
In this discussion we assume that all finite-precision quantities are represented using fixed-point 2's complement arithmetic, so the value F of a normalized number u represented using m binary digits $(u_{m-1}u_{u-2}\ldots u_0)$ is

$$F = -u_{m-1} + \sum_{j=0}^{m-2} u_j \cdot 2^{-m+j+1} \tag{25.18}$$

As will be presented next, there is a requirement in the CORDIC algorithm to accommodate bit growth in both the integer and fractional fields of the x and y variables. To accommodate this, the data format is enhanced with an additional G_I and G_F integer and fractional guard bits, respectively, so that a number with $B_I + G_I$ and $B_F + G_F$ bits allocated to the integer and fractional fields s and r, respectively $(s_{B_I+G_I-1}s_{B_I+G_I-2}\cdots s_0 r_{B_F+G_F-1}r_{B_F+G_F-2}\cdots r_0)$, is expressed as

$$F = -r_{B_I+G_I-1} \cdot 2^{B_I+G_I-1} + \sum_{j=0}^{B_I+G_I-2} s_j \cdot 2^j + \sum_{j=0}^{B_F+G_F-1} r_j \cdot 2^{-(B_F+G_F)+j} \tag{25.19}$$

Figure 25.5 illustrates the extended data format. The integer guard bits are necessary to accommodate the vector growth experienced when operating in circular coordinates. The fractional guard bits are required to support the word growth that occurs in the fractional field of the x and y registers due to the successive arithmetic shift-right operations employed in the iterative updates. It is assumed that the input samples are represented as normalized $(1 \cdot B_F)$ quantities.

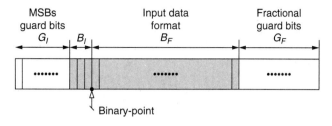

MSBs guard bits G_I — B_I — Input data format B_F — Fractional guard bits G_F

Binary-point

FIGURE 25.5 ■ The fractional fixed-point data format used for internal storage in the quantized CORDIC algorithm.

There are n fixed rotation angles $\alpha_{m,i}$ employed to approximate a desired angle of rotation θ. Neglecting all other error sources, the accuracy of the calculation is governed by the nth and final rotation, which limits the angle approximation error to $\alpha_{m,n-1}$. Because $\alpha_{m,n-1} = \frac{1}{\sqrt{m}}\tan^{-1}\left(\sqrt{m}\cdot 2^{-s_{m,n-1}}\right)$, the angle approximation error can be made arbitrarily small by increasing the number of micro-rotations n. Of course, the number of bits allocated to represent the elemental angles $\alpha_{m,i}$ needs to be sufficient to support the smallest angle $\alpha_{m,n-1}$. The number representation defined in equation 25.19 results in a least significant digit weighting of $2^{-(B_F+G_F)}$. Therefore, $\alpha_{m,n-1} \geq 2^{-(B_F+G_F)}$ must hold in order to represent $\alpha_{m,n-1}$. Approximately $n+1$ iterations are required to generate B_F significant fractional bits.

Datapath rounding error
As discussed earlier, most FPGA realizations of CORDIC processors employ fixed-point arithmetic. The update of the x, y, and z state variables according to equation 25.12 produces a dynamic range expansion, which is ideally supported by precisions that accommodate the worst-case bit growth. The number of additional guard bits beyond the original precision of the input operands can be very large, and carrying these additional bits in the datapath is generally impractical. For example, in the circular mode of operation the number of additional fractional bits required to support a full-precision calculation is determined by the sum of the shift sequence $s_{m,i}$.

If the input operands are presented as a 16.15 value (a 16-bit field width with 15 fractional bits) and 16 micro-rotations are performed, the bit growth for the fractional component of the datapath is $\sum_{i=0}^{15} i = 120$ bits. Thus, the total number of fractional bits required for a full-precision calculation is $120 + 15 = 135$. While FPGAs certainly provide the capability to support arbitrary precision arithmetic, it would be highly unusual to construct a CORDIC processor with such a wide datapath. In fact, the error in the CORDIC result vector can be maintained to a desired value using far few fractional guard bits, as discussed next.

Rather than by accommodating the bit growth implied in the algorithm, the dynamic range expansion is better handled by rounding the newly computed state variables. Control over wordlength can be achieved using unbiased rounding, simple truncation, or other techniques [26]. True rounding, while the preferred approach because of the smaller error introduced when compared to truncation, can be the most area consuming because a second addition is potentially required. In some cases, the cost of rounding can be significantly reduced by exploiting the carry-in port of the adders used in the implementation. Truncation is obviously the simplest approach, requiring only the extraction of a bit field from the full-precision value, but it introduces an undesirable positive bias in the final result and an error component that is twice the magnitude of unbiased rounding. Nevertheless, truncation arithmetic is the option most frequently employed in FPGA CORDIC datapath design.

A simple approach to understanding the quantization effects of the CORDIC algorithm was first presented by Walther [36]. A very complete analysis was later published by Hu [16], with further work reported by Park and Cho [28] and Hu and Bass [17].

For many practical applications Walther's method produces acceptable results, and this is the approach we will use to design the FPGA implementations. A brief summary of the method is presented here.

Analysis of the rounding error for the z variable is straightforward because there are no data shifts involved in the state update, as there are with the x and y variables. The rounding error is simply due to the quantization of the rotation angles. The upper bound on the error is then the accumulation of the absolute values of the rounding errors for the quantized angles $\alpha_{m,i}$.

Datapath pruning and its associated quantization effects for the x and y variables is certainly a more challenging analysis than that for the angle variable because the scaling term involved in the cross-addition update. Nevertheless, several extensive treatments have been published. The effects of error propagation in the algorithm were reported by Hu in a Cray Research publication [5] and later extended by Hu and Bass [17]. Walther's treatment takes a slightly simplified approach and assumes that the maximum rounding error for n iterations is the sum of the absolute value of the maximum rounding error associated with each micro-rotation and the subsequent quantization that is performed to control word growth.

The format for the CORDIC variables was shown in Figure 25.5. $B = B_I + B_F + G_F + G_I$ bits are used to for internal storage, with $B_F + G_F$ of these bits assigned to the fractional component of the representation. The maximum error for one iteration is therefore of magnitude $2^{-(B_F+G_F)}$. In the simplified analysis, the rounding error $e(n)$ in the final result, and after all n iterations, is simply n times this quantity, which is $e(n) = n2^{-(B_F+G_F)}$. If B_F accurate fractional bits are required in the result word, the required resolution is $2^{-(B_F-1)}$. If B_F is selected such that $e(n) \leq 2^{-B_F}$, the datapath quantization can effectively be ignored. This implies that $n2^{-(B_F+G_F)} \leq 2^{-B_F}$, which requires $B_F \geq \log_2(n)$. Therefore, $G_F = \lceil \log_2(n) \rceil$ fractional guard bits are required to produce a result that has an accuracy of B_F fractional bits. This simplified treatment of the computation noise is a reasonable approximation that can help guide the definition of the datapath width required to meet a specified numerical fidelity.

Figure 25.6 shows the results of a simulation using different data representations for the x, y, and z variables of a CORDIC vectoring algorithm in circular

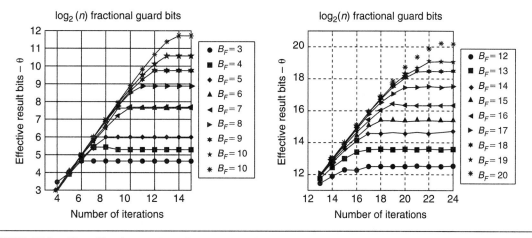

FIGURE 25.6 ■ The effiective number of result bites for a CORDIC vector processor (circular coordinates). The number of fractional guard bites is $G_F = \lceil log_2(n) \rceil$.

coordinates. Unit modulus complex vectors with random angles were generated and projected onto the CORDIC input sample (x_0, y_0). Each sample point in the plot represents the maximum absolute error of the angle estimate resulting from 4000 trials. We note that in all of the simulations the effective number of fractional output bits is matched to the number of fractional bits in the input operand.

The simplified treatment of the rounding noise generated in the update equations is certainly pessimistic and produces a requirement on the number of guard bits that is biased slightly higher than what might typically be required.

Selecting $G_F = \lceil \log_2(n) \rceil$ is certainly a safe, if not a slightly overengineered, choice. In the context of an FPGA realization, an additional bit of precision carried by the variables has almost negligible impact on the area and maximum operating clock frequency of the design.

An additional observation from the plots in Figure 25.6 is that the production of B_F effective output digits requires more iterations than the $B_F + 1$ iterations required for a full floating-point implementation—an additional three iterations are, in general, necessary. The implication of this is that two additional bits must be allocated to represent the elemental angles to provide the angle resolution implied by the adjusted iteration count.

Defining the number of guard bits G_I is very straightforward based on the number of integer bits B_I in the input operands, the coordinate system to be employed (e.g., circular, hyperbolic, or linear), and the mode (vectoring or rotation). For example, if the input data is in standard 2's complement format and bounded by ± 1, then $B_I = 1$. This means that the l^2 norm of the input (x_0, y_0) is $\sqrt{2}$. For the CORDIC vectoring mode, the range extension introduced by the iterations is approximately $K_1 \approx 1.6468$ for any reasonable number of iterations. The maximum that the final value of the x register can assume is approximately $\sqrt{2} \cdot 1.6468 \approx 2.3289$, which requires that $G_I = 2$.

TABLE 25.3 ■ Number of rotations and required CORDIC processor datapath format required to achieve a desired number of effective output bits

Number of effective fractional result bits	Micro-rotations: n	Internal storage data format: x and y	Internal storage data format: z
8	10	(15.12)	(15.14)
12	15	(19.16)	(19.18)
16	19	(24.21)	(24.23)
24	27	(32.29)	(32.31)

Based on this approach, a reasonable procedure for selecting the number of CORDIC micro-rotations and a suitable quantization for the x, y, and z variables, given the effective number of fractional bits required in the output, is the following:

1. Define the number of iterations as $n = B_F + 3$.
2. Select the field width for the x and y variables as $2 + B_I + B_F + \log_2(n)$ for the vectoring mode in circular coordinates—$B_F + \log_2(n)$ of these bits are of course allocated to the fractional component of the register.
3. Select the fractional precision of the angle register z to be $B_F + \log_2(n) + 2$, while maintaining 1 bit for the integer portion of the register.
4. Apply similar reasoning to select n and G_I for the other coordinate systems and modes.

Based on this approach, Table 25.3 shows the number of micro-rotations n and the internal data storage format corresponding to 8, 12, 16, 24, and 32 effective fractional result bits. The notation $(p \cdot q)$ indicates a bit field width of p bits, with q of these bits allocated to the fractional component of the value.

25.2 ARCHITECTURAL DESIGN

There are many hardware architecture options to evaluate when considering FPGA CORDIC datapath implementation. A particular choice is determined by the design specifications of numerical accuracy, throughput, and latency. At the highest level are key architectural decisions on whether a folded [27] or fully parallel [27] pipelined (or nonpipelined) architecture is to be used. At a lower, technology-specific level, FPGA features associated with a particular FPGA family are also a factor in the decision process. For example, later-generation FPGAs such as the Virtex-4 family [41] include an array of arithmetic units called the XtremeDSP Slice [43] (referred to as the DSP48 in the remainder of the chapter).

As discussed later, a CORDIC implementation can be realized that is mostly based on the DSP48 embedded tile. Thus, with this particular family of devices the designer has a choice of producing an implementation that is completely logic slice based [40] or biased toward the use of DSP48 elements. The process that guides such decisions is elaborated in the next section.

25.3 FPGA IMPLEMENTATION OF CORDIC PROCESSORS

One of the elegant properties of FPGA computing is the ability to construct a compute engine closely tailored to the problem specifications, including processing throughput, latency, and numerical accuracy. Consider, for example, the throughput requirement. At one end of the architecture spectrum, and when modest processing rates are involved, a fully folded [27] implementation, where the same logic is used for all iterations (folding factor = n), is one option. In this case, new operands are delivered, and a new result vector is produced, every n clock cycles. This choice of implementation results in the smallest FPGA footprint at the expense of processing rate. If a high-throughput unit is required, a fully parallel, or completely unfolded implementation (folding factor = 1) that allocates a complete hardware PE to each iteration is appropriate. This will of course result in the largest area, but provides the highest compute rate.

25.3.1 Convergence

One of the design considerations for the CORDIC engine is the region of convergence that needs to be supported by the implementation, as the basic form of the algorithm does not converge for all input coordinates. For the rotation mode, the CORDIC algorithm converges provided that the absolute value of the rotation angle is no larger than $\theta_{MAX} \approx 1.7433$ radians, or approximately $99.88°$.

In many applications we need to support input arguments that span all four quadrants of the complex plane—that is, a so-called *full-range* CORDIC. Much published work addresses this requirement [8, 19, 25], and many elegant extensions to the basic set of CORDIC iterations have been produced. Some of them introduce additional iterations and, while maintaining the basic shift-and-add property of the algorithm, result in a significant time or area penalty.

The most straightforward approach for handling the convergence issue in FPGA hardware is to first note that the natural range of convergence extends beyond the angle $\pi/2$. That is, the basic set of equations converges over the interval $[-\pi/2, \pi/2]$. To extend the implementation to converge over $[-\pi, \pi]$, we can simply detect when the input angle extends beyond the first quadrant, map that angle to either the first or fourth quadrants, and make a post-micro-rotation correction to account for the input angle mapping. This architecture is illustrated in Figure 25.7.

The input mapping is particularly simple. Referring to Figure 25.7, if x_0 is negative, the quadrants must be changed by applying $a \pm \pi/2$ ($\pm 90°$) rotation. Whether it is a positive or negative rotation is determined by the sign of y_0. To compensate for the input mapping, an angle rotation is conditionally applied to the micro-rotation engine result z_n' to produce the final output value z_n. Details

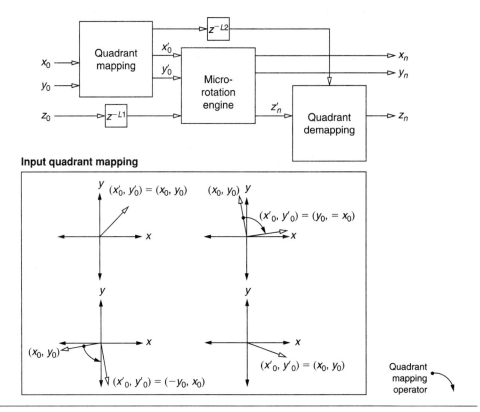

FIGURE 25.7 ▪ A full-range CORDIC processor showing input quadrant mapping, micro-rotation engine, and quadrant correction.

of the course angle rotator and matching quadrant correction circuit are shown in Figure 25.8. The area cost for an FPGA implementation of the circuits is modest [40].

25.3.2 Folded CORDIC

The folded CORDIC architecture allocates a single PE to service all of the required micro-rotations. At one architectural extreme a bit-serial implementation employing a single 3-2 full adder, with appropriate control circuitry and state storage, can address all of the required updates for x, y, and z. However, our treatment employs a word-oriented architecture that associates unique functional units (FU) with each of the x, y, and z processing engines, as shown in Figure 25.9.

Multiple mapping options are available when projecting the dependency graph onto an FPGA architecture. In the Xilinx Virtex-4 family [41], one option for supporting the adder/subtractor FUs is to utilize the logic fabric and realize these modules at the cost of one lookup table (LUT) per result digit. So for example, the addition of two 16-bit operands to generate a 17-bit sum requires 17 LUTs. An alternative is to use the 48-bit adder in the DSP48 tile.

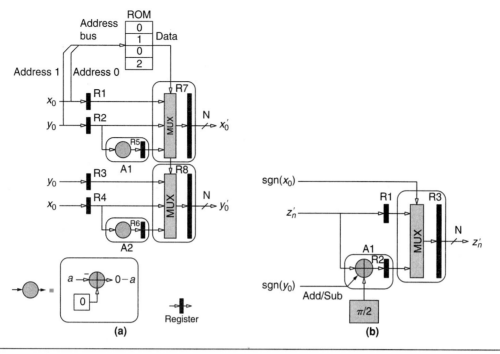

FIGURE 25.8 ■ A course angle rotator preceding a micro-rotation engine for a full-range CORDIC processor (a). A post-micro-rotation quadrant correction circuit (b).

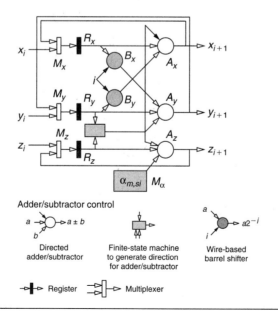

FIGURE 25.9 ■ A folded CORDIC architecture with separate functional units for each of the x, y, and z updates. Only the micro-rotation engine is shown.

There are also several mapping options for the barrel shifter: It can be realized in the logic fabric, with the multiplier in the DSP48 tile, or, for that matter, using an embedded multiplier in any FPGA family that supports this architectural component (e.g., Virtex-II Pro [39] or Spartan-3E [37]).

Consider a fabric-only implementation of a vectoring CORDIC algorithm in circular coordinates. In this case all of the FUs are implemented directly in the logic fabric. The FPGA area, A_F, can be expressed as

$$A_F = 3 \cdot a_{add} + 2 \cdot a_{barrel} + 3 \cdot a_{mux} + a_{LUT} + a_Q + a_{Q-1} \qquad (25.20)$$

where a_{add}, a_{barrel}, a_{mux}, a_{LUT}, a_Q, and a_{Q-1} correspond to the area of an adder, barrel shifter, input multiplexer, elementary angle LUT, quadrant input mapper, and output mapper circuits, respectively. The FPGA logic fabric is designed to efficiently support the implementation of arbitrary-precision high-speed adder/subtractors. Each configurable logic block (CLB) [41] includes dedicated circuitry that provides fast carry resolution, with the LUT itself producing the half-sum.

The component that can be costly in terms of area is the barrel shifter. The barrel shifter area cost can be much more significant than the aggregate cost of the adder/subtractors used for updating the x, y, and z variables. For example, in a design that supplies 16 effective result digits, the 2 barrel shifters occupy an aggregate area of 226 LUTs while the adders occupy 74 LUTs in total. Here, the barrel shifters have a footprint approximately three times that of the adders.

The barrel shifter area can be reduced if a multiplier-based barrel shifter is used rather than a purely logic fabric–based implementation. FPGA families such as Spartan-3E [37], Virtex-II Pro [39], and Virtex-4 [40] include an array of embedded multipliers, which are useful for realizing arithmetic shifts. The multiplier accepts 18-bit precision operands and produces a 36-bit result. When used as a barrel shifter, one port of the multiplier is supplied with the input operand that is to experience the arithmetic shift, while the second port accepts the shift value 2^i, where i is the iteration index. In a typical hardware implementation the iteration index rather than the exponentiated value is usually available in the control plane that coordinates the operation of the circuit. The exponentiation can be done via a small LUT implemented using distributed memory [40]. Multiple multiplier primitives can be combined with an adder to form a barrel shifter that can support a wider datapath. For the previous example, multiplier realization of the barrel shifter results in an FPGA footprint that is less than half that of an entirely fabric-based implementation.

The folded CORDIC architecture is a recursive graph, which means that deep pipelining cannot be employed to reduce the critical path. The structure can accept a new set of operands, and produces a result every n clock cycles.

25.3.3 Parallel Linear Array

When throughput is the overriding design consideration, a fully parallel pipelined CORDIC realization is the preferred architecture. With this approach

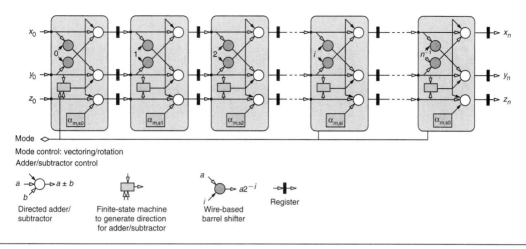

FIGURE 25.10 ■ A programmable parallel pipelined CORDIC array. In a completely unfolded implementation, the barrel shifters are realized as FPGA routing and so consume no resources other than interconnect.

the CORDIC algorithm is completely unrolled and each operation is projected onto a unique hardware resource, as shown in Figure 25.10.

One interesting effect of the unrolling is that the data shifts required in the cross-addition update can be realized as wiring between successive CORDIC processing elements (PEs). Unlike the folded architecture, where either LUTs or embedded multipliers are consumed to realize the barrel shifter, no resources other than interconnect are required to implement the shift in the linear array architecture. The only functional units required for each PE with this approach are three adder/subtractors and a small amount of logic to implement the control circuit that steers the add/subtract FUs. The micro-rotation angle for each PE is encoded as a constant supplied on one arm of the adder/subtractor that performs the angle update—no LUT resources are required for this. Note in Figure 25.10 that the sign bit of the y and z variables is supplied to the control circuit that is local to each processing engine. This permits the architecture to operate in the y- or z-reduction configuration under the control of the Mode input control signal, and thus support vectoring or rotation, respectively.

Figure 25.11(a) shows a comparison of the area functions for the parallel and folded architectures. The folded implementation is entirely fabric based. As expected, the area of the parallel design exhibits modest exponential growth and, for an effective number of result digits greater than 15, occupies more than three times the area of the folded architecture. For the case of 24 effective result digits, the parallel design is larger by a factor of approximately 5. Figure 25.11(b) contrasts the throughput of the two architectures. Naturally, the parallel design has a constant throughput of one CORDIC operation per second for a normalized clock rate of 1, while the throughput for the folded design falls off as the inverse of the number of iterations.

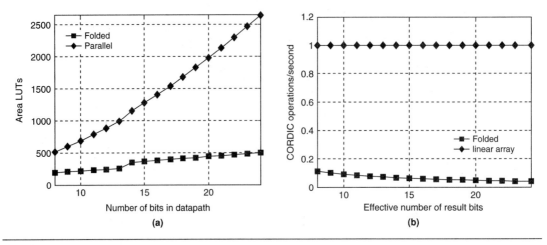

FIGURE 25.11 ■ (a) Comparison of the FPGA resource requirements for folded and linear array CORDIC architectures—circular coordinates. (b) Throughput in rotations/vectoring operations per second for the two architectures. A normalized clock rate of 1 is assumed.

The parallel design has a performance advantage of approximately an order of magnitude for the number of effective result bits great than 10. In an FPGA implementation the advantage is significantly more than this because of the higher clock frequency that can be supported by the linear array compared to the folded processor. With its heavy pipelining, the linear array typically achieves an operating frequency approximately twice that of the folded architecture, so for high-precision calculations—for example, on the order of 24 effective fractional bits or greater—the parallel implementation has a throughput advantage of approximately 50, which is delivered in a footprint that is only five times that of the folded design.

The add/subtract FUs can be realized using the logic fabric or the 48-bit adder that is resident in each DSP48 tile in the Virtex-4 class of FPGAs. The DSP48 [42] is a dynamically configurable embedded processing block that supports over 40 different op-codes, optimized for signal-processing tasks. The logic fabric approach tends to result in an implementation that operates at a lower clock frequency than a fully pipelined version based on the DSP48. The DSP48-based implementations can operate at very high clock frequencies—in the region of 500 MHz in the fastest "–12" speed-grade parts [40]. However, for a datapath precision of up to 36 bits, three DSP48 tiles are required for each CORDIC iteration (see Figures 25.12 and 25.13). For scenarios where throughput is the overarching requirement, these resource requirements are acceptable.

A potential downside to the use of the DSP48 in this application is that the multiplier colocated with the high-precision adder is not available for use by another function if the adder is used by the CORDIC PE. This is because the input and output ports of the block are occupied supporting the addition/subtraction and there is no I/O available to access other functions (such as the multiplier) in the tile.

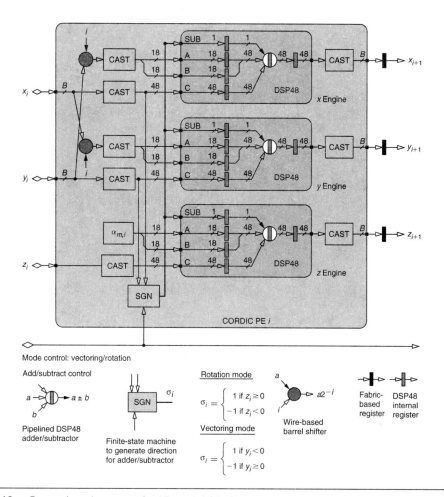

FIGURE 25.12 ■ Processing element i of a Virtex-4 DSP48-based CORDIC processor.

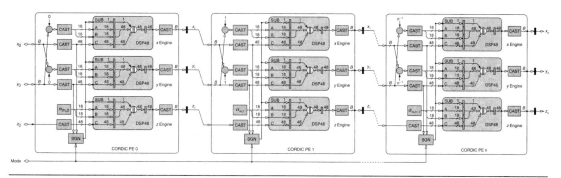

FIGURE 25.13 ■ A programmable parallel pipelined CORDIC array based almost entirely on the Virtex-4 DSP48 embedded tile. Each DSP48 has three levels of pipelining. Additional fabric-based registers are included to pipeline the routing between DSP48 tiles.

25.3.4 Scaling Compensation

As highlighted earlier, the rotation mode of the CORDIC algorithm produces a rotation extension (i.e., it increases or decreases the distance of the point from the origin) rather than a pure rotation. The growth associated with circular and hyperbolic coordinate systems is approximately $K_{1,n} \approx 1.6468$ and $K_{-1,n} \approx 0.8382$, respectively. In some applications this growth can be tolerated, and there is no need to perform any compensation. For example, if the vectoring mode is used to map the output vector of a discrete Fourier transform (DFT) from Cartesian to polar coordinates in order to compute a magnitude spectrum, the CORDIC scaling may not be an issue because all terms are similarly scaled. If the CORDIC output is to be further processed, there might be an opportunity to absorb the CORDIC scale factor in the postprocessing circuit. Continuing with the DFT example, if the magnitude spectrum is to be compared with a threshold in order to make a decision about a particular spectral bin, the CORDIC scaling can be absorbed into the threshold value.

If the scaling cannot be tolerated, several scaling compensation techniques are possible. Some approaches employ modified iterations [20, 32, 33] while others exploit alternatives such as online arithmetic [6]. Some methods merge scaling iterations with the basic CORDIC iterations [15], which result in either an area penalty or a time penalty if the basic CORDIC hardware is to be used for both the fundamental updates and the scaling iterations. It is also possible to employ a modified set of elemental angles [9].

The problem of scaling compensation has been examined by many researchers, and many creative and elegant results have been produced; however, the most direct way to accommodate the problem in an FPGA is to employ its embedded multipliers. The architecture of a programmable and scale-compensated CORDIC engine is shown in Figure 25.14. The `Mode` control signal defines if a vectoring or rotation operation is to be performed. It essentially controls if the iteration update is guided by the sign of the y or z variable for vectoring or rotation, respectively. The `Coordinate_System` signal selects the coordinate system for the processor: circular, hyperbolic, or linear. This control line selects the page in memory where the elemental angles are stored: $\tan^{-1}\left(2^{-i}\right)$, $i = 0, \ldots, n-1$ for circular; $\tanh^{-1}\left(2^{-i}\right)$, $i = 1, \ldots, n$ for hyperbolic; and $\left(2^{-i}\right)$, $i = 0, \ldots, n-1$ for linear. `Coordinate_System` also indexes a small memory located in FPGA distributed memory that stores the values $1/K_{m,n}$ for use by the scaling compensation multiplier $M1$. Naturally, the precision of these constants should be commensurate with the number of effective result bits.

25.4 SUMMARY

This chapter provided an overview of the CORDIC algorithm and its implementation in current-generation FPGAs such as the Xilinx Virtex-4 family. The basic set of CORDIC equations was first reviewed, and the utility of this simple shift-and-add-type algorithm was highlighted by the many functions that can be accessed through it. We also highlighted the fact that, while there are many options for architecting math functions in hardware, the CORDIC approach

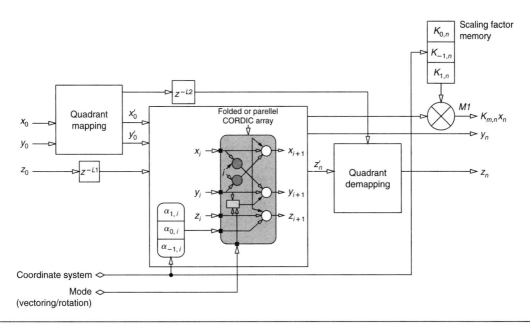

FIGURE 25.14 ■ A programmable CORDIC processor with multiplier-based scaling compensation.

comes into its own when multi-element input and output vectors are involved. The functional requirements of the angle and cross-addition updates make it an excellent match for FPGAs because of the utility and efficiency with which these devices realize addition and subtraction.

Most hardware realizations of the CORDIC algorithm employ fixed-point arithmetic, and this is certainly true of nearly all FPGA implementations. We showed that it is therefore important to understand the effects of quantizing the datapath. While this analysis can be complex [16], for most applications the simplified approach first described by Walther [36] is suitable for most cases and provides excellent results.

The FPGA implementation of a CORDIC processor would appear to be straightforward. However, FPGA-embedded functions such as multipliers and the DSP48 provide opportunities for architectural innovation and for design trade-offs that satisfy design requirements. For example, embedded multipliers can be exchanged for logic fabric with the implementation of the barrel shifter. The wide 48-bit adder in the DSP48 can be used almost as the sole arithmetic building block of a complete fully parallel CORDIC array.

References

[1] J. R. Cavallaro, F. T. Luk. CORDIC arithmetic for an SVD processor. *Journal of Parallel and Distributed Computing* 5, 1988.

[2] J. R. Cavallaro, F. T. Luk. Floating-point CORDIC for matrix computations. *Proceedings of the IEEE International Conference on Computer Design: VLSI in Computers and Processors*, October 1988.

[3] L. W. Chang, S. W. Lee. Systolic arrays for the discrete Hartley transform. *IEEE Transactions on Signal Processing* 29(11), November 1991.

[4] W. H. Chen, C. H. Smith, S. C. Fralick. A fast computational algorithm for the discrete cosine Transform. *IEEE Transactions on Communications* C-25, September 1977.

[5] Cray Research. *Cray XD1 Supercomputer, http://www.cray.com/products/xd1/ index.html*.

[6] H. Dawid, H. Meyer. The differential CORDIC algorithm: Constant scale factor redundant implementation without correcting iterations. *IEEE Transactions on Computers* 45(3), March 1996.

[7] A. A. J. de Lange, A. J. van der Hoeven, E. F. Deprettere, J. Bu. An optimal floating-point pipeline CMOS CORDIC processor. *IEEE Symposium on Circuits and Systems*, June 1988.

[8] J. M. Delsme. VLSI implementation of rotations in pseudo-Euclidean spaces. *Proceedings of the IEEE International Conference on Acoustics, Speech, and Signal Processing* 2, 1983.

[9] E. Deprettere, P. Dewilde, R. Udo. Pipelined CORDIC architectures for fast VLSI filtering and array processing. *Proceedings of the ICASSP'84*, 1984.

[10] A. M. Despain. Very fast Fourier transform algorithms for hardware implementation. *IEEE Transactions on Computers* C-28, May 1979.

[11] A. M. Despain. Fourier transform computers using CORDIC iterations. *IEEE Transactions on Computers* 23, October 1974.

[12] C. Dick, F. Harris, M. Rice. FPGA implementation of carrier phase synchronization for QAM demodulators. *Journal of VLSI Signal Processing, Special Issue on Field-Programmable Logic* (R. Woods, R. Tessier, eds.), Kluwer Academic, January 2004.

[13] D. Ercegovac, T. Lang. *Digital Arithmetic*, Morgan Kaufmann, 2004.

[14] B. Haller, J. Gotze, J. Cavallaro. Efficient implementation of rotation operations for high-performance QRD-RLS filtering. *Proceedings of the International Conference on Application-Specific Systems, Arthictectures and Processors*, July 1997.

[15] G. H. Haviland, A. A. Tuszinsky. A CORDIC arithmetic processor chip. *IEEE Transactions on Computers* c-29(2), February 1980.

[16] Y. H. Hu. The quantization effects of the CORDIC algorithm. *IEEE Transactions on Signal Processing* 40, July 1992.

[17] X. Hu, S. C. Bass. A neglected error source in the CORDIC algorithm. *IEEE International Symposium on Circuits and Systems* 1, May 1993.

[18] X. Hu, S. C. Bass. A neglected error source in the CORDIC algorithm. *Proceedings of the IEEE ISCAS*, 1993.

[19] X. Hu, R. G. Garber, S. C. Bass. Expanding the range of convergence of the CORDIC algorithm. *IEEE Transactions on Computers* 40(1), January 1991.

[20] J. Lee. Constant-factor redundant CORDIC for angle calculation and rotation. *IEEE Transactions on Computers* 41(8), August 1992.

[21] Y. H. Liao, H. E. Liao. CALF: A CORDIC adaptive lattice filter. *IEEE Transactions on Signal Processing* 40(4), April 1992.

[22] Mathworks, The, *http://www.mathworks.com/*.

[23] U. Mengali, A. N. D'Andrea. *Synchronization Techniques for Digital Receivers*, Plenum Press, 1997.

[24] J. Mia, K. K. Parhi, E. F. Deprettere. Pipelined implementation of CORDIC-based QRD-MVDR adaptive beamforming. *IEEE Fourth International Conference on Signal Processing*, October 1998.

[25] J. M. Muller. Discrete basis and computation of elementary functions. *IEEE Transactions on Computers* C-34(9), September 1985.

[26] B. Parhami. *Computer Arithmetic: Algorithms and Hardware Designs*, Oxford University Press, 2000.

[27] K. K. Parhi. *VLSI Digital Signal Processing Systems Design and Implementation*, John Wiley, 1999.

[28] S. Y. Park, N. I. Cho. Fixed-point error analysis of CORDIC processor based on the Variance Propagation Formula. *IEEE Transactions on Circuits and Systems* 51(3), March 2004.

[29] J. G. Proakis, M. Salehi. *Communication Systems Engineering*, Prentice-Hall, 1994.

[30] C. M. Rader. VLSI systolic arrays for adaptive nulling. *IEEE Signal Processing Magazine* 13(4), July 1996.

[31] T. Y. Sung, Y. H. Hu. Parallel VLSI implementation of Kalman filter. *IEEE Transactions on Aerospace and Electronic Systems* AES 23(2), March 1987.

[32] N. Takagi. Redundant CORDIC methods with a constant scale factor for sine and cosine computation. *IEEE Transactions on Computers* 40(9), September 1991.

[33] D. H. Timmerman, B. J. Hosticka, B. Rix. A new addition scheme and fast scaling factor compensation methods for CORDIC algorithms. *Integration, the VLSI Journal* (11), 1991.

[34] D. H. Timmerman, B. J. Hosticka, G. Schmidt. A programmable CORDIC chip for digital signal processing applications. *IEEE Journal of Solid-State Circuits* 26(9), September 1991.

[35] J. E. Volder. The CORDIC trigonometric computing technique. *IRE Transactions on Electronic Computers* 3, September 1959.

[36] J. S. Walther. A unified algorithm for the elementary functions. *AFIPS Spring Joint Computer Conference* 38, 1971.

[37] Xilinx Inc. Spartan-3E Datasheet, *http://www.xilinx.com/xlnx/xweb/xil_publications_display.jsp?iLanguageID=1&category= /Data+Sheets/FPGA+Device+Families/Spartan-3E.*

[38] Xilinx Inc. System Generator for DSP, *http://www.xilinx.com/ise/optional_prod/system_generator.htm.*

[39] Xilinx Inc. Virtex-II Pro Datasheet, *http://www.xilinx.com/xlnx/xweb/xil_publications_display.jsp?category=Publications/FPGA+Device+Families/Virtex-II+Pro&iLanguageID=1.*

[40] Xilinx Inc. Virtex-4 Datasheet, *http://www.xilinx.com/xlnx/xweb/xil_publications_display.jsp?sGlobalNavPick=&sSecondaryNavPick=&category=-1210771&iLanguageID=1.*

[41] Xilinx Inc. Virtex-4 Multi-Platform FPGA, *http://www.xilinx.com/products/silicon_solutions/fpgas/virtex/virtex4/index.htm.*

[42] Xilinx Inc. XtremeDSP Design Considerations Guide, *http://www.xilinx.com/products/silicon_solutions/fpgas/virtex/virtex4/capabilities/xtremedsp.htm.*

[43] Xilinx Inc. XtremeDSP Slice, *http://www.xilinx.com/products/silicon_solutions/fpgas/virtex/virtex4/capabilities/xtremedsp.htm.*

CHAPTER 26

Hardware/Software Partitioning

Frank Vahid, Greg Stitt
Department of Computer Science and Engineering
University of California–Riverside

Field-programmable gate arrays (FPGAs) excel at implementing applications as highly parallel custom circuits, thus yielding fast performance. However, large applications implemented on a microprocessor may be more size efficient and require less designer effort, at the expense of slower performance. In some cases, mapping an entire application to a microprocessor satisfies performance requirements and so is preferred. In other cases, mapping an application entirely to custom circuits on FPGAs may be necessary to meet performance requirements. In many cases, though, the best implementation lies somewhere between these two extremes.

Hardware/software partitioning, illustrated in Figure 26.1, is the process of dividing an application between a microprocessor component ("software") and one or more custom coprocessor components ("hardware") to achieve an implementation that best satisfies requirements of performance, size, designer effort, and other metrics.[1] A custom coprocessor is a processing circuit that is tailor-made to execute critical application computations far faster than if those computations had been executed on a microprocessor.

FPGA technology encourages hardware/software (HW/SW) partitioning by simplifying the job of implementing custom coprocessors, which can be done just by downloading bits onto an FPGA rather than by manufacturing a new integrated circuit or by wiring a printed-circuit board. In fact, new FPGAs even support integration of microprocessors within an FPGA itself, either as separate physical components alongside the FPGA fabric ("hard-core microprocessors") or as circuits mapped onto the FPGA fabric just like any other circuit ("soft-core microprocessors"). High-end computers have also begun integrating microprocessors and FPGAs on boards, allowing application designers to make use of both resources when implementing applications.

Hardware/software partitioning is a hard problem in part because of the large number of possible partitions. In its simplest form, hardware/software partitioning considers an application as comprising a set of *regions* and maps

---

[1] The terms *software*, to represent microprocessor implementation, and *hardware*, to represent coprocessor implementation, are common and so appear in this chapter. However, when implemented on FPGAs, coprocessors are actually just as "soft" as programs implemented on a microprocessor, with both consisting merely of a sequence of bits downloaded into a physical device, leading to a broader concept of "software."

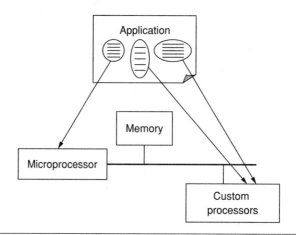

FIGURE 26.1 ■ A diagram of hardware/software partitioning, which divides an application between a microprocessor component ("software") and custom processor components ("hardware").

each region to either software or hardware such that some cost criteria (e.g., performance) is optimized while some constraints (e.g., size) are satisfied.

A *partition* is a complete mapping of every region to either hardware or software. Even in this simple formulation, the number of possible partitions can be enormous. If there are n regions and there are two choices (software or hardware) for each one, then there are 2^n possible partitions. A mere 32 regions yield over 4 billion possibilities. Finding the optimal partition of this simple form is known to be NP-hard in general. Many other factors contribute to making the problem even harder, as will be discussed.

This chapter discusses issues involved in partitioning an application among microprocessor and coprocessor components. It considers two application categories: *sequential programs*, where an application is a program written in a sequential programming language such as C, C++, or Java and where partitioning maps critical functions and/or loops to coprocessors; and *parallel programs*, where an application is a set of concurrently executing tasks and where partitioning maps some of those tasks to coprocessors.

While designers today do mostly manual partitioning, automating the process has been an area of active study since the early 1990s (e.g., [10, 15, 26]) and continues to be intensively researched and developed. For that reason, we will begin the chapter with a discussion of the trend toward automatic partitioning.

26.1 THE TREND TOWARD AUTOMATIC PARTITIONING

Traditionally, designers have manually partitioned applications between microprocessors and custom coprocessors. Manual partitioning was in part necessitated by radically different design flows for microprocessors versus coprocessors. A microprocessor design flow typically involved developing code in programming languages such as C, C++, or Java. In sharp contrast, a coprocessor design flow may have involved developing cleverly parallelized and/or pipelined datapath circuits, control circuits to sequence data through the datapath, memory circuits to enable rapid data access by the datapath, and then mapping those circuits to a particular ASIC technology. Thus, manual partitioning was necessary because partitioning was done early in the design process, well before a machine-readable or executable description of an application's desired behavior existed. It resulted in specifications for both the software design and the hardware design teams, both of which might then have worked for many months developing their respective implementations.

However, the evolution of synthesis and FPGA technologies is leading toward automated partitioning because the starting point of FPGA design has been elevated to the same level as that for microprocessors, as shown in Figure 26.2.

Current technology enables coprocessors to be realized merely by downloading bits onto an FPGA. Downloading takes just seconds and eliminates the months-long and expensive design step of mapping circuits to an ASIC. Furthermore, synthesis tools have evolved to automatically design coprocessors from high-level descriptions in hardware description languages (HDLs), such as VHDL or Verilog, or even in languages traditionally used to program microprocessors, such as C, C++, or Java. Thus, designers may develop a single machine-readable high-level executable description of an application's desired behavior and then partition that description between microprocessor and coprocessor parts, in a process sometimes called hardware/software codesign. New

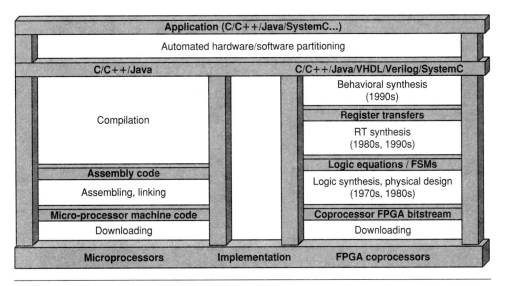

FIGURE 26.2 ■ The codesign ladder: evolution toward automated hardware/software partitioning due to synthesis tools and FPGA technologies enabling a similar design starting point, and similar implementation manner of downloading bits into a prefabricated device.

approaches, such as SystemC [14], which supports HDL concepts using C++, have evolved specifically to support it. With a single behavior description of an application, and automated tools to convert partitioned applications to coprocessors, automating partitioning is a logical next step in tool evolution. Some commercial automated hardware/software partitioning products are just beginning to appear [4, 7, 21, 27].

In the remainder of the chapter, many of the issues discussed relate to both manual and automatic partitioning, while some relate to automatic partitioning alone.

26.2   PARTITIONING OF SEQUENTIAL PROGRAMS

In a sequential program, the regions comprising an application's behavior are defined to execute sequentially rather than concurrently. For example, the semantics of the C programming language are such that its functions execute sequentially (though parallel execution is allowed as long as the results of the computation stay the same). Hardware/software partitioning of a sequential program involves speeding up certain regions by moving them to faster-executing FPGA coprocessors, yielding overall application speedup.

Hardware/software partitioning of sequential programs is governed to a large extent by the well-known Amdahl's Law [1] (described in 1967 by Gene Amdahl of IBM in the context of discussing the limits of parallel architectures for speeding up sequential programs). Informally, Amdahl's Law states that application speedup is limited by the part of the program *not* being parallelized. For example, if 75 percent of a program can be parallelized, the remaining nonparallelized 25 percent of the program limits the speedup to 100/25 = 4 times speedup (usually written as 4x) in the best possible case, even in the ideal situation of zero-time execution of the other 75 percent.

Amdahl's Law has been described more formally using the equation `max_speedup` = $1/(s + p/n)$, where p is the fraction of the program execution that can be parallelized; s is the fraction that remains sequential, $s + p = 1$; n is the number of parallel processors being used to speed up the parallelizable fraction; and `max_speedup` is the ideal speedup. In the 75 percent example, assuming that n is very large, we obtain `max_speedup` = $1/(0.25 + 0.75/n) = 1/(0.25 + {\sim}0) = 4x$.

Amdahl's Law applies to hardware/software partitioning by providing speedup limits based on the regions *not* mapped to hardware. For example, if a region accounts for 25 percent of execution but is not mapped to hardware, then the maximum possible speedup obtainable by partitioning is 4x. Figure 26.3 illustrates that only when regions accounting for a large percentage of execution are mapped to hardware might partitioning yield substantial results. For example, to obtain 10x speedup, partitioning *must* map to hardware those regions accounting for *at least* 90 percent of an application's execution time.

Fortunately, most of the execution time for many applications comes from just a few regions. For example, Figure 26.4 shows the average execution time

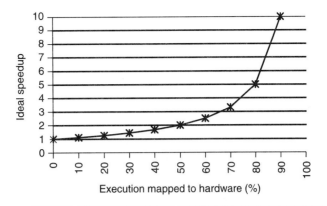

FIGURE 26.3 ■ Hardware/software partitioning speedup following Amdahl's Law.

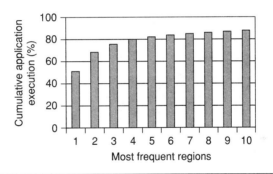

FIGURE 26.4 ■ Ideal speedups achievable by moving regions (loops) to hardware, averaged for a variety of embedded system benchmark suites (MediaBench, Powerstone, and Netbench).

contribution for the first n regions (in this case loops) for several dozen standard embedded system application benchmarks, all sequential programs. Note that the first few regions account for 75 to 80 percent of the execution time. The regions are roughly equal in size following the well-known informal "90–10" rule, which states that that 90 percent of a program's execution time is spent in 10 percent of its code. Thus, hardware/software partitioning of sequential programs generally must sort regions by their execution percentage and then consider moving the highest contributing regions to hardware.

A corollary to Amdahl's Law is that if a region is moved to hardware, its actual speedup limits the remaining possible speedup. For example, consider a region accounting for 80 percent of execution time that, when moved to hardware, runs only 2x faster than in software. Such a situation is equivalent to 40 percent of the region being sped up ideally and the other 40 percent not being sped up at all. With 40 percent not sped up, the ideal speedup obtainable by partitioning of the remaining regions (the other 20 percent) is limited to a mere 100 percent/40 percent = 2.5x. For this reason, hardware/software partitioning of sequential programs generally must focus on obtaining very large speedups of the highest-contributing regions.

Amdahl's Law therefore greatly prunes the solution space that partitioning of sequential programs must consider—good solutions must move the biggest-contributing regions to hardware and greatly speed them up to yield good overall application speedups.

Even with this relatively simple view, several issues make the problem of hardware/software partitioning of sequential programs quite challenging. Those issues, illustrated in Figure 26.5(a–e), include determining critical region

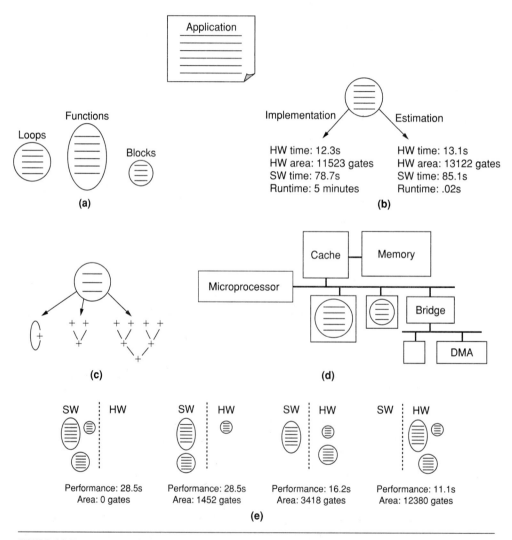

FIGURE 26.5 ■ Hardware/software partitioning: (a) granularity; (b) partition evaluation; (c) alternative region implementations; (d) implementation models; (e) exploration.

granularity (a), evaluating partitions (b), considering multiple alternative implementations of a region (c), determining implementation models (d), and exploring the partitioning solution space (e).

26.2.1 Granularity

Partitioning moves some code regions from a microprocessor to coprocessors. A first issue in defining a partitioning approach is thus to determine the granularity of the regions to be considered. *Granularity* is a measure of the amount of functionality encapsulated by a region, which is illustrated in Figure 26.6.

A key trade-off involves coarse versus fine region granularity [11]. Coarser granularity simplifies partitioning by reducing the number of possible partitions, enables more accurate estimates during partitioning by considering more computations when creating those estimates (and thus reducing inaccuracy when combining multiple estimates for different regions into one), and reduces inter-region communication. On the other hand, finer granularity may expose better

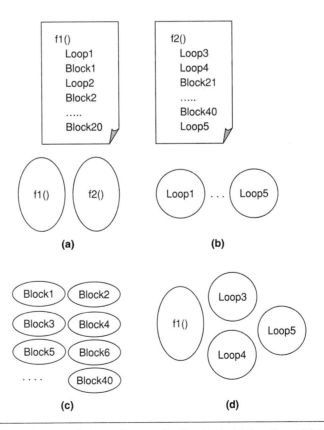

FIGURE 26.6 ■ The region granularities of an application (*top*): (a) functions; (b) loops; (c) blocks; (d) heterogeneous combination. Finer granularities may expose better solutions, at the expense of a more complex partitioning problem and more difficult estimation challenges.

partitions that would not otherwise be possible. Early automated partitioning research considered fine granularities of arithmetic operations or statements, while more recent work typically considers coarser granularities involving basic blocks, loops, or entire functions.

Coarse granularity simplifies the partitioning problem by reducing the number of possible partitions. Take, for example, an application with two 1000-line C functions, like the one shown in Figure 26.6 (*top*), and consider partitioning at the granularity of functions, loops, or basic blocks. The granularity of functions involves only two regions, as shown in Figure 26.6(a), and the granularity of loops involves five regions, as shown Figure 26.6(b). However, the granularity of the basic block may involve many tens or hundreds of regions, as shown in Figure 26.6(c). If partitioning simply chooses between hardware and software, then two regions would yield $2*2 = 4$ possible partitions, while just 32 regions would involve $2*2*2*...*2$ (32 times) possible partitions, or over four billion.

Coarse granularity also enables more accurate early estimations of a region's performance, size, power, and so forth. For example, an approach using function granularity could individually presynthesize the two previously mentioned functions to FPGAs before partitioning, gathering performance and size data. During partitioning, it could simply estimate that, for the case of partitioning both functions to the FPGA, the two functions' performances would stay the same and their sizes would add. This estimate is not entirely accurate because synthesizing both functions could involve interactions between the function's implementations that would impact performance and size, but it is likely *reasonably* accurate. In contrast, similar presynthesis and performance/size estimates for basic blocks would yield grossly inaccurate values because multiple basic blocks would actually be synthesized into a combined circuit having extensive sharing among the blocks, bearing little resemblance to the individual circuits presynthesized for each block.

However, finer granularity may expose better partitions that otherwise would not be possible. In the two-function example just described, perhaps the best partition would move only half of one function to hardware—an option not possible at the coarse granularity of functions but possible at finer granularities of loops or basic blocks.

Manual partitioning often involves initially considering a "natural" granularity for an application. An application may consist of dozens of functions, but a designer may naturally categorize them into just a few key high-level functions. A data-processing application, for example, may naturally consist of several key high-level functions: acquire, decompress, transform, compress, and transmit. The designer may first try to partition at that natural granularity before considering finer granularities.

Granularity may be restricted to one region type, but can instead be *heterogeneous*, as shown in Figure 26.6(d). For example, in the previous two-function example from Figure 26.6 (*top*), one function may be treated as a region while the other may be broken down so that its loops are each considered as a region. A particular loop may even be broken down so that its basic blocks are individually considered as regions. Thus, for a single application, regions considered for movement to hardware may include functions, loops, and basic blocks. With heterogeneous granularity, preanalysis of the code may select regions based on execution time and size, breaking down a region with very high execution time or large size.

Furthermore, while granularity can be predetermined statically, it can also be determined *dynamically* during partitioning [16]. Thus, an approach might start with coarse-grained regions and then decompose specific regions deemed to be critical during partitioning.

Granularity need not be restricted to regions defined by the language constructs such as functions or loops, used in the original application description. Transformations, some being well-known compiler transformations, may be applied to significantly change the original description. They include function inlining (replacing a function call with that function's statements), function "exlining" (replacing statements with a function call), function cloning (making multiple copies of a function for use in different places), function specialization (creating versions of a function with constant parameters), loop unrolling (expanding a loop's body to incorporate multiple iterations), loop fusion (merging two loops into one), loop splitting (splitting one loop into two), code hoisting and sinking (moving code out of and into loops), and so on.

26.2.2   Partition Evaluation

The process of finding a good partition is typically iterative, involving consideration and evaluation of certain partitions and then decisions as to which partitions to consider next. *Evaluation* determines a partition's design metric values. A *design metric* is a measure of a partition. Common metrics include performance, size, and power/energy. Other metrics include implementation cost, engineering cost, reliability, maintainability, and so on.

Some design metrics may need to be *optimized*, meaning that partitioning should seek the best possible value of a metric. Other design metrics may be *constrained*, meaning that partitioning must meet some threshold value for a metric. An *objective function* is one that combines multiple metric values into a single number, known as *cost*, which the partitioning may seek to minimize. A partitioning approach must define the metrics and constraints that can be considered, and define or allow a user to define an objective function.

Evaluation can be a complex problem because it must consider several implementation factors in order to obtain accurate design metric values. Among others, these factors include determining the communication time between regions that transfer data (thus requiring knowledge of the communication structure), considering clock cycle lengthening caused by multiple application regions sharing hardware resources (which may introduce multiplexers or longer wires), and the like.

The key trade-off in evaluation involves estimation versus implementation. Estimating design metric values is faster and so enables consideration of more possible partitions. Obtaining the values through implementation is more accurate and thus ensures that partitioning decisions are based on sound evaluations.

Estimation involves some characterization of an application's regions before partitioning and then, during partitioning, quickly combining the characterizations into design metric values. The previous section on granularity discussed how two C function regions could be characterized for hardware by synthesizing each region individually to an FPGA, resulting in a characterization of each region consisting of performance and size data. Then a partition with multiple regions in hardware could be evaluated simply by assuming that each region's performance is the same as the predetermined performance and by adding any hardware-mapped region sizes together to obtain total hardware size. Estimation for software can be done similarly, using compilation rather than synthesis for characterization.

Nevertheless, while estimation typically works well for software [24], the nature of hardware may introduce significant inaccuracy into an estimation approach because multiple regions may actually share hardware resources, thus intertwining their performance and size values [9,18]. Alternatively, implementation as a means of evaluation involves synthesizing actual hardware circuits for a given partition's hardware regions. Such synthesis thus accounts for hardware sharing and other interdependencies among the regions. However, synthesis is time consuming, requiring perhaps tens of seconds, minutes, or even hours, restricting the number of partitions that can be evaluated.

Many approaches exist between the two extremes just described. Estimation can be improved with more extensive characterization, incorporating much more detail than just performance and size. Characterization may, for example, describe what hardware resources a region utilizes, such as two multipliers or 2 Kbytes of RAM. Then estimation can use more complex algorithms to combine region characterizations into actual design metric values, such as that the regions may share resources such as multipliers (possibly introducing multiplexers to carry out such sharing) or RAM. These algorithms yield higher accuracy but are still much faster than synthesis. Alternatively, synthesis approaches can be improved by performing a "rough" rather than a complete synthesis, using faster heuristics rather than slower, but higher-optimizing heuristics, for example.

Evaluation need not be done in a single exploration loop of partitioning, but can be *heterogeneous*. An outer exploration loop may be added to partitioning that is traversed less frequently, with the inner exploration loop considering thousands of partitions (if automated) and using estimation for evaluation, while the outer exploration loop considers only tens of partitions that are evaluated more extensively using synthesis. The inner/outer loop concept can of course be extended to even more loops, with the inner loops examining more partitions evaluated quickly and the outer loops performing increasingly in-depth synthesis on fewer partitions.

Furthermore, evaluation methods can change *dynamically* during partitioning. Early stages in the partitioning process may use fast estimation techniques to map out the solution space and narrow in on particular sections of it, while later stages may utilize more accurate synthesis techniques to fine-tune the solution.

26.2.3 Alternative Region Implementations

Further adding to the partitioning challenge is the fact that a given region may have *alternative region implementations* in hardware rather than just one implementation, as assumed in the previous sections. For example, Figure 26.7 (*top*) shows a particular function that performs 100 multiplications. A fast but large hardware implementation may use 100 multipliers, as shown in Figure 26.7(a). The much smaller but much slower hardware implementation in Figure 26.7(b) uses only 1 multiplier. Numerous implementation alternatives exist between those two extremes, such as having 2 multipliers as in Figure 26.7(c), 10 multipliers, and so on. Furthermore, the function may be implemented in a pipelined or non-pipelined manner. Utilized components may be fast and large (e.g., array-style multipliers or carry-lookahead adders) or small and slow (e.g., shift-and-add multipliers or carry-ripple adders). Many other alternatives exist.

A key trade-off involves deciding how many alternative implementations to consider during partitioning. More alternatives greatly expand the number of possible partitions and thus may possibly lead to improved results. However, they also expand the solution space tremendously. For example, 8 regions each with one hardware implementation yield $2^8 = 256$ possible partitions. If each

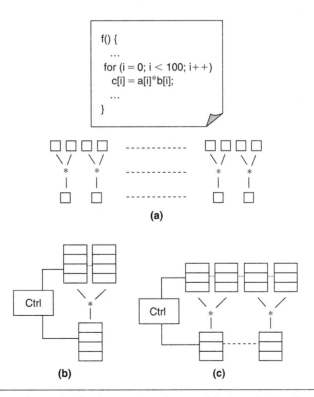

FIGURE 26.7 ■ Alternative region implementations for an original application (*top*) requiring 100 multiplications: (a) 100 multipliers; (b) 1 multiplier; (c) 2 multipliers. Alternative region implementations may have hugely different performances and sizes.

region instead has 4 possible hardware implementations, then it has 5 possible implementations (1 software and 4 hardware implementations), yielding 5^8, or more than 300,000, possible partitions.

Most automated hardware/software partitioning approaches consider one possible hardware implementation per region. Even then, a question exists as to which one to consider for that region: the fastest, the smallest, or some alternative in the middle? Some approaches do consider multiple alternative implementations, perhaps selecting a small number that span the possible space, such as small, medium, and large [5].

As we saw with granularity and evaluation, the number of alternative implementations considered can also be *heterogeneous*. Partitioning may consider only one alternative for particular regions and multiple alternatives for other regions deemed more critical.

Furthermore, as we saw with granularity and evaluation, the number of alternative implementations can change *dynamically* as well. Partitioning may start by considering only a few alternatives per region and then consider more for particular regions as partitioning narrows in on a solution.

Sometimes obtaining alternative implementations of an application region may require the designer to write several versions of it, each leading to one or more alternatives. In fact, a designer may have to write different region versions for software and hardware because a version that executes fast in software may execute slow in hardware, and vice versa. That difference is due to software's fundamental sequential execution model that demands clever sequential algorithms, while hardware's inherently parallel model demands parallelizable algorithms.

26.2.4 Implementation Models

Partitioning moves critical microprocessor software regions to hardware coprocessors. Different *implementation models* define how the coprocessors are integrated with the microprocessor and with one another [6], enlarging the possible solution space for partitioning and greatly impacting performance and size.

One implementation model parameter is whether coprocessor execution and microprocessor execution overlap or are mutually exclusive. In the overlapping model, the microprocessor activates a coprocessor and may then continue to execute concurrently with it (if the data dependencies of the application allow). In the mutually exclusive model, the microprocessor waits idly until the coprocessor finishes, at which time the microprocessor resumes execution.

Figure 26.8(a) illustrates the execution of both models. Overlapping may improve overall performance, but mutual exclusivity simplifies implementation by eliminating issues related to memory contention, cache coherency, and synchronization—the coprocessor may even access cache directly. In many partitioned implementations, the coprocessor executes for only a small fraction of the total application cycles, meaning that overlapping gains little performance improvement. When the microprocessor and coprocessor cycles are closer to

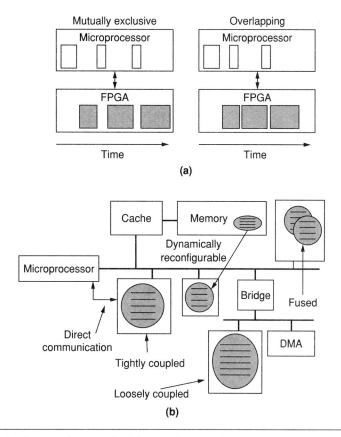

FIGURE 26.8 ■ Implementation models: (a) mutually exclusive and overlapping. (b) implementation model parameters.

being equal, overlapping may improve performance, up to a limit of 2 times, of course. Similarly, the execution of coprocessors relative to one another may be overlapped or mutually exclusive.

A second implementation model parameter involves communication methods. The microprocessor and coprocessors may communicate through memory and share the same data cache, or the microprocessor may communicate directly with the FPGA through memory-mapped registers, queues, fast serial links, or some combination of those mechanisms.

Another implementation model parameter is whether multiple coprocessors are implemented separately or are fused. In a separate coprocessor model, each critical region is synthesized to its own controller and datapath. In a fused model, the critical regions are synthesized into a single controller and datapath. The fused model may reduce size because the hardware resources are shared, but it may result in performance overhead because of a longer critical path as well as the need to run at the slowest clock frequency of all the regions.

Certain coprocessors can be fused and others left separate. Furthermore, fusing need not be complete—two coprocessors can share key components, such as a floating-point unit, but otherwise be implemented separately.

Yet another model parameter is whether coprocessors and the microprocessor are tightly or loosely coupled. Tightly coupled coprocessors may coexist on the microprocessor memory bus or may even have direct access to microprocessor registers. Loosely coupled, they may access microprocessor memory through a bridge, adding several cycles to data accesses. Both couplings can coexist in a single implementation.

FPGAs add a particularly interesting model parameter to partitioning—dynamic reconfiguration—which replaces an FPGA circuit with another circuit during runtime by swapping in a new FPGA configuration bitstream [2]. In this way, not all of an application's coprocessors need to simultaneously coexist in the FPGA. Instead, one subset of the application's required coprocessors may initially be loaded into the FPGA, but, as the application continues to execute, that subset may be replaced by another subset needed later in the application's execution. Reconfiguration increases the effective size of an FPGA, thus enabling better performance when more application regions are partitioned to it or, alternatively, enabling use of a smaller and hence cheaper FPGA with a runtime overhead required to swap in new bitstreams. In some cases, this overhead may limit the benefits of reconfiguration and should therefore be considered during partition evaluation.

Figure 26.8(b) illustrates some of the different implementation model parameters, including communication methods, fused regions, and tightly/loosely coupled coprocessors. Often these parameters are fixed prior to partitioning, but can also be explored dynamically during partitioning to determine the best implementation model for a given application and given constraints.

26.2.5 Exploration

Exploration is the searching of the partition solution space for a good partition. As mentioned before, it is at present mostly a manual task, but automated techniques are beginning to mature. This section discusses automated exploration techniques for various formulations of the partitioning problem.

Simple formulation

A simple and common form of the hardware/software partitioning problem consists of *n* regions, each having a software runtime value, a hardware runtime value, and a hardware size. It assumes that all values are independent of one another (so if two regions are mapped to hardware, their hardware runtime and size values are unchanged); it assumes that communication times are constant regardless of whether a region is implemented as software or hardware (such as when all regions use the same interface to a shared memory); and it seeks to minimize total application runtime subject to a hardware size constraint (assuming no dynamic reconfiguration).

Although this problem is known to be NP-hard, it can be solved by first mapping it to the well-known *0-1 knapsack problem* [20]. The 0-1 knapsack problem involves a knapsack with a specified weight capacity and a set of items, each with a weight and a profit. The goal is to select which items to place in the knapsack such that the total profit is maximized without violating the weight capacity. For hardware/software partitioning, regions correspond to items, the FPGA size constraint corresponds to the knapsack capacity, an implementation's size corresponds to an item's weight, and the speedup obtained by implementing a region in hardware instead of software corresponds to an item's profit.

Thus, algorithms that solve the 0-1 knapsack problem solve the simple form of the hardware/software partitioning problem. The 0-1 knapsack problem is NP-hard, but efficient optimal algorithms exist for relatively large problem sizes. One of these is a well-known dynamic programming algorithm [12] having runtime complexity of $O(A^*n)$, where A is the capacity and n is the number of items. Alternatively, integer linear programming (ILP) [22] may be used. ILP solvers perform extensive solution space pruning to reduce exploration time.

For problems too big for either such optimal technique, heuristics may be utilized. A *heuristic* finds a good, but not necessarily the optimal, solution, while an *algorithm* finds the optimal solution. A common heuristic for the 0-1 knapsack problem is a greedy one. A greedy heuristic starts with an initial solution and then makes changes only if they seem to improve the solution. It sorts each item based on the ratio of profit to weight and then traverses the sorted list, placing an item in the knapsack if it fits and skipping it otherwise, terminating when reaching the knapsack capacity or when all items have been considered. This heuristic has $O(nlgn)$ time complexity, allowing for fast automated partitioning of thousands of regions or feasible manual partitioning of tens of regions. Furthermore, the heuristic has been shown to commonly obtain near-optimal results in the situation when a few items have a high profit to weight ratio. In hardware/software partitioning terms, that situation corresponds to the existence of regions that are responsible for the majority of execution time and require little hardware area, which is often the case.

Formulation with asymmetric communication and greedy/nongreedy automated heuristics

A slightly more complex form of the hardware/software partitioning problem considers cases where communication times between regions change depending on the partitioning, with different required times for communication depending on whether the regions are both in software or both in hardware, or are separated, with one in software and one in hardware. This form of the problem can be mapped to the well-known graph bipartitioning problem.

Graph bipartitioning divides a graph into two sets in order to minimize an objective function. Each graph node has two weights, one for each set. Edges may have three different weights: two weights associated with nodes connected in the same set (one weight for each set) and one for nodes connected between sets. Typically, the objective function is to minimize the sum of all node and edge weights using the appropriate weights for a given partition. Graph bipartitioning is NP-hard.

ILP approaches may be used for automatically obtaining optimal solutions to the graph bipartitioning problem. Heuristics may be used when ILP is too time consuming. A simple greedy heuristic for graph bipartitioning starts with some initial partition, perhaps random or all software. It then determines the cost improvement of moving each node from its present set to the opposite set and then moves the node yielding the best improvement. The heuristic repeats these steps until no move yielding an improvement is found. Given n nodes, a basic form of such a heuristic has $O(n^2)$ runtime complexity. Techniques to update the existing cost improvement values can reduce the complexity to $O(n)$ in practice [25].

More advanced heuristics seek to overcome what are known as "local minima," accepting solution-worsening moves in the hope that they will eventually lead to an even better solution. For example, Figure 26.9 illustrates a heuristic that accepts some solution-worsening changes to escape a local minimum and eventually reach a better solution. A common situation causing a local minimum involves two items such that moving only one item worsens the solution but moving both improves it.

A well-known category of nongreedy heuristic used in partitioning is known as *group migration* [11], which evolved from an initial heuristic by Kernighan–Lin. Like the previous greedy heuristic, group migration starts with an initial partition and determines the cost improvement of moving each node from its present set to the opposite set. The group migration heuristic then moves the node yielding the best improvement (like the greedy heuristic) or yielding the *least worsening* (including zero cost change) if no improving move exists. Accepting such worsening moves enables local minima to be overcome. Of course, such a heuristic would never terminate, so group migration ensures termination by locking a node after it is moved. Group migration moves each node exactly once in what is referred to as an iteration, and an iteration has complexity of $O(n^2)$ (or $O(n)$ if clever techniques are used to update cost improvements after each

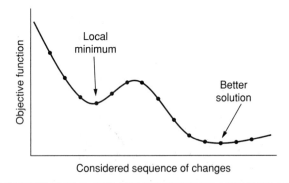

FIGURE 26.9 ■ Solution-worsening moves accepted by a nongreedy heuristic to escape local minima and find better solutions.

move). If an iteration ultimately leads to an improvement, then group migration runs another iteration. In practice, only a few iterations, typically less than five, can be run before no further improvement can be found.

The previous discussions of heuristics ignore the time required by partition evaluation. The heuristics therefore may have even higher runtime complexity unless care is taken to incorporate fast incremental evaluation updates during exploration.

Complex formulations and powerful automated heuristics

Increasingly complex forms of the hardware/software partitioning problem integrate more parameters related to the earlier mentioned issues of exploration—granularity, evaluation, alternative region implementation, and implementation models. For example, the earlier mentioned dynamic granularity modifications, such as decomposing a given region into smaller regions, or even applying transformations to an application such as function inlining, can be applied during partitioning. The partitioning problem can consider different couplings of coprocessors, may also consider coprocessor fusing, and can support dynamic reconfiguration. When one considers the multitude of possible parameters that can be integrated with partitioning, the size of the solution space is mind-boggling. Searching that space for the best solution becomes a tremendous combinatorial optimization challenge, likely requiring long-running search heuristics.

At this point, it may be interesting to note that hardware/software partitioning brings together two previously separate research fields: compilers and CAD (computer-aided design). Compilation techniques tend to emphasize a quick series of *transformations* applied to an application's description. In contrast, CAD techniques tend to emphasize a long-running iterative *search* of enormous solution spaces. One possible reason for these different perspectives is that compilers were generally expected to run quickly, in seconds or at most minutes, because they were part of a design loop in which compilation was applied perhaps dozens or hundreds of times a day as programs were developed. In contrast, CAD optimization techniques were part of a much longer design loop. Running CAD optimization tools for hours or even days was perfectly acceptable because that time was still small compared to the weeks or months required to manufacture chips. Furthermore, the very nature of coprocessor design meant that a designer was extremely interested in high performance, so longer tool runtimes were acceptable if they optimized an implementation.

Hardware/software partitioning merges compilation and synthesis into a single framework. In some cases, compiler-like runtimes of seconds must be achieved. In other cases, CAD-like runtimes of hours may be acceptable. Approaches to partitioning may span that range. Highly complex partitioning formulations will likely require moving away from the fast linear time algorithms and heuristics described earlier and toward longer-running powerful search heuristics.

A popular powerful and general search heuristic is *simulated annealing* [17]. The simulated annealing heuristic starts with a random solution and then randomly makes some change to it, perhaps moving a region between software and hardware, choosing an alternative implementation for a particular region, decomposing a particular region into finer-grained regions, performing a transformation on the original regions, and so forth, and evaluates the cost (as determined by an objective function) of the new partition obtained from that change. If the change improves the cost, it is accepted (i.e., the change is made). If the change worsens the cost, the seemingly "bad" change is accepted with some probability. The key feature of simulated annealing is that the probability of accepting a seemingly bad move decreases as the approach proceeds, with the pattern of decrease determined by some parameters provided to the annealing process that eventually causes it to narrow in on a good solution. Simulated annealing typically must evaluate many thousands or millions of solutions in order to arrive at a good one and thus requires very fast evaluation methods.

The complexity of simulated annealing is generally dependent on the problem instance. With properly set parameters, it can achieve near-optimal solutions on very large problems in long but acceptable runtimes. Faster machines have made simulated annealing an increasingly acceptable search heuristic for a wider variety of problems—it can complete in just seconds for many problem instances.

The simulated annealing heuristic is known as a neighborhood search heuristic because it makes local changes to an existing solution. Tabu search [13] is an effective method for improving neighborhood search. Meaning "forbidden," Tabu maintains a list of recently seen, Tabu, solutions. When considering a change to an existing solution, it disregards any change that would yield a solution on the Tabu list. This prevents cycling among the same solutions and has been shown to yield improved results in less time. The Tabu list concept can also be applied on a broader scale, maintaining a long-term history of considered solutions in order to increase solution diversity. Tabu search can improve neighborhood search heuristic runtimes during hardware/software partitioning by a factor of 20x [8].

Other issues

Because implementing an application as software generally requires a smaller size and less designer effort, most approaches to exploration start with an all-software implementation and then explore the mapping of critical application regions to hardware. However, in some cases, such as when the application is written specifically for hardware, an approach may start with an all-hardware implementation and then move noncritical application regions to software to reduce hardware size.

Furthermore, when an application is originally written for software implementation, some of its regions may not be suitable for hardware implementation. For example, application regions that utilize recursive function calls, pointer-based data structures, or dynamic memory allocation may not be easy to implement as a hardware circuit. Some research efforts are beginning to address these problems by developing new synthesis techniques that support a wider range of program constructs and behavior. Alternatively, designers sometimes write (or rewrite) critical regions such that those regions are well suited for circuit implementation.

26.3 PARTITIONING OF PARALLEL PROGRAMS

In parallel programs, the regions that make up an application are defined to execute concurrently, as opposed to sequentially. Such regions are often called *tasks* or *processes*. For some applications, expressing behavior using tasks may result in a more parallel implementation and hence in faster application performance. For example, an MPEG2 decoder may be described as several tasks, such as motion compensation, dequantization, or inverse discrete cosine transform, that can be implemented in a pipelined manner.

Numerous parallel programming models have been considered for hardware/software partitioning, among others, synchronous dataflow, dynamic dataflow, Kahn process networks, and communicating sequential processes.

26.3.1 Differences among Parallel Programming Models

While hardware/software partitioning of parallel programs has many similarities to partitioning for sequential programs, several key differences exist.

Granularity
Partitioning of parallel programs typically treats each task as a region, meaning that the granularity is quite coarse. In some cases, decomposing a task into finer granularity may be considered.

Evaluation
Parallel programs often involve multiple performance constraints, with particular tasks or sets of tasks having unique performance constraints of their own. Furthermore, estimations of performance must consider the scheduling of tasks on processors, which is not an issue for sequential programs because regions in these programs are not concurrent.

Alternative region implementations
Given the coarse granularity of tasks, considering alternative implementations becomes even more important, as the variations among the alternatives can be huge.

Implementation models
Because tasks are inherently concurrent, partitioning of parallel programs typically uses parallel execution models in their implementations, meaning that microprocessors and coprocessors run concurrently rather than mutually exclusively and meaning that coprocessors may be arranged to form high-level pipelines. Partitioning of parallel programs is less likely to consider fusing multiple coprocessors into one because fusing eliminates concurrency.

Parallel program partitioning introduces a new aspect to exploration—scheduling. When mapping multiple tasks to a single microprocessor, partitioning must carry out the additional step of scheduling to determine when each task will execute. Scheduling tasks to meet performance constraints is known as *real-time scheduling* and is a heavily studied problem [3].

Including partitioning during scheduling results in a more complex problem. Such partitioning often considers more than just one microprocessor as well and even different types of microprocessors. It may even consider different numbers and types of memories and different bus structures connecting memories to processors.

Parallel partitioning must also pay more attention to the data storage requirements between processors. Queues may be introduced between processors, the sizes of those queues must be determined, and their implementation (e.g., in shared memory or in separate hardware components) must be decided.

Exploration

More complex issues in the hardware/software partitioning problem—such as scheduling, different granularities, different evaluation methods, alternative region implementations, and different numbers and connections of microprocessors/memories/buses—require more complex solution approaches. Most modern automatic partitioning research considers one or a few extensions to basic hardware/software partitioning and develops custom heuristics to solve the new formulations in fast compiler-like runtimes. However, as more complex forms of partitioning are considered, more powerful search heuristics with longer runtimes, such as simulated annealing or search algorithms tuned to the problem formulation, may be necessary.

26.4 SUMMARY AND DIRECTIONS

Developing an approach for hardware/software partitioning requires the consideration of granularity, evaluation, alternative region implementations, implementation models, exploration, and so forth, and each such issue involves numerous options. The result is a tremendously large partition solution space and a huge variety of approaches to finding good partitions. While much research into automated hardware/software partitioning has occurred over the past decades, most of the problem's more complex formulations have yet to be considered. A key future challenge will be the development of effective partitioning approaches for these increasingly complex formulations.

As FPGAs continue to enter mainstream embedded, desktop, and server computing, incorporating automated hardware/software partitioning into standard software design flows becomes increasingly important. One approach to minimizing the disruption of standard software design flows is to incorporate partitioning as a backend tool that operates on a final binary, allowing continued use of existing programming languages and compilers and supporting the use of assembly and even object code. Such binary-level partitioning [23] requires powerful decompilation methods to recover high-level regions such as functions and loops. Binary-level partitioning even opens the door for dynamic partitioning, wherein on-chip tools transparently move software regions to FPGA coprocessors, making use of new lean, just-in-time compilers for FPGAs [19].

References

[1] G. Amdahl. Validity of the single processor approach to achieving large-scale computing capabilities. *Proceedings of the AFIPS Spring Joint Computer Conference*, 1967.

[2] J. Burns, A. Donlin, J. Hogg, S. Singh, M. De Wit. A dynamic reconfiguration run-time system. *Proceedings of the Symposium on FPGA-Based Custom Computing Machines*, 1997.

[3] G. Buttazzo. *Hard Real-time Computing Systems: Predictable Scheduling Algorithms and Applications*, Kluwer Academic, 1997.

[4] S. Chappell, C. Sullivan. Handel-C for co-processing and co-design of field programmable system on chip. *Proceedings of Workshop on Reconfigurable Computing and Applications*, 2002.

[5] K. Chatha, R. Vemuri. An iterative algorithm for partitioning, hardware design space exploration and scheduling of hardware-software systems. *Design Automation for Embedded Systems* 5(3–4), 2000.

[6] K. Compton, S. Hauck. Reconfigurable computing: A survey of systems and software. *ACM Computing Surveys* 34(2), 2002.

[7] CriticalBlue. *http://www.criticalblue.com*.

[8] P. Eles, Z. Peng, K. Kuchchinski, A. Doboli. System level hardware/software partitioning based on simulated annealing and tabu search. *Design Automation for Embedded Systems* 2(1), 1997.

[9] R. Enzler, T. Jeger, D. Cottet, G. Tröster. High-level area and performance estimation of hardware building blocks on FPGAs. *Lecture Notes in Computer Science* 1896, 2000.

[10] R. Ernst, J. Henkel. Hardware-software codesign of embedded controllers based on hardware extraction. *Proceedings of the International Workshop on Hardware/Software Codesign*, 1992.

[11] D. Gajski, F. Vahid, S. Narayan, J. Gong. *Specification and Design of Embedded Systems*, Prentice-Hall, 1994.

[12] P. C Gilmore, R. E Gomory. The theory and computation of knapsack functions. *Operations Research* 14, 1966.

[13] F. Glover. Tabu search, part I. *Operations Research Society of America Journal on Computing* 1, 1989.

[14] T. Grotker, S. Liao, G. Martin, S. Swan. *System Design with System C*. Springer-Verlag, 2002.

[15] R. Gupta, G. De Micheli. System-level synthesis using re-programmable components. *Proceedings of the European Design Automation Conference*, 1992.

[16] J. Henkel, R. Ernst. A hardware/software partitioner using a dynamically determined granularity. *Design Automation Conference*, 1997.

[17] S. Kirkpatrick, C. Gelatt, M. Vecchi. Optimization by simulated annealing. *Science* 220(4598), May 1983.

[18] Y. Li, J. Henkel. A framework for estimation and minimizing energy dissipation of embedded HW/SW systems. *Design Automation Conference*, 1998.

[19] R. Lysecky, G. Stitt, F. Vahid. Warp processors. *Transactions on Design Automation of Electronic Systems* 11(3), 2006.

[20] S. Martello, P. Toth. *Knapsack Problems: Algorithms and Computer Implementations*, Wiley, 1990.

[21] Poseidon Design Systems, Inc. *http://www.poseidon-systems.com/index.htm*.

[22] A. Schrijver. *Theory of Linear and Integer Programming*, Wiley, 1998.

[23] G. Stitt, F. Vahid. New decompilation techniques for binary-level co-processor generation. *Proceedings of the International Conference on Computer-Aided Design*, 2005.

[24] K. Suzuki, A. Sangiovanni-Vincentelli. Efficient software performance estimation methods for hardware/software codesign. *Design Automation Conference*, 1996.

[25] F. Vahid, D. Gajski. Incremental hardware estimation during hardware/software functional partitioning. *IEEE Transactions on VLSI Systems* 3(3), 1995.

[26] F. Vahid, D. Gajski. Specification partitioning for system design. *Design Automation Conference*, 1992.

[27] XPRES Compiler. *http://www.tensilica.com/products/xpres.htm*.

PART V

CASE STUDIES OF FPGA APPLICATIONS

Parts I through IV covered technologies and techniques for creating efficient FPGA-based solutions to important problems. Part V focuses on specific, important field-programmable gate array (FPGA) applications, presenting case studies of interesting uses of reconfigurable technology. While this is by no means an exhaustive survey of all applications done on FPGAs, these chapters do contain several very interesting representative points in this space. They can be read in any order, and can even be interspersed with other chapters of this book.

This introduction should help readers identify the concepts the case studies cover and the chapters each help to illustrate. To understand the case studies, a basic knowledge of FPGAs (Chapter 1), CAD tools (Chapters 6, 13, 14, and 17), and application development (Chapter 21) is required.

Chapter 27 presents a high-performance image compression engine optimized for satellite imagery. This is a streaming signal-processing application (Chapters 5, 8, and 9), a type of computation that typically maps well to reconfigurable devices. In this case, the system saw speedups of approximately 400 times, for which the authors had to optimize the algorithm carefully, considering memory bandwidth (Chapter 21), conversion to fixed point (Chapter 23), and alteration of the algorithm to eliminate sequential dependencies.

Chapter 28 focuses on automatic target recognition, which is the detection of regions of interest in military synthetic aperture radar (SAR) images. Like the compression engine in Chapter 27, this represents a very complex, streaming signal-processing application. It also is one of the most influential applications of runtime-reconfiguration (Chapters 4 and 21), where a large circuit is time-multiplexed onto a single FPGA, enabling it to reuse the same silicon multiple times. This was necessary because the possible targets to be detected were represented by individual custom, instance-specific circuits (Chapter 22), the huge number of which was too large for the available FPGAs.

Chapter 29 discusses Boolean satisfiability (SAT) solving—the determination of whether there is an assignment of values to variables that makes a given Boolean equation true (satisfied). SAT is a fairly general optimization technique that is useful in, for example, chip testing, formal verification, and even FPGA CAD flows. This work on solving Boolean equations via FPGAs is an interesting application of instance-specific circuitry (Chapter 3) because each equation to be solved was compiled directly into FPGA logic. However, this meant that the runtime of the CAD tools was part of the time needed to solve a given Boolean equation, creating a strong push toward faster CAD algorithms for FPGAs (Chapter 20).

Chapter 30 covers logic emulation—the prototyping of complex integrated circuits on huge boxes filled with FPGAs and programmable interconnect chips. This is one of the most successful applications of multi-FPGA systems (Chapter 3) because the translation of a single ASIC into FPGA logic necessitates hundreds to thousands of FPGAs to provide adequate logic capacity. Fast mapping tools for such systems are also important (Chapter 20).

In Chapter 23 we discussed methods for eliminating (or at least minimizing) the amount of floating-point computation in FPGA designs by converting floating-point operations to fixed point. However, there are situations where floating point is unavoidable. Scientific computing codes often depend on floating-point values, and many users require that the FPGA-based implementation provide *exactly* the same results as those of a processor-based solution. These situations require full floating-point support. In other cases, the high dynamic range of values might make fixed-point computations untenable. Chapter 31 considers the development of a library of floating-point units and their use in applications such as FFTs.

Chapter 32 covers a complex physical simulation application—the finite difference time domain (FDTD) method, which is a way of modeling electromagnetic signals in complex situations that can be very useful in applications such as antenna design and breast cancer detection. The solution involves a large-scale cellular automata (Chapter 5) representation of the space to be modeled and an iterative solver. The key to achieving a high-performance implementation on FPGAs, however, involves conversion to fixed-point arithmetic (Chapter 23), simplification of complex mathematical equations, and careful consideration of the memory bottlenecks in the system (Chapter 21).

Chapter 33 discusses an alternative to traditional design flow for creating FPGA mappings in which the FPGA is allowed to evolve its own configuration. Because the FPGA is reprogrammable, a genetic optimization system can simply load into it random configurations and see how well they function. Those that show promise are retained; those that do not are removed. Through mutation and breeding, new configurations are created and evaluated in the same way, slowly evolving better and better computations. The hope is that such a system can support important classes of computation with circuits significantly more efficient than standard design flows. This design strategy exploits special features of the FPGA's reprogrammability and flexibility (Chapter 4).

Some of the chapters in this section focus on streaming digital signal processing (DSP) applications. Such applications often benefit from FPGA logic because of their amenability to pipelining and because of the large amount of data parallelism inherent in the computation. Network processing and routing is another such application domain. Chapter 34 considers packet processing, the application of FPGA logic to network filtering, and related tasks. Heavy pipelining of circuits onto the reconfigurable fabric and optimization of custom boards to network processing (Chapter 3) support very high-bandwidth networking. However, because the system retains the flexibility of FPGA logic, new computations and new filtering techniques can be easily accommodated within the system. This ability to incrementally adjust, tune, and invent new circuits provides a valuable capability even in a field as rapidly evolving as network security.

For many applications, memory access to a large set of state, rather than computational, throughput can be the bottleneck. Chapter 35 explores an object-oriented, data-centric model (Chapter 5) based on adding programmable or reprogrammable logic into DRAM memories. The chapter emphasizes custom-reprogrammable chips (Chapter 2) and explores both FPGA and VLIW implementation for the programmable logic. Nevertheless, much of the analysis and techniques employed can also be applied to modern FPGAs with large, on-chip memories.

CHAPTER 27

SPIHT IMAGE COMPRESSION

Thomas W. Fry
Samsung, Global Strategy Group

Scott Hauck
Department of Electrical Engineering
University of Washington

This chapter describes the process of mapping the image compression algorithm SPIHT onto a reconfigurable logic architecture. A discussion of why adaptive logic is required, as opposed to an ASIC, is provided, along with background material on SPIHT. Several discrete wavelet transform hardware architectures are analyzed and evaluated. In addition, two major modifications to the original image compression algorithm, which are required in order to build a reconfigurable hardware implementation, are presented: (1) the storage elements necessary for each wavelet coefficient, and (2) a modification to the original SPIHT algorithm created to parallelize the computation. Also discussed are the effects these modifications have on the final compression results and the trade-offs involved.

The chapter then describes how the updated SPIHT algorithm is mapped onto the Annapolis Microsystems WildStar reconfigurable hardware system. This system is populated with three Virtex-E field-programmable gate array (FPGA) parts and several memory ports. The issues of how the modified algorithm is divided between individual FPGA parts and how data flows through the memories are discussed. Lastly, final results and speedups are presented and evaluated against a comparable microprocessor solution from the time the Annapolis Microsystems WildStar was released.

27.1 BACKGROUND

As NASA deploys each new generation of satellites with more sensors, capturing an ever-larger number of spectral bands, the volume of data being collected begins to outstrip a satellite's ability to transmit data back to Earth. For example, the Terra satellite contains five separate sensors, each collecting up to 36 individual spectral bands. The Tracking and Data Relay Satellite System (TDRSS) ground terminal in White Sands, New Mexico, captures data from these sensors at a limited rate of 150 Mbps [19]. As the number of sensors on a satellite grows and the transmission rates increase, this bandwidth limitation became a driving force for NASA to study methods of compressing images prior to downlinking.

FPGAs are an attractive implementation medium for such a system. Software solutions suffer from performance limitations and power requirements. At the same time, traditional hardware platforms lack the required flexibility needed for postlaunch modifications. After launch, such fixed hardware systems cannot be modified to use newer compression schemes or even to implement bug fixes. In the past, modification of fixed systems in satellites proved to be very expensive [4].

By implementing an image compression kernel in a reconfigurable system, we overcame these shortcomings. Because such a system may be reprogrammed after launch, it does not suffer from conventional hardware's inherit inflexibility. At the same time, the algorithm is computing in custom hardware and can perform at the required processing rates while consuming less power than a traditional software implementation.

This chapter describes the work performed as part of a NASA-sponsored investigation into the design and implementation of a space-bound FPGA-based hyperspectral image compression machine. For this work, the Set Partitioning in Hierarchical Trees (SPIHT) routine was selected as the image compression algorithm. First, we describe the algorithm and discuss the reasons for its selection. Then we describe how the algorithm was optimized for implementation in a specific hardware platform and we present the results.

27.2 SPIHT ALGORITHM

SPIHT is a wavelet-based image compression coder. It first converts an image into its wavelet transform and then transmits information about the wavelet coefficients. The decoder uses the received signal to reconstruct the wavelet and then performs an inverse transform to recover the image. SPIHT was selected because both it and its predecessor, the embedded zerotree wavelet coder, were significant breakthroughs in still-image compression. Both offered significantly improved quality over other image compression techniques such as vector quantization, JPEG, and wavelets combined with quantization, while not requiring training that would have been more difficult to implement in hardware. In short, SPIHT displays exceptional characteristics over several properties all at once [15]:

- Good image quality with a high peak-signal-to-noise ratio (PSNR).
- Fast coding and decoding.
- A fully progressive bitstream.
- Can be used for lossless compression.
- May be combined with error protection (useful in satellite transmissions).
- Ability to code for an exact bitrate or PSNR.

In addition, since the SPIHT algorithm processes an image in two distinct steps—the discrete wavelet transform phase and the coding phase—it provides a natural point at which a hardware implementation may be divided. (The advantage of this property will be seen in Section 27.4.) The rest of this section describes the basics of wavelets, the discrete wavelet transform, and the SPIHT coding engine.

27.2.1 Wavelets and the Discrete Wavelet Transform

The wavelet transform is a reversible transform on spatial data. The discrete wavelet transform (DWT) is a form appropriate to discrete data, such as the individual points or pixels in an image. DWT runs a high-pass and low-pass filter over the signal in one dimension. This produces a low-pass ("average") version of the data and a high-pass (rapid changes within the average) version. Every other result from each pass is then sampled, yielding two subbands, each of which is one-half the size of the input stream. The result is a new image comprising of a high- and a low-pass subband. These two subbands can be used to fully recover the original image. In the case of a multidimensional signal such as an image, this procedure is repeated in each dimension (Figure 27.1).

The vertical and horizontal transformations break up the image into four distinct subbands. The wavelet coefficients that correspond to the fine details are the LH, HL, and HH subbands. Lower frequencies are represented by the LL subband, which is a low-pass filtered version of the original image [17].

The next wavelet level is calculated by repeating the horizontal and vertical transformations on the LL subband from the previous level. Four new subbands are created from the transformations. The LH, HL, and HH subbands in the next level represent coarser-scale coefficients and the new LL subband is an even smoother version of the original image. It is possible to obtain coarser and coarser scales of the LH, HL, and HH subbands by iteratively repeating the wavelet transformation on the LL subband of each level. Figure 27.2 displays the subband components of an image with three scales of wavelet transformation.

The reverse transformation uses an inverse filter on the final LL subband and the LH, HL, and HH subbands at the same level to recreate the LL subband of the previous level. By iteratively processing each level, the original image may be restored. Figure 27.3 displays a satellite image of San Francisco and its corresponding 3-level DWT. By processing either the wavelet transform or the inverse wavelet transform, these two images may be converted from one into the other and thus may be viewed as equivalent.

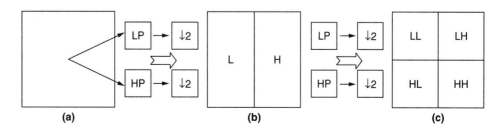

FIGURE 27.1 ■ A 1-level wavelet built by two one-dimensional passes: (a) original image, (b) horizontal pass, and (c) vertical pass.

| LL₃ | LH₃ | LH₂ | LH₁ |

The figure shows a 3-level wavelet transform subband layout with regions labeled LL₃, LH₃, HL₃, HH₃ in the top-left quadrant, LH₂, HL₂, HH₂ in the next level, and LH₁, HL₁, HH₁ in the outer level.

FIGURE 27.2 ■ A 3-level wavelet transform.

FIGURE 27.3 ■ An image of San Francisco (a) and the resulting 3-level DWT (b).

27.2.2 SPIHT Coding Engine

SPIHT is a method of coding and decoding the wavelet transform of an image. As discussed in the previous section, by coding and transmitting information about the wavelet coefficients, it is possible for a decoder to perform an inverse transformation on the wavelet and reconstruct the original image. A useful property of SPIHT is that the entire wavelet does not need to be transmitted in order to recover the image. Instead, as the decoder receives more information about the original wavelet transform, the inverse transformation yields a better-quality reconstruction (i.e., a higher PSNR) of the original image. SPIHT generates excellent image quality and performance due to three properties of the coding algorithm: partial ordering by coefficient value, taking advantage

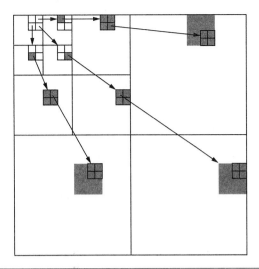

FIGURE 27.4 ■ Spatial orientation trees.

of the redundancies between different wavelet scales, and transmitting data in bit-plane order [14].

Following a wavelet transformation, SPIHT divides the wavelet into *spatial orientation trees* (Figure 27.4). Each node in a tree corresponds to an individual pixel. The offspring of a pixel are the four pixels in the same spatial location of the same subband at the next finer scale of the wavelet. Pixels at the finest scale of the wavelet are the leaves of the tree and have no children. Every pixel is part of a 2×2 block with its adjacent pixels. Blocks are a natural result of the hierarchical trees because every pixel in a block shares the same parent pixel. Also, the upper-left pixel of each 2×2 block at the root of the tree has no children since there are only three subbands at each scale and not four. Figure 27.4 shows how the pyramid is defined. Arrows point to the offspring of an individual pixel and the grayed blocks show all of the descendents for a specific pixel at every scale.

SPIHT codes a wavelet by transmitting information about the significance of a pixel. By stating whether or not a pixel is above some threshold, information about that pixel's value is implied. Furthermore, SPIHT transmits information stating whether a pixel or any of its descendents are above a threshold. If the statement proves false, all of the pixel's descendants are known to be below that threshold level and they do not need to be considered during the rest of the current pass. At the end of each pass, the threshold is divided by two and the algorithm continues. In this manner, information about the most significant bits of the wavelet coefficients will always precede information on lower-order significant bits, which is referred to as *bit-plane ordering*.

Information stating whether or not a pixel is above the current threshold or is being processed at the current threshold is contained in three lists: the *list of insignificant pixels* (LIP), the *list of insignificant sets* (LIS) and the *list of significant pixels* (LSP). The LIP are pixels that are currently being processed but are not yet above the threshold. The LIS are pixels that are currently being processed but none of their descendents are yet above the current threshold and so they are not being processed. Lastly, the LSP are pixels that were already stated to be above a previous threshold level and whose value at each bit plane is now transmitted.

Figure 27.5 is the algorithm from the original SPIHT paper [14], modified to reflect changes (discussed later in the chapter) referring to 2×2 block information. $S_n(i, j)$ represents if the pixel (i, j) is greater than the current threshold, and $S_n(D(i, j))$ states if any of the pixel's (i, j) descendents are greater than the current threshold.

There are three important concepts to take from the SPIHT algorithm. First, as the encoder sequentially steps through the image, it inserts or deletes pixels from the three lists. All of the information required to keep track of the lists is output to the decoder, allowing the decoder to generate and maintain an identical list order as the encoder. For the decoder to reproduce the steps taken by the encoder we merely need to replace the output statements in the encoder's algorithm with input for the decoder's algorithm.

Second, the bitstream produced is naturally progressive. A progressive bitstream is one that can be cut off at any point and still be valid. As the decoder steps through the coding algorithm, it gathers finer and finer detail about the original wavelet transform. The decoder can stop at any point and perform an inverse transform with the wavelet coefficients it has currently reconstructed. Progressive bitstreams can also be reduced to an arbitrary size or be cut off during transmission and still produce a valid image. Such a property is very useful in satellite transmissions.

---

1. **Initialization: output** n = floor[log$_2$(max$_{(i,j)}${|$c_{i,j}$|})]; clear the LSP list, add the root pixels to the LIP list and root pixels with descendants to LIS.
2. **Sorting Pass:**
    2.1 for each entry (i,j) in the LIP:
        2.1.1 **output** $S_n(i,j)$;
        2.1.2 If $S_n(i,j)$ = 1, move (i,j) to the LSP list and **output** its sign
    2.2 for each entry (i,j) in the LIS:
        2.2.1 If one of the pixels in (i,j)'s block is not in LIP but all are in LIS:
                output S_n(all descendants of the current block);
                if none are significant, skip 2.2.2.
        2.2.2 **Output** $S_n(D(i,j))$
                if $S_n(D(i,j))$ = 1, then
                    for each of (i,j) immediate children (k,l):
                        output $S_n(k,l)$;
                        add (k,l) to the LIS for the current pass
                        if $S_n(k,l)$ = 1, add (k,l) to the LSP and **output** its sign
                                    else add (k,l) to the LIP
3. **Refinement Pass:** for each entry (i,j) in LSP, except ones inserted in the current pass, **output** the nth most significant bit of (i,j).
4. **Quantization-step Update:** decrement n by 1 and go to Step **2**.

FIGURE 27.5 ▪ SPIHT coding algorithm.

Third, and the concept that has the largest impact on building a hardware platform, the **SPIHT** algorithm develops an individual list order to transmit information within each bit plane. This ordering is implicitly created from the threshold information discussed before—the order in which each pixel enters each list determines the transmission order for each image. As a result, each image will transmit wavelet coefficients in an entirely different order. Slightly better PSNRs are achieved with this dynamic ordering of the wavelet coefficients.

The **SPIHT** algorithm in Figure 27.5, which creates the individual list ordering, is inherently sequential. As a result, SPIHT cannot be significantly parallelized in hardware. This drawback greatly limits the performance of any SPIHT implementation in hardware. To get around this limitation and improve performance, it was necessary to parallelize the SPIHT algorithm and essentially create a new image compression algorithm. These changes and the trade-offs involved are described in Section 27.3.3.

27.3   DESIGN CONSIDERATIONS AND MODIFICATIONS

To fully take advantage of the high performance a custom hardware implementation of SPIHT could yield, the software specifications had to be examined and adjusted where they either performed poorly in hardware or did not make the most of the resources available. Here we review the three major factors taken under consideration while evaluating how to create a hardware implementation of the SPIHT algorithm on an adaptive computing platform.

The first factor was to determine what discrete wavelet transform architecture to use. Section 27.3.1 provides a summary of the DWTs considered, showing how memory and communication requirements helped dictate the structure chosen. Section 27.3.2 describes the fixed-point precision optimization performed for each wavelet coefficient and the final data representation employed. Section 27.3.3 explains how the SPIHT algorithm was altered to vastly speed up the hardware implementation.

27.3.1   Discrete Wavelet Transform Architectures

One of the benefits of the SPIHT algorithm is its use of the discrete wavelet transform, which had existed for several years prior to this work. As a result, numerous studies on how to create a DWT hardware implementation were available for review. Much of this work on DWTs involved parallel platforms to save both memory access and computations [5, 12, 16].

The most basic architecture is the basic folded architecture. The one-dimensional DWT entails demanding computations, which involve significant hardware resources. Since the horizontal and vertical passes use identical finite impulse response (FIR) filters, most two-dimensional DWT architectures implement folding to reuse logic for each dimension [6]. Figure 27.6 illustrates how folded architectures use a one-dimensional DWT to realize a two-dimensional DWT.

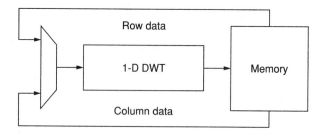

FIGURE 27.6 ▪ A folded architecture.

Although the folded architecture saves hardware resources, it suffers from high memory bandwidth. For an $N \times N$ image there are at least $2N^2$ read-and-write cycles for the first wavelet level. Additional levels require rereading previously computed coefficients, further reducing efficiency.

To lower the memory bandwidth requirements needed to compute the DWT, we considered several alternative architectures. The first was the Recursive Pyramid Algorithm (RPA) [21]. RPA takes advantage of the fact that the various wavelet levels run at different clock rates. Each wavelet level requires one-quarter of the time that the previous level needed because at each level the size of the area under computation is reduced by one-half in both the horizontal and vertical dimensions. Thus, it is possible to store previously computed coefficients on-chip and intermix the next level's computations with the current level's. A careful analysis of the runtime yields $(4^*N^2)/3$ individual memory load and store operations for an image. However, the algorithm has huge on-chip memory requirements and demands a thorough scheduling process to interleave the various wavelet levels.

Another method to reduce memory accesses is the partitioned DWT, which breaks the image into smaller blocks and computes several scales of the DWT at once for each block [13]. In addition, the algorithm made use of wavelet lifting to reduce the DWT's computational complexity [18]. By partitioning an image into smaller blocks, the amount of on-chip memory storage required was significantly reduced because only the coefficients in the block needed to be stored. This approach was similar to the RPA, except that it computed over sections of the image at a time instead of the entire image at once. Figure 27.7, from Ritter and Molitor [13], illustrates how the partitioned wavelet was constructed.

Unfortunately, the partitioned approach suffers from blocking artifacts along the partition boundaries if the boundaries were treated with reflection.[1] Thus, pixels from neighboring partitions were required to smooth out these boundaries. The number of wavelet levels determined how many pixels beyond a subimage's boundary were needed, since higher wavelet levels represent data

---

[1] An FIR filter generally computes over several pixels at once and generates a result for the middle pixel. To calculate pixels close to an image's edge, data points are required beyond the edge of the image. Reflection is a method that takes pixels toward the image's edge and copies them beyond the edge of the actual image for calculation purposes.

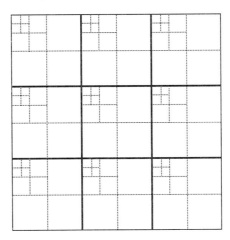

FIGURE 27.7 ■ The partitioned DWT.

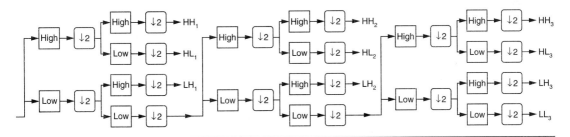

FIGURE 27.8 ■ A generic 2D biorthogonal DWT.

from a larger image region. To compensate for the partition boundaries, the algorithm processed subimages along a single row to eliminate multiple reads in the horizontal direction. Overall data throughputs of up to 152 Mbytes/second were reported with the partitioned DWT.

The last architecture we considered was the generic 2D biorthogonal DWT [3]. Unlike previous designs, the generic 2D biorthogonal DWT did not require FIR filter folding or on-chip memories as the Recursive Pyramid design. Nor did it involve partitioning an image into subimages. Instead, the architecture created separate structures to calculate each wavelet level as data were presented to it, as shown in Figure 27.8. The design sequentially read in the image and computed the four DWT subbands. As the LL_1 subband became available, the coefficients were passed to the next stage, which calculated the next coarser level subbands, and so on.

For larger images that required several individual wavelet scales, the generic 2D biorthogonal DWT architecture consumed a tremendous amount of on-chip resources. With SPIHT, a 1024×1024 pixel image computes seven separate wavelet scales. The proposed architecture would employ 21 individual high- and low-pass FIR filters. Since each wavelet scale processed data at different rates, some control complexity would be inevitable. The advantage of the architecture was much lower on-chip memory requirements and full utilization of the memory's bandwidth, since each pixel was read and written only once.

To select a DWT, each of the architectures discussed before were reevaluated against our target hardware platform (discussed below). The parallel versions of the DWT saved some memory bandwidth. However, additional resources and more complex scheduling algorithms became necessary. In addition, some of the savings were minimal since each higher wavelet level is one-quarter the size of the previous wavelet level. In a 7-level DWT, the highest 4 levels compute in just 2 percent of the time it takes to compute the first level. Other factors considered were that the more complex DWT architectures simply required more resources than a single Xilinx Virtex 2000E FPGA (our target device) could accommodate, and that enough memory ports were available in our board to read and write four coefficients at a time in parallel.

For these reasons, we did not select a more complex parallel DWT architecture, but instead designed a simple folded architecture that processes one dimension of a single wavelet level at a time. In the architecture created, pixels are read in horizontally from one memory port and written directly to a second memory port. In addition, pixels are written to memory in columns, inverting the image along the 45-degree line. By utilizing the same addressing logic, pixels are again read in horizontally and written vertically. However, since the image was inverted along its diagonal, the second pass will calculate the vertical dimension of the wavelet and restore the image to its original orientation.

Each dimension of the image is reduced by half, and the process iteratively continues for each wavelet level. Finally, the mean of the LL subband is calculated and subtracted from itself. To speed up the DWT, the design reads and writes four rows at a time. Figure 27.9 illustrates the architecture of the DWT phase.

Since every pixel is read and written once and the design processes four rows at a time, for an $N \times N$-size image both dimensions in the lowest wavelet level compute in $2*N^2/4$ clock cycles. Similarly, the next wavelet level processes the image in one-quarter the number of clock cycles as the previous level. With an infinite number of wavelet levels, the image processes in:

$$\sum_{l=1}^{\infty} \frac{2 \cdot N^2}{4^l} = \frac{3}{4} \cdot N^2 \qquad (27.1)$$

Thus, the runtime of the DWT engine is bounded by three-quarters of a clock cycle per pixel in the image. This was made possible because the memory ports in the system allowed four pixels to be read and written in a single clock cycle.

It is very important to note that many of the parallel architectures designed to process multiple wavelet levels simultaneously run in more than one clock cycle per image. Also, because of the additional resources required by a parallel implementation, computing multiple rows at once becomes impractical. Given more resources, the parallel architectures discussed previously could process multiple rows at once and yield runtimes lower than three-quarters of a clock cycle per pixel. However, the FPGAs available in the system used, although state of the art at the time, did not have such extensive resources.

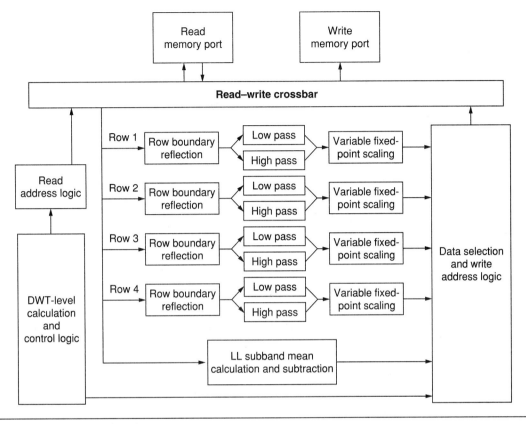

FIGURE 27.9 ■ A discrete wavelet transform architecture.

By keeping the address and control logic simple, there were enough resources on the FPGA to implement 8 distributed arithmetic FIR filters [23] from the Xilinx Core library. The FIR filters required significant FPGA resources, approximately 8 percent of the Virtex 2000E FPGA for each high- and low-pass FIR filter. We chose the distributed arithmetic FIR filters because they calculate a new coefficient every clock cycle, and this contributed to the system being able to process an image in three-quarters of a clock cycle per pixel.

27.3.2 Fixed-point Precision Analysis

The next major consideration was how to represent the wavelet coefficients in hardware. The discrete wavelet transform produces real numbers as the wavelet coefficients, which general-purpose computers realize as floating-point numbers. Traditionally, FPGAs have not employed floating-point numbers for several reasons:

- Floating-point numbers require variable shifts based on the exponential description, and variable shifters perform poorly in FPGAs.

- Floating-point numbers consume enormous hardware resources on a limited-resource FPGA.
- Floating point is often unnecessary for a known dataset.

At each wavelet level of the DWT, coefficients have a fixed range. Therefore, we opted for a fixed-point numerical representation—that is, one where the decimal point's position is predefined. With the decimal point locked at a specific location, each bit contributes a known value to the number, which eliminates the need for variable shifters. However, the DWT's filter bank was unbounded, meaning that the range of possible numbers increases with each additional wavelet level.

We chose to use the FIR filter set from the original SPIHT implementation. An analysis of the coefficients of each filter bank showed that the two-dimensional low-pass FIR filter at most increases the range of possible numbers by a factor of 2.9054. This number is the increase found from both the horizontal and the vertical directions. It represents how much larger a coefficient at the next wavelet level could be if the previous level's input wavelet coefficients were the maximum possible value and the correct sign to create the largest possible filter output. As a result, the coefficients at various wavelet levels require a variable number of bits above the decimal point to cover their possible ranges.

Table 27.1 illustrates the various requirements placed on a numerical representation for each wavelet level. The Factor and Maximum Magnitude columns demonstrate how the range of possible numbers increases with each level for an image starting with 1 byte per pixel. The Maximum Bits column shows the maximum number of bits (with a sign bit) necessary to represent the numeric range at each wavelet level. The Maximum Bits from Data column represents the maximum number of bits required to encode over one hundred sample images obtained from NASA. These numbers were produced via software simulation on this sample dataset.

In practice, the magnitude of the wavelet coefficients does not grow at the maximum theoretical rate. To maximize efficiency, the Maximum Bits from Data values were used to determine what position the most significant bit must stand for. Since the theoretical maximum is not used, an overflow situation may occur.

TABLE 27.1 ▪ Fixed-point magnitude calculations

Wavelet level	Factor	Maximum magnitude	Maximum bits	Maximum bits from data
Input image	1	255	8	8
0	2.9054	741	11	11
1	8.4412	2152	13	12
2	24.525	6254	14	13
3	71.253	18170	16	14
4	207.02	52789	17	15
5	601.46	153373	19	16
6	1747.5	445605	20	17

To compensate, the system flags overflow occurrences as an error and truncates the data. However, after examining hundreds of sample images, no instances of overflow occurred, and the data scheme used provided enough space to capture all the required data.

If each wavelet level used the same numerical representation, they would all be required to handle numbers as large as the highest wavelet level to prevent overflow. However, since the lowest wavelet levels never encounter numbers in that range, several bits at these levels would not be used and therefore wasted.

To fully utilize all of the bits for each wavelet coefficient, we introduced the concept of *variable fixed-point* representation. With variable fixed-point we assigned a fixed-point numerical representation for each wavelet level optimized for that level's expected data size. In addition, each representation differed from one another, meaning that we employed a different fixed-point scheme for each wavelet level. Doing so allowed us to optimize both memory storage and I/O at each wavelet level to yield maximum performance.

Once the position of the most significant bit was found for each wavelet level, the number of precision bits needed to accurately represent the wavelet coefficients had to be determined. Our goal was to provide enough bits to fully recover the image and no more. Figure 27.10 displays the average PSNRs for several recovered images from SPIHT using a range of bit widths for each coefficient.

An assignment of 16 bits per coefficient most accurately matched the full-precision floating-point coefficients used in software, up through perfect reconstruction. Previous wavelet designs we looked at focused on bitrates less than 4 bits per pixel (bpp) and did not consider rounding effects on the wavelet transformation for bitrates greater than 4 bpp. These studies found this lower bitrate acceptable for lossy SPIHT compression [3].

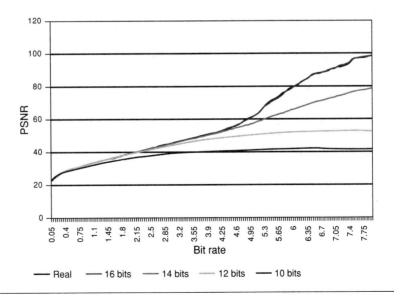

FIGURE 27.10 ■ PSNR versus bitrate for various coefficient sizes.

TABLE 27.2 ■ Final variable fixed-point representation

Wavelet level	Integer bits	Fractional bits
Input image	10	6
0	11	5
1	12	4
2	13	3
3	14	2
4	15	1
5	16	0
6	17	−1

Instead, we chose a numerical representation that retains the equivalent amount of information as a full floating-point number during wavelet transformation. By doing so, it was possible to perfectly reconstruct an image given a high enough bitrate. In other words, we allowed for a lossless implementation. Table 27.2 provides the number of integer and fractional bits allocated for each wavelet level. The number of integer bits also includes 1 extra bit for the sign value. The highest wavelet level's 16 integer bits represent positions 17 to 1, with no bit assigned for the 0 position.

27.3.3 Fixed Order SPIHT

The last major factor we took under consideration was how to parallelize the SPIHT algorithm for use in hardware. As discussed in Section 27.2, SPIHT computes a dynamic ordering of the wavelet coefficients as it progresses. By always adding pixels to the end of the LIP, LIS, and LSP, coefficients most critical to constructing a valid wavelet are generally sent first, while less critical coefficients are placed later in the lists. Such an ordering yields better image quality for bitstreams that end in the middle of a bit plane. The drawback of this ordering is that every image has a unique list order determined by the image's wavelet coefficient values.

By analyzing the SPIHT algorithm, we were able to conclude that the data a block of coefficients contributes to the final SPIHT bitstream is fully determined by the following set of localized information:

- The 2×2 block of coefficients
- Their immediate children
- The maximum magnitude of the four subtrees

As a result, we were able to show that every block of coefficients could be calculated independently and in parallel of one another. We were also able to determine that, if we could parallelize the computation of these coefficients, the final hardware implementation would operate at a much higher throughput. However, we were not able to take advantage of this parallelism because in SPIHT the order in which a block's data is inserted into the bitstream is not known, since it depends on the image's unique ordering. Only once the order is determined is it possible to produce a valid SPIHT bitstream from the information listed previously.

Unfortunately, the algorithm employed to calculate the SPIHT ordering of coefficients is sequential. The computation steps over the coefficients of the image multiple times within each bit plane and dynamically inserts and removes coefficients from the LIP and LIS lists. Such an algorithm is not parallelizable in hardware. As a result, many of the speedups a custom hardware implementation may produce would be lost. Instead, any hardware implementation we could develop would need to create the lists in an identical manner as the software implementation. This process would require many clock cycles per block of coefficients, which would significantly limit the throughput of any SPIHT implementation in hardware.

To remove this limitation and design a faster system, we created a modification to the original algorithm called *Fixed Order SPIHT*. Fixed Order SPIHT is similar to the SPIHT algorithm shown in Figure 27.5, except that the order of the LIP, LIS, and LSP lists is fixed and known beforehand. Instead of inserting blocks of coefficients at the end of the lists, they are inserted in a predetermined order. For example, block A will always appear before block B, which is always before block C, regardless of the order in which A, B, and C were added to the lists. The order of Fixed Order SPIHT is based upon the Morton scan ordering discussed in Algazi and Estes [1].

Fixed Order SPIHT removed the need to calculate the ordering of coefficients within each bit plane and allowed us to create a fully parallel version of the original SPIHT algorithm. Such a modification increased the throughput of a hardware encoder by more than an order of magnitude at the cost of a slightly lower PSNR within each bit plane. Figure 27.11 outlines the new version of SPIHT we created. The final bitstream generated is precisely the same as the bitstream generated from the original SPIHT algorithm except that data will appear in a different order within each bit plane.

By using the algorithm in Figure 27.11 instead of the original sequential algorithm in Figure 27.8, the final datastream can be computed in one pass through the image instead of multiple passes. In addition, each pixel block is coded in parallel, which yields significantly faster compression times with FPGAs.

The advantage of this method is that at the end of each bit plane, the exact same data will have been transmitted, just in a different order. Thus, at the end of each bit plane the PSNR of Fixed Order SPIHT will match that of the original SPIHT algorithm, as shown in Figure 27.12. Since the length of each bitstream is fairly short within the transmitted datastream, the PSNR curve of Fixed Order SPIHT very closely matches that of the original algorithm. The maximum loss in quality between Fixed Order SPIHT and the original SPIHT algorithm found was 0.2 dB. This is the maximum loss any image in our sample set displayed over any bitrate from 0.05 to 8.00 bpp.

For a more complete discussion on Fixed Order SPIHT, refer to Fry [8].

1. **Bit-plane calculation**: for each 2×2 block of pixels (i,j) in a *Morton Scan Ordering*
   1.1 for each threshold level n from the highest level to the lowest
      1.1.1 if (i,j) is a root and Max$((i,j))$ >= n
         add all four pixels to the LIP
      1.1.2 if (i,j) is not a root and Max$((i,j))$ >= previous n
         for each pixel p in the block
           if p < previous n
             add p to the LIP
           else
             add p to the LSP
      1.1.3 if (i,j) is not a leaf and Max$((i,j))$ >= n
         add all four pixel to the LIS unless (i,j) is a root, then just add the three with children
      1.1.4 if all four pixels are in LIS and at least one is not in the LIP
         if at least one pixel will be removed from the LIS at this level
           output a '0' to the LIS stream
         else
           output a '1' to the LIS stream
      1.1.5 for each pixel p in the LIP
         if p >= n
           output a '1' and the sign of p to the LIP stream
           remove p from the LIP and add it to the LSP
         else
           output a '0' to the LIP stream
      1.1.6 for each pixel p in the LIS
         if child max(p) >= n
           output a '1' to the LIS stream
           remove p from the LIS
           for each child (k,l) of p
             if (k,l) >= n
               output a '1' and the sign of (k,l) to the LIS stream
             else
               output a '0' to the LIS stream
         else
           output a '0' to the LIS stream
      1.1.7 for each pixel p in the LSP
         output the value of p at the bit plane n to the LSP stream
2. **Grouping phase**: for each threshold level n from the highest level to the lowest
   2.1 **output** the LIP stream at threshold level n to the final data stream
   2.2 **output** the LIS stream at threshold level n to the final data stream
   2.3 **output** the LSP stream at threshold level n to the final data stream

FIGURE 27.11 ▪ Fixed Order SPIHT.

27.4   HARDWARE IMPLEMENTATION

In the following subsections we first describe the target hardware platform that the SPIHT algorithm was mapped onto. Next, we present an overview of the implementation and a detailed description of the three major steps of the

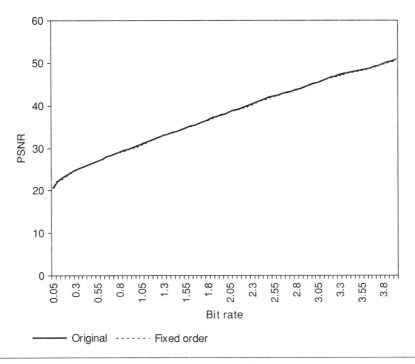

FIGURE 27.12 ■ A comparison of original SPIHT and Fixed Order SPIHT.

computation. A thorough understanding of the target platform is required because it strongly influenced the SPIHT implementation created.

27.4.1   Target Hardware Platform

The target platform was the WildStar FPGA processor board developed by Annapolis Microsystems [2]. Shown in Figure 27.13, it consists of three Xilinx Virtex 2000E FPGAs—PE 0, PE 1, and PE 2—and operates at rates of up to 133 MHz. The board makes available 48 MBytes of memory through 12 individual memory ports, between 32 and 64 bits wide, yielding a throughput of up to 8.5 GBytes/sec. Four shared memory blocks connect the Virtex chips through a crossbar. By switching a crossbar, several MBytes of data are passed between the chips in just a few clock cycles.

The Xilinx Virtex 2000E FPGA allows for 2 million gate designs [22]. For extra on-chip memory, the FPGAs contain 160 asynchronous dual-ported BlockRAMs. Each BlockRAM stores 4096 bits of data and is accessible in 1-, 2-, 4-, 8-, or 16-bit-wide words. Because they are dual ported, the BlockRAMs function well as first in, first outs (FIFOs). A PCI bus connects the board to a host computer.

27.4.2   Design Overview

The architecture constructed consisted of three phases: wavelet transform, maximum magnitude calculation, and Fixed Order SPIHT coding. Each phase

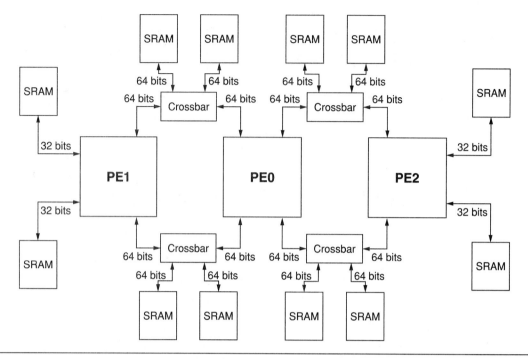

FIGURE 27.13 ■ A block diagram of the Annapolis Microsystems WildStar board.

was implemented in one of the three Virtex chips. By instantiating each phase on a separate chip, separate images could be operated on in parallel. Data was transferred from one phase by the next through the shared memories. The decision on how to break up the phases came naturally from the resources available in each FPGA and the requirements of each section. The DWT and the SPIHT coding phases each required close to the full resources of a single FPGA, and the maximum magnitude phase needed to be completed prior to the SPIHT coding phase. These characteristics of the algorithm and system naturally lead to placing the three phases on the three separate FPGAs.

The architecture was also designed in this manner because once processing in a phase is complete, the crossbar mode could be switched and the data calculated would be accessible to the next chip. By coding a different image in each phase simultaneously, the throughput of the system is determined by the slowest phase, while the latency of the architecture is the sum of the three phases. Figure 27.14 illustrates the architecture of the system.

27.4.3   Discrete Wavelet Transform Phase

As discussed in Section 27.3.1, after implementing each algorithm in hardware we chose a simple folded architecture, which matched the bandwidth, memory, and chip capacities of the target board well. The results of this phase are stored into memory and passed to the maximum magnitude phase.

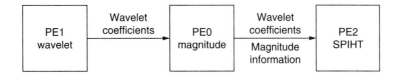

FIGURE 27.14 ■ An overview of the architecture.

27.4.4 Maximum Magnitude Phase

Once the DWT is complete, the next phase prepares and organizes the image into a form easily readable by the parallel version of the SPIHT coder. Specifically, the maximum magnitude phase calculates and rearranges the following information for the next phase:

- The maximum magnitude of each of the four child trees
- The absolute value of the 2×2 block of coefficients
- A sign value for each coefficient in the block
- The threshold level when the block is first inserted into the LIS by its parent
- Threshold and sign data of each of the 16 child coefficients
- Reorder the wavelet coefficients into a Morton Scan Ordering

The SPIHT coding phase shares two 64-bit memory ports with the maximum magnitude phase, allowing it to read 128 bits on each clock cycle. The data just listed can fit into these two memory ports. By doing so on every clock cycle the SPIHT coding phase will be able to read and process an entire block of data. The data that the maximum magnitude phase calculates is shown in Figure 27.15.

To calculate the maximum magnitude of all coefficients below a node in the spatial orientation trees, the image must be scanned in depth-first search order [7]. With a depth-first search, whenever a new coefficient is read and considered, all of its children will have already been read and the maximum coefficient so far is known. On every clock cycle the new coefficient is compared to and updates the current maximum. Because PE 0 (the maximum magnitude phase) uses 32-bit-wide memory ports, it can read half a block at a time.

The state machine, which controls how the spatial orientation trees are traversed, reads one-half of a block as it descends the tree, and the other half as it ascends the tree. By doing so all of the data needed to compute the maximum magnitude for the current block is available as the state machine ascends back up the spatial orientation tree. In addition, the four most recent blocks of each level are saved onto a stack so that all 16 child coefficients are available to the parent block.

Figure 27.16 demonstrates the algorithm. The current block, maximum magnitude for each child, and 16 child coefficients are shown on the stack. Light gray blocks are coefficients previously read and processed. Dark gray blocks are coefficients currently being read. In this example, the state machine has just finished reading the lowest level and has ascended to the second wavelet level.

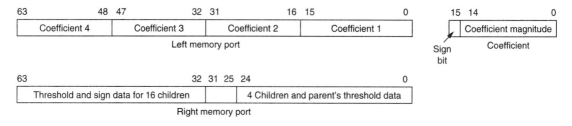

FIGURE 27.15 ▪ Data passed to the SPIHT coder to calculate a single block.

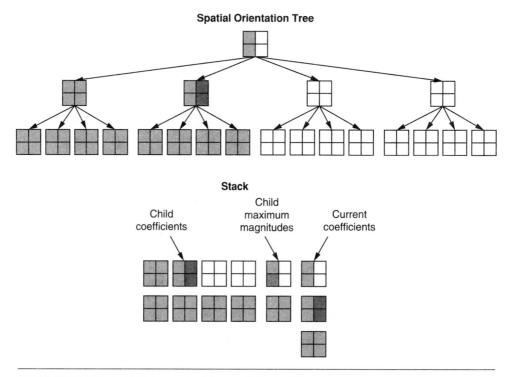

FIGURE 27.16 ▪ A depth-first search of the spatial orientation trees.

The second block in the second level is now complete, and its maximum magnitude can now be calculated, shown as the dark gray block in the stack's highest level. In addition, the 16 child coefficients in the lowest level were saved and are available. There are no child values for the lowest level since there are no children.

Another benefit of scanning the image in a depth-first search order is that Morton Scan Ordering is naturally realized within each level, although it is intermixed between levels. By writing data from each level to a separate area of memory and later reading the data from the highest wavelet level to the lowest, the Morton

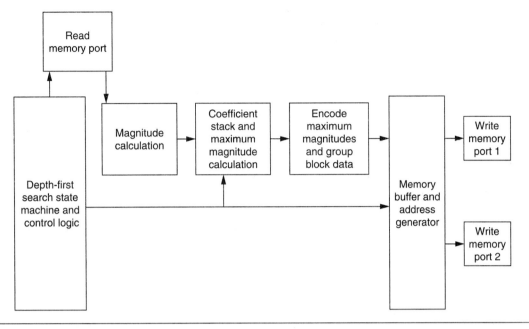

FIGURE 27.17 ▪ A block diagram of the SPIHT maximum magnitude phase.

Scan Ordering is naturally realized. A block diagram of the maximum magnitude phase is provided in Figure 27.17. Since two pixels are read together and the image is scanned only once, the runtime of this phase is half a clock cycle per pixel. Because the maximum magnitude phase computes in less time than the wavelet phase, the throughput of the overall system is not affected.

27.4.5 The SPIHT Coding Phase

The final SPIHT coding phase performs the Fixed Order SPIHT encoding in parallel, based on the data from the maximum magnitude phase. Coefficient blocks are read from the highest wavelet level to the lowest. As information is loaded from memory it is shifted from the variable fixed-point representation to a common fixed-point representation for every wavelet level. Once each block has been adjusted to an identical numerical representation, the parallel version of SPIHT is used to calculate what information each block will contribute to each bit plane.

The information is grouped and counted before being added to three separate variable FIFOs for each bit plane. The data that the variable FIFO components receive range in size from 0 to 37 bits, and the variable FIFOs arrange the block data into regular sized 32-bit words for memory access. Care is also taken to stall the algorithm if any of the variable FIFOs becomes too full.

Data from each buffer is output to a fixed location in memory and the number of bits in each bitstream is output as well. Given that data is added dynamically to each bitstream, there needs to be a dynamic scheduler to select which buffer should be written to memory. Since there are a large number of FIFOs that all require a BlockRAM, the FIFOs are spread across the FPGA, and some type of staging is required to prevent a signal from traveling too far. The scheduler selects which FIFO to read based on both how full a FIFO is and when it was last accessed.

Our studies showed that the LSP bitstream is roughly the same size of the LIP and LIS streams combined. Because of this the LSP bitstreams transfer more data to memory than the other two lists. In our design the LIP and LIS bitstreams share a memory port while the LSP stream writes to a separate memory port. Since a 2×2 block of coefficients is processed every clock cycle, the design takes one-quarter of a clock cycle per pixel, which is far less than the three-quarters of a clock cycle per pixel for the DWT. The block diagram for the SPIHT coding phase is given in Figure 27.18.

With 22 total bit planes to calculate, the design involves 66 individual data grouping and variable FIFO blocks. Although none consume a significant amount of FPGA resources individually, 66 blocks do. The entire design required 160 percent of the resources in a Virtex 2000E, and would not fit in the target system. However, by removing the lower bit planes, less FPGA resources are needed, and the architecture can easily be adjusted to fit the FPGA being used. Depending on the size of the final bitstream required, the FPGA size used in the SPIHT phase can be varied to handle the number of intermediate bitstreams generated.

Removing lower bit planes is possible since the final bitstream transmits data from the highest bit plane to the lowest. In our design the lower 9-bit planes

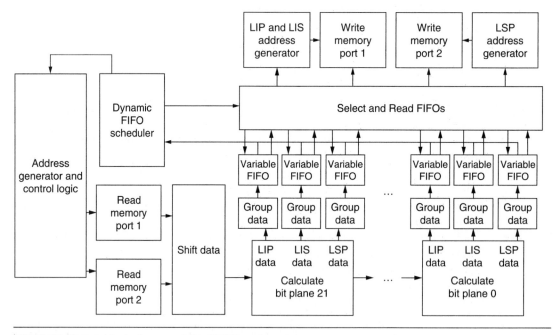

FIGURE 27.18 ■ A block diagram of the SPIHT coding phase.

were eliminated. Yet, without these lower planes, bitrates of up to 6 bpp can still be achieved. We found the constraint to be acceptable because we are interested in high compression ratios using low bitrates, and 6 bpp is practically a lossless signal. Since SPIHT is optimized for lower bitrates, the ability to calculate higher bitrates was not considered necessary. Alternatively, the use of a larger FPGA would alleviate the size constraint.

27.5 DESIGN RESULTS

The system was designed using VHDL with models provided by Annapolis Micro Systems to access the PCI bus and memory ports. Simulations for debugging purposes were carried out with ModelSim EE 5.4e from Mentor Graphics. Synplify 6.2 from Synplicity was used to compile the VHDL code and generate a netlist. The Xilinx Foundation Series 3.1i tool set was used to place and route the design. Lastly, the `peutil.exe` utility from Annapolis Micro Systems generated the FPGA configuration streams.

Table 27.3 shows the speed and runtime specifications of the final architecture. All performance numbers are measured results from the actual hardware implementation. Each phase computes on separate memory blocks, which can operate at different clock rates. The design can process any square image where the dimensions are a power of 2: 16×16, 32×32, up to 1024×1024.

Since the WildStar board is connected to the host computer by a relatively slow PCI bus, the throughput of the entire system we built is constrained by the throughput of the PCI bus. However, since the study is on how image compression routines could be implemented on a satellite, such a system would be designed differently, and would not contain a reconfigurable board connected to some host platform though a PCI bus. Instead, the image compression routines would be inserted directly into the data path and the data transfer times would not be the bottleneck of the system. For this reason we analyzed the throughput of just the SPIHT compression engine and analyzed how quickly the FPGAs can process the images.

The throughput of the system was constrained by the discrete wavelet transform at 100 MPixels/sec. One method to increase this rate is to compute more rows in parallel. If the available memory ports accessed 128 bits of data instead of the 64 bits with our WildStar board, the number of clock cycles per pixel could be reduced by half and the throughput could double.

TABLE 27.3 ■ Performance numbers

Phase	Clock cycles per 512×512 image	Clock cycles per pixel	Clock rate	Throughput	FPGA area (%)
Wavelet	182465	3/4	75 MHz	100 MPixels/sec	62
Magnitude	131132	1/2	73 MHz	146 MPixels/sec	34
SPIHT	65793	1/4	56 MHz	224 MPixels/sec	98

Assuming the original image consists of 8 bpp, images are processed at a rate of 800 Mbits/sec.

The entire throughput of the architecture is less than one clock cycle for every pixel, which is lower than parallel versions of the DWT. Parallel versions of the DWT used complex scheduling to compute multiple wavelet levels simultaneously, which left limited resources to process multiple rows at a time. Given more resources though, they would obtain higher data rates than our architecture by processing multiple rows simultaneously. In the future, a DWT architecture other than the one we implemented could be selected for additional speed improvements.

We compared our results to the original software version of SPIHT provided on the SPIHT web site [15]. The comparison was made without arithmetic coding since our hardware implementation does not perform any arithmetic coding on the final bitstream. Additionally, in our testing on sample NASA images, arithmetic coding added little to overall compression rates and thus was dropped [11]. An IBM RS/6000 Model 270 workstation was used for the comparison, and we used a combination of standard image compression benchmark images and satellite images from NASA's web site. The software version of SPIHT compressed a 512×512 image in 1.101 seconds on average without including disk access. The wavelet phase, which constrains the hardware implementation, computes in 2.48 milliseconds, yielding a speedup of 443 times for the SPIHT engine. In addition, by creating a parallel implementation of the wavelet phase, further improvements to the runtimes of the SPIHT engine are possible.

While this is the speedup we will obtain if the data transfer times are not a factor, the design may be used to speed up SPIHT on a general-purpose processor. On such a system the time to read and write data must be included as well. Our WildStar board is connected to the host processor over a PCI bus, which writes images in 13 milliseconds and reads the final datastream in 20.75 milliseconds. Even with the data transfer delay, the total speedup still yields an improvement of 31.4 times.

Both the magnitude and SPIHT phases yield higher throughputs than the wavelet phase, even though they operate at lower clock rates. The reason for the higher throughputs is that both of these phases need fewer clock cycles per pixel to compute an image. The magnitude phase takes half a clock cycle per pixel and the SPIHT phase requires just a quarter. The fact that the SPIHT phase computes in less than one clock cycle per pixel, let alone a quarter, is a striking result considering that the original SPIHT algorithm is very sequential in nature and had to consider each pixel in an image multiple times per bit plane.

27.6   SUMMARY AND FUTURE WORK

In this chapter we demonstrated a viable image compression routine on a reconfigurable platform. We showed how by analyzing the range of data processed by each section of the algorithm, it is advantageous to create optimized memory structures as with our variable fixed-point work. Doing so minimizes memory usages and yields efficient data transfers. Here each bit transferred between memory and the processor board directly impacted the final results. In addition, our Fixed Order SPIHT modifications illustrate how by making slight adjustments to an existing algorithm, it is possible to dramatically increase the performance in a custom hardware implementation and simultaneously yield essentially identical results. With Fixed Order SPIHT the throughput of the system increased by over an order of magnitude while still matching the original algorithm's PSNR curve.

This SPIHT work was part of a development effort funded by NASA.

References

[1] V. R. Algazi, R. R. Estes. Analysis-based coding of image transform and subband coefficients. *Applications of Digital Image Processing XVIII, SPIE Proceedings* 2564, 1995.

[2] Annapolis Microsystems. *WildStar Reference Manual*, Annapolis Microsystems, 2000.

[3] A. Benkrid, D. Crookes, K. Benkrid. Design and implementation of generic 2D biorthogonal discrete wavelet transform on an FPGA. *IEEE Symposium on Field-Programmable Custom Computing Machines*, April 2001.

[4] M. Carraeu. Hubble Servicing Mission: Hubble is fitted with a new "eye." *http://www.chron.com/content/interactive/space/missions/sts-103/hubble/archive/931207.html*, December 7, 1993.

[5] C. M. Chakrabarti, M. Vishwanath. Efficient realization of the discrete and continuous wavelet transforms: From single chip implementations to mappings in SIMD array computers. *IEEE Transactions on Signal Processing* 43, March 1995.

[6] C. M. Chakrabarti, M. Vishwanath, R. M. Owens. Architectures for wavelet transforms: A survey. *Journal of VLSI Signal Processing* 14, 1996.

[7] T. Cormen, C. Leiserson, R. Rivest. *Introduction to Algorithms*, MIT Press, 1997.

[8] T. W. Fry. *Hyper Spectral Image Compression on Reconfigurable Platforms*, Master's thesis, University of Washington, Seattle, 2001.

[9] R. C. Gonzalez, R. E. Woods. *Digital Image Processing*, Addison-Wesley, 1993.

[10] A. Graps. An introduction to wavelets. *IEEE Computational Science and Engineering* 2(2), 1995.

[11] T. Owen, S. Hauck. *Arithmetic Compression on SPITH Encoded Images*, Technical report UWEETR-2002–2007, Department of Electrical Engineering, University of Washington, Seattle, 2002.

[12] K. K. Parhi, T. Nishitani. VLSI architectures for discrete wavelet transforms. *IEEE Transactions on VLSI Systems* 1(2), 1993.

[13] J. Ritter, P. Molitor. A pipelined architecture for partitioned DWT based lossy image compression using FPGAs. *ACM/SIGDA Ninth International Symposium on Field-Programmable Gate Arrays*, February 2001.

[14] A. Said, W. A. Pearlman. A new fast and efficient image codec based on set partitioning in hierarchical trees. *IEEE Transactions on Circuits and Systems for Video Technology* 6, June 1996.

[15] A. Said, W. A. Pearlman. SPIHT image compression: Properties of the method. *http://www.cipr.rpi.edu/research/SPIHT/spiht1.html*.

[16] H. Sava, M. Fleury, A. C. Downton, A. Clark. Parallel pipeline implementations of wavelet transforms. *IEEE Proceedings Part 1 (Vision, Image and Signal Processing)* 144(6), 1997.

[17] J. M. Shapiro. Embedded image coding using zero trees of wavelet coefficients. *IEEE Transactions on Signal Processing* 41(12), 1993.

[18] W. Sweldens. The Lifting Scheme: A new philosophy in biorthogonal wavelet constructions. *Wavelet Applications in Signal and Image Processing* 3, 1995.

[19] NASA. TERRA: The EOS flagship. The EOS Data and Information System (EOS-DIS). *http://terra.nasa.gov/Brochure/Sect_5-1.html*.

[20] C. Valens. A really friendly guide to wavelets. *http://perso.wanadoo.fr/polyvalens/clemens/wavelets/wavelets.html*.

[21] M. Vishwanath, R. M. Owens, M. J. Irwin. VLSI architectures for the discrete wavelet transform. *IEEE Transactions on Circuits and Systems, Part II*, May 1995.

[22] Xilinx, Inc. *The Programmable Logic Data Book*, Xilinx, Inc., 2000.

[23] Xilinx, Inc. *Serial Distributed Arithmetic FIR Filter*, Xilinx, Inc., 1998.

CHAPTER 28

AUTOMATIC TARGET RECOGNITION SYSTEMS ON RECONFIGURABLE DEVICES

Young H. Cho
Open Acceleration Systems Research

An Automatic Target Recognition (ATR) system analyzes a digital image or video sequence to locate and identify all objects of a certain class. There are several ways to implement ATR systems, and the right one is dependent, in large part, on the operating environment and the signal source. In this chapter we focus on the implementations of reconfigurable ATR designs based on the algorithms from Sandia National Laboratories (SNL) for the U.S. Department of Defense Joint STARS airborne radar imaging platform. STARS is similar to an aircraft AWACS system, but detects ground targets.

ATR in Synthetic Aperture Radar (SAR) imagery requires tremendous processing throughput. In this application, data come from high-bandwidth sensors, and the processing is time critical. On the other hand, there is limited space and power for processing the data in the sensor platforms. One way to meet the high computational requirement is to build custom circuits as an ASIC. However, very high nonrecurring engineering (NRE) costs for low-volume ASICs, and often evolving algorithms, limit the feasibility of using custom hardware. Therefore, reconfigurable devices can play a prominent role in meeting the challenges with greater flexibility and lower costs.

This chapter is organized as follows: Section 28.1 describes a highly parallelizable Automatic Target Recognition (ATR) algorithm. The system based on it is implemented using a mix of software and hardware processing, where the most computationally demanding tasks are accelerated using field-programmable gate arrays (FPGAs). We present two high-performance implementations that exercise the FPGA's benefits. Section 28.2 describes the system that automatically builds algorithm-specific and resource-efficient "hardwired" accelerators. It relies on the dynamic reconfiguration feature of FPGAs to obtain high performance using limited logic resources.

The system in Section 28.3 is based on an architecture that does not require frequent reconfiguration. The architecture is modular, easily scalable, and highly tuned for the ATR application. These application-specific processors are automatically generated based on application and environment parameters. In Section 28.4 we compare the implementations to discuss the benefits and the trade-offs of designing ATR systems using FPGAs. In Section 28.5, we draw our conclusions on FPGA-based ATR system design.

28.1 AUTOMATIC TARGET RECOGNITION ALGORITHMS

Sandia real-time SAR ATR systems use a hierarchy of algorithms to reduce the processing demands for SAR images in order to yield a high probability of detection (PD) and a low false alarm rate (FAR).

28.1.1 Focus of Attention

As shown in Figure 28.1, the first step in the SNL algorithm is a Focus of Attention (FOA) algorithm that runs over a downsampled version of the entire image to find regions of interest that are of approximately the right size and brightness. These regions are then extracted and processed by an indexing stage to further reduce the datastream, which includes target hypotheses, orientation estimations, and target center locations. The surviving hypotheses have the full resolution data sent to an identification executive that schedules multiple identification algorithms and then fuses their results.

The FOA stage identifies interesting image areas called "chips." Then it composes a list of targets suspected to be in a chip. Having access to range and altitude information, the FOA algorithm also determines the elevation for the chip, without having to identify the target first. It then tasks the next stage with evaluating the likelihood that the suspected targets are actually in the given image chip and exactly where.

28.1.2 Second-level Detection

The next stage of the algorithm, called Second Level Detection (SLD), takes the extracted imagery (an image chip), matches it against a list of provided target

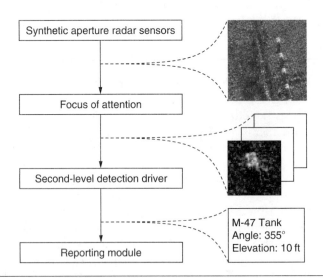

FIGURE 28.1 ▪ The Sandia Automatic Target Recognition algorithm.

hypotheses, and returns the hit information for each image chip consisting of the best two orientation matches and other relevant information.

The system has a database of target models. For each target, and for each of its three different elevations, 72 templates are defined corresponding to its all-around views. The orientations of adjacent views are separated by 5 degrees.

SLD is a binary silhouette matcher that has a bright mask and a surround mask that are mutually exclusive. Each template is composed of several parameters along with a "bright mask" and a "surround mask," where the former defines the image pixels that should be bright for a match, and the latter defines the ones that should not. The bright and surround masks are 32×32 bitmaps, each with about 100 asserted bits. "Bright" is defined relative to a dynamic threshold.

On receiving tasks from the FOA, the SLD unit compares all of the stored templates for this target and elevation and the applicable orientations with the image chip, and computes the level of matching (the "hit quality"). The two hits with the highest quality are reported to the SLD driver as the most likely candidates to include targets. For each hit, the template index number, the exact position of the hit in the search area, and the hit quality are provided. After receiving this information, the SLD driver reports it to the ATR system.

The purpose of the first step in the SLD algorithm, called the shape sum, is to distinguish the target from its surrounding background. This consists of adaptively estimating the illumination for each position in the search area, assuming that the target is at that orientation and location. If the energy is too little or too much, no further processing for that position for that template match is required. Hence, for each mask position in the search area, a specific threshold value is computed as in equation 28.1.

$$SM_{x,y} = \sum_{u=0}^{31} \sum_{v=0}^{31} B_{u,v} M_{x+u,y+v} \tag{28.1}$$

$$TH_{x,y} = \frac{SM_{x,y}}{BC} - Bias \tag{28.2}$$

The next step in the algorithm distinguishes the target from the background by thresholding each image pixel with respect to the threshold of the current mask position, as computed before. The same pixel may be above the threshold for some mask positions but below it for others. This threshold calculation determines the actual bright and surround pixel for each position. As shown in equation 28.2, it consists of dividing the shape sum by the number of pixels in the bright mask and subtracting a template-specific *Bias* constant.

As shown in equation 28.3, the pixel values under the bright mask that are greater than or equal to the threshold are counted; if this count exceeds the minimal bright sum, the processing continues. On the other hand, the pixel values under the surround mask that are less than the threshold are counted to calculate the surround sum as shown in equation 28.4. If this count exceeds the minimal surround sum, it is declared a hit.

$$BS_{x,y} = \sum_{u=0}^{31} \sum_{v=0}^{31} B_{u,v} \left[M_{x+u,y+v} \geq TH_{x,y} \right] \tag{28.3}$$

$$SS_{x,y} = \sum_{u=0}^{31} \sum_{v=0}^{31} S_{u,v} \left[M_{x+u,y+v} < TH_{x,y} \right] \tag{28.4}$$

Once the position of the hit is determined, we can calculate its quality by taking the average of bright and surround pixels that were correct, as shown in equation 28.5. This quality value is sent back to the driver with the position to determine the two best targets.

$$Q_{x,y} = \frac{1}{2} \left(\frac{BS_{x,y}}{BC} + \frac{SS_{x,y}}{SC} \right) \tag{28.5}$$

28.2   DYNAMICALLY RECONFIGURABLE DESIGNS

FPGAs can be reconfigured to perform multiple functions with the same logic resources by providing a number of corresponding configuration bit files. This ability allows us to develop dynamically reconfigurable designs. In this section, we present an ATR system implementation of UCLA's Mojave project that uses an FPGA's dynamic reconfigurability.

28.2.1   Algorithm Modifications

As described previously, the current Sandia system uses 64×64 pixel chips and 32×32 pixel templates. However, the Mojave system uses chip sizes of 128×128 pixels and template sizes of 8×8 pixels. It uses different chip and template sizes in order to map into existing FPGA devices that are relatively small. A single template moves through a single chip to yield 14,641 (121×121) image correlation results. Assuming that each output can be represented with 6 bits, the 87,846 bits are produced by the system.

There is also a divide step in the Sandia algorithm that follows the shape sum operation and guides the selection of threshold bin for the chip. This system does not implement the divide, mainly because it is expensive relative to available FPGA resources for the design platform.

28.2.2   Image Correlation Circuit

FPGAs offer an extremely attractive solution to the correlation problem. First of all, the operations being performed occur directly at the bit level and are dominated by shifts and adds, making them easy to map into the hardware provided by the FPGA. This contrasts, for example, with multiply-intensive algorithms that would make relatively poor utilization of FPGA resources. More important, the sparse nature of the templates can be utilized to achieve a far more efficient implementation in the FPGA than could be realized in a general-purpose correlation device. This can be illustrated using the example of the simple template shown in Figure 28.2.

In the example template shown in the figure, only 5 of the 20 pixels are asserted. At any given relative offset between the template and the chip, the correlation output is the sum of the 5 binary pixels in the chip that match the asserted bits in the template. The template can therefore be implemented in the FPGA as a simple multiple-port adder. The chip pixel values can be stored in flip-flops and are shifted to the right by one flip-flop with each clock cycle. Though correlation of a large image with a small mask is often understood conceptually in terms of the mask being scanned across the image, in this case the opposite is occurring—the template is hardwired into the FPGA while the image pixels are clocked past it.

Another important opportunity for increased efficiency lies in the potential to combine multiple templates on a single FPGA. The simplest way to do this is to spatially partition the FPGA into several smaller blocks, each of which handles the logic for a single template. Alternatively, we can try to identify templates that have some topological commonality and can therefore share parts of their adder trees. This is illustrated in Figure 28.3, which shows two templates sharing several pixels that can be mapped using a set of adder trees to leverage this overlap.

A potential advantage FPGAs have over ASICs is that they can be dynamically optimized at the gate level to exploit template characteristics. For our application, a programmable ASIC design would need to provide large general-purpose adder trees to handle the worst-case condition of summing all possible template bits, as shown in Figure 28.4. In constrast, an FPGA exploits the sparse nature of the templates and constructs only the small adder trees required. Additionally, FPGAs can optimize the design based on other application-specific characteristics.

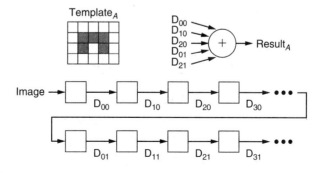

FIGURE 28.2 ■ An example template and a corresponding register chain with an adder tree.

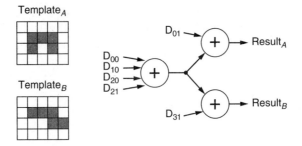

FIGURE 28.3 ■ Common hardware shared between two templates.

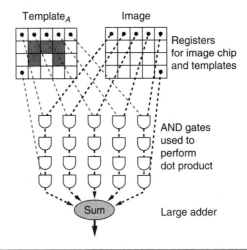

FIGURE 28.4 ■ The ASIC version of the equivalent function.

28.2.3 Performance Analysis

Using a template-specific adder tree achieves significant reduction in routing complexity over a general correlation device, which must include logic to support arbitrary templates. The extent of this reduction is inversely proportional to the fraction of asserted pixels in the template. While this complexity reduction is important, alone it is not sufficient to lead to efficient implementations on FPGAs. The number of D-flip-flops required for storing the data points can cause inefficiencies in the design. Implementing these on the FPGA using the usual flip-flop–based shift registers is inefficient.

This problem can be resolved by collapsing the long strings of image pixels—those not being actively correlated against a template—into shift registers, which can be implemented very efficiently on some lookup table (LUT)–based FPGAs. For example, LUTs in the Xilinx XC4000 library can be used as shift registers that delay data by some predetermined number of clock cycles. Each 16×1-bit

LUT can implement an element that is effectively a 16-bit shift register in which the internal bits cannot be accessed. A flip-flop is also needed at the output of each RAM to act as a buffer and synchronizer. A single control circuit is used to control the stepping of the address lines and the timely assertion of the write-enable and output-enable signals for all RAM-based shift register elements. This is a small price to pay for the savings in configurable logic block (CLB) usage relative to a brute-force implementation using flip-flops.

In contrast, the 256-pixel template images, like those shown in Figure 28.5, can be stored easily using flip-flop–based registers. This is because sufficient flip-flops are available to do this, and the adder tree structures do not consume them. Also, using standard flip-flop–based shift registers for image pixels in the template simplifies the mapping process by allowing every pixel to be accessed. New templates can be implemented by simply connecting the template pixels of concern to the inputs of the adder tree structures. This leads to significant simplification of automated template-mapping tools.

The resources used by the two components of target correlation—namely, storage of active pixels on the FPGA and implementation of the adder tree corresponding to the templates—are independent of each other. The resources used by the pixel storage are determined by the template size and are independent of the number of templates being implemented. Adding templates involves adding new adder tree structures and hence increases the number of function generators being used. The total number of templates on an FPGA is bounded by the number of usable function generators.

The experimental results suggest that in practice we can expect to fit 6 to 10 surround templates having a higher number of overlapping pixels onto a 13,000-gate FPGA. However, intelligent grouping of compatible templates is important. Because the bright templates are less populated than the surround templates, we estimate that 15 to 20 of them can be mapped onto the same FPGA.

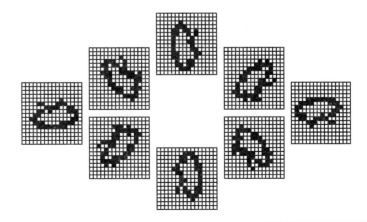

FIGURE 28.5 ■ Example of eight rotation templates of a SAR 16×16 bitmap image.

28.2.4 Template Partitioning

To minimize the number of FPGA reconfigurations necessary to correlate a given target image against the entire set of templates, it is necessary to maximize the number of templates in every configuration of the FPGA. To accomplish this optimization goal, we want to partition the set of templates into groups that can share adder trees so that fewer resources are used per template. The set of templates may number in the thousands, and the goal may be to place 10 to 20 of them per configuration; thus, exhaustive enumeration of all of the possible groupings is not an option. Instead, we use a heuristic method that furnishes a good, although perhaps suboptimal, solution.

Correlation between two templates can establish the number of pixels in common, and it is a good starting point for comparing and selecting templates. However, some extra analysis, beyond iterative correlations on the template set, is necessary. For example, a template with many pixels correlates well with several smaller templates, perhaps even completely subsuming them, but the smaller templates may not correlate with each other and involve no redundant computations. There are two possible solutions to this. The first is to ensure that any template added to an existing group is approximately the same size as the templates already in it. The second is to compute the number of additions required each time a new template is brought in—effectively recomputing the adder tree each time.

Recomputing the entire adder tree is computationally expensive and not a good method of partitioning a set of templates into subsets. However, one of the heuristics used in deciding whether or not to include a template in a newly formed partition is to determine the number of new terms that its inclusion would create in the partition's adder tree. The assumption is that more terms would result in a significant number of new additions, resulting in a wider and deeper adder tree. Thus, by keeping to a minimum the number of new terms created, newly added templates do not increase the number of additions by a significant amount.

Using C++, we have created a design tool to implement the partitioning process that uses an iterative approach to partitioning templates. Templates that compare well to a chosen "base" template (usually selected by largest area) are removed from the main template set and placed in a separate partition. This process is repeated until all templates are partitioned. After the partitions have been selected, the tool computes the adder tree for each partition.

Figure 28.6 shows the creation of an adder tree from the templates in a partition. Within each partition, the templates are searched for shared subsets of pixels. Called *terms*, these subsets can be automatically added together, leading to a template description that uses terms instead of pixels.

The most common addition of two terms is chosen to be grouped together, to form a new term that can be used by the templates. In this way, each template is rebuilt by combining terms in such a way that the most redundant additions are shared between templates; the final result is terms that compute entire templates. For the sample templates shown in Figure 28.6, 39 additions would be required to compute the correlations for all 5 in a naive approach. However,

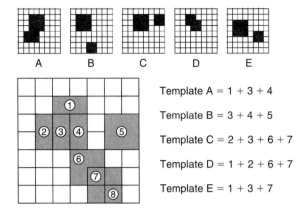

Template A = 1 + 3 + 4

Template B = 3 + 4 + 5

Template C = 2 + 3 + 6 + 7

Template D = 1 + 2 + 6 + 7

Template E = 1 + 3 + 7

FIGURE 28.6 ■ Example of template grouping and rewritten as sums of terms.

after combining the templates through the process just described, only 17 additions are required.

28.2.5 Implementation Method

For a configurable computing system, the problem of dividing hardware and software is particularly interesting because it is both a hardware and a software issue. Consider the two methods for performing addition shown in Figure 28.7. Method A, a straightforward parallel implementation requiring several FPGAs, has several drawbacks. First, the outputs from several FPGAs converge at the addition operation, which may create a severe I/O bottleneck. Second, the system is not scalable—if it requires more precision, and therefore more bit planes, more FPGAs must be added.

Method B in Figure 28.7 illustrates our approach. Each bit plane is correlated individually and then added to the previous results in temporary storage. It is completely scalable to any image or template precision, and it can implement all correlation, normalization, and peak detection routines required for ATR. One drawback of method B is the cost and power required for the resulting wide temporary SRAM. Another possible drawback is the extra execution time required to run ATR correlations in serial. The ratio of performance to number of FPGAs is roughly equivalent for the two methods, and the performance gap can be closed simply by using more of the smaller method B boards.

The approach of a reconfigurable FPGA connected to an intermediate memory allows us a fairly complicated flow of control. For example, the sum calculation in ATR tends to be more difficult than the image–template correlation. Thus, we may want a program that performs two sum operations and forwards the results to a single correlation.

Reconfigurations for 10K-gate FPGAs are typically around 20 kB in length. Reconfiguring every 20 milliseconds gives a reconfiguration bandwidth of approximately 1 MB per FPGA per second. Coupled with the complexity of the

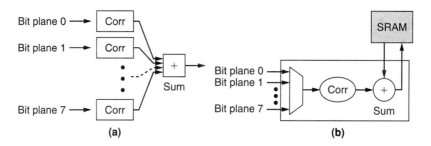

FIGURE 28.7 ■ Each of eight FPGAs correlating each bit plane of the template (a). A single FPGA correlating bit planes and adding the partial sums serially (b).

flow control, this reconfiguration bandwidth can be handled by placing a small microcontroller and configuration RAM next to every FPGA. The microcontroller permits complicated flow of control, and since it addresses the configuration RAM, it frees up valuable I/O on the FPGA. The microcontroller is also important for debugging, which is a major issue in configurable systems because the many different hardware configurations can make it difficult to isolate problems.

The principal components include a "dynamic" FPGA, which is reconfigured on the fly and performs most of the computing functions, and a "static" FPGA, which is configured only once and performs control and some computational functions. The EPROM holds configuration bitstreams, and the SRAM holds the input image data (e.g., the chip). Because the correlation operation involves the application of a small target template to a large chip, a first in, first out (FIFO) is needed to hold the pixels being wrapped around to the next row of the template mask. The templates used in this implementation are of size 8×8, whereas the correlation image is 128×128. Each configuration of the dynamic FPGA implements a total of four template pairs (four bright templates and four surround templates).

The large amount of sum in the algorithm can be performed in parallel. This requires a total of D clock cycles, where D is each pixel's depth of representation. Once the sum results are obtained, the correlation outputs are produced at the rate of 1 per clock cycle. Parallelism cannot be as directly exploited in this step because different pixels are asserted for different templates. However, in the limit of very large FPGAs the number of clock cycles to compute the correlation is upper-bounded by the number of possible thresholds, as opposed to the number of templates.

28.3   RECONFIGURABLE STATIC DESIGN

Although the idea of reusing reconfigurable hardware to dynamically perform different functions is unique to FPGAs, the main weaknesses of dynamic FPGA reconfiguration are the lengthy time and additional resources required for FPGA reconfiguration and design compilation. Although reconfiguration time has improved dramatically over the years, any time spent on reconfiguration is time that could be used to process more data.

Unlike the dynamic reconfigurable architecture describe in the previous section, we describe another efficient FPGA design that does not require complete design reconfiguration. However, like the previous system, it uses a number of parameters to design a highly pipelined custom design to maximize utilization of the design space to exploit the parallelism in the algorithm.

28.3.1 Design-specific Parameters

To verify our understanding of the algorithm, we first implemented a software simulator and ran it on a sample dataset. Our simulations reproduced the expected results. Over time this algorithm simulator became a full hardware simulator and verifier. It also allowed us to investigate various design options before implementing them in hardware.

The dataset includes 2 targets, each with 72 templates for 5-degree orientation intervals. In total, then, we have 144 bright masks and 144 surround masks, each a 32×32 bitmap. The dataset also includes 16 image chips, each with 64×64 pixels at 1 byte per pixel. Given a template and an image, there are 441 matrix correlations that must take place for each mask. This corresponds to 21 search rows, each 21 positions wide. The total number of search row correlations for the sample data and templates is thus 48,384. The behavior of the simulator on the sample dataset revealed a number of algorithm-specific characteristics. Because the design architecture was developed for reconfigurable devices, these characteristics are incorporated to tune the hardware engine for the best cost and performance.

28.3.2 Order of Correlation Tasks

Correlation tasks for threshold calculation (equation 28.2), bright sum (equation 28.3), and surround sum (equation 28.4) are very closely related. Valid results for all three must exist in order to calculate the quality of the hit, so invalid results from any one of them make other calculations unnecessary.

For the data samples, about 60 percent of the surround sums and 40 percent of the threshold results were invalid, while all of the bright sum results were valid. The low rejection rate by bright sum is the result of the threshold being computed using only the bright mask, regardless of the surround mask. The threshold is computed by the same pixels used for computing bright sum, so we find that, for a typical dataset, checking for invalid surround sums before the other calculations drastically reduces the total number of calculations needed.

Zero mask rows

Each mask has 32 rows. However, many have all-zero rows that can be skipped. By storing with each template a pointer to its first nonzero row we can skip directly to that row "for free." Embedded all-zero rows are also skipped.

The simulation tools showed that, for our template set, this optimization significantly reduces the total computational requirements. For the sample template set, there are total of 4608 bitmap rows to use in the correlation tasks. Out of 4608 bright rows, only 2206 are nonzero, and out of 4608 surround rows, 2815 are nonzero. Since the bright mask is used for both threshold and bright sum calculations, and the surround mask is used once, skipping the zero rows reduces the number of row operations from 13,824 to 7227, which produces a savings of about 52 percent.

It is also possible to reduce the computation by skipping zero columns. However, as will be described in following section, the FPGA implementation works on an entire search row concurrently. Hence, skipping rows reduces time but skipping columns reduces the number of active elements that work in parallel, yielding no savings.

28.3.3   Reconfigurable Image Correlator

Although it is possible to reconfigure FPGAs dynamically, the time spent on context switching and reconfiguration could be used instead to process data on a register-based static design. For this reason, minimizing reconfiguration time during computation is essential in effective FPGA use. Nevertheless, when we use FPGAs as compute engines, reconfiguration allows the hardware to take on a large range of task parameters.

The SLD tasks represented in equations 28.1, 28.3, and 28.4 are image correlation calculations on sliding template masks with radar images. To explain our design strategies, we examine each equation by applying the algorithm on a small dataset consisting of a 6×6 pixel image, a 3×3 mask bitmap, and a 4×4 result matrix.

For this dataset, the shape sum calculation for a mask requires multiplying all 9 mask bits with the corresponding image pixels and summing them to find 1 of 16 results. To build an efficient circuit for the sum equations 28.3 and 28.4, we write out the subset of both equations as shown in Table 28.1. By expanding the summation equations, we expose opportunities for hardware to optimize the calculations. First, the same B_{uv} is used to calculate the nth term of all of the shape sum results. Thus, when the summation calculations are done in parallel, the B_{uv} coefficient can be broadcast to all of the units that calculate each result. Second, the image data in the nth term of the SM_{xy} is in the $(n+1)$th term of SM_{xy-1}, except when v returns to 0, the image pixel is located in the subsequent row. This is useful in implementing the pipeline datapath for the image pixels through the parallel summation units.

TABLE 28.1 ■ Expanded sum equations 28.3 and 28.4

Term	1	2	3	4	5	6	7	8	9
u	0	0	0	1	1	1	2	2	2
v	0	1	2	0	1	2	0	1	2
$SM_{00} =$	$B_{00}M_{00}+$	$B_{01}M_{01}+$	$B_{02}M_{02}+$	$B_{10}M_{10}+$	$B_{11}M_{11}+$	$B_{12}M_{12}+$	$B_{20}M_{20}+$	$B_{21}M_{21}+$	$B_{22}M_{22}$
$SM_{01} =$	$B_{00}M_{01}+$	$B_{01}M_{02}+$	$B_{02}M_{03}+$	$B_{10}M_{11}+$	$B_{11}M_{12}+$	$B_{12}M_{13}+$	$B_{20}M_{21}+$	$B_{21}M_{22}+$	$B_{22}M_{23}$
$SM_{02} =$	$B_{00}M_{02}+$	$B_{01}M_{03}+$	$B_{02}M_{04}+$	$B_{10}M_{12}+$	$B_{11}M_{13}+$	$B_{12}M_{14}+$	$B_{20}M_{22}+$	$B_{21}M_{23}+$	$B_{22}M_{24}$
$SM_{03} =$	$B_{00}M_{03}+$	$B_{01}M_{04}+$	$B_{02}M_{05}+$	$B_{10}M_{13}+$	$B_{11}M_{14}+$	$B_{12}M_{15}+$	$B_{20}M_{23}+$	$B_{21}M_{24}+$	$B_{22}M_{25}$

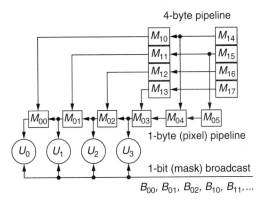

FIGURE 28.8 ■ A systolic image array pipeline.

Based on the characteristics of the expanded equations, we can build a systolic computation unit as in Figure 28.8. To save time while changing the rows of pixels, the pixel pipeline can either operate as a pipeline or be directly loaded from another set of registers. At every clock cycle, each U_y unit performs one operation, v is incremented modulo 3, and the pixel pipeline shifts by one stage (U_1 to U_0, U_2 to U_1, ...). When v returns to 0, u is incremented modulo 3, and the pixel pipeline is loaded with the entire $(u+x)$th row of the image. When u returns to 0, the results are offloaded from the U_y stage, their accumulators are cleared, and x is incremented modulo 4. When x returns to 0, this computing task is completed.

The initial loading of the image pixel pipeline is from the image word pipeline, which is word wide and so four times faster than the image pixel pipeline. This speed advantage guarantees that the pipeline will be ready with the next image row data when u returns to 0.

28.3.4 Application-specific Computation Unit

Developing different FPGA mappings for equations 28.1, 28.3, and 28.4 in parallel processing unit is one way to implement the design. At the end of each stage, the FPGA device is reconfigured with the optimal structure for the next task. As appealing as this may sound, current FPGA devices have typical reconfiguration times of tens of milliseconds, during which the reconfiguring logic cannot be used for computation.

As presented in Section 28.3, each set of template configurations also has to be designed and compiled before any computation can take place. This can be a time-consuming procedure that does not allow dynamic template sets to be immediately used in the system.

Fortunately, we can rely on the fact that FPGAs can be tuned to target-specific applications. From the equations, we derived one compact structure, shown in Figure 28.9, that can efficiently perform all ATR tasks. Since the target ATR

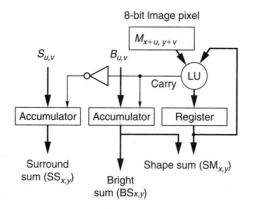

FIGURE 28.9 ■ Computation logic for equations 28.1, 28.3, and 28.4.

system can be seen as "embarrassingly parallel," the performance of the FPGA design is linearly scalable to the number of the application-specific units.

28.4 ATR IMPLEMENTATIONS

In this section we present the implementation results of two reconfigurable Sandia ATR systems, researched and developed on different reconfigurable platforms. Both designs leverage the unique characteristics of reconfigurable devices to accelerate ATR algorithms while making efficient use of available resources. Therefore, they both outperformed existing software as well as custom ASIC solutions. By analyzing the results of the reconfigurable solutions, we examine design trade-offs in cost and performance.

28.4.1 A Dynamically Reconfigurable System

All of the component technologies described in this chapter have been designed, implemented, tested, and debugged using the Mojave board shown in Figure 28.10. This section discusses various performance aspects of the complete system, from abstract template sets through application-specific CAD tools and finally down to the embedded processor and dynamic FPGA. The current hardware is connected to a video camera rather than a SAR data source, though this is only necessary for testing and early evaluation.

The results presented here are based on routing circuits to two devices: the Xilinx 4013PG223-4 FPGA and the Xilinx 4036. Xilinx rates the capacity of these parts as 13K and 36K equivalent gates.

Table 28.2 presents data on the effectiveness of the template-partitioning phase. Twelve templates were considered for this comparison: in one case they were randomly divided into three partitions; in the other, the CAD tool was used to guide the process. The randomly selected partitions required 33 percent more CLBs than those produced by the intelligent partitioning tool. These numbers

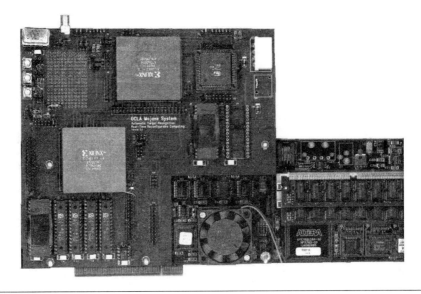

FIGURE 28.10 ■ Photograph of second-generation Mojave ATR system.

Table 28.2 ■ Comparison of scored and random partitioning on an Xilinx 4036

Random grouping CLB count	Initial partitioning CLB count
1961	1491
1959	1449
1958	1487

Table 28.3 ■ Comparison of resources used for the dynamic and static FPGAs

	Flip-flops	Function generators	I/O pins
Dynamic FPGA	532	939	54
Support FPGA	196	217	96
Available	1536	1536	192

account for the hardware requirements of the entire design, including the control hardware that is common to all designs as well as the template-specific adder trees. Relative savings in the adder trees alone are higher.

Table 28.3 lists the overall resources used for both FPGAs in the system, the dynamic devices used for correlation, and the static support device used to implement system control features. Because the image source is a standard video camera rather than a SAR sensor, the surround template is the complement of the bright template, resulting in more hardware than would be required for true SAR templates. The majority of the flip-flops in the dynamic FPGA are assigned to holding the 8-bit chip data in a set of shift registers. This load increases as a linear function of the template size.

Each configuration of the dynamic FPGA requires 16 milliseconds to complete an evaluation of the entire chip for four template pairs. The Xilinx 4013PG223-4 requires 30 milliseconds for reconfiguration. Thus, a total of 4 template pairs can be evaluated in 46 milliseconds, or 84 template pairs per second. This timing will increase logarithmically with the template size.

Comparing configurable machines with traditional ASIC solutions is necessary but complicated. Clearly, for almost any application, a bank of ASICs could be designed that used the same techniques as the multiple configurations of the FPGA and would likely achieve higher performance and consume less power. The principal advantage of configurable computing is that a single FPGA may act as many ASICs without the cost of manufacturing each device. If the comparison is restricted to a single IC (e.g., a single FPGA against a single ASIC of similar size), relative performance becomes a function of the hardware savings enabled by data specificity. For example, in the ATR application the templates used are quite sparse—only 5 to 10 percent of the pixels are important in the computation—which translates directly into a hardware savings that is much more difficult to realize in an ASIC. Further savings in the ATR application are possible by leveraging topological similarities across templates. Again, this is an advantage that ASICs cannot easily exploit.

If the power and speed advantages of ASICs over FPGAs are estimated at a factor of 10, the configurable computing approach achieves a factor of improvement anywhere from 2 and 10 (depending on sparseness and topological properties) for the ATR application.

28.4.2   A Statically Reconfigurable System

The FPGA nodes developed by Myricom integrate reconfigurable computing with a 2-level multicomputer to promote flexibility of programmable computational components in a highly scalable network architecture. The Myricom FPGA nodes and its motherboard are shown in Figure 28.11. The daughter nodes are 2-level multicomputers whose first level provides the general-purpose infrastructure of the Myrinet network using the LANai RISC microprocessor. The FPGA functions as a second-level processor responsible for application-specific tasks.

The host is a SparcStation IPX running SunOS 4.1.3 with a Myrinet interface board having a 512K memory. The FPGA node—consisting of Lucent Technologies' ORCA FPGA 40K and Myricom's LANai 4.1 running in 3.3 V at 40 MHz—communicates with the host through an 8-port Myrinet switch.

Without additional optimization, static implementation of the complete ATR algorithm on one FPGA node processes more than 900 templates per second. Each template requires about 450,000 iterations of 1-bit conditional accumulate for the complete shape sum calculation. The threshold calculation requires one division followed by subtraction. The bright and surround sum compares all the image pixels against the threshold results. Next, 1-bit conditional accumulate is

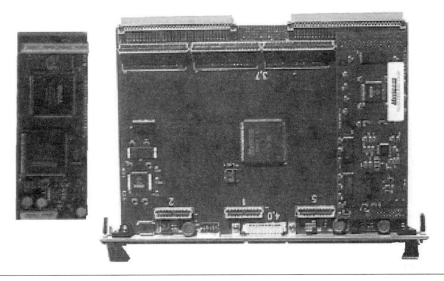

FIGURE 28.11 ■ A Myrinet 8-port switch motherboard with Myricom ORCA FPGA daughter nodes. Four FPGA nodes can be plugged into a single motherboard.

executed for each sum. And then the quality values are calculated using two divides, an add, and a multiply.

Given that 1-bit conditional accumulate, subtract, divide, multiply, and 8-bit compare are one operation each, the total number of 8-bit operations to process one 32×32 template over a 64×64 image is approximately 3.1 million. Each FPGA node executes over 2.8 billion 8-bit operations per second (GOPS).

After the simulations, we found that the sparseness of the actual templates reduced their average valid rows to approximately one-half the number of total template rows. This optimization was implemented to increase the throughput by 40 percent. Further simulations revealed more room for improvements, such as dividing the shape sum in the FPGA, transposing narrow template masks, and skipping invalid threshold lines. Although these optimizations were not implemented in the FPGA, the simulation results indicated an additional 94 percent increase in throughput. Implementing all optimizations would yield a result equivalent to about a 7.75 GOPS correlator.

28.4.3 Reconfigurable Computing Models

The increased performance of configurable systems comes with several costs. These include the time and bandwidth required for reconfiguration, the memory and I/O required for intermediate results, and the additional hardware required for efficient implementation and debugging. Minimizing these costs requires innovative approaches to system design.

Figure 28.12 illustrates the fundamental difference between a traditional computing model and the two reconfigurable computing architectures discussed in this chapter. The traditional processor receives simple operands from data

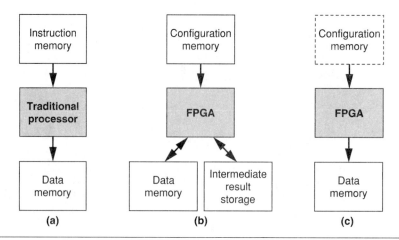

FIGURE 28.12 ■ A comparison of a traditional computing model (a) with a dynamically reconfigurable model (b) and a statically reconfigurable custom model (c).

memory, performs a simple operation in the program, and returns the result to data memory. Similarly, dynamic computing uses a small number of rapidly reconfiguring FPGAs tightly coupled to an intermediate result memory, data memory, and configuration memory. A reconfigurable custom computer is similar to a fixed ASIC device in that, usually, only one highly tuned design is configured on the FPGA—there is no need to reconfigure to perform a needed function.

In most cases, a custom ASIC performs far better than a traditional processor. However, traditional processors continue to be used for their programmability. FPGAs attempts to bridge the gap between custom ASICs and software by allowing designers to build custom hardware using programmable firmware. Therefore, unlike in pure ASIC designs, configuration memory is used to program the reconfigurable hardware as instructions in a traditional processor would dictate the functionality of a program. Unlike software, once the FPGA is configured, it can function just like a custom device.

As shown in previous sections, an ATR was implemented in an FPGA using two different methods. The first implementation uses the dynamic computer model, where parts of the entire algorithm are dynamically configured to produce the final results. The second design uses simulation results to produce a highly tuned fixed design in the FPGA that does not require more than a single reconfiguration. Because of algorithm modifications made to the first design, there is no clear way to compare the two designs. However, looking deeper, we find that there is not a drastic difference in the subcomponents or the algorithm; in fact, the number of required operations for the algorithm in either design should be the same.

The adders make up the critical path of both designs. Because both designs are reconfigurable, we expect the adders used to have approximately the same performance as long as pipelining is done properly. Clever use of adders in the static design allows it to execute more than one calculation simultaneously. However, it is possible to make similar use of the hardware to increase performance in the dynamic design.

The first design optimizes the use of adders to skip all unnecessary calculations, also making each configuration completely custom. The second design has to be more general to allow some programmability. Therefore, depending on the template data, not all of the adders may be in use at all times. If all of the templates for the first design can be mapped onto a single FPGA, the first method results in more resource efficiency than the second. The detrimental effect of idle adders in the static design becomes increasingly more prominent as template bitmap rows grow more sparse.

On the other hand, if the templates do not all fit in a single FPGA, the first method adds a relatively large overhead because of reconfiguration latency. Unfortunately, the customized method of the second design works against making the design smaller. Every bit in the template maps to a port of the adder engine, so the total size of the design is proportional to the number of total bits in all of the templates. Therefore, as the number of templates increases, the total design size must also increase. Ultimately, the design must be divided into several smaller configurations that are dynamically reconfigured to share a single device.

From these results, we observe the strengths and weaknesses of dynamic reconfiguration in such applications. Dynamic reconfiguration allows a large custom design to successfully run in a smaller FPGA device. The trade-off is significant time overhead in the system.

28.5 SUMMARY

Like many streaming image correlation algorithms, the Sandia ATR system discussed in this chapter can be efficiently implemented on an FPGA. Because of the high degree of parallelism in the algorithm, designers can take full advantage of parallel processing in hardware while linearly scaling total throughput with available hardware resources. In this chapter we presented two different ways of implementing such a system.

The first system employs a dynamic computing model to effectively implement a large custom design using a smaller reconfigurable device. To fit, high-performance custom designs can be divided into subcomponents, which can then share a single FPGA to execute parts of the algorithm at a high speed. For the ATR algorithm, this process produced a resource-efficient design that exceeded the performance of previous custom ASIC-based systems.

The second system is based on a more generic architecture highly tuned for a given set of templates. Through extensive simulations, many parameters of the algorithm are tuned to efficiently process the incoming data. With algorithm-specific optimizations, the throughput of the system increased threefold from an initial naive implementation. Because of the highly pipelined structure of the design, the maximum clock frequency is more than three times that of the dynamic computer design. Furthermore, a larger FPGA on the platform allowed the generic processing architecture to duplicate the specifications of the original algorithm. Therefore, the raw performance of the static design was faster than the dynamically reconfigurable system.

Although the second system is a static design, it is best suited for reconfigurable platforms because of its highly tuned parameters. Since this system is reconfigurable, it is conceivable that the dynamic computational model can be applied on top of it. Thus, the highly tuned design may be implemented efficiently, even on a device with enough resources for only a fraction of the entire design.

Acknowledgments   I would like to acknowledge Professor William H. Mangione-Smith for permission to integrate publications on the Mojave project into this chapter.

References

[1] P. M. Athanas, H. F. Silverman. Processor reconfiguration through instruction-set metamorphosis. *IEEE Computer* 26, 1993.

[2] J. G. Eldredge, B. L. Hutchings. Run-time reconfiguration: A method for enhancing the functional density of SRAM-based FPGAs. *Journal of VLSI Signal Processing* 12, 1996.

[3] J. Villasenor, W. H. Mangione-Smith. Configurable computing. *Scientific American* 276, 1997.

[4] E. Mirsky, A. DeHon. MATRIX: A reconfigurable computing architecture with configurable instruction distribution and deployable resources. *Proceedings of the IEEE International Symposium on Field-Programmable Custom Computing Machines*, 1996.

[5] R. Razdan, M. D. Smith. A high-performance microarchitecture with hardware-programmable functional units. *Proceedings of the 27th Annual International Symposium on Microarchitecture*, pp. 172–180, 1994.

[6] G. Estrin. Organization of computer systems—the fixed plus variable structure computer. *Proceedings of the Western Joint Computer Conference*, 1960.

[7] M. Shand, J. Vuillemin. Fast implementations of RSA cryptography. *Proceedings of the Symposium on Computer Arithmetic*, 1993.

[8] K. W. Tse, T. I. Yuk, S. S. Chan. Implementation of the data encryption standard algorithm with FPGAs. *Proceedings of International Symposium on Field-Programmable Logic and Applications*, 1993.

[9] J. Leonard, W. H. Mangione-Smith. A case study of partially evaluated hardware circuits: Key-specific DES. *Proceedings of the 7th International Workshop on Field-Programmable Logic and Applications* 1304:151–160, 1997.

[10] P. M. Athanas, A. L. Abbott. Real-time image processing on a custom computing platform. *IEEE Computer* 28, 1995.

[11] J. G. Eldredge, B. L. Hutchings. Density enhancement of a neural network using FPGAs and run-time reconfiguration. *Proceedings of the IEEE International Symposium on Field-Programmable Custom Computing Machines*, 1994.

[12] J. G. Eldredge, B. L. Hutchings. RRANN: The run-time reconfiguration artificial neural network. *Proceedings of the Custom Integrated Circuits Conference*, 1994.

[13] B. Schoner, C. Jones, J. Villasenor. Issues in wireless coding using run-time-reconfigurable FPGAs. *Proceedings of the IEEE International Symposium on Field-Programmable Custom Computing Machines*, 1995.

[14] C. Chou, S. Mohanakrishnan, J. B. Evans. FPGA implementation of digital filters. *Proceedings of the Fourth International Conference on Signal Processing Applications and Technology*, pp. 80–88, 1993.

[15] G. Estrin, B. Bussell, R. Turn, J. Bibb. Parallel processing in a restructurable computer system. *IEEE Transactions on Electronic Computers* EC-12(5):747–755, December 1963.

[16] G. Estrin, R. Turn. Automatic assignment of computations in a variable structure computer system. *IEEE Transactions on Electronic Computers* EC-12(6):755–773, December 1963.

[17] M. J. Wirthlin, B. L. Hutchings. Improving functional density through run-time constant propagation. *Proceedings of the 1997 ACM Fifth International Symposium on Field-Programmable Gate Arrays*, 1997.

[18] P. Lee, M. Leone. Optimizing ML with run-time code generation. *Proceedings of Programming Language Design and Implementation*, 1996.

[19] D. R. Engler, T. A. Proebsting. DCG: An efficient, retargetable dynamic code generation system. *Proceedings of the Sixth International Symposium on Architectural Support for Programming Languages and Operating Systems*, 1994.

[20] H. Massalin. *Synthesis: An Efficient Implementation of Fundamental Operating System Services*, Ph.D. thesis, Columbia University, Department of Computer Science, 1992.

[21] W. H. Mangione-Smith, B. Hutchings. Configurable computing: The road ahead. *Proceedings of the Reconfigurable Architectures Workshop*, 1997.

[22] P. Bertin, H. Touati. PAM programming environments: Practice and experience. *Proceedings of the International Symposium on Field-Programmable Custom Computing Machines*, April 1994.

[23] Y. H. Cho. Optimized automatic target recognition algorithm on scalable Myrinet/field programmable array nodes. *Thirty-fourth IEEE Asilomar Conference on Signals, Systems, and Computers*, October 2000.

[24] K. N. Chia, H. J. Kim, S. Lansing, W. H. Mangione-Smith, J. Villasenor. High-performance automatic target recognition through data-specific very large scale integration. *IEEE Transactions on Very Large Scale Integration Systems* 6(3), 1998.

[25] J. Villasenor, B. Schoner, K. N. Chia, C. Zapata, H. J. Kim, C. Jones, S. Lansing, W. H. Mangione-Smith. Configurable computing solutions for automatic target recognition. *Proceedings of the IEEE International Symposium on FPGAs for Custom Computing Machines*, April 1996.

[26] R. Sivilotti, Y. Cho, D. Cohen, W. Su, B. Bray. Scalable network based FPGA accelerators for an automatic target recognition application. *Proceedings of the International Symposium on Field-Programmable Custom Computing Machines*, April 1998.

[27] R. Sivilotti, Y. Cho, W. Su, D. Cohen. *Scalable, Network-connected, Reconfigurable, Hardware Accelerators for an Automatic-Target-Recognition Application*, Myricom technical report, May 1998.

[28] R. Sivilotti, Y. Cho, W. Su, D. Cohen. *Myricom's FPGA-based Approach to ATR/SLD*, DARPA ACS PI meeting slide presentation, November 1997.

[29] R. Sivilotti, Y. Cho, W. Su, D. Cohen. Production-quality, LANai-4-based quad-FPGA-node VME boards. *http://www.myri.com/research/darpa/97a-fpga.html*, October 1997.

[30] C. L. Seitz, Tactical network and multicomputer technology. *http://www.myri.com/ research/darpa/index.html*, March 1997, July 1997, August 1998.

[31] C. L. Seitz. Two-level-multicomputer project: Summary. *http://www.myri.com/ research/darpa/96summary.html*, July 1996.

[32] W. C. Athas, L. Seitz. Multicomputers: Message-passing concurrent computers. *IEEE Computer* 21, 1988.

[33] M. Shand, J. Vullemin. Fast implementations of RSA cryptography. *Proceedings of 11th Symposium on Computer Arithmetic*, 1993.

[34] J. G. Eldredge, B. L. Hutchings. RRANN: The run-time reconfiguration artificial neural network. *Proceedings of the IEEE Custom Integrated Circuits Conference*, 1994.

[35] Xilinx, Inc. *RAM-based Shift Register v9.0, LogiCORE Datasheet*, Xilinx, Inc., July 13, 2006.

CHAPTER 29

BOOLEAN SATISFIABILITY: CREATING SOLVERS OPTIMIZED FOR SPECIFIC PROBLEM INSTANCES

Peixin Zhong
Department of Electrical and Computer Engineering
Michigan State University
Margaret Martonosi, Sharad Malik
Department of Electrical Engineering
Princeton University

Boolean satisfiability (SAT) is a classic NP-complete problem with a broad range of applications. There have been many projects that use reconfigurable computing to solve it. This chapter presents a review of the subject with emphasis on a particular approach that employs a backtrack search algorithm and generates solver hardware according to the problem instance. This approach utilizes the reconfigurability and fine-grained parallelism provided by FPGAs.

The chapter is organized as follows: Section 29.1 is an introduction to the SAT formulation and applications. Section 29.2 describes the algorithms to solve the SAT problem. Sections 29.3 and 29.4 describe in detail two SAT solvers that use reconfigurable computing, and Section 29.5 provides a broader discussion.

29.1 BOOLEAN SATISFIABILITY BASICS

The Boolean satisfiability problem is well known in computer science [1]. Given a Boolean formula, the goal is to find an assignment to the variables so that the formula evaluates to true or 1 (it satisfies the formula), or to prove that such an assignment does not exist (the formula is not satisfiable). It has many applications, including theorem proving [5], automatic test pattern generation [2], and formal verification [3,4].

29.1.1 Problem Formulation

The Boolean formula in an SAT problem is typically represented in conjunctive normal form (CNF), also known as product-of-sums. Each sum of literals is called a clause. A literal is either a variable or the negation of a variable, denoted with a negation symbol or a bar (such as $\neg v_1$ or $\bar{v}_1$). Equations 29.1 and 29.2 are examples of simple CNFs.

$$(v_1 + v_2 + v_3)(\bar{v}_1 + v_2 + v_3)(v_1 + v_2 + \bar{v}_3)(\bar{v}_2 + \bar{v}_3) \tag{29.1}$$

or

$$(v_1 \lor v_2 \lor v_3) \land (\neg v_1 \lor v_2 \lor v_3) \land (v_1 \lor v_2 \lor \neg v_3) \land (\neg v_2 \lor \neg v_3) \qquad (29.2)$$

Each sum term, such as $(v_1 + v_2 + v_3)$, is a clause. In the clause, v_1 or $\neg v_1$ is called a literal. It can be easily tested that $v_1 = 1, v_2 = 1, v_3 = 0$ is a solution to the problem.

The SAT clauses represent implication relationships between variables. To satisfy the CNF, each clause should be satisfied (i.e., at least one literal in each clause should be 1). For a given partial assignment, if only one literal in a clause is not assigned but all others are assigned to 0, the unassigned literal is implied to be 1 to satisfy the clause. The first clause in equation 29.1 contains three possible implications. If $v_1 = 0$ and $v_2 = 0, v_3$ is implied to be 1, denoted as $\neg v_1 \neg v_2 \supset v_3$. Similarly, $v_1 = 0$ and $v_3 = 0$ imply $v_2 = 1$, and $v_2 = 0$ and $v_3 = 0$ imply $v_1 = 1$. Such implications can be used to construct powerful logic expressions. They are also the key to SAT-solving algorithms.

29.1.2   SAT Applications

The many applications of SAT include test pattern generation [2] and model checking [3, 4]. The logic relations of a digital circuit can also be represented in SAT CNF. Each logic gate is represented by a group of clauses, with each signal represented by a variable with two possible values, 1 or 0. A circuit is represented by a conjunction of clauses representing all gates in the circuit. What follows is the transformation from simple gates to clauses:

AND gate, $z <= ab$, maps to $(a + \neg z)(b + \neg z)(\neg a + \neg b + z)$
NAND gate, $z <= \neg(ab)$, maps to $(a + z)(b + z)(\neg a + \neg b + \neg z)$
OR gate, $z <= a + b$, maps to $(\neg a + z)(\neg b + z)(a + b + \neg z)$
NOR gate, $z <= \neg(a + b)$, maps to $(\neg a + \neg z)(\neg b + \neg z)(a + b + z)$
XOR gate, $z <= a \oplus b$, maps to $(\neg a + \neg b + \neg z)(\neg a + b + z)(a + \neg b + z)(a + b + \neg z)$
Buffer gate, $z <= a$, maps to $(\neg a + z)(a + \neg z)$
Inverter gate, $z <= \neg a$, maps to $(a + z)(\neg a + \neg z)$

SAT can be used in test pattern generation or to verify the equivalence of two combinational circuits. The circuit construction is shown in Figure 29.1. In equivalence checking, the two representations of the circuit are fed with the same primary inputs signals, and the corresponding primary outputs feed into an exclusive-or (XOR) gate. If an assignment of primary inputs can be found such that any of the XOR gates has 1 as an output, the circuits are different. If no such assignment can be found, the circuits are functionally identical.

For test pattern generation, instead of using two representations of one circuit, we use two copies of the same circuit. However, one copy has a fault introduced into the design, which we can detect by searching for some pattern of inputs. In this case any input pattern that can generate a 1 on an XOR output is a test for that fault. If no such assignment is possible, that fault is untestable.

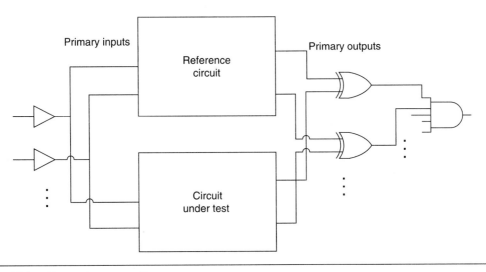

FIGURE 29.1 ■ Test pattern generation.

29.2 SAT-SOLVING ALGORITHMS

29.2.1 Basic Backtrack Algorithm

There are many algorithms to solve the SAT problem. They can be divided into two categories: complete and incomplete. A complete algorithm guarantees either to find a solution on termination or to prove that there is no solution. Complete algorithms typically employ a methodical search of the variable assignment space. For hard problems, the runtime may well exceed acceptable levels. An incomplete algorithm does not guarantee to find the solution and typically involves greedy or randomized search [22]. It can often find a solution of an easy problem very quickly, but if it fails to do so within a given time, it does not prove that no solution exists. Many applications require a complete algorithm to provide a definite answer, so this chapter concentrates on such algorithms for SAT.

An early SAT algorithm was proposed by Davis and Putnam [5]. Like theirs, most complete SAT algorithms are based on backtrack search [6–9], which is similar to depth-first search in traversing a tree. The pseudo-code of the basic algorithm, shown in Figure 29.2, starts with an empty variable partial assignment (i.e., every variable value is assumed to be unknown, or free). The search level is increased by branching—that is, assigning a value for a free variable. The algorithm checks if the incremented partial assignment can be part of a solution. If not, we say a conflict is detected. If there is no conflict, the algorithm will choose another free variable and branch on it; if a conflict is detected, it will backtrack to the most recently assigned variable and choose the opposite value. All decisions made after that backtrack point will be undone.

```
Solve_SAT()
{
  assign all variables to unknown;
  while (true) {
    if (implications force an unknown variable to a specific value)
      set that variable to that specific value;
    if (the current assignment has a conflict) {
      undo all implications and branches up to most recent untoggled branch;
      if (all branches undone)
        return No_solution;
      toggle value assigned to the variable of last untoggled branch;
    }
    if (no unassigned variables remain)
      return Solved;
    } else {
      start new branch by assigning a value to the next free variable;
    }
  }
}
```

FIGURE 29.2 ▪ The basic backtrack algorithm to solve SAT.

The algorithm has two possible terminating conditions. If all variables values are known and the formula is satisfied, a solution is found. If all branches fail to find a solution and the algorithm must backtrack beyond the first branch variable, there is no solution and the formula is unsatisfiable.

The key to the efficiency of the backtrack algorithm is effectively pruning the search space. Early detection of a conflict assignment avoids useless searches along this branch. The following are some basic rules and techniques used in the algorithm. At each stage of the search, a variable can have one of three possible values: 1, 0, and free (unassigned).

1. If at least one literal of a clause evaluates to 1, this clause is satisfied. There is no need to check other literals in the clause.
2. If all literals of a clause evaluate to 0, the partial assignment is a conflict and cannot be part of the solution.
3. If only one literal of a clause is free and all other literals evaluate to 0, the free literal is implied to be 1. This is called unit resolution or implication. Implication is a powerful mechanism because it can deduce implied values of variables not yet branched on. However, it can create another case of conflict if a variable is implied by two clauses to be of opposite values.
4. If all of the literals of a free variable in the as yet unsatisfied clauses are all of the same polarity (i.e., inverted or not inverted), a value can be chosen for this variable that safely satisfies these clauses.
5. Because the variable ordering of branches has a large impact on the efficiency of the algorithm, different dynamic or static ordering schemes have been investigated. A simple heuristic orders the variables based on the number of clauses they appear in. A variable with the most appearances

often has more influence than others. Therefore, branching on it early typically prunes the search space more quickly.

A basic algorithm can use a static variable ordering. It can also use a fixed branching scheme, such as always branching with value 1, in which, after each branch or backtrack, implication is checked exhaustively. This basic algorithm corresponds to the reconfigurable SAT solver described in Section 29.2.

29.2.2 Improving the Backtrack Algorithm

Among the advanced features explored to further improve the efficiency of the backtrack search algorithm [6, 7], an effective one is learning based on conflict analysis. With the search algorithm moving back and forth by branching and backtracking, similar spaces are explored many times. Consider a problem, as in equation 29.3, where some of the clauses are

$$(\neg v_i + v_j + v_k)(\neg v_i + v_j + \neg v_k)(\neg v_i + \neg v_j + v_k)(\neg v_i + \neg v_j + \neg v_k)\ldots\ldots \qquad (29.3)$$

The variable v_i is branched to be 1, and many other variables may have been tested before v_j is branched on. When v_j is branched on and 1 is tested, a conflict on v_k is detected. Then v_j is switched to 0, which again causes a conflict. Thus, the algorithm will backtrack to the previous branch variable. However, switching variable assignments other than v_i will not help. The algorithm may reenter the same region many times before it backtracks to v_i. Conflict analysis would be helpful in this situation.

A new variable value is implied by the value choices of all other literals in this clause being 0. Each literal has obtained its value either from branch decisions or from earlier implications. Therefore, we can create a transitive implication graph where an implied variable is ultimately implied by a set of branch decisions. A conflict is detected when a variable is implied to be of opposite values. It can be identified by backtracking the implication graph to identify the complete set of branch assignments that led to it. This set of decisions is responsible for the conflict.

In the example just given, the first conflict is caused by $v_i = 1$ and $v_j = 1$. A new clause can be derived as $(\neg v_i + \neg v_j)$. This is a redundant clause that can be added to the formula without changing the solution. It can also be viewed as applying the following consensus theorem to clauses 3 and 4 in equation 29.4:

$$(x + y)(\neg x + z) = (x + y)(\neg x + z)(y + z) \qquad (29.4)$$

With the conflict on $v_j = 1$ detected, it can be interpreted as v_j is implied to be 0. In this case, it is implied by $v_i = 1$. Another round of implication will render a conflict because of the first two clauses in the original formula. From the second conflict, a new clause can be derived as $(\neg v_i + v_j)$. Combined with the conflict analysis result of the previous conflict, the resulting clause is $(\neg v_i)$, which dictates $v_i = 0$.

The algorithm should instead directly backtrack to v_i, in what is called nonchronological backtracking by Marques-Silva and Sakallah [6]. The new clause can be added to the problem and thus help prune the future search space.

This example is extremely simple, but the principle is applicable to all conflicts and can reduce runtime by several orders of magnitude on many problems. For example, for the AIM200 group of problems, GRASP takes 10.8 seconds, whereas many other SAT solvers take more than 10,000 seconds. However, because of the heuristic nature of the algorithms, they show different performance characteristics with different problems.

Learning also has its trade-offs. Every conflict will generate one redundant clause, and storage will explode if every such clause is recorded permanently. Heuristics for discarding long or unused redundant clauses can keep the storage size manageable and still achieve significant speedup.

29.3 A RECONFIGURABLE SAT SOLVER GENERATED ACCORDING TO AN SAT INSTANCE

This section presents an example of generating an SAT solver according to the SAT instance [10–12]. That is, instead of creating a generic, hardware SAT solver, we generate a new configuration for the reconfigurable computing machine for each SAT equation being solved.

29.3.1 Problem Analysis

A hard SAT problem can take a very long time to solve, limiting the application of the formula and the solvers' powerful formalism. Therefore, we will look at the use of reconfigurable computing techniques to accelerate SAT solutions. For this it is necessary to compare the relative merit of FPGAs and CPUs and look at the characteristics of SAT algorithms to identify an efficient solution.

FPGAs allow the full customization of control and datapaths. In particular, they make it efficient to perform bit-level operations. Also, by allocating more computing resources for bottleneck operations, they can provide massive parallelism and deep pipelining for suitable applications. However, FPGA clock rates are lower than those for microprocessors of the same technology generation, so raw chip performance may suffer.

Two opportunities for parallel processing in the SAT algorithm stand out, one of which is the parallelism in the vast search space. For a problem with n variables, there are 2^n possible assignments (though with the backtrack algorithm pruning the search space, that number is actually much smaller). It is possible to split at the branch choices and allocate each subspace to its own processor. However, because the search space is typically unbalanced, such parallelization requires rebalancing the load and this would be very complex to implement in hardware. Another source of potential performance gain is implication and conflict checking. Whenever a new value is assigned to a variable, all clauses containing the variable should be checked for implication and conflict. New implied values will trigger further checking and implication. Additionally, the variables are Boolean and suitable for low-level processing by logic circuits, and thus implication and conflict checking are good candidates for hardware acceleration. It has also been confirmed through software profiling that implication and conflict checking take up the majority of computing time.

The basic backtrack search includes branch, implication, and backtrack functions, which are relatively simple and can be implemented with finite-state machines. Many projects implement a full SAT solver on one or multiple FPGAs. The next section describes one of them.

29.3.2 Implementing a Basic Backtrack Algorithm with Reconfigurable Hardware

Since implication and conflict checking are time-consuming processes, they are good candidates for hardware acceleration. Checking all clauses in parallel is one approach enabled by reconfigurable computing techniques. The circuit used for such parallel checking is presented as follows.

During the search, a variable can take one of three possible values: unknown, 1 (true), and 0 (false). A 2-bit encoding, denoted $(v, \bar{v})$, is used for the three variable values because it can conveniently represent them: $(0, 0)$ is an unknown (free) variable; $(1, 0)$ is value 1; and $(0, 1)$ is value 0. The fourth combination, $(1, 1)$, is used for conflict. The 2-bit encoding can be easily used for implication as well. For example, a clause with three literals $(v_i + \neg v_j + v_k)$ represents three possible implications that can be expressed with the 2-bit encoding as logical assignments, as shown in equation 29.5:

$$
\begin{aligned}
v_i &<= v_j \bar{v}_k \\
\bar{v}_j &<= \bar{v}_i v_k \\
v_k &<= \bar{v}_i v_j
\end{aligned}
\tag{29.5}
$$

When a literal appears in multiple clauses, its value is 1 if any one of the clauses implies it to be 1. The general form can be written as

$$
v_{inew} <= \sum_{\substack{each\ clause\ v_i \\ appears\ in}} \left(\prod_{\substack{each\ uninverted \\ literal\ v_k}} \bar{v}_k \prod_{\substack{each\ inverted \\ literal\ \neg v_l}} v_l \right)
$$

$$
\bar{v}_{inew} <= \sum_{\substack{each\ clause\ \bar{v}_i \\ appears\ in}} \left(\prod_{\substack{each\ uninverted \\ literal\ v_k}} \bar{v}_k \prod_{\substack{each\ inverted \\ literal\ \neg v_l}} v_l \right)
$$

The summation $\sum$ is a logic OR over the set of clauses in which the implied literal appears. The production $\prod$ is a logic AND over all other literals in the clause. Note that the literal in the formula is inverted from the one in the clause, meaning that the implication is effective if and only if all other literals are known to be 0. With this formula, a complete CNF can be converted to circuits that evaluate all possible implications in parallel.

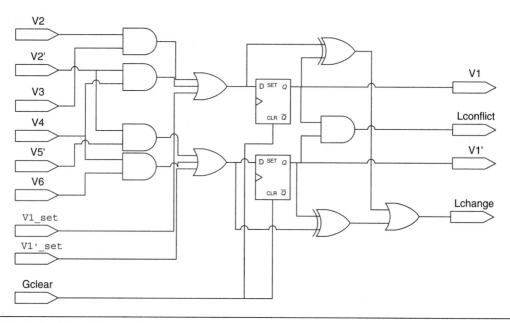

FIGURE 29.3 ▪ The implication circuit for one variable, V1.

The implication circuit for V1, shown in Figure 29.3, corresponds to the partial CNF of $(v_1 + \neg v_2 + \neg v_3)(v_1 + v_2 + \neg v_4)(\neg v_1 + v_2 + v_5)(\neg v_1 + \neg v_4 + \neg v_6)$, and is directly derived from the implication equation. A variable may assume a value because of either a branch decision or implication. An OR gate adds the assigned value. Since a newly implied variable may take part in generating new implications, registering the newly implied values allows implication to propagate one level in each clock cycle and avoids combinational cycles. To determine when implications have settled, an XOR gate checks the difference between the current and the next value. An AND gate checks if both literals of a variable are assigned to 1. If such a situation exists, the conflict (also called contradiction) signal is raised.

The other part of the algorithm is the control for the backtrack search. A distributed control architecture is used, with each finite-state machine (FSM) controlling one variable. Using a predetermined variable ordering, the architecture can be implemented by a linear array of communicating FSMs, as shown in Figure 29.4. Other than a few global signals, each FSM communicates only with the two neighboring FSMs. During the SAT-solving process, only one variable is active in terms of branching and backtracking. Its active status is represented by an active token. Two wires connect each pair of FSMs to pass the active token back and forth. Only one variable is the owner of the token at any given time.

In addition to the basic clock and reset signals, there are three global control signals. Gconflict is asserted when a conflict is detected. It is the wide OR function of all local conflicts, Lconflict. A local conflict is asserted when both

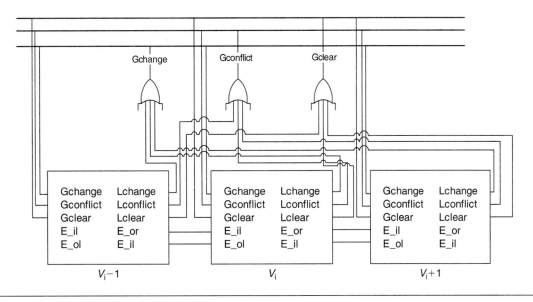

FIGURE 29.4 ■ The global topology for a basic SAT solver circuit.

v_i and $\bar{v}_i$ are assigned or implied to be 1. Gchange is asserted when any variable has changed value. It is the wide OR function of all local changes, Lchange. A local change is asserted when v_{inew} is different from v_i or when $\bar{v}_{inew}$ is different from $\bar{v}_i$. Gclear tells each state machine to clear the implied values. It is issued when the algorithm needs to backtrack and erase earlier implications.

With the external interface defined, each FSM should hold the assigned value, the implied value, and its state of backtrack search. The state machine is designed as registers for the implied value and an FSM combining the assigned value and state in the backtrack search. The state diagram of the latter FSM, shown in Figure 29.5, contains five states:

■ *Idle:* This is the initial state, in which the internal variable value is (0, 0). The FSM will stay in the idle state unless it has received the active token from its neighbor through branching or backtracking. When the token is received, if this variable already has an implied value, there is no need to branch, and the FSM will simply pass the token to the next variable at the next clock. If this variable has no implied value and the token has been passed from the left, it will branch and choose the branch value as 1 (the active 1 state).

■ *Active 1:* This state is the result of branching from the idle state, in which the variable value is chosen to be 1. The new value will be available for implication and conflict checking. The FSM will keep the token until there is no more change or until a conflict is detected. In the case of no conflict, it will pass the token to the right and will transition to the

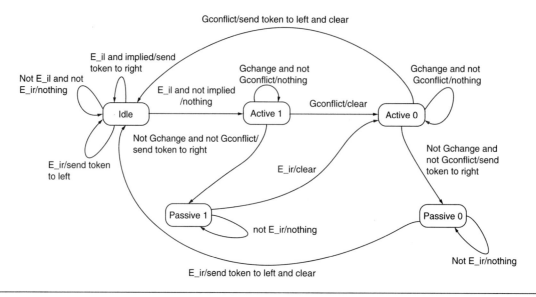

FIGURE 29.5 ▪ The FSM associated with one variable.

passive 1 state. If a conflict is detected, it will transition to the active 0 state and restart the implication and conflict checking.

- *Active 0:* This state is the result of a conflict in the active 1 state or of the token being passed to passive 1 by backtracking. The variable value is set to 0. Implication and conflict are checked. If there is no conflict, the FSM passes the token to the right and transitions to passive 0. If there is a conflict, it will transition to the idle state and pass the token to the left.
- *Passive 1:* This state is the result of branching further from active 1. If the FSM receives a token from the right because of backtracking, it will transition to active 0.
- *Passive 0:* This state is the result of branching further from active 0. If the FSM receives a token from the right because of backtracking, it will transition to idle and pass the token to the left.

With these FSMs logically forming a linear chain, the branching of the algorithm corresponds to passing the token to the right and performing implications during the process. When a conflict is detected, backtracking is needed. Backtrack switches a value from 1 to 0. If it is already 0, the token is passed to the left. Whenever a conflict is detected, all of the implied values are cleared by the global clear signal and reset to free. The termination condition is easy to test: If the token is passed to the left of the first variable, the problem is unsatisfiable; if it is passed to the right of the last variable, a solution has been found. In addition to the regular problem-solving mode, the linear chain of variables can also be configured as a shift register. When a solution is found, it can be shifted out as a bitstream.

At the time of the design of this SAT solver (1997–1998), a single FPGA chip provided a very limited number of logic gates, and so for typical problems a multi-FPGA solution was needed. The algorithm was implemented on an IKOS (now part of Mentor Graphics) VirtualLogic SLI Emulator, which contained one to six FPGA boards, each containing 64 Xilinx XC4013E FPGA chips to form an 8×8 mesh. Thus, it provided the logic capacity to handle a midsize to large SAT problem. While the FPGA itself could support a clock rate of about 20 MHz, the Ikos system used a time-multiplexing I/O scheme called VirtualWire to overcome the pin limitation (see Section 6.4). Thus, the system clock rate was reduced to the 1-MHz range. An HP logic analyzer/function generator was connected to provide the initial input signal and collect the result.

To provide perspective, in 1992 the mainstream FPGA XC4013E had 1368 logic cells. In 2006, the large XC4VLX200 FPGA had 200,448 logic cells (i.e., about 146 times the logic capacity), which was more than what two big Ikos boards could provide.

To solve an SAT problem on this platform, the following steps are needed:

1. *Generate VHDL.* A software tool written in C++ reads in the problem CNF file and generates the VHDL code that models the SAT solver circuit. The FSM is manually coded in VHDL and reused for each SAT problem.
2. *Compile the FPGA.* The VHDL is compiled to bitstream files for programming the FPGAs. For a single FPGA implementation, this can be done by the FPGA tools. For the Ikos emulator, in contrast, this process takes three steps: (1) the design is synthesized into a netlist and partitioned to multiple FPGAs by the IKOS tool; (2) the partitioned netlist is generated; and (3) the netlist is compiled by Xilinx tools into bitstream files. The main function of the Xilinx tools is placement and routing.
3. *Configure the FPGA.* The bitstream is downloaded to the FPGA board, and the FPGA is configured with these files.
4. *Run the problem solver in the FPGA and load the result.* The logic analyzer/function generator creates the initial signals to start the computation. When the problem is solved, the solution is shifted out, where it can be captured by a logic analyzer.

The runtime performance of the FPGA SAT accelerator is shown in Figure 29.6 as a histogram of speedup ratios. This test was carried out in 1998 using the problem set from the DIMACS SAT challenge benchmark. The software runtime basis was obtained by running GRASP with parameter settings close to those of the basic backtrack algorithm. GRASP was run on a Sun 5 workstation with a 110-MHz processor and 64 MB of RAM. The hardware performance was normalized to a 1.33-MHz system clock rate, which is representative of implementations on the IKOS emulator. In the figure, the x-axis is the ratio of software solver runtime to reconfigurable hardware runtime. It does not include the compilation time and the time to configure the FPGAs.

As we see from Figure 29.6, the result indicates that even though the reconfigurable solution has a clock rate 82 times slower than that of the microprocessor-based system, it can still achieve 20 times or greater speedup

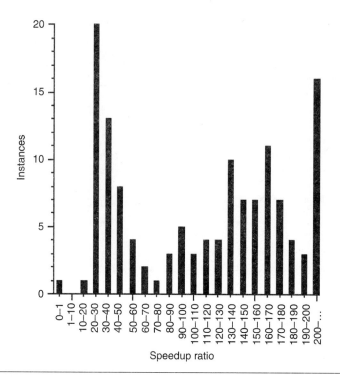

FIGURE 29.6 ■ A performance comparision of the FPGA SAT accelerator and the software version implementing the same algorithm as hardware.

for many problems. It should be noted that the comparison is based on runtime alone. The reconfigurable approach suffers from compilation overhead, which in 1998 required hours to perform logic synthesis and placement and route for the FPGAs. Current FPGA tools can perform such compilation within a minute. Ways to ameliorate compilation issues will be discussed in later sections.

For an understanding of the speedup results, Table 29.1 shows the speedup ratios for different problems. The average number of clause evaluations per cycle serves as a rough measure of the utilization of parallelism. It is defined as the number of clauses that contain at least one literal from the variables newly assigned in the previous clock cycle. There is a correlation between parallelism in clause evaluation and speedup ratio. Another factor in the speedup is that custom hardware effectively reduces a complex operation into single-cycle implication.

29.3.3 Implementing an Improved Backtrack Algorithm with Reconfigurable Hardware

The example in the previous section shows the performance benefit of reconfigurable computing. However, the hardware solution was implemented with the

TABLE 29.1 ■ Speedup ratios for different problems

Problem	Number of clauses	Average clause evaluations/cycle	Clock rate (MHz)	Speedup ratio
aim-50-2_0-yes1-2	100	7.1	1.78	44.5
aim-100-2_0-yes1-4	200	8.4	0.95	20.9
aim-200-6_0-yes1-1	1200	62.3	0.92	101
dubois20	160	8.0	1.78	13.9
hole7	204	18.3	1.78	44.5
hole8	297	21.9	1.78	45.6
hole9	415	25.9	1.57	40.2
hole10	561	30.1	1.48	41.4
ii8a2	800	15.8	1.07	923
par-8-1-c	254	29.4	1.57	174
par-16-1-c	1264	60.4	0.99	153
pret60_40	160	8.5	2.05	39
ssa0432-003	1027	11.0	0.95	24.7

basic backtrack algorithm, and improvements to the algorithm have brought thousands of times speedup in the software solution. The following example shows a more sophisticated backtrack algorithm with reconfigurable computing. As demonstrated by GRASP, conflict analysis helps identify the true reasons for conflict. Nonchronological backtracking and learning based on the analysis can greatly improve search efficiency.

Knowing that the hardware can perform fast implication checking, an alternative to conflict analysis-based backtracking was developed through trial assignments. When a conflict is detected, there are two possible scenarios regarding the most recently assigned variable. In the first, the variable has just been assigned by branching—it will be assigned the alternative value and tested. In the second, the variable has been assigned to an alternative value because of previous conflicts, so backtracking is needed. GRASP shows that conflict analysis can identify the reasons for conflict and may backtrack multiple levels, saving search time.

In the reconfigurable hardware approach, trial backtrack is performed. The algorithm moves back one decision level at a time and flips the assigned variable. Unlike a real backtrack, the most recent assignment is not turned to unknown. Instead, two implication/conflict tests are run for both value 0 and value 1. If both lead to conflict, we can trial-backtrack another level. If either case leads to no conflict, we have seen the real backtrack destination and the search reverts to regular search mode. This leads to much improved performance, with the only drawback being an increase in finite-state machine complexity.

Figure 29.7 is a diagram of the state machine for this enhanced algorithm. It is an extension of the basic backtrack algorithm, but with nine states instead of five.

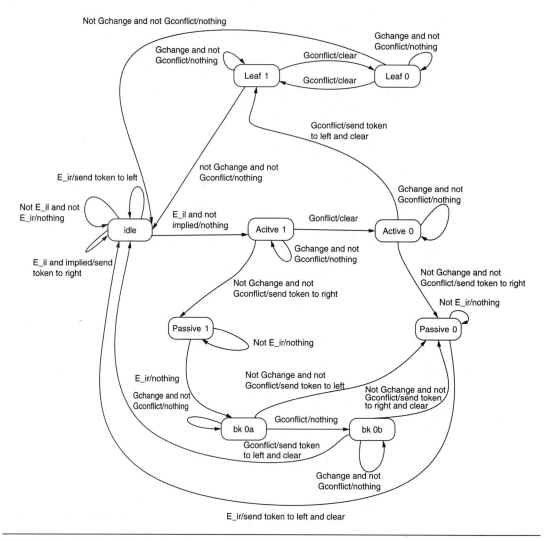

FIGURE 29.7 ▪ A state diagram of the improved algorithm.

- *Idle:* This is the state before branch; it is also the state if the value is already determined by implication.
- *Active 1:* This is the state after branch on value 1.
- *Active 0:* This is the state after backtrack on the branched value 1. When a conflict is detected, instead of a simple backtrack, a new phase of testing is added. It passes the token to the left and transitions to leaf 1.
- *Passive 1:* The variable value is 1 because of branching, and active control has been passed to the right in branching.
- *Passive 0:* The variable value is 0 because of backtracking, and active control has been passed to the right in branching.

- *Leaf 1:* Leaves 1 and 0 are testing states after conflict is detected with value 0. If the testing settles with no conflict, we have found the most recent branch assignment that contributes to the conflict. The FSM will backtrack directly to that variable. If a conflict is detected, it will try a 0 value in the leaf 0 state.
- *Leaf 0:* This is also a testing state. If the testing settles with no conflict, we have found the most recent branch assignment that contributes to the conflict. The FSM will backtrack directly to that variable. If a conflict is detected, it will switch to 1 and continue the testing.
- *bk0a:* This state works in coordination with the leaf 0 state. It is reached through testing backtrack to the passive 1 state. If the test results in no conflict, this variable is the backtrack target.
- *bk0b:* This state works in coordination with the leaf 1 state. If the test results in no conflict, this variable is the backtrack target. If the conflict persists, FSM passes the token to the left and returns to idle.

29.4 A DIFFERENT APPROACH TO REDUCE COMPILATION TIME AND IMPROVE ALGORITHM EFFICIENCY

A practical issue in creating an FPGA-based SAT solver circuit optimized to a specific problem instance is the time needed to generate the circuit. While the VHDL for the solver circuit can be generated in less than a second, the process of FPGA compilation is quite long. It can take at least 10 to 20 minutes to compile the mapping for a single FPGA. FPGA hardware and software have improved to the point that a compilation may take a few minutes; however, compilation time still cannot be ignored. In the next section ᵂ⁻ describe an SAT solver with redu--⁴ -- ⁱ⁻ algorithm.

29.4.1 System Architecture

The solution described in the pre into an SAT solver circuit. It does

- The circuit design does not t. The implication circuit inclu(may be placed far away from that generate global control s resources, and the system clo
- The circuit is a complex netli: to compile into FPGA configu
- The solver implements the ba: an improved nonchronologica architecture does not support

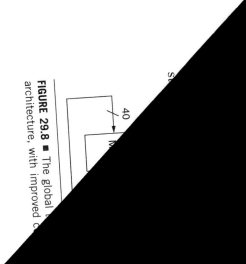

FIGURE 29.8 ■ The global architecture, with improved c

To deal with these issues, we developed a follow-on SAT solver with lessons learned from the previous design [13, 14]. The following characteristics of the new design address the previous design's shortcomings:

▪ Structural regularity is a high priority. A regular structure allows easier physical design. Specially designed processing elements allow regular placement and distributed processing. Overall, modular approaches can improve clock speed and allow fast circuit generation.

▪ Shared-wire global signaling is used to distribute data across the system. For example, a pipelined ring-style bus replaces the random interconnects. The bus allows a faster clock rate, a low pin count between chips, and a regular structure.

▪ The algorithm control is separated from the parallel data processing in the architecture. This allows the development of sophisticated control algorithms.

▪ Algorithm improvements have been implemented. In addition to implication, the circuit is capable of conflict analysis. Therefore, nonchronological backtracking and learning can be implemented.

The core of the new design is an optimized pipelined bus system, in which the bus width can be customized according to the hardware resources. The bus includes both control and data bits. The control bits notify the processing elements of actions to take; the data bits utilize a fixed sequence to encode the variable values. The system uses the same 2-bit encoding for variable values. Thus, a width of 32 data bits supports 16 variables. Also, the variables are encoded with a fixed order. For example, if at clock t the variables are v_1 through v_{16}, then, at $t+1$, the variables are v_{17} through v_{32}. In n clock cycles, $w*n$ variables pass through a stage, where $2w$ is the bit width of the data bus. The bus only propagates the variable value. There is no need to propagate the variable identification because it is inferred from the sequence. At each stage, the data bit may be OR'ed with a local signal, allowing it to be set to 1.

Figure 29.8 shows the global topology. The bus width is 40 bits, with 32 bits for data and 8 bits for control. Figure 29.9 shows one stage of the bus. The value is accessible to the PE as `Vi_in`. The propagated value can be set or reset through the signals `Vi_set` and `Vi_reset_n`. The main control block is the core of the algorithm control. It maintains an internal copy of the variable states and controls the backtrack algorithm.

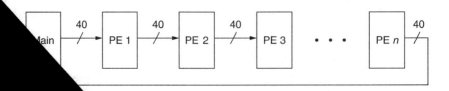

topology for processing and communication in the new SAT
onflict analysis and nonchronological backtracking.

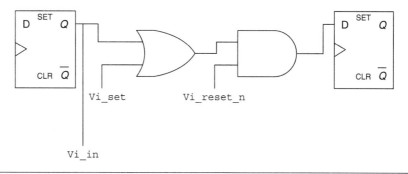

FIGURE 29.9 ■ One stage of the pipelined bus.

Multiclause modules can be placed in one processing element (PE). The total number of PEs depends on the total number of clauses in the CNF and the number of clauses per PE. Each PE contains a resettable counter to count the sequence of variables. The clause modules use the counter to identify variables on the bus.

A clause module holds the data corresponding to one clause. To simplify the hardware design, a 3-SAT formula is assumed (i.e., each clause has at most three literals). This assumption does not lose generality, because any SAT formula can be transformed into a 3-SAT formula in polynomial time by introducing new variables and breaking up long clauses. Each clause module has the following functions:

- *Implication.* Each clause should check for implication and put implied values onto the bus.
- *Conflict analysis.* This is the reversal of the implication process. Given an implied variable, the module finds the variables that lead to the implication.
- *Storage and interface.* The module interfaces with the bus, taking commands and variable values from it. It also sends new values and flags for value updates to the bus. It needs to store the values of variables related to the clause as well as the implication information.

Clause modules have three basic states: reset, implication, and analysis. The reset state will reset variables to (0, 0) if the corresponding value on the bus is (0, 0) and the state bus dictates reset. It is used during backtrack to undo the decisions and implications made after the backtrack point. Implication uses the same algorithm defined in the previous section. However, because the variable value is propagated on the bus, the clause module should also hold variable values locally. The data latching takes place when the PE counter matches the count stored in the module. The implied value is also stored locally until the correct bit passes through. The module will update the bus value at that moment. An internal flag denotes the implied value. It will be used in the analysis phase.

The analysis phase is the reverse of implication. The goal is to find the list of branch decisions that are transitive predecessors. This can be easily obtained if the history is stored. When the clause module is in analysis mode, it will be idle if it has not generated an implication. If it has generated an implication, it will check if the implied literal is asserted on the bus during analysis. If so, the module will reset this literal on the bus and set the complement of other literals in the clause. In this way it signals to the units that generated the values of these other literals. For example, in the clause $(v_i + v_j + \neg v_k)$, if v_i is implied, the implying predecessors are $v_j = 0$ and $v_k = 1$. These variables may in turn be implied by other variables.

The main control unit handles flow control and decision making. It has the following major states and functions:

- *Branch.* Branch chooses the next free variable and assigns a value to it. Using a fixed variable order and always choosing 1 simplifies the function. A priority encoder can quickly select the first row with a free variable and assign it to 1. The branch state is associated with the first round of broadcasting the variable values. The next state is implication.
- *Implication.* The controller checks for conflicts, in which case it performs conflict analysis. Alternatively, if in two cycles of data movement no new values have been found, all iterative implications have settled. It then performs the next round of branching.
- *Conflict analysis.* This step identifies the variable assignments leading to the conflict. The control bus shows the analysis state. The conflict variable is set to $(1, 1)$, while all other variables are set to $(0, 0)$. When a clause that implied a variable currently asserted on the bus is found, that implied literal is reset to 0 and the implying literals are all set to 1.

When a conflict arises from a branch, a list of variable assignments contributing to it can be collected through conflict analysis. The current branching variable is considered to be implied by this set of literals. The implication is stored in the main control unit and can be expressed as a redundant clause. For example, if assignments $v_i = 1$, $v_j = 1$, $v_k = 1$, $v_l = 1$ lead to conflict, the new clause is $(\neg v_i + \neg v_j + \neg v_k + \neg v_l)$. If v_l is the current branch variable, it is implied to be 0 by this new clause. Conceptually, the new value is not a branch decision. Rather, it is forced to be the opposite value because of the recent conflict. It is a redundant implication not explicitly visible from the original formula. Adding the new clause to the database is a learning process that has been used in modern SAT solvers to prune future search space. Such learning can be carried out in hardware by reserving some FPGAs for this purpose and generating new compilations during runtime.

29.4.2 Performance

The performance of the new design is shown in Table 29.2. It should be noted that the table lists the cycle counts, but the clock rates of the two designs are different. The new design has a regular structure, and communication is pipelined. It is therefore easy to achieve a much higher clock rate. Based on the same Xilinx XC4000 FPGAs, the earlier design, implemented on the IKOS

TABLE 29.2 ■ Performance comparison

Problem	Acceleration of new design without added clauses	Acceleration of new design with added clauses
aim-50_2_0-yes1-2	33.00	65.87
aim-200-6_0-yes1-1	1.32	3.66
aim-50-1_6-no-1	8.10	487.19
aim-50-2_0-no-1	4.95	2449.26
aim-50-2_0-no-4	13.89	1121.68
aim-100-1_6-yes1-1	20.57	4354.04
aim-100-3_4-yes1-4	2.81	10.58
hole7	4.63	4.63
hole8	3.95	3.95
hole9	3.46	3.46
par8-1-c	5.03	5.03
par16-1-c	1.29	1.29
pret60_40	4.05	2154.23
ssa0432-003	0.65	2.04

Note: The comparison is based on normalized speedup against the old design, assuming $20 \times$ clock speed improvement in the new design.

Logic Emulator, achieved a 1- to 2-MHz clock rate. The new design could easily achieve a 20-MHz clock rate in 1998. In 2006, the achievable clock rate was in the range of 200 MHz. This shows that the new design will likely achieve better performance even without added clauses. Still, added clauses can bring dramatic improvement in many problems.

29.4.3 Implementation Issues

One of the objectives of the new design is to reduce compilation time by exploiting its regular structure. However, typical FPGA tools use simulated annealing or similar algorithms to place the components. They are not capable of utilizing the regular structure automatically, and so a regular structure will not yield faster compilation times. It is necessary to bypass the automated tool and directly generate the system layout.

JBits is a tool set that allows direct programming of Xilinx FPGAs. It is an application programming interface (API) to the Xilinx configuration bitstream file that permits Java applications to dynamically modify Xilinx XC4000EX/XL bitstream configurations quickly.

A two-step approach can take advantage of the JBits tool and effectively reduce compilation time. The first step is to create a generic SAT solver template mapped to the FPGAs. The second step is customization to modify the configuration according to a specific problem instance. For each instance, only the second step is needed to compile the SAT solver. It can be performed quickly if the number of changes is small.

The architecture described in the previous section is used with additional constraints to minimize the customization. At each pipelined stage of the bus, multiple clause modules are connected to the bus. By limiting the problem formulation to 3-SAT, all clause modules are the same. The only difference is the variable identification of these three variables and the bus connection. The variable identification is expressed as a constant that can be programmed as a ROM that feeds a comparator. The connection to the bus also depends on the variable identity and polarity.

The points where a clause module wire interconnects with the bus wire should be programmed in the second step. Another simple constraint, that each bus wire connect to no more than one clause module, can be met with a simple greedy assignment algorithm.

The complete methodology to create an SAT solver is as follows:

1. *Design of a single clause module.* An SAT clause module is designed in VHDL. The synthesized netlist is further optimized manually. The design is expressed by schematic capture, which provides a more direct correspondence between design and implementation.
2. *Placement and routing of the module in a bounding box.* Placement constraints/floorplanning sets the bounding box of the clause module. The Xilinx tool automatically places and routes within the bounding box.
3. *Manual improvement.* The Xilinx EPIC tool provides a graphical user interface to manually edit the placement and routing on the FPGA.
4. *Solver generation.* With the bounding box constraints, a sample SAT solver is generated. Additional manual editing creates a regular layout.
5. *Template extraction.* The JBits tool reads the configuration bitstream and identifies the modification points.
6. *Java generator.* The SAT solver generator is created in Java with the JBits library and templates.
7. *Instance-specific bitstream.* The SAT solver generator is run with the problem instance, and the bitstream files are created.
8. *Load/run.* The programming is loaded to the FPGAs and the solver is run.

Only steps 7 and 8 are needed for each problem instance. For this reason, the compilation time is reduced from hours to merely seconds compared to the logic emulator implementation.

The target implementation is the Xilinx XC4036EX FPGA. Each FPGA contains 36×36 CLBs, and each clause module takes 4×16 CLBs. Sixteen clauses are placed in each FPGA. Each FPGA forms a stage of the pipeline, and multiple FPGAs can form a ring. The Sun Java 1.1.7 tool is used to compile and run the Java program. The host computer is an Intel Pentium Pro running Microsoft NT 4.0. The CPU clock rate is 200 MHz, and the main memory is 128 MB.

Table 29.3 shows the performance comparison, with times given in seconds. The Old Hardware and New Hardware columns include the time to create the FPGA mapping (CAD) and the time to find the solution on the hardware engine (HW). Numbers in parentheses are speedups as compared to the GRASP software.

Table 29.3 ■ Performance comparison between the standard GRASP software and two versions of the hardware SAT solver

Problem	GRASP SW	Old hardware CAD	HW	Total	New hardware CAD	HW	Total
a50-2_0-y1-2	0.05	10783	0.0011 (45x)	10783	1.9	0.0004 (125x)	19 (<1x)
a100-2_0-y1-4	894	89530	42 (21x)	89572	2.4	9.7 (92x)	12.1 (74x)
a200-6_0-y1-1	128	>100K	1.35 (94x)	>100K	7.9	0.89 (144x)	8.8 (14x)
dubois20	986	11377	70.8 (14x)	11447	2.3	8.44 (117x)	10.7 (92x)
par8-1-c	0.02	12834	0.000011 (1818x)	12834	2.7	0.000035 (571x)	2.7 (<1x)
par16-1-c	202	83191	1.3 (155x)	83192	9.4	2.2 (92x)	11.6 (17x)
pret60_40	705	12396	18 (39x)	12414	2.3	9 (78x)	11.3 (62x)
Geometric Mean			75.6x	<1x		(134x)	(4.14x) (27.6x speedup problems only)

29.5 DISCUSSION

Many groups have demonstrated that reconfigurable computing, compared to software, can achieve speedups of about 100 times in solving SAT problems. The main reasons are massive parallelism and fine-grained operation due to customized hardware. Software/hardware solutions have been explored to reduce hardware complexity and allow larger problems to be solved. A recent survey of these systems is presented by Skliarova and Ferrari [15].

In each of the software/hardware systems, the massive computation to find unit resolutions/implications and conflicts is the target of hardware acceleration. However, there are several differences among these SAT solvers:

- *Algorithms.* The base algorithms are different. Several of them are based on backtracking similar to that of GRASP. Some use a full variable assignment and employ flipping during the search. Some use matrix representations.
- *Logic engine implementation.* Different styles are used to implement the massively parallel engine. Some use circuit translation, where the SAT formula is translated into logical circuits. This means that the FPGA configuration must be compiled for each problem instance, which is slow. Alternatively, the formula is translated into memory, often distributed into small blocks, which can avoid the compilation time.
- *HW/SW organization.* Some implementations are all hardware, where the entire solver is mapped onto one or multiple FPGAs. Some implementations are SW/HW, in which part of the problem is handled by software.

While there has been significant progress in reconfigurable SAT solvers, we do not see them replacing software solvers in real applications for several reasons:

- *The need for flexibility.* The SAT problem is NP-complete—that is, the worst case is assumed to be exponential to the problem size. However, sophisticated heuristics make many large problems solvable in practice. Modern software SAT solvers typically contain many heuristics and allow the user to choose different heuristic combinations to tackle especially hard problems. Reconfigurable solvers generally have only a few heuristics, and there is little flexibility on which ones to use.
- *Algorithm efficiency.* Most reconfigurable SAT solvers have algorithm efficiencies similar to that of the basic backtrack algorithm with some simple heuristics. In the meantime, software algorithms have made significant efficiency gains. More elaborate analysis, such as conflict analysis, leads to more efficient backtracking and learning. Learning can improve SAT solver speed by several orders of magnitude. Reconfigurable SAT solvers generally lag in algorithm sophistication.
- *The scalability of hardware.* The implementations of reconfigurable SAT solvers are generally limited to moderate-size problems. However, large problems are more likely to benefit from hardware acceleration.

Many projects have designed Boolean satisfiability solvers with reconfigurable computing. These projects demonstrate the performance potential of these solvers through fine-grained custom hardware and massively parallel processing. Significant progress has been made in software algorithms as well, and recently, reconfigurable computing solutions have not kept up in incorporating these innovations. This is partly because the tools for reconfigurable computing are not yet mature.

Future research may result in a breakthrough by studying these issues:

- *Hardware/software solution.* The complex algorithms are difficult to implement and verify in hardware. It is more efficient to partition the problem and allocate only the massively parallel portion to the reconfigurable hardware. With microprocessors embedded in FPGAs, such as Xilinx Virtex-II Pro and Virtex-4, communication between the processor and the FPGA is greatly improved. The proliferation of multicore processors and high-bandwidth interconnects enables the exploitation of parallelism at different levels with heterogeneous processing technologies.
- *System-level design and synthesis methodologies.* Models of computation that preserve concurrency can be mapped to heterogeneous multicore architectures. The designer can decide the trade-off between parallelism and hardware usage. FPGA-based fabrics provide the massive parallelism and low-level customization, while other components, such as embedded processor or controller, can be chosen for their desirable characteristics.
- *Distribution of data and customization of hardware.* Mapping SAT formulas to FPGA circuits generates random routing and requires long compilation times. Mapping problem instances into distributed memory

blocks can solve the time issue but it forces some degree of sequential access. Learning from the design of content addressable memory may lead to hardware architectures better able to solve SAT and other Boolean problems.

- Simultaneous exploration of multiple states. Creating an algorithm that can efficiently explore multiple states in the assignment space simultaneously will allow the utilization of large amounts of computing resources. A simplified approach is to simultaneously run the search on multiple machines with different heuristics. However, efficient utilization of learning across different searches remains an open problem.

References

[1] T. H. Cormen, C. E. Leiserson, R. L. Rivest. *Introduction to Algorithms*, MIT Press, 1990.

[2] T. Larrabee. Test pattern generation using Boolean satisfiability. *IEEE Transactions on Computer-Aided Design* 11, January 1992.

[3] A. Biere, A. Cimatti, E. M. Clarke, Y. Zhu. Symbolic model checking without BDDs. *Proceedings of the Workshop on Tools and Algorithms for Analysis and Construction of Systems (TACAS)* 1579, LNCS, 1999.

[4] A. Gupta, M. Ganai, C. Wang, Z. Yang, P. Ashar. Learning from BDDs in SAT-based bounded model checking. *Proceedings of the Design Automation Conference*, 2003.

[5] M. Davis, H. Putnam. A computing procedure for quantification theory. *Journal of the ACM* 7, 1960.

[6] J. P. Marques-Silva, K. A. Sakallah. GRASP: A search algorithm for propositional satisfiability. *IEEE Transactions on Computers* 48(5), May 1999.

[7] R. J. Bayardo Jr., R. C. Schrag. Using CSP look-back techniques to solve real-world SAT instances. *Proceedings of the 14th International Conference on Artificial Intelligence*, 1997.

[8] E. Goldberg, Y. Novikov. BerkMin: A fast and robust SAT-solver. *Design, Automation and Test in Europe*, 2002.

[9] M. W. Moskewicz, C. F. Madigan, Y. Zhao, L. Zhang, S. Malik. Chaff: Engineering an efficient SAT solver. *Proceedings of the 38th Design Automation Conference*, 2001.

[10] P. Zhong, M. Martonosi, P. Ashar, S. Malik. Using configurable computing to accelerate Boolean satisfiability. *IEEE Transactions on Computer-Aided Design of Integrated Circuits and Systems* 18(6), June 1999.

[11] P. Zhong, P. Ashar, S. Malik, M. Martonosi. Using reconfigurable computing techniques to accelerate problems in the CAD domain: A case study with Boolean satisfiability. *Proceedings of the 35th Design and Automation Conference*, June 1998.

[12] P. Zhong, M. Martonosi, P. Ashar, S. Malik. Accelerating Boolean satisfiability with configurable hardware. *Proceedings of the IEEE Symposium on FPGAs for Custom Computing Machines*, April 1998.

[13] P. Zhong, M. Martonosi, P. Ashar, S. Malik. Solving Boolean satisfiability with dynamic hardware configurations. *Proceedings of the Eighth International Workshop on Field-Programmable Logic and Applications: From FPGAs to Computing Paradigms*, August–September 1998.

[14] P. Zhong, M. Martonosi, P. Ashar. FPGA-based SAT solver architecture with near-zero synthesis and layout overhead. *IEE Proceedings on Computer and Digital Techniques* 147(3), May 2000.

[15] I. Skliarova, A. B. Ferrari. Reconfigurable hardware SAT solvers: A survey of systems. *IEEE Transactions on Computers* 53(11), November 2004.

[16] M. Yokoo, T. Suyama, H. Sawada. Solving satisfiability problems using field-programmable gate arrays: First results. *Proceedings of the Second International Conference on Principles and Practice of Constraint Programming*, 1996.

[17] T. Suyama, M. Yokoo, H. Sawada, A. Nagoya. Solving satisfiability problems using reconfigurable computing. *IEEE Transactions on VLSI Systems* 9(1), 2001.

[18] T. Suyama, M. Yokoo, A. Nagoya. Solving satisfiability problems on FPGAs using experimental unit propagation. *Proceedings of the Fifth International Conference on Principles and Practice of Constraint Programming*, 1999.

[19] T. Suyama, M. Yokoo, H. Sawada. Solving satisfiability problems using logic synthesis and reconfigurable hardware. *Proceedings of the 31st Hawaii International Conference on System Sciences* 7, 1998.

[20] J. de Sousa, J. P. Marques-Silva, M. Abramovici. A configware/software approach to SAT solving. *Proceedings of the Ninth IEEE International Symposium on Field-Programmable Custom Computing Machines*, 2001.

[21] I. Skliarova, A. B. Ferrari. A software/reconfigurable hardware SAT solver. *IEEE Transactions on Very Large Scale Integration (VLSI) Systems* 12(4), April 2004.

[22] J. Gu. Local search for satisfiability (SAT) problem. *IEEE Transactions on Systems, Man, and Cybernetics* 23(4), July 1993.

[23] H. Zhang, M. Stickel. An efficient algorithm for unit-propagation. *Proceedings of the Fourth International Symposium on Artificial Intelligence and Mathematics*, 1996.

[24] H. Zhang. SATO: An efficient propositional prover. *Proceedings of the International Conference on Automated Deduction*, 1997.

[25] L. Zhang, S. Malik. The quest for efficient Boolean satisfiability solvers. *Proceedings of the Eighth International Conference on Computer-Aided Deduction; Proceedings of 14th Conference on Computer-Aided Verification*, July 2002.

[26] L. Zhang, S. Malik. Validating SAT solvers using an independent resolution-based checker: Practical implementations and other applications. *DATE2003*, March 2003.

[27] F. A. Aloul, A. Ramani, I. L. Markov, K. A. Sakallah. Solving difficult instances of Boolean satisfiability in the presence of symmetry. *IEEE Transactions on Computer-Aided Design of Integrated Circuits and Systems* 22(9), September 2003.

[28] P. T. Darga, M. H. Liffiton, K. A. Sakallah, I. L. Markov. Exploiting structure in symmetry detection for CNF. *Proceedings of the 41st IEEE/ACM Design Automation Conference*, 2004.

[29] Y. Oh, M. N. Mneimneh, Z. S. Andraus, K. A. Sakallah, I. L. Markov. AMUSE: A minimally-unsatisfiable subformula extractor. *Proceedings of the 41st IEEE/ACM Design Automation Conference, 2004.*

MULTI-FPGA SYSTEMS: LOGIC EMULATION

Russell Tessier
Department of Electrical and Computer Engineering
University of Massachusetts, Amherst

Application specific integrated circuit (ASIC) verification has been an important and commercially successful application of field-programmable gate arrays (FPGAs) for over a decade. By mapping the logic of a new chip design onto a system of FPGAs, logic emulation systems provide a high-speed simulation of the design under development. As FPGA technology has matured and FPGA logic capacity has grown, the use of FPGAs for functional logic emulation has increased. Contemporary emulation systems often include a sizable number of FPGA and memory devices organized in topologies that allow for efficient logic evaluation and inter-FPGA communication.

Although the hardware architecture of an emulator plays an important role in defining its effectiveness, system usability is often most closely tied to an emulator's compilation environment. To successfully map a complete ASIC design to an emulation system, emulators require optimized compilation steps that effectively distribute design logic across available FPGA resources and coordinate intra-FPGA computation and inter-FPGA communication.

To illustrate contemporary approaches to FPGA-based logic emulation, we profile here the hardware and software systems of a commercial FPGA-based emulator. We show that, although off-the-shelf FPGAs have been used effectively in a number of commercial logic emulators, several issues related to FPGA compile time, design debugging, and emulator host interfacing must be addressed to maintain their commercial viability.

30.1 BACKGROUND

Research in reconfigurable computing has been active for well over a decade, but the widespread commercial use of FPGAs as computing devices has been limited. A notable commercial success story for reconfigurable computing has been the use of FPGAs in ASIC logic verification. Over the past decade, the number of transistors that can be integrated into application-specific devices has grown exponentially with Moore's Law, leading to an increased need to verify design functionality prior to device fabrication. Currently, it is estimated that 60 to 80 percent of ASIC design time is spent performing verification [29], primarily because of the high nonrecurring engineering (NRE) cost associated with ASIC fabrication. The flexibility, parallelism, and reprogrammability of FPGAs make them an ideal platform for verifying, prior to fabrication, the functionality of ASIC designs. The availability of automatic FPGA mapping tools, such as those described in Chapters 13, 14, and 17, have streamlined the design conversion process, making the path from ASIC design to FPGA implementation more straightforward.

FPGA-based logic verification is often used to augment or replace microprocessor-based simulation of register transfer level (RTL) or gate-level designs. The primary source of emulation speed improvement versus simulation is the parallel implementation of circuit logic in the FPGA. While the amount of logic evaluated per clock cycle in a microprocessor-based simulator is constrained by a limited number of ALUs (typically four or five at most), the number of per-cycle FPGA operations per emulation system is constrained only by the available amount of total FPGA resources. This increase in logic evaluation capacity comes at a cost. Unlike its simulation counterparts, FPGA-based emulation can provide only functional verification for designs. Because the fundamental technology used to implement the emulated logic differs from the source ASIC technology, postlayout timing information cannot be replicated. As a result, FPGA-based emulators support only cycle-accurate logic evaluation that is synchronized to design clock edges of the emulated design. Additionally, circuit debugging for emulation systems is often more complex than debugging with simulators. The sequential nature of simulation-based verification facilitates debugging and logic tracing. Logic analysis in a parallel verification environment requires the use of specialized hardware resources and debugging tools.

FPGA-based emulators take on a variety of forms, ranging from single-device systems to commercial emulation systems that include hundreds of devices. Although specific system implementations vary, most FPGA-based logic emulators contain a tightly connected collection of FPGA devices. These systems can be distinguished by their component FPGA and memory devices, interconnection topology, design-mapping software, and external interfaces. The system topology defines the positions of FPGAs and inter-FPGA communication resources. The need for multiple devices to emulate many ASIC designs is due to the cost of FPGA reconfigurability. Because the silicon area overhead of FPGA versus ASIC technology has been measured to be about 40x [15], FPGA programming technology requires that an ASIC logic design be partitioned across multiple FPGA devices to achieve the necessary device logic capacity.

For most emulators, there is a strong association between the physical architecture of the FPGA system and the compiler used to map user designs to the emulator. Like the intra-FPGA mapping flow outlined in Chapters 13, 14, and 17, emulation mapping for multi-FPGA emulators requires a series of complex and interrelated algorithms. As we will see later in this section, emulation system compilation is complicated by the variety of design features in contemporary ASICs. These features include multiple asynchronous clock domains, multiported memories, and testing and debugging interfaces, which are playing an increasingly important role. In assessing modern emulation, the interfaces between emulators, simulators, logic analyzers, and prototype systems must be considered. It will be shown that, in the future of FPGA-based logic emulation, both design compilation and testing interfaces will play a critical role.

To illustrate the complexity of contemporary FPGA-based emulation, the hardware, compilation, and testing components of a VirtuaLogic VLE-2M emulation system from Mentor Graphics [21] will be profiled. This commercially successful system demonstrates not only the benefits of FPGA-based emulation, but also some of its limitations.

30.2 USES OF LOGIC EMULATION SYSTEMS

Logic emulation systems are typically used in one of two verification scenarios: (1) as a physical replacement for an ASIC in a target system, or (2) as a simulation accelerator. The ASIC replacement approach requires the use of a physical connection between the emulator and the target system. As shown in Figure 30.1, one end of the connection typically plugs into connectors on the emulation system that are interfaced to selected FPGA I/O pins. The other end of the connection plugs into the location on the target system that would normally hold the package of the emulated device. This emulation pod typically has the same pin configuration as the emulated device package. The use of in-circuit emulation allows for complete target system verification, including the emulated design and surrounding interfaces and peripherals. Although many times the target system is forced to operate at clock speeds of 0.5 to 5 MHz, a substantial amount of system functionality can generally be evaluated via in-circuit emulation. An attached logic analyzer is often used to probe specific design signals.

An alternative to in-circuit emulation is coverification (sometimes called cosimulation). In this mode of operation, the logic emulator works in concert with a host workstation to verify an emulated design without the use of

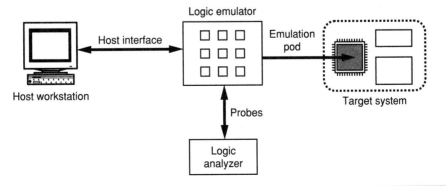

FIGURE 30.1 ■ A typical configuration of a logic emulation system.

a physical target system. Typically, the host workstation (Figure 30.1) performs the simulation of target system components and provides inputs to the emulated design via a host interface such as a backplane bus or cable. Design outputs are returned to the host workstation via the same path. In most cases, only the most time-consuming portion of the design under test is mapped to the emulator. The rest is simulated on the companion processor located in the host workstation. Coverification is often used to concurrently verify software components running on both the processor in the host workstation and in the emulated design.

In contrast to simulation, the use of in-circuit emulation and coverification allows for exhaustive prefabrication functional testing [3]. Typically, logic emulation can provide about five to six orders of magnitude speedup versus simulation for a logic design [2, 14]. Numerous commercial ASIC projects have used coverification to confirm the functionality of end applications with billions of test vectors prior to chip fabrication [3]. The speed of in-circuit emulation often allows for complete software system design verification as soon as a functionally specified ASIC design is complete. In the case of microprocessor design, a significant fraction of the emulated processor's software system can be tested long before processor fabrication, ensuring the functionality of both hardware and software. For example, Unix was successfully booted on an emulated M68060 microprocessor in about two hours [14]. This value represents a 40,000 times speedup over RTL simulation for the same processor operation.

30.3   TYPES OF LOGIC EMULATION SYSTEMS

For many designers of small ASICs, a large, expensive multi-FPGA emulation system may be unnecessary because one large FPGA and some associated external memory may be sufficient to implement the entire ASIC design.

30.3.1   Single-FPGA Emulation

The use of a single FPGA simplifies emulation system mapping because design partitioning and inter-FPGA routing are unneeded. Often, an unmodified RTL description of the ASIC design can be resynthesized for the FPGA with the use of an alternate synthesis library. Standard FPGA compilation tools are then used to complete the design mapping. As shown in Figure 30.2, the FPGA used for prototyping is typically mounted on a custom board that receives design inputs either from a target system where the completed ASIC design eventually will be located or from a workstation that provides input test vectors via a download cable. Additional interfaces are usually provided to allow for connections to a power supply and a logic analyzer. Since most FPGAs used for prototyping are SRAM based, resources must be provided to store and download the configuration bitstream to the FPGA at power-up.

As the logic capacity of FPGAs grows, it may appear that an increasing number of ASIC designs could be prototyped using a single FPGA. However, since both FPGA and ASIC gate counts follow the same VLSI process trends,

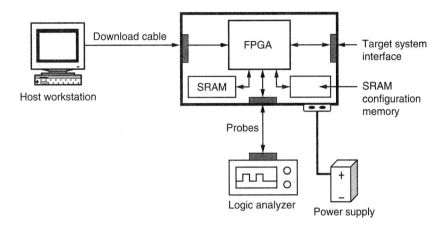

FIGURE 30.2 ▪ An example of a single-FPGA logic emulation system.

it is likely that most ASIC designs will continue to require multiple FPGAs for verification.

30.3.2 Multi-FPGA Emulation

Contemporary multi-FPGA emulation systems are complex verification platforms containing hundreds of FPGA and memory chips, high-speed interfaces to target systems, hosts, logic analyzers, and support for interactive debugging [11]. Since their initial commercial introduction in 1988, these systems have evolved into important functional verification platforms [7]. Typical systems include multiple boards each containing tens of FPGA devices interconnected in a fixed topology. Interboard communication is performed via fixed connections or a backplane bus. Because of the need to communicate signals between FPGAs, the typical frequency of an emulated design is in the range of 0.5 to 5 MHz.

Two distinguishing characteristics of a multi-FPGA logic emulator are the topology used to interconnect FPGAs and the approach used to communicate interpartition logic signals between them. Before addressing the issues of topology, two possible approaches for assigning logical signals to inter-FPGA wires will be analyzed.

Consider the mapping of a simple circuit shown in Figure 30.3(a) to two FPGAs as shown in Figure 30.3(b). For this circuit, two interpartition signals (x and y) exist. One approach to mapping these signals to inter-FPGA wires is to dedicate them to inter-FPGA wires A and B, respectively, as shown in Figure 30.3(b). This *dedicated-wire* mapping preserves the original structure of the circuit and does not require the inclusion of any additional logic. In contrast, the mapping shown in Figure 30.3(c), adds pipeline flip-flops and a multiplexer to interpartition signals so that inter-FPGA wire A can be shared. From the figure it can be seen that wire A is multiplexed to transport both x and y. This *multiplexed-wire* approach allows for more efficient use of FPGA pins and inter-FPGA wires, at the cost of additional FPGA logic and flip-flops. However, in most emulation systems I/O pins are a more precious resource than logic and flip-flops.

Both dedicated-wire and multiplexed-wire FPGA-based emulators are commercially available. Dedicated-wire systems include the SystemRealizer [24] and Mercury [25] families from Cadence; multiplexed-wire systems include Cadence Xcite [36] and the Mentor Graphics VirtuaLogic [21] and VStation [22] families. For dedicated-wire systems, design logic partitions must meet both the pin and gate count requirements of the target FPGAs. In virtually all cases, the FPGAs are pin limited, constraining the amount of logic and associated I/O that can be assigned to each FPGA. Rent's Rule [17], an empirical relationship that quantifies the growth of pin requirements as logic capacity increases, indicates that this problem is likely to get worse as FPGA logic capacity increases. As a result,

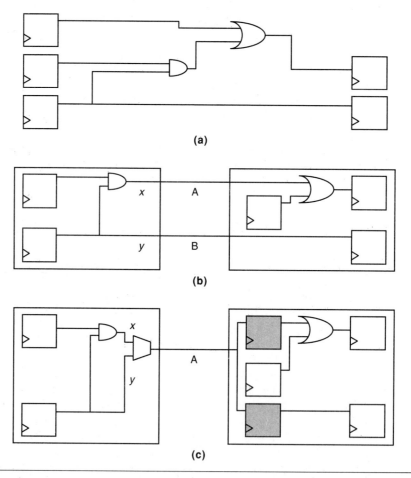

FIGURE 30.3 ■ The mapping of a simple circuit (a) by dedicated-wire(b) and multiplexed-wire (c) assignment.

the time-multiplexed use of pin resources is prevalent in contemporary emulation systems.

A series of topologies for FPGA interconnection have been investigated for both dedicated-wire and multiplexed-wire emulators. A number of early commercial dedicated-wire emulation systems organized FPGAs primarily in a near-neighbor or low-dimensional mesh topology, as illustrated in Figure 30.4(a). Although these topologies are easy to build, their lack of routing flexibility complicates design partitioning. Since many interpartition connections may not have direct FPGA-to-FPGA connections, one or more FPGAs are required to provide through-hop connectivity. Not only does this make the timing along interpartition connections unpredictable, but scarce FPGA pin resources must be dedicated to through-hop connections. As a result, direct-connect dedicated-wire systems are now used only for emulation systems with a very small number of FPGAs (typically four or less) [4]. These systems often allow direct connections between all FPGAs, eliminating the need for through-hops.

In an attempt to provide predictable FPGA delay and eliminate the need for through-hops, a series of emulation systems were developed that use specialized crossbar devices called field-programmable interconnect chips (FPICs) in addition to FPGAs [7]. These systems route most or all inter-FPGA connections through the FPICs so that the length of each inter-FPGA path is predictable. For basic systems, such as the one shown in Figure 30.4(b), some of each FPGA's I/O pins are dedicated to bidirectional connections on each FPIC device forming a crossbar. As a result, any inter-FPGA connection can be made by passing through a single FPIC, leading to predictable timing. Multiple levels of FPIC interconnect allow for system scaling to hundreds of FPGAs. The delay for each individual path is predictable because the FPIC's timing is predictable, although the number of FPICs traversed by different inter-FPGA paths may vary.

Most multiplexed-wire systems use meshes with primarily near-neighbor connectivity [7, 34]. Inter-FPGA paths are pipelined, so each path has a predictable

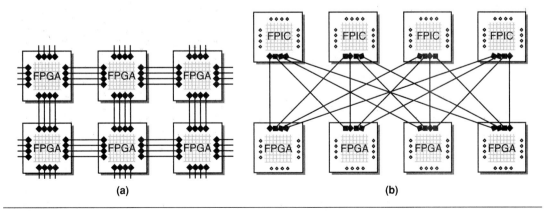

(a)   **(b)**

FIGURE 30.4 ■ Example FPGA-based logic emulator topologies: (a) mesh; (b) crossbar. *Source:* Adapted from Hauck [7].

delay, which is a multiple of the system clock frequency. Additionally, inter-FPGA routing congestion is overcome by the reuse of inter-FPGA routing resources, eliminating the restrictions created by through-hops. Although some multiplexed-wire systems that use partial or full crossbars (FPICs) have been proposed [19], the need for these expensive devices in time-multiplexed systems is unclear.

30.3.3   Design-mapping Overview

Several key issues drive the use of logic emulation systems. For most emulation products, system ease of use and resource utilization are important factors in system design. The translation of designs from ASIC netlist to multi-FPGA implementation must be fully or nearly automatic. These ease-of-use issues require sophisticated multi-FPGA computer-aided design approaches to process netlists in addition to the per-FPGA processing for numerous individual FPGAs.

A high-level flow for multi-FPGA logic emulation similar to the flow outlined by Hauck and Agarwal [8] is shown in Figure 30.5. It starts with a circuit description that is specified at the behavioral or register transfer level. Design translation, which typically includes logic synthesis, converts the high-level netlist to a gate-level structural equivalent. Following design translation, design logic is partitioned into pieces that will fit within the logic resources of individual FPGA devices. Partitioning is often performed to minimize required inter-FPGA interconnect, control system-wide critical path delay, and localize memory access. For some systems, partitioning must be performed so that inter-FPGA routing restrictions in terms of available FPGA pin count and system topology are considered. If the logic emulator contains memory chips that are external to the FPGA, design memory must be partitioned across memory resources to meet memory chip capacity constraints.

Partitioned design logic and memory structures are subsequently assigned to specific system devices via global placement. For some systems, swap-based placement algorithms, which are similar to the FPGA placement approaches described in Chapter 14, are used. A placement cost metric based on distance and delay is often iteratively used to judge placement quality. Partitioning and placement are sometimes combined into a single step to concurrently optimize interpartition bandwidth and inter-FPGA signal delay and distance [8]. The communication of interpartition signals between FPGAs is determined based on routing algorithms. For most multi-FPGA emulators, routing involves the determination of the shortest feasible path between FPGAs using available board interconnect resources for each inter-FPGA signal [2]. Topology constraints often require these signals to pass through intermediate (through-hop) FPGAs.

The last mapping step in logic emulation involves the individual compilation of the FPGAs. Multi-FPGA emulation systems have a number of constraints that can lead to less-than-efficient FPGA use. The FPGA compilation step may require hundreds of individual compiles. If even one design partition fails to successfully map to its target FPGA, the emulation flow shown in Figure 30.5 must be restarted from the design partitioning step. As a result, design partitions are often sized conservatively to ensure successful compilation.

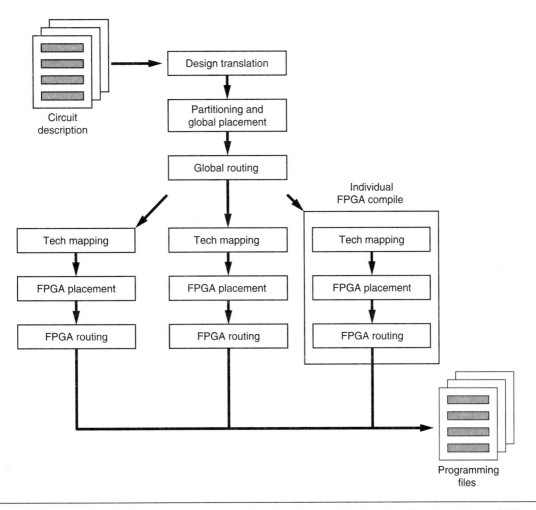

FIGURE 30.5 ■ A typical multi-FPGA emulator mapping flow. *Source:* Adapted from Hauck and Agarwal [8].

Although the steps just described define the high-level mapping flow for FPGA-based logic emulators, the specific partitioning, placement, and routing approaches used by individual emulators are heavily influenced by the approach used to communicate intermediate data signals between FPGAs. Although similar, dedicated-wire and multiplexed-wire emulators require specialized partitioning, placement, and routing algorithms.

30.3.4 Multi-FPGA Partitioning and Placement Approaches

Design partitioning and placement play an important role in system performance for dedicated-wire FPGA-based logic emulators. Because FPGA pins are such critical resources for these systems, the primary goal of partitioning is to minimize communication between partitions. A large number of algorithms have been developed that split logic into two pieces (bipartitioning) and multiple pieces (multiway partitioning) based on both logic and I/O constraints. Unfortunately, the need to satisfy dual constraints complicates their application to dedicated-wire emulation systems.

One way to address the partitioning and placement problem is to perform both operations simultaneously [8]. For example, a multiway partitioning algorithm can be used to simultaneously generate multiple partitions while respecting inter-FPGA routing limitations [28]. Unfortunately, multiway partitioning algorithms are computationally expensive (often exhibiting exponential runtime in the number of partitions), which makes them infeasible for systems containing tens or hundreds of FPGA devices. As a result of inter-FPGA bandwidth limitations and the need for reasonable CAD tool runtime, most dedicated-wire FPGA emulation systems use iterative bipartitioning for combined partitioning and placement [6]. This approach has been effectively applied to both crossbar and mesh topologies [31].

The use of recursive bipartitioning for dedicated-wire emulators creates several problems. Although it can be used effectively to locate an initial cut, it is inherently greedy. The bandwidth of the initial cut is optimized, but may not serve as an effective start point for further cuts. This issue may be resolved by ordering hierarchical bipartition cuts based on criticality [5].

Partitioning for multiplexed-wire systems is simple compared to the dedicated-wire case, because it must meet only FPGA logic constraints, rather than both logic and pin constraints. Unlike the dedicated-wire case, partitioning and placement are generally performed not simultaneously but rather sequentially [2]. First, recursive bipartitioning successively divides the original design into a series of logic partitions that meet the logic capacity requirements of the target FPGAs. During partitioning, the amount of logic required to multiplex inter-FPGA signals must be estimated because both design partition logic and multiplexing logic must be included in the logic capacity analysis. Following partitioning, individual partitions are assigned to individual FPGAs. Placement typically attempts to minimize system-wide communication by minimizing inter-FPGA distance, particularly on critical paths. To fully explore placement choices, simulated annealing is frequently used for multi-FPGA placement [2].

30.3.5 Multi-FPGA Routing Approaches

The global routing step determines which FPGAs are used to route inter-FPGA signals. Inter-FPGA routes may directly connect source and destination FPGAs, or intermediate through-hops may be necessary. Global routing algorithms typically attempt to minimize distance and inter-FPGA routing resource usage while ensuring that no routing resources are overused.

The routing problem for dedicated-wire systems is similar to the intra-FPGA routing problem described in Chapter 17. In dedicated-wire systems, the amount of available inter-FPGA wiring is fixed, possibly leading to infeasible or inefficient routes if an effective routing algorithm is not employed. Groups of wires between FPGAs are considered a communication channel, and inter-FPGA routing channels can be represented as a directed channel graph. As seen in Figure 30.6, for a direct-connect topology, the edge weight in the channel graph represents the number of physical wires in the channel [8]. Prior to routing, the channel graph for the system topology in Figure 30.6(a) can be represented as in Figure 30.6(b).

As routing is performed, inter-FPGA connections are assigned to wires, reducing the available capacity in each channel. A variant of maze routing [18] is typically used to assign inter-FPGA signals to specific system wires. Like the maze-routing algorithms used for intra-FPGA connections, multiple router iterations are often necessary. The maze-routing algorithm works by selecting a wire and finding the shortest feasible path from its source to its destination partition. Multiple iterations involving rip-up may be necessary to complete all routes.

The example mapping in Figure 30.7 provides an overview of the use of channel graph representation. Following the assignment of logical signals from the mapped design in Figure 30.7(a) to inter-FPGA wires, the channel availability is modified to take used wires into account. The effects of this assignment are shown in Figure 30.7(b), where the modified channels are shown with dashed lines.

For multiplexed-wire systems, both intra-FPGA computation and inter-FPGA communication are synchronized by a global system clock. This clock provides control over the sequence of events in the time-multiplexed system. Because many combinational evaluations and signal transfers occur in a single design (emulation) clock cycle, the system clock must operate at a faster speed than that of the design clock of the emulated design. Thus, routing in multiplexed-wire

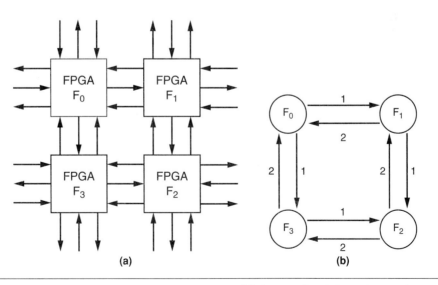

(a)   (b)

FIGURE 30.6 ■ (a) A multi-FPGA interconnection and (b) the associated channel graph for dedicated-wire routing. *Source:* Adapted from Hauck and Agarwal [8].

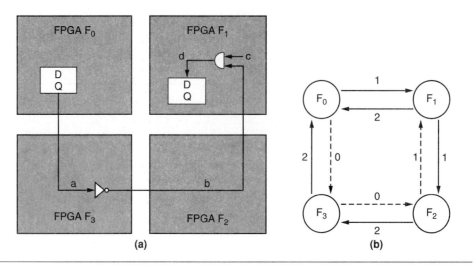

FIGURE 30.7 ▪ Assignment of logic signals to inter-FPGA wires in a dedicated-wire system (a), and the resultant mapping (b).

systems assigns each interpartition wire a source–destination path schedule in both time and space.

Routing for multiplexed-wire systems generally requires two routing steps to connect an inter-FPGA signal: the determination of a feasible path between FPGAs and the scheduling of multiplexed signal transport along the path [2]. Initially, a path between source and destination FPGAs is determined using a shortest-path algorithm. Unlike dedicated-wire routing, the utilization of wires in the channel is less restrictive because a different signal may be assigned to each wire on each clock cycle. Following path selection, a data signal can be transmitted along an inter-FPGA path as soon as it is assigned a valid logic value by the flip-flop or logic gate that drives it. To complete the transmission, the signal is assigned to a series of inter-FPGA wires along the path until it reaches the destination FPGA. One clock cycle of the system clock is allowed for each inter-FPGA hop along the path. Because inter-FPGA paths are synchronized at FPGA boundaries with pipeline flip-flops, long combinational paths are effectively broken into a series of discrete timesteps. A number of scheduling algorithms that perform the assignment of interpartition signals to inter-FPGA wires have been developed [2, 32].

The result of routing using multiplexed wires is illustrated in the following example taken from Tessier and Jana [34]. In Figure 30.8, the circuit shown in Figure 30.7(a) has once again been partitioned onto FPGAs interconnected using the direct-connect FPGA topology shown in Figure 30.6(a). Each inter-FPGA signal can travel only between two FPGAs during each system clock cycle. In the figure, pipeline flip-flops, which have been added to allow multiplexed communication on each path, are shaded. Circuit communication and computation in terms of system clock cycles can be determined by evaluating the critical path from signal a to signal d, as shown in Figure 30.9. In both Figures 30.8 and 30.9, system clock cycles are labeled V_1 through V_5. In Figure 30.8, communication delays

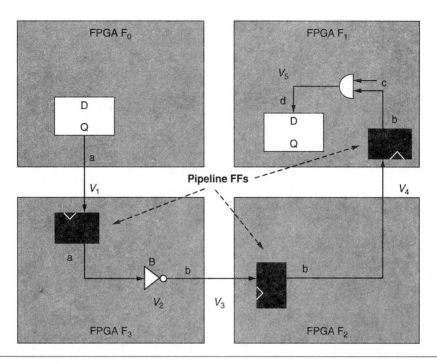

FIGURE 30.8 ■ Circuit mapping to FPGAs for a multiplexed-wire system.

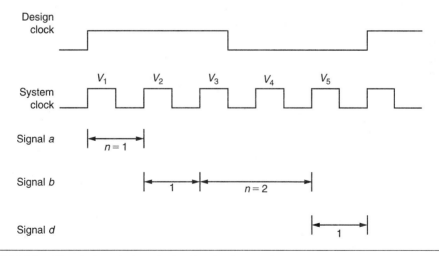

FIGURE 30.9 ■ The design clock cycle for the circuit mapping shown in Figure 30.8. Spans labeled n indicate a communication delay of n system clock cycles.

are listed, with n equal to the number of system clock cycles required for communication. Combinational evaluations are listed, with a number (e.g., 1). After system cycle V_5, signal d is latched into a design flip-flop, completing the design clock cycle.

The schedule for this example does not depend on the binary value of individual signals. Each interpartition signal is transmitted during each design cycle, whether or not it has changed. Alternative, dynamic scheduling approaches, which only transmit changed signals, have also been proposed [16]. For dynamic scheduling, the availability of the communication resources must be determined at *runtime*, which can significantly increase the amount of communication control circuitry needed in each FPGA. Kwon and Kyung [16] used a global controller and a shared bus to control dynamically scheduled data movement.

30.4 ISSUES RELATED TO CONTEMPORARY LOGIC EMULATION

30.4.1 In-circuit Emulation

As discussed in Section 30.2, a logic emulation system is often used to replace design logic in a target system. In-circuit emulation presents a series of challenges that often must be addressed by the user of the emulation system [11]. Since emulated designs operate at relatively slow clock rates, all or a portion of the target system must be modified to operate at a clock rate that is substantially less than the planned product clock rate. Special care must be taken to ensure that actions such as DRAM refresh and device phase-locked loop activity are not adversely affected. The clock for the target system must be interfaced to the emulator to control emulator logic evaluation. In some cases, the emulator provides the target system clock, simplifying synchronization.

30.4.2 Coverification

As described in Section 30.2, coverification requires the logic emulator to verify a portion of a design at the same time the rest of the design is simulated on a host workstation. Typically, the physical interface between the host and the emulator is the limiting factor to coverification performance [12]. A cycle-based approach to coverification requires a data exchange between the host and the FPGA-based emulator during each design clock cycle edge. This exchange includes collating inputs for the emulated design from the simulation database, transferring the inputs to the host interface via the appropriate software driver, collecting the generated results from the emulator, and returning the values to the simulator. The amount of time needed by the host to perform these transfer operations is often significantly longer than the time to evaluate the logic for a single design clock cycle on the emulator.

Transaction-based host–emulator interfacing has been introduced as a way to reduce interface time [12]. In transaction-based interfacing, the host-based simulator and FPGA-based emulator operate independently for a number of design clock cycles, limiting the amount of data that must be transferred across the host–emulator interface. Transaction-based interfacing often works best for stream-based computations where dependencies between the simulated and emulated designs are minimal, allowing independent operation [27]. A detailed example of transaction-based coverification will be presented in Section 30.7.

For coverification environments, the simulation performed on the host workstation can take a variety of forms. Most commonly, an RTL or behavioral representation of a system component written in a hardware description language is simulated with a commercial HDL simulation tool. Following preliminary verification, some simulated components may then be synthesized and mapped to the logic emulator. Alternately, a software version of the simulated system components (typically in C/C++) may be used [27].

30.4.3 Logic Analysis

Logic analysis, the capturing of signal state around specific events of interest, plays an important role in FPGA-based logic emulation for both in-circuit emulation and coverification. Unlike processor-based logic simulation, which stores intermediate logic signals in a centralized memory, intermediate signals in FPGA-based emulation are physically distributed throughout the emulation system. As a result, for emulation the signal set of interest usually must be selected prior to compilation so that probing circuitry can be added to the design under test. The data collected by this circuitry can then be connected to an external logic analyzer or sent back to the host workstation for display. In some cases, combinational signals can be reconstructed from saved design flip-flop values via simulation once emulation is complete [20]. Signal reconstruction allows for a significant reduction in the amount of probe circuitry required within the logic emulator, and limits the amount of signal data transferred from the emulator after each design clock cycle.

Because of their cycle-accurate operation, logic analysis for FPGA-based emulators has several additional, unique characteristics:

- FPGA-based emulators can only perform functional verification, so only combinational and flip-flop values captured on design clock edges accurately indicate design behavior.
- If the set of design signals selected for probing is changed, one or more FPGAs may need to be recompiled to implement the change.
- Logic analysis for a design can be triggered by prespecified logic conditions in the design. This triggering circuitry can be added to the design under test.

Logic emulators can be used to evaluate millions of design clock cycles, so there often has to be a trade-off between the number of probes and the number of consecutive clock cycles probing is performed. If emulation can be stopped, intermediate probe values can be offloaded to the host workstation or to a disk. Emulation can then be restarted [20].

30.5   THE NEED FOR FAST FPGA MAPPING

Commercially available FPGAs are optimized to provide good performance and mapping efficiency to a wide range of user designs. As seen in Chapter 1, contemporary off-the-shelf FPGAs offer a diverse and flexible routing network to reach this goal. To achieve modest to high logic resource utilization (e.g., greater than 75 percent lookup table [LUT] usage) and high design performance, an FPGA's mapping tools must perform a detailed evaluation of FPGA placement and routing choices, typically requiring 30 minutes to several hours of compile time per device. As a result, most FPGA-based logic emulators suffer from long compile times, which is a major limitation to their widespread deployment. The presence in an emulator of hundreds of FPGAs with significant compile times can considerably delay the debug, redesign, and retest cycle for a design under test. As noted in Chapter 20, several research projects have investigated accelerated FPGA mapping to solve this problem.

There are several reasons why fast FPGA design mapping for logic emulation is important:

1. The sheer number of FPGAs needed for logic emulation necessitates fast compilation. If compilation can be accelerated by an order of magnitude, so too, roughly, can the turnaround time from design change to emulator implementation. For many systems, faster design turnaround time can make a substantial difference in emulator usability, especially early in the design cycle when design errors are more prevalent.

2. A fast mapping is useful for determining if all logic partitions will fit within emulation system FPGA devices. If any partition fails to map into the emulator, the entire emulation mapping flow typically must be restarted from scratch.

3. Because multiplexed-wire emulation systems require the use of a synchronous global clock to coordinate computation and communication, the overall system clock speed is dependent on the slowest FPGA. A fast evaluation of achievable clock speed is therefore important. A fast mapping helps identify if the partitions are likely to meet the emulator's target system clock speed.

4. The inclusion of probes, which are frequently changed, necessitates a fast design compilation turnaround. Changes generally affect only a small number of FPGAs, which usually can be recompiled quickly.

Of the emulation system mapping steps shown in Figure 30.5, the individual FPGA compiles collectively require over 90 percent of the total compilation time. However, unlike the other steps, individual FPGA compiles can be easily distributed to multiple PCs and workstations for parallel compilation [9]. A centralized server is used to control distribution of the compiles to the client workstations, collect the resulting FPGA configuration bitstreams, and verify that all compilation constraints have been met.

It will be difficult to significantly accelerate compilation for FPGAs with existing commercial architectures without a substantial increase in the ratio of routing resources to logic resources per device or improved parallel mapping approaches for individual FPGAs. Fundamentally, FPGA placement and routing are dedicated resource assignment problems, and the search for a mapping solution is accelerated only through additional available resources or a parallel search. Although compile times for logic emulation can be significantly reduced by underpopulating commercial FPGA device logic in emulators, the hardware cost involved is prohibitive. Therefore, parallel FPGA placement and routing offer the most promise in improving compile times for existing FPGA architectures.

In many ways, FPGA compilation for a partition of an emulated design under test is more difficult than FPGA compilation for a single-chip design specifically created for an FPGA. All FPGA compiles for logic emulators must be performed with constrained pin assignments because inter-FPGA channel assignments are determined prior to individual FPGA compilation. Forced pin assignments make designs more difficult to map and require extended FPGA compilation times. Since partitions were not specifically designed for an FPGA, performance or utilization issues may sometimes arise during mapping.

30.6   CASE STUDY: THE VIRTUALOGIC VLE EMULATION SYSTEM

To illustrate many of the issues in logic emulation, we consider the VirtuaLogic VLE emulator from Mentor Graphics [9]. This system represents one point in a spectrum of similar FPGA-based emulation systems from Mentor Graphics, including the Avatar and the VStation [23]. The following analysis illustrates the basic approaches used by this family for system architecture, design compilation, external system interfacing, and coverification.

30.6.1   The VirtuaLogic VLE Emulation System Structure

Figure 30.10 illustrates the components of the VLE emulation system hardware, including its interfaces to a host workstation and target system [9]. The system chassis, shown on the right, can contain up to six multi-FPGA array boards, which emulate the logic and memory of a design under test. Two array boards are shown in the configuration in the figure. Each board contains 64 Xilinx XC4036XL FPGAs, arranged in an 8×8 array, and 32 32K $\times$ 32 single-port synchronous SRAM chips. As shown in Figure 30.11, each FPGA connects to its four nearest neighbors in both horizontal and vertical directions and to FPGAs two hops away in the horizontal and vertical directions. A single memory device is shared between each pair of FPGAs. Direct connections between each FPGA and the six I/O connectors on the array board provide an interface for in-circuit emulation connections, logic analysis, and host interfacing. As shown in Figure 30.10, these connectors are located at the front of each board.

The FPGA array boards connect to a passive backplane in the system chassis to create a scalable system. Each FPGA has direct connections through the backplane to FPGAs on other array boards. All intra-FPGA computation and inter-FPGA communication throughout the system is coordinated via a global

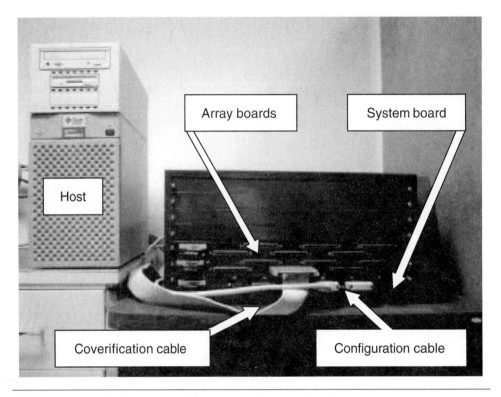

FIGURE 30.10 ■ A VirtuaLogic VLE-2M logic emulation system with two array boards.

system clock. The system board in the emulator controls the configuration of array board FPGAs and coordinates the distribution of the global system clock. Configuration bitstreams are loaded into the system board from the host workstation via an SCSI-2 cable.

30.6.2 The VirtuaLogic Emulation Software Flow

The emulation mapping flow for the VirtuaLogic VLE system follows the flow outlined earlier in this section. During design translation, an RTL netlist is converted to a gate-level design through the use of RTL synthesis. The mapped netlist is then partitioned into pieces appropriate for the logic capacity of each FPGA using algorithms that attempt to minimize bandwidth and encapsulate critical design paths within individual FPGAs.

Partitioning is performed so that the logic capacity of the FPGA is considered while partitioning to minimize bandwidth [1, 8]. For the multiplexed-wire VLE system, the number of logic gates required per partition can be represented as

$$G \geq G_P + c^* P$$

where G is the number of available gates in the FPGA, G_P is the number of user design logic gates in the partition, c is a constant representing the amount of

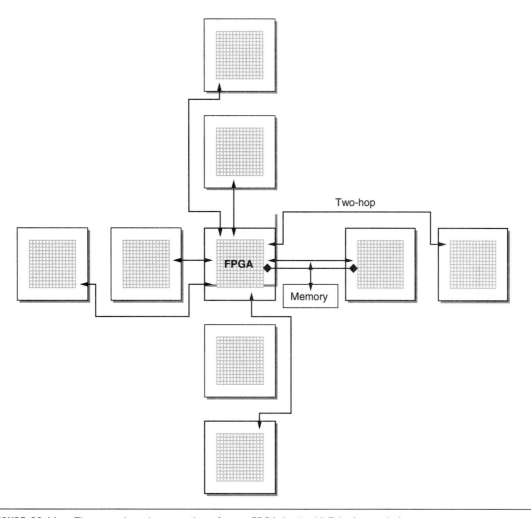

FIGURE 30.11 ■ The array board connections for an FPGA in the VLE logic emulation system.

logic required to multiplex a pin, and P is the number of I/O signals associated with the partition.

Design partitions assigned to an FPGA have a required gate count that is less than G. The partitioning process for the VLE system starts with an initial assignment of logic to partitions. Iterative mincut swapping is then performed to reduce the amount of I/O needed by each partition (the value P in the equation). Not only does this optimization reduce the amount of subsequent pin multiplexing for I/Os, but the amount of required logic per device is also reduced because G depends on P [8]. Partitions for this emulation system are subsequently placed using a simulated annealing placement algorithm [30]. In general, placement is performed to minimize the overall distance of inter-FPGA connections assuming that all connections will be scheduled along shortest paths. The logic partition to FPGA assignment formulation is similar to the one used to place clusters inside an island-style FPGA.

A distinctive aspect of the VLE system is the statically scheduled routing approach used to make connections between signal sources and destinations. The approach used by the VirtuaLogic compiler follows that described in Section 30.4 [8, 34]. All intra-FPGA computation and inter-FPGA communication is synchronized to the global system clock cycle so that multiple system clock cycles are required to complete an emulation clock cycle. A signal may be routed between FPGAs on a specific system clock cycle once it is known to be valid for the current emulation cycle based on signal dependencies. The following steps are then taken to perform the statically scheduled routing of the signal between a source FPGA s_f and a destination FPGA d_f [34]:

1. The shortest feasible path P_{sd} between FPGAs s_f and d_f in terms of inter-FPGA channels is determined.
2. The send time T_s of the signal is determined. This is the system clock time slot at which the signal leaves s_f.
3. The signal arrives at FPGA d_f at the arrival time T_a of the signal. The arrival time is defined as $T_a = T_s + n$, where n is the number of FPGA chip boundaries (hops) between source FPGA s_f and destination FPGA d_f.

To illustrate the use of T_s and T_a, the schedule of the circuit shown in Figure 30.8 can be augmented to include send and arrival times. The communication schedule, including T_s and T_a values, is shown in Figure 30.12. Note that in Figure 30.8 signal b passes unchanged through FPGA F_2 on the path from

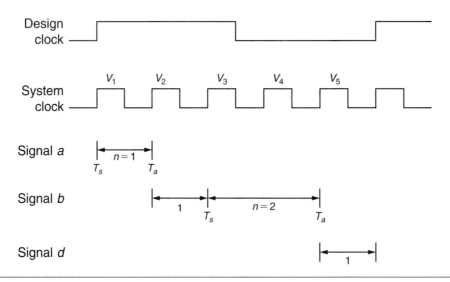

FIGURE 30.12 ■ The design clock cycle for the circuit mapping shown in Figure 30.8, including send times T_s and arrive times T_a.

FPGA F_3 to FPGA F_1. This through-hop is necessary given the lack of a direct FPGA F_3 to FPGA F_1 connection.

After each interpartition signal is scheduled for communication, the chosen schedule is implemented by synthesizing multiplexers, registers, and state machines that are added to the circuit partition for each FPGA. The resulting circuits are then applied to standard Xilinx Foundation design-mapping tools [37].

Most ASIC designs that are targeted for emulation contain complex logic and memory structures that require specialized processing outside the standard emulation mapping flow. For VLE systems, specialized mapping techniques have been developed to map complex design memories to emulation system memory chips [1], to map designs that contain multiple asynchronous design clocks [13], and to incrementally map design changes [34]. The algorithms created to address these mapping issues are important keys to system usability.

30.6.3 Multiported Memory Mapping

In a VLE system, multiple accesses to a $32K \times 32$ synchronous single-ported SRAM can be scheduled within a design (emulation) cycle to emulate the behavior of a multiport RAM. For example, Figure 30.13(a) shows a user-specified dual-port memory with two read ports and a single write port. During an emulation cycle access that requires reads from both read ports, both reads can be performed in sequence from the single-ported SRAM chip. As shown in Figure 30.13(b), a state machine can be used to sequence the application of the addresses to the single-ported SRAMs, and the storage of the read data in the output registers.

The VirtuaLogic compiler determines the schedule for data accesses in conjunction with routing address, data, and control signals to the on-board physical memory devices. Although not shown in the Figure 30.13, for data wider than the width of the physical memory, memory accesses can be made by sequentially accessing consecutive memory locations. For example, a read of a 128-bit value requires four system clock cycles. Dependency relationships for multiported RAMs (e.g., read-after-write) can be handled via the sequential scheduling of RAM accesses.

30.6.4 Design Mapping with Multiple Asynchronous Clocks

In Section 30.4 it was shown that for multiplexed-wire systems both intra-FPGA computation and inter-FPGA communication are coordinated to a global system clock. Because multiple system clock cycles are required to perform computation and communication for a single emulation clock cycle, a fixed relationship must exist between the clocks. Many contemporary ASIC designs contain multiple design clocks that operate asynchronously to each other. While synchronization between a system clock and a single design clock can be addressed by rising design clock edges that delineate functional evaluations, deriving a relationship between multiple asynchronous design clocks and a system clock is more difficult.

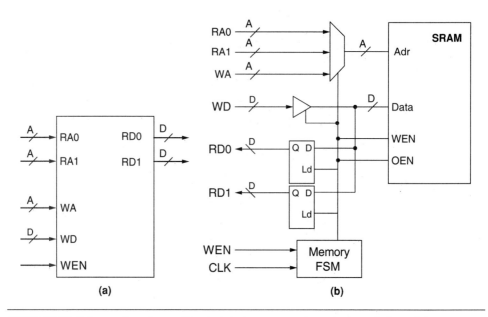

FIGURE 30.13 ■ A mapping of a multiported design memory to a single-ported emulator memory: (a) parallel-accessed multiport memory; (b) sequentially accessed single-port multiplexed memory. *Source:* Adapted from Agarwal [1].

In the circuitry shown in Figure 30.14, taken from Kudlugi and Tessier [13], the asynchronous clocks CLK1 and CLK2 drive state elements. It can be seen that signal N5 is a multidomain signal because it changes value and is sampled as a result of both CLK1 and CLK2 clock transitions. Now consider a situation where the circuit in Figure 30.14 is partitioned so the multidomain signal N5 must be transported from FPGA 1 to FPGA 4 as shown in Figure 30.15. In a multi-FPGA VLE system, the physical wires that connect FPGAs are grouped into unidirectional channels, where each physical wire is capable of carrying multiple signals that belong to the same emulation clock domain (e.g., CLK1 or CLK2).

Signal routing may include several intermediate FPGA hops. To simplify scheduling, logical signals assigned to the same inter-FPGA wire must be associated with the same clock domain. For designs with multidomain signals, this restriction requires that each multidomain signal be logically split into separate single-domain versions prior to transport. These single-domain values are then transmitted separately along separate physical channel links and combined at the destination to support multidomain behavior. Unfortunately, this approach of separately routing copies of the same signal along different links can lead to scheduling problems because each copy may arrive at the destination at different system clock cycles.

This issue is best illustrated through an example. As shown in Figure 30.15, communication for each asynchronous clock domain takes place over a different

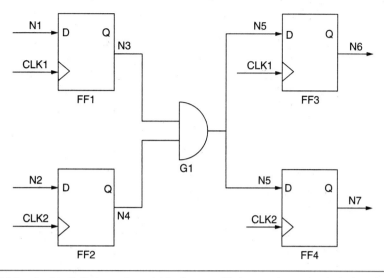

FIGURE 30.14 ■ A circuit that requires clocks from multiple asynchronous clock domains.

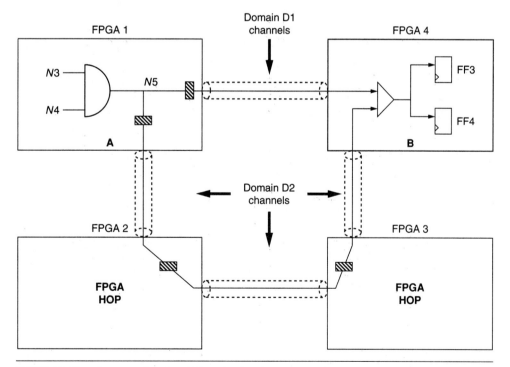

FIGURE 30.15 ■ An example of multidomain signal transport. *Source:* Adapted from Kudlugi and Tessier [13].

set of inter-FPGA channels. In the case of N5, paths using both domain 1 (D1) and domain 2 (D2) channels are needed to transport N5 between FPGA 1 and FPGA 2. The disjoint nature of multiple routing paths for the same logical signal can lead to differing arrival times for the copies of signal N5 at the destination FPGA. If both copies of signal N5 leave FPGA 1 at the same time, the D1 version of the signal will arrive at FPGA 2 two system clock cycles before the D2 version. This arrival order can lead to an incorrect logic evaluation if an attempt is made to use the D1 version of the signal before the D2 version arrives.

A requirement in transporting multidomain signals is to ensure that causality of events is guaranteed irrespective of routing delays. Causality can be preserved by ensuring that the length of the route for each domain from the source to the destination requires exactly the same number of system clock cycles. This can be accomplished by requiring the scheduler to use the same number of system clock cycles to communicate versions of the same signal to a destination FPGA. In Figure 30.16, for example, the scheduler must determine a path from FPGA 1 to FPGA 2 of length 3 for domain D1, since this is the path length of the domain D2 version. Each path now contains three pipeline flip-flops. The determination of the specific schedule may require several scheduling iterations because the length of the longest path is not known until each path is initially scheduled.

The scheduler used by the VirtuaLogic compiler takes multidomain paths into account and can handle designs with any number of asynchronous clock

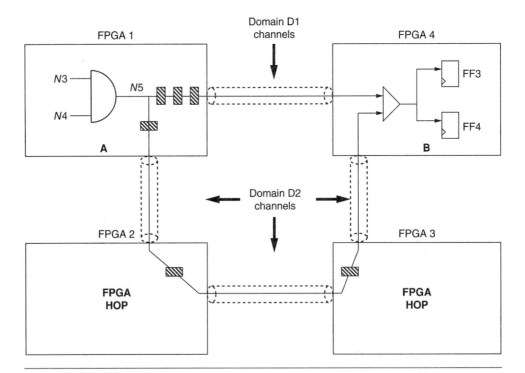

FIGURE 30.16 ▪ A retimed version of the multidomain signal transport shown in Figure 30.15.

domains. The mapping of this multidomain logic to the emulator takes place automatically. The asynchronous design clock signals may be interfaced to the emulator from outside the system through the system board.

30.6.5 Incremental Compilation of Designs

The need for incremental design support in VLE systems is a result of recent interest in core-based design and system-on-a-chip integration. Most ASIC verification flows involve numerous iterations of design test, debug, and recompilation. As modifications are evaluated and errors are identified, the original design is subjected to a series of minor modifications. Often, a change may be isolated to a component that was originally spread across two or more FPGAs in the emulator. If emulator recompilation can be limited primarily to those FPGAs that contain logic affected by the change, the compilation process can be greatly accelerated. The ability to support design changes in a small set of FPGAs is crucial to avoid the need to recompile all FPGAs in the system from scratch. In addition to providing fast design turnaround, the resulting emulation performance of the incrementally compiled design should be the same or close to the same as the performance of the original design mapping [34].

The use of scheduling for VirtuaLogic inter-FPGA routing facilitates the management of incremental design compilation. A series of steps are required to address changes in the design and map them to the FPGA-based emulator [34]:

1. *Netlist comparison.* The first step in the incremental compilation process is to identify the logic and interconnect associated with the initial design that is no longer in the modified design. Subsequently, the logic and interconnect added to the initial design to create the modified design are identified. Logic removed from the initial design was assigned to a set of FPGAs as a result of initial design mapping. These modified FPGAs provide a possible destination for added logic.

2. *Incremental path identification.* In the VLE system, individual FPGAs may serve as through-hop steps for intermediate routes. Thus, even if a given FPGA does not contain logic that has changed, these FPGAs will require recompilation if they are used as through-hops for the modified logic. To limit compile time, the number of unmodified FPGAs selected to perform through-hop routing should be minimized.

3. *Incremental partitioning.* Once the modified and required through-hop FPGAs have been identified, newly added design logic can be partitioned onto them subject to processor logic and memory capacity constraints.

4. *Incremental routing.* Following incremental partitioning, routing is performed to create a path for the added design signals connecting the modified FPGAs. Because FPGAs surrounding the modified FPGAs are unaltered, this incremental routing must be performed using board-level routing resources that have not been consumed by unchanged design routes. Feasible shortest paths between FPGAs are evaluated and then incremental scheduling is used to form a communication pipeline.

The most important part of incremental compilation for multiplexed-wire systems is the scheduling of added signals onto available inter-FPGA wires (incremental routing). In some cases, portions of previously routed inter-FPGA links may need to be rerouted as a result of changed logic depth and dependency. Consider the circuit shown in Figure 30.17, taken from Tessier and Jana [34]. The circuit is the same as the one assigned to FPGAs in Figure 30.8 except that the OR gate F and signals e and f have been added. One potential incremental mapping for the modified circuit appears in Figure 30.18. A design clock

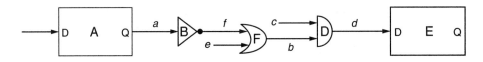

FIGURE 30.17 ▪ A modified version of the circuit assigned to FPGAs in Figure 30.8.
Source: Adapted from Tessier and Jana [34].

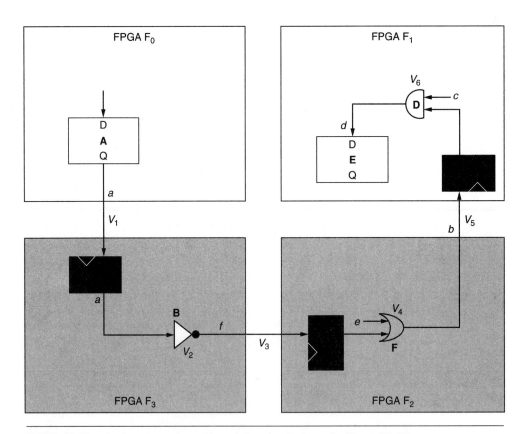

FIGURE 30.18 ▪ An incremental mapping of the circuit shown in Figure 30.17.

cycle associated with the scheduled route of the circuit mapping in Figure 30.17 is shown in Figure 30.19.

When these waveforms are compared to the waveforms in Figure 30.12, it can be seen that an extra cycle of combinational delay has been added because of the OR gate evaluation in FPGA F_2, extending the number of system clock cycles needed to evaluate the design. Closer examination of the two sets of waveforms indicates that although signal b was previously routed between FPGA F_2 and FPGA F_1 in the initial design, it will have to be rerouted for the modified mapping. For the initial design, signal b has been routed between FPGA F_2 and FPGA F_1 on system clock cycle V_4. As a result of the mapping shown in Figure 30.18, signal b cannot be routed until system clock cycle V_5 because of combinational dependencies. This results in a need to recompile both FPGA F_2 to transmit the signal on cycle V_5 and FPGA F_1 to receive the value on system clock cycle V_5.

After dependencies are determined, the new links are scheduled for communication using the VirtuaLogic compiler two-step routing approach described earlier. Only added interpartition signals are routed; previously routed signals that are unchanged are left in place. Incremental routing of added signals may lead to an emulation system performance loss. For example, the waveforms shown in Figure 30.19 represent the schedule of the incrementally modified design shown in Figure 30.17. The new schedule requires six system clock cycles to complete a design clock cycle as opposed to the five required for the original design. Although not shown in Figure 30.19, a global control signal distributed to all FPGAs indicates the end of the design clock cycle. Following recompilation, this signal can be asserted every six rather than five system clock cycles. This requires FPGAs

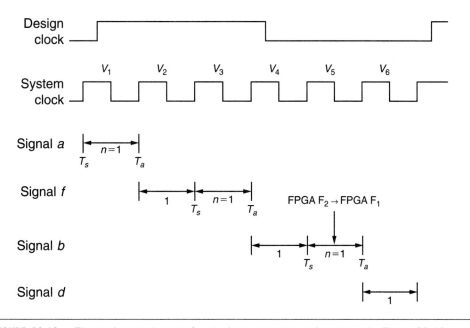

FIGURE 30.19 ■ The design clock cycle for the incremental mapping shown in Figure 30.18.

that were not recompiled to hold data values for an extra system clock cycle while the recompiled FPGAs complete computation. All results are then clocked into design flip-flops system-wide after six clock cycles by the design clock.

30.6.6 VLE Interfaces for Coverification

The VLE system has a number of interfaces to support both in-circuit emulation and coverification. For in-circuit emulation, an emulation pod can be interfaced to one of six connectors on each of the array boards shown in Figure 30.10. These signals are directly connected to FPGAs and drive/receive I/O signals on the emulated design. Tuned clock cables are used to control clocking both on the target system and in the emulator when the emulator has completed evaluation for an emulation clock. To permit in-circuit emulation the target system must be slowed to accommodate the 0.5- to 2-MHz design emulation rate.

In addition to support for in-circuit emulation, the VLE emulator has significant support for a variety of coverification modes. This support is primarily provided through a series of software interfaces created at the host workstation and on the emulator. These interfaces allow the emulator to be used in a variety of coverification scenarios [9]. Designers initiate ASIC verification by representing the ASIC using a high-level language such as C or SystemC (a C-compatible language that represents the concurrency and clocking associated with hardware implementations). As a design matures, portions of it are migrated to hardware. Inputs and outputs to the portion of the design on the emulator are interfaced to the emulator via an application programming interface (API).

The transfer, execution, and collection of results using the emulator can be represented as shown in Figure 30.20. This implementation of coverification is performed with a series of components. The software test environment interacts with an application adapter—that is, an interface to a series of library-based drivers that packetize the data and prepare it for transfer via a PCI-based board. The use of library-based drivers allows for communication at functional, bus-cycle-accurate, and cycle-accurate levels [27].

An interface circuit is required at the destination to reassemble data for subsequent use as input to the design. A transactor accepts the reassembled data, generates an emulation clock for use with the design under test, and coordinates per-cycle data transfer to and from the design. Generally, the interface circuit and transactor are created in RTL and added to the design. VLE systems use the transaction-based approach described earlier in this section. Transactions contain both data and synchronization information. A single transaction results in multiple verification cycles of work being performed by the emulator. The transaction can be as simple as a memory read or as complex as the transfer of an entire structured packet through a channel. To support coverification, the host for the VLE emulator contains an SPCI (Springtime PCI) card [27]. This custom PCI card implements the physical layer of transaction-based interfacing between the host and the emulator via a cable.

The transaction application protocol interface (TAPI) forms the application adapter for the VLE system [27]. TAPI consists of a library of C functions. The

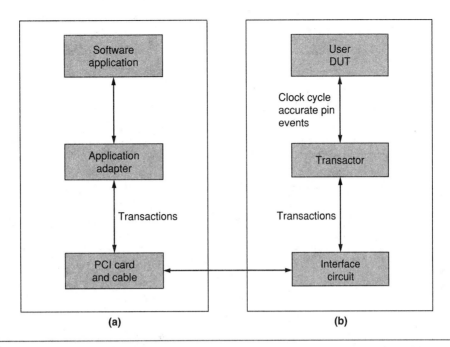

FIGURE 30.20 ■ The coverification flow between the workstation (a) and the emulator (b).

adapter is a utility package that converts raw signals into transactions by making calls to the C function library. It supports a verification environment that allows a C model to interact with an RTL model running on the emulator. The transfer of data across the host–emulator cable can be aided by buffering data in memory and transferring it as a block. This approach is preferable to the individual transfer of values from discrete memory locations in a file. Data buffering in arrays can be implemented in the same C modules that contain the TAPI driver calls for the emulator.

For the VLE system, the emulator system clock speed is set to 30 MHz. The same six multi-FPGA board connectors used for interfacing to an in-circuit emulation pod can also be used as an interface for coverification. The remaining connectors on the multi-FPGA boards can allow for direct access to logic analyzers for signal probing.

30.6.7   Parallel FPGA Compilation for the VLE System

Given the number of FPGAs in the VLE system, parallel compilation of the individual devices is a necessity. An FPGA compile server is used to distribute the numerous Xilinx XC4036XL compiles out to a number of available workstations that can perform the needed operations [9]. Unfinished compiles are held in a queue until compilation resources become available. Following design compilation, configuration bitstream information and status reports are returned to the server for subsequent transfer to the emulation system.

30.7   FUTURE TRENDS

Although FPGAs have played an important role in the development and success of commercial logic emulation hardware, current trends indicate a possibly reduced role for them in future emulation systems. Over the past few years, special-purpose custom logic processors have replaced FPGAs in a number of commercial emulation systems [26, 35]. Processor-based emulators generally contain a series of logic resources that perform a different Boolean function during every system clock cycle [10]. Data values, which are stored in on-chip RAM, are supplied to the logic resources every cycle via time-multiplexed on-chip routing resources. The per-cycle logic function definition and routing configuration information form instructions that are stored in on-chip instruction memory.

The depth of the memory constitutes the amount of multiplexing that can be performed both on the processor and in the interprocessor interconnect structure. Like multiplexed-wire FPGAs, interprocessor communications are time-sliced based on combinational logic dependencies so that processor pins are reused.

In general, the compile time for processor-based emulation is very fast compared to FPGA-based emulation. This disparity is a result of the assignment of intra-FPGA (processor) logic to interconnect resources. In multiplexed- and dedicated-wire emulation systems, internal FPGA logic and interconnect are *dedicated* to specific design resources. This has three implications:

1. For long combinational paths, each logic block and intra-FPGA wire is used only a small fraction of the time, effectively limiting system efficiency.
2. The dedicated assignment of signals to intra-FPGA wires is a problem of limited resource allocation. To significantly reduce compile time, a substantial increase in routing resources is needed relative to available logic to make FPGA routing linear time (a value of at least 20 percent is reported by Swartz et al. [33]). According to Rent's Rule, this disparity is likely to become worse as designs and FPGAs increase in size.
3. Because FPGA routers are unpredictable, it is impossible to determine both whether a device will route and what the per-FPGA (and hence global system) performance will be until all FPGAs have been successfully mapped.

In contrast, in processor-based emulator hardware, internal logic and routing structures are time-multiplexed. As a result, simpler routing structures with fixed memory to processor delays for all intra-processor paths are set. This, too, has implications:

1. Logic and interconnect resources are multiplexed over time to increase resource use efficiency per clock cycle.
2. The assignment of both inter- and intra-FPGA resources is a scheduling problem. Unlike search-based FPGA routing, scheduling algorithms

typically can be performed quickly and have runtimes largely proportional to circuit combinational depth.

3. The global system clock period is fixed by the architecture of the device, not by individual designs.

Specialized logic processors have other potential benefits. Specialized circuitry for signal probing and coverification transactions do not have to be fashioned out of generic FPGA logic, but rather can be customized to limit silicon overhead and optimize speed.

FPGA-based emulators do have some advantages. In some cases, they may provide more parallelism for certain designs that have shallow combinational depth. Rather than multiplexing logic resources, FPGAs can perform all logic operations simultaneously. The use of specialized logic processors in emulation introduces additional overhead for the emulation system provider. Because FPGAs typically use the newest silicon fabrication processes, specialized logic processors are likely to be at least one silicon generation behind the state of the art. Additionally, mapping tools for the logic processors must be developed and maintained by the emulation company rather than by the FPGA vendor. Recent trends indicate that despite these issues, the benefits of orders of magnitude faster compile time are driving emulation vendors in the direction of special-purpose logic processors.

Several developments in the design of FPGAs may swing this trend back in their favor. Recent FPGAs provide high-speed I/Os such as low-voltage differential signaling (LVDS) that support rapid I/O multiplexing. Additionally, the introduction of fixed cores, such as multipliers and microprocessors, may provide faster mapping and higher performance for emulation once they are integrated in the emulator compilation flow.

30.8 SUMMARY

FPGA-based logic emulation is a distinct example of a commercially successful reconfigurable computing application. A key aspect of its success has been the development of sophisticated software systems that can seamlessly map a large ASIC design to hundreds of FPGAs with minimal or no designer intervention. An important characteristic of most multi-FPGA emulators is the scheduling of both intra-FPGA computation and inter-FPGA communication in concert with a global system clock. The use of scheduling overcomes limited FPGA pin resources and takes advantage of signal dependencies, so that only portions of a design are active at a given time. Contemporary multi-FPGA logic emulators are used as both physical replacements in circuit and as coverification engines to accelerate design simulation. These supporting environments have advanced in recent years to include multiple asynchronous clock domains and support for incremental design changes.

Extended compile times are quickly becoming a dominant issue for FPGA-based emulators, and have motivated the development of fast FPGA compile approaches. Although emulation systems with custom-designed logic processors have been developed, recent FPGA trends and faster compile approaches may spur renewed interest in FPGA-based emulation.

References

[1] A. Agarwal. *VirtualWires: A Technology for Massive Multi-FPGA Systems*, Mentor Graphics Corp., 2002.

[2] J. Babb, R. Tessier, M. Dahl, S. Hanano, D. Hoki, A. Agarwal. Logic emulation with virtual wires. *IEEE Transactions on Computer-Aided Design of Integrated Circuits and Systems* 16(6), June 1997.

[3] M. Butts. Future directions of dynamically reprogrammable systems. *IEEE Custom Integrated Circuits Conference*, May 1995.

[4] C. Chang, K. Kuusilinna, B. Richards, R. Broderson. Implementation of BEE: A real-time, large-scale hardware emulation engine. *ACM/SIGDA International Symposium on Field-Programmable Gate Arrays*, February 2003.

[5] S. Hauck, G. Borriello. Logic partition orderings for multi-FPGA systems. *ACM/SIGDA International Symposium on Field-Programmable Gate Arrays*, February 1995.

[6] S. Hauck, G. Borriello. An evaluation of bipartitioning techniques. *IEEE Transactions on Computer-Aided Design of Integrated Circuits and Systems* 16(8), August 1997.

[7] S. Hauck. The role of FPGAs in reprogrammable systems. *Proceedings of the IEEE* 86(4), April 1998.

[8] S. Hauck, A. Agarwal. *Software Technologies for Reconfigurable Systems*, Technical report, Department of ECE, Northwestern University, 1996.

[9] IKOS Systems. *VirtuaLogic VLE Emulation System Manual*, 2001.

[10] D. Jones, D. Lewis. A time-multiplexed FPGA architecture for logic emulation. *IEEE Custom Integrated Circuits Conference*, May 1995.

[11] H. Krupnova, G. Saucier. FPGA-based emulation: Industrial and custom prototyping solutions. *International Conference on Field-Programmable Logic and Applications*, August 2000.

[12] M. Kudlugi, S. Hassoun, C. Selvidge, D. Pryor. A transaction-based unified simulation/emulation architecture for functional verification. *ACM/IEEE Design Automation Conference*, June 2001.

[13] M. Kudlugi, R. Tessier. Static scheduling and multidomain circuits for fast functional verification. *IEEE Transactions on Computer-Aided Design of Integrated Circuits and Systems* 21(11), November 2002.

[14] J. Kumar. Prototyping the M68060 for concurrent verification. *IEEE Design and Test of Computers* 24(1), January 1997.

[15] I. Kuon, J. Rose. Measuring the gap between FPGAs and ASICs. *International Symposium on Field-Programmable Gate Arrays*, February 2006.

[16] Y. Kwon, C. Kyung. Performance-driven event-based synchronization for multi-FPGA simulation accelerator with event time-multiplexing bus. *IEEE Transactions on Computer-Aided Design of Integrated Circuits and Systems* 24(9), September 2005.

[17] B. Landman, R. Russo. On a pin versus block relationship for partitioning of logic graphs. *IEEE Transactions on Computers* C20(12), December 1971.

[18] C. Lee. An algorithm for path connections and its applications. *IRE Transactions on Electronic Computers* EC-10(2), September 1961.

[19] J. Li, C.-K Cheng. Routability improvement using dynamic interconnect architecture. *IEEE Workshop on FPGA-Based Custom Computing Machines*, April 1995.

[20] J. Marantz. Enhanced visibility and performance in functional verification by reconstruction. *ACM/IEEE Design Automation Conference*, June 1998.

[21] Mentor Graphics Corp. *VirtuaLogic Datasheet*, 2002.

[22] Mentor Graphics Corp. *VStation Datasheet*, 2004.

[23] Mentor Graphics. Emulation products web page: *http://www.mentor.com/emulation*, April 2006.

[24] Quickturn Design Systems. *System Realizer Data Sheet*, 1998.

[25] Quickturn Design Systems. *Mercury Data Sheet*, 1999.

[26] Quickturn Design Systems. *Cobalt Systems User Guide*, 2001.

[27] R. Ramaswamy, R. Tessier. The integration of SystemC and hardware-assisted verification. *International Conference on Field-Programmable Logic and Applications*, September 2002.

[28] K. Roy-Neogi, C. Sechen. Multiple FPGA partitioning with performance optimization. *ACM/SIGDA International Symposium on Field-Programmable Gate Arrays*, February 1995.

[29] M. Santarini. ASIC prototyping: Make versus buy. *EDN*, November 21, 2005.

[30] K. Shahookar, P. Mazumder. VLSI cell placement techniques. *ACM Computing Surveys* 23(1), June 1991.

[31] G. Snider, P. Kuekes, W. Culbertson, R. Carter, A. Berger, R. Amerson. The Teramac configurable compute engine. *International Conference on Field-Programmable Logic and Applications*, August 1995.

[32] H. Su, Y. Lin. A phase assignment method for virtual-wire-based hardware emulation. *IEEE Transactions on Computer-Aided Design of Integrated Circuits and Systems* 16(7), July 1997.

[33] J. S. Swartz, V. Betz, J. Rose. A fast routability-driven router for FPGAs. *ACM/SIGDA International Symposium on Field-Programmable Gate Arrays*, February 1998.

[34] R. Tessier, S. Jana. Incremental compilation for parallel verification systems. *IEEE Transactions on VLSI Systems* 10(5), October 2002.

[35] Tharas Systems. *Tharas Hammer Product Brief*, 2002.

[36] P. Tseng. Reconfigured engines REV simulation. *EE Times*, July 10, 2000.

[37] Xilinx, Inc. *Xilinx Foundation Tools User Guide*, 2002.

CHAPTER 31

THE IMPLICATIONS OF FLOATING POINT FOR FPGAS

Keith D. Underwood, K. Scott Hemmert
Sandia National Laboratories

FPGA-based computing has a long history of accelerating assorted types of computations in integer and fixed-point arithmetic. Until recently, however, applications based on floating-point arithmetic have been a relative rarity. This stems from early work [6, 12, 13] that indicated that IEEE-754 standard [11] floating point was a poor match for field-programmable gate array (FPGA) technology. This led directly to numerous efforts that created libraries using specialized floating-point formats [1, 3, 7], where the width of the exponent and the width of the mantissa could be specified. Unfortunately, many scientific applications require compliance with the IEEE standard. While seemingly an arbitrary requirement, it is driven by several factors. Foremost, some scientific applications have data with high dynamic ranges and high precision requirements. A good example is a typical linear solver that needs high precision to guarantee convergence of the algorithm. Second, application developers rely on the portability of their applications and the reproducibility of their results. Put another way, it is difficult to trust results that differ on every platform that runs them.

Fortunately, recent work indicates that FPGAs are viable competitors in IEEE-compliant floating-point arithmetic [14], and there has been an explosion of interest in mapping floating-point kernels to FPGA platforms [2, 5, 8–10, 15, 17, 18]. However, while FPGAs are now capable of implementing floating-point applications, the use of floating point in FPGAs still requires a great deal of care. This chapter introduces the IEEE floating-point standard and discusses implementations of compliant floating-point units for FPGAs. Section 31.2 contains case studies of three floating-point application kernels and their implementation on FPGAs.

31.1 WHY IS FLOATING POINT DIFFICULT?

Floating-point arithmetic is fundamentally different from typical integer or fixed-point arithmetic. Where integer and fixed-point values are typically stored in 2's

Note: Sandia is a multiprogram laboratory operated by Sandia Corporation, a Lockheed Martin Company, for the United States Department of Energy's National Nuclear Security Administration under contract DE-AC04-94AL85000.

complement, floating-point numbers are typically stored in signed-magnitude format. Floating-point numbers also add an exponent field to control the position of the decimal point in the value. The most widely used floating-point format is the IEEE-754 standard. As an example, the IEEE double-precision floating-point format is shown in Figure 31.1. The mantissa (fraction part) is 52 bits, the exponent is 11 bits, and the sign is a single bit. A simple picture, however, cannot tell the full story of the complexities of the IEEE format.

First, as the figure suggests, the exponent in the IEEE format is maintained in *biased* notation. That is, rather than being in a signed-magnitude or 2's complement format, a *bias* is added to the true exponent to store it. For double precision, the bias is 1023 (approximately half the range). This means that an exponent of -1022 is stored as a 1. The second complication in the format is the use of an *implied 1*. An implied 1 means that the stored number is maintained in a normalized format such that there is a 1 immediately to the left of the decimal and the decimal is immediately to the left of the stored value. This allows the format to have an extra bit of precision without having to store it. Thus, the value can be extracted as shown in equation 31.1.

$$(-1)^S \times 2^{exp-bias} \times 1.mantissa \tag{31.1}$$

The format, as discussed so far, would have a major shortcoming. The number 0 would be impossible to represent. Since humanity has had the use of 0 for a few millennia now, the format inventors thought it best to include it by reserving a special value. They also saw fit to include representations for ∞, $-\infty$, and not-a-number (NaN), which is used as the result of meaningless operations (e.g., $\infty \times 0$). The reserved special values are summarized in Table 31.1.

As the table implies, both positive and negative 0 are possible (0 and 1 for the sign bit, respectively) as are positive and negative infinity. Several values require that the maximum possible value be loaded into the exponent field (i.e., all bits are set to 1 in the field). Finally, there is a set of values known as denormals.

S	exp (+1023)	Mantissa
1	11	52

FIGURE 31.1 ■ IEEE double-precision floating-point format.

TABLE 31.1 ■ Special values in the IEEE-754 format

Special value	Sign	Exponent	Mantissa
Zero	0/1	0	0
∞	0	MAX	0
$-\infty$	1	MAX	0
NaN	0/1	MAX	nonzero
Denormal	0/1	0	nonzero

Denormals are a special form of IEEE floating-point numbers that provide a small amount of extra precision as the result of an operation approaches underflow. Unlike most IEEE floating-point numbers, they do not include the implied 1. Instead, they have an exponent of 0, keep the decimal immediately to the left of the stored value, and allow the first 1 to fall anywhere in the stored value. Denormals are particularly useful for code such as: if (x != y) z = 1/ (x - y). This code should never cause an exception, but without denormal support it can easily cause a divide by 0 when *x* and *y* are small enough and close enough that the format cannot represent the difference. Floating-point hardware within a microprocessor typically implements denormals with an exception that then computes the value via software. However, in an FPGA-based implementation, to support full IEEE floating point we must generally add denormal support into the hardware itself. Thus, for denormal numbers, the value is extracted as in equation 31.2.

$$(-1)^S \times 2^{exp-bias} \times 0.mantissa \qquad (31.2)$$

31.1.1 General Implementation Considerations

To produce the smallest, fastest circuits, it is necessary to efficiently use the structure of the FPGA. This comes up in two areas: (1) It is necessary to fully utilize every lookup table (LUT), whenever possible and (2) it is advantageous to provide an optimized layout for each unit. The floating-point units presented here have been written using JHDL—a structural design tool that provides a clean mechanism for mapping and relationally placing logic.

The units were optimized by identifying opportunities to combine logic into the LUT architecture of the FPGA. This can be challenging, particularly for operations that use the carry-chain logic. However, the special values in the IEEE format make it vital that carry-chain and other logic be mixed. For example, there are many instances where the output of the exponent logic is either the result of an arithmetic operation or a constant. For FPGA architectures, such as the Xilinx Virtex family, it is possible to map the arithmetic operation and the constant generation into the same LUT (along with its associated carry logic).

Take, for example, the passAddOrConstant circuit. It has four possible outputs: $a+b$, a, $c0$, or $c1$, where a and b are variables and $c0$ and $c1$ are constants. The inputs to the circuit are a, b, s, and c_n. When $c\_n = 0$, the output is one of the two constants, which is selected by the s input. Otherwise, the result is $a+b$ when $s = 1$ and a when $s = 0$. The logic used for each bit is shown in Figure 31.2(a). The circuit is only possible because of the mult_and added in the Virtex family of FPGAs. mult_and was originally intended for use in multipliers built from logic, but it enables many other useful optimizations. The same basic logic can also create a passSubOrConstant, and if the AND gate before the arithmetic operation is left off, the circuit is simply an addOrConstant or subOrConstant. These circuits are used to reduce the amount of logic and the logic delay required to compute the exponents. The JHDL code used to generate each bit of this circuit is shown in Figure 31.2(b). Note that all the logic is

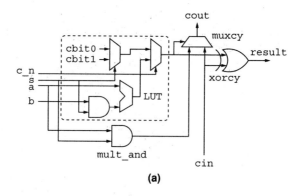

(a)

```
// Produce the constant bit. The Xilinx tools believe
// that gnd and vcc are inputs to the LUT, so we can't
// use them. Instead, use c_n, which will be 0
// when the constant is selected.
Wire cbit0 = ((c0 >> i) & 1) == 1 ? not(c_n) : c_n;
Wire cbit1 = ((c1 >> i) & 1) == 1 ? not(c_n) : c_n;
Wire constant_result = mux(cbit0,cbit1,s);

// Generate the sum bit.
Wire sum = mux(constant_result,
          xor(a.gw(i),and(s,b.gw(i))),c_n);

// Map all the above logic in a single LUT
Cell x = map(c_n,s,a.gw(i),b.gw(i),s_partial);
place(x,0,virtex ? maxrow - i/2 : i/2);

Wire mult_and_out = wire(1,"mult_and_out" +i);
x = new mult_and(this,c_n,a.gw(i),mult_and_out);
place(x,0,virtex ? maxrow - i/2 : i/2);

x = new muxcy(this,mult_and_out,cin,s_partial,cout);
place(x,0,i/2);

x = new xorcy(this,s_partial, cin, output.gw(i));
place(x,0,i/2);
```
(b)

FIGURE 31.2 ■ Logic (a) and JHDL code (b) for the i th bit of the passAddOrConstant.

first mapped into LUTs using the map function, then relationally placed, using the place function. The same place function is used to relationally place the lower-level blocks at each level of hierarchy. The overall unit is placed into a rectangular area so that it can be easily tiled in a design (see the descriptions of the adder and multiplier in Sections 31.1.2 and 31.1.3).

In addition to concerns about efficiently using the LUT and providing good placement directives, there are concerns about where to pipeline the units. The major concern that largely determined the pipelining of the units presented here involves the carry-chain logic. In the Virtex family, the times to initalize and finalize the carry chain are large relative to the per-bit propagation time on the carry chain. Thus, it is necessary to avoid having cascaded carry chains in the same stage. In most cases, this constraint determines the stage mapping.

31.1.2 Adder Implementation

The most noticeable difference between integer operations and floating-point operations is in the implementation of the adder. A 64-bit registered integer adder requires 64 4-LUTs, 64 flip-flops, and the associated carry-chain logic. It can be packed into 32 *slices* in a Xilinx Virtex-4[1] or similar family. In stark contrast, a 64-bit floating-point adder requires hundreds of 4-LUTs, hundreds of flip-flops, and nearly 700 *slices*. The core of the differences can be seen in Figure 31.3(a).

The fundamental problem is that two numbers of the form

$$(-1)^{S0} \times 2^{exp0-bias} \times 1.mantissa0 \tag{31.3}$$

and

$$(-1)^{S1} \times 2^{exp1-bias} \times 1.mantissa1 \tag{31.4}$$

must be added together. The signs can be the same or different, so the actual operation may be an addition or a subtraction. Worse, the exponents can differ (dramatically), so the two mantissas must be aligned before the operation can proceed. When the two are combined (different signs and different exponents), it becomes necessary to determine which number is larger so that they are subtracted in the right order. If the exponents are the same but the signs are different, the result can yield a very small mantissa, which must be normalized (i.e., the leftmost one is moved to the leftmost position) before it can be stored.

Looking again at Figure 31.3(a), we can see the impact of the extra format. Each horizontal dashed line represents a register, and the vertical dashed line separates the exponent path from the mantissa path. Note that the first two stages are spent inspecting and preparing the numbers and determining whether either of the inputs is one of the special values. The third and fourth stages are needed to align the mantissas, and it is not until the fifth stage that the actual *operation* occurs. In the exponent path, stages six through nine clean up the exponent to handle a variety of exception conditions. The sixth and seventh mantissa stages have two parallel paths: one for rounding the result and one for computing the shift value if the result must be renormalized. The last two stages are used to renormalize the result (if needed).

Figure 31.3(b) shows the approximate layout of the logic used in an implementation of the floating-point adder. For the adder implementation, it is possible to place all pipelining registers in the same slices as the logic, though some registers are placed in slices with unrelated logic. Of the total area, approximately 39 percent is used to align the mantissas prior to the actual add or subtract operation; this area includes right-shift logic and swap logic. These operations would be required for any floating-point format; however, the left-shift on the backend is only required because of the existence of the implicit 1 in the format. This case arises during a loss of precision when two numbers with

---

[1] A slice is two 4-LUTs, two flip-flops, and the associated carry-chain logic in this generation.

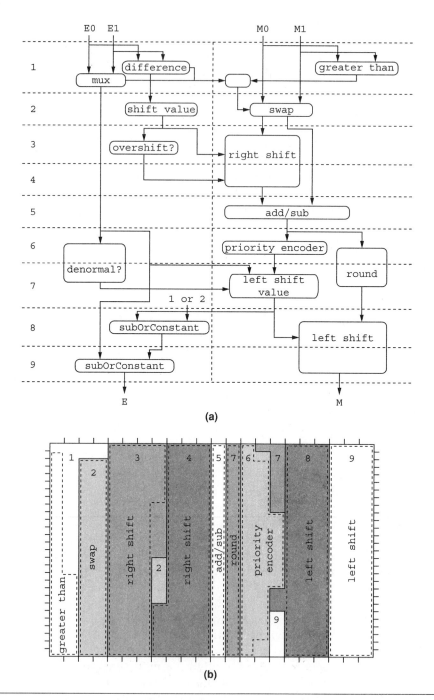

FIGURE 31.3 ■ Adder block (a) and adder layout (b) diagrams.

identical, or very close, exponents are subtracted and require normalization. The normalization logic, including a priority encoder to locate the first 1, uses another 39 percent of the logic. For comparison, the actual add and round logic consumes only 9 percent of the area.

31.1.3 Multiplier Implementation

The relationship between a floating-point multiplication and a fixed-point multiplication is a little more unusual. A fixed-point multiplier grows with the square of the width of the input. At the core of a floating-point multiplier is a fixed-point multiplier that multiplies the mantissas. Since the mantissa is significantly narrower than the floating-point number, a 64-bit fixed-point multiplier actually has a much larger core operation than a 64-bit floating-point multiplier because the floating-point multiplier only has to multiply two 53-bit mantissas. It does, however, have a lot of other work to do that more than makes up for the difference.

Floating-point multiplication starts with two numbers:

$$(-1)^{S0} \times 2^{exp0-bias} \times 1.mantissa0 \tag{31.5}$$

and

$$(-1)^{S1} \times 2^{exp1-bias} \times 1.mantissa1 \tag{31.6}$$

that produce the result:

$$(-1)^{(S0 \oplus S1)} \times 2^{(exp0-bias)+(exp1-bias)} \times 1.mantissa0 \times 1.mantissa1 \tag{31.7}$$

Conceptually, the dataflow shown in Figure 31.4(a) is quite simple. The first three stages unpack the IEEE format looking for special cases and preparing a possible denormal mantissa for the multiplier core. Stages F4 through F6 operate concurrently with the multiplier core and compute the resulting exponent and determine whether the result is denormal. The four backend stages provide shifting for creating denormal numbers, rounding, and normalization, which includes adjusting the exponent when required.

Figure 31.4(b) gives the approximate layout of the logic for the front- and backends of the multiplier. The multiplier core (not shown in the figure) uses nine 17×17 multiplier blocks plus additional logic to sum the partial products to create a 53×53 multiplier core. The logic used in the core is about 40 percent of the total multiplier logic. Unlike the adder, it is not possible to place all of the required pipelining registers in slices used by the logic. The black regions in Figure 31.4(b) are either unused or used by pipelining registers.

The logic required to support the IEEE format is nontrivial. Support for denormals consumes 40 percent of the multiplier area and includes logic to gather information about the mantissa, swap the mantissa, and shift the mantissa. Thus, supporting denormals requires approximately the same amount of logic resources as the multiplier core. An additional 7 percent of the area is used for rounding and normalization to put the number back into the IEEE format.

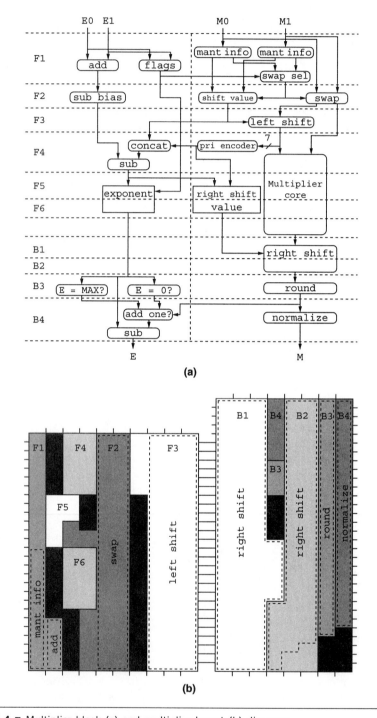

FIGURE 31.4 ■ Multiplier block (a) and multiplier layout (b) diagrams.

31.2 FLOATING-POINT APPLICATION CASE STUDIES

Floating-point applications that are appropriate to map to FPGAs differ dramatically from integer applications that are typically mapped to FPGAs. The differences can be understood by realizing that a single floating-point operation can easily consist of 30 integer operations; thus, where a 2005-era FPGA can easily implement 1000 integer operations, it is more likely that it can only implement 32 double-precision floating-point operations. Furthermore, floating-point operations are much higher latency than corresponding integer operations, which significantly affects designs.

This section considers three kernel operations implemented with double-precision floating point to demonstrate three important considerations when using floating point operations on FPGAs. The first operation is matrix multiply, which demonstrates the FPGA's ability to exploit high degrees of parallelism and to programmably manage local storage to significantly reduce the amount of external RAM bandwidth needed. The second kernel is a vector dot product, which highlights the ability of the FPGA to provide large amounts of RAM bandwidth; plus it highlights limitations introduced by the high latency of the floating-point units. The third kernel is the fast Fourier transform (FFT), which can find similar advantages in mitigating the need for memory bandwidth as the matrix multiply, but has similar limitations from the latency of the floating-point units to the dot product.

31.2.1 Matrix Multiply

The standard matrix multiply (the DGEMM BLAS routine) is defined as:

$$\mathbf{C}_{ij}+ = \sum_{k=0}^{N-1} \mathbf{A}_{ik}\mathbf{B}_{kj} \tag{31.8}$$

The operation multiplies two matrices and adds it to a third (in place). Conceptually, this means performing the dot product of a single row of A with a single column of B and adding the result to a single point of C. Each dot product is completely independent, which means there are N^2 independent dot products. In practice, neither microprocessors nor FPGAs implement it this way because of the nature of modern memory hierarchies. In all modern systems (including FPGAs), main memory is "far away" and there is one or more caches significantly "closer."

The primary performance characteristic of matrix multiply is that it does $O(N^3)$ operations on $O(N^2)$ data. Thus, for every data item loaded from memory, it should be hypothetically possible to do $O(N)$ operations. Performing matrix multiplication as a series of independent dot products would throw away this advantage; thus, all matrix multiply implementations attempt to exploit some form of locality within the cache structure.

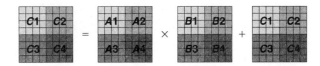

FIGURE 31.5 ▪ Block decomposition of a matrix multiply.

FPGA implementation

To understand an FPGA implementation of matrix multiply, it helps to first understand how it is done on a microprocessor. To exploit (or rather compensate for) the nature of modern memory hierarchies, the typical approach to matrix multiplication on a microprocessor breaks the matrices into smaller $S \times S$ blocks [16]. A given block from each matrix is loaded into the processor, a matrix multiply is performed on the block, and partial results are stored. An example for an 8×8 matrix multiply is shown in Figure 31.5. Each matrix is broken into four regions that are 4×4. A row of these blocks is then multiplied by a column of these blocks to create a 4×4 block of the result; thus, $C1 = A1 * B1 + A2 * B3 + C1$. In the process, the partial result (a 4×4 block) is updated two times (although typically in local storage or cache).

The same approach can be used on FPGAs. After all, FPGAs and microprocessors are similar in that they have a small amount of local memory with high bandwidth and a large amount of external, slower memory. FPGAs differ, however, in that they have a drastically large number of floating-point units that should be kept fully utilized. Whereas microprocessors must supply inputs to two functional units per cycle, FPGAs must supply inputs to 32 functional units (in a 2005 FPGA).

A matrix multiply can be decomposed into a series of multiply–accumulate (MACC) operations that multiply the individual elements of a row with elements of a column and accumulate the result into one element of the final matrix. The MACC unit has a multiplier, an adder, and a feedback path. In an FPGA, 16 MACC units are operating concurrently. Unfortunately, the latency of the adder is very high (10 cycles). This means that we must keep at least 10 concurrent operations (*row × column* operations) in progress at all times to hide the latency of the adder. In a perfect world, each unit could work on a block of the matrix, with the concurrent operations happening on the independent row–column dot product in that block. Unfortunately, this would require far more internal memory than is available in typical FPGAs.

To exploit the parallelism available in FPGAs without exhausting the limited internal memory, we can further decompose the view of the problem. A simple way to view one block-level matrix multiplication is as a collection of S matrix–vector multiplications. As such, significantly more parallelism is obvious. Figure 31.6 shows an FPGA-based implementation that first decomposes the problem into blocks and then distributes portions of the work to multiply the two blocks as matrix–vector multiplications.

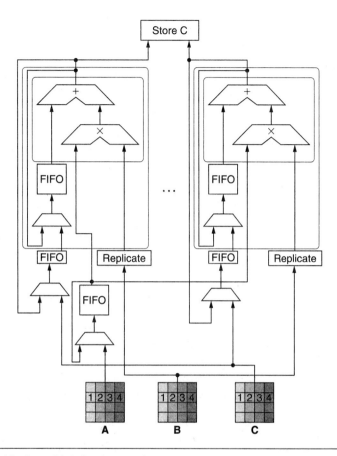

FIGURE 31.6 ■ Matrix multiply implementation.

To perform the full matrix multiplication, each matrix is decomposed into $S \times S$ blocks. In Figure 31.6, S is 4, but in practice, S is typically set large enough to cover the adder's latency (currently 10 cycles). Blocks of **B** are broken into m columns, where m is the number of MACC units (m is assumed to be 4 in the figure); thus, independent columns of a block of **B** go to each MACC unit. All the blocks of **A** are *broadcast* to all MACC units. Thus, in Figure 31.6, one column of block **B** is multplied by all four rows from the **A** block. This requires that four copies (in the general case S copies) of the **B** block be made by the replicate unit. This creates the concurrency needed to cover the latency of the adder.

Matrix **C** is managed similarly. A block of **C** is loaded and distributed in the same *order* as the block of **B**, but there is no need to replicate it. In addition, taking the example from Figure 31.5, two **A** blocks and two **B** blocks are needed for each **C** block. Thus, $A1$, $B1$, and $C1$ are loaded and used to create an intermediate product $C1 - 2$ that is used as the C block when $A2$ and $B2$ are multiplied. Overall, this requires no more than $6S^2$ elements of storage at 8 bytes per element. This includes two copies of each matrix block—one to operate on and one to change it from row-major to column-major order.

Performance

By nature, a matrix multiply requires at least $4N^2$ memory accesses[2] and performs $2N^3$ floating-point operations. This yields $\frac{N}{2}$ floating-point operations for each element retrieved from memory, but it assumes that two matrices (**A** and **B**) can be kept resident in the chip (processor or FPGA) for the entire operation. In the perfect scenario, the maximum sustainable floating-point rate would be

$$FLOPs = \frac{\frac{N}{2} \times BW}{8} \qquad (31.9)$$

where BW is the memory bandwidth in bytes per second, N is the dimension of the matrix, and 8 bytes are required to store a double-precision floating-point number.

While this is unrealistic for all but relatively small matrices, using blocking techniques [16] to manage the local storage makes it possible to sustain a high percentage of peak performance with relatively low memory bandwidth. The result is that the matrices are fetched several times more than would otherwise be necessary. For blocks of dimension S, this yields a factor of $\frac{N}{S}$ increase in accesses to the **A** and **B** matrices, leading to $2N^2 + \frac{2N^3}{S}$ memory accesses. For large matrices, this approaches a floating-point rate of

$$FLOPs = \frac{S \times BW}{8} \qquad (31.10)$$

This is shown in Figure 31.7(a) as MFLOP/s versus MB/s on a log–log graph. Delineations that map memory bandwidth needs to the generation of FPGAs are provided for clarity, based on earlier work [14,15].

A slightly different perspective is presented in Figure 31.7(b) where the total amount of on-chip memory needed to sustain peak performance is graphed. What is notable about these graphs is the relatively small amount of memory and relatively small amount of memory bandwidth needed to sustain peak performance on FPGAs. This stands in stark contrast to modern microprocessors (2005 era) that only sustain 85 to 90 percent of peak performance on a matrix multiply using several times as much on-chip memory and off-chip memory bandwidth. This is a product of the ability of the FPGA to directly manage local storage and to separate data prefetching from computation.

We can also compare performance over time using data from 2004 [see 14,15]. Table 31.2 shows parts used for comparison. The performance of FPGAs gained rapidly on microprocessors during this era, as shown in Figure 31.8.

---

[2] This assumes square matrices and includes retrieving three matrices and storing one matrix.

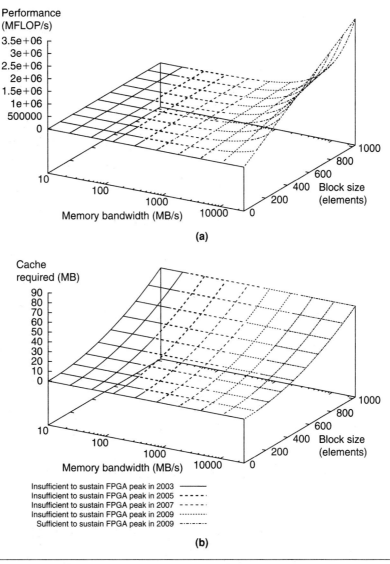

FIGURE 31.7 ■ Maximum achievable performance versus memory bandwidth and block size (a); on-chip memory needed versus memory bandwidth and block size (b).

31.2.2 Dot Product

The standard vector dot product (the `DDOT` BLAS routine) is the sum of the pairwise products of two vectors, or

$$p = \sum_{i=0}^{N-1} \mathbf{x}_i \mathbf{y}_i \tag{31.11}$$

TABLE 31.2 ■ Parts used for performance comparison

Year	FPGA	CPU
1997	XC4085XLA-09	Pentium 266 MHz
1999	Virtex 1000-5	
2000	Virtex-E 3200-7	Athlon 1.2 GHz
2001	Virtex-II 6000-5	
2003	Virtex-II Pro 100-6	Pentium-4 3.2 GHz

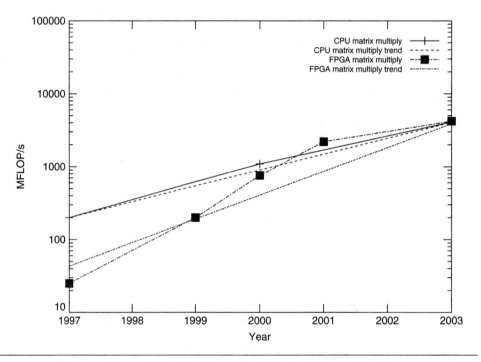

FIGURE 31.8 ■ Matrix multiply performance of FPGAs and microprocessors from 1997–2003.

which requires 2N memory accesses to perform 2N floating-point operations. This means that a double-precision floating-point number (8 bytes) must be fetched from memory for every floating-point operation that will be done. Modern processors are not built with this type of balance between memory bandwidth and floating-point capability. A processor capable of providing five GFLOP/s may only have 6.4 GB/s of memory bandwidth. Streaming problems (like this one) provide FPGAs an opportunity to excel—processors have a fixed-memory bandwidth that is configured based on a balance between the requirements for various markets and the cost of providing that bandwidth. In contrast, each board containing an FPGA can decide how many FPGA pins are used for memory bandwidth, including dedicating almost all available user pins to memory connections.

FPGA implementation

Although the potential for increased memory bandwidth on an FPGA gives it a distinct advantage, it also faces significant challenges imposed by the large number of functional units and the high latency of the units. Like many BLAS routines, DDOT is based on multiply–accumulate operations; however, it differs from many BLAS routines in that it exposes a relatively limited amount of parallelism. Where a DGEMM operation computes N^2 independent results and a DGEMV operation computes N independent results, a DDOT operation produces a single number as the final result. This means than any partial products must be reduced through a long, slow pipeline. The nature of the problem is best realized through a comparison to microprocessors.

Current microprocessors typically have a floating-point pipeline depth of four to six cycles for the functional unit running at 2 GHz or more. Obviously, we would not want every addition to depend on the previous addition, so the microprocessor can easily keep six running sums in progress and then reduce those sums to one result. This leads to several pipeline stalls in the final reduction, but the total time is a small number of nanoseconds. In contrast, FPGAs differ in three dramatic ways:

- The adder pipeline is deeper.
- Multiple MACC units are required to fully utilize high bandwidth memory.
- The clock rate is lower.

A modern FPGA would have tens of functional units with a pipeline depth of 10-cycles running at approximately 300 MHz. Assuming 16 adders with a pipeline depth of 10 cycles means that there must be 160 concurrent summations. This is impossible for short vectors and challenging even for longer vectors. Furthermore, the process of reducing these partial sums to a single result is slow and cumbersome.

To achieve reasonable performance, additional control logic is required inside and outside the multiply–add and MACC units. First, a multiplier bypass multiplexer (labeled MB) is required in the multiply–add (Figure 31.9(b)) to reuse the adder for portions of the final summation. Second, the adder has a 10-cycle latency; thus, the MACC must perform 10 concurrent operations to keep the adder pipeline filled. This requires a second feedback path (with associated control) through the FP multiplexer in the MACC (Figure 31.9(c)) to sum the 10 results. The added logic is shown with dashed lines in Figure 31.9(b) and (c).

Performance

If we work from the memory bandwidth as the typical limiting factor, the maximum sustainable floating-point rate is

$$FLOPs = \frac{BW}{8} \tag{31.12}$$

where BW is the memory bandwidth in bytes per second and 8 bytes are required to store a floating-point number. This is graphed in Figure 31.10(a)

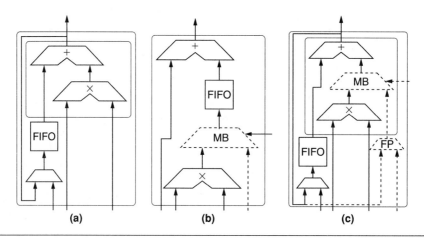

FIGURE 31.9 ▪ A standard multiply–accumulate (a); a modified multiply–add for the dot product (b); a modified multiply–accumulate for the dot product (c).

on a log–log graph. Like Figure 31.8, Figure 31.10(b) compares performance projections for both FPGAs and microprocessors [14, 15]. In this case, however, the FPGA shows a much more dramatic advantage over a microprocessor. This is because large FPGAs provide sufficient I/O resources to obtain much higher memory bandwidths than commodity microprocessors offer. Since this is a memory bandwidth-limited problem, the platform with the most memory bandwidth wins.

The other notable feature of Figure 31.10(b) is that it is somewhat more crowded than the matrix–multiply comparison. This is because FPGAs face a second challenge in implementing the dot product operation: the latency of the floating-point unit. Thus, the size of the vector has a much greater impact on sustained performance on the FPGA than the microprocessor. The top FPGA line represents a scenario whereby the FPGA achieves 90 percent of its peak performance, but this requires a nearly 6000-element vector.[3] The second FPGA line shows the FPGA achieving 50 percent of peak performance by using an 800-element vector. Despite this hefty penalty, the FPGA still has a remarkable advantage (4× in 2003) over the microprocessor.

31.2.3   Fast Fourier Transform

The fast Fourier transform (FFT) is a reduced-complexity implementation of the discrete Fourier transform (DFT), which takes as input N complex numbers and returns as output N complex numbers where each of the outputs is determined by the following equation:

---

[3] Earlier work by Underwood and Hemmert [15] specified a 7500-element vector, but the floating-point unit latency has been optimized since then.

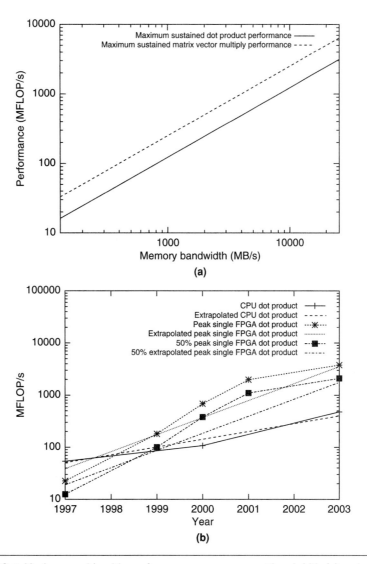

FIGURE 31.10 ■ Maximum achievable performance versus memory bandwidth (a) and dot product performance on FPGAs and microprocessors from 1997–2003 (b).

$$Y[j] = \sum_{k=0}^{N-1} X[k] W_N^{jk} \tag{31.13}$$

where $W_N^{jk} = e^{\frac{-i2\pi jk}{N}}$.

The FFT exploits symmetries in the DFT and is implemented in stages, where each stage combines r items to create r outputs. The value r is known as the *radix*. For the implementation discussed here, $r = 2$ (radix-2). For the radix-2

FFT, each stage operates pairwise on the data, although there are different for-mulations of the algorithm that determine how the data are combined. These operations are commonly referred to as *butterflies* and in the formulation used in this example, each pairwise operation is identical and consists of one complex multiply and two complex adds. This is shown graphically in Figure 31.11(a).

Even after selecting the formulation that gives the structure of the butterfly, there is some flexibility in the structure of the stages. The basic stage structures are shown in Figure 31.12. Both structures require data reordering, either on

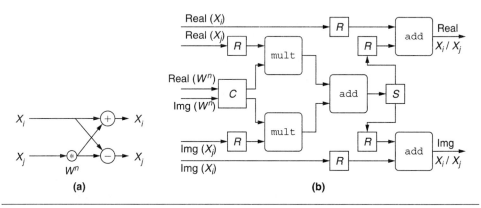

FIGURE 31.11 ▪ Basic butterfly operation (a) and basic butterfly datapath (b). The component S is a switch that directs inputs to alternate outputs. The components marked as R replicate the input once and C is a crossover to facilitate the complex multiply.

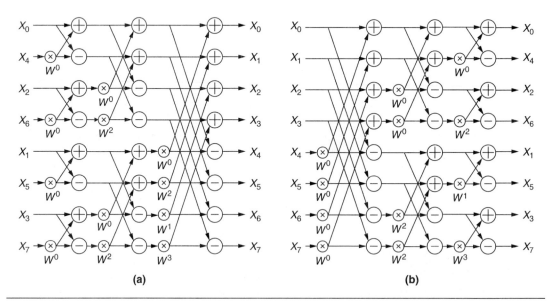

FIGURE 31.12 ▪ Variations of the 8-point, radix-2 FFTs with reordered inputs (a) and reordered outputs (b).

the frontend or backend, and produce the identical set of computations (though in different orders). This example uses the ordering shown in Figure 31.12(b), because this structure provides an increasing number of independent datasets as the computation progresses. This approach is easier for implementations that use units in parallel to process data within a single stage since all interunit communication can reside at the front of the pipeline.

FPGA implementation
The butterfly computation requires four multiplications and six additions to implement one complex multiply and two complex adds. The hardware presented here uses two double-precision multiplies and three double-precision adds (see Figure 31.11(b)). Each floating-point unit is used twice for each set of inputs, which results in an average throughput of one data item per clock cycle. Although it is possible to design a datapath that accepts two data items per clock cycle, this design was chosen because it matches the available bandwidth of internal RAM blocks in the target architecture and because it provides the greatest flexibility when scaling the parallelism of the final implementation.

Parallelism in the FFT computation can be exploited in two ways: (1) pipelined units, or parallelism in the stages (S), and (2) parallel units, or parallelism (P) within a stage. Three architectures, which exploit the two types of parallelism to differing degrees, are explored.

Parallel architecture   The *parallel implementation* exploits only parallelism within a stage (P). This is shown in Figure 31.13(a). In this implementation, data are read from external memory, processed iteratively, and written back to external memory. Each of the butterfly units operates on a subset of the data and is able to work independently of the other units for a large part of the computation (the datasets are completely independent after $log_2(P)$ stages).

The advantages of this architecture are that the utilization of the units is high because the pipeline depth is short. The parallel version can also take advantage of higher-memory bandwidths. The disadvantages of this architecture as implemented are that it requires a large amount of internal memory and it requires a parallelism that is a power of 2. This second restriction is important because it can limit the number of butterfly units that can be used. For example, if six butterfly units fit in an FPGA, the parallel architecture is still only able to use four.

Pipelined architecture   At the other extreme, one butterfly unit can be dedicated to each of the stages of the FFT in a pipelined fashion, as illustrated in Figure 31.13(c). Data is read from memory and passed through a series of butterfly units before being written back to memory. Data delays and permutations are needed between each of the stages and between the pipelined FFT unit and DRAM memory. When the number of stages, S, that can be implemented in the FPGA is less than the number of stages needed by the FFT ($log_2(N)$), then $\frac{log_2(N)}{S}$ passes to memory are needed, with the final pass using a subset, R, of the stages. For each pass to memory, data must be read and written in a particular permutation to optimize the delay and storage requirements in the pipeline.

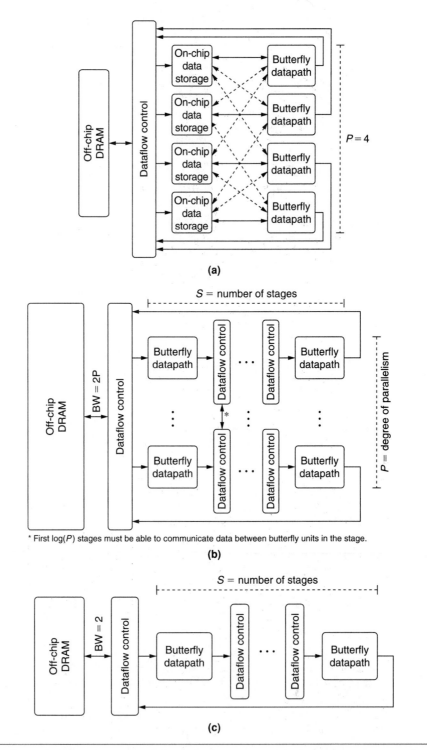

FIGURE 31.13 ■ Three architectures: (a) parallel, (b) parallel–pipelined, and (c) pipelined for exploiting parallelism in the FFT—from using all parallelism within a single stage to using all parallelism in the stages.

The pipelined architecture works well when streaming a large number of small FFTs. This is because the architecture gets good performance with minimal memory bandwidth requirements. Another benefit of this architecture is that it can take advantage of parallelism at a finer granularity than the parallel version (i.e., it can use a nonpower of 2 number of processors). However, there are some major disadvantages to this architecture. First, for single FFTs, the unit utilization is low because of the depth of the overall pipeline. Second, it is unable to take advantage of higher-memory bandwidth. Last, the buffer space required between stages for data reordering grow as 2^S, where S is the number of stages in the circuit. For a large number of stages, the memory required for buffering can easily exceed available on-chip memory.

Parallel–pipelined architecture   Figure 31.13(b) is a cross between the two previous architectures. Data moves from external memory, through a set of P parallel pipelines—each with S stages—and back to external memory. The first $log_2(P)$ stages must have additional data exchange circuits (for the first pass through the pipeline) because these stages have data dependencies between the pipelines. This approach leverages the ability of the pipelined architecture to reduce bandwidth demands and the ability of the parallel architecture to tolerate shorter input vectors (as well as a wider variety of vector lengths) than the pure pipelined approach. In contrast, the parallel–pipelined hybrid has a higher bandwidth demand than the purely pipelined approach and less tolerance of short vectors than the parallel approach.

Performance

In evaluating the performance of the FFT, the floating-point operation count that is typically used is $5Nlog_2(N)$; there are $log_2(N)$ stages that each contain $5N$ computations (four multiplies and six additions for each pair of data). To determine performance, it is necessary to know how long it will take the FPGA to compute the FFT. For the parallel version, the number of cycles required to complete the FFT is given by the following equation:

$$T = \frac{32N}{BW} + BL + (\frac{N}{P} + BL)(log_2(N) - 2) \qquad (31.14)$$

The first term of equation 31.14 is the time to read and then write N items based on the memory bandwidth, BW, in bytes per cycle. The usable bandwidth is limited to the number of units, P. The second term is the latency of passing through the butterfly units during the read from memory. The third term is the time to perform the iterations—using P butterfly units of latency BL for $log_2(N) - 2$ iterations, assuming that the first and last iterations are performed as part of reading and writing the data.

The pipelined and parallel–pipelined architectures share the same equation for determining the number of clock cycles required to complete the operation. The only difference is that the pipelined architecture is limited to a bandwidth (*BW*) of 2. The number of cycles to compute the FFT for these architectures is

$$T = P(S) \times \left\lfloor \frac{log_2(N)}{S} \right\rfloor + P(R) \tag{31.15}$$

$$P(J) = BL \times J + I(J) + \frac{2N}{BW} + (B-1) \times 2^J \tag{31.16}$$

$$I(K) = \sum_{i=0}^{K-1} B \times 2^i \approx B \times 2^K \tag{31.17}$$

$$R = log_2(N) \bmod S \tag{31.18}$$

Each pass, $P(J)$, through J butterfly stages (each having a latency of *BL*) requires the time shown in equation 31.16.

Data dependencies between the stages introduce a delay that doubles at each stage, and create a total interstage delay given by $I(K)$. Using standard DRAM memories introduces a penalty associated with the burst length (*B*) required to maintain full memory bandwidth to both the interstage delay and a backend reordering time. The time to retrieve the data from memory and write them back is defined by $\frac{2N}{BW}$. The final term represents the final pass through a subset of the stages, *R*, with the corresponding delays.

The preceding equations point to the fact that the *best* implementation for the FFT depends on many factors: memory bandwidth, size of the FFT, and size of the FPGA. The performance (in FLOPs per cycle) for a single FFT of the different FPGA architectures on a Xilinx Virtex-II Pro (a late 2005 part) are shown in Figure 31.14(a). For single short vectors, the parallel architecture provides the best performance. This is because of the high utilization of the floating-point units. For longer FFTs, all three units provide good performance, though the pipelined version requires less external memory bandwidth. Figure 31.14(b) shows that the FPGA implementations (running at 160 MHz) compare favorably to microprocessors for large FFTs.

31.3 SUMMARY

Implementing floating-point arithmetic on FPGAs requires significant effort. Supporting the IEEE-754 standard poses particularly unique challenges, but much of the effort is expended in coping with the interaction between exponent logic and mantissa logic. Great care is required to minimize the latency through the unit without significantly decreasing clock rate by having two dependent carry chains in a single pipeline stage. Even with effort, floating-point operations are significantly bigger and have significantly deeper pipelines than their fixed-point counterparts. This adds additional challenges to the design of applications.

Although FPGAs can now deliver impressive performance on double-precision floating-point operations, it requires a very different mind-set from working with fixed-point arithmetic. Increased operation latency leads to a need to find more parallelism to exploit in paths with the cyclic data dependencies typical of

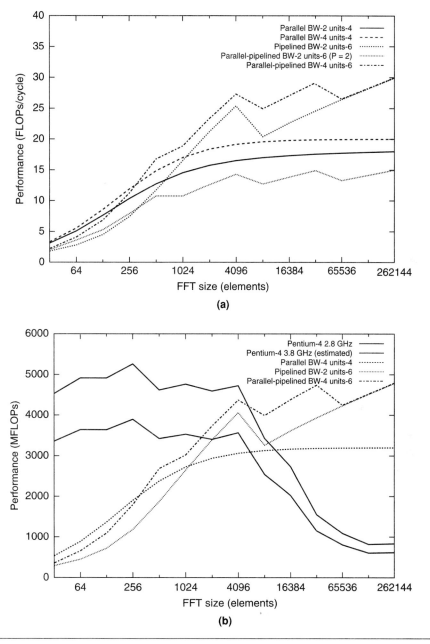

FIGURE 31.14 ■ A comparison of performance for different FFT architectures in FLOPs per cycle (a) and a comparison of FFT implementation on FPGAs and CPUs (b).

iterative solutions. Simultaneously, the increased size of a single operation reduces the portion of a given dataflow graph that can be implemented directly and pushes a designer toward more iterative solutions. The dot product is an excellent example because it is forced to reuse adders to compute a summation that would typically be done as a tree of adders in a fixed-point solution. The result is that only longer vectors make sense.[4]

Even simple feedforward paths incur a penalty from the high latency of the floating-point units. The FFT provides an example whereby the latency of a single butterfly path can approach the length of a short vector. Thus, if the FFT implementation in an FPGA is not used for a long FFT or a series of short FFTs, it cannot offer competitive performance.

There are, however, floating-point kernels that offer abundant parallelism for the FPGAs to exploit. Matrix–multiply (DGEMM), for example, is an N^3 operation with minimal data dependencies. Similar things can be said about LU solvers, which form the basis of the traditional Linpack benchmark [4]. Three-dimensional FFTs are another example in which hundreds of one-dimensional FFTs can be carried out simultaneously.

References

[1] P. Belanovic, M. Leeser. A library of parameterized floating-point modules and their use. *Proceedings of the International Conference on Field-Programmable Logic and Applications*, 2002.

[2] M. deLorimier, A. DeHon. Floating point sparse matrix-vector multiply for FPGAs. *Proceedings of the ACM International Symposium on Field-Programmable Gate Arrays*, February 2005.

[3] J. Dido, N. Geraudie, L. Loiseau, O. Payeur, Y. Savaria, D. Poirier. A flexible floating-point format for optimizing data-paths and operators in FPGA based DSPs. *Proceedings of the ACM International Symposium on Field-Programmable Gate Arrays*, February 2002.

[4] J. J. Dongarra. The linpack benchmark: An explanation. *First International Conference on Supercomputing*, June 1987.

[5] Y. Dou, S. Vassiliadis, G. Kuzmanov, G. Gaydadjiev. 64-bit floating-point FPGA matrix multiplication. *Proceedings of the ACM International Symposium on Field-Programmable Gate Arrays*, February 2005.

[6] B. Fagin, C. Renard. Field-programmable gate arrays and floating point arithmetic. *IEEE Transactions on VLSI* 2(3), 1994.

[7] A. A. Gaar, W. Luk, P. Y. Cheung, N. Shirazi, J. Hwang. Automating customisation of floating-point designs. *Proceedings of the International Conference on Field-Programmable Logic and Applications*, 2002.

[8] G. Govindu, S. Choi, V. K. Prasanna, V. Daga, S. Gangadharpalli, V. Sridhar. A high-performance and energy-efficient architecture for floating-point based LU decomposition on FPGAs. *Proceedings of the 11th Reconfigurable Architectures Workshop (RAW)*, April 2004.

[9] G. Govindu, L. Zhuo, S. Choi, P. Gundala, V. K. Prasanna. Area and power performance analysis of a floating-point based application on FPGAs. *Proceedings of the Seventh Annual Workshop on High-Performance Embedded Computing*, September 2003.

[10] K. S. Hemmert, K. D. Underwood. An analysis of the double-precision floating-point FFT on FPGAs. *Proceedings of the IEEE Symposium on Field-Programmable Custom Computing Machines*, April 2005.

---

[4] A long series of short vectors can also be made to work using an appropriate architecture.

[11] IEEE Standards Board. *IEEE Standard for Binary Floating-Point Arithmetic*. Technical Report ANSI/IEEE Std. 754-1985, The Institute of Electrical and Electronics Engineers, 1985.

[12] L. Louca, T. A. Cook, W. H. Johnson. Implementation of IEEE single precision floating point addition and multiplication on FPGAs. *Proceedings of the IEEE Symposium on FPGAs for Custom Computing Machines*, 1996.

[13] N. Shirazi, A. Walters, P. Athanas. Quantitative analysis of floating-point arithmetic on FPGA based custom computing machines. *Proceedings of the IEEE Symposium on FPGAs for Custom Computing Machines*, 1995.

[14] K. D. Underwood. FPGAs vs. CPUs: Trends in peak floating-point performance. *Proceedings of the ACM International Symposium on Field-Programmable Gate Arrays*, February 2004.

[15] K. D. Underwood, K. S. Hemmert. Closing the gap: CPU and FPGA trends in sustainable floating-point BLAS performance. *Proceedings of the IEEE Symposium on Field-Programmable Custom Computing Machines*, April 2004.

[16] R. C. Whaley, A. Petitet, J. J. Dongarra. Automated empirical optimizations of software and the ATLAS project. *Parallel Computing* 27(1–2), 2001.

[17] L. Zhuo, V. K. Prasanna. Scalable and modular algorithms for floating-point matrix multiplication on FPGAs. *18th International Parallel and Distributed Processing Symposium*, April 2004.

[18] L. Zhuo, V. K. Prasanna. Sparse matrix–vector multiplication on FPGAs. *Proceedings of the ACM International Symposium on Field-Programmable Gate Arrays*, February 2005.

CHAPTER 32

FINITE DIFFERENCE TIME DOMAIN: A CASE STUDY USING FPGAS

Wang Chen, Miriam Leeser
Department of Electrical and Computer Engineering
Northeastern University

This chapter presents a reconfigurable hardware accelerator that implements the FDTD method. We first present background, including applications of the FDTD method. We then provide analysis and design details of the FPGA accelerator for FDTD.

32.1 THE FDTD METHOD

Modeling electromagnetic behavior has become a requirement for key technologies such as cellular phones, mobile computing, lasers, and photonic circuits. The finite-difference time-domain (FDTD) method, which provides a direct, time domain solution to Maxwell's equations in differential form with relatively good accuracy and flexibility, has become a powerful method for solving a wide variety of electromagnetic problems [1–3]. The main drawback to FDTD is its high computational complexity.

32.1.1 Background

The discovery of Maxwell's equations was one of the outstanding achievements of nineteenth-century science. The equations give a unified and complete theory for understanding electromagnetic (EM) wave phenomena. Solving Maxwell's equations is an important method for investigating the propagation, radiation, and scattering of EM waves.

The FDTD method, first introduced by Yee in 1966 [4], is a way to solve Maxwell's equations. The differential form of these equations and constitutive relations can be written as follows:

$$\nabla \times \vec{E} = -\frac{\partial \vec{B}}{\partial t} - \sigma_m \vec{H} - \vec{M} \tag{32.1}$$

$$\nabla \times \vec{H} = \frac{\partial \vec{D}}{\partial t} + \sigma_e \vec{E} + \vec{J} \tag{32.2}$$

$$\nabla \cdot \vec{D} = \rho_e; \quad \nabla \cdot \vec{B} = \rho_m \tag{32.3}$$

$$\vec{D} = \epsilon\vec{E}; \quad \vec{B} = \mu\vec{H} \tag{32.4}$$

In equations 32.1 through 32.4, the following symbols are used:

$\vec{E}$: electric field $\vec{H}$: magnetic field

$\vec{D}$: electric flux density $\vec{B}$: magnetic flux density

$\vec{J}$: electric current density $\vec{M}$: equivalent magnetic current density

ϵ: electrical permittivity μ: magnetic permeability

σ_e: electric conductivity σ_m: equivalent magnetic conductivity

First, the FDTD method replaces $\vec{D}$ and $\vec{B}$ in equations 32.1 and 32.2 with $\vec{E}$ and $\vec{H}$ according to the constitutive relations in equation 32.4, which yields Maxwell's curl equation.

$$\mu\frac{\partial \vec{H}}{\partial t} = -\nabla \times \vec{E} - \sigma_m\vec{H} - \vec{M}; \quad \epsilon\frac{\partial \vec{E}}{\partial t} = \nabla \times \vec{H} - \sigma_e\vec{E} - \vec{J} \tag{32.5}$$

All of the curl operators are then written in differential form and replaced by partial derivative operators, as shown in equation 32.6, with the $\vec{E}$ and $\vec{H}$ vectors separated into three vectors in three dimensions (i.e., $\vec{E}$ is separated into E_x, E_y, E_z, and $\vec{H}$ is separated into H_x, H_y, H_z):

$$curl\vec{F} = \nabla \times \vec{F} = \hat{x}(\frac{\partial F_z}{\partial y} - \frac{\partial F_y}{\partial z}) + \hat{y}(\frac{\partial F_x}{\partial z} - \frac{\partial F_z}{\partial x}) + \hat{z}(\frac{\partial F_y}{\partial x} - \frac{\partial F_x}{\partial y}) \tag{32.6}$$

We then can rewrite Maxwell's curl equations into six equations in differential form in rectangular coordinates.

$$\mu\frac{\partial H_x}{\partial t} = \frac{\partial E_y}{\partial z} - \frac{\partial E_z}{\partial y} - \sigma_m H_x - M_x; \quad \epsilon\frac{\partial E_x}{\partial t} = \frac{\partial H_z}{\partial y} - \frac{\partial H_y}{\partial z} - \sigma_e E_x - J_x \tag{32.7}$$

$$\mu\frac{\partial H_y}{\partial t} = \frac{\partial E_z}{\partial x} - \frac{\partial E_x}{\partial z} - \sigma_m H_y - M_y; \quad \epsilon\frac{\partial E_y}{\partial t} = \frac{\partial H_x}{\partial z} - \frac{\partial H_z}{\partial x} - \sigma_e E_y - J_y \tag{32.8}$$

$$\mu\frac{\partial H_z}{\partial t} = \frac{\partial E_x}{\partial y} - \frac{\partial E_y}{\partial x} - \sigma_m H_z - M_z; \quad \epsilon\frac{\partial E_z}{\partial t} = \frac{\partial H_y}{\partial x} - \frac{\partial H_x}{\partial y} - \sigma_e E_z - J_z \tag{32.9}$$

Second, in preparation for "discretizing" the model in the next step, the model size, unit size, and unit timestep must be determined. The FDTD method establishes a model space, which is the physical region where Maxwell's equations are solved or the simulation is performed. The model space is then discretized to a number of cells, and the time duration, t, is discretized to a number of timesteps. The unit cell size should be small enough to ensure the accuracy of the result, but large enough to minimize the number of cells in order to save computation resources.

Although half of the EM wavelength is an upper bound of the cell size by the Nyquist sampling theorem, the cell size is often set to less than one-tenth of the EM wavelength for better results [1]. The model size depends on the number of cells in the model space, which is usually inversely proportional to the size of the unit cell. The unit timestep is calculated by following the Courant condition, which states that it must be less than the time the EM wave spends traveling to the adjacent unit cell. For a ground-penetrating radar example, assuming a central frequency of 1.25 GHz, the central wave length is 0.24 m. We set the unit cell size to 0.012 m, which is one-twentieth of the central wave length, for good simulation quality. The timestep can be set to 0.02 ns, which meets the Courant condition.

Every cell in the model space has its associated electric and magnetic fields. The material type of each cell is specified by its permittivity ϵ, permeability μ, and conductivity σ. The three-dimensional grid shown in Figure 32.1, the "Yee cell" [4], is helpful for understanding the discretized EM model space. The Yee cell is a small cube that can be treated as a single cell picked from the discretized model space; Δx, Δy, and Δz are the three dimensions of this cube. We use (i,j,k) to denote the point whose real coordinate is $(i\Delta x, j\Delta y, k\Delta z)$ in the model space. Instead of placing the E and H components in the center of each cell, the E and H field components are interlaced so that every E component is surrounded by four circulating H components and every H component is surrounded by four circulating E components.

Maxwell's equations in rectangular coordinates—equations 32.7 through 32.9—can be clearly illustrated by Yee's cell. For example, the H_x component located at point $(i, j+\frac{1}{2}, k+\frac{1}{2})$ is surrounded by four circulating E components, two E_y components, and two E_z components, matching equation 32.7, which states that the H_x component increases directly in response to a curl of E components in the x direction. Similarly, the E_x component increases directly in response to the curl of the H components, as shown in Figure 32.2, also matching equation 32.7. We represent an electric component E_z at the discretized three-dimensional coordinate $(i\Delta x, j\Delta y, (k + \frac{1}{2})\Delta z)$ as $E_z|_{i,j,k+\frac{1}{2}}$, and when the

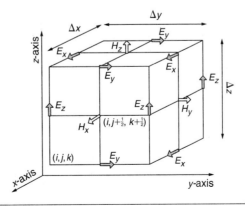

FIGURE 32.1 ■ The geometrical representation of the three-dimensional Yee cell.

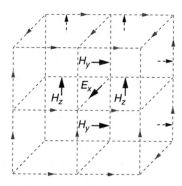

FIGURE 32.2 ▪ Example of electric and magnetic components on a 4-cell grid.

current time is in the discretized N^{th} timestep, we denote the same component as $E_z|_{i,j,k+\frac{1}{2}}^{N}$.

Third, all of the partial derivative operators in equations 32.7 through 32.9 are replaced by their central difference approximations, as illustrated in equation 32.10. The second-order part of the Taylor series expansion is discarded to keep the algorithm simple and reduce the computational cost. Also, the variable without partial derivative can be approximated by time averaging, as shown in equation 32.11, which has a similar structure to the central difference approximation.

$$\frac{\partial f(u_o)}{\partial u} = \frac{f(u_o + \Delta u) - f(u_o - \Delta u)}{2\Delta u} + O[(\Delta u)^2] \tag{32.10}$$

$$f(u_o) = \frac{f(u_o + \Delta u) + f(u_o - \Delta u)}{2} \tag{32.11}$$

For example, equation 32.7 is changed to

$$\mu \frac{H_x(t_0 + \frac{\Delta t}{2}) - H_x(t_0 - \frac{\Delta t}{2})}{\Delta t} = \frac{E_y(z_0 + \frac{\Delta z}{2}) - E_y(z_0 - \frac{\Delta z}{2})}{\Delta z} \tag{32.12}$$

$$-\frac{E_z(y_0 + \frac{\Delta y}{2}) - E_z(y_0 - \frac{\Delta y}{2})}{\Delta y} - \sigma_m \frac{H_x(t_0 + \frac{\Delta t}{2}) + H_x(t_0 - \frac{\Delta t}{2})}{2} - M_x$$

After these modifications, the FDTD method turns Maxwell's equations into a set of linear equations from which we can calculate the electric and magnetic fields in every cell in the model space. We call these equations *the electric and magnetic field updating algorithms*. Six field-updating algorithms form the basis of the FDTD method. For example, the field-updating algorithm for the H_x

component, derived from equation 32.12 or equation 32.7, is given by

$$\left(\frac{\mu}{\Delta t} + \frac{\sigma_m}{2}\right) H_x \Bigg|_{i,j+\frac{1}{2},k+\frac{1}{2}}^{N+\frac{1}{2}} = \left(\frac{\mu}{\Delta t} - \frac{\sigma_m}{2}\right) H_x \Bigg|_{i,j+\frac{1}{2},k+\frac{1}{2}}^{N-\frac{1}{2}} \qquad (32.13)$$

$$+ \frac{1}{\Delta z}\left[E_y \Bigg|_{i,j+\frac{1}{2},k+1}^{N} - E_y \Bigg|_{i,j+\frac{1}{2},k}^{N}\right] - \frac{1}{\Delta y}\left[E_z \Bigg|_{i,j+1,k+\frac{1}{2}}^{N}\right.$$

$$\left. - E_z \Bigg|_{i,j,k+\frac{1}{2}}^{N}\right] - M_x \Bigg|_{i,j+\frac{1}{2},k+\frac{1}{2}}^{N}$$

32.1.2 The FDTD Algorithm

The FDTD algorithm, whose flow diagram is shown in Figure 32.3, is based on these equations. It first establishes the model space and specifies the material properties and the excitation source. The source can be a point source, a plane wave, an electric field, or another option depending on the application. The algorithm then runs through the electric and magnetic updating algorithms on every cell in the model space and loops through every timestep. The output of the FDTD algorithm can be any electric or magnetic field data from any cell in any timestep.

The electric and magnetic fields depend on each other. As we can see from equation 32.13, the current timestep's magnetic field depends on the electric fields in the surrounding cells. Similarly, the current timestep's electric field depends on the magnetic fields in the surrounding cells. Because of this dependence between the electric and magnetic fields, we cannot update them

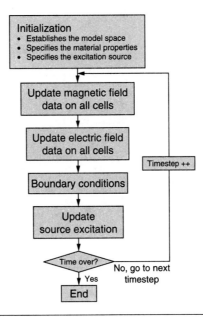

FIGURE 32.3 ■ The flow diagram of the FDTD algorithm.

in parallel. So the FDTD algorithm updates the electric and magnetic fields in an interlaced manner, timestep by timestep, until the job finishes. First, all the magnetic fields in all cells in the model space are updated; next, all the electric fields in all cells, then the source excitation and boundary conditions, are given to the model space; finally the algorithm goes to the next timestep and starts from the magnetic fields again.

The boundary condition computation consists of special algorithms to deal with the unit cells located on the boundary of the model space. The preceding electric and magnetic updating algorithms work accurately in the interior of the model space; however, because the cells on the boundary do not have the adjacent cells needed, the algorithm does not work properly and, as a result, there are algorithm-introduced reflections on the boundary. Special techniques, called absorbing boundary conditions (ABC), are necessary to deal with boundary cells, to prevent nonphysical reflections from outgoing waves, and to simulate the extension of the model space to infinity. The development of efficient ABCs is very important for the FDTD method.

The perfect matched layers (PMLs) ABC [5] sets the outer boundary of the model space to an absorbing material medium layer, which absorbs most of the impinging wave and has low reflection for most incidence angles. The UPML (uniaxial PML) ABC [3]—a modification of PML—uses a generalized formulation on the entire FDTD model space that integrates the boundary condition and electric field updating algorithms, simplifies the FDTD algorithm, and makes a good model for hardware datapath design. Although UPML introduces extra computation and memory consumption, the quality of the uniaxial PML is especially good for dispersive media, which is useful in solving many realistic problems (e.g., the dispersive soil found in modeling ground-penetrating radar and medical studies of EM waves' effects on dispersive human tissue).

The FDTD algorithm is an accurate and successful modeling technique for computational electromagnetics. It is flexible, allowing the user to model a wide variety of EM materials and environments on most scales. It is also easy to understand, with its clear structure and direct time domain calculation. However, FDTD is data and computationally intense. It needs to visit all the cells in every step of the calculation, forcing a large working set. The amount of data in the FDTD model space can be very large for large model sizes, creating a heavy burden on both memory storage and access. The computation is also intense for each cell in the FDTD model space, including updating six electric and magnetic fields and the boundary conditions. This complexity makes the FDTD algorithm run slowly on a single processor—modeling an electromagnetic problem using the FDTD method can easily require several hours. Without powerful computational resources, FDTD models are too time consuming to be implemented on a single computer node. Accelerating FDTD with inexpensive and compact hardware will greatly expand its application and popularity, which is the purpose of an FPGA implementation.

The FDTD algorithm can be viewed as a cellular automata (CA) (see Section 5.2.5). A cellular automaton is a discrete model that consists of an infinite or finite grid of cells, where the state of every cell at discrete time t is a function of the states of a finite number of neighborhood cells at discrete time $t-1$. Every cell has the same rule for updating. The updating algorithm loops through the whole discrete model and then goes to the next discrete time $t+1$. The FDTD algorithm exactly fits the definition of a CA. First, it creates a discrete model space, discretizing both physical space and time with a uniform grid. Second, every cell in the model space follows the same rule (six uniform updating algorithms) for updating the electric and magnetic fields. Finally, the calculation loops though cells to simulate the phenomenon of the whole model space through time. A hardware implementation of the FDTD method is thus a template hardware design for most CA problems.

32.1.3 FDTD Applications

The FDTD method is an important tool for investigating the propagation, radiation, and scattering of EM waves. Before the 1990s the cost of solving Maxwell's equations directly was high and most of the related research was for military–defense purposes. For example, engineers used huge parallel supercomputing arrays to model the radar wave reflection of airplanes by solving Maxwell's equations, trying to develop an airplane with a low radar cross-section [6]. The difficult task of solving Maxwell's equations has had more economical solutions since 1990 with the development of fast computing resources applied to the FDTD method. Now FDTD has spread to many areas, including discrete scattering analysis, antenna and radar design [3], EM wave phenomena analysis on multilayer circuit boards [6], subsurface sensing and ground-penetrating radar (GPR) detection [7,8], studies of EM wave phenomena in the human body, and the study of breast cancer detection using EM waves [9,10]. We apply our FDTD solution to landmine detection using GPR, breast cancer detection, and spiral antenna modeling.

Ground-penetrating radar

The FDTD method has been used to simulate GPR applications for buried landmine detection [7,8]. A three-dimensional FDTD model, as shown in Figure 32.4, simulates the wave propagation and scatter response of three-dimensional GPR geometries with realistic dispersive soil along with air, metal, and dielectric media. The UPML ABC produces good results for this application. The three-dimensional model has been validated by experiments performed with a commercially available GPR system and realistic soil.

Breast cancer detection

Because of the large difference in electromagnetic properties between malignant tumor tissue and normal fatty breast tissue, microwave breast cancer detection has attracted much interest because it may overcome some of the shortcomings of X-ray detection. Accurate computational modeling of microwaves in human tissue with the FDTD method is promising for breast cancer detection research. Researchers built a three-dimensional model of the human breast [9,10], shown in Figure 32.5, that includes a semi-ellipsoid geometric representation of the

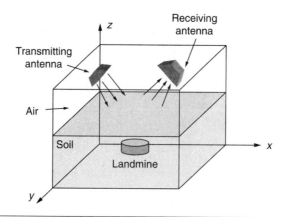

FIGURE 32.4 ▪ A three-dimensional FDTD application of landmine detection using GPR.

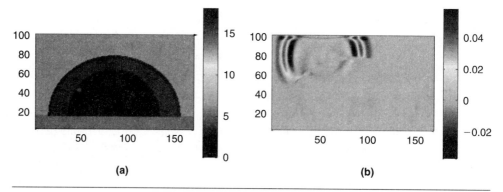

FIGURE 32.5 ▪ Three-dimensional FDTD application of microwave breast cancer detection: (a) geometry map; (b) simulated model space.

breast and a planar chest wall. The modeling is in the range of 30 MHz to 20 GHz, and the UPML ABC is implemented.

Spiral antenna model

The spiral antenna is a popular frequency-independent antenna. As shown in Figure 32.6, we use the FDTD method to simulate the radiation of the Archimedean spiral antenna as an example of its application to antenna design.

Clearly, FDTD is a powerful tool that can be used in many different applications. However, its data-intense and computationally intense properties make it run slowly on a single processor.

The reconfigurable hardware implementation of the FDTD method can greatly accelerate the running speed of the algorithm and maintain its accuracy and flexibility. For example, the breast cancer detection FDTD algorithm running on a single processor may require hours, while the hardware implementation delivers results in minutes, enabling a medical device that

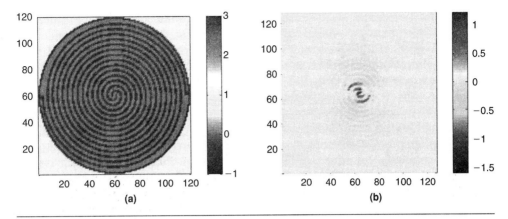

FIGURE 32.6 ■ (a) The floorplan of the spiral antenna model; (b) an FDTD-simulated two-dimensional space.

delivers an answer during the examination. With the help of faster computing technology, the FDTD method will be applied to more research areas and applications.

32.1.4 The Advantages of FDTD on an FPGA

Compared to software running on a general-purpose processor, the advantages of an FPGA implementation are evident—faster speed, smaller size, lower power consumption; the last two advantages are significant, especially compared to a large computer cluster.

Compared to an ASIC finite-difference time-domain design, the FDTD field-programmable gate array (FPGA) implementation has the advantage of flexibility while accelerating the algorithm. The FDTD method models a wide variety of electromagnetic problems that are difficult to cover with a single hardware design. With an FPGA, a designer can modify the model size, the materials, and the parameters and even introduce new updating algorithms and boundary conditions easily. While the ASIC may outperform the FPGA as to speed, size, and power, the reconfigurable property of an FPGA makes it more suitable for the FDTD algorithm.

We can achieve fast computation in an FPGA for finite-difference time-domain because FDTD has properties that make it very suitable for hardware implementation. These properties are its favorable structure for pipelining and parallelism and its constrained data ranges, which are good for fixed-point representation. They make the FDTD method especially suitable for FPGA implementation.

Parallelism and deep pipelining

The FDTD algorithm repeats the same electric and magnetic updating algorithms on every cell of the model space. These calculations are independent between each cell. As long as there are adequate hardware resources, the fields for several cells can be calculated in parallel. Also, although the electric and magnetic updating algorithms depend on each other, the hardware design can still run these calculations in parallel with a carefully designed memory interface. The parallelism between electrical and magnetic fields and the parallelism between space cells make the FDTD algorithm very suitable for parallel hardware implementation, which is a key method for hardware acceleration.

The six electric and magnetic updating algorithms can also be constructed with deep pipelining because they repeat the same calculation on each cell. *Deep pipelining*, another key method for hardware acceleration, maximizes data throughput and greatly increases overall design performance.

Most cellular automata have properties similar to the FDTD algorithm with repeated, independent computation on every cell of the model space. The CA computation can be constructed with deep pipelining, and the parallelism between discrete cells is the same as that available in any CA problem.

Fixed-point arithmetic

Floating-point representation provides high resolution and large dynamic range, but it can be costly. In hardware design, floating point uses slower arithmetic components and consumes more area. In contrast, fixed-point components have much faster speed and occupy less area. In applications where data resolution and dynamic range can be constrained, such as the FDTD algorithm, fixed-point arithmetic can provide similar precision and much faster speed than floating-point arithmetic.

The majority of the data in the FDTD algorithm is the six EM field variables and nine intermediate field variables for each cell in the model space. Since all the calculations in the FDTD method are linear, we can maintain the EM field data at a certain level of magnitude by normalizing the incoming source field magnitude. For example, if the source fields are between −1 and 1, all the EM field variables are between −1 and 1. In rare cases, we simulate the model space with a focus lens to magnify the EM field data. In this case we can estimate the EM data range and still keep the variables between −1 and 1 by normalizing the source field. Since all the EM field variables can be controlled in a fixed range, a fixed-point representation can be used for better performance with a relatively low error rate.

The uniaxial PML FDTD algorithm must be optimized for fixed-point representation. Several parameters in the algorithm have a much different order of magnitude than the EM fields. They may not be representable in fixed point directly or may result in a large error when quantized. Additional error can arise from arithmetic calculations with these parameters in fixed point. These errors can be canceled by making a few changes to the original FDTD algorithm. For example, very large and small coefficients can be multiplied together to create a medium-value coefficient to be used in the new equation. The modification has no effect on the result of the algorithm.

Careful analysis is important for fixed-point quantization to avoid errors. For normalized EM field values that range between −1 and 1, the data tends to be accurate to a relative error of 0.5 percent. The resolution of the fixed-point representation is determined by its data bit width. The longer the bit width, the higher the resolution, so the smaller the error. However, longer bit-width data uses more hardware resources. After careful study of the FDTD algorithm and representative data, we can pick a suitable bit-width with relatively small error (see also Chapter 23).

In conclusion, the FDTD algorithm is very suitable for hardware implementation. The FPGA implementation of the finite-difference time-domain method will empower many FDTD applications in medical, military, and other areas by providing fast, small, low-power, and inexpensive implementations. Many cellular automata, which share similar properties, are also suitable for FPGA hardware implementation. The FDTD hardware design we present in the next section is a good example of hardware implementations for CA.

32.2 FDTD HARDWARE DESIGN CASE STUDY

The FDTD algorithm has a clear structure for hardware design. For each cell in the model space, it reads the electric and magnetic data out of the memories, passes them through the updating algorithms, and writes the results back to the memories. The algorithm repeats this processing until it completes the model space; then it goes to the next timestep and does the same calculations again.

It is easy to separate any hardware design into datapath, memory interface, and control logic. For FDTD, the datapath implements all the electric and magnetic updating algorithms; the memory interface controls data reading, writing, and caching; and the control logic uses a finite-state machine (FSM) to control the progress of the whole design. However, because of its complexity, an efficient hardware implementation of FDTD is not straightforward. The FDTD algorithm is data intense. The electric and magnetic updating algorithms interface a lot with the input and output memories, which creates a heavy burden on the memory interface and data bandwidth. Also, the EM field dataset for the whole model space can be very large for a large model size (a $100 \times 100 \times 100$ model may require 60 MB of memory space), meaning that local FPGA memory is insufficient to contain the entire problem.

The FDTD algorithm is also computationally intense. Every EM field has its own updating algorithms and boundary conditions. A special interlaced mechanism is used between the electric and magnetic updating algorithms, making them depend on each other. Many problems arise when considering the pipelining and parallelism of the datapaths. The FDTD algorithm is complex enough to reach the resource limits of most advanced FPGAs available on the market. Consideration of fixed-point quantization and resource performance trade-offs is very important for efficient hardware design.

One of the main purposes of a hardware implementation is to achieve better performance. To implement the FDTD algorithm on an FPGA efficiently, we need to consider the following:

- Determining the right precision for fixed-point representation (Section 32.2.2)
- Determining the memory hierarchy and designing the memory interface and cache module (see Memory hierarchy and memory interface subsection of Section 32.2.3)
- Determining the pipelining and parallelism by considering the trade-off between resources and performance (see Pipelining and parallelism subsection of Section 32.2.3)

It is important to analyze the data structures, algorithm structure, hardware architecture, and resource limits before design of hardware implementation. This section introduces a target reconfigurable platform, the WildStar-II Pro FPGA board, and lists its detailed specifications. Then we choose the suitable fixed-point representation by analyzing the quantization error of a fixed-point FDTD algorithm and the hardware resource limits. Then we go through the problems in the FDTD hardware implementation and provide detailed solutions and analyses. By carefully considering the trade-offs between hardware resources and performance, we can design the FDTD accelerator with the memory interface, pipelining, and parallelism optimal to the current FPGA computing board.

32.2.1   The WildStar-II Pro FPGA Computing Board

The FPGA board used here is a WildStar-II Pro/PCI reconfigurable FPGA computing board from Annapolis Micro Systems [12]. Its main features are summarized in Table 32.1; a block diagram of this board is shown in Figure 32.7. There are two Xilinx Virtex-II Pro FPGAs, each with 328 embedded 18×18 signed multipliers and 328×18-Kb BlockRAMs.

The embedded multipliers are much faster than a multiplier component implemented with reconfigurable logic, so it is best to use them if possible. The BlockRAMs are the fastest memory the designer can use in an FPGA design, operating as fast as 200+ MHz on the Virtex-II Pro chip. Critical data interchange and interfacing can be programmed using the BlockRAMs. A pair consisting of an embedded multiplier and a BlockRAM shares the same data and address buses in the Xilinx Virtex-II architecture, so once the embedded multiplier is used, we cannot use its

TABLE 32.1 ■ The main features of the WildStar-II Pro FPGA board

FPGA chips	Two Xilinx Virtex-II Pro XC2V70 FPGAs (33,088 slices, 328 embedded multipliers, and 5904 Kb BlockRAM)
Memory ports	Twelve DDRII SRAM ports totaling 54 MBytes (6×4.5 MBytes for each FPGA chip)
Memory bandwidth	Eleven GB/s memory bandwidth (6×72 bits for each FPGA chip)
PCI interface	133 MHz/64-bit PCI-X up to 1.03 GB/s

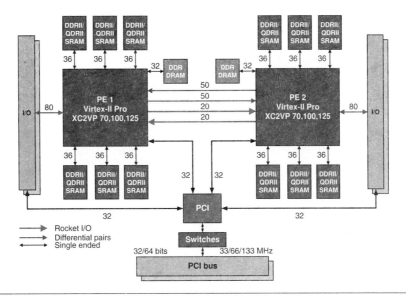

FIGURE 32.7 ■ A block diagram of the WildStar-II Pro FPGA board.

corresponding BlockRAM, and vice versa. Thus, the sum of the total number of embedded multipliers and BlockRAMs used must be less than 328.

Each FPGA is connected to six independent onboard memories, which are 1-M×36-bit DDRII SRAM that have 72-bit data bandwidth and speeds up to 200 MHz. The size of each SRAM is 36 Mbits, or 4.5 MBytes, so the total SRAM attached to each FPGA is 27 MBytes. The WildStar-II Pro board is connected to the desktop computer via a PCI-X interface, with a DMA data transfer rate up to 1 GB/s between the host PC and the FPGA.

The WildStar-II Pro is a typical commercial off-the-shelf (COTS) FPGA computing board, which is widely available and easy to set up. These boards normally contain one or two FPGA chips. Each FPGA chip may be connected to several onboard memories consisting of SRAM or DRAM. The computing boards are often PCI boards for a desktop computer or PCMCIA cards for a laptop. Data and control signals can be transferred between the FPGA computing board and the host PC via either standard PCI transfer or fast DMA transfer. The FDTD hardware design is based on the WildStar-II Pro board but can be easily modified for other COTS FPGA boards.

32.2.2 Data Analysis and Fixed-point Quantization

Because of its limited data range and favorable algorithm properties, the FDTD method is suitable for fixed-point arithmetic (see Section 32.1.4). To use fixed-point representation with the algorithm, we need to first decide its representation and the right data precision.

For simplicity, we use a 2's complement fixed-point representation that has a fixed number of digits before and after the binary point. Because the EM

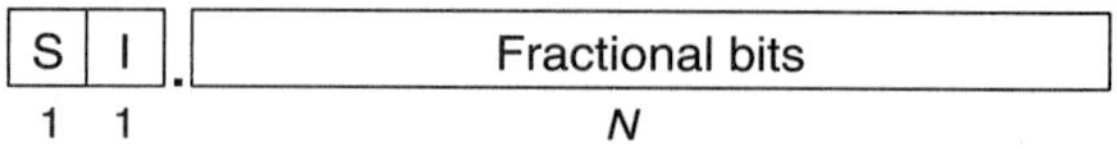

| S | I | . | Fractional bits |
| 1 | 1 | | N |

FIGURE 32.8 ▪ The data structure of the fixed-point representation.

field data in the FDTD algorithm fits in the range −1 to 1, and the results of the intermediate calculations (i.e., add, subtract, and multiply) fit in the range −2 to 2, we set the fixed-point data structure as one sign bit S, one integer bit I before the binary point, and N fractional bits F_i after the binary point, as shown in Figure 32.8. The fixed-point data value is $V = -S \cdot 2 + I + \frac{1}{2^N} \sum_{i=0}^{N-1} 2^i F_i$. The data range given by this representation is between −2.0 and 1.999.

The data precision depends on the smallest absolute value that can be represented. Because the binary point position is fixed, the smallest absolute value is 2^{-N}, which depends solely on the bit width N of the fractional part. To determine the right value for N, we need to consider the trade-off between quantization error and resource costs. To avoid quantization error, which is the difference between the fixed-point and corresponding floating-point data, a longer data bit width is preferable. However, longer data bit widths require larger and slower arithmetic components and put more burden on memory bandwidth and data storage. The problem is how to pick the optimal data bit width such that the fixed-point FDTD algorithm generates acceptable quantization error and consumes a reasonable amount of hardware resources.

To determine this, we wrote the FDTD algorithm in C code both in double-precision floating-point and fixed-point arithmetic and compared the results. Fixed-point representation is simulated by long integers in C, which have a 32-bit maximum bit width. We used two long integer variables to represent one fixed-point datum up to 64 bits. Based on this representation, we created add, subtract, and multiply components for each fixed-point bit width. The C code simulates the fixed-point arithmetic and produces results that are exactly the same as the hardware output. Thus, this C code also can be used for hardware results verification.

By comparing floating-point and the corresponding fixed-point data results for the same model space, we can calculate the relative error, defined in equation 32.14, over the time period that the algorithm runs.

$$Relative\ error = \frac{|floating\text{-}point\ data - fixed\text{-}point\ data|}{|floating\text{-}point\ data|} \quad (32.14)$$

We studied the following six experimental FDTD models to investigate quantization errors:

- The two-dimensional and three-dimensional soil media–based GPR landmine detection models
- The two-dimensional and three-dimensional human tissue media–based tumor detection models
- The two-dimensional and three-dimensional spiral antenna models

TABLE 32.2 ■ Detailed specifications of the experimental FDTD models

	2D landmine detection	3D landmine detection	2D breast detection	3D breast detection	2D spiral antenna	3D spiral antenna
Size	150×100	50×50×50	240×140	80×60×40	120×120	120×120×25
Time duration	2000	2000	2000	2000	2000	2000
Source	Plane wave		Point source		Point source	
Media	Soil, air, dielectric		Human tissue, dielectric		Metal, air, dielectric	

TABLE 32.3 ■ Relative error between fixed-point and floating-point representation

Bit width	Field	Timestep (%) 400	600	1000	1400	1600	Average across timestep (%)
29	E_x	9.187	3.503	0.280	0.182	0.558	2.742
	H_y	12.440	0.124	1.431	0.244	0.264	2.901
	H_z	2.706	1.925	0.472	0.200	0.235	1.108
31	E_x	3.861	0.941	0.058	0.032	0.110	1.001
	H_y	3.681	0.025	0.295	0.042	0.001	0.809
	H_z	1.905	0.461	0.105	0.039	0.046	0.511
33	E_x	2.155	0.209	0.016	0.010	0.031	0.484
	H_y	2.101	0.007	0.077	0.012	0.014	0.442
	H_z	1.479	0.120	0.029	0.010	0.013	0.330
35	E_x	1.729	0.063	0.004	0.002	0.008	0.361
	H_y	1.420	0.002	0.021	0.003	0.004	0.290
	H_z	1.314	0.030	0.007	0.003	0.003	0.271

The specifications of these models are listed in Table 32.2. For all of them, we studied the average relative errors between the floating-point and the fixed-point results. This section analyzes the GPR model results. The other model spaces are similar.

Table 32.3 shows average relative errors for the fractional data bit-width range from 29 to 35 bits in the two-dimensional GPR landmine detection model. E_x, H_y, and H_z are electric and magnetic field data. The relative errors are plotted in Figure 32.9. Those of both electric and magnetic field data decrease as bit widths increase. However, the rate of decrease slows as the bit widths increase. Considering both the relative error and the bit-width cost, a 33-bit fractional part is a good choice for the trade-off between data precision and hardware resources. The average absolute error for this representation is on the order of 10^{-8} for magnetic field data and on the order of 10^{-6} for electric field data; the average relative error is about 0.3 to 0.5 percent. Thus, this representation satisfies the accuracy requirement that the relative error is less than 0.5 percent.

In addition to quantization error analysis, we need to consider the resource limits of the real hardware device in determining the fixed-point data bit width. The FDTD model space will be stored in the onboard SRAMs on the WildStar-II

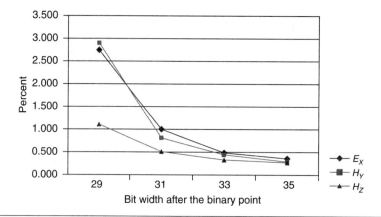

FIGURE 32.9 ■ The relative error between fixed-point and floating-point arithmetic for different bit widths.

Pro FPGA board. The SRAM memory chip we used has size $512K \times 36$ bit. The data is stored in the memory in units of 36 bits. Any data more than 36 bits wide will take two memory units. To keep the memory interface working efficiently, we want to set the data bit width less than or equal to 36 bits.

The embedded multiplier provided on the Xilinx Virtex II-Pro FPGA chip, an 18×18-bit 2's complement signed multiplier, is much faster than the multiplier component implemented by normal reconfigurable logic. Four embedded multipliers can form a 35×35-bit signed multiplier. However, to construct a 36×36-bit signed multiplier, nine embedded multipliers are needed. Because the number of multipliers is limited and very useful in the FDTD algorithm, it is uneconomical to use a 36×36 multiplier or 36-bit data. A data bit width of 35 bits is more efficient for the embedded multiplier. Because the fixed-point quantization error analysis performed in the last section also recommends a data bit width of 35, we choose 35 bits of data as the fixed-point data structure based on both quantization error and resource limits.

32.2.3 Hardware Implementation

After choosing the fixed-point data representation, we then study two very important problems in the FDTD hardware implementation: memory interfacing and pipelining and parallelism.

Memory hierarchy and memory interface

Because the EM field data is proportional to the number of cells in the FDTD model space, the dataset can be very large. Every cell in the FDTD model space has 6 EM field data and 9 intermediate field data for the UPML computation, adding up to 15 field data. An FDTD model space may have millions of cells, require hundreds of megabytes of memory space, and easily exceed the limits of the memory available inside the FPGA chip. Therefore, the data must be stored in larger memories, which are normally slower than the fast on-chip memories, outside the FPGA chip.

The data stored in the slower memories needs to be transferred to the processing core in the FPGA. The processing core is composed of six electric and magnetic updating algorithms, which require very large amounts of input data. In the worst case, three electric updating algorithms require 36 input data and three magnetic ones require 18, adding up to 54 input data for each dispersive UPML FDTD cell. In other words, to make sure that the processing core works at full speed, we need to transfer 54 input data from off-chip memory to the FPGA for each cell. The data transfer puts a heavy burden on the interface between the off-chip memories and the FPGA design. To provide the necessary data at the right time and to optimize the efficiency of the memory interface, we need to determine how to organize the memory resources efficiently by considering the size, speed, and interface bandwidth of each memory resource.

There are three levels of memory hierarchy, based on the WildStar-II Pro/PCI FPGA computing board:

- The fast and wide data-width on-chip memory (BlockRAM) integrated on the FPGA chip
- The fast but limited data-width onboard memory located on the FPGA computing board
- The slow memory for the FPGA to access located in the host PC

BlockRAMs are programmable memories that are integrated inside modern FPGA chips. A Xilinx Virtex-II Pro XC2V70 FPGA contains 328 BlockRAMs, 18 Kb each, with a maximum data width of 36 bits. They can be implemented as small memory blocks or cascaded to form large memory blocks. They also can be programmed to be different depths and widths to fit the hardware design and data structures. They are fast memory units in terms of latency, with only one clock cycle delay for clock cycles up to 200 MHz.

Although BlockRAMs are fast and flexible memory resources, there is much less BlockRAM available compared to off-chip memory. So normally we do not fit the entire model space's data into BlockRAMs. Instead, they are used to build cache modules that read from and write to off-chip memories continuously and feed data to the processing core. What's more, the BlockRAMs are true dual-ported RAM units, and a group of BlockRAMs can provide a very wide data width to the processing core when aggregated together. For example, 54 Block-RAMs on the input side can provide a 54×36-bit data width every clock cycle, which allows the FDTD processing core to run at full speed. The *data width* is the number of bits that can be transferred in one clock cycle. Along with clock frequency, data width determines the data transfer speed (bandwidth) of the memory interface.

Onboard memories, which directly communicate with the FPGA chip, are relatively slower than BlockRAMs in terms of latency, but they are usually much larger in size, varying from megabytes to hundreds of megabytes. The interface between the memory chips and the FPGA chips follows the read/write cycles of the specific memory chips, which are normally single-ported data access with limited data transfer width. Because of the heavy data access required by the FDTD algorithm, the onboard memory bandwidth is very important to the performance of the FDTD design.

As discussed before, the six electric and magnetic updating algorithms need 54 input data for each FDTD cell, which is around $54 \times 36\text{-bit} \times 100$ MHz = 194 Gb/s—far beyond the onboard memory bandwidth of typical FPGA boards. The input data of a single cell have to be transferred to the updating algorithms in several clock cycles, while the updating algorithms can calculate results with a throughput of one cell per clock cycle. So, the onboard memory data transfer bandwidth is the bottleneck of the FDTD design. Memory bandwidth is an important specification in choosing the FPGA computing board for a finite-difference time-domain implementation. To solve this bottleneck, we introduce the managed-cache module that is explained in the next subsection.

The memories in the host PC can be accessed by the FPGA via the PCI or other interfaces. These interfaces are normally slower than the two memory interfaces we have discussed, so we treat the memories in the host PC as the slowest memory, no matter what the actual speed. This memory can be used for data initialization at design startup and data retrieval at the end. At the start of processing, the model space data are loaded from the host PC to the onboard memory and loaded back to memory in the PC at the end of the design. If the onboard memory is not big enough to hold the whole model space, the memory in the host PC will be the primary memory and the data need to be transferred to and from the onboard memory throughout the entire calculation, slowing down the whole design. The size of onboard memories is thus another critical specification in choosing an FPGA computing board.

The memory hierarchy and memory interface structure used in this design is shown in Figure 32.10. We use one FPGA and six onboard memories on the WildStar-II FPGA board. The FDTD field data stored in the onboard memories are sent to the electric and magnetic field–processing cores for calculation via

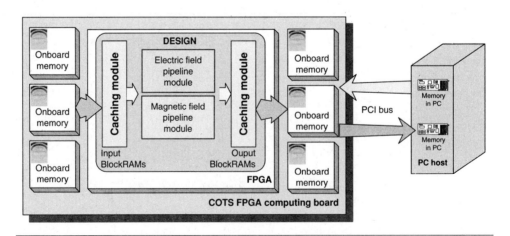

FIGURE 32.10 ■ A structural diagram of the memory interface.

the caching modules built using the BlockRAMs on the FPGA chip. The 3-level memory hierarchy formed from the host PC, the onboard memories, and the BlockRAM caching modules ensure that the electric and magnetic field updating algorithms work at optimal speed.

As shown in Figure 32.10, the BlockRAM caching modules are split into two parts: input and output. The six onboard memories, which are used to store EM field data, are split into two parts also. The entire FDTD model space of the previous timestep is stored in the input onboard memories, and the calculation results, which comprises the data in the current timestep, will be stored in the output onboard memories. In the next timestep, the role of the onboard memories is swapped. The original output onboard memories, which store the current timestep's data, will be connected to the input caching module and the original input onboard memories will be connected to the output module to store the next timestep's result.

The separation of the input and output onboard memories eliminates the need for simultaneous read/write access to the same memory. Because the onboard memories are single ported, shifting between reading and writing to the same memory will create overhead and greatly reduce the speed of the design. By separating input and output memory, we can read from and write to the onboard memories at the same clock cycle, and continue reading and writing a group of data on every clock cycle. So, although the separation of the memory interface does not change the memory bandwidth, the data-transfer rate of the memory interface is increased. Also, the separation makes the structure of the memory interface clearer and the swapping mechanism avoids the extra effort of transferring data from output memories to input memories at the end of every timestep. This swapping of input and output memories is a common hardware design technique to increase throughput.

Managed-cache module

As introduced in the previous section, onboard memory data bandwidth is limited on the FPGA computing board, so the EM field data cannot be transferred to the FPGA fast enough to allow the processing core to run at full speed. To solve this memory transfer bottleneck, we need to introduce the managed-cache module, which is an important part of the memory interface design.

Memory transfer bottleneck   Although the FDTD processing core requires a large amount of input data, the input data for each cell are the EM field data in their nearest-neighbor cells. For two cells located near each other in the FDTD model space, some of the nearest-neighbor cells are the same. The cache module between the onboard memories and the hardware processing cores is designed to avoid reading the same data multiple times from onboard memories.

All of the input data for each cell are from their near neighbors, which means the data are located in a small cubic window around the current cell. If the managed-cache module is designed to be larger than this cubic window, when we calculate the fields of the next cell, the processing core can get all the necessary input data from the cache module. Among the input data, only a little is new, so we only need to fetch the new data from the onboard memories every clock cycle, which greatly reduces the data-transfer burden. At the same time, some of the old data becomes obsolete. In the managed-cache module, we can replace the obsolete data with the new data fetched from onboard memory.

Ideally, we keep the processing core running at full speed so that it calculates one cell's EM data per clock cycle. The managed-cache module needs to be designed to provide all the necessary input data for the processing core, while fetching only one new cell's data from onboard memory every clock cycle. Since every UPML FDTD cell has 15 field data and the processing core needs up to 54 field data inputs, an ideal managed-cache module will fetch 15 field data from onboard memory every clock cycle and provide a data width of 54 field data to the processing core, solving the memory bandwidth bottleneck problem by reducing the number of fetches to 15 every clock cycle, which is 15×36-bit×100 MHz = 54 Gb/s. This rate can be supported by the WildStar-II Pro FPGA computing board. We explain how to realize this ideal cache module in the next two subsections.

Dataflow and processing core optimization   To simplify the explanation of how to optimize the dataflow and how to optimize the processing core, we start from a two-dimensional FDTD algorithm, which can be directly reduced from the three-dimensional FDTD algorithm by considering only one plane in the three-dimensional model. The two-dimensional algorithm updates three EM field data instead of six, handling much less data transfer and calculation, but it keeps the same algorithm structure and datapath. For a two-dimensional model plane of size $N \times N$, we assume that each N cell row is a basic processing unit. Calculating one row of data means updating all EM field data for this row.

The cache modules separate the whole dataflow of the FDTD design into three processes: (1) READ from the input onboard memory and store to the input cache module; (2) read from the input cache module, CALCULATE, and write the result to the output cache module; (3) read from the output cache module and WRITE to the output onboard memory. These three processes can be run in parallel since the cache module can be read from and written to at the same time (i.e., because the cache modules are built from dual-ported BlockRAMs). The parallelism of READ, CALCULATE, and WRITE means that the FDTD design can, at the same time, READ one row of data, CALCULATE the previous loaded row, and WRITE out the results of the row before that. We can understand this as systemwide pipelining in the dataflow. Each process is a pipeline stage. Rows of data are pushed into this 3-stage pipeline, one at a time. Compared to running the three processes serially, this optimized dataflow structure increases the throughput by a factor of 3.

For a two-dimensional plane of size $N \times N$, a simple 2-row cache module (size $2 \times N$) realizes the READ/CALCULATE/WRITE pipelining. As shown in Figure 32.11, the data can be READ from input onboard memory and stored in the second input cache row while the CALCULATE process works on the previously loaded data in the first input cache row. The result is stored in the first output cache

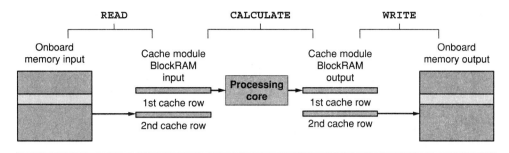

FIGURE 32.11 ■ A structural diagram of the simple 2-row cache module.

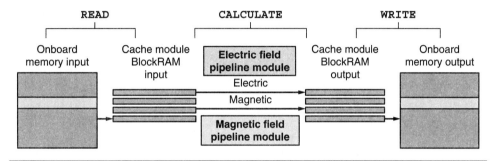

FIGURE 32.12 ■ A structural diagram of the two-dimensional managed-cache module.

row while the previous row's result is read from the second output cache row and WRITTEN to output onboard memory. This cache module structure can be applied to other CA designs.

Furthermore, for FDTD implementation the managed-cache module enables parallel implementation of the electric and magnetic updating algorithms in the implementation of the processing core. Because of the data dependency of the electric updating algorithm on the magnetic updating algorithm—the former needs the current result of the latter—we cannot directly update the M-field and E-field in parallel until we introduce two extra rows in the managed-cache module (see Section 32.1.2). Why two extra rows?

The electric updating algorithm needs to have newly updated magnetic data in the current cell and newly updated magnetic data in the cell below as inputs. So, the electric updating algorithm needs to wait until the magnetic updating algorithm finishes two rows of computation. As long as the cache has two extra rows to save the newly calculated magnetic data, we can run the magnetic updating algorithms two rows ahead of the electric updating algorithms and partially overlap their computation. This is illustrated in Figure 32.12.

For a two-dimensional model space of size $N \times N$, the managed-cache module stores four rows ($4 \times N$) of field data. While the READ process is working on the fourth cache row, the magnetic updating algorithm can work on the data in the third row, which was just read from the memories by the last READ. At the same time, the electric updating algorithm can work on the first cache row, which is two rows after the magnetic algorithm. Finally, WRITE also works on the fourth row, sending out both calculation results from the electric and magnetic updating algorithms. The four rows of field data roll over in the cache modules until the entire model space is calculated. This 4-row cache module improves the total computation time by a factor of almost 2, or $(N+2)/(2N+2)$, by partially parallelizing the electric and magnetic updating implementations.

Thus, the managed-cache module optimizes the design here in two ways: (1) systemwide pipelining of the design dataflow, and (2) processing-level parallelism of the electric and magnetic updating algorithms.

Expansion to three dimensions Here we expand the two-dimensional cache module design to three dimensions. The memory interface and the cache modules are more complex in the three-dimensional FDTD hardware implementation, which handles many more data transfers and calculations. There are two possible approaches for upgrading the cache module to three dimensional. The first is a direct upgrade of the two-dimensional memory interface, as shown in Figure 32.13. Instead of a 4-row cache module, we need to build a 4-slice cache module. Here we READ one slice, CALCULATE one slice, and WRITE out one slice of data at each time interval. However, a $4 \times 100 \times 100$ cache module consumes more than 1200 18-Kb BlockRAMs, which is over three times all the BlockRAMs on the targeted Virtex-II Pro XC2V70. This approach is not feasible for large three-dimensional model spaces.

The second approach reduces the size of the cache module to 4×3 rows of field data by cutting the model space into slices and then into rows. As shown in Figure 32.14, the cache module reads three rows of field data at each time interval, goes through the current vertical slice until it finishes, and then goes to the next vertical slice in the model space. Instead of a 4-slice cache module, we only need to build a 4×3 row cache module. This method minimizes Block-RAM consumption; however, it sacrifices overall design speed to achieve larger model space compatibility. We READ three rows of data at each time interval to CALCULATE only one row of results. This is because we need the current row

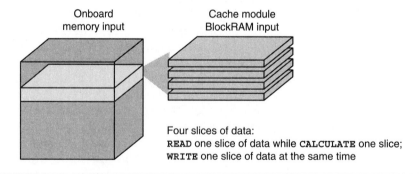

Onboard memory input

Cache module BlockRAM input

Four slices of data:
READ one slice of data while CALCULATE one slice;
WRITE one slice of data at the same time

FIGURE 32.13 ■ A structural diagram of the 4-slice caching design.

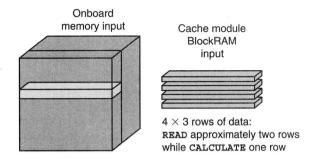

Onboard
memory input

Cache module
BlockRAM
input

4 × 3 rows of data:
READ approximately two rows
while **CALCULATE** one row

FIGURE 32.14 ■ A structural diagram of the 4×3 row caching module.

and adjacent two rows of data to calculate the current row's results. Because only one row of results is calculated from the field-updating pipelines, the READ process is longer than the CALCULATE and WRITE processes. At this point the other two processes need to wait for the READ process.

This waiting process slows down hardware design. Fortunately, we do not need to READ all three rows (45 data per cell) to start processing since the field-updating algorithm only needs part of the data in adjacent rows. We only need to READ approximately two rows of data (36 data per cell), CALCULATE one row, and WRITE one row at each time interval. Due to the limited number of BlockRAMs, the second approach is more practical. From the preceding analysis of the managed-cache modules, we conclude that the efficiency of the memory interface plays a key role in the performance of the complete FPGA design. The speed and manner in which the memory interface handles the input data often limits the speed of the entire design.

Pipelining and parallelism

Given an efficient memory interface and proper fixed-point data representations, the designer next needs to adjust the architecture and optimize design performance by considering pipelining and parallelism.

As discussed before, we can implement the electric and magnetic updating algorithms in parallel with the correct cache structure. We can also implement the three key processes—READ, CALCULATE, and WRITE—in parallel by separating the input and output memory interfaces and building dual-ported cache modules. In hardware design, parallelism translates to faster speed; however, it also "costs" more in hardware resources. The FDTD algorithm is large enough to reach the resource limits of the most advanced FPGAs on the market. One of the important problems in FDTD hardware design is determining the design architecture by considering the trade-offs between resources and performance. The hardware resource limit of each FPGA chip and computing board is different. The resource–performance trade-off analysis here is based on the targeted WildStar-II Pro FPGA computing board.

Pipelining   The FDTD algorithm repeats the same electric and magnetic updating algorithms, which are independent of each other, on every cell of the model space. The algorithms can be implemented with complex combinational logic with long delay. Building them with deep pipelining helps reduce the clock cycle and increase the throughput of the hardware design. Because of the advantages, we pipeline all the updating algorithms. The embedded multipliers, which are the slowest components in the datapath, can also be pipelined to several stages to reduce delay. Because the lengths of the electric and magnetic updating pipelines are different, state machines are used to control the start and end of the pipelines and to synchronize them.

Parallelism   Because the updating calculations on every cell in the FDTD model space are independent of each other, as long as there are adequate hardware resources, the computation of two or more FDTD cells can be implemented in parallel. However (see Section 32.2.3), the bandwidth of the memory interface is the bottleneck of the FDTD hardware design. The memory data width here is 3×72 bits, which can transfer six 35-bit field data inputs at each clock cycle. This memory bandwidth needs 6 clock cycles to prepare one cell's 36 input data when using the 4×3 row cache module. Can this memory interface handle the increased parallelism?

Running two cells in parallel actually saves memory bandwidth per cell. As shown in Figure 32.15, two adjacent FDTD cells share a portion of their nearest-neighbor cells. For each single cell, we need to read three rows of data (36 field data per cell) from the onboard memories, which is when running two cells in parallel, we only need to read four rows of data, or 24 data per cell. Because the bottleneck of the design is the memory bandwidth, the 2-cell parallelism mechanism improves the performance of the whole design. We can use the ratio between input data and result data as a metric to measure the efficiency of the memory interface. After implementing 2-cell parallelism, the input–result ratio decreases from 6:1 to 4:1.

Running two cells in parallel creates an extra burden on the cache size and the calculation pipelines, however. The cache module needs to hold 4×4 rows of data at the same time instead of 3×4 rows. Fortunately, the Virtex-II Pro XC2V70 FPGA has adequate BlockRAMs for the 4×4 row cache, but there is no space for increasing the cache beyond this, which is why we choose not to run three cells in parallel, even though this would further save memory bandwidth per cell and improve the input–result ratio.

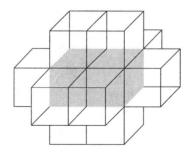

FIGURE 32.15 ▪ Running two cells in parallel.

Also, the Virtex-II Pro FPGA XC2V70 does not have enough reconfigurable logic to implement all the updating pipelines in parallel. Instead, because the memory interface takes four clock cycles to transfer enough input data for one cell's calculation, the number of parallel updating pipelines can be reduced. The calculation core can run several updating algorithms serially in one updating pipeline, taking more than one clock cycle to finish the calculation for one cell. The serial calculation reduces the level of parallelism, saves reconfigurable logic, and still maintains the performance of the hardware design.

Two hardware implementations   The preceding input–result ratio is calculated based on the input data needed for the uniaxial PML FDTD algorithm. This algorithm treats the whole model space as UPML cells and provides a uniform structure for both the UPML cells and the non-UPML center cells, as shown in Figure 32.16. However, the UPML FDTD algorithm requires nine extra field data for each cell in the model space, which adds overhead to the memory interface. The cells in the center of the model space that are not located in the UPML layer can be calculated by the normal FDTD algorithm, which has only six field data for each cell. Small modifications to the UPML updating pipelines can make the new updating pipelines work on both the UPML cells and non-UPML center cells.

Therefore, we can save memory bandwidth and memory space on the center cells by combining the UPML and center cell algorithms in the hardware design. The input–result ratio of a center cell is 3:1 and will be 2:1 after applying 2-cell parallelism. For the normal model space, where half the cells are center cells and the other half are UPML cells, the overall input–result ratio will decrease to approximately (4:1 + 2:1)/2 = 3:1, raising the performance of the hardware design.

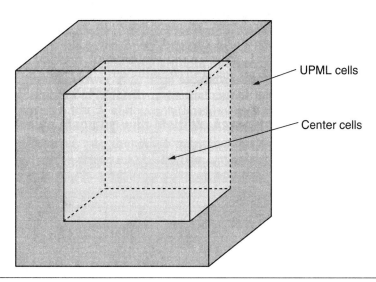

FIGURE 32.16 ■ Uniaxial PML boundary condition cells and non-uniaxial PML center cells in the model space.

We have two hardware implementations for the uniaxial PML FDTD algorithm. The first implementation treats the whole model space as UPML cells, with a simpler design structure and an input–result ratio of 4:1. The second implementation, which includes center cell and UPML cell calculations, has a more complex memory interface and better performance (the input–result ratio depends on the number of center cells and UPML cells).

The analysis of resources and performance trade-offs here is based on the WildStar-II Pro FPGA computing board. For other FPGA devices, the analysis is similar. A wider onboard memory data width, which can ease the memory bottleneck, will raise the design performance proportionally. A bigger FPGA chip, which can hold larger cache modules and more updating pipelines, will speed up the hardware design by calculating more cells in parallel.

32.2.4 Performance Results

A comparison of performance results for three-dimensional FDTD software and hardware implementations is shown in Table 32.4. The sample model is a $50 \times 50 \times 50$ three-dimensional uniaxial PML FDTD algorithm model with 500 timesteps of FDTD iteration. The fixed-point FDTD hardware design, which treats all cells as UPML boundary cells, runs at 90 MHz on the WildStar-II Pro FPGA board. The UPML FDTD FPGA implementation is 16 times faster than the floating-point Fortran software implementation running on a 3.0-GHz PC. Hardware times are measured on the board and include the time to transfer data between the FPGA board and the host PC at the start and end of computation. The hardware design speedup can increase to 25 times with the implementation that combines the center and UPML region. The Virtex-II Pro XC2V70 FPGA chip is almost fully utilized because the FDTD hardware design occupies 99 percent of the reconfigurable slices, 51 percent of the BlockRAMs, and 46 percent of the embedded multipliers. There are two Xilinx Virtex-II Pro FPGAs on a WildStar-II Pro FPGA board. Dual-FPGA parallel implementations of the FDTD algorithm are expected to double the speedup.

TABLE 32.4 ■ Three-dimensional FDTD hardware implementation performance results

	Software floating-point Fortran code on 3.0 GHz PC	Hardware fixed-point design running at 90 MHz	Hardware fixed-point design running at 90 MHz	Hardware fixed-point design running at 90 MHz
		All cells as center cells	All cells as UPML boundary cells	Combined center and UPML region
Runtime (sec)	49	1.59	2.985	1.89
Million nodes/sec	1.27	39.31	20.93	33.07
Speedup	1	30.9	16.5	25.9

32.3 SUMMARY

Implementing the FDTD algorithm in hardware greatly increases its computational speed. The speedup is due to three major factors: fixed-point representation, custom memory interface design, and pipelining and parallelism. FDTD is a data-intense algorithm; the bottleneck of the hardware design is its memory interface. With the limited bandwidth between the FPGA and data memories, a carefully designed custom memory interface allows for full utilization of the memory bandwidth and greatly improves performance. The FDTD algorithm is also a computationally intense algorithm; by considering the trade-offs between resources and performance, we implement as much pipelining and parallelism as possible to speed up the design.

The FDTD algorithm is also a cellular automata, sharing a similar algorithmic structure with many other CA problems. The hardware design techniques and memory interface architecture presented in this chapter can be applied to a wide range of other CA problems to achieve speedup on an FPGA and to provide fast, small, low-power, and inexpensive implementations.

References

[1] K. S. Kunz, R. J. Luebbers. *The Finite Difference Time Domain Method for Electromagnetics*, CRC Press, 1993.

[2] A. Taflove, S. C. Hagness. *Computational Electrodynamics: The Finite-Difference Time-Domain Method*, 2nd ed., Artech House, 2000.

[3] A. Taflove. *Advances in Computational Electrodynamics: The Finite-Difference Time-Domain Method*, Artech House, 1998.

[4] K. Yee. Numerical solution of initial boundary value problems involving Maxwell's equations in isotropic media. *IEEE Transactions on Antennas and Propagation* 16, 1966.

[5] J. P. Berenger. Three-dimensional perfectly matched layer for the absorption of electromagnetic waves. *Journal of Computational Physics* 127, 1996.

[6] A. Taflove. Reinventing electromagnetics: Emerging applications for FD–TD computation. *IEEE Computational Science and Engineering* 2(4), 1995.

[7] B. Yang, C. Rappaport. Response of realistic soil for GPR applications with two-dimensional FDTD. *IEEE Transactions on Geoscience and Remote Sensing*, June 2001.

[8] P. Kosmas, Y. Wang, C. Rappaport. Three-dimensional FDTD model for GPR detection of objects buried in realistic dispersive soil. *SPIE Proceedings* 4742, April 2002.

[9] P. Kosmas, C. Rappaport. Modeling with the FDTD method for microwave breast cancer detection. *IEEE Transactions on Microwave Theory and Technology* 52(8), 2004.

[10] P. Kosmas, C. Rappaport. Use of the FDTD method for time reversal: Application to microwave breast cancer detection. *SPIE Proceedings Computational Imaginary* 5299, 2004.

[11] Xilinx, Inc. *Virtex-II Pro and Virtex-II Pro X Platform FPGAs: Complete Data Sheet*, 2004.

[12] Annapolis Micro Systems. *WildStar-II Hardware Reference Manual*, 2004.

CHAPTER 33

Evolvable FPGAs

Andres Upegui, Eduardo Sanchez
School of Computer and Communication Sciences
Ecole Polytechnique Fédérale de Lausanne

Reconfigurable and Embedded Digital Systems Institute
Haute Ecole d'Ingénierie et de Gestion du Canton de Vaud

One of the main advantages of living beings over engineered computing systems is their capacity to adapt. While computers are tied to a fixed architecture predefined at design time, the human brain exhibits an impressive structural plasticity whereby interconnections are constantly being reinforced or destroyed according to environmental interactions. This and other comparisons between computers and living beings have given rise to what we know today as bioinspired hardware design.

Evolvable hardware is a bioinspired technique that has enjoyed impressive growth during the last decade. In 1993 Higuchi et al. and de Garis proposed an analogy between living beings and programmable hardware devices [1, 2]: In both cases specification of the system is by means of a finite string of symbols. In the case of living beings, DNA determines how the organism develops into its final phenotypic representation; in programmable hardware devices, a configuration bitstream drives behavior. This parallel suggests the utilization of so-called *evolutionary algorithms* in the design of hardware systems.

33.1 THE POE MODEL OF BIOINSPIRED DESIGN METHODOLOGIES

Living organisms, from microscopic bacteria to giant sequoias, including animals such as butterflies and humans, have successfully survived on Earth for millions of years. If we had to propose but one key to explain this success, it certainly would be *adaptation*. In contrast with nature, adaptation has been very elusive to human technology. The model examples of adaptive systems are not among human's creations but among nature's—natural organisms show a striking capacity to adapt to changing circumstances, thus ensuring their continued functionality.

During the last few years, computer scientists, inspired by certain biological processes, have given birth to domains such as artificial neural networks and evolutionary computation.

Living organisms are complex systems exhibiting a range of desirable characteristics, such as evolution, adaptation, and fault tolerance, which have proved difficult to realize using traditional engineering methodologies. Such systems are characterized by a genetic program—the genome—that guides their development, their functioning, and their death. If one considers life on Earth from its very beginning, the following three levels of organization can be distinguished [3].

Phylogeny: The first level is the temporal evolution of the genetic program, the hallmark of which is the evolution of species, or *phylogeny*. The multiplication of living organisms is based on the reproduction of the program, subject to an extremely low error rate at the individual level to ensure that the species of the offspring remains unchanged. Mutation (asexual reproduction) or mutation with recombination (sexual reproduction) gives rise to new organisms. The phylogenetic mechanisms are fundamentally nondeterministic, with the mutation and recombination rate providing a major source of diversity. This diversity is indispensable for the survival of living species, for their continuous adaptation to a changing environment, and for the appearance of new species.

Ontogeny: This level constitutes the developmental process of multicellular organisms. The successive divisions of the mother cell, the zygote, into newly formed cells, each possessing a copy of the original genome, is followed by a specialization of the daughter cells in accordance with their surroundings (i.e., their position within the ensemble). This latter phase is known as cellular differentiation. The ontogenetic process is essentially deterministic: An error in a single base within the genome can provoke an ontogenetic sequence that results in notable, possibly lethal, malformations.

Epigenesis: The ontogenetic program is limited in the amount of information it can store, rendering the complete specification of the organism impossible. A well-known example is the human brain, whose some 10^{10} neurons and 10^{14} connections are far too many to be completely specified in the 4-character genome with a length of approximately 3×10^9. Therefore, when a certain level of complexity is reached, there must emerge a different process that permits the individual to integrate its vast quantity of interactions with the outside world. This is known as *epigenesis*, which primarily includes the nervous, immune, and endocrine systems. These systems are characterized by a basic structure that is entirely defined by the genome (the innate part), which is then subjected to modification through the individual's lifetime interactions with the environment (the acquired part). The epigenetic processes can be grouped under the heading of *learning* systems.

Analogous to nature, the space of bio-inspired hardware systems can be partitioned along the phylogenic, ontogenic, and epigenetic axes; we refer to this as the POE model [3, 4]. The distinction between the axes cannot be easily drawn where nature is concerned. We therefore define each axis within the model's framework as follows:

- The phylogenetic axis involves *evolution*.
- The ontogenetic axis involves the *development* of a single individual from its own genetic material, essentially without environmental interactions.
- The epigenetic axis involves *learning* through environmental interactions that take place after the individual is formed.

As an example, consider the following three paradigms, whose hardware implementations can be positioned along the POE axes:

- *P*—evolutionary algorithms are the simplified artificial counterpart of phylogeny.
- *O*—self-replicating and self-repairing cellular automata are based on the concept of ontogeny, where a single mother cell gives rise through multiple divisions to a multicellular organism.
- *E*—artificial neural networks embody the epigenetic process, where the system's synaptic weights and perhaps topological structure change through interactions with the environment.

The domains collectively referred to as soft computing [5] often involve the solution of ill-defined problems coupled with the need for continual adaptation or evolution. The paradigms listed yield impressive results, frequently rivaling those of traditional methods.

We will talk about the phylogenetic axis of hardware bio-inspired systems, most known as evolvable hardware (EHW). The scope of EHW covers diverse areas ranging from analog circuits to antenna design, but this chapter focuses on evolution of digital circuits using reconfigurable computing devices, more precisely, field-programmable gate arrays (FPGAs).

33.2 ARTIFICIAL EVOLUTION

The idea of applying the biological principle of natural evolution to artificial systems, introduced more than three decades ago, has seen impressive growth in the past few years. Usually grouped under the term *evolutionary algorithms* (EAs) or *evolutionary computation*, we find the domains of genetic algorithms, evolution strategies, evolutionary programming, and genetic programming [6–9].

33.2.1 Genetic Algorithms

As a generic example of artificial evolution, we consider genetic algorithms (GAs) [10]. As illustrated in Figure 33.1, a GA is an iterative procedure applied to a constant-size population of individuals. Each individual represents a possible

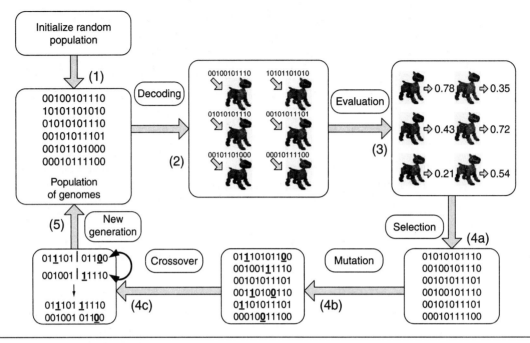

FIGURE 33.1 ▪ A genetic algorithm.

solution to the given problem, and eventually one is chosen as the searched solution.

Each individual is coded by a finite string of symbols from a given alphabet, known as the *genome*. Each genome gives rise to the individual's *phenotype*, which constitutes the actual solution (a program or a circuit) to the problem at hand (e.g., a robot controller for the example in Figure 33.1). The individual receives a score (better known as fitness) depending on the performance exhibited during its evaluation. The process from the genome to a fitness value can be seen as an n-dimensional function (where n is the genome size), and the set of all possible solutions can be seen as an n-dimensional *search space*.

A GA can be summarized in the following steps:

1. *Initialization:* Create an initial population of individuals by defining a set of genomes in a random or heuristic manner.
2. *Decoding:* Generate the phenotypes for the individuals in the current population by decoding (mapping) the genotypes.
3. *Fitness evaluation:* Evaluate individuals according to some predefined quality criterion, referred to as *fitness* or *fitness function*.
4. *Genetic operators:* Apply genetically inspired operators to the current population:

    (a) *Selection:* Individuals are selected into a mating pool for reproduction according to their fitness. With stochastic or deterministic selection mechanisms, the fittest individuals have more chances to transmit their genetic material to the next generation.

(b) *Mutation:* The genome is randomly changed; and

(c) *Crossover:* Two genomes are selected to be split and swapped at a random position.

5. If a predefined convergence condition has not been met, go back to step 2 to evaluate a new generation. Otherwise, deliver the best individual evaluated.

The basic components of GAs are always the same: a population of individuals, a decoding mechanism from a genotype to a phenotype, a fitness evaluation, genetic operators, and an iterative process. However, GAs allow variants: There exist several methods for defining each of the steps just listed. By running a large enough number of generations, the GA should eventually find an acceptable solution (i.e., one with high fitness).

EAs can be considered as a family of stochastic global optimization algorithms, mainly differing from their deterministic counterparts [11] by the lower knowledge of the problem they require and by the absence of mathematical proofs of convergence due to their stochastic nature. For highly nonlinear search spaces, EAs have exhibited faster convergence than deterministic methods, given their population-based approach. In most cases, the applications solved by EAs can also be tackled with deterministic optimization methods.

EAs are very common, having been successfully applied to numerous problems from domains as diverse as optimization, circuit design, disease diagnosis assistance, precision agriculture, self-organizing systems, automatic programming, machine learning, economics, immune systems, ecology, population genetics, studies of evolution and learning, and social systems [9].

33.3 EVOLVABLE HARDWARE

In the case of humans, adaptation due to evolution comes about through modifications in our DNA (deoxyribonucleic acid), which constitutes the encoding of every living being on Earth. DNA is a double-stranded molecule composed of two sugar-phosphate chains linked together by pairs of the bases adenine, cytocine, guanine, and thymine, constituting a string of symbols from a quaternary alphabet (A, C, G, T). Similarly, reconfigurable logic devices are configured by a string of symbols (the configuration bitstream) from a binary alphabet (0, 1). This string determines the function implemented by each of the programmable components and the connectionism of each of the switch matrices.

With this description, a rough analogy arises naturally between DNA and a configuration bitstream and between a living being and a circuit (Figure 33.2). In both cases there is a mapping from a string representation to an entity that will perform one or more actions: growing, moving, reproducing, and so forth, for living beings; computing a function for circuits.

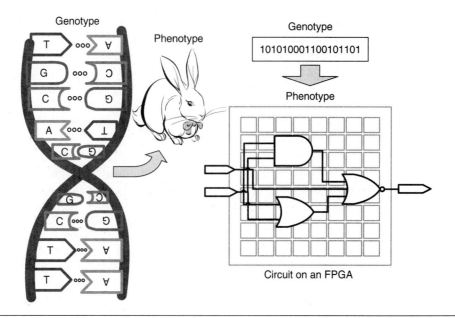

FIGURE 33.2 ▪ The analogy between living beings and digital circuits.

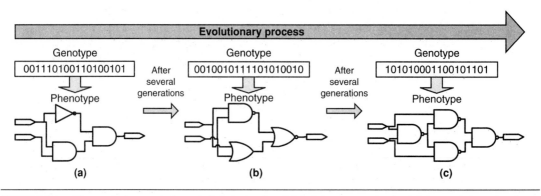

FIGURE 33.3 ▪ The evolutionary design of digital circuits: (a) intial random circuit, (b) intermediate circuit, and (c) final circuit.

This analogy between living beings and digital circuits suggests the possibility of applying the principles of artificial evolution to circuit design (Figure 33.3). Designing analog and digital electrical circuits is, by tradition, a hard engineering task vulnerable to human error, and for large circuits the optimality of a solution cannot be guaranteed. Design automation has become a challenge for tool designers, and given the increasing complexity of circuits, higher abstraction levels are needed. Evolvable hardware arises as a promising solution to this problem: From a given behavior specification of a circuit, an EA will search for a bitstream describing a circuit that satisfies it.

If we carefully examine the EHW work carried out to date, it becomes evident that it mostly involves the application of EAs to the synthesis of digital systems [12–23]. From this perspective, EHW is simply a subdomain of artificial evolution, where the final goal is the synthesis of an electronic circuit. The work of Koza [8], which includes the application of genetic programming to the evolution of a 3-variable multiplexer and a 2-bit adder, may be considered an early precursor along this line. It should be noted that, in Koza's time, the main goal was to demonstrate the capabilities of the genetic programming methodology rather than to design actual circuits. We argue that the term *evolutionary circuit design* would be more descriptive of such work than the term *evolvable hardware* [24]. For now, we will stay with the latter (popular) term; however, we will return to the issue of definitions in Section 33.4.

Taken as a design methodology, EHW offers a major advantage over classical methods. The designer's job is reduced to constructing the evolutionary setup, which involves specifying the circuit requirements, the basic elements, a decoding mechanism, and the testing scheme used to assign fitness (this last phase is often the most difficult). If the setup has been well designed, evolution may then (automatically) generate the desired circuit. Currently, most evolved digital designs are suboptimal with respect to traditional methodologies; however, improved results are regularly demonstrated.

There are two critical questions to ask when setting up a system to be evolved: how to map a phenotype from a genotype and how to compute the fitness of a circuit. The answers to these questions are critical and can make the difference between a successful and an unsuccessful evolution.

33.3.1 Genome Encoding

In examining the EHW work carried out to date, we can derive a classification of current EHW in accordance with genome encoding (i.e., the circuit description) and the calculation of a circuit's fitness.

High-level languages

Using a high-level functional language to encode the evolving population implies an additional step to obtain the final circuit implementation: The chosen individual must be synthesized. Koza's evolved solution [8] was a program that described the (desired) multiplexer or adder rather than an interconnection diagram of logic elements (the actual hardware representation). Mermoud et al. [25] used fuzzy rules as evolvable components, and Murakawa et al. [26] and Upegui et al. [27] proposed the evolution of artificial neural network topologies at the neuron and layer levels. Hemmi et al. [28] used a high-level HDL to represent the genomes. Koza et al. [29] used the rewriting operator, in addition to crossover and mutation, to form a hierarchical structure.

Low-level languages

The idea of directly incorporating the bit string representing the configuration of a programmable circuit within the genome was presented early on by Atmar [30] and more recently by Higuchi et al. [1] and de Garis [2]. As a first step, a set of basic logic gates must be chosen (e.g., AND, OR, and NOT) and suitably codified, along with the interconnections between gates, to produce the genome encoding. For example, Higuchi et al. [31] used a low-level bit-string representation of the system's logic diagram to describe small-scale programmable array logics (PALs), where the circuit is restricted to a logic sum of products. The limitations of PAL circuits have been overcome to a large extent by the introduction of FPGAs, as used initially by Thompson [32,33] and later by a number of research groups.

The use of a low-level circuit description that requires no further transformation is an important step forward because it potentially enabled the placing of the genome directly into the actual circuit and thus paved the way toward true EHW (we will elaborate on this in Section 33.4). However, FPGAs presented two major problems: (1) The genome's length was on the order of tens of thousands of bits, rendering evolution practically impossible using current technology, and (2) within the circuit space, consisting of all representable circuits, many circuits were invalid.

With the introduction of the Xilinx XC6200 [34] family of FPGAs, these problems were reduced. As with previous FPGA families, there was a direct correspondence between the bit string of a cell and the actual logic circuit; however, because the XC6200 was completely multiplexer based, the result was always a viable system with no short circuits. Moreover, as opposed to previous FPGAs where the entire system had to be configured, the XC6200 family permitted the separate configuration of each cell, which was markedly faster and more flexible. Thompson [32] employed this feature to reduce the genome's size, although he did not introduce real-time, partial system reconfigurations. Unfortunately, the XC6200 was discontinued after a few years; however, the results achieved by directly evolving its bitstream led to increased visibility for the EHW community and made possible the growth of this research field.

Fitness calculation

Note the following with regard to calculations for fitness with evolvable hardware.

- *Off-chip*. The use of a high-level language for genome representation means that we have to transform the encoded system to evaluate its fitness. This is usually carried out by simulation, and only the final solution found by evolution is actually implemented in hardware.
- *On-chip*. As noted previously, the low-level genome representation enables a direct configuration (and reconfiguration) of the circuit, which leads to the possibility of using real hardware during the evolutionary process. An example of *on-chip fitness calculation* is presented in the next section in the form of an intrinsic evolvable system.

33.4 EVOLVABLE HARDWARE: A TAXONOMY

In EHW, the phylogenetic axis admits four qualitative subdivisions of evolution (Figure 33.4) according to the level of bio-inspiration: extrinsic, intrinsic, complete, and open ended.

33.4.1 Extrinsic Evolution

At the bottom of this axis, we find what is in essence *evolutionary circuit design*, where all operations are carried out in software, and the resulting solution may be loaded onto a real circuit. Though a potentially useful design methodology, this falls completely within the realm of traditional evolutionary techniques. This category is also widely known as *extrinsic* EHW.

Extrinsic EHW has typically targeted the synthesis of circuits—that is, from a desired behavior specification, an EA finds a schematic of a circuit implementing a function that satisfies the specification [29]. This category supports different levels of abstraction, allowing to evolve logical gates, arithmetic operations, more complex functional blocks, or HDL code; however, it is not suited for evolving circuits at the bitstream level. Evolution has also been used in other extrinsic aspects of circuit design such as placement and routing [35, 36] and scheduling and allocation [37].

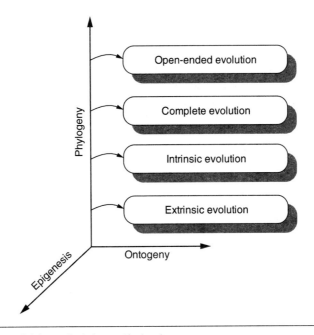

FIGURE 33.4 ■ The divisions of phylogenetic hardware.

33.4.2 Intrinsic Evolution

Moving upward along the axis, we find research in which a real circuit is used during the evolutionary process for fitness computation, although most operations are still carried out offline, in software, as depicted in Figure 33.5.

The very first intrinsic evolution was reported by Thompson [32]. He evolved a section of an XC6216 FPGA, consisting of 10×10 cells (the full array size was 64 × 64), to discriminate between square waves of 1 kHz and 10 kHz presented as inputs. His complete system setup is depicted in Figure 33.6 (see Thompson [33]). From a PC, he configured the FPGA with a configuration bitstream generated by a GA, which used a genome of 1800 bits (18 configuration bits per cell) to represent a possible circuit. Then the individual's fitness was automatically evaluated as follows:

1. The tone generator, driven by the PC, presented five bursts each of both waves (1 kHz and 10 kHz) to the circuit. The analog integrator was reset before the generation of each burst, and it then integrated the circuit's output during the presentation of the burst.
2. Back in the PC, the individual's fitness was computed by a function aiming to maximize the difference between the average output voltages when presenting both waves.
3. After running the experiment for 2 to 3 weeks, during which 5000 generations of 50 individuals were evaluated, the resulting circuit achieved successful discrimination of the waves. However, the perfect desired behavior was obtained around generation 4100.

In another interesting project, Thompson et al. [38] evolved a hardware controller for a two-wheeled autonomous mobile robot that was required to display simple wall avoidance behavior in an empty rectangular arena.

A very important aspect of Thompson's work is the unconstrained use of hardware. Conventional (human) design requires that constraints be applied to the circuit's spatial structure and dynamic behavior, but evolution can do away with

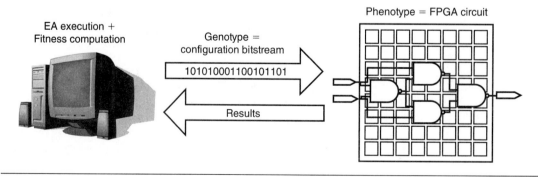

FIGURE 33.5 ▪ Intrinsic evolution.

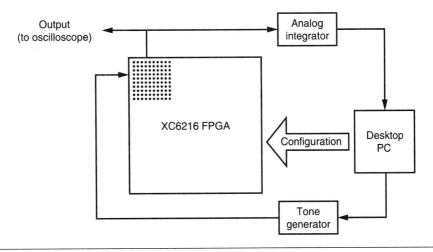

FIGURE 33.6 ■ Adrian Thompson's intrinsic evolvable system setup.

these. The circuits evolved by Thompson [33, 38] and Ly and Mowchenko [37] had no enforced spatial structure (e.g., limitations on recurrent connections), no impositions upon modularity, and no dynamic constraints such as a synchronizing clock or handshaking between modules. Unconstrained circuit design can better exploit the dynamics of the circuit supporting it; however, such circuits exhibit two main drawbacks. One is the impossibility of reproducing a solution: The same bitstream does not behave in the same manner in two different devices. The other is the circuit's high sensitivity to external conditions: Slight temperature changes can modify its behavior.

Two more examples from this subdivision of the phylogenetic axis are the works of Murakawa et al. [39] and Iwata et al. [40]. One of the major obstacles these researchers hoped to overcome was large genome size (defining the FPGA's full configuration). They suggested two solutions:

1. Variable-length chromosome GAs (VGA), where the genome does not directly represent the configuration bit string but rather codifies the possible logical operations and interconnections [40].
2. Evolution at the function level, where the basic units are not elementary logic gates (e.g., AND, OR, and NOT) but rather higher-level functions (e.g., sine-wave generator, multiplier) [39].

Because no such commercial FPGA currently exists, Murakawa and Iwata and their colleagues proposed a novel architecture, dubbed F^2PGA (function-based FPGA).

It is important to note that while experiments of the above type have been referred to by some as intrinsic evolution, they have a prominent extrinsic aspect because the population is stored in an external computer, which also controls the evolutionary process.

33.4.3 Complete Evolution

Still further along the phylogenetic axis, we find systems in which all operations (selection, crossover, mutation), as well as fitness evaluation, are carried out intrinsically, in hardware (Figure 33.7). This category, called *complete* evolution by Haddow and Tufte [41], has as its main motivation attaining adaptive systems that are able to accomplish difficult tasks, possibly involving real-time behavior in a complex, dynamic environment. The major aspect missing here, compared with biological evolution, is that the evolution is not open ended (i.e., there is a predefined goal and no dynamic environment to speak of).

Within the category of complete evolution, we find two subdivisions: *centralized* and *population oriented*.

Centralized evolution

The main characteristic of centralized evolution is the existence of a single evolvable circuit and a single evolvable algorithm computation (Figure 33.7(a)). With this approach an on-chip genetic machine, a hardwired EA, is implemented. The approach also comprises implementations where the EA is executed in an on-chip processor. Centralized evolution holds special interest because it greatly enhances the autonomy of the circuit, allowing the EHW to adapt to a changing environment during its lifetime. Implementations of EAs in general-purpose processors, in spite of their lower performance compared to their fully hardwired counterparts, exhibit several important advantages that permit them to benefit from a more general framework: They provide a more user-friendly interface for implementing chromosome manipulations, fitness evaluations, and memory access; they support easier algorithm upgrades; and they enhance the possibilities of immediately using the evolving circuit for useful computations.

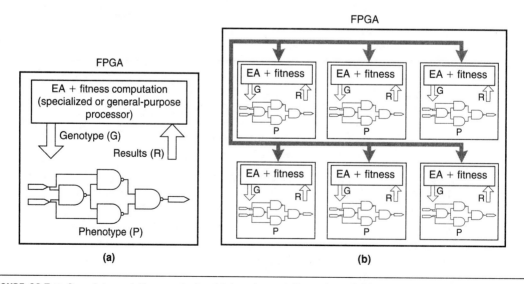

FIGURE 33.7 ▪ Complete evolution: centralized (a) and population oriented (b).

One example of a self-reconfigurable platform that performs online and on-chip evolution is that of Upegui and Sanchez [42, 43]. Their standalone platform consists of a MicroBlaze processor with memory access control, ICAP (internal configuration access port) access, and a reconfigurable evolvable section, as depicted in Figure 33.8. The full system, implemented in a Virtex-II FPGA, runs an EA on the MicroBlaze processor, reads a section of the configuration bitstream through the ICAP, modifies the bitstream according to the genome currently evaluated in the MicroBlaze, sends back the bitstream though the ICAP for partially reconfiguring the FPGA, and evaluates the fitness of the current individual by interacting with the reconfigurable evolvable section through the standard OPB bus. Upegui and Sanchez [42] evolve nonuniform cellular rules and FPGA lookup table (LUT) configurations with fixed interconnectivity. In Upegui and Sanchez [43], Boolean networks are evolved as well, but in this case the interconnectivity is not fixed, so the system topology is also driven by the evolutionary algorithm.

Other interesting experiments were carried out by Haddow and Tufte [41] in which a hardware implementation of a GA, the "GA pipeline," evolves a robot controller. Glette and Torresen [44] report the implementation of a GA on an embedded PowerPC processor in a Virtex-II Pro FPGA that evolves a circuit in the same FPGA.

Population-oriented evolution

A hardware implementation of the *full population*, not only of one individual (as was the case in previous categories), is the distinctive feature of the population-oriented approach (Figure 33.7(b)). A significant example is the work of Goeke et al. [45], where an evolving cellular system was implemented in which evolution takes place completely on-chip. This system is based on the cellular automata model—a discrete dynamic system that performs computations in

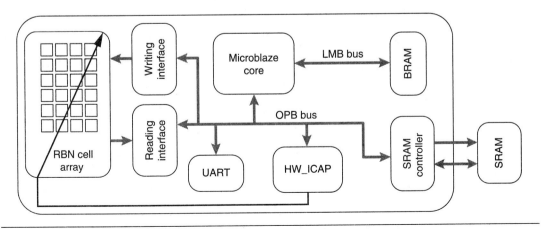

FIGURE 33.8 ■ The setup of a complete and centralized self-reconfigurable evolvable platform.

a distributed fashion on a spatially extended grid. A cellular automaton consists of an array of cells, each of which can be in one of a finite number of possible states, updated synchronously in discrete timesteps according to a *local, identical* interaction rule [46]. The *state* of a cell at the next timestep is determined by the current state of a surrounding neighborhood of cells. This transition is usually specified in the form of a *rule table*, which delineates the cell's next state for each possible neighborhood configuration. The cellular array (grid) is n-dimensional, where typically $n = 1, 2, 3$. Nonuniform cellular automata have also been considered in which the local update rule need not be identical for all grid cells [47].

Based on the *cellular programming* EA of Sipper [47], Goeke et al. [45] implemented an evolving, one-dimensional, nonuniform cellular automaton. The main feature of the cellular programming algorithm is the fact that genetic operators are computed in a distributed way: Each automaton modifies its own rule based on its own and its neighbors' fitness. Each of the system's 56 binary-state cells contains a genome that represents its rule table. These genomes are initialized at random and then are subjected to evolution.

The environment imposed on the system specifies the resolution of a global synchronization task: On presentation of a random initial configuration of cellular states, the system must reach, after a bounded number of timesteps, a configuration for which the states of the cells oscillate between all zeros and all ones on successive timesteps. This may be compared to a swarm of fireflies, thousands of which may flash on and off in unison, having started from totally uncoordinated flickerings. Each insect has its own rhythm, which changes only through local interactions with its neighbors'. Because of the local connectivity of the system, this global behavior, which involves the entire grid, makes for a difficult task. Nonetheless, applying the evolutionary process of Sipper [47], the system evolves (i.e., the genomes change) such that the task is completed.

The evolving cellular system described here exhibits complete on-chip evolution in that all operations are performed in hardware in a distributed population-based manner with no reference to an external computer.

33.4.4 Open-ended Evolution

The last subdivision, situated at the top of the phylogenetic axis, involves a population of hardware entities evolving in an open-ended environment. When the fitness criterion is imposed by the user in accordance with the task to be performed (currently the rule with artificial evolution techniques), we attain a form of guided, or directed, evolution. This is to be contrasted with the open-ended evolution that occurs in nature, which admits no externally imposed fitness criterion but rather an implicit, emergent, dynamic one (which can arguably be summed up as reproducibility). Open-ended undirected evolution is the only form of evolution known to produce such devices as eyes, wings, and nervous systems and to give rise to the formation of species. Undirectedness may have to be applied to artificial evolution if we want to observe the emergence of completely novel systems.

We argue that only open-ended evolution can be truly considered EHW, which is still an elusive goal at present. We point out that a more correct term would probably be *evolving hardware*. A natural application area for such systems is the field of autonomous robots—that is, machines capable of operating in unknown environments without human intervention [48]. Specifically, collective robotics exhibits a population of individuals interacting in a common environment, in which they can learn to cooperate or to compete for achieving their goals [49]. In their interactions the individuals exhibit a high level of emergence as a first step to open endedness. Modular robotics, a subtype of collective robotics, also offers a promising open-ended real environment.

A modular robotic platform well suited for evolving distributed hardware is YaMoR. This is a modular robot composed of mechanically homogeneous modules [50], each of which contains an FPGA-based system that allows wireless FPGA configuration and on-board self-reconfiguration. Another interesting example is what we call Hard-Tierra. This involves the hardware implementation (e.g., FPGA circuits) of the Tierra "world," which consists of an open-ended environment of evolving computer programs [51]. Hard-Tierra is important because it demonstrates that open-endedness does not necessarily imply a real, biological environment.

33.5 EVOLVABLE HARDWARE DIGITAL PLATFORMS

The hardware substrate that supports evolution is one of the most important initial decisions to make when evolving hardware. The hardware architecture is closely related to the type of solution being evolved. Hardware platforms usually have a cellular structure composed of uniform or nonuniform components. In some cases, we can evolve the components' functionality; in others, the connectivity; or sometimes both, with the most powerful ones. FPGAs fit well into this third category because they are composed of configurable logic elements interconnected by configurable switch matrices. FPGA configuration is contained in a configuration bitstream, which holds every function and switch position to be configured for implementing a given design. Current FPGAs allow the processing of partial bitstreams, reconfiguring just a sector of the FPGA while the remaining logic stays the same.

When evolving a circuit on an FPGA, we consider the logic cell as the basic element. The logic cells' configuration and their interconnectivity are defined by the evolution. However, this implies a huge search space to explore and can prevent the EA from finding a solution. A common technique to constrain the search space is to define a basic block as a set of logic cells. In this way each basic block can be an artificial neuron, a fuzzy rule, or a more complex cell in general. Another option is to constrain the connectionism, using layered architectures, to a certain neighborhood, or by just defining it as fixed.

The most basic requirement when evolving hardware is to have a set of high- or low-level evolvable components and a hardware substrate supporting them.

These evolvable components are the basic elements from which the evolved circuits will be built (transistors, logic gates, arithmetic functions, functional cells, etc.), and the evolvable substrate must be a flexible hardware platform that allows arbitrary configurations mapped from a genome. FPGAs constitute the perfect hardware substrate, given their connectivity and functional flexibility. The evolvable substrate can be implemented using one of two main techniques: (1) exploiting the flexibility provided by the FPGA's configuration logic and (2) building a virtual flexible substrate on top of the logic.

In the first approach the configuration bitstream of the FPGA is directly generated. In this way, we can make better use of FPGA resources—logic functions are directly mapped into the FPGAs LUTs, and connections are directly mapped to routing switch matrices and multiplexers—but the penalty is very low-level circuit descriptions [33, 38, 52]. In the second approach a virtual reconfigurable circuit is built on top of the actual circuit [53]. In this way the designer can also define the configuration bitstream and determine which features of the circuit to evolve. This approach has been widely used by several groups, as it produces enhanced flexibility and ease of implementation. The penalty here is the cost of an inefficient use of logic resources [25, 27, 42, 45, 53–60].

Different custom chips have been proposed for this purpose with very interesting results: The main interest in proposing an architecture is that commercial FPGAs are designed for general-purpose applications, so they do not necessarily fit the requirements for evolvable architectures. For example, commercial devices may have illegal configurations that cause short circuits; this is reasonable for standard FPGA users who rely on the CAD flow to create the design, but it can be disastrous for genetically evolved bitstreams. Custom evolvable chips generally provide dynamic and partial reconfiguration, contain multi-context configuration memories, and can be configured with arbitrary bitstreams. However, although the custom chips are better suited to EHW applications, the commodity devices benefit from economies of scale and access to more advanced fabrication processes.

Different chips and platforms have been developed to provide the flexibility necessary for evolving analog, digital, and mixed circuits; some of them have been designed specifically for EHW, while for others EHW is just another application field. Among them we find different levels of granularity, different types of reconfiguration including dynamic and static reconfigurations, and the possibility of loading partial configuration bitstreams, and the utilization of context memories.

33.5.1 Xilinx XC6200 Family

The obsolete Xilinx XC6200 family [61] deserves a special mention in a discussion of EHW platforms. For several years, the XC6200 family constituted the perfect platform for intrinsic EHW, because it made possible downloading any arbitrary bitstream without risking contention given its multiplexer-based connection architecture. It also allowed dynamic reconfiguration, making it more flexible for adaptive algorithms in a general sense. The results reported by Thompson [32, 33, 38, 62], discussed previously, are a very good example of the XC6200's potential for evolving circuits.

The XC6200 represents an important initial stepping-stone in the EHW field. It has also been used for implementing several types of applications, among them cooperative robot controllers [63], sorting networks [64], and image-processing algorithms [65].

33.5.2 Evolution on Commercial FPGAs

After the XC6200 disappeared, many research groups turned to the Xilinx XC4000 family. However, these FPGAs had an important drawback for evolving hardware: They were not partially reconfigurable, and no arbitrary bitstreams were allowed. When the Virtex FPGAs appeared, they exhibited two well-appreciated features for the EHW community: partial and dynamic reconfiguration. However, not all the evolution-friendly features from the XC6200 were kept. Specifically, the connection mechanism does not support arbitrary bitstreams, making these FPGAs susceptible to damage by internal short circuits.

Recent work on evolvable circuits in commercial FPGAs has focused on the Virtex and Virtex-II architectures from Xilinx [66] and will extend its focus to Virtex-4 in the near future. Two main approaches have been used for evolving Virtex circuits: using virtual reconfigurable circuits [67] and partially reconfiguring the FPGA.

Virtual reconfiguration

Two solutions were used in order to replace the obsolete XC6200 family: implementing an ASIC evolvable circuit (only achievable by some privileged groups, summarized in Section 33.5.3) and building a reconfigurable circuit on top of another reconfigurable circuit (i.e., a virtual reconfigurable device [53]). The concept of a virtual reconfigurable circuit is depicted in Figure 33.9, where a reconfigurable neuron cell constitutes the device's basic logic cell.

In the beginning, the most intuitive method was to reconstruct the XC6200 architecture. At the University of York, a virtual XC6200 CLB was implemented in Virtex FPGAs [68, 69]. Slorach and Sharman [54] also used virtual XC6200 cells in the Xilinx XC4010 and Altera EPF6010A, evolving configuration bitstreams that configured not the FPGA itself but the virtual XC6200 CLBs. Afterward, other research groups developed different reconfigurable architectures with enhanced features, several of which had the goals of flexibility and easy reconfiguration [54–59, 70–72]. For example, Sekanina and Drabek [70] developed a virtual reconfigurable cell called a *functional block* (FB) and used an array of FBs for image compression. Durbeck and Macias [71] implemented an 8×8 cell matrix using a Xilinx Spartan-2 FPGA.

With this approach came the possibility of designing any desired reconfigurable fabric. In most cases the architecture consists of a fine-grained cellular array in which a general-purpose evolvable architecture is proposed. However,

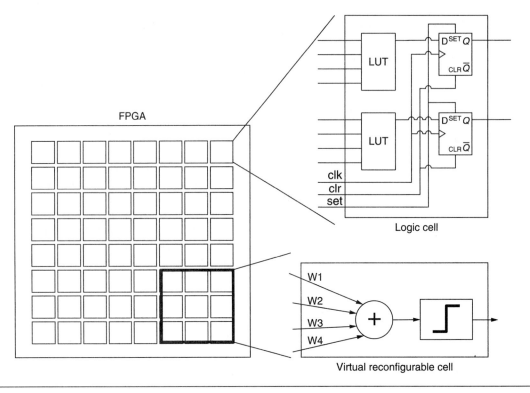

FIGURE 33.9 ▪ A virtual reconfigurable circuit with a reconfigurable neuron.

problem-oriented reconfigurable fabrics can use coarser-grained architectures, where a reduced set of features is evolved.

Dynamic partial reconfiguration

In addition to the Xilinx XC6200, other commercial platforms have been partially reconfigured for evolving circuits, with the main focus on the Xilinx Virtex families. However, there are two main issues in evolving circuits by partially reconfiguring Virtex architectures. The first is the size of their configuration bitstreams, which implies a huge search space for the EA. The second is the generation of invalid bitstreams—that is, bitstreams that cause internal contentions. Different solutions to these problems have been suggested.

Haddow and Tufte proposed a two-dimensional array of Sblocks [72], each containing a flip-flop, a 5-input LUT, and some routing resources. Sblocks provide a reduced configurability compared to Virtex cells in order to reduce the search space size and to guarantee contention-free configurations. Even though the Sblock array is virtually reconfigurable, the functionality is reconfigured by partially reconfiguring a Virtex FPGA. Haddow and Tufte used a partial bitstream for reconfiguring only the LUT contents.

At the University of York, JBits [73] has been used for evolving circuits. JBits is a Java API for describing circuits and manipulating configuration bitstreams. It allows safe generation of partial bitstreams, permitting the modification of internal modules in the FPGA design. At York, LUT contents have been mapped from a genome for evolving simple combinatorial functions [74], fault tolerance circuits [69], and robot controllers for obstacle avoidance [75]. Also using JBits, Levi and Guccione from Xilinx developed a tool called GeneticFPGA [76], which translates a configuration bitstream from a chromosome, making it easy to generate legal bitstreams.

Even though JBits provides interesting features for EHW, it has several limitations, such as the impossibility of running on an embedded platform (for on-chip evolution), dependence on supported FPGA families and supported boards, incompatibility with other hardware description languages (HDLs), and limited support from Xilinx, mainly reflected in insufficient documentation.

Several ways to overcome these limitations have been proposed at the EPFL. Upegui and Sanchez [52] summarize three techniques for EHW by partially reconfiguring Virtex and Virtex-II families dynamically, without using JBits. The first is a coarse-grained high-level solution based on the modular partial reconfiguration flow proposed by Xilinx [77]. It defines large evolvable functions, implemented as modules, that are well suited for architecture exploration [27].

The second and third techniques are fine-grained low-level solutions. In both of the cases, hard-macros are used to define an evolvable component. Then by placing the hard-macros they modify, the bitstream partially reconfigures components of the hard macros. The second technique uses the difference-based partial reconfiguration flow proposed by Xilinx [77]. The third technique directly manipulates the bitstream in a manner similar to the XC6200, by adding some constraints (only LUT and multiplexer configuration modifications are allowed). These techniques are well suited for fine-tuning. With the difference-based approach, Mermoud et al. [25] report the intrinsic evolution of a fuzzy classifier; and with the bitstream manipulation, they report a complete evolution of cellular automata [42] and Boolean networks [43].

33.5.3 Custom Evolvable FPGAs

One of the more recent evolvable chips is the POEtic tissue [78,79], a computational substrate optimized for the implementation of digital systems inspired by the POE model presented in the introduction to this chapter. The POEtic tissue is a self-contained, flexible physical substrate designed (1) to interact with the environment through spatially distributed sensors and actuators; (2) to develop and adapt its functionality through a process of evolution, growth, and learning to a dynamic and partially unpredictable environment; and (3) to self-repair parts damaged by aging or environmental factors in order to remain viable and retain the same functionality.

The POEtic tissue is composed of a two-dimensional array of POEtic cells, each designed as a 3-layer structure following the three axes of bio-inspiration (Figure 33.10):

■ The phylogenetic layer acts on a cell's genetic material. It can be used to find and select the genes of the cells for the genotype layer, which is conceptually the simplest of the three tissue layers as it is mainly a memory containing the genetic information of the organism.

■ Ontogeny concerns the development of the individual and thus the mapping or configuration layer of the cell, which implements cellular differentiation and growth. In addition, it has an impact on the system as a whole for self-repair. The configuration layer selects which gene will be expressed depending on a user-defined differentiation algorithm.

■ The epigenetic axis modifies the behavior of the organism during its operation and is therefore best applied to the phenotype, which is probably the most application-dependent layer. If the final application is a neural network, the phenotype layer will consist of an artificial neuron.

A key aspect of the applicability of the POEtic tissue, in addition to its architecture, is its reconfigurability. A molecule can be partially reconfigured by an on-chip microprocessor or by neighbor molecules. For EHW, this feature is

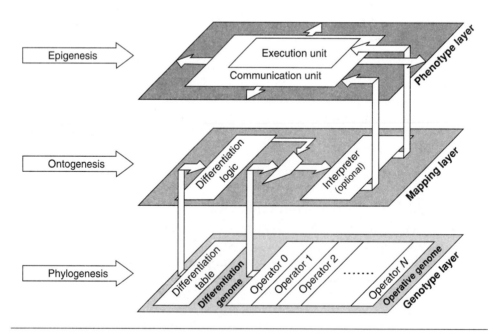

FIGURE 33.10 ▪ The organizational layers of the POEtic cell.

very important in terms of execution time. Because only two clock cycles are needed for a write, and three words of 32 bits define a complete molecule, the configuration of the entire array (or a part of it) is very fast. In comparison with commercial FPGAs, such as the Virtex-II, in which at least a full configuration frame must be sent each time, reconfiguration takes place in parallel, allowing a huge speedup.

A distinctive feature of the POEtic tissue is its two-dimensional array of routing units that implement a dynamic routing algorithm [80]. It is used for intercellular communication, allowing the tissue to dynamically create paths between cells. The dynamic routing can be performed by a distributed algorithm [80] or by the on-chip processor.

Another very important circuit is the evolvable LSI chip developed by Higuchi's group [81]. It includes a GA unit and has the ability to process two chromosomes in parallel. Higuchi's group is famous for the large number of applications implemented in their chips [82, 83]. They have implemented an adaptive prosthetic hand controller [84, 85] that can adapt to the user's electromyographic signals in less than 10 minutes with a much more compact circuit than required with a neural network (before that, the user had to adapt to the hand instead of the hand to the user, requiring more than a month of training). They have also evolved data compressors for electrophotographic printing [86, 87], often attaining compression ratios twice those obtained with international standard compression algorithms such as Lempel-Ziv, JBIG, and JBIG2. It must be noted that Higuchi's applications often finish as part of a commercial product. Other interesting applications implemented by the same group include robot navigation controllers [88] and low-power integrated circuits [89].

This chapter focused primarily on evolution for digital devices; however, several platforms have been proposed for analog and mixed-signal circuit evolution. At the Jet Propulsion Laboratory of the California Institute of Technology, a field-programmable transistor array (FPTA) [90] has been developed that is the basis of the Standalone Board-level Evolvable System (SABLES) [91]. Layzell [92] proposed the evolvable motherboard: a diagonal matrix of analog switches connected to up to six plug-in daughter boards, which contain the desired basic elements for evolution.

33.6 CONCLUSIONS AND FUTURE DIRECTIONS

EHW has been shown to be effective at finding solutions [82, 83] for real-world applications. Additionally, some solutions have proven to perform better than their engineered counterparts [83, 89, 93]. On the other hand, EHW generally performs poorly, as a system-level solution: Microprocessor architectures, for example, are not among evolution results. As a matter of fact, evolution works better when the target is a complex cellular architecture: cellular automata, neural networks, or gate arrays.

If we look at the EHW work carried so far, we find many common characteristics spanning most current systems that often differ from biological evolution (this difference is not necessarily disparaging):

- Evolution pursues a predefined goal: The design of an electronic circuit is subject to precise specifications. On finding the desired circuit, the evolutionary process terminates.
- The population has no material existence. At best, in what has been called intrinsic and complete evolution, there is one circuit available onto which individuals from the population are loaded *one at a time* to evaluate their fitness.
- The absence of a real population in which individuals coexist simultaneously entails notable difficulties in the realization of interactions between "organisms." This usually results in a completely independent fitness calculation, contrary to nature, which exhibits a coevolutionary scenario.
- The different phases of evolution are carried out sequentially, controlled by a central unit.

These limitations suggest that the simple application of EAs to hardware design is not enough and that future research in EHW must not be limited to exploration of architectures and substrates; there is also much to do at the algorithmic level. Human-made adaptable systems are still far from exhibiting an adaptation comparable to living beings, and even though we have yet to attain circuits of equivalent complexity, limitations are not just a matter of magnitude. Only by modeling together the three axes of life (phylogeny, ontogeny, and epigenesis) will we be able to build systems featuring naturelike adaptation.

Future trends in nanotechnology are also guiding us toward "Avogadro computers"—that is, massively parallel devices with 10^{23} transistors. What to do with such huge number of transistors, and how to use, interconnect, and program them, goes beyond present engineering knowledge; however, EHW architectures and algorithms arise as a promising solution for dealing with the design complexity of these machines.

In this chapter we focused on evolving silicon circuits, which constitute the main developments achieved by the EHW community. However, other types of substrates have been evolved that extend the domain and represent new directions for evolvable hardware. For example, NASA researchers have been working on evolving antennas for space missions [94, 95]. Miller and Downing are currently working on evolving liquid crystals (LC) [96]—by applying electric fields mapped from a genome, they modify the LC molecular alignment to implement a desired function. Molecular circuit design is another promising evolvable substrate. Masiero et al. [97] report the use of a GA for tuning component parameters in a molecular circuit. Quantum circuit synthesis, too, is a potential field for EHW [98], given that designing circuits in such a substrate will require new design paradigms.

References

[1] T. Higuchi, T. Niwa, T. Tanaka, H. Iba, H. de Garis, T. Furuya. Evolving hardware with genetic learning: A first step towards building a Darwin Machine. From animals to animals 2. *Proceedings of the International Conference on Simulation of Adaptive Behavior*, 1993.

[2] H. de Garis. Evolvable hardware: Genetic programming of a Darwin Machine. *Proceedings of the International Conference on Artificial Neural Nets and Genetic Algorithms*, 1993.

[3] E. Sanchez, D. Mange, M. Sipper, M. Tomassini, A. Perez-Uribe, A. Stauffer. Phylogeny, ontogeny, and epigenesis: Three sources of biological inspiration for softening hardware. *Evolvable Systems: From Biology to Hardware, LNCS* 1259, 1997.

[4] M. Sipper, E. Sanchez, D. Mange, M. Tomassini, A. Perez-Uribe, A. Stauffer. A phylogenetic, ontogenetic, and epigenetic view of bio-inspired hardware systems. *IEEE Transactions on Evolutionary Computation* 1(1), 1997.

[5] S. Mitra, Y. Hayashi. Neuro-fuzzy rule generation: Survey in soft computing framework. *IEEE Transactions on Neural Networks* 11(3), 2000.

[6] T. Bäck. *Evolutionary Algorithms in Theory and Practice: Evolution Strategies, Evolutionary Programming, Genetic Algorithms*, Oxford University Press, 1996.

[7] D. B. Fogel. *Evolutionary Computation: Toward a New Philosophy of Machine Intelligence*, 2nd ed., IEEE Press, 2000.

[8] J. R. Koza. *Genetic Programming: On the Programming of Computers by Means of Natural Selection*, MIT Press, 1992.

[9] M. Mitchell. *An Introduction to Genetic Algorithms*, MIT Press, 1996.

[10] M. D. Vose. *The Simple Genetic Algorithm: Foundations and Theory*, MIT Press, 1999.

[11] J. Pinter. *Global Optimization in Action (Continuous and Lipschitz Optimization: Algorithms, Implementations and Applications)*, Kluwer Academic Press, 1996.

[12] E. Sanchez, M. Tomassini. Towards evolvable hardware. *LNCS* 1062. Springer-Verlag, 1996.

[13] Y. Liu. Evolvable systems: from biology to hardware. *Proceedings of the Fourth International Conference, ICES*, October 2001.

[14] A. M. Tyrrell, P. C. Haddow, J. Torresen. Evolvable systems: From biology to hardware. *Proceedings of the 5th International Conference, LNCS*, March 2003.

[15] J. M. Moreno, J. Madrenas, J. Cosp. Evolvable systems: From biology to hardware. *Proceedings of the Sixth International Conference, ICES 2005*, September 2005.

[16] T. Higuchi, M. Iwata, W. Liu. Evolvable systems: From biology to hardware. *Proceedings of the First International Conference*, October 7–8, 1996. *LNCS* 1259, Heidelberg: Springer-Verlag, 1997.

[17] M. Sipper, D. Mange, A. Pérez-Uribe. Evolvable systems: From biology to hardware. *Proceedings of the Second International Conference*, September, *LNCS* 1478, Heidelberg: Springer, 1998.

[18] J. Miller. Evolvable systems: From biology to hardware. *Proceedings of the Third International Conference, ICES 2000*, April 17–19, 2000. *LNCS* 1801, Heidelberg: Springer, 2000.

[19] A. Stoica, D. Keymeulen, J. D. Lohn. *Proceedings of the First NASA/DOD Workshop on Evolvable Hardware*, July. IEEE Computer Society, 1999.

[20] A. Stoica, J. D. Lohn, R. Katz, D. Keymeulen, R. Zebulum. *Proceedings of the 2002 NASA/DOD Conference on Evolvable Hardware*, July. IEEE Computer Society, 2002.

[21] J. D. Lohn, R. Zebulum, J. Steincamp, D. Keymeulen, A. Stoica, M. Ferguson. *Proceedings of the 2003 NASA/DOD Conference on Evolvable Hardware*, July. IEEE Computer Society, 2003.

[22] R. Zebulum, D. Gwaltney, G. Hornby, D. Keymeulen, J. D. Lohn. A. Stoica. *Proceedings of the 2004 NASA/DOD Conference on Evolvable Hardware*, July 2004. IEEE Computer Society.

[23] J. D. Lohn, D. Gwaltney, G. Hornby, R. Zebulum, D. Keymeulen. A. Stoica. *Proceedings of the 2005 NASA/DOD Conference on Evolvable Hardware*, June 2005. IEEE Computer Society.

[24] X. Yao, T. Higuchi. Promises and challenges of evolvable hardware. *IEEE Transactions on Systems, Man, and Cybernetics, Part C: Applications and Reviews* 29(1), 1999.

[25] G. Mermoud, A. Upegui, C. A. Pena. E. Sanchez. A dynamically-reconfigurable FPGA platform for evolving fuzzy systems. *Computational Intelligence and Bioinspired Systems, LNCS* 3512, 2005.

[26] M. Murakawa, S. Yoshizawa, I. Kajitani, X. Yao, N. Kajihara, M. Iwata, T. Higuchi. The GRD chip: Genetic reconfiguration of DSPs for neural network processing. *IEEE Transactions on Computers* 48(6), 1999.

[27] A. Upegui, C. A. Peña-Reyes, E. Sanchez. An FPGA platform for on-line topology exploration of spiking neural networks. *Microprocessors and Microsystems* 29(5), 2005.

[28] H. Hemmi, J. Mizoguchi, K. Shimohara. Development and evolution of hardware behaviors. *Towards Evolvable Hardware, LNCS* 1062, 1996.

[29] J. R. Koza, F. H. Bennett, D. Andre, M. A. Keane. Synthesis of topology and sizing of analog electrical circuits by means of genetic programming. *Computer Methods in Applied Mechanics and Engineering* 186(2), 2000.

[30] J. W. Atmar. Speculation on the Evolution of Intelligence and Its Possible Realization in Machine Form, Ph.D. dissertation, New Mexico State University, Las Cruces, 1976.

[31] T. Higuchi, M. Iwata, I. Kajitani, H. Iba, Y. Hirao, F. T. Furuya, B. Manderick. Evolvable hardware and its application to pattern recognition and fault-tolerant systems. *Towards Evolvable Hardware, LNCS* 1062, 1996.

[32] A. Thompson. Silicon evolution. *Proceedings of Genetic Programming*, J. R. Koza et al. (eds.), MIT Press, 1996.

[33] A. Thompson. An evolved circuit, intrinsic in silicon, entwined with physics. *Evolvable Systems: From Biology to Hardware, LNCS* 1259, 1997.

[34] Xilinx, Inc. *The Programmable Logic Data Book*, 1996.

[35] G. K. Venayagamoorthy, V. G. Gudise. Swarm intelligence for digital circuits implementation on field-programmable gate array platforms. *Proceedings of the 2004 NASA/DOD Conference on Evolvable Hardware*, July 2004.

[36] B. C. Kahne. *A Genetic Algorithm-Based Place-and-Route Compiler for a Run-time Reconfigurable Computing System*, Master's thesis, Virginia Polytechnic Institute and State University, Blacksburg, VA, 1997.

[37] T. A. Ly, J. T. Mowchenko. Applying simulated evolution to high-level synthesis. *IEEE Transactions on Computer-Aided Design of Integrated Circuits and Systems* 12(3), 1993.

[38] A. Thompson, I. Harvey, P. Husbands. Unconstrained evolution and hard consequences. *Towards Evolvable Hardware, LNCS*, 1996.

[39] M. Murakawa, S. Yoshizawa, I. Kajitani, T. Furuya, M. Iwata, T. Higuchi. Hardware evolution at function level. *Parallel Problem Solving from Nature (PPSN IV), LNCS* 1141, 1996.

[40] M. Iwata, I. Kajitani, H. Yamada, H. Iba, T. Higuchi. A pattern recognition system using evolvable hardware. *Parallel Problem Solving from Nature (PPSN IV), LNCS* 1141, 1996.

[41] P. Haddow, G. Tufte. Evolving a robot controller in hardware. *Proceedings of the Norwegian Computer Science Conference*, 1999.

[42] A. Upegui, E. Sanchez. On-chip and on-line self-reconfigurable adaptable platform: The non-uniform cellular automata case. *Proceedings of the 20th IEEE International Parallel and Distributed Processing Symposium*, 2006.

[43] A. Upegui, E. Sanchez. Evolving hardware with self-reconfigurable connectivity in Xilinx FPGAs. *Proceedings of the First NASA/ESA Conference on Adaptive Hardware and Systems*, 2006.

[44] K. Glette, J. Torresen. A flexible on-chip evolution system implemented on a Xilinx Virtex-II Pro device. *Evolvable Systems: From Biology to Hardware, LNCS* 3637, 2005.

[45] M. Goeke, M. Sipper, D. Mange, A. Stauffer, E. Sanchez, M. Tomassini. Online autonomous evolware. *Evolvable Systems: From Biology to Hardware, LNCS* 1259, 1997.

[46] T. Toffoli, N. Margolus. *Cellular Automata Machines: A New Environment for Modeling*. MIT Press Series in Scientific Computation, 1987.

[47] M. Sipper. *Evolution of Parallel Cellular Machines: The Cellular Programming Approach*, Springer, 1997.

[48] R. A. Brooks. New approaches to robotics. *Science* 253, 1991.

[49] Y. U. Cao, A. S. Fukunaga, A. B. Kahng. Cooperative mobile robotics: Antecedents and directions. *Autonomous Robots* 4(1), 1997.

[50] R. Moeckel, C. Jaquier, K. Drapel, E. Dittrich, A. Upegui, A. Ijspeert. YaMoR and Bluemove: An autonomous modular robot with Bluetooth interface for exploring adaptive locomotion. *Proceedings of the 8th International Conference on Climbing and Walking Robots (CLAWAR)*, 2005.

[51] T. S. Ray. An approach to the synthesis of life. *Artificial Life II, SFI Studies in the Sciences of Complexity* 10, 1992.

[52] A. Upegui, E. Sanchez. Evolving hardware by dynamically reconfiguring Xilinx FPGAs. *Evolvable Systems: From Biology to Hardware, LNCS* 3637, 2005.

[53] L. Sekanina. *Evolvable Components: From Theory to Hardware Implementations*, Springer, 2004.

[54] C. Slorach, K. Sharman. The design and implementation of custom architectures for evolvable hardware using off-the-shelf programmable devices. *Evolvable Systems: From Biology to Hardware, LNCS*, 2000.

[55] Y. Zhang, S. Smith, A. Tyrrell. Digital circuit design using intrinsic evolvable hardware. *Proceedings of the 2004 NASA/DOD Conference on Evolvable Hardware*, July 2004.

[56] L. Sekanina, S. Friedl. On routine implementation of virtual evolvable devices using COMBO6. *Proceedings of the 2004 NASA/DOD Conference on Evolvable Hardware*, July 2004.

[57] K. Vinger, J. Torresen. Implementing evolution of FIR-filters efficiently in an FPGA. *Proceedings of the 2003 NASA/DOD Conference on Evolvable Hardware*, July 2003.

[58] L. Sekanina. Towards evolvable IP cores for FPGAs. *Proceedings of the 2003 NASA/DOD Conference on Evolvable Hardware*, July 2003.

[59] P. C. Haddow, G. Tufte. An evolvable hardware FPGA for adaptive hardware. *Proceedings of the 2000 Congress on Evolutionary Computation*, 2000.

[60] M. Sipper, M. Goeke, D. Mange, A. Stauffer, E. Sanchez, M. Tomassini. The firefly machine: Online evolware. *Proceedings of the IEEE International Conference on Evolutionary Computation*, 1997.

[61] Xilinx, Inc. *The XC6200 Data Sheet v.1.7*, 1996.

[62] A. Thompson, P. Layzell. Evolution of robustness in an electronics design. *Evolvable Systems: From Biology to Hardware, LNCS* 1801, 2000.

[63] D.-W. Lee, C.-B. Ban, K.-B. Sim, H.-S. Seok, L. Kwang-Ju, B.-T. Zhang. Behavior evolution of autonomous mobile robot using genetic programming based on evolvable hardware. *Proceeding of the 2000 IEEE International Conference on Systems, Man, Cybernetics*, 2000.

[64] J. R. Koza, F. H. Bennett, J. Hutchings, S. L. Bade, M. A. Keane, D. Andre. Evolving sorting networks using genetic programming and rapidly reconfigurable field-programmable gate arrays. *Workshop on Evolvable Systems. International Joint Conference on Artificial Intelligence*, 1997.

[65] J. Dumoulin, J. A. Foster, J. F. Frenzel, S. McGrew. Special purpose image convolution with evolvable hardware. *Real-World Applications of Evolutionary Computing, EvoWorkshops 2000, LNCS*, 2000.

[66] Xilinx, Inc. *Virtex-II Platform FPGA User Guide* (*www.xilinx.com*), March 2005.

[67] L. Sekanina. Virtual reconfigurable circuits for real-world applications of evolvable hardware. *Evolvable Systems: From Biology to Hardware, LNCS* 2606, 2003.

[68] G. Hollingworth, S. Smith, A. Tyrrell. Safe intrinsic evolution of Virtex devices. *Proceedings of the Second NASA/DoD Workshop on Evolvable Hardware*, 2000.

[69] R. O. Canham, A. Tyrrell. Evolved fault tolerance in evolvable hardware. *Proceedings of the Congress on Evolutionary Computation*, 2002.

[70] L. Sekanina, V. Drabek. The concept of pseudo evolvable hardware. *Proceedings of the IFAC Workshop on Programmable Devices and Systems*, 2000.

[71] L. Durbeck, N. J. Macias. Defect-tolerant, fine-grained parallel testing of a cell matrix. *Proceedings of SPIE ITCom* 4867, 2002.

[72] P. Haddow, G. Tufte. Bridging the genotype-phenotype mapping for digital FPGAs. *Proceedings of the Third NASA/DoD Workshop on Evolvable Hardware*, 2001.

[73] S. A. Guccione, D. Levi, P. Sundararajan. JBits: A Java-based interface for reconfigurable computing. *Proceedings of the Second Annual Military and Aerospace Applications of Programmable Devices and Technologies Conference*, 1999.

[74] G. Hollingworth, S. Smith, A. Tyrrell. The intrinsic evolution of Virtex devices through Internet reconfigurable logic. *Evolvable Systems: From Biology to Hardware, LNCS* 1801, 2000.

[75] A. M. Tyrrell, R. A. Krohling, Y. Zhou. Evolutionary algorithm for the promotion of evolvable hardware. *IEE Proceedings—Computers and Digital Techniques* 151(4), 2004.

[76] D. Levi, S. A. Guccione. Genetic FPGA: Evolving stable circuits on mainstream FPGA devices. *Proceedings of the First NASA/DOD Workshop on Evolvable Hardware*, 1999.

[77] Xilinx, Inc. *XAPP 290: Two Flows for Partial Reconfiguration: Module Based or Difference Based* (*www.xilinx.com*), September 2004.

[78] Y. Thoma, E. Sanchez. A reconfigurable chip for evolvable hardware. *Proceedings of the Genetic and Evolutionary Computation Conference*, 2004.

[79] Y. Thoma, G. Tempesti, E. Sanchez, J.M.M. Arostegui. POEtic: An electronic tissue for bio-inspired cellular applications. *Biosystems* 76(1–3), 2004.

[80] Y. Thoma, E. Sanchez, J.M.M. Arostegui, G. Tempesti. A dynamic routing algorithm for a bio-inspired reconfigurable circuit. *Proceedings of the International Conference on Field-Programmable Logic and Applications* 2778, 2003.

[81] M. Iwata, I. Kajitani, Y. Liu, N. Kajihara, T. Higuchi. Implementation of a gate-level evolvable hardware chip. *Evolvable Systems: From Biology to Hardware, LNCS* 2210, 2001.

[82] T. Higuchi, M. Iwata, H. Sakanashi, E. Takahashi, M. Murakawa, I. Kajitani. Dynamic adaptive devices and their applications. *Bulletin of the Electrotechnical Laboratory, Special Issue: RWC Research Toward Realization of Real World Intelligence* 64(4/5), 2000.

[83] T. Higuchi, M. Iwata, D. Keymeulen, H. Sakanashi, M. Murakawa, I. Kajitani, E. Takahashi, K. Toda, M. Salami, N. Kajihara, N. Otsu. Real-world applications of analog and digital evolvable hardware. *IEEE Transactions on Evolutionary Computation* 3(3), 1999.

[84] I. Kajitani, M. Iwata, M. Harada, T. Higuchi. A myoelectric controlled prosthetic hand with an evolvable hardware LSI chip. *Technology and Disability, Special Issue: Advances in the Control of Prosthetic Arms* 15(2), 2003.

[85] I. Kajitani, T. Hoshino, N. Kajihara, M. Iwata, T. Higuchi. An evolvable hardware chip and its application as a multi-function prosthetic hand controller. *Proceedings of the 16th National Conference on Artificial Intelligence*, 1999.

[86] H. Sakanashi, M. Iwata, T. Higuchi. Evolvable hardware for lossless compression of very high resolution bi-level images. *IEE Proceedings—Computers and Digital Techniques* 151(4), 2004.

[87] H. Sakanashi, M. Iwata, D. Keymulen, M. Murakawa, I. Kajitani, M. Tanaka, T. Higuchi. Evolvable hardware chips and their applications. *Proceedings of the International Conference on Systems, Man, and Cybernetics*, 1999.

[88] D. Keymeulen, M. Iwata, Y. Kuniyoshi, T. Higuchi. Online evolution for a self-adapting robotic navigation system using evolvable hardware. *Artificial Life* 4, 1998.

[89] E. Takahashi, M. Murakawa, Y. Kasai, T. Higuchi. Power dissipation reductions with genetic algorithms. *Proceedings of the 2003 NASA/DoD Conference on Evolvable Hardware*, 2003.

[90] A. Stoica, R. Zebulum, D. Keymeulen, R. Tawel, T. Daud, A. Thakoor. Reconfigurable VLSI architectures for evolvable hardware: From experimental field-programmable transistor arrays to evolution-oriented chips. *IEEE Transactions on Very Large Scale Integration (VLSI) Systems* 9(1), 2001.

[91] A. Stoica, R. Zebulum, M. Ferguson, D. Keymeulen, V. Duong. Evolving circuits in seconds: Experiments with a stand-alone board-level evolvable system. *Proceedings of the 2002 NASA/DOD Conference on Evolvable Hardware*, July 2002.

[92] P. Layzell. A new research tool for intrinsic hardware evolution. *Evolvable Systems: From Biology to Hardware, LNCS*, 1998.

[93] L. Sekanina, R. Ruzicka. Easily testable image operators: The class of circuits where evolution beats engineers. *Proceedings of the 2003 NASA/DOD Conference on Evolvable Hardware*, July 2003.

[94] J. Lohn, J. Crawford, A. Globus, G. Hornby, W. Kraus, G. Larchev, A. Pryor, D. Srivastava. Evolvable systems for space applications. *Proceedings of the International Conference on Space Mission Challenges for Information Technology*, 2003.

[95] J. Lohn, D. Linden, G. Hornby, W. Kraus, A. Rodriguez-Arroyo. Evolutionary design of an X-band antenna for NASA's space technology 5 mission. *Proceedings of the 2003 NASA/DoD Conference on Evolvable Hardware*, 2003.

[96] J. F. Miller, K. Downing. Evolution in materio: Looking beyond the silicon box. *Proceedings of the 2002 NASA/DoD Conference on Evolvable Hardware*, 2002.

[97] L. P. Masiero, M. Pacheco, C. R. Hall, C. Santini. Molecular circuit design. *Proceedings of the 2005 NASA/DOD Conference on Evolvable Hardware*. June–July, 2005.

[98] L. Spector, H. Barnum, H. J. Bernstein, N. Swamy. Quantum computing applications of genetic programming. *Advances in Genetic Programming*, MIT Press, 1999.

CHAPTER 34

NETWORK PACKET PROCESSING IN RECONFIGURABLE HARDWARE

John W. Lockwood
Washington University in St. Louis and Stanford University

This chapter will show, through an example, how networking systems have been built with reconfigurable hardware. It will describe how data can be switched, routed, buffered, processed, scanned, and filtered over networks using field-programmable gate arrays (FPGAs).

The chapter begins by describing the mechanisms by which Internet packets are segmented into frames and cells for transmission across a network. Internet Protocol (IP) wrappers are introduced, and it is shown how they simplify the implementation of large packet-processing systems. Next, a framework for building modular systems that implement Internet firewalls and intrusion prevention systems is presented. The chapter continues with a detailed explanation of how Bloom filters can scan streams of data for fixed strings and how finite automata can be used to scan for regular expressions.

Case studies are provided that show how deep packet inspection systems are implemented in reconfigurable hardware. One circuit detects the spread of worms and viruses across an Internet link. Another circuit analyzes the semantics of the text in traffic flows to determine which language is used within attached documents. A hardware-accelerated version of the popular SNORT intrusion detection system is illustrated, and it is shown how the FPGA hardware works with the software on a host to analyze packets.

34.1 NETWORKING WITH RECONFIGURABLE HARDWARE

34.1.1 The Motivation for Building Networks with Reconfigurable Hardware

Although modern microprocessors continue to improve their performance, they are not improving as fast as the rate at which data flows over Internet connections. As the limits of Moore's Law are reached, alternative computational methods are needed to route, process, filter, and transform Internet datastreams.

Networking systems created with reconfigurable hardware are flexible and easily modified to provide new functionality. Reconfigurable hardware enables features on networking platforms to be implemented in ways that are quite different from current platform implementations. It allows new modular components to be created and then dynamically installed in remote networksystems.

By processing network packets in hardware rather than in software, networking applications do not suffer the performance penalty caused by sequential data processing.

The Internet evolves as new protocols, features, and capabilities are added to the routers that implement the underlying network. Protocols, such as IP version 6 (IPv6), allow more devices to be individually addressed. Added features, such as per-flow queuing, allow voice and video to be reliably delivered in real time. Firewalls and intrusion prevention systems (IPSs) enhance Internet security.

Network platforms have been built to route network traffic, filter packets, and queue data in reprogrammable hardware. With reconfigurable hardware, networking platform operation can change over time as packet-processing algorithms and protocols evolve. With FPGAs, all features of the packet-processing system are configurable down to the logic gates. These systems enable new services to deploy and operate at the rate of the highest-speed backbone links.

34.1.2 Hardware and Software for Packet Processing

For their packet-processing operations, today's fastest routers use network processing elements implemented in custom silicon or in application-specific integrated circuits (ASICs). As shown in Figure 34.1, network processing elements reside between the line card where packets are transmitted and received and the Gigabit/second rate switch fabric that interconnects ports. They contain hundreds to thousands of parallel logic circuits and finite-state machines that are optimized to route, filter, queue, and/or process Internet datagrams in hardware.

Several platform types have been developed, many of which use standard microprocessors such as the Intel Pentium, AMD Athlon, or Motorola/IBM PowerPC. Others use ASICs from vendors such as Agere, Intel, Motorola, Cavium, Broadcom and Vitesse. Although software-based systems have outstanding flexibility, their packet processing is limited because of the sequential nature of their instruction execution. ASICs and custom silicon networking chips have high performance, but they offer little flexibility as measured by their ability to reprogram. Figure 34.2 illustrates the trade-offs between flexibility and performance.

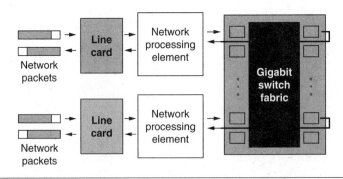

FIGURE 34.1 ■ A reconfigurable network processing element located between a line card and switch fabric.

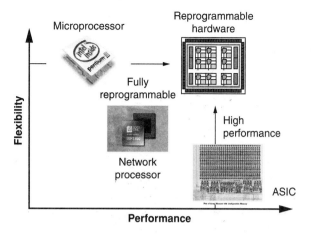

FIGURE 34.2 ■ Flexibility and performance trade-offs for networking systems that use microprocessors, network processors, ASICs, and reprogrammable hardware.

34.1.3 Network Data Processing with FPGAs

Reconfigurable hardware devices share the performance advantage of ASICs because they can implement parallel logic functions in hardware. However, they also share the flexibility of microprocessors and network processors because they can be dynamically reconfigured.

Using FPGAs for high-performance asynchronous transfer mode (ATM) networking was explored during the development of the Illinois Pular-based Optical Interconnect (iPOINT) testbed. In this project, an ATM switch with FPGAs [2] was developed and an advanced queuing module was implemented that provided per-flow queuing functionality in FPGA hardware. The FPGAs were used to implement the datapath of the switch and to control the state machines that buffered the ATM cells as they arrived on each switch port of the switch. The lookup tables (LUTs) in the FPGA fabric were used to build the multiplexers that switched the data between the ports. Finally, combinational logic was used to implement the state machines that controlled how packets were written to and read from SRAM [3].

FPGAs have also proven effective for implementation of bit-intensive function networking, such as forward error correction (FEC), and for boosting the performance of networking protocols [4]. The bitwise processing function maps well into the fine-grained logic on an FPGA. On-chip LUTs are used to encode data patterns as symbols with redundant bits of information. When the symbols are decoded, the redundant bits allow the receiver to reconstruct the data even with a few bits in error. Reconfigurable logic allows algorithms that use varying amounts and types of error correction to be programmed on-chip.

Through the development of the Field-Programmable Port Extender (FPX) platform [1], it was demonstrated that high-performance network packet-processing systems implemented with FPGAs are both useful and practical. The

FPX platform used two multi-Gigabit/second network interfaces, four banks of off-chip memory, and two FPGAs to implement over 30 networking applications. Applications developed for the FPX platform included modules that performed Internet Protocol IP address lookup for routing [7]; payload scanning for detection of fixed strings and regular expressions within the body of a packet; data queuing to provide quality of service (QoS); intrusion detection to determine when a network may be under attack; intrusion prevention to halt such attacks; and semantic processing of network data.

34.1.4   Network Processing System Modularity

Modularity is a key feature of networking systems. Network developers need standard interfaces to interface high-level network processing components to the underlying network infrastructure. In systems with reconfigurable hardware, modules can be implemented in regions of an FPGA and bound by a well-defined interface to the datapath and to external memory. Multiple modular data-processing components can be integrated to compose systems. Memory interfaces can connect logic to off-chip memory in order to buffer data and hold large lookup tables LUTs.

For the FPX platform modules, data was received and transmitted via a series of ATM cells carried over a 32-bit-wide Utopia interface. ATM cells contained 48 bytes of payload data and 4 bytes of a header that included a virtual path identifier (VPI) and a virtual circuit identifier (VCI). Each ATM cell also included an 8-bit checksum that covered the ATM cell header. Larger IP datagrams were sent between modules using layered protocol wrappers that segmented and reassembled multiple cells into ATM adaptation layer 5 (AAL5) frames. These frames contained data from a series of ATM cells and a 32-bit checksum at the end that covered all bytes of the payload. Segmentation and reassembly of cells into frames were performed to transfer packets over the network.

The FPX platform (Figure 34.3) stored and loaded data from two types of off-chip memory. Two interfaces supported transfer of 36-bit-wide data to and from an on-chip SRAM. SDRAM interfaces provided 64-bit-wide interfaces to multiple banks of high-capacity, off-chip memory. In the implementation of the IP lookup module, the off-chip SRAM was used to store data structures for IP lookup, while the SDRAM was used to buffer packets. The lower latency of SRAM access was important for the implementation of lookup functions where there was a data dependency for the result; the larger capacity of the SDRAM was beneficial for reducing the cost of storing bulk data, including buffering dataflows.

A switch was implemented using the reprogrammable application device (RAD) FPGA logic that allowed traffic to be routed to extensible modules. Layered protocol wrappers performed the segmentation and reassembly of AAL5 frames so that full packets could be processed by the FPGA hardware. To reprogram the RAD FPGA that contained the extensible modules, configuration and control logic was implemented on the network interface device (NID) FPGA.

The FPX platform was integrated into the Washington University Gigabit Switch (WUGS) to process packets as they passed into and out of the networking

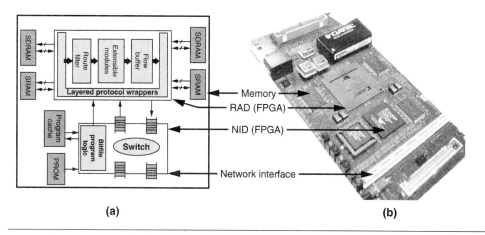

(a)   (b)

FIGURE 34.3 ■ A block diagram and a physical implementation of the FPX platform.

ports of a scalable network switch. The WUGS switching platform provided a backplane for transferring ATM cells between ports. By adding the FPX between the line cards and the switch fabric, the system was able to analyze, process, route, and filter IP packets as they flowed through the system. OC-3 to OC-48 line cards were used to directly send and receive ATM cells, while Gigabit Ethernet line cards were used to segment frames into multiple ATM cells and reassemble them. After data passed through the FPX, they were forwarded to the switch fabric, where cells were forwarded to other FPX modules in the chassis based on their VPI and VCI values.

34.2 NETWORK PROTOCOL PROCESSING

The Open Systems Interconnection (OSI) Reference Model defines how multiple layers can be used to transport data over a computer network. OSI divides the functions of a protocol into a series of layers, each of which has two properties: (1) It uses only the functions of the layer below, and (2) it exports functionality only to the layer above. A system that implements protocol behavior consisting of a series of these layers is known as a protocol stack. Protocol stacks can be implemented in hardware, in software, or in a mixture of the two (typically, only the lower layers are implemented in hardware; the higher layers, in software). This logical separation makes reasoning about the behavior of protocol stacks much easier and allows their design to be elaborate but highly reliable. Each layer performs services for the next highest layer and makes requests for the next lowest layer [5].

For real systems that process Internet data, the OSI model is not directly implemented but instead serves as a reference for implementation of the real protocols. Layers are important for processing IP data, however, because they permit application-processing modules to abstract details of the lower-layer

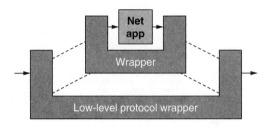

FIGURE 34.4 ■ Integration of a network application within one or more wrappers.

network protocols. At the lowest layer, networks modify raw cells of data that move between interfaces. At higher layers, the applications process variable-length frames or IP packets. To send and receive data at the user level, a network application may transmit directly or receive user datagram protocol (UDP) messages by instantiating all wrappers and sending data from a network application down through a series of wrappers [6] (see Figure 34.4).

34.2.1   Internet Protocol Wrappers

Hundreds of millions of computers deployed throughout the world communicate over the Internet. Traffic from these machines is concentrated to flow over a smaller number of routers that forward traffic through the Internet core. Currently, Internet backbones operate over communication links ranging in speed from OC-3 (155 Mbps) to OC-768 (40 Gbps). Fast links that process small packets have the ability to process millions of IP packets per second.

A library of layered protocol wrappers (see Figure 34.5) was developed to process Internet packets in reconfigurable hardware. Collectively, the wrappers simplified and streamlined the implementation of high-level networking functions by abstracting the operation of lower-level packet-processing functions. The library infrastructure was synthesized into FPGA logic and integrated into an FPX network platform. At the lowest levels, the library processes ATM cells. Complete frames of data are segmented and reassembled using ATM adaptation layer 5 (AAL5), over which IP messages are then transported.

When only a single message needs to be transmitted, the UDP can send one packet over the Internet. UDP encapsulates a variable-length message into an IP packet and allows the system to specify source and destination port numbers that identify from which application on a machine the data was sent and to which application it should be delivered. UDP/IP also provides a checksum to ensure the integrity of the data. Using the FPX protocol-processing library, this checksum is automatically computed, using FPGA hardware, as the sum over the payload bytes of the message.

34.2.2   TCP Wrappers

Over 85 percent of all traffic on the Internet today uses the Transmission Control Protocol (TCP). TCP is stream oriented and guarantees delivery of data with

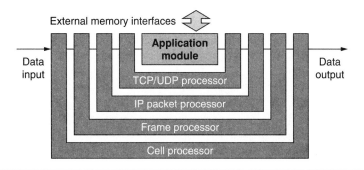

FIGURE 34.5 ■ Implementation of layered protocol wrappers on the FPX platform.

an ordered byte flow. Processing TCP dataflows in the middle of the network is extremely difficult because network packets can be dropped, duplicated, and reordered. Packet sequences observed within the interior of the network may be different from packets received and processed at the connection endpoints. The complexities associated with tracking the state of end systems and reconstructing byte sequences based on observed traffic are significant.

A TCP processing circuit was developed that handles the complexities associated with flow classification and TCP stream reassembly. It provided the FPGA logic with a view of network traffic flow data through a simple client interface. The TCP wrapper enabled other high-performance data-processing subsystems to operate on TCP network content without needing to implement their own state-tracking operations. The TCP module used a state store to track the status of each TCP/IP flow and, using a hash function, assigned a unique flow number to each session [8].

Figure 34.6 is a block diagram of the TCP processor. Internet packets arrive as frames of data to the input state machine of the TCP processing engine. The input state machine forwards the frames to a first in, first out (FIFO) that buffers the packet; a checksum engine that computes and verifies the correctness of the TCP checksum; and a flow classifier that computes a flow identifier (flow ID) using a hash over fields in the packet header.

The flow ID is passed to the state store manager that retrieves the state associated with the particular flow. Results are written to the control and state FIFO, and the state store is updated with the current flow state. The output state machine reads data from the frame and control FIFO buffers and passes data to the packet-routing engine. Most traffic flows through the content-scanning engines, which scan the data. Packet retransmissions bypass these engines and go directly to the flow-blocking module.

Data returning from the content-scanning engines also goes to the flow-blocking module. This stage updates the per-flow state store with application-specific state information. If a content-scanning engine indicates that it has a need to block a flow, the flow-blocking module can enforce this rule by comparing the packet's sequence number with the sequence numbers for which flow blocking should take place. If the packet meets the blocking criteria, the

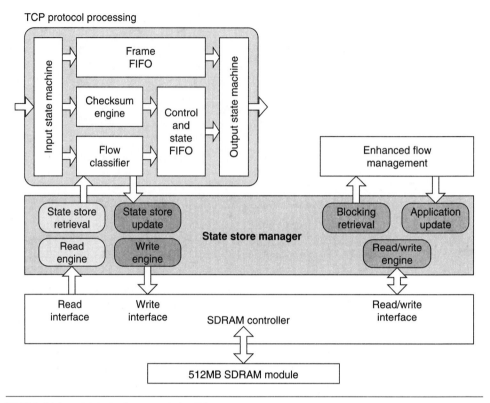

FIGURE 34.6 ▪ A block diagram of the TCP processor.

flow-blocking module drops it from the network. Any remaining packets go to the outbound protocol wrapper.

The state store manager processes requests to read and write flow state records. It also handles all interactions with SDRAM memory and caches recently accessed flow state information. The SDRAM controller exposes three memory access interfaces: a read/write, a write-only, and a read-only. The controller prioritizes requests in that order, with the read/write interface having the highest priority.

34.2.3 Payload-processing Modules

Many network applications have a common requirement for string matching in the payload of packets or flows. Once the data being transported over the network has been reconstructed using the IP and TCP modules, it can be examined in the payload. For example, the presence of a string of bytes (or a signature) can identify the presence of a media file, an attachment, or a security exploit. Well-known Internet worms, such as Nimda, Code Red, and Slammer, propagate by sending malicious executable programs identifiable by certain byte sequences in payloads [14]. Because the location (or offset) of such strings and their length are unknown, such applications must be able to detect strings of different lengths starting at arbitrary packet payload locations.

Packet inspection applications, when deployed at router ports, must operate at wire speeds. As network rates increase, the implementation of packet monitors that process data at Gigabit/second line rates has become increasingly difficult. Thus, the growth in network traffic has motivated specialized packet- and payload-processing modules in hardware.

34.2.4 Payload Processing with Regular Expression Scanning

A regular expression (RE) is a pattern that describes a set of strings. The basic building blocks for these patterns consist of individual characters, such as {a, b, and c}. These characters can be combined with meta-characters, such as: {*, |, and ?}, to form regular expressions with wildcards. For two regular expressions, r1 and r2, rules define that r1* matches any string composed of zero or more occurrences of r1; r1? matches any string composed of zero or one occurrence of r1; r1|r2 matches any string composed of r1 or r2; and r1r2 matches any string composed of r1 concatenated with r2. For instance, a is an RE that denotes the singleton set {a}, while a|b denotes the set {a, b} and a* denotes the infinite set {null, a, aa, aaa, . . .}. REs can be identified using nondeterministic finite automata (NFA).

Research on RE matching in hardware has been performed by Sidhu and Prasanna [16] and Franklin et al. [17]. Sidhu and Prasanna were primarily concerned with minimizing the time and space required to construct NFAs. They ran their NFA construction algorithm in hardware as opposed to software. Franklin et al. followed with an analysis of this approach for the large set of expressions found in a SNORT database [18].

The search function FPgrep was implemented by Moscola et al. to search packet payloads for substrings that belong to the language defined by the RE [15]. When FPgrep matched a substring in a packet, it transmitted information about the packet to a monitoring host system. The information sent for network intrusion detection functions specified the content found and the sender's and receiver's IP addresses. The search ran in linear time (proportional to packet size), $O(n)$ (where n was the number of bytes in a packet), and in constant space. That is, there was never a need to examine a character more than once and the amount of hardware was proportional to the size of the RE. Approximately one flip-flop was required per character.

A streaming content editor, FPsed, was implemented as a module on the FPX platform. The FPsed module selectively replaced content in packet payloads. String replacement for an RE is not as straightforward or efficient as searching. It requires that the machine do more than simply determine the presence of matching substrings in a record—it must also determine the position of the first and last character of all complete substrings that are matched by it. It is this requirement that makes RE search and replace more complicated and less efficient than a simple search. Searching for the complete substring is logical when the goal is to replace it.

Consider the replacement of every occurrence of a certain hexadecimal string associated with a computer virus, 3n*4n*5n*B, with the text Virus Pattern Detected. For the sake of brevity, the previous expression uses *n* as shorthand for any hexadecimal character (i.e., 0|1|2|3|4|5|6|7|8|9|A|B|C|D|E|F). For the input string 3172F34435B6B7B8, the substring can be replaced from the point where the machine starts running, 34, to the point where the substring is accepted, just before B6 (i.e., substring 34435B). However, this would allow a portion of the virus to remain in the content stream. In most situations, it is preferable to replace complete substrings; here the complete substring match starts with 31 and includes everything to just before B8 (i.e., the substring 3172F34435B6B7B).

34.2.5   Payload Scanning with Bloom Filters

A hash table is one of the most attractive choices for quick lookups. Hash tables require only constant time, $O(1)$, average memory accesses per lookup. Because of their versatile applicability in network packet processing, it is useful to implement these hashing functions in hardware [19, 20].

Bloom filters can detect strings of characters that appear in streaming data moving at very high data rates. A Bloom filter is a data structure that stores a set of signatures compactly by computing multiple hash functions on each member of the set. It queries a database of strings to check for the membership of a particular string. The answer to this query can be false positive but never false negative. The average computation time to perform a query remains constant so long as the sizes of the hash tables scale linearly with the number of strings they store. Because each table entry stores only a hashed version of the content, the amount of storage required by the Bloom filter for each string is independent of its length.

34.3   INTRUSION DETECTION AND PREVENTION

Existing firewalls that examine only the packet headers do little to protect against many types of attack. Multiple new worms transport their malicious software, or *malware*, over trusted services and cannot be detected without examining the payload. Intrusion detection systems (IDSs) perform deep scanning of the payload to detect malware, but do nothing to impede the attack because they only operate passively. An intrusion prevention system (IPS), on the other hand, can intervene and stop malware from spreading. The configuration of a network intrusion prevention system is shown in Figure 34.7.

One problem with software-based IDSs is that they cannot keep pace with the high volume of traffic that transits high-speed networks. Existing systems that implement IPS functions in software limit the bandwidth of the network and delay the end-to-end connection.

A reconfigurable system that can keep pace with high-speed network traffic has been developed. It scans data quickly, reconfigures to search for new attack

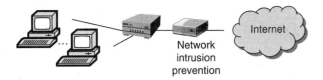

FIGURE 34.7 ■ Configuration of an in-line network IPS situated between two hosts attached to a router and to the Internet.

patterns, and takes immediate action when attacks occur. By processing the content of Internet traffic in real time within an extensible network, data that contains computer viruses or Internet worms can be detected and prevented. By adding only a few filtering devices at key network aggregation points, Internet worms and computer viruses can be quarantined to the subnets where they were introduced.

A complete system has been designed and implemented that scans the full payload of packets to route, block, and track the packets in the flow based on their content. The result is an intelligent gateway that provides Internet worm and virus protection in both local and wide area networks.

Network intrusion detection and prevention systems search for predefined virus or worm signatures in network traffic flows (see Section 34.2.3). Such signatures can be loaded into the system manually by an operator or automatically by a signature detection system. (Note that *string* is synonymous with *signature* throughout the chapter.)

Once a signature is found, an intrusion detection and prevention system (IDPS) can use it to block traffic containing infected data from spreading throughout a network. To perform this operation on a high-speed network, the signature scanning and data blocking must operate quickly. Comparing a variety of systems running the SNORT rule-based NID sensor reveals that most general-purpose computer systems are inadequate as NID sensor platforms even for moderate-speed networks. Factors such as microprocessor, operating system, main memory bandwidth, and latency limit the performance that an NIDS sensor platform can achieve [22].

34.3.1   Worm and Virus Protection

Computer virus and Internet worm attacks are pervasive, aggravating, and expensive, both in terms of lost productivity and consumption of network bandwidth. Attacks by Nimba, Code Red, Slammer, SoBig.F, and MSBlast have infected computers globally, clogged large computer networks, and degraded corporate productivity. It can take weeks to months for information technology professionals to sanitize infected computers in a network after an outbreak [24].

In the same way that a human virus spreads among people coming in contact with each other, computer viruses and Internet worms spread when computers communicate electronically [25]. Once a few systems are compromised, they infect other machines, which in turn quickly spread the infection throughout a network. As is the case with the spread of a contagious disease, the number of infected computers grows exponentially unless contained. Computer systems spread contagion much more quickly than humans do because they can communicate instantaneously over large geographical distances. The Blaster worm, for example, infected over 400,000 computers in less than five days. In fact, about one in three Internet users are infected with some type of virus or worm every year.

Malware can propagate as a computer virus, an Internet worm, or a hybrid of both. Viruses spread when a computer user downloads unsafe software, opens a malicious attachment, or exchanges infected computer programs over a network. An Internet worm spreads over the network automatically when malware exploits one or more vulnerabilities in an operating system, a web server, a database application, or an email exchange system.

Malware can appear as a virus embedded in software that a user has downloaded. It can also take the form of a Trojan that is embedded in what appears to be benign freeware. Alternatively, it can spread as content attached to an email message, as content downloadable from a web site, or in files transferred over peer-to-peer systems. Modern attacks typically use multiple mechanisms to execute. Malware, for example, can spoof messages that lure users to submit personal financial information to cloaked servers. In the future, malware is likely to spread much faster and cause much more damage.

Today, most anti-virus solutions run in software on end systems. To ensure that an entire network is secure from known attacks, integrated systems were developed that can perform multiple network processing functions.

34.3.2   An Integrated Header, Payload, and Queuing System

An integrated system that incorporated the payload-scanning function, a ternary content addressable memory (TCAM) for header matching, and a flow buffer and queue manager for packet storage was implemented [13]. It is shown as a block diagram in Figure 34.8.

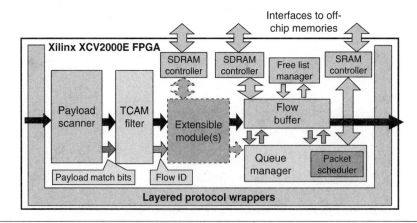

FIGURE 34.8 ■ Complete on-chip networking header and payload processing integrated with a flow buffer and a queue manager.

SNORT is a lightweight NID sensor that can filter packets based on predefined rules over packet headers and payloads [18]. With the TCP option enabled, SNORT matches strings that appear anywhere within traffic flows. Each SNORT rule operates first on the packet header to verify that the packet is from a source or to a destination network address and/or port of interest. If the packet matches a certain header rule, its payload is scanned against a set of predefined patterns associated with that rule. Matching of one or multiple patterns implies a complete match of a rule, and further action can be taken on either the packet or the TCP flow.

To provide complete detection of all known attacks, an intrusion system must process all packets. Several thousand patterns appeared in the version 2.2 rule set for SNORT. SNORT's rule database continually expands as new threats are observed. As the number of headers and signatures to match increases, the CPU on a PC running SNORT becomes overloaded and not all packets are processed.

A SNORT intrusion filter for TCP (SIFT) was implemented in reconfigurable hardware and is illustrated in Figure 34.9. SIFT data entered the system via the TCP de-serialize wrapper. Control signals marked specific locations in the

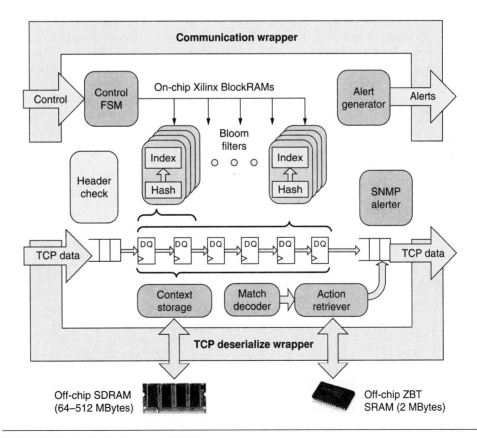

FIGURE 34.9 ■ A block diagram of SIFT.

packet that included the starts of the IP header, the TCP header, and the payload. The value of the header was sent to a header check component to determine if the packet matches a header-only rule. The payload was sent through an 8-stage pipeline where each byte offset is searched for signatures by Bloom filters. If a match was detected, the match decoder determines the string identifier (ID), which was next sent to the action retriever to determine what to do with the packet. Suspect packets were forwarded to software for further inspection. Those that had no match were not inspected further; those that did need additional processing were sent to the outgoing side of the TCP de-serialized wrapper.

To match payloads, SIFT used Bloom filters to allow signatures to be incrementally programmed into hardware. Signatures could be added or deleted via messages embedded in UDP control packets. These packets were sent through the communication wrapper to a control finite-state machine (FSM). In turn, the FSM set the appropriate bits in BlockRAM memories on the FPGA to add the signature to the Bloom filter. To achieve high throughput, four engines ran in parallel [21].

34.3.3 Automated Worm Detection

Outbreaks of new worms constitute a major threat to Internet security. IDPSs described previously only filter traffic that contain known worms. Systems that automatically detect new worms in real time by monitoring traffic on a network allow detection and protection from new outbreaks.

Internet worms spread by exploiting vulnerabilities in operating systems and application software that run on end systems. Once they infect a machine, they use it to attack other hosts; these attacks compromise security and degrade network performance, causing large economic losses for businesses resulting from system downtime and lowered worker productivity. The Susceptible/Infective (SI) model illustrates the spread of Internet worms [25]. With this model, a well-known equation can be used to estimate how fast a worm will infect vulnerable machines.

Worms can be prevented by writing code that has no vulnerabilities, and the computer security community has made great strides toward this goal. Programmers analyze the vulnerability that the worm exploits and release a "patch" to fix it. However, it takes time to analyze and patch software. In addition, many end users may never apply the patch, and as a result a significant number of machines in the network remain vulnerable.

Another way to prevent the spread of worms is to have the network contain them. When intrusion prevention systems scan traffic for a predetermined signature and filter the flows that match, the spread of a known worm can be blocked. The EarlyBird System [26, 27] detects the signatures for unknown worms in real time, identifying them by their repeating content. Because worms consist of malicious code, frequently repeated content on the network can be a useful warning of worm activity. Large flows are identified by computing a hash of packet content in combination with a destination port.

A hardware-accelerated worm detection circuit implemented in reconfigurable hardware draws from two ideas presented in the EarlyBird system [23]. To detect commonly occurring content, a hash is computed over 10-byte windows of streaming data. The hash value is used to identify a counter in a vector that is instructed to increment by one. At periodic intervals (called timeouts), the counts in each of the vectors are decremented by the average number of arrivals due to normal traffic. When a counter reaches a predetermined threshold, an alert is generated and its value is reset to zero.

For the implementation of the circuit on an FPGA, the count vector was implemented by configuring dual-ported, on-chip BlockRAMs as an array of memory locations. Each memory afforded one read operation and one write operation every clock cycle, which allowed a 3-stage pipeline to be implemented that reads, increments, and writes memory every clock cycle. Because the signature changes every clock cycle and because every occurrence of every signature must be counted, the dual-ported memories allow the occurrence count to be written back while another count is being read.

When an on-chip counter crosses the threshold, the corresponding signature is hashed to a table in off-chip SRAM. The next time the same string causes the counter to exceed the threshold, it is hashed to the same location in SRAM and the two strings are compared. If they are the same, it is determined that the match is not a false positive and the counter is incremented. If they are different, the contents of the string stored in SRAM is overwritten with the value of the new string and the count is reset.

On receiving confirmation from the SRAM analyzer that a signature frequently occurs, a UDP control packet is sent to an external computer. The packet contains the offending signature, which is the string of bytes by which the hash was computed. The computer, in turn, programs other IDS/IDP systems to filter traffic that contains this signature.

34.4 SEMANTIC PROCESSING

Next-generation networks route and forward data based on the semantics of the data within documents. Rather than assigning arbitrary headers to packets, routers use the meaning of the text itself to determine the packet routing.

34.4.1 Language Identification

As of 2004, nearly two-thirds of the world's Internet users spoke a non-English native language [29], and nearly one-third of the pages available on the Internet were written in a non-English language [29, 30]. As the rate at which data is transferred over the Internet increases, the rapid identification of languages becomes an increasingly difficult problem. A system capable of quickly identifying the primary language or languages used in documents can be useful as a preprocessor for document classification and translation services. It can also be used as a mechanism for language-based document routing.

A hardware-accelerated algorithm was designed to automatically identify the primary languages used in documents transferred over the Internet [28]. The module was implemented in hardware on the FPX platform. Referred to as Hardware-Accelerated Identification of Languages (HAIL), this complete system identified the primary languages used in content transferred over TCP/IP networks. It operated on streaming data at a rate of 2.4 Gigabits/second using FPGA hardware. This level of performance far outstripped software algorithms running on microprocessors.

Several methods have been shown to be effective for the classification of document characteristics based on principles from linguistics and artificial intelligence. Some methods used dictionary-building techniques [31], while others used Markov Models, trigram frequency vectors [32], and/or n-gram–based text categorization [33, 34]. Although these methods are capable of achieving high degrees of accuracy, most require floating-point mathematics, large amounts of memory, and/or generous amounts of processing time.

HAIL uses n-grams to determine the language of a document. These are sequential patterns of exactly n characters that are found in written documents, and when they are used as indicators of language, the primary language or languages of a document can be reliably determined. HAIL can use any n-gram length, although experiments have shown that n-grams of length 3 (trigrams) and length 4 (tetragrams) provide the most accurate results.

Before processing data with HAIL, the target system is trained with information on languages. Training is performed by scanning a set of documents in the languages of interest. When an n-gram appears significantly more frequently in the documents of one language than in any other, it is associated with that language. After training has established which n-grams best correspond to particular languages, memory modules on the hardware platform implementing HAIL have to be programmed. Memory is populated by using a hash to map each n-gram to a particular memory location. The memory location that corresponds to a particular n-gram is labeled with the associated language. Once data processing begins, the n-grams are sampled from the datastream and used as addresses into memory to discern the language associated with the n-gram. The final language is determined by the statistics of the words that appear in each language.

34.4.2 Semantic Processing of TCP Data

Within the intelligence community, there is a need to search through massive amounts of multilingual documents that are encoded using different character sets. It has been shown that computational linguistics and text-processing techniques are effective for sorting through large information sets, extracting relevant documents, and discovering new concepts [33]. There is a problem, however, in that the computational complexity of the text-processing algorithms is such that the document ingest rate is too slow to keep up with the high rate of information flow [34].

To overcome this problem, a system using FPGA hardware was developed for accelerated concept discovery and classification algorithms [35, 36].

Circuits were implemented as reconfigurable hardware modules that dramatically increased data ingest rates. It was found that text analysis algorithms that perform "bag of words" processing were widely used and appropriate for many types of computational linguistics tasks. To investigate the utility of hardware-accelerated text analysis algorithms, a reconfigurable FPGA-based semantic-processing system was developed. The hardware tested a variety of target problems involving concept classification, concept discovery, and language identification [36].

A blend of high-speed network devices and reconfigurable hardware was used to rapidly ingest and process data [35]. Data were received from the network as text or HTML documents and carried over standard TCP/IP packets. The TCP processor decoded the packets that contained the document in one or more TCP/IP input flows. Every word (baseword) in the document was analyzed for its semantic meaning. All words in each document were then counted to determine their frequency of occurrence. A document vector was generated that characterized the document content. It was then scored against a set of vectors that represented known or emerging concepts. Thresholds were used to determine if content could be classified as existing or if a new cluster should be formed.

Figure 34.10 diagrams the dataflow of the semantic-processing system. The FPGAs enabled streaming, computationally intensive semantic-processing functions to be performed in constant time. They performed all of the

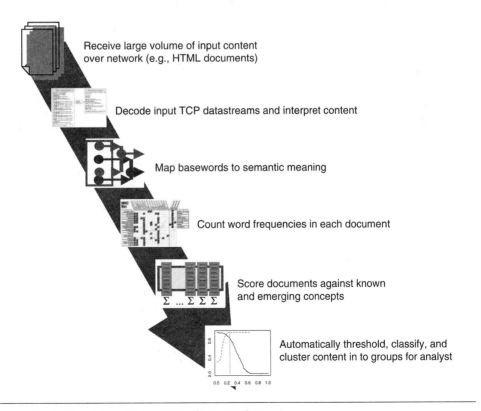

FIGURE 34.10 ■ Dataflow for the semantic processing system.

data-processing functions for the system shown in the figure except for threshold and classification (which were performed and displayed on a computer console). By using FPGAs to implement all parts of the text processing, the entire system could be dynamically reconfigured to allow variations of algorithms to be evaluated for their content classification or concept-clustering ability. Massive volumes of data were streamed through the system, and the system's precision, recall, throughput, and latency were measured [36].

The RAD circuits on the FPX (shown in Figure 34.3) were used to implement the TCP processor, the baseword module, the count module, the score module, and the report module. All were implemented as modular hardware components on individual FPX platforms connected in a vertical stack. The high-speed network interfaces allowed the FPX platforms to communicate intermediate results of processing to other modules in the system and to send reports to software running on a computer outside the system using standard IP datagrams. Multiple copies of the FPX platform were stacked on each other to implement network intrusion detection and network intrusion prevention. Figure 34.11 is a photograph displaying how five FPX cards were stacked to implement the semantic processing system. Additional modules were added to tag tokens in a context-free grammar [37].

34.5   COMPLETE NETWORKING SYSTEM ISSUES

To deploy complete network systems, additional issues must be considered. First, the hardware must be placed in a form factor appropriate for use in remote network closets. Second, the control and configuration of the hardware must be secure. And third, reconfiguration mechanisms are needed so that entire FPGAs, or (as needed) only parts, can be reconfigured over the network. With dynamic hardware plug-ins, most of the system can remain operational while parts of it are reconfigured. Partial bitfile reconfiguration allows the system itself to remain operational 24 hours a day (which is necessary to maintain a good network uptime) while individual components can still be modified quickly and efficiently. The PARBIT tool allows precompiled partial bitfile configurations to be generated and then quickly deployed into regions of FPGA networking hardware.

34.5.1   The Rack-mount Chassis Form Factor

Networking equipment is typically deployed in the form factor of a chassis that can be mounted into a 19-inch rack. Each unit (U) of a rack is 1.75 inches tall. In a 3U rack-mount chassis, up to four FPX modules could be stacked on each of two ports in the system. Data entered and left the system through the Gigabit Ethernet ports on the front panel. Figure 34.12 is a photograph of FPX modules integrated in a rack-mount chassis.

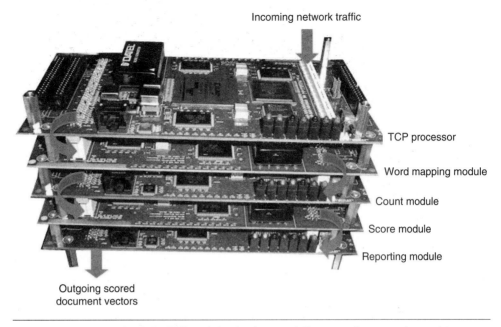

Incoming network traffic

TCP processor

Word mapping module

Count module

Score module

Reporting module

Outgoing scored
document vectors

FIGURE 34.11 ■ A stack of the FPX modules implemented the semantic processing system.

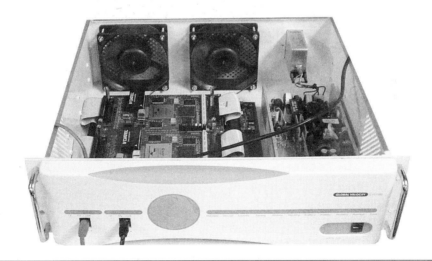

FIGURE 34.12 ■ FPX modules integrated in a rack-mount chassis.

34.5.2 Network Control and Configuration

Reconfigurable hardware circuits perform a variety of functions in the networking system. Some parts of the system implemented the infrastructure while others implemented the dynamically reconfigurable logic. Static circuits are used to switch cells between modules. The extensible modules implemented as plug-ins perform the reconfigurable features. The FPX used a combination of statically configured and dynamically configurable logic to implement the complete platform.

On the FPX, the NID was statically configured using a bitfile stored in a PROM. It controlled how data was routed between network modules. and included switching modules that forwarded traffic flows based on virtual paths and circuits found in the ATM cell headers. The NID also contained the logic that enabled other hardware modules to be dynamically loaded over the network. This logic implemented a circuit that used a reliable network protocol to receive full and partial bitfiles over the network. The NID, in turn, buffered this data in a configuration cache and streamed the bitstream into the programming port of the attached FPGA.

The RAD on the FPX was a Xilinx VirtexE-2000E FPGA that received the configuration data and performed application-specific functions implemented as dynamic hardware plug-in (DHP) modules. A DHP consisted of a region of FPGA gates and internal memory bound by the well-defined interface. For bitfiles that used all of the logic on the RAD, the interface was defined by user constraints file (UCF) pins. For partial bitfiles that used less than the entire FPGA, a standard on-chip interface was developed to transmit and receive packet data between modules. A full or partial bitfile was built using standard CAD tools [11].

34.5.3 A Reconfiguration Mechanism

The NID allowed modules created for the FPX platform to be remotely and dynamically loaded into the RAD. This bitstream was sent over the network into the configuration cache, which was implemented by a circuit that controlled an off-chip SRAM. Once a full or partial bitfile was received, a command was sent to the NID to initiate the RAD reconfiguration. On a Xilinx Virtex, the SelectMAP interface loaded a new bitstream into the FPGA. To reprogram the RAD, the NID read the configuration memory and wrote a preprogrammable number of configuration bytes into the RAD FPGA's SelectMAP interface. Figure 34.13 illustrates this process.

The NCHARGE API [9] was developed for debugging, programming, and configuring an FPX. Specifically, it included commands to check the status of an FPX, configure routing on the NID, and perform memory updates and full and partial RAD reprogramming.

NCHARGE provided a mechanism for applications to define their own custom control interface. Control cells were transmitted by NCHARGE and processed by control cell processors (CCPs) on the RAD or NID. To configure routes for the traffic flowing through the system, NCHARGE sent control cells with commands that modified routing tables on the Gigabit switch or on the NID. To check the status of the FPX, NCHARGE sent a control cell to the NID on the FPX, the NID updated fields in the cell, and the software process received the response.

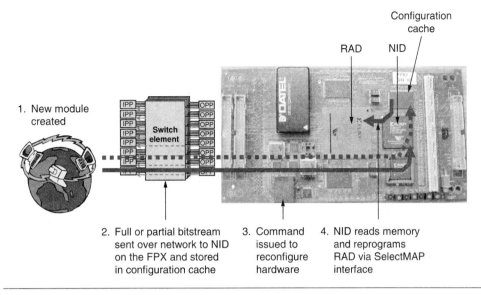

FIGURE 34.13 ■ Remote reconfiguration of the FPX platform.

34.5.4 Dynamic Hardware Plug-ins

Use of runtime reconfiguration in networking systems enables developers of hardware packet-processing applications to achieve a capability similar to that of the dynamically linked libraries (DLLs) used in software applications. Just as a DLL is a software module that can be attached to or removed from a running program as an application demands, DHPs can be loaded into or removed from a running FPGA without disturbing other circuits operating in it. The ability to change the hardware feature set in a running system is particularly useful in packet-processing applications such as firewalls and routers where it is not desirable to suspend the network operation during reprogramming.

A practical system for implementing DHPs was implemented on the FPX and provided sufficient resources for networking, well-defined interfaces to hardware, a complete design methodology, scripts that ran physical implementation tools to place and route logic, and tools that allowed selective reconfiguration of portions of the bitstream. These five elements were analogous to an operating system platform, application programming interface, modular programming methodology, compiler, and linker needed to implement DLLs in the software domain.

34.5.5 Partial Bitfile Generation

Tools and a design methodology were developed to support partial runtime reconfiguration of DHP modules on the FPX platform. The PARBIT tool was developed to transform and restructure bitstreams created by standard computer-aided design tools into partial bitstreams that programmed DHPs.

The methodology allowed the platform to hot-swap application-specific DHP modules without disturbing the operation of the rest of the system [12].

To partially reconfigure an FPGA, it is necessary to isolate a specific area in it and download the configuration only for the bits related to that area. PARBIT transformed and restructured the Xilinx bitstreams to extract and merge data from the bitfile's regions. To restructure the configuration bitfile, it read the original bitfile, a target bitfile, and parameters given by the user that specified the block coordinates of the logic implemented on a source FPGA, the coordinates of the area for a partially programmed target FPGA, and the programming options. After reading these data, PARBIT copied to the target bitstream only the part of the original bitstream related to the area defined by the user.

The target bitstream was used by PARBIT to preserve the part of the configuration data that was in a column specified by the user but outside the partial reconfigurable area. On a Xilinx VirtexE FPGA, the use of the target bitstream was necessary because one reconfiguration frame could span all rows of a column but have a partial reconfigurable area smaller than the column's height. PARBIT allowed arbitrary block regions of a compiled design to be retargeted into any similarly sized region of an FPGA.

To relocate blocks from the original bitfile, a user defined the start and end columns and rows for the block in the original design. Then the user defined where to put this block in a target bitfile of the same device type. The tool generated the partial bitfile containing the area selected by the user (from the original bitfile). This data was used to reconfigure the target device. The configuration bits for the top and bottom input/output blocks (IOBs) from the target device did not change after the partial bitfile was loaded. Those for the columns from the original and target bitfile were merged according to the rows defined by the user.

34.5.6   Control Channel Security

For devices deployed remotely on the Internet, security of the control channel is critical. Remote systems need to be safe from both passive and active network attacks by malicious users. In passive attacks, malicious users glean information by monitoring the system. In active attacks, they attempt to change the system's behavior or paralyze it. Access control mechanisms have been developed to protect remotely configured systems from unauthorized use.

Common attacks include passive eavesdropping, active tampering, replay, and denial of service (DoS). For a passive eavesdropping attack, a malicious user taps the network to copy and analyze its traffic. If the attacker can see clear text control and configuration information, he or she may discover how to control and configure the system. In an active tampering attack, an unauthorized user attempts to gain control of the remote system by issuing bogus control packets. For a replay attack, a malicious user passively captures legitimate traffic and then attempts to change the operation of the system by resending the captured traffic at a later time. For an active DoS attack, the user paralyzes the system by overloading the network with massive amounts of traffic.

Remotely configurable network systems can be made safe by mechanisms that ensure confidentiality of data, provide authentication of the administrator, and guarantee integrity of the messaging. By encrypting messages with the Advanced Encryption Standard (AES) or other secure encryption algorithms, data confidentiality can be protected. With digital signatures generated by public key algorithms, the administrator of the system can be authenticated to guarantee that no one else attempts to modify its operation. The integrity of messages can be ensured by verifying that exactly what is transmitted by the administrator is received by the system. Use of a message authentication code (MAC) can assure users that data are not modified and that no additional control messages are inserted.

The Internet Protocol Security (IPSec) standard provides a mechanism to secure communications across the Internet. Many companies, such as Cisco, have implemented IPSec capability in their networking products. To secure a remotely reconfigurable FPGA, an IPSec in transport mode was designed for a Xilinx Virtex-II Pro FPGA [10]. Security policies at network access points defined who could gain access and under what conditions access was granted. Encryption keys and hash keys remained secret using the security services previously described. The Internet key exchange (IKE) protocol negotiated and exchanged shared secrets between communication entities.

34.6 SUMMARY

As the limits of processor clock scaling are reached, systems that route, process, filter, and transform Internet data scale better in reconfigurable hardware than in software alone. Networking platforms created with FPGA hardware are both fast and flexible. The FPX platform was used to implement over 30 core networking functions.

The combination of Gigabit network interfaces, parallel banks of SRAM and SDRAM, and a large array of reconfigurable logic on the FPX platform enabled it to perform a wide range of networking applications. Modules and protocol wrappers created in reconfigurable hardware were developed on the FPX and provided functionality similar to the procedures and DLLs in software for network processing. Reconfiguration of the modules over the network proved to be as effective for remotely loading new functionality on the FPX as the reprogramming of software on remote PCs.

By using IP wrappers, the FPX platform provided the ability to process ATM cells, AAL5 frames, IP packets, UDP datagrams, and/or TCP/IP flows. Parallel finite automata engines proved useful in detecting regular expressions in packet payloads and TCP traffic flows. Bloom filters that performed parallel hash lookups also proved to be effective for detecting fixed strings in packets and TCP flows. A complete IDS system was implemented that performed a large subset of SNORT using a combination of protocol-processing wrappers, IP header matching circuits, and Bloom filter payload-scanning circuits. A worm and virus detection and blocking system was built using an FPX that demonstrated its utility in providing Internet security.

Reconfigurable hardware holds great promise for new types of networking applications. A language detection circuit was demonstrated that routed traffic based on the language used in a document. A semantic-processing circuit was demonstrated that allowed documents to be classified based on their topic.

Going forward, reconfigurable hardware is becoming the technology of choice for future networking systems. Reconfigurable hardware is the key feature of a new platform, called the NetFPGA. This open platform enables switching and routing of network packets on Gigabit Ethernet links. Because the NetFPGA has many of the same resources as the FPX, it can implement most of the features first prototyped on the FPX [38, 39].

References

[1] J. W. Lockwood. Evolvable Internet hardware platforms. *NASA/DoD Workshop on Evolvable Hardware*, July 2001.

[2] J. W. Lockwood, H. Duan, J. M. Morikuni, S. M. Kang, S. Akkineni, R. H. Campbell. Scalable optoelectronic ATM networks: The iPOINT fully functional testbed. *IEEE Journal of Lightwave Technology*, June 1995.

[3] H. Duan, J. W. Lockwood, S. M. Kang, J. D. Will. A high-performance OC-12/OC-48 queue design prototype for input-buffered ATM switches. *IEEE Infocom '97*, April 1997.

[4] W. Marcus, I. Hadzic, A. McAuley, J. Smith. Protocol boosters: Applying programmability to network infrastructures. *IEEE Communications Magazine* 36(10), 1998.

[5] Wikipedia. OSI model. *http://wikipedia.org/wiki/OSI_model*, July 2006.

[6] F. Braun, J. W. Lockwood, M. Waldvogel. Protocol wrappers for layered network packet processing in reconfigurable hardware. *IEEE Micro* 22(3), February 2002.

[7] D. E. Taylor, J. S. Turner, J. W. Lockwood, T. S. Sproull, D. B. Parlour. Scalable IP lookup for Internet routers. *IEEE Journal on Selected Areas in Communications* 21(4), May 2003.

[8] D. Schuehler, J. W. Lockwood. A modular system for FPGA-based TCP flow processing in high-speed networks. *Proceedings of the 14th International Conference on Field-Programmable Logic and Applications*, August 2004.

[9] T. S. Sproull, J. W. Lockwood, D. E. Taylor. Control and configuration software for a reconfigurable networking hardware platform. *IEEE Symposium on Field-Programmable Custom Computing Machines*, April 2002.

[10] J. Lu, J. W. Lockwood. IPSec implementation on Xilinx Virtex-II Pro FPGA and its application. *Reconfigurable Architectures Workshop*, April 2005.

[11] E. D. Horta, J. W. Lockwood, D. E. Taylor, D. Parlour. Dynamic hardware plugins in an FPGA with partial run-time reconfiguration. *Design Automation Conference*, June 2002.

[12] E. Horta, J. W. Lockwood. Automated method to generate bitstream intellectual property cores for Virtex FPGAs. *Proceedings of the 14th International Conference on Field-Programmable Logic and Applications*, August 2004.

[13] J. W. Lockwood, C. Neely, C. Zuver, D. Lim. Automated tools to implement and test Internet systems in reconfigurable hardware. *SIGCOMM Computer Communications Review* 33(3), July 2003.

[14] J. W. Lockwood, J. Moscola, D. Reddick, M. Kulig, T. Brooks. Application of hardware accelerated extensible network nodes for Internet worm and virus protection. *International Working Conference on Active Networks*, December 2003.

[15] J. Moscola, J. W. Lockwood, R. P. Loui, M. Pachos. Implementation of a content-scanning module for an Internet firewall. *IEEE Symposium on Field-Programmable Custom Computing Machines*, April 2003.

[16] R. Sidhu, V. K. Prasanna. Fast regular expression matching using FPGAs. *IEEE Symposium on Field-Programmable Custom Computing Machines*, April 2001.

[17] R. Franklin, D. Carver, B. L. Hutchings. Assisting network intrusion detection with reconfigurable hardware. *IEEE Symposium on Field-Programmable Custom Computing Machines*, April 2002.

[18] M. Roesch. Snort: Lightweight intrusion detection for networks. *Proceedings of the 13th Administration Conference, LISA*, November 1999.

[19] S. Dharmapurikar, P. Krishnamurthy, T. S. Sproull, J. W. Lockwood. Deep packet inspection using parallel Bloom filters. *IEEE Micro* 24(1), January 2004.

[20] H. Song, S. Dharmapurikar, J. Turner, J. W. Lockwood. Fast hash table lookup using extended Bloom filter: An aid to network processing. *ACM SIGCOMM*, August 2005.

[21] M. Attig, J. W. Lockwood. SIFT: SNORT intrusion filter for TCP. *IEEE Symposium on High Performance Interconnects (Hot Interconnects-13)*, August 2005.

[22] L. Schaelicke, T. Slabach, B. Moore, C. Freeland. Characterizing the performance of network intrusion detection sensors. *Proceedings of the Sixth International Symposium on Recent Advances in Intrusion Detection*, September 2003.

[23] B. Madhusudan, J. W. Lockwood. A hardware-accelerated system for real-time worm detection. *IEEE Micro* 25(1), January 2005.

[24] D. Moore, C. Shannon, G. Voelker, S. Savage. Internet quarantine: Requirements for containing self-propagating code. *IEEE INFOCOM*, 2002.

[25] S. Staniford, V. Paxson, N. Weaver. How to own the Internet in your spare time. *Usenix Security Symposium*, August 2002.

[26] S. Singh, C. Estan, G. Varghese, S. Savage. *The Earlybird System for the Real-time Detection of Unknown Worms*, Technical report CS2003-0761, University of California, San Diego, Department of Computer Science, 2003.

[27] C. Estan, G. Varghese. New directions in traffic measurement and accounting. *ACM SIGCOMM*, August 2002.

[28] C. M. Kastner, G. A. Covington, A. A. Levine, J. W. Lockwood. HAIL: A hardware-accelerated algorithm for language identification. *Proceedings of the 15th Annual Conference on Field-Programmable Logic and Applications*, August 2005.

[29] Global Reach. Global Internet statistics by language. *http://www.glreach.com/globstats/index.php3*, December 2004.

[30] Global Reach. Global Internet statistics: Sources and references. *http://www.glreach.com/globstats/refs.php3*, December 2004.

[31] R. Paulsen, M. Martino. *Word Counting Natural Language Determination*, U.S. Patent 6,704,698, 1996.

[32] J. Schmitt. *Trigram-based Method of Language Identification*, U.S. Patent 5,062,143, 1990.

[33] M. Damashek. *Method of Retrieving Documents that Concern the Same Topic*, U.S. Patent 5,418,951, 1994.

[34] J. B. Sharkey, D. Weishar, J. W. Lookwood, R. Loui, R. Rohwer, J. Byrnes, K. Pattipati, D. Cousins, M. Nicolletti, S. Eick. Information processing at very

high-speed data ingestion rates. In *Emergent Information Technologies and Enabling Policies for Counter Terrosiom*, edited by R. Popp and J. Yin. IEEE Press/Wiley, 2006.

[35] J. W. Lockwood, S. G. Eick, D. J. Weishar, R. Loui, J. Moscola, C. Kastner, A. Levine, M. Attig. Transformation algorithms for datastreams. *IEEE Aerospace Conference*, March 2005.

[36] J. W. Lockwood, S. G. Eick, J. Mauger, J. Byrnes, R. Loui, A. Levine, D. J. Weishar, A. Ratner. Hardware accelerated algorithms for semantic processing of document streams. *IEEE Aerospace Conference*, March 2006.

[37] Y. H. Cho, J. Moscola, J. W. Lockwood. Context-free grammar based token tagger in reconfigurable devices. *Proceedings of the International Workshop on Data Engineering*, April 2006.

[38] J. W. Lockwood, N. McKeown, G. Watson, G. Gibb, P. Hartke, J. Naous, R. Raghuraman, J. Luo. NetFPGA—An open platform for Gigabit-rate network switching and routing. *IEEE International Conference on Microelectronic Systems Education (MSE2007)*, June 2007.

[39] J. Luo, J. Pettit, M. Casado, N. McKeown, J. W. Lockwood. Prototyping fast, simple, secure switches for ethane. *IEEE Symposium on High-Performance Interconnects (Hot Interconnects-15)*, August 2007.

CHAPTER 35

ACTIVE PAGES: MEMORY-CENTRIC COMPUTATION

Diana Franklin
Department of Computer Science
California Polytechnic State University

Although field-programmable gate arrays (FPGAs) excel at tailoring the computation and interconnect to an application's needs, we can go one step further. In many applications, regardless of the speed of the computation, memory performance always will be the limiting factor. This problem, referred to as the *memory wall*, is broken up into two parts—memory latency and bandwidth. For large-scale data-parallel applications, the computation can be moved to memory. This allows for both parallel computation and increased bandwidth. The replication of small computation units provides parallelism, and the sum of their memory ports provides increased bandwidth. Because they are located in memory, there is no shared-bus resource to serialize communication.

One such system, Active Pages, places computation with each page of DRAM. It is unique in that it targets the commodity DRAM market. This decision has both advantages and disadvantages. One advantage is that it supports both data streaming and general-purpose computation, and the computational resources scale automatically with memory allocation. One disadvantage is that, to keep costs low, there is no additional interconnect, and parallelism is only at the page level.

Many of the characteristics of Active Pages are present in any memory-centric system. This case study explores several characteristics of the Active Pages design. It begins, in Section 35.1, with an overview of the Active Pages architecture and programming model. Section 35.2 shows the performance potential of a scalable, memory-centric design. Section 35.3 then looks at how this scaling of computational resources, but not the interconnect resources, affects the asymptotic properties of several algorithms. Finally, Sections 35.4 and 35.5, explore the parallelism properties and the defect tolerance provided by the Active Pages design. Active Pages is just one of many projects in this realm, and Section 35.6 presents related work, followed by some conclusions in Section 35.7.

35.1 ACTIVE PAGES

This section gives a brief description of the Active Pages system. We present three aspects of the design: the hardware design, the interface between Active

Pages and the Central Processor, and the programming model that arises naturally from the design and interface.

35.1.1   DRAM Hardware Design

High-density DRAMs are divided into subarrays, complete with row and column decoders, to minimize column capacitance and decrease power consumption [1]. The proposed Active Pages implementation exploits this natural structure, treating each subarray as an Active Page. As shown in Figure 35.1, a small computational unit and cache—a *Page Processor* and *Page Cache*—are embedded next to each subarray to implement Active Page functions [2]. Using commodity 1-Gb DRAM technology as a target [3], we expect subarray size to be 512 KB and the embedded processing to consume less than 31 percent of the chip area.

To minimize DRAM modification and reduce hardware overhead, the Active Pages implementations do not provide hardware support for communication between Active Pages. If two Active Pages need to share data, the Central Processor reads the data from one and writes to the other. The disadvantage of this *process-mediated approach* is that interpage communication must be infrequent to maintain performance with a single processor.

35.1.2   Hardware Interface

To interface with the Central Processor, Active Pages leverage conventional page-based memory mechanisms to "virtualize" hardware for memory-based computation. Computations for each page can be suspended, restarted, and even swapped to disk. Computations for several pages can be multiplexed on a single embedded processing element.

Further, Active Pages use the same interface as conventional memory systems. Active Pages data are modified with conventional memory reads and writes; Active Pages functions are invoked through memory-mapped writes. Synchronization is accomplished through user-defined memory locations.

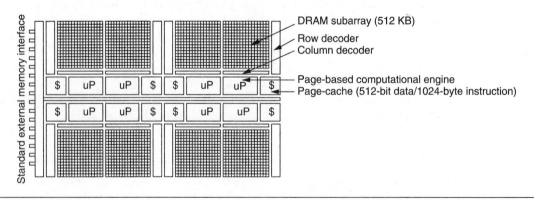

FIGURE 35.1 ▪ The Active Pages architecture (8 pages).

35.1.3 Programming Model

The programming model of Active Pages was determined by several design decisions. First, communication between Active Pages and the Central Processor is accomplished through traditional reads and writes, allowing the Central Processor to operate on Active Pages data just as it does on any other data. Second, Active Pages were intended for commodity DRAM systems, which may be running general-purpose applications. Thus, we could not assume a traditional data parallel, streaming model. Third, there is no interconnect between Active Pages processors. The model needs to limit the Pages to their own data, with no knowledge of neighboring cells. Finally, each Active Page has computation associated with it. This is a direct association of data with computation. For these two reasons, the model of computation here is object-oriented programming.

To program a Page Processor, the programmer creates an object in C++. The choice of C++ is not critical; it is used because it has no runtime system associated with it and has well-defined interfaces for object manipulation. The 512 KB allocated to each Page Processor is divided between code, stack, and data. These 512 KB, larger-than-typical operating systems' virtual pages are referred to as superpages. The code must fit within the code segment, and the data size of the object is padded appropriately.

The operating system (OS) is responsible for allocating Active Pages memory and loading the code into the correct region. The Page Processor begins on activation, first performing any initialization similarly to a C++ object constructor, and then polling a variable waiting for an invocation of a function. To maintain pin compatibility, all Active Pages functions are designed to use conventional reads and writes. The Central Processor invokes Active Pages functions by writing the parameters into appropriate places in the Active Pages memory. The Central Processor then changes the `Running` variable, on which the Page Processor is polling, indicating which function to execute next.

When the Page Processor has completed the function, it resets the looping variable (`Running`) and waits for the next invocation. Figure 35.2 shows the object declaration and implementation for execution on a Page Processor for LCS. More details on the LCS algorithm can be found in Section 35.3.3. In the LCS algorithm, the application requires only a single function, so the event loop is not actually necessary. It is shown, however, to illustrate how an application with many functions would use the Central Processor to invoke functions on the Page Processors. The main function run on the Central Processor is not shown. The Central Processor can poll the `Running` variable to determine whether a Page Processor has completed a particular function.

35.2 PERFORMANCE RESULTS

Now that we have an idea of what the Active Pages architecture looks like and how it is programmed, this section presents performance results for several applications using a simulated Active Pages system. A more detailed study can be found in Oskin et al. [4].

```
Class LCS{
  //int    CodeAndStack[8192];   // added by compiler
  public:
    int Running, Data[WIDTH-1][LENGTH-1];
    char X[WIDTH], Y[LENGTH];
    LCS(){ Running = AP_WAIT; }
    void Start();
    void DoLCS();
} ;
void LCS::DoLCS() {
  int i, j;
  for(i=1;i<LENGTH;i++) // row 0, column 0 initialized by Central Processor
    for(j=1;j<WIDTH;j++) {
        if (X[i] == Y[j])
            Data[i][j] = Data[i-1][j-1] + 1;
        else if (Data[i-1][j] > Data[i][j-1])
            Data[i][j] = Data[i-1][j];
        else
            Data[i][j] = Data[i][j-1];
  }
}
void LCS::Start() {
    volatile int *act = &(Running);
    while(*act != AP_STOP) {
        while(*act == AP_WAIT) ;   // wait for Central Processor
        switch (*act) {
        case(AP_LCS):
            DoLCS(Val);
            *act = AP_WAIT;  // it is done
            break;
      }
    }
}
```

FIGURE 35.2 ■ A code example of an Active Pages object. Each Page Processor initializes its own space on allocation using the constructor. The Central Processor starts the Page Processor by writing to the `Running` variable. When the call is finished, the Page Processor sets `Running` back to `AP_WAIT`.

To estimate the performance of Active Pages configurations, each Active Pages function was hand-coded in a high-level circuit-description language, such as VHDL (see Chapter 6 and [5]), and synthesized to an Altera 10K FPGA. The mapping was carried out all the way to placed and routed designs [6].

To demonstrate effective partitioning of applications between the Central Processor and Active Pages, we chose a range of applications representing both memory- and processor-centric partitioning. Table 35.1 summarizes the attributes of these applications.

35.2.1 Speedup over Conventional Systems

To evaluate performance of the Active Pages memory system, each application was executed on a range of problem sizes. The speedup of the applications

TABLE 35.1 ■ Summary of the partitioning of applications between the Central Processor and Active Pages

		Memory-centric applications	
Name	**Application**	**Central Processor computation**	**Active Pages computation**
Array	C++ standard template library array class	C++ code using array class cross-page moves	Array insert, delete, and find
Database	Address database	Initiates queries summarizes results	Searches unindexed data
Median	Median filter for images	Image I/O	Median of neighboring pixels
Dynamic program	Protein sequence matching	Backtracking	Compute MINs and fills table
		Processor-centric applications	
Matrix	Matrix multiply for Simplex and finite element	Floating-point multiplies	Index comparison and data gathering and scattering
MPEG-MMX	MPEG decoder using MMX instructions	MMX dispatch Discrete cosine transform	MMX instructions

running on an Active Pages memory system compared to a conventional memory system is shown in Figure 35.3. Each application was run on a range of problem sizes, given in terms of number of Active Pages (512-KB superpages). The following are two primary observations about this graph.

First, the performance results qualitatively scale as expected. This shows the advantage of memory-centric computation. We observe that most applications show little growth in speedup as data size grows within the subpage region (below one page). In this region, Active Pages applications have little parallelism to offset activation costs. When leaving this region, however, we enter the scalable region and see that performance on all applications grows as data size increases. Four applications—database, MMX, matrix-simplex, matrix-boeing, and median-filtering—also reach the saturated region. Here, Active Pages performance is limited by the progress of the Central Processor. This limitation may be because of either too much work for a given-speed Central Processor or too much data travelling between the Central Processor and Active Pages across the memory bus. Performance can actually decrease as coordination costs dominate performance. Given a large enough problem size, all applications would eventually reach the saturated region.

Second, we see that the array-delete primitive performs poorly in the subpage region. This is because of the difference between the FPGA implementation and the instruction set used to implement the Central Processor. The Central Processor's instruction set is especially well suited for the array-delete primitive. Thus, unless there is sufficient parallelism to justify using Active Pages, it is faster to use the Central Processor. So, for small deletes, we use only the Central Processor. This benchmark was a combination of small deletes and large deletes.

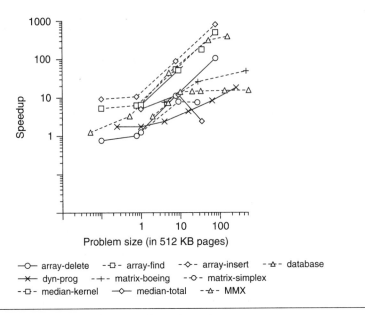

FIGURE 35.3 ▪ Active Pages speedup as problem size varies.

As problem size grows, and the Central Processor is used for both the coordination of large deletes and the complete execution of small deletes, the Central Processor becomes the limiting factor in performance and the performance gets closer to that of the uniprocessor. This shows an interesting trade-off between the FPGA and the Central Processor. Some computations, though not many, will perform better on the Central Processor. If this coincides with a part of the application that does not require parallelism, then the advantage of the memory-centric FPGA implementation will be reduced.

35.2.2 Processor–Memory Nonoverlap

The saturated region of Active Pages performance emphasizes the importance of partitioning applications to efficiently use the Central Processor in a system. For processor-centric applications, this dependence is obvious. The goal is to keep the Central Processor computing by providing a steady stream of useful data from the memory system. For memory-centric partitions, however, the Central Processor is still a vital resource. Active Pages cannot compute without activation and interpage communication, both provided by the Central Processor.

As data size grows in an Active Pages application, so does the load on the Central Processor. We measure the remaining capacity of a Central Processor to handle this load with a metric, *processor–memory nonoverlap* time. Nonoverlap is the time the Central Processor spends waiting for the memory system and can be used to estimate the boundary between the scalable and saturated regions of application performance.

The relative percentage of time the Central Processor is stalled, waiting for memory system computation, is shown in Figure 35.4. As described in

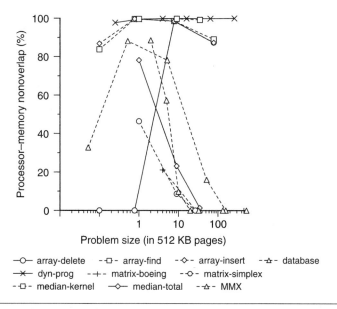

FIGURE 35.4 ■ The percent of cycles that the Central Processor is stalled on Active Pages as problem size varies.

the previous section, the applications that reached the saturated region of speedup were database, matrix-simplex, matrix-boeing, and median-filtering. As Figure 35.4 shows, these applications also reach a point of complete processor–memory overlap.

We also observe that for the array primitives and the dynamic programming application, the nonoverlap percentage remains relatively high. These applications are largely memory-centric with very little Central Processor activity. In fact, the array primitives operate asynchronously to the end of the application and are artificially forced into synchronous operation for this study. This means that an application can use the array-insert and array-delete primitives with only the cost of Active Pages function invocation. Modulo dependencies on the array, the time spent by the memory system shifting data, can be overlapped with operations outside of the STL array class. This overlap occurs in a natural way with no additional effort required by the programmer who uses the Active Pages STL array class. Opportunities for overlapping execution of data structure operations with data structure usage are intriguing and are being investigated further.

The dynamic programming example maintains a very high processor–memory nonoverlap; however, preliminary results indicate that processor-mediated communication required by the Active Pages memory system eventually dominates performance. This occurs for extremely large problems that are well beyond the range of problem sizes presented in this study. Dedicating more resources to the interconnect increases the range of problems that Active Pages can help solve.

35.2.3 Summary

Memory-centric computation provides a scalable source of performance for large-scale applications. Active Pages provides a large number of simple, reconfigurable computational elements that can achieve speedups up to 1000 times faster than conventional systems. Systems with rich interconnects have the potential for scalable gains on an even wider range of applications.

35.3 ALGORITHMIC COMPLEXITY

Although the simulated results show great promise, to truly understand how Active Pages improves runtimes as problem sizes grow, we need to explore asymptotic properties of algorithms in conventional systems as well as Active Pages systems [7]. For this study, we use a set of kernels whose asymptotic properties are well known in algorithmic literature.

While it is unrealistic to expect the number of processors in a conventional multiprocessor to scale arbitrarily, the amount of DRAM in a system is expected to scale with problem size for a majority of problems. With Active Pages DRAMs, computational hardware also scales. This scaling provides parallelism that can improve asymptotic performance. Table 35.2 gives a preview of such gains for a variety of algorithms. Note that Active Pages execution times rely on the optimal page size given in the table. In practice, we expect Active Pages hardware to support a small range of page sizes designed to support target applications and problem sizes.

The challenge in the analysis is to take communication costs into account. In any system, the interconnect will affect the asymptotic properties of the performance as the problem scales. Active Pages, in particular, requires careful consideration of the communication between Page Processors as well as between the Central Processor and the Page Processors. The partitioned computations and restricted communication model here differ substantially from traditional parallel models such as PRAM [8]. This section presents an analysis of each algorithm that considers these issues. These analyses are also validated with simulation results.

TABLE 35.2 ■ Algorithmic complexity (summary)

Application	Conventional	Execution time within Active Pages	Page size
Array insert	$O(n)$	$O(\sqrt{n})$	$O(\sqrt{n})$
2D LCS	$O(n^2)$	$O(n\sqrt{n})$	$O(n)$
3D LCS	$O(n^3)$	$O(n^{7/3})$	$O(n^2)$
All-pairs shortest path	$O(n^3)$	$O(n^{7/3})$	$O(n^{4/3})$
Sorting	$O(n \cdot \log_2(n))$	$O(n \cdot \log_2(\log_2(n)))$	$O(n/z)$ where $n = z \cdot e^z$
Volume rendering	$O(n^3)$	$O(n^{5/2})$	$O(n^{3/2})$

35.3.1 Algorithms

Active Pages can dramatically improve the performance of many algorithms. This section maps several common algorithms to an Active Pages system and analyzes performance gains. Figure 35.5 introduces the notation used here. With these conventions, we analyze the worst-case execution time of the algorithms: insertion of an element into a linear array of elements, longest common subsequence of two- and three-dimensional sequences using a dynamic programming formulation, all-pairs shortest path using a dynamic programming formulation, sorting of a linear array of elements, and volume rendering using ray-tracing and linear absorption coefficients [7, 9].

Each analysis is provided by first presenting a general model for the algorithm's execution time. Next, various model-specific parameters are assumed to be constants. After this simplification, the derivative of execution time with respect to page size is used to find an optimal page size. This page size is then substituted back into the model, and execution time is expressed again as a function of problem size.

These results are then validated with a high-level simulator. The simulator models Active Pages execution using parameters based on execution of the cycle-level simulator. The parameters used are given in Table 35.3. *Typical* parameters correspond to the target architecture studied here and often exhibit better performance than a purely asymptotic analysis would suggest. *Asymptotic* parameters emphasize the dominant terms in asymptotic performance while remaining within realistic problem sizes. These exaggerated parameters are used to validate the more conservative analyses.

Table 35.3 summarizes the parameters used in the high-level simulator. T_a is the amount of time required by the processor to invoke a function on a memory-based

---

n is the size of the input.

p is the number of data elements in an Active Page.

q is a problem-specific function of p that is used for most algorithms to define p. For instance, for dynamic programming algorithms where a two-dimensional result set is generated, it is convenient to describe p as equal to $p = q^2$.

k is a function of the number of Active Pages used for the problem—usually $k = n/q$.

FIGURE 35.5 ■ The notation used for algorithmic analysis.

TABLE 35.3 ■ Summary of simulation parameters

Parameter	APSP*	Sort	Array insert	LCS*	LCS3	Render
Activation time (T_a)	100/0	0	2058	100/100	100	100
Central Processor per-page processing time (T_p)	–	1	387	–	–	5
Page processing per-element processing time (T_c)	10/10	1	2	–	10	10
Fixed communication overhead (T_{sa})	1/1	–	–	10/10	1	–
Per-element communication cost (T_{sb})	1/1	–	–	1/100	1	–

∗ Typical/asymptotic.

processor. This includes setup, argument passing, and invocation. This constant is per page. T_p is the amount of time required by the processor to complete execution of an algorithm associated with a particular page. Generally, the "focus" of execution traverses from the Central Processor to the Active Pages and then back again. This may proceed many times and involve overlap throughout the execution of the algorithm. However, for the analysis presented here the focus is on a single set of transitions from host to memory and back. Hence, T_p is the time spent by the Central Processor per page when completing the Central Processor portion of the computation for that page. T_c is the amount of time required by the memory-based processing element to compute its portion of the algorithm for a single data item within the page. For instance, on a conventional processor and memory system, an $O(n)$ algorithm requires some time, T_c, to compute the solution for each element; hence, the execution time is described as $T = T_c \cdot n$. T_{sa} is the amount of time that corresponds to the "fixed overhead" associated with each interpage communication. Inter–Active Pages communication is a necessarily expensive process, and this constant quantifies the relatively large fixed overhead associated with each such communication request. T_{sb} is the amount of time, per data item, associated with an interpage communication. Not all algorithms use interpage communication, and some use portions of T_a or T_p to perform such communication as part of activation and postprocessing, respectively.

This short section can present detailed analysis only of the array and LCS applications. We refer the reader to a technical report by Oskin et al. for the full set of analyses and results [9].

35.3.2 Array-Insert

The analysis begins with a simple array library. Specifically, we examine an insertion operation performed on an array of elements arranged in a linear fashion. A conventional system requires $O(n)$ execution to complete this task. In an Active Pages memory system, we partition these n elements into k pages, with each Active Page managing n/k elements. To insert an element at position j within the array, each Active Page from the page containing j up to the last page of the array shifts the elements up by one to make room for the new element. These shifts proceed in parallel, however, since each Active Page operates independently. Note, though, that some form of communication between pages is required to migrate elements across page boundaries. This communication is grouped within the activation portion of each Active Page. The algorithm can be expressed as shown in Figure 35.6.

```
for j=1 to k
    communicate the last element of
    page j to page j+1
    activate page j informing it to
    shift elements upward
```

FIGURE 35.6 ■ The array-insert algorithm.

The analysis begins with $s(i)$, the nonoverlap (*stall*) time for page i. The nonoverlap time, discussed in Section 35.2.2, is the amount of time spent by the processor waiting for the Active Pages memory system to finish. Essentially, this algorithm (and many other Active Pages algorithms) proceeds by having the Central Processor set up and activate memory-based processing, then wait for a page to complete computing. After the memory-based computation section is complete, the processor can return to finish its section of the computation. It turns out that quantifying how much a processor stalls while waiting for memory-based computation to complete, for traditionally linear algorithms, is an important and measurable quantity that can be used to tune applications to achieve maximum performance. We use it to quantify execution time.

Three functions—Ta, Tp, and Tc—are used to quantify portions of the execution time. These are expressed as functions because several linear-based algorithms can be mapped to an execution time analysis similar to that presented here. The functions correspond to activation time, host processor postexecution time, and per-page memory-based computation time, respectively.

For array insertion, these are essentially constant functions; hence, $Tc(i) = T_c$, $Ta(i) = T_a$, and $Tp(i) = T_p$. Figure 35.7 shows the timing of the array-insert operation (or any other linear-based function) on the Active Pages system using Ta, Tc, and Tp. Next, note that $\sum_{i=1}^{k} s(i) \leq T_c \cdot p$ allows us to simplify execution time and take the derivative of T with respect to p. This gives us a new expression for T given the optimal value for p:

$$T = \sum_{i=1}^{k} \left[T_a + T_p + s(i) \right] = k \left(T_a + T_p \right) + \sum_{i=1}^{k} s(i)$$

$$\leq k \left(T_a + T_p \right) + T_c \cdot p = \frac{n}{p} \left(T_a + T_p \right) + T_c \cdot p$$

$$\frac{dT}{dp} = \frac{-n}{p^2} \left(T_a + T_p \right) + T_c \Rightarrow p = \sqrt{\frac{n \left(T_a + T_p \right)}{T_c}}$$

$$T_{opt} = \frac{n}{p} \left(T_a + T_p \right) + T_c \cdot p = 2 \cdot \sqrt{n \cdot \left(T_a + T_p \right) \cdot T_c} = O(\sqrt{n}) \qquad (35.1)$$

$$T = \sum_{i=1}^{k} \left[Ta(i) + Tp(i) + s(i) \right]$$

$$s(i) = \max \begin{cases} 0 \\ s'(i) \end{cases}$$

$$s'(i) = Tc(i) - \left(\sum_{j=i+1}^{k} Ta(j) + \sum_{j=1}^{i-1} \left(Tp(j) + s(j) \right) \right)$$

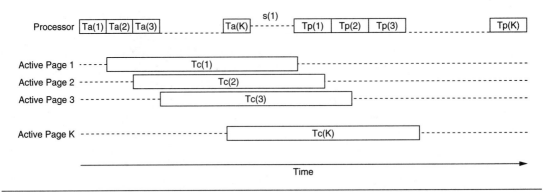

FIGURE 35.7 ■ An array-insert operation demonstrating processor and Active Page computations.

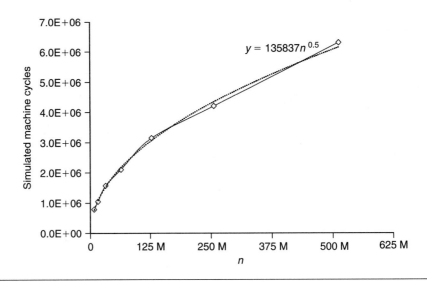

FIGURE 35.8 ■ Simulation results for the array-insert operation.

This analysis makes the conservative assumption that computation proceeds in serializable steps. First, all pages are activated; then all pages compute; finally, all pages finish and the processor performs some minimal postpage computation for each page. In reality, there is substantial overlap of these functions, and only during asymptotic performance is this serializing behavior observed. During practical application of this algorithm, the dominant term is $T_c \cdot p$, and execution time is held relatively constant. This behavior is observed until the point at which the number of pages times the activation and postpage processing per page starts to significantly approach $T_c \cdot p$. Figure 35.8 depicts simulated application performance versus problem size. As can be seen from the graph, simulated performance follows an $O(\sqrt{n})$ growth curve, as predicted by the analytical model here.

35.3.3 LCS (Two-dimensional Dynamic Programming)

Moving to a more complex algorithm, we examine a dynamic programming formulation for computing the longest common subsequence in a protein. The conventional execution time of this algorithm is $O(n^2)$. Figure 35.9 outlines the algorithm. For a more in-depth discussion of the LCS algorithm with fine-grained parallel execution in a systolic model, see Hoang [10].

Parallel execution of this algorithm proceeds in "wave-fronts," as depicted in Figure 35.10. Once the first subproblem is solved and the results have been dispatched, two other problems can immediately start computing, and when they are done, three other Active Pages can start their computation in parallel. The processor is responsible for activating a wave-front. When processor-mediated communication is used, the wave-front is uneven, with certain pages of the computation executing slightly ahead of other pages. This is because of the overlapping nature of Active Pages computation and processor activity. In the model of computation here, this overlap is very important to performance, and we take advantage of it to lower overall execution time. Also note that the subproblem solution that an Active Page will make available consists only of the items on two edges of the page.

For this problem we assume the following constants. T_c is the time required by the Active Pages processor to compute the result of a single item of the LCS computation. T_{sa} is the fixed overhead cost associated with an interpage communication. T_{sb} is the cost to transfer items between pages on a per-item basis.

```
partition x and y into k segments
divide the computation into x/q and y/q smaller computations
initialize page (i,j) with the corresponding component i of string x
          and with component j of string y.
let page (i, j) perform the conventional LCS algorithm after subproblems
          (i, j-1), (i-1, j), and (i-1, j-1) have been solved.
page (i,j) dispatches results to neighboring subproblems.
```

FIGURE 35.9 ■ The two-dimensional LCS algorithm.

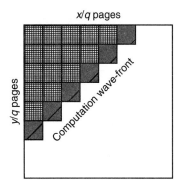

FIGURE 35.10 ■ Parallel execution of two-dimensional LCS on Active Pages.

Further, since the dynamic programming model dictates that the number of items in a page be quadratic in terms of the length of sequence x and the length of sequence y, we define the page size p to be equal to q^2, where q is a variable.

This makes the reasonable analytical assumption that x and y are of similar lengths. We can express application execution time as

$$T < 2 \cdot \sum_{i=1}^{j} \left[T_c \cdot q^2 + T_{sa} + q \cdot T_{sb} \right] + 2 \cdot \sum_{i=j+1}^{n/q} i \cdot \left[3 \cdot T_{sa} + (2 \cdot q + 1) \cdot T_{sb} \right] \tag{35.2}$$

where j represents the particular wave-front in which the overall execution switches from being bounded by computation to being bounded by communication. Focusing on the first half of the computation-bound area, each wave-front has an ever-increasing cost of communication. This is because more Active Pages are involved in each wave-front.

At first, the communication is hidden by computation, but eventually the cost of communicating the required data between wave-fronts exceeds the cost of computation for the wave-front. At this point, the algorithm crosses over from being bounded by computation to being bounded by communication; thus, computation completely overlaps with communication. We denote the wave-front where this occurs as j. This chapter presents an analysis that achieves a better theoretical upper-bound than the conventional sequential solution. Based on particular protein sequence sizes, computer-assisted analysis can reveal the ideal j and q, which minimize the execution time of this algorithm, thus tailoring the behavior of Active Pages in terms of the given problem size. The simulation results show that computer-calculated ideal page sizes entail even a slightly better performance than the theoretical analysis. As will be seen, this is because of a simplification in the analysis.

Suppose we force $j \geq n/q$. This implies that the algorithm will never become bounded by communication resources. We can do this by carefully selecting q and then demonstrating that this q does indeed force $j \geq n/q$. To find a q that satisfies these conditions, we require that the communication always weighs less than computation:

$$\frac{n}{q} \cdot \left[3 \cdot T_{sa} + (2 \cdot q + 1) \cdot T_{sb} \right] \leq \left[T_c \cdot q^2 + T_{sa} + q \cdot T_{sb} \right] \tag{35.3}$$

Then simplify this inequality by:

$$\frac{n}{q} \cdot \left[3 \cdot T_{sa} + (2 \cdot q + 1) \cdot T_{sb} \right] \leq \left[T_c \cdot q^2 + T_{sa} + q \cdot T_{sb} \right]$$

$$\frac{n}{q} \cdot \left[3 \cdot q \cdot (T_{sa} + T_{sb} + 1) \right] \leq \left[T_c \cdot q^2 + T_{sa} + q \cdot T_{sb} \right] \tag{35.4}$$

$$T_c \cdot q^2 \leq \left[T_c \cdot q^2 + T_{sa} + q \cdot T_{sb} \right]$$

This simplification will not lead to an absolute lower-bound on execution time, but it does present a tractable alternative that can be used to find an "ideal" q:

$$q \geq \sqrt{n} \cdot \sqrt{\frac{3 \cdot (T_{sa} + T_{sb} + 1)}{T_c}} = \alpha \cdot \sqrt{n} \tag{35.5}$$

Then use this q to drop j from the equation, since the algorithm will never be bound by communication:

$$T < 2 \cdot \sum_{i=1}^{n/q} \left[T_c \cdot q^2 + T_{sa} + q \cdot T_{sb} \right] = 2 \cdot \frac{n}{q} \cdot \left[T_c \cdot q^2 + T_{sa} + q \cdot T_{sb} \right] \tag{35.6}$$

$$= 2 \cdot \frac{\sqrt{n}}{\alpha} \cdot \left[T_c \cdot n \cdot \alpha^2 + T_{sa} + \sqrt{n} \cdot T_{sb} + \alpha \right] = O(n\sqrt{n})$$

While $O(n\sqrt{n})$ is a loose upper-bound, it is faster than the conventional runtime of $O(n^2)$. The simulation results concurred with the findings and suggested a slightly better than $O(n\sqrt{n})$ lower worst-case execution bound.

Figure 35.11 depicts simulated performance of the LCS algorithm; two curves are shown. The first curve depicts the predicted performance of $O(n\sqrt{n})$ (using *asymptotic* parameters from Table 35.3). The second curve predicts a more realistic performance of $O(n^{4/3})$ (using *typical* parameters). The discrepancy is because of communication performance. If communication were more expensive, then the ideal page size would shift away from communication requirements and toward increased computational requirements, amplifying that term in the execution time expression. This in turn would reveal the asymptotic order of the LCS algorithm.

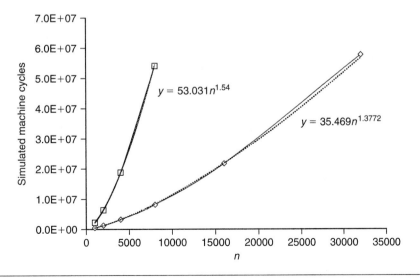

FIGURE 35.11 ■ Simulation results for the two-dimensional LCS.

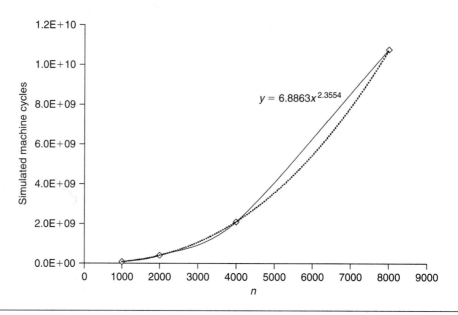

FIGURE 35.12 ▪ Simulation results for the three-dimensional LCS.

A more realistic depiction of application performance follows an $O(n^{4/3})$ trend. A similar analysis predicts performance of $O(n^{7/3})$ for three-dimensional LCS. Figure 35.12 shows that the simulated performance for three-dimensional LCS closely matches this prediction.

35.3.4 Summary

We can see that with a memory-centric architecture such as Active Pages, in which the computation scales with the communication, the asymptotic complexity can be reduced. We also see that it is a much more complex equation than one might think. The overhead of the Active Pages, the delay of any communication, and the page size need to be taken into account. Two algorithms, along with validated simulations, have been presented to show their new asymptotic properties. We have found that the inexpensive parallelism provided by page-based intelligent memories can have a significant affect on asymptotic performance. We have also found the optimal page sizes that are required to maximize performance.

35.4 EXPLORING PARALLELISM

In any memory-centric system, we must decide the proper balance between memory resources and computation power. To save money, we could share a single computational element with twice as much memory. Allowing sharing can potentially even out the computational requirements of two processing elements because their needs may not always be identical.

This section looks at virtualizing the computational logic across superpages in the Active Pages chip. Virtualization is accomplished by time-slicing a VLIW processor (see VLIW datapath control subsection of Section 5.2.2) across one to eight Active Pages. We refer to this time-slicing as the *multiplexing* of the computational logic. This study presents an analysis of multiplexing and its effects on performance in a multiprocess environment. In addition, it looks at how varying individual processor widths affects performance. By combining these approaches, we demonstrate that multiplexing is a more effective technique for reducing logic area requirements than reducing individual Page Processor performance.

In this study, we chose to use VLIW computational elements rather than an FPGA so that we could explore the trade-off between instruction-level parallelism and task-level parallelism. The results hold for FPGAs as well. From a high level, it is merely the trade-off between smaller dedicated resources per memory segment and shared resources between memory segments. The study is cleaner when using processor width rather than FPGA area.

35.4.1 Speedup over Conventional

We begin with the raw speedups of a commodity workload that is used for this study. Because the focus is on multi-programmed systems, we are using a slightly different workload than before.

Figure 35.13 depicts application speedup when applications use an Active Pages memory system. Speedup is measured in terms of wall-clock time for the application in a conventional memory system divided by its wall-clock time

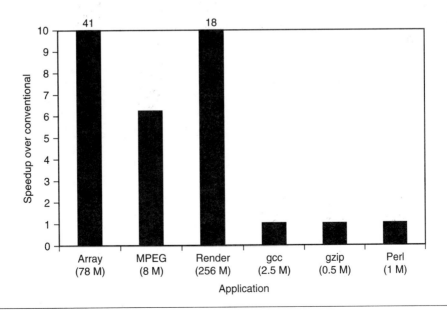

FIGURE 35.13 ■ Speedup over conventional.

using an Active Pages memory system. We observe that Active Pages applications continue to show substantial speedups when executed in a multiprocess environment. That is, even when many independent applications are executed at once, the applications experience speedup.

35.4.2 Multiplexing Performance

We continue by exploring how much performance degradation occurs as resources are shared between Active Pages. Figure 35.14 depicts relative application performance as the degree of multiplexing is increased. We normalize the results to a configuration with no multiplexing, where a one-to-one relationship exists between 4-wide VLIW processors and DRAM subarrays. Multiplexing factors of two, four, and eight make up the remaining data points. Note that hardware multiplexing of eight incurs no more than a 17 percent performance penalty, and a multiplexing factor of four incurs no more than a 6 percent performance penalty for all Active Page applications in the workload.

35.4.3 Processor Width Performance

It is promising that with a 4-wide VLIW, performance does not degrade substantially, as it is shared between Active Pages. Is this because the VLIW processor is not being used efficiently? We now examine the inherent instruction-level parallelism (ILP) in our applications. Figure 35.15 depicts relative application performance as VLIW processor width is varied. Here, processor widths of one, two, four, and eight were evaluated. We observe that half of the applications show a 20 to 80 percent increase in performance from increasing processor width, but the other half do not. It should be noted that MPEG suffers adverse

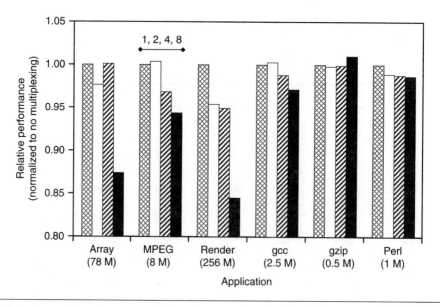

FIGURE 35.14 ▪ Performance versus hardware multiplexing.

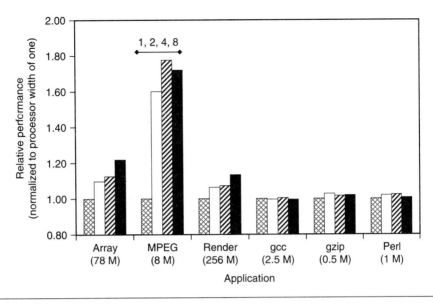

FIGURE 35.15 ■ Performance of multiplexing versus VLIW processor width.

cache effects with a VLIW width of eight, thus lowering performance relative to a 4-wide VLIW. We note that the largest performance gains because of VLIW processor width are achieved with processor widths of two and four, and not with eight.

35.4.4 Processor Width versus Multiplexing

Taking another look at Figure 35.15, we find that the Active Pages applications do not have the static instruction-level parallelism to use much beyond a 4-wide VLIW processor. In addition, Figure 35.14 shows that degradation because of multiplexing is superlinear, suggesting that too much coarse-grained parallelism exists within the application workloads to substantially multiplex processor resources.

An experiment designed to compare these two forms of parallelism is depicted in Figure 35.16. Here we compare an Active Pages device using a single-issue processor with no multiplexing against a device using a 2-wide VLIW with two-way multiplexing, a 4-wide VLIW with four-way multiplexing, and an 8-wide VLIW with eight-way multiplexing.

In the Active Pages applications, a 2-wide VLIW with two-way multiplexing shows a performance gain. This implies that the gain from the increased ILP outweighs the reduced coarse-grained parallelism. Because several conventional applications are active in the workloads, this makes sense because many of the pages do not need the page processors. A 4-wide VLIW with four-way multiplexing is the best configuration studied. Hence, we use this configuration in the remainder of this study.

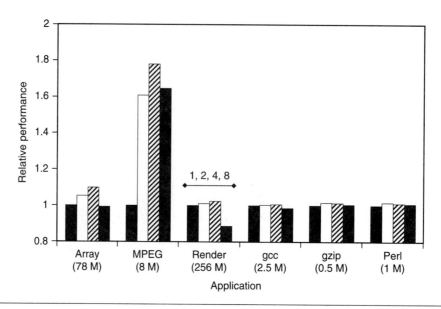

FIGURE 35.16 ■ Performance versus processor width.

To describe why multiplexing performs well in a multiprocess environment, we identify three key factors: nonactive memory, Active Pages processing time, and partitioning.

Nonactive memory

This helps mask the performance degradation because of multiplexing. By definition, all pages of memory in a conventional application require no computation in memory. Some pages in an Active Pages application also require no memory computation.

Active Pages processing time

This is the amount of time spent by the Active Pages computing without main processor intervention. The time varies with Page Processor performance. Simple data manipulations are easily offloaded to the memory system. This leads to longer per-page computation times, most notably MPEG, with Active Pages processing time on the order of seconds.

The combination of low Active Pages processing times and context switching in the Central Processor hides the effects of multiplexing in the memory system. In the absence of multiplexed Active Pages, when the main processor switches to another process, the Active Pages associated with the previous process quickly finish their work and stall until the process regains control of the Central Processor. Multiplexing allows efficient utilization of Page Processors by context-switching them to another Active Pages process when they would otherwise be idle.

In an environment with Active Pages processing times longer than a Central Processor time slice, such as those observed in MPEG, we would expect multiplexing to degrade performance. Within this study, however, degradation is minimal due to the relatively low memory requirements of MPEG and the effects of conventional memory (without computational capability).

Partitioning
This is the process of dividing an application into work done in Active Pages and work done in the Central Processor. As long as the main processor can keep up with the Active Pages, an application is *scalable* and will exhibit linear speedup as its dataset grows and more Active Pages are used. Once the main processor becomes *saturated* with work, however, performance will no longer increase as more Active Pages are used.

We find that multiprocess environments change the position at which an application transitions from scalable to saturated. Multiprocessing time slices the Central Processor, which may be viewed as artificially slowing down the processor from the perspective of a single process. This will shift the scalable-saturated point toward smaller problem sizes. We may use multiplexing to reverse this shift. Essentially, multiplexing slows down the Active Pages computation, shifting the scalable-saturated point back toward larger problem sizes.

Because of the preceding properties of multi-programming environments, we observe that multiplexing is an efficient mechanism for reducing logic area requirements in an Active Pages memory device. A four-way multiplexed 4-wide VLIW Active Pages device is estimated to require 12 percent of the available chip area for computational logic while still providing substantial performance gains. This estimate is based on the reduced logic area coupled with a 20 percent logic area increase because of additional interconnect requirements.

35.4.5 Summary

This study has looked at a promising method for reducing the computational logic area requirements of an Active Pages memory device. Such an approach could be exploited by any memory-centric device. By multiplexing the computational logic among one to four Active Pages, hardware cost can be reduced by four times with little performance impact in a multiprogrammed environment. Further, we find that it is more important to have fewer, faster computational logic elements that are time-shared across pages than more abundant, slower ones available for direct computation at each page. With a 4-wide VLIW processor multiplexed with every four Active Pages, computational logic area can be reduced to 12 percent of total chip area in a gigabit DRAM.

35.5 DEFECT TOLERANCE

The previous section explored the parallelism trade-offs gained by sharing computational units between pages. This section focuses on another major factor in cost: manufacturing defects. DRAM architectures use redundant cells to tolerate defects, dramatically increasing chip yields and reducing cost. Embedded processors, however, do not have an analogous unit of redundancy. While multiplexing several Active Pages with one embedded processor reduces chip area, multiplexing each group of pages with two processors allows each group to tolerate a processor defect. This *associativity* requires some additional interconnect, but tolerance to randomly distributed processor defects increases from 33 percent to more than 50 percent.

In this section, we use associativity to increase the defect tolerance of an Active Pages system. The focus is on manufacturing defects that render embedded processors inoperative. The goal is to provide some degree of processor redundancy under the assumption that memory cells already have their own redundancy techniques.

Instead of four Active Pages sharing one 4-wide VLIW processor, we allow eight pages to share two processors. We study the effect of randomly distributed processor defects on this associative system. If a group suffers two defects, the operating system will only map conventional pages to that group (pages with no computation).

The performance degradation because of randomly distributed processor defects is depicted in Figure 35.17. We note that up to a 50-percent defect rate is tolerated. Increasing the defect rate to 60 percent decreased the number of functional Active Pages below that required by the workload without page swapping. Virtualizing Active Pages to disk was studied by Oskin et al. [11], and a similar mechanism can be used to further increase defect tolerance.

Associativity creates an increased tolerance to defects. The benefits are straightforward. Two processors must fail instead of one in order to disable any Active Pages. If 50 percent of embedded processors fail in the test system, we see that with two-way associativity up to 75 percent of the memory will still be available for Active Pages use.

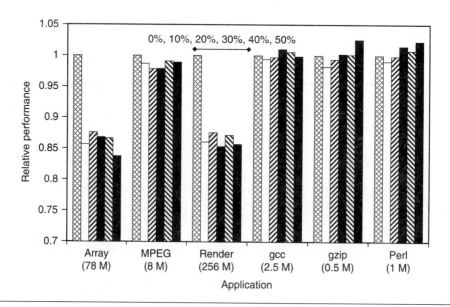

FIGURE 35.17 ■ Performance versus random processor defects.

Second, not all of the system memory is required to be "active" at the same time. This allows the OS to map around defect areas and use fully defective functional groups for conventional applications. Further, the workloads do not require the full 512 MB available to the system, and the unutilized memory is available to map into defective regions. The OS can tolerate some defects without associativity by taking advantage of underutilization and conventional applications.

As noted in this section, multiplexing, associativity, and clever OS resource allocation can map around manufacturing defects with only a 20 percent performance penalty with 50 percent random logic defects. An Active Pages–aware OS can be defect tolerant and allow a lower-cost system to be developed by increasing manufacturing chip yield. These incremental costs make Active Pages an attractive memory-based computation model, though the same principles would hold for FPGA-based systems (see Chapter 37).

35.6 RELATED WORK

DRAM densities have made intelligent memory attractive as commodity components. Intelligent memory, however, was proposed well before the current commodity thrust. The SWIM project [12] combined reconfigurable logic and memory to perform fast protocol computations. The J-Machine integrated processor, memory, and network router in a single chip to form building blocks for a fine-grained multiprocessor [13]. The RAW [14], MORPH [15], and RaPiD [16] projects continue to explore the use of reconfigurable technology to exploit parallelism. The RAW project, in particular, has also examined issues of processor width, dynamically trading off ILP and speculation. The HPAM project [17] takes a hierarchical approach to intelligent memory.

The project that is most similar to Active Pages is FlexRAM [18], which targeted general-purpose computation. The goal was to find computation that could take advantage of the bandwidth provided within a DRAM chip. FlexRAM proposed a hierarchical solution with simple computational elements within each page and a more complex processor for each DRAM. This allowed communication to be handled by an on-chip processor rather than the Central Processor. This had the disadvantage of adding pins to commodity DRAM packaging.

Several other projects explored placing processors in DRAM for more massively parallel computation. IRAM [19] solved this problem by placing a single-vector processor in DRAM. For applications amenable to vectorization, this is an excellent match between a high, bandwidth memory and a processing element. Notre Dame's PIM [20] project uses SIMD functional units to consume the extra bandwidth. DIVA [21] has the most sophisticated design, allowing for a kernel to run on the PIM processors. It also features a dedicated PIM communication network, allowing for communication between PIM processors without host processor intervention. Currently, there is a single computational element in each DRAM.

The Impulse project [22] has similar goals to Active Pages but focuses on adding address manipulation functions to the memory controller. Its applications, such as gather-scatter for multiplying a sparse matrix by a dense vector, are also enhanced by more efficiently feeding the microprocessor with data. All the Active Pages applications, however, require some small computations that cannot be supported without more generalized computation in the memory system than Impulse provides.

35.7 SUMMARY

This chapter presented the enormous potential for memory-centric computation, along with several issues specific to the Active Pages DRAM environment. The potential for all memory-centric designs is the bandwidth between memory and the nearest computational unit. The challenge, just as in Active Pages, is how to communicate between units. As the ratio of memory to processing units decreases, the total bandwidth increases, but the communication needs increase. This different balance between computation and communication can affect the asymptotic properties of algorithms.

The barriers for intelligent memory, in particular, are the need for explicit parallel programming and the buy-in by manufacturers to put it in commodity production to lower the price. DIVA is working on a migration path for this technology. The advent of multicore commodity processors pushes the field in two directions. First, it provides performance improvements in multi-programmed environments without the need for parallel programming. This hurts the case for intelligent memory. The prevalence of parallel processors on the market, however, increases the utility of parallel programming so that this may not be such a rare skill in the future. If parallel programming becomes commonplace, then intelligent memory will be poised for success in the commodity market.

Acknowledgments   Like any large-scale project, Active Pages was the work of several people over several years. Fred Chong and Mark Oskin were the driving force behind the project. Matt Farrens provided valuable advice. Several graduate and undergraduate students contributed to the project, including Justin Hensley, Lucian Vlad-Lita, Tim Sherwood, Ravishankar Rao, Aneet Chopra, Paul Sultana, and Jennifer Hollfelder.

References

[1] K. Itoh et al. Limitations and challenges of multigigabit DRAM chip design. *IEEE Journal of Solid-State Circuits* 32(5), 1997.

[2] M. Oskin, J. Hensley, D. Keen, F. T. Chong, M. K. Farrens, A. Chopra. Exploiting ILP in page-based intelligent memory. *International Symposium on Microarchitecture*, 1999.

[3] Semiconductor Industry Association. The national technology roadmap for semiconductors. *http://www.sematech.org/public/roadmap/*, 1994.

[4] M. Oskin, F. T. Chong, T. Sherwood. Active pages: A computation model for intelligent memory. *Proceedings of the 25th Annual International Symposium on Computer Architecture*, 1998.

[5] P. Ashenden. *The Designer's Guide to VHDL*, 2nd ed., Morgan Kaufmann, 2002.

[6] Altera Corporation. *FLEX 10K Embedded Programmable Logic Family*, May 1998.

[7] M. Oskin, L. V. Lita, F. T. Chong, J. Hensley, D. K. Franklin. Algorithmic complexity with page-based intelligent memory. *Parallel Processing Letters* 10(1), 2000.

[8] A. Kautonen, V. Leppnen, M. Penttonen. PRAM model. *http//www.cs.joensuu.fi/pages/penttonen/parallel/pram.pram.html*.

[9] M. Oskin, L.-V. Lita, F. T. Chong, J. Hensley, D. K. Franklin. Algorithmic Complexity with Page-Based Intelligent Memory. Technical Report CS-01-00, Department of Computer Science, University of California, Davis, February 2000.

[10] D. T. Hoang. Searching genetic database on Splash 2. In D. Buell, J. Arnold, W. Kleinfelder, *Splash 2: FPGAs in a Custom Computing Machine*, IEEE Computer Society Press, 1996.

[11] M. Oskin, F. T. Chong, T. Sherwood. ActiveOS: Virtualizing intelligent memory. *Proceedings of the IEEE International Conference on Computer Design*, 1999.

[12] A. Asthana, M. Cravatts, P. Krzyzanowski. Design of an active memory system for network applications. *International Workshop on Memory Technology, Design and Testing*, IEEE Computer Society Press, 1994.

[13] M. Noakes, D. Wallach, W. Dally. The J-Machine multicomputer: An architectural evaluation. *Proceedings of the 20th Annual ACM International Symposium on Computer Architecture*, May 1993.

[14] W. Lee. Space-time scheduling of instruction-level parallelism on a Raw machine. *Proceedings of the 8th International Conference on Architectural Support for Programming Languages and Operating Systems*, October 1998.

[15] A. A. Chien, R. K. Gupta. MORPH: A system architecture for robust high performance using customization. *Frontiers*, 1996.

[16] C. Ebeling et al. Mapping applications to the RaPiD configurable architecture. *Symposium on FPGAs for Custom Computing Machines*, April 1997.

[17] Z. Miled, R. Eigenmann, J. Fortes, V. Taylor. Hierarchical processors-and-memory architecture for high performance computing. *Sixth Symposium on the Frontiers of Massively Parallel Computation*, October 1996.

[18] Y. Kang, M. Huang, S. Yoon, Z. Ge, D. K. Franklin, V. Lam, P. Pattnaik, J. Torrellas. FlexRAM: An advanced intelligent memory system. *International Conference on Computer Design*, October 1999.

[19] D. Patterson. Microprocessors in 2020. *Scientific American*, September 1995.

[20] P. M. Kogge, T. Sunaga, E. A. E. Retter. Combined DRAM and logic chip for massively parallel applications. *16th IEEE Conference on Advanced Research in VLSI*, 1995.

[21] J. Draper, J. Chame, M. Hall, C. Steele, T. Barrett, J. LaCoss, J. Granacki, J. Shin, C. Chen, C. W. Kang, I. Kim, G. Daglikoca. Architecture: The architecture of the DIVA processing-in-memory chip. *International Conference on Supercomputing*, 2002.

[22] J. Carter, et al. Impulse: Building a smarter memory controller. *Proceedings of the International Symposium on High-Performance Computer Architecture*, January 1999.

PART VI

Theoretical Underpinnings and Future Directions

Parts I through V addressed what reconfigurable architectures look like (Part I), how we can develop reconfigurable solutions (Parts I, II, IV, V), and, by example, where reconfigurable solutions can be particularly beneficial (Part V). In this, the final part of the book, we examine why reconfigurable architectures are beneficial and we gain insight into the areas where the benefits of reconfigurable solutions lie. We also observe technology trends and examine why reconfigurable architectures may become increasingly important over time. To support and ground these discussions, the following chapters delve into the technology basis from which we build these architectures, and their alternatives, and discuss physical issues including area, defects, faults, and manufacturing trends.

Chapter 36 constructs a simplified model of the architectural design space in which postfabrication programmable architectures (e.g., processors, FPGAs, VLIWs, SIMD arrays) are built. Using this model, the chapter illustrates the trade-offs inherent in different architectures and the impact these trade-offs have on the architectures' efficiency in implementing various applications. This simple analysis illuminates the appropriate roles for processors and FPGAs, underscores how we can use FPGAs efficiently, and suggests why, as component capacities continue to grow, reconfigurable architectures may be important for carrying out an ever-enlarging set of high-throughput tasks.

Chapters 37 and 38 explore how continued feature size scaling will influence the design of integrated circuits. As device feature sizes approach the atomic scale, our traditional techniques, abstractions, and solutions may no longer be appropriate. Manufacturing at the atomic scale demands higher regularity and produces less controlled structures. At the same time, physical imperfections (e.g., defects, faults, wear) occur at significantly higher rates. Postfabrication configurability appears to be an essential tool for dealing with these atomic-scale effects. This, too, suggests the growing importance of reconfigurable architectures for future technologies.

Chapter 37 addresses defect and fault tolerance. It shows how configurable designs can accommodate defects and suggests in what directions our design and usage paradigms should evolve in order to deal with increasing defect rates. The chapter also examines how transient faults will affect future configurable systems.

Chapter 38 further explores the impact of technologies in which feature sizes are measured in single-digit atomic widths. It reviews emerging atomic-scale technologies and shows how they can be assembled into a complete reconfigurable architecture.

CHAPTER 36

THEORETICAL UNDERPINNINGS

André DeHon

Department of Electrical and Systems Engineering
University of Pennsylvania

Throughout this book there are examples for which reconfigurable designs offer superior performance to processor-based solutions. The reconfigurable implementation is typically orders of magnitude faster than the processor-based system. Even when we normalize the performance advantage to the number of components used in the solution, or to the number of square millimeters of silicon in the same process technology, we often see the reconfigurable solution providing one to two orders of magnitude higher computational capacity per square millimeter. These observations raise questions about reconfigurable computing systems.

- Why do we see this greater computational capacity per unit area?
- How can we predict when reconfigurable systems can deliver significantly higher performance than processor-based implementations?
- What does this tell us about how we should engineer reconfigurable designs?

This computational density advantage is not an accident. It occurs for real, structural reasons resulting from where silicon is allocated in reconfigurable architectures. Field-programmable gate arrays (FPGAs) and reconfigurable architectures organize their instructions differently from processors, making different trade-offs between instruction and computational density. Processors give up raw computational capacity for the ability to support large and irregular computations robustly, while FPGAs give up the ability to switch rapidly among diverse tasks to maximize available compute density and spatial parallelism. This chapter develops a simple model of programmable devices and uses it to illustrate the gross design space, which includes processors and FPGAs, the trade-offs each makes, and the consequences of those trade-offs.

36.1 GENERAL COMPUTATIONAL ARRAY MODEL

Let us start by focusing exclusively on a capabilities viewpoint, ignoring, for the moment, costs. *What would be good to have for a general-purpose programmable computing architecture?*

The most general and flexible programmable architecture we might build would have:

- Computational operators (e.g., programmable gates) that compute an output bit from some number of input bits
- Full, bit-level interconnect among computational operators
- Local data storage for each bit operator
- The ability to issue a unique instruction to each bit-level computational operator on every cycle; this instruction should indicate:
  - Which computational function the operator should perform on each cycle
  - Where the inputs for the operator should come from, including both spatially from any other operator and temporally from local memory
  - Where the output of the operator on this cycle should go into local memory

Figure 36.1 shows a diagram of this architecture. For this simple model, we assume that all the programmable blocks are identical. We call the instruction that controls each programmable block (including interconnect and memory, as just summarized) a *primitive instruction*, or *pinst* for short (see Figure 36.2). With an array of N blocks, the full instruction word issued on every cycle to control the computational array is the composition of N pinsts.

This array provides a computational capacity of N-bit operations (*bitops*) on each cycle. We have great flexibility in using this array since every bitop can have a unique pinst on every cycle. So, if we need to process an irregular collection of operations, such as a 17-bit add, an 8-bit subtract, a 13-bit exclusive-or (XOR), the next state evaluation on a 23-state finite-state machine (FSM), and a 5-bit shift left by 3, we can direct each bitop independently to keep all bitops performing exactly the operations needed for the computation. Further, if the following cycle needs a very different set of operations, such as a 9-bit multiply by the constant 27, a 12-bit AND, the next state evaluation on a 23-state FSM,

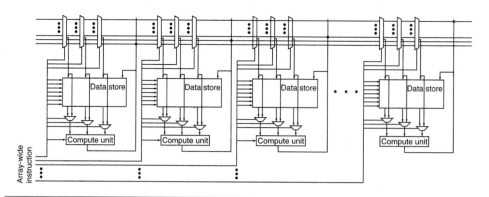

FIGURE 36.1 ▪ The general computational array model.

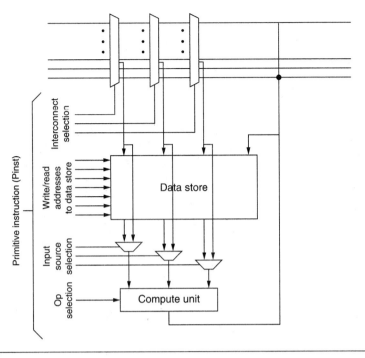

FIGURE 36.2 ■ Primitive instruction (pinst) for programmable bitops.

and an 11-bit shift right by 2, we can issue the next array-wide instruction to control the computational array accordingly.

We get to use all the bitops all the time. Mapping designs to this array is simply a matter of scheduling the bit-level computational needs onto the N-bit operations provided by the array. With this full ability to control the cycle-by-cycle operation of each bitop independently, scheduling is relatively easy. (Strictly speaking, optimal scheduling remains NP-hard, but it can be approximated within a factor of 2 of optimal using a variant of Johnson's Algorithm [1].) So, why is it that we do not have a popular architecture that provides this model?

36.2 IMPLICATIONS OF THE GENERAL MODEL

From a purely logical standpoint, we cannot fault the general computational array model. However, we must implement any architecture in a physical computational medium (e.g., out of a number of discrete vacuum tubes or transistors, on a silicon die, ultimately out of molecules and atoms). To support the architecture, we must commit physical resources. Those resources have a cost in terms of area, delay, and energy. The general computational array model turns out to be extravagant—so much so that we are generally willing to compromise its power to build more practical architectures.

This section illustrates two ways in which the instruction organization of the general model is unreasonably expensive. The focus here is on silicon VLSI implementations, and we discuss the sizes and areas of components in VLSI. To make the discussion general, resource areas are measured in terms of technology-normalized units. In particular, we will measure widths in units of F—the minimum feature size in a VLSI process; as a consequence, areas are measured in units of F^2. VLSI technologies are normally named by their minimum feature size, so when we talk about a 45 nm technology, we are talking about a technology with $F = 45$ nm. Ideally, when we scale from a larger technology to a smaller technology, everything scales as F. Features 900 nm wide in a 90 nm technology are $10F$ wide and should become 450 nm wide in a 45 nm technology. Features do not always scale perfectly linearly like this, but they scale close enough for illustrative purposes. Details and estimates on how the industry expects silicon technology to scale are summarized by the ITRS [2]; the industry collaborates to produce an updated or revised version of this document annually.

36.2.1   Instruction Distribution

This section starts by considering the resource implications of delivering a separate pinst to every bitop. We assume the following:

- The bitops are arranged in a dense $\sqrt{N} \times \sqrt{N}$ array (see Figure 36.3).
- The area required for each bitop, including compute, storage, and interconnect, is $A_{bop} = 250{,}000\,F^2$; we further assume that the bit operator itself is laid out as a square $500F$ on a side. This size assumes that the interconnect has also been designed in a more restrictive way than the most general model (see Section 36.1), perhaps resembling something closer to traditional FPGA interconnect capabilities.
- The metal pitch available for distributing an instruction bit is $W_{metal} = 4F$. The minimum pitch possible in a given technology is $2F$ because we need to leave one feature size worth of space between features so that they do not short together. The smallest feature sizes tend to be polysilicon for transistor gate widths, with metal pitches being a little wider. A modern VLSI process has many metal layers, and the ones higher in the stack (farther from the silicon base) tend to be wider.
- We have one complete horizontal metal layer and one complete vertical metal layer available to distribute instructions. As noted, modern VLSI processes generally have many metal layers; for example, an $F = 65$ nm process might have 11 metal layers. Some of the layers will be needed for local wiring in the cell, some for power and clock distribution, and some for interconnect. Dedicating two complete metal layers to instruction distribution is extravagant even with 11 metal layers.
- Each pinst requires $I_{bits} = 64$ to specify its instruction. This may seem small if we think about how many bits are required per 4-LUT in an FPGA, or large if you think about 32-bit processor instructions. Encoded densely, FPGA configurations could be much smaller [3]. The capabilities of the pinst might be closer to two processor instructions than one.

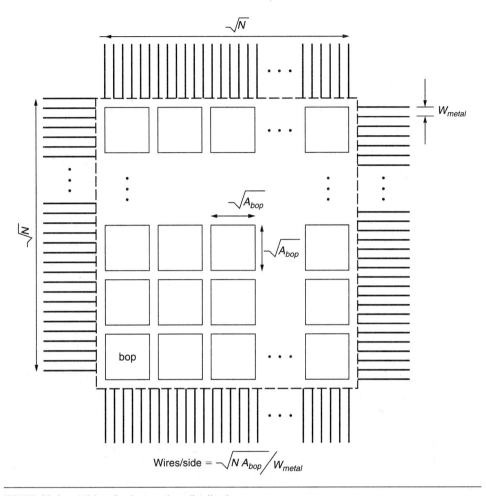

FIGURE 36.3 ■ Wiring for instruction distribution.

As we will see, the preceding assumptions only affect the particular quantitative conclusion we reach. The qualitative effect remains even if we assume two or four times as many metal layers, half the metal pitch, more compact instruction encodings, or larger bitop cell sizes.

If the instructions must all come into the computational array, then the total wiring capacity available for instruction distribution is equal to the perimeter of the array.

$$A_{side}(N) = \sqrt{N} \times \sqrt{A_{bop}} \qquad (36.1)$$

$$L_{perimeter}(N) = 4 \times A_{side}(N) \qquad (36.2)$$

Note that the two metal layers allow the connections on the top and bottom layers to cross over each other to reach into the array. However, if the lower layer is completely dense, we will have trouble making connections between the upper layer and the bit operations (i.e., we need to reserve space for vias through the lower level). To keep the math simple, general, and illustrative, we will not model that effect, which will only tend to make the problem more severe than the simple model indicates.

To feed the N-bit operators into the array, we need:

$$I_{total\_bits}(N) = N \times I_{bits} \tag{36.3}$$

$$L_{instr\_dist}(N) = W_{metal} \times I_{total\_bits}(N) \tag{36.4}$$

For the distribution to be viable, we need:

$$L_{perimeter}(N) > L_{instr\_dist}(N) \tag{36.5}$$

Substituting into the previous equations, this results in:

$$4 \times \sqrt{N} \times \sqrt{A_{bop}} > W_{metal} \times N \times I_{bits} \tag{36.6}$$

$$\frac{4 \times \sqrt{A_{bop}}}{W_{metal} \times I_{bits}} > \sqrt{N} \tag{36.7}$$

$$N < \left(\frac{4 \times \sqrt{A_{bop}}}{W_{metal} \times I_{bits}} \right)^2 \tag{36.8}$$

Using the preceding assumptions:

$$N < \left(\frac{4 \times 500F}{4F \times 64} \right)^2 = 61 \tag{36.9}$$

This says that we cannot afford to feed more than about 60 bit-processing units without saturating available instruction distribution bandwidth. If we want to support more bit-processing elements, we must increase the perimeter and effectively make the bitops larger. Rearranging equation 36.6 with A_{bop} as the variable:

$$\sqrt{A_{bop}(N)} > \frac{W_{metal} \times \sqrt{N} \times I_{bits}}{4} \tag{36.10}$$

$$A_{bop}(N) = \left(\frac{W_{metal} \times \sqrt{N} \times I_{bits}}{4} \right)^2 \tag{36.11}$$

$$A_{bop}(N) = 4096 \times NF^2 \tag{36.12}$$

That is, the area of each bitop needs to grow linearly with N, meaning that the array area is actually growing quadratically with N.

Equivalently, we can recognize this effect as a difference between the growth rate of the area and the perimeter. If we assume the bitop area is constant, then the total area in the array is growing linearly in the number of bitops. However, the perimeter of the array is only growing as the square root of the array area. So it is not surprising that we reach a point where the array's need for instructions, which is also growing linearly with bitops, exceeds the ability to feed instructions into the array that grows only as the square root of the number of bitops in it. The particular assumptions used for this example starkly illustrate that this effect is already an issue for very small arrays. You can substitute your favorite assumptions about instruction bits, metal pitch, metal layers, or bit-operator area, but the qualitative conclusion remains as follows:

> *If we support this model, either we are limited in the size of the arrays we can build, or instruction distribution wiring ends up dominating all other resources and forces us to scale only as the square root of the area we spend on the computational array.*

36.2.2 Instruction Storage

The previous section illustrated that instruction distribution from outside the computational array is not scalable to large computations. Alternately, consider storing the instructions inside the array. In particular, each bitop could include an instruction memory that holds its instruction (see Figure 36.4). We would

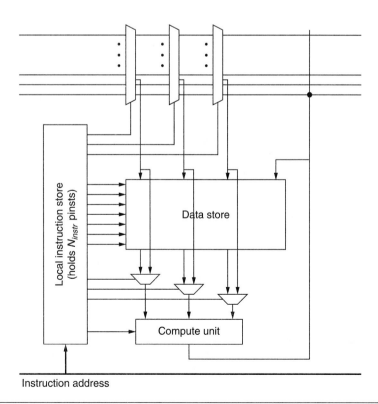

FIGURE 36.4 ■ A bitop with local instruction memory.

then only need to broadcast an address into the array, and each bitop could translate that through the instruction memory to its instruction. Even a 64-bit address is small compared to $L_{perimeter}(1)$, so this solution does not challenge wiring capacity. However, it does raise the question of how large the instruction memory should be to begin to approximate the general model.

In any case, storing the instructions requires area. So we should assess the cost of storing these instructions. Assume that the instruction memory lives in SRAM, and that the area of an SRAM cell to hold an instruction bit is $A_{bit} = 200\,F^2$. This means that the area per instruction is:

$$A_{pinst} = A_{bit} \times I_{bits} \tag{36.13}$$

$$A_{pinst} = 200\,F^2 \times 64 = 12{,}800\,F^2 \tag{36.14}$$

The total area per bitop is now:

$$A_{bitop\_w\_imem} = A_{bop} + N_{instrs} \times A_{pinst} \tag{36.15}$$

$$A_{bitop\_w\_imem} = 250{,}000\,F^2 + N_{instrs} \times 12{,}800\,F^2 \tag{36.16}$$

Equation 36.16 now tells a very interesting story. The area required to store a single instruction is small compared to the area required for compute and interconnect in the bit operator (one-twentieth the area). If we store 20 instructions locally, we place half of the area into instruction memory. When we store 200 instructions locally, the instruction memory area ends up dominating (i.e., is 10 times the size of) the area required for computation. That is, given fixed area, the design with 200 instructions will only fit one-tenth the number of bitops as the design with a single local instruction.

Unless we can limit the number of different, array-wide instructions we need to issue, the instruction memory needed to approximate the general model will end up dominating the computational area. Taken together with the result on instruction distribution, these examples illustrate why the general model is not typically supported:

> *To support the general model, instruction resources would dominate all other resources, forcing limited computational density.*

We are left with the choice of either accepting very low computational density or looking for compromises in the general model that will allow us to avoid the huge instruction expense it implies.

36.3 INDUCED ARCHITECTURAL MODELS

If the general model was viable, we would not have the varied set of computer architectures that exist. That is, computer architectures arise because (1) the general model is too expensive, and (2) there is structure in typical computational tasks that permits more economical implementations. Having identified that it is unreasonable to support the general computational array model, we ask: Which structure exists in typical computations that can be exploited to provide a more economical implementation?

36.3.1 Fixed Instructions (FPGA)

If the instructions never change, we do not need to distribute them into the computational array, nor do we need to allocate instruction memory area to store more than a single instruction. We still allow each bitop a pinst, so each can perform a unique operation; however, we do not allow the pinst to change from cycle to cycle. Unchanging instructions is an extreme form of temporal locality, where computation remains the same over time. This allows us to build large arrays and keep the computation dense. If we need to, or can arrange to, perform the same computation on every cycle, then we use the array efficiently. This restriction on the general model effectively gives us an FPGA or spatially reconfigurable architecture. In Chapter 5, Section 5.2, we saw many system architectures that illustrate how we might organize computation to enhance this kind of structure.

36.3.2 Shared Instructions (SIMD Processors)

Another structure common to applications is SIMD datapaths (see Single program, multiple data subsection of Section 5.2.4)—that is, it is common for us to identify sequences of bit-level operations that are the same across a number of data bits. The most common case is word-wide operations, such as multibit adds or bitwise logical operations (e.g., OR, AND, XOR). At a higher level, we would perform a number of identical word-wide operations on different data (e.g., performing a component-wise multiplication on the elements of two arrays as part of a dot product). Here we perform the same operation across many bitops. Rather than providing a unique instruction for each bitop, we can arrange to share a single instruction across a large number of bit operators, amortizing the instruction distribution or storage expense.

In the extreme, we would distribute a single instruction to all the bitops in the array. This is the opposite of the simplification used in the FPGA. Here, all bitops in the array must perform the same operation on a given cycle, but this operation may change from cycle to cycle.

We can view conventional, word-wide processors as exploiting this idea. A processor instruction typically only tells the datapath to do one homogeneous thing—that is, the processor instruction asks every bit in the arithmetic logic unit (ALU) bit slice to perform the same computation (e.g., perform a full adder bit, perform an XOR, perform a shift). For example, a 32-bit processor datapath could perform many more operations if each individual bit slice of the ALU could operate independently; instead, ALUs are constrained to operate in SIMD fashion to keep the cycle-by-cycle instruction size small.

In the general computational array model, we saw that the instruction memory took up the same area as the computation when we stored only 20 instructions in the array (equation 36.16). If we instead share each instruction across

W_{simd} = 32 bitops to form a SIMD datapath, it takes 625 instructions for the instruction memory to reach parity with the computation—that is:

$$A_{bitop\_w\_imem}(W_{simd}, N_{instrs}) = A_{bop} + \left(\frac{N_{instrs}}{W_{simd}} \right) \times A_{pinst} \qquad (36.17)$$

$$A_{bitop\_w\_imem}(N_{instrs}, 32) = 250,000 F^2 + N_{instrs} \times 400 F^2 \qquad (36.18)$$

From these illustrations, we can see how the more familiar FPGA and processor architectures fall out as simplifications of the general computational array model that exploits different kinds of structures that exist in typical computations.

36.4 MODELING ARCHITECTURAL SPACE

The demonstrations in Sections 36.2 and 36.3 highlight the fact that choices about instruction architecture can have a first-order impact on the area, and hence density, of programmable computing components. We can take this a step farther and build models of the density, and ultimately relative efficiency, of architectural design points.

Table 36.1 summarizes where some familiar architectures fall in the (W_{simd}, N_{isntr}) architectural space. Nonetheless, remember that we are using a deliberately simple model and that many other effects and issues are associated with each architecture, some of which are mentioned in Section 36.4.3.

36.4.1 Raw Density from Architecture

Using equation 36.17, we can plot the relative densities of each bit operator as a function of the local instruction memory, N_{instr}, and the SIMD instruction width, W_{simd}. Figure 36.5 shows plots of the computational density for the instruction memory from 1 to 16,384 and the instruction width from 1 to 1024. Here, note that peak densities vary over three orders of magnitude. As we increase instruction depth (N_{instr}), we shift area into instructions rather than compute, often significantly reducing computational density. Wide-word architectures can reduce the memory costs at a particular instruction depth, but there also may be significant computational density reductions as instruction depth grows.

TABLE 36.1 ▪ Placement of sample architectures in (W_{simd}, N_{instr}) space

Architecture	W_{simd}	N_{instr}	Reference
FPGA	1	1	
GARP fabric	2	4	Chapter 2, Section 2.1.1
KiloCore256	8	16	Chapter 2, Section 2.1.2
MIPS-X	32	512	[4]
IA-64 (Montecito)	64	200,000	[5]
Cell SPU	128	65,536	[6]

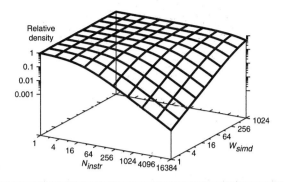

FIGURE 36.5 ■ Relative peak computational density from the model (normalized to the density of $N_{instr} = 1$, $W_{simd} = 1024$ design points).

36.4.2 Efficiency

The previous section showed peak raw densities achievable at various architectural points. If peak raw density was all that mattered, we would build SIMD designs with shallow instruction memories, as Figure 36.5 illustrates. However, it is seldom the case today that we can keep the millions of SIMD bit-processing elements we might be able to put on a die performing useful computations. When we cannot match the structure assumed by the architecture, the yield is only a fraction of the potential density—that is, another architecture, perhaps one with lower peak density, often can deliver more net density to the application. In particular, the architectural point whose structure assumptions exactly match the application will deliver the highest net density on that application. This leads to an interesting set of questions:

- How does the efficiency of an architecture fall off as it becomes mismatched to the structure of the application?
- How does the net density compare between various matched and mismatched architectures?

Since there is a model for the area of architectural design points in the (W_{simd}, N_{instr}) design space (equation 36.17), we can use that to measure efficiency. In particular, it is possible to measure the efficiency of an architecture design point $(\text{Arch}(W_{simd}, N_{instr}))$ processing applications with a particular structure $(\text{App}(W_{app}, L_{path}))$ as the ratio of the area of the architecture that exactly matches the application structure to the area of the point being evaluated:

$$\text{Efficiency}\left(\text{Arch}(W_{simd}, N_{instr}), \text{App}\left(W_{app}, L_{path}\right)\right)$$

$$= \frac{Area\left(\text{Arch}\left(W_{app}, L_{path}\right), \text{App}\left(W_{app}, L_{path}\right)\right)}{Area\left(\text{Arch}(W_{simd}, N_{instr}), \text{App}\left(W_{app}, L_{path}\right)\right)} \quad (36.19)$$

TABLE 36.2 ■ Sample applications in the (W_{app}, L_{path}) space

Application	W_{app}	$L_{critpath}$	L_{path}	Comments
Conway's Game of "Life"	1	1	1	Bit-level CA [7]
Error correcting codes	1	1	1–10,000	At memory interface, need one per cycle; on audio-rate, real-time data can be low throughput
Entropy coding	1	1–10	1–10,000	(similar to previous)
Video processing of pixel data	8	1–6	12	1024×1024 at 30 frames per second on a 500 MHz cycle can afford approximately 12 cycles per pixel
CD audio	16	1–10	10,000	44 kHz real-time vs. 500 MHz cycle
SPIHT image compression	16	10	10+	Chapter 27
FDTD	35	1–5	1–5	Chapter 32

To characterize the structure of the architecture separately from the structure of the application, equation 36.19 keeps W_{simd} and N_{instr} as parameters characterizing the architecture and adds the dual parameters W_{app} and L_{path} to characterize the application structure. W_{app} is simply the natural SIMD datapath width of the application, while L_{path} is the path length of the application (see the Mismatch in N_{instr} subsection).

For illustrative purposes, Table 36.2 summarizes where several applications appear in the (W_{app}, L_{path}) space. The area of the mismatched design is always larger, so the efficiency metric in equation 36.19 effectively tells us how much lower the mismatched point's net density is than the matched point's net density.

To develop the intuition and keep the explanation simple, we stay with the assumption that applications have homogeneous structure (i.e., single-characteristic W_{app} and L_{path}). One of the reasons we are interested in how well an architecture deals with different, mismatched structures is that a real application will typically contain heterogeneity in the structure it exhibits.

Mismatch in W_{simd}

What happens when the application width W_{app} is mismatched to the architectural width W_{simd}?

- $W_{simd} > W_{app}$: Here we do not have as fine-grained control of the bit operators as the application requires. Consequently, bitops go unused. In particular, we will actually need a larger array so that we match the instruction control needs of the application. For example, if $W_{app} = 5$ and $W_{simd} = 8$, then three bitops in every architectural SIMD datapath will go idle. To satisfy the application requirements, we end up needing $\frac{W_{simd}}{W_{app}} = \frac{8}{5} = 1.6$ times as many physical bitops as the application actually requires.

- $W_{simd} < W_{app}$: There are two effects that can work to make implementations in this architecture larger than the optimally matched architecture:

  1. We have finer-grained control, but may still need more physical bit operators because of granularity problems. For example, when $W_{app} = 8$ and $W_{simd} = 5$, we need $\left\lceil \frac{W_{app}}{W_{simd}} \right\rceil = 2$ groups of W_{simd} bitops to cover each application group, or $\left\lceil \frac{8}{5} \right\rceil \times W_{arch} = 10$ bitops, of which only $W_{app} = 8$ are doing useful work.

  2. Since we have more control than necessary for the application, the area of each bitop is larger than necessary in order to accommodate additional instruction memory; this extra instruction memory holds redundant information. Continuing the $W_{app} = 8$ and $W_{simd} = 5$ example, each bit operator effectively pays for $\frac{W_{app}}{W_{simd}} = \frac{8}{5} = 1.6$ times as many instructions as necessary for the application.

Assuming that instruction storage depth is matched to application path length ($N_{instr} = L_{path}$) to focus on the width mismatch, we can show this in an area model as:

$$Area\left(\mathrm{Arch}\left(W_{simd}, L_{path}\right), \mathrm{App}\left(W_{app}, L_{path}\right)\right)$$

$$= \left(\frac{W_{simd}}{W_{app}}\right) \times \left\lceil \frac{W_{app}}{W_{simd}} \right\rceil \times A_{bitop\_w\_imem}\left(W_{simd}, L_{path}\right) \quad (36.20)$$

$$= \left(\frac{W_{simd}}{W_{app}}\right) \times \left\lceil \frac{W_{app}}{W_{simd}} \right\rceil \times \left(A_{bop} + \left(\frac{L_{path}}{W_{simd}}\right) \times A_{pinst}\right)$$

This allows us to compute the efficiency of the mismatched SIMD datapath width at a matched L_{path} as:

$$\mathrm{Efficiency}\ [L_{path}]\left(W_{simd}, W_{app}\right)$$

$$= \frac{\left(A_{bop} + \left(\frac{L_{path}}{W_{app}}\right) \times A_{pinst}\right)}{\left(\frac{W_{simd}}{W_{app}}\right) \times \left\lceil \frac{W_{app}}{W_{simd}} \right\rceil \times \left(A_{bop} + \left(\frac{L_{path}}{W_{simd}}\right) \times A_{pinst}\right)} \quad (36.21)$$

Figure 36.6 shows plots of the efficiency from equation 36.21 versus W_{app} for a collection of W_{simd}'s and L_{path}'s. Perhaps more significant than the large density range shown in Figure 36.5, we see that SIMD width mismatches can cost us orders of magnitude in net density delivered to an application. Interestingly, we see some SIMD width selections that do not show orders of magnitude efficiency losses (e.g., $W_{simd} = 1$ for $L_{path} = 1$, $W_{simd} = 3$ for $L_{path} = 64$, $W_{simd} = 32$ for $L_{path} = 640$). These robust points occur when the instruction area is equal to the compute and interconnect area. That is:

$$A_{bop} = \left(\frac{L_{path}}{W_{simd}} \right) \times A_{pinst} \qquad (36.22)$$

In these cases, half the area is allocated to storing instructions and half to compute. For illustration, consider the $L_{path} = 640$ and $W_{simd} = 32$ case. Here, if we are processing $W_{app} = 1$ data, then we use only one-thirty-second of the compute

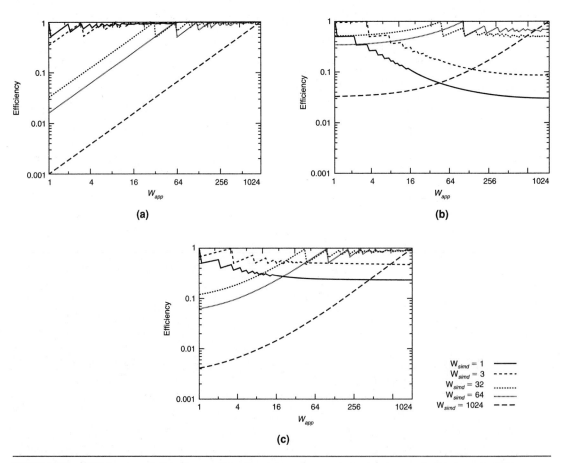

(a)

(b)

(c)

$W_{simd} = 1$ ———
$W_{simd} = 3$ – – – –
$W_{simd} = 32$ ··········
$W_{simd} = 64$ ··········
$W_{simd} = 1024$ – – –

FIGURE 36.6 ▪ Efficiency as a function of W_{app} for various L_{path} values: (a) $L_{path} = 1$, (b) $L_{path} = 640$, and (c) $L_{path} = 64$.

area. However, we are able to use all the memory area; a matched architecture can, at most, be half the size of this design point since it still requires the 640 instructions, even if they drive a smaller datapath. At the opposite extreme, if W_{app} = 16,384, we can use all the compute operators but we underutilize the instructions. Here, a matched architecture could have used a factor of 512 lower instruction area; however, since half the area is in compute, the matched architecture is, at best, only half the size of this robust point.

It should be clear that this observation holds for any choice of W_{app} when the area is allocated evenly between compute and instruction memory. In contrast, if we make W_{simd} = 1 for this L_{path} = 640 case, then 97 percent of the area goes into memory; if this W_{simd} = 1 architecture now has a task with W_{app} = 16,384, it is much larger (at least 33 times larger) than a design with matched width, which can put significantly less area into instruction memory.

If we can design to a single application width, or a small range of widths, it is best to select a matched width, or the width that provides the highest average efficiency over the range. However, if we don't have tight bounds on the application width, these robust points show how we can select organizations that remain fairly efficient for any application width.

Mismatch in N_{instr}

A similar phenomenon occurs when N_{instr} does not match the structure of the application. First, we need to understand L_{path}—the application demand for N_{instr}. In particular, let us consider an inner loop in a kernel or the computation required for each invocation of a transform operator (see Transform or object subsection of Section 5.1.2). To compute each inner loop iteration, or each operator invocation, we need to evaluate a set of N_{ops} bitops. In general, there may be a set of cyclic sequential dependencies, or a critical path, of depth $L_{critpath}$ among the bitops in the computation that prevent us from starting the next iteration of the loop or invocation of the operator until the $L_{critpath}$ array cycles have completed. For example, consider the loop body of a saturated accumulation:

$$y[i] = \max(\min(x[i] + y[i-1], 255), 0)$$

Before performing the next addition to compute $y[i+1]$ from $y[i]$, we must complete the computation of $y[i]$, including both the addition and the selection of maximum or minimum bound limits (see Figure 36.7).[1] Assume the following:

- The addition requires a path length of six sequential bitops.
- The comparisons can be performed in parallel.
- Each comparison requires a path of three sequential bitops.
- The final selection requires a single bitop.

The critical path $L_{critpath}$ is 10 for this computation. With a path length of $L_{critpath}$, we can schedule the N_{ops} required to evaluate the application into $L_{critpath}$ cycles

---

[1] With care, this actually can be avoided using sophisticated transformations [8].

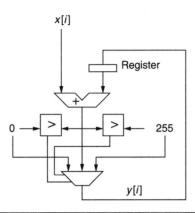

FIGURE 36.7 ■ Saturated accumulator cyclic dependency.

on the array without slowing down the application, the sequentially dependent paths guarantee that it will always take at least $L_{critpath}$ cycles to perform the operation.

The application may not actually demand that the computation be performed every $L_{critpath}$ cycle. Perhaps the data throughput is lower and new samples, $x[i]$, are arriving every 20 ns while the array cycle time is 1 ns. Here, evaluating with $L_{critpath} = 10$ leaves the array sitting idle for 10 cycles before the next input sample is available to compute. Consequently, it would be possible to schedule to $L_{path} = 20 > L_{critpath}$ and cut the number of bitops needed by at least a factor of 2. In this way, the loop or transform body is efficiently implemented by scheduling the computations onto a minimum number of bitops in a period of L_{path} cycles, with each operator potentially getting a unique instruction on each cycle $N_{instr} = L_{path}$. For examples, see Table 36.2, which summarizes the throughput L_{path} required in a few applications.

Now consider the two mismatched cases:

- $N_{instr} > L_{path}$: In this case, by scheduling the computation into L_{path} cycles, $(N_{instr} - L_{path})$ instruction memory slots in each bitop go unused. The matched architecture is smaller because it does not spend area on these unused instruction memories. In the aforementioned saturated accumulation, if $L_{path} = 20$ and an array with $N_{instr} = 100$ is used, then 80 instruction slots go unused.
- $N_{instr} < L_{path}$: In this case, we cannot necessarily reuse each bit operator in L_{path} in different ways on each of the L_{path} cycles. Since we can only use each operator in N_{instr} ways, to solve the entire problem we may need a total of $\left\lceil \dfrac{L_{path}}{N_{instr}} \right\rceil$ times as many bitops to perform the computation. Continuing with the example, if $N_{instr} = 5$ and there is an $L_{path} = 20$, we may need four times as many bitops as the optimally matched architecture. The total amount of memory is the same between these cases; however, an $N_{instr} = 5$ architecture pays for four times as many

compute blocks (A_{bop}). There is also a granularity effect here; for example, we still need four times as many bitops even when $N_{instr} = 6$.

Assuming that the datapath width is matched ($W_{simd} = W_{app}$), allows us to focus on the instruction mismatch; we can show this in an area model as:

$$Area\left(\text{Arch}\left(W_{app}, N_{instr}\right),\ \text{App}\left(W_{app}, L_{path}\right)\right)$$

$$= \left\lceil \frac{L_{path}}{N_{instr}} \right\rceil \times A_{bitop\_w\_imem}\left(W_{app}, N_{instr}\right) \qquad (36.23)$$

$$= \left\lceil \frac{L_{path}}{N_{instr}} \right\rceil \times \left(A_{bop} + \left(\frac{N_{instr}}{W_{app}}\right) \times A_{pinst}\right)$$

This allows us to compute the efficiency of the mismatched instruction store at a matched W_{app} as:

$$\text{Efficiency}\left[W_{app}\right]\left(N_{instr}, L_{path}\right)$$

$$= \frac{\left(A_{bop} + \left(\dfrac{L_{path}}{W_{app}}\right) \times A_{pinst}\right)}{\left\lceil \dfrac{L_{path}}{N_{instr}} \right\rceil \times \left(A_{bop} + \left(\dfrac{N_{instr}}{W_{app}}\right) \times A_{pinst}\right)} \qquad (36.24)$$

Figure 36.8 plots the efficiency from equation 36.24 versus L_{path} for a collection of N_{instrs}'s and W_{apps}'s. Again, note that instruction store mismatches can cost orders of magnitude in net density. We also see robust points here where the net density remains within 50 percent of the matched architecture. The effect is the same as for datapath width mismatch (see previous section), and the efficient points are governed by an analogous equation:

$$A_{bop} = \left(\frac{N_{instr}}{W_{app}}\right) \times A_{pinst} \qquad (36.25)$$

For any of these robust points, at the minimum value, $L_{path} = 1$, we are using all the compute area and only a fraction of the instruction memory area, so an optimally matched architecture could, at best, be implemented in half the area. Similarly, for arbitrarily large L_{path}, if $N_{instr} < L_{path}$, all the instruction memory area is used to hold instructions, but this may leave the compute area idle most of the time. Here, again, with only 50 percent of the area in compute, the design is, at most, twice the size of an optimally matched architecture with less area allocated to computation. In contrast, if we put 90 percent of the area into compute, then we could end up wasting 90 percent of the area in scenarios where $L_{path} \gg N_{instr}$; matched architectures can be an order of magnitude smaller in such cases. Similarly, if 90 percent of the area is put into instruction memory, we can end up wasting almost 90 percent of the area when L_{path} is small.

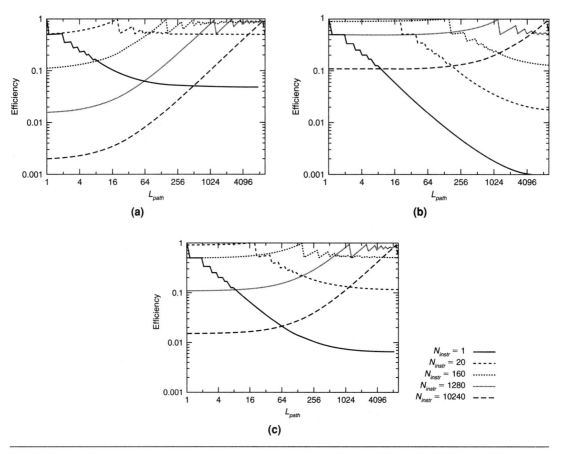

FIGURE 36.8 ▪ Efficiency as a function of L_{path} for various W_{app} values: (a) $W_{app} = 1$, (b) $W_{app} = 64$, and (c) $W_{app} = 8$.

Composite effects

Combining the effects of SIMD width mismatch and local instruction storage mismatch, we get the total efficiency:

$$\text{Efficiency} \left(\text{Arch} \left(W_{simd}, N_{instr} \right), \text{App} \left(W_{app}, L_{path} \right) \right)$$

$$= \frac{\left(A_{bop} + \left(\frac{L_{path}}{W_{app}} \right) \times A_{pinst} \right)}{\left(\frac{W_{simd}}{W_{app}} \right) \times \left\lceil \frac{W_{app}}{W_{simd}} \right\rceil \times \left\lceil \frac{L_{path}}{N_{instr}} \right\rceil \times \left(A_{bop} + \left(\frac{N_{instr}}{W_{simd}} \right) \times A_{pinst} \right)} \tag{36.26}$$

Unfortunately, if both the SIMD width and the local instruction storage mismatch, it is not possible to pick a robust point as we did in previous sections.

Returning to equations 36.22 and 36.25, we note that the robust points occur when we can match the instruction storage area, $\left(\frac{N_{instr}}{W_{simd}} \right) \times A_{pinst}$, and the computation and interconnect area, A_{bop}. However, when both W_{app} and L_{path} vary, even when the area is matched, we can have cases where the allocation of width versus storage size within that area can prevent us from using the computational units efficiently.

Efficiency of processors and FPGAs

The previous section suggests that we will not find an architectural point in this (W_{simd}, N_{instr}) design space that is efficient across a wide range of application structures. To understand where processors and FPGAs are efficient, we can use the composite efficiency relation (equation 36.26) and estimate how efficient they each can be across a portion of the design space (see Figure 36.9). Here the FPGA is naturally modeled with $N_{instr} = 1$ and $W_{simd} = 1$. We model a processor as $W_{simd} = 64$ and $N_{instr} = 16,384$.

Figure 36.9 shows starkly that the FPGA and processor are both designed for different points in the application space. Notice that each can be less than 1 percent efficient in some portions of the space. Further, we note that *in the places where the processor is very inefficient (< 1 percent), the FPGA is highly efficient; the reverse is true as well.* This effect, coupled with the heterogeneous nature of applications, explains why it is often useful to have reconfigurable systems that mix FPGA or reconfigurable fabrics along with processors (e.g., Instruction augmentation subsection of Section 5.2.2 and Chapter 26).

36.4.3 Caveats

As noted in the introduction to this chapter, we are deliberately using a simple model to illustrate key effects in instruction organization. There are many other application structural opportunities and architectural variables that can also have a large effect on resource balance and efficiency, including interconnect richness (e.g., [9]) and organization, data storage and memory hierarchy capacities, bandwidth and latencies, threads of control, dynamic instruction selection, and integration of hardware functional units (e.g., multipliers [10,11]

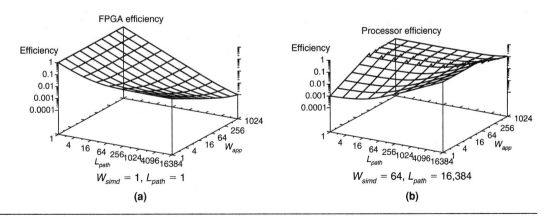

FIGURE 36.9 ■ Efficiency of FPGA-like (a) and processor-like (b) designs across both L_{path} and W_{app}.

and floating-point units [12]). In processors, the SIMD control of ALUs is coupled with fast logic to support carries in arithmetic (e.g., [13]), which serves to reduce $L_{critpath}$; FPGAs also employ fast cascade structures for similar reasons (e.g., [14], Chapter 1) but do not tie them to SIMD datapaths. Nonetheless, the simple model shows that these instruction organization decisions can have a significant impact on computational density, and it illustrates why FPGAs can be more efficient than processors for important classes of applications.

36.5   IMPLICATIONS

36.5.1   Density of Computation versus Description

From this model, we can clearly see a trade-off between computational density and instruction density. Equation 36.16 illustrates that the instruction store area for a single bitop can be an order of magnitude smaller than the computation to support it. This means an $N_{instr} = 1$ design stores instructions an order of magnitude less densely than an $N_{instr} = 200$ design, and an $N_{instr} = 200$ design packs computation an order of magnitude less densely than an $N_{instr} = 1$ design.

When the goal is to simply pack a large, irregular computation into a small area, we are best off focusing on instruction density; this minimizes the area for the implementation, at the expense of lower performance. When the goal is to perform the computation at high throughput, designs with high computational density allow us to meet the throughput with the least area.

36.5.2   Historical Appropriateness

When we first started building programmable integrated circuits, the premium for describing large computations was high. The capacity on a single integrated circuit was very low when they were built with $F = 3\,\mu m$ technology. In the mid-1980s, with $N_{instr} = 1$ and $W_{simd} = 1$, we could put only 64 bitops on a die [15], limiting computations to those that could be described by 64 instructions. At roughly the same time, one could put $N_{instr} = 512$ instructions on the die along with 32 bitops controlled in an SIMD fashion by a single pinst on each cycle ($W_{simd} = 32$) [4]. The struggle at this point in history was to fit an entire computational kernel onto a single die, and the deep instruction, word-wide processor design could begin to fit interesting kernels while the FPGA designs could fit only the most trivial computations.

By 2005, however, with $F \leq 0.1\,\mu m$, the landscape had changed. Moore's Law process scaling has given us more than a 10,000-fold increase in capacity per integrated circuit. Modern processors, still built with ever-deeper memories, have large enough instruction stores to contain large applications. At the same time, FPGAs hold hundreds of thousands of active bitops. Even kernels with thousands of 64-bit-wide operations can fit spatially on the FPGA and exploit the higher computational density.

The question with today's silicon is less "Can we get the application to fit on the die?" and more "How do we turn the available die area into performance?" Consequently, as we continue to scale feature sizes, the fraction of tasks where high instruction density remains the premium is shrinking, while the fraction where the application fits on the die and high computational density offers a benefit is increasing.

36.5.3 Reconfigurable Applications

Understanding why FPGAs can be efficient and where they are most efficient (e.g., Figure 36.9) provides additional insight into where we should use FPGAs and how to fully exploit their strengths. Certainly, if the task has low throughput requirements (i.e., large L_{path}), then FPGAs are often not an efficient implementation. The FPGA is efficient when we operate at minimum path length, preferably $L_{path} = 1$, where we are performing the same operation over and over and keeping all the bitops active during the operation. For FPGAs with a variable clock cycle, we want to keep the cycle time to the minimum, maximizing the reuse rate of each operation. This underscores why retiming operations such as pipelining and C-slow (see Chapter 18) are important for optimizing FPGA efficiency, as well as behavioral transformations that reduce $L_{critpath}$.

When L_{path} is large simply because of a low throughput demand, we can often turn the SIMD structure, W_{app}, into additional operation regularity. In particular, when $W_{app} > 1$, that is an indication that a number of bit-level operators do perform the same operation. By moving this regularity into time rather than space, we can reduce the number of unique instruction combinations needed and hence reduce the N_{instr} required. For example, if $W_{app} = 16$ and $L_{path} \gg L_{critpath}$, we can implement the SIMD datapath bit serially so that the necessary instruction storage depth is a factor of 16 smaller ($N'_{instr} \approx \frac{L_{path}}{W_{app}}$). As shown in Figure 36.10, this can increase the FPGA's domain of efficiency.

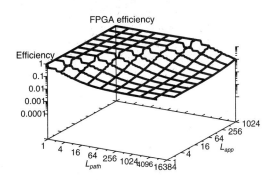

FIGURE 36.10 ■ FPGA efficiency when datapath regularity can be used to increase temporal regularity.

References

[1] D. S. Hochbaum, ed. *Approximation Algorithms for NP-Hard Problems*, PWS Publishing, 1997.

[2] International technology roadmap for semiconductors. *http://www.itrs.net/Links/2005ITRS/Home2005.htm*, 2005.

[3] A. DeHon. Entropy, counting, and programmable interconnect. *Proceedings of the International Symposium on Field-Programmable Gate Arrays*, ACM/SIGDA, 1996.

[4] M. Horowitz, J. Hennessy, P. Chow, G. Gulak, J. Acken, A. Agarwal, C.-Y. Chu, S. McFarling, S. Przybylski, S. Richardson, A. Salz, R. Simoni, D. Stark, P. Steenkiste, S. Tjiang, M. Wing. A 32b microprocessor with on-chip 2 Kbyte instruction cache. *IEEE International Solid-State Circuits Conference, Digest of Technical Papers*, IEEE, 1987.

[5] C. McNairy, R. Bhatia. Montecito: A dual-core, dual-thread Titanium processor. *IEEE Micro* 25(2), 2005.

[6] M. Gschwind, H. P. Hofstee, B. Flachs, M. Hopkins, Y. Watanabe, T. Yamazaki. Synergistic processing in cells multicore architecture. *IEEE Micro* 26(2), 2006.

[7] M. Gardner. The fantastic combinations of John Conway's new solitaire game "Life." *Scientific American* 223, 1970.

[8] K. Papadantonakis, N. Kapre, S. Chan, A. DeHon. Pipelining saturated accumulation. *Proceedings of the International Conference on Field-Programmable Technology*, 2005.

[9] A. DeHon. Balancing interconnect and computation in a reconfigurable computing array (or, why you don't really want 100% LUT utilization). *Proceedings of the International Symposium on Field-Programmable Gate Arrays*, 1999.

[10] A. DeHon. The density advantage of configurable computing. *IEEE Computer* 33(4), 2000.

[11] I. Kuon, J. Rose. Measuring the gap between FPGAs and ASICs. *IEEE Transactions on Computer-Aided Design of Integrated Circuits and Systems* 26(2), 2007.

[12] M. J. Beauchamp, S. Hauck, K. D. Underwood, K. S. Hemmert. Embedded floating-point units in FPGAs. *Proceedings of the International Symposium on Field-Programmable Gate Arrays*, 2006.

[13] R. P. Brent, H. T. Kung. A regular layout for parallel adders. *IEEE Transactions on Computers* 31(3), 1982.

[14] S. Hauck, M. M. Hosler, T. W. Fry. High-performance carry chains for FPGAs. *IEEE Transactions on Very Large Scale Integration (VLSI) Systems* 8(2), 2000.

[15] W. S. Carter, K. Duong, R. H. Freeman, H.-C. Hsieh, J. Y. Ja, J. E. Mahoney, L. T. Ngo, S. L. Sze. A user programmable reconfigurable logic array. *Proceedings of the IEEE Custom Integrated Circuits Conference*, 1986.

CHAPTER 37

DEFECT AND FAULT TOLERANCE

André DeHon
Department of Electrical and Systems Engineering
University of Pennsylvania

As device size *F* continues to shrink, it approaches the scale of individual atoms and molecules. In 2007, 65-nm integrated circuits are in volume production for processors and field-programmable gate arrays (FPGAs). With atom spacing in a silicon lattice around 0.5 nm, *F* = 65-nm drawn features are a little more than 100 atoms wide. Key features, such as gate lengths, are effectively half or a third this size. Continued geometric scaling (e.g., reducing the feature size by a factor of 2 every six years) will take us to the realm where feature sizes are measured in single-digit atoms sometime in the next couple of decades.

Very small feature sizes will have several effects on integrated circuits, including:

- *Increased defect rates:* Smaller devices and wires made of fewer atoms and bonds are less likely to be "good enough" to function properly.
- *Increased device variation:* When dimensions are a few atoms wide, the addition, absence, or exact position of each atom has a significant affect on device parameters.
- *Increased change in device parameters during operational lifetime:* With only a few atoms making up the width of wires or devices, small changes have large impacts on performance, and the likelihood of a complete failure grows. The fragility of small devices reduces traditional opportunities to overstress them as a means of forcing weak devices to fail before the component is integrated into an end system. This means many weak devices will only turn into defects during operation.
- *Increased single die capacity:* Smaller devices allow integration of more devices per die. Thus, not only do we have devices that are more likely to fail, but there also are more of them, meaning more chances that some device on the die will fail.
- *Increased susceptibility to transient upsets:* Smaller nodes use less charge to hold state or configuration data, making them more susceptible to upset by noise, including ionizing particles, thermal noise, and shot noise. Coupled with the greater capacity, which means more nodes that can be upset, dies will have significantly increased upset rates.

Accommodating and exploiting these effects will demand an increasing role for postfabrication configurable architectures. Nonetheless, some usage paradigms will need to shift to fully exploit the potential benefits of reconfigurable architectures at the atomic scale.

This chapter reviews defect tolerance approaches and points out how the configurability available in reconfigurable architectures is a key tool for coping with defects. It also touches briefly on lifetime and transient faults and their impact on configurable designs.

37.1   DEFECTS AND FAULTS

A *defect* is a persistent error in a component. Because defects are persistent, we can test for defect occurrences and record their locations. We contrast defects with transient faults that may produce the wrong value on one or a few cycles but do not continue to corrupt calculations. For the sake of simple discussion here, we classify any persistent problem that causes the circuitry to work incorrectly for some inputs and environments as defects. Defects are often modeled as stuck-at-1, stuck-at-0, or shorted nodes. They can also be nodes that are excessively slow, such that they compute correctly but not in a timely fashion, or excessively leaky, such that they do not hold their value properly. A large number of physical effects and causes may lead to these manifestations, including broken wires, shorts or bridging between nodes that should be distinct, excessive or inadequate doping in a device, poor contacts between materials or features, or excessive variation in device size.

A *transient fault* is a temporary error in a circuit result. Transient faults can occur at random times. A transient fault may cause a gate output or node to take on the incorrect value on some cycle of operation. Examples of transient faults include ionizing particles (e.g., α-particles), thermal noise, and shot noise.

37.2   DEFECT TOLERANCE

37.2.1   Basic Idea

An FPGA or reconfigurable array is a set of identical (programmable) bit-processing operators with postfabrication configurable interconnect. When a device failure renders a bitop or an interconnect segment unusable, we can configure the computation to avoid the failing bitop or segment (see Figure 37.1). If the bitop is part of a larger SIMD word (Chapter 36, Section 36.3.2) or other structure that does not allow its independent use, we may be forced to avoid the entire structure. In any case, as long as all the resources on the reconfigurable array are not being used, we can substitute good resources for the bad ones. As defect rates increase, this suggests a need to strategically reserve spare resources on the die so that we can guarantee there are enough good resources to compensate for the unusable elements.

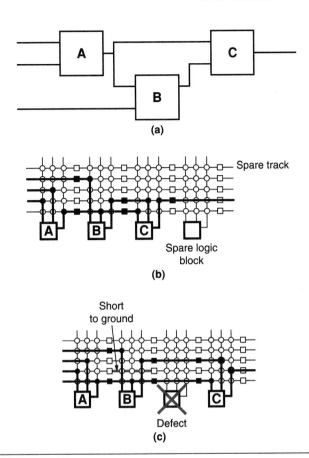

FIGURE 37.1 ■ Configuring computation to avoid defective elements in a reconfigurable array: (a) logical computation graph, (b) mapping to a defect-free array with spare, and (c) mapping to an array with defects.

This basic strategy of (1) provisioning spare resources, (2) identifying and avoiding bad resources, and (3) substituting spare resources for bad resources is well developed for data storage. DRAM and SRAM dies include spare rows and columns and substitute the spare rows and/or columns for defective rows and columns (e.g., see [1, 2]). Magnetic data storage (e.g., hard disk) routinely has bad sectors; the operating system (OS) maps the bad sectors and takes care not to allocate data to those sectors. These two forms of storage actually illustrate two models for dealing with defects:

1. *Perfect component:* In the perfect component model, the component has to look perfect; that is, we require every address visible to the user to perform correctly. The spare resources are added beyond those required to deliver the promised memory capacity and are substituted out behind the scenes so that users never see that there are defective elements in the component. DRAM and SRAM components are the traditional example of the perfect component model.

2. *Defect map:* The defect map model allows elements to be bad. We expose these defects to higher levels of software, typically the OS, which is responsible for tracking where the defects occur and avoiding them. Magnetic disks are a familiar example of the defect map model—we permit sectors to be bad and format the disk to avoid them.

37.2.2 Substitutable Resources

Some defects will be catastrophic for the entire component. While a reconfigurable array is composed largely of repeated copies of identical instances, the device infrastructure is typically unique; defects in this infrastructure may not be repairable by substitution. Common infrastructures include power and ground distribution, clocking, and configuration loading or instruction distribution. It is useful to separate the resources in the component into *nonrepairable* and *repairable* resources. Then we can quantify the fraction of resources that are nonrepairable.

We can minimize the impact of nonrepairable resources either by reducing the fraction of things that cannot be repaired or by increasing the reliability of the constituent devices in the nonrepairable structures. Many of the infrastructure items, such as power and ground networks, are built with larger devices, wires, and feature sizes. As such, they are less susceptible to the failures that impact small features. Memory components (e.g., DRAMs) also have distinct repairable and nonrepairable components; they typically use coarser feature sizes for the nonrepairable infrastructure. Memory designs only use the smallest features for the dense memory array, where row and column sparing can be used to repair defects. In FPGAs, it may be reasonable to provide spares for some of the traditional infrastructure items to reduce the size of the nonrepairable region. For example, modern FPGAs already include multiple clock generators and configurable clock trees; as such, it becomes feasible to repair defective clock generators or portions of the clock tree by substitution. We simply need to guarantee that there are sufficient alternative resources to use instead of the defective elements.

For any design there will be a minimum *substitutable unit* that defines the granularity of substitution. For example, in a memory array we cannot substitute out individual RAM cells. Rather, with a technique like row sparing, the substitutable unit is an entire row. In the simplest sparing schemes, a defect anywhere within a substitutable unit may force the discard of the entire element. Consequently, the granularity of substitution can play a big role in the viable yield of a component (see the Perfect yield subsection that follows). Section 37.2.5 examines more sophisticated sparing schemes that relax this constraint.

37.2.3 Yield

This section reviews simple calculations for the yield of components and substitutable units. We assume uniform device defect rates and independent, random failure (i.e., identical, independently distributed—iid). Using these simple models, we can illustrate the kinds of calculations involved and build intuition on the major trends.

Perfect yield

A component with no substitutable units will be nondefective only if all the devices in the unit are not defective. Similarly, in the simplest models each substitutable unit is nondefective only when all of its constituent devices are not defective. If we have a device defect probability P_d and if a unit contains N devices, the probability that the entire component or unit is nondefective is:

$$P_{defect-free}(N, P_d) = (1 - P_d)^N \qquad (37.1)$$

We can expand this as a binomial:

$$P_{defect-free}(N, P_d) = \sum_i \left(\binom{N}{i}(-P_d)^i \right) = 1 - N \cdot P_d + \binom{N}{2}(P_d)^2 - \dots \qquad (37.2)$$

If $N \times P_d \ll 1$, then we observe that each successive power of P_d is much smaller than the previous term. We can approximate this yield as:

$$P_{defect-free}(N, P_d) \approx 1 - N \cdot P_d \qquad (37.3)$$

This tells us we have a substitutable unit defect rate, P_{sd}, or a component defect rate, roughly equal to the product of the number of devices and the device defect rate:

$$P_{sd}(N, P_d) \approx N \cdot P_d \qquad (37.4)$$

This simple equation indicates several things:

- For today's large chips with $N > 10^9$ devices, the defect rate P_d must be below 10^{-10} to expect 90 percent or greater chip yield.
- To maintain constant yield ($P_{defect-free}$) for a chip as N scales, we must continually decrease P_d at the same rate. For example, a $10\times$ increase in device count, N, must be accompanied by a $10\times$ decrease in per-device defect rate.
- As noted in this chapter's introduction, we expect the opposite effect for atomic-scale devices; smaller devices mean a higher likelihood of defects. This exacerbates the challenge of increasing device counts.
- At the same defect rate, P_d, a finer-grained substitutable unit (e.g., an individual LUT or bitop) will have a higher unit yield rate than a coarser-grained unit (e.g., a cluster of 10 LUTs, such as an Altera LAB (Section 1.5.1) or an SIMD collection of 32 bitops). Alternatively, if one reasons about defect rates of the substitutable units, a defect rate of $P_{sd} = 0.05$ for a coarse-grained block corresponds to a much lower device defect rate, P_d, than the same P_{sd} for a fine-grained substitutable unit.

- To keep substitutable unit yield rates at some high value, we must decrease unit size, N, as P_d increases. For example, if we design for a $P_{sd} = 10^{-4}$ and the device defect rate doubles, we need to cut the substitutable block size in half to achieve the same block yield; this suggests a trend toward fine-grained resource sparing as defect rates increase (e.g., see Fine-grained Pterm matching subsection of Section 37.2.5 and Section 38.6).

Yield with sparing

We can significantly increase overall yield by providing spares so that there is no need to demand that every substitutable unit be nondefective. Assume for now that all substitutable units are interchangeable. The probability that we will have exactly i nondefective substitutable units is:

$$P_{yield}(N, i) = \left(\binom{N}{i} (P_{sd})^i (1 - P_{sd})^{N-i} \right) \tag{37.5}$$

That is, there are $\binom{N}{i}$ ways to select i nondefective blocks from N total blocks, and the yield probability of each case is $(P_{sd})^i (1 - P_{or})^{N-i}$. An ensemble with at least M items is obtained whenever M or more items yield, so the ensemble yield is actually the cumulative distribution function, as follows:

$$P_{yield}(N, M) = \sum_{M \leq i \leq N} \left(\binom{N}{i} (P_{sd})^i (1 - P_{sd})^{N-i} \right) \tag{37.6}$$

As an example, consider an Island-style FPGA cluster (see Figure 37.2) composed of 10 LUTs (e.g., Altera LAB, Chapter 1). Assume that each LUT, along with its associated interconnect and configuration, is a substitutable unit and that the LUTs are interchangeable. Further, assume $P_{sd} = 10^{-4}$. The probability of yielding all 10 LUTs is:

$$P_{yield}(10, 10) = \left(10^{-4} \right)^{10} \left(1 - 10^{-4} \right)^0 \approx 0.9990005 \tag{37.7}$$

Now, if we add two spare lookup tables, the probability of yielding at least 10 LUTs is:

$$\begin{aligned} P_{yield}(12, 10) = &\left(10^{-4} \right)^{12} \left(1 - 10^{-4} \right)^0 + 12 \left(10^{-4} \right)^{11} \left(1 - 10^{-4} \right)^1 \\ &+ \frac{12 \cdot 11}{2} \left(10^{-4} \right)^{10} \left(1 - 10^{-4} \right)^2 \\ = &\, 0.99880065978 + 0.0011986806598 + 0.0000006593402969 \\ \approx &\, 0.9999999998 > 1 - 10^{-9} \end{aligned} \tag{37.8}$$

Without the spares, a component with only 1000 such clusters would be difficult to yield. With the spares, components with 1,000,000 such clusters yield more than 99.9 percent of the time.

Cluster inputs   Cluster outputs

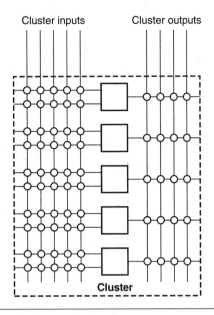

Cluster

FIGURE 37.2 ■ An island-style FPGA cluster with five interchangeable 2-LUTs.

The assumption that all substitutable units are interchangeable is not directly applicable to logic blocks in an FPGA since their location strongly impacts the interconnections available to other logic block positions. Nonetheless, the sparing yield is illustrative of the trends even when considering interconnect requirements.

To minimize the required spares, it would be preferable to have fewer large pools of mostly interchangeable resources rather than many smaller pools of interchangeable resources. This results from Bernoulli's Law of Large Numbers (the Central Limit Theorem) effects [3, 4], where the variance of a sum of random variables decreases as the number of variables increases. For a more detailed development of the impact of the Law of Large Numbers on defect yield statistics and strategies see DeHon [5].

37.2.4 Defect Tolerance through Sparing

To exploit substitution, we need to locate the defects and then avoid them. Both testing (see next subsection) and avoidance could require considerable time for each individual device. This section reviews several design approaches, including approaches that exploit full mapping (see the Global sparing subsection) to minimize defect tolerance overhead, approaches that avoid any extra mapping (see the Perfect component model subsection), and approaches that require only minimal, local component-specific mapping (see the Local sparing subsection).

Testing

Traditional acceptance testing for FPGAs (e.g., [6]) attempts to validate that the FPGA is defect free. Locating the position of any defect is generally not important if any chip with defects is discarded. Identifying the location of all defects is more difficult and potentially more time consuming. Recent work on group testing [7–9] has demonstrated that it is possible to identify most of the nondefective resources on a chip with N substitutable components in time proportional to $\sqrt{N}$.

In group testing, substitutable blocks are configured together and given a self-test computation to perform. If the group comes back with the correct result, this is evidence that everything in the group is good. Conversely, if the result is wrong, this is evidence that something in the group may be bad. By arranging multiple tests where substitutable blocks participate in different groups (e.g., one test set groups blocks around rows while another groups them along columns), it is possible to identify which substitutable units are causing the failures.

For example, if there is only one failure in each of two groupings, and the failing groups in each grouping contain a single, common unit, this is strong evidence that the common unit is defective while the rest of the substitutable units are good. As the failure rates increase such that multiple elements in each group fail in a grouping, it can be more challenging to precisely identify failing components with a small number of groupings. As a result, some group testing is conservative, marking some good components as potential defects; this is a trade-off that may be worthwhile to keep testing time down to a manageably low level as defect rates increase.

In both group testing and normal FPGA acceptance testing, array regularity and homogeneity make it possible to run tests in parallel for all substitutable units on the component. Consequently, testing time does not need to scale as the number of substitutable units, N. If the test infrastructure is reliable, group tests can run completely independently. However, if we rely on the configurable logic itself to manage tests and route results to the test manager, it may be necessary to validate portions of the array before continuing with later tests. In such cases, testing can be performed as a parallel wave from a core test manager, testing the entire two-dimensional device in time proportional to the square root of the number of substitutable units (e.g., [8]).

Global sparing

A defect map approach coupled with component-specific mapping imposes low overhead for defect tolerance. Given a complete map of the defects, we perform a component-specific design mapping to avoid the defects. Defective substitutable units are marked as bad, and scheduling, placement, and routing are performed to avoid these resources. An annealing placer (Chapter 14) can mark the physical location of the defective units as invalid or expensive and penalize any attempts to assign computations to them. Similarly, a router (Chapter 17) can mark defective wires and switches as "in use" or very costly so that they are avoided. The Teramac custom-computing machine tolerated a 10 percent defect rate in logic cells ($P_{sd_{logic}} = 0.10$) and a 3 percent defect rate in on-chip interconnect ($P_{sd_{interconnect}} = 0.03$) using group testing and component-specific mapping [7].

With place-and-route times sometimes running into hours or days, the component-specific mapping approach achieves low overhead for defect tolerance at the expense of longer mapping times. As introduced in Chapter 20, there are several techniques we could employ to reduce this mapping time, including:

- Tuning architectures to facilitate faster mapping by overprovisioning resources and using simple architectures that admit simple mapping; the Plasma chip—an FPGA-like component, which was the basis of the Teramac architecture—takes this approach and was highlighted in Chapter 20.
- Trading mapping quality in order to reduce mapping time.
- Using hardware to accelerate placement and routing (also illustrated in Sections 9.4.2 and 9.4.3).

Perfect component model

To avoid the cost of component-specific mapping, an alternate technique to use is the perfect component model (Section 37.2.1). Here, the goal is to use the defect map to preconfigure the allocation of spares so that the component looks to the user like a perfect component. Like row or column sparing in memory, entire rows or columns may be the substitutable units. Since reconfigurable arrays, unlike memories, have communication lines between blocks, row or column sparing is much more expensive to support than in memories. All interconnect lines must be longer, and consequently slower, to allow configuration to reach across defective rows or columns. The interconnect architecture must be designed such that this stretching across a defective row is possible, which can be difficult in interconnects with many short wires (see Figure 37.3).

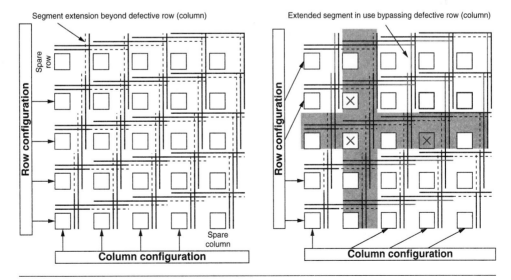

FIGURE 37.3 ■ Arrays designed to support row and column sparing.

A row of FPGA logic blocks is a much coarser substitutable unit than a memory row. FPGAs from Altera have used this kind of sparing to improve component yield [10, 11], including the Apex 20KE series.

Local sparing

With appropriate architecture or stylized design methodology, it is possible to avoid the need to fully remap the user design to accommodate the defect map. The idea here is to guarantee that it is possible to locally transform the design to avoid defects. For example, in cases where all the LUTs in a cluster are interchangeable, if we provision spares within each cluster as illustrated earlier in the Yield with sparing subsection of Section 37.2.3, it is simply a matter of locally reassigning the functions to LUTs to avoid the defective LUTs.

For regular arrays, Lach et al. [12] show how to support local interchange at a higher level without demanding that the LUTs exist in a locally interchangeable cluster. Consider a $k \times k$ tile in the regular array. Reserve s spares within each $k \times k$ tile so that we only populate $(k^2 - s)$ LUTs in each such region. We can now compute placements for the $(k^2 - s)$ LUTs for each of the possible combinations of s defects. In the simplest case, $s = 1$, we precalculate k^2 placements for each region (e.g., see Figure 37.4). Once we have a defect map, as long as each region has fewer than s errors, we simply assemble the entire configuration by selecting an appropriate configuration for each tile.

When a routing channel provides full crossbar connectivity, similarly, it may be possible to locally swap interconnect assignments. However, typical FPGA routing architectures do not use fully populated switching; as a result, interconnect sparing is not a local change. Yu and Lemieux [13, 14] show that FPGA switchboxes can be augmented to allow local sparing at the expense of 10 to 50 percent of area overhead. The key idea is to add flexibility to each switchbox that allows a route to shift one (or more) wire track(s) up or down; this allows routes to be locally redirected around broken tracks or switches and then restored to their normal track (see Figure 37.5).

To accommodate a particular defect rate and yield target, local interchange will require more spares than global mapping (see the Global sparing subsection). Consider any of the local strategies discussed in this section where we allocate one spare in each local interchange region (e.g., cluster, tile, or channel). If there are two defects in one such region, the component will not be repairable. However, the component may well have adequate spares; they are just assigned to different interchange regions. With the same number of resources, a global remapping would be able to accommodate the design. Consequently, to achieve the same yield rate as the global scheme, the local scheme always has to allocate more spares. This is another consequence of the Law of Large Numbers (see the Yield with sparing subsection):

> *The more locally we try to contain replacement, the higher variance we must accommodate, and the larger overhead we pay to guarantee adequate yield.*

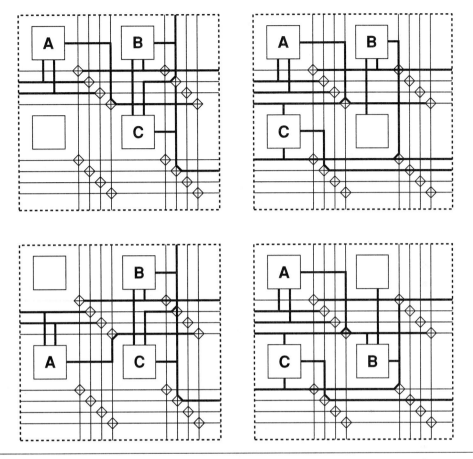

FIGURE 37.4 ■ Four placements of a three-gate subgraph on a 2 × 2 tile.

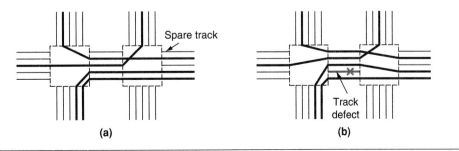

FIGURE 37.5 ■ Added switchbox flexibility allows local routing around interconnect defects: (a) defect free with spare and (b) configuration avoiding defective track.

37.2.5 Defect Tolerance with Matching

In the simple sparing case (Section 37.2.4), we test to see whether each substitutable unit is defect free. Substitutable units with defects are then avoided. This works well for low-defect rates such that P_{sd} remains low. However, it can also be highly conservative. In particular, not all capabilities of the substitutable unit are always needed. A configuration of the substitutable unit that avoids the particular defect may still work correctly. Examples where we may not need to use all the devices inside a substitutable unit include the following:

■ A typical FPGA logic block, logic element, or slice includes an optional flip-flop and carry-chain logic. Many of the logic blocks in the user's design leave the flip-flop or carry chain unused. Consequently, these "defective" blocks may still be usable, just for a subset of the logical blocks in the user's design.

■ When the substitutable unit is a collection of W_{simd} bitops, a defect in one of the bitops leaves the unit imperfect. However, the unit may work fine on smaller data. For example, maybe a $W_{simd} = 8$ substitutable unit has a defect in bit position 5. If the application requires some computations on $W_{app} = 4$ bit data elements, the defective 8-bit unit may still perform adequately to support 4 bitops.

■ A product term (Pterm) in a programmable logic array (PLA) or programmable array logic (PAL) is typically a substitutable unit. Each Pterm can be configured to compute the AND of any of the inputs to the array (see Figure 37.6). However, all the Pterms configured in the array will never need to be connected to all the inputs. Consequently, defects that prevent a Pterm from connecting to a subset of the inputs may not inhibit it from being configured to implement some of the Pterms required to configure the user's logic.

Instead of discarding substitutable units with defects, we characterize their capabilities. Then, for each logical configuration of the substitutable unit

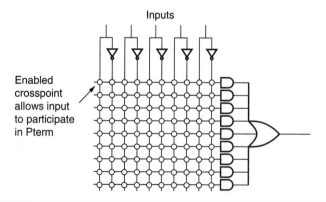

FIGURE 37.6 ■ A PAL OR-term with a collection of substitutable Pterm inputs.

demanded by the user's application, we can identify the set of (potentially defective) substitutable units capable of supporting the required configuration. Our mapping then needs to ensure that assignments of logical configurations to physical substitutable units obey the compatibility requirements.

Matching formulation

To support the use of partially defective units as substitutable elements, we can formulate the mapping between logical configurations and substitutable units as a bipartite matching problem. For simplicity and exposition, it is assumed that all the substitutable units are interchangeable. This is likely to be an accurate assumption for LUTs in a cluster or Pterms in a PAL or PLA, but it is not an accurate assumption for clusters in a two-dimensional FPGA routing array. Nonetheless, this assumption allows precise formulation of the simplest version of the problem.

We start by creating two sets of nodes. One set, $R = \{r_0, r_1, r_2 \ldots\}$, represents the physical substitutable resources. The second set, $L = \{l_0, l_1, l_2 \ldots\}$, represents the logic computations from the user's design that must be mapped to these substitutable units. We add a link (l_i, r_j) if-and-only-if logical configuration l_i can be supported by physical resource r_j. This results in a bipartite graph, with L being one side of the graph and R being the other. What we want to find is a *complete matching* between nodes in L and nodes in R—that is, we want every $l_i \in L$ to be matched with exactly one node $r_j \in R$, and every node $r_j \in R$ to be matched with at most one node $l_i \in L$.

We can optimally compute the *maximal matching* between L and R in polynomial time using the Ford–Fulkerson maximum flow algorithm [15] with time complexity $O(|V| \cdot |E|)$ or a Hopcroft–Karp algorithm [16] with time complexity $O\left(\sqrt{|V|} \cdot |E|\right)$. In the graph, $|V| = |L| + |R|$ and $|E| = O(|L| \cdot |R|)$. Since there must be at least as many resources as logical configurations, $|L| \leq |R|$, the Hopcroft–Karp algorithm is thus $O(|R|^{2.5})$; for local sparing schemes, $|R|$ might be reasonably in the 10 to 100 range, meaning that the matching problem is neither large nor growing with array size. If the maximal matching fails to be a complete matching (i.e., assign each l_i to a unique match in r_i), we know that it is not possible to support the design on a particular set of defective resources.

Fine-grained Pterm matching

Naeimi and DeHon use this matching to assign logical Pterms to physical nanowires in a nanoPLA (Chapter 38, Section 38.6) [17, 18]. Before considering defects, all the Pterm nanowires in the PLA are freely interchangeable. Each nanowire that implements a Pterm has a programmable diode between the input nanowires and the nanowire itself. If the diode is programmed into an off state, it disconnects the input from the nanowire Pterm. If the diode is in the on state, it connects the input to the nanowire, allowing it to participate in the AND that the Pterm is computing.

The most common defect anticipated in this technology is that the programmable diode is stuck in an off state—that is, it cannot be programmed into a valid on state. Consequently, a Pterm nanowire with a stuck-off diode at a particular input location cannot be programmed to include that input in the AND it is performing.

A typical PLA will have 100 inputs, meaning each product-term nanowire is connected to 100 programmable diodes. A plausible failure rate for the product-term diodes is 5% ($P_d = 0.05$). If we demanded that each Pterm be defect free in order to use it, the yield of product terms would be:

$$P_{nwpterm}(100, 0.05) = (1 - 0.05)^{100} \approx 0.006 \qquad (37.9)$$

However, since none of the product terms use all 100 inputs, the probability that a particular Pterm nanowire can support a logical Pterm is much higher. For example, if the Pterm only uses 10 inputs, then the probability that a particular Pterm nanowire can support it is:

$$P_{nwpterm}(10, 0.05) = (1 - 0.05)^{10} \approx 0.599 \qquad (37.10)$$

Further, typical arrays will have 100 product-term nanowires. This suggests that, on average, this Pterm will be compatible with roughly 60 of the Pterm nanowires in the array—that is, the l_i for this Pterm will end up with compatibility edges to 60 r_j's in the bipartite matching graph described before.

As a result, DeHon and Naeimi [18] were able to demonstrate that we can tolerate stuck-off diode defects at $P_d = 0.05$ with no allocated spare nanowires. In other words, we can have $|L|$ as large as $|R|$ and, in practice, always find a complete matching for every PLA. This is true even though the probability of a perfect nanowire is below 1 percent (equation 37.9), suggesting that most arrays of 100 nanowires contain no perfect Pterm nanowires.

This strategy follows the defect map model and does demand component-specific mapping. Nonetheless, the required mapping is local (see the Local sparing section) and can be fast. Naeimi and DeHon [17] demonstrate the results quoted previously using a greedy, linear-time assignment algorithm rather than the slower, optimal algorithm. Further, if it is possible to test the compatibility of each Pterm as part of the trial assignment, it is not necessary to know the defect map prior to mapping.

FPGA component level

It is also possible to apply this matching idea at the component level. Here, the substitutable unit is an entire FPGA component. Unused resources will be switches, wires, and LUTs that are not used by a specific user design. Certainly, if the specific design does not fill the logic blocks in the component, there will be unused logic blocks whose failure may be irrelevant to the proper functioning of the design. Even if the specific design uses all the logic blocks, it will not use all the wires or all the features of every logic block. So, as long as the defects in the component do not intersect with the resources used by an particular FPGA configuration, the FPGA can perfectly support the configuration.

Xilinx's EasyPath series is one manifestation of this idea. At a reduced cost compared to perfect FPGAs, Xilinx sells FPGAs that are only guaranteed to work with a particular user design, or a particular set of user designs. The user provides their designs, and Xilinx checks to see whether any of their defective devices will successfully implement those designs. Here, Xilinx's resource set, R, is the nonperfect FPGAs that do not have defects in the nonrepairable portion of the logic. The logical set, L, is the set of customer designs destined for Easy-Path. Xilinx effectively performs the matching and then supplies each customer with FPGA components compatible with their respective designs.

Hyder and Wawrzynek [19] demonstrate that the same idea can be exploited in board-level FPGA systems. Here, their resource set, R, is the set of FPGAs on a particular board with multiple FPGAs. Their logical set is the set of FPGA configurations intended for the board. If all the FPGAs on the board were interchangeable, this would also reduce to the previous simple matching problem. However, in practice, the FPGAs on a board typically have different connections. This provides an additional set of topological constraints that must be considered along with resource compatibility during assignment. Rather than creating and maintaining a full defect map of each FPGA in the system, they also use application-specific testing (e.g., Tahoori [20]) to determine whether a particular FPGA configuration is compatible with a specific component on the FPGA board.

37.3 TRANSIENT FAULT TOLERANCE

Recall that transient faults are randomly occurring, temporary deviations from the correct circuit behavior. It is not possible to test for transient faults and configure around them as we did with defects. The impact of a transient fault depends on the structure of the logic and the location of the transient fault. The fault may be masked (hidden by downstream gates that are not currently sensitive to this input), may simply affect the circuit output temporarily, or may corrupt state so that the effect of the transient error persists in the computation long after the fault has occurred. Examples include the following:

- If both inputs to an OR gate should be 1, but one of the inputs is erroneously 0, the output of the OR gate will still have the correct value.
- If the transient fault impacts the combinational output from a circuit, only the output on that cycle is affected; subsequent output cycles will be correct until another transient fault occurs.
- If the transient fault results in the circuit incorrectly calculating the next state transition in a finite-state machine (FSM), the computation may proceed in the incorrect state for an indefinite period of time.

To deal with the general case where transient faults impact the observable behavior of the computation, we must be able to prevent the errors from propagating into critical state or to observable outputs from the computation. This demands that we add or exploit some form of redundancy in the calculation to detect or correct errors as they occur. This section reviews two general approaches to transient fault tolerance: feedforward correction (Section 37.3.1) and rollback error recovery (Section 37.3.2).

37.3.1 Feedforward Correction

One common strategy to tolerate transient faults is to provide adequate redundancy to correct any errors that occur. This allows the computation to continue without interruption. The simplest example of this redundancy is replication. That is, we arrange to perform the intended computation R times and vote on the result, using the majority result as the value allowed to update state or to be sent to the output. The smallest example uses $R = 3$ and is known as triple modular redundancy (TMR) (see Figure 37.7). In general, for there to be a clear majority, R must be odd, and a system with R replicas can tolerate at least $\frac{R-1}{2}$ simultaneous transient faults. We can perform the multiple calculations either in space, by concurrently placing R copies of the computation on the reconfigurable array, or in time, by performing the computation multiple times on the same datapath.

In the simple design in Figure 37.7, a failure in the voter may still corrupt the computation. This can be treated similarly to nonrepairable area in defect-tolerance schemes:

- If the computation is large compared to the voter, the probability of voter failure may be sufficiently small so that it is acceptable.
- The voter can be implemented in a more reliable technology, such as a coarser-grained feature size.
- The voter can be replicated as well. For example, von Neumann [21] and Pippenger [22] showed that one can tolerate high transient fault rates (up to 0.4 percent) using a gate-level TMR scheme with replicated voters.

TMR strategies have been applied to Xilinx's Virtex series [23]. Rollins et al. [24] evaluate various TMR schemes on Virtex components, including strategies with replicated voters and replicated clock distribution.

A key design choice in modular redundancy schemes is the granularity at which voting occurs. At the coarsest grain, the entire computational circuit could be the unit of replication and voting. At the opposite extreme, we can replicate and vote individual gates as the Von Neumann design suggests. The appropriate choice will balance area overhead and fault rate. From an area

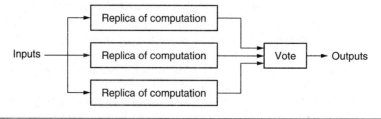

FIGURE 37.7 ▪ A simple TMR design.

overhead standpoint, we would prefer to vote on large blocks; this allows the area of the voters to be amortized across large logic blocks so that the total area grows roughly as the replication factor, R. From an area overhead standpoint, we also want to keep R low. From a reliability standpoint, we want to make it sufficiently unlikely that more than $\frac{R-1}{2}$ replicas are corrupted by transient errors in a single cycle. Similar to defects (equation 37.4), the failure rate of a computation, and hence a replica, scales with the number of devices in the computation and the transient fault rate per device; consequently, we want to scale the unit of replication down as fault rate increases to achieve a target reliability with low R.

Memory

A common form of feedforward correction is in use today in memories. Memories have traditionally been the most fault-sensitive portions of components because: (1) A value in a memory may not be updated for a large number of cycles; as such, memories integrate faults over many cycles. (2) Memories are optimized for density; as such, they often have low capacitance and drive strength, making them more susceptible to errors.

We could simply replicate memories, storing each value in R memories or memory slots and voting the results. However, over the years information theory research has developed clever encoding schemes that are much more efficient for protecting groups of data bits than simple replication [25, 26]. For example, DRAMs used in main memory applications generally tolerate a single-bit fault in a 64-bit data-word using a 72-bit error correcting code. Like the nonrepairable area in DRAMs, the error correcting circuitry in memories is generally built from coarser technology than the RAM memory array and is assumed to be fault free.

37.3.2 Rollback Error Recovery

An alternative technique to feedforward correction is to simply detect when errors occur and repeat the computation when an error is detected. We can detect errors with less redundancy than we need to correct errors (e.g., two copies of a computation are sufficient to detect a single error, while three are required for correction); consequently, detection schemes generally require lower overhead than feedforward correction schemes. If fault rates are low, it is uncommon for errors to occur in the logic. In most cycles, no errors occur and the normal computation proceeds uninterrupted. In the uncommon case in which a transient fault does occur, we stop processing and repeat the computation in time without additional hardware. With reasonably low transient-fault rates, it is highly unlikely that repeated computation will also be in error; in any case, detection guards against errors in the repeated computation as well.

To be viable, the rollback technique demands that the application tolerate stalls in computation during rollback. This is easily accommodated in streaming models (Chapter 5, Section 5.1.3) that exploit data-presence signaling (see Data presence subsection of Section 5.2.1) to tolerate variable timing for operator implementations. When detection and rollback are performed on an operator level, stream buffers between operator datapaths can isolate and minimize the performance impact of rollback.

Detection

To detect errors we use some form of redundancy. Again, this can be either temporal or spatial redundancy.

To minimize the performance impact, we can employ a *concurrent-error detection* (CED) technique—that is, in parallel with the normal logic, we compute some additional function or property of the output (see Figure 37.8). We continuously check consistency between the logical output and this concurrent calculation. If the concurrent calculation ever disagrees with the base computation, this means there is an error in the logic.

In the simplest case, the parallel function could be a duplicate copy of the intended logic (see Figure 37.8(b)). Checking then consists of verifying that the two computations obtained the equivalent results. However, it is often possible to avoid recomputing the entire function and, instead, compute a property of the output, such as its parity (see Figure 37.8(c)) [27].

The choice of detection granularity is based on the same basic considerations discussed before for feedforward replica granularity. Larger blocks can amortize out comparison overhead but will increase block error rates and hence the rate of rollback. For a given fault rate, we reduce comparison block granularity until the rollback rate is sufficiently low so that it has little impact on system throughput.

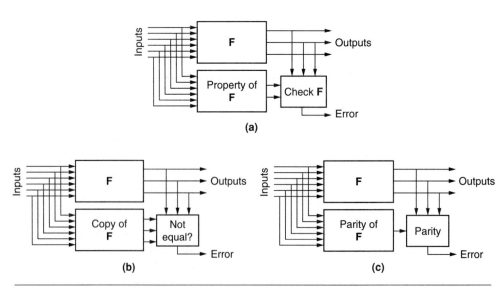

FIGURE 37.8 ▪ A concurrent error-detection strategy and options: (a) generic formulation, (b) duplication, and (c) parity.

Recovery

When we do detect an error, it is necessary to repeat the computation. This typically means making sure to preserve the inputs to a computation until we can be certain that we have reliably produced a correct result. Conceptually, we read inputs and current state, calculate outputs, detect errors, then produce outputs and save state if no errors are detected. In practice, we often want to pipeline this computation so that we detect errors from a previous cycle while the computation continues, and we may not save state to a reliable storage on every calculation. However, even in sequential cases, it may be more efficient to perform a sequence of computations between error checks.

A common idiom is to periodically store, or *snapshot*, state to reliable memory, store inputs as they arrive into reliable memory, perform a series of data computations, and store results to reliable memory. If no errors are detected between snapshots, then we continue to compute with the new state and discard the inputs used to produce it. If errors are detected, we discard the new state, restore the old state, and rerun the computation using the inputs stored in reliable memory. As noted earlier in the Memory subsection, we have particularly compact techniques for storing data reliably in fault-prone memories; this efficient protection of memories allows rollback recovery techniques to be robust and efficient.

In streaming systems, we already have FIFO streams of data between operators. We can exploit these memories to support rollback and retry. Rather than discarding the data as soon as the operator reads it, we keep it in the FIFO but advance the head pointer past it. If the operator needs to rollback, we effectively reset the head pointer in the FIFO to recover the data for reexecution. When an output is correctly produced and stored in an output FIFO, we can then discard the associated inputs from the input FIFOs. For operators that have bounded depth from input to output, we typically know that we can discard an input set for every output produced.

Communications

Data transmission between two distant points, especially when it involves crossing between chips and computers, is highly susceptible to external noise (e.g., crosstalk from nearby wires, power supply noise, clock jitter, interference from RF devices). As such, for a long time we have protected communication channels with redundancy. As with memories, we simply need to reliably deliver the data sent to the destination.

Unlike memories, we do not necessarily need to guarantee that the correct data can be recovered from the potentially corrupted data that arrive at the destination. When the data are corrupted in transmission, it suffices to detect the error. The sender holds onto a copy of the data until the receiver indicates they have been successfully received. When an error is detected, the sender can retransmit the data. The detection and retransmission are effectively a rollback technique.

When the error rates on the communication link are low, such that error detection is the uncommon event, this allows data to be protected with low overhead error-detecting codes, or *checksums*, instead of more expensive error correcting codes. The Transmission Control Protocol (TCP) used for communication across the Internet includes packet checksums and retransmission when data fail to arrive error free at the intended destination [28].

37.4   LIFETIME DEFECTS

Over the lifetime of a component, the physical device will change and degrade, potentially introducing new defects into the device. Individual atomic bonds may break or metal may migrate, increasing the resistance of the path or even breaking a connection completely. Device characteristics may shift because of hot-carrier injection (e.g., [29, 30]), NBTI (e.g., [31]), or even accumulated radiation doses (e.g., [32, 33]). These effects become more acute as feature sizes shrink. To maintain correct operation, we must detect the errors (Section 37.4.1) and repair them (Section 37.4.2) during the lifetime of the component.

37.4.1   Detection

One way to detect lifetime failures is to periodically retest the device—that is, we stop normal operation, run a testing routine (see the Testing subsection in Section 37.2.4), then resume normal operation if there are no errors. It can be an application-specific test, determining whether the FPGA can still support the user's mapping [20], or an application-independent test of the FPGA substrate. Application-specific tests have the advantage of both being more compact and ignoring new defects that do not impact the current design. Substrate tests may require additional computation to determine whether the newly defective devices will impact the design. While two consecutive, successful tests generally mean that the computation between these two points was correct, the component may begin producing errors at any time inside the interval between tests and the error will not be detected until the next test is run.

Testing can also be interleaved more directly with operation. In partially reconfigurable components (see Section 4.2.3), it is possible to reconfigure portions of a component while the rest of the component continues operating. This allows the reservation of a fraction of the component for testing. If we then arrange to change the specific portions of the component assigned to testing and operation over time, we can incrementally test the entire component without completely pulling it out of service (e.g., [34, 35]).

In some scenarios, the component may need to stall operation during the partial reconfiguration, but the component only needs to stall for the reconfiguration period and not the entire testing period. When the total partial reconfiguration time is significantly shorter than the testing time, this can reduce the fraction of cycles the application must be removed from normal operation. This still means that we may not detect the presence of a new defect until long after it occurred and started corrupting data.

If it is necessary to detect an error immediately, we must employ one of the fault tolerance techniques reviewed in Section 37.3. CED (see the Detection subsection in Section 37.3.2) can identify an error as soon as it occurs and stall computation. TMR (Section 37.3.1) can continue correct operation if only a single replica is affected; the TMR scheme can be augmented to signal higher-level control mechanisms when the voters detect disagreement.

37.4.2 Repair

Once a new error has occurred, we can repeat global (see the Global sparing subsection in Section 37.2.4) or local mapping (see the Local sparing subsection in Section 37.2.4) to avoid the new error. However, since the new defect map is most likely to differ from the old defect map by only one or a few defects, it is often easier and faster to incrementally repair the configuration. In local mapping schemes, we only need to perform local remapping in the interchangeable region(s) where the new defect(s) have occurred. This may mean that we only need to move LUTs in a single cluster, wires in channel, or remap a single tile. Even in global schemes the incremental work required may be modest. Lakamraju and Tessier [36] show that incrementally rerouting connections severed by new lifetime defects can be orders of magnitude faster than performing a complete reroute from scratch.

A rollback scheme (Section 37.3.2) can stall execution during the repair. A replicated, feedforward scheme (Section 37.3.1) with partial reconfiguration may be able to continue operating on the functional replicas while the newly defective replica is being repaired.

Lifetime repair strategies depend on the ability to perform defect mapping and reconfiguration. Consequently, the perfect component model cannot support lifetime repair. Even if the component retains spare redundancy, redundancy and remapping mechanisms are not exposed to the user for in-field use.

37.5 CONFIGURATION UPSETS

Many reconfigurable components, such as FPGAs, rely on volatile memory cells to hold their configuration, typically static memory cells (e.g., SRAM). Dynamic memory cells have long had to cope with upsets from ionizing particles (e.g., α-particles). As the feature sizes shrink, even static RAM cells can be upset by ionizing particles (e.g., Harel et al. [37]). In storage applications, we can typically cope with memory soft errors using error correcting codes (see the Memory subsection in Section 37.3.1) so that bit upsets can be detected and corrected. However, in reconfigurable components, we use the memory cells directly and continuously as configuration bits to define logic and interconnect. Upsets of these configuration memories will change, and potentially corrupt, the logic operation.

Unfortunately, although memories can amortize the cost of a large error correction unit across a deep memory, FPGA configurations are shallow (i.e., $N_{instr} = 1$); an error correction scheme similar to DRAM memories would end up being as large as or larger than the configuration memory it protects. Data and projections from Quinn and Graham [38] suggest that ionizing radiation upsets can be a real concern for current, large FPGA-based systems and will be an ongoing concern even for modest systems as capacity continues to increase.

Because these are transient upsets of configuration memories, they can be corrected simply by reloading the correct bitstream once we detect that the bitstream has been corrupted. Logic corruption can be detected using any of the strategies described earlier for lifetime defects (Section 37.4.1). Alternatively, we can check the bitstream directly for errors. That is, we can compute a checksum for the correct bitstream, read the bitstream back periodically, compute the checksum of the readback bitstream, and compare it to the intended bitstream checksum to detect when errors have occurred. When an error has occurred, the bitstream can be reloaded [38, 39]. Like interleaved testing, bitstream readback introduces a latency, which can be seconds long, between configuration corruption and correction. If the application can tolerate infrequent corruption, this may be acceptable.

Asadi and Tahoori [40] detail a rollback scheme for tolerating configuration upsets. Pratt et al. [41] use TMR and partial TMR schemes to tolerate configuration upsets; their partial TMR scheme uses less area than a full TMR scheme in cases where it is acceptable for the outputs to be erroneous for a number of cycles as long as the state is protected so that the results return to the correct values when the configuration is repaired.

37.6 OUTLOOK

The regularity in reconfigurable arrays, coupled with the resource configurability they already possess, allow these architectures to tolerate defects. As features shrink and defect rates increase, all devices, including ASICs, are likely to need some level of regularity and configurability; this will be one factor that serves to narrow the density and cost gap between FPGAs and ASICs. Further, at increased defect rates, it will likely make sense to ship components with defects and defect maps. Since each component will be different, some form of component-specific mapping will be necessary.

Transient upsets and lifetime defects further suggest that we should continuously monitor the computation to detect errors. To tolerate lifetime defects, repair will become part of the support system for components throughout their operational lifetime. Increasing defect rates further drive us toward architectures with finer-grained substitutable units. FPGAs are already fairly fine grained, with each bit-processing operator potentially serving as a substitutable unit, but finer-grained architectures that substitute individual wires, Pterms, or LUTs may be necessary to exploit the most aggressive technologies.

References

[1] S. E. Schuster. Multiple word/bit line redundancy for semiconductor memories. *IEEE Journal of Solid State Circuits* 13(5), 1978.

[2] B. Keeth, R. J. Baker. *DRAM Circuit Design: A Tutorial*. Microelectronic Systems, IEEE Press, 2001.

[3] J. Bernoulli. *Ars Conjectandi*. Impensis thurnisiorum, fratrum, Basel, Switzerland, 1713.

[4] A. W. Drake. *Fundamentals of Applied Probability Theory*, McGraw-Hill, 1988.

[5] A. DeHon. Law of large numbers system design. *Nano, Quantum and Molecular Computing: Implications to High Level Design and Validation*, S. K. Shukla, R. I. Bahar (eds.), Kluwer Academic, 2004.

[6] W. K. Huang, F. J. Meyer, X.-T. Chen, F. Lombardi. Testing configurable LUT-based FPGAs. *IEEE Transactions on Very Large Scale Integration (VLSI) Systems* 6(2), 1998.

[7] W. B. Culbertson, R. Amerson, R. Carter, P. Kuekes, G. Snider. Defect tolerance on the TERAMAC custom computer. *Proceedings of the IEEE Symposium on FPGAs for Custom Computing Machines*, 1997.

[8] M. Mishra, S. C. Goldstein. Defect tolerance at the end of the roadmap. *Proceedings of the International Test Conference (ITC)*, 2003.

[9] M. Mishra, S. C. Goldstein. Defect tolerance at the end of the roadmap. *Nano, Quantum and Molecular Computing: Implications to High Level Design and Validation*, S. K. Shukla, R. I. Bahar (Eds.), Kluwer Academic, 2004.

[10] R. G. Cliff, R. Raman, S. T. Reddy. Programmable logic devices with spare circuits for replacement of defects. U.S. Patent number 5,434,514, July 18, 1995.

[11] C. McClintock, A. L. Lee, R. G. Cliff. Redundancy circuitry for logic circuits. U.S. Patent number 6,034,536, March 7, 2000.

[12] J. Lach, W. H. Mangione-Smith, M. Potkonjak. Low overhead fault-tolerant FPGA systems. *IEEE Transactions on Very Large Scale Integration (VLSI) Systems* 26(2), 1998.

[13] A. J. Yu, G. G. Lemieux. Defect-tolerant FPGA switch block and connection block with fine-grain redundancy for yield enhancement. *Proceedings of the International Conference on Field-Programmable Logic and Applications*, 2005.

[14] A. J. Yu, G. G. Lemieux. FPGA defect tolerance: Impact of granularity. *Proceedings of the International Conference on Field-Programmable Technology*, 2005.

[15] T. Cormen, C. Leiserson, R. Rivest. *Introduction to Algorithms*. MIT Press, 1990.

[16] J. E. Hopcroft, R. M. Karp. An $n^{2.5}$ algorithm for maximum matching in bipartite graphs. *SIAM Journal on Computing* 2(4), 1973.

[17] H. Naeimi, A. DeHon. A greedy algorithm for tolerating defective crosspoints in nanoPLA design. *Proceedings of the International Conference on Field-Programmable Technology*, IEEE, 2004.

[18] A. DeHon, H. Naeimi. Seven strategies for tolerating highly defective fabrication. *IEEE Design and Test of Computers* 22(4), 2005.

[19] Z. Hyder, J. Wawrzynek. Defect tolerance in multiple-FPGA systems. *Proceedings of the International Conference on Field-Programmable Logic and Applications*, 2005.

[20] M. B. Tahoori. Application-dependent testing of FPGAs. *IEEE Transactions on Very Large Scale Integration (VLSI) Systems* 14(9), 2006.

[21] J. von Neumann. Probabilistic logic and the synthesis of reliable organisms from unreliable components. *Automata Studies* C. Shannon, J. McCarthy (ed.), Princeton University Press, 1956.

[22] N. Pippenger. Developments in "the synthesis of reliable organisms from unreliable components." *Proceedings of the Symposia of Pure Mathematics* 50, 1990.

[23] C. Carmichael. *Triple Module Redundancy Design Techniques for Virtex FPGAs*. San Jose, 2006 (XAPP 197—*http://www.xilinx.com/bvdocs/appnotes/xapp197.pdf*).

[24] N. Rollins, M. Wirthlin, P. Graham, M. Caffrey. Evaluating TMR techniques in the presence of single event upsets. *Proceedings of the International Conference on Military and Aerospace Programmable*, 2003.

[25] G. C. Clark Jr., J. B. Cain. *Error-Correction Coding for Digital Communications*, Plenum Press, 1981.

[26] R. J. McEliece. *The Theory of Information and Coding*, Cambridge University Press, 2002.

[27] S. Mitra, E. J. McCluskey. Which concurrent error detection scheme to choose? *Proceedings of the International Test Conference*, 2000.

[28] J. Postel (ed.). Transmission Control Protocol—DARPA Internet Program Protocol Specification, RFC 793, Information Sciences Institute, University of Southern California, Marina del Rey, 1981.

[29] E. Takeda, N. Suzuki, T. Hagiwara. Device performance degradation to hot-carrier injection at energies below the Si-SiO2 energy barrier. *Proceedings of the International Electron Devices Meeting*, 1983.

[30] S.-H. Renn, C. Raynaud, J.-L. Pelloie, F. Balestra. A thorough investigation of the degradation induced by hot-carrier injection in deep submicron N- and P-channel partially and fully depleted unibond and SIMOX MOSFETs. *IEEE Transactions on Electron Devices* 45(10), 1998.

[31] D. K. Schroder, J. A. Babcock. Negative bias temperature instability: Road to cross in deep submicron silicon semiconductor manufacturing, *Journal of Applied Physics* 94(1), 2003.

[32] J. Osborn, R. Lacoe, D. Mayer, G. Yabiku. Total dose hardness of three commercial CMOS microelectronics foundries. *Proceedings of the European Conference on Radiation and Its Effects on Components and Systems*, 1997.

[33] C. Brothers, R. Pugh, P. Duggan, J. Chavez, D. Schepis, D. Yee, S. Wu. Total-dose and SEU characterization of 0.25 micron CMOS/SOI integrated circuit memory technologies. *IEEE Transactions on Nuclear Science* 44(6) 1997.

[34] J. Emmert, C. Stroud, B. Skaggs, M. Abramovici. Dynamic fault tolerance in FPGAs via partial reconfiguration. *Proceedings of the IEEE Symposium on Field-Programmable Custom Computing Machines*, 2000.

[35] S. K. Sinha, P. M. Kamarchik, S. C. Goldstein. Tunable fault tolerance for run-time reconfigurable architectures. *Proceedings of the IEEE Symposium on Field-Programmable Custom Computing Machines*, 2000.

[36] V. Lakamraju, R. Tessier. Tolerating operational faults in cluster-based FPGAs. *Proceedings of the International Symposium on Field-Programmable Gate Arrays*, 2000.

[37] S. Harel, J. Maiz, M. Alavi, K. Mistry, S. Walsta, C. Dai Impact of CMOS process scaling and SOI on the soft error rates of logic processes. *Proceedings of Symposium on VLSI Digest of Technology Papers*, 2001.

[38] H. Quinn, P. Graham. Terrestrial-based radiation upsets: A cautionary tale. *Proceedings of the IEEE Symposium on Field-Programmable Custom Computing Machines*, 2005.

[39] C. Carmichael, M. Caffrey, A. Salazar. *Correcting Single-Event Upsets Through Virtex Partial Configuration*. Xilinx, Inc., San Jose, 2000 (XAPP 216—*http://www.xilinx.com/bvdocs/appnotes/xapp216.pdf*).

[40] G.-H. Asadi, M. B. Tahoori. Soft error mitigation for SRAM-based FPGAs. *Proceedings of the VLSI Test Symposium*, 2005.

[41] B. Pratt, M. Caffrey, P. Graham, K. Morgan, M. Wirthlin. Improving FPGA design robustness with partial TMR. *Proceedings of the IEEE International Reliability Physics Symposium*, 2006.

CHAPTER 38

RECONFIGURABLE COMPUTING AND NANOSCALE ARCHITECTURE

André DeHon
Department of Electrical and Systems Engineering
University of Pennsylvania

For roughly four decades integrated circuits have been patterned top down with optical lithography, and feature sizes, F, have shrunk in a predictable, geometric fashion. With feature sizes now far below optical wavelengths (c.f. 400 nm violet light and 65 nm feature sizes) and approaching atomic lattice spacings (c.f. 65 nm feature sizes and 0.5 nm silicon lattice), it becomes more difficult and more expensive to pattern arbitrary features.

At the same time, fundamental advances in synthetic chemistry allow the assembly of structures made of a small and precise number of atoms, providing an alternate, bottom-up approach to constructing nanometer-scale devices. Rather than relying on ever-finer precision and control of lithography, bottom-up techniques exploit physical phenomena (e.g., molecular dimensions, film thicknesses composed of a precise number of atomic layers, nanoparticles constructed by self-limiting chemical processes) to directly define key feature sizes at the nanometer scale. Bottom-up fabrication gives us access to smaller feature sizes and promises more economical construction of atomic-scale devices and wires.

Both bottom-up structure synthesis and extreme subwavelength top-down lithography can produce small feature sizes only for very regular topologies. In optical lithography, regular interference patterns can produce regular structures with finer resolution than arbitrary topologies [1]. Bottom-up syntheses are limited to regular structures amenable to physical self-assembly.

Further, as noted in Chapter 37, construction at this scale, whether by top-down or bottom-up fabrication, exhibit high defect rates. High defect rates also drive increasing demand for regularity to support resource substitution.

At the same time, new technologies offer configurable switchpoints that can fit in the space of a nanoscale wire crossing (Section 38.2.3). The switches are much smaller than current SRAM configurable switches and can reduce the cost of reconfigurable architectures relative to ASICs. Smaller configurable switchpoints are particularly fortuitous because they make fine-grained configurability for defect tolerance viable.

High demand for regularity and fine-grained defect tolerance coupled with less expensive configurations increase the importance of reconfigurable architectures. Reconfigurable architectures can accommodate the requirements of these atomic-scale technologies and exploit the density benefits they offer. Nonetheless, to fully accommodate and exploit these cost shifts, reconfigurable architectures continue to evolve.

This chapter reviews proposals for nanoscale configurable architectures that address the demands and opportunities of atomic-scale, bottom-up fabrication. It focuses on the nanoPLA architecture (see Section 38.6 and DeHon [2]), which has been specifically designed to exploit nanowires (Section 38.2.1) as the key building block. Despite the concrete focus on nanowires, many of the design solutions employed by the nanoPLA are applicable to other atomic-scale technologies. The chapter also briefly reviews nanoscale architectures (Section 38.7), which offer alternative solutions to key challenges in atomic-scale design.

38.1   TRENDS IN LITHOGRAPHIC SCALING

In the conventional, top-down lithographic model, we define a minimum, lithographically imageable feature size (i.e., half pitch, F) and build devices that are multiples of this imageable feature size. Within the limits of this feature size, VLSI layout can perfectly specify the size of features and their location relative to each other in three dimensions—both in the two-dimensional plane of each lithographic layer and with adequate registration between layers. This gives complete flexibility in the layout of circuit structures as long as we adhere to the minimum imageable and repeatable feature size rules.

Two simplifying assumptions effectively made this possible: (1) Feature size was large compared to atoms, and (2) feature size was large compared to the wavelength of light used for imaging. With micron feature sizes, features were thousands of atoms wide and multiple optical wavelengths. As long as the two assumptions held, we did not need to worry about the discreteness of atoms nor the limits of optical lithography.

Today, however, we have long since passed the point where optical wavelengths are large compared to feature sizes, and we are rapidly approaching the point where feature sizes are measured in single-digit atom widths. We have made the transition to optical lithography below visible light (e.g., 193 nm wavelengths) and subwavelength imaging. Phase shift masking exploits interference of multiple light sources with different phases in order to define feature sizes finer than the wavelength of the source. This has allowed continued feature size scaling but increases the complexity and, hence, the cost of lithographic imaging.

Topology in the regions surrounding a pattern now impacts the fidelity of reproduction of the circuit or interconnect, creating the demand for optical proximity correction. As a result, we see an increase both in the complexity of lithographic mask generation and in the number of masks required. Region-based topology effects also limit the structures we can build. Because of both limitations in patterning and limitations in the analysis of region-based patterning effects, even in "full-custom" designs, we are driven to compose functions from a small palette of regular structures.

Rock's Law is a well-known rule of thumb in the semiconductor industry that suggests that semiconductor processing equipment costs increase geometrically as feature sizes shrink geometrically. One version of Rock's Law estimates that the cost of a semiconductor fabrication plant doubles every four years. Fabrication plants for the 90 nm generation were reported to cost $2 to 3 billion.

The increasing cost comes from several sources, including the following:

- *Increasing demand for accuracy:* Alignment of features must scale with feature sizes.
- *Increasing demand for purity:* Smaller features mean that even smaller foreign particles (e.g., dust and debris) must be eliminated to prevent defects.
- *Increasing demand for device yield:* As noted in Chapter 37 (see Perfect yield, Section 37.2.3), to keep component yield constant, the per-device defect rate, P_d, must decrease as more devices are integrated onto each component.
- *Increasing processing steps:* More metal layers plus increasingly complex masks for optical resolution enhancement (described before) demand more equipment and processing.

It is already the case that few manufacturers can afford the capital investment required to develop and deploy the most advanced fabrication plants. Rising fabrication costs continue to raise the bar, forcing consolidation and centralization in integrated circuit manufacturing.

Starting at around 90 nm feature sizes, the mask cost per component typically exceeds $1 million. This rising cost comes from the effects previously noted: more masks per component and greater complexity per mask. Coupled with rising component design and verification complexity, this raises the nonrecurring engineering (NRE) costs per chip design.

The economics of rising NRE ultimately lead to fewer unique designs. That is, if we hope to keep NRE costs to a small fraction—for example 10 percent—of the potential revenue for a chip, the market must be at least 10 times the NRE cost. With total NRE costs typically requiring tens of millions of dollars for 90 nm designs, each chip needs a revenue potential in the hundreds of millions of dollars to be viable. The bar continues to rise with NRE costs, decreasing the number of unique designs that the industry can support. This decrease in unique designs creates an increasing demand for differentiation after fabrication (i.e., reconfigurability).

38.2 BOTTOM-UP TECHNOLOGY

In contrast, bottom-up synthesis techniques give us a way to build devices and wires without relying on masks and lithography to define their atomic-scale features. They potentially provide an alternative path to device construction that may provide access to these atomic-scale features more economically than traditional lithography.

This section briefly reviews the bottom-up technology building blocks exploited by the nanoPLA, including nanowires (Section 38.2.1), ordered assembly of nanowires (Section 38.2.2), and programmable crosspoints (Section 38.2.3). These technologies are sufficient for constructing and understanding the basic nanoPLA design. For a roundup of additional nanoscale wire and crosspoint technologies, see the appendix in DeHon's 2005 article [2].

38.2.1 Nanowires

Chemists and material scientists are now regularly producing semiconducting and metallic wires that are nanometers in diameter and microns long using bottom-up synthesis techniques. To bootstrap the process and define the smallest dimensions, self-limiting chemical processes (e.g., Tan et al. [3]) can be used to produce nanoparticles of controlled diameter. From these nanoparticle seed catalysts, we can grow nanowires with diameters down to 3 nm [4]. The nanowire self-assembles into a crystalline lattice similar to planar silicon; however, growth is only enabled in the vicinity of the nanoparticle's catalyst. As a result, catalyst size defines the diameter of the grown nanowires [5]. Nanowires can be grown to millimeters in length [6], although it is more typical to work with nanowires tens of microns long [7].

Bottom-up synthesis techniques also allow the definition of atomic-scale features within a single nanowire. Using timed growth, features such as composition of different materials and different doping levels can be grown along the axis of the nanowire [8–10]. This effectively allows the placement of device features into nanowires, such as a field effect gateable region in the middle of an otherwise ungateable wire (see Figure 38.1). Further, radial shells of different materials can be grown around nanowires with controlled thickness using timed growth [11, 12] or atomic-layer deposition [13, 14] (see Figure 38.2). These shells can be used to force the spacing between device and wire features, to act as dielectrics for field effect gating, or to build devices integrating heterogeneous materials with atomic-scale dimensions.

After a nanowire has been grown, it can be converted into a metal–silicon compound with lower resistance. For example, by coating select regions of

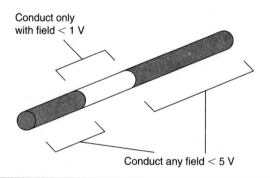

Conduct only
with field < 1 V

Conduct any field < 5 V

FIGURE 38.1 ■ An axial doping profile. By varying doping along the axis of the nanowire, selectively gateable regions can be integrated into the nanowire.

FIGURE 38.2 ■ A radial doping profile.

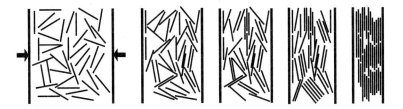

FIGURE 38.3 ■ The Langmuir–Blodgett alignment of nanowires.

the nanowire with nickle and annealing, we can form a nickle–silicide (NiSi) nanowire [15]. The NiSi resistivity is much lower than the resistivity of heavily doped bulk silicon. Since nanowires have a very small cross-sectional area, this conversion is very important to keep the resistance, and hence the delay, of nanowires low. Further, this conversion is particularly important in reducing contact resistance between nanowires and lithographic-scale power supplies.

38.2.2 Nanowire Assembly

Langmuir–Blodgett (LB) flow techniques can be used to align a set of nanowires into a single orientation, close-pack them, and transfer them onto a surface [16, 17] (see Figure 38.3). The resulting wires are all parallel, but their ends may not be aligned. By using wires with an oxide sheath around the conducting core, the wires can be packed tightly without shorting together. The oxide sheath defines the spacing between conductors and can, optionally, be etched away after assembly. The LB step can be rotated and repeated so that we get multiple layers of nanowires [16, 18], such as crossed nanowires for building a wired-OR plane (Section 38.4.1).

38.2.3 Crosspoints

Many technologies have been demonstrated for nonvolatile, switched crosspoints. Common features include the following:

- Resistance that changes significantly between on and off states
- Ability to be made rectifying (i.e., to act as diodes)
- Ability to turn the device on or off by applying a voltage differential across the junction
- Ability to be placed within the area of a crossed nanowire junction

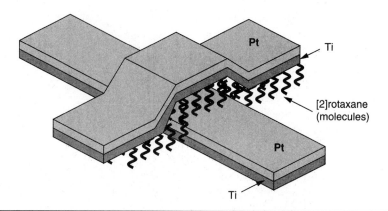

FIGURE 38.4 ■ Switchable molecules sandwiched between nanoscale wires.

Chen et al. [19, 20] demonstrate a nanoscale Ti/Pt-[2]rotaxane-Ti/Pt sandwich (see Figure 38.4), which exhibits hysteresis and nonvolatile state storage showing an order of magnitude resistance difference between on and off states. The state of these devices can be switched at $\pm 2\,V$ and read at $\pm 0.2\,V$. The basic hysteretic molecular memory effect is not unique to the [2]rotaxane, and the junction resistance is continuously tunable [21]. The exact nature of the physical phenomena involved is the subject of active investigation. LB techniques also can be used to place the switchable molecules between crossed nanowires (e.g., Collier et al. [22], Brown et al. [23]).

In conventional VLSI, the area of an SRAM-based programmable crosspoint switch is much larger than the area of a wire crossing. A typical CMOS switch might be $600\,F^2$ [24], compared to a $3F \times 3F$ bottom-level metal wire crossing, making the crosspoint more than 60 times the area of the wire crossing. Consequently, the nanoscale crosspoints offer an additional device size reduction beyond that implied by the smaller nanowire feature sizes. This particular device size benefit reduces the overhead for configurability associated with programmable architectures (e.g., FPGAs, PLAs) in this technology, compared to conventional CMOS.

38.3 CHALLENGES

Although the techniques reviewed in the previous section provide the ability to create very small feature sizes using the basic physical properties of materials to define dimensions, they also bring with them a number of challenges that any nanoscale architecture must address, including the following:

■ *Required regularity in assembly and architecture:* These techniques do not allow the construction of arbitrary topologies; the assembly techniques limit us to regular arrays and crossbars of nanowires.

- *Lack of correlation in features:* The correlation between features is limited. It is possible to have correlated features within a nanowire, but only in a single nanowire; we cannot control which nanowire is placed next to which other nanowire or how they are aligned.
- *Differentiation:* If all the nanowires in a regular crossbar assembly behaved identically (e.g., were gated by the same inputs or were diode-connected to the same inputs), we would not get a benefit out of the nanoscale pitch. It is necessary to differentiate the function performed by the individual nanowires in order to exploit the benefits of their nanoscale pitch.
- *Signal restoration:* The diode crosspoints described in the previous section are typically nonrestoring; consequently, it is necessary to provide signal restoration for diode logic stages.
- *Defect tolerance:* We expect a high rate of defects in nanowires and crosspoints. Nanowires may break or make poor contacts. Crosspoints may have poor contact to the nanowires or contain too few molecules to be switched into a low-resistance state.

38.4 NANOWIRE CIRCUITS

It is possible to build a number of key circuits from the nanoscale building blocks introduced in the previous section, including a diode-based wired-OR logic array (Section 38.4.1) and a restoring nanoscale inverter (Section 38.4.2).

38.4.1 Wired-OR Diode Logic Array

The primary configurable structure we can build is a set of tight-pitched, crossed nanowires. With a programmable diode crosspoint at each nanowire intersection, this crossed nanowire array can serve as a programmable OR-plane. Assuming the diodes point from columns to rows (see Figure 38.5), each row output nanowire serves as a wired-OR for all of the inputs programmed into the low-resistance state. In the figure, programmed on crosspoints are shown in black; off crosspoints are shown in gray. Bold lines represent a nanowire pulled high, while gray lines remain low. Output nanowires are shown bold starting at the diode that pulls them high to illustrate current flow; the entire output nanowire would be pulled high in actual operation. Separate circuitry, not shown, is responsible for pulling wires low or precharging them low so that an output remains low when no inputs can pull it high.

Consider a single-row nanowire, and assume for the moment that there is a way to pull a nondriven nanowire down to ground. If any of the column nanowires that cross this row nanowire are connected with low-resistance crosspoint junctions and are driven to a high voltage level, the current into the column nanowire will be able to flow into the row nanowire and charge it up to a higher voltage value (see O1, O3, O4, and O5 in Figure 38.5). However, if none of

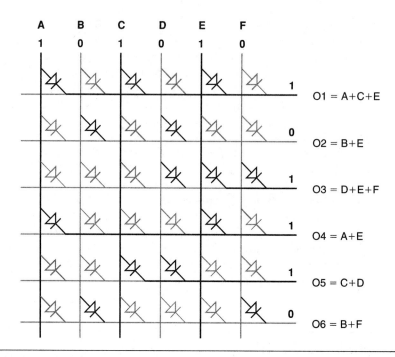

FIGURE 38.5 ■ The wired-OR plane operation.

the connected column nanowires is high, the row nanowire will remain low (see O2 and O6 in the figure). Consequently, the row nanowire effectively computes the OR of its programmed inputs.

The output nanowires do pull their current directly off the inputs and may not be driven as high as the input voltage. Consequently, these outputs will require restoration (Section 38.4.2).

A special use of the wired-OR programmable array is for interconnect. That is, if we restrict ourselves to connecting a *single* row wire to each column wire, the crosspoint array can serve as a crossbar switch. This allows any input (column) to be routed to any output (row) (see Figure 38.6). This structure is useful for postfabrication programmable routing to connect logic functions and to avoid defective resources. In the figure, programmed on crosspoints are shown in black; off crosspoints are shown in gray. This means that the crossbar shown in the figure is programmed to connect A→T, B→Q, C→V, D→S, E→U, and F→R.

38.4.2   Restoration

As noted in Section 38.4.1, the programmable, wired-OR logic is passive and nonrestoring, drawing current from the input. Further, OR logic is not universal. To build a good, composable logic family, we need to be able to isolate inputs from output loads, restore signal strength and current drive, and invert signals.

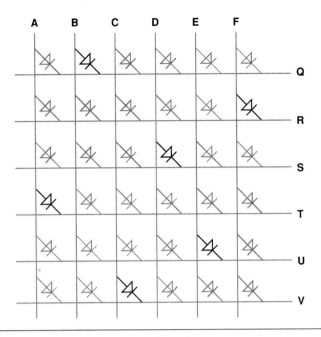

FIGURE 38.6 ■ An example crossbar routing configuration.

Fortunately, nanowires can be field effect controlled. This provides the potential to build gates that behave like field effect transistors (FETs) for restoration. However, to realize them, we must find ways to create the appropriate gate topology within regular assembly constraints (Section 38.5).

If two nanowires are separated by an insulator, perhaps using an oxide core shell, we can use the field from one nanowire to control the other nanowire. Figure 38.7 shows an inverter built using this basic idea. The horizontal nanowire serves as the input and the vertical nanowire as the output. This gives a voltage transfer equation of

$$V_{out} = V_{high} \left(\frac{R_{pd}}{R_{pd} + R_{fet}(\text{Input}) + R_{pu}} \right) \tag{38.1}$$

For the sake of illustration, the vertical nanowire has a lightly doped P-type depletion-mode region at the input crossing that forms a FET controlled by the input voltage ($R_{fet}(\text{Input})$). Consequently, a low voltage on the input nanowire allows conduction through the vertical nanowire ($R_{fet} = R_{\text{on-fet}}$ is small), and a high input depletes the carriers from the vertical nanowire and prevents conduction ($R_{fet} = R_{\text{off-fet}}$ is large). As a result, a low input allows the nanowire to conduct and pull the output region of the vertical nanowire up to a high voltage. A high input prevents conduction and the output region remains low. A second crossed region on the nanowire is used for the pulldown (R_{pd}). This region can be used as a gate for predischarging the output so that the inverter is pulled low

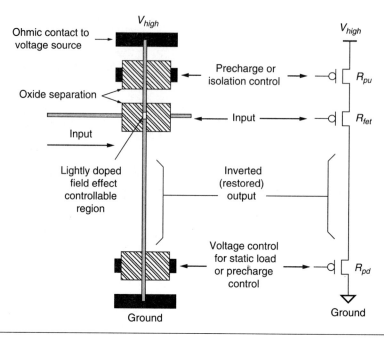

FIGURE 38.7 ■ A nanowire inverter.

before the input is applied, then left high to disconnect the pulldown voltage during evaluation. Alternatively, it can be used as a static load for **PMOS**-like ratioed logic. By swapping the location of the high- and low-power supplies, this same arrangement can be used to buffer rather than invert the input.

Note that the gate only loads the input capacitively. Consequently, the output current is isolated from the input current at this inverter or buffer. Further, nanowire field effect gating has sufficient nonlinearity so that this gate provides gain to restore logic signal levels [25].

38.5 STATISTICAL ASSEMBLY

One challenge posed by regular structures, such as tight-pitch nanowire crossbars, is differentiation. If all the wires are the same and are fabricated at a pitch smaller than we can build arbitrary topologies lithographically, how can we selectively address a single nanowire? If we had enough control to produce arbitrary patterns at the nanometer scale, we could build a decoder (see Figure 38.8) to provide pitch-matching between this scale and the scale at which we could define arbitrary topologies.

The trick is to build the decoder statistically. That is, differentiate the nanowires by giving each one an address, randomly select the nanowires that go into each array, and carefully engineer the statistics to guarantee a high

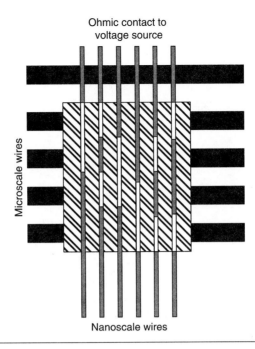

Ohmic contact to
voltage source

Microscale wires

Nanoscale wires

FIGURE 38.8 ■ A decoder for addressing individual nanowires assembled at nanoscale pitch.

probability that there will be a unique address associated with each nanowire in each nanowire array. We can use axial doping to integrate the address into each nanowire [26].

If we pick the address space sparsely enough, Law of Large Numbers statistics can guarantee unique addressability of the nanowires. For example, if we select 10 nanowires out of a large pool with 10^6 different nanowire types, we get a unique set of nanowires more than 99.99 percent of the time. In general, we can guarantee more than 99 percent probability of uniqueness of N nanowires using only $100 N^2$ addresses [26]. By allowing a few duplications, the address space can be much smaller [27].

Statistical selection of coded nanowires can also be used to assemble nanoscale wires for restoration [2]. As shown in Figure 38.9(a), if coded nanowires can be perfectly placed in an array, we can build the restoration circuit shown in Section 38.4.2 (Figure 38.7) and arrange them to restore the outputs of a wired-OR array. However, the bottom-up techniques that can assemble these tight-pitch feature sizes cannot order or place individual nanowires and cannot provide correlation between nanowires. As shown in Figure 38.9(b), statistical alignment and placement of the restoration nanowires can be used to construct the restoration array. Here, not every input will be restored, but the Law of Large Numbers guarantees that we can restore a reliably predictable fraction of the inputs. For further details, see DeHon [2, 27].

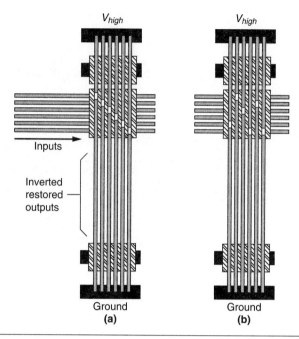

FIGURE 38.9 ■ A restoration array: (a) ideal and (b) stochastic.

38.6   NANOPLA ARCHITECTURE

With these building blocks we can assemble a complete reconfigurable architecture. This section starts by describing the PLA-based logic block (Section 38.6.1), then shows how PLAs are connected together into an array of interconnected logic blocks (Section 38.6.2). It also notes that nanoscale memories can be integrated with this array (Section 38.6.3), reviews the defect tolerance approach for this architecture (Section 38.6.4), describes how designs are mapped to nanoPLA designs (Section 38.6.5), and highlights the density benefits offered by the technology (Section 38.6.6).

38.6.1   Basic Logic Block

The nanoPLA architecture combines the wired-OR plane, the stochastically assembled restoration array, and the stochastic address decoder to build a simple, regular PLA array (see Figure 38.10). The stochastic decoder described in Section 38.5 allows individual nanowires to be addressed from the lithographic scale for testing and programming (see Figures 38.11 and 38.12). The output of the programmable, wired-OR plane is restored via a restoration plane using field effect gating of the crossed nanowire set as described in Section 38.5 and shown in Figure 38.9.

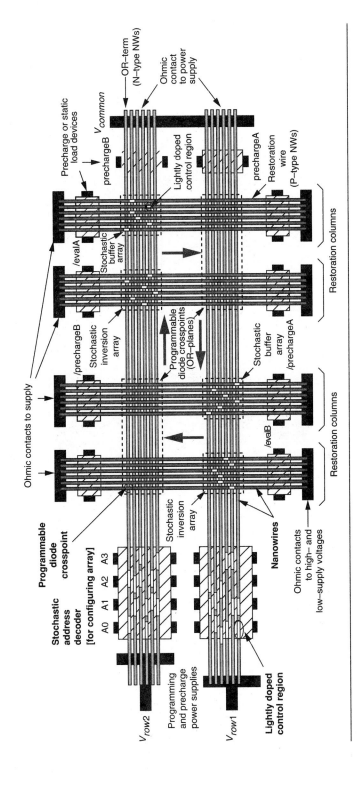

FIGURE 38.10 ■ A simple nanoPLA block.

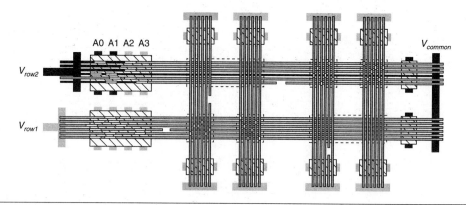

FIGURE 38.11 ▪ Addressing a single nanowire.

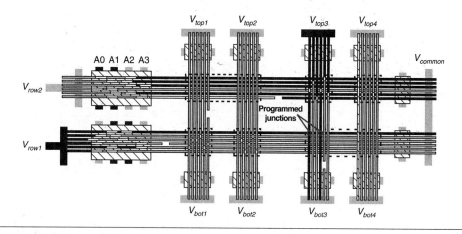

FIGURE 38.12 ▪ Programming a nanowire–nanowire crosspoint.

As shown in Figure 38.11, an address is applied on the lithographic-scale address lines (A0 ... A3). The applied address (1100) allows conduction through only a single nanowire. By monitoring the voltage at the common lithographic node at the far end of the nanowire (V_{common}), it is possible to determine whether the address is present and whether the wire is functional (e.g., not broken). By monitoring the timing of the signal on V_{common}, we may be able to determine the resistance of the nanowire.

As shown in Figure 38.12, addresses are applied to the lithographic-scale address lines of both the top and bottom planes to select individual nanowires in each plane. We use the stochastic restoration columns to turn the corner between the top plane and the restoration inputs to the bottom plane. Note that since column 3 is an inverting column, we arrange for the single, selected signal on the top plane to be a low value. Since the stochastic assembly resulted in two restoration wires for this input, both nanowire inputs are activated. As a result, we place the designated voltage across the two marked crosspoints to turn on the crosspoint junctions between the restored inputs and the selected nanowire in the bottom plane.

The restoration planes can provide inversion such that the pair of planes serve as a programmable NOR. The two back-to-back NOR planes can be viewed as a traditional AND–OR PLA with suitable application of DeMorgan's Law. A second set of restoration wires provides buffered, noninverted inputs to the next wired-OR plane; in this manner, each plane gets the true and complement version of each logical signal just as is normally provided at the inputs to a VLSI PLA. Microscale field effect gates (e.g., /evalA and /evalB) control when nanowire logic can evaluate, allowing the use of a familiar 2-phase clocking discipline. As such, the PLA cycle shown in Figure 38.10 can directly implement an FSM. Programmable crosspoints can be used to personalize the array, avoid defective wires and crosspoints (Section 38.6.4), and implement a deterministic function despite fabrication defects and stochastic assembly.

38.6.2 Interconnect Architecture

To construct larger components using the previously described structures, we can build an array of nanoPLA blocks, where each block drives outputs that cross the input (wired) regions of many other blocks (Figure 38.13) [2, 28]. This allows the construction of modest-size PLAs (e.g., 100 Pterms), which are efficient for logic mapping and keep the nanowire runs short (e.g., 10 μm) in order to increase yield and avoid the high resistance of long nanowires. The nanoPLA blocks provide logic units, signal switching, and signal buffering for long wire runs. With an appropriate overlap topology, such nanoPLAs can support Manhattan (orthogonal X–Y) routing similar to conventional, island-style FPGA architectures (Chapter 1).

By stacking additional layers of nanowires, the structure can be extended vertically into the third dimension [29]. Programmable and gateable junctions between adjacent nanowire layers allow routing up and down the nanowire stack. This provides a path to continue scaling logic density when nanowire diameters can shrink no further.

The resulting nanoPLA structure is simple and very regular. Its high-density features are built entirely from tight-pitched nanowire arrays. All the nanowire array features are defined using bottom-up techniques. The overlap topology between nanowires is carefully arranged so that the output of a function (e.g., wired-OR, restoration, routing) is a segment of a nanowire that then crosses the active or input portion of another function. Regions (e.g., wired-OR, restoration) are differentiated at a lithographic scale. Small-scale differentiation features are built into the nanowires and statistically populated (e.g., addressing, restoration).

In the nanoPLA, the wired-OR planes combine the roles of switchbox, connection box, and logic block into one unified logic and switching plane. The wired-OR plane naturally provides the logic block in a nanoPLA block. It also serves

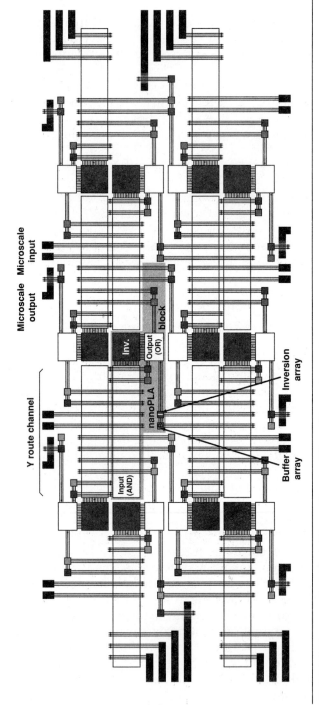

FIGURE 38.13 ■ nanoPLA block tiling with edge I/O to lithographic scale.

to select inputs from the routing channel that participate in the logic. Signals that must be rebuffered or switched through a block are also routed through the same wired-OR plane. Since the configurable switchpoints fit within the space of a nanowire crossing, the wired-OR plane (hence the interconnect switching) can be fully populated unlike traditional FPGA switch blocks that have a very limited population to reduce their area requirements.

38.6.3 Memories

The same basic crosspoints and nanowire crossbar used for the wired-OR plane (Section 38.4.1) can also serve as the core of a memory bank. An address decoder similar to the one used for programming the wired-OR array (see Section 38.5 and Figure 38.8) supports read/write operations on the memory core [26, 30]. Unique, random addresses can be used to configure deterministic memory addresses, avoiding defective memory rows and columns [31]. A full-component architecture would interleave these memory blocks with the nanoPLA logic blocks similar to the way memory blocks are embedded in conventional FPGAs (Chapter 1).

38.6.4 Defect Tolerance

Nanowires in each wired-OR plane and interconnect channel are locally substitutable (see the Local sparing subsection in Section 37.2.4). The full population of the wired-OR crossbar planes guarantees this is true even for the interconnect channels. We provision spare nanowires based on their defect rate, as suggested in the Yield with sparing subsection of Section 37.2.3. For each array, we test for functional wires as illustrated in Section 38.6.1. Logical Pterms are assigned to nanowires using the matching approach described in the Fine-grained Pterm matching subsection of Section 37.2.5. For a detailed description of nanoPLA defect tolerance, see DeHon and Naeimi [32].

38.6.5 Design Mapping

Logic-level designs can be mapped to the nanoPLA. The logic and physical mapping for the nanoPLA uses similar techniques to those introduced in Part III. Starting from a logic netlist, technology mapping can be performed using PLAmap (see Section 13.3.4) to generate two-level clusters for each nanoPLA block, which can then be placed using an annealing-based placer (Chapter 14). Routing is performed with a PathFinder-based router (Chapter 17). Because of the full population of the switchboxes, the nanoPLA router need only perform global routing. Since nanoPLA blocks provide both logic and routing, the router must also account for the logic assigned to each nanoPLA block when determining congestion. As noted before, at design loadtime, logical Pterms are assigned to specific nanowires using a greedy matching approach (see the Fine-grained Pterm matching subsection of Section 37.2.5).

38.6.6 Density Benefits

Despite statistical assembly, lithographic overheads for nanowire addressing, and high defect rates, small feature sizes, and compact crosspoints can offer a significant density advantage compared to lithographic FPGAs. When mapping the Toronto 20 benchmark suite [33] to 10-nm full-pitch nanowires (e.g., 5-nm-diameter nanowires with 5-nm spacing between nanowires), we typically see two orders of magnitude greater density than with defect-free 22-nm lithographic FPGAs [2]. As noted earlier, areal density can be further increased by using additional layers of nanowires [29].

38.7 NANOSCALE DESIGN ALTERNATIVES

Several architectures have been proposed for nanoscale logic. A large number are also based on regular crossbar arrays and look similar to the nanoPLA at a gross level (see Table 38.1). Like the nanoPLA, all these schemes employ fine-grained configurability to tolerate defects. Within these architectures there are different ways to address the key challenges (Section 38.3). These architectures enrich the palette of available component solutions, increasing the likelihood of assembling a complementary set of technology and design elements to practically realize nanoscale configurable logic.

38.7.1 Imprint Lithography

In the concrete technology described in Section 38.2, seeded nanowire growth was used to obtain small feature sizes and LB flow to assemble them into parallel arrays. Another emerging technique for producing regular, nanoscale structures (e.g., a set of parallel, tight-pitched wires) is imprint lithography. The masks for imprint lithography can be generated using bottom-up techniques.

TABLE 38.1 ▪ A comparison of nano-electronic programmable logic designs

Component element	HP/UCLA crossbar architecture	CMU nanoFabric	nanoPLA	Stony Brook CMOL	Hewlett-Packard FPNI
Crosspoint technology	Programmable diode	Programmable diode	Programmable diode	Programmable diode	Programmable diode
Nanowire technology	Nano-imprint lithography	Nanopore templates	Catalyst nanowires	Nano-imprint lithography	Nano-imprint lithography
Logic implementation	Nanoscale wired-OR	Nanoscale wired-OR	Nanoscale wired-OR	Nanoscale wired-OR	Lithoscale (N)AND2
CMOS↔Nanowire interface	Random particles	–	Coded nanowires	Crossbar tilt	Crossbar tilt
Restoration	CMOS	RTD latch	nanowire FET	CMOS	CMOS
References	[34, 35, 36]	[37, 38]	[28, 39]	[40]	[41]

In one scheme, timed vertical growth or atomic-layer deposition on planar semiconductors is used to define nanometer-scale layers of differentially etchable materials. Cut orthogonally, the vertical cross-section can be etched to produce a comblike structure where the teeth, as well as the spacing between them, are single-digit nanometers wide (e.g., 8 nm). The resulting structure can serve as a pattern for nanoscale imprint lithography [42,43] to produce a set of tight-pitched, parallel lines. That is, the long parallel lines resulting from the differential etch can be stamped into a resist mask [43], which is then etched to produce a pattern in a polymer or coated with metal to directly transfer metallic lines to a substrate [42]. These techniques can produce regular nanostructures but cannot produce arbitrary topologies.

38.7.2 Interfacing

When nanowires are fabricated together using imprint lithography, it is not possible to uniquely construct and code nanowires as exploited for addressing in the nanoPLA (Section 38.5). Williams and Kuekes [36] propose the first randomized decoder scheme for differentiating nanoscale wires and interfacing between lithographic and nanoscale feature sizes. They use a physical process to randomly deposit metal particles between the lithographic-scale address lines and the nanoscale wires. A nanowire is controllable by an address wire only if it has a metal particle bridging it to the address line. Unlike the nanowire-coding scheme where addresses are selected from a carefully chosen address space and grown into each nanowire (Section 38.5), in this scheme the address on each nanowire is randomly generated. As a result, this scheme requires 2 to 2.5 times as many address wires as the statistically assembled nanowire-coding scheme.

Alternately, Strukov and Likharev [40, 44] observe that it should be possible to directly connect each long crossbar nanowire by a nanovia to lithographic-scale circuitry that exists below the nanoscale circuits. The *nanovia* is a semiconductor pin spaced at lithographic distances and grown with a taper to a nanoscale tip for interfacing with individual nanowires. An array of these pins (e.g., Jensen [45]) can provide nanovia interfaces.

The key idea is to pitch-match the lithographically spaced nanovia pins with the nanoscale pitch nanowires and guarantee that there is space in the CMOS below the nanoscale circuitry for the CMOS restoration and programming circuits. Note of the following:

- Nanoscale wires can be angled relative to the CMOS circuitry to match the pitch of the CMOS nanovias to the nanoscale wires. Figure 38.14 shows this tilt interfacing to a single nanowire array layer. Nanovias that connect to the CMOS are arranged in a square array with side $2\beta F_{CMOS}$, where F_{CMOS} is the half-pitch of the CMOS subsystem, and β is a dimensionless factor larger than 1 that depends on CMOS cell complexity. The nanowire crossbar is turned by an angle $\alpha = \arcsin\left(F_{nano}/\beta F_{CMOS}\right)$ relative to the CMOS pin array, where F_{nano} is the nanowire half-pitch.

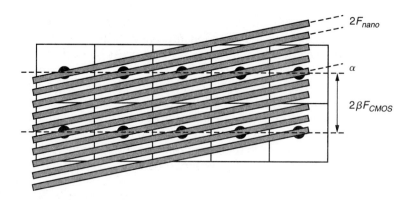

FIGURE 38.14 ■ Nanoscale and CMOS pitch matching via tilt.

■ If sufficiently long nanowires are used, the area per nanowire can be as large as each CMOS cell (e.g., restoration buffer and programming transistors). For example, if we use $10\,\mu m$ nanowires at $10\,nm$ pitch, each nanowire occupies $10^5\,nm^2$; each such nanowire could have its own $300\,nm \times 300\,nm$ CMOS cell ($\beta \approx 3$ for $F_{CMOS} = 45\,nm$) and keep the CMOS area contained below the nanowire area.

For detailed development of this interface scheme, see Likharev and Strukov [44]. Hewlett-Packard employs a variant of the tilt scheme for their field-programmable nanowire interconnect (FPNI) architecture [41].

38.7.3 Restoration

Enabled by the array-tilt scheme that allows each nanowire to be directly connected to CMOS circuitry, the hybrid semiconductor–molecular electronics (CMOL) and FPNI nanoscale array designs use lithographic-scale CMOS buffers to perform signal restoration and inversion. CMOS buffers with large feature sizes will be larger than nanowire FETs and have less variation. The FPNI scheme uses nanoscale configurability only to provide programmable interconnect, using a nonconfigurable 2-input CMOS NAND/AND gate for logic.

Alternatively, it may be possible to build latches that provide gain and isolation from 2-terminal molecular devices [38]. Specifically, molecules that serve as resonant-tunneling diodes (RTDs) or negative differential resistors have been synthesized [46, 47]. These devices are characterized by a region of negative resistance in their IV-curve. The CMU nanoFabric design shows how to build and integrate latches based on RTD devices. The latches draw their power from the clock and provide restoration and isolation.

38.8 SUMMARY

Between highly regular structures and high defect rates, atomic-scale design appears to demand postfabrication configurability. This chapter shows how configurable architectures can accommodate the extreme regularity required. It further shows that configurable architectures can tolerate extremely limited control during the fabrication process by exploiting large-scale assembly statistics. Consequently, we obtain a path to denser logic using building blocks roughly 10 atoms wide, as well as a path to continued integration in the third dimension.

Spatially configurable design styles become even more important when all substrates are configurable at their base level. We can always configure sequential processors on top of these nanoscale substrates when tasks are irregular and low throughput (see Chapter 36 and the Processor subsection of Section 5.2.2). However, when tasks can be factored into regular subtasks, direct spatial implementation on the configurable substrate will be more efficient, reducing both runtime and energy consumption.

References

[1] S. R. J. Brueck. There are no fundamental limits to optical lithography. *International Trends in Applied Optics*, SPIE Press, 2002.

[2] A. DeHon. Nanowire-based programmable architectures. *ACM Journal on Emerging Technologies in Computing Systems* 1(2), 2005.

[3] Y. Tan, X. Dai, Y. Li, D. Zhu. Preparation of gold, platinum, palladium and silver nanoparticles by the reduction of their salts with a weak reductant–potassium bitartrate. *Journal of Material Chemistry* 13, 2003.

[4] Y. Wu, Y. Cui, L. Huynh, C. J. Barrelet, D. C. Bell, C. M. Lieber. Controlled growth and structures of molecular-scale silicon nanowires. *Nanoletters* 4(3), 2004.

[5] Y. Cui, L. J. Lauhon, M. S. Gudiksen, J. Wang, C. M. Lieber. Diameter-controlled synthesis of single crystal silicon nanowires. *Applied Physics Letters* 78(15), 2001.

[6] B. Zheng, Y. Wu, P. Yang, J. Liu. Synthesis of ultra-long and highly-oriented silicon oxide nanowires from alloy liquid. *Advanced Materials* 14, 2002.

[7] M. S. Gudiksen, J. Wang, C. M. Lieber. Synthetic control of the diameter and length of semiconductor nanowires. *Journal of Physical Chemistry B* 105, 2001.

[8] M. S. Gudiksen, L. J. Lauhon, J. Wang, D. C. Smith, C. M. Lieber. Growth of nanowire superlattice structures for nanoscale photonics and electronics. *Nature* 415, 2002.

[9] Y. Wu, R. Fan, P. Yang. Block-by-block growth of single-crystalline Si/SiGe superlattice nanowires. *Nanoletters* 2(2), 2002.

[10] M. T. Björk, B. J. Ohlsson, T. Sass, A. I. Persson, C. Thelander, M. H. Magnusson, K. Depper, L. R. Wallenberg, L. Samuelson. One-dimensional steeplechase for electrons realized. *Nanoletters* 2(2), 2002.

[11] L. J. Lauhon, M. S. Gudiksen, D. Wang, C. M. Lieber. Epitaxial core-shell and core-multi-shell nanowire heterostructures. *Nature* 420, 2002.

[12] M. Law, J. Goldberger, P. Yang., Semiconductor nanowires and nanotubes. *Annual Review of Material Science* 34, 2004.

[13] M. Ritala. Advanced ALE processes of amorphous and polycrystalline films. *Applied Surface Science* 112, 1997.

[14] M. Ritala, K. Kukli, A. Rahtu, P. I. Räisänen, M. Leskelä, T. Sajavaara, J. Keinonen. Atomic layer deposition of oxide thin films with metal alkoxides as oxygen sources. *Science* 288, 2000.

[15] Y. Wu, J. Xiang, C. Yang, W. Lu, C. M. Lieber. Single-crystal metallic nanowires and metal/semiconductor nanowire heterostructures. *Nature* 430, 2004.

[16] Y. Huang, X. Duan, Q. Wei, C. M. Lieber. Directed assembly of one-dimensional nanostructures into functional networks. *Science* 291, 2001.

[17] D. Whang, S. Jin, C. M. Lieber. Nanolithography using hierarchically assembled nanowire masks. *Nanoletters* 3(7), 2003.

[18] D. Whang, S. Jin, Y. Wu, C. M. Lieber. Large-scale hierarchical organization of nanowire arrays for integrated nanosystems. *Nanoletters* 3(9), 2003.

[19] Y. Chen, D. A. A. Ohlberg, X. Li, D. R. Stewart, R. S. Williams, J. O. Jeppesen, K. A. Nielsen, J. F. Stoddart, D. L. Olynick, E. Anderson. Nanoscale molecular-switch devices fabricated by imprint lithography. *Applied Physics Letters* 82(10), 2003.

[20] Y. Chen, G.-Y. Jung, D. A. A. Ohlberg, X. Li, D. R. Stewart, J. O. Jeppesen, K. A. Nielsen, J. F. Stoddart, R. S. Williams. Nanoscale molecular-switch crossbar circuits. *Nanotechnology* 14, 2003.

[21] D. R. Stewart, D. A. A. Ohlberg, P. A. Beck, Y. Chen, R. S. Williams, J. O. Jeppesen, K. A. Nielsen, J. F. Stoddart. Molecule-independent electrical switching in Pt/organic monolayer/Ti devices. *Nanoletters* 4(1), 2004.

[22] C. Collier, G. Mattersteig, E. Wong, Y. Luo, K. Beverly, J. Sampaio, F. Raymo, J. Stoddart, J. Heath. A [2]catenane-based solid state reconfigurable switch. *Science* 289, 2000.

[23] C. L. Brown, U. Jonas, J. A. Preece, H. Ringsdorf, M. Seitz, J. F. Stoddart. Introduction of [2]catenanes into Langmuir films and Langmuir–Blodgett multilayers: A possible strategy for molecular information storage materials. *Langmuir* 16(4), 2000.

[24] A. DeHon. Reconfigurable Architectures for General-Purpose Computing. AI Technical Report 1586, MIT Artificial Intelligence Laboratory, Cambridge, MA, 1996.

[25] A. DeHon. Array-based architecture for FET-based, nanoscale electronics. *IEEE Transactions on Nanotechnology* 2(1), 2003.

[26] A. DeHon, P. Lincoln, J. Savage. Stochastic assembly of sublithographic nanoscale interfaces. *IEEE Transactions on Nanotechnology* 2(3), 2003.

[27] A. DeHon. Law of Large Numbers system design. In *Nano, Quantum and Molecular Computing: Implications to High Level Design and Validation*, Kluwer Academic, 2004.

[28] A. DeHon. Design of programmable interconnect for sublithographic programmable logic arrays. *Proceedings of the International Symposium on Field-Programmable Gate Arrays*, 2005.

[29] B. Gojman, R. Rubin, C. Pilotto, T. Tanamoto, A. DeHon. 3D nanowire-based programmable logic. *Proceedings of the International Conference on Nano-Networks* 2006.

[30] A. DeHon, S. C. Goldstein, P. J. Kuekes, P. Lincoln. Non-photolithographic nanoscale memory density prospects. *IEEE Transactions on Nanotechnology* 4(2), 2005.

[31] A. DeHon. Deterministic addressing of nanoscale devices assembled at sublithographic pitches. *IEEE Transactions on Nanotechnology* 4(6), 2005.

[32] A. DeHon, H. Naeimi. Seven strategies for tolerating highly defective fabrication. *IEEE Design and Test of Computers* 22(4), 2005.

[33] V. Betz, J. Rose. FPGA Place-and-Route Challenge. *http://www.eecg.toronto.edu/~vaughn/challenge/challenge.html*, 1999.

[34] J. R. Heath, P. J. Kuekes, G. S. Snider, R. S. Williams. A defect-tolerant computer architecture: Opportunities for nanotechnology. *Science* 280(5370), 1998.

[35] Y. Luo, P. Collier, J. O. Jeppesen, K. A. Nielsen, E. Delonno, G. Ho, J. Perkins, H.-R. Tseng, T. Yamamoto, J. F. Stoddart, J. R. Heath. Two-dimensional molecular electronics circuits. *ChemPhysChem* 3(6), 2002.

[36] S. Williams, P. Kuekes. Demultiplexer for a molecular wire crossbar network. U.S. Patent number 6,256,767, July 3, 2001.

[37] S. C. Goldstein, M. Budiu. NanoFabrics: Spatial computing using molecular electronics. *Proceedings of the International Symposium on Computer Architecture* 178–189, 2001.

[38] S. C. Goldstein, D. Rosewater. Digital logic using molecular electronics. *ISSCC Digest of Technical Papers*, IEEE, 2002.

[39] A. DeHon, M. J. Wilson. Nanowire-based sublithographic programmable logic arrays. *Proceedings of the International Symposium on Field-Programmable Gate Arrays*, 2004.

[40] D. B. Strukov, K. K. Likharev. CMOL FPGA: A reconfigurable architecture for hybrid digital circuits with two-terminal nanodevices. *Nanotechnology* 16(6), 2005.

[41] G. S. Snider, R. S. Williams. Nano/CMOS architectures using a field-programmable nanowire interconnect. *Nanotechnology* 18(3), 2007.

[42] N. A. Melosh, A. Boukai, F. Diana, B. Gerardot, A. Badolato, P. M. Petroff, J. R. Heath. Ultra high-density nanowire lattices and circuits. *Science* 300, 2003.

[43] M. D. Austin, H. Ge, W. Wu, M. Li, Z. Yu, D. Wasserman, S. A. Lyon, S. Y. Chou. Fabrication of 5 nm linewidth and 14 nm pitch features by nanoimprint lithography. *Applied Physics Letters* 84(26), 2004.

[44] K. K. Likharev, D. B. Strukov. CMOL: Devices, circuits, and architectures. In *Introducing Molecular Electronics*, Springer, 2005.

[45] K. L. Jensen. Field emitter arrays for plasma and microwave source applications. *Physics of Plasmas* 6(5), 1999.

[46] J. Chen, M. Reed, A. Rawlett, J. Tour. Large on-off ratios and negative differential resistance in a molecular electronic device. *Science* 286, 1999.

[47] J. Chen, W. Wang, M. A. Reed, M. Rawlett, D. W. Price, J. M. Tour. Room-temperature negative differential resistance in nanoscale molecular junctions. *Applied Physics Letters* 77, 2000.

INDEX